BARBARA A. BABCOCK
COMPARATIVE CULTURAL
& LITERARY STUDIES
1249 NORTH HIGHLAND
UNIVERSITY OF ARIZONA
TUCSON, ARIZONA 85721
602-626-8694 (3)

THE TYPES OF THE FOLKTALE

FF COMMUNICATIONS No. 184

THE TYPES OF THE FOLKTALE

A CLASSIFICATION AND BIBLIOGRAPHY

ANTTI AARNE'S

Verzeichnis der Märchentypen
(FF Communications No. 3)

Translated and Enlarged by

STITH THOMPSON

Indiana University

Second Revision

HELSINKI 1987
SUOMALAINEN TIEDEAKATEMIA
ACADEMIA SCIENTIARUM FENNICA

First published, 1961
Second printing, 1963
Third printing, 1973
Fourth printing, 1987

Presented at the Academia Scientiarum Fennica
by Martti Haavio and Lauri Hakulinen
on May 12, 1961

Copyright © 1961 by
Academia Scientiarum Fennica

ISSN 0014-5815
ISBN 951-41-0132-4

Pieksämäki 1987
Sisälähetysseuran kirjapaino Raamattutalo

PREFACE TO THE SECOND REVISION

Almost immediately after the appearance of the first revision of this work, regional and national indexes of folktales from Russia, Spain, Iceland, and Lithuania brought suggestions of many new types which should be included in any future edition, if it is to be usable and adequate. And during all the years since, as new surveys have appeared from various parts of the world, it has become clear that although the *Types of the Folktale*, both in its original form of 1910 and in its revision of 1928, has served as a basis for nearly all the classifications, it could be made much more valuable if it were revised so as to take better account of the actual body of narrative material present in the various countries.

At the Congress for the Study of the Folktale at Lund in 1935, the question of the revision of *The Types of the Folktale* was discussed at some length. The usefulness of the index for bringing the great mass of folktales of various countries into a single classification was clear enough, as was the desirability of its eventual improvement. It was shown that Aarne in his original classification had proceeded primarily from the practical necessity of arranging the great Finnish collections of tales, and that his classification had also covered the countries of northern Europe reasonably well. Although some attempt was later made, in the first revision, to extend the coverage of the index to southern Europe, it was still true that most of the countries of southern and southeast Europe and of Asia over to India were left practically unnoticed. And this was in spite of the fact that for any comparative studies of folktales the versions from the Mediterranean, the near East, and India are of prime importance.

The extent of the area to be covered in the revision was discussed, and it was agreed that India itself demanded special consideration. Before the end of the congress, I had agreed that, with the help of my colleagues, I would undertake to revise the index in due time. Meanwhile, I wished to make a special study of the tales of India so as to balance the index between east and west.

At that time, no systematic study had been made of the folktales of any of the countries of southeast Europe or of the near east. Even today there are large areas almost completely unexplored, such as Arabia, Iraq, and Iran. But within the last twenty years, much has been done to make available oral narratives from many different countries, including the south and east, so that the balance between east and west is no longer as uneven as it was in Aarne's day. Good indexes are now available for Russia, Spain, Iceland, Lithuania, Latvia, Sweden, Germany, Italy, Turkey, France, India, Czechoslovakia, Hungary, Rumania, and Spanish America. All of these have appeared since the publication of the first revision, and several others are nearly ready for publication — Greece, French Canada, Scotland, and Ireland.

In addition to these various surveys, the last years have witnessed the development of various folktale archives, some of them of first-rate importance. In preparing the present revision, I have attempted to visit all of these possible, and I have actually spent some weeks in most of them — Quebec, Edinburgh, Dublin, Marburg, Copenhagen, Lund, Stockholm, Uppsala, Oslo, Helsinki, Ljubljana, Zagreb, and Athens. My purpose in visiting these was to see how far the archives were finding the 1928 revision adequate for their use. For tales already in that revision, I secured an inventory of the holdings of the archives and learned of the need of additions and changes.

During the last years, many important studies of individual tales have appeared, and it is my hope that none of these have been overlooked. A number of notable articles appeared in the *Handwörterbuch des deutschen Märchens*, although its publication was interrupted midway. Within the last few years, an important event in folktale study has been the establishment of the periodical *Fabula*. Here many collections of folktales have been arranged according to types. And since some of these collections are in languages difficult for the ordinary student, these analyses frequently serve as keys to unlock otherwise impenetrable doors. Since the surveys for such countries as Lithuania, Poland, Latvia, Czechoslovakia, and Hungary appear in the original languages, I have had to secure the help of native speakers in order to use these surveys. It has been helpful afterward to check my results with these reviews in *Fabula* and other journals. I am particularly grateful for help in this respect from Professor Walter Anderson.

The title of the present work, either in its original German form or in its English form, is certainly not quite accurate. The German word *Märchen* is in some ways better than the English word *folktale*, although there are certainly many things in the index which are by no means *Märchen*. At any rate, neither the Märchen, nor the folktales of all the world are considered in this index. Students of the tale have long realized that the lands from Ireland to India form an important tradition area where the same stories are found, some of them extending over the entire territory, and some following these peoples as they migrate to distant continents. Strictly then, this work might be called »The Types of the Folk-Tale of Europe, West Asia, and the Lands Settled by These Peoples.»

Another limitation has to do with the type of tradition concerned. On the one hand, this index does not include local legends (German *Sagen*), nor unless they also appear in oral tradition, the great literary traditional collections. Thus, Aesop's Fables, the Panchatantra, the Thousand and One Nights, the Renaissance Novelle – these have been considered only when they have been encountered as oral tales and been recorded by those who have heard them. As to the *Sagen*, attention is called to Professor R. Th. Christiansen's *The Migratory Legends* (FFC No. 175), in which an extension of the number system of the present catalog is used.

For several reasons, the abbreviation »Mt.» used in the earlier editions has been abandoned in this. »Type» has been used instead, so as to contrast with »motif.» Aside from the fact that this is an English translation, »type» is almost an international word and is easily understood.

Within the last few years, I have completed a revision of the *Motif-Index of Folk-Literature* and have checked carefully all of the references to that work. For some of the long and complicated tales, I have felt it desirable to make a motif analysis so as to display the anatomy of the tale.

The first revision had a considerable supplement consisting of »Tales Not Included», usually those appearing very rarely or in a single country. With many new archives and new surveys, the number of such tales has greatly increased. It has no longer seemed desirable to print these as a supplement, but rather adjacent to the corresponding regular numbers and in a smaller type-face. Generally, if a tale is found in several countries, it has been placed in the main index. Normally, if I have known of only one appearance of a story, it has not been used at all. But I have frequently broken this rule when I have felt it likely that the tale is actually known but not recorded, and when its presence in the index might be useful in the future.

With the fewest exceptions, I have made no changes in numbers. If a number appeared with a star in the 1928 edition, it has sometimes been changed to a regular type, but a notice is always given of such a change. One difficulty in the old edition was that when supplementary numbers were added, each with its proper star, it was often necessary to use four or five stars. With the same system used in the present edition, these asterisks might occasionally increase to twelve or fifteen. To avoid such awkwardness, letters have been added to the number before the star, thus 879A*, 879B*, 879C*, etc.

In the bibliographical references for the various types the general plan of the earlier edition has been followed. After each of the surveys and archives, I have noted in italics the approximate number now found for the particular type. Though these figures are subject to continual change, they should give an idea of the distribution of the tale.

A word is perhaps desirable about the difference between an index such as this and the *Motif-Index of Folk-Literature*. This classification is concerned with whole tales, those that have an independent tradition. And they are confined to narratives of a certain area. On the other hand, the motif-index attempts a theoretical classification of motifs covering the whole world. Sometimes, indeed, these are equivalent to types, since many tales consist of only a single motif. But the approach of the two works is entirely different. The present index is merely a practical listing of tales for a certain area, so that collectors and scholars can have a common base of reference. From the purely theoretical point of view it is certain that faults can be found with this classification, but in practice, fifty years of experience have shown that for the area covered it works satisfactorily. It would be a mistake to think that it could be extended to tales of such areas as central Africa, the North American Indians, or Oceania. Each of those would need an index based strictly upon its own traditions.

In the preparation of this work I have had the help of many colleagues and friends, and it would be impossible to acknowledge properly all help received. Some have made my visits to their archives both profitable and pleasant; some have answered repeated queries; and some have helped with their advice at various stages of the task. My thanks for such help go to the following: Walter Anderson; Jonas Balys; Laurits Bødker; Maja Bošković-Stulli; Katherine Briggs; Reidar Th. Christiansen; Gianfranco D'Aronco; Linda Dégh; Maartje Draak; Ivan Grafenauer; Fritz Harkort; Martti Haavio; Gottfried Henssen; Hiroko Ikeda; Agnes Kovács; Luc Lacourcière; Waldemar Liungman; Sebastiano Lo Nigro; Calum Maclean; Milko Matičetov; Georgios Megas; Dov Noy; Åsa Nyman; Seamus O'Duilearga; Sean O'Suilleabhain; Vlajko Palavestra; Kurt Ranke; Georg-Henri Rivière; Warren E. Roberts; Anna Birgitta Rooth; Einar Ó. Sveinsson; J. Ö. Swahn; Archer Taylor; Marie-Louise Tenèze; and Carl-Herman Tillhagen.

Finally, I am thankful for financial support from the John Simon Guggenheim Foundation, the American Philosophical Society, and Indiana University. Without such aid this work, extending as it has over five years, could hardly have been undertaken.

Stith Thompson

Bloomington, Indiana

June, 1960

ABBREVIATIONS AND BIBLIOGRAPHY

For those entries which are arranged in accordance with the numbering of this catalogue no page indications have been necessary. An effort has been made to give an approximate inventory of versions accessible for each entry or for a group of entries, and these numbers have been printed in italics. The sources for the totals for various countries or regions and the order in which these are presented follow:

Finnish. (1) A. Aarne. Finnische Märchenvarianten (FFC V and XXXIII). (2) Archive: Suomalaisen Kirjallisuuden Seura, Helsinki.
Finnish-Swedish. O. Hackman. Katalog der Märchen der finnländischen Schweden (FFC VI).
Estonian. A. Aarne. Estnische Märchen- und Sagenvarianten (FFC XXV).
Livonian. O. Loorits. Livische Märchen- und Sagenvarianten (FFC LXVI).
Latvian. Alma Medne. Latviešu dzīvnieku pasakas. Riga, 1940. (Latvian animal tales. Made accessible through kindness of Professor Walter Anderson.)
Lithuanian. J. Balys. Lietuviu Pasakojamosios Tautosakos Motyvu Katalogas. Motif-Index of Lithuanian Narrative Folk-Lore. Kaunas, 1936.
Lappish. J. Qvigstad. Lappische Märchen- und Sagenvarianten (FFC LX).
Swedish. (1) W. Liungman. Sveriges Samtliga Folksagor, 3 vols. Stockholm, 1949. (Special title for Volume 3: Varifrån Kommer Våra Sagor? Unless otherwise indicated, all references are to Volume 3.) Supplementary references have been secured from (2) Landsmåls och Folkminnesarkivet, Uppsala, and (3) Folklivsarkivet, Lund.
Norwegian. (1) R. Th. Christiansen. Norske Eventyr utgit av den Norske Historiske Kildeskriftskommission. Kristiania, 1921. (English summary: FFC XLVI). (2) S. Solheim. Register til Norsk Folkminnelags skrifter Nos. 1—49 (Norsk Folkminnelag No. 50). Oslo, 1943.
Danish. (1) A. Lunding. The System of Tales in the Folklore Collection of Copenhagen (FFC II). (2) Archive: Dansk Folkmindesamling, Copenhagen. (The inventory of tales in this archive is complete for this index only down to Type 1350.)
Icelandic. E. Ó. Sveinsson. Verzeichnis isländischer Märchenvarianten (FFC LXXXIII).
Scottish. (1) Archive: School of Scottish Studies, Edinburgh. (2) J. G. McKay. More West Highland Tales, Vol. 1 (cited: Campbell-MacKay). Edinburgh and London, 1940.
Irish. (1) Archive: Irish Folklore Commission, Dublin. Catalogue of types in preparation. (2) S. O'Suilleabhain. Handbook of Irish Folklore. Dublin, 1942.
English. E. W. Baughman. A Comparative Study of the Folktales of England and North America. (Indiana University dissertation, 1953). University Microfilms, Ann Arbor, Michigan.
French. (1) P. Delarue. Le Conte Populaire Français, tome I. Paris, 1957. (2)

Manuscript for the rest of this work consulted in the Musée des Arts et Traditions Populaires.

Spanish. (1) R. S. Boggs. Index of Spanish Folktales (FFC XC). (2) A. M. Espinosa (Sr.). Cuentos Populares Españoles, 3 vols. Second edition, Madrid, 1946—47.

Catalan. J. Amades. Folklore de Catalunya: Rondallistica. Barcelona, 1950. (Notes by W. Anderson in Schweiz. Archiv für Volkskunde L (1954) 57ff.

Dutch. J. R. W. Sinninghe. Katalog der niederländischen Märchen, Ursprungssagen-, Sagen- und Legendenvarianten (FFC CXXXII).

Flemish. (1) M. de Meyer. Les Contes Populaires de la Flandre (FFC XXXVII). (2) A. J. Witteryck. Oude Westvlaamsche Volksvertelsels. Brugge-Brussel, 1946.

Walloon. G. Laport. Les Contes Populaires Wallons (FFC CI).

German. (1) Archive: Zentralarchiv der deutschen Volkserzählungen in Marburg/Lahn. (2) K. Ranke. Schleswig-Holsteinische Volksmärchen, Vols. 1, 2. Kiel, 1955, 1957. (3) See also Henssen Jül., Henssen Meckl., Henssen Volk, Merk. in bibliography.

Italian. (1) Basile, Pentamerone (see Penzer). (2) G. D'Aronco. Le *Fiabe* di magia in Italia. Udine, 1957. (3) Tuscan = G. D'Aronco. Indice delle fiabe toscane (with notes by W. Anderson in Hessische Blätter für Volkskunde XLV). (4) Friuli = G. D'Aronco.»Folklore friulano» in *Folklore* (Napoli) IX (1954—55). (5) Trieste = G. Pinguentini. Fiabe, leggende, etc. in dialetto triestino. Trieste, 1955. (6) Sicilian = S. Lo Nigro. Racconti popolari Siciliani. Firenze, 1958. See also Gonzenbach in bibliography.

Rumanian. A. Schullerus. Verzeichnis der rumänischen Märchen und Märchenvarianten (FFC LXXVIII).

Hungarian. (1) H. Honti. Verzeichnis der publizierten ungarischen Volksmärchen (FFC LXXXI). (2) J. Berze Nagy, Magyar Népmesetipusok, 2 vols. Pecs, 1957 (Notes by W. Anderson in Fabula II 281ff.). (3) Linda Dégh. Kakasdi Népmesék. Budapest, 1955. (4) Agnes Kovács. Magyar Allatmesék Tipusmutatoja. Budapest, 1958.

Czech. (1) V. Tille. Verzeichnis der bömischen Märchen (FFC XXXIV). (2) V. Tille. Soupis Českijch Pohádek, 2 vols. Praha, 1929—37. (Notes by W. Anderson in Zeitschrift für slavische Philologie IX 509ff., XIV 227ff., XVIII 245ff.).

Slovenian. Archive: Slovenska Akademija znanosti in Umetnosti, Ljubljana.

Serbocroatian. (1) Archives: Insitut za Narodnu Umjetnost, Zagreb, and Zemaljski Muzey, Sarajevo. (2) Istria = M. Bošković-Stulli. Istarske Narodne Priče. Zagreb, 1959.

Polish. J. Krżyzanowski. Polska Bajka Ludowa w Układzie Systematycznym, Vols. 1, 2. Warszawa, 1947.

Russian. (1) N. P. Andrejev. Ukazatel' Skazocnich Sjuzhetov po Sisteme Aarne. Leningrad, 1929. (2) A. N. Afanasiev. Narodnije Russikije Skazki, 3 vols. Moskva, 1957 (Type-index by V. Y. Propp). (3) Andrejev Ukraine = N. P. Andrejev.»A Characterization of the Ukrainian tale corpus,» translated by Barbara Krader, Fabula I 228ff.

Greek. (1) Archive: Laographikon Archeion (Manuscript collection of the Folklore Archives of the Athens Academy). (2) See also in bibliography: Hahn, Loukatos, Dawkins.

Turkish. W. Eberhard and P. N. Boratav. Typen türkischer Volksmärchen. Wiesbaden, 1953. (Type-index by W. Anderson in Hessische Blätter für Volkskunde XLIV 112ff.)

India. (1) S. Thompson and W. E. Roberts. Types of Indic Oral Tales. (FFC CLXXX). (2) Thompson-Balys = S. Thompson and J. Balys. The Oral Tales of India. Bloomington, Indiana, 1958.

Indonesian. J. DeVries.»Typen-Register der Indonesische Fabels en Sprookjes» in Volksverhalen uit Oost-Indië (Leiden, 1925, 1928) II 398ff.

Japanese. Hiroko Ikeda. Type and Motif Index of Japanese Folktales. (Indiana University dissertation). University Microfilms, Ann Arbor, Michigan, 1955.
Chinese. (1) W. Eberhard. Typen chinesischer Volksmärchen (FFC CXX). (2) W. Eberhard. Volksmärchen aus Südost-China (FFC CXXVIII).
Franco-American. (1) Archive: Les Archives de Folklore, Université Laval, Quebec. Type-index in preparation by L. Lacourcière.
English-American. E. W. Baughman. A Comparative Study of the Folktales of England and North America. (Indiana University dissertation, 1953). University Microfilms, Ann Arbor, Michigan.
Spanish-American. T. L. Hansen. The Types of the Folktale in Cuba, Puerto Rico, the Dominican Republic and Spanish South America. Berkeley and Los Angeles, 1957.
African. May A. Klipple. African Tales with Foreign Analogues. (Indiana University dissertation, 1938). University Microfilms, Ann Arbor, Michigan.

Alphabet Banks, M. M. An Alphabet of Tales, an English 15th century translation of the Alphabetum Narrationum of Etienne de Besancon (EETS Nos. 126, 127). 2 vols. London, 1904—05.
Anderson, W. Novelline popolari sammarinesi. 3 vols. Tartu, 1927, 1929, 1933.
— Zu Albert Wesselski's Angriffen auf der finnischen folkloristischen Forschungsmethode. Tartu, 1935.
Anesaki, Masaharu. Japanese Mythology (The Mythology of all Races VIII). Boston, 1928.
Arfert, P. Das Motiv von der unterschobenen Braut. Rostock, 1897.
Argenti-Rose = Argenti, P. P. and Rose, H. J. The Folk-lore of Chios. Cambridge (Eng.), 1949.
Artin = Artin Pacha, Yacoub. Contes populaires inédits de la vallée du Nil. Paris, 1895.
Arv. (Tidskrift for Nordisk Folkminnesforskning). Uppsala, 1944 ff.
Azadovsky, M. K. Russkaya Skazka. 2 vols. Moskva, 1932.
Balys, Jonas. Motif-Index of Lithuanian Narrative Folklore. Tautosakos Darbai Vol. II, Publication of the Lithuanian Folklore Archives. Kaunas, 1936.
— Lithuanian Folk Legends. Publication of the Lithuanian Folklore Archives I. Kaunas, 1940.
Barker, W. N. and Sinclair, C. West African Folk-tales. London, 1917.
Basden, G. T. Among the Ibos of Nigeria. London, 1921.
Basile, G. The Pentamerone (trans. and edited by Benedetto Croce and N. M. Penzer). 2 vols. London, 1932.
Basset, René. Contes populaires berbères. 2 vols. Paris, 1887.
— Mille et un contes, récits et légendes arabes. 3 vols. Paris, 1925—27.
— Nouveaux contes berbères. Paris, 1897.
Beal = Bealoideas: Journal of the Folklore of Ireland Society.
Beckwith, Martha. Hawaiian Mythology. New Haven, 1940.
Bédier, Joseph. Les Fabliaux. 2d edition. Paris, 1893.
Benfey, T. Pantschatantra: fünf Bücher indischer Fabeln, Märchen und Erzählungen. Leipzig, 1859.
Bergsträsser = Bergsträsser, G. Neuaramäische Märchen. Leipzig, 1915.
BFIF = Bulletin Folklorique d'Ile-de-France.
Bin Gorion, M. J. Der Born Judas: Legenden, Märchen und Erzählungen. 6 vols. Leipzig, 1918 ff. (Vols. 1—4 cited are second edition, 5 and 6 are first edition).
Bladé, J. F. Contes populaires de Gascogne (Les Littératures Populaires, Nos. 19, 20, 21). 3 vols. Paris, 1886.
Bødker, Laurits. Christen Nielssen, De Gamle Vijses Exempler oc Hoffsprock. København, 1951, 1953.

Bolte, J. Jakob Freys Gartengesellschaft (Bibliothek des Literarischen Vereins in Stuttgart, No. 209). Tübingen, 1896.
— Martin Montanus Schwankbücher (Bibliothek des Literarischen Vereins in Stuttgart, No. 217). Tübingen, 1899.
— See BP.
— See Fischer.
— See Pauli.
Boratav, P. N. Contes turcs. Paris, 1955.
BP = Bolte, J. and Polivka, G. Anmerkungen zu den Kinder- und Hausmärchen der Brüder Grimm. 5 vols. Leipzig, 1913—31.
Braga, T. Contos tradicionaes do provo portuguez. Porto, 1883.
Brown Collection = The Frank C. Brown Collection of North Carolina Folklore. 5 vols. Durham, N.C., 1952—.
Bryan, William F. and Dempster, Germaine. Sources and Analogues of Chaucer's Canterbury Tales. Chicago, 1941.
Callaway, N. Nursery Tales, Traditions, and Histories of the Zulus. Natal and London, 1868.
Campbell Arab = Campbell, C. G. Tales from the Arab Tribes. London, 1949.
Campbell, J. F. Popular Tales of the West Highlands. 4 vols. 2d edition. London, 1890—93.
Campbell, K. The Seven Sages of Rome. Boston, 1907.
Campbell-McKay = John G. McKay. More West Highland Tales, transcribed and translated from the original Gaelic manuscript of John Francis Campbell. Edinburgh and London, 1940.
Camara Cascudo, Luis da. Trinta estorias brasileiras. Porto, 1955.
Carrière = J. M. Carrière, Tales from the French Folk-Lore of Missouri. Evanston and Chicago, 1937.
CColl = Colorado College Publications, Language Series.
Les Cent Nouvelles Nouvelles. 2 vols. (ed. Pierre Champion). Paris, 1928.
Chauvin, Victor. Bibliographie des ouvrages arabes. 12 vols. Liege, 1892—1922.
Chavannes, Edouard. Cinq cent contes et apologues extraits du Tripitaka chinois. 4 vols. Paris, 1910—34.
Child, Francis James. The English and Scottish Popular Ballads. 5 vols. in 10. Boston, 1882—98.
Christensen, Arthur. Dumme Folk (DF No. 50). København, 1941.
— Molboernes vise Gerninger (DF No. 47). Kobenhavn, 1939.
Christensen Iran = Christensen, A. Märchen aus Iran. Jena, 1939.
Clodd, Edward. Tom-Tit-Tot. London, 1898.
Clouston, W. A. The Book of Noodles. London, 1888.
— Popular Tales and Fictions. 2 vols. Edinburgh, London, 1887.
Coelho, A. Contos populares portuguezes. Lisboa, 1879.
Coffin = Coffin, T. P. Analytical Index to the Journal of American Folklore. Philadelphia, 1958.
Cosquin, E. Contes populaires de Lorraine. 2 vols. Paris, 1887.
— Etudes folkloriques. Paris, 1922.
— Les contes indiens et l'occident. Paris, 1922.
Coster-Wijsman, L. N. Uilespiegel-Verhalen in Indonesië. Santpoort, 1929.
Cowell, E. B. and others. The Jātaka or Stories of the Buddha's Former Births. 6 vols. and index. Cambridge, 1895—1913.
Cox, Marian R. Cinderella (PFLS XXXI). London, 1893.
Crane, T. F. The Exempla of Jacques de Vitry (PFLS XXVI). London, 1890.
Dähnhardt = Dähnhardt, Oskar. Natursagen. 4 vols. Leipzig, 1909—12.
Dawkins, Richard M. Forty-five Stories from the Dodekanese. Cambridge (England), 1950.
— Modern Greek Folktales. Oxford, 1953.
— Modern Greek in Asia Minor. London, 1916.

De Cock, Alfons. Studien en Essays over oude Volksvertelsels. Antwerp, 1919.
— *Volkssage*, Volksgeloof en Volksgebruik. Antwerp, 1918.
DF = Danmarks Folkeminder. København, 1908—.
DFS = Dansk Folkemindesamling (Copenhagen).
Dickson, Arthur. Valentine and Orson, a study in late Medieval Romance. New York, 1929.
Dirr. = Dirr, A. Kaukasische Märchen. Jena. 1922.
Dittmaier, W. Sagen, Märchen und Schwänke von der unteren Sieg. Bonn, 1950.
Dixon, Roland B. Oceanic Mythology (The Mythology of all Races IX). Boston, 1916.
Dorson, R. M. Negro Folktales from Michigan. Cambridge, Mass., 1956.
Ellis (Yoruba) = Ellis, A. B. The Yoruba-speaking Peoples of the Slave Coast of West Africa. London, 1894.
Espinosa, Aurelio M. Cuentos populares españoles. 3 vols. 2d edition. Madrid, 1946—47.
Feilberg = Feilberg, N. F. Bidrag til en *Ordbog* over jyske Almuesmål. 4 vols. København, 1886—1914.
Felice, A. de. Contes de Haute-Bretagne. Paris, 1954.
FFC = FF Communications, published by the Folklore Fellows. Helsinki, 1907ff.
Field, John E. The Myth of the Pent Cuckoo. London, 1913.
Fischer, H. and Bolte, J. Die Reise der Söhne Giaffers (Bibliothek des Litterarischen Vereins in Stuttgart No. 208). Tübingen, 1895.
FL = Folklore. London, 1890 ff.
FM = Publications of the Field Columbian Museum, Anthropological Series, Chicago, 1895ff.
Frazer, J. G. Pausanias's Description of Greece. 6 vols. London, 1898.
Frobenius, Leo. Atlantis: Volksdichtung und Volksmärchen Afrikas. 12 vols. Jena, 1921—28.
Gaster, Moses. The Exempla of the Rabbis. London, Leipzig, 1924.
— Studies and Texts in Folklore, Magic, Medieval Romance, Hebrew Apocrypha and Samaritan Archaeology. 3 vols. London, 1925—28.
Gayton, A. H. and Newman, Stanley S. Yokuts and Western Mono Myths. Berkeley (Calif.), 1940.
Georgeakis, G. et Pineau, L. Le folk-lore de Lesbos. Paris, 1894.
Gerber = Gerber, Adolph. Great Russian Animal Tales. PMLA VI. Baltimore, 1891.
Gesta Romanum. See Oesterley.
Gonzenbach, Laura. Sicilianische Märchen. 2 vols. Leipzig, 1870.
Graham (Chinese) = Graham, David Crockett. Songs and Stories of the Ch'uan Miao (Smithsonian Miscellaneous Publications CXXXIII No. 1). Washington, D.C., 1954.
Grimm = Grimm, J. and W. Kinder- und Hausmärchen. Various editions.
Grundtvig. = Lunding, A. The System of Tales in the Folklore Collection of Copenhagen (FFC II).
GSCan = Publications of the Geological Survey of Canada, Anthropological Series.
Hahn = Hahn, J. G. Griechische und albanesische Märchen. 2 vols. Leipzig, 1864.
Halm, K. von. Aisōpeiōn Mythōn Synagōgē. Lipsiae, 1852.
Harris, Joel C. Uncle Remus: his Songs and Sayings. New York, 1880.
— Uncle Remus and his Friends. Boston, 1892.
— Nights with Uncle Remus. Boston, 1883.
Hartland, E. S. The Legend of Perseus. 3 vols. London, 1894ff.
— The Science of Fairy Tales. London, 1891.
Hartmann, E. Die Trollvorstellungen in den Sagen und Märchen der skandinavischen Völker. Stuttgart, 1936.
Hazlitt, W. C. Shakespeare Jest-books London, 1881.

Hdwb. d. März. = Mackensen, L. and others. Handwörterbuch des deutschen Märchens. Berlin, 1931 ff.
Henssen Jül. = Henssen, Gottfried. Sagen, Märchen und Schwänke des jülicher Landes. Bonn, 1955.
Henssen Meck. = Wossidlo, R. and Henssen, G. Mecklenburger Erzählen. Berlin, 1957.
Henssen Volk = Henssen, G. Volk Erzählt. Münster, 1935, 1954.
Herbert, J. A. Catalogue of Romances in the Department of Manuscripts in the British Museum. London, 1910. (Vol. 3 only; for vols. 1 and 2 see Ward, H. L. D.).
Hertz, Wilhelm. Gesammelte Abhandlungen (ed. F. v.d. Leyen). Stuttgart and Berlin, 1905.
Hervieux, L. Les fabulistes latins. 2d ed. 2 vols. Paris, 1893—4.
Hessisch Blätter. Hessische Blätter für Volkskunde.
Hibbard, Laura A. Mediaeval Romance in England. New York, 1924.
Holmberg, Uno. Siberian Mythology (The Mythology of all Races IV). Boston, 1927.
Holmström, Helge. Studier över svanjungfrumotivet. Malmö, 1919.
Huber, P. Michael. Die Wanderlegende von den Siebenschläfern. Leipzig, 1910.
Jacobs, Joseph. The Fables of Aesop. New York, 1894.
— Eng.ish Fairy Tales. London, 1890.
— More English Fairy Tales. London, 1895.
JAFL = Journal of American Folk-Lore. Boston, etc., 1888ff.
Jahn = Jahn, A. Die Mehri-Sprache in Sudarabien. Wien, 1902.
JAI = Journal of the Royal Anthropological Institute of Great Britain and Ireland. London, 1871ff.
JAOS = Journal of the American Oriental Society. Boston, etc., 1849ff.
JE = Publications of the Jesup North Pacific Expedition. New York, etc., 1898ff.
Jegerlehner, Johannes. Sagen und Märchen aus dem Oberwallis. Basel, 1909.
JSFO = Journal de la Société Finno-ougrienne. Helsingfors, 1886ff.
Jungbauer, G. Das Volk Erzählt. Karlsbad and Leipzig, 1943.
Keller, John Esten. Motif-Index of Mediaeval Spanish Exempla. Knoxville (Tenn.), 1949.
Khatchatrianz = Khatchatrianz, I. Armenian Folk-Tales (trans. N. W. Orloff). Philadelphia, 1946.
Kirchhof, H. W. Wendunmuth, ed. H. Oesterley. 5 vols. Tübingen, 1865.
Kittredge, G. L. Arthur and Gorlagon (Harvard Studies and Notes in Philology and Literature VIII). Boston, 1903.
— Witchcraft in Old and New England. Cambridge (Mass.), 1929.
Knowles, J. H. Folk-Tales of Kashmir. London, 1893.
Köhler, Reinhold. Aufsätze über Märchen und Volkslieder (ed. J. Bolte and E. Schmidt). Berlin, 1894.
Köhler-Bolte = Köhler, R. Kleinere Schriften (ed. J. Bolte). 3 vols. Weimar, 1898—1900.
Krauss, F. Sagen und Märchen der Südslaven. 2 vols. Leipzig, 1883—84.
— Zigeunerhumor. Leipzig, 1907.
Kretschmer, P. Neugriechische Märchen. Jena, 1919.
Kristensen, E. T. Danske *Dyrefabler* og Kjæderemser. Aarhus, 1896.
— Jyske Folkeminder. 13 vols. Kjøbenhavn, 1871—97.
— Vore Fædres *Kirketjeneste.* Aarhus, 1899.
Krohn, Kaarle. Mann und Fuchs. Helsingfors, 1891.
Kunike = Kunike, H. Märchen aus Sibirien. Jena, 1940.
Lambertz = Lambertz, M. Die geflügelte Schwester . . ., albanesische Volksmärchen. Eisenach, 1952.
Laoust = Laoust, E. Contes berbères du Maroc. 2 vols. Paris, 1949.
Le Braz, A. La Légende de la Mort chez les Bretons armoricains. 2 vols. Paris, 1902.

Lee, A. C. The Decameron, its Sources and Analogues. London, 1909.
Legrand, E. Recueil de contes populaires grecs. Paris, 1881.
Lescot = Lescot, R. Textes kurdes. Pt. I, Paris, 1940.
Liebrecht, Felix. Zur Volkskunde. Heilbronn, 1879.
Liljeblad, Sven. Die Tobiasgeschichte und andere Märchen mit toten Helfern. Lund, 1927.
Littmann = Littmann, Enno. Arabische Märchen. Leipzig, n.d.
Liungman SSF = Sveriges Samtliga Folksagor. 3 vols. Djursholm (Sweden), 1950—52.
Loomis, C. Grant. White Magic: an Introduction to the Folklore of Christian Legend. Cambridge (Mass.), 1948.
Lorimer, D. L. R. and E. O. Persian Tales. London, 1919.
Loukatos = Loukatos, D. S. Neoellenika Laographika Keimena. Athēnai, 1957.
Luzel, F. M. Contes populaires de Basse-Bretagne. 3 vols. Paris, 1887.
MAFLS = Memoirs of the American Folk-Lore Society.
Malalasekera, George Peiris. Dictionary of Pali Proper Names. 2 vols. London, 1937.
Massé = Massé, H. Contes en persan populaire (Journal Asiatique, Paris, 1925, pp. 71—157).
Megas Paramythia = Mega, G. A. Ellēnika Paramythia. Athēnai, 1956.
Meinhof, Carl. Afrikanische Märchen. Jena, 1921.
Mensa Philosophica = T. F. Dunn. The Facetiae of the Mensa Philosophica (Washington University Studies, new series, Lang. and Lit. No. 5). St. Louis, 1934.
Merk. = Merkelbach, A. Lothringer Volksmärchen. Kassel, 1940.
Merkens, H. Was sich das Volk erzählt. 3 Bde. Jena, 1892—1900.
Meyer, G. F. Plattdeutsche Volksmärchen und Schwänke. Neumünster, 1925.
Meyer, M. de. Vlaamsche Sprookjethemas. Leuven, 1942.
Meyere, V. de. De Vlaamsche Vertelselschat. 3 vols. Antwerp, 1925—29.
Millien, A. and Delarue, P. Contes du Nivernais et du Morvan. Paris, 1953.
Mitford, A. B. F. Tales of Old Japan. 3d edition. London, 1876.
MLN = Modern Language Notes. Baltimore, 1886ff.
Moe, Moltke. Samlede Skrifter. 4 vols. Oslo, 1925 ff.
Montaiglon-Raynaud = Montaiglon, A. and Raynaud, G. Recueil général et complet de fabliaux. 6 vols. Paris, 1872—90.
Motif = Thompson, S. Motif-Index of Folk-Literature. 6 vols. Copenhagen and Bloomington, Ind., 1955—58.
MSFO = Mémoires de la Société Finno-ougrienne, Helsingfors.
MPh = Modern Philology. Chicago, 1903ff.
Munchhausen, [Baron]. Wunderbare Reisen (many editions).
Nassau, R. H. Where Animals Talk: West African Folklore Tales. London, 1914.
Neuman, Dov. Motif-index to the Talmudic-Midrashic Literature. (Indiana University Ph.D. thesis). University Microfilms, Ann Arbor, Mich., 1954.
Norlind, T. Svenska Allmogens Liv. 2d ed. Stockholm, 1952.
Nouvelles recreations et joyeaux devis (in Oeuvres francoises de Bonaventure des Périers). Vol. II. Paris, 1856.
Nouvelles de Sens (ed. E. Langlois). Paris, 1908.
Oesterley, H. Gesta Romanorum. Berlin, 1872.
O'Suilleabhain, S. Handbook of Irish Folklore. Dublin, 1942.
PaAm = Anthropological Papers of the American Museum of Natural History.
PAES = Publications of the American Ethnological Society.
Panchatantra (tr. A. Ryder). Chicago, 1925.
Panzer, F. Beowulf (Studien zur germanischen Sagengeschichte I). München, 1910.
Patch, H. R. The Other World According to Descriptions in Medieval Literature. Cambridge (Mass.), 1950.
Pauli = Johannes Pauli. Schimpf und Ernst (ed. Johannes Bolte). 2 vols. Berlin, 1924.

Penzer, N. M. The Ocean of Story: being C. H. Tawney's translation of Somadeva's Kathā Sarit Sāgara. 10 vols. London, 1923 ff.
— Poison-Damsels and other essays in Folklore and Anthropology. London, 1952.
Perbosc, A. Contes de Gascogne. Paris, 1954.
Peuckert Festschrift = Festschrift für Will-Erich Peuckert. Berlin-München, 1955.
Pierre Faifeu = Charles de Bourdigné. Le Légende de Maistre Pierre Faifeu. Paris, 1880.
Plenzat, Karl. Die ost- und westpreussischen Märchen und Schwänke nach Typen geordnet (Veröffentlichungen des volkskundlichen Archivs der pädagogischen Akademie Elbing I). Königsberg, 1927.
PMLA = Publications of the Modern Language Association of America.
Radloff = Radloff, W. Proben der Volksliteratur der türkischen Stämme Südsiberiens. St. Petersburg, 1866ff.
Rael, Juan B. Cuentos Españoles de Colorado y de Nuevo Méjico. 2 vols. Stanford University, n.d.
Randolph, Vance. The Devil's Pretty Daughter. New York, 1955.
— The Talking Turtle. New York, 1957.
— Who Blowed Up the Church House. New York, 1952.
Rattray (Ashanti) = Rattray, R. Sutherland. Akan-Ashanti Folk Tales. Oxford, 1930.
RBAE = Annual Report of the Bureau of American Ethnology.
Rittershaus, Adeline. Die neuisländischen Volksmärchen. Halle, 1902.
Roberts, W. E. The Tale of the Kind and the Unkind Girls. Berlin, 1958.
Rooth, Anna Birgitta. The Cinderella Cycle. Lund, 1951.
Rosen, G. Tuti-Nameh, das Papageienbuch. Leipzig, 1858.
Rotunda, D. P. Motif-Index of the Italian Novella. Bloomington, Ind., 1942.
Roy, Carmen. La littérature orale en Gaspésie. Musée national du Canada, Bulletin No. 134. Ottawa, 1955.
RTP = Revue des Traditions Populaires. Paris, 1886—1917.
Saintyves, P. Les Contes de Perrault et les recits paralleles. Paris, 1923.
Scala Celi = Johannes Gobii junior. Scala Celi. Lübeck, 1476.
Schmidt-Kahle = Schmidt, H. and P. Kahle. Volkserzählungen aus Palästina. Göttingen 1918.
Schoolcraft, H. R. Algic Researches. New York, 1839.
Schott, Arthur and Albert. Walachische Märchen. Stuttgart and Tübingen, 1845.
Sebeok-Nyerges = Sebeok, T. A. Studies in Cheremis Folklore. (The folktale by A. N. Nyerges). Bloomington, Ind., 1952.
Sebillot, P. Contes populaires de la Haute-Bretagne. 3 vols. Paris, 1881—82.
— Les incidents des contes populaires de la Haute-Bretagne. Vannes, 1892. (= RTP VII 411 ff, 515 ff.)
Smith, E. W. and Dale, A. The Ila-speaking People of Northern Rhodesia, vol. 2. London, 1920.
Spitta = Spitta-Bey, G. Contes arabes modernes. Paris, 1883.
Steere, E. Swahili Tales as told by the Natives of Zanzibar. London, 1922.
Swahn, J. Ö. The Tale of Cupid and Psyche. Lund, 1955.
Sydow, C. W. von. Två Spinnsagor. Lund, 1909.
Talbot, P. A. In the Shadow of the Bush. New York and London, 1912.
Tauscher Volksmärchen = Tauscher, R. Volksmärchen aus dem Jeyporeland. Berlin, 1959.
Tegethoff, Ernst. Studien zum Märchentypus von Amor und Psyche. Bonn und Leipzig, 1922.
Thien, J. Uebereinstimmende und verwandte Motive in den deutschen Spielmannsepen im Anschluss an König Rother. Hamburg, 1882.
Thomas, Northcote W. Anthropological Report on the Ibo-Speaking Peoples of Nigeria. 2 vols. London, 1913—14.

Thompson Festschrift = Studies in Folklore in honor of . . . Stith Thompson. Bloomington, Ind., 1957.
Thompson, Stith. European Tales among the North American Indians (CColl II). Colorado Springs, 1919.
— Tales of the North American Indians. Cambridge (Mass.), 1929.
— The Folktale. New York, 1946.
Tuti-Nameh. See Rosen.
Voorhoeve, Petrus. Overzicht van de Volksverhalen der Bataks. Vlissingen, 1927.
Vuk = Wuk, S. Karadschitch. Volksmärchen der Serben. Berlin, 1854.
Ward, H. L. D. Catalogue of Romances in the Department of Manuscripts in the British Museum. London, 1883, 1893. (Vols. 1 and 2 only; for vol. 3 see Herbert, J. A.).
Werner, Alice. African Mythology (The Mythology of all Races VII). Boston, 1925.
Wesselski, Albert. Die Schwänke und Schnurren des Pfarrers Arlotto. 2 vols. Berlin, 1910.
— Heinrich Bebels Schwänke. 2 vols. München, 1907.
— Die Begebenheiten der beiden *Gonnella.* Weimar, 1920.
— Der Hodscha Nasreddin. 2 vols. Weimar, 1911.
— *Märchen* des Mittelalters. Berlin, 1925.
— Mönchslatein. Leipzig, 1909.
— Die Novellen Girolamo *Morlinis.* München, n.d.
— Versuch einer *Theorie* des Märchens. Reichenberg i.B., 1931.
Wisser, W. Plattdeutsche Volksmärchen. 2 vols. Jena, 1922, 1927.
Wünsche, A. Der Sagenkreis vom geprellten Teufel. Leipzig and Wien, 1905.
Zachariae, Theodor. Kleine Schriften. Bonn and Leipzig, 1920.
Zender, M. Volksmärchen und Schwänke aus der Westeifel. Bonn, 1935.
Zong in-Sob. Folk Tales from Korea. London, 1952.
ZsEs = Zeitschrift für Eingeborenen-Sprachen.
Zs.f.Vksk. = Zeitschrift des Vereins für Volkskunde. 38 vols. Berlin, 1891—1928.
— Continued as Zeitschrift für Volkskunde. Berlin, 1929ff.

OUTLINE OF THE CLASSIFICATION OF TALES

I. ANIMAL TALES

No.		
1—99	Wild Animals	21
100—149	Wild Animals and Domestic Animals	42
150—199	Man and Wild Animals	54
200—219	Domestic Animals	66
220—249	Birds	71
250—274	Fish	80
275—299	Other Animals and Objects	80

II. ORDINARY FOLK-TALES

300—749	A. Tales of Magic	88
300—399	Supernatural Adversaries	88
400—459	Supernatural or Enchanted Husband (Wife) or Other Relatives	128
460—499	Supernatural Tasks	156
500—559	Supernatural Helpers	167
560—649	Magic Objects	202
650—699	Supernatural Power or Knowledge	225
700—749	Other Tales of the Supernatural	239
750—849	B. Religious Tales	254
850—999	C. Novelle (Romantic Tales)	284
1000—1199	D. Tales of the Stupid Ogre	346

III. JOKES AND ANECDOTES

1200—1349	Numskull Stories	374
1350—1439	Stories about Married Couples	400
1440—1524	Stories about a Woman (Girl)	423
1525—1874	Stories about a Man (Boy)	431
1525—1639	The Clever Man	431
1640—1674	Lucky Accidents	464

1675—1724	The Stupid Man	474
1725—1849	Jokes about Parsons and Religious Orders	486
1850—1874	Anecdotes about Other Groups of People	507
1875—1999	Tales of Lying	509

IV. FORMULA TALES

2000—2199	Cumulative Tales	522
2200—2249	Catch Tales	536
2300—2399	Other Formula Tales	537

V. UNCLASSIFIED TALES

2400—2499	Unclassified Tales	539

I ANIMAL TALES

WILD ANIMALS

1—69 The Fox (sometimes jackal) = the Clever Animal

1 *The Theft of Fish.* The fox plays dead; a man throws him on his wagon of fish. The fox throws the fish off and carries them away. The wolf imitates and is caught.

Motifs: K341.2 Thief shams death and steals. K371.1 Trickster throws fish off the wagon. K1026 Dupe imitates trickster's theft and is caught.

**Krohn *Bär (Wolf) und Fuchs* (JSFO VI) 46ff.; *BP II 116; *Anderson *Novelline* No. 115; *Dähnhardt IV 225, 304; Coffin *11;* Gerber 47 No. 1. — Finnish *100;* Finnish-Swedish *3;* Estonian *22;* Livonian *1;* Latvian *136;* Lithuanian *38;* Lappish *16;* Swedish *9* (Uppsala *2*, Stockholm *1*, Göteborg *2*, Lund *2*, Liungman *2*); Norwegian *3;* Danish *2;* Irish *59* (Archive *58*, Beal XIII 233); French *9;* Spanish *4;* Catalan: Amades No. 265; German *65* (Archive *62*, Merk. p. 308, Meckl. No. 8, Henssen Volk No. 113); Italian *5* (Tuscan No. [1] a, Sicilian *4*); Rumanian *1;* Hungarian *10;* Slovenian *4;* Serbocroatian *36;* Polish *25;* Russian *23;* Greek Archive *9*, Loukatos No. 1; Turkish: Eberhard-Boratav No. 5 *2*. — Franco-American *7;* West Indies (Negro) *2*. — African *5*.

1* *The Fox Steals the Basket.* The rabbit plays dead. The girl lays her basket down to pick up the rabbit. The fox steals the basket. [K341.2].
Coffin *2*. — Finnish-Swedish *1;* Latvian *14;* Slovenia (1b); India *6*. — Spanish-American: Hansen (1A*) (Puerto Rico) *1*.

1** *Rabbit (Wolf) Makes Hole in Basket* and steals cheese.
— Spanish-American: Hansen (Puerto Rico) *2*.

2 *The Tail-Fisher.* The bear (wolf) is persuaded to fish with his tail through a hole in the ice. His tail freezes fast. When he is attacked and tries to escape, he loses his tail. [K 1021].

**Krohn *Bär (Wolf) und Fuchs* (JSFO VI) 46ff.; *BP II 111;Coffin *14;* Gerber 48 No. 2; *Anderson *Novelline* Nos. 24, 65. — Finnish *156;* Finnish-Swedish *3;* Estonian *20;* Livonian *6;* Latvian *142;* Lithuanian *44;* Lappish *26;* Swedish *96* (Uppsala *30*, Stockholm *8*, Göteborg *27*, Lund *5*, Liungman *5*, misc. *19*); Norwegian *14;* Danish *10;* Icelandic *1;*

Scottish *1;* Irish *12* (Archive *11*, Beal III 240f. No. 1); French *24;* Spanish *4;* Catalan: Amades Nos. 263, 304; Dutch *1;* Flemish *8;* Walloon *1;* German *86* (Archive *83*, Henssen Jül. Nos. 438, 110, Merk. p. 308, 308, Meckl. No. 8); Italian (Sicilian *3*); Rumanian *3;* Hungarian *10;* Slovenian *6;* Serbocroatian *2;* Polish *9;* Russian: Afanasiev *18;* Greek: Loukatos No. 11; Turkish: Eberhard-Boratav No. 5 *2;* India *2;* Japanese. — Franco-American *6;* Spanish-American: Hansen (Puerto Rico) *1;* American Negro: Dorson No. 5.

2A *The Buried Tail.* Dupe's tail is buried or hair tied. He is then attacked. [K1021.1].
*Motif K1021.1. — Spanish: Espinosa III Nos. 199—201, 204. — India *3;* Indonesia: DeVries Nos. 35, 88. — West Indies (Negro) *2.* — African *7.*

2B *Basket Tied to Wolf's Tail* and filled with stones. Wolf persuaded that it is filled with fish. [K1021.1].
— Spanish: Boggs No. 2, Espinosa III Nos. 199—204, 209, 211, 223; Greek *6.*

2C *Bear Persuaded to Jump over Fire* three times. Basket of rocks tied to his tail. He loses his tail. Cf. German: Merk. p. 310.

2D *Wolf (Bear) Persuaded to Turn in Wind* so that his tail of flax is burned.
— French *11* (Gascony) Perbosc No. 24; French-Canadian *2*, Walloon (2A*) *1;* German: Merk. p. 310; Hungarian (8') *1.*

3 *Sham Blood and Brains.* The fox covers his head with buttermilk (blood, urine, etc.) and says that his brains have been knocked out. Frightens the bear.
Motifs: K473 Sham blood and brains. K522.1 Escape by shaming death: blood and brains. K1818 Disguise as sick man. K1875 Deception by sham blood.
**Krohn *Bär (Wolf) und Fuchs* (JSFO VI) 55ff.; *Anderson *Novelline* No. 65, 66; *Dähnhardt IV, 243; Coffin *1;* Gerber 49, No. 3. — Finnish *58;* Finnish-Swedish *2;* Estonian *2;* Latvian *38;* Lithuanian *4;* Swedish *3* (Göteborg *3*); Spanish *1;* Catalan: Amades Nos. 261, 266; Flemish *1;* German *8;* Italian (Sicilian *4*, Tuscan No. 41 b); Hungarian (3 I, 3 II) *4;* Slovenian *3;* Serbocroatian *4;* Polish *26;* Russian: Afanasiev *8;* Turkish: Eberhard-Boratav No. 5 *2;* Greek *1.* — Spanish-American: Rael No. 381 (U.S. *1*).

3* *The Bear Throws Hens to the Fox.* As he throws them from the roof-beam, he falls into the room and is beaten [K1022.3]. The fox pretends to have received even worse punishment.
Finnish-Swedish *1;* Latvian *18;* Flemish *1.*

4 *Carrying the Sham-Sick Trickster.* The fox shams sickness and is carried by the wolf. Cf. Type 72.
Motifs: K1818 Disguise as sick man. K1241 Trickster rides dupe horseback.

**Krohn *Bär (Wolf) und Fuchs* (JSFO VI 59ff.); *BP II 117; *Anderson *Novelline* Nos. 27, 65, 66; Gerber 51 No. 4. — Finnish *57;* Finnish-Swedish *3;* Estonian *15;* Latvian *26;* Lithuanian *1;* Lappish *2;* Swedish *2* (Uppsala *2*); French *2;* Catalan: Amades No. 261; German *48* (Archive *46,* Meckl. Nos. 5, 16); Italian (Sicilian *4*); Hungarian *12;* Slovenian *2;* Serbocroatian *8;* Polish *1;* Russian *8;* Greek *1;* Turkish: Eberhard-Boratav No. 5 *2;* India *1.* — Franco-American *1;* Spanish-American: Hansen (Chile) *3,* (Dominican Republic) *1;* Rael Nos. 380, 381 (U.S. *2*); West Indies (Negro) *4.* — African *6.*

4* *Fox Pollutes Wolf ho is Carrying Him.* Says that cones are dropping from the trees.
Latvian *3.*

5 *Biting the Foot.* The fox to the bear, who is biting his foot: »You are biting the tree root.» The bear lets loose! [K543].
**Krohn *Bär (Wolf) und Fuchs* (JSFO VI) 62ff.; *BP II 117 n. 2; Pauli No. 743. — Finnish *54;* Finnish-Swedish *6;* Lappish *9;* Swedish *10* (Uppsala *2,* Stockholm *1,* Göteborg *1,* Lund *4,* misc. *3*); Norwegian *14;* French *11;* Spanish *1;* Catalan: Amades No. 274; German *5;* Hungarian *3;* Polish *1;* Russian: Andrejev; Greek *6,* Hahn No. 89, Loukatos No. 2; Turkish: Eberhard-Boratav No. 6 *3;* India *22;* Indonesian: DeVries No. 1. — Spanish-American: Hansen (Argentina) *2,* (Chile) *1,* (Dominican Republic) *1,* (Puerto Rico) *1.* — African *16.*

6 *Animal Captor Persuaded to Talk* and release victim from his mouth. Usually cock and fox, fox and wolf, or mouse and cat. [K561.1]. Cf. Type 61A.
Dargan MPh IV 39; *BP II 207; Coffin *2;* Pauli (ed. Bolte) No. 743. — Finnish *70;* Finnish-Swedish *2;* Livonian *3;* Latvian (122*D) *25,* (*242A) *4;* Lithuanian: Balys No. 239*; Lappish *4;* Swedish *1* (Uppsala *1*); Irish *2* (Archive *1,* Beal IV 204); French *31;* Spanish *1;* Flemish (6*) *3;* German *5;* Hungarian *2;* Serbocroatian *2;* Russian: Andrejev (*242 I) *1;* India *3.* — Cf. Franco-American *1;* Spanish-American: Hansen (Argentina) *1,* (Puerto Rico, 6**A) *1,* Rael No. 369 (U.S. *1*). — Literary Treatments: Chauvin II 200 No. 39; Graf, FFC XXXVIII 26ff., 39f.; Wienert FFC LVI 52.

6* *The Wolf Catches a Goose* and the fox a chicken. Fox asks wolf: »Where did you get that goose?» Wolf answers and goose flies out of his mouth. Fox avoids answering wolf and keeps chicken.
Hungarian (44*) *1.*

7 *The Calling of Three Tree Names.* The bear and the fox wager as to which can name three trees first. The bear names different varieties of the same tree. The fox wins the wager. [N51].
**Krohn *Bär (Wolf) und Fuchs* (JSFO VI) 65ff.; *Dähnhardt I 193. — Finnish *53;* Finnish-Swedish *3;* Swedish *43* (Uppsala *7,* Stockholm *1,* Göteborg *14,* Lund *4,* Liungman *3*); Norwegian *10;* German *1;* Russian: Andrejev. — American Indian (San Carlos Apache): Goddard PaAM XXIV 24. — African *1.*

8 »*Painting*» *on the Haycock*. The bear (wolf) wants to be painted like the birds. The fox persuades him to lie on a haycock and sets fire to it. [K1013.2].

**Krohn *Bär (Wolf) und Fuchs* (JSFO VI) 67ff.; *Dähnhardt IV 239; Gerber 58 No. 12. — Finnish *23;* Estonian *5;* Lappish *17;* Swedish *1* (Uppsala *1*); Russian: Andrejev; Indonesian: DeVries Nos. 72—74. — Franco-American *1;* Spanish-American: Hansen (Puerto Rico) *1;* American Negro: Harris Friends 60ff. No. 8.

8* *The Fox Trades the Burned Bones of the Bear for Reindeer.*
Lappish *17.*

8** *The Fox Summons the Animals to the Reindeer Slaughter* and scares them away.
Lappish *13.*

8**** *The Fox Burns his Eyes* and trades them for the eyes of a tree [E781.1].
Lappish *4.*

8**** *The Bear Catches a Reindeer;* the animals shoot it; the fox drives them away.
Lappish *1.*

8A *False Beauty-doctor.* The trickster pretends to make the dupe beautiful. Injures him. [K1013].

*Cosquin *Etudes* 385ff.; India: Thompson-Balys (K1013) *4;* Chinese: Graham; Indonesia: DeVries Nos. 73, 74; Eskimo (Bering Strait): Nelson RBAE XVIII 467; N. A. Indian: *Thompson *Tales* 352 n. 271, (California): Gayton and Newman 83. — African (Ekoi): Talbot 387, (Kaffir): Theal 99, (Wute): Sieber ZsEs XII 69 f., 172.

9 *The Unjust Partner.* In the field and in the stable. The bear works: the idle fox cheats the bear. [K472].

**Krohn *Bär (Wolf) und Fuchs* (JSFO VI 97ff.; *BP III 335, 363 n. 1; Dähnhardt IV 249ff. — Finnish *183;* Finnish-Swedish *6;* Estonian *2;* Lappish *1;* Swedish *28* (Uppsala *10,* Stockholm *1,* Göteborg *7,* Liungman *2*); Irish *4;* French *4;* Catalan: Amades No. 321; German *2* (Archive *1,* Henssen Jül. No. 437a); Russian: Andrejev; Greek *4* (Archive *4*); India *1.* — Spanish-American: cf. Hansen **74F (Puerto Rico) *4;* West Indies (Negro) *3.* — African *8.*

9A *In the Stable the Bear Threshes.* The fox pretends to hold up the roof so that it will not fall on the bear's head. [K1251.1].
Swedish *4* (Uppsala *4*).

9B *In the Division of the Crop the Fox Takes the Corn,* the bear the more bulky chaff [K171.1]. At the mill the fox's grain makes a different sound from the bear's [K171.2]. Cf. Type 1030.
Serbocroatian *1.*

9C *In Cooking Dinner the Fox's Porridge Is Light,* the bear's black. At dinner the fox steals a spoonful of bear's porridge and lets bear taste it. The bear believes the fox's porridge is as bad as his own. [K471].
Swedish *1* (Uppsala *1*).

10* *The Fox Forces the Bear upon Weak Ice;* the bear drowns [K893].
Lappish *1.*
10** *The He-goat Pushes the Fox into the Lake* [K892].
Lappish *1.*
10*** *Over the Edge.* Fox, bear, and wolf lie sleeping close to the edge of a precipice. The fox crowds the others over the edge. [K891.5.2].
Norwegian (10*)*2,* Solheim *1.*

15 *The Theft of Butter (Honey) by Playing Godfather.* The fox (the hen) pretends that he has been invited to be godfather and steals the butter stored by him and the bear (the cock) for the winter. He smears butter on the mouth (tail) of the sleeping bear.
Motifs: K372 Playing godfather. K401.1 Dupe's food eaten and then blame fastened on him.
**Krohn *Bär (Wolf) und Fuchs* (JSFO VI) 74ff.; *BP I 9; Dähnhardt IV 241; Gerber 52 No. 5; *Coffin *16;* Beckwith MAFIS 238. — Finnish *48;* Finnish-Swedish *6;* Estonian *20;* Livonian *2;* Latvian *77;* Lithuanian *3;* Lappish *6;* Swedish *23* (Uppsala *8,* Stockholm *1,* Göteborg *6*); Norwegian *12;* Danish *2;* Icelandic *3;* Irish *16* (Archive *13,* Beal III 339ff., XX 3f. No. 1, IV 204ff.; French *50;* Spanish *4;* Catalan: Amades No. 269; Dutch *2;* Flemish *5;* Walloon *1;* German *41* (Archive *39,* Henssen Volk No. 112, Meckl. No. 5); Rumanian *1;* Hungarian *2;* Slovenian *8;* Serbocroatian *5;* Russian: Andrejev *5,* Afanasiev *16;* Greek: Archive *3,* Argenti-Rose I 530ff., Loukatos No. 2, Hahn II 89; Turkish: Eberhard-Boratav Nos. 6, 16 *3;* India *1.* — Franco-American *27;* Spanish-American: Hansen (Puerto Rico) *1,* Rael No. 402 (U.S. *1*); Cape Verde Islands: Parsons MAFLS XV (1) 66 n. 1, 359 n. 1; West Indies (Negro) *20;* American Negro: Dorson No. 1. — African *5.*

15* *The Fox Entices the Wolf away from his Booty* and eats it himself [K 341]. Finnish-Swedish *1.*
15** *The Cock Entices the Jay from his Booty* [K 341]. Then he eats it himself, Flemish*2.*

20 *Animals Eat One Another Up.* The fox persuades them to begin with the smallest. [K1024]. Cf. Type 231*.
**Krohn *Bär (Wolf) und Fuchs* (JSFO VI) 81ff.; Coffin *1.* — Finnish *48;* Estonian *3;* Norwegian *1;* Irish *5.* — Franco-American *1;* West Indies (Negro) *1.*

20A *The Animals are Caught in a Pit.* To eat one another up. (Cf. Type 20).
Finnish *10;* Finnish-Swedish *1;* Estonian *9;* Livonian *1;* Latvian *62;* Lithuanian *4;* Hungarian *7;* Slovenian *1;* Russian: Afanasiev *12;* Turkish: Eberhard-Boratav Anlage No. C 7.

20B *An Old Man is Caught in a Trap and Dies.* The animals carry his body home, eat him up, and have nothing left to eat.
Finnish *5;* Russian: Andrejev.

20C *The Animals Flee in Fear of the End of the World* or of a war. A leaf has fallen into the sea or a nut has fallen on the cock's head. [J1812]. The big ones eat the small ones. Cf. Type 2033.

BP I 237 n. 1; Taylor JAFL XLVI 78. — Finnish *32;* Estonian *12;* Lithuanian *4;* Latvian *31;* Swedish 2 (Uppsala *1*); Norwegian *13;* Danish *3;* Scottish *3* (Archive 2, Campbell-McKay No. 4); Catalan: Amades No. 298; German *14;* Hungarian *7;* Russian: Andrejev *2;* Greek: Loukatos No. 1; Turkish: Eberhard-Boratav No. 20.

20D* *Cock and Other Animals Journey to Rome to become Pope.* Fox invites them into his den where he eats them after each has sung. The sparrow will sing only before an open window. Escapes. [B296.1, K563].
Danish *1*; Polish (84) *1.*

20E* *The Animals Leap across a River.* The hare, the wolf, and the bear fall into it with some of their legs — and get out again. The fox rushes in with all his legs and is drowned.
Latvian (20*E) *4.*

21 *Eating his own Entrails.* The fox persuades the wolf (bear) to do so [K1025]. Usually with Type 20.
**Krohn *Bär (Wolf) und Fuchs* (JSFO VI) 85; *Anderson in Tauscher *Volksmärchen* 187; *Gerber 58, No. 14. — Finnish *10;* Estonian *12;* Latvian *30;* Lithuanian *7;* Hungarian *15;* Slovenian *1;* Russian: Afanasiev *12;* Greek *1;* India *3;* Indonesian: DeVries No. 16. — African *1.*

21* *The She-fox Declares she is Eating her own Brains.* The wolf, wanting to get his brains out, strikes his head against a tree. [K1025.1].
Latvian *5*; Lithuanian (*21A) *5.*

23*. *Fox (Man) Induces Wolf (Bear) to Impale Himself.*
Hungarian: Berze Nagy (23*) *3*; Serbocroatian *2.*

30—35 The Rescue from the Pit

30 *The Fox Tricks the Wolf into Falling into a Pit.* Race. [K1171].
Finnish *16;* Estonian *3;* Lithuanian *2;* Latvian (*30) *8;* Irish *2;* German *2;* Hungarian (30^I, 30^{II}, 30^{III}) *3;* Serbocroatian *2;* Russian: Afanasiev *1*, Andrejev. — Franco-American *1.* — African *1.*

31 *The Fox Climbs from the Pit on the Wolf's Back* [K652].
Finnish *40;* Finnish-Swedish *1;* Estonian *5;* Livonian *2;* Latvian *32;* Lappish *1;* Swedish *1* (Uppsala *1*); Irish *19;* German *2;* Hungarian *3;* Slovenian *1;* Russian: Andrejev; India *5;* Indonesian: DeVries No. 4. — African *1.* — Literary Treatment: Wienert FFC LVI 52 (ET 119), 97, 108, 114, (ST 117, 206, 250).

31* *The Fox (Birds) Pulls the Wolf Out of the Pit.*
Hungarian: Kovács (31B*) *2.*

32 *The Wolf Descends into the Well in one Bucket and Rescues the Fox in the Other* [K651].
*BP III 192 n. 3, IV 320; Fischer-Bolte 213; *Dähnhardt IV 230f.; Krappe. Bulletin Hispanique XXXIX 43; *Coffin 5. — Finnish *32;* Finnish-Swedish *1;* Swedish *5* (Uppsala *2*, Liungman *1*, misc. *2*); Danish

3; Irish *1;* French *5;* Spanish *2;* Catalan: Amades No. 263; Flemish *6;* Walloon *1;* German *5* (Archive *4*, Meckl. No. 9); Italian (Tuscan [cf. 41b]); Hungarian *2;* Slovenian *1;* Russian: Andrejev; Greek: Argenti-Rose I 578f. — Spanish-American: Hansen (Chile) *1.* — Literary Treatment: Chauvin III 78 No. 57.

32* *The Fox Persuades the Wolf that Beef is not Suitable for a Christening.* The wolf who is going to the hens falls into a well.
Latvian *3.*

33 *The Fox Plays Dead and is Thrown out of the Pit and Escapes* [K522].
*BP II 120 345. — Finnish *41;* Estonian *9;* Latvian *2;* Lithuanian *4;* Irish *105;* German *1;* Serbocroatian *1;* Russian: Andrejev; Greek *7*, Loukatos Nos. 3, 4; Turkish: Eberhard-Boratav No. 5 V, Anlage C 7; Indonesian: DeVries No. 5. — African *4.*

33* *Fox Overeats in Cellar;* thrown on dunghill and escapes. Cf. Type 41.
Irish *11.*

33** *Fox Overeats, is Caught, Feigns Death,* escapes in boat to island.
Irish *20.*

34 *The Wolf Dives into the Water for Reflected Cheese* [J1791.3].
*Christensen DF XLVII 217f. No. 78; Clouston *Noodles* 44; *Dähnhardt IV 230ff.; Köhler-Bolte I 107. — Latvian *2;* Swedish *13* (Uppsala *4*, Stockholm *1*, Liungman *2*); Danish *4;* Irish *11;* English *6;* French *4;* Spanish *4*, (*64) *1*, Espinosa III Nos. 206ff.; Catalan: Amades No. 276; Flemish (32*) *3;* German *4* (Archive *3*, Meckl. No. 7); Hungarian *1;* Slovenian *4;* Serbocroatian *8;* Polish (11) *1;* Turkish: cf. Eberhard-Boratav No. 237 ½. — Franco-American *2;*Spanish-American:Hansen (Puerto Rico) *3*, Rael Nos. 371, 374—76, 379—381; West Indies (Negro) *3;* American Indian: Thompson *Tales* 295 n. 81. — African *2.* — Literary Testament: Wienert FFC LVI 64 (ET 270), *105 (ST 178).

34A *Dog Drops his Meat for the Reflection.* Crossing the stream with the meat in his mouth he sees his reflection; thinking it another dog with meat he dives for it and loses his meat [J1791.4] Cf. Types 92, 1168A, 1383.
*Pauli (ed., Bolte) No. 426; Chauvin II 85; Bødker *Exempler* 275 No. 13; Wienert FFC LVI 64 (ET 270), *105 (ST 178); Aesop (Halm No. 233, Jacobs 199 No. 3); Crane *Vitry* 140 No. 18; *Scala Celi* 19a No. 111. — Spanish Exempla: Keller; Livonian (201') *1;* India: Thompson-Balys (J1791.4) *1;* Africa (Zulu): Callaway 357 (cf. J1791.3).

34B *Wolf Drinks Water to Get Cheese.* Fox puts stopper in him to keep water from escaping but takes it out when they come to a tavern.
Spanish (64*) *1;* Polish (11) *1.*

34B* *Hare Asks Enemy where he has Found Cheese.* Enemy tells him to tie rope around his neck, fasten rock to it, and jump into pond. Hare does as told and disappears.
Spanish-American: Hansen (34**A) (Dominican Republic) *1.*

35A* *The Fox Asks the Wolf for Meat,* but gets nothing. In the evening the fox breaks into the wolf's house and steals the meat.
Latvian (**35) *3.*

35B* *Fox Gets Bait from Trap by Luring Wolf into it* [K1115.1].
Latvian (*35) *2;* Lithuanian (35*) *3;* German: Plenzat p. 6; Serbocroatian *1;* Russian: Andrejev (30*).

35C* *Fox and Hedgehog.* »No other justice than that of the stomach.» [U31.1].
Rumanian (35*) *1.*

36 *The Fox in Disguise Violates the She-Bear.* The she-bear is caught in a tree-cleft or hole in the hedge. To avoid later recognition the fox covers himself with soot and is taken for the pastor. Variant: the hare, the she-fox.

Motifs: K521.3 Disguise by painting (covering with soot, etc.) so as to escape. K1384 Female overpowered when caught in tree cleft (hole in hedge).

****Krohn *Bär (Wolf) und Fuchs* (JSFO VI) 89ff.; *Gerber 53 No. 5A. — Finnish *14;* Livonian (2015') *1;* Latvian *4;* French *2;* Russian: Andrejev; Turkish: Eberhard-Boratav No. 1 V *4;* Indonesian: DeVries No. 45; India *3.*

37 *Fox as Nursemaid for Bear.* Search for a nursemaid (or mourning-woman). Fox takes service and eats up the young bears. [K931].

****Krohn *Bär (Wolf) und Fuchs* (JSFO VI) 93ff.; *Dähnhardt IV 247; Gerber 54 No. 6; Aarne FFC XIII 80. — Finnish *54;* Finnish-Swedish *1;* Estonian *8;* Lithuanian *1;* Norwegian *1;* German *2;* Polish *1;* Russian: Afanasiev *10;* India: Thompson-Balys (K931) *3;* Indonesian: DeVries No. 23; Chinese: Eberhard FFC CXXX 19ff. — African *30.*

37* *The Fox as Shepherd.* A woman seeks a shepherd. Tries voices. The wolf and the bear are rejected, the fox accepted. [K934].
Latvian *3;* Norwegian *1.*

38 *Claw in Split Tree.* The fox (or man) persuades the bear to stick his claw in the cleft of a split tree [K1111]. Cf. Type 151.

*BP I 68, II 99 n. 1; *Dähnhardt IV 231ff.; Coffin *2.* — Finnish *17;* Estonian *3;* Latvian *4;* Lithuanian *1;* Lappish *1;* Swedish *8* (Uppsala *2,* Stockholm *2,* misc. *4*); Norwegian *9;* Danish *1;* Irish *28;* French *4;* Catalan: Amades No. 328; Flemish *2;* Dutch: *Volkskunde* (1956) 123; German *2* (Archive *1,* Meckl. No. 6); Italian (Trieste); Pinguentini No. 13; Hungarian *5;* Slovenian *4;* Polish *3;* Russian: Andrejev; Turkish: Eberhard-Boratav No. 13 *1,* Giese *Türkische Märchen* 273; Indonesian: DeVries No. 9; India *1.* — Spanish-American: Hansen (Puerto Rico) *1,* Rael No. 398 (U.S. *1*); American Negro: Harris Nights 33 No. 7. — Oceania (New Britain): Dixon 195 n. 30. — Literary Treatment: Chauvin II 86 No. 20, III 77.

39 *The Bear Pulls Mountain Ashes apart so that the Fox's Old Mother can Get Berries.* The fox eats the berries himself. [K461.1].
Finnish *1;* Russian: Andrejev.
(*Carrying the Tree;* see Type 1052).
(*The Crop Division;* see Type 1030).

40 (formerly 40*) *The Fox Rings the Bell.* The bear eats a horse which has a bell tied around his neck. The fox rings the bell. [K1114].
Finnish *1;* Serbocroatian *1;* Russian: Andrejev No. 40.

40A* *Wolf Has Tail Attached to Bell.* Rings alarm. Cf. Type 160***.
French *3.*

40B* *Bear Persuaded to Have New Tail Made by Blacksmith.* It is of glowing iron.
RTP XXII 326. — French *5,* French Canadian *1.*

41 *The Wolf Overeats in the Cellar.* The fox persuades the wolf to enter a cellar (smokehouse or kitchen) and steal food. The wolf eats so much that he cannot escape through the hole he has entered by. He is killed. [K1022.1]. Cf. Types 33*, 33**.
*BP II 109 (Grimm No. 73); Coffin *3;* *Anderson *Novelline* Nos. 27, 65, 66; Dähnhardt IV 232. — Estonian *1;* Livonian *2;* Latvian *10;* Lithuanian *4;* Swedish *2* (Lund *1,* misc. *1*); Danish *2;* Irish *15;* French *26;* Spanish *1;* Catalan: cf. Amades Nos. 259, 264; Flemish *2;* Walloon *2;* German *99* (Archive *93,* Henssen Volk No. 111, Henssen Jül. No. 437b, Meckl. No. 14A and B, No. 5, Merk. p. 308); Italian (Tuscan *2*); Hungarian *9;* Slovenian *4;* Serbocroatian *1;* Russian: Andrejev *1;* Greek: Hahn *2,* Argenti-Rose I 576, Loukatos No. 6; Turkish: Eberhard-Boratav No. 1 *4;* India *1.* — Franco-American *6;* Spanish-American: Hansen **74S (Puerto Rico) *1;* Cape Verde Islands: Parsons MAFLS XV (1) 16 n. 3; West Indies (Negro) *1.* — Literary Treatment: Wienert FFC LVI 60 (ET 226).

41* *Fox in the Orchard.* Has overeaten and must fast six days so as to get back through the hole.
Rumanian (35 I*).

41** *Fox Persuades Wolf to go Help Priest so as to Get Bread as Reward.* Chased away.
Greek (2*) *3.*

42* *Laughter Contest between the Fox and the Bear* [K87].
Finnish *1;* Russian: Andrejev (42).

43 *The Bear Builds a House of Wood; the Fox, of Ice.* In summer the fox wants to drive the bear out of his house [J741.1]. Cf. Types 81, 1097, 1238.
**Krohn *Bär (Wolf) und Fuchs* (JSFO VI) 109ff.; *Gerber 54 No. 7.
— Finnish *1;* Estonian *2;* Latvian *8;* Lithuanian *2;* Slovenian *10;* Russian: Afanasiev *10;* India *3.*

44 *The Oath on the Iron.* In a dispute between the fox, the wolf, and the bear concerning the theft of their winter supplies, the fox denies the guilt and swears by touching iron (a trap). The bear follows his example but hits the iron so hard that his paws are caught. [K1115].
*Köhler-Bolte I 408f.; Gerber 61 No. 17. — Latvian (122*C) *1;* French *2;* Italian: (cf. Tuscan [1]a); Slovenian *6;* Serbocroatian *8.* — Franco-American *1;* Spanish-American: cf. Hansen **167A (Chile) *1.*

44* *The Wolf Claims the Sheep's Fleece.* The fox rescues the sheep causing the wolf to kiss the trap as a symbol of his oath. The wolf falls into it.
Latvian (122*C) *41;* Russian: Afanasiev *1.*

47A *The Fox (Bear, etc) Hangs by his Teeth to the Horse's Tail, Hare's Lip.* The bear is persuaded to bite the seemingly dead horse's tail. Is dragged off by the horse. The hare asks the destination and laughs till his lip splits.

Motifs: K1047 The bear bites the seemingly dead horse's tail. A2211.2 Rabbit laughs: cause of hare-lip.

**Krohn *Bär (Wolf) und Fuchs* (JSFO VI) 70; *BP III 75 (Grimm No. 132); Coffin *6;* Dähnhardt II 22f., 492, IV 98f., 235. — Finnish *90;* Finnish-Swedish *4;* Estonian *15;* Latvian *16;* Lappish *2;* Swedish *12* (Uppsala *4,* Stockholm *1,* Göteborg *2,* misc. *5*); Norwegian *7;* Irish *19;* Spanish: Espinosa III Nos. 163—167, 172—174; Catalan: Amades cf. No. 289; Dutch *1;* German *33* (Archive *31,* Henssen Jül No. 439, Henssen Volk No. 11); Italian (Tuscan cf. [205]); Hungarian *3;* Polish *2,* cf. (46) *3;* Russian: Andrejev (47); Greek (47A*) *7;* India *3.* — Franco-American *2;* Portuguese-American (Brazil): Camara Cascudo p. 131; West Indies (Negro) *6;* American Negro: Harris *Nights* p. 6 No. 2; American Indian (Chickasaw): Speck JAFL XXVI 292. — African *2.*

47B *The Horse Kicks the Wolf in the Teeth.* The wolf was not expecting an attack from that end [K1121].

*BP III 77; Baum *MLN* XXXVII 350ff.; Crane *Vitry* 147f. No. 33, 197 No. 152. — Latvian *22;* Lappish (47*) *1;* Danish *4;* French *4;* German: Merk. p. 308; Hungarian *1;* Slovenian *2;* Polish *13.* — Spanish-American: Rael No. 396 (U.S. *1*); West Indies (Negro) *6.*

47C *Fox Ties One End of the Rope around Wolf's Neck and other End to Horns of Cow They Intend to Eat.* Cow drags wolf to house where man skins it [K1022.2].

Spanish: Espinosa III, 272—276, Boggs (47C*) *1;* Polish *1.* — Spanish-American: Hansen (Chile) *2.*

47D *The Dog Imitating a Wolf Wants to Slay a Horse.* He asks the cat: »Is my back bristled, etc.?« The horse kills him with a kick.

Lithuanian (*106) *7;* Russian: Afanasiev (*119) *4;* India *2.*

47E *Ass's Charter in his Hoof.* The ass absents himself from the parliament of beasts. The lion sends the fox and the wolf to summon him. He pleads his charter of exemption and invites the fox to read it in his hoof. (Cf. K551.18.)

Baum MLN XXVII 350; Herbert III 53. — Rumanian (122 D) *2;* Literary Treatments: Crane *Vitry* 147 No. 33; Italian Novella: Rotunda.

47* *Horse Kicks Wolf and Fox.* Wolf bites horse's nose and fox catches his tail. They finally kill horse. A hunter passes and shoots wolf and fox.
Hungarian: Berze Nagy (163*) *1.*

48* *The Bear who Went to the Monkey for the Gold Chain.* The fox flatters the monkey into giving him a gold chain, food, etc. The bear (wolf) goes, tells the truth about what he sees and gets nothing. [J815].
Norwegian (48**) *3.*

49 *The Bear and the Honey.* The fox leads the bear to a wasp-nest. [K1023]. Cf. Type 1785C.
 Lappish (49*) *3;* Swedish *2* (Uppsala *1,* Liungman *1*); Norwegian (49**) *2;* Danish: DF XLV 138 No. 16; German *1;* Slovenian *3;* Polish *1,* (176) 1. — Spanish-American: Hansen (Argentina 51**A) *2,* (Peru) *1,* Rael Nos. 373, 376, 381 (U.S. *3*); American Indian (Menomini): Skinner JAFL XXVI 75.

49A *The Wasp Nest as King's Drum.* Two animals steal food together but one eats it all. The clever animal pursued by the dupe sits beside a waspnest which he says is the king's drum he has been ordered to guard. The dupe insists upon playing the »drum» and is badly stung, etc.
 I. *Characters:* (a) tiger, (b) hare, (c) monkey, (d) fox or jackal, (e) man.
 II. *Incidents:* (a) The wasp nest said to be drum, (b) Snake said to be flute, scepter, etc., (c) Prickly plants said to be king's sugar cane, (d) Top of well, etc., said to be king's bed. [J1761.6, K1023.1, K1078, K1056, K1023.5].
 India *9;* Java: Dixon 188 n. 5; Indonesian: DeVries No. 12.

50 *The Sick Lion.* The fox pretends to seek a remedy for the lion; advises him to skin the wolf [K961].
 **Krohn *Bär (Wolf) und Fuchs* (JSFO VI) 21ff. — Finnish *2;* Latvian *10;* Lithuanian *4;* Irish *2;* French *2;* Spanish *3;* Catalan: Amades No. 275; Walloon *1;* German *1;* Italian (Sicilian *2*); Slovenian *2;* Serbo-croatian *1;* Russian: Andrejev; Greek: Hahn *2;* Indonesian: DeVries No. 39. — Spanish-American: Rael No. 367 (U.S. *1*); Cape Verde Islands: Parsons MAFLS XV (1) 57 n. 20. — African *5.* — Literary Treatment: Chauvin III 78; Graf FFC XXXVIII 20ff.; Pauli (ed. Bolte) No. 494; Wienert FFC LVI 47, 50 (ET 55, 102), 99, 100 (ST 129, 133).

50A *Fox Sees all Tracks going into Lion's Den but none coming out* [J644.1].
 Latvian *4;* Lithuanian *1;* Catalan: Amades No. 313; India *1.* — West Indies (Negro) *1;* North American Indian *1.* — African *2.* — Literary Treatment: Aesop (Halm No. 246, Jacobs No. 73).

50B *Fox Leads Ass to Lion's Den but is Himself Eaten* [K1632].
 Spanish: Espinosa III Nos. 210f.

50C *The Ass Boasts of Having Kicked the Sick Lion.* The fox praises him for his courage.
 Latvian (*51) *1.*

50* *Lion Holds Celebration for all Animals with Horns.* Dog makes horns and wears them. Cat cannot get horns to stay on. Cat tells lion that not all animals attending celebration have real horns. Dog is discovered and thrown into water.
 Spanish-American: Hansen (Puerto Rico) *1.*

51 *The Lion's Share.* The ass divides booty equally between himself, the fox, and the lion. The lion eats the ass. The fox then divides: gives the lion meat and keeps bones. [J811.1].

Crane *Vitry* 198—200 Nos. 156—158. — Flemish (50*) *1;* Slovenian *4;* Greek: Loukatos No. 7. — Franco-American *1;* Spanish-American: Hansen (Argentina 51**A) *1;* American Negro: Harris *Nights* 338 No. 58. — African *6.* — Literary Treatment: Wienert FFC LVI 59 (ET 213), 110 (ST 220).

51A *Fox Refuses to be Mediator.* Lion decides to abandon lioness because of her bad odor. Ass, hog, and fox as judges. Ass says she has bad odor: lioness slaps him. Hog says she has not: lion slaps him. Fox says he has a bad cold and cannot smell. [J811.2]. Cf. Type 68*.

*BP IV 360 No. 13. — Latvian (**50) *4;* Spanish: Boggs (52*) *1;* Catalan: Amades No. 313; Slovenian *1.*

51* *Bear Will Eat Butter.* Fox suggests to bear that pot of butter they have found be divided. Bear tells him to be quiet; he will eat the butter.
Finnish *3.*

51** *Wolf Takes Best Parts.* Hedgehog seeks a butcher who will cut up the slain deer. Hare and fox unsuccessful; wolf takes all best parts for himself.
Serbocroatian *2.*

51*** *Fox as Umpire to Divide Cheese* between bear's quarreling sons; eats all the cheese [K452]. Cf. Types 518*, 926 D.
Hungarian *2.*

52 *The Ass without a Heart.* The ass as toll-gatherer is killed by the lion for asking for toll. The fox eats the ass's heart. When the lion asks for it, the fox replies that the ass could have had no heart since he was such a fool as to ask the lion for toll. [K402.3].

**Keidel »Die Eselherz Fabel» Zs. f. vgl. Litgsch. n. ser. VII No. 58; Gaster *Exempla* 229 No. 244; Penzer V 130 n. 1; *Chauvin II 99 No. 58; Bødker *Exempler* 299 No. 63. — Spanish Exempla: Keller (K402.3); Jewish: *Neuman (K402.3); India *4.*

53 *Reynard the Fox at Court.* The fox is summoned to appear before the court of justice, but he does not come and laughs at the messengers. When he is caught at last and about to be hanged, he escapes again.
Graf FFC XXVIII 13ff. — Latvian (*50A) *7.*

53* *The Fox and the Hare Hear Screaming.* The hare runs away, the fox goes to look and finds a frog.
Latvian *4.*

55 *The Animals Build a Road (Dig Well).* The fox as overseer punishes lazy animals. [A2233.1, Q321].
*Dähnhardt III 321ff., 323; *Motifs A2233.1.1, A2233.1.2, A2233.1.3 (Estonian, Livonian, Lithuanian). — Finnish *30;* Russian: Andrejev. — American Indian (Cherokee): Mooney RBAE XIX 272.

56 *The Fox through Sleight Steals the Young Magpies.*
L. Sudre *Les sources du Roman de Renard* (Paris, 1893) 301—10; Gerber 61 No. 18. — Livonian *1;* Irish *5;* Spanish (57*) *1;* Turkish: Eberhard-Boratav No. 9 *1.* — Spanish-American: Rael No. 369 (U.S.) *1;* West Indies (Negro) *1.* — African: Meinhof 67.

56A *The Fox Threatens to Push Down the Tree.* The crow gives good advice to the magpies. The fox avenges himself, plays dead, and catches the crow. [K751].
*BP I 579; Dähnhardt IV 279. — Finnish *39;* Finnish-Swedish *1;* Estonian *6;* Latvian *40;* Lithuanian *9;* Lappish *9;* Swedish *1* (Göteborg *1*); Spanish: Espinosa III 258f.; German *13;* Hungarian *6;* Cheremis: Sebeok-Nyerges (K1788); Slovenian *1;* Russian: Andrejev; Turkish: Eberhard-Boratav No. 9. — African *7.* — Literary Treatment: Chauvin II 112 No. 81; Bødker *Exempler* 306 No. 82.

56B *The Fox Persuades the Magpies into Bringing their Young into his House.* The young foxes eat the young magpies. The magpies avenge themselves, with the help of the dog, who plays dead and kills the fox.
Motifs: K811. Victim lured into house and killed. K1788. Fox threatens to catch bird, who feeds him her young as appeasement. K911. Feigning death to kill enemy.
Finnish *1;* Estonian *1;* Latvian *9;* Swedish *3* (Uppsala *1*, Göteborg *1*, Lund *1*); Danish *9;* French *22;* Catalan: Amades Nos. 318, 319; Hungarian *3;* Russian: Andrejev *Ukraine 5*, Afanasiev *1.* — Franco-American *1.* — African *4.*

56C *The Jackal as Schoolmaster.* The jackal will educate the children of the crocodile if they are left in his care. The jackal eats one child each day; but by showing the crocodile the same child over and over, convinces him all is well. [K931.1, K1822.2].
India *5.*

56D *Fox Asks Bird what She Does when Wind Blows.* Bird puts head below breast and fox seizes her. [K827.1].
Dähnhardt IV 279. — German (61) *2.* — West Indies (Negro) *1.* — African *2.* — Literary Treatment: Chauvin II 112 No. 81.

56A* *Fox Plays Dead and Catches Bird.* (This episode alone). [K911].
Hungarian: Kovács (1 I—1 III) *4.*

56B* *The Fox Drinks and Laughs.* The bird feeds the fox, gives him something to drink and makes him laugh when the fox threatens to eat the bird's young. The bird perches on the barrel on the man's head. They come to strike the bird, but hit the barrel and the man.
Latvian *21.*

56C* *The Fox Sits in a Pit and Threatens to Eat the Bird's Young,* if the bird will not help him to get out, to feed him, to give him drink, to make him laugh and to heal him.
Latvian (56*C) *32* (+ Latvian *248A) *21.*

56D* *Fox Promises to Help Hen and Chickens.* He baptizes chickens to gain confidence of hen. She sends chickens to his school and he eats them. When she comes to see their progress, he eats her. Cf. Type 37.
Spanish-American: Hansen (Argentina) *1.*

56E* *Fox Forces Another Animal to Procure food and Pleasure for him* but finally is betrayed into hands of threshers and beaten.
Danish *1.*

57 *Raven with Cheese in his Mouth.* The fox flatters the raven into singing. He drops his cheese and the fox gets it. [K334.1].

*Crane *Vitry* 172f. No. 91; Basset RTP VI 244; Krappe Bulletin Hispanique XXXIX 17 No. 11. — Finnish *24;* Finnish-Swedish *3;* Livonian *1;* Latvian *18;* Lithuanian *3;* Lappish *2;* Swedish *8* (Uppsala *6,* Göteborg *1,* misc. *1*); Danish *1;* Irish *10;* Spanish *1;* Catalan: Amades No. 308, cf. No. 340; Dutch *1;* German *7* (Archive *6,* Henssen Volk No. 107); Hungarian *1* (+ 239* *1*); Slovenian *1;* Russian: Andrejev, Andrejev *Ukraine 5;* India *2;* Korean: Zong in-Sob 29 No. 12. — Franco-American *3;* American Indian: Thompson *C Coll* II 451. — African *1.* — Literary Treatment: Chauvin III 76 No. 49; Wienert FFC LVI (ET 121), 97 (ST 115); Halm *Aesop* No. 204.

57* *The Fox Flatters the Cock, the Squirrel and others.*
Latvian (**57) *4.*

58 *The Crocodile Carries the Jackal.* The jackal, who wants to eat fruit or carrion on the other bank, persuades a crocodile to carry him across the river by saying he will find a bride for the crocodile. He makes a dummy and, safe back on shore, sends the crocodile to that.
India *7.*

58* *Birds Break Rope and Let Fox Fall to Earth* [K963].
Spanish-American: Hansen (59**A, B) (Argentina) *1,* (Peru) *1.*

58** *Fox Asks Thrush to Teach him to Sing.* Thrush consents if fox will bring needle and thread. Thrush sews up snout of fox and he sings. While hunting quail he shouts too loud and breaks thread.
Spanish-American: Hansen (Argentina) *1,* (Chile) *1,* (Peru) *1.*

59 *Fox and the Sour Grapes.* Pretends that the grapes he cannot reach are sour. [J871].
*Liungman SSF III 23, 425. — Latvian (***64) *6;* Swedish (GS 59) *4;* Spanish: Boggs (66*A) *1;* Hungarian: Kovács (66*) *1;* India (64 IIa) *4.* — Literary Treatment: Aesop (Halm No. 33, Jacobs No. 31).

59* *The Jackal as Trouble-Maker.* The jackal carries false challenges, etc., between the lion and the bull so that they kill each other [K2131.2].
India *4.*

60 *Fox and Crane Invite Each Other.* The crane (heron) has his food in a deep dish, the fox his on a flat plate. The crane injures his beak. [J1565].
*Crane *Vitry* 202 No. 165; *Anderson *Novelline* No. 10; Gerber 68. — Finnish *25;* Finnish-Swedish *1;* Estonian *1;* Livonian *1;* Latvian *17;* Lithuanian *1;* Swedish *6* (Uppsala *3,* Lund *1,* misc. *2*); Danish *5;* Irish *6;* Spanish *1;* Catalan: Amades Nos. 315, 517; German *4;* Russian: Afanasiev *2;* Greek *5,* Loukatos No. 8. — Spanish-American: Hansen (Puerto Rico) *1,* Rael Nos. 377, 378 (U.S.) *2;* West Indies (Negro) *1;* American Indian: Thompson C Coll II 450. — African *10.* — Literary Treatment: Halm Aesop No. 34; Wienert FFC LVI 54 (ET 123).

61 *The Fox Persuades the Cock to Crow with Closed Eyes.* Captures him. Often followed by: the cock persuades the fox to ask a blessing before eating him. Cf. Types 6, 122.

Motifs: K721. Cock persuaded to crow with closed eyes. K551.1 Respite from death granted until prayer is finished.

*BP II 207; Coffin *2;* *Anderson *Novelline* Nos. 20, 67; Dargan MPh IV 39. — Estonian *1;* Latvian *2;* Swedish *8* (Uppsala *3,* Göteborg *1,* misc. *4*); Norwegian *5;* Scottish *1;* Irish *19* (Archive *17,* Beal IV 204f. No. 7, X 38; French *9;* Spanish: Espinosa III 225, 258; Catalan: Amades No. 309; Flemish *2;* Walloon *2* + *61B, *61C *3;* German *2;* Italian (Tuscan 2); Slovenian *7;* Serbocroatian *4;* Russian: Andrejev *2;* Turkish: Eberhard-Boratav No. 2 *2;* Japanese. — Literary Treatment: Chaucer's Nuns Priest's Tale; Graf FFC XXXVIII 26ff.; Wienert FFC LVI 52 (ET 122), 97 (ST 116).

61A *Fox as Confessor.* Fox persuades cock to come down from a tree and confess sins to him. When cock comes down, fox seizes him. Cock begs to be released and tempts fox by saying that he will lead him to a feast of a rich bishop. Fox believes it, and the cock flies away and mocks him. Cf. Type 6.

*Anderson in Tauscher *Volksmärchen* 184. — Polish (84) *1;* Russian: (61 I*) *10;* Greek: Loukatos Nos. 15, 16.

61B *Cat, Cock, and Fox live together.* When cat goes away into the forest, fox carries cock off. Cock screams for help; cat rescues him. By playing music cat lures young foxes from den and kills them. [K815.15].

Lithuanian (*133) *40;* Lappish (133*) *1;* Serbocroatian *1;* Russian: (*61 II) *15.*

62 *Peace among the Animals — the Fox and the Cock.* The fox tries to beguile the cock by reporting a new law establishing peace among the animals. Dogs appear and the fox flees saying that the dogs have not yet heard of the new law. [J1421].

**Lancaster »The Peace Fable» PMLA XXII 33; Coffin *3;* Espinosa III 321 No. 225; *BP II 207 (Grimm No. 86). — Finnish *3;* Estonian *2;* Livonian *1;* Latvian *13;* Norwegian *1;* Danish *1;* Irish *23;* French *4;* Spanish *36* (Espinosa); Catalan: Amades No. 322, cf. 311; German *6* (Archive *5,* Meckl. No. 10); Slovenian *6;* Serbocroatian *2;* Polish *2;* Russian: Afanasiev *2;* Greek *2,* Loukatos Nos. 9, 16; Turkish: Eberhard-Boratav No. 2 *2;* India *2.* — Franco-American *2;* Spanish-American: Rael No. 370 (U.S.); American Indian: Thompson C Coll II 450. — African *4.* — Literary Treatment: Halm Aesop No. 225; Jacobs Aesop 214 No. 59; Graf FFC XXXVIII 26ff.; Wienert FFC LVI 52, 98.

62* *Forbidden to Sit in Trees.* Fox tries to convince grouse of a new law forbidding them to sit in trees.

Latvian *13;* Lithuanian (*62A) *2.*

63 (formerly 63*) *The Fox Rids himself of Fleas.* He lets himself sink somewhat in water with a bundle of hay. The fleas gather on the haybundle. Finally the fox dives under the water. [K921].

Estonian *1;* Catalan: Amades No. 316; Flemish *1;* Danish *1;* Hungarian *1;* Polish (63*) *2;* Russian: Andrejev (63*); Slovenian *12;* India *2.* — U.S.A. (Texas): Boatright et al. *Mesquite and Willow* (1957) 107.

64 *Tailless Fox Tries in Vain to Get Foxes to Cut off Tails* [J758.1]. Cf. Type 1707.
Aesop (Jacobs No. 65, Halm No. 5); *Basset RTP XXVI 267. — Rumanian (16*) *3;* India *1.*

64* *The Jackal Domineers Over the Tigers* [K1715.14, J873.1, J873.2].
I. (a) The jackal steals food from the tiger cubs. (b) The tiger pursues him, is caught between two trees, or in a hole, and dies (cf. Type 36). (c) The jackal overawes the tigress and tries to take the place of the tiger.

II. (a) On the hunt, he is unable to kill deer but says they were too small, etc. (b) Falls into river and claims to be fishing, etc. (cf. Type 67).
India *6.*

64** *The Fox Puts his Head in the Sand* to protect himself from the rain.
Latvian (**64) *2.*

65 *The She-fox's Suitors.* The widowed she-fox proves her faithfulness by rejecting suitors who do not resemble her deceased husband. [T211.6].
*BP I 362 (Grimm No. 38); Taylor JAFL XLVI 78; *Schmidt Zs f. Vksk XLVII 177ff. — Norwegian *3;* Danish *2;* German *34* (Archive *33,* Meckl. No. 27); Hungarian: Berze Nagy 65* *1;* Russian: Andrejev.

65* *The Fox Fries a Beetle by the River.* The fire is on the opposite bank. The fox says of the beetle, »It is quite good, only too crisp.« Cf. Type 1262.
Latvian *22.*

66A »*Hello, house!*« The Cave Call. Monkey (jackal) pretends that his house always answers him: thus discovers his enemy. [K607.1, K1722].
**M. Bloomfield JAOS XXXVI 58; Louisiana Creole: Fortier MAFLS II 110; Mexican Spanish: Espinosa JAFL XXIV 419ff.; Panchatantra (tr. Ryder) III 15, 361; Indonesian: DeVries No. 31; India *7.* — Spanish-American: Hansen **74B (Chile) *2,* (Dominican Republic) *1,* (Puerto Rico) *7;* American Indian (Oaxaca, Mexico): Boas JAFL XXV 208; American Negro (Georgia): Harris Friends 142 No. 19; Jamaica: Beckwith MAFLS XVII 247 No. 23; West Indies: Flowers 517. — African (Zanzibar): Bateman 41.

66B *Sham-dead (Hidden) Animal Betrays Self.* I. The jackal says that dead animals wiggle their tails, etc. The crocodile moves his tail. II. The crocodile in hiding hears a bell the jackal has found. Thinking it a goat, the crocodile cries out for the goat to go away. III. Crocodile hiding in piles of leaves makes them rustle when jackal says leaves always rustle. [H248.2.1, K607.2.1, K607.3, K607.3.2, K1860].
India *12.* — U.S.: Baughman (K607.3) *1;* American Negro (Georgia): Harris Remus 53 No. 11; West Indies: Flowers 517ff.

66* *The Fox Seeks Food.* Tries the courage of the animals.
Lappish *2;* Swedish (Lund) *3;* German *8.*

66** *The Fox Caught in the Bakehouse.* »I should be caught if there were not an escape at the back.» When his captors run to the rear, he escapes in front [K542.1]. The wolf tries the same trick and is caught [K1026].
Flemish (66*) 2.

66A* *The Fox buys himself a Pipe* and goes into the barn to smoke. The hay begins to burn. The fox extinguishes the fire with his tail, and singes himself.
Latvian (*66) 6.

66B* *Fox Eats Puma's Meat and Goes to Sleep.* Puma wakes him and devours him.
Spanish-American: Hansen (66**C) 1.

67 *Fox in Swollen River Claims to be Swimming to Distant Town* [J873].
Spanish: Boggs (66B*) 1; India (64 IIb) 3. — Literary Treatment: Aesop (Halm No. 30).

67* *Fox as Seaman.*
Lappish 1.

67** *Fox Caught by Butcher.* Throws butcher's smock on the fire and escapes. [K634.1].
Flemish 1.

67*** *Measuring the Land with the Tail.* Fox saves himself in this manner from pursuing dogs and escapes into the wood.
Livonian (67') 1.

67A* *Game Taken from Fox's Bag and Trash Substituted.* [Cf. K526].
Spanish-American: Hansen **67CDE (Peru) 3, (Argentina) 1, (Puerto Rico) 2.

68 *The Jackal Trapped in the Animal Hide* [F929.1, J2136.6.1, K565.2, K952.1.1, K1022.1.1, K1973].
I. *Entering the Elephant.* (a) An elephant lets his friend the jackal enter his body to drink water. The jackal eats the internal organs and the elephant dies. The jackal is trapped in the carcass. (b) A jackal eats its way into a carcass which it finds and is trapped inside when the skin dries.
II. *Jackal and the God.* (a) A god passes and the jackal challenges him to a rain-making contest. The god sends rain, the carcass swells, and the jackal escapes. (b) The jackal pretends to be a god and frightens people into bringing sacrifice and pouring water over the carcass.
India 12.

68A *The Jug as Trap.* The animal puts his head into the jug in which there is some food; he cannot get it out of the trap and is caught or killed.
Polish (163) 1.

68B *The Fox Drowns the Pot.* Puts the pot on his head and is himself drowned. [J2131.5.7].
Latvian (*64) 20; Lithuanian (*66) 3; Russian: Andrejev (64) 3; Greek (2B*) 5.

68* *The Fox Jeers at the Fox-trap.* Is caught. [J656]. Cf. Livonian 68**.
Lappish 1.

68** *The Wolf and the Fox Punished by the Siren.* The fox praises the siren's children, who are very ugly. The wolf says that they are ugly, and is punished. [J815]. Cf. Type 51A.
Latvian 1; Flemish 1.

69*   *The Race of the Fox and the Polar Bear.*
        Lappish *1.*
69**   *Escape by Asking a Last Kiss.* Uses the opportunity to attack adversary. [K551.10].
        Spanish (69*) *1.*

70—99 Other Wild Animals than the Fox

70   *More Cowardly than the Hare.* The hare finds one (sheep, fish, frog, etc.) who is afraid of him and laughs till his lip splits. [J881.1, A2342.1]. Cf. Type 47A.

       Dähnhardt IV 97ff. — Finnish *95;* Finnish-Swedish *4;* Estonian *27;* Livonian *1;* Latvian *51;* Lithuanian *5;* Lappish *1;* Swedish *18* (Uppsala *13,* Stockholm *1,* Göteborg *1,* misc. *3*); Norwegian *5;* Danish *1;* Irish *9;* Flemish *5;* Walloon (*70A) *1;* German *8* (Archive *7,* Henssen Jül. No. 444); Italian (Sicilian *1*); Rumanian (92*) *2;* Slovenian *2;* Polish *5;* Russian: Afanasiev *2;* Greek: Loukatos No. 11; Turkish: Eberhard-Boratav No. 18. — Literary Treatment: Halm Aesop No. 237; Jacobs Aesop No. 15; Wienert FFC LVI 63 (ET 245), 116 (ST 266).

70*   *The Hare Is Dressed up as a Hunter,* but the dog chases him.
        Latvian (**70) *4.*

71   *Contest of Frost and the Hare.* The hare lies on the frozen snow and says, »Oh, how warm!» [H1541.1].

       Dähnhardt III 23. — Finnish *48;* Estonian *4;* Latvian *11;* Slovenian *2;* Russian: Andrejev.

71*   *When it Rains, the Hare Creeps under the Spear-grass* and is glad not to be wet by the rain.
        Latvian (*71) *2.* Also known in Russia.

72   *Rabbit Rides Fox A-courting.* The fox is the favorite suitor of the girl the rabbit wants. The rabbit tells the girl that the fox is his horse. She refuses to believe him. She agrees to marry if he will ride to her house. He persuades fox to carry him — usually by feigning lameness — and wins the girl. (Sometimes told of human beings.) [K1241, K1241.1]. Cf. Type 4.

       *Parsons MAFLS XV (1) 66; Beckwith MAFLS XVII 235; Coffin *16;* Gerber 51 No. 4. — Latvian *3;* Norwegian (72*) *1;* Indonesian: DeVries No. 40. — Franco-American *8;* Spanish-American: Hansen (Dominican Republic) *3,* (Puerto Rico) *9;* American Negro (See K1241.1); West Indies (Negro) *17;* American Indian: Thompson *C Coll* II 440, 447 (L).

72*   *The Hare Instructs his Sons.* »You have as large eyes as I have.» [J61].
        Finnish *1;* Estonian *3;* cf. Lappish (94*) *1.*
72**   changed to Type 81.
72A*   *Dupe Digs till he Dies of Exhaustion* [K1061].
        Spanish: Boggs *1.*
72B*   *Fox to Hare: Why do you Jump over the Path?* — Because I cannot get under it.
        Finnish *4.*

72C* **Hare in Trap Complains** that he must stay there all day. The fox tells him he is there for the rest of his life.
Finnish *5*.

73 **Blinding the Guard.** The rabbit, imprisoned in a hollow tree, induces his guard to look up at him. He spits tobacco juice into the guard's eyes and blinds the guard, and thus effects his escape.
*Motif K621; Dähnhardt IV 184; Coffin *10;* Beckwith MAFLS XVII 240. — Spanish: Espinosa, Jr. No. 2 *2;* Slovenian *1;* India *1*. — Franco-American *2;* Spanish-American: Hansen (Argentina) *2*, (Chile) *2*, (Colombia) *2*, (Venezuela) *1;* West Indies (Negro) *3;* American Indian: Thompson *C Coll* II 440—441. — African *10*.

74* changed to Type 156A.

74A* **Lion and Dog.** For a whole year the lion lives quite peacefully in his cage together with a dog. When the dog dies, the lion mourns and soon dies too.
Latvian (*74) *2*.

74B* **Tiger Gives Dance** for all animals. He recites a couplet telling all guests to enter cooking vessel. Rabbit recites couplet telling guests to depart.
Spanish-American: Hansen 74**I (Puerto Rico) *3*.

74C* **Rabbit Throws Coconut.** Rabbit is eating coconuts in tree. Wolf asks rabbit to throw one down. Rabbit throws one that almost kills wolf. Cf. Type 22.
Spanish-American: Hansen 74**M (Puerto Rico) *2*, (Chile) *1*, (Peru) *1*.

74D* **Rabbit's Tail as Stick.** Rabbit digs hole on river bank and jumps leaving tail exposed. Tiger thinks tail is stick and throws rabbit across river.
Spanish-American: Hansen 74**O (Puerto Rico) *6*.

75 **The Help of the Weak.** The mouse gnaws the net and liberates the captured bear (fox, lion).
Motifs: B371.1. Lion spares mouse: mouse grateful. Later releases lion from net. B363. Animal grateful for rescue from net.
Crane *Vitry* 194 No. 145. — Finnish *3;* Livonian (75*) *1;* Latvian *16;* Irish *3;* Catalan: Amades No. 331; Dutch *1;* Flemish *1;* Hungarian *1;* Slovenian *4;* Russian: Andrejev; Greek: Loukatos No. 7; India *5*. — West Indies (Negro) *5*. — African *11*. — Literary Treatment: Halm Aesop 256; Jacobs Aesop 203 No. 11; Wienert FFC LVI (ET 215, 113, 355).

75* **Wolf Waits in Vain for the Nurse to Throw away the Child.** She has threatened to throw the child to the wolf. [J2066.5].
Wienert FFC LVI 68 (ET 320), 102 (ST 156); Aesop (Halm No. 275, Jacobs 211 No. 46). — Finnish *5;* Japanese: Ikeda [J2066.5].

76 **The Wolf and the Crane.** The crane pulls a bone from the wolf's windpipe. When he asks for payment the wolf says, »That you were allowed to take your beak from my throat is payment enough.» [W154.3].
Crane *Vitry* 192 No. 136. — Finnish (73*) *1;* Estonian (73*) *3;* Latvian *4;* Lithuanian *1;* Irish *2;* Catalan: Amades No. 291; German *3;* Russian: Andrejev. — West Indies (Negro) *3*. — African *2*. — Literary Treatment: Wienert FFC LVI 54 and note 3 (ET 145), (ST 517); Halm Aesop No. 276, Jacobs Aesop 200 No. 5; Italian Novella: Rotunda (W154.3).

76* *Vulture and Sparrow.* Have caught a hare together. »Be glad that I don't eat you.» [J811.1.1].
Rumanian (243 II*) *1.*

76A* *The Wolf Hurts his Paw.* The raven wants to peck out the wolf's eyes. The wolf catches the raven and is about to eat him. The raven promises to heal the wolf's paw, if he is set free. He does so.
Latvian (*76) *6.*

77 *The Stag Admires Himself in a Spring.* He is proud of his horns, ashamed of his legs. In flight his horns are caught and the dogs overtake him. [L461].
Crane *Vitry* 254 No. 274. — Estonian (75*) *1;* Latvian *5;* Lithuanian *2;* Swedish *1* (Stockholm *1*); Irish *1;* Catalan: Amades No. 287; German *3;* Slovenian *3;* Russian: Andrejev. — Literary Treatment: Halm Aesop No. 128; Jacobs Aesop No. 25; Wienert FFC LVI 65 (ET 265), 140 (ST 465).

77* *The Wolf Confesses his Sins to God* before his death. He has eaten a thousand sheep, five hundred hogs, a hundred cows, and fifty horses.
Livonian (77') *1;* Swedish *2* (Uppsala *1*, Göteborg *1*).

78 *Animal Allows himself to be Tied to Another for Safety.* Carried to his death. [K713.1.2].
*BP III 75 n. 2; Spanish: Espinosa Jr. No. 28; India: *Thompson-Balys (K713.1.2); Indonesian: DeVries No. 87.

78A *Animal Allows Himself to be Tied so as to Avoid Being Carried off by Storm* [K713.1.1].
Spanish-American: Hansen (74**A) (Argentina) *1*, (Peru) *1*, (Puerto Rico) *14*, (Venezuela) *1;* American Negro (Georgia): Harris Friends 12ff. No. 2, Harris Nights 325ff. No. 56; West Indies: Flowers 523f.; Cape Verde Islands: *Parsons MAFLS XV (1) 324 n. 2; Jamaica: Beckwith MAFLS XVII 233 No. 1. — African (Wute): Sieber ZsEs XII 215.

78* *The Mill Speaks to the Wolf.* To the lazy wolf the mill seems to say: »It is good to live in Riga.» The wolf sets out for Riga. Now he hears the mill say: »It is the same there as here» — and returns.
Latvian (*78) *2.*

79* *The Wolf Dominates the Hare.* The Wolf orders the hare to dress himself, to put on boots, to get a coat made, to buy a cap and to feed the wolf. The hare gets nothing. He hatches a young hare out of an egg. The wolf devours them both.
Latvian (*79) *2.*

80 (formerly 80*) *The Hedgehog in the Badger's Den.* Befouls it so that badger abandons it.
*Henssen Jül. 321 No. 442. — Livonian (80') *1;* Irish *1;* Catalan: Amades No. 865; German Archive *2*, Henssen Jül. No. 442; Italian (Sicilian) *1*.

80A* *Who Gets the Beehive.* Badger: »I was a hundred years old when grama grass first grew.» Crane: »My daughter was a hundred years old when grama grass first grew.» Wolf: »I am only eight years old, but we shall see who gets the beehive.»

Latvian (*86) *1;* Spanish: Boggs FFC XC 31 No. *80, Espinosa III Nos. 268—270, Espinosa Jr. Nos. 26, 27.

81 (formerly 72**) *Too Cold for Hare to Build House in Winter*, not necessary in summer: must go without house. [A2233.2.1]. Cf. Types 43, 1238.
 *Dähnhardt *Natursagen* III 203; Wienert FFC LVI 64 (ET 269). — Finnish *2;* Lithuanian (72*) *1;* Swedish *21;* Hungarian (205*B) *1;* Serbocroatian *1;* Polish (72A) *1;* Russian: Andrejev *1.* — American Negro (Michigan): Dorson No. 13.

85 *The Mouse, the Bird, and the Sausage* keep house together each with appropriate duties. When they exchange roles, all goes ill. [J512.7].
 *BP I 204 (Grimm No. 23), III 558. — Latvian *7;* Danish *4;* French *4;* Catalan: Amades Nos. 239, 240, 241; German *12;* Italian (Tuscan [2022 d, e]); Polish *1;* Russian: Andrejev; Turkish: Eberhard-Boratav No. 21; Indonesian: DeVries No. 135. — Franco-American *1.*

87A* *The Bear Stands on a Heap of Wood* and pelts the wolves with logs.
 Latvian (*87A) *36.*

87B* *Why Squirrel Is Gay.* The wolf catches the squirrel and asks him why he is always so gay. The squirrel begs to be set free before answering the question. He climbs up a tree and says that the wolf cannot be gay because of his wicked heart.
 Latvian (*82) *7.* Also known in Russia.

88* *The Bear Climbs on to a Tree* to get at the honey, but he fails.
 Latvian (*88) *2.*

90 *The Needle, the Glove, and the Squirrel.* The needle at first has little success; receives blows from the others. Finally it slips into an elk's stomach and kills the elk. [L391].
 Finnish *6;* Russian: Andrejev; Turkish: Eberhard-Boratav No. 18 *1.*

91 *Monkey (Cat) who Left his Heart at Home.* Monkey when caught for his heart (as remedy) makes his captor believe that he has left his heart home. Is released. [K544].
 Dähnhardt IV 1ff. — Latvian (***288) *1;* Hungarian (Kovács 122^{II}/$_1$, 122^{II}/$_2$, Berze Nagy 136*) *2;* Jewish: Neumann (K544); India *3;* Indonesian: DeVries No. 3, Dixon 193; Japanese: Ikeda (K544); Philippine: Fansler MAFLS XII 374 No. 56. — Spanish-American: Hansen (**283) (Puerto Rico) *1.* — African (Zanzibar): Bateman 17 No. 1. — Literary Treatments: Chauvin II 99 No. 57; Penzer V 127 n. 1; Buddhist myth: Malalasekera II 852; *Bødker 298 No. 62.

91* *The Wolf Carries off a Pig.* The lion takes it.
 Flemish *1.*

91A* *Wolf and Wildboar.* Latter asks to cry out once. Wildboar comes to help. [K551.3.4]. Cf. Types 312, 959*.
 Bolte Zs. f. Vksk. IX 87. — Rumanian *1;* Flemish *1;* India *1.* — Literary Treatment: Pauli (ed., Bolte) No. 87.

91B* *The Wolf's and the Bear's (She-fox's) Wedding* [B281.3].
 Lithuanian (*91) *6.*

91C* *The Death of the Gnat.* Bugs are fighting and gnat dies. Others dismember gnat until nothing is left.
Hungarian (91*) *18.*

92 *Lion Dives for his own Reflection.* The hare, sent to be the lion's dinner, says he has been detained by a more powerful enemy and shows the lion his own reflection in a well. The lion leaps in and is drowned. [K1715.1]. Cf. Types 34, 34A, 1168A, 1336, 1383.
*Anderson in Tauscher *Volksmärchen* 193. — India *15;* Indonesia: DeVries No. 17. — American Negro (Georgia): Harris Friends 134 No. 18, (Virginia): Parsons JAFL XXXV 264 No. 12. — Literary Treatments: *Penzer V 49 n. 1; Chauvin II 88 No. 25.

92A *Hare as Ambassador of the Moon.* Hare claiming to be ambassador of moon shows elephant the moon irritated in a spring. Elephant is persuaded that the moon is angry. [K1716].
*Penzer V 101 n. 1; Chauvin II 96 No. 49; Panchatantra III 2 (tr. Ryder 308); Bødker Exempler 294 No. 54; Spanish Exempla: Keller; India: Thompson-Balys (K1716).

93 *The Master Taken Seriously.* She-fox and her children do not flee from the vineyard until owner begins in earnest to root it out. [J1031]. (Also told of other animals.)
*Pauli (ed. Bolte) No. 867. — Latvian (*113) *2,* (*244) *4;* Lithuanian (*848) *3;* Rumanian (93*) *1;* Hungarian *3.* — Literary Treatment: Halm Aesop No. 210.

95* *The Wolf and the Reindeer.*
Lappish *1.*

96* *When the Hare Was Married.*
Norwegian *4.*

WILD ANIMALS AND DOMESTIC ANIMALS

100 *The Wolf as the Dog's Guest Sings.* Has drunk too much. Sings in spite of the dog's objections. Is killed. [J581.1].
*BP II 111 (Grimm No. 73). — Finnish *27;* Estonian *10;* Latvian *72;* Lithuanian *31;* Irish *2;* French *1;* Spanish *2;* Catalan: Amades No. 282, cf. No. 262, 286; German *1;* Russian: Andrejev *Ukraine 15,* Afanasiev *6;* Greek: Loukatos No. 16. — Spanish-American: Rael No. 376 (U.S.); American Indian (Jicarilla Apache): Goddard PaAm VIII 236 No. 44.

100* *The Parrot Abuses the Dog.* He is taken and imagines to himself that they are going with him to the fair. He is killed.
Flemish *1.*

101 *The Old Dog as Rescuer of the Child (Sheep).* A farmer plans to kill a faithful old dog. The wolf makes a plan to save the dog. The latter is to rescue the farmer's child from the wolf. The plan succeeds. The wolf

in return wants to steal the farmer's sheep. The dog objects and loses the wolf's friendship. [K231.3].
*BP I 424 (Grimm No. 48). — Finnish *11;* Estonian *8;* Latvian *81;* Lithuanian *28;* Swedish *1;* Irish *5;* Catalan: Amades No. 282; Flemish *1;* German *10;* Hungarian *3;* Slovenian *8;* Serbocroatian *3;* Polish *11;* Russian: Andrejev *Ukraine 16,* Afanasiev *2;* Japanese: Ikeda. — American Indian (Jicarilla Apache): Goddard PaAm VIII 236 No. 44.

101* *The Dog Wants to Imitate the Wolf.* The old dog, the helper of the wolf, wants to imitate it; he attacks the horse and perishes from his hooves. Cf. Type 47A.
Polish *4.*

102 *The Dog as Wolf's Shoemaker.* He demands material for the shoes and then successively eats up the cow, hog, etc. furnished him. [K254.1].
*Parsons MAFLS XV (1) 10, 11. — Finnish *10;* Finnish-Swedish *2;* Estonian *2;* Latvian *25;* Lithuanian *7;* German *2;* Hungarian *1;* Polish *11;* Russian: Andrejev. — Franco-American *1;* Cape Verde Islands: Parsons MAFLS (1) 10, 11.

103 *The Wild Animals Hide from the Unfamiliar Animal.* The cat shrieks; the bear falls out of the tree and breaks his backbone. [K2324].
*BP I 425 (Grimm No. 48); Gerber 77 No. 37. Finnish *156;* Finnish-Swedish *8;* Estonian *23;* Livonian *2;* Latvian *8;* Lithuanian *37;* Lappish *2;* Swedish *1* (Liungman *1*); Danish *2;* Spanish *2;* German *15* (Archive *14,* Henssen Jül. No. 437b); Italian; Rumanian *8;* Hungarian *5;* Slovenian *5;* Serbocroatian *27,* (Istrian) No. 1; Russian: Andrejev *Ukraine 16,* Afanasiev *16;* Greek *3;* Turkish: Eberhard-Boratav Nos. 15, 45 III, Anlage C 2.

103A *The Cat as She-fox's Husband.* Frightens the other wild animals invited by her. [B281.9.1].
Latvian (*103A) *43;* Lithuanian (*103A) *8.*

103A* *Cat Claims to be King and Receives Food from other Animals* who flee from him in fright.
Hungarian: Kovács (103') *3.*

103B* *The Cat Goes Hunting* with the huntsman. The tom-cat remains beside the shot stag, while the huntsman goes for a cart. The tom-cat licks the stag's blood. The other animals, thinking that he is a mighty beast, bring him food.
Latvian (*103B) *7* (continues as Type 103).

103C* *Old Ass Turned out by Master Meets Bear or Lion.* They have various contests. Ass frightens his opponent with dung called cannonballs, or by braying. This marvelous animal is described to fox or wolf. Cf. Types 1060, 1114.
Catalan: Amades No. 329.

103D* *Flight of the Animals.* Half-skinned goat frightened by man's (woman's) breaking wind.
Rumanian *5.*

104 *The Cowardly Duelers.* War between the domestic and wild animals. The cat raises her tail; the wild animals think it is a gun and flee. [K2323]. Cf. Type 222.

*BP I 425 (Grimm No. 48); Coffin *1;* Dähnhardt IV 209. — Finnish *6;* Finnish-Swedish *4;* Estonian *8;* Latvian *71;* Lithuanian *7;* Swedish *3* (Liungman *1,* misc. *2*); Danish *2;* Spanish: Espinosa III Nos. 246—248; Flemish *1;* German *25* (Archive *22,* Henssen Jül. No. 437b, Merk. p. 308, Meckl. No. 12); Hungarian *1;* Slovenian *4;* Polish *5;* Russian: Andrejev *Ukraine 6.* — Franco-American *1;* American Indian: Thompson *C Coll* II 439ff.

105 *The Cat's Only Trick.* She saves herself on a tree. The fox who knows a hundred tricks is captured. [J1662].
*BP II 119 (Grimm No. 75). — Finnish *25;* Finnish-Swedish *3;* Latvian *6;* Lappish *1;* Swedish *6* (Uppsala *3,* Göteborg *2,* Liungman *1*); Norwegian *1;* Danish *4;* Irish *9;* French *5;* Spanish *1;* Catalan: Amades No. 320; German *18* (Archive *17,* Meckl. No. 13); Hungarian *1;* Slovenian *4;* Polish *3;* Russian: Andrejev; India *1.* — Spanish-American: Hansen (Argentina) *2,* (Dominican Republic) *1;* West Indies (Negro): Beckwith MAFLS XVII 239. — African *2.*

105* *The Hedgehog's only Trick.*
Greek *5,* Hahn No. 91, Laographia I 322ff.

105A* *Cat's Curiosity and Single Trick.* Cat wants to know what a predicament is. Cat is given suitcase and sent to plains where there are no trees. He opens suitcase and dog jumps out. The Lord places a tree for cat to climb. Cat does not want to know any more about a predicament. (Sometimes told of monkey and his desire for misery.) Cf. Type 326.
Spanish-American: Hansen (*218A, B), (Dominican Republic) *3,* (Puerto Rico) *2.*

105B* *Fox and Hawk.* Hawk plays dead. Thereby fox is also saved from the hunters. Better simple than sevenfold understanding.
Rumanian (331*) *2;* Slovenian *2.*

106 *Animals' Conversation* (imitation of animal sounds). Cf. Types 206, 236*, 2075.
**Aarne FFC IX. — Hungarian (106*) *2,* (106 I) *1;* Slovenian *2;* Serbocroatian *1.*

106* *The Wolf and the Hog.* The hog disregards advice; at night he goes out beyond the gate. The wolf eats him.
Russian: Afanasiev *3.*

107 *Dog Leader Fears Defeat Because his Forces are of Different Breeds.* Wolves are all of one kind. [J1023].
*BP II 545f.; *Dähnhardt IV 104f., 290. — Lithuanian (*107) *2.* — Literary Treatment: Wienert FFC LVI 47 (ET 57), *48 (ET 68), 112 (ST 230); Aesop (Halm No. 267).

110 *Belling the Cat.* The mice buy a bell for the cat but no one dares tie it on her. [J671.1].
**Baum MLN XXXIV 462; *Pauli (ed. Bolte) No. 694; Dähnhardt *Natursagen* IV 145ff. — Finnish *5;* Finnish-Swedish *3;* Estonian *3;* Livonian *1;* Latvian *6;* Swedish *3* (Stockholm *1,* misc. *2*); Irish *7;*

Catalan: Amades No. 549; Italian *3* (Tuscan *2*, Sicilian *1*); Hungarian *2;* Russian: Andrejev; Greek: Loukatos No. 4; Turkish· Eberhard-Boratav No. 41 *1*. — Spanish-American: Rael No. 497 (U.S.). — Literary Treatment: Wesselski *Hodscha Nasreddin* I 260 No. 213; Wesselski *Arlotto* II 226 No. 93; Aesop (Halm No. 15, Jacobs No. 67); Pauli (ed. Bolte) No. 634.

110* *Is the Cat at Home?* The mouse asks the cricket if the cat is at home. The cricket says, »No,» but that is a lie. The cat devours the mouse.
Latvian *24*.

111 *The Cat and the Mouse Converse.* The mouse tells the cat a tale. The cat answers, »Even so, I eat you up.» [K561.1.1].

Finnish *3;* Norwegian *25;* Danish *21;* Flemish *1;* Russian:Andrejev; Greek: Loukatos Nos. 2, 3; Indonesian: DeVries No. 96. — Franco-American *1*.

111A *Wolf Unjustly Accuses Lamb and Eats him.* When all the lamb's defenses are good the wolf asserts the right of the strong over the weak. (Usually accused of stirring up water lower in stream.) [U31].

*Crane *Vitry* 191 No. 135. — Latvian (*128) *4;* Russian: Andrejev; India *4;* Indonesian: DeVries No. 83. — Literary Treatment: Aesop (Halm No. 274, Jacobs No. 2); Wienert FFC LVI 50 (ET 97), 148 (ST 526); Italian Novella: Rotunda.

111A* *A Drunkard's Promise.* A drunken mouse challenges a cat to fight. The cat is about to kill him when the mouse reminds the cat that, when the cat was drunk, he had promised the mouse never to kill him. »That was a drunkard's promise,» says the cat. Kills the mouse.
Irish.

112 *Country Mouse Visits Town Mouse.* Former prefers poverty with safety. [J211.2]. Cf. Type 245.

*Anderson in Tauscher *Volksmärchen* 184; *Crane *Vitry* 199 No. 157.
— Finnish *3;* Finnish-Swedish *3;* Latvian *5;* Lithuanian *1;* Swedish *5* (Uppsala *1*, Göteborg *3*, Liungman *1*); Norwegian *2;* Danish *3;* Catalan: Amades No. 344; German *5* (Archive *4*, Meckl. No. 15); Italian (Sicilian *3*); Rumanian *2;* Hungarian *3;* Serbocroatian *2;* Polish *2;* Russian: Andrejev; Greek *1*, Loukatos No. 5; Turkish: Eberhard-Boratav No. 14 *1;* India *1*. — Chinese: Eberhard FFC CXX 15 No. 5, CXXVIII 19f. No. 3. — Spanish-American: Rael Nos. (394), 407, 408, (409) (U.S.). — Literary Treatment: Aesop (Halm No. 297, Jacobs No. 7); Wienert FFC LVI 59 (ET 208 and note 4).

112* *Mice Carry the Egg.* One mouse takes an egg between her legs, while the other pulls her into the cave by her tail.
Latvian (*112) *1*.

112** *The Mice and the Cock.* The little mice ask their mother: »Who is he that cries Doodle-do in the morning?» (The cock.) The mother answers: »That is a friend». »And he who stands in the hall and has a sword behind?» »That is an enemy». (The cat.)
Latvian (**112) *1;* (old Russian fable).

113 *Mice Choose Cat as King.*
Hungarian (113*): Kovács 2.

113A *King of the Cats Is Dead.* Cat leaves house when report is made of death of one of his companions. His master has been told to say »Robert is dead». As soon as this is said, the cat leaves. [B342].
*Boberg *Sagnet om den store Pans død,* København 1934; Taylor *Washington University Studies* X (Hum. Ser.) 60ff. — Estonian (FFC XXV 123 No. 45) *16;* Irish: Beal III 66; German (common); Czech: Tille Soupis II (2) 435f. — U.S.: Baughman (B342).

113B *The Cat as Sham Holy Man.* Cat pretends to be a holy man, enlists mice as disciples, and eats them one by one as they file by or listen to sermons. [K815.13]. Cf. Type 61.
*Anderson in Tauscher *Volksmärchen* 184; Bødker *Exempler* 306 No. 81. — Spanish Exempla: Keller (K815.13); Polish (113) *1;* Greek: Loukatos Nos. 2, 3; India 9.

113* *The Cat's Funeral.* Mice preparing to bury cat find that she is only sleeping. She kills them.
Spanish-American: Hansen (113**ABC) (Puerto Rico) *3.*

114 *Chanticleer Believes that his Crowing Makes the Sun Rise.* Disappointed when it rises without his aid. [J2272.1].
*Vossische Zeitung 17 Sept. 1910; India: *Thompson-Balys (J2272.1) *3;* N.A. Indian (Hopi): Voth FM VIII 176 No. 55. — Rostand's Chanticleer.

115 *The Hungry Fox Waits in Vain for the Horse's Lips (Scrotum) to Fall Off* [J2066.1].
Finnish *27;* Finnish-Swedish *19;* Latvian *9;* Lithuanian *1;* Swedish *12* (Uppsala *9,* Stockholm *1,* Göteborg *2*); Irish *3;* Russian: Andrejev; Greek: Loukatos No. 2.

116 *The Bear on the Hay-Wagon* (or on the horse) is mistaken for the preacher [J1762.2].
Finnish *40;* Finnish-Swedish *36;* Estonian *3;* Livonian (2015') *1;* Latvian (*87A) *36;* Lithuanian *11;* Swedish *4* (Uppsala *1,* Liungman *1,* misc. *2*); Norwegian *4;* Hungarian: cf. Berze Nagy (1322*) *1;* Russian: Andrejev.

117 (formerly 117*) *The Bear Riding the Horse* lets his claws sink into the horse's flanks. He is caught on a tree and leaves his claws in the horse's flesh. [J2187].
Finnish *15;* Swedish (Uppsala) *1;* Russian: Andrejev.

117* *A Dog Imitates a Bear (Wolf).* A dog tries to frighten a mare, by imitating a wolf: he digs up the earth with his paws, howls. The mare does not fear him and strikes him with her hoof.
Lithuanian (*106) *7;* Russian: Afanasiev (*119) *4.*

118 *The Lion Frightened by the Horse.* The horse strikes sparks with his hooves.

The wolf (bear) boasts of having eaten horses. [J2351.4]. The lion thereupon picks up the wolf to show him the horse and squeezes him to death.
Finnish *15;* Finnish-Swedish *1;* Latvian *18;* Lithuanian *20;* Irish *3;* Spanish: Espinosa Jr. No. 28; Italian (Tuscan cf. [101], Sicilian *2*); Hungarian *6;* Serbocroatian *2;* Russian: Andrejev *Ukraine 6.*

119A* *Dog's Feet Shaven.* Dog angry with hare for shaving the soles of his feet.
Dähnhardt III 129, 324; Aesop (Halm Nos. 71, 166—173. — Rumanian (131) *4;* Hungarian: Kovács (119^I A *6*, 119^I B *4*, 119^{II} *1*) *11.*

119B* *Horse's Defense against Wolves.* The horses protect themselves from the wolves by putting their foals in the middle and turning their hindquarters toward their enemies.
Latvian (**119B) *3.*

119C* *The Wolf Goes Three Times Round the Horses* and asks the dog if his eyes are red. Then he kills one horse and leaves it to the dog to feed on. The dog wants to do the same, but cannot.
Latvian (*119) *5.* Also Russian.

120 *The First to See the Sunrise.* Wager between the fox and the hog. In the contest the fox places himself on a hill facing the east; the hog in a lower place facing the high trees to the west. The sun shines on the top of the trees and the hog wins. (Sometimes told with human actors.) [K52].
Dähnhardt *Natursagen* III 150f. — Finnish *71;* Finnish-Swedish *29;* Estonian *3;* Swedish *24* (Uppsala *23*, Lund *1*); Norwegian *6;* Danish: Kristensen *Jyske Folkeminder* XIII No. 48; Irish *2* (IFC *1*, Jackson FL XLVII 285); Catalan: Amades No. 268; Russian: Andrejev; Japanese: Ikeda. — American Negro: Harris Friends 3 No. 1. — Literary Treatment: Pauli (ed. Bolte) No. 269.

120* *Mock Sunrise.* Contract is to be fulfilled at dawn. Wolf makes fire as mock sunrise. Is caught. [K1886.3].
Cape Verde Islands: *Parsons MAFlS XV (1) 6 n. 1.

120** *Wolf Announces Dawn Prematurely to Collect Debt.* The contract is to be fulfilled at daybreak. The wolf imitates the cock and crows, but is caught. [K494].
Cape Verde Islands: *Parsons MAFLS XV (1) 6 n. 1.

121 *Wolves Climb on Top of One Another to Tree.* The hog (or man) in the tree. The lowest wolf runs away and all fall. [J2133.6]. Cf. Type 1250.
*Anderson in Tauscher *Volksmärchen* 183; *BP I 40f., II 530 note 3; Köhler-Bolte I 113. — Finnish *7;* Finnish-Swedish *1;* Estonian *5;* Latvian (*121A) *75;* Lithuanian *18;* Spanish: Espinosa III 386f. No. 255 *1;* Catalan: Amades No. 290; Flemish *4;* German *1;* Hungarian *8;* Russian: Afanasiev *3;* India *8.* — Franco-American *2.*

121A* *The Wolf and the Pig Run a Race.* The loser is to have a tooth pulled out. The wolf bites off the pig's head.
Latvian (**121B) *3.*

121B* *The Wolf Chases the Sheep through a Window.* God has ordained that sheep shall be eaten by the wolf. The farmer is frightened and leaves the door open. The wolf gets the sheep.
Latvian (*121B) *1.*

121C* *The Wolf Pursues the Pig.* Both fall into a well. The wolf is killed.
Latvian (*121C) *2.*

122 *The Wolf Loses his Prey.* Escape by false plea. [K550].
Wesselski *Märchen* 250 No. 96; Coffin *1.* — Finnish *22;* Finnish-Swedish *2;* Estonian *37;* Livonian *2;* Irish *6;* French *34;* Walloon (61B*, 61C*) *2;* German *43* (Archive *40*, Merk. 308, 334, Meckl. No. 16); Italian (Tuscan [122a—e], [1003] *6*, Sicilian *3*); Hungarian *1;* Slovenian *2;* Serbocroatian *6;* Polish *2;* Russian: Andrejev *Ukraine 27*, Afanasiev *8;* Greek: Loukatos No. 10 (1). — Franco-American: *1;* Spanish-American: Hansen (122**D—122**M) (Puerto Rico) *4*, (Chile) *1*, (Venezuela) *1*, (Peru) *3*, (Paraguay) *1;* West Indies (Negro) *11.* — African *1.*

122A *The Wolf (Fox) Seeks Breakfast.* He threatens to eat various animals (the hog, the sheep, the horse, etc.). At their request he waits till the passport has been examined, the children have been baptized, and the like. He loses his feast. Cf. Type 227.
Motifs: K551. Respite from death granted until particular act is performed. K551.1. Respite from death granted until prayer is finished. K551.3.4. Wild boar given permission to squeal before wolf eats him up. Rescue arrives. K551.8. Wolf kept at door until children have been christened. K562.1. Captive trickster persuades captor to pray before eating.
*BP II 207 (Grimm No. 86); Wesselski *Märchen* 250 No. 58; Beckwith MAFLS XVII 240. — Estonian (227A) *1;* Latvian *3;* Lithuanian *5;* Swedish *28* (Uppsala *6*, Stockholm *1*, Göteborg *6*, Lund *3*); Danish *15;* French (122D) *7;* Spanish *12;* Catalan: Amades Nos. 272, 299; Italian *5* (Sicilian *3*); Serbocroatian *2;* Turkish: Eberhard-Boratav No. 11 V, 13 V, Anlage C 4, C 5. — Spanish-American: Hansen (Puerto Rico) *2;* American Negro (Michigan): Dorson No. 3.

122B *The Rat Persuades the Cat to Wash her Face Before Eating.* He escapes. [K562].
*Anderson in Tauscher *Volksmärchen* 187; Dähnhardt III 237. — Latvian *18;* Lithuanian *7;* Irish; Flemish (6**) *4;* cf. Walloon *61B; Rumanian (58*) *1;* Slovenian; India *2.* — African *5.*

122C *The Sheep Persuades the Wolf to Sing.* The dogs are thus summoned. [K561.2].
*Bolte Zs. f. Vksk. IX 87. — Danish *2;* Spanish *1;* Catalan: Amades No. 295; Flemish (6****) *1;* Serbocroatian *2;* Greek *2;* India *3.* — Spanish-American: Hansen (Puerto Rico) *2.*

122D »*Let me Catch you Better Game.*» Captured animal pretends to help captor bring more desirable victim. Escapes. [K553.1].
French (Gascony): Bladé III 203; India *2.* — American Negro (Georgia): Harris Nights 286 No. 48. — African (Kaffir): Theal 188, (Basuto): Jacottet 40. — Literary Treatment: Chauvin II 116 No. 94.

122E (formerly 123*) *Wait for the Fat Goat (Three Billy-goats Gruff).* Three goats (rams) have to pass a bridge where a troll keeps guard. He lets the two small ones pass in order to take the biggest one; but is thrown into the river [K553.2].

Norwegian (213*) *9;* Swedish: Liungman *1;* Walloon (138*) *2;* Hungarian (122') *1;* India *1.*

122F »*Wait till I Am Fat Enough.*» Captured person (animal) persuades his captor to wait and fatten him before eating him. [K553].

Spanish: Espinosa III 446; India *8.* — American Negro (Georgia): Harris Nights 366ff. No. 65 (variant); West Indies: Flowers 516. — African (Zulu): Callaway 164. — Literary Treatments: Wienert FFC LVI 53 (ET 117), 105 (ST 179); Halm Aesop No. 231.

122G »*Wash Me*» (»*Soak Me*») *before Eating* [K553.5]. I. Trickster tells captor he must be washed before captor eats him. Escapes. II. Turtle tells jackal he must be soaked in water to soften his shell.

India *5.*

122H »*Wait Until I Get Dry.*» Monkey pulled from mud by tiger asks to dry in sun before being eaten. Escapes. [K551.12].

India *3.*

122J *Ass begs Wolf to Pull Thorn out of Foot before Eating him:* kicks wolf in mouth [K566].

Wienert FFC LVI 52 (ET 115), 114 (ST 244); Halm Aesop No. 334. — Spanish: Espinosa Jr. Nos. 30, 31; Japanese: Ikeda.

122Z *Other Tricks to Escape from Captor* [K561ff.].

India *7.*

122B* *The Squirrel Persuades the Fox to Pray before Eating.* Escapes. [K562.1].

Walloon (*61B, *61C) *2.*

122D* *To Make Bird Tastier.* The fox puts the bird into the hub of a wheel to make it tastier.

Latvian (122*B) *40.*

122K* *Wolf Acts as Judge before Eating the Rams.* They are to go to the end of field and run to him. They run at him and kill him. [K579.5.1].

*Wesselski *Märchen* 251 No. 58. — Spanish: Espinosa Jr. Nos. 30, 31.

122L* *Blind Wolf Keeps Guard over a Captive Ox,* holding his legs, which are tied fast. The ox begs the wolf to free his legs, as they were tied too tightly. Then the ox gives the wolf wooden sticks to hold, instead of his feet, and runs away.

Latvian (122*F) *2.*

122M* *The Ram Runs Straight into the Wolf's Stomach.*

Latvian (122*E) *41.*

122N* *The Donkey Persuades the Wolf to Ride on his Back* to the village, because the villagers want him as their mayor. They run after him carrying sticks.

Greek *3,* Hahn No. 93.

122P* *Goat Entices Wolf to Farmhouse.* By making the wolf believe that he is wanted to

look after the herd, the goat entices him into coming near the farmhouse, and so saves herself.
Lithuanian 2.

123 *The Wolf and the Kids.* The wolf comes in the absence of the mother and eats up the kids [K971]. The old goat cuts the wolf open and rescues them [F931]. Cf. Type 333.

Motifs: K1832. Disguise by changing voice. K311.3. Thief disguises voice and is allowed access to goods (children). K1839.1. Wolf puts flour on his paws to disguise himself. J144. Well-trained kid does not open door to wolf. F913. Victims rescued from swallower's belly.

**Olrik *Folkelige Afhandlinger* I (1919) 140ff.; *BP I 37 (Grimm No. 5); Coffin *1;* Beckwith MAFLS XVII 116, 2780; *Anderson *Novelline* No. 2; *Parsons MAFLS XV (1) 21 n. 1. — Finnish *5;* Estonian *2;* Livonian *1;* Latvian *64;* Lithuanian *35;* Lappish *2;* Swedish (Uppsala) *1;* Norwegian *4* (Archive *3,* Solheim (123*) *1*); Danish: Grundtvig *Gamle Danske Minder* II 322; Irish *20;* French *52;* Catalan: Amades Nos. 279, 296, 297; Dutch *4;* Flemish *2;* Walloon (123A*, 123B*, 123C*) *3;* German *24* (Archive *22,* Merk. 321, Meckl. No. 17); Hungarian *5;* Slovenian *3;* Serbocroatian *3;* Russian *8;* Greek *9,* Loukatos Nos. 6, 22; Turkish: Eberhard-Boratav No. 8 *10;* India *1;* Chinese: Eberhard FFC CXX 19ff. No. 11, FFC CXXVIII 27ff. No. 8. — Franco-American *6;* Spanish-American: Hansen (Argentina) *1,* (Puerto Rico) *1;* Cape Verde Islands: Parsons MAFLS XV (1) 197 No. 1; West Indies (Negro) *14;* Jamaica: Beckwith MAFLS XVII 260 No. 58; American Indian: Thompson *C Coll* II 439. — African (letter from P. D. Swart, Johannesburg) *11.*

123A *Fox Buys Colt and Leaves it at Home.* Wolf changes voice and devours colt.

Hungarian: Berze Nagy (124*) 1; Serbian: Vuk 264 No. 50, Krauss *Sagen und Märchen der Südslaven* I 28 No. 8.

123B *Wolf in Sheep's Clothing Gains Admission to the Fold* [K828.1]. Cf. Type 214B.

*Herbert III 36ff.; Hervieux IV 222 No. 51; Jacobs Aesop 209 No. 39; Wienert FFC LVI 45 (ET 35), 68 (ET 325), 96 (ST 100); Halm Aesop No. 376. — Latvian (*166A) *3;* Spanish Exempla: Keller (K828.1); Catalan: Amades No. 542.

123* changed to 122E.

124 *Blowing the House In.* The goose builds a house of feathers; the hog one of stone. The wolf blows the goose's house in and eats her. Cannot blow down the hog's house. Finally he is allowed to enter. He is tricked into the chimney (or churn) where he is burned up.

Motifs: Z81. Blowing the house in. K891.1. Intruding wolf tricked into jumping down chimney and killing himself. J2133.7. Intruding wolf falls down chimney and kills himself.

*BP I 40f.; *Jacobs *English* (London 1908); Coffin *11;* *Taylor JAFL

XLVI 78; *Anderson *Novelline* Nos. 11, 26, 72—78. — Danish *3;* Irish *3;* English *1;* French *47;* Spanish *3;* Catalan: Amades Nos. 292, 294, 298, 355, cf, 267; German *8;* Italian (Trieste: Pinguentini No. 21); Hungarian: Berze Nagy (23*) *3;* Slovenian *1;* Serbocroatian *1;* Turkish: Eberhard-Boratav No. 8 III, cf. 17 *3.* — Japanese: Ikeda. — Franco-American *11;* English-American: Baughman *7;* Spanish-American: Hansen (Cuba *3*); West Indies (Negro) *3;* American Negro (Georgia): Harris Nights 38 No. 8, (South Carolina): Parsons JAFL XXXIV 17, (Virginia): Parsons JAFL XXXV 267.

124A* *Pigs Build Houses of Straw, Sticks and Iron.* Wolf destroys the first two by breaking wind. On the third try, he tears his skin. The shoe-maker repairs it but leaves no vent. When the error is corrected, the explosion destroys the shoe-maker and his house.
Waloon *1.*

125 *The Wolf Flees from the Wolf-head.* The sheep have found a sack and wolf-head. They make the wolf believe that they have killed a wolf. He flees in terror. [K1715.3]. Cf. Type 1149.

*BP I 237ff., especially 254 (Grimm No. 27); Coffin *1.* — Finnish *212;* Irish: Beal I 90—94; French *1;* Catalan: Amades Nos. 300, 301; Russian *6;* Turkish: Eberhard-Boratav No. 11 *5.* — Chinese: Eberhard FFC CXX 14 Nos. 3, 10, CXXVIII 19ff. No. 3, 25ff. No. 7. — Spanish-American: Hansen (Puerto Rico *1*); West Indies (Negro) *2.* — African *12.*

125A* *Ram Scratches Wolf.* The ram wants to scratch the wolf's side with his horns to rid him of lice. He horns the wolf to death.
Latvian (*125) *4.*

125B* *Ass Overawes Lion.* Ass tells lion that he carries the shepherds around and he is the king of the lambs. Deceives lion in contest in bringing water from ground.
Hungarian: Berze Nagy (133*) *2.*

125C* *Lion and Ass Contest in Pulling down Treetop.* Lion pulls down top of tree and challenges ass to do the same thing. Tree branch picks up the ass and throws him into a bush, where he falls on rabbit and kills him. Ass boasts that he can pull the top of a tree down and kill a rabbit at the same time.
Hungarian: Berze Nagy (134*) *2.*

125D* *Ass Frightens Lion by Turning his Ears Back.*
Hungarian: Berze Nagy (135*) *3.*

126 (formerly 126*) *The Sheep Chases the Wolf.* »Yesterday I ate seven wolves; today I eat the eighth.» [K1715]. Cf. Type 1149.

*BP I 160 n. 1; *Krappe *Neophilologus* XV 274ff. — Estonian (126*) *1;* Spanish: Espinosa III Nos. 249f.; Russian: Andrejev (126*) *1;* India: *Thompson-Balys (K1715); Indonesian: *Dixon 191 nn. 15, 16, 192 n. 17. — Cape Verde Islands: Parsons MAFLS XV (1) 317, 320, 322; West Indies: Flowers 543; American Negro (Georgia): Harris Nights 44 No. 9, 291 No. 49. — African: Weeks Jungle 394, Werner African 223, (Kaffir): Kidd 230 No. 2, (Vai): Ellis 191 No. 7, (Hottentot): Bleek 24.

126A* *The Frightened Wolves.* A he-goat, a cat and a ram are running from people. They meet some wolves and a bear and take refuge in a tree. While sitting in the tree, they (the wolves) threaten to eat them. The billygoat falls on the wolf with his horns. The wolves in fear run in all directions.
Latvian *1;* Russian: Afanasiev *1.*

126B* *The Wolf Carries the He-goat Away.* The goats ask: »Michael, when will you come back?» The he-goat replies: »Who knows what will happen? Perhaps never.» Cf. Type 47A.
Latvian (*126) *7.*

126C* *The Ram Promises that he himself will Jump into the Wolf's Jaws.* Runs straight to the wolf and gives him a hard knock. Stunned by the shock, the wolfs thinks he has swallowed the ram.
Lithuanian (122*E) *12.*

127A* *Wolf Induces Goat to Come down from Cliff and Devours it.* (Or goat refuses to come.) [K815].
Spanish *3.*

127B* *Goat Eats in Garden and is Caught.* Fox says, »If your sense were as long as your beard, you would have looked for exits as well as entrances.» [J2136.3].
Spanish: Boggs (*128) *1.*

129A* *Sheep Licks her Newly-born.* Wolf says, »Such is bad conduct; if I were to do that they would say I was eating it.» [J1909.5].
Spanish (129*) *1.* — Literary Treatment: Pauli (ed. Bolte) No. 587; Aesop (Halm Nos. 282, 330).

130 *The Animals in Night Quarters* (Bremen City Musicians). They drive away an intruder. [K1161]. Cf. Type 210.

Motifs: B296. Animals go a-journeying. N776. Light seen from tree lodging place by night leads to adventures. K335.1.4. Animals climb on one another's backs and cry out; frighten robbers. K1161. Animals hidden in various parts of a house attack owner with their characteristic powers and kill him when he enters.

**Aarne *Die Tiere auf der Wanderschaft* (FFC XI); *BP I 237 (Grimm No. 27); *Beckwith MAFLS XVII 260 No. 58; Coffin *8;* Parsons MAFLS XV (1) 187 n. 1. — Livonian *1;* Lappish *8;* Swedish *46* (Uppsala *14,* Stockholm *3,* Göteborg *9,* Lund *2,* Liungman *2,* misc. *16*); Norwegian *15;* Danish *46;* Scottish *1;* Irish *63,* Beal XI 83f. No. 37, XVII 204; French *45;* Spanish *3;* Catalan: Amades No. 301; Dutch *4;* Flemish *10,* Witteryck p. 295 *15;* Walloon (130D, 130E) *2;* German *49* (Archive *48,* Henssen Jül 437b); Italian: Crane No. 88 (Tuscan *1,* Sicilian *2*); Rumanian *3;* Slovenian *9;* Serbocroatian *15,* (Istrian) No. 2; Polish *3;* Russian: Afanesiev *11;* Greek *4,* Loukatos No. 7; Turkish: Eberhard-Boratav No. 11 *5;* India *1;* Chinese: Eberhard FFC CXX No. 3, CXXVIII Nos. 2, 7; Japanese: Ikeda, Anesaki 331; Franco-American *12;* English-American: Baughman *8;* Spanish-American: Hansen (Puerto Rico) *5,* Rael Nos. 361—366 (U.S.); West Indies (Negro) *1;* American Negro: Dorson No. 152. — African *1.*

130A *Animals Build themselves a House.*
Finnish *8;* Estonian *3;* Latvian *61;* Lithuanian *18.*

130B *Animals in Flight after Threatened Death.*
Finnish *51;* Finnish-Swedish *12;* Livonian *3;* Estonian *18;* Latvian *46;* Lithuanian *9;* Hungarian *5.*

130C *Animals in Company of a Man.*
Finnish *39;* Finnish-Swedish *14;* Livonian *2;* Latvian *11;* Lithuanian *14.*

130D* *Animals Warm Themselves.* The domestic animals flee because they have been bad, or they feel cold. To get warm the tom-cat advises the goat to wind some birch bark round his head and to have a fight with the ram. The bark begins to burn. The bear also comes to the fire, to warm himself. After that they all creep into a haystack. Seven wolves come along wanting to fight. The ram frightens the wolves, and they run away. Cf. Type 159A.
Latvian (130*D) *1.*

131 *Tiger as False Friend to the Cow.* A tiger and a cow become friends and both bear offspring. The tiger drinks water downstream from the cow, decides her flesh would be sweet, and kills and devours her. The calf has been forewarned (life-token: cup of milk). The cub, ashamed of its mother, accompanies the calf on adventures. [J427].
India *4.*

132 *Goat Admires his Horns in the Water,* and says, »I needn't be afraid of the wolf.» Wolf behind him asks him what he was saying. Goat: »One talks such foolishness when one is drinking.» [K1775].
Latvian (*127) *14;* Swedish *3* (Uppsala *1,* Göteborg *1,* Liungman *1*); Walloon (79*) *1;* Hungarian: Kovács (79*) *1.* — Spanish-American: Hansen 246**A (Puerto Rico) *1.*

132* *Quarrel between the Cow and the Reindeer.*
Lappish *1.*

133* *Goat Carries Snake over Stream.* Snake threatens goat, who then kills snake. [K952.1]. Cf. Type 155.
Liebrecht 123. — Rumanian *4;* Hungarian (59*) *1.*

134* *The Mouse and the Cat.*
Lappish *1.*

135* *The Mouse Makes a Boat of a Bread-crust.* Takes animals and birds into the boat. It capsizes. The animals quarrel. [B295.1].
Lappish *1.*

135A* *Fox Stumbles over Violin.* Chased from chicken coop by dogs. When he stumbles he says, »What a fine opportunity to dance if I have the time!» [J864.1].
Spanish (*135A) *2,* Espinosa Jr. No. 24; Spanish-American: Hansen (Argentina) *1.*

135B* *Fleeing Fox Loses an Eye in the Briars.* Returns the next day and eats it, thinking that it tastes like chicken.
Spanish (*135) *1.*

135C* *The Hare Teaches the Dog to Whistle* by widening his muzzle with a saw. The dog gets angry and bites off the hare's tail.
Latvian (*135) *3.*

136 *Wolf Surprises Pig in Apple Tree.* Will release him in return for one of his hams. Pig throws down a piece of thorny wood instead, which splits wolf's gullet. [K1043]

Walloon (136*, 78*) *2;* Catalan: Amades No. 293; Slovenian *1.* — American Indian: JAFL XV (1902) 63ff.

136A* *Confession of Animals.* Cat at ditch across which pole is laid: »He who will safely cross it shall be without sin.» Only the cat crosses the ditch; the other animals fall in.
Lithuanian *9.*

136B* *The Hare and the Ram in Contest.* The hare pushes his head down his neck; the ram pulls the hare by the ears. That is why the hare has such long ears.
Latvian (*136) *2.*

137 *The Filthy Hog and the Clean Fish.* The hog: »People will spit when they eat you, whereas in my case all will lick their fingers.»
Latvian (*251A) *8;* Lithuanian (*137) *3;* Rumanian (255*) *1;* Hungarian (255*) *1.*

137* *Chicken Hides from Wolf in Pail which Wolf Thinks is a Chapel.* Other misadventures of wolf.
Walloon *1.*

MAN AND WILD ANIMALS

150 *Advice of the Fox.* A man releases a fox (bird) if the latter will give him three counsels: »When you have a fox, don't let him loose.»
Motifs: K604. The three teachings of the bird (fox). J21.12. »Rue not not a thing that is past»: counsel proved wise by experience. J21.13. »Never believe what is beyond belief»: counsel proved wise by experience. J21.14. »Never try to reach the unattainable»: counsel proved wise by experience.
*BP III 230, IV 149 n. 2; DeCock *Studien* 51ff.; Crane *Vitry* 144 No. 28; Coffin *1;* Gaster *Exempla* 256 No. 390; Basset *1001 Contes* II 276f.; Hdwb. d. Märchens I 95a. — Finnish *30;* Finnish-Swedish *3;* Estonian *30;* Irish *1;* French *2;* Flemish (150*) *1;* Italian (Tuscan [206] *1*); Czech: Tille Soupis II (2) p. 424 *1;* Russian: Andrejev; Greek (150*) *4;* Turkish: Eberhard-Boratav No. 55 *1;* Arab: Basset *1001 Contes* II No. 39; Jewish: Bin Gorion *Born Judas* IV No. 174; India *1;* Indonesian: DeVries No. 231. — Literary Treatment: Pauli (ed. Bolte) No. 380; Aesop (Halm No. 271).

150* included in 150.

150A* *The Frog's Counsels.* A farmer agrees to take in a frog for the winter, and in return gets three counsels from it. [K604].
Livonian (670B*) *2;* Lithuanian (*286) *3.*

151 *The Man Teaches Bears to Play the Fiddle.* He tricks them by catching their claws in a cleft tree [K1111.0.1]. Similarly betrays many other animals [K1111.1]. The freed animals try in vain for revenge. Cf. Types 38, 1159.
*BP I 68 (Grimm No. 8). — Finnish *14;* Finnish-Swedish *4;* Estonian *2;* Livonian *1;* Latvian *15;* Lithuanian *17;* Irish *5;* French *10;* Catalan: Amades cf. No. 278; Dutch *1;* Flemish *4,* Witteryck p. 297 *5;* German *7*

(Archive 6, Henssen Volk. No. 140); Hungarian *1;* Slovenian *2;* cf. Serbocroatian *1;* Polish *3;* Russian: Andrejev *1;* Greek: Loukatos Nos. 8, 12; India *1.* — Franco-American *9.*

152 (formerly 152*) *The Man Paints the Bear.* Burns him with red hot iron. The hare and gadfly keep up the punishment. [K1013.3]. Cf. Types 8, 153.

Finnish *11;* Estonian *1;* Latvian *14;* German *2;* Serbocroatian *3;* Russian: Afanasiev *4.*

152A* *The Wife Scalds the Wolf.* At a signal from her husband, the wife scalds the wolf with boiling water. Next day, the man is beset by the wolf. He escapes by shouting »Pour, Catherine!» at which the wolf flees.
Latvian (*179B) *9;* Walloon (*152, *152A) *2.*

152B* *The Wicked Plowman.* With a hot iron he traces patterns on the wolf's flanks, twists the crow's foot, sticks a stalk of grass into the gadfly's hindmost; a farm girl brings him his lunch and he begins to play with her; the wolf: »He is making a pattern on her sides.» The crow: »He is twisting her foot.» The gadfly: »He is sticking a stalk of grass into her hindmost.» [J2211].
Lithuanian *3;* Polish (152) *1.*

153 *The Gelding of the Bear and the Fetching of Salve.* The man tells the bear that the horse is strong because he is gelded. The bear has the man geld him to make him strong. He is to geld the man the next day. The man substitutes his wife and sends her with salve; the bear in disgust throws the salve into the tree. Cf. Type 1133.

Motifs: K1012.1. Making the dupe strong — by castration. K241. The castrarion bargain: wife sent.

*BP III 633. — Finnish *93;* Finnish-Swedish *2;* Estonian *10;* Livonian *2;* Latvian *3;* Lappish *2;* Swedish *8* (Uppsala *1,* Göteborg *7*); Norwegian *8;* Danish: Kristensen *Danske Sagn* I (1892) 441, (1928) 276—81; German *24* (Archive *23,* Meckl. No. 19); Hungarian *3;* Serbocroatian *1,* cf. *1;* Polish *1;* Russian: Andrejev.

154 »*Bear-food.*» The fox helps the man; his reward. He converses with his members.

I. The man in anger calls his horse »bear-food». The bear comes and threatens to eat the horse. [C25].

II. A fox agrees to help the man in return for geese. The fox goes into the woods, imitates the barking of dogs. The bear is intimidated, betrayed, and killed.

III. The man goes for the geese but instead brings dogs back in his bag [K235]. The dogs chase the fox to his hole.

IV. Here the fox asks his feet, eyes, ears, and tail how they have helped him in his flight. His tail admits that it did not help. He sticks out his tail, which is attacked by dogs. [J2351.1].

**Krohn *Mann und Fuchs* 11; *BP I 518 n. 1, III 361f.; Gerber 56 No. 9, 57 Nos. 10, 11; Coffin *2;* Espinosa III 310ff. — Finnish *78;* Finnish-Swedish *4;* Estonian *30;* Livonian *2;* Latvian *35;* Lithuanian *29;* Lappish

3; Swedish *4* (Uppsala *2,* Göteborg *1,* misc. *1*); Norwegian *6;* Spanish: Espinosa *23;* Catalan: Amades No. 271, cf. 323; German (155') *22;* Rumanian *4;* Hungarian *3* (+ [Kovács 54*] *3*); Slovenian *5;* Serbocroatian *2;* Polish *2;* Russian: Afanasiev *10;* Greek *8,* Loukatos No. 13; Turkish: Eberhard-Boratav Nos. 1 IV, V, 39, 40, 48 IV. — Spanish-American: Rael No. 370 (U.S.), Hansen (Argentina) *1,* (Chile) *2,* (Puerto Rico) *1;* Portuguese-American (Brazil): Camara Cascudo p. 129; American Indian (Tepoztlan-Mexican): Boas JAFL XXV 257 No. 2. — African *6.* — Literary Treatment: Disciplina Clericalis No. 24; Aesop (Hervieux II 205f.). References for 154 IV only:

Lappish (5*) *1;* Spanish (135C*) *1;* Walloon (79*) *1;* Rumanian (54^{III}) *2;* Hungarian: Berze Nagy (63*) *1;* Russian (154 I) *10.*

154* *Present to the Wolf.* Losing his temper, the man promises the wolf to give him a cow or a horse. The wolf comes to fetch what is promised. The man is frightened and shouts for help. The wolf goes away, but warns the man not to call him by name.
Latvian *1.*

155 *The Ungrateful Serpent Returned to Captivity.* A man rescues a serpent (or a bear), who in return seeks to kill the rescuer. Fox, as judge, advises the man to put the serpent back into captivity. [J1172.3].
Motifs: W154.2.1 Rescued animal threatens rescuer. J1172.3 Ungrateful animal returned to captivity.

**McKenzie MPh I 497ff.; *Anderson in Tauscher *Volksmärchen* 170: **Krohn *Mann und Fuchs* 38; **Espinosa III 420; *BP II 420; *Cosquin Etudes 613ff.; Coffin *12;* *Gaster *Exempla* 268 No. 441; Liungman SSF III 426f.; *Köhler-Bolte I 50; *Krappe Bulletin Hispanique XXXIX 39. — Finnish *52;* Finnish-Swedish *2;* Estonian *7;* Livonian *1;* Lithuanian *39;* Lappish *1;* Swedish *8* (Uppsala *1,* Göteborg *1,* misc. *6*); Norwegian *7,* Solheim *1;* Danish *8;* Irish *76;* French *12;* Spanish *3* + (290*) *1;* Catalan: Amades No. 325; Flemish *3;* German *13* (Archive *12,* Meckl. No. 18); Italian (Crane Nos. 38, 49, Sicilian *4,* Gonzenbach No. 69); Rumanian *9* + (133*) *4;* Hungarian *4;* Slovenian *7;* Serbocroatian *5;* Polish *8;* Russian: Andrejev *Ukraine* 15, Afanasiev *6;* Greek *11;* Turkish: Eberhard-Boratav No. 48 *8;* India *36;* Indonesian: DeVries No. 5 *10;* Chinese: Eberhard FFC CXX No. 15. — Spanish-American: Rael Nos. 386, 387 (U.S.), Hansen (Argentina) *3,* (Chile) *3,* (Dominican Republic) *1,* (Peru) *1,* (Puerto Rico) *3;* West Indies (Negro) *4;* Portuguese-American (Brazil): Camara Cascudo 193; American Negro (Michigan): Dorson No. 161, Harris *Nights* No. 46. — African *49.* — Literary Treatment: Aesop (Halm No. 97); Crane *Vitry* No. 160; Pauli (ed. Bolte) No. 745.

156 *Thorn Removed from Lion's Paw (Androcles and the Lion).* In gratitude the lion later rewards the man. [B381].
**Brodeur »The Grateful Lion,» PMLA XXXIX 485; Pauli (ed. Bolte) No. 745; *BP III 1 n. 2; *Krappe Bulletin Hispanique XXXIX

29. — Finnish *31;* Finnish-Swedish *2;* Estonian (74* + 156) *8;* Latvian *6;* Lithuanian *7;* Swedish *6* (Göteborg *4,* misc. *2*); Danish *2;* Irish *15;* Dutch *1;* Slovenian *1;* Serbocroatian *2;* Polish *2;* Russian: Andrejev; Turkish: Eberhard-Boratav Nos. 37, 42 *3;* Chinese: Eberhard FFC CXX 27 Nos. 15, 17; Graham pp. 183ff. — Franco-American *3;* American Indian (Wyandot): Barbeau GSCan XI 106 No. 29. — African *1.* — Literary Treatment: Aesop (Jacobs No. 23); Gesta Romanorum No. 278.

156A (formerly 74*) *The Faith of the Lion.* He follows the man in thankfulness for his deed. On the grave. [B381].
Estonian (74*) *2;* Latvian *4;* Slovenian *1;* Russian: Andrejev (72**). Cf. German legend of Henry the Lion.

156* *Man Shares Sheep with Wolf.* The man sees the wolf carrying off a sheep He addresses him saying, »Let us share it.» The wolf drops the sheep, and every year he carries away a lamb. When the man kills the sheep, he gives half of it to the wolf, who comes back for half of the skin as well.
Latvian (**156) *9.*

156A* *Wolf Fetches a Man to Remove Thorn from his Children's Paws.* Does not attack the man's livestock. [B381.1].
Latvian *17;* Lithuanian *2.*

156B* *Woman as Snake's Midwife.* The woman sees a snake bring forth her young ones, and assists her. The snake rewards the woman with money.
Latvian (*156B) *9.*

156C* *The Boy and the Bear in Pit.* The boy falls into a pit on top of the bear, and helps him to get out of the pit. The bear too helps the boy and shows him where to find money. Cf. Type 160A.
Latvian (*156C) *4.*

157 *Learning to Fear Men.* The fox undertakes to persuade the wolf of the frightfulness of men. They see an old man. The fox says this was a man but is no longer one. Likewise a boy (will be a man). Next a man with a gun. The wolf approaches and is shot. He tells the fox he could have defeated the man but for the man's spitting fire. [J17].
*BP II 96 (Grimm No. 72); cf. III 239 (Grimm No. 157); *Espinosa III 411. — Finnish *113;* Finnish-Swedish *10;* Estonian *6;* Livonian *1;* Latvian *21;* Lithuanian *19;* Lappish *3;* Swedish *11* (Uppsala *4,* Göteborg *4,* Lund *2*); Norwegian: Solheim *1;* Danish *2;* Irish *1;* French *16;* Spanish *3;* Catalan: Amades Nos. 317, 1950, cf. 327; Dutch *2;* Flemish *12;* German *2* (Henssen Volk No. 109, Archive *1,* Meckl. No. 21); Italian (Trieste) Pinguentini No. 13; Hungarian *6;* Slovenian *7;* Serbocroatian *6;* Polish *14;* Russian: Andrejev *1;* Greek *2,* Loukatos Nos. 8, 14; Turkish: Eberhard-Boratav No. 13; India *1;* Chinese: Eberhard FFC CXX 29 No. 17. — Franco-American *4;* Spanish-American: Hansen (Chile *2,* Puerto Rico *1*), Rael 397—400 (U.S.); West Indies (Negro) *2;* American Negro: Dorson No. 7, Harris Nights Nos. 7, 57; American Indian: Thompson *C Coll* II 439. — African *1.*

157A *The Lion Searches for Man.* A young lion, warned by parents to shun man, asks other large animals if they are man. He meets a man and is scornful of him, but man tricks him into entering a cage and leaves him to starve. [J17].
   India *4*.

157*** *The Wolf with the Tail Torn off.* The peasant surrounded by wolves protects himself in a tree with a hole and tears off the tail of a wolf; caught again unsuspectedly by wolves, he repeats the same movement with his hand; they flee.
   Polish (162) *2*.

157B* *The Sheep, the Fox, and the Hunter.* The sheep makes the fox believe that the hunter is a priest, the dog his servant, and the gun a holy sprinkler. [K1178].
   Lithuanian (*140) *2*.

157C* *Hiding from Man.* The animals want to hide themselves from man. The wild beasts hide in the forest, the birds in the air, the fish in the water. However, man gets them all with his gun, his noose and his fishing-rod.
   Latvian (*157) *4*.

157D* *Fox Entices Wolf to Attack Man* and thus get killed. Fox thus saves himself from man.
   Walloon *2*.

158 *The Wild Animals on the Sleigh.* The sleigh comes in two. The animals get unsatisfactory material for repairs from the forest. [B831]. While the owner goes for good material they eat the horse.
   *Gerber 59 No. 15. — Finnish *15;* Estonian *14;* Latvian *63;* Lithuanian (cf. Type 2025); German *39;* Rumanian *4;* Russian: Andrejev *Ukraine 11,* Afanasiev *14;* Turkish: Eberhard-Boratav No. 35.

159 *Captured Wild Animals Ransom Themselves.* Bring horses, cows, etc. to the man. [B278]. Cf. Type 130.
   Finnish *3;* Latvian *1;* Lithuanian *5;* German *1;* Russian: Andrejev.

159A *Animals Warm Selves at Charcoal Burner's Fire.* Sent after food for dinner, each brings back booty, but charcoal burner tricks them and kills them. Cf. Type 130D*.
   French *8;* Catalan: Amades No. 278.

159B *Enmity of Lion and Man.* Lion allows man to strike him behind the head with an axe. After a year: The wound is healed but not the ache. Devours man. [W185.6]. Cf. Type 285D.

159* *Quarrel over the Stag.* The man, sitting in a tree hears the lion, the dog, the cat and the eagle quarreling over a dead stag. They beg the man to arbitrate. [B392]. Cf. Type 554.
   Latvian *2*.

160 *Grateful Animals; Ungrateful Man.* The rescue from the pit.
   A traveler saves a monkey, a snake, a tiger, and a jeweler from a pit. The monkey gives him fruit; the tiger a necklace of the princess he has killed. The jeweler accuses the rescuer before the king. The serpent saves him by biting the prince and then showing the man the proper remedy.

Motifs: W154.8. Grateful animals; ungrateful man. K735. Capture in pitfall. B522.1. Serpent shows condemned man how to save prince's life. Bites the prince and then shows the man the proper remedy. By thus ingratiating himself the man is freed from false accusation. B522.2. Kite steals jewels and thus saves condemned man. Innocent man in possession of stolen jewels, is about to be apprehended. Kite carries off jewels and saves him. B512. Medicine shown by animal. It heals another animal with a medicine (herb, water, etc.) and thus shows the man the remedy. Sometimes the medicine resuscitates the dead. (The animal is most frequently the serpent.)

*Bolte-Polívka IV 139; *Hilka Mittheilungen der Schlesischen Gesellschaft für Volkskunde XVII 1; *Wesselski *Märchen* 246 No. 56; Coffin *2;* Cosquin *Etudes* 22ff. — Finnish *2;* Latvian *1;* Norwegian (160**) *1,* Solheim *1;* Danish *6;* French *2;* Catalan: Amades No. 266; German *1;* Italian (Sicilian 1); Hungarian *1;* Polish *1;* Greek *1;* Turkish: Eberhard-Boratav cf. No. 65 *2;* India *10.* — African *9.* Literary Treatments: Gesta Romanorum (Oesterley No. 119); *Bin Gorion *Born Judas,* IV 51, 277; Penzer *Ocean of Story* V 157 n. 1.; Chauvin II 106 No. 71.

160A *The Travelers and the Animals in the Wolf's Hole.* The violinist falls into the wolf's hole together with the bear and the wolf. He plays to them and in the morning he helps the bear to get out; the bear then saves him, leaving the wolf who had hindered the violinist from getting out. Cf. Latvian *156C. Cf. Type 168.

Polish *3.*

160* *The Woman Betrays the Bears.* Lays her head-covering on a stump of a tree and slips away [K525].
Estonian *2;* Finnish *2;* Danish (160**) *1;* Slovenian *3.*

160** *The Fox Steals from the Man's Storehouse.* Is caught and killed.
Lappish (160*) *1.*

160*** *The Wolf Rings the Bell.* The wolf threatens to tear the fox to pieces if he does not bring him some food. The fox brings cake from the window-sill. When the wolf tries it, he rings a bell and wakes the people. He is beaten [K1022.4]. Cf. Types 1, 40*, and 60.
Livonian (160**) *2;* Italian (Tuscan [4] *1).*

160A* *The Pike Caught by the Fox.* The fox catches the pike's tail and the pike catches the fox's tail. Peasant captures both.
Hungarian: Berze Nagy 160** *1.*

160B* *The Hare's Last Will.* Summoned by hunters, the hare considers which of his members he will allot to each of them. [U242.1]. Cf. Type 154 IV.
Lithuanian *2;* Prussian: Plenzat No. 8.

161 *Peasant Betrays Fox by Pointing.* The peasant has hidden the fox in a basket, and promised not to tell. When the hunters come, he says, »The fox just went over the hill,» but points to the basket. [K2315].
**Krohn *Mann und Fuchs* 61ff.; *Köhler-Bolte I 1. — Swedish *6* (GS 132 *4,* Göteborg *1,* Lund *1*); Danish (150B) *1;* French *4;* Spanish: Boggs 161* *1,* Espinosa Jr. No. 24; Catalan: Amades No. 312; German

2 (Archive 149' *1*, Meckl. No. 20); Polish (154A) *1;* Jewish: BP IV 340 No. 75. — Literary Treatment: Wienert FFC LVI 69 (ET 324), 102 (ST 150); Aesop (Halm No. 35).

161* *The Fox Betrays the Playing Children in Regard to a Cloth.*
Lappish *1.*

161A* *The Bear with the Wooden Leg.* Old man cuts off sleeping bear's leg with axe. Bear makes himself leg from linden wood. At night he comes to the house and eats the old man up.
Russian *5.*

161B* *The Lion Made Drunk.* The lion leads the man, who has lost his way, out of the forest and insist on his telling nobody about it. The man gets drunk and blabs. The lion attacks him. The man says it was the fault of the oats and barley. He makes the lion drunk and shears him. Now the lion knows that the man was right. Cf. Type 485.
Latvian (*161) *1.*

162 (formerly 162**) *The Master Looks more Closely than the Servant.* A stag is hidden in the stable. The servant had not noticed him, but the master finds him. [J1032].
Flemish (162*) *1.* — Literary Treatments: Aesop (Jacobs No. 30).

162* *The Man Punishes the Wolf.* The wolf gathers wild animals and pursues the man. The latter climbs a tree and saves himself. [R311].
Lappish *2.*

162A* *Wolf Steals and Eats One Sheep,* then two, finally the whole herd and the shepherd. The wolf dies.
Latvian (**162B) *3.*

163 *The Singing Wolf.* By his singing the wolf compels the old man to surrender his cattle, his children and grandchildren, and finally his wife. The old woman goes into the wolf's service. She returns home bringing butter, etc. [Z33.4.2].
Latvian (*762) *48;* Lithuanian *23;* Russian: Andrejev (162*) *11.*

163* *Numskull, the Poor Hero, and Fox go Hunting and Fishing.*
Lappish *1.*

163A* *The Bear Chases away the Flies* that annoy his master. By chance he strikes his master dead. Cf. Type 1586.
Latvian (**163) *5.* Also Russian fable.

163B* *She-Bear Demands her Wool and Flesh from Old Woman;* comes to the window and sings: »All the people are asleep; so are the little birds. Only one old woman is awake — she is spinning my wool and boiling my flesh.»
Lithuanian (163*) *7;* Russian: Andrejev (*160 I) *3.*

163C* *Bear Pursues Boy across Bridge.* An old man shows the boy the way across a bridge. After that the bear breaks his leg and begs the boy to bandage it. The bear again pursues the boy who runs across the bridge again. The bear breaks his other leg.
Latvian (*163B) *2.*

164* *The Bear's Testament.* The bear commands his son (his wife) to ask for his skin (a piece of his flesh) when he is dead.
Lappish *3.*

164A* *Wolf in the Bath House.* The wolf drags the sheep away. The shepherds ask him to come to the sweat bath where it is heated with aspen and birch or fir wood; the wolf does not come. He comes only when it is heated with the wood of apple tree. The shepherds give the wolf a good thrashing.
Latvian (*164) 3.

165 *The Wolf in the Company of Saints.* Promises to give up slaying animals. After wringing the gander's neck, excuses himself, saying: »He should not have hissed at the saint.« [K2055.1].
Lithuanian 8; Serbocroatian 1. Cf. French (Gascony): Bladé III 149.

165* *The Man Makes a Son of Wood.* The fox throws him down from a cliff.
Lappish 1.

165A* *The Wolf Grows Angry with the Farmer's Wife* for chasing him from the calves' paddock. »Am I not allowed to look into your garden because of your calves?«
Latvian (*165) 13.

165B* *Wolf Punished by Being Married.* After debate it is decided that marriage is the greatest punishment. [K583].
Spanish: Boggs (*165) 1.

166* *The Crow Receives Reindeer Meat from the Boys.* He advises them to go to the woods to protect the reindeer from the bears.
Lappish 1.

166A* *The Wolf Puts his Tail through the Window* of the stable and alarms the sheep. The farmer snatches at it and tears the tail off.
Latvian (*166A) 29.

166B* *Wolf and Horses.*

166B$_1$* In the night the wolf comes near the horses and the sleeping drivers. One of them awakes, seizes the wolf's tail, and tears it off.
Latvian (*166C) 1.

166B$_2$* In the night the wolf comes to the horses, plunges into the river, and then shakes himself by the bonfire to extinguish it.
Latvian (*166D) 11.

166B$_3$* The wolf wallows in the mud, then splashes it at the horses in order to get at them.
Latvian (*166E) 2.

166B$_4$* The bear devours the horse. The horse collar falls on his neck and he has to draw the cart.
Münchhausen. — Latvian (*168C) 1.

167* *A Mouse Frightens a Man to Death.* His wife also dies. [N384.1].
Lappish 1.

167A* *The Peasant Catches a Bear* that has swallowed a stick smeared with honey, till it comes out of him at the other end. The man drives a peg into it.
Münchhausen. — Latvian (***168) 2.

168 *The Musician in the Wolf-Trap.* There he encounters a wolf already trapped, and saves himself by playing music. [B848.1]. Cf. Types 160A, 1652.
Estonian (2002) 5; Latvian (**167) 11; Lithuanian (168*) 3.

168A *Old Woman and Wolf Fall into Pit Together.* »Sit still.« [K735]. Sometimes other animals also. She commands the fox to sit still since the father (the wolf) is at home.

Swedish (GS 169) *18* (Göteborg *16*, misc. *2*); Danish *6*.

169* *Miscellaneous Stories of Wolves.*
Latvian (*168G) *20*.

169A* *On the Road the Wolf does not Touch the Man.* (1) The wolf causes man to clear the way for him. He says: »Half of the way for me, the other half for you.» He lashes with his tail as he passes. (2) The girl gives the wolf some bread and says: »Man, go your way.» (The wolf brings a sheep.) (3) The lad calls the wolf a lamb-stealer and is attacked by him. (Variant: The wolf is called broad-head, tapped on the forehead and driven off to a swamp to sleep.) (4) The beggar calls the wolf »God's dog» and sends him to the ducks in the pond. The wolf disappears. On his way the beggar finds money. (5) The man wants to beat the wolf, but abstains from doing so and throws his stick away, which the wolf tears to pieces. (6) The bear (wolf) does not touch man when he pretends to be dead. (7) The bear will not allow the housewife to cross the road. She lifts her dress. The bear clears off.
Latvian *18*.

169B* *The Wolf (Bear) does not Touch Children.* (1) The children have lost their way. The she-wolf (she-bear) takes them to her lair, and feeds them with meat. The parents find the children. (2) The wolf (bear) carries off a child. The child threatens to prick the wolf's cubs with a puncheon, or to beat them with a spoon. (3) The she-bear gives suck to the man's child, and it grows very strong. (4) The wolves attack and tear the man and his wife (or only the man) to pieces. They do not touch the child.
Latvian (*167B) *18*.

169C* *The Wolves Urinate on the Man.* (1) The Jew meets 99 wolves that one after another urinate on him. (They do the same to the man when he pretends to be dead.) (2) Twelve wolves pass the woman. The last urinates on her, who is much astonished at this. The wolves fall on one another.
Latvian (*167C) *6*.

169D* (1) *The Wolf Devours the Foal* and lies down beside the shepherd to sleep. The latter leaps upon the wolf's back and rides on him. (2) The wolf-hunter falls asleep. When he awakes, there is a wolf sleeping between his legs. (3) A child that has lost its way sleeps beside the wolf during the night. (4) When it rains, the wolf creeps under the fir-tree and sits down on the man's lap.
Latvian (*167D) *15*.

169E* *The Wolf Comes into the Room* and is taken for a dog or a neighbor.
Latvian (*167E) *4*.

169F* *The Wolf Wants some Tobacco*, follows the man and wags his tail. The man strews tobacco on the ground and sets it on fire. The wolf snuffs at it.
Latvian (*167F) *3*.

169G* *The Wolves and the Hayrick.* The bear, persecuted by wolves, runs to the hayrick where a man is hidden and pelts them with bunches of hay. [B855].
Lithuanian (*167) *11*.

169H* *The Man in the Wolves' Den* with the wolves' cubs. Another man mounts guard before the den. He snatches the tail of the she-wolf. The man in the den wonders at the darkness around him. Cf. Types 1229, 1875, 1896.
Latvian (*169) *2*.

169J* *The Wolf and the Wheel.* The man goes along carrying a wheel. The wolf leaps on

him and puts his head into the wheel. Running he cannot get rid of it, and is caught by the bushes.
Latvian (*168B) *1*.

169K* *The Man Drives with a Tub and Little Pigs.* The wolves attack him. The man pulls the tub on himself and also on the pigs. With a knife he gashes the wolves' paws, which they put under the tub.
Latvian (*168D) *3*.

169L* *The Wolf Dies of Fright, Soils Man.* (Different variants.)
Latvian (**168) *11*.

170 *The Fox Eats his Fellow-lodger.* The fox spends the night with a cock in a house. He eats the cock but in the morning he accuses the sheep of having eaten it. In the next inn likewise the ox has eaten the sheep, etc. In compensation he demands a larger animal each time. [K443.7]. Cf. Type 1655.
*Anderson *Novelline* Nos. 4, 28. — Finnish (170*) *2;* Estonian (170*) *6;* Latvian *38;* Russian: Afanasiev *15;* Turkish: Eberhard-Boratav No. 35. — West Indies (Negro) *1*.

170A *The Clever Animal and the Fortunate Exchanges* [Z39.9, Z47.1]. Cf. Types 1655, 2029C*. I. A jackal, (b) a monkey, (c) a mouse is given a razor when the barber cuts its tail in trying to remove a thorn. II. A mouse catches or is given a fish. III. A series of fortunate exchanges follows: (a) pot, (b) firewood, (c) drum, (d) food, (e) goat, cow, etc., (f) bride.
India *14*.

171A* *Bear Plays with the Boar's Young.* The boar pursues him. The bear climbs up a tree. But the game keeper has cut a notch in the branch. It breaks; the bear falls down on the boar. They fight each other and die.
Latvian (*168E) *7*.

171B* *Various Conflicts with Bears.* (1) The bear pushes the man into the swamp, pulls him out again, sucks his blood and listens to his breathing. (The bear sucks the blood of cows.) (2) The bear carries his guardian across the water, throws him into the middle of it, and torments him. (3) The bear climbs up a tree after the man. The latter hits the bear on its muzzle. The bear dies (or falls down and is killed.) (4) The bear holds a girl in front of him in order to protect himself from his pursuers. The girl tells them to shoot, as the bear will not set her free without injuring her. The bear throws the girl down on a stone. (5) The bear rolls the hunter into a pit. The latter comes out of it, and shoots the bear who comes along with a stump.
Latvian (*168F) *8*.

172A* *The Shepherd always Takes a Tame Fox with Him.* In an ancient castle the shepherd loses himself, the fox shows him the way out.
Latvian (**172) *2*.

173 *Men and Animals Readjust Span of Life.* At first, 30 years are given to all animals and to man. For the animals it is too long, for man too short. Man is given a portion of animal's lives. [A1321].
*BP III 290. — German: Grimm No. 176.

175 *The Tarbaby and the Rabbit.* The rabbit, who has been stealing fruit from a garden, is captured by means of a tarbaby, an image with tar. The rab-

bit tries to make the tarbaby talk and finally becomes so angry that he strikes it. He sticks to the tarbaby and is captured. Usually followed by briar-patch punishment for rabbit. (Cf. Type 1310.)

Motifs: K741. Capture by tarbaby. K581.2. Briar-patch punishment for rabbit.

**Espinosa JAFL XLIII 129, LVI 31ff.; *Espinosa FL (1930); **Espinosa II 163—227; **Cline *American Literature* II 72ff.; **Parsons FL XXX 227, JAFL XXXV 330; Dähnhardt IV 26; *Taylor JAOS LXIV 4ff.; Brown *Scientific Monthly* XV 228; Coffin *55;* Werner Folklore X 282; — Latvian *2;* French *2;* Spanish: Espinosa *8*, Boggs FFC XC 77 No. 650; India *11;* Japanese: Ikeda. — Spanish-American: Hansen (Argentina *4*, Chile *2*, Colombia *4*, Cuba *3*, Dominican Republic *5*, Puerto Rico *10*, Venezuela 1), Rael No. 373, 374 (U.S.); Portuguese American: Parsons MAFLS XV (1) 95 No. 1; West Indies (Negro) *35;* North American Indian: *Thompson *C Coll* II 440, 444ff. — African *35*. — Philippine: Fansler MAFLS XII 336, 442.

176 *The Farmer Tricks the Jackals.*

1. *Farmer vs. jackal*. (a) A jackal forces a woman carrying food to her husband to give him food. (b) The husband disguises as a woman carrying food and beats the jackal, etc. (c) The jackal threatens to defecate on the man's plow. The man affixes knives to his plow and the jackal is cut. (d) The man tricks the vengeful jackal in other ways. (e) The jackals tell the farmer to cook his seed before sowing it. The jackals come at night and eat the seed.

II. *The funeral feast*. The man feigns death and his wife invites the jackals to a funeral feast. When the jackals are all in the house or all tied, the man rises from his bier and beats the jackals, etc. [K751, K811.1].

III. *Jackal's punishment and escape*. The jackal is tied by a path and beaten daily until his body is swollen [K713.1]. He gets another jackal to take his place by saying he is plump from good feeding [K842.3].

India *19*.

176* *Hare Outwits Man and Fox*. The hare and the fox want to deprive the man of his meat. The hare tells the man that the meat smells bad, that he ought to tie it to a string, and draw it behind him. The hare stealthily unties the meat and fastens a stone to the string. The hare tells the fox that the man has taken the meat away.

Latvian (*176) *2*.

176** *Man and Animals Brew Beer*. A man, a wolf, a bear, etc. brew beer in a lake; in turn they keep watch. Baba-Yaga beats the wolf and the bear unmercifully; the man kills her.

Russian: Andrejev *2*.

177 *The Thief and the Tiger* [J1758ff., J1769.3, J2132.4, N392, N691.1ff.]. (a) A tiger overhears a person saying that he fears the dripping (of rain), or some other unusual term, worse than he does a tiger. (b) A tiger has come to a sheepfold to steal a sheep and overhears the farmer warning the guard to watch out for tigers and »botiyas» (or some other word, often an »echo word»). (c) The tiger hides among the sheep (goats, etc.). A thief comes, thinks the tiger is a big sheep, and carries it off. (d) Tiger hides elsewhere. A man (who is blind or drunk) thinks the tiger is his horse or ass, and rides it off. (e) The tiger, believing the term he has overheard refers to a mighty animal or ogre, thinks the man is the mighty one and meekly submits to various indignities. (f) The man flees when dawn comes, or ties his »horse» to a post and discovers next morning he was riding a tiger. (g) The tale involves a demon rather than a tiger. Cf. Type 1692.

India 25. — Spanish Exempla: Keller. — Korean: Zong in-Sob 149 No. 65.

178 *The Faithful Animal Rashly Killed* [B331].

178A *Llewellyn and His Dog (The Brahman and the Mongoose).* Dog has saved child from serpent. Father sees bloody mouth, thinks the dog has eaten the child, and kills the dog. [B331.2]. (Sometimes told of mongoose).

*BP I 425 n. 1; Köhler-Bolte I 534; *Emeneau *Proceedings of the American Philosophical Society* LXXXIII 503ff.; Chauvin II 100 No. 59, VIII 66 No. 31; Penzer V 138 n. 1; K. Campbell *Sages* lxxviii ff.; Benfey *Panschatantra* I 479ff.; Bødker Exempler 299 No. 64; Pauli (ed. Bolte) No. 257; Clouston *Tales* II 167. — Spanish Exempla: Keller; Irish myth: Cross; Polish (520) *3;* India *16.* — U.S.: Baughman. — Literary Treatments: Pauli (ed. Bolte) No. 257; Ward *Catalogue of Romances* II 170; Chauvin II 100 No. 59, VIII 67 No. 31; Kittredge *Arthur* 223 n. 1; Frazer *Pausanias* V 421.

178B *The Faithful Dog as Security for a Debt.* A poor man leaves his dog with a wealthy man as security for a large loan. The dog shows the wealthy man where thieves have hidden goods stolen from him and drives off thieves when they come to ransack the house. The grateful wealthy man sends the dog back to its owner with a letter saying the debt is cancelled. The owner, thinking the dog has run away, kills it only to find the letter. Cf. Type 916. [B331.2.2, B579.6].

*Emeneau »The Faithful Dog as Security for a Debt; A Companion to the Brahman and Mongoose Story-Type» JAOS LXI 1—17. — India 27.

179 *What the Bear Whispered in his Ear.* Paid guide climbs tree and leaves traveler to mercy of a bear. Traveler feigns death and the bear sniffs at him and leaves. The guide: »What did the bear say to you?» »He said, never trust a coward like you.» [J1488].

*Anderson in Tauscher *Volksmärchen* 177; Wienert FFC LVI 68 (ET 319), 126 (ST 349); Aesop (Halm No. 311); Pauli (ed. Bolte) No. 422. — Irish; French Canadian; Polish (169) *1;* India *4.*

179* *Men and Bear* — miscellaneous.

179A* (1) *The Bear Pursues the Man who Hides in a Bush.* The bear puts his paws round the bush. The man rips open the bear's belly. 2) The man and the bear take hold of each other round a tree and do not let go. Another man hurries home for help. He is long coming back. When he comes at last, his comrade, who is holding the bear's paws, cause him to take his place and goes away. He stays away for a long time, taking his revenge on his friend's thoughtlessness.
Latvian (*168A) *12.*

179B* *An Old Man Carrying a Kneading Trough* goes through the woods. He lies down to rest a little, and draws the trough over himself. Now come the hare, the wolf, the fox, and the bear, and admire the fine little table. All of them bring something to eat: a cabbage, a lamb, a goose, some honey. The man under the table moves; the animals run away, and the man gets all.
Latvian (*179) *29.*

180 *The Rebounding Bow.* A hunter kills several animals but is in turn bitten by a snake. A jackal comes by, nibbles at the hunter's bow, and is killed when the bow rebounds. [J514.2].

Chauvin II 95 No. 47; Bødker *Exempler* 292 No. 51; Spanish Exempla: Keller (J514.2). — India *5.*

181 *The Man Tells the Tiger's Secret.* (Sometimes leopard's.) Cf. Type 534.

I. *The Tiger's Secret.* A lizard and leopard are playing hide and seek. The lizard fastens onto the leopard's tail or rump [J411.10]. (b) The lizard coats himself with mud to withstand tiger's claws. (c) A crab fastens onto a tiger's tail (nose).

II. *Silence Demanded.* A man has seen the contest or removes the lizard, and the tiger threatens him unless he maintains silence.

III. *Punishment.* The man tells his friends and the tiger carries him off. (a) The man makes a noise and frightens the tiger by saying it is the lizard coming [K1715.5]. (b) The man says he has eggs from which lizards will soon hatch. (c) The man escapes by swinging up into a tree. Cf. Type 1149.

India *14.* — Polynesian (Hawaiian): Beckwith 442.

182 *The Helpful Animal and the Snake.* The helpful animal sees a snake bite his master. He catches the crow, who is the snake's confederate, and forces the snake to revive his master by sucking out the poison. [B449.1, B478, B511.1.3].

India *8.* — African (Mpongwe): Nassau 41 No. 6.

183* *The Hare Promises to Dance.* First asks the gate to be opened, then he will dance nicely; escapes. [K571.1].
Lithuanian (*180) *2;* Ceylon: Parker I 352.

DOMESTIC ANIMALS

200 *The Dog's Certificate.* Through the cat's carelessness it is lost. Since then dogs and cats are enemies. [A2281.1].

*BP III 542, 544 (Grimm No. 223); Dähnhardt IV 117ff., 142ff. — Finnish *34;* Finnish-Swedish *5;* Estonian *12;* Livonian *4;* Latvian

(*200A, *200B, *200C) *14;* Lithuanian *21;* Swedish *1* (Uppsala *1*); Irish *1*, Beal III 467f. No. 40; Catalan: Amades No. 339; Walloon *1;* Flemish *5;* German *18;* Italian (Tuscan 2 [762] a, b); Hungarian *6;* Slovenian *11;* Serbocroatian *1;* Polish *12;* Russian: Andrejev *Ukraine 8*, Andrejev *1;* Greek: Loukatos Nos. 9, 10, 11, 12; Turkish: Eberhard-Boratav No. 7. — Franco-American *2;* Spanish-American: Hansen (Chile) *1*, (cf. Dominican Republic **202) *1*.

200A *Dog Loses his Patent Right;* seeks it: why dogs look at one another under the tail [A2275.5.5]. (Cf. A2471.1).

*BP III 543 (Grimm No. 223); *Dähnhardt IV 129. — Lithuanian (202*) *5;* Catalan: Amades No. 834; Walloon (*200C, *200D, *200E) *3;* German: Plenzat 10; Hungarian (200^{I}/$_{2}$) *1;* U.S.; Baughman (A2275.5.5).

200B *Why Dogs Sniff at One Another.* They are looking for a dog that was sent to Prussia for pepper and has never returned since.

BP III 543 (Grimm No. 223). — Latvian *4;* Lithuanian (*202) *5;* Hungarian (200^{I}/$_{3}$) *1;* Polish (202) *3;* Prussian: Plenzat *10*.

200B* *False Horns at Horned Animals' Dance.* Cause of cat's and dog's enmity. [A2326.2.2]. India (200 Ind.) *1.* — Spanish-American: Hansen (**203A, B) (Puerto Rico) *2.*

200C* *Hare and Hunting Dog Conduct a Store* (inn) together. Quarrel. Hare chased henceforth by dog.
Rumanian (131*) *4.*

200D* *Why Cat is Indoors and Dog Outside in Cold.* In race, dog delays to attack beggar and cat wins.
Irish; Rumanian (202*) *2.*

200E* *Dogs must Go to Next Village for Water.* Are thirsty again before they reach home.
Hungarian: Kovács (203*) *3.*

201 *The Lean Dog Prefers Liberty to Abundant Food and a Chain* [J211, L451.3].
*Pauli (ed. Bolte) No. 433. — Flemish *1;* Hungarian *1.* — Franco-American *1.* — African *2.* — Literary Treatment: Crane *Vitry* 221 No. 217; Wienert FFC LVI 61 (ET 238), 124 (ST 326); Aesop (Halm No. 278, Jacobs No. 28).

201A* *Dog Carries a Basket with a Sausage.* Another dog wants to take it away from him. The first dog eats the sausage himself, so that his enemy may not get it.
Latvian (**201A) *6.*

201B* *Clever Dog Milks Cows,* cooks the food, threshes the corn in the threshing machine. Envious people feed the dog with needles, and he dies.
Latvian (**201B) *4.*

201C* *Dog Learns to Herd Cattle,* another is the children's playmate, and learns nothing that is useful. When the children are tired of him, he is not able to herd the cattle.
Latvian (***201) *2.*

201D* *Dog Barks at the Thieves.*
Latvian (**201D) *2.*

201E* *Dog does not Spare his Life* to render services to men.
Latvian (**201E) *2.*

202 (formerly 202*) *The Two Stubborn Goats.* They meet each other on a bridge and neither will step aside. Both fall into the water. [W167.1].
 *Wienert FFC LVI 56 (ET 171). — Livonian (202') *1;* Turkish: Eberhard-Boratav No. 1 *4.*

203 (formerly 203*) *Sheep and Horse Have Eating Contest.* Sheep thinks he lost contest because his legs were too weak. [J2228].
 Finnish *3;* Russian: Andrejev.

203A* *The Sheep Drive their Shepherds Away,* and become victims of the wolves.
 Latvian (*203) *2.*

204 *Sheep, Duck, and Cock in Peril at Sea.* The duck swims; the cock flies to the mast and crows that he sees the shore. [J1711.1].
 Finnish *1;* Norwegian: Solheim *1;* Danish *11,* Kristensen *Dyrefabler* 27ff.; German *2;* Russian: Andrejev.

206 *Straw Threshed a Second Time.* The animals eating at night say they have good food because the straw has not been well threshed. The master hears and threshes it a second time. They grow hungry. (Animals' voices imitated in telling story.) [J2362]. Cf. Types 106, 2075.
 Finnish *6;* Finnish-Swedish *1;* Estonian *1;* Latvian *7;* Lithuanian *1;* Swedish *58* (Uppsala *41,* Göteborg *11,* Liungman *4,* misc. *2);* Danish *3;* Russian: Andrejev *1.* Common in French Canada.

207 *Rebellion of the Work Animals.* Cock as leader punished. [K1633].
 Coffin *2.* — Spanish: Espinosa III 410 No. 260, Boggs (207*) *1;* Mexican: JAFL XXXIII 13; Spanish-American: Hansen (*207) (Dominican Republic) *1,* (Peru) *1,* (Puerto Rico) *2.*

207A *Ass Induces Overworked Bullock to Feign Sickness.* Ass must do bullock's work and persuades bullock to return.
 Irish; Walloon (*218) *1.* — Spanish-American: Hansen *207 (Dominican Republic) *1,* (Peru) *1,* (Puerto Rico) *2.*

207B *Hard-hearted Horse and Ass.* Allows ass to be overburdened until it is crushed. Horse must then assume load. [W155.1].
 Wienert FFC LVI *56 (ET 170), 144 (ST 397); Halm Aesop No. 177. — Catalan: Amades No. 333; Hungarian (216*) *1.*

207C *Animals Ring Bell and Demand Justice.* A king has a bell which petitioners for justice may ring and thus summon him. The bell is rung by a serpent which is being menaced by a turtle (or by an old horse who wishes to complain against a cruel master). [B271.3].
 *Pauli (ed., Bolte) No. 648. — Latvian (**207) *1.* — Literary Treatments: *Wesselski *Theorie* 20; Italian Novella: Rotunda [B271.3].

207A* *Lazy Horse is Always Waiting* for the next season; the diligent one is pleased with any season.
 Latvian (*208) *2.*

208* *Duck Persuades Cock to Cut off his Crest and Spurs.* The cat attacks the duck, who cries, »peace, gentlemen, peace.» [K1065].
 Spanish *1.*

210 *Cock, Hen, Duck, Pin, and Needle on a Journey.* The animals and objects hide themselves in various parts of a house. They punish with their characteristic powers the owner of the house and finally kill him. Cf. Type 130.

Motifs: B296. Animals go a-journeying. (Cf. F1025.) K1161. Animals hidden in various parts of a house attack owner with their characteristic powers and kill him when he enters.

**Aarne *Die Tiere auf der Wanderschaft* (FFC XI); *BP I 75, 135 (Grimm Nos. 10, 41). — Finnish-Swedish *1;* Estonian *1;* Livonian *1;* Latvian *22;* Lithuanian *1;* Swedish *9* (Uppsala *1,* Stockholm *4,* Göteborg *3,* Lund *1*); Danish *4;* Irish *11;* French *2;* Dutch *5;* Walloon *4;* German *24;* Hungarian *10;* Slovenian *1;* Serbocroatian *1;* Russian: Andrejev (210A); Turkish: Eberhard-Boratav No. 11 V; India *9;* Indonesian: DeVries No. 99; Chinese: Eberhardt FFC CXX 25ff. No. 14, FFC CXXVIII 33ff. Nos. 8, 9. — Franco-American *4;* Spanish-American: Hansen (Dominican Republic) *1,* (Puerto Rico) *6;* West Indies (Negro) *1.*

210* *Verlioka.* The terrible monster, Verlioka, kills an old woman and her little grandson. The old man sets out for his hut to punish him. The old man is aided by a drake, a string, a beetle and an acorn. They destroy Verlioka.

Russian: Afanasiev (210*B) *3.*

211 (formerly 211***) *The Two Asses.* One of them loaded with salt, the other with feathers. They must pass through the water. The salt melts and the first is relieved of his weight. The second adds to his. [J1612].

Wienert FFC LVI 72 (ET 372), 98 (ST 126); Flemish (211*) *1;* Hungarian *1.* — West Indies (Negro) *1.*

211* *The Hog who Was so Tired of his Daily Food.* Goes to the judge and gets a better food assigned to him. The fox deceives him out of it. [W128.1].

Norwegian (211**) *1.* Also known in French Canada (information from Luc Lacourcière).

211** *One Dog is to Remain* with good master; the other is to leave the stingy master.

Lappish (211*) *1.*

211A* *The Cock Laughs at the Duck* because of her awkwardness. When the cock falls into the water and cannot swim, the duck laughs.

Latvian (**211) *5.*

211B* *The Gander, the Drake, and the Boar Go into the Tavern,* but they have no money to pay the bill.

Latvian (*211) *7.*

212 *The Lying Goat.* A father sends his sons one after the other to pasture the goat. The goat always declares he has had nothing to eat. The father angrily sends his sons from home and learns, when he himself tries to pasture the goat, that he has been deceived. [K1151, Q488.1]. Cf. Type 2015.

*BP I 346; *Anderson *Novelline* No. 41. — Latvian *39;* Lithuanian *29;* Swedish *2* (Liungman *1,* misc. *1*); Danish *3;* French *27;* Catalan: Amades No. 297; German *10;* Italian (Tuscan [200] a, c; cf. [2015a—d]

2); Hungarian *13;* Serbocroatian *3;* Russian: Afanasiev *10,* Andrejev Ukraine *15.* — Franco-American *3.*

212* *Selling Goat and Cabbage.* The man drives to market to sell a goat and cabbage. The goat eats the cabbage and escapes. Cf. Type 1579.
Latvian (*212) *1.*

214 *Ass Tries to Caress his Master like a Dog.* He is driven off. [J2413.1].
Aesop (Halm No. 331, Jacobs No. 10); Crane *Vitry* 139 No. 15; Wienert FFC LVI 46 (ET 45), *90 (ST 19); Oesterley *Gesta Romanorum* No. 79; Spanish Exempla: Keller. — Hungarian (202*) *2;* India *6.* — West Indies: Flowers 489f.

214A *Camel and Ass Together Captured because of Ass's Singing.* [J2137.6].
*Chauvin III 49 No. 1; Spanish: Espinosa III Nos. 199—201, 204—5; India: Thompson-Balys (J2137.6) *2.*

214B *Ass in Lion's Skin Unmasked when he Raises his Voice* [J951.1].
**DeCock *Volkssage* 184ff., BP IV 337 No. 47; Wienert FFC LVI 57 (ET 175, 176), *91 (ST 38), 93 (ST 69); Halm Aesop Nos. 333, 336; Jacobs Aesop 211 No. 49; *Chauvin II 224 No. 22. — Lappish (109) *2;* Spanish Exempla: Keller (J951.1); Catalan: Amades No. 283; India: Penzer V 99 n. 3.

214* *Ass Envies Horse in Fine Trappings.* Horse killed in battle; ass content. [J212.1].
Jacobs Aesop 220 No. 78; *Scala Celi* 135a No. 744. — Hungarian (215*) *1;* India: Thompson-Balys (J212.1) *1.*

217 *The Cat and the Candle.* A man has a cat trained to hold up lighted candles on its head. The king has a mouse let loose. The cat drops the candle and chases the mouse. [J1908.1]. (Often used as a method of cheating in a game [N7].)
**Cosquin *Le conte du chat et de la chandelle* (Paris, 1912); Basset RTP XXVII 330; Köhler-Bolte II 639; Wesselski *Arlotto* II 238 No. 131. — Latvian *1;* Swedish *4* (Stockholm *1,* misc. *3*); Irish *47;* French *2;* Italian (Sicilian *1*); Serbocroatian *1;* India *20.* — West Indies (Negro) *2.*

217* *Devil-cat which Holds Candle* in minister's or landlord's house is banished by a priest.
Irish.

218* *Cock and Hen Plant Bean.*

218A* The cock and the hen plant a bean, which grows up into the sky. The cock climbs up to gather the harvest. The hen below calls to him, and he falls. The cock imprisons the hen in the stove, and climbs up into the sky again. However, the hen gets out of the stove, cannot keep on her feet and again calls the cock. The latter falls down and is killed.
Latvian (*219A) *1.*

218B* The cock and the hen plant a pea or a bean which grows very long. The man puts his wife into his trousers, and climbs up with her. She falls down, and is killed. The wolf, the fox, the bear, and the cat help the man to mourn his wife. Cf. Type 2022.
Latvian (*219B) *21;* Russian: Andrejev (*1960G I).

219* *Miscellaneous Tales of Domestic Animals.*

219A* *The Cat Asks the Gypsy why he Has a Hanging Lip*, then causes him to bend a little and bites his throat.
Latvian (*213) 2.

219B* *The Industrious Chicken* is hatched from a woman's armpit. Brings everything desired. [K366]. Cf. Type 1735.
Rumanian (213 I*) 1.

219C* *Five Cats Go to the Forest for Firewood*. They come home, cook the porridge, and go to sleep.
Latvian (*215) 6.

219D* *The Hog with Broken Leg*. The sick hog (leg broken for rooting peas) is asked to tell another where the peas are to be found. »No, I shall not tell you. I intend to go there myself as soon as I get well again.» [W151.6].
Lithuanian (*215) 2.

219E* The old man has a cock, the old woman a hen. The old man loves his cock, who brings him some money from the tavern. The old woman does not love the hen who dirties the house.
Latvian (*218) 1. — Also Russian *Märchen*.

219F* *Dog and Hog Dispute* over their children: worth lies not in speed [J243.1].
Wienert FFC LVI 44 (ET 19), 142 (ST 478); Halm Aesop No. 409. — Hungarian (218*) 1.

219G* *The Cat, the Dog, the Cock and the Sheep Quarrel* about whose food is best.
Latvian (*217) 2.

BIRDS

See also 15**.

220 *The Council of Birds*. The eagle as judge assigns each his place and work. [B238.1].
*Cosquin *Etudes* 401ff. — Finnish *4;* Irish *1;* Russian: Andrejev (220A). — Literary Treatment: cf. Chaucer »Parlement of Foules».

220A *The Trial of the Crow by the Eagle*. The crow is tried and punished for various crimes. In order to avenge himself, the crow slanders other birds who are then also punished.
Russian: Afanasiev *1*.

221 *The Election of Bird-king*. Wren wins by cleverness.
Motifs: B236.0.1. Animal king chosen as result of a contest. B236.1. Election of king of birds. B242.1.2. Wren king of birds. Wins contest for kingship.
*BP III 278 (Grimm No. 171); Dähnhardt IV 169ff. — Finnish-Swedish *1;* Latvian *2;* Lithuanian *10;* Swedish *7* (Uppsala *3,* Stockholm *1,* misc. *3*); Norwegian *1,* Solheim *1;* Scottish *2;* Irish *39,* Beal III 467f. No. 44; French *10;* Catalan: Amades No. 822; Dutch *6;* Flemish *14;* German *42* (Archive *41,* Henssen Volk No. 117); Italian (Sicilian *3*); Rumanian *3;* Hungarian *2;* Polish *6;* Russian: Andrejev *1,* Andrejev *Ukraine 5;* Greek *2,* Loukatos Nos. 1, 2; Indonesian: DeVries No. 102. — Franco-American *1.* — African *12.* — Literary Treatments: Wienert FFC 54 (ET 139), 114 (ST 248).

221A *Test: who can Fly Highest?* Wren hides in eagle's wings. [K25.1].
Danish *12.*

221B *Test: who can Go Deepest in Earth?* Wren goes into mouse-hole. To be starved out. [K17.1.1]. Owl as watchman [A2233.3].
Danish *1.*

222 *War of Birds and Quadrupeds* [B261]. Birds win by cleverness. The fox's lifted tail is to be the signal. The gnats stick him under the tail. He drops it and the quadrupeds flee [K2323.1]. Cf. Type 104. It often serves as introduction to Type 313.
*BP II 435 (Grimm No. 102). — Finnish *3;* Estonian *4;* Latvian *4;* Lappish *1;* Norwegian *1;* Scottish *1;* Irish *25;* French *13;* Spanish *4;* Catalan: Amades No. 332; Flemish *3;* Hungarian *2;* Russian: Andrejev (222A); Greek: Loukatos No. 9; Turkish: Eberhard-Boratav No. 2 *2;* India *1;* Japanese: Ikeda. — Franco-American *1;* Spanish-American: Hansen (Argentina) *1,* (Dominican Republic) *1,* (Peru) *1.* — African *4.*

222A *Bat in War of Birds and Quadrupeds.* Because of ambiguous form joins first one side and then the other. Discredited. [B261.1].
Wienert FFC LVI *48 (ET 66, 67), *52 (ET 166), 134 (ST 398, 399); Halm Aesop Nos. 307, 391; Dähnhardt IV 197ff. — Latvian (**222) *5;* Slovenian; India: Thompson-Balys (B261.1); Japanese: Ikeda (B261.1). — African (Benga): Nassau 163 No. 21, (Ibo, Nigeria): Basden 281, Thomas 161 (hornbill), (Mpongwe): Nassau 53 No. 8 (crocodile), (Yoruba): Ellis 252 No. 3.

222B *War between Mouse and Sparrow.* Eagle and dragon act as champions.
Livonian (99') *2;* Hungarian (222 I) *1;* Serbocroatian *1;* Russian: Andrejev *12.*

222A* *The Lion Wages War with the Eagle,* having eaten the eagle's eggs. The animals attack the birds that hover high in the air and cover the sun. The animals flee.
Latvian *1.*

222B* *The Sparrow and the Mouse.* The sparrow quarrels with the mouse about a grain or ear of corn. The eagle as arbitrator decides in favor of the sparrow, and is thrashed by the friends of the mouse. (Very often there follows Type 313.) (Cf. 313 I [d].)
Livonian (99') *2;* Latvian *22;* Russian: Andrejev *12.*

223 *The Bird and the Jackal as Friends.* I. The jackal asks the bird to obtain food. The bird flies near men carrying baskets of food. They drop them to pursue bird and jackal eats food. See Type 1*. II. The jackal asks the bird to make him laugh. The bird alights on the men's heads so that they strike one another. [K1082.3]. III. The jackal asks the bird to make him cry. The bird leads men or dogs to his hiding place. IV. The jackal asks the bird to save its life. The bird entices the jackal into power of the crocodile, then strikes crocodile so that jackal escapes.
India *5.*

223 *Wedding of the Turkey and the Peacock.* All birds are invited to the wedding except the eagle. This omission starts a great conflict. [B282].
****Kunstmann *Hdwb. d. Märchens* s.v. »Vogelhochzeit»; *Bolte Zs. f. Vksk. XII 169; *RTP V 15. — Livonian (224') *2;* Latvian *1.*

224* *The Crow on her Wedding Borrows Feathers* from other birds to adorn herself. She begins to boast and to laugh at others. At that the stork laughs so much that he falls into a tar-barrel and gets black wings.
Latvian *2.*

225 *The Crane Teaches the Fox to Fly.* Lets him fall to the earth [K1041].
*Dähnhardt IV 269; *Espinosa III Nos. 218—220. — Finnish *4;* Estonian *3;* Latvian *24;* Lithuanian *1;* Danish *3;* Spanish *4;* Catalan: Amades No. 307; German Archive *26;* Hungarian *4;* Polish *3;* Russian: Andrejev *3.* — Spanish-American: Rael No. 377 (U.S.); West Indies (Negro) *2;* American Indian: Thompson *C Coll* II 441, 449. — Literary Treatment: Aesop (Halm No. 419).

225A *Tortoise Lets self be Carried by Eagle.* Dropped and eaten. [J657.2].
Wienert FFC LVI 46, 50 Nos. 51, 98. — Spanish Exempla: Keller. — India *5.*

226 *The Goose Teaches the Fox to Swim.* Shakes him off in the water. [K1042].
Swedish (Uppsala) *1;* Danish *2;* German *3;* Polish *3;* Russian: Andrejev; Indonesian: DeVries No. 69. — Franco-American *2.* — Oceanic: Dixon 193 n. 20.

227 *Geese Ask for Respite for Prayer* before the fox eats them. They cackle continuously and finally escape. [K551.1]. Cf. Types 6, 122.
*BP II 206 (Grimm No. 86). — Livonian (227A) *2;* Latvian *13;* Swedish *2* (Uppsala *1,* Lund *1*); Irish *2;* French *9;* German *28* (Archive 27, Merk. p. 334); Slovenian; Serbocroatian *2;* Russian: Andrejev; Greek *1,* Loukatos Nos. 15, 16; India *1.* — West Indies (Negro) *1.*

227* *The Crayfish Entices the Crow into Talking.* When the crow opens its mouth, the crayfish drops into water, and so saves his life. Cf. Types 6, 122.
*BP II 207. — Lithuanian (*239) *2;* Russian: Andrejev (*242 I) *1;* India: Panchatantra I 7.

228 *The Titmouse Tries to be as Big as a Bear.* She ruffles up her feathers but does not succeed in fooling her young. But in her own form she flies into the bear's ear and kills him. [L315.1].
*BP II 437. — Finnish *39;* Finnish-Swedish *1;* Estonian *5;* Latvian *8;* Russian: Andrejev; Greek: Loukatos No. 17; Indonesian: DeVries No. 115. — Franco-American *1;* West Indies (Negro) *1.* — African *8.*

229 (formerly 229*) *The Hawk Frightened at the Snipe's Bill.* The snipe: »It is a bill, but it is good for nothing (weak).» The hawk is no longer afraid. [J2616].
Finnish *4;* Russian: Andrejev.

229A* *The Birds' Court.*
I. *The Jay (Sparrow) has Wronged the Magpie (Wagtail).* He is to be hanged.

The wren (fox) says that a respectable man cannot be so severely punished for such a trifle. The jay is acquitted.

II. *The Starling Beats the Magpie*, the stranger, who complains to the court. The judge — the eagle — asks for the oldest of the birds, the sparrow. Jumping about, the latter says that the starling is guilty.

III. *The Snipe Tramples on the Crow*. The snipe is to be hanged. The woodstarling defends her. The snipe is forbidden to fly during the day.

IV. *The Crow Insults the Cuckoo*. The judge says that henceforth the cuckoo is allowed to insult the crow.

V. *The Crow Accuses the Nightingale*. The witnesses are the magpie and the oriole. The court decides that the crow must not hurt the nightingale.
Latvian 9.

229B* *Eagle Warns Shepherd that Wolf is Eating Sheep*. Crow rebukes eagle for thus imperiling his own food supply. [J715.1].
Spanish (229*) *1*.

230 *The Rearing of the Large-headed and Large-eyed Bird*. When the one rearing the owl learns its great age he kills it. [K1985].
Finnish *18;* Russian: Andrejev; Greek *2*, Loukatos No. 3.

230* *The Race of the Cock, the Birch-cock and the Birch-hen*. Winner to live in town. Dupe's attention distracted so that he loses race. [A2250.1].
Finnish-Swedish *1;* Swedish 22 (Stockholm *4*, Lund *2*, misc. *16*).

230** *The Race of the Birch-cock and the Cat*.
Finnish-Swedish *1*.

230A* *The Bird (the Owl) Snatches the Hare with one Foot*, while with the other he holds to the tree. The hare disengaging himself, tears the bird.
Latvian *6*.

230B* *The Falcon Tears the Hare*. The sparrow laughs. But the falcon snatches the sparrow too, and eats him up.
Latvian *4*.

231 *The Heron (Crane) Transports the Fish*. A heron (crane) tells the fish in a lake that is drying up that it will transport them one by one to another lake, but eats them instead. A crab sees through the deception, seizes the heron by the throat and kills it. [J657.3, K815.14].
Bødker Exempler 281 No. 26; Spanish Exempla: Keller; India *5;* Buddhist myth: Malalasekera II 260.

231* *Animals Eat Each Other*. Cf. Type 20.
I. The animals eat part of the toad's bread. The toad is eaten by the falcon, and the latter is shot by the hunter.
II. The falcon eats the cock, the fox eats the falcon, and the hunter shoots the fox.
III. The eagle tears the man to pieces, the wolf kills the eagle, the bear — the wolf, and the bear bursts.
Latvian *11*.

231** *The Eagle Wants to Tear the Dove to Pieces*. The dove begs the falcon to help her, but he eats the dove and her young.
Latvian *2*.

232 *The Heathcock and the Birds of Passage*. The former prefers to remain at home amid hardships than to go to foreign lands. [J215.3].
Finnish *10;* Polish *1;* Russian: Andrejev.

232A* *Crow Bespatters Swan.* The crow, envying the swan's white color, bespatters him with mud. The swan washes herself, and is white again. The crow never becomes white.
Latvian 5.

232B* *Crane as Traveler.* The crow says that the crane in spite of his frequent traveling has not become clever. The magpie says: »Stupid people do not grow wiser by traveling.»
Latvian 4.

232C* *Which Bird Is Father.* A very small bird goes to God with his adult son, and asks God to guess which of them is the father and which the son. God: »There is a spot on the father's nose.» Immediately the father rubs his nose, and now God knows which is the father, and which the son. [J1141.1]. Cf. Type 66A.
Latvian (*228) 1.

232D* *Crow Drops Pebbles into Water Jug so as to be Able to Drink* [J101].
Wienert FFC LVI 64 (ET 272), 106 (ST 186, 246); Jacobs Aesop 213 No. 55. — Latvian (*226) 4.

233 *The Birds and the Net.*

233A *Birds Escape by Shamming Death.* Birds, caught in a fowler's net, follow the advice of an old bird and sham death. After the fowler has thrown them out on the ground, they fly away. [K522.4].
India 5.

233B *The Birds Fly Off with the Net.* Birds, caught in a fowler's net, all work together and fly off with the net. They fly to a mouse (rat) who gnaws the net asunder. [K581.4.1].
India 6.

233C *The Swallow and the Hemp-seeds.* Swallow in vain urges other birds to eat seeds as fast as it is sowed. Ridiculed, he builds nest among the dwellings of men. Later birds are caught in nets made from the hemp. [J621.1].
*Dähnhardt IV 275; Wienert FFC LVI 62 (ET 248), 118 (ST 277); Aesop (Haim Nos. 105, 106, Jacobs 203 No. 12); Herbert III 8; Crane Vitry 176 No. 101. — Africa (Fang): Tessman 27ff., (Pangwe): *ibid.* 362ff.

234 *The Nightingale and the Blindworm* each have one eye. The nightingale borrows the blindworm's eye and then refuses to return it. Since then, she has two eyes, the blindworm none. The latter is always on a tree where a nightingale has her nest and in revenge bores holes in the nightingale's eggs. [A2247.5].
*Köhler-Bolte I 72; Dähnhardt II 136ff. — Finnish: Aarne FFC XXXIII 55 No. 110**; Irish 3; French 21; Catalan: Amades No. 995; German 4 (Archive 3, Meckl. No. 26); Polish 2. — Spanish-American: Hansen (Puerto Rico) 1.

234A* *The Birds Brew Beer* and rejoice that it is excellent.
Latvian (*234) 25.

234B* *The Crow Complaints of Pains* in her belly because of having eaten sour milk. The raven marvels and asks who has dug up the dung.
Latvian (**234) 3.

235 *The Jay Borrows the Cuckoo's Skin* and fails to return it [A2313.1, A2241].
Dähnhardt III 131ff., especially 140. — Finnish *15;* Finnish-Swedish *1;* Lithuanian *3;* Irish *3;* German *1;* Russian: Andrejev. — Indonesian: DeVries No. 117.

235A* *The Cat Eats some Rat Poison and Dies.* The woodpecker makes a cross, the raven delivers the sermon and the little birds sing. [B257]. Cf. Type 2021.
Latvian (*235) *13.*

235B* *The Thrush Gets a Pretty Coat of Feathers* from the peacock whom she has fed when hungry. [A2222.1].
Livonian (235) *1.*

235C* *Bird has New Clothes Made:* flies away without paying [K233.1].
Spanish: Boggs (244) *1.*

236 *The Thrush Teaches the Doves (etc.) to Build Small Nests.* The dove keeps saying »I know» and persists in building her small nest. (Imitation of bird's sounds.) Cf. Type 2075. [A2271.1].
Dähnhardt III 191ff. — Finnish *9;* Lithuanian *1;* Latvian *28;* Swedish *2* (Uppsala *1,* misc. *1*); Danish *7;* Irish *10;* Flemish: De Meyer FFC XXXVII 88 No. 93; German *45* (Archive *44,* Henssen Volk No. 118); Hungarian *2;* Polish *1;* Russian: Andrejev.

236* Other tales with imitation of bird sounds. Cf. Type 206.
Hungarian: Kovács (236 II—236 V) *11;* Polish (233).

237 *Magpie Tells why Sow is Muddy.* A magpie is punished by his master, who throws him into a mud puddle. The magpie sees a muddy sow. He says, »You also must have had a quarrel with your master.» [J2211.2].
*Pauli (ed. Bolte) No. 669; French *3;* U.S.: Baughman (J2211.2) *3;* Spanish-American: Hansen (**237A—E) (Puerto Rico) *9,* (Argentina) *1.*

238 *The Keen Sight of the Dove and the Keen Hearing of the Frog.* They boast to each other. [K85, K86].
Finnish *9;* Latvian *1;* Lithuanian *2;* French *7;* Russian: Andrejev.

239 *The Crow Helps the Deer Escape from the Snare.* The deer aids the jackal, but when the deer is caught in a snare the jackal refuses to help him. On the advice of the crow the deer feigns death. When the hunter releases him, he bounds away. [K642.1].
India *7.*

240 *The Dove's Egg-substitution:* two for seven. The dove persuaded by the magpie to exchange eggs, the seven dove's eggs for two of the magpie. Since then the dove lays but two eggs. [A2247.4].
Dähnhardt *Natursagen* III 127. — Finnish *94;* Finnish-Swedish *1;* Estonian *11;* Swedish *52* (Uppsala *30,* Stockholm *5,* Göteborg *7,* Lund *3,* misc. *7*); Russian: Andrejev.

240A *The Cuckoo Lays her Egg into the Wren's Nest.*
Latvian (*239 A—C) *15.*

240* *The Egg-substitution: Race.* The hen lays two eggs, the dove more than half a

bushel of eggs. They contend by running for the sake of the eggs. The hen shouts to the dove that its trousers are opened. The dove puts them right, and falls. The hen wins the race, and now she lays a bushel full of eggs, whereas the dove has only two.
Estonian: (FFC XXV 147 No. 49) *1;* Latvian (*238) *3.*

240A* *The Bee Falls into the Water.* The dove saves her. The hunter wants to shoot the dove. The bee stings the hunter. Cf. Type 75.
Latvian (*240) *3.*

241 *The Officious Bird and the Monkey.* A bird, sitting in its nest during a cold rain, asks shivering monkey why it doesn't build a house since it has hands like a man. The enraged monkey destroys the bird's nest. [B275.4, L462, Q295].
India *4.*

241* changed to 2021B.

242 *The Frog Enticed out of his Hole.* Crow (or other bird) swears not to eat him. Breaks his oath. [K815].
Finnish *24;* Estonian *1;* Lappish *1;* Swedish *7* (Uppsala *2* Göteborg *1* misc. *2*); Danish *3;* Flemish *6;* Russian: Andrejev.

242B* *The Crow Catches a Crayfish.* The crayfish begs to be set free, promising to sew her a warm coat for winter. In winter the crow looks for »the tailor» and calls him, but nobody answers.
Latvian *3.*

242C* *The Crow Calls the Frog from the Dike,* threatening to hack his back. The frog answers, »Wait, wait!»
Latvian *4.*

243 *The Parrot Pretends to be God.* Cf. Types 1380, 1422. [B131.3, J1154.1, K1971].

I. *The Tell-tale Parrot.* (a) A parrot decides a lawsuit against a woman, or (b) reports a woman's infidelity to her husband. (c) The woman orders the parrot killed, cooked, and served to her, but the parrot escapes the cook (after it is plucked) and the cook substitutes a chicken.

II. *The Parrot as God.* (a) The parrot hides in a temple and advises the woman, when she comes to worship, to shave her head, give away all her goods, or the like, and she will go directly to heaven. The woman thinks it is a god speaking and obeys. (b) When she has done as ordered and has called the people to witness her ascent into heaven, the parrot ridicules her.
India *4.*

243A *Cock who Crows about Mistress's Adultery Killed.* Discreet cock saves his life. [J551.1].
Pauli (ed. Bolte) No. 9; Oesterley *Gesta Romanorum* No. 68; Herbert III 206. — Spanish (1829*) *1.*

243* *The Crow Marries.* As the grain is being harvested in the autumn, the wife calls out, »Iaak, they are stealing the grain.» [J953.7.].
Finnish *1;* Estonian *23;* Livonian *2;* Latvian *5;* West Indies (Negro) *1.*

243A* *Peace for the Frogs.* The frog has been in church. The clergyman has said that big ones must not hurt little ones. All at once the stork swallows the frog. Cf. Type 62.
Latvian *2.*

243B* *Lark Reminisces with Stork* about old times. Stork eats her up.
Rumanian *4.*

244 (formerly 244*) *The Raven in Borrowed Feathers.* He puts on swan feathers. Other birds take them from him and leave him cold and disgraced. [J951.2].
Livonian (249') *1;* Spanish *1;* Hungarian: Berze Nagy (249**) *1.* — Spanish-American: Hansen (Puerto Rico) *2;* West Indies (Negro) *15.* — Literary Treatments: Crane *Vitry* 239 No. 249; Wienert FFC 46 (ET 49); Aesop (Halm Nos. 200, 201, 201b, Jacobs No. 21).

244** *The Crow and the Titmouse.* The crow refuses to marry the titmouse since he has heard that she is a hundred years old. The titmouse has lived through cold that made dough freeze in women's hands. [B282.22.1.].
Estonian *1.*

244*** *The Raven Carries his Young across a Lake.* The last one promises to carry his young over in like manner.
Finnish *4.*

244A* *Crane's Courtship of Heron.* Crane proposes to heron. She refuses him. After some meditation she goes to the crane, but he sends her away. Then he regrets it. Again he goes to her and receives a refusal, etc.
Lithuanian (*223) *1;* Latvian (224*) *1;* Russian: Andrejev (*244) *1.* — Also reported from East Prussia by Professor Ranke.

244B* *The Two Starving Sparrows.* Two sparrows are starving. One flies away to look for food, and finds some cherries. He eats his fill and flies back to his companion with some cherries. His companion is already dead.
Latvian (**244) *3.*

244C* *Raven Drowns his Young who Promise to Aid him when he Becomes Old.* He saves one who admits he will not help, because he will have to carry his own young. (Cf. Type 510 I.) [J267.1].
Lithuanian (*244) *3.*

244D* *The Bird and the Hunter's Skull.* Hunter dies chasing bird. Later bird is caught when she enters hunter's skull and cannot escape.
Hungarian: Kovács (244*) *2.*

245 *Tame Bird and Wild Bird.* The tame bird advises the wild bird to look about him. The wild bird is shot. [L451.1]. Cf. Type 112.
Finnish *22;* Estonian *2;* Russian: Andrejev.

245* *The Birds Discuss the Trap.* The magpie, the crow, and the raven talk about the trap. The raven gets caught. [J655.1]. Cf. Type 44.
Lappish *1;* Indonesian: DeVries No. 110.

246 *The Hunter Bends the Bow.* One bird escapes; other remains and is shot. (Told also of fish.) [J641.1].
Finnish *5;* Russian: Andrejev. —Spanish-American: Hansen (246**A) (Puerto Rico) *1.* — Literary Treatment: Chauvin III 59 No. 21.

246* *The Swan and the Swallow* want to live and die together. At the moment of danger only the swallow can fly away. [J429.1].
Flemish *1.*

247 *Each Likes his Own Children Best.* The snipe asks the sportsman to spare its small ones, easily recognized as being the prettiest in the forest. To be on the safe side the man shoots only the ugliest he can find. They are the young snipes. (Often told of the ape.) [T681].

Dähnhardt II 242ff. — Latvian *5;* Lithuanian *1;* Swedish *7* (Uppsala 1, Göteborg *1,* Lund *2,* misc. *3*); Norwegian *4;* Danish *3;* Irish *3;* German *4;* Italian (Sicilian *1*); Hungarian *2;* Polish *3;* India *1.* — Literary Treatments: Wienert FFC LVI 77 (ET 426), 146 (ST 509); Herbert *Catalogue of Romances* III 39ff.

247* *The Crow and the Seal Keep House Together.* The crow burnt up.
Lappish *2.*

247A* *Sandpiper and Thrush Converse.* »What do people say of my song?» The thrush: »No one praises it.» — »Then I will praise it myself.»
Estonian *2.*

247B* *The Falcon Praises the Owl's Young.* The latter shuts her eyes with joy, and the falcon captures the young.
Latvian (*247A) *3.*

247B** The falcon praises the owl's young and asks if they have had something to eat. The mother: »What does a man know about children?»
Latvian (*247B) *5.*

247B*** »Owl, you have fine children!» — »Just like their mother.» — »With big heads and broad feet.» — »Just like their father.»
Latvian (*247C) *5.*

248 *The Dog and the Sparrow.* A man runs over the dog, friend of the sparrow. The sparrow takes vengeance. The man loses his horse, his property, and finally his life. [N261].

*BP I 515 (Grimm No. 58); *Beckwith MAFLS XVII 254. — Finnish *14;* Estonian *1;* Latvian *10;* Lithuanian *12;* Swedish (Uppsala) *1;* Scottish *1;* Irish *9;* French *4;* Catalan: Amades No. 318; Dutch *1;* Flemish (160*) *1;* German *8;* Italian (Tuscan [201] *1*); Rumanian *2;* Hungarian *3;* Slovenian; Polish *4;* Russian: Afanasiev (248A) *3.* — Spanish-American: Hansen (Dominican Republic) *1,* (Puerto Rico) *1.*

248A *The Elephant and the Lark.* The elephant tramples the lark's nest. The lark gets the aid of the frog, who croaks and leads the elephant to fall into a dry pool; of the crow, who pecks out the elephant's eyes; and of bees, which sting the elephant to death. [N261].
India *3.*

248A* *The Clever Bird.* The sparrow (thrush) provides for his friend, the wolf (fox). He cleverly procures meat and beer (pecks at a barrel of beer; an axe thrown at him breaks the barrel.)
Lithuanian *3;* Russian: Andrejev (*56C, *248B) *8.*

249 changed to 280A.

249* *The Fox and the Bird Build a Boat.*
Lappish *1.*

249** *The Wagtail and the Water Ousel Float Wood for the Thrush.*
Lappish *1.*

FISH

250 *Swimming Match of the Fish.* The perch hangs on to the tail of the salmon and wins. [K11.2]. Cf. Types 221, 275.
*BP III 339, 354; Dähnhardt *Natursagen* IV 72ff., 91, 160ff. — Finnish *49;* Finnish-Swedish *1;* Latvian *8;* Lappish *2;* Catalan: Amades No. 349; German *1;* Russian: Andrejev. — West Indies (Negro) *3.* — Literary Treatment: Wienert FFC LVI *54 (ET 139).

250A *Flounder's Crooked Mouth.* In race between fish he cries out in jealousy because herring is winning [A2252.4] (or he makes a discourteous answer to God [A2231.1.2]). He is punished by having his mouth turned around.
*BP II 284 (Grimm No. 172); *Dähnhardt IV 192—197, III 24f. — Finnish: Aarne FFC VIII 21 No. 117; Livonian: Loorits FFC LXVI 91 No. 92; Lithuanian (3178).

252 *The Pike and the Snake Race to Land.* The winner is to remain on land. [A2252.1].
Dähnhardt III 145. — Finnish *7;* Lappish *2;* Russian: Andrejev.

253 *The Fish in the Net.* The little fish slip through the meshes; the big ones are caught. [L331].
*BP III 355. — Finnish *4;* Rumanian (254*) *1;* Russian: Andrejev. — Literary Treatment: Wienert FFC LVI 66 (ET 290), 113 (ST 240); Aesop (Halm No. 26).

253* *The Old Salmon Advises the Young* how they may slip through the net. [L331].
*BP III 355; Aesop (Halm No. 26). — Lappish *1.*

254* *Conversation of the Fish.*
Lappish *7.*

254** *The Trial of Yorsh Yorshovich* (»Perch Perchovich«). Yorsh settles in a foreign lake and drives everyone away. When they call him in for trial before the fish he mocks them all. He ends in the fish soup of a peasant fisherman.
Russian: Afanasiev (254*) *11.*

OTHER ANIMALS AND OBJECTS

275 *The Race of the Fox and the Crayfish.* The latter hangs on to the fox's tail and wins. [K11.2]. Cf. Types 250, 1074.
*BP III 339, 355 (Grimm No. 187); Coffin *4;* *Anderson *Novelline* No. 42; Dähnhardt IV 46—97. — Finnish *10;* Estonian *3;* Livonian *3;* Latvian *26;* Lappish *1;* Swedish *4* (Liungman *2,* Misc. *2*); Irish *19;* French *19;* Spanish *3;* Catalan: Amades Nos. 277, 306, cf. 337; Walloon (275C) *2;* German *23* (Archive *22,* Henssen Volk No. 106); Italian (Tuscan [100] *1*); Hungarian *4;* Slovenian *4;* Polish *8;* Russian: Afanesiev *1;* Greek *2,* Loukatos Nos. 10, 12, 13, 14, 17; Turkish: Eberhard-

Boratav No. 4 *2;* Indonesian: DeVries Nos. 120, 121. — Franco-American *2;* West Indies (Negro) *6;* American Negro: Parsons JAFL XXX 189, 209; Beckwith MAFLS XVII 261; American Indian: Thompson *C Coll* II 441. — African *6.*
(*The Keen Sight of the Dove and the Keen Hearing of the Frog.* See Type 238.)

275A *Hare and Tortoise Race: Sleeping Hare.* In a race between the fast and the slow animal, the fast animal sleeps on the road and allows the slow animal to pass him. [K11.3].

Dähnhardt IV 66ff.; *BP III 341ff.; Jacobs Aesop 162 No. 68; Haupt Zs. f. deutsches Altertum XII (1865) 527; *Wienert FFC LVI 44 (ET 22), 135 (ST 412); Halm Aesop No. 420. — Japanese: Ikeda; Ainu: Chamberlain, *Aino Folktales* (London, 1888) No. 14; N. A. Indian (Ojibwa): Schoolcraft *Algic Researches* 181, (Cherokee): Mooney RBAE XIX 290 No. 43; Africa (West Africa): Cronise and Ward *Cunnie Rabbit, Mr. Spider and the Other Beef* (London, 1903) 155f.; West Indies: Flowers 494; Bahama: Parsons MAFLS XIII 102; American Negro (Pennsylvania): Parsons JAFL XXX 214, (North Carolina): Parsons JAFL XXX 174, (South Carolina): Parsons MAFLS XVI 79, (Florida): Parsons JAFL XXX 226.

275A* *Race between Hedgehog and Hare.*
Latvian (*275) *17.*

275B* *Race of Wolf and Bee.* Other bees sting wolf under tail. While he chases them away, the bee wins. Cf. Type 1074.
Spanish *1.*

275C* *Race of Frog and Snail.* Snail wins race because frog cannot pass a barrier on the road; the snail crawls over it.
Walloon (*275D) *1.*

276 *Crab Walks Backward: Learned from his Parents* [U121.1].
*Crane *Vitry* 152 No. 44; Wienert FFC LVI *63 (ET 258), *103 (ST 159); Halm Aesop No. 187. — Latvian (*276) *1.*

276* *The Frog Turns a Somersault in Front of the Harrow.* Says he has danced at a wedding.
Estonian *1.*

276** *The Flea, the Louse, and the Bug.* Flea by jumping about betrays others to man, who kills them.
Lappish *2;* Hungarian *2.*

277 (formerly 277*) *The King of the Frogs.* When the frogs ask God for a king, God throws a log into the water. They are unhappy. God sends a crane and he eats them up. They regret that they were not satisfied with their first king. [K643.1].
Estonian (277*) *1;* Latvian *3;* Lithuanian (277*) *1;* Russian: Andrejev (277*) *1.* — Literary Treatment: Aesop (Halm No. 76); Crane *Vitry* No. 24.

277A *The Frog Tries in Vain to be as Big as the Ox*, puffs and bursts [J955.1].
Jacobs Aesop 205 No. 22; Wienert FFC LVI 58 (ET 192), 93 (ST 61);

Halm Aesop No. 84; *Crane *Vitry* 145 No. 29. — Finnish *2;* Latvian (*277) *2;* Hungarian (278*) *1;* India: Thompson-Balys (J955.1) *1.*

278 *Rat and Frog Tie Paws Together to Cross Marsh.* Carried off by falcon. [J681.1].
*Chauvin II 123 No. 117; Scala Celi 73a No. 416; *Crane *Vitry* 135 No. 3; Latvian (*277) *3;* Spanish Exempla: Keller (J681.1); India: Thompson-Balys (J681.1) *1;* Indonesian: DeVries No. 124, cf. No. 125.

278A *Frog Persists in Living in Puddle on Road.* Disregards advice of another frog and is run over. [J652.1].
Wienert FFC LVI 59 (ET 203), 118 (ST 279); Halm Aesop No. 75; North Carolina: Brown Collection I 704.

278A* *Frogs Decide Not to Jump into the Well.* Their spring having dried up, they consider jumping into a well. They decide that the well may also dry up. [J752.1].
Wienert FFC LVI 59 (ET 202), 108 (ST 201); Halm Aesop No. 74; Latvian (***279) *2;* Italian Novella: Rotunda (J742).

278B* *The Frog's Names.* The frogs or the toads rejoice, when the cock (stag) gives them pretty names: »High leaper» — »Fine leaf» — »Golden leaf».
Latvian (*280B) *13.*

278C* *Advice of the Frog.* A man takes care of the frog during the winter. In spring the frog gives him advice. That is not enough for the rescuer. He beats the frog. That is why the frog is hunchbacked. [A2356.2.1]. Cf. Type 150.
Dähnhardt III 42ff., 493f. — Estonian: Loorits *Estnische Märchen* No. 48; Livonian (670B*) *1;* Latvian (*278) *9;* Lithuanian (*286) *3.*

278D* *The Frog's Names.* The frog or the toad rejoice, when the cock (stag) gives them pretty names: »High leaper» — »Fine leaf» — »Golden leaf».
Latvian (*280B) *13.*

279* *Snake Trying to surround Crab Refuses to straighten himself out.* Is seized by crab and killed. Now must be straight and can finally be friends. [J1053].
Greek: Megas *Paramythia* No. 24. — Literary Treatment: Aesop (Halm No. 346).

280 *The Ant Carries a Load as Large as Himself.* The contest of the raven (or other bird) with the ant. [A2251.1].
Dähnhardt *Natursagen* III 143. — Finnish *41;* Lithuanian *7;* Serbocroatian *1;* Polish *2;* Russian: Andrejev *1;* Greek: Loukatos Nos. 10, 12, 13.

280A (formerly 249). *The Ant and the Lazy Cricket.* The lazy creature is put to shame by the thrift of the industrious creature. In the winter he is in distress. [J711].
Aesop (Halm Nos, 295, 405, Jacobs No. 36); Pauli (ed. Bolte) No. 845; *Chauvin III 58 No. 19. — Latvian (*281) *8;* Swedish (Uppsala) *5;* Norwegian *1;* Flemish (249*) *2;* Italian (Sicilian *2);* Hungarian *1;* Serbocroatian *5,* (Istrian) No. 4; Polish *1.* — Spanish-American: Rael No. 406 (U.S.); American Indian: Thompson *C Coll* II 451. — African *2.*

281 (formerly 281*) *The Gnats and the Horse.* The gnats want to kill the horse. They think they have thrown him when the horse rolls over. Cf. Type 243*. [J953.6].

Finnish (281*) ; Estonian (281*) *8;* Russian: Andrejev; India *1;* Indonesian: DeVries No. 136. — Literary Treatment: Aesop (Halm No. 235).

281A* *Buffalo and Gnat.* Man cannot chase buffalo from mud hole. Gnat does it. [L315.6].
Rumanian (212) *2.* — Literary Treatment: Aesop (Halm No. 234).

282* *Wedding of Cricket and Fly.* Cf. Type 224.
Hungarian: Berze Nagy (131*) *17.*

282A* *The Flea and the Fly:* the flea unhappy in the country; the fly in the city; they switch their places.
Polish (299) *6;* Russian: Andrejev (*284).

282B* *Conversation of Fly and Flea.* Flea is hunchbacked because he raises lumps all night on sleeping man. Fly has swollen eyes since he laughs so much over man's unsuccessful efforts to catch him. [J612.1].
*Bolte Zs. f. Vksk. XV 105; *Dähnhardt III 19, 126. — Rumanian (288*) *3;* Hungarian (288*) *2.*

282C* *The Louse Invites the Flea.* The flea bites the man and jumps away. The bed is searched and the louse is killed. [J2137.1].
Chauvin II 89 No. 27; Spanish Exempla: Keller; Bødker Exempler 283 No. 29; India: *Thompson-Balys (J2137.1) *3.*

283 Spider Invites Fly to Rest on her Curtain. Eats her. [K815.2].
Spanish Exempla: Keller; Herbert *Catalogue of Romances* III 40ff.

283A* *The Spider is Dead.* Spider catches some flies and gnats. He releases a fly, in order that it may spread the rumor he is dead. The insects believe it, rejoice, are careless, and fall into the web of the spider.
Russian: Afanasiev *2.*

283B* *The House of the Fly.* A fly, a mouse, a hare, a fox, and a wolf gather in a mitten. A bear sits on the house (mitten) and crushes it.
Russian: Andrejev (*283).

283C* *The Spider Grows Thin* in the house of the very saving housewife [W152.7].
Flemish *4.*

283D* *The Spider Laughs at the Silkworm* working so slowly. The silkworm says that his work is valuable, whereas that of the spider is of no good.
Latvian (***285B) *3.*

283E* *The Spider Marvels at the Order in the Beehive.* The bee says that they have a queen to rule the house, and the spiders have none.
Latvian (***285A) *3.*

283F* *Dungbeetle and Dung.* The bee wonders at the dungbeetle's wallowing in the dung. The dungbeetle does not want anything better.
Latvian (*286) *2.*

283G* *The Spiders Catch Fish in their Webs.*
Lappish (287*) *1.*

285 *The Child and the Snake.* The snake drinks from the child's milk-bottle.
**B. Waugh »The Child and the Snake» *Norweg* VII 153ff.; *BP II 459 (Grimm No. 105); Coffin *4.* Cf. Type 672B, C. — Finnish *6;* Finnish-Swedish *1;* Latvian *1;* Lithuanian *29;* Swedish *73* (Uppsala *11,* Stockholm *5,* Göteborg *50,* Lund *3,* misc. *4*); Danish *14;* English *1;*

French *3;* Spanish *2;* German *15;* Hungarian: Berze Nagy (285*) *1;* Czech: Tille (1937) p. 385f. *5;* Russian: Andrejev; India *1.* — English American: Baughman *8;* West Indies (Negro) *1;* American Negro: (Michigan) *Dorson No. 101.

285A *The Dead Child and the Snake's Tail.* White snake brings luck to house. He is fed milk. People kill snake and thereafter have bad luck. [B335.1].
**BP II 461; Aesop (Halm No. 96). — *Oesterley *Gesta Romanorum* No. 141; Hungarian: Berze Nagy (285*) *1;* Greek (285*), Megas No. 27; India: *Thompson-Balys.

285B *Falling Nut Saves Man from Serpent.* Farmer sleeps under tree. Snake is about to crawl into his mouth. Nut drops from tree, wakens the farmer who kills snake and eats nut. [N652].
Spanish *2.* — Spanish-American: Espinosa Jr. No. 57 (U.S.).

285C *Farmer Feeds Serpent so that it will not Eat Cattle.* Feeds it hot stones (pins) so that it dies. [K951.1, K951.2].
Spanish (285*A) *3.*

285D *Serpent (bird) Refuses Reconciliation.* Snake is given milk. Gives gold from tail as reward. Later man's son wants all gold at once and cuts the tail off. Boy is bitten by snake. Man tries to give snake milk again, but they can't be reconciled for each has injuries that cannot be forgotten. Cf. Type 159*. [J15].
*Anderson in Tauscher *Volksmärchen* 171 No. 4; *BP II 459; Chauvin II 94 No. 43, 102 No. 62. — Serbocroatian *2;* Greek (285*) *3,* Megas *Paramythia* No. 7, Loukatos No. 15; Turkish: Eberhard-Boratav No. 49 *2.* — Literary Treatment: Aesop (Halm Nos. 96, 251, 350).

285A* *The Adder Poisons the Children's Food* because the mother has thrown away her eggs. The mother puts the eggs back. The adder upsets the pot of porridge. Latvian *2;* Polish (168) *3.*

285B* *Snake Enticed out of Man's Stomach.* Patient fed salt: animal comes out for water. The patient is fed salt or heavily salted food and allowed no water for several days. He then stands with mouth open before a supply of fresh water, often a running brook. The thirsty animal emerges to get fresh water. [B784.2.1].
Ireland, U.S.: *Baughman (B784.2.1); Italian Novella: Rotunda (J1115.2.3); Polish (286) *3.*

286* *The Turtle's Wedding.* Mud turtle invites friends to daughter's wedding, but forgets to send invitation to toad. Conflict ensues. Cf. Type 224.
Spanish-American: Hansen **289 (Cuba) *1.*

287** *Frogs Refuse Fire to Arrogant Mole.* They give it to the polite quail. [Q2].
Flemish (287*) *1.*

288A* »*But by a Fine Fellow!*« Dying toad thus comforts his paramour, the frog, whom he is leaving neither married nor widow nor maiden and pregnant. [J865.1].
Spanish *4.*

288B* *The Over-hasty Toad (Beetle).* Is years ascending steps. On last step falls and curses haste. [X1862].
Latvian (**276AB) *2;* Spanish (288C) *1,* Espinosa Jr. Nos. 59, 60; Italian (Sicilian *288 *2*). — West Indies (Negro): Flowers 585.

288C* *The Deliberate Turtle.* Turtle is sent by animals to ask God for rain. After two months animals go in search of her. When they speak ill of her, she raises her head from under a rock and rebukes them.
Spanish-American: Hansen 288**D (Puerto Rico) *1.*

289 *Bat, Diver, and Thornbush Shipwrecked.* Bat brought money, bush put on clothes, and diver brought leather. All shipwrecked. Diver is looking for his leather. Bush looks for his clothes and holds fast to all passers-by. Bat is abroad only at night to escape creditors. (Cf. A2471.4, A2491.1). [A2275.5.3].
*Dähnhardt IV 273f.; *BP I 137 (Grimm No. 18); Wienert FFC LVI 35; Halm Aesop No. 306. — Latvian (**249) *3.*

291 *Deceptive Tug-of-war.* Small animal challenges two large animals to a tug-of-war. Arranges it so that they unwittingly pull against each other (or one end of rope is tied to a tree). [K22].
Spanish-American: Hansen (Peru) *1;* American Negro (Georgia): Harris Remus 124 No. 26; Bahama: Parsons MAFLS XIII 74 No. 34, Edwards MAFLS III 65; South American Negro: Cf. Hartt *Amazonian Tortoise Myths* (Rio de Janeiro, 1875) 20, Cape Verde Islands: Parsons MAFLS XV (1) 83 No. 27; West Indies (Negro): Flowers 495ff. *2.* — Africa *3.*

291* *The Tragic Death of the Three Gnats.* One of them meets his death between the oxen's horns, another due to two restless stallions, the third during a tussle between two giants. [X1295.1].
Lithuanian *2.*

292 *Ass Tries to Get a Cricket's Voice.* Asks cricket what they eat to get such a voice. They answer, »dew.» He tries it and starves. [J512.8].
Hungarian (292*) *1.* — Literary Treatments: Wienert FFC LVI 46 (ET 43), 90 (ST 24); Halm Aesop No. 337.

292* *The Cricket and the Coin.* Finds a coin but has it immediately stolen. — »So goes it always with the poor.» (Imitation of cricket sound.) Cf. Types 106, 206, 236*.
Hungarian (291*) *2.*

293 *Debate of the Belly and the Members.* Debate as to their usefulness. All are mutually useful. [J461.1].
*Prato *Archivio per lo studio della tradizioni popolari* IV (1885) 25ff.; Penzer V 135 n.; *Pauli (ed. Bolte) No. 399; Wienert FFC LVI *43 (ET 6), 92 (ST 59); Halm Aesop No. 197; Jacobs Aesop 206 No. 29; *Crane *Vitry* 167 No. 73; *H. Gombel *Die Fabel vom Magen und den Gliedern* (Beihefte zur Zs. f. romanische Philologie LXXX [Halle, 1934]). — French *1;* Jewish: bin Gorion *Born Judas* III 71, *301f., *Neuman; Indonesia: DeVries No. 139. — African (Ekoi): Talbot 393.

293A* *The Spring and the Wood.* The spring reproaches the wood with depriving it of light and warmth. Men hew the wood down, the spring dries up.
Latvian (*292) *3.*

293B* *The Mushroom Reviles the Young Oak* for clinging to it. After three days the mushroom collapses. The oak keeps on growing. [J953].
Latvian (**291) *19.*

293C* *Man and his Associates.* Animals, insects, and inanimate things: each tells of the place it best likes to live in. (Flea chats with fly, one disease with another, bread with boot, etc.)
Lithuanian (*290) *6.*

293D* *The Hops and the Turnips Quarrel.* »You tear the children's bellies.» — »Murderer of men.» Later on they are reconciled. »Supporter of the poor.» — »Comforter of men.»
Latvian (*289) *5.*

293E* *The Grains Talk with One Another.* The barley: »We go where gold is to be found.» The wheat: »We ourselves are gold.» Cf. Russian tale: two kinds of porridge talk. One: »I am good with milk.» The other: »I am good in and for myself.»
Latvian (*288) *1.*

293F* *Human Mucus and Excrement Converse.* The former prospers better in town, the latter in the country.
Latvian (*287) *2;* Hungarian: Kovács (287^{II}) *1.*

293G* *The Hedgehog, the Shilling, and the Gentleman.* The hedgehog finds a shilling. The young gentleman takes it away from him, then throws it back again. The hedgehog muses: »Having much, I go along the roadside. He who had nothing, took all away from me ... feeling ashamed, returned it.» [J953].
Latvian (*281) *8;* Lithuanian (*278) *3.*

294 *The Months and the Seasons.* Symbolic actions.
*Roberts *Kind and Unkind Girls* 75 (9 v.). — Latvian (**299A—D) *7.*

295 *The Bean, the Straw, and the Coal.* The coal burns the straw in two and falls into the water. The bean laughs till it splits.
Motifs: F1025.1. Bean, straw and coal go journeying. Coal burns straw in two and falls into the water. Bean laughs until it splits. A2741.1. Bean laughs till it splits: cause of black stripe.
BP I 135 (Grimm No. 18). — Estonian (295) *4;* Livonian (295*) *4;* Latvian *39;* Lithuanian *2;* Danish *2;* French *3;* Flemish (295*) *6;* German *6;* Hungarian *4;* Russian: Afanasiev *2;* India *1.* — Franco-American *7;* West Indies (Negro) *27;* American Negro: Beckwith MAFLS XVII 260, *285; American Indian (Ojibwa): Jones-Michelson PAES VII (II) 131 No. 11, 701 No. 71; (San Carlos Apache): Goddard PaAM XXIV 75.

297 *Objects go on Warpath.*

297A *Turtle's war-party.* Turtle recruits war-party of strange objects (knife, brush, awl, etc.) and animals. Because of their nature the companions get into trouble. [F1025.2, F601.7].
American Indian: *Thompson *Tales* 302 n. 108. — Japanese: Mitford 185ff., Ikeda.

297B *The War of the Mushrooms.* A mushroom summons the mushrooms to war. All refuse except the brown mushrooms.
Russian: Afanasiev *1.*

298 *Contest of Wind and Sun.* Sun by warmth causes traveler to remove coat, while the wind by violent blowing causes him to pull it closer around him. [A287.0.1].

Finnish-Swedish (1097*) *1;* Estonian: Loorits *Grundzüge* I 381ff.; Latvian (*298C) *10;* Lithuanian (3900); Catalan: Amades No. 663; Hungarian: Berze Nagy (729*) *1;* Polish (276) *4;* Russian: Andrejev *1;* Indonesian: DeVries Nos. 95, 140. — Literary Treatment: Wienert FFC LVI 43 (ET 7), 80 (ET 457), 136 (ST 419); Aesop (Halm No. 82).

298A *The Frostgod and his Son.* Two frosts agree to make the gentleman in his fur-coat and the peasant shiver. The gentleman suffers much from the frost. The other frost creeps into the peasant's old fur coat. The peasant quickly takes it off and hews wood. The fur is frozen hard. The peasant beats it, and so the frost also gets a thrashing.

Finnish *2;* Estonian: Loorits *Estnische Märchen* No. 68; Latvian (**298A) *3;* Russian: Andrejev (298 I) *1.*

298A* *The Man Greets the Wind.* The latter protects him from severe heat and cold.
Finnish *2;* Latvian *8;* Russian: Andrejev (*298) *1.*

298B* *The Cold and the Wind Compete* with each other for mastery. A passing peasant greets the wind. Now they contend about the peasant's barley field. The cold decides that the peasant shall reap only as many bushels of barley as there are cart-loads brought home from the field. The wind causes the peasant to have the corn carried in very small carts.
Latvian *1.*

298C* *Reeds Bend before Wind (Flood).* Save themselves while oak is uprooted. [J832].
*Pauli (ed. Bolte) No. 174; Wienert FFC LVI 73 (ET 387), 107 (ST 190, 243); Halm Aesop No. 179; **E. Grawi *Die Fabel vom Baum und dem Schilfrohr in der Weltliteratur* (Rostock Diss., 1911). — India: Thompson-Balys (J832) *1;* Jewish: Neumann (J832).

298D* *The Wind and the Whirlwind* go out into the world with the money given them by their father. The wind works useful things, gains more money; the whirlwind causes only losses and loses all.
Latvian (**297) *9.*

II ORDINARY FOLK-TALES

A. TALES OF MAGIC

SUPERNATURAL ADVERSARIES[1]

300—359 The Ogre (Giant, Dragon, Devil, Cobold, etc.) is Defeated

300 *The Dragon-Slayer.* Rescue of the princess. Cf. Types 301, 303, 305*, 315, 466, 466*, 466**, 502, 530, 532, 553.

I. *The Hero and his Dogs.* (a) A shepherd, (b) with a sister who afterwards proves to be faithless, or (c) other hero (d) acquires helpful dogs, (e) through exchange or (f) because they were born with the hero; or (g) through kindness he receives the help of animals; (h) he also receives a magic stick or sword.

II. *The Sacrifice.* (a) A princess is demanded as a sacrifice and (b) exposed to a dragon. She is offered to her rescuer in marriage.

III. *The Dragon* (a) breathes fire and (b) has seven heads (c) which magically return when cut off.

IV. *The Fight.* (a) While waiting for the dragon, the hero is loused by the princess and (b) falls into a magic sleep. (c) She awakens him by (d) cutting off a finger or (e) letting a tear fall on him. (f) In the fight, the hero is assisted by his dogs, or (g) his horse.

V. *The Tongues.* (a) The hero cuts out the tongues of the dragon and keeps them as proof of the rescue. (b) An impostor cuts off the dragon's heads, which he later seeks to use as proof.

VI. *Impostor.* (a) The hero leaves the princess (b) with an injunction of silence as to his identity; or (c) he is murdered and (d) resuscitated by his dogs. (e) The impostor forces an oath of secrecy from the princess.

VII. *Recognition.* (a) The hero intercepts the impostor on the wedding day, when he secures recognition (b) through the theft of the wedding cake by his dogs, or the presentation of (c) the dragon tongues, (d) of a ring, or (e) of another token.

---

[1] Cf. also Tales of the Stupid Orge, Types 1000—1199.

Motifs:

I. L100. Unpromising hero. P412.1. Shepherd as hero. K2212. Treacherous sister. B421. Helpful dog. B312.2. Helpful animals obtained by exchange. B311. Congenital helpful animal. Born at same time as master and (usually) by same magic means. B350. Grateful animals. B391. Animal grateful for food. B392. Hero divides spoil for animals. B312.1. Helpful animals a gift. D1254. Magic stick. D1081. Magic sword.

II. B11.10. Sacrifice of human being to dragon. S262. Periodic sacrifices to a monster. T68.1. Princess offered as prize to rescuer. Q112. Half of kingdom as reward.

III. B11. Dragon. G346. Devastating monster. Lays waste to the land. B11.2.11. Fire-breathing dragon. B11.2.3.1. Seven-headed dragon. B11.5.5. Self-returning dragon's head.

IV. D1962.2. Magic sleep by lousing. Picking the lice from the head of an old person or an ogre is used to put him to sleep. D1975. Dragon-fighter's magic sleep. While waiting for fight with dragon, hero falls into magic sleep. D1978.1. Waking from magic sleep by cutting off finger. D1978.2. Waking from magic sleep by letting tear fall on sleeper. B11.11. Fight with dragon. B11.11.1. Dragon fight: respite granted and dragon returns with renewed strength. B11.11.2. Hero's dogs (horse) prevent dragon's heads from rejoining body. B524.1.1. Dogs kill attacking cannibal (dragon). K1052. Dragon attacks own image in mirror. R111.1.3. Rescue of princess (maiden) from dragon.

V. H105.1. Dragon-tongue proof. Dragon-slayer cuts out the tongues and uses them later to prove his identity as slayer. R111.6. Girl rescued and then abandoned. K2262. Treacherous charcoal-burner. K2265. Treacherous red knight.

VI. C422.1. Tabu: revealing dragon-fighter's identity. Dragon-fighter forbids princess whom he has rescued to tell who he is. B515. Resuscitation by animals. K1933. Impostor forces oath of secrecy. K1932. Impostor claims reward (prize) earned by hero. N681. Lover arrives home just as mistress is to marry another. T151. Year's respite from unwelcome marriage. H151.2. Attention drawn by helpful animals' theft of food from wedding table: recognition follows. H83. Rescue tokens. Proof that hero has succeeded in rescue. H105.1. Dragon-tongue proof. H80. Identification by tokens. H113. Identification by handkerchief. K1816.0.3.1. Hero in menial disguise at heroine's wedding.

**Krappe FL XXXIV 141 (under Type 511); **Ranke *Die Zwei Brüder* (FFC CXIV) (368 versions); **Hartland *Legend of Perseus* III 1—65; *BP I 303, 534 (incident C), 547, II 22 (for I g as introduction); Coffin *21;* Anderson *Novelline* No. 29; Köhler-Bolte I 57. — Finnish *168;* Finnish-Swedish *13;* Estonian *61;* Livonian *6;* Lithuanian *88;* Lappish *8;* Swedish *37* (Uppsala *5,* Stockholm *1,* Göteborg 1, Lund *5,* Liungman *5,* misc. *20);* Norwegian *38,* Solheim *6;* Danish *129,* Grundtvig

No. 13B, cf. No. 14; Scottish *5;* Irish *527,* Beal I 388ff., IV 214—227, 300—306, VII 10, VIII 201—211, IX 124, XVIII 128—141, XIX 185—87, XX 167—176; French *30;* Spanish *6;* Catalan: Amades No. 82; Dutch *2;* Flemish *25,* Witteryck p. 292: *9;* Walloon *1;* German (Archive *125,* Henssen Jül. No. 451, Meckl. Nos. 28, 29, 30, 31, 34, Henssen Volk No. 212); Austrian: Haiding Nos. 59, 70; Italian: D'Aronco *Fiabe 42* (Pentamerone I No. 7, Tuscan [300 a—g, i—m], [852], cf. [902] *14,* Sicilian *5,* Gonzenbach Nos. 40, 44, Friuli *2);* Rumanian *17,* *Sainenu 334, 347, 481; Hungarian *33;* Czech *27* (FFC XXXIV 9—17, Soupis I 290—305 *11);* Slovenian *18;* Serbocroatian *7;* Polish *29,* 300A: *1,* 300B: *1;* Russian: Azadowsky *Russkaya Skazka* Nos. 5, 37, Andrejev *Ukraine* (300A) *22,* Afanasiev *67;* Greek *55,* Hahn Nos. 58, 70, 98; Turkish: Eberhard-Boratav Nos. 215 IV, 216, 220 *7;* India *35;* Indonesian: DeVries No. 141. — Franco-American *66;* English-American: Baughman *1;* Spanish-American: Hansen (Chile) *4,* (Colombia) *1,* (Dominican Republic) *6,* (Puerto Rico) *9,* Rael Nos. 246, 247, 338 (U.S.); Portuguese-American (Cape Verde Islands): Parson MAFLS XV (1) 261 n. 1; West Indies (Negro) *36;* American Indian: Thompson *C Coll* II 323ff. — African *12* (See Ranke FFC CXIV 106ff.).

300A *The Fight on the Bridge.* Aided by his filly, the strong youth defeats three dragons and their wives, in spite of his sleeping helpers.

*Ranke FFC CXIV 10 (German, Rumanian, Czech, Latvian, Estonian, White Russian, Great Russian, Ukraine, Vogul, Tatar, Chuvasian, Hungarian). — Finnish *2;* Livonian (300B) *2;* Lithuanian (*651) *7;* Czech: Tille Soupis I 283ff. *4;* Russian: Afanasiev (300*B) *29.*

300B *King of the Snakes.* King of the snakes is offended and devastates the country and carries off girls. The magically conceived hero is advised by a maiden and given an aspen stick with which he defeats the snake and later a dragon. Marriage with the maiden-helper.

Polish (678) *3.*

300* *The Boy Rescues the Princess [R112] through her Magic Power.* She changes herself into a golden bird [D150].

Lappish *1.*

300A* *The Princess is Won.* (Often mixed with Types 303, 304, 315, 316, 550, 552). (For detailed analysis see Rumanian 300 I* with its subdivisions.)

Rumanian *56.*

301 *The Three Stolen Princesses.*

1. *The Hero* is of supernatural origin and strength: (a) son of a bear who has stolen his mother; (b) of a dwarf or robber from whom the boy rescues himself and his mother; (c) the son of a man and a she-bear or cow; or (e) engendered by the eating of fruit, (f) by the wind or (g) from a burning piece of wood. (h) He grows supernaturally strong and is unruly.

II. *The Descent.* (a) With two extraordinary companions (b) he comes to a house in the woods, or (b¹) a bridge; the monster who owns it punishes the companions but is defeated by the hero, (c) who is let down through a well into a lower world. — Alternative beginning of the tale: (d) The third prince, where his elder brothers have failed, (e) overcomes at night the monster who steals from the king's apple-tree, and (f) follows him through a hole into the lower world.

III. *Stolen Maidens.* (a) Three princesses are stolen by a monster. (b) The hero goes to rescue them.

IV. *Rescue.* (a) In the lower world, with a sword which he finds there, he conquers several monsters and rescues three maidens. (b) The maidens are pulled up by the hero's companions and stolen.

V. *Betrayal of Hero.* (a) He himself is left below by his treacherous companions, but he reaches the upper world through the help of (b) a spirit whose ear he bites to get magic power to fly or (c) a bird, (d) to whom he feeds his own flesh; or (e) he is pulled up.

VI. *Recognition.* He is recognized by the princesses when he arrives on the wedding day. (b) He is in disguise and (c) sends his dogs to steal from the wedding feast; or (d) he presents rings, (e) clothing, or (f) other tokens, secures the punishment of the impostors and marries one of the princesses. — Adapted from BP.

Motifs:

I. L114. Hero (heroine) of unpromising habits. F610. Remarkably strong man. B631. Human offspring from marriage to animal. B635.1. The Bear's Son. Human son of woman who marries a bear acquires bear charasteristics. F611.1.1. Strong man son of bear who has stolen his mother. F611.1.2. Strong man son of woman and dwarf. F611.1.5. Strong man son of man and she-bear. F611.1.6. Strong man son of man and mare. F611.1.8. Strong hero engendered by eating fruit. F611.1.9. Strong hero engendered by the wind. F611.1.10. Strong hero engendered from burning brand. F611.2.1. Strong hero suckled by animal. T615. Supernatural growth. L114.3. Unruly hero.

II. F601. Extraordinary companions. A group of men with extraordinary powers travels together. G475.1. Ogre attacks intruders in house in woods. G475.2. Ogre attacks intruders on bridge. H1471. Watch for devastating monster. Youngest alone successful. F451.5.2. Malevolent dwarf. F102.1. Hero shoots monster (or animal) and follows it into lower world. N773. Adventure from following animal to cave (lower world). F92. Pit entrance to lower world. Entrance through pit, hole, spring or cavern. F96. Rope to lower world. F80. Journey to lower world.

III. R11.1. Princess (maiden) abducted by monster (ogre). H1385.1. Quest for stolen princess.

IV. R111.2.1. Princess(es) rescued from lower world. F601.3. Extraordinary companions betray hero. K1935. Impostors steal rescued princess.

V. K1931.2. Impostors abandon hero in lower world. K677. Hero tests the rope on which he is to be pulled to upper world. K963. Rope cut and victim dropped. K1932. Impostors claim reward (prize) earned by hero. K1933. Impostor forces oath of secrecy. D2135.2. Magic air journey from biting ear. B542.1.1. Eagle carries men to safety. F101.3. Return from lower world on eagle. B322.1. Hero feeds own flesh to helpful animal. The hero is carried on the back of an eagle who demands food. The hero finally feeds part of his own flesh.

VI. K1816.0.3.1. Hero in menial disguise at heroine's wedding. T68.1. Princess offered as prize to rescuer. T161. Year's respite from unwelcome marriage. N681. Husband (lover) arrives home just as wife (mistress) is to marry another. H151.2. Attention drawn by helpful animal's theft of food from wedding table; recognition follows. H83. Rescue tokens. Proof that hero has succeeded in rescue. H80. Identification by tokens. H94. Identification by ring. H111. Identification by garment. H113. Identification by handkerchief. Q262. Impostor punished. L161. Lowly hero marries princess.

**Delarue *Nouvelle Revue des Traditions Populaires* I (Sept.-Oct. 1949) 312ff., II 275; **A. Irving Hollowell »John the Bear in the New World» JAFL LXV 418; **Panzer *Beowulf* 1—246; *BP II 300 (Grimm No. 91); *M. de Meyer *Vlaamsche Sprookjesthemas* 20ff.; *Parsons MAFLS XV (1) 30 n. 3, 43 n. 1; Coffin *24;* *Anderson *Novelline* No. 57; *Tille FFC XXXIV 66ff.; Espinosa II 498ff.; *Liungman SSF III 428. — Livonian (531B') *1;* Lappish *5;* Swedish *65* (Uppsala *16,* Stockholm *2,* Göteborg *19,* Lund *6,* Liungman *7,* misc. *15*); Norwegian *35,* Solheim *4;* Danish *130;* Scottish *4;* Irish *150,* Beal IV 414—424, IX 66f. No. 6, XI supplement 14, XII 86ff.; English *1;* Catalan: Amades No. 39, cf. No. 16; Flemish *4;* Walloon (*301DE) *2;* German: Meckl. Nos. 31, 32, 33, 34; Austrian: Haiding Nos. 10, 24, 38; Hungarian (334) *5* (only 301 IIe); Czech: Tille Soupis II (1) 387ff., FFC XXXIV 66ff. *37;* Slovenian *19;* Serbocroatian *12;* Polish *37;* Russian: Andrejev *Ukraine 31,* Afanasiev *83;* Chinese: Graham (301 I and II) No. 155 p. 222, 504 p. 229. — Franco-American *57;* English-American: Baughman *4;* Spanish-American: Rael Nos. 170—175, 236 (U.S.). — West Indies (Negro) *11.* — African *2;* Swahili: Steere 199ff., 217. See also references to Types 301A and 301B.

301A *Quest for a Vanished Princess.* Turns in cooking dinner. Episode with the dwarf. The hole in the lower world and the rescue of the princesses (from a dragon or the like; cf. Type 300). The treacherous companions. Parts II, III, IV, V of the analysis above.

Finnish *85;* Finnish-Swedish *9;* Estonian *23;* Livonian *4;* Lithuanian *61;* Danish: Grundtvig No. 5A; French *10;* Spanish *1;* Catalan: Amades Nos. 9, 71, 111, 164, cf. Nos. 16, 39; Flemish *18;* German *105* (Archive *102,* Henssen Volk No. 122a + 122b); Italian: D'Aronco *Fiabe 75* (Tuscan [301 a, c, e—h, n, s, t] *9,* Sicilian *10,* Gonzenbach Nos. 58, 59,

61—64); Rumanian *15;* Hungarian *55;* Slovenian *1;* Serbocroatian *3;* Polish *1;* Russian: Azadowsky *Russkaya Skazka* Nos. 10, 21; Greek *48,* Hahn Nos. 26, 70, Dawkins *Modern Greek Folktales* No. 26; Turkish: Eberhard-Boratav No. 72 *38;* Arab: Littman 136ff.; India *1;.* — Spanish-American: Hansen (Chile) *1,* (Puerto Rico) *1,* cf. 301**C (Puerto Rico) *1;* American Indian: Thompson *C Coll* II 409ff., cf. also (Zuni) Boas JAFL XXXV 76 No. 4.

301B The same, preceded by: *The Strong Man and his Companions* (Pine-twister, Cliff-breaker). Cf. Types 513A, 650, and Parts I, II, III, IV, V of the analysis above.

Finnish *171;* Finnish-Swedish *5;* Estonian *50;* Livonian *5* + (300B') *2;* Lithuanian *67;* Lappish *2;* Swedish (Lund) *3;* Danish: Grundtvig No. 5B; Icelandic *2;* Basque *2;* French *86;* Spanish *5;* Catalan: Amades No. 1; Flemish *6;* German: Henssen Volk No. 123; Italian (Tuscan [300], [883] *2,* Sicilian *3*); Hungarian (301B, 301 I *Berze Nagy) *14;* Slovenian *4;* Serbocroatian *5;* Greek *16;* Turkish: Eberhard-Boratav Nos. 72 III, 77 IV, 146 V, 215 III, Anl. C3, cf. 252, Anl. C 4; India *10;* Chinese: Eberhard FFC CXX 179ff. No. 122, FFC CXXVIII 140ff. No. 81. — Spanish-American: Hansen (Chile) *1;* American Indian: Thompson *C Coll* II 409ff., cf. also (Zuni) Boas JAFL XXXV 76 No. 4.

301B* *The Strong Man and his Strong Companions Journey to the Land of Gold.* The Giant and his Son are overcome.
Lappish *4.*

301C* *The Magic Objects.* The youngest brother [L10] rescues a stolen princess [R112] and on the way receives magic objects: a lamp [D1162] (candle [D1162.1[), a loaf of bread [D1036.1], and a roast [D1035] (cup [D1176]). The brothers [K2211] throw him into prison [K1931.5]. Here he lives with aid of his magic objects [D1470] from year to year until he is rescued by his son [R156].
Livonian *2.*

301D* *Dragons Ravish Princesses.* The hero on a voyage in quest of the princesses. The forgotten ring and the faithless captain. The hero, abandoned on the island, takes service with a wizard; for payment gets magic objects, with the help of which he recovers the princesses.
Lithuanian (*301C) *21.*

302 *The Ogre's (Devil's) Heart in the Egg.* The youth who can turn himself into a lion, ant, etc. Sometimes the ogre's heart in the egg appears alone. Cf. Type 665. Sometimes introduced as in Type 400, or 425.

I. *Magic Help.* The hero receives magic help (a) from grateful animals for whom he has made an equable division of food, (b) from giants whom he has by trickery traded out of magic objects, or (c) from his animal brothers-in-law. Cf. Type 552.

II. *The Captive Princess.* (a) A princess has been carried off by an ogre. From her the hero learns (b) where his heart (soul, life) is, (c) what his life is bound up with, or (d) how he may be slain.

III. *The External Soul.* The hero follows instructions, finds the ogre's soul hidden away, and kills the ogre by destroying the external soul.

Motifs:

I. B393. Hero divides spoil for animals. B500. Magic power from animals. D1834. Magic strength from helpful animals. D831. Magic object acquired by trick exchange. By means of second magic object hero recovers first. B314. Helpful animal brothers-in-law. D630. Transformation and disenchantment at will. D532. Transformation by putting on claw, feather, etc. of helpful animal. D112.1. Transformation: man to lion. D182 2. Transformation: man to ant.

II. R11.1. Princess (maiden) abducted by monster (ogre). T68.1. Princess offered as prize to rescuer. K975.2. Secret of external soul learned by deception. G530.1. Help from ogre's wife (mistress). E710. External soul. A person (often a giant or ogre) keeps his soul or life separate from the rest of his body. E711.1. Soul in egg. E713. Soul hidden in a series of coverings. E715. Separable soul kept in animal. E765. Life dependent on external object or event.

III. B571.1. Animals help man overcome monster with external soul. Discover where he keeps his soul. K956. Murder by destroying external soul. R111.1. Princess (maiden) rescued from captor. L161. Lowly hero marries princess.

*BP III 434 (Grimm No. 197), II 22 n. 1; Espinosa III 33ff.; Coffin *10;* *Liungman SSF III 428. — Finnish *92;* Finnish-Swedish *7;* Estonian *26;* Livonian (*302) *3;* Lithuanian (*302) *41;* Lappish *8;* Swedish *54* (Uppsala *8,* Stockholm *4,* Göteborg *5,* Lund *5,* Liungman *8,* misc. *24*); Norwegian *26;* Danish *104;* Icelandic *2;* Irish *254,* Beal V 111f. No. 2, IV 214—227; French *41;* Spanish *5;* Catalan: Amades No. 82, cf. Nos. 14, 157; Flemish *5;* German *46* (Archive *31,* BP *10,* Merk. 114, 228, 287, 354, Meckl. No. 36); Austria: Haiding Nos. 30, 38; Italian *12* (Tuscan 425A f, [302] a—c, [864], [916], [933], [934] *8,* Sicilian *6,* Gonzenbach Nos. 6—12); Rumanian *10;* Hungarian *20;* Czech: Tille FFC XXXIV 114, Soupis II (1) 119—135 *2;* Slovenian *9;* Serbocroatian *12;* Polish *11;* Russian: Azadowsky *Russkaya Skazka* Nos. 14, 17, Andrejev *Ukraine 6,* Afanasiev *81;* Greek *18,* Hahn No. 5; Turkish: Eberhard-Boratav Nos. 213, 214 IV, 215 III, IV, 216, 217, 256 V, cf. 163 *26;* India *47;* Indonesian: DeVries No. 142. — Franco-American *43;* Spanish-American: Rael Nos. 187, 188, 194, 202, 261 (U.S.), Hansen (Argentina) *1,* (Chile) *2,* (Dominican Republic) *10,* (Puerto Rico) *7;* Cape Verde Islands: Parsons MAFLS XV (1) 220 No. 74; West Indies (Negro) *5;* American Indian: Thompson *C Coll* II 409ff., cf. also (Zuni) Boas JAFL XXXV 76 No. 4. — African *1.* — Mauritius *1* (Delarue).

302A *The Youth Sent to the Land of the Ogres.* A youth is sent to the land of the ogres by his stepmother who is, herself, an ogress. Uriah letter changed. Youth finds out where lives of ogres are kept (usually in bees) and destroys them. Returns home and destroys stepmother. [Usually as part of 462].

Serbocroatian *1;* India *12.*

302B *Hero with Life Dependent on his Sword.* A neighboring king covets the hero's wife and sends an old woman to secure her for him. The emissary steals the sword, burns it, and escapes with the wife. The hero's friend discovers what has happened (usually through a life token), recovers the sword, restores it to its original condition, resuscitates the hero, and rescues the wife. [E142, E711.10].
    India *12*.

302A* [Combined with 301A, 301B, 303, 304, 513A, 516, 531, 552, 566, 612]. Fight with wild animals which contain the pigeons with the devil's external soul.
    Greek: Hahn II 259 No. 64, variant Nos. 1, 3.

302B* *The Red Bull.* Cf. Type 300 and 511A.
    I. *Stepmother Demands Bull's Blood* (heart) as remedy for feigned sickness [K961]. A prince brings her some of it but she knows that bull still lives and demands his death. The stepmother is killed by bull's horns. Bull and prince leave.
    II. *Fight with Giant.* (a) They meet and fight giant. They find the life-egg [E710] of the giant and kill him. (b) Prince receives magic wishing objects.
    III. *Impostor.* Princess promised to giant. »Dragon fight». Red Knight as impostor. Token given prince.
    IV. *Life Egg.* Rescue of princess from giant by having magic bull kill another bull in which the life-egg is. Egg thrown on giant's forehead kills him [K956].
    V. *Red Knight as Impostor* [K2265]. Recognition through tokens or by princess talking to stove. Bull disenchanted.
    Icelandic (302 I*) *9*.

303 *The Twins or Blood-Brothers.* Two boys, horses, and dogs are born (from the eating of a magic fish, or in other magic fashion; cf. Type 705). One frees princesses from a dragon; cf. Type 300. A witch turns him into stone. The second brother sleeps with his brother's wife and rescues him from enchantment. (As frequent introduction: Type 567, The Magic Bird-heart.)
    I. *The Twins' Origin.* (a) A magic fish, which a man has returned to the water twice, when caught the third time tells the man to cut him up and give parts of it to his wife, his dog, and his mare to eat; each of these bears twins; — or (b) they are born after their mother has drunk a magic water or (c) eaten an apple or (d) in other magic fashion. (e) A mother of a child finds another identical and adopts him. (f) Magic swords and trees for each of the brothers. (g) The twins mature miraculously.
    II. *The Life-Tokens.* As the boys leave on their adventures at a crossroads, each with his dog and horse, they set up a life-token which will in the case of trouble to one notify the other: sometimes (a) a knife in a tree which will become rusty, (b) a track which will fill with blood.
    III. *The Transformation by Witch.* Having rescued and married a princess (as in Type 300), the first brother (a) goes hunting or, (b) goes in search of another princess, or (c) follows a fire which on his bridal evening he sees out the window. (d) He falls into the power of a witch who turns him into stone.
    IV. *The Chaste Brother.* (a) When the second brother sees from the life-token that the first is in trouble he seeks him and (b) is greeted by the

brother's wife as her husband. (c) At night he lays a naked sword between himself and her.

V. *Disenchantment.* (a) He disenchants his brother. (b) The first brother is jealous and kills his rescuer but when he finds the truth, he kills the witch and (c) resuscitates him with magic roots received from animals.

Motifs:

I. B375.1. Fish returned to water: grateful. B211.5. Speaking fish. B243. King of fishes. T511.5.1. Conception from eating fish. T512. Conception from drinking. T511.1.1. Conception from eating apple. T589.7.1. Simultaneous birth of (domestic) animal and child. B311. Congenital helpful animal. Born at same time as master and (usually) by same magic means. F577.2. Brothers identical in appearance. Z210. Brothers as heroes. T685.1. Twin adventurers. T589.3. Birth trees. F611.3.2. Hero's precocious strength.

II. N772. Parting at crossroads to go on adventures. E761. Life token. Object (animal, person) has mystic connection with the life of a person, so that changes in the life-token indicates changes in the person, usually disaster or death. E761.3. Life-token: flower fades. E761.4.1. Life-token: knife stuck in tree rusts (becomes bloody). E761.1.3. Life-token: track fills with blood.

III. T68.1. Princess offered as prize to rescuer. R111.1.3. Rescue of princess (maiden) from dragon. R111.6. Girl rescued and then abandoned. K1932. Impostors claim reward (prize) earned by hero. K1935. Impostors steal rescued princess. H105.1. Dragon-tongue proof. Dragon slayer cuts out the tongues and uses them later to prove his identity as slayer. H105.1.1. False dragon-head proof. Impostor cuts off dragon heads (after tongues have been removed) and attempts to use them as proof of slaying the dragon. K1816.0.3.1. Hero in menial disguise at heroine's wedding. L161. Lowly hero marries princess. L225. Hero refuses reward. G451. Following witch's fire into her power. G263. Witch injures, enchants or transforms. D231. Transformation: man to stone.

IV. G551.4. One brother rescues another from ogre. K1311.1. Husband's twin brother mistaken by woman for her husband. T351. Sword of chastity.

V. D700. Disenchantment. N342.3. Jealous and overhasty man kills his rescuing twin brother. B512. Medicine shown by animal.

**Ranke *Die Zwei Brüder* (FFC CXIV) (770 versions); *BP I 528 (Grimm Nos. 60, 85); *M. de Meyer *Vlaamsche Sprookjethemas* 39ff.; *J. R. Caldwell, »The Origin of the Story of Bothvar-Bjarki,» Arkiv f. Nord. Filologi LV 223—275; Coffin 7. — Finnish *139;* Finnish-Swedish *5;* Estonian *21;* Livonian *3;* Lithuanian *47;* Lappish *3;* Swedish *28* (Uppsala *10,* Stockholm *1,* Lund *1,* Liungman *2,* misc. *14*); Norwegian *38,* Solheim *2;* Danish: *67,* Grundtvig Nos. 25 A—B; Scottish *4;* Irish *236,* Beal II 363 f. No. 1, IV 431—39, XIX 75ff.; French *68;* Spanish *4;* Catalan: Amades Nos. 118, 156; Dutch *1;* Flemish *15,* Witteryck p. 279

14; Walloon *2;* German *101* (Archive *97,* Merk. p. 69, Henssen Volk No. 124, Meckl. Nos. 31, 35); Austrian: Haiding Nos. 32, 54; Italian *15* (Pentamerone I Nos. 7, 9, Tuscan [300a—d, h] *5,* Sicilian *8,* Gonzenbach Nos. 39, 40); Rumanian *13;* Hungarian *47;* Czech: Tille FFC XXXIV 22ff., Soupis I 335—351, II (2) 243ff. *14;* Polish *3;* Russian: Azadowsky *Russkaya Skazka* Nos. 5, 10, Andrejev *Ukraine 11,* Afanasiev *41;* Greek *18,* Hahn No. 22; Turkish: Eberhard-Boratav No. 220, cf. 108 IV *6;* India *8;* Indonesian: DeVries No. 143. — Franco-American *15;* English-American: Baughman *1;* Spanish-American: Hansen (Argentina) *2,* (Dominican Republic) *4,* [333**A] *1,* (Puerto Rico) *5,* Rael Nos. 248—250 (U.S.); Cape Verde Islands: Parsons MAFLS XV (1) 263 n. 2; West Indies (Negro) *14;* American Indian: Thompson *C Coll* II 323ff. — African *3,* Fjort: Dennett 64 No. 12.

303A (formerly 303*) *Six Brothers Seek Seven Sisters as Wives.* On the way the devil steals the seventh, who was meant for the youngest brother who remained at home, and transforms the brothers into stone [D231]. The youngest brother rescues them [L11].

Motifs: T69.1. 100 brothers seek 100 sisters as wives. R11.1. Maiden abducted by ogre. D231. Transformation: man to stone. R155.1. Youngest brother rescues his elder brothers.

*BP III 431ff.; *Ranke *Schleswig-Holsteinische Märchen* I 100. — Estonian *6;* Rumanian (303 I*) *7;* Hungarian: Honti 728 *11;* Slovenian *4.*

304 *The Hunter.* The magic gun; the rescued princess; the impostor. (Often combined with Types 300, 302, 400, 554, 555, 675 or 950.)

I. *The Magic Gun.* A youth receives a magic gun, (a) from a green clad huntsman or (b) from an old woman.

II. *Killing of Giants.* (a) The boy shows his skill by shooting meat out of the hands of giants and (b) goes with them to carry off a queen. (e) He enters a palace and calls the giants in, and as they enter he cuts off their heads one at a time.

III. *The Sleeping Princess.* (a) He sees a sleeping princess in the castle and lies with her without waking her. (b) He takes various tokens, handkerchief, ring, etc.

IV. *Search for Father of Princess's Child.* (a) An impostor claims to be the father of the princess's child. (b) She refuses to marry him and is made to live in a house in the woods and cook for everyone or in an inn where all comers must tell their life histories.

V. *Recognition.* The hero appears and proves his identity by means of the tokens, and marries the princess.

Motifs:

I. D1096.1. Magic gun. D1653.1.7. Infallible gun. D823.1. Magic object received from green-clad huntsman. D821. Magic object received from old woman.

II. F661.1. Skillful marksman shoots meat from giant's hands.

F771.4.1. Castle inhabited by ogres. K912. Robbers' (giants') heads cut off one by one as they enter house.

III. N711.2. Hero finds maiden in (magic) castle. F771.14.4. Castle in which everyone is asleep. H81.1. Hero lies by sleeping girl and leaves identification token with her. H81.1.1. Hero takes token from sleeping princess. T475.2. Hero lies by princess in magic sleep and begets child. H83. Rescue tokens. Proof that hero has succeeded in rescue. H94. Identification by ring. H113. Identification by handkerchief. H117. Identification by cut garment. Garment is cut and fragment taken as token.

IV. K1936. Impostor claims to be father of princess's child. Q481. Princess (queen) compelled to keep an inn. H11.1.1. Recognition at inn (hospital, etc.) where all must tell their life histories. Q483. Princess must sell goods on market as punishment.

V. H81. Clandestine lover recognized by token. H80. Identification by tokens. T68.1. Princess offered as prize to rescuer. L161. Lowly hero marries princess.

*BP II 503 (Grimm No. 111); *Ranke *Schleswig-Holsteinische Volksmärchen* I 138. — Finnish *14;* Swedish *7* (Göteborg *1,* Lund *2,* misc. *4*); Norwegian *2,* Solheim *2;* Danish *11;* Irish *12;* French *11;* Flemish *2;* German *31* (Ranke *30,* Meckl. No. 37); Austrian: Haiding No. 69; Rumanian *22,* *Sainenu 466; Hungarian *10,* Dégh No. 1; Czech: Tille FFC XXXIV 56, Soupis II (1) 264—276 *11;* Serbocroatian *5;* Polish *9;* Russian: Andrejev *1;* Greek *12;* Turkish: Eberhard-Boratav Nos. 213, 247 III *26;* Albanian: Lambertz 21f.; Berber: Laoust No. 120. — Franco-American *12.* — African *1.*

304* *The Magic Staff* [D1254]. Animals as helpers. Two noble lords steals the rescued princess [K1935]. The hero recovers her with help of the animals [B544].
Lappish *1.*

305 (formerly 305*) *The Dragon's Heart-blood as Remedy for the King* [D1500.1.7.3.3]. Hero kills the dragon and brings the heart [B11.11]. Nobleman overpowers him and receives the princess [K1935]. As last the truth comes to light.

Danish: Grundtvig No. 14; Serbocroatian *1;* Polish *7;* Russian: Andrejev.

306 *The Danced-out Shoes.* The princess's nightly visits to the supernatural being. A youth who follows her and wins her hand. Cf. Type 507.

I. *Princess as Prize.* (a) A princess is offered to the man who can find why her shoes are danced to pieces each morning.

II. *Discovery of the Secret.* (a) By refusing a narcotic the hero succeeds where others have failed in keeping awake. (b) By making himself invisible, he accompanies the princess on a magic underground journey through enchanted woods of copper, silver, and gold, (d) where she dances with a supernatural being.

III. *Recognition.* (a) Tokens from the supernatural realm corroborate his tale and he marries the princess.

Motifs:

I. T68. Princess offered as prize. H508.2. Bride offered to man who can find answer to question. F1015.1.1. The danced-out shoes.

II. D1364.7. Sleeping potion. K625.1. Escape of girl foiled by hero's refusal to take narcotic. D1980. Magic invisibility. D2131. Magic underground journey. F811.1.3. Copper tree. F811.1.2. Silver tree. F811.1.1. Golden tree. T118. Girl (man) married to (enamored of) a monster. D2174. Magic dancing. Enchanted persons dance till released.

III. H80. Identification by tokens. H83. Rescue tokens. Proof that hero has succeeded in rescue. L161. Lowly hero marries princess.

*BP III 78 (Grimm No. 133); *Liungman SSF III 429; Krohn FFC XCVI 89; Köhler-Bolte I 412, 437. — Finnish *4;* Finnish-Swedish *1;* Estonian *9;* Livonian *3;* Lithuanian *17;* Lappish *1;* Danish *13;* Norwegian *2;* Icelandic *14;* Irish *33;* French *3,* Spanish cf. *1;* German: Ranke *12;* Austrian: Haiding No. 53; Rumanian 6, Sainenu 777; Hungarian *14;* Czech: Tille FFC XXXIV 311—318, Soupis II (1) 337—347 *12;* Slovenian *2;* Serbocroatian *1;* Polish *8;* Russian: Afanasiev *13;* Greek *6,* Loukatos No. 1; Turkish: Eberhard-Boratav No. 183 *10.* — Franco-American *4,* Antilles *5;* Cape Verde Islands: Parsons MAFLS XV (I) 291 No. 95, 293 No. 96; West Indies (Negro) *5.* — African *1.*

306A *The Pursuit of the Heavenly Maiden.*

I. *The Heavenly Maiden.* The prince sees a lovely maiden and wishes to marry her. (a) She agrees but stipulates that she must be allowed to return to her parent's home each evening.

II. *Following to the Other World.* The prince is given a magic object which makes him invisible [D1980] and follows his wife. (a) A flying tree (b) or other flying object carries her and other fairies to heaven to dance before Indra or some other god or supernatural being. The prince is able to seize the flying object and to remain unnoticed in Indra's court. (c) While the fairies are dancing, he takes the place of one of the musicians.

III. *Winning his Wife.* (a) He plays so well that Indra grants him a boon and he demands his wife [F81.1]. Or (b) he is told he must pick out his wife from among others similarly clad.

India *12.*

307 *The Princess in the Shroud.* Each morning the watchers are found dead. A youth overcomes the enchantment; the dead girl comes out of the shroud. He wins her hand. (Not always a princess). Sometimes combined with Type 506 (I b, V).

I. *The Parents' Hasty Wish.* (a) Barren parents wish for a child even if she is a devil. (b) A daughter is born who is diabolical.

II. *Vampire.* After her death she leaves her grave in the church at night like a vampire and kills the soldiers who keep watch.

III. *Disenchantment.* At last she is disenchanted by a youth, on the advice of an old man, when for three nights in prayer, once kneeling before the altar, once prone before the altar, and once lying in her grave, he endures her punishments. The other watchers are resuscitated. Happy marriage.

Motifs:

I. T548.1. Child born in answer to prayer. S223. Childless couple promise child to the devil if they may only have one. C758.1. Monster born because of hasty wish of parents. T556. Woman gives birth to demon.

II. E251. Vampire. Corpse which comes from grave at night and sucks blood.

III. D701. Gradual disenchantment. N825.2. Old man helper. M241. Bargain: to divide all winnings. V52.2. Continuous prayer sustains man through frightful vigil. C401.1. Tabu: speaking during vigil. H1451. Test: speechless vigil in church. D758.1. Disenchantment by three nights' silence under punishment. E251.1.1. Vampire's power overcome by endurance and prayer. Hero continues to pray without looking or speaking while vampire punishes him. E251.2.1. Vampire brought to life through endurance of punishment by her victim. E0. Resuscitation. L161. Lowly hero marries princess.

**Christiansen in *Festskrift til H. P. Hansen* (Aarhus) 213ff.; *BP III 534 (Grimm No. 219). — Finnish *13;* Estonian *37;* Livonian *1;* Lithuanian (*369) *11;* Norwegian *1,* Solheim *1;* Danish *13,* Grundtvig No. 23 B; French *13;* Walloon (*307A) *1;* German *51* (Archive *39,* Merk. p. 187, Henssen Volk No. 176); Austrian: Haiding No. 53; Rumanian 11; Hungarian *10;* Czech: Tille Soupis II (1) 326—337 *14;* Slovenian *14;* Serbocroatian *14;* Polish *30;* Russian: Andrejev Ukraine *22,* Afanasiev *31;* India *1.* — Franco-American *2.* — African *1.*

307A* *Ring from the Dead.* A soldier who watches the grave of a queen receives from the dead a ring, which she had stolen from her sister; the sister forgives the dead woman and the dead ceases to frighten.
Polish (309) *1.*

307B* *The Conquered Ghost.* A soldier watches in a haunted castle, and thrice conquers the ghost and closes him in the grave. The black daughter of the king becomes white and marries her deliverer.
Hungarian: Berze Nagy (419).

307C* *Ten Nights' Resistance.* A young man delivers an enchanted princess by resisting her temptations for ten nights. [H1272, D750].
Polish (453) *2.*

308* *The Magic Hammers.* The rejected hero triumphs through the aid of a magic hammer [D1209.4] (sabre [D1082]) and marries the princess [L161].
Flemish *2.*

308** *Watching the Supposed Corpse.* A stepmother asks her stepson to watch three nights over her corpse. An old man, however, acts as watch. They frighten each other in dragon form. He conquers her but lets her go. She explains her plan to him.

She transforms herself into a child and is adopted by a king. The old man takes service with the king and the child must beg his food from him. She kills the queen, takes her clothes and passes as queen. She falsely accuses the old man of the murder. (Various endings.)
Icelandic 3.

310 *The Maiden in the Tower.* Rapunzel. The hair ladder for the witch. The prince is blinded.

I. *Promise of Child.* To appease a witch whom he has offended, a man promises her his child when it is born.

II. *The Hair Ladder.* (a) The girl is imprisoned in a windowless tower which the witch enters by climbing on her hair as a ladder. (b) The king's son watches and does likewise.

III. *Abandonment and Blinding.* (a) When the witch discovers the deceit, she cuts off the girl's hair and abandons her in a desert. (b) When the prince comes, he saves himself by jumping from the tower, and is blinded.

IV. *Blindness cured.* Finally his wife's tears falling on his eyes heal them.

Motifs:

I. S222. Man promises (sells) child in order to save himself from danger or death. G204. Girl in service of witch.

II. R41.2. Captivity in tower. T381. Imprisoned virgin to prevent knowledge of men (marriage, impregnation). F848.1. Girl's long hair as ladder into tower. L162. Lowly heroine marries prince (king).

III. S144. Abandonment in desert. S165. Mutilation: putting out eyes.

IV. F952.1. Blindness cured by tears.

Lüthi »Die Herkunft des Grimmschen Rapunzelmärchens» Fabula III 95ff.; *BP I 97 (Grimm No. 12); *Parsons MAFLS XV (1) 228 n. 1. — Lithuanian *6;* Irish *1;* French *17;* Catalan: Amades Nos. 34, 160, 172; Flemish *1;* German: Ranke *8;* Italian *15* (Pentamerone II No. 1, Tuscan 310 a, b, 313 a—d, [306], [858], [859] *9*, Sicilian *5*, Gonzenbach Nos. 20, 53); Serbocroatian *3;* Polish *2;* Russian: Andrejev; Greek *11;* Turkish: Eberhard-Boratav No. 200 V, Anlage C 12. — Franco-American *2;* Spanish-American: Hansen (Cuba) *1*, (Puerto Rico) *1*, (Dominican Republic) (310A) 1; West Indies (Negro) *4*.

311, 312 *Three Sisters Rescued* from the power of an ogre.

311 *Rescue by the Sister*, who deceives the ogre into carrying the girls in a sack (chest) back to their home. Cf. Types 312, 1132.

I. *The Forbidden Chamber.* (a) Two sisters, one after the other, fall into an ogre's power, and are taken into a subterranean castle. (b) They are forbidden entrance into one room or (b[1]) to see souls in torment or (b[2]) to eat a human bone. (c) They disobey and an egg or key becomes bloody.

II. *Punishment.* The ogre kills them for disobedience.

III. *Rescue by youngest suster.* (a) The youngest sister finds the bodies and (b) resuscitates them by putting their members together or (c) otherwise, and hides them.

VI. *Carrying the Sacks.* (a) The girls are put into sacks and the ogre is persuaded to carry the sacks home without looking into them.

V. *Disguise as Bird.* (a) The youngest sister leaves a skull dressed as a bride to deceive the ogre. (b) She smears herself with honey and feathers and escapes as a strange bird.

VI. *Punishment of the Murderer.*

Motifs:

I. G400. Person falls into ogre's power. R11.1. Princess (maiden) abducted by monster (ogre). G81. Unwitting marriage to cannibal. T721.5. Subterranean castle. C611. Forbidden chamber. Person allowed to enter all chambers except one. C311.1.1. Tabu: looking at ghosts. C227. Tabu: eating human flesh. C913. Bloody key as sign of disobedience.

II. C920. Death for breaking tabu.

III. R157.1. Youngest sister rescues elder. G551.2. Rescue of sister from ogre by another sister. E30. Resuscitation by arrangement of members. E0. Resuscitation.

IV. G501. Stupid ogre. G561. Ogre tricked into carrying his prisoners home in bag on his own back.

V. K525. Escape by use of substituted object. K521.1. Escape by dressing in animal (bird, human) skin.

VI. Q211. Murder punished.

*BP I 398 (Grimm Nos. 46, 66), III 483; **Christiansen in *Thompson Festschrift* 24ff.; *Anderson *Novelline* No. 80; *Lo Nigro *30;* Coffin *8.* — Finnish *55;* Finnish-Swedish *1;* Estonian *28;* Livonian *6;* Lithuanian *19;* Lappish *1;* Swedish *11,* Göteborg *5,* Lund *3,* Liungman *1,* misc. *2*); Norwegian *54,* Solheim *3;* Danish *37,* (Christiansen l. c. 38 n. 14; Icelandic *11;* Scottish: Campbell-McKay No. 31a; Irish *44,* Beal IV 396; Basque *1;* French *2;* Spanish *4;* Catalan: Amades Nos. 72, 125, cf. 31, 162; German *36* (Ranke *33,* Meckl. No. 38, 39, 40); Austrian: Haiding Nos. 22, 459ff.; Italian: D'Aronco *Fiabe* 24 (Pentamerone I No. 5, Fruili *2,* Tuscan 311 a—d, 955 a, f, h, p, q, [863] *10,* Sicilian *11,* Gonzenbach Nos. 22, 23); Rumanian *1,* (365*) *5;* Hungarian *6;* Czech: Tille Soupis II (1) 80ff. *10;* Slovenian *14;* Serbocroatian *8;* Polish *18;* Russian: Andrejev *6;* Greek *18,* Hahn No. 19; Turkish: Eberhard-Boratav No. 152 III, 157 III, cf. 157 *36.* — Franco-American *18;* English-American *1;* Spanish-American: Rael No. 157 (U.S.), Hansen (Dominican Republic) *2,* (311*B) (Cuba) *1,* (Puerto Rico) *2,* (311**C) (Puerto Rico) *2;* **West Indies (Negro)** *8,* Beckwith MAFLS XVII 150, 284.

311A* *Escape in Glass Gourd.* Two sisters murdered by Bluebeard. Third escapes on glass gourd to island where she marries prince. Bluebeard comes and attempts to kill her but touches gourd which makes noise so that he is caught.
Polish (322*) *5.*

311B* *The Singing Bag.* Girl put in bag and made to sing. »Singing bag» exhibited. Comes to girl's home. Voice recognized. Dog or cat substituted in bag. Man scratched or bitten. [K526].
Spanish *3;* Espinosa II 233ff.; Catalan: Amades No. 381. Spanish-American: Hansen (311*B) (Cuba) *1,* (Puerto Rico) *1,* (311**C) (Puerto Rico) *2.*

312 *The Giant-killer and his Dog (Bluebeard).* The brother rescues his sisters.
See analysis of Type 311 (I a, b, c; II; III a) for introduction.
The youngest sister threatened with death for disobedience asks respite for prayer. Her brother with the aid of animals kills the ogre (cf. Type 300) and rescues his sisters.

Motifs:
For introductory motifs, see Type 311. S62.1. Bluebeard. K551. Respite from death granted until prayer is finished. G551.1. Rescue of sister from ogre by brother. G652. Rescue from ogre by helpful animals.
*BP I 400ff. (Grimm Nos. 46, 66) *Anderson in Tauscher *Volksmärchen* 170. — Finnish *1;* Finnish-Swedish *3* (955*); Livonian *1* (964); Lithuanian (*454) *13;* Lappish (55*) *1;* Swedish *9* (Uppsala *1,* Göteborg *2,* Liungman *3,* misc. *3*); Norwegian *8,* Solheim *1;* Danish *8;* Irish *26,* Beal II 221f. No. 3, 346f. No. 3; Basque *3;* French A *28,* B *3;* Catalan: Amades cf. No. 1968; Dutch *2;* Flemish (955*) *3;* German *24;* Austrian: Haiding No. 55; Hungarian *4;* Slovenian *3;* Serbocroatian *1;* Polish *7* (312A) *1;* Wend: Nedo No. 27; Greek *1,* Hahn No. 19; Turkish: Eberhard-Boratav No. 157 III. — Franco-American *18,* Antilles *4;* English-American: Baughman *4;* Spanish-American: Hansen (Dominican Republic) *1,* (Puerto Rico) *1;* West Indies (Negro) *39.* — African *2.*

312A *The Brother Rescues His Sister from the Tiger.*
I. *A Man Promises his Daughter to a Tiger.* (a) Rash vow spoken in anger. (b) Tiger carries load of wood for man in forest and demands his daughter in payment. (c) Tiger comes in guise of man and marries girl. Or (d) Tiger threatens the man.
II. *The Tiger Eats the Girl* and demands her sister, whom he also eats.
III. *Killing the Tiger.* (a) The brother follows the third girl and (b) kills the tiger. (c) The girl herself kills the tiger, or (d) The girl escapes and the tiger is lured back to town and killed.
Slovenian; Serbocroatian *3;* India *10.*

312B *Two Sisters Carried off by a Diabolic Being* and condemned to perish, are rescued through the intervention of divine beings.
French: Delarue p. 182, *3.*

312C *Devil's Bride Rescued by Brother.* Frequently with his dogs. Cf. Type 452*.
Spanish (340*A) *1;* Spanish-American: Hansen (340*A—340*H) (Puerto Rico) *3,* (Dominican Republic) *3,* (Cuba) *2.*

312D *Brother Saves his Sister and Brothers from the Dragon.* The sister has been carried off by the dragon (raven, etc.). The elder brothers look for her and perish; the youngest saves his sister and revives his brothers. Cf. Type 550.

*BP III 429ff. No. 197; Russian: Afanasiev (*312) *10*.

313, 314 *The Magic Flight.* From the ogre's house. The fugitives throw magic objects behind them which become mountains, wood, or sea; or they change themselves into various animals or objects.

**Aarne *Die magische Flucht* (FFC XCII). — Catalan: Amades No. 43.

313 *The Girl as Helper in the Hero's Flight.*

I. *Hero Comes into Ogre's Power.* (a) A boy promises himself to an ogre in settlement of a gambling debt, or (b) he sees girls (transformed swans) bathing in a lake and steals the swan coat of one of them; she agrees to marry him and takes him to her father's house (cf. Types 400, 465A); — or (c) the hero pursues a bird to the ogre's house; — or (d) after war of birds and quadrupeds (Type 222) a wounded eagle is cared for by a man. Eagle (eagle's sister, father) gives man box not to be opened until he arrives at home. Man disobeys and castle appears. Man must get help of ogre to close box and must promise ogre his unborn son (Type 537).

II. *The Ogre's Tasks.* (a) The ogre forbids the hero to enter one certain chamber; — or (b) the ogre assigns the hero impossible tasks, e.g., planting a vineyard, cleaning a stable, washing black yarn white, cutting down a forest, catching a magic horse, sorting grains, etc., which are (c) performed with the magic help of the ogre's daughter. (d) He must choose his wife from her sisters who look magically like her; by means of a missing finger (lost in the process of killing and resuscitating her) the hero chooses correctly.

III *The Flight.* (a) In preparation for the flight they leave behind them magic speaking objects. (b) In their flight they transform themselves into various persons and things to deceive the ogre; e.g., rose and thornbush, church and priest, etc., or (c) they throw behind them magic objects (comb, stone, flint) which become obstacles (forest, mountain, fire) in the path of the pursuer, and (d) escape over a magic bridge which folds up behind them.

IV. *The Forgotten Fiancée.* The hero forgets his bride when, against her warning, he kisses his mother (or his dog) or tastes food on his visit home.

V. *Waking from Magic Forgetfulness.* (a) The bride buys a place for three nights in the bridal bed from her husband's new bride: not till the third night does he wake, — or (b) the girl attracts attention to herself by magically placing three lovers in embarrassing positions, (c) by magically stopping the wedding carriage, (d) by a conversation between herself and objects or animals, (e) by the conversation of two magic birds displayed at the wedding, (f) by transformation or (g) otherwise.

VI. *The Old Bride Chosen.* Between the new and the old bride the choice is made according to the adage about the old key that has been found again.

Motifs:

I. S22.3. Youth sells himself to an ogre in settlement of a gambling debt. G461. Youth promised to ogre visits ogre's home. D361.1. Swan Maiden. A swan transforms herself at will into a maiden. She resumes her swan form by putting on her swan coat. D531. Transformation by putting on skin (feathers). D721. Disenchantment by removing skin (covering). B653.9. Marriage to swan maiden. K1335. Seduction (or wooing) by stealing clothes of bathing girl. G402.1. Pursuit of bird leads to ogre's house. S222. Man promises (sells) child in order to save himself from danger or death. C915.1. Troubles escape when forbidden casket is opened.

II. C611. Forbidden chamber. Person allowed to enter all chambers of house except one. G465. Ogre sets impossible tasks. H335. Tasks assigned suitors. Bride as prize for accomplishment. H1010. Impossible tasks. H1103. Task: setting out vineyard in one night. H1102. Task: cleaning Augean stable. Stable has not been cleaned in years. Must be done in one night. River turned through it. H1023.6. Task: washing black wool white. H1095. Task: felling a forest in one night. H1154.8. Task: capturing magic horse. H1091. Task: sorting a large amount of grain (beads, beans, peas) in one night. H1097. Task: draining sea-covered land in one night. H1113. Task: bailing out a pond. H1101. Task: removing mountain (mound) in one night. H1104. Task: building castle in one night. H335.0.1. Bride helps suitor perform his tasks. H161. Recognition of transformed person among identical companions. Prearranged signals. E33. Resuscitation with missing member. In reassembling the members, one has been inadvertently omitted. The resuscitated person or animal lacks this member. H57.0.1. Recognition of resuscitated person by missing member.

III. G550. Rescue from ogre. D1611. Magic object answers for fugitive. Left behind to impersonate fugitive and delay pursuit. (D1611.5. Spittle; D1611.6. Blood-drops; D1611.14. Magic apple, etc.). D671. Transformation flight. Fugitives transform themselves in order to escape detection by pursuer. D672. Obstacle flight. Fugitives throw objects behind them which magically become obstacles in pursuer's path. D1258.1. Birdge made by magic. D1642.1. Self-folding bridge prevents pursuit.

IV. D2003. Forgotten fiancée. Young husband visiting his home breaks tabu and forgets his wife. Later she succeeds in reawakening his memory. D2004.2. Kiss of forgetfulness. D2004.2.1. Dog's licking of man produces forgetfulness. C234. Tabu: eating while on visit home. D2004.3. Forgetfulness by eating. D2006.1.4. Forgotten fiancée buys place in husband's bed and reawakens his memory. D1978.4. Hero wakened from magic sleep by wife who has purchased place in his bed from false bride.

V. D1971. Three-fold magic sleep. Husband (lover) put to sleep by false bride. Only on the third night (the last chance) he wakes. D2006.1.1. Forgotten fiancée reawakens husband's memory by detaining lovers through magic. H151.1. Attention drawn by magic objects: recognition follows. D1649.1.2. Magic birds keep falling off perch. D2006.1.2. Forgotten fiancée reawakens husband's memory by serving as milk-maid and talking to calf. D2006.1.5. Forgotten fiancée attracts attention by magically stopping wedding carriage of new bride. H13. Recognition by overheard conversation (usually with animal or objects). Person not daring to reveal self directly thus attracts attention and recognition. D2006.1.3. Forgotten fiancée reawakens husband's memory by having magic doves converse.

VI. The old and the new keys.

**Aarne FFC XCII 102ff.[1]; **Grace Knapp »The Motifs of the Jason and Medea Myth in Modern Tradition (a study of Märchentypus 313)» Abstracts of Dissertations, Stanford University VIII 59—67; *BP I 442, II 516ff.; Coffin 20; Christiansen »A Gaelic Fairytale in Norway» Beal I 107ff.; *Parsons MAFLS XV (1) 142 n. 1; *Liungman SSF III 77. — Lithuanian 37; Swedish 7 (Uppsala 2, Lund 5); Norwegian 48, Solheim 3; Scottish 4; Irish 515, Beal II 10ff., III 31—35, V 111f. No. 3, VII 197f. No. 9, VIII 214—222, IX 106, XI Supp. 25, XX 130ff.; French 85; Basque 3; Spanish 13; Catalan (313 III): Amades cf. Nos. 104, 1231; Dutch 3; Walloon 1, *313D 1; German 4 (Henssen Volk No. 125, Meckl Nos. 41, 42, 43); Austrian: Haiding No. 11; Hungarian 53; Czech: Tille (Soupis I 246f.) 4; Slovenian 17; Serbocroatian 5; Russian: Andrejev Ukraine 37, Afanasiev 74; Greek: Loukatos Nos. 5, 9; India 6; Chinese: Eberhard FFC CXX 80f. No. 46, Graham No. 413 p. 279, (313 I b, II b c). — Franco-American 79, French Antilles 22; English-American: Baughman 1; Spanish-American: Rael Nos. 144, 145, 147—152, 157 (U.S.); West Indies (Negro) 39. — African 3. — Other: French Mauritius (Delarue) 1.

Three forms of the type follow:

313A *The Girl as Helper* of the hero on his flight. The youth has been promised to the devil. See analysis: I; II b, c, (d); III.

*BP I 442 (Grimm Nos. 51, 79). — Finnish *101;* Finnish-Swedish *1,* (cf. also 463*) *1;* Estonian *35;* Livonian *2;* Lithuanian *44;* Lappish *3;* Swedish (Uppsala) *8;* Danish *82,* Grundtvig No. 28; Irish: Christiansen Beal. III 355; Spanish *3;* Catalan: Amades Nos. 49, 69, 120, 155; Flemish *4,* (cf. also 463*) *4;* German *67;* Italian *10* (Tuscan 313 d, [301], [302] c, [889], [901], [903], [915] *7,* Sicilian *3,* Gonzenbach No. 53); Rumanian *26,* Sainenu 376; Hungarian *12;* Czech: Tille Soupis I 219 *11;* Slovenian *10;* Serbocroatian *26;* Istrian No. 5; Polish *15;* Russian: Azadowsky *Russkaya Skazka* Nos. 19, 36; Greek *29,* Hahn No. 1;

---

[1] Not all annotators or archivists have used the divisions of the tale suggested below, but have made references simply to Type 313.

Turkish: Eberhard-Boratav Nos. 84, 87, 98, 102 III, 104 IV, 212 III 9.
— Spanish-American: Hansen (Cuba) 2, (Dominican Republic) 4, (Puerto Rico) 2, (Venezuela) 1, (Uruguay) 1, (313*E) (Cuba) 1; American Negro (Michigan): Dorson No. 153; American Indian: Thompson C Coll II 34ff.

313B The same, introduced by *The Forbidden Box* in which a magic castle is hidden. (This introduction is Type 222, War of Birds and Quadrupeds + Type 537, The Marvelous Eagle Gives the Hero a Box which he must not Open.) See analysis I d; II; III; IV.

I. Levin (Leningrad) has a study in preparation. — **Haavio *Der Etanamythos in Finnland* (FFC CLIV); *BP II 516ff. (Grimm Nos. 56, 113, 186, 193); Anderson FFC XLII 165; Anderson *Archives Suisses des Traditions Populaires* XLV 224. — Finnish 3; Estonian 7; Livonian 2; Lithuanian (320) 22; Scottish: Campbell I p. 25; Irish; French 1; Flemish 3; Czech: Tille FFC XXXIV 143; Serbocroatian 2; Russian: Afanasiev (222*B) 19. — Cape Verde Islands: Parsons MAFLS XV (1) 142; American Indian: Thompson C Coll II 347ff.

313C The same, followed by the episode of *The Forgotten Fiancée*. See analysis: I; II; III; IV; V; VI.

*BP II 516ff. (Grimm Nos. 56, 113, 186, 193). — Finnish 3; Finnish-Swedish 6; Estonian 3; Lithuanian 33; Lappish 4; Swedish (Uppsala) 2; Danish: Grundtvig No. 27; Icelandic 5; Catalan: Amades Nos. 5, 165, 175, cf. 120; Walloon (*313D) 1; Flemish 1; Italian 16 (Pentamerone II No. 7, III No, 9, Tuscan 313 a—c, [302] a, b, [874], [882] 7, Sicilian 8, Gonzenbach Nos. 13, 14, 55); Hungarian 11; Czech: Tille Soupis I 241 7; Slovenian 1; Serbocroatian 1; Polish 1; Greek 17, Hahn No. 54; Turkish: Eberhard-Boratav No. 249. — Spanish-American: Hansen (Argentina) 1, (Chile) 3, (Dominican Republic) 7, (313*D) 1; Jamaica Negro: Beckwith MAFLS XVII 135, *281.

313* *The Hero Goes to the Land of the Immortals* [F116]. Flees with a maiden. Fight with the immortals.
Lappish 1.

313** *A Princess is Promised to the Sea Giant.* The hero conquers the three giants [R112].
Lappish 1.

313*** *A Youth has Been Promised to an Ogre.* He visits the ogre's home [G461]. Three sisters and the north wind help him back to the princess.
Lappish 1.

313D* *Magic Flight and Transformation to Bird.* Girl having escaped from ogress by leaving speaking objects and by magic flight (cf. Type 313 III), is transformed to a bird. Disenchanted by king who, an old woman's counsel, throws handkerchief over bird [D 777.1]. Marriage to king.
Polish 4.

313E* *Girl Flees from Brother who Wants to Marry her* (cf. Type 510B) and arrives in lower world at house of sorceress. She and sorceress's daughter who resembles her escape by magic flight. Girls change into birds but are disenchanted by fright

when the brother appears about to kill himself. Marriage of brother and sorceress's daughter.
Lithuanian (*314A) *9;* Polish (317A) *9;* Russian: Afanasiev (*722) *7.*

313F* *Escape by Help of Sheep* who answer for her and by magic flight.
Polish (323*) *1.*

313G* *Three Brothers Search for Stolen Cow.* Cow bellows when they call her and find her in a giant's cave. First two brothers killed. While giant sleeps youngest brother leaves behind magic owl which answers for him. Magic flight with help of cow's hair. Cf. Type 511A, The Little Red Ox.
Icelandic (313*) *4.*

313H* *Flight from the Witch.* Children escape from a witch or sorceress, throwing behind themselves a brush, pebbles, towel, etc., transforming themselves into a forest, mountains, or river.
*BP II No. 79; Russian: Afanasiev (*313 I) *23.*

313J* *The Sorceress and the Sunshine Fairy* (sister). The prince, fleeing from the sorceress, runs to the Sunshine Fairy. The sorceress pursues him, but Oakborer and the Mountainborer and others save him. (Cf. Type 513 III.) He remains with the Sunshine Fairy.
Hungarian: Berze Nagy (343*) *1;* Russian: Afanaseiv (313 II*) *2.*

314 *The Youth Transformed to a Horse.* (Goldener). The horse as helper on the flight (cf. Types 530—533). Usually: the goldenhaired youth at a king's court. (Cf. Type 502 for a closely related tale.)

I. *In the Devil's Service.* (a) A boy, sold to the devil in return for his services as godfather or (b) for pay, (c) goes at the time agreed to the devil's castle; — or (d) a boy is servant in the devil's house.

II. *Forbidden Chamber.* (a) The boy breaks the prohibition against entering a certain chamber and as a mark of disobedience his hair turns to gold.

III. *Magic Horse.* (a) The boy is commanded to care for certain horses and to abuse others. The abused horse is an enchanted prince.

IV. *Obstacle Flight.* (a) The hero flees on the magic horse, and as the devil approaches he throws magic objects behind him (stone, comb, flint, etc.), which become obstacles in the pursuer's path (mountain, forest, fire, etc. — Cf. Type 313, III c).

V. *Gardener Disguise.* (a) The hero covers his gold hair with a cap or cloth, (b) saying that he has the scaldhead, and takes service in the king's court as gardener. (c) The princess falls in love with him. (d) They marry and are put in a pigsty to live.

VI. *Conquests.* (a) With the magic horse's help, (b) he wins a tournament for three days in succession, but remains unknown until after the third, or (c) shows his prowess in battle, as a dragon-slayer (cf. Type 300), or as a bringer of a magic remedy for the king (cf. Type 551). (d) He brands his haughty brothers-in-law and puts them to shame.

VII. *Disenchantment.* The magic horse is disenchanted. — Adapted from BP.

Motifs:

I. S240. Children unwittingly promised (sold). S211. Child sold (promised) to devil (ogre). S224. Child promised to devil for acting as godfather. G461. Youth promised to ogre visits ogre's home. G462. Person as servant in ogre's house.

II. C611. Forbidden chamber. Person allowed to enter all chambers of house except one. C912. Hair turns to gold as punishment in forbidden chamber.

III. B316. Abused and pampered horses. Hero is ordered by ogre to feed and care for certain horse and to neglect other horse. Hero disobeys and feeds neglected horse. Latter is enchanted prince and helps hero. D131. Transformation: man to horse. B313. Helpful animal an enchanted person. B184.1. Magic horse.

IV. G550. Rescue from ogre. B184.1.6. Flight on magic horse. D672. Obstacle flight. Fugitives throw objects behind them which magically become obstacles in pursuer's path. D1258.1. Bridge made by magic.

V. K1816.0.3. Menial disguise of princess's lover. K1816.1. Gardener disguise. H75.4. Recognition by golden hair. T91.6.4. Princess falls in love with lowly boy. T55.1. Princess declares her love for lowly hero. T31.1. Lovers' meeting: hero in service of lady's father. L132. Pig-sty abode for unpromising hero (heroine). L113.1.0.1. Heroine endures hardships with menial husband.

VI. B184.1. Magic horse. B401. Helpful horse. D1868.1. Broken down nag becomes magnificent riding horse. H1561.1. Test of valor: tournament. R222. Unknown knight: (the three-days' tournament). H55. Recognition by wound. H51. Recognition by scar. H55. Recognition through branding. H55:1. Recognition through branding with hoofmarks. H101. Identification by broken weapon. Point of weapon broken off. Later found to match rest of weapon.

VII. Disenchantment by decapitation.

**Aarne *Die magische Flucht* FFC XCII 94ff.; *BP III 94ff. (Grimm No. 136): incidents A 3 B 2 CDEF); *Ranke *Schleswig-Holsteinische Volksmärchen* I 169; Coffin *4;* *Liungman SSF III 81, 429. — Finnish *115;* Finnish-Swedish *18;* Estonian *40;* Livonian *1;* Lithuanian *37;* Lappish *1;* Swedish *3* (Uppsala *2*, Lund *1*); Norwegian *10*, Solheim *1;* Danish *67*, Grundtvig Nos. 8A, 28; Irish *21*, Beal II 268ff., IV 300ff., XIX 55ff.; French *34;* Basque *3;* Catalan: Amades Nos. 20, 40, 46, cf. 120; Dutch *1;* Flemish *7;* German *110* (Merk. p. 109, Ranke *81*, Meckl. No. 43, 44); Austrian: Haiding Nos. 1, 23, 43; Italian *11* (Pentamerone cf. III No. 1, Tuscan [309], [896] *2*, Sicilian *8*, Gonzenbach Nos. 26, 61, 64, 67); Hungarian *35*, Dégh No. 2; Czech: FFC XXXIV 32ff. *14*, 54ff. *3;* Slovenian *5;* Serbocroatian *8;* Polish *29;* Russian: Andrejev *2;* Greek *12*, Hahn Nos. 45, 68, Dawkins *Modern Greek Folktales* No. 49 *6;* Turkish: Eberhard-Boratav No. 158 *4;* India *12;* Indonesian: DeVries No. 145. — Franco-American *58;* Spanish-American: Rael Nos. 164, 176, 211, 230—232, 235, 236, 238, 239, Hansen (Chile) *1*, (Dominican Republic) *1*, (Puerto Rico) *6;* Cape Verde Islands: Parsons MAFLS XV (1) 164 n. 1;

West Indies (Negro) *1;* American Indian: Thompson *C Coll* II 347ff. — African *4.*

314A *The Shepherd and the Three Giants.* He overcomes three giants, gets three horses at their castles and with these wins a tournament three times, defeats three ogres or helps the king thrice in battle.

Motifs: L113.1.4. Shepherd as hero. G500. Ogre defeated. Z71.1. Formulistic number: three. B184.1. Magic horse. B401. Helpful horse. R222. Unknown knight (Three days' tournament).

*Ranke *Schleswig-Holsteinische Volksmärchen* I 175; *BP III 113 n. 4. — Lithuanian (*530A) *9;* French (317) *9;* Basque (Delarue 317) *2;* German: Ranke *26;* French Canadian (Delarue 317) *3;* Slovenian.

314* *The Ogre's Wife's Child.* The little hero pretends to be the child of the ogre's wife [G610]. Steals a jewel [K347]. The magic flight [D670].
Lappish *1.*

314** *The Magic Flight of the Youth* from the giant's house [D670].
Lappish *1.*

314A* *The Bullock-savior.* A bullock helps children escape from their kidnapper (bear, witch). Cf. Type 327.
Russian: Afanasiev (*314 I) *16.*

314B* *The Magic Flight with the Help of a Kid.* The kid saves the girl promised to the devil. [D674].
Lithuanian (314B*) *15.*

315 *The Faithless Sister.* The children promised to the water-spirit. The maiden wife of the water-spirit (devil). At his advice she feigns sickness and sends her brother for a remedy (or the like) [K2212.0.2]. Imprisoned animals break loose and save the boy. See analysis under Type 590. Frequent as introduction to Type 300.

See Ranke *Schleswig-Holsteinische Volksmärchen* 185; *Delarue p. 268. — Finnish *89;* Finnish-Swedish *4;* Estonian *20;* Lithuanian *62;* Lappish *1;* Danish *2;* Irish *36;* French *8;* Spanish: Espinosa Cuentos II 18; Catalan: Amades No. 158; Dutch *1;* Flemish *1;* German: Ranke *3;* Italian *2* (Tuscan [300f] *1,* Sicilian *1*); Rumanian *7,* (315A) *22,* Sainenu 642; Hungarian *12;* Czech: Tille Soupis I 320—334 *10,* cf. II (1) 252—260, FFC XXXIV 17 *4;* Slovenian *6;* Serbocroatian *5;* Polish *10;* Russian: Azadowsky *Russkaya Skazka* No. 19, Andrejev *Ukraine* (No. 315A) *22,* Afanasiev (315A) *46;* Greek *48;* Turkish: Eberhard-Boratav No. 149 (cf. 148) *3;* India *8.* — Franco-American *7;* Spanish-American: Rael No. 247 (U.S.), Hansen (Chile) *1,* (Dominican Republic) *3,* (Puerto Rico) *3;* West Indies (Negro) *1.*

315A *The Cannibal Sister.*

I. *A Princess Becomes a Cannibalistic Ogress* and devours the animals, then the people at the court, and finally all the inhabitants of the city [G30, G346]. Her brother alone escapes.

II. *The Captive Brother.* (a) The brother returns to the city and is captured by his sister. (b) He gains a respite by sending her to sharpen her teeth or the like [K550]. (c) A helpful animal takes his place or warns him [B521].

III. *Magic Flight.* He flees, throwing behind magic obstacles.

IV. *Escape on the Tree.* (a) He climbs a tree but the sister gnaws it down. He escapes to another tree [R251]. (b) He calls his dogs who have been imprisoned. They break loose and kill the sister. [B524.1.2].

India 5.

316 *The Nix of the Mill-pond.* The youth promised to the nix is pulled into the water by her.

I. *Promise to the Water-Nix.* A boy is unwittingly promised to a water-nix.

II. *Grateful Animals.* A youth receives from grateful animals the power of transforming himself into their shapes.

III. *Rescue from the Water-Nix.* He falls into the power of the water-nix but is rescued (a) by his wife who received advice from an old woman and (b) through his power to transform himself.

IV. *Recognition.* After many years recognition is brought about, and he is united to his wife.

Motifs:

I. S240. Children unwittingly promised. F420.1.2. Water-spirit as woman (water-nymph, water-nix).

II. B500. Magic power from animals.

III. F420.5.2.2. Water-spirits kidnap mortals and keep them under water. R152. Wife rescues husband. N825.3. Old woman helper. H923.1. Task assigned before wife may rescue husband from supernatural power. D642.2. Transformation to escape death. D659.2. Transformation to animals to fight.

IV. H0. Recognition: identity tests. N730. Accidental reunion of families.

*BP III 322 (Grimm No. 181). — Lappish *3;* Norwegian *1;* Danish *1;* Scottish *2;* Irish *140,* Beal XI Suppl. 35ff., VII 47ff., 51ff., IX 66f. No. 7; French *4;* Spanish *2;* Catalan: Amades No. 17; German: Ranke *10;* Polish *1;* Russian:Andrejev; Greek *11.* — Franco-American *1,* French-Antilles *1;* Spanish-American: Rael Nos. 16, 251 (U.S.), Hansen (Dominican Republic) *1;* West Indies (Negro) *2,* (Jamaica): Beckwith MAFLS XVII 147, 283.

317 *The Stretching Tree.* A youth climbs on a magic stretching tree into the upper world [F54]. There he rescues a princess from an ogre. Cf. Type 328A.

*Köhler-Bolte I 437f.; *Solymossy »Elements Orientaux dans les Contes Populaires Hongroises,» Revue des Etudes Hongroises VI (1928) 16f. — German Archive (317*) *2;* Hungarian: Berze Nagy (530 I*) *17;* Serbocroatian *2.*

317A* *Peasant Girl Seeks Prince.* A prince disappears. Reward offered for rescue (sometimes half a kingdom [Q112] and marriage with prince). A peasant girl goes on the quest. On the way she receives magic objects and help because of helpfulness [D817] — magic ship, etc. Finds prince asleep on bed but cannot waken him. She hides. A giantess comes and wakens him with formula [D1978]. Woos him but he refuses. She puts him back to sleep. Girl wakens him and they plan. Next night he promises to marry giantess but she must tell him her secrets: magic flying cloak [D1053], magic runes, life-egg, sword, etc. The lovers make a magic alarm but flee on cloak. Kill giantess by (a) life-egg [E711.1], or (b) reading runes, or magic flight on magic boat. — Forgotten fiancée [D2003]. — Recognition.

Icelandic (317* I) *7*, (317* II) *1*.

318 *The Faithless Wife*. Batu: the Egyptian »Two Brothers» Tale. Plots with paramour against life of her husband. Cf. Types 303, 315, 590, 590A.

I. *Rescue of a Princess from a Dragon*. [R111.1.3].

II. *Treacherous Wife*. The hero marries the princess, but she falls in love with another man [T232]. She deceives her husband into giving up his magic weapons and plots against his life [K2213].

III. *Transformations*. A magician, or the hero's brother who has been warned by a life-token [E761] (cf. Type 303), teaches the hero how to take the form of a horse, a tree, a duck. The wife always recognizes him and orders the horse to be killed, the tree to be cut down, etc. [D610ff.].

IV. *Vengeance*. Through the help of a servant girl, the husband regains the magic weapons, avenges himself on his wife and her lover and marries the servant girl.

**Liungman SSF III 69, 102f., *Sagan om Bata och Anubis och den orientalisk-europeiska undersagans ursprung*, Djursholm, 1946 (= Bäckahästen I 101ff., II 66ff., 128ff.); **Von Sydow *Den fornegyptiska Sagan om de två Bröderna* (Yearbook of the New Society of Letters of Lund, 1930) pp. 53ff.; *Ranke FFC CXIV 187. — Finnish *2;* Lithuanian (315B*) *37;* Swedish (GS 367) *5;* Danish: Kristensen *Jyske Folkeminder* XII 23 No. 3; German: Plenzat p. 25, *Henssen Jül. No. 443; French: Luzel *Contes populaires de Basse Bretagne* III 262 No. 6; Rumanian (315B*) *3;* Hungarian: Berze Nagy 568* *14;* Czech: Tille FFC XXXIV 293ff.; Slovenian *1;* Polish (568) *7;* Russian: Afanasiev (315B*) *18;* Turkish: Eberhard-Boratav No. 221 *1*. — Franco-American (Missouri): Carrière 177 No. 36. — Literary Treatment: Ancient Egyptian: »The Two Brothers».

319A* *Magic Hare Changes into a Hawk*. Shoots a forester and escapes the chase.
Polish (319) *2*.

319B* *Three Wanderes each Kill a Dragon at Night*. They disagree and part company.
Polish (320) *3*.

321 *Eyes Recovered from Witch*. A boy takes service with a blind couple. Warned not to let goats (sheep) wander beyond certain point, he does so and there defeats the witch who has stolen the blind couple's eyes. He restores the eyes. [D2161.3.1.1].

*Köhler-Bolte I 432ff.; *Cosquin Lorraine II 89—97; *Delarue I 275. — French (317') *9;* Basque *2;* French Canadian *3;* Rumanian: Schott *Walachische Märchen* p. 85ff.; Hungarian (321*) *9;* Czech: Tille

Soupis I 83—87 *6;* Serbocroatian *4;* Armenian: Wlislocki *Märchen und Sagen der Bukovinaer und Siebenbürger Armenier* No. 52.

321* *The Bewitched Palace.* Mother of three girls murders suitors; king in armor escapes death and bewitches palace so that it collapses. Attempted rescue fails, because rescuer does not endure certain tortures.
Polish (321) *2.*

322* *Magnetic Mountain Pulls Everything to it* [F754]. Rescue by help of Giant bird. Princess won.
*Chauvin V 202 No. 117, VII 86 No. 373 n. 1. — Hungarian: Honti (320) *2,* Berze Nagy (728*) *4.*

325 *The Magician and his Pupil.* The father put to a test recognizes his son. The son as horse, ring, etc. rescues himself from the power of his master.

I. *Learning Magic.* (a) A father gives his son to a magician to teach, (b) but must be able to recognize him in his animal form at the end of a year.

II. *Magic Flight.* The hero learns magic secretly and flees (a) in various forms or by means of magic obstacles.

III. *Trick Sale of Son.* (a) He has his father sell him as dog, ox, horse. (b) At last, he is sold to the magician to whom the father, contrary to instructions, also gives the bridle.

IV. (a) The boy succeeds in stripping off the bridle and (b) conquers the magician in a transformation combat (to hare, fish, bird, etc.) (c) Usually it happens that the prince has flown to a princess in the form of a bird and is hidden by her in the guise of a ring; the magician as physician of the sick king asks for the ring. As the princess throws the ring, a great number of grains of corn fall on the ground. When the magician as cock is about to eat the corn the youth becomes a fox and bites off the cock's head. — Adapted from BP.

Motifs:

I. D1711.0.1. Magician's apprentice. S212. Child sold to magician. D1721. Magic power from magician. H62.1. Recognition of person transformed to animal. H161. Recognition of transformed person among identical companions. Prearranged signals.

II. D671. Transformation flight. Fugitives transform themselves in order to escape detection by pursuer. D672. Obstacle flight. Fugitives throw objects behind them which magically become obstacles in pursuer's path.

III. D612. Protean sale: man sells youth in successive transformations. K252. Selling oneself and escaping. D100. Transformation: man to animal. C837. Tabu: loosing bridle in selling man transformed to horse. Disenchantment follows. D722. Disenchantment by taking off bridle. Man transformed to horse (ass) thus released.

IV. D615.2. Transformation contest between master and pupil. D610. Repeated transformation. Transformation into one form after another. D641.1. Lover as bird visits mistress. L142.2. Pupil surpasses magician.

**Cosquin *Etudes* 502ff.; *BP II 60 (Grimm No. 68); Coffin *3*. — Finnish *35;* Finnish-Swedish *3;* Estonian *30;* Livonian *1;* Lithuanian *72;* Lappish *1;* Norwegian *4*, Solheim *1;* Danish *46*, Grundtvig No. 56; Icelandic *3;* Scottish *2*, Campbell-McKay No. 16; Irish *189*, Beal VII 197f. No. 4, VIII 3ff., IX 92ff.; French *4;* Spanish *3*, (cf. 325*A) *1;* Dutch *1;* Flemish *5;* German *45* (Archive *44*, Merk. 277); Austrian: Haiding No. 469; Italian: D'Aronco *Fiabe 10* (Tuscan 325 a—d, [870] *5*, Sicilian *2*); Rumanian *9*, Sainenu 376; Hungarian *9*, Dégh No. 3; Czech: Tille FFC XXXIV 299, Soupis I 132 *12;* Slovenian *9;* Serbocroatian *20;* Polish *24*, (380*) *1;* Russian: Azadovsky *Russkaya Skazka* No. 18, Andrejev *Ukraine 11*, Afanasiev *24;* Greek *19*, Hahn No. 68, Loukatos No. 2; Turkish: Eberhard-Boratav No. 169 *36;* Albanian: Lambertz 9ff.; Berber: Laoust 103; India *13;* Indonesian: DeVries No. 146. — Franco-American *8*, French Antilles *2;* Spanish-American: Rael No. 259 (U.S.), Hansen (Argentina) *2*, (Dominican Republic) *1*, (Puerto Rico) *1;* Cape Verde Islands: Parsons MAFLS XV (1) 337 n. 1; West Indies (Negro) *5*, Jamaica: Beckwith MAFLS XVII 153, *284; American Negro (Michigan): Dorson No. 29.

325* *Apprentice and Ghost.* Sorcerer's apprentice having read verse from forbidden book evokes ghost, but cannot make him disappear. When sorcerer reads verse backwards, ghost disappears.
Polish (337A*) *2*.

325** *Sorcerer Punished* for evil deeds by magic means learned from another sorcerer.
Polish (342) *20*.

326 *The Youth Who Wanted to Learn What Fear Is.* Various episodes: in the church tower, under the gallows, etc. Cf. Types 1159, 1160.

I. *Quest: To Meet Fear.* A youth who does not know what fear is goes out to find it.

II. *Experiences.* He tries various frightful experiences: (a) playing cards with devil in church; (b) stealing clothes from a ghost; (c) staying at night under a gallows, (d) in a cemetery, or (e) in a haunted house where a dead man's members fall down the chimney; (f) vanquishing ghost-like cats; (g) playing ninepins with a reassembled dead man; (h) being shaved by barber-ghost; (i) cutting devil's finger nails.

III. *Learning Fear.* After his wedding he learns fear when cold water is thrown on him or eels are put down his back while he is asleep.

Motifs:

I. H1376.2. Quest: learning what fear is. H1400. Fear test. A person is put to various tests in the attempt to make him show fear. Q82. Reward for fearlessness.

II. H1421. Fear test: playing cards with devil in church. E577.2. Dead person plays cards. H1431. Fear test: stealing clothes from ghosts. H1415. Fear test: staying under gallows at night. H1416. Fear test: spending night by grave. H1411.1. Fear test: staying in haunted house where corpse drops piecemeal down chimney. F982.2. Four cats carry coffin. H1411.2. Fear test: staying in haunted house infested by cats. E423.1.2. Revenant as cat. H1433. Fear test: playing game with reassembled dead man. E577.3. Dead persons bowl. H1422. Fear test: cutting devil's fingernails. E571. Ghostly barber. E281. Ghosts haunt house. E283. Ghosts haunt church. E578. Dead person builds fires. E578.1. Revenants want to warm themselves.

III. H1441. Fearless hero frightened by being awakened with cold water. H1441.1. Fearless hero frightened by being awakened by eels put down his back.

*See Ranke *Schleswig-Holsteinische Volksmärchen* 203 for analysis; **Wisser »Das Märchen von einem der auszog das Fürchten zu lernen« (cf. Zs. f. Vksk. XXXIV 177); O'Suilleabhainn *Handbook* under cf. 326; Coffin *6*. — Finnish *47;* Finnish-Swedish *10;* Estonian *15;* Livonian *2;* Lithuanian *37;* Swedish *13* (Uppsala *1*, Lund *12*); Norwegian *22*, Solheim *2;* Danish *124*, Grundtvig No. 11; Icelandic *3;* Scottish *8;* Irish *495*, Beal I 398, IV 228f. No. 2, V 25, VII 50, X 188, XI suppl. 75, XVII 203, XIX 29; French *55;* Spanish *3;* Catalan: Amades No. 95; Dutch *9;* Flemish *4*, Witteryck (p. 289) *5;* German *134* (Archive *128*, Merk. 287, Henssen Volk No. 44, Henssen Jül. No. 454, Meckl. Nos. 45, 47, 48); Austrian: Haiding No. 59; Italian: D'Aronco *Fiabe 17* (Trieste: Pinguentini No. 12, Friuli 2, Tuscan 326a—d, 1000 *5*, Sicilian *6*, Gonzenbach No. 57); Rumanian *9*, Sainenu 826; Hungarian *23;* Czech: Tille Soupis II (1) 103ff. *20;* Slovenian *14;* Serbocroatian *21;* Polish *53;* Russian: Andrejev *Ukraine* (326 III) *8*, Afanasiev (326A) *2;* Greek *5*, Dawkins *Modern Greek Folktales* No. 78; Turkish: Eberhard-Boratav No. 284 *6;* India *1*. — Franco-American *38;* English-American *5;* Spanish-American: Rael Nos. 176, 177, 276, 478 (U.S.), Hansen (Chile) *3*, cf. 326*A (Chile) *1*, (Puerto Rico) *1*, (326*B) (Puerto Rico) *1;* Portuguese-American: Parsons MAFLS XV (1) 241; West Indies (Negro) *6;* American Negro (Michigan): Dorson No. 85; American Indian: (Zuni): Boas JAFL XXXV 84 No. 5; New Mexico: Espinosa JAFL XXIV 428 No. 10.

326* *The Fearless Boy.* The boy escapes from the murderers' house.
Lappish *2*.

326A* *Soul Released from Torment.* Poor soldier spends night in haunted house to earn reward offered. He is not afraid of the dragging chains, falling members, etc. He releases soul from punishment by giving its ill-gotten gains to charity. He may keep part of the revealed treasure for himself.
Spanish *4*.

326B* *The Fearless Youth* takes up a corpse and frightens some robbers with it [K335.1.1.1]. Cf. Type 1653B; he overpowers the evil spirits and frees a princess, marries her.
Lithuanian *15;* Russian (326B*) *1*.

326C* *Magician and Dragon.* Magician enchants dragon out of the swamp. Is killed with his tail by latter.
Rumanian (326 I*) *1*.

326D* *Fearless Boy and Witches.* Boy goes unfrightened at midnight to place where witches were burned and to a church.
   Polish (354*) 2.

327 *The Children and the Ogre.*

   I. *Arrival at Ogre's House.* (a) Children are abandoned by poor parents in a wood. (b) but they find their way back by cloth shreds or pebbles that they have dropped; (c) the third time birds eat their breadcrumbs, or grain clue and (d) they wander until they come to a gingerbread house which belongs to a witch; or (e) a very small hero (thumbling) and his brothers stay at night at the ogre's house; or (f) the ogre carries the child home in a sack; (g) the child substitutes a stone in the sack twice but is finally captured.

   II. *The Ogre Deceived.* The ogre smells human flesh and has the children imprisoned and fattened. (b) When his finger is to be cut to test his fatness the hero sticks out a bone or piece of wood. (c) The exchange of caps, (d) the ogre's wife or child burned in his own oven (Type 1121), or (e) the hero by singing induces the ogre to free them, or (f) the hero to be hanged feigns ignorance and has ogre show him how, or (g) hero feigns inability to sleep until ogre brings certain objects and escapes while ogre hunts the object.

   III. *Escape.* (a) The children are carried across the water by ducks (or angels), or (b) they throw back magic objects which become obstacles in the ogre's path, or (c) they transform themselves, or (d) the ogre (ogress) tries to drink the pond empty and bursts, or (e) the ogre is misdirected and loses them.

   Motifs:

   I. S321. Destitute parents abandon children. S301. Children abandoned (exposed). S143. Abandonment in forest. R135. Abandoned children (wife, etc.) find way back by clue (breadcrumbs, grain, pebble, etc.). R135.1. Crumb (grain) trail eaten by birds. F1045. Night spent in tree. Hero goes into tree to spend the night. N776. Light seen from tree lodging place at night leads to adventures. F771.1.10. Gingerbread house. House made of cake. G412.1. Ogre's gingerbread house lures child. G100. Giant ogre. Polyphemus. G501. Stupid ogre. G10. Cannibalism. G401. Children wander into ogre's house. F535.1. Thumbling. Person the size of a thumb. G441. Ogre carries victim in bag (basket). K526. Captor's bag filled with animals or objects while captives escape. G422. Ogre imprisons victim.

   II. G532. Hero hidden and ogre deceived by his wife (daughter) when he smells human blood. G84. Fee-fi-fo-fum. Cannibal returning home smells human flesh and makes exclamation. G82. Cannibal fattens victim. G82.1. Cannibal cuts captive's finger to test fatness. G82.1.1. Captive sticks out bone instead of finger when cannibal tries to test his fatness. G83. Cannibal sharpens knife to kill captive. G83.1. Ogress whets teeth to kill captive. K1611. Substituted caps cause ogre to kill own children. G526. Ogre deceived by feigned ignorance of hero. Hero must be shown how to get into oven (or the like). Ogre shows him and permits himself to be burnt. G512.3.2. Ogre burned in his own oven. G512.3.2.1. Ogre's wife (daughter) burned in his own oven.

III. K550. Escape by false plea. G555. Rescue from ogre by means of singing. D1612.1. Magic objects betray fugitive. Give alarm when fugitive escapes. D1317.7. Magic bell gives alarm. D671. Transformation flight. Fugitives transform themselves in order to escape detection by pursuer. D672. Obstacle flight. Fugitives throw objects behind them which magically become obstacles in pursuer's path. K646. Confederate misdirects pursuer. G522. Ogre persuaded to drink pond dry bursts.

Finnish[1] *137;* Swedish *21* (Göteborg *19*, Lund *2*); Norwegian *1*, Solheim (327*) *1;* Irish *86;* Basque *2;* French (327A, 327B) *82*, Flemish: Witteryck p. 291 *4;* Walloon *1;* Austrian: Haiding No. 68; Slovenian *4;* Serbocroatian *15;* Polish (324*) *2;* Indonesian: DeVries Nos. 148, 149. — Franco-American 57, French Antilles *8;* English-American: Baughman *1;* West Indies (Negro) *37*. — African *2*.

Three forms of the type follow:

327A *Hansel and Gretel.* The parents abandon their children in the wood. The gingerbread house. The boy fattened; the witch thrown into the oven. Cf. Type 1121. The children acquire her treasure. See analysis: I a, b, c, d; II a, b, d; III.

*Anderson in Tauscher *Volksmärchen 175;* *Anderson *Novelline* Nos. 43, 83; *BP I 115 (Grimm No. 15). — Finnish-Swedish *17;* Estonian *51;* Livonian *4;* Lithuanian *12* + *31* (*327D); Lappish *2;* Swedish *37* (Uppsala *10*, Lund *7*, Liungman *12*, misc. *8*); Norwegian *8*, Solheim *3;* Danish *35*, Grundtvig No. 53; Icelandic *9;* Spanish *1;* Catalan: Amades Nos. 68, 182, cf. No. 42; Dutch *1;* Flemish *5;* Walloon (327A, *327G) *2;* German *61*, Ranke *70;* Italian: D'Aronco *Fiabe 33* (Sicilian *7*, Gonzenbach No. 2); Rumanian *4;* Hungarian *15;* Czech: Tille Soupis I 381—393, II (1) 213—217 *11;* Slovenian *3;* Serbocroatian *3;* Polish *29*, (327E*) *3;* Sorb: Nedo No. 31, cf. No. 28; Russian: Afanasiev *3;* Greek *3;* India *3;* Indonesian: DeVries No. 148. — Spanish-American: Hansen (Chile) *1*, (Colombia) *1*, (Cuba) *3*, (Dominican Republic) *5*, (Peru) *4*, (Puerto Rico) *11;* Portuguese-American (Brazil): Camara Cascudo 89, 232; West Indies (Negro) *3;* American Indian: Thompson *C Coll* II 357ff.

327B *The Dwarf and the Giant.* The dwarf and his brother in the giant's house. The nightcaps of the children are exchanged. Cf. Types 700, 1119. See analysis: I e; II; IV.

*Anderson in Tauscher *Volksmärchen* 175; *BP I 124 No. 15, 499 No. 56. — Finnish-Swedish *4;* Estonian *13;* Livonian *1;* Lithuanian *6;*

---

[1] Not all annotators or archivists have used the divisions of the tale suggested below, but have made references simply to Type 327.

Lappish *2;* Swedish *20* (Uppsala *17,* Lund *1,* Liungman 2); French: Perrault »Le Petit Poucet»; Catalan: Amades Nos. 21, 32, 38; Flemish *4;* German: Ranke *15;* Italian *5* (Tuscan [321 bis], [884], cf. 425A f., [304] a *4,* Sicilian *1,* Gonzenbach No. 83); San Marino: Anderson *Novelline* No. 44; Rumanian *8;* Czech: Tille II (1) 170—173, II (2) 195—209 *10,* FFC XXXIV 162—169, 172—175, 224; Slovenian *1;* Russian: Afanasiev *10,* Andrejev *Ukraine 11;* Turkish: Eberhard-Boratav Nos. 160, 161 III, 288 IV; India *3;* Indonesian: DeVries No. 49. — English-American: Baughman *3;* Spanish-American: Hansen (Dominican Republic) *2,* (Puerto Rico) *1,* Rael Nos. 333, 495 (U.S.); Portuguese-American (Brazil): Camara Cascudo 237; West Indies (Negro) *2;* American Indian: Thompson *C Coll* II 357ff.

327C *The Devil (Witch) Carries the Hero Home in a Sack.* The wife or daughter are to cook him, but are thrown into the oven themselves. Cf. Type 1121. See analysis: I f; II d.

*Ranke *Schleswig-Holsteinische Volksmärchen* 239; *Anderson in Tauscher *Volksmärchen 175;* *BP I 115ff.; *Delarue Bulletin Folklorique d'Ile de France XV 514f. — Finnish-Swedish (327**) *1;* Lithuanian (*327C) *61;* Swedish *8* (Uppsala *6,* Liungman 2); Norwegian (327**) *21;* Faroe: Jacobsen *Færøske Folkesagn* (1899) 227ff.; Icelandic *4;* English: Jacobs *English Fairy Tales* (London 1898) 164 *3;* Irish (hen and fox); French *1;* Catalan: Amades Nos. 54, 124; Dutch *7;* Flemish (327**) *5;* Walloon (333A) *1;* German *6;* Italian *9* (Tuscan 8, Friuli *3,* Trieste: Pinguentini No. 19; San Marino: Anderson *Novelline* Nos. 43, 83; Hungarian (162*) *4;* Slovenian *1;* Serbocroatian *2;* Polish *4;* Russian: Andrejev *Ukraine 6,* Afanasiev *25;* Turkish: Eberhard-Boratav No. 160 III, IV, 161 *29.* — English-American: Baughman *1.* — African *3.*

327D *The Kiddelkaddelkar.* The children in the ogre's house are protected by his wife but discovered. They are to be hanged, but the ogre is persuaded to show them how it is done. He is released only when he promises them a »kiddelkadderlkar» and much treasure. They flee. The ogre is misdirected and defeated. See analysis I a—e, II a, f, III e.

*Ranke *Schleswig-Holsteinische Volksmärchen* I 244; Cosquin RTP XXV 1, 65, 126; Penzer I 157 n. 2, VII 123, 263; Saintyves *Perrault* 276; German *2;* India: *Thompson-Balys (G526); Indonesian: DeVries No. 244; African (Benga): Nassau 121ff. No. 12, (Zanzibar): Bateman 187 No. 9.

327E *Abandoned Children Escape from Burning Barn.* Return after long time and astonish parents.

Irish *2;* French Canadian *5.*

327F *The Witch and the Fisher Boy.* Witch has her tongue made thin by a blacksmith so as to change her voice [F556.2, K1832]. She thus entices the fisher boy [G413].

*BP I 42 (Russian, Ukrainian, Bulgarian, Lithuanian).

327G (formerly 327*) *The Boy at the Devil's (Witch's) House.* The daughters are to cook him, but are killed by him. The devil is then killed. With his corpse the robbers are frightened from the tree. [G512.3.2.1, K335.1.2.1]. Cf. Type 334.

Finnish-Swedish *3*.

327* changed to Type 327G.
327** changed to Type 327C.
327*** changed to Type 327*.
327* *A Giant Carries off a Girl.* He is beheaded by the girl.
Lappish *1*.

327B* *Thumbling as Rescuer.* Thumbling (born of peppercorn) rescues stolen sister (sisters, brothers). He extorts the secret of the stolen sisters (or the slain brothers) by squeezing breasts under the door sill.
Rumanian (327D*) *4*.

327D* *The Hill-Woman and the Peasants.* A peasant couple is robbed continually by a hill-woman. Foolish wife tells hill-woman not to take hens, cow, etc. which are hidden. Hill-woman does. Finally man kills hill-woman from ambush. Cf. Type 1703.
Icelandic *1*.

328 *The Boy Steals the Giant's Treasure.* Jack and the Beanstalk. The horse, the light, etc. Finally the giant is killed. Sometimes joined with Type 327. Cf. also Types 531, 1525.

I. *Expeditions to the Giant.* (a) The hero sets out to steal from a giant in order to get revenge for former ill-treatment, or (b) to help a friendly king, or (c) as a task suggested by jealous rivals, or (d) he ascends to sky on magic beanstalk and finds the giant's house.

II. *Giant Robbed.* (a) By threatening the giant with an approach of an overwhelming army and locking him up to protect him or (b) putting too much salt in the giant's food, so that he goes outside to get water, or (c) by fishing through the chimney — (d) he steals from the giant a light, a horse, a violin, etc. (e) He tricks the giant into giving him magic objects; e.g., a cap of knowledge, an invincible sword, a cloak of invisibility, and seven-league boots.

III. *The Giant Captured.* (a) The giant is beguiled into a cage and taken to court. (b) The giant is tricked into killing himself.

Motifs:

I. G610. Theft from ogre. G610.1. Stealing from ogre for revenge. G610.2. Stealing from ogre to help a friendly king. G610.3. Stealing from ogre as task. H1151. Theft as task. H911. Tasks assigned at suggestion of jealous rivals. F54.2. Plant grows to sky. L10.1.1. »Thirteen» name of victorious youngest son.

II. K335.0.1. Owner frightened from goods by report of approaching enemy. K337. Oversalting food of giant so that he must go outside for water. K316.1. Theft from giant by fishing through chimney. D833. Magic object acquired by tricking giant. Giant persuaded to give the objects to the hero. D1162. Magic light. H1151.9. Task: stealing troll's golden horse. D1233. Magic violin. D1300.2. Cap gives magic wisdom. D1400.1.4.1. Magic sword conquers enemy. D1361.12. Magic cloak of invisibility. D1521.1. Seven-league boots. Boots with miraculous speed.

III. G520. Ogre deceived into self-injury. G514.1. Ogre trapped in box (cage). H1172. Task: bringing an ogre to court.

*BP II 511, III 33f.; Köhler-Bolte I 305; *Christiansen *Maal og Minne* 1926, p. 188ff., *Studia Septentrionalia* II 69ff. — Finnish *54;* Finnish-Swedish *10;* Estonian *6;* Lappish *1;* Swedish *11* (Uppsala *5,* Lund *6*); Norwegian *24,* Solheim *4;* Danish: Grundtvig No. 52; Icelandic *9;* Irish *89,* Beal II 10f., III 342ff., VII 65, IX 60ff., XVII 206; English: Baughman (328A) *1;* Basque *2;* French *12;* Spanish (328A*) *2;* Catalan: Amades Nos. 32, 38, 84; Dutch *5;* Walloon *1* (cf. 569A); German: Ranke *5;* Italian *13* (Tuscan [317] b, c bis, d—h, [884] *8,* Sicilian *5,* Gonzenbach Nos. 30, 83); Rumanian (461A*) *4;* Hungarian *14;* Dégh (328 I, No. 4); Czech: Tille FFC XXXIV 224, Soupis II (1) 206ff. *3;* Slovenian *3;* Serbocroatian *14;* Polish *4;* Russian *1,* Andrejev *Ukraine 5;* Greek *30,* Dawkins *Modern Greek Folktales* No. 3; Turkish: Eberhard-Boratav Nos. 160, 288 IV *11;* Albanian: Lambertz 9ff.; India *6.* — Franco-American *58,* French Antilles *1;* English-American: Baughman (328A) *6,* (328C) *1;* Spanish-American: Rael Nos. 333, 335, 336 (U.S.), Hansen (328, 328**A, 328**B) (Dominican Republic) *3,* (Chile) *1;* West Indies (Negro) *8.*

328* *A Boy Guards the King's Garden.* Steals the one eye of the three giants. [G121.1, G612].
Lappish *2;* Danish *6.*

328A* *Three Brothers Steal Back the Sun, Moon, and Star* which they have carried off from the three dragons.
Hungarian (319*) *30.*

328B* *Theft of Magic Objects from Monkeys.* Obstacle flight.
Polish (339*) *1.*

329 *Hiding from the Devil.* A man hides himself three times (in the belly of the fish, etc.). (Sometimes combined with Types 301 or 313.)

I. *The Task.* (a) A princess (devil) assigns her suitors the task of hiding themselves. (b) She has magic windows that give her magic sight. (c) Unsuccessful suitors have their heads placed on stakes before her palace.

II. *Youngest Brother Undertakes Task.* After his elder brothers have lost their lives the youngest undertakes the task. (b) He receives the help of grateful animals or (c) of an old man.

III. *Accomplishment.* (a) After hiding himself through the animal's help in a raven's egg and in the belly of a fish and being discovered, the hero is turned into an insect (or the like) under the princess' hair; in her anger she breaks her magic window. (b) He is disenchanted and they marry.

Motifs:

I. H321. Suitor test: hiding from princess. She has magic sight. D1323.3. Magic clairvoyant windows. Twelve, each more powerful than the next. H901.1. Heads placed on stakes for failure in performance of task.

II. L13. Compassionate youngest son. D684. Transformation by helpful animals. H982. Animals help man perform task. N825.2. Old man helper.

III. D641. Transformation to reach difficult place. D700. Disenchantment. L161. Lowly hero marries princess.

**Ingrid Hartmann *Das Meerhäschen: eine vergleichende Märchenuntersuchung* (Diss. Göttingen), 1953; *Rörich *Deutsches Jahrbuch für Volkskunde* II 285f.; *BP III 365 (Grimm No. 191); Carmen Roy *La Littérature orale en Gaspésie* 222. — Finnish *5;* Lithuanian *1;* Danish *4,* Grundtvig No. 51; Irish *137,* Beal IV 439ff., XI 14ff., XIX 53ff.; French *1;* Catalan: Amades No. 46; Rumanian *2,* Sainenu 770; Hungarian *3;* Serbocroatian *2;* Polish (329, 329A*) *2;* Russian: Azadowsky *Russkaya Skazka* Nos. 1, 13; Andrejev *Ukraine 2,* Afanasiev *23;* Greek *4,* Hahn No. 59; Turkish: Eberhard-Boratav No. 64 *4.* — Franco-American *13,* French Antilles *1;* Spanish-American: Rael Nos. 258, 261 (U.S.).

329A* *Man Gives (Sells) his Shadow to the Devil.* (Cf. Q552.9 and Type 775.)
French *2.*

330 *The Smith Outwits the Devil.*

I. *Contract with Devil.* A smith has made a contract with the devil so that in return for becoming a master-smith he is to belong to the devil after a certain time.

II. *Receipt of Magic Objects.* (a) The Lord (St. Peter) visits the smith and teaches him how to be more skillful; (b) the smith is granted three wishes: (c) a tree that causes people to stick to it; (d) a bench with the same power, (e) a knapsack that forces persons into it, and (f) a pack of cards with which he will always win.

III. *Deceiving the Devil.* (a) The devil (Death) is made to stick to the bench and the tree and meantime no one can die. (b) He is put into the knapsack and pounded on the anvil by the smith until he gives up his power over him.

IV. *Expulsion from Hell and Heaven.* (a) The smith goes to hell but is not admitted since the devil has lost power over him; (b) he goes to heaven but is not known there and is refused admittance; (c) he gets his knapsack inside and then has it pull him into it, or (d) he defeats the devil at cards; or (e) he throws his cards inside the gate of heaven and is permitted inside to pick them up. — (f) Explanation of Will-o-the-Wisp (ignus fatuus) or continuance of suffering on earth.

Motifs:

I. M211. Man sells soul to devil.

II. K1811. Gods (saints) in disguise visit mortals. Q115. Reward: any boon that may be asked. J2071. Three foolish wishes. D1413.1. Tree from which one cannot descend. D1413.4. Stairs to which person sticks. D1413.5. Bench to which person sticks. D1412.1. Magic bag draws person into it. D1413.9.1. Wallet (sack) from which one cannot escape. N221. Man granted power of winning at cards.

III. Z111.2. Death magically bound to tree. While he is bound no one can die. K213. Devil pounded in knapsack until he releases man.

IV. Q565. Man admitted to neither heaven nor hell. K2371.1. Heaven entered by a trick. K2371.1.3. Heaven entered by trick: »wishing sack» thrown in. E756.2. Soul won from devil in card game. A2817. Origin of Will-o'-the-Wisp (Jack o' Lantern).

**M. de Meyer *Vlaamsche Sprookjesthemas* 51ff. No. 330; *BP II 149ff., 163ff. (Grimm Nos. 81, 82); *Ranke *Schleswig-Holsteinische Volksmärchen* I 245; *Parsons MAFLS XV (1) 182 n. 1; *Espinosa III 140—150. — Finnish *146;* Finnish-Swedish *11;* Estonian *54;* Swedish (Lund) *12;* Norwegian *4;* Danish *71,* Grundtvig No. 64; Scottish *3;* Irish *359,* Beal VII 197ff. No. 5, X 160, XI suppl. 45, XVIII 114f. No. 7; Basque *2;* French *90,* Perbosc *Contes de Gascogne* 256; Spanish *1;* Dutch 6: Walloon 2; German *201* (Ranke *200,* Henssen Volk No. 26); Italian: D'Aronco *Fiabe 23;* Hungarian *33;* Slovenian *40;* Serbocroatian *25.* — Franco-American *23,* French Antilles *3;* English-American: McIntosh *Midwest Folklore* I 51—54; Spanish-American: Rael Nos. 274, 285, 294, 296, 297, 300, 301 (U.S.), Hansen (Argentina) *1,* (Chile) *2,* (Colombia) *1,* (Dominican Republic) *1,* (Puerto Rico) *6;* West Indies (Negro) *10*.

330A *The Smith and the Devil (Death).* The Savior and Peter; the three wishes; cf. Type 750. Sticking to the bench, to the apple tree, etc. The smith is admitted neither into heaven nor hell. See analysis: I; II a, b, c, d; III a; IV a, b.

Livonian *1;* Lithuanian *75;* Icelandic *3* (cf. *2*); English *1;* Spanish *6;* Catalan: Amades Nos. 212, cf. 202, 204; Flemish *11,* Witteryck p. 287 *14;* German: Merk. 242, 265, 287, Henssen Jül. No. 456; Italian *9* (Tuscan [333 b—h] *6,* Sicilian *3*); Hungarian *6;* Czech: Tille Soupis I 590—600 *18;* Istrian No. 8; Polish *31;* Russian *10;* Greek *2,* Loukatos No. 17; India *1.* — English-American *5*.

30B *The Devil in the Knapsack (Bottle, Cask).* The smith hammers on the knapsack. The devil flees to an island, whither his adversary comes, or the latter is admitted into neither heaven nor hell. See analysis: II (a), (b), e; III a; IV a, b, (c).

— Livonian *2;* Lithuanian *73,* (*330C) *21;* Lappish *2;* Swedish (Lund) *2;* Spanish *2;* Catalan: Amades Nos. 204. 205; Flemish *16;* German: Meckl. No. 48; Italian *4* (Trieste: Pinguentini No. 49, Tuscan [333 a] *1,* Sicilian *2*); Hungarian *2;* Czech: Tille Soupis I 505ff. *12;* Istrian No. 9; Polish *25;* Russian: Andrejev Ukraine *11,* Afanasiev *11.* — English-American: Baughman *1*.

330C *The Winning Cards.* Grant of magic pack of cards. Devil defeated and heaven entered with these. See analysis: II b, f; IV d, e.
  *De Meyer *Vlaamsche Sprookjesthemas* 65ff. No. 330C. — French: Delarue I 348ff.

330D *Bonhomme Misère.* Magic pear tree on which Death is caught. Misère must remain on earth. See analysis: II a, b, c; III a; IV a, b, f. Cf. Type 1186*.
  *Delarue I 348ff.; *De Meyer *Vlaamsche Sprookjesthemas* 69ff. — Walloon *330CD *2*.

330* *Heaven Entered by Trick* [K2371.1].
  *BP I 343, II 189, III 303. — French *10*.

331 *The Spirit in the Bottle.* The man frees the evil spirit from the bottle and receives in reward a wonderful remedy or the power to turn iron into silver (gold). He tricks the spirit into the bottle again. (Often combined with Types 330 or 332.)

Motifs:

K717. Deception into bottle (vessel). D2177.1. Demon enclosed in bottle. R181. Demon enclosed in bottle released. D1240. Magic waters and medicines. D2102. Gold magically produced.
  *BP II 414 (Grimm No. 99). — Finnish *4;* Finnish-Swedish *2;* Estonian *2;* Lithuanian *6;* Swedish *9* (Uppsala *3,* Lund *6*); Danish *2;* Irish *1;* French *9;* Spanish *3;* Catalan: Amades cf. Nos. 202, 204; German: Ranke *20;* Italian *2* (Tuscan [336] *1*, Sicilian *1*); Hungarian *3;* Czech: Tille Soupis II (2) 30—34 *4;* Slovenian *10;* Serbocroatian *1;* Polish *11* (331A *7*, 331B *4*); Russian: Andrejev *1;* Greek *1;* India *3*. — Franco-American *5;* Spanish-American: Hansen (Puerto Rico) *1*, (Argentina 340) *1;* American Indian (Pochulta): Boas JAFL XXV 223 No. 6. — Literary Treatment: Chauvin VI 25 No. 195.

331* *Devil as Flies in Knapsack.* Soldier defeats devils by means of iron automaton: he changes the devils into flies, and encloses them in his knapsack.
  Polish (355*) *1*.

332 *Godfather Death.* The man as doctor. Death at the feet of the sick man (the bed or the sick man turned around).

  I. *Death as Godfather.* (a) A poor man chooses death as godfather, (b) since he considers him juster than either God or the Devil.

  II. *Death's Gifts.* (a) Death gives him or (b) the son the (c) power of seeing Death standing at the head or foot of the bed and thus forecasting the progress of sickness.

  III. *Death Tricked.* (a) The doctor betrays Death by not finishing the Paternoster he had been granted time to say or (b) by turning the bed around when Death is standing at the foot.

  IV. *Death Avenges Self* (a) by tricking the man into finishing the prayer or (b) by putting out the man's life-light which he shows the man in a lower-world of lights.

Motifs:

I. Z111. Death personified. J486. Death preferred above God and Justice.

II. D1724. Magic power from Death. Death as godfather. D1825.3.1. Magic power of seeing Death at head or foot of bed and thus forecasting progress of sickness.

III. K551.1. Respite from death granted until prayer is finished. K557. Death cheated by moving bed.

IV. E765.1.3. Life-lights in lower world. Each light mystically connected with the life of a person. When light is extinguished, person dies.

**R. Th. Christiansen *Danske Studier* (1915) 71ff.; *BP I 377 (Grimm No. 44; cf. No. 42); *Köhler-Bolte I 291; *Liungman SSF II 430; *Espinosa III 140—150. — Finnish *57;* Finnish-Swedish *2;* Estonian *16;* Lithuanian *48;* Lappish *1;* Swedish (Uppsala) *1;* Norwegian *7,* Solheim *1;* Danish *34,* Grundtvig No. 122; Icelandic *1;* Scottish *1;* Irish *186,* Beal XII 165ff.; French *26;* Spanish *3;* Catalan: Amades Nos. 99, 202, 203, cf. 204; Dutch *2;* Flemish *11;* German *46* (Ranke *45,* Henssen Volk No. 127); Italian *4* (Sicilian *4,* Gonzenbach No. 19); Rumanian *4,* Sainenu 888; Hungarian *6,* Dégh No. 5; Czech: Tille Soupis II (2) 95—103 *12;* Slovenian *9;* Serbocroatian *7;* Polish *25,* (332A) *1;* Russian: Andrejev *5,* Andrejev *Ukraine 11;* Greek *5;* Turkish: Eberhard-Boratav No. 112 *1;* India *1.* — Franco-American *6;* Spanish-American: Rael No. 83—86 (U.S.), Hansen (Dominican Republic) *2;* Cape Verde Islands: Parsons MAFLS XV (1) 182 n. 1; West Indies (Negro) *4.*

332A* *Visit in the House of the Dead.* The man's own life-light. At last Death awaits the sacrifice as a beggar. (Often mixed with Type 332.)
Laographia XVII 110ff., 146f. — Rumanian *7;* Greek (1191*) *3.*

332B* *Death and Luck.* Poor coal miner asks God for enough money to buy chicken to eat. He obtains chicken and prepares to eat it. Luck visits him and asks for some of chicken. He says no, since Luck follows only the rich. Death visits him and he shares the chicken, since Death comes to rich and poor alike.
Spanish-American: Hansen (332**A) (Puerto Rico) *1.*

332C* *Immortality Won through Betrayal of Death.*
Hungarian (332 I) *3.*

332D* *Death Held off by Magic Formula.* Cf. Type 1183*.
Polish (336*) *1.*

332E* *Frog as Godfather.* Woman invited to baptism finds the souls of the drowned.
Hungarian (332 II*) *4.*

332F* *Poverty Locked Up.* Poverty lives with a poor man who worked very hard, but must live with Poverty. The poor man by a trick locks Poverty up and afterwards lives happily.
Hungarian (332 I*) *2.*

332G* *Woman Tries to Induce Death to Take her Husband* but Death refuses and chokes her.
Polish (338*) *1.*

332H* *The Treacherous Cat.* The cat entices a little girl, a little boy, an old man, and an old woman to the old man. He devours them.
Russian: Andrejev *1.*

333 *The Glutton. (Red Riding Hood).* The wolf or other monster devours human beings until all of them are rescued alive from his belly. Cf. Types 123, 2027, 2028.

I. *Wolf's Feast.* (a) By masking as mother or grandmother the wolf deceives and devours (b) a little girl (Red Riding Hood) whom he meets on his way to her grandmother's.

II. *Rescue.* (a) The wolf is cut open and his victims rescued alive; (b) his belly is sewed full of stones and he drowns; (c) he jumps to his death.

Motifs:

I. K2011. Wolf poses as »grandmother» and kills child. Z18.1. What makes your ears so big? F911.3. Animal swallows man (not fatally).

II. F913. Victims rescued from swallower's belly. Q426. Wolf cut open and filled with stones as punishment.

**Delarue BFIF 1951 pp. 221ff., 251ff., 288ff., 1953 pp. 511ff.; **Mariann Rumpf *Rotkäppchen: eine vergleichende Märchenuntersuchung* (Dissertation Göttingen, 1951, cf. Delarue BFIF 1953 pp. 514f.); *BP I 40, 234 Nos. 5, 26; *Anderson *Novelline* Nos. 30, 31, 45, 84—86. — Finnish *5;* Finnish-Swedish *10;* Estonian *3;* Swedish (Uppsala) *1;* Norwegian *5,* Solheim *4;* Danish *17;* Irish *34;* Beal II 228f.; French *32;* Spanish *2;* Flemish *11,* Witteryck p. 277 *9;* Walloon (333A) *1;* German *7;* Italian: Friuli *2;* Hungarian *13;* Slovenian *1;* Serbocroatian *1;* Polish *11;* Russian: Andrejév (333A, 333*B) *8;* Greek *8;* Turkish: Eberhard-Boratav Anlage Aa *3.* — Franco-American *10;* English-American *4;* Spanish-American: Hansen (Puerto Rico) *1;* West Indies (Negro) *3.*

333A *Caterinella.* Little girl goes to wolf (ogre) to borrow a pan in which to prepare pancake. On the way back to return pan with fritters, she eats them and substitutes horse dung (dirt). She then hides from the wolf. He unties the horse and eats her. (Sometimes she is rescued from the wolf's stomach.)

Italian: Rumpf Fabula I 76ff. *9;* cf. also Fabula I 287.

333* changed to Type 934B.

333B *The Cannibal Godfather (Godmother).* The little girl disregards the warning of friendly animals and visits the godfather (godmother). She is devoured.

Russian: Andrejev (*333 I) *4.*

334 *Household of the Witch.* Visit to house of a witch (or other horrible creature). Many gruesome and marvelous happenings. Lucky escape. Cf. Type 327G.

*Ranke *Schleswig-Holsteinische Volksmärchen* I 272 *31;* *BP I 375. — Lithuanian (2027B) *21;* German: Plenzat p. 19.

335 *Death's Messengers.* Death promises the man to indicate his future. He gives him a blow, blindness, etc. But the man does not understand the signs and lives happily throughout.

*BP III 293; *H. Schwartzbaum *Numen* IV (1937) 63 n. 20. — Estonian (332*) *2;* Slovenian *1.*

336 *Death Washes His Feet.* When death visits a house the youngest daughter is sent by her mother and her elder sisters for light to make a fire. On her way she meets a ghost. When she returns home, Death is washing his feet. The daughter asks about Death's strange looking feet, arms, legs, etc. [Z18.1]. Death never answers, but eats her.
Hungarian: Berze Nagy (345*) *7.*

360 *Bargain of the Three Brothers with the Devil.* They receive money in return for the devil's power over them [M211]. The host of the inn kills a man and the boys are accused. They have pledged themselves always to say the same words: »we three,» »for gold» »that was right» [C495.2.1, M175]. The devil rescues them from the gallows [R175], the host is hanged in their place, and the devil is satisfied to take his soul and leave them [K217]. Cf. Types 475, 1697.

*BP II 561 (Grimm No. 120). — Finnish-Swedish *2;* Estonian *1;* Norwegian *1;* Danish *19,* Grundtvig No. 57A; Irish: Beal I 299f.; Catalan: Amades No. 360; Flemish *1;* German *21* (Ranke *20,* Henssen Volk No. 128); Austrian: Haiding 469; Italian *1* (Tuscan *1*); Rumanian *1;* Hungarian *2;* Slovenian *6;* Polish *5,* (360A) *1;* Russian: Andrejev. — Franco-American *1;* Spanish-American: Rael No. 69 (U.S.).

361 *Bear-skin* [F821.1.3.1]. A soldier bargains with the devil [M211]. For seven years he must neither wash nor comb himself [C721.1, C723.1]. He receives much money. He marries the youngest of three sisters [L54.1], the two elder of which have made sport of him [Q2]. The elder sisters hang themselves. The devil: »I got two; you one» [K217]. Cf. Type 475.

*BP II 427 (Grimm No. 101). — Finnish *72;* Finnish-Swedish *10;* Estonian *25;* Livonian *1;* Lithuanian *44;* Swedish (Uppsala) *5;* Norwegian *2,* Solheim *1;* Danish *22,* Grundtvig No. 57B; Icelandic *1;* Scottish *2;* Irish *1,* Beal VII 51; Spanish *1;* German *27* (Archive *25,* Merk. p. 274, Meckl. No. 49); Austrian: Haiding No. 60; Italian *1* (Sicilian *1,* Gonzenbach No. 72); Hungarian *3;* Czech: Tille Soupis I 201 *8;* Slovenian *2;* Serbocroatian *1;* Polish *16;* Russian: Afanasiev *3;* — Franco-American *3.*

361* *Wolf Threatens to Eat Hero* unless he lives as a »bear's skin» when he marries. Hero breaks prohibition and kills the wolf with help of his dogs.
Hungarian: Berze Nagy (340*), Honti (361 I*) *21.*

362* *The Devil's Kindness.* The devil helps one boy with his work. The second boy hangs himself out of envy and thus the devil receives his payment. [K217].
Danish *2,* Grundtvig No. 77; Russian: Andrejev.

363 *The Vampire.* The bridegroom eats corpses in three churches [E251.3.1, G20]. He appears to his bride in the form of her father, her mother, etc. [D40, D610] and when she tells about his habit he devours her.

*BP III 534 note 1. — Finnish *54;* Finnish-Swedish *9;* Estonian *12;* Livonian *3;* Lithuanian *12;* Norwegian *8,* Solheim *1;* Danish *11,* Grundtvig No. 85, Kristensen *Skattegraveren* XII 118 No. 246; Irish *10;* Catalan:

Amades cf. No. 155, 1968; Italian *1* (Tuscan [cf. 709 n] *1*); Czech: Tille Soupis II (2) 336—344 *10;* Serbocroatian *1;* Polish *7;* Russian: Afanasiev *1;* Turkish: Eberhard-Boratav Nos. 152, 153 III, 154 *11*.

365 *The Dead Bridegroom Carries off his Bride (Lenore).* He carries her behind on his horse. Says, »The moon shines bright, the dead ride fast,» etc. She is pulled into the grave [E215].

Child *English and Scottish Popular Ballads* V 60—61; M. Böhm »Der Lenorenstoff in der lettischen Volksüberlieferung» Hessische Blätter XVII (1918) 15—25. — Finnish *174;* Finnish-Swedish *1;* Estonian *10;* Livonian *2;* Lithuanian *42;* Lappish *3;* Norwegian *1;* Danish *10;* Icelandic *5;* Irish *13;* French *7;* Dutch *4;* Flemish *4;* German *76* (Archive *70*, Meckl. No. 130 a—f); Italian *1* (Trieste: Pinguentini No. ·14); Rumanian *12;* Slovenian *7;* Serbocroatian 37, (Istrian) Nos. 10, 11; Hungarian *7*, Dégh Nos. 6, 7; Czech: Tille Soupis II (2) 330—336 *14;* Polish *15;* Russian: Andrejev *3*, Andrejev *Ukraine 11*. — Franco-American *3*.

365A* *Wizard Youth (Vampire) Entices Maiden into his Grave.*
Rumanian *2*.

365B* »*Young Men, Who Lie in these Graves, Come Dance with Us.*» The girls at the dancing-party, with great difficulties free themselves from the dead who have come to dance with them.
Lithuanian (*365B) *15*.

366 *The Man from the Gallows.* A man steals the heart, (liver, stomach, clothing) of one who has been hanged [E235.4, E236.1]. Gives it to his wife to eat. The ghost comes to claim his property and carries off the man.

*BP III 478 (Grimm No. 211); Ranke *Schleswig-Holsteinische Volksmärchen* 277; Coffin *3*. — Finnish-Swedish *1;* Estonian *1;* Lithuanian *4;* Swedish (Uppsala) *4;* Norwegian *1;* Danish *39*, Grundtvig No. 87, Kristensen *Skattegraveren* II 166; English *3;* French *23;* Spanish *1*, Espinosa III 116—121; Catalan: Amades Nos. 23, 2101; Dutch *14;* Flemish *2;* German: Ranke *33;* Italian *3* (Trieste: Pinguentini No. 11, Tuscan [323], [1443 b] *2*); Hungarian *6;* Czech: Tille Soupis II (2) 401 *3;* Slovenian *1;* Serbocroatian *6;* Polish *9;* Russian: Andrejev *1*. — Franco-American *3;* English-American: Baughman *8;* Spanish-American: Hansen (Puerto Rico) *1*.

366* *Thief Steals from Corpse and Prevents its Resuscitation.*
Polish (340*) *1*.

367* *The Earl-king* [G305].
Flemish *1*.

368* *The Punishment of the Lazy Woman* [Q321]. The bread changed to stone [D471.1, D661]; the corpse in the bed, etc.
Flemish *2;* Slovenian *1*.

368A* *Old Woman (Monster) Entices and Punishes Lazy Spinning Woman.* Kills hunter and hounds.
Rumanian *6*.

368B* *Holy Friday, Tuesday, Thursday.* Old woman punishes the girls who spin on their Saint's day or haven't spun enough in the winter.
Rumanian *4*.

368C* *Baba Dochia.* Cruel stepmother sends stepdaughter in March to the river to wash wool clean. Two wanderers — God and Peter — help her. She brings the first flower. Evil stepmother is thus led astray into the mountains with shepherd, and freezes to stone.
Rumanian *7*.

369 *The Youth on a Quest for his Lost Father* [H1381.2.2.1.1].

I. *The Quest.* (a) Village boys taunt boy without a father. (b) The boy sets out to find his father. Cf. Type 873.

II. *At Old Woman's House.* (a) He stays overnight with an old woman (Cf. Type 334) (b) who, during the night chews up his bows and arrows. (c) He has iron bow and arrows made and the old woman loses her teeth.

III. *Discovery of Father's Body.* He finds (a) a rhinoceros or other animal or (b) a bird with the corpse of his father on its horn and shoots it.

IV. *Resuscitation.* (a) A god overhears the boy weeping and restores his father to life.
India *8*.

382* *Quest to the Devil.* Three sons sent by their father »to the devil.» Come to the devil's palace. He throws them into a stove and two of them perish. An angel opens the door for the third. He is tempted by the devil's walking-stick. His hand cleaves to this stick, but he cuts it with axe and escapes.
Polish *2*.

SUPERNATURAL OR ENCHANTED HUSBAND (WIFE) OR OTHER RELATIVES

400—424 Wife

400 *The Man on a Quest for his Lost Wife.* Magic objects or animals as helpers (as introduction frequently the Swan Maiden).

I. *The Hero.* (a) A father unwittingly promises his son to a sea monster (giant, etc.). (b) The boy is adopted by a king. (c) The ogre wants to take the boy but cannot since he has a bible under his arm (see Type 810); — or (d) A field is tramped down; the brothers keep watch, but only the youngest remains by his post; — or (e) A prince is on a hunt.

II. *The Enchanted Princess.* (a) The hero goes in a self-moving boat to a foreign land or castle; or (b) The hero and another find a bewitched princess in the castle. (c) They are rescued by the hero's enduring in silence three frightful nights in the castle or (d) by his sleeping by the princess three nights without looking at her or disturbing her. — (e) Girls in swan coats: the hero steals one coat and will give it back to the to the owner only if she will marry him (see IV d). (f) The hero marries the princess or the girl.

III. *His Visit Home.* (a) The hero wants to go home on a visit. (b) The princess gives him a wishing ring, or (c) three wishes. (d) She forbids him: to call for her to come to him, or (e) to utter her name, or (f) to sleep, (g) to eat, or (h) to drink. (i) She has promised to meet the hero, but an enemy by means of a magic pin makes him sleep when she comes.

IV. *Loss of the Wife.* (a) He calls upon her to come so as to show how beautiful she is, or (b) breaks one of the other prohibitions. (c) She comes, takes the ring and disappears and gives him iron shoes which he must wear out before he finds her again; — or (d) The swan-maiden (see II e) finds her swan coat and flies away.

V. *The Search.* (a) He sets out in search of her and (b) meets people who rule over wild animals, birds, and fish. (c) An old eagle gives him advice. (d) He asks his way of the sun and moon, who know nothing, (e) but the wind shows him his way. (f) Three old women help him; (g) he must climb up a steep mountain without looking back. (h) He meets people who are fighting over magic objects and gets the objects in a trick trade; e.g. saddle, hat, mantle, boots, sword.

VI. *The Recovery.* (a) He meets the north wind and (b) by means of his magic objects reaches the castle where the princess is about to be married. (c) The new bridegroom is killed. (d) Recognition by ring in cake. — (e) Sometimes followed by tasks to be performed and transformation flight (Type 313). — Adapted from Christiansen *Norske Eventyr.*

Motifs:

I. S211. Child sold (promised) to devil (ogre). S240. Children unwittingly promised (sold). N836.1. King adopts hero. K218.2. Devil cheated of his victim by boy having a bible under his arm. H1471. Watch for devastating monster. Youngest alone successful. N771. Prince lost on hunt has adventures.

II. D1523.2. Self-propelling boat. D5. Enchanted person. N711.2. Hero finds maiden in (magic) castle. D758.1. Disenchantment by three nights' silence under punishment. H1472. Test: sleeping by princess three nights without looking at her or disturbing her. L161. Lowly hero marries princess. D361.1. Swan Maiden. A swan transforms herself at will into a maiden. She resumes her swan form by putting on her swan coat. K1335. Seduction (or wooing) by stealing clothes of bathing girl (swan maiden). D721.2. Disenchantment by hiding skin (covering). When the enchanted person has temporarily removed the covering, it is stolen and the victim remains disenchanted until it is found. B652.1. Marriage to swan-maiden.

III. D1470.1.15. Magic wishing ring. D1426.2. Magic ring causes woman to come to man. D1761.0.2. Limited number of wishes given. C31.6. Tabu: calling on supernatural wife. C31.5. Tabu: boasting of supernatural wife. C430. Name tabu: prohibition against uttering the name of a person or thing. C735.1. Tabu: sleeping during certain time. C234. Tabu: eating while on visit home. C250. Tabu: drinking. D1364.15. Pin causes magic sleep. D1364.4.1. Apple causes magic sleep. D1972. Lover's magic sleep at rendezvous. A lover (husband) is to meet his mistress but magically oversleeps.

IV. D2074.2.3.1. Mistress summoned by wish. C932. Loss of wife (husband) for breaking tabu. Q502.2. Punishment: wandering till iron shoes are worn out. D361.1.1. Swan Maiden finds her hidden wings and resumes her form.

V. H1385.3. Quest for vanished wife (mistress). B221. Animal kingdom. B222. Kingdom of birds. B223. Kingdom of fishes. B541. Helpful eagle. B560. Animals advise man. B563. Animals direct man on journey. H1232. Directions on quest given by sun, moon, wind, and stars. H1233.1.1. Old woman helps on quest. H1235. Succession of helpers on quest. One helper sends to another, who sends to another, etc. H1114. Task: climbing glass mountain. D831. Magic object acquired by trick exchange. By means of second magic object hero recovers first. D832. Magic objects acquired by acting as umpire for fighting heirs. When hero gets hold of objects he refuses to return them. D1209.2. Magic saddle. D1361.14. Magic cap renders invisible. D1521.1. Seven-league boots. D1400.1.4. Automatic sword.

VI. D1520. Magic objects transports. D2121. Magic journey. N681. Husband (lover) arrives home just as wife (mistress) is to marry another. H94.1. Identification by ring baked in cake. H94.4. Identification by ring dropped in glass (cup) of wine.

**Holmström; *BP II 318, 335, III 406 (Grimm Nos. 92, 93, 193); Köhler-Bolte I 444; de Raille RTP IV 312ff.; H. Ellekilde *Danske Studier* (1919) 166 ff.; E. Moór »Über das Märchen von der verwünschten Königstochter» *Gragger-Gedenkbuch*, 1927; Coffin *10;* *L.Hibbard *Medieval Romance in England* 200ff., *FFC LXXXIII xv, li, lxxi, 35. — Finnish *81;* Finnish-Swedish *6;* Estonian *25;* Lithuanian *23*, (*422 A) *8;* Lappish *4;* Swedish *49* (Uppsala *19*, Stockholm *1*, Göteborg *7*, Lund *1;* Liungman *4*, misc. *17*); Norwegian *51*, Solheim *4;* Danish *113*, Grundtvig No 1; Icelandic *2* (II e, f, IV d) *7;* Scottish *4;* Irish *162*, Beal VII 53ff.; French *17;* Spanish (400*A, 400*B) *2;* Catalan: Amades No. 18, cf. 107; Flemish *6;* German *138* (Archive *129*, Merk. 114, 228, Meckl. Nos. 50, 51, 52, 53, 89, Henssen Volk Nos. 125, 149); Austrian: Haiding Nos. 2, 5, 19, 21; Italian *9* (Tuscan [307] b, c, *2*, Sicilian *7*, Gonzenbach No. 60); Rumanian *12*, Sainenu 265; Hungarian *18*, (Berze Nagy 400 I*) *46;* Czech: Tille FFC XXXIV 124—127, Soupis I 72ff., 363ff., II (1) 348ff., 368ff., II (2) 209ff. *15;* Slovenian *15;* Serbocroatian *41;* Polish (400 A B C D) *34;* Russian: Andrejev *Ukraine* (400A) *22*, Afanasiev (400A) *58*, (400B) *16;* Greek *16*, Dawkins *45 Stories* 436 Nos. 7, 40, Dawkins *Modern Greek Folktales* No. 19; Turkish: Eberhard-Boratav Nos. 83, 84, 105, 198 III, 205, cf. 204 III, V, *18;* India *28;* Indonesian:

DeVries No. 151; Chinese: Eberhard FFC CXX 55ff. Nos. 34f., FFC CXXVIII 6ff. Nos. 21ff. — Franco-American *69;* English-American: Baughman *1;* Spanish-American: Rael Nos. 191, 192, 195, 196, 198 (U.S.), Hansen (Chile) 1, (Dominican Republic) *5,* (Puerto Rico) *9;* Portuguese-American: Parsons MAFLS XV (1) 305 n. 2, cf. 361; West Indies (Negro) *2;* American Indian: Thompson *Tales* No. 54, and note 206 (III d, IV b, V f, g, VI E tasks). — African *1.*
(*The Man Envied for his Beautiful Wife.* See Type 465.)

400* *The Swan Maid.* When her feathers are burned, she becomes a beautiful girl. The prince marries her. Some years later her swan relatives about to migrate, entice her to accompany them on their flight. Her lover throws feathers to her and she flies off; only from time to time she secretly returns to visit her son.
Lithuanian (*404) *5.*

401 *The Princess Transformed into Deer.* The prince a-hunting. Disenchants princess by spending three nights in a deserted castle. Quest for departed wife, as in Type 400. Cf. Type 400 (I e, II b, c, III i, V, VI). [H1222].
*BP II 218 (Grimm No. 93), II 330f. (Grimm No. 137); Köhler-Bolte Zs. f. Vksk. VI 164; Coffin *1.* — Danish *21,* Grundtvig No. 2; Icelandic *1;* Scottish *2,* Campbell-McKay No. 24; Irish *3;* Catalan: Amades Nos. 53, 63; Flemish *5;* German *4;* Austrian: Haiding No. 16; Italian *10* (Tuscan [317] c, [932] b, cf, [325], [918] *5,* Sicilian *5,* Gonzenbach No. 60); Hungarian: Berze Nagy *40;* Czech: Tille FFC XXXIV 127—135, Soupis II (1) 357ff. *9;* Polish (406) *1;* Russian: Afanasiev *14.* — Franco-American *4;* English-American: Baughman *2;* Spanish-American: Rael No. 190 (U.S.). — African *1.*

401A *Enchanted Princesses and their Castles.* The heroes rescue the princesses by keeping awake for three nights in succession, keeping silent, or refraining from looking into secret chambers, or otherwise. [D753]. (Various episodes.)
Lithuanian (*422) *71;* Rumanian (308*) *1;* Hungarian: Berze Nagy (400 I*) *45,* (411*) *2;* Serbocroatian *8.*

401A* *The Three Soldiers in the Enchanted Manor.* Curiosity overcoming them, they forfeit the power of disenchanting the princesses. Seven seven-year-old children break the spell and save the princesses. [D759.9, D759.10].
Lithuanian (*422B) *2.*

402 *The Mouse (Cat, Frog, etc.) as Bride.* The youngest of three brothers succeeds best in the quests set by his father. He brings the best cloth, the most beautiful bride, etc. The mouse (cat) who has helped him changes herself into a beautiful maiden.
Motifs:
I. H1242. Youngest brother alone succeeds on quest. H1210.1. Quest assigned by father. H1306. Quest for the finest of linen. H1305. Quest for the best of bread. H1307. Quest for the smallest of dogs. H1303. Quest for for the finest of chains. H1301.1. Quest for the most beautiful bride. B313. Helpful animal an enchanted person. B437.2. Helpful

mouse. B422. Helpful cat. B493.1. Helpful frog. B493.2. Helpful toad. D700. Person disenchanted. D735.1. Beauty and the beast. Disenchantment of animal by being kissed by woman (man). D711. Disenchantment by decapitation.

W. Wisser *Niederdeutsche Zeitschrift für Volkskunde* V 8ff.; *Anderson *Novelline* Nos. 58, 88, 118; *BP II 30, 466 (Grimm Nos. 63, 106); *Tegethoff *Amor u. Psyche* 27ff.; *Homenaje a Fritz Kruger* I (1952) 399f.; *Arts et Traditions Populaires* I 274; Coffin *3;* Köhler-Bolte I 407. — Finnish *103;* Finnish-Swedish *10;* Estonian *16;* Livonian *1;* Lithuanian *48;* Lappish *3;* Swedish *41* (Uppsala *9*, Stockholm *2*, Göteborg *2*, Lund *4*, Liungman *6*); Danish *55*, Grundtvig No. 15; Irish *38;* French *31;* Spanish *1*, (557*) *1;* Catalan: Amades Nos. 33, 34, 89, 91, 119, 127, 172; Flemish *1;* German *96* (Archive *92*, Merk. p. 140, Meckl. Nos. 54,55, 66); Austrian: Haiding No. 37, 75; Italian: D'Aronco *Fiabe 40* (Trieste: Pinguentini No. 18, Tuscan 313 d, 402 a—r, t—v *20*, Sicilian *1*); Rumanian (402 A*) *7;* Hungarian *4;* Czech: Tille FFC XXXIV 248ff., Soupis II (1) 181ff. *12;* Slovenian *13;* Serbocroatian *1;* Polish *10*, (414) *6;* Russian: Afanasiev *25;* Greek *6*, Hahn No. 67, Loukatos No. 3, *Dawkins *Modern Greek Folktales* No. 18; Turkish: Eberhard-Boratav Nos. 85, 86, 87, 88 *60;* India *1*, (402A Ind.) *8*. — Franco-American *12;* Spanish-American Rael Nos. 183—186 (U.S.), Hansen (Chile) *1*, (Dominican Republic) *1*, (Dominican Republic 402A) *1;* American Portuguese (Brazil): Camara Cascudo 160; West Indies (Negro) *1*. — Literary Treatment: Chauvin VI 133 No. 286.

402* *The Princess who Scorned an Unloved Suitor* [T75.1] is turned into a frog [D661].
Finnish-Swedish *1*.

402A* *Princess Transformed to Toad* is disenchanted by hero's kiss and marries him. Cf. Type 440.
Polish (420) *2*.

403 *The Black and the White Bride.* Cf. Types 450, 480, 510, 511.

I. *Cruel Stepmother.* A stepmother hates her stepchildren.

II. *Kind and Unkind.* (a) The stepdaughter is kind to a person she meets (witch, the Lord, etc.) or (b) is sent after strawberries in winter, where she meets dwarfs who help her in gratitude. (c) She receives as gift great beauty and the power of dropping gold or jewels from her mouth. (d) The woman's own daughter is unkind under these conditions and is made ugly and made to drop toads from her mouth.

III. *The Prince as Lover.* (a) The heroine is seen by the king (prince), who marries her; — or (b) her brother is in service at the court of a king who sees her picture and falls in love with her and sends the brother for her.

IV. *The Substituted Bride.* (a) After marriage with the king the stepmother throws the heroine and her child into the water; — or (b) On the voyage of the brother and sister to the king, the stepmother or stepsister casts the heroine overboard. (c) The woman's daughter is substituted for the bride without detection. (d) The brother is thrown into prison or a pit of snakes.

V. *Disenchantment.* (a) The true bride who is transformed to a goose comes to the king's court three times (sometimes to suckle her child). (b) The last night the king wakes and disenchants her by cutting her finger and drawing blood or by holding her while she changes form.

VI. *Conclusion.* (a) The brother, unharmed in the den of snakes, is rescued, the true bride married or reinstated, and punishment executed.

Motifs:

I. G205. Witch stepmother. S31. Cruel stepmother. L55. Stepdaughter heroine.

II. Q2. Kind and unkind. Churlish person disregards requests of old person (animal) and is punished. Courteous person (often youngest brother or sister) complies and is rewarded. H1023.3. Task: bringing berries (fruit, roses) in winter. F451.5.1. Helpful dwarfs. D1723. Magic power from fairy. D1860. Magic beautification. D1454.2. Treasure falls from mouth. D1454.1.2. Jewels from hair. D1870. Magic hideousness. M431.2. Curse: toads from mouth.

III. N711. King (prince) accidentally finds maiden in woods (tree) and marries her. T11.2. Love through sight of picture. T51. Wooing by emissary. L162. Lowly heroine marries prince (king).

IV. S432. Cast-off wife thrown into water. K2212.1. Treacherous stepsisters. K1911. The false bride (substituted bride). K1911.1.2. False bride takes true bride's place when child is born. Q465.1. Throwing into pit of snakes as punishment.

V. D683.2. Transformation by witch (sorceress). K1911.2.1. True bride transformed by false. D161.2. Transformation: man to goose. D688. Transformed mother suckles child. D762. Disenchantment by proper person waking from magic sleep. The enchanted person appears three times and if the sleeper does not wake by the third time the enchantment must last. D712.4. Disenchantment by holding enchanted person during successive transformation.

VI. B848. Man unharmed in den of animals. Q261. Treachery punished.

**Arfert; *Anderson *Novelline* No. 5; Coffin *10*. — Finnish *79;* Lvonian *1;* Swedish *10* (Göteborg *1,* Lund *4,* misc. *5*); Norwegian *6;* Danish *85;* Irish *74,* Beal I 349ff., II 97f. No. 5, 221 f. No. 4, III 257f. No. 3, VII 197f. No. 6, VIII 3f. No. 2; French *31;* Walloon (*403EF) *2;* German *52* (Archive *51,* Meckl. No. 56); Austrian: Haiding No. 18; Italian: D'Aronco *Fiabe 61* (Pentamerone III No. 10, IV No. 7, cf. V No. 2, Friuli *3,* Tuscan [403A b, f—l, s, q, u, 510 b, [304] b, c, [316] c, [894], [895] b, [897] *19,* Sicilian *8,* Gonzenbach Nos. 32, 33, 34); Czech: Tille Soupis II (1) 225ff. *10;* Slovenian *9;* Serbocroatian (403, 403 I, II) *14;* Polish *11;* Turkish: Eberhard-Boratav No. 240 *29;* India *22.* — Franco-American *22;* Spanish-American: Rael Nos. 106, 108, 113, 117 (U.S.),

Hansen (Chile) *3*, (Dominican Republic) *1*, (Puerto Rico) *7;* Cape Verde Islands: Parsons MAFLS XV (1) 170 n. 1; West Indies (Negro) *9*. — African *17*.
The three forms of the type follows:

403A *The Wishes* (the Savior and Peter, etc.). The man's own daughter becomes beautiful (gold from her mouth), the stepdaughter ugly (frogs), or the clanging tree. The brother of the real daughter in the service of the king. The sister's picture. The voyage to the castle. The girl thrown overboard. Transformation to a duck. Stepsister as the king's bride in her place. See analysis: I; II a, c, d; III b; IV b, c, d; V a, b; VI.
*Parsons MAFLS XV (1) 234 n. 1; *Liungman SSF III 112, 431f. — Finnish-Swedish *6;* Estonian *9;* Lithuanian *19;* Lappish *9;* Swedish *17* (Uppsala *9,* Liungman *2,* misc. *6*); Norwegian *32;* Danish: Grundtvig No. 35; Icelandic *3;* Catalan: Amades Nos. 117, 1515, cf. No. 140; Flemish *6;* German *60;* Rumanian *24;* Hungarian *16;* Serbocroatian *3;* Russian: Afanasiev *9;* Greek *22;* Turkish: Eberhard-Boratav No. 60, IV 90.

403B As introduction: Three dwarfs. Strawberries under the snow, etc. The real daughter bride of the king. A child born. The stepmother throws the child into the water, etc. See analysis: I, II b, c, d; III a; IV a, c; V a, b; VI.
*BP I 99 (Grimm No. 13); *Liungman SSF III 114, 431f. — Finnish-Swedish *7;* Estonian *6;* Swedish *18* (Uppsala *2,* Liungman *2,* misc. *14*); Catalan: Amades No. 83; Hungarian *1;* Russian: Andrejev *Ukraine 11,* Afanasiev *6;* Greek *19*. — American Indian: Thompson *C Coll* II 385ff. — African: Werner *African Mythology* 230 (2 versions).

403C *The Witch Secretly Substitutes her own Daughter* for the bride. The husband throws the witch's daughter under the bridge. From the girl's navel grows a reed in which the witch recognizes her own daughter.
Estonian (403C*) *32;* Lithuanian *1*.

403* *The Stepmother's Dream.* Worried by a prophetic dream, the stepmother drowns the orphan in a well at full moon [S432]. The drowned comes out with a gold crown at full moon to sing [E546]. A prince comes to marry the real daughter of the stepmother. The night before the wedding he rescues the orphan and marries her.
Livonian (403') *1*.

403** *The Snake-girdle.* An ugly girl helps an old woman and gets a girdle and becomes beautiful [Q2, L145]. Two pretty girls steal the girdle, which changes into a snake.
Livonian (403$_2$) *1*.

404* *Girl Transformed by Jealous Stepmother into Cow's Stomach.* Disenchantment only by marrying a prince. Rolling cow-stomach as shepherd on king's estate. Prince tries to drive her off but he magically sticks to the cow's stomach and can be released only by marrying her. Disenchantment.
Icelandic *6*.

405 *Jorinde and Joringel.* A witch turns the girl into a bird [D683.2, D150]. The youth with the help of a magic object changes her back into her former shape [D771].
  *BP II 69 (Grimm No. 69); Coffin *1*. — Finnish *1*; Swedish (misc.) *1*; Irish *3*; German *2*; Serbocroatian *1*; Polish *3*; Russian: Andrejev. — Franco-American *1*.

405A* *Enchanted Girl Disenchanted by Lover.* Killing her serpent guard and other means.
  Spanish *1*.

406 (formerly 406*) *The Cannibal.* A couple have a child who is a cannibal [G33]. It eats everyone up except its conqueror. The latter succeeds in breaking the enchantment [D716], and the cannibal is transformed into a maiden [D11.1]. They are married [T101]. Cf. Type 307.
  *BP II 236 n. 2. — Danish *1*, Grundtvig No. 33; Russian: Andrejev.

406A* *The Defeated King Regains the Throne.* (a) A king, who has been defeated, receives help from an old woman in the woods, (b) to whom he promised marriage; (c) to a sound of the trumpet, which he received from the old woman, appears an army which defeats the enemy; (d) the king forgets about his promise, but admonished, submits himself to the punishment; (e) then the old woman changes into the young girl, forgives him and becomes his wife.
  Polish (521) *4*.

407 *The Girl as Flower.* A maiden is transformed into a flower [D212]. A man breaks a stalk of the flower and she becomes human again [D711.4]. He takes her as his wife [T101]. Cf. Type 652.
  *Anderson in Tauscher *Volksmärchen* 190; *BP I 501, II 121, III 259 (Grimm Nos. 56, 78, 160). — Estonian *1*; Lithuanian *2*; Danish *1*, Grundtvig No. 42; German *5*; Rumanian *1*; Hungarian *16*; Czech: Tille Soupis II (2) 336—343 *10*; Slovenian *2*; Polish *1*; Russian: Afanasiev *2*; Greek *7*, Loukatos No. 4; Turkish: Eberhard-Boratav No. 215 III; India *2*; Chinese: Graham 245 No. 308.

407A *The Bayberry Child.* Because of hasty wish of a barren mother she bears a bayberry. Eventual disenchantment and marriage to prince (as in Type 409A).
  Greek (407*) *7*, Hahn I 163 No. 21.

407B *The Devil's (Dead Man's) Mistress.* Her mother, father, brother and sister die; to be rid of her supernatural husband, she, too, dies. From her grave a flower springs up which changes into a girl. The prince (gentleman) rescues the girl from her former lover and weds her.
  *BP II 126. — Lithuanian (*368) *16*; Hungarian (365[I]) *16*; Serbocroatian *4*.

408 *The Three Oranges.* The quest for the Orange Princess. The false bride.
  I. *The Old Woman's Curse.* A young prince insolently throws a stone and breaks an old woman's oil jar. She utters a curse: he is to fall in love with the three oranges (lemons, pomegranates, eggs).
  II. *The Winning of the Orange Princess.* The prince sets out on the quest.

An old woman (or other person) gives him good advice and after overcoming various obstacles he finds the three oranges. He may open them only near a water. He disobeys this warning. Out of the first orange comes a beautiful maiden, calls for water and dies. The same thing happens with the second orange. For the third orange the prince has water ready and she remains alive. Since she is naked the prince leaves her hidden among the branches of a tree and he goes to bring clothes for her.

III. *The Substitution of a Negress for the Orange Princess.* Under the tree there is a spring. A hideous negro slave (gypsy) comes to get water, thinks that the reflection of the heroine is her own and breaks her water jar since she is too beautiful to carry water. Orange Princess laughs and thus draws attention. The slave learns her story and turns her into a dove (fish, etc.) and takes her place. The prince returns and though astonished at the sudden change marries the false bride.

IV. *The Orange Princess as Dove.* The dove flies to a castle and asks the gardener (cook) about the prince and the false bride. The dove is captured and the prince is much pleased but the negress has the bird killed.

V. *The Orange Princess as Tree.* From the remains of the bird arises a tree. The prince is pleased but the false bride has it cut down.

VI. *The Disenchantment of the Heroine.* A chip of the tree comes into the hands of an old woman. During her absence the orange Princess assumes her earlier form and does the old woman's house work. Eventually she is surprised by the old woman.

VII. *The Lovers' Reunion.* The prince finds the Orange Princess again; the false bride is hanged.

— Analysis furnished by Professor Walter Anderson.

Motifs:

I. S375. Old woman's maledictions inform abandoned hero of his future. M301.2.1. Enraged old woman prophecies for youth.

II. Q40. Kindness rewarded. N825.3. Old woman helper. B350. Grateful animals. N711.2. Hero finds maiden in (magic) castle. D211.1. Transformation: man (woman) to orange. L51. Favorite youngest daughter. D721.5. Disenchantment from fruit (flower) by opening it. L50. Victorious youngest daughter.

III. K2252. Treacherous maidservant. J1791.6.1. Ugly woman sees beautiful woman reflected in water and thinks it is herself. R351. Fugitive discovered by reflection in water. K1911. The false bride (substituted bride). K1911.2.2. True bride pushed into water by false one. K1911.1.3. False bride takes true bride's place at fountain. K1934. Impostor forces hero (heroine) to change places with him (her). D170. Transformation to fish. D150. Transformation to bird.

IV. D610. Repeated transformation. K1911.3. Reinstatement of true bride.

**W. Anderson forthcoming monograph (Kiel); *BP II 125 n., IV 257 n. 1; *Penzer Basile II 158ff.; Köhler-Bolte I *61, 346, 369; Köhler to

Gonzenbach No. 13 and Zs. f. Vksk. VI 63; Coffin *2*. — Swedish (misc.) *1;* Norwegian (408**) *1;* French *8;* Spanish *14*, (cf. 408A*) *1;* Catalan: Amades Nos. 62, 93, 116, 1998, cf. Nos. 12, 165, 173; German *5;* Austrian: Haiding No. 26; Italian: D'Aronco *Fiabe 77* (Trieste: Pinguentini No. 22, Friuli *3*, Pentamerone V No. 9, Tuscan *12*, Sicilian *3*, Gonzenbach No. 13); Hungarian *23*, Dégh No. 14; Czech: Tille Soupis II (1) 222ff. *4;* Slovenian *3;* Serbocroatian *19*, cf. *1;* Russian: Andrejev *1*, Andrejev *Ukraine 7;* Greek *29*, Loukatos No. 5, Dawkins *Modern Greek Folktales* No. 1, Hahn No. 49; Turkish: Eberhard-Boratav Nos. 89, 167 III, IV, 168 III, 290 V *55*, Menzel *Türkische Märchen* (Hanover, 1942) II 63; India *17*. — Franco-American *2;* Spanish-American: Rael Nos. 115, 179—182 (U.S.), Hansen (Argentina) *1*, (Chile) *2*, (Cuba) *2*, (Dominican Republic) *4*, (Puerto Rico) *9;* West Indies (Negro) *13*.

408A* *Devil to Help Gambler in Exchange for One Task Yearly* [M214, N6.1]. On visit to magic castle, men find gold and provisions [D145.7.1, D1422.1.5] and dig hole to underground enchanted palace [D1132]. Forbidden chamber entered. Escape from guardian animals by throwing objects so that they fight over them [K671, K672]. Sleeping girl awakened by kiss [D565.5]. She becomes dove [D154.1] and tells hero to meet her at fountain of three oranges. At fountain treacherous black man [K2261] feeds him figs and gives him cigar which causes magic sleep [D1363.4.2, D1364.19]. Eventual arrival as girl is to marry another. Recognition.
Spanish: Boggs *1*.

409 *The Girl in the Form of a Wolf* [D113.1]. Suckles her child on a stove. On the advice of a magician the stove is made hot and when the girl lays her wolf-clothing on the stove she is restored to human form [D721.3].

Estonian (408*) *56;* Livonian (408*) *2;* Russian: Andrejev *6;* Slovenian *3;* Serbocroatian *1*.

409A *The Girl as Goat (Jackdaw)*. A childless woman wants a child even if it be an animal: she bears a goat-child (jackdaw). When she sends the goat-child to get water for its father, the goat lays off goat-skin and plays. A prince sees her and sends wooers to her house. The prince marries her and she stays as goat and causes trouble in the palace. At a wedding she appears in her human form and is admired and dances. She throws a golden apple and twice escapes and assumes her goat form. The last time the prince burns the goat covering and disenchants her.

Serbocroatian *1;* Greek (409*) *8*, Hahn I 127 No. 14, I 305 No. 57 (daw).

409A* *Snake Princess is Disenchanted* by being thrown on fire. Marries deliverer.
Polish (421) *2*.

409B* *Child Weeping in his Mother's Womb is Promised Supernatural Wife*. After adventures he receives her.
Hungarian: Berze Nagy (409*) *8*.

410 *Sleeping Beauty*. The king's daughter falls into a magic sleep. A prince breaks through the hedge surrounding the castle and disenchants the maiden.

I. *The Wished-for Child.* A frog announces the birth of the much desired daughter of the king.

II. *The Fairies' Gifts.* (a) A fairy who has not been invited to the celebration (christening) makes a wish that the princess shall die of a wound from a spindle. (b) Another fairy changes the death into a hundred-year sleep.

III. *The Enchanted Princess.* (a) The prophecy is fulfilled: with the maiden all the dwellers in the castle sink into a magic sleep and all about grows a hedge of thorn.

IV. *The Disenchantment.* After a hundred years a prince breaks through the hedge, awakes the princess with a kiss and holds a happy marriage.
— Adapted from BP.

Motifs:

I. B211.7.1. Speaking frog. B493.1. Helpful frog.

II. F312. Fairy presides at child's birth. F361.1.1. Fairy takes revenge for not being invited to feast. G269.4. Curse by disappointed witch. M412.1. Curse given at birth of child. F316. Fairy lays curse on child. M341.2.13. Prophecy: death through spindle wound. F316.1. Fairy's curse partially overcome by another fairy's amendment.

III. M370. Vain attempts to escape fulfillment of prophecy. D1962.1. Magic sleep through curse. D1364.17. Spindle causes magic sleep. D6. Enchanted castle. D1960.3. Sleeping Beauty. Magic sleep for definite period (e.g., a hundred years). D1967.1. Person in magic sleep surrounded by protecting hedge. F771.4.4. Castle in which everyone is asleep. F771.4.7. Castle inhabited by enchanted princess.

IV. N711.2. Hero finds maiden in (magic) castle. D1978.5. Waking from magic sleep by kiss. D735. Disenchantment by kiss.

**DeVries »Dornröschen» Fabula II 110ff.; **Romain Zs f. Vksk. XLII 84ff.; *BP I 434 (Grimm No. 50). — Livonian *1;* Lithuanian *3;* Swedish *2* (Uppsala *1,* misc. *1*); Danish *3;* Irish *10;* French *5;* Spanish *1;* Flemish *1,* Witteryck p. 299 *1;* German: Ranke *5;* Austrian: Haiding No. 31; Italian *10* (Pentamerone II No. 8, V No. 5, Tuscan 707 q, 709 r, [876] *3,* Sicilian *5,* Gonzenbach No. 3); Slovenian *2;* Serbocroatian *1;* Polish *1;* Russian: Andrejev; Greek *1;* India *1.* — Franco-American *4* (from Perrault); Spanish-American: Hansen (Dominican Republic) *1;* Portuguese-American (Brazil): Camara Cascudo p. 144; West Indies (Negro) *1.*

410* *The Petrified Kingdom.* A soldier comes to a kingdom where everything has turned to stone. He spends three successive nights in the castle without surrendering to fear of the evil spirits. All the kingdom revives; the soldier marries the princess.
*BP II 330f. — Russian: Afanasiev *9.*

411 *The King and the Lamia.*

I. *The Snake-Wife.* A king sees, falls in love with, and marries a lovely girl who is actually a snake-woman [B29.1].

II. *Overcoming her Power.* (a) His health deteriorates. (b) A fakir tells him to feed her salty food and to stay at night and watch her. (c) She assumes her snake form and goes for water.

III. *The Ashes.* (a) An oven is heated red-hot and she is pushed in. (b) Among the ashes is found a pebble capable of turning anything it touches into gold [D1469.10.1].

India *8.*

412 *The Maiden (Youth) with a Separable Soul in a Necklace* [E711.4]. Cf. Types 302, 403, 425.

I. *Maiden's Life in Necklace.* A maiden's life depends upon her necklace which always must be kept in her possession. She marries a prince. A jealous girl steals the heroine's necklace so that the heroine seemingly dies and the jealous girl takes her place. The body of the heroine is placed in a temple. She comes to life whenever her rival removes the necklace. The prince finds her body and recovers the necklace, or a son is born who recovers the necklace. The impostor is punished, or

II. *A Prince whose Soul is in a Necklace,* seemingly dies when the necklace is stolen (by his stepmother). A maiden marries the prince and recovers the necklace.

*Cosquin *Contes Indines* 27—29. — India *7.*

412A* *Young Man Bathes Successively in Springs* of health, wealth, and wisdom and marries a fairy woman.
Hungarian (412*) *1.*

412B* *Unbaptized Child Stolen by Fairies* found in barn, rescued, and married.
Lithuanian (412*) *12.*

412C* *Enchanted Nymph shows man Treasure in Woods.* Disenchantment.
Spanish *15.*

413 *Marriage by Stealing Clothing.* A youth comes upon a holy man (old woman) in the forest [N825]. He is told not to go in a certain direction but does so [Z211] and sees three lovely maidens bathing. The holy man agrees to help him, turns him into a bird, tells him to steal the clothes of one of the bathing girls [H1335], and warns him not to look back, no matter what the provocation [C311]. The first time he does look back and is burned to a pile of ashes. The holy man restores him [E121.5] and he succeeds on the second attempt. Cf. Types 400, 408.
India *11.*

413A* *Childless Woman Bears Pig* which is disenchanted by witch taking off pig's skin. Witch becomes pig and girl marries prince.
Polish (413*) *1.*

413B* *Girl Transformed to Fish as Mysterious Housekeeper.* Hero burns her fish-skin and disenchants her.
Spanish-American: Hansen (**416) (Cuba) *1.*

413C* *The Elephant Man.* The hero goes hunting with a friend, but becomes tired and falls asleep. Beautiful enchanted princess speaks to him. The hero's father arranges his marriage with another girl. The enchanted princess changes hero to

an elephant for six months, at end of which time enchantment is broken and they are married.
Spanish-American: Hansen (**414) (Dominican Republic) *1*.

422* *Intoxicated Dragon Abducts Queen.* A king intoxicates a dragon chained in a castle. The dragon breaks loose and carries off the queen, telling the king that he will have to shed a barrel of tears to recover his queen.
Polish *1*.

424* *The Youth Wed to a She-Devil.* The youth is worried by a succubus. He catches and marries her. Some years later his wife's brothers, in the form of ravens, come to invite them to a feast (wedding). There he is forbidden to laugh, look into a secret chamber, etc. As gifts (wife's dowry) he gets two bags of coal which, taken home, turn to gold and a pair of horses, which turn out to be sinners transformed to horses.
Lithuanian (*424) *16*.

425—449 Husband

425 *The Search for the Lost Husband.* Cf. also Types 430, 432, and 441.

I. *The Monster as Husband.* (a) A monster is born because of a hasty wish of the parents. (b) He is a man at night. (c) A girl promises herself as bride to the monster, (c^1) to recover stolen clothes or jewels, (c^2) to escape from captivity in spring or well, (c^3) or a girl seeks out or accidentally discovers a supernatural husband, (d) or her father promises her (d^1) in order to secure a flower (lark) his daughter has asked him to bring from journey, (d^2) to pay a gambling debt, or (d^3) to escape from danger. (e) The father and daughter try in vain to send another girl as the monster's bride.

II. *Disenchantment of the Monster.* (a) The girl disenchants the monster (dwarf, bear, wolf, ass, snake, hog, hedgehog, frog, bird, or tree) by means of a kiss and tears, or (b) by burning the animal skin or (c) by decapitation, or (d) by other means.

III. *Loss of the Husband.* (a) But she loses him because she has burned the animals skin too soon, or (b) has revealed his secret to her sisters, or (c) has broken other prohibitions, (c^1) looking at him, (c^2) kissing him, or (c^3) staying too long at home.

IV. *Search for Husband.* (a) She undergoes a sorrowful wandering in iron shoes, (b) gets magic objects from an old woman or from her own child, (c) asks her directions from the wind and stars, (d) climbs a steep glass mountain, (e) takes service as maid with witch who gives her impossible or dangerous tasks to perform, or (f) deceives importunate suitors.

V. *Recovery of Husband.* (a) She buys with three jewels three nights by the side of her lost husband, and wins him back, or (b) disenchants him by affectionate treatment. (c) Sometimes she must go on a journey (as in Type 480) and be compassionate to people and objects.

Motifs:

I. C758.1. Monster born because of hasty (inconsiderate) wish of parents. D621.1. Animal by day; man by night. T111. Marriage of mortal and supernatural being. B640.1. Marriage to beast by day and man by night. S215.1. Girl promises herself to animal suitor. K1335. Seduction (or wooing) by stealing clothes of bathing girl (swan maiden). S240.1. Girl promised unwittingly by her parents to ogre. B620.1. Daughter promised to animal suitor. L221. Modest request: present from the journey. S228. Daughter promised to monster as bride to secure flower (bird) she asked for. S221.1. Bankrupt father sells his daughters in marriage to animals. S221.2. Youth sells himself to an ogre in settlement of a gambling debt. S222. Man promises (sells) child in order to save himself from danger or death. S241. Child unwittingly promised: »first thing you meet.» S252. Vain attempt to save promised child. L54.1. Youngest daughter agrees to marry monster; later the sisters are jealous.

II. D735.1. Beauty and the beast. Disenchantment of animal by being kissed by woman (man). D711. Disenchantment by decapitation. D766.3. Disenchantment by tears. D721.3. Disenchantment by destroying skin (covering).

III. C32. Tabu: offending supernatural husband. C932. Loss of wife (husband) for breaking tabu. C757.1. Tabu: destroying animal skin of enchanted person too soon. C421. Tabu: revealing secret of supernatural husband. C32.1. Tabu: looking at supernatural husband. C916.1. Trespass betrayed by dripping candle. C121. Tabu: kissing supernatural husband. C761.2. Tabu: staying too long at home.

IV. H1385.4. Quest for vanished husband. Q502.2. Punishment: wandering till iron shoes are worn out. H1125. Task: traveling till iron shoes are worn out. D1313.1. Magic ball indicates road. N825.3. Old woman helper. H1233.1.1. Old woman helps on quest. H1235. Succession of helpers on quest. One helper sends to another, who sends to another, etc. H1232. Directions on quest given by sun, moon, wind and stars. H1114. Task: climbing glass mountain. Q482.1. Princess serves as menial. H1010. Impossible tasks. D2006.1.1. Forgotten fiancée reawakens husband's memory by detaining lovers through magic.

V. N681.1. Wife finds lost husband just as he is to marry another. D2006.1.4. Forgotten fiancée buys place in husband's bed and reawakens his memory. D735.1. Disenchantment of animal by being kissed by woman. Q41. Politeness rewarded.

**Swahn *The Tale of Cupid and Psyche* (Lund, 1955). For list and evaluation of other monographs on this cycle, see Swahn 395—418. See also references for 425A. — Finnish *8;* Swedish *54* (Uppsala *13*, Stockholm *1*, Göteborg *8*, Liungman *5*, misc. *27*); Norwegian *64*, Solheim *4;* Icelandic *3* (cf. *6*); Scottish *1;* Irish *220*, Beal II 157ff., VI 72ff., VII 59ff., IX 66f. No. 4, XII suppl. 95—102, XX 3f. Nos. 2, 3, XXI 319; Basque (Delarue) *4;* French *66;* Spanish *7* (cf. *445 A, B) *2;* Catalan:

cf. Amades No. 6; German: Ranke *123*, Meckl. No. 57, 58; Austrian: Haiding Nos. 17, 49, 42, 35; Italian D'Aronco *Fabia 53*, Pentamerone Introduction V No. 3, (Sicilian *13*, Gonzenbach Nos. 15, 42, 43); Slovenian *5;* Serbocroatian *9;* Polish *12;* Indonesian: DeVries No. 154. — Franco-American *43;* Spanish-American: Rael Nos. 153—156, 163, 166, 299 (U.S.); West Indies (Negro) *13*. — African *5.* Various forms of the type follow.[1]

425A *The Monster (Animal) as Bridegroom* (Cupid and Psyche). The maiden on quest for her vanished bridegroom. Various introductions: Present from journey, father promises daughter or daughter promises self. Jephthah's vow. Attempt to evade promise. Sometimes: louse fattened (Cf. Type 621). Sometimes the husband is a vivified image. Tabu: looking, skin burning, gossip. Long wearisome search. Buying three nights to sleep with husband. Formula: old and new key.

Note: Many references given for 425 undoubtedly belong here.
**Swahn *The Tale of Cupid and Psyche* (Lund, 1955) (425B) 31, 278ff.; **E. Tegethoff *Amor und Psyche;* **Stumfall *Das Märchen von Amor und Psyche* (Leipzig, 1907); **I. M. Boberg »The Tale of Cupid and Psyche» Classica et Mediaevalia I (1938) 177—216; **M. de Meyer »Amor et Psyche, étude comparée de variants recueillis en France, en Belgique et en Allemagne» *Folk-Liv* II (1938) 197—210; *BP II 229ff., especially 245ff., III 37ff. (Grimm No. 127), IV 250 n.; *Delarue *Arts et Traditions Populaires* I 274. — Finnish *8* (425A, B); Finnish-Swedish *3* (425A and B); Estonian *16* (425A, B); Livonian *1;* Lithuanian *15* (425A, B); Lappish *2* (425A, B); Swedish (misc.) *5* (425A, B); Danish *87*, Grundtvig No. 26A; English *4;* Spanish *1;* Catalan: Amades Nos. 15, 47, 58, 129, 147, 187, cf. Nos. 22, 130, 131, 154, 157, 162, 173; German Archive *65;* Italian: D'Aronco *Fiabe 38* (Pentamerone I No. 5, II No. 5, II No. 9, V No. 4, Tuscan 425A b—e, i—p, u—aa, cc, dd, [879] a, b, [893], [897], cf. 425A t *19*, Sicilian *15*); Rumanian *29;* Hungarian *28* (425A, B), Dégh No. 15; Czech: Tille Soupis II (2) 247—257 *10;* Slovenian *2;* Serbocroatian *12;* Polish (458) *2;* Albanian: Lambertz No. 16; Greek *71*, Loukatos No. 6, Dawkins *Modern Greek Folktales* No. 16, Dawkins *45 Stories* 114f.; Turkish: Eberhard-Boratav Nos. 90, 92, 95, 98, 102 III, 103, 104 III, 105 *46;* India *7*. — English-American: Baughman (425A, B) *7;* Spanish-American: Hansen (Chile) *4;* (Dominican Republic) *4*, (Puerto Rico) *5;* American Indian: cf. (Zuni): Boas JAFL XXXV 66 No. 2; American Negro (Jamaica): Beckwith MAFLS XVII 130.

425B *The Disenchanted Husband: the Witch's Tasks.* Present from journey or other promise to supernatural husband, marriage. Tabu broken. Search

---

[1] In general I have followed the divisions suggested by Swahn in his study, but because so many regional surveys have listed the Cupid and Psyche as 425A, that number has been retained and includes both Types 425A and B. Swahn's type 425A is here called 425B. The rest of the series corresponds with Swahn's numbering.

for vanished husband leads to house of witch who has enchanted him. Heroine as servant, given difficult or impossible tasks. Sometimes visits to second witch where objects or beings are to be treated with kindness (Cf. Type 480). Box not to be opened. Disenchantment by kiss or affectionate treatment. (Swahn's 425A.)

**Swahn 29ff., 251ff. — Russian: Andrejev (425C) *5*. — Spanish-American: Hansen (Venezuela 425*D) *1*, (Puerto Rico **429) *1*.

425C *Beauty and the Beast.* Father stays overnight in mysterious palace and takes a rose. Must promise daughter to animal (or she goes voluntarily). Tabu: overstaying at home. She finds the husband almost dead. Disenchants him by embrace. (No search, no tasks.) Analysis I b, c, d, II, III c³, V b.

Swahn 32, 296ff.; *BP II 229ff., especially 34ff. (Grimm No. 88); *De Meyer *Vlaamsche Sprookjesthemas* 76ff.; *Anderson *Novelline* No. 89; Coffin *12*. — Finnish *12;* Finnish-Swedish *3;* Estonian *3;* Lithuanian *30;* Swedish (misc.) *2;* Spanish *3;* Catalan: Amades Nos. 72, 125; Dutch *1;* Flemish *8*, Witteryck p. 301 *8;* German *24;* Italian: D'Aronco *Fiabe 39* (Tuscan 425A a, f—h, q—s, v, z, bb *10*, Sicilian 2, Gonzenbach No. 9); Rumanian *1;* Hungarian *7*, (Berze Nagy 434) *12;* Czech: Tille Soupis I 550ff. *10;* Slovenian *1;* Serbocroatian *1;* Polish *15*, (436) *1;* Russian: Afanasiev *8;* Greek *13*, Dawkins *Modern Greek Folktales* No 13, Dawkins *45 Stories* p. 222, Loukatos No. 7, Garnett *Greek Folk Poesy* II 3ff.; India *1*. — Franco-American *3;* English-American: Baughman *4;* West Indies (Negro) *5*.

425D *Vanished Husband Learned of by Keeping Inn (Bath-house).*
I. *Introductions:* (a) A prince learns from an old woman's malediction about his birth and his future [M301.2.1, S375]. He masks as stable boy at the palace [K1816.0.3]. He and the princess elope [T91.6.4]. A bird steals a jewel and he pursues, leaving his fiancée [N352], or (b) an ape makes daughter laugh. A childless couple adopts an animal or object, who wants to marry. (Cf. Type 433). Marriage to animal husband. When tabu is broken he departs.

II. *Recognition.* Heroine sets up inn or bath-house where all must tell stories [H11.1.1]. She thus hears of her husband and finds him.

**Swahn 32, 313ff.; Köhler to Gonzenbach Nos. 12, 13. — Italian (Sicilian **516 *6*, Gonzenbach Nos. 12, 13, 14); Polish (458) *2*.

425E *Enchanted Husband Sings Lullaby.* Enchanted husband (not animal) found in underground palace. Tabu: looking, keyhole or padlock on body which discloses strange objects. She cries out and awakens the husband. Search following ball of yarn [H1226.4]. She gives birth to child in a castle. Husband visits her and sings a lullaby to the child and thus tells how he may be disenchanted. Cf. 425L.

**Swahn 32, 318ff.; Basile Pentamerone II No. 9; Catalan: Amades Nos. 22, 162; Serbocroatian *5*.

425F *Bird Steals Jewel from Girl.* (Sometimes resembles Type 432.) Princess is to be made to laugh (see Types 425D, 559) and she laughs at old woman at a well who tells her that the bird is an enchanted prince. She helps disenchant him by starving or exposing herself. Fairies help her build castle. She rejects his wooing. He feigns death and she reveals her sorrow.
**Swahn 32, 325f.

425G *False Bride Takes Heroine's Place* as she tries to stay awake [K1911.1.4]. Search with iron shoes. Attempted disenchantment of husband by refraining from sleep (or otherwise). Substitute bride. Recognition when true bride tells story to persons or objects. [H13]. Cf. Type 437.
**Swahn 33, 321ff.

425H *Short form of the tale.* Girl promised to animal: Jepththah's vow [S241]. Gift from the journey or king lost in forest. Girl rides away on animal's tail.
**Swahn 33, 327f.

425J *Service in Hell to Release Enchanted Husband.* Looking tabu. Various tests in hell.
**Swahn 33, 329ff.

425K *Search in Men's Clothing.* Gift from the journey. Snake husband. At separation she is given magic hairs and a ring or jewel as life index. She wanders disguised as a man. Tested as to whether she is man or woman [H1578.1]. Attempted seduction by queen. Husband arrives at execution and saves her. Cf. Types 881*, 884, 884A.
**Swahn 34, 334ff. — Italian (Sicilian *515 *1*).

425L *The Padlock on the Enchanted Husband.* Looking tabu. Padlock or keyhole in husband's body with extraordinary things within. Wife cries out and wakes him. At separation wife is pregnant. Spell broken at birth of child. Cf. 425E.
**Swahn 34, 338f.; *Penzer Basile I 201 to Pentamerone II No. 9. — Catalan: Amades No. 22, Rumanian (425A) *28;* Turkish: Eberhard-Boratav No. 104 *14.*

425M *Bathing Girl's Garments Kept* until promise of marriage. Husband usually serpent or water-being. After reunion: visit home after performing tasks set by husband. Formula for calling on him learned by others, who kill him.
**Swahn 34, 340ff. — Lithuanian (*425D) *27;* German: Plenzat p. 24.

425N *Bird Husband.* Tabus: skin burning, looking, gossiping. Heroine in service at palace given difficult tasks (cf. Type 425B). Would-be seducers enchanted (cf. Type 313).
**Swahn 34, 343ff.

425P *Enchanted Wife Lost and Found.* (Cf. Type 400). Looking tabu. Princess must go to a giant. (Cf. Types 301, 302).

*Swahn 35, 346ff. — Catalan: Amades No. 1632; Italian *1* (Tuscan [932] a *1*).

425* *Enchanted Animal Husband Insulted by Guests.* Palace disappears. Heroine helped by hermit finds husband in subterranean palace. Disenchantment.
Italian (Sicilian *552C 2, Gonzenbach No. 77).

426 *The Two Girls, the Bear, and the Dwarf.* The girls let the bear into the hut. They rescue an ungrateful dwarf from death. The bear kills the dwarf. The bear changes into a prince who has been enchanted by the dwarf.

Motifs:

F451.2.3.1. Long-bearded dwarf. K1111.1. Ogre's (dwarf's) beard caught fast. F451.6.1. Dwarf caught by beard in cleft of tree. F451.5.2.1. Ungrateful dwarf. W154.2. Monster ungrateful for rescue. D113.2. Transformation to bear. D763. Disenchantment by destroying enchanter.

*BP III 259 (Grimm No. 161). — Finnish *3;* German *5,* Henssen Volk No. 130; Polish *1;* Russian: Andrejev 2.

428 *The Wolf.* A maiden in the service of a witch. Assigned seemingly impossible tasks, among others to deliver to another witch a letter with instructions to kill the maiden. A wolf helps her to escape. The wolf is thereby disenchanted and becomes a prince who marries the girl.

Motifs:

G204. Girl in service of witch. H1010. Impossible tasks. G462. Person as servant in ogre's house. H931. Tasks assigned in order to get rid of hero. K978. Uriah letter. K511. Uriah letter changed. Falsified order of execution. B435.3. Helpful wolf. D113.1. Transformation: man to wolf.

See Swahn 361ff.[1]; Köhler, notes to Gonzenbach No. 15 (II 214). — Finnish *6;* Finnish-Swedish *1;* Swedish *27;* Danish *34;* French *1;* Catalan: Amades No. 141, cf. 58, 79, 104, 150; German Archive *1;* Italian (Tuscan [858], [859], [879] a, b, [922] *5*); Serbocroatian *1;* Russian: Afanasiev *7;* Turkish: Eberhard-Boratav Nos. 98, 102 III, 188 III, 257 IV. — Spanish-American: Hansen (428**A) (Chile) *1*.

430 *The Ass.* The prince transformed to an ass. Plays a lyre and is entertained at king's court. Becomes husband of a princess who disenchants him. For analysis see Type 425 (I a, II b).

Motifs:

C758.1. Monster born because of hasty (inconsiderate) wish of parents. D132.1. Transformation: man to ass. D963. Man transformed to ass plays the lyre. B641.4. Marriage to peson in ass form. D721.3. Disenchantment by destroying skin (covering).

*BP II 234, III 152 (Grimm No. 144). — Swedish (misc.) *2;* Danish

---

[1] In spite of Dr. Swahn's convincing argument that this is no real tale-type, but only a part of Type 425, so many annotators and archivists have used Type 428 that it has been retained.

5, Grundtvig No. 34, Irish *2;* German *3;* Serbocroatian *1;* Russian: Afanasiev *4;* Italian (cf. Gonzenbach No. 43).

431 *The House in the Wood.* Three maidens one after the other sent into the wood. Kind and unkind. Animals disenchanted. (Cf. Type 480.) Their clue of grain (lentils) is eaten by birds [R135, R135.1]. They come to a house where they find an old man [D1890], a cock [D166.1.1.], a hen [D166.1], and a cow [D133.1]. The elder sisters are unkind [Q2] and are thrown into the cellar. The youngest [L54] feeds the animals and thus disenchants them all [D731]. The old man is a prince, the animals the servants. He marries the girl [L162].

*BP III 276 (Grimm No. 169); Coffin *1*. — Irish *50;* French *1;* German *9;* Austrian: Haiding No. 49; Hungarian *5;* Czech: Tille Soupis I 455ff. *5;* Serbocroatian *1;* Russian: Andrejev; Greek: Dawkins *Modern Greek Folktales* No. 11, *Modern Greek in Asia Minor* 334ff., 385ff.; Turkish: Eberhard-Boratav cf. Nos. 46, 59, 67 V, 118 V *45;* Berber: Laoust No. 124; Palestine: Schmidt-Kahle No. 45. — Franco-American *1;* Spanish-American: Rael No. 107 (U.S.). — African *1*.

431A* *Girls Follow Balls.* Two girls leave home and meet a stranger when they lose their way. He gives them two small balls to roll in front of them to guide them [D1313.1]; the balls roll into a hole in the ground in a wood. They follow the balls, and meet an old woman. That night the robber sons of the old woman enter with a dead sheep: one of them is the man who had given the children the balls. He does not disclose the presence of the girls and they succeed in escaping that night. He asks one of them to marry him and she cuts a bit from his coat as token [H100]. They return home, and later the stranger comes and is recognized by the token; marries the girl; the magic spell is removed from him.
Irish *2*.

432B* *Girls Follow Breadloaf.* Princess sees rabbit herd that forms wheel. Rabbits disappear. Peasant woman and daughter come to comfort princess. On road they drop loaf of bread which rolls to cave where they see rabbits become men. Princess goes there. Their castle disappears. She marries one of them.
Spanish-American: Hansen (**438) *1*.

431C* *The Fish Lover.* Girl on beach finds fish who turns to prince. They are spied upon and fish is killed. (Various denouements.)
Spanish-American: Hansen (**439 A—F) (Puerto Rico) *5*, Dominican Republic) *3*, (Haiti) *1*, (Cuba) *1*.

432 *The Prince as Bird.* Visits to the princess. The wicked stepmother. The wound on the window ledge.

I. *The Bird Lover.* (a) A prince in the form of a bird flies to a beautiful maiden. (b) When in her presence he becomes a man.

II. *The Lover Wounded.* The cruel stepmother (sister) severely wounds him with a knife, a thorn, or glass placed on the window-ledge.

III. *The Lover Healed.* (a). The maiden follows her lover and (b) on the way overhears in a conversation of animals or witches how he may be healed. (c) She follows their directions and heals him.

Motifs:

I. L221. Modest request: present from the journey. Asked what her father shall bring her as a present, the heroine chooses a modest gift. It is usually a flower but sometimes does not turn out to be such a simple gift after all (golden cloak, golden apple). D150. Transformation: man to bird. D641.1. Lover as bird visits mistress. D620. Periodic transformation. A person or thing is transformed at definite intervals. B642. Marriage to person in bird-form.

II. S31. Cruel stepmother. L55. Stepdaughter heroine. K2212.1. Treacherous stepsisters. S181. Wounding by trapping with sharp knives (glass).

III. H1385.5. Quest for vanished lover. H1232.1. Directions on quest given by herdsmen (peasants). N452. Secret remedy overheard in conversation of animals (witches).

*BP II 261ff. — Finnish *1;* Finnish-Swedish *2;* Lithuanian *1;* Lappish *1;* Swedish *12* (Uppsala *1,* Stockholm *1,* Liungman *3,* misc. *7*); Norwegian *6;* Danish *11;* Irish *22;* Spanish *2;* Catalan: Amades Nos. 13, 97, 138; German *3;* Italian: D'Aronco *Fiabe 15* (Pentamerone II No. 2, cf. V No. 3, Tuscan 432 a, [880], [891 sexies], [900] *3,* Sicilian *4*); Hungarian *1,* (666*) *1;* Czech: Tille Soupis II (2) 356f. *1;* Slovenian *1;* Serbocroatian *1;* Russian: Afanasiev *8;* Greek *10,* Dawkins *Modern Greek Folktales* Nos. 15, 16, 17; Turkish: Eberhard-Boratav No. 46 IV, 93, 102 *48;* India *8.* — Franco-American *2;* Spanish-American: Hansen (432** A, B, C) (Chile) *1,* (Puerto Rico) *1,* (**429) *1,* (Dominican Republic) *1,* (Cuba) *1.* — African *1.*

432* *Bird Lover Disenchanted.* Boy is pledged by mother to pigeons (magicians). He learns from them how to change to a bird. Flies as bird to princess. When she is ready to give birth he sends her to his father's home. Boy's mother hides at night and takes his feathers and burns them. He is disenchanted. [Variant: Princess confined in glass tower. From hole in glass tower prince as dove steal ring from princess. Later (H11.1.1), she learns where doves are and thus finds the prince as dove, removes nail from head and disenchants him.)
Greek *4.*

433 *The Prince as Serpent* [D191].
Liungman SSF III 125, 432. — Livonian *2;* Italian (Pentamerone II No. 5, Sicilian *3,* Gonzenbach No. 27); Slovenian *3;* Serbocroatian *1.* — Literary Treatment: Straparola II 1.

433A *A Serpent Carries a Princess into its Castle* [R13.4.1, R16.1]. The maiden kisses and disenchants the youth [D735.1]. See analysis of Type 425: I c (or e); II a.
Cosquin *Lorraine* II 228 (No. 63). — Estonian *1;* Lithuanian *3;* Swedish *11* (Uppsala *3,* Stockholm *1,* Göteborg 1, Lund *1,* Liungman *1,* misc. *4*); Norwegian *1;* Danish *12,* Grundtvig No. 30; Irish *1;* Catalan: Amades No. 60; German *6;* Austrian: Haiding No. 3; Hungarian *2;* Czech: Tille Soupis II (2) cf. 346f. *1;* Slovenian *1;* Russian: **Andrejev;** Greek: Laographia X 433 ff., Loukatos No. 7. — West Indies (Negro) *1.* — African *3.*

433B *King Lindorm.* A childless queen bears a boy who stays in serpent form. When he grows up he demands a wife and his father finds a maiden who is willing. (In some versions, he devours the bride and only after several have tried does the bride survive). She (or her father) disenchants him by bathing [D766.1], or by burning his serpent skin while he is transformed [D721.3]. Cf. Type 711.

A. Olrik »Kung Lindorm» *Danske Studier* I 1—34; **Anna Birgitta Waldemarson-Rooth »Kung Lindorm, en orientalisk saga i Danske-Skånsk Sagotradition» *Folkkultur* (1942) 172—245. — Swedish (misc.) *5;* Danish *4,* Grundtvig No. 31B; Catalan: Amades No. 174, 176—245; German *3;* Italian *7* (Tuscan 425A b, d, i, m—o, cf. 707v 7); Slovenian *2;* Serbocroatian *3;* Russian: Andrejev, Andrejev *Ukraine 8;* Greek *7,* Dawkins *Modern Greek Folktales* No. 14, *45 Stories* No. 36; Turkish: Eberhard-Boratav No. 101, 106 *14;* India *2;* Chinese: Eberhard FFC CXX 76ff. Nos. 72f., FFC CXXVIII 67f. No. 27. — Spanish-American: Hansen (425D) (Venezuela) *1,* (425**F) (Puerto Rico) *1,* (425**E) (Dominican Republic) *1;* African *1.*

433C *The Serpent Husband and the Jealous Girl.* A girl marries a serpent. She is given many jewels and ornaments. The serpent becomes a handsome youth; the girl burns the snake skin and lives happily with the youth. A jealous girl demands that her father marry her to a serpent. One is caught and the girl and serpent are left together. The girl is killed. Cf. Types 425D, 441, 480.

India *5.*

434 *The Stolen Mirror.* The princess as doctor cures the lovesick prince. A youth receives magic power from his teacher. Through its use he goes to a distant land where he steals from a beautiful princess her mirror and her picture. He returns home and takes sick from love. The princess sets out in search for her mirror. Masking as a doctor she magically cures the princess and a prince. She finally reaches the land where the love-sick hero is prince. She reveals herself. Cf. Types 425K, 514**, 881*.

Motifs:

D1711. Magician. D2121. Magic journey. T24.1. Love-sickness. H1346.1. Quest for stolen mirror. D2161. Magic healing power. K1825.1.4. Girl masks as doctor to find departed lover. L161. Lowly hero marries princess.

*Köhler-Bolte I 335. — Catalan: Amades No. 90; Italian *7* (Tuscan [854], [892], cf. 310 c *3,* Sicilian *4*); Turkish: Eberhard-Boratav Nos. 92, 93.

434* *The Diver and the Princess.* A skillful diver loves the king's daughter. The prince who is in love with the princess advises her [H911] to throw a strap into the sea and to order the diver to bring it back [H1132.2]. The diver transforms himself into a duck with the strap around his neck [D165, D641]. Finally he is restored to human form [D700] and marries the princess [L161].

Estonian *2.*

435* *The Dumb Princess Disenchants the Prince.* Princess cures sick princess and then dumb princess disenchants a prince — all by getting rid of enchanters. (Introduced by Tales of a Parrot, Type 1352A)

Motifs: K2261. Treacherous negro. D2065.4. Insanity of princess dependent on height of fire. K925. Victim pushed into fire. D582. Transformation by sticking magic pin into head. D765.1.2. Disenchantment by removal of enchanting pin (thorn).

Spanish *2.*

435A* *Cow Helps Disenchant the Prince.* Girl, following advice of cow, goes to enchanted castle, where she stays for a night between terrifying ghosts; due to her prayers she disenchants a prince who has been transformed into a horse.

Polish *1.*

437 *The Supplanted Bride (The Needle Prince).* The maiden finds a seemingly dead prince whose body is covered with pins and needles and begins to remove them, or she must weep a jug full of tears or spend three sleepless nights by the coffin [D762, D759.7]. As the task is almost completed she leaves the side of the prince for a moment or falls asleep. A servant girl takes her place, completes the task and marries the restored prince [K1911.1.4]. The mistake is afterwards explained. Cf. Type 425G.

*Type 403, 450; *Arfert *Unterschobene Braut.* — Lithuanian: Balys Index No. *422A, 446*; Spanish (445*A) *1,* (449*) *1;* Italian: Pentamerone Introduction; Russian: Andrejev (*533B) *2;* India *5.* — African (Angola): Chatelain 35, 43.

440 *The Frog King or Iron Henry.* A maiden promises herself to a frog in a spring. The frog comes to the door, the table, the bed. Turns into a prince.

I. *Promise to Marry the Frog.* (a) To the youngest of three sisters a frog in a spring gives clear water (a ball thrown into the water). (b) In return he exacts the promise that the girl shall marry him.

II. *Reception of the Frog.* (a) Though the girl has forgotten her promise, the frog appears at her door and requests entrance. (b) He then sleeps at the door, on the table, and finally in her bed.

III. *Disenchantment.* The frog is disenchanted and becomes a prince (a) by being allowed to sleep in the girl's bed, (b) by a kiss, (c) by decapitation, (d) by being thrown against the wall, or (e) by having his frog-skin burnt.

IV. *Iron Henry.* His faithful servant has three iron bands around his heart to keep it from breaking; at his master's rescue the bands snap one by one.

Motifs:

I. L50. Victorious youngest daughter. C41.2. Tabu: letting ball fall into water. G423. Ball falling into water puts person into ogre's (witch's, water spirit's) power. B211.7.1. Speaking frog. S215.1. Girl promised herself to animal suitor.

II. D195. Transformation: man to frog. K1361.1. Transformed person sleeps before girl's door, at foot of bed, in the bed. B654.1.2. Marriage to person in frog form.

III. D734. Disenchantment of animal by admission to woman's bed. D735.1. Disenchantment of animal by being kissed by woman. D711. Disenchantment by decapitation. D712.2. Disenchantment by slinging against something. D721.3. Disenchantment by destroying skin (covering). L162. Lowly heroine marries prince (king).

IV. F875. Iron bands around heart to keep it from breaking. When master is disenchanted, bands around heart of faithful servant snap one by one.

*BP I 1 (Grimm No. 1). — Finnish *1;* Finnish-Swedish *1;* Estonian *2;* Livonian *2;* Lithuanian *1;* Swedish *11* (Uppsala *4,* Stockholm *2,* Göteborg *3,* misc. *2*); Danish *27,* Grundtvig No. 124; Irish *13;* French *1;* Spanish *1;* Dutch *1;* Flemish *1;* German: Ranke *27,* Meckl. Nos. 59, 60; Hungarian *1;* Czech: Tille Soupis II (2) 344—346 *4;* Slovenian *1;* Polish *12;* Russian: Andrejev; Turkish: Eberhard-Boratav Anlage Ae *3.* — Franco-American *4;* English-American: Baughman *1;* West Indies (Negro) *3.*

441 *Hans my Hedgehog.* A childless woman gives birth to a hedgehog [C758.1, T554]. The king unwittingly promises the hedgehog his daughter when the latter shows him the way out of the forest [S226]. The hedgehog takes the bride [B641.5]. His hedgehog's skin is burnt, and he changes into a handsome youth [D721.3].

For analysis see Type 425: I a, d³; II b or c.

*BP II 234, 482 (Grimm No. 108). — Estonian *5;* Lithuanian *19;* Swedish *4* (Lund *1,* misc. *3*); Norwegian *1;* Flemish *1;* German *4;* Hungarian *10;* Czech: Tille Soupis II (2) 229—301 *4;* Slovenian *11;* Serbocroatian *5;* Polish *2;* Russian: Andrejev. — West Indies (Negro) *1.* — Literary Treatment: Straparola II 1.

442 *The Old Man in the Forest.* The maiden disenchants [D700] a prince whom an evil woman [G263] has transformed into a tree [D215]. She gets the magic ring [D1076] from the old woman's house. Marriage [L162].

BP III 9 (Grimm No. 123). — Scottish *1;* Irish *5;* German *3;* Polish *3;* Russian: Andrejev. — Franco-American *1.*

444* *Enchanted Prince Disenchanted — miscellaneous.*

444A* *Prince Transformed to a Pike,* helps a stepdaughter in performing tasks given her by stepmother. After having drowned the stepmother he marries the girl.
Polish (444) *1.*

444B* *Guessing the Girls' Names.* A sorcerer kidnaps two beautiful princesses, takes them to a distant country, and offers them in marriage to anyone, including animals, who can guess their names. Many men try without success. A toad and a turtle overhear princesses talking, learn their names (cf. Type 500 III, Type 812 III), and win them in marriage. At midnight princesses become angry at animals and throw them against the wall. Animals are disenchanted and become princes. They marry.
Spanish-American: Hansen (**444) (Cuba) *1.*

444C* *The Girl in the Lagoon.* A girl is sad because every day she has to frighten birds away from cornfield. A handsome young man, mounted on a beautiful horse with a gold saddle, appears, proposes to her, and offers her untold wealth. He asks her to get on his horse but to close her eyes. They go toward the lagoon; when the girl opens eyes she is in a rich palace. The girl's father searches for her in vain. One morning he sees her on the banks of the lagoon beautifully dressed. He tries to catch her but she flees into the lagoon. The priest tells him to lasso her. He takes her to the priest who prays for her, but she escapes and returns to the lagoon.

Spanish-American: Hansen (**448) (Peru) *1*.

444D* *The Cat Husband.* A princess spends three nights in a house where a cat sleeps at the foot of her bed. The cat-husband arrives in a coach: he has been disenchanted by sleeping three nights with a princess (cf. Type 440). They marry. Her sisters arrive. Through them (or another woman) the princess is poisoned through a key hole. The husbands preserves the body and remarries. The princess is revived by the removal of a poison pin (cf. Type 709) or by a dog licking her body.

Irish.

444E* *Wild Boar as Husband.* A wild boar demands the daughter of a poor fisher in return for good things to eat. The boar carries the daughter to the bottom of the sea to an enchanted city. She remains silent for three days. With drops of water she disenchants the city and all inhabitants. The boar becomes a prince. He marries the girl and invites her parents to live in their palace.

Spanish-American: Hansen (**446) (Argentina) *1*.

445* *Wife Undoes Curse on Husband.* An angry mother curses a son who, in obedience to his father's jestingly given command, has struck her with a switch. Returning home from church on his wedding day, he disappears. A beggar sees him doing penance in the forest. The father and mother endeavor to save their son: only his wife saves him.

Lithuanian (*445) *31;* cf. Greek: Loukatos No. 8, Dawkins *Modern Greek Folktales* No. 32, *More Greek Folktales* No. 5; Polish (443*) *1;* Russian: Afanasiev (*813B) *6*.

449 (formerly 449*) *The Tsar's Dog (Sidi Numan).*

I. *The Unfaithful Wife* (witch) transforms her husband into a dog [D141].

II. *The Clever Dog* (really a transformed man) [D682.3] in the service of the Tsar [B292].

III. *Transformation.* When he comes home, the wife transforms him into a sparrow [D151.8].

IV. *The Wife's Punishment.* A magician catches him as bird and disenchants him [N845, D700], and gives advice how to transform the wicked wife into a mare [D535].

*BP III 7f. No. 122; *Anderson *Zu Wesselski* 17; Malone PMLA XLIII 418, 421, 441; Kittredge *Arthur* 170 n. 3; Anderson *Roman apuleja i narodnaja skazka* I 376—487, 612—633. — Finnish *1;* Livonian (449) *1;* Lithuanian (3655) *15;* Scottish: Campbell-McKay No. 21; Irish: Larminie p. 18; French (449*); Hungarian: Berze Nagy (589*) *2;* Polish *2;* Russian: Afanasiev (*449) *18;* Turkish: Eberhard-Boratav No. 204 *8;* India *3*. — Literary Treatment: *Chauvin V 315f., VI 198 No. 371, VII 129f.

450—459 Brother or Sister

450 *Little Brother and Little Sister.* The boy is turned into a roe by the cruel stepmother. Lives with his sister in the forest. The king marries the sister. Her stepmother usurps her place as wife. Disclosure, punishment, and reunion. Cf. Types 403, 480, 533.

I. *Cruel Stepmother.* A widower yields to the persuasion of his daughter and marries again. The new wife is cruel to the stepchildren.

II. *Kind and Unkind.* The good maiden is granted beauty and other gifts but her evil sister receives ugliness as a gift. Cf. Types 403, 480.

III. *The Children's Flight from Home.* (a) Brother and sister escape together. (b) The brother is transformed by the stepmother into a roe or sheep, (c) when he drinks from an animal's track; — or (d) the brother takes service with a king whom he tells about his beautiful sister.

IV. *False Bride.* The sister marries a king but is replaced by another: (a) on the way to the wedding, (b) when a child is born; — or (c) she is thrown into the water and abandoned, or (d) transformed by the stepmother into a bird or fish, or (e) caught by a mermaid or swallowed by a fish. (f) The impostor is usually a stepsister.

V. *Persecuted Brother.* The king (a) has the brother thrown into a snake pit and (b) marries the false bride.

VI. *Denouement.* (a) Conversation of brother and sister overheard by a servant or the king. (b) The queen returns at night in her animal form to learn about her family and is disenchanted by decapitation or by cutting of the chain which binds her. (c) The dead queen returns at night from the grave to suckle her child.

VII. *Punishment.* The villain is given the punishment she has unwittingly suggested.

Motifs:

I. S31.5. Girl persuades her father to marry a widow who has treated her kindly. S31. Cruel stepmother. L55. Stepdaughter heroine.

II. Q2. Kind and unkind.

III. P253. Sister and brother. S301. Children abandoned (exposed). S143. Abandonment in forest. D683.2. Transformation by witch (sorceress). D555.1. Transformation by drinking from animal's track. D135. Transformation: man to sheep. D114.1.1. Transformation: man to deer. P253.2. Sister faithful to transformed brother. T11.1. Love from description.

IV. N711.1. King (prince) finds maiden in woods (tree) and marries her. L162. Lowly heroine marries prince (king). K1911. The false bride (substituted bride). K2212.1. Treacherous stepsisters. K1911.1.1. False bride takes true bride's place on way to wedding. K1911.1.2. False bride takes true bride's place when child is born. S142. Person thrown into the water and abandoned. S432. Cast-off wife thrown into water. K1911.2.2. True bride pushed into water by false. K1911.2.1. True bride transformed by false. D150. Transformation to bird. D170. Transformation to fish. B82. Mermaid. K1911.2.2.1. True bride lives in fish's belly. F913. Victims rescued from swallower's belly.

V. Q465.1. Throwing into pit of snakes as punishment.

VI. H13. Recognition by overheard conversation. E322.2. Dead wife returns to wake husband. E323.1.1. Dead mother returns to suckle child. D688. Transformed mother suckles child. D711. Disenchantment by decapitation. D757. Disenchantment by holding enchanted person during successive transformation. D762. Disenchantment by proper person waking from magic sleep. The enchanted person appears three times and if the sleeper does not wake by the third times the enchantment must last.

VII. Q581. Villain nemesis.

*BP I 79 (Grimm No. 11; cf. No. 141). — Finnish *21;* Estonian *4;* Livonian *1;* Lithuanian *43;* Swedish *6* (Stockholm *1*, misc. *5*); Danish *2*, Grundtvig No. 38; Irish *1;* French *12;* Spanish *1;* German *20;* Italian *7* (Pentamerone cf. V No. 8, Tuscan 451 a, d, e *3*, Sicilian *3*, Gonzenbach Nos. 48, 49); Rumanian *11;* Hungarian *20*, Dégh No. 16; Czech: Tille Soupis I 106 *3;* Serbocroatian *5;* Russian: Afanasiev *15*, Greek *6*, Loukatos Nos. 9, 10; Turkish: Eberhard-Boratav No. 168 *32;* South Arabia: Jahn 28. — Franco-American *3;* Spanish-American: Hansen (Puerto Rico) *1*, (Chile **425A) *1;* West Indies (Negro) *6*. — African *1*.

450A *The Brother Transformed to a Snake.* See analysis of 450.

III. (c) A brother and sister are driven forth by their stepmother. The boy kills a snake. A flowering tree grows from its body. The girl puts one of the flowers on her brother and he is changed into a snake.

IV. (b) The brother is disenchanted.

India *4.*

451 *The Maiden Who Seeks her Brothers.* The twelve brothers are changed into ravens. Cf. The Speechless Princess, Types 705, 710.

I. *The Brothers and their Sister.* (a) Seven (twelve) brothers have a younger sister. (b) The parents have promised the death of the brothers if a daughter is born; the brothers discover this; the mother lets them know by a sign if a girl is born; the brothers flee; the sister finds them; or (c) the boys leave home out of fear of their father or stepmother.

II. *Transformation of Brothers to Ravens.* (a) Through a wish of their father or (b) stepmother or (c) because their younger sister has plucked twelve flowers from an enchanted garden, the brothers are transformed to ravens.

III. *The Sister's Quest.* (a) The sister seeks for them and asks direction of sun, moon, and stars and finds them on a glass mountain (and they are thereby disenchanted) or (b) the sister must remain speechless for years and make shirts.

IV. *The Calumniated Wife.* (a) A king sees the speechless girl and marries her. (b) On the birth of her children they are stolen and she is accused of killing them.

V. *Disenchantment.* (a) As she is about to be executed her period of silence is over, the ravens fly down, are disenchanted and all is cleared up.

Motifs:

I. Z71.5.1. Seven brothers and one sister. P253.0.5. One sister and six (seven, eleven, twelve) brothers. P251.6.7. Twelve brothers. S272. Sacrifice of brothers promised if girl is born. T595. Sign hung out informing brothers whether mother has borne boy or girl. N344.1. Wrong sign put out leads to boys' leaving home. S272.1. Flight of brothers from home to avoid being sacrificed.

II. S11. Cruel father. S31. Cruel stepmother. D521. Transformation through wish. D515. Transformation by plucking flowers in enchanted garden. C515. Tabu: touching (plucking) flowers. D151.5. Transformation to raven. D161.1. Transformation to swan.

III. P253.2. Sister faithful to transformed brothers. H1385.8. Quest for lost brothers. H1232. Directions on quest given by sun, moon, and stars. H1114. Task: Climbing glass mountain. D783. Disenchantment by being found when lost. D753. Disenchantment by accomplishment of tasks. D753.1. Disenchantment by sewing shirts for enchanted brothers. D758. Disenchantment by maintaining silence. Z72.2. Seven years, seven months, seven days.

IV. N711. King (prince) accidentally finds maiden in woods (tree) and marries her. K2116.1.1. Innocent woman accused of killing her new-born children.

V. H215. Magic manifestation at execution proves innocence.

*BP I 70, 227, 427 (Grimm Nos. 9, 49, cf. No. 25); Coffin 2. — Finnish *46;* Finnish-Swedish *4;* Estonian *6;* Livonian *5;* Lithuanian *43;* Lappish *3;* Swedish *18* (Uppsala *11,* Stockholm *1,* Göteborg *2,* Lund *2,* Liungman *2,* misc. *3*); Norwegian *8,* Solheim *1;* Danish *21,* Grundtvig No. 40; Icelandic *2;* Scottish *4,* Campbell-McKay No. 22; Irish *96,* Beal I 115ff.; Basque: Delarue *2;* French *14;* Spanish *2;* Catalan: Amades No. 45, cf. Nos. 11, 32, 163; Flemish *2;* German: Ranke *57,* Meckl. No. 61, Henssen Volk No. 131; Italian: D'Aronco *Fiabe 21* (Pentamerone IV No. 8, Tuscan 451 h, [310] a, b, [869] *4*); Rumanian *1;* Hungarian *9;* Czech: Tille Soupis II (2) 45—55 *12;* Slovenian *10,* Istrian No. 14; Polish *20;* Russian *15,* Andrejev *Ukraine 3;* Greek *1, Laographia* XI 452ff.; Turkish: Eberhard-Boratav No. 165, cf. 166 *15;* India *3.* — Franco-American *6;* Spanish-American: Hansen (Dominican Republic) *2,* (Puerto Rico) *7;* West Indies (Negro) *7.*

451A *The Sister Seeking her Nine Brothers.* She sets forth with the mare whose offspring are the steeds of her nine brothers. Contrary to warning the girl obeys a fairy and goes bathing. The fairy takes the girl's clothes and carriage and leaves in their place her own rags and a hog harnessed to a trough. She claims to be the sister of the brothers [K1934], and they

entertain her. Meanwhile the real sister of the brothers, tending to the grazing horses, relates her sad fate in song [H12]. The brothers hear the song, understand the trickery, and recognize her for their sister. The wicked fairy is torn to pieces by a horse smeared with pitch [Q416].
Lithuanian (*452) *20;* Prussian: Plenzat p. 21.

451* *Sister as Mysterious Housekeeper.* Two brothers leave home. A bird carries off sister's necklace or ring [N774.1], telling her she can find it at her brothers' house. After wandering she arrives, puts their house in order and hides [N331.1]; on the third day they discover her. She keeps house for them.
Spanish (327*D) *2.*

452A* *Sister Rescued from Devil.* The hero enchants his sister and wishes that the devil may take her. This happens. He goes, finds her and rescues her. Cf. Type 312C.
Hungarian: Honti *4,* Berze Nagy (468*) *6.*

452B* *The Sisters as Oxen.* Witch and daughter are jealous of three beautiful orphan girls who are in the king's favor. The witch puts magic powder in the girls' soup and two elder girls eat it and are transformed into oxen. The king asks the youngest girl to marry him and she accepts on condition that the oxen be cared for in the king's palace. The witch visits the palace and sticks two pins in the queen's head and she becomes a dove (cf. Type 408 III). The witch's daughter pretends to be queen. The dove comes to the palace and is caught by a gardener when he hears it speak. The king removes the pins from its head and it regains human form (cf. Type 408 IV). Witch and daughter are burned to death.
Spanish-American: Hansen (**452B) (Puerto Rico) *1.*

452C* *The Sister as Duck.* While the brother is serving in the army, the stepmother ill-treats his sister [S31] (commands her to spin an impossible quantity of flax [H1092] and to tend cattle at the same time). The girl is helped by a cow [H1092.1.]. The witch prepares under the doorstep a pit of burning coals, but the little dog gives timely warning [B521.3.1] After it is killed, the girl falls into the pit and is burned. The cow licks the ashes: a little duck appears therefrom and flies away into the woods [B613.1]. Returning home, the brother hears the little duck relating her sad fate in song [H12]. Smears his horse with pitch and punishes the witch [Q416.2].
Lithuanian (*453) *4.*

452D* *Parents as Birds.* The hero's parents and sisters are enchanted by a dwarf and they become birds. The hero receives ointment from an old man, disenchants his parents, and kills the dwarf.
Spanish-American: Hansen (**459) (Dominican Republic) *1.*

454* *Girl who Must Remain Small* because she has not made her fairy godmother laugh. (Sometimes told of a boy.)
French *4.*

455* *Jealous Queen Blinds Nieces.* She has the eyes of twelve beautiful nieces put out, and has them imprisoned. Their brother helper is sent on dangerous quests (for lion's milk, etc.). Cf. Type 590.
Spanish *1;* Spanish-American: Hansen (455**A) (Chile) *1.*

459 *The Make-Believe Son (Daughter).* The king turns out his eldest queen because she is childless. The maidservant informs the king that the queen has borne (a) a son or (b) a daughter but that the king must not see it. The queen is supplied a house and food. After some years the king arranges a marriage for his »son». The maidservant makes (c) an image of a youth or (d) puts an animal in the sedan-chair. A god pities the

queen and vivifies the image or turns the animal into a handsome youth (maiden). The king is reconciled with the queen.
India 5.

SUPERNATURAL TASKS

460—462 Questions

460A *The Journey to God to Receive Reward.*
A youth has heard that God returns the alms given to a poor man [J1262.5.1]; cf. Type 1735. He sets out on a journey to God [H1263] and receives his reward (see Type 461 [V]) along with the answers to questions which have been asked him on his journey [H1291, H1292, H544]). See Type 461 (III).
**Aarne FFC XXIII 127; *Anderson in Tauscher *Volksmärchen* 183; *BP I 292 (Grimm No. 29); Coffin *1*. — Estonian *25;* Livonian *1;* Lithuanian *4;* Icelandic *7;* Irish *1*, (460A, B); French *15* (460, 416); German: Plenzat (460) *1;* Italian *5* (Sicilian *5*, Gonzenbach No. 47); Rumanian *7;* Czech: Tille FFC XXXIV 327; Slovenian *1;* Russian: Andrejev; Greek *2;* Turkish: Eberhard-Boratav No. 126; India *1;* Indonesian: DeVries No. 166; Chinese: Eberhard FFC CXX 183f. No. 125, FFC CXXVIII 145ff. No. 83. — Spanish-American: Hansen (Argentina) *1.*

460B *The Journey in Search of Fortune.* A poor man has no good luck. He wanders abroad to see Fortune [H1281] from whom he receives answers to questions which have been asked on his journey [H544]. He learns that his ill-luck came because he was born on a luckless day [N127.0.1]. Later after marrying into wealth he loses all. See Types 461 (III), 735.
*Aarne FFC XXIII 124; **Megas *Laographia* XV (1953) 3ff.; **Megas *Makedonikē Parallagē tēs pros tēn Tychēn Odoiporias* (Athenai 1956); Dawkins *Laographia* XV 147ff.; Coffin *1*. — Finnish *1;* Estonian; Lithuanian *11;* Lappish *3;* Catalan: Amades cf. No. 188; Italian (Sicilian: Gonzenbach No. 47); Slovenian *3;* Russian: Afanasiev *2;* Greek *2*, Dawkins *Modern Greek Folktales* No. 79, *45 Stories* 351ff., *More Greek Folktales* 77f. *6*, Loukatos No. 1; Turkish: Eberhard-Boratav No. 127, cf. 130 *1;* India *6.*

461 *Three Hairs from the Devil's Beard.* Prophecy, Urias letter, and resultant marriage; cf. Type 930.
I. *Introduction.* Prophecy that a youth is to become the king's son-in-law. Vain attempts to prevent the marriage.
II. *Quest for Devil's Hairs.* (a) The hero is sent on a quest to hell to bring three hairs from the devil's beard or (b) to find who is the strongest (cleverest) person in the world.
III. *The Questions.* On his way various questions are given to which the

youth is asked to find the answers; e.g., (a) why a tree does not flourish, (b) when a ferryman will be freed from his duties (a water-animal be freed from some annoyance), (c) how the sick prince (princess) can be cured, (d) why a spring has gone dry, (e) where is the lost princess, (f) where is the lost key, (g) how can a girl thus far avoided by suitors marry, (h) why the live stock die.

IV. *Success of the Quest.* (a) The youth is aided by the devil's wife. (b) He transforms himself into an insect and hides. (c) The devil smells human flesh but fails to find the hero. (d) By help of the wife he learns the answers to the questions; i.e., (d^1) gold or a serpent is hidden under the tree and must be removed, (d^2) the ferryman must pass the oar to someone else, who will have to assume his duties, (d^3) the princess can be cured when the consecrated wafer stolen at her first communion by a rat is returned (the prince when he removes the stone he has spit out in the church), (d^4) the spring will start again when the animal or stone is removed from its vein, and (e) he receives the three hairs.

V. *Rewards.* (a) On the homeward journey he answers the questions and receives a large reward.

VI. *King as Ferryman.* (a) The envious king attempts to imitate the youth's exploits. (b) The ferryman puts the oar into his hand and he must remain ferryman.

Motifs:

I. M312. Prophecy of future greatness for youth. M312.1. Prophecy: wealthy marriage for poor boy. H1510. Tests of power to survive. Vain attempts to kill hero. M370. Vain attempts to escape fulfillment of prophecy.

II. H1211. Quests assigned in order to get rid of hero. H1210.2. Quest assigned by king. H1273.2. Quest for three hairs from devil's beard. G303.4.1.8.2. Devil has three golden hairs. H105.4.1. Monster's beard as proof of visit. H1316. Quest for the strongest.

III. H1291. Questions asked on way to other world. H1292. Answers found in other world to questions propounded on the way.

IV. G530.1. Help from ogre's wife. D642. Transformation to escape difficult situation. G532. Hero hidden and ogre deceived by his wife (daughter) when he says he smells human blood.

V. H1243. Riches the reward of questions solved on quests. N471. Foolish attempt of second man to overhear secrets (from animals, demons, etc.). He is punished. P413.1.1. Ferryman puts oar into king's hand and he must remain ferryman. Q521.5. Penance: ferryman setting people over a stream until relieved by another.

Tille Zs. f. Vksk. XXIX 22ff.; **Aarne *Der reiche Mann und sein Schwiegersohn* FFC XXIII 115—194 (Bibliography of studies p. 17); *BP I 276 (Grimm No. 29); Coffin *1*. — Finnish *176;* Finnish-Swedish *10;* Estonian; Livonian *4;* Lithuanian *21;* Lappish *1;* Swedish *54* (Uppsala *8*, Stockholm *2*, Göteborg *10*, Liungman *5*, misc. *23*); **Norwegian *24;*

Danish *47*, Grundtvig No. 68; Icelandic *1;* Irish *202*, Beal IX 62ff., 66f. Nos. 3, 98, XVIII 85ff., XXI 318f.; French (460+461) *15;* Spanish *1;* Catalan: Amades No. 213; Flemish *4;* German: Ranke *44*, Meckl. No. 62; Austrian: Haiding No. 33, 64, cf. 65; Italian (Pentamerone cf. IV No. 8, Tuscan [324] *1*); Hungarian *13;* Czech: Tille FFC XXXIV p. 327, Tille Soupis I 141—162 *21;* Slovenian *2;* Polish *18;* Russian: Andrejev *Ukraine 11*, Afanasiev *14;* Greek (936*) *12;* Turkish: Eberhard-Boratav No. 125 IV; Indonesian: DeVries No. 167; Chinese: Graham No. 26 p. 237. — Franco-American *12;* Spanish-American: Rael No. 494 (U.S.), Hansen (Dominican Republic) *1*, (Puerto Rico) *1;* Cape Verde Islands: Parsons MAFLS XV (1) 304 n. 3; West Indies (Negro) *2;* American Indian: Thompson *C Coll* II 387f.

461A *The Journey to the Deity for Advice or Repayment.* Cf. Type 460A.

I. *The Quest.* A poor man sets out to seek a deity to recover lost gold, to seek advice, or for other reasons.

II. *The Questions.* On his way, various questions are given to which he is asked to find the answers: (a) Persons with various objects stuck to their bodies ask how they can be removed. (b) A crocodile or fish suffering great pain asks how it can be relieved. (c) Why a tank leaks or will not fill. (d) Why the fruit of a tree is bitter or why no one will eat the fruit or why the tree is withered. (e) Why a man cannot die or why a corpse cannot find rest. (f) Why a palace, bridge, etc., continually collapses. (g) Why no one will ride a horse. (h) Why a king is blind. (j) Other questions.

III. *The Reward.* After finding the deity and receiving the answers, he returns. On his way he supplies the answers to the questions and is rewarded; i.e., the fruit of the tree is bitter because gold is buried at its foot. The man digs up the gold and takes it with him.

India *14.*

462 *The Outcast Queens and the Ogress Queen.* Cf. Type 590.

I. *The Ogress Queen.* (a) Men in a forest are pursued by an ogress who takes on the form of a lovely girl [G264, G369.1.5]. (b) A king hunting in the forest [G405] sees the lovely girl and takes her as his queen.

II. *The Blinded Queens.* (a) The ogress at night eats the palace horses [G264.3.1] or some other animals and piles the bones by the beds of the seven (twelve, etc.) other queens. (b) At the insistence of the ogress, the seven queens are blinded [S413, S438] and thrown into a pit [S435]. (c) Each queen bears a son and, to avoid starvation, the babies are eaten [G72.2]. The youngest queen saves her son [L71], who provides food for the queens. [Z215].

III. *The Tasks.* The son of the blinded queen attracts the attention of the ogress [D369.1.5], who tries to destroy him by setting tasks [H1212]: (a) To bring tiger's milk [H1361.1]. He befriends the cubs [H1361.0.1] or removes a thorn from the tigress's foot and is given the milk (Cf.

Type 156). (b) The ogress sends the youth to the land of demons on a pretext with a Uriah letter, which is changed by a helper [K511]. In the land of demons he finds where their lives are kept and slays them [K956] as well as the ogress queen. (c) Other tasks.

IV. *Recognition.* The youth is recognized as the prince, the ogress slain, and the blinded queens' eyesight restored, and the queens reinstated.

India *24.*

463A* *Quest for Father's Friend.* Prince goes on quest for his father's old friend who lives far away beyond the Glass Mountains.

Hungarian: Berze Nagy (320*) *13.*

463B* *The Black Princess* may be disenchanted by youth who for certain time spends on himself the money which he receives from her. The hero fails because at the last moment he hands the remaining coin to a beggar. The gradually whitening princess becomes black again.

Polish (464*) *2.*

465 *The Man Persecuted Because of his Beautiful Wife.*

I. *Obtaining the Beautiful Wife.* (a) The hero steals the clothing of a bathing girl (swan maiden) and gives them back only if she will marry him [D361.1, K1335], or (b) he receives his wife from God.

II. *The Tasks.* (a) The envious king covets the wife [H931.1] and on the advice of an evil counselor [H911] (usually a barber [H919.1.1]) he is given impossible quests or tasks [H1211]: (a^1) to find the unknown food [H1382], (a^2) to find the living harp [H1335], (a^3) to find God in the other world [H1262], (a^4) to find the wonderful flower [H1333.5], (a^5) to bring tiger's milk to cure feigned sickness [H1212], (a^6) to reap field of grain (or the like) in one night [H1090], or (a^7) other tasks. (b) He accomplishes these with the help of his wife [H1233.2.1]. Cf. Type 313,

III. *The Punishments.* (a) The king is overcome, and (b) the barber punished by being sent to heaven as he had advised be done to the hero [K964].

465A *The Quest for the Unknown.* The Swan Maidens. The envious king covets the wife and gives the man impossible tasks, among others to find the unknown (food). The exchange of objects [D831], cf. Type 569. With the help of his wife he succeeds. See analysis (465): Ia; IIa, a^1, b; III.

**Helge Holmström *Studier över svanjungfrumotivet* (Malmö, 1919), **G. A. Megas *Hessische Blätter* XLIX—L 135ff.; Coffin *1.* — Finnish *13;* Finnish-Swedish *7* (465); Estonian *15* (465); Lithuanian *18;* Lappish *4* (465); Irish *3* (465); Dutch *1* (465); Rumanian *8;* Hungarian *5,* Dégh No. 17; Polish *10* (465); Russian: Andrejev *Ukraine 5;* Afanasiev *40;* Greek *27,* Dawkins *Modern Greek Folktales* No. 18; Turkish: Eberhard-Boratav Nos. 86, 87, 216, 248, cf. 280 *32;* India *23;* Chinese: Eberhard FFC CXXVIII 63f. — Franco-American *2;* Spanish-American: Rael (465) Nos. 191, 192 (U.S.); West Indies (Negro) *1* (465).

465B *The Quest for the Living Harp.* An animal as wife [B642]. A king assigns (among others) a quest for the living harp. With the help of his wife the man succeeds. See analysis (465): I; II a, a², b; III.
**Cf. Holmström 172. — Finnish *10;* Polish *1;* Russian: Afanasiev *6.*

465C *A Journey to the Other World.* A man receives his wife from God. A king sends him on a quest to the other world [H1260] (to bring God from heaven, etc.). The man succeeds with the help of his wife. See analysis (465): I b; II a, a³; III.
**Cf. Holmström 172. — Finnish *5;* Livonian *1;* Lithuanian *11;* Russian: Andrejev *Ukraine 16,* Afanasiev *9;* Turkish: Eberhard-Boratav Nos. 86 IV, 256 V.
(*The Heartblood of the Dragon as Remedy for the King;* see Type 305.)

465D *Animal Brothers Help the Hero.* They steal the clothes of a bathing girl (cf. Swan Maiden). Tasks: (a) To bring the tiger's milk; (b) The hero's bull, etc., must fight the king's animals. The youth's helpers perform the tasks; or the king is overcome and the youth becomes king. See analysis (465): Ia; IIa, a⁵, a⁶, a⁷, b; III.
India *4.*

465A* *The Fickle Wife and the General.* The general elopes with another man's wife. As a conscript, the betrayed husband is assigned to the general's regiment. A charge is brought against him for theft, and his life is attempted [H931.1]. The truth, however, comes to light.
Lithuanian (*782) *7.*

465B* *Quest for Golden Hair.* The hero finds golden hair, golden feather and golden horseshoe (or the like). His master commands him to bring back the princess, the bird or the steed from which these objects come. Hero accomplishes this and the greedy master is punished. (Cf. Type 531.)
Hungarian (465 I) *11.*

466* *The Knotted Handkerchief.* The hero wins the hand of a maiden. For three nights he holds a handkerchief tied in knots and keeps it from the ogre [D758.1].
Finnish-Swedish *1;* Danish *7.*

466** *The Journey to Hell.* The hero rescues three maidens from the dragon (see Type 300); disenchants a princess who has been turned into a dragon and wins the hand of the princess. Cf. Type 871.
Estonian (466) *1;* Danish *3,* Grundtvig No. 12; Russian: Andrejev (466).

466A* *The Giant's Servant and the Queen.* The giant sends his servant for golden apples, whose bringer is to be rewarded by marriage to the queen; the servant, thanks to his magic golden ring, plucks the apples, knocks down the giant, and marries the queen.
Polish (466) *1.*

467 *The Quest for the Wonderful Flower (Jewel)* [H1335.5]. (Cf. Types 402, 407, 465.)

I. *Obtaining the Flower.* A youth finds a lovely (a) flower or (b) jewel and takes it to a king. The king demands another [H1218] (c) at the request of his queen or daughter.

II. *The Quest.* After many adventures on the way, the youth finds a princess who produces the flowers (jewels) magically [D457.1.3], marries her, and returns in triumph.

India *18*.

468 *The Princess on the Sky-Tree.* Ascent on a tree which reaches the sky. On its branches lives a princess.

Hungarian: Honti (467) *11*, Berze Nagy (530 I) *18*, Dégh No. 18; German (317') *6*.

470 *Friends in Life and Death.* The deceased friend followed into the other world. Cf. Type 471.

I. *The Visit to the Other World.* (a) Two friends pledge themselves never to part. One of them dies. (b) The living friend invites the dead to visit him on Christmas and goes with him when he returns; or (c) a man in a churchyard invites a skull to dinner and then goes off with the skull.

II. *The Journey.* (a) On the way they see many strange sights; among them: (b) fat and lean kine; (c) a broad and narrow road; (d) people and things that strike one another. (e) The living goes to sleep by a water; when he wakes he is covered with moss. (f) They see houses of feast and of mourning.

III. *The Return.* (a) When the living man returns he has been away many centuries; all is changed and he knows no one.

IV. *Death.* (a) He dies the next day by falling from a tree (or high place). (b) He vanishes after prayer.

Motifs:

I. M253. Friends in life and death. M252. Promise of dying man to bring news of other world. E238. Dinner with the dead. Dead man is invited to dinner. Takes his host to other world. C13. The offended skull (statue) (Festin de Pierre). A skull (statue) is invited to dinner. Attends the dinner and takes his host off to the other world. C954. Person carried off to other world for breaking tabu.

II. E481. Land of the dead. F171. Extraordinary sights in otherworld. F171.0.1. Enigmatic happenings in otherworld which are later explained. F171.1. Fat and lean kine in otherworld. F162.2. Rivers in otherworld. F171.2. Broad and narrow road in otherworld. F171.3. People and things that strike one another in otherworld. D1960. Magic sleep.

III. D2011. Years thought days. Years spent in the otherworld or sleep seem as days because of magic forgetfulness.

IV. F2. Translation to otherworld without dying.

**DeCock *Studien* 108ff., 308f.; *Pauli (ed. Bolte) No. 561; *Köhler-Bolte I 52, cf. II 224ff., and to Gonzenbach No. 88; *Espinosa II 313f. — Finnish *15;* Finnish-Swedish (470*) *5;* Estonian *9;* Livonian *3;* Lithuanian *7;* Lappish *1;* Swedish *18* (Uppsala *3*, Stockholm *1*, Göteborg *1*, Liungman *1*, misc. *12*); Norwegian *8*, Solheim *1;* Danish: Grundtvig No. 82; Icelandic *3;* Scottish *3;* Irish (470—471) *58*, Beal X 25; French *23;* Spanish *9;* Flemish (471*) *2;* German: Ranke *27*, Meckl.

No. 63; Italian *4* (Tuscan [1529 a, b] *2*, Sicilian *2*, Gonzenbach No. 88); Rumanian: Dima *Rumänische Märchen* 43f.; Czech: Tille Soupis II (2) 127—129 *3;* Slovenian *16;* Polish *13*, (470A) *1;* Russian: Afanasiev *1;* Turkish: Eberhard-Boratav No. 62 IV; Chinese (Part III only): Eberhard FFC CXX 156 No. 103, FFC CXXVIII 110f. No. 65. — Franco-American *11*.

470A *The Offended Skull (Statue).* Festin de Pierre. A skull (statue) is invited to dinner. Attends the dinner and takes his host off to the other world [C13]. (Type 470 Ic as independent tale.)
  **D. E. Mackay *The Double Invitation in the Legend of Don Juan* (Stanford University 1943); **Espinosa II 313ff.; *BP III 483 n. 1. — Lithuanian (*470A) *9;* Estonian (472*) *6;* Spanish (*835) *4;* Polish (470*) . — Spanish-American: Hansen (*835) (Chile) *1*, (Dominican Republic).

470B (formerly 825*) *The Land where No One Dies* [F116].
  *BP IV 269 n.; Köhler-Bolte II 406, 413, 434; Groome *Gypsy Fairy Tales* 58 No. 14; Penzer Ocean VI 209, 278; Ruben FFC CXXXIII 74. — Estonian (471*) *1;* Flemish (471*) *2;* French *5;* Hungarian: (Berze Nagy 342*) *4;* Serbocroatian (425*) *4*.

470* *The Hero Visits the Land of the Immortals* and marries its queen. Allowed to visit his home. He must not get off his horse. He breaks the prohibition and dies. [F116].
  Finnish-Swedish *5;* Hungarian: Berze Nagy (342*) *3;* Polish (469) *1*.

471 *The Bridge to the Other World.* The youngest of three brothers crosses into the other world and sees extraordinary things which are later explained.
  I. *The Quest.* Three brothers one after the other set out to search for their lost sister. (b) On the way they are appointed to herd seven foals (oxen) and at the end of the day they are to bring back a sample of the animals' food; or (c) the three brothers go on some other quest.
  II. *Successful Youngest Brother.* (a) The elder brothers are lured away by a bird; (b) they are persuaded by an old woman to rest; (c) they turn aside from a certain bridge which they should have crossed and they are transformed to stone. (d) The youngest brother follows instructions and passes across the bridge.
  III. *Across the Bridge.* (a) The youngest leads into another world where extraordinary things happen: (b) animals pass in and out of a church and become human beings; (c) stones strike on each other; (d) wild boars fight; (e) he sees fat and lean kine; (f) and other strange sights.
  IV. *The Return Home.* (a) He takes bread and wine from the altar in the church. (b) The animals follow him back and he cuts off their heads and disenchants them. (c) A (religious) explanation of all he has seen is given. (d) His brothers are disenchanted.

  Motifs:
  I. H1385.6. Quest for lost sister. H1251. Quest to other world for samples of magic animals' food.

II. N744. Adventures from pursuing enchanted bird. C730. Tabu: resting. D231. Transformation: man to stone. H1242. Youngest brother alone succeeds on quest.

III. F152. Bridge to otherworld. E481.2.1. Bridge to land of dead. F171. Extraordinary sights in otherworld.

IV. R155.1. Youngest brother rescues his elder brothers. D711. Disenchantment by decapitation. F171.0.1. Enigmatic happenings in otherworld, which are later explained.

*Chauvin VIII 160 No. 168; Cosquin *Romania* V 333, VII 571, IX 381; Köhler-Bolte I 52, 132, notes to Gonzenbach No. 88, Zs. f. Vksk. VI 173; XVI 460; H. Oertel *Studien zur vergleichenden Litteraturgeschichte* VIII 113; Coffin *1.* — Lithuanian (*806) *2*, (*472) *54;* Swedish *14* (Uppsala *5*, Stockholm *1*, Liungman *1*, misc. *7*); Norwegian (471*) *9;* Danish *2;* Icelandic *5;* Irish *47*, Beal VI 97, 99, XXI 320; French *32;* Spanish *2;* Catalan: Amades No. 249; Portuguese: Pedroso *Revue Hispanique* XIV 148; German *5;* Hungarian: Honti (829) *6,* Berze Nagy (758*) *8;* Slovenian *5;* Serbocroatian *14;* Polish *8;* Russian: Andrejev (*804 I) *10;* India *1.* — Franco-American *12;* Spanish-American: Real Nos. 206—210 (U.S.), Hansen (Argentina) *3,* (Chile) *2,* (Puerto Rico) *2;* West Indies (Negro) *7;* American Indian (Pochulata): Boas JAFL XXV No. 3. — Oceanic (Philippine): Gardener JAFL XX 111; Siberian: Holmberg *Siberian Mythology* 488ff. — Literary Treatment: Chavannes No. 498.

471A *The Monk and the Bird.* Years seem moments while man listens to song of bird [D2011.1].

**Hammerich *Munken og Fuglen* (København, 1933); *Pauli (ed., Bolte) No. 562; *Herbert *Catalogue of Romances* III 67. — Estonian (471*) *2;* Lithuanian (472A*) *3;* Slovenian *7;* Russian: Andrejev (471*) *3;* Welsh: MacCulloch Celtic 104; Polish (470B) *3.*

471* *Footbridge to Heaven.* A soldier is looking for a traitor in hell; he sees sufferings of the condemned and then passes through the footbridge to heaven.

Polish (472) *1.*

471A* *The Trip to Hell.* A peasant driving a landlord to hell; in three days finds that he has spent three years there.

Polish (474) *1.*

473 (Changed to Type 750C).

475 *The Man as Heater of Hell's Kettle.* Bargain with the devil: seven years' service without washing or combing. In the kettle in hell are his former masters. In payment he receives the sweepings which change into gold. The host at the inn robs him of his gold, but with the devil's help he recovers it. Cf. Types 360, 361.

Motifs:

M210. Bargain with the devil. C721.1. Tabu: bathing during certain time. E755.2.1. Souls in heated kettle in hell. C325. Tabu: looking into

the pots in hell. D475.1. Transformation: objects to gold. D861.1. Magic object stolen by host (at inn). D885. Magic object recovered with devil's help.
*BP II 423 (Grimm No. 100); Aarne FFC XCII 97. — Finnish *45;* Finnish-Swedish *1;* Estonian *6;* Lithuanian *15;* Swedish *6* (Uppsala *2,* Stockholm *1,* Liungman *1,* misc. *2*); Norwegian *3;* Danish *6,* Grundtvig No. 57 C; Irish *1;* French *17;* German *18;* Austrian: Haiding No. 60 n.; Hungarian *10;* Czech: Tille (Soupis I 201) *8;* Slovenian *2;* Serbo-croatian *1;* Polish *4;* Russian: Andrejev *2.* — Franco-American *2.*

475* A *Youth Promises the Ogre the Sun* in return for gold; is saved by the devil. Serves as the heater of the kettle of hell. Cf. Type 361.
Lappish *1.*

476* In *the Frog's House.* A woman promises to be the frog's friend and is able to free the souls he keeps in his house. She does many favors for the frog's wife: takes the frog's child to be christened, sweeps the dust in the frog's house and takes the garbage home with her. The garbage becomes gold.
Hungarian: Berze Nagy *8* (= Honti 332 II).

480 *The Spinning-Women by the Spring. The Kind and the Unkind Girls.* The real daughter and the stepdaughter by the spring, or the rolling cake. Cf. Types 403, 510A.

I. *Kind and Unkind Girls.* (a) A real daughter and a stepdaughter or (b) two sisters or (c) other girls, one kind and one unkind, go from home, the kind girl first.

II. *Start of the Journey.* (a) She falls into a well or climbs down or is pushed in for losing a spinning contest; or (b) she is sent for water to a well, spring, or river or (c) to gather wood (get food); or (d) she leaves home to seek service or (e) she is sent to a secluded spot or otherwise abandoned; or (f) she is assigned difficult or impossible tasks (gathering flowers at midwinter, etc.); or (g) she is sent from home for other reasons.

III. *The Pursuit.* She pursues (a) objects which a river carries off (animal intestines which she must wash, etc.) or (b) cotton which the wind has blown away or (c) a bird which has flown away with an object or is lost, or (d) a rolling cake or ball.

IV. *Encounters en Route.* In the course of the pursuit she encounters: (a) various animals which ask her help: (a^1) cow (goat) to be milked (with pail on its horns), (a^2) sheep to be sheared, (a^3) horse (donkey) to be groomed, (a^4) etc. (b) She is kind to an old man or old woman (louses or feeds them). (c) She obeys requests of objects, e.g. (c^1) removes bread from oven, (c^2) oils or treats gently a gate or door, (c^3) cleans or repairs a spring, (c^4) shakes an apple tree. (d) She maintains silence about unusual sights. — (e) The grateful animals, persons or objects, (e^1) help her later in her flight, (e^2) reward her on her return, or (e^3) forward her journey.

V. *End of the Journey.* She arrives at the abode of (a) an old woman, (b) old man, (c) witch, (d) animals, (e) supernatural person (fairy, devil, giant, the twelve months) or (f) religious personage (Virgin Mary). (g)

This is usually in the lower world, though sometimes (h) on the earth by a river, a spring or in a forest.

VI. *The Old Woman's Tasks.* Here she remains and is assigned tasks: (a) doing household or farm work; (b) cleaning, tending or feeding a person or supernatural being, e.g., (b^1) lousing, (b^2) giving drink of water, (b^3) feeding, (b^4) dealing gently with heads in a well; (c) cleaning or attending to animals; (d) maintaining polite conduct under difficult conditions; (e) doing impossible things, e.g., (e^1) bringing water in a sieve, (e^2) washing black wool white; (f) observing tabus (forbidden room, etc.). (g) She is given enigmatic commands and must do the opposite. (h) She is helped with the tasks, usually by animals.

VII. *The Reward.* (a) She is offered as a reward for success with the tasks the choice (a^1) between fine or common things or (a^2) between attractive or ugly caskets, or (a^3) objects which say »take me» and those which say »don't take me»; (a^4) she makes the modest choice and is rewarded. (b) Gold, gems, flowers fall from her mouth or hair and (c) she is made more lovely. (d) She is given wealth, jewels, clothes, etc. or (e) other good things.

VIII. *Kind and Unkind.* When on her return home her sister learns of her success she attempts to have the same adventures, but is unkind and disobedient to everything and everyone and is punished (a) by disfigurements, e.g., (a^1) frogs, etc. falling from her mouth, (a^2) horse's tail on her forehead, (a^3) horns on her head; or (b) she is killed or severely beaten; (c) or she is made hideous. (d) When she makes the wrong choice of caskets she finds it filled with fire or snakes, or the like.

— Analysis based on Roberts.

Motifs:

I. S31.5. Girl persuades her father to marry a widow who has treated her kindly. S31. Cruel stepmother. L55. Stepdaughter heroine. L102. Unpromising heroine. L50. Victorious youngest daughter.

II. S146. Abandonment in pit. S143. Abandonment in forest. S338. Father abandons his daughter in forest and leaves axes tied so that they move in wind. S322. Children abandoned (driven forth) by hostile relative. H934.3. Tasks assigned by stepmother. H1020. Tasks contrary to laws of nature. H1023.3. Task: bringing berries (fruit, roses) in winter.

III. D1313. Magic objects point out road. N791. Adventures from pursuing object carried off by river. N777.2. Bucket dropped into well leads to adventures. N777.3. Flax dropped into well leads to adventures. N777.4. Spindle dropped into well leads to adventures. N777.1. Adventures encountered in running after cotton being blown away by wind. N792. Adventures from pursuing objects carried off by bird. H1226. Pursuit of rolling cake leads to quest. H1226.3. Pursuit of rolling golden apple leads to quest. H1226.4. Pursuit of rolling ball of yarn leads to quest.

IV. B350. Grateful animals. B344. Cow grateful for being milked. D1658. Grateful objects. D1658.1. Objects repay kindness. D1658.1.4. Continually slamming doors grateful for being fastened. D1658.1.5. Apple tree grateful for being shaken. D1658.1.1. River grateful for being praised even when ugly. D1658.1.3. Bitter water grateful for being praised. D1658.1.2. Figs grateful for being praised even when ill-tasting. N825.2. Old man helper. N825.3. Old woman helper.

V. F93.1. River entrance to lower world. F92. Pit entrance to lower world. Z122.3. The Twelve Months seated about a fire. G204. Girl in service of witch.

VI. H935. Witch assigns tasks. Q41. Politeness rewarded. Q41.2. Reward for cleansing loathsome person. G466. Lousing as task set by ogre. H1192. Task: combing hair of fairies. G219.9. Witch's back covered with nails and broken glass. Q42.1.1. Child divides last loaf with fairy (witch, etc.). H 1537.1. Bear demands that heroine play Blindman's Buff. H1010. Impossible tasks. H1023.2. Task: carrying water in a sieve. H1023.6. Task: washing black wool (cloth. cattle) white. C611. Forbidden chamber. C337. Tabu: looking up chimney. Q62. Reward for ability to keep secrets. H580.1. Girl given enigmatic commands must do the opposite. H982. Animals help man perform task.

VII. L211. Modest choice: three caskets type. J229.3. Choice: a big piece of cake with my curse or a small piece with my blessing. L215. Unpromising magic object chosen. C811.1. Tabu: heeding persuasive voice of magic drum. Not to pick up the drum that says »take me». L220. Modest request best. D1454.2. Treasure falls from mouth. D1860. Magic beautification. Q111. Riches as reward.

VIII. Q2. Kind and unkind. M431.2. Curse: toads from mouth. D1870. Magic hideousness.

**Roberts *The Tale of the Kind and the Unkind Girls* (Berlin, 1958); **Christiansen »A Norwegian Fairytale in Ireland?» Beal II 235ff.; *BP I 207 (Grimm No. 24); *Anderson *Novelline* No. 6; *Cosquin *Contes indiens* 509ff. — Finnish *108;* Finnish-Swedish *17;* Estonian *130;* Livonian *7;* Lithuanian *20,* (*482) *63;* Lappish *1;* Swedish *129* (Uppsala *33,* Stockholm *3,* Göteborg *27,* Lund *7,* Liungman *22,* misc. *37*); Norwegian *45,* Solheim *2;* Danish *41,* Grundtvig No. 37; Icelandic *8;* Irish *81;* English *5;* French *29;* Spanish: Espinosa Cuentos III 89—93; Catalan: Amades Nos. 24, 122; Flemish *3;* German: Ranke *78;* Austrian: Haiding Nos. 56, 72; Italian (Pentamerone IV No. 7, V No. 2, Tuscan 403A b—l, o, q, r, t—z, cf. 403A s. *17,* Sicilian *5,* Gonzenbach Nos. 32, 34); Rumanian *9,* (480A) *5,* Sainenu 706; Hungarian *12,* (Berze Nagy 481*, 403B*, 546) *21;* Czech: Tille Soupis I 436—449, 458f., cf. II (2) 415f. *16;* Slovenian *21;* Serbocroatian *9;* Polish (431A) *8;* Russian: Andrejev *Ukraine 16* (480B), Afanasiev (480*B, *C, *E, *F) *53;* Greek *19;* Turkish: Eberhard-Boratav cf. No. 68; India (480A + 480B) *18;* Indonesian: DeVries I 365 No. 23. — Franco-American *8,* English-American *9;*

Spanish-American: Hansen (**778) (Dominican Republic **447, **597, 806**A) *1*, (Puerto Rico) *3*, Rael No. 114 (U.S.); West Indies (Negro) *22*. — African *25*.

480* *The Youth who Sold the Devil a Sausage with Blood* [K141].
Lappish *1*.

480A* *Three Sisters Set out to Save their Little Brother.* Two of the sisters pay no heed to the requests of the tree, the oven, etc., and are overtaken by the witch, who takes back their brother with her. The third does all she is asked to do; therefore, the grateful objects help her to recover her little brother from the clutches of the witch. Cf. Type 480.
Lithuanian (*314C) *30*.

480B* *Girl Sent to Watch for Fire.* Kind and Unkind.
Hungarian: Berze Nagy (344I*) *4*; Russian: Andrejev (480F*) *2*.

480C* *Transporting White Bread to Hell.* The poor brother brings his wealthy brother a gift of coarse white bread. — »Go to hell with your bread.» On his way to hell, he meets an old man who tells him what he is to do there. He saves many souls from hell and is rewarded by the old man. (He buys the sheep — redeemed souls). The wealthy brother also takes bread to hell, but through discourtesy to the old man he gets no counsel, and so falls a victim to the devils.
Lithuanian *25*; German: Plenzat p. 45.

485 *Borma Jarizhka.* On instructions of the tsar the hero sets off to Babylon to get the crown. He steals the crown and burns the snakes which were sent after him. He comes to a one-eyed giant, blinds him, and escapes from the cave under the belly of the giant (Cf. Type 1137). With a wild woman he begets a child and when he leaves her she breaks the baby in two. He helps a lion who brings him home. In spite of the lion's prohibitions, the drunkard boasts of his journey. In justification he shows the lion the power of intoxication, and gets him drunk.
Russian: Andrejev (485A) *11*.

485A* Only the episode with the woman on the island.
Russian: Afanasiev (485B) *1*.

485B* *The Power of Hops.* The magic helper of the hero, (bear, lion, etc.) forbids him, on pain of death, to praise him. The hero while drunk breaks this rule. In order to justify and save himself, he makes his helper drunk; while drunk the helper lets himself be bound. He acknowledges the power of hops and forgives the hero.
Russian: Afanasiev (*485C) *8*.

SUPERNATURAL HELPERS

500—501 The Spinning-Women

500 *The Name of the Helper* (Titeliture, Rumpelstilzchen, Tom-Tit-Tot). The maiden learns the name of her supernatural helper.

I. *Impossible Task.* (a) A girl wedded to prince is compelled (to fulfill her mother's false boasting) to spin an impossible amount of yarn or (b) to spin gold. Cf. Type 501.

II. *Bargain with the Helper.* (a) A supernatural being agrees to help the girl (b) or to reward a man (c) but she must give him her child or (d) herself, (e) if she cannot within a certain time guess his name or (f) his age.

III. *The Helper Overcome.* (a) By chance the name (age) is discovered, (b) the name is pronounced, and the helper vanishes.

Motifs:

I. H914. Tasks assigned because of mother's foolish boasting. H1092. Task: spinning impossible amount in one night. H1021.8. Task: spinning gold.

II. D2183. Magic spinning. Usually performed by a supernatural helper. S222. Man promises (sells) child in order to save himself from danger or death. S222.1. Woman promises her unborn child to appease offended witch. H512. Guessing with life as wager. H521. Test: guessing unknown propounder's name. H521.1. Test: guessing unknown propounder's age.

III. N475. Secret name overheard by eavesdropper. C432.1. Guessing name of supernatural creature gives power over him.

**Clodd *Tom-Tit-Tot;* **Polívka Zs. f. Vksk. X 254—272, 325, 382—396, 438f.; **von Sydow *Tvâ Spinnsagor;* Liungman *Rig* (1941) 89ff., and *Folkminnen och Folktankar* (1943) 94ff.; Hartmann *Trollvorstellungen* 170; Boberg FFC CLI 10ff.; Coffin *3;* *BP I 490 (Grimm No. 55). — Finnish *70;* Finnish-Swedish *3;* Estonian *16;* Lithuanian *8;* Swedish *47* (Uppsala *13,* Stockholm *5,* Göteborg *12,* Lund *4,* Liungman *3,* misc. *10*); Norwegian *4,* Solheim *2;* Danish *90,* Grundtvig No. 50A; Icelandic *4;* Irish *171,* Beal I 301f., III 467f. No. 10, V 221, VII 105, VIII 150, X 44ff., XII 165; English *3;* Basque *2;* French *39;* Spanish *1;* Flemish *4;* German: Ranke *96;* Austrian: Haiding No. 46; Italian *3* (Tuscan [908] *1,* Sicilian *2,* Gonzenbach No. 84); Hungarian *6;* Czech: Tille Soupis II (2) 129—131 *4;* Slovenian *5;* Serbocroatian *2;* Polish *3;* Russian: Andrejev; Turkish: Eberhard-Boratav Anlage A c *4.* — Franco-American *9;* Spanish-American: Hansen (Puerto Rico) *2;* West Indies (Negro) *26.*

500* *The Monster Reveals the Riddle.* Students must count the peaks of a mountain; they go to sleep; the monster comes and thinks they are a many-headed monster; says that he walked through all the peaks of the mountain and tells their number. Thus they hear and solve the riddle.

Polish (377*) *3.*

501 *The Three Old Women Helpers.* Invited to the wedding.

I. *Spinning Assigned to Girl.* (a) Through false boast of a girl's mother, or (b) of the girl herself, or (c) false reports by jealous servants a girl is compelled to spin an impossible amount (cf. Type 500). (d) She is to marry the prince if successful.

II. *Bargain with Helpers.* (a) She receives help from three old women spinners who have become deformed from their much spinning. (b) In payment she must invite them to her wedding.

III. *Guests at Wedding.* (a) The three old women appear by invitation to the wedding. The prince exclaims in disgust. They tell him that spinning has deformed them. He says that he will never let his wife spin.

Motifs:

I. H914. Tasks assigned because of mother's foolish boasting. H915. Task assigned because of girl's (boy's) own foolish boast. H911. Task assigned at suggestion of jealous rivals. H1092. Task: spinning impossible amount in one night. T67. Prince offered as prize.

II. G201.1. Three witches (hags) deformed from much spinning. G244. Witch spins. D2183. Magic spinning. Usually performed by a supernatural helper. N233. Three deformed witches invited to wedding in exchange for help.

III. H51. Sight of deformed witches causes man to release wife from spinning duty. They tell that their deformity has come from too much spinning.

**von Sydow *Två Spinnsagor.* — Finnish *72;* Finnish-Swedish *2;* Estonian *2;* Livonian *3;* Lappish *1;* Lithuanian *15;* Swedish *18* (Uppsala *4,* Stockholm *5,* Göteborg *3,* Lund *1,* Liungman *2,* misc. *3*); Norwegian *8;* Danish *14,* Grundtvig No. 50B; Irish *97,* Beal IX 58ff.; English *2;* French *12;* Spanish *3;* Catalan: Amades No. 181; Flemish *1;* German: Ranke *32,* Meckl. No. 67; Italian *2* (Pentamerone IV No. 4, Tuscan [860] *1,* Sicilian *1*); Rumanian (1405 I = 501 III) *3;* Hungarian *2;* Czech: Tille Soupis II (2) 131—134 *4;* Slovenian *1;* Serbocroatian *1;* Polish *15;* Russian: Andrejev *1,* Andrejev Ukraine *2;* Greek *5;* Turkish: Eberhard-Boratav No. 371 *6.* — Spanish-American: Hansen (Puerto Rico) *1;* West Indies (Negro) *1.*

502 *The Wild Man.* The prince sets the prisoner free. The latter becomes his servant and helper. (The Ride on the Glass Mountain; cf. Type 530. Rescue of the Princess from the Dragon, cf. Type 300. Service as Shepherd; War or Other Adventures). The youth wins the princess. (For the whole tale cf. Type 314.)

I. *In the Wild Man's Service.* (a) A prince frees a wild man (Iron John) out of the cage wherein he has been confined by the king; or (b) the prince flees from his cruel stepmother; or (c) the wild man brings about the birth of a son to childless parents and receives the promises to give him the boy at a specified time.

II. *Escape from the Wild Man.* (a) At the wild man's house where he has disobeyed instructions, the youth acquires golden hair and (b) is freely let go, or (c) flees on a speaking horse.

III. *Gardener Disguise.* (a) He covers his gold hair with a hat or cloth and serves as gardener at the palace. (b) The princess falls in love with him.

IV. *The Tournament.* At a tournament he appears three times on a splendid horse which the wild man has furnished him and wins the hand of the princess.

V. *Other Accomplishments.* He shows his noble qualities (a) as victor in a battle, (b) as dragon-slayer (cf. Types 300, 303), (c) as bringer of a remedy for the sick king (cf. Type 551), or (d) in a hunt in which he humiliates his proud brothers-in-law.

VI. *Disenchantment.* The wild man or the helpful horse is disenchaned.

Motifs:

I. F567. Wild man lives alone in wood like beast. G671. Wild man released from captivity aids hero. S31. Cruel stepmother. S211. Child sold (promised) to devil (ogre). S223. Childless couple promise child to devil if they may only have one.

II. C611. Forbidden chamber. Person allowed to enter all chambers of house except one. B316. Abused and pampered horses. Hero is ordered by ogre to feed and care for certain horse and to neglect other horse. Latter is enchanted prince and helps hero. D672. Obstacle flight. Fugitives throw objects behind them which magically become obstacles in pursuer's path.

II. K1818.2. Scald-head disguise. K1816.1. Gardener disguise. H311. Inspection test for suitors. Suitors for princess's hand must present themselves for public inspection. H316. Suitor test: apple thrown indicates princess's choice. (Often golden apple). H75.4. Recognition by golden hair.

IV. H335. Tasks assigned suitors. Bride as prize for accomplishment. R222. Unknown knight. (Three Days' Tournament).

V. H55.1. Recognition through branding with hoof-marks. H56. Recognition by wound.

VI. D700. Person disenchanted. L161. Lowly hero marries princess.

**Hartmann *Trollvorstellungen* 172; *BP III 94 (Grimm No. 136); See Comment in Ranke *Schleswig-Holsteinische Volksmärchen* I 169; *Arts et Traditions Populaires* I 279. — Finnish *28;* Finnish-Swedish *2;* Estonian *11;* Livonian *2;* Lithuanian *15;* Lappish *1;* Swedish *16* (Uppsala *5,* Lund *1,* misc. *10*); Norwegian *1;* Danish *17,* Grundtvig No. 8B; Irish *1;* French *16;* Dutch *2;* Flemish *2;* German *16;* Rumanian *10;* Hungarian *10;* Czech: Tille FFC XXXIV 29—32 *2,* (also pp. 5ff.) *6,* (pp. 48ff.) *2,* Soupis I 290ff., II (2) 278—281 *16;* Serbocroatian *1;* Polish *5;* Russian: Andrejev *Ukraine 7,* Afanasiev *16;* Greek *4.* — Franco-American *12;* West Indies (Negro) *3.*

503 *The Gifts of the Little People.* Dwarfs take hump from hunchback and place it on another man.

I. *The Dwarfs' Favor.* (a) A wanderer takes part in a dance of the witches or people from below the earth (elves, dwarfs) or plays for them; or (b) adds to their song by naming more days of the week; or (c) complacently lets them cut his hair and shave him.

II. *The Reward.* (a) They remove his hump; or (b) give him gold.

III. *The Companion Punished.* (a) His avaricious and bungling companion is given the hump or (b) receives coal instead of gold. — Adapted from BP.

Motifs:

I. F261. Fairies dance. F340. Gifts from fairies. F331.1. Mortal wins fairies' gratitude by joining in their dance. F331.2. Mortal wins fairies' gratitude by letting them cut his hair and shave him. F331.3. Mortal wins fairies' gratitude by joining in their song and completing it by adding the names of the days of the week. F331.4. Mortal wins fairies' gratitude by playing for their dance.

II. F344.1. Fairies remove hunchback's hump (or replace it). F342. Fairies give mortal money. F451.5.1.4. Dwarfs' gold. Seemingly worthless gift given by dwarfs turns to gold. F342.1. Fairy gold. Fairies give coals (wood, earth) that turns to gold.

III. N471. Foolish attempt of second man to overhear secrets (from animals, demons, etc.). He is punished. J2415. Foolish imitation of lucky man. Because one man has had good luck a numskull imitates and thinks he will have equal luck. He is disappointed.

**Greverus *Die Geschenke des kleinen Volkes* Fabula I 263ff.; *BP III 324 (Grimm No. 182); *De Meyer *Vlaamsche Sprookjesthemas* 91ff.; Coffin *1.* — Finnish-Swedish (502*) *1;* Lithuanian *5;* Lappish (502*) *1;* Swedish *5* (Uppsala *3,* misc. *2*); Danish *2;* Scottish *7;* Irish *279,* Beal I 65f., II 10, III 211, VI 169ff. No. 161, VII 62; French *43;* Spanish *1;* Catalan: Amades No. 1444; Dutch *7;* Flemish (502*) *12,* Witteryck (p. 273) *15;* Walloon *2;* German: Ranke *22;* Italian *10* (Tuscan *6,* Fruili *3,* Sicilian *1*); Czech: Tille Soupis II (2) 126f. *1;* Slovenian *3;* Polish *1;* Greek: Dawkins *45 Stories* No 25; Turkish: Eberhard-Boratav No. 118, cf. 117 *3;* Persian: Massé No. 10; India *3;* Japanese: Anesaki 283, Mitford 191. — Franco-American *4;* English-American *1;* Spanish-American: Rael Nos. 255, 256 (U.S.), Hansen (Chile) *6;* West Indies (Negro) *2.*

503* *Series of Helpful Dwarfs.*
Icelandic (505*) *3.*

505—508 The Grateful Dead

Danish *30;* Irish *283,* Beal I 46ff., 167ff., 283ff., IV 292ff., VI 275ff., VII 62ff., 180ff. XI 50ff., XV 157ff., 263ff., XIX 134ff.; Czech: Tille FFC XXXIV 22f.; Turkish: Eberhard-Boratav No. 63, 215 IV.

505 *Dead Man as Helper.* Through the assistance of the dead man the hero wins the princess and the castle [E341.1]. (For detailed relationship see Types 506—508. Cf. also Types 513—514, and 545A and B.)

**Liljeblad *Die Tobiasgeschichte und andere Märchen mit toten Helfern*

(Lund, 1927); **Gerould *The Grateful Dead* (London, 1908); *BP III 490 (Grimm No. 217); Coffin *1*. — Finnish *1;* Estonian *7;* Lappish *3;* Danish *3*, Grundtvig No. 67A; Scottish *1;* Catalan: Amades No. 149, German *4;* Hungarian *1*, Dégh No. 19; Slovenian *1;* Russian: Andrejev; Greek *2;* Dawkins *Kyriakides Volume* 154ff.; India (505A Ind) *3*. — Franco-American *9;* West Indies (Negro) *6*.

506 *The Rescued Princess.*

I. *The Grateful Dead Man.* (a) The hero ransoms a corpse from creditors who refuse its burial. (b) The grateful dead man in the form of an old man, a servant, or a fox later helps the hero on condition that they are to divide all winnings.

II. *The Princess in Slavery.* (a) The hero ransoms a princess from slavery and marries her. (b) The king has learned her whereabouts by means of a cloth or flag which she has sewed, and has sent the hero for her; or (c) the hero rescues a princess from robbers and flees with her to her father's home.

III. *Overboard.* The hero is thrown overboard by a rival but is rescued by a dead man and finally brought to the princess.

IV. *Recognition.* He is recognized by means of (a) a ring thrown into a cup, (b) by recounting his life history by means of a picture, (c) or otherwise.

V. *The Dividing in Halves.* The dead man demands has half and exacts the dividing of the princess (or the child), but relents and reveals his identity. — Adapted from Liljeblad *Tobiasgeschichte* pp. 39f.

Motifs:

I. Q271.1. Debtor deprived of burial. E341.1. Dead grateful for having corpse ransomed. Corpse is being held unburied because of nonpayment of debts. Hero pays debt and secures burial of corpse. M241. Bargain: to divide all winnings. T66.1. Grateful dead man helps hero win princess.

II. R61. Person sold into slavery. R111.1.6. Princess ransomed from slavery. L161. Lowly hero marries princess. H35.3. Recognition by unique needlework. H1385.1. Quest for stolen princess. R111.1.2. Princess rescued from robbers.

III. S142. Person thrown into the water and abandoned. K1931.1. Impostors throw hero overboard into sea. S145. Abandonment on an island. R163. Rescue by grateful dead man. B541.2. Fox rescues man from sea. T68.1. Princess offered as prize to rescuer.

IV. H94.4. Identification by ring dropped in glass (cup) of wine. H11.1. Recognition by telling life history.

V. M241.1. Dividing the winnings: half the bride demanded.

Most of the following references to Type 506 refer to 506B.

**Liljeblad *Tobiasgeschichte; Arts et Traditions Populaires* I 274; Coffin *6*. — Finnish *108;* Finnish-Swedish *15;* Lithuanian *19;* Lappish *4;* Norwegian *7*, Solheim *1;* Icelandic *2;* Scottish *3;* French *31;* Spanish *4;*

Catalan: Amades No. 197; Flemish 7; German: Ranke *41;* Austrian: Haiding No. 6; Hungarian *6;* Slovenian *3;* Serbocroatian *4;* Polish *6;* Greek *5;* Indonesian: DeVries No. 173. — Spanish-American: Rael Nos. 98, 99 (U.S.), Hansen (Chile) *3*, (Dominican Republic) *2*, (Puerto Rico) *2;* Cape Verde Islands: Parsons MAFLS XV (1) 344 n. 1—2; West Indies (Negro) *3.*

The two forms of the type follow:

506A *The Princess Rescued from Slavery.* See analysis: I a, b; II a; III; IV; V.

Swedish *5* (Uppsala *3*, Liungman *1*, misc. *1*); Danish *13;* Catalan: Amades No. 87; Czech: Tille FFC XXXIV 210ff., Soupis I 468ff. *9;* Serbocroatian *6;* Russian: Andrejev; India *1.* — Franco-American *30.*

506B *The Princess Rescued from Robbers.* See analysis: I a, b; II c; III; IV.

Swedish *11* (Uppsala *4*, Stockholm *1*, Lund *1*, Liungman *1*); Danish *11*, Grundtvig No. 67B; Dutch *2;* Czech: Tille FFC XXXIV 210; Russian: Andrejev. — Franco-American *10;* American Indian: Thompson *C Coll* II 404ff.; Jamaica Negro: Beckwith MAFLS XVII 152, 284.

506* *Prophecy Escaped.* A child is born in answer to prayer [T548.1]. Prophecy: hanging when 20 years old [M341.1.4]. Is helped by companion whom he chooses because of his modest choice (or by a saint). Helper demands half of winnings. Princess is to be divided [M241.1]. Cf. Type 934B.

Spanish (*936) *1;* Catalan: Amades No. 379.

506** *The Grateful Saint.* The hero redeems a saint's maltreated picture and is afterwards rewarded by the grateful saint [N848.1].

Lithuanian *12.*

507A *The Monster's Bride.*

I. *The Grateful Dead Man.* See Type 506 I.

II. *The Monster Husband.* The hero woos a princess whose former suitors have all come to misfortune and whose heads have been stuck on poles. With the help of the dead man who has taken the necessary magic means from three giants, he succeeds in the tests assigned: finding objects which she hides, and in killing the evil monster with whom she is enamored.

III. *Rendering the Princess Harmless.* The dead man by means of beating, burning, or bathing takes from her the remaining magic power.

IV. *The Dividing in Half.* See Type 506 V.

Motifs:

II. T172.0.1. All husbands have perished on bridal night. H901.1. Heads placed on stakes for failure in performance of task. H972. Tasks accomplished with help of grateful dead. D833. Magic object acquired by tricking the giant. D381. Magic object acquired by trick exchange. By means of second magic object hero recovers first. H322.1. Suitor test: finding object hidden by princess. T118. Girl (man) married to (enamored of) a monster. T172.2.1. Grateful dead man kills princess's monster husband. L161. Lowly hero marries princess.

III. D712.5. Disenchantment by beating. D766.1. Disenchantment by bathing.
**Liljeblad *Tobiasgeschichte;* **Hartmann *Trollvorstellungen* 160; *BP III 83. — Finnish (507) *8;* Finnish-Swedish (507) *4;* Lithuanian *3;* Lappish (507) *1;* Swedish *10* (Uppsala *2,* Göteborg *2,* Lund *1,* Liungman *1,* misc. *4)*; Norwegian (507) *16,* Solheim (507) *2;* Danish (507) *27,* Grundtvig No. 68; English *2;* Catalan: Amades No. 126; German: Ranke *7;* Austrian: Haiding No. 53 (507); Hungarian (507) *13;* Czech: Tille FFC XXXIV 210, cf. 220; Polish (507) *10;* Russian: Andrejev *1;* Greek: Hahn No. 114; Turkish: Eberhard-Boratav No. 63 III *10.* — Franco-American *4.*

507B *The Monster in the Bridal Chamber.*
I. *The Grateful Dead Man.* See Type 506 (I).
II. *The Monster in the Bridal Chamber.* All bridegrooms of a princess have perished during the bridal night [T172.0.1]. The hero marries her on advice of the grateful dead man who kills the dragon (or serpent) who comes into the chamber to kill the bridegroom [T172.2.1].
III. *The Dividing in Half.* See Type 506 (V). The dead man cleanses the princess of enchantment by cutting her in two so that her serpent brood is driven from her body.
**Liljeblad *Tobiasgeschichte;* BP III 490ff., 494; *Wesselski *Märchen* 201ff., No. 12. — Lithuanian *1;* Italian (Sicilian *1,* Gonzenbach No. 89); Rumanian (507 I*) *3;* Russian: Afanasiev *5;* Greek: Dawkins *Modern Greek Folktales* Nos. 36, 48, *45 Stories* No. 14; India *2.*

507C *The Serpent Maiden.*
I. *The Grateful Dead Man.* See Type 506 (I).
II. *The Serpent Maiden* [F582]. All bridegrooms of a princess have perished during the bridal night. The hero marries her and the dead man saves his life by killing the serpent (serpents) that creeps from the mouth of the bride to strangle the bridegroom [T172.2].
*Liljeblad *Tobiasgeschichte.* See also references to Type 507 A and B. — Lithuanian (*306A) *3;* Catalan: Amades No. 10; Rumanian (306A*); Czech: Tille FFC XXXIV 217ff., Soupis I 481ff. *7;* Russian: Andrejev *2;* Greek *7,* Dawkins *Kyriakides Volume* 164, Dawkins *Modern Greek Folktales* Nos. 36, 48, *45 Stories* No. 14; Turkish: Eberhard-Boratav No. 62 *12;* Aramaic: Bergsträsser No. 17; Arab (lower Euphrates): C. G. Campbell *11;* India *18.* — Franco-American *1;* Spanish-American: Rael Nos. 317—320 (U.S.), Hansen (Argentina) *1;* American Indian (Thompson River): Teit JE VIII 385 No. 93.

508 *The Bride won in a Tournament.*
I. *The Grateful Dead Man.* See Type 506 (I).
II. *The Tournament.* The hero wins a bride in a tournament [H331.2] by means of a horse or of weapons which he has received from the dead man [H972].

III. *The Dividing in Half.* See Type 506 (V).

**Liljeblad *Tobiasgeschichte.* — Lithuanian *3;* Swedish (misc.) *2;* Danish *1;* Spanish *1* (508*A); Slovenian *9;* Russian: Andrejev (508A) *3.*

508* *Dead Man Performs Difficult Tasks.* He builds a church, etc.
Russian: Andrejev (508*B) *2.*

510 *Cinderella and Cap o' Rushes.*

I. *The Persecuted Heroine.* (a) The heroine is abused by her stepmother and stepsisters and (a¹) stays on the hearth or in the ashes and, (a²) is dressed in rough clothing — cap of rushes, wooden cloak, etc., (b) flees in disguise from her father who wants to marry her, or (c) is cast out by him because she has said that she loved him like salt, or (d) is to be killed by a servant.

II. *Magic Help.* While she is acting as servant (at home or among strangers) she is advised, provided for, and fed (a) by her dead mother, (b) by a tree on the mother's grave, or (c) by a supernatural being or (d) by birds, or (e) by a goat, a sheep, or a cow. (f) When the goat (cow) is killed, there springs up from her remains a magic tree.

III. *Meeting the Prince.* (a) She dances in beautiful clothing several times with a prince who seeks in vain to keep her, or she is seen by him in church. (b) She gives hints of the abuse she has endured as servant girl, or (c) she is seen in her beautiful clothing in her room or in the church.

IV. *Proof of Identity.* (a) She is discovered through the slipper-test or (b) through a ring which she throws into the prince's drink or bakes in his bread. (c) She alone is able to pluck the gold apple desired by the knight.

V. *Marriage with the Prince.*

VI. *Value of Salt.* Her father is served unsalted food and thus learns the meaning of her earlier answer. — Adapted from BP.

Motifs:

I. S31. Cruel stepmother. L55. Stepdaughter heroine. L52. Abused youngest daughter. L102. Unpromising heroine. L131. Hearth abode of unpromising hero (heroine). K521.1. Escape by dressing in animal (bird, human) skin. K1821.9. Disguise in wooden covering. F821.1.4. Wooden coat. F821.1.3. Dress of raw fur. M255. Deathbed promise concerning the second wife. H363.1. Bride test: wearing deceased wife's clothes. T411.1. Lecherous father. S322.1.2. Father casts daughter forth when she will not marry him. T311.1. Flight of maiden to escape marriage. H592.1. Love like salt. K512. Compassionate executioner. Servant charged with killing the heroine arranges her escape.

II. E323.2. Dead mother returns to aid persecuted daughter. E366. Return from dead to give counsel. D815.1. Magic object received from mother. D842.1. Magic object found on mother's grave. E631. Reincarnation in plant (tree) growing from grave. N810. Supernatural helpers. F311.1. Fairy godmother. N815. Fairy as helper. D813. Magic object received from fairy. D1473.1. Magic wand furnishes clothes. D1050.1. Clothes produced by magic. D1111.1. Carriage produced by magic. F861.4.3. Carriage from pumpkin. D411.6.1. Transformation: mouse to horse. D315.1. Transformation: rat to person. B313. Helpful animal an enchanted person. B313.1. Helpful animal reincarnation of parent. The dead mother appears to the heroine in the form of an animal. B450. Helpful bird. E611.4. Man reincarnated as goat. B413. Helpful goat. B400. Helpful sheep. B411. Helpful cow. B394. Cow grateful for being milked. E611.2. Reincarnation as cow. D1470.1. Magic wishing object causes wishes to be fulfilled. D1470.2. Provisions received from magic object. D1470.2.1. Provisions received from magic tree. D1470.2.3. Horn of plenty (cornucopia). B115.1. Ear-cornucopia. Animal furnishes treasure or supplies from its ears. B100.2. Magic animal supplies treasure. D842.3. Magic object found on grave of slain helpful animal. B100.1. Treasure found in slain helpful animal. B335. Helpful animal killed by hero's enemy. E631. Reincarnation in plant (tree) growing from grave. D950. Magic tree. D1658. Grateful objects. D1658.1. Objects repay kindness (cf. Type 480).

III. N711.6. Prince sees heroine at ball and is enamored. C761.3. Tabu: staying too long at ball. Must leave before certain hour. R221. Heroine's three-fold flight from ball. R255. Formula for girl fleeing: behind me night, etc. N711.4. Prince sees maiden at church and is enamored. N712. Prince first sees heroine as she comes forth from her hiding-box. H151.6.2. Recognition because of imperfection of disguise. H151.5. Attention attracted by hints dropped by heroine as menial: recognition follows. H151.6. Heroine in menial disguise discovered in her beautiful clothes: recognition follows.

IV. K2212.1. Treacherous stepsisters. H111. Identification by garment. H36.1. Slipper test. Identification by fitting of slipper. K1911.3.3.1. False bride's mutilated feet. F823.2. Glass shoes. J1146.1. Detection by pitch-trap. Pitch is spread so that footprints are left in it, or that shoe is left behind as clue. H94.4. Identification by ring dropped in glass of wine. H94.2. Identification by ring baked in bread. D1648.1.1. Tree bends only to heroine. H31.12. Only one person able to pluck fruits from tree.

V. L162. Lowly heroine marries prince.

VI. H592.1. Love like salt: the value of salt.

**Rooth *The Cinderella Cycle* (Lund, 1951); **Cox *Cinderella* (London, 1893); *R. Th. Christiansen »Cinderella in Ireland» Beal XX 96—107; Coffin *17*. — Finnish-Swedish *23;* Swedish *46* (Uppsala *19,* Göteborg *19,* Lund *9*); Norwegian: Solheim *5;* Danish *68;* Irish *293,* Beal I 366ff., II 333, 363f. No. 3, III 69ff., 457f. No. 3, VI 293ff., VII 65, VIII 3f. No. 2, IX 66f. No. 5, XI 83f. No. 35, XX 3f. No. 3; Dutch *1;* Austrian: Haiding

No. 52; Slovenian *10;* Serbocroatian *3;* Chinese: Graham No. 76 p. 266.
— West Indies (Negro) *30.*
Two forms of the type follow. See also Type 511.

510A *Cinderella.* The two stepsisters. The stepdaughter at the grave of her own mother, who helps her (milks the cow, shakes the apple-tree, helps the old man; cf. Type 480). Three-fold visit to church (dance). Slipper test.

See analysis: I a; II a, b; III a; IV a; V.

**Rooth *The Cinderella Cycle* (Lund, 1951); **Cox *Cinderella* (London, 1893); *BP I 165 (Grimm No. 21); *Loukatos in *Parnassos* (Athenai, 1959) I 463—485; *Arts et Traditions Populaires* I 280; *Parsons MAFLS XV (2) 170; S. Morosoli *A Theoretical Reconstruction of the Original Cinderella Story* (Stanford University, 1930); M. J. Woods *A Study of the Cinderella Story in the Spanish Folklore of New Mexico and Colorado* (Stanford University, 1948); Arthur Waley »The Chinese Cinderella Story» *Folklore* LVIII 226ff.; *Anderson *Novelline* No. 12; *Espinosa II 414—421. — Finnish *141;* Estonian *17;* Livonian *3;* Lithuanian *15;* Lappish *14;* Swedish *25* (Stockholm *1,* Liungman *13,* misc. *11*); Norwegian *43;* Danish: Grundtvig No. 47; Basque *1;* French *37;* Spanish *3;* Catalan: Amades No. 4; Flemish *5,* Witteryck p. 294 *13;* German: Ranke *47;* Italian: D'Aronco *Fiabe 27* (Tuscan 403A m, n, 510 a—c *5,* Pentamerone I No. 6, Fruili *1,* Sicilian *3,* Gonzenbach No. 32); Rumanian *11,* Sainenu 725; Hungarian *21;* Czech: Tille Soupis I 381ff., II (1) 242ff. *22;* Slovenian *1;* Serbocroatian *21;* Polish *18;* Russian: Afanasiev *6;* Greek *29,* Hahn No. 2, Loukatos No. 12, Dawkins *Modern Greek Folktales* No. 21, *45 Stories* No. 14; Turkish: Eberhard-Boratav Nos. 60, 240 III *23;* Armenian: Khatchatrianz 83ff.; India *8;* Indonesian: DeVries No. 174; Chinese: Eberhard FFC CXX 52ff. No. 32. — Franco-American *21;* English-American: Baughman *2;* Spanish-American: Rael Nos. 106—108, 109, 110, 111, 114, 116—118, 237 (U.S.), Hansen (Chile) *1,* (Cuba) *4,* (Puerto Rico) *8;* West Indies (Negro) *1;* American Indian: Thompson *C Coll* II 382ff.

510B *The Dress of Gold, of Silver, and of Stars.* (Cap o' Rushes). Present of the father who wants to marry his own daughter. The maiden as servant of the prince, who throws various objects at her. The three-fold visit to the church and the forgotten shoe. Marriage. Cf. Type 451.

See analysis: I b, III a; IV (a), b; V.

**Rooth *The Cinderella Cycle;* **Cox *Cinderella* (London, 1893); *BP II 45 (Grimm No. 65); *Arts et Traditions Populaires* I 275; Espinosa II 406—421; *Anderson *Novelline* Nos. 90, 91. — Finnish *2;* Livonian *2;* Lithuanian *39;* Swedish *46* (Uppsala *8,* Stockholm *2,* Göteborg *19,* Liungman *3,* misc. *14*); Norwegian *3;* Danish: Grundtvig No. 47; English *2;* Basque *3;* French *26;* Spanish *7;* Catalan: Amades Nos. 4, 24, 65, 133, 139 n., cf. 48, 106, 134, 369; German: Ranke *27;* Italian: D'Aronco *Fiabe* (Pentamerone II No. 6, Tuscan 403A a, 510 VIa, 923 a—s *19,* Sicilian *5,* Gonzenbach No. 38); Rumanian (871*) *6;* Hungarian *12,*

Dégh No. 20; Czech: Tille Soupis II (I) 91ff. *8;* Slovenian *2;* Serbocroatian *10;* Polish *15;* Russian: Afanasiev *13;* Greek: Archive *16*, *Laographia* XV 323ff., *45 Stories* No. 14; Argenti-Rose *Chios* I 445ff., Loukatos No. 13, Hahn No. 27; Turkish Eberhard-Boratav No. 188 III, 189, 244, 245 III *35;* India *11;* Franco-American *15;* English-American: Baughman *4;* Spanish-American: Rael Nos. 106—108, 109, 110, 111, 114, 116—118, 237 (U.S.), Hansen (Cuba) *2*, (Dominican Republic) *3*, (Puerto Rico) *5;* West Indies (Negro) *4*.

510A* *The Golden Shoe in the Cave.* A girl buries her only lamb in a cave and leaves there a golden shoe. A prince sees it and will marry none but the owner of the shoe. The girl presents three such shoes and wins the prince. [H36.1].
Italian (Sicilian 512* *1*).

511 *One-Eye, Two-Eyes, Three-Eyes* [F512.1, F512.2.1.1]. Two-Eyes (or a stepdaughter) is abused by her mother [S12]. She has to act as goatherd and she becomes hungry. A wise old woman [N825.3] provides the maiden with a magic table [D1153] and food [D1031]. The sisters spy upon her [D830.1]. Gold-producing tree from animal's entrails [B100.1, D1461, D1470.2.1]. The wonderful tree whose fruit Two-Eyes alone can pluck [D590, H31.12]. She becomes the wife of a lord [L162]. Cf. Type 403.

For analysis see Type 510: I a; II c, e, f; IV c; V.

**Rooth *The Cinderella Cycle;* **Cox *Cinderella;* *BP III 60 (Grimm No. 130); *Krappe FL XXXIV (1923) 141ff.; Coffin *1;* *Wesselski *Deutsche Märchen vor Grimm* 7ff., 91ff, 304ff. — Finnish *16;* Finnish-Swedish *1;* Estonian *10;* Livonian *3;* Lithuanian (*481) *55;* Swedish *18* (Uppsala *1*, Stockholm *1*, Liungman *2*, misc. *14*); Danish *4;* Scottish *1,* Irish *130,* Beal VII 197f. No. 3; French *21;* Dutch *1;* German: Ranke *16;* Austrian: Haiding No. 50; Hungarian *3;* Serbocroatian *2;* Polish *8;* Russian: Afanasiev *11;* Greek *3;* India *13.* — Franco-American *2;* English-American: Baughman *1;* Spanish-American: Rael No. 112 (U.S.); West Indies (Negro) *2*.

511A *The Little Red Ox.* Cf. Type 302 I*.

I. *The Ox Helper.* A stepbrother of One-Eye, Two-Eyes and Three-Eyes is cruelly treated by his stepmother and stepsisters. He is assisted by a magic ox which furnishes him food from his removable horn.

II. *Spying on the Ox.* The stepsisters try to spy on him, but he puts them to sleep except for a single eye. The stepmother feigns illness and demands the meat of the ox.

III. *Flight.* The ox carries the boy on his horns through woods of copper, silver, and gold, where they pick twigs and must fight successive animal guardians. The ox is eventually killed.

IV. *Magic Horn.* The boy takes the ox's horn, which furnishes him property and leads to success.

(The tale may lead into Type 590.)

Motifs:

I. S31. Cruel stepmother. S34. Cruel stepsisters. F512.1. One-eyed person. F512.2.1.1. Three-eyed person. B411.2. Helpful ox. D1470.2.3. Horn of plenty. B115.1. Ear-cornucopia. Animal furnishes treasure or supplies from its ears (horn). B184.2.3.1. Magic bull to be flayed.

II. D830.1. Attempt to learn about magic object by spying. D1961. Magic watchful eye remains awake while many other eyes sleep. B335.2. Feigned illness to take life of helpful animal.

III. B551.1. Man carried on animal's horns. F811.1. Trees of extraordinary material (copper, silver, gold). C513. Tabu: breaking twig. B576. Animal as guard.

IV. B505. Magic object received from animals. B115. Animal with horns of plenty.

*BP III 65; *Cox *Cinderella* p. 455; A. Kovács »The Hungarian Folktale Catalogue in Preparation» *Acta Ethnographica* (Budapest) IV (1955) 457ff.; Thompson *Folktale* p. 129; *Rooth *The Cinderella Cycle* 135ff.; *Arts et Traditions Populaires* I 178. — Icelandic (302 I*) *9;* French (511*) *2;* Hungarian: Honti (535) *4,* Berze Nagy (469*, 340*) *23;* Serbocroatian *2;* Egypt (modern): Artin Pascha I 111; Gypsy: Groome 203 No. 53; India *8.* — Franco-American *18;* American Indian (Wyandot): Thompson *C Coll* II 415.

511A* *The Helpful Cow.* A girl is treated cruelly by an old woman with whom she lives. For lack of food she faints in the stable. When she revives, a cow is licking her face. The latter tells her to pull off her right horn and she will find whatever she wants. From the horn come many good things to eat. The girl forgets to cut wood and the old woman beats her. The cow tells her that the old woman is a witch and is going to kill her. The cow carries the girl to an enchanted field guarded by serpents and lions belonging to a fairy. They pass through it successfully. The next field is much the same but they make noise and are attacked. Both are wounded but they manage to escape. The cow dies and becomes an angel and flies to Heaven.

Spanish-American: Hansen (**542) (Cuba) *1.*

512* *The Sister Driven from Home.* The elder sisters [K2212] drive the youngest away. On the advice of an old man [N825] she takes service at a castle. The old man in the chest gives good advice. The son of the lord of the castle pledges himself to the girl [L162]; wants to see her castle. The old man shows her how to provide the castle [D1131.1]. Cf. Type 545.

Finnish (512); Russian: Andrejev.

512A* *The Stepdaughter Driven from Home.* A stepfather forces a girl to leave home and tells her never to return. She finds refuge in the home of another couple. One day while his wife is away the husband asks her to marry him. She flees (cf. Type 510 I c). She wanders to an old woman's house in the woods. The latter gives her a hunter's suit, with which she disguises as man and travels through the woods unrecognized by bandits. She acts as page for a queen who falls in love with her. She is assigned task of securing a feather of a certain bird. An old man tells her that the queen is a witch and how to secure the feather. She returns with it to he queen who proposes marriage again and asks her to kill the king. When the girl refuses, the queen tells the king that the girl is a witch. The king orders her burned. The feather becomes a bird that tells the queen that the page

is a girl and the king that the queen is a witch. The queen is burned and the king marries the girl. Cf. Types 425K, 434, 514, 514**, 881*.
Spanish-American: Hansen (Cuba) *1*.

512B* *The Ghost is Avenged.* Youngest of three sisters follows a mysterious dog into a deserted palace. The sisters watch in turn and hear voice crying »I am coming» [H1411.1, E373.1]. The youngest answers and ghost comes and begs to have her murder avenged. The girl entices the murderer, gives him a soporific and kills him. She is rewarded with the palace. Cf. Type 326 II e.
Italian (Sicilian **512 *3*, Gonzenbach No. 78).

513, 514 *The Helpers.* (Cf. Type 653).

I. *The Hero.* (a) The hero unlike his elder brothers has been kind to an old man (b) who helps him provide a ship that goes both on land and water (c) for the building of which the king will give his daughter in marriage. — (d) The hero is aided by a grateful dead man (cf. Type 506).

II. *The Companions.* The hero is joined one after the other by extraordinary companions: (a) a man so strong that he pulls up trees, (b) one who shoots the left eye of a fly at two miles' distance, (c) a great blower, (d) a great hearer, (e) great runner, (f) a withstander of cold, (g) etc.

III. *Help of the Companions.* They help the hero (a) defeat the princess in a race for her hand, (b) perform tasks set by the king or enchantress: (c) eating, (d) drinking, (e) withstanding cold, (f) carrying off money, (g) bringing a ring from the sea, (h) guarding a maiden, (i) bringing a maiden, (j) bringing a magic remedy, (k) annihilating a pursuing army, etc.

Motifs:

I. Q2. Kind and unkind. L13. Compassionate youngest son. N825.2. Help from old man. D1533.1.1. Magic land and water ship. H335. Tasks assigned suitors. Bride as prize for accomplishment. H331. Suitor contest: bride offered as prize. H972. Tasks accomplished with help of grateful dead.

II. F601. Extraordinary companions. A group of men with extraordinary powers travel together. F621. Strong man: tree-puller. Can uproot all trees. F622. Mighty blower. Man turns mill with his blowing. F661.5.3. Skillful marksman shoots left eye of fly at two miles. F641.1. Man can hear grass (wool) grow. F641.2. Man can hear ant leave nest fifty miles away. F641.3. Man can hear one sleeping by putting ear to ground. F681.1. Marvellous runner keeps leg tied up. To prevent him him from running away. F685. Marvellous withstander of cold. F633. Mighty drinker. Drinks up whole pool of water, or the like. F632. Mighty eater. Eats whole ox at a time, or the like. D2144.1.2. Man with power to make everything freeze wears cap over his ear to prevent this.

III. F601.2. Extraordinary companions help hero in suitor tests. H331.5.1. Race with princess for her hand. F601.1. Extraordinary companions perform hero's tasks. H1450.1. Waking contest. H1114.

Task: eating enormous amount. H1142. Task: drinking enormous amount. H1512. Cold test. Attempt to freeze hero to death. H1511. Heat test. Attempt to kill hero by burning him in fire. H1127. Task: carrying off huge quantity of money. H1132.1. Task: recovering lost object from sea. H1132.1.1. Task: recovering lost ring from sea. H1324. Quest for marvelous remedy. D1240. Magic waters and medicines. H1135. Task: annihilating (overcoming) army single-handed. L161. Lowly hero marries princess.

513 *The Extraordinary Companions.* Cf. Types 301B, 571.
*BP II 79ff., 95; Coffin *8;* *Motif-Index F601. — Lappish *2;* Swedish *56* (Uppsala *13,* Göteborg *12,* Lund *5,* Liungman *6,* misc. *20*); Norwegian *24,* Solheim *1;* Danish *48;* Scottish *1,* Campbell-McKay No. 3; Irish *353,* Beal IV 228f. No. 1, VII 180ff., XVIII 79ff.; French *31;* Dutch *3;* Austrian: Haiding p. 470; Czech: Tille Soupis I 253—257, II (1) 303—308, 373f., FFC XXXIV 225—229, 231—234 *9;* Slovenian *8;* Serbocroatian *2;* Polish *15;* Turkish: Eberhard-Boratav No. 207 III. — African *4.*

513A *Six Go through the Whole World.* The helpers perform various deeds for the hero at the king's court.
See analysis (513, 514): II; III. See also references to Type 513.
*Anderson in Tauscher *Volksmärchen* 191; *BP II 79ff., III 84f., 556ff. (Grimm Nos. 134, 224); Wesselski *Märchen vor Grimm* No. 2; Chauvin VII 124 No. 392; Espinosa II 89 No. 9; Liungman SSF III 434; Anderson *Novelline* No. 92. — Finnish *164;* Finnish-Swedish *4;* Estonian *7;* Livonian *1;* Lithuanian *10;* Danish: Grundtvig No. 9 A B; Spanish *3;* Catalan: Amades Nos. 25, 76, 145, cf. 164; Flemish *14,* Witteryck p. 299 *18;* Walloon (*513C) *1;* German: Henssen Volk No. 132a, 132b, Ranke *57;* Italian *4* (Pentamerone cf. I No. 5, Tuscan 571b, cf. [855] a, b *3*); Rumanian *7,* Sainenu 557; Hungarian *12;* Czech: Tille Soupis I 248, 253, II (1) 303ff., FFC XXXIV 225ff., 231 *24;* Slovenian *1;* Serbocroatian *4;* Russian: Andrejev Ukraine 16, Afanasiev *21;* Greek *14,* Hahn No. 63; Turkish: Eberhard-Boratav Nos. 77, 86 IV, 197 III, 215 III *8;* India *6.* — Spanish-American: Rael Nos. 10, 11, 16, 267 (U.S.), Hansen (Chile) *1,* (Dominican Republic) *2,* (Puerto Rico) *1;* Cape Verde Islands: Parsons MAFLS XV (1) 244 n. 4; West Indies (Negro) *5;* American Indian: Thompson *C Coll* II 345ff.

513B *The Land and Water Ship.*
See analysis (513, 514): I a, b, c, (d); II; III.
*BP II 79ff. (Grimm No. 71), III 272. — Finnish *4;* Finnish-Swedish *9;* Estonian *9;* Lithuanian *2;* Swedish (Lund) *4;* Icelandic *1;* Catalan: Amades No. 170; Flemish *6;* German *13,* Merk. p. 251; Italian (Sicilian *1,* Gonzenbach No. 74); Czech: Tille FFC XXXIV 229, Soupis II (1) 307ff., 373f. *6;* Slovenian *1;* Serbocroatian *4;* Russian: Afanasiev *5.* — Franco-American *23;* English-American *2;* West Indies (Negro) *2.*

513C *The Son of the Hunter.*
I. *The Worker's Secret.* A mother reluctantly lets her son know that his father has been a hunter. The son becomes a hunter and is persecuted by a courtier who hated his father.
II. *The Tasks.* The boy is assigned difficult tasks at the courtier's suggestion [H911]: (a) to build a castle of ivory (done by pouring wine in lake where elephants bathe and intoxicating them); (b) other tasks; (c) bringing a distant object to the king (done with the help of extraordinary companions [F601.1]).
III. *Marriage to Princess.*

Greek: Dawkins *Modern Greek Folktales* Nos. 42a, 42b *10;* Turkish: Eberhard-Boratav No. 207 *6;* Armenian: Khatchatrianz 32ff.; Kurd: Lescot No. 2.

513C* *The Seven Magic Talents.* A king offers daughter for marriage to gain an heir to his throne. The princess chooses a handsome prince who is killed by a Moor. The princess is taken captive, but she plans to get the better of the Moor and returns his love. She sends word to her father by birds that she is still alive, but will have to be rescued by a widow's seven sons. An orphan finds a widow and seven sons, each of whom has a magic talent. With the help of the seven sons, the orphan rescues the princess. The Moor recovers her, but he and the princess are killed. The princess is revived by one of the seven sons and returned to the king. The prince who was killed by the Moor is also revived and marries the princess. The king rewards the orphan and the seven sons.

Spanish-American: Hansen (513**C) (Chile) *1.*

514 *The Shift of Sex.* The sister becomes a soldier in place of her brother. Marries the daughter of the king [K1837, K1322]. She is driven away and rescued by her companions. The change of sex in the ogress' house [D11]. Marriage with the princess [L161].

*Anderson in Tauscher *Volksmärchen* 174; *BP II 58, 79ff., 87, *III 24f., 84; *Espinosa III 97ff.; Chauvin VIII 43f. No. 11. — Finnish *17;* Lithuanian *10;* Norwegian *1;* Danish *9;* Scottish *1,* Campbell-McKay No 3; Irish *10;* Spanish *4;* Walloon (*514) *1;* German *1;* Austrian: Haiding p. 470; Italian (Tuscan [312], cf. [317] a *2*); Rumanian *4;* Serbocroatian *2;* Polish *6;* Russian: Andrejev; Greek *6;* Turkish: Eberhard-Boratav No, 97, 374 III *13;* Indonesian: DeVries No. 175. — Franco-American *1;* Cape Verde Islands: cf. Parsons MAFLS XV (1) 281 n. 2; West Indies (Negro) *3.*

514* *The Unlaughing Fate.* Old woman becomes a lizard who becomes a girl and marries a king. The girl again becomes a lizard. The lizard climbs on a cock. The unlaughing fate sees this and laughs. This causes disenchantment: the cock becomes a horse; the lizard becomes a girl with roses issuing from her mouth (or the old woman becomes a young girl, or the unlaughing fates are made to laugh and cause other transformations).

Greek *6.*

514** *The Court Physician.* A poor girl masks as a doctor and is made court physician [K1825.1.2]. The queen falsely accuses her of attempted seduction [K2111]. Tasks are imposed which are performed with the help of a saint [H984]. The truth comes to light. Cf. Types 425K, 434, 881*, 884A.

Spanish: *Espinosa No. 146.

515 (formerly 515**) *The Shepherd Boy*. The boy finds three objects (shoes, cap, etc. [D1065.2, D1067]) which he in turn gives to a little girl [N827] and an old man [N821]. They promise to be his helpers [Q42]. With their aid he brings back the lost princess [R111] and wins her hand [L161].

Livonian *2;* Swedish *2;* Flemish *1;* Russian: Andrejev; Turkish: Eberhard-Boratav No. 177 *4.*

515* *The Magic Pipe*. A boy gives an old man the first fish he catches. In return he receives a pipe that gives him power over all wild animals [D1441.1.2].

Lappish *1.*

516 *Faithful John*. The picture of the princess. She is carried off on a ship. The conversation of the ravens. The true servant transformed to stone. Brought back to life.

I. *The Prince Falls in Love.* (a) A prince becomes enamored of a faraway princess by seeing her picture or (b) by dreaming of her.

II. *The Princess is Carried Off.* With the help of a faithful servant, brother or foster brother, he carries her off (a) by enticing her aboard a merchant ship, (b) by stealing into her presence in women's clothes, or (c) through an underground passage, or by other means. — (d) The servant woos her as adviser of the prince.

III. *Perils on the Voyage.* (a) On the return voyage the prince and his bride are submitted to three perils, such as (a^1) poisoned food, (a^2) poisoned clothing, (a^3) meeting with robbers or a drowning person, (a^4) crossing a stream or passing through a door, etc. (a^5) The last peril is the entrance of a snake into the bedchamber of the bridal pair. (b) These perils are arranged (b^1) by the father of the princess, (b^2) by the father, or (b^3) the stepmother of the prince.

IV. *The Misunderstood Servant.* (a) Through the conversation of birds (ghosts), (b) the faithful servant learns of the dangers and strives to prevent them. (c) Since he has touched the prince's sleeping wife, he is thought to be treacherous to his master and must justify himself by an explanation of the circumstances. (d) Immediately following the explanation, the servant is turned to stone.

V. *Disenchantment of the Servant.* (a) The servant can be brought to life only by the blood of a prince's child or (b) through a remedy which the prince must fetch from afar. (c) The prince kills his own child and restores the servant. The children are then resuscitated. — Adapted from BP.

Motifs:

I. T11.2. Love through sight of picture. F674. Skillful painter. Can paint from description of a dream. T11.2.1. Love through sight of statue. T11.1. Love from mere mention or description. T11.3. Love through dream. T24.2. Swooning for love. M301.2.1. Enraged old woman prophesies for youth. T12. Love through prophecy that prince shall marry the fairest. T381.1. Guarded maiden first seen by hero in church.

II. P361. Faithful servant. N801. Helper grateful for being bought from slavery. N861. Foundling helper. L31. Youngest brother helps elder. P311. Sworn brethren. P273.1. Faithful foster brother. T381. Imprisoned virgin to prevent knowledge of men (marriage, impregnation). R10.1. Princess abducted. R16.1. Maiden abducted by transformed hero. K1332. Seduction by taking aboard ship to inspect wares. K1321.2. Man disguised as woman abducts princess. R25.1. Princess abducted through underground passage. R225.1. Elopement on winged horse. T51. Wooing by emissary.

III. B211.3. Speaking bird. B143. Prophetic bird. M352. Prophecy of particular perils to prince on wedding journey. M302.1. Prophesying through knowledge of animal languages. N451. Secrets overheard from animal (demon) conversation. H1515. Poisoned food test. H1516. Poisoned clothing test. T175. Magic perils threaten bridal couple. T172.2. Bridal chamber invaded by magic dragon (serpent). B176.1. Magic serpent. H1510. Vain attempts to kill hero. S11. Cruel father. S31. Cruel stepmother. S52. Cruel father-in-law.

IV. R169.4.1. Rescue of bride from mysterious perils by hidden faithful servant. N342.1. Faithful servant guarding master's wife from danger falsely condemned for betraying his master. C423.4. Tabu:uttering secrets heard from spirits. C961.2. Transformation to stone for breaking tabu.

V. H1558. Test of friendship. E114. Resuscitation by spittle. E113. Resuscitation by blood. D766.2. Disenchantment by application of blood. D1818. Magic remedy learned by magic. S268. Child sacrificed to provide blood for cure of friend. E0. Resuscitation.

**Rösch *Der Getreue Johannes* (FFC LXXVII); **Krohn FFC XCVI 82ff.; *BP I 46 (Grimm No. 6); *Liungman SSF III 435. — Finnish *24;* Finnish-Swedish *1;* Estonian *2;* Livonian *2;* Lithuanian *49;* Swedish *6* (Göteborg *1,* Lund *1,* Liungman *1,* misc. *3*); Danish *5;* Scottish *1;* Irish *211;* French *6;* Spanish *2;* Catalan: Amades Nos. 44, 123, 171, 189; Flemish *1;* German: Ranke *16,* Meckl. No. 68; Austrian: Haiding No. 67; Italian: D'Aronco *Fiabe 14* (Pentamerone IV No. 9, Tuscan 425A a—-g, [305] a, b *9,* Sicilian *1*); Rumanian *13,* Sainenu 598; Hungarian *19,* (520*) *2;* Czech: Tille FFC XXXIV 201—206, Soupis II (2) 173—180 *3;* Slovenian *1;* Serbocroatian *5;* Polish *13;* Russian: Andrejev *Ukraine 2,* Afanasiev *9;* Greek *12,* Dawkins *45 Stories* No. 2, *Modern Greek Folktales* No. 37; Turkish: Eberhard-Boratav No. 125 V, 214 *16;* Albanian: Lambertz 24ff.; Arab: Littmann 159f; India *22.* — Franco-American *8;* Spanish-American: Rael No. 205 (U.S.), Hansen (Argentina) *1,* (Chile) *2,* (Dominican Republic) *1,* (Puerto Rico) *2;* Portuguese-American (Brazil): Camara Cascudo p. 148; Cape Verde Islands: Parsons MAFLS XV (1) 223 n. 1, 229; West Indies (Negro) *4.* — Literary Treatment: Chauvin IV 8, 57, VII 98.

516A *The Sign Language of the Princess.*

I. *The Friends.* A prince and a youth of lower rank (vizier's son, etc.) are close friends. (a) The Old Woman as Trouble-Maker [M301.2.1, T12]; (this element appears sometimes as a separate tale). (b) For other false reasons the prince commands that his friend be executed. Compassionate executioner. Later, the friend appears to interpret signs. (c) The two friends are banished. (They break the villager's water pots, etc.) (d) The prince dreams of a princess [T11.3] and he and his friend search for her.

II. *The Princess and her Sign Language.* The prince sees a lovely princess who makes signs to him [H607.3]. The friend interprets them [H611.2]. (Example: the princess strikes her teeth with a rose [Z175.1, Z175.2], signifying that her father's name is Rajaj Tooth).

III. *Winning the Princess* [K1300]. They travel to the city where dwells the princess. (a) Through the help of an old woman (flower-seller, etc.) they gain access to the princess. (b) The prince, disguised as a girl, gains access to the princess [K1321.2]. (c) The princess tries to poison the friend, but fails. (d) The friend drugs the princess and brands her back. In the guise of a fakir he then tells the king he has driven a witch away from a human corpse which the witch was eating and has branded the back of the witch. The king, believing the princess to be a witch, drives her out and his friend carries her off. (e) The prince, disguised as a woman, is left in the care of the king by the friend. The prince then escapes. The friend returns and demands the »woman.» The king is forced to give the princess instead. (f) Other means of winning the princess.

India *20*.

516B *The Abducted Princess* (Love Through Sight of Floating Hair).

I. *A Hero Wins a Princess.* After the marriage, the princess (a) loses a hair or (b) a shoe, which floats down the river, or (c) which is swallowed by a fish. A strange prince sees the hair [T11.4.1] (shoe) [T11.4.2] and falls in love with the princess. Or (d) the strange prince falls in love with the princess in other ways [T10].

II. *The Abduction.* An old woman, sent by the strange prince, ingratiates herself with the princess and abducts her [R39.2] (a) by using a flying bedstead [D1520.17.1], (b) by killing the hero, (c) or by stealing the hero's magic object.

III. *The Recovery.* The princess refuses to marry the strange prince for a period of time, using as an excuse a vow. The hero's helper [P361] in disguise recovers the princess, (a) kills the old woman and (b) restores the hero to life. Or (c) the hero's helpers recover the magic object. See Type 560.

Note: This story rarely appears as a separate tale. Instead it is usually found combined with other tale types such as 516, 534, 560.

India *11*.

516C *St. James of Galicia.* Amicus and Amelius. To carry out the vow of parents who have prayed for a child [T548.1] the hero goes to a shrine accompanied by a man who has chosen the smallest of three apples offered [H1558.0.1.1.]. At court the king poisons the companion. He is restored by blood of the hero's children [S268].

*Köhler to Gonzenbach No. 90; *BP II 39 n. 2, III 236. — Italian (Sicilian *1*, Gonzenbach No. 90).

517 *The Boy who Learned Many Things.* Vaticinium. The learning of the speech of birds; cf. Types 670, 671. The princess who has destroyed her child; cf. Type 781. A boy understands the language of birds. The birds prophesy that the parents shall humble themselves before him. On repetition of the prophecy, the parents drive him away. The boy becomes great, returns unknown to his parents, and the prophecy is fulfilled. Cf. Type 725.

Motifs:

B215.1. Bird language. B216. Knowledge of animal languages. B143. Prophetic bird. N451. Secrets overheard from animal (demon) conversation. M312.0.2. Prophecy of future greatness given by animals. S10. Cruel parents. M373. Expulsion to avoid fulfillment of prophecy. N682. Prophecy of future greatness fulfilled when hero returns home unknown.

*BP I 322f., 323 n. 1; *Wesselski *Märchen* 221 No. 35; Coffin *1;* Liungman SSF III 173f., 435. — Finnish *82;* Finnish-Swedish *3;* Estonian *6;* Swedish *7* (Uppsala *1*, Stockholm *1*, misc. *5*); Danish *3;* Scottish *5*, Campbell-McKay No. 14; Irish *27;* Basque *2;* French *6* (often with Type 671); German *1;* Italian: D'Aronco *Fiabe 9*, Fruili *1;* Hungarian: Dégh No. 21; Czech: Tille Soupis I 30ff. *7;* Russian: Andrejev; Greek: *Laographia* XI 444ff.; Turkish: Eberhard-Boratav No. 214 IV; Jewish: Gaster *Rabbis* 248 No. 352. — Franco-American *2;* Spanish-American: Rael Nos. 100, 101 (U.S.); West Indies (Negro) *1*.

518 *Devils (Giants) Fight over Magic Objects,* which the hero gets by trickery (cf. Type 400, incident V g) [D832], and with the help of which he performs the tasks imposed on the suitors of the princess [H335] and frees her from an enchantment [D753]. Cf. Types 51***, 302, 552, 926 D.

*BP III 424 (Grimm No. 197); cf. BP II 331ff. (Grimm No. 92) for the fighting over the magic objects. — Finnish *6;* Estonian *2;* Livonian *3;* Lithuanian *19;* Swedish *7* (Göteborg 1, Liungman *3*, misc. *3*); Danish *1;* Catalan: Amades No. 154, cf. No. 37; Flemish *1;* German *6;* Italian *4* (Tuscan [307] b, c, [901] *3*, Sicilian *1*); Rumanian *6;* Hungarian *10;* Czech: FFC XXXIV 126f., Soupis II (1) 416f., II (2) 209f. *4;* Slovenian *2;* Serbocroatian *1;* Russian: Andrejev *Ukraine 11*, Afanasiev *15;* Turkish: Eberhard-Boratav Nos. 84 IV, 97 III, 174 IV, 205, 212 III, 213 III; India *3*. — Franco-American *5;* Spanish-American: Hansen (Dominican

Republic) *1;* Cape Verde Islands: Parsons MAFLS XV (1) 293 n. 1; West Indies (Negro) *1.* — African *1.*

518* *Unjust Umpire Misappropriates Disputed Goods.* [K452]. Cf. Types 51***, 926D. Chauvin VII 38ff.; Wesselski *Arlotto* II 254 No. 171. — Spanish (*1593) *1;* India: Thompson-Balys; U.S.: Baughman.

519 *The Strong Woman as Bride (Brunhilde).* The helper in the suitor test. Cf. Type 513A.

I. *The Suitor.* A prince with his extraordinary companion woos a bride who is beautiful, strong, and warlike, and who will have as husband no man who is not her equal in strength.

II. *Suitor Tests.* (a) The prince must wield her gigantic weapons and ride her untamed steed. (b) By substitution of his companion this is accomplished.

III. *The Bridal Night.* (a) In the bridal night she lays her feet and hands on the prince and almost stifles him. (b) He asks permission to go outside and in the darkness the helper substitutes himself and overcomes the princess.

IV. *The Princess's Revenge.* (a) When on the return to the prince's home she discovers the betrayal, she cuts off the feet of the helper and drives forth the prince, who becomes a swineherd. (b) The lamed helper joins a blind man and they assist each other. (c) They overcome a giant and compel him to show healing water. (d) The helper with his feet restored returns and compels the restoration of his master.

Motifs:

I. F601.2. Extraordinary companion helps hero in suitor test. T58. Wooing the strong and beautiful bride. H345. Suitor test: overcoming princess in strength.

II. H345.1. Suitor test: Lifting strong princess's giant weapon. H345.2. Suitor test: riding strong princess's horse. K3. Substitute in contest.

III. T173.1. Strong bride tries to stifle husband in bed. K1844.1. Husband has his strong servant substitute in bed with strong wife.

IV. Q261. Treachery punished. Q451.2. Laming as punishment. S162. Mutilation: cutting off legs (feet). K1816.6. Disguise as herdsman. N886. Blind man carries lame man. D1500.1.18. Magic healing water. R169.4. Hero rescued by servant.

**A. von Löwis of Menar *Die Brünhildsage in Russland* (Leipzig, 1923); See Anderson Zeitschrift für slavische Philologie XXV (1956) 311f. — Estonian (519*) *3;* Lithuanian *2;* Swedish *2* (Lund *1,* misc. *1*); German *1;* Hungarian (523*) *9;* Czech: Tille Soupis I 101—104 *2;* Polish *1;* Russian: Afanasiev *18.* — Franco-American *1.*

520* *Poor Man and Rich Travel.* Poor agrees to let rich always seem the more skillful. Poor does deeds, rich gets credit. — Kills robbers, giant, etc. In a tournament the poor refrains and shows up the rich.
Icelandic *1.*

524* *The Stupid Prince in the Cave.* An enchanted queen rescues a stupid prince whom his brother has pushed into a cave. The queen gives him her daughter for wife and he forgives his brothers.
Polish *1*.

530—559 Animals as Helpers

530 *The Princess on the Glass Mountain.* Cf. Types 300, 329, 502, 550.

I. *Reward for the Vigil.* (a) Three brothers one after the other are sent to guard a meadow which is devastated at night by a monster or (b) they must in turns keep vigil for their dead father. (c) The elder brothers are frightened away but the youngest umpromising brother succeeds and secures three fine horses with saddle and bridle and armor of copper, of silver, and of gold. (d) He tells no one of this.

II. *The Glass Mountain.* (a) The king offers the princess to one who can take three golden apples from her as she sits on top of a glass mountain or (b) one who can ride to the fourth story of a tower, or (c) up a mast or (d) over a pit. (e) The hero rides with his three horses ever higher and at last to the top. (f) The hero alone succeeds.

III. *Unknown Knight.* (a) The hero disappears without telling who he is. (b) All suitors are summoned but only he can show the golden apples. (c) He marries the princess.

Motifs:

I. G346. Devastating monster. H1471. Watch for devastating monster. Youngest alone successful. H1462. Vigil for dead father. L10. Victorious youngest son. L131. Hearth abode of unpromising hero. B315. Animal helpful after being conquered. B401. Helpful horse. B181. Magic horse. F824. Extraordinary armor.

II. F751. Glass mountain. H331.1.1. Suitor contest: riding up glass mountain. H331.1.2. Suitor contest: riding to fourth story of tower. F1071. Prodigious jump. To fourth story (or the like). R111.2.2. Rescue of princess from mountain. F989.1. Horse jumps over high wall. H331.1.3. Suitor contest: riding up mast (spear). H331.1.4. Suitor contest: riding across pit.

III. R222. Unknown knight. H311. Inspection test for suitors. H80. Identification by tokens. L161. Lowly hero marries princess.

**Boberg *Danske Studier* 1928 pp. 16—53; *BP III *111, 340; *Hartmann *Trollvorstellungen* 172f.; *Honti Beal VI 34; *Ranke *Schleswig-Holsteinische Volksmärchen* II 146; Köhler-Bolte I 55, 67, Coffin *1*. — Finnish *208;* Finnish-Swedish *10;* Estonian *33;* Livonian *5;* Lithuanian *11;* Swedish *21* (Uppsala *6*, Göteborg *4*, Lund *2*, Liungman *2*, misc. *7*); Norwegian *20;* Danish *41*, Grundtvig No. 3A; Irish *56;* French *3;* Flemish *1;* German: Ranke *56*, Meckl. No. 50, 51; Rumanian (300 I*C) *21;* Hungarian *32*, (530 I*) *18;* Czech: Tille FFC XXXIV 52ff. *6*, Soupis II (1) 148ff. *6;* Slovenian *2;* Serbocroatian *18;* Polish *40*, (530A)

6, (530B) *1*, (536) *1;* Russian: Andrejev *Ukraine* (530A) *16*, Afanasiev (530A) *20;* Albanian: Lambertz 83ff.; Turkish: Eberhard-Boratav Nos. 73, 257 IV, 258 *11;* Caucasus: Dirr 30; Arab: Littmann 183f., Spitta 152; India *8.* — Franco-American *9;* English-American: Baughman *2;* Spanish-American: Rael No. 229 (U.S.).

530A *The Pig with the Golden Bristles.* A tsar commands his sons-in-law to get a pig with golden bristles, a golden-horned stag, etc. A foolish boy gets these wonders, but yields them to the sons-in-law, when they cut off his fingers and cut the skin from his back. At the feast they are exposed by the fool and the mutilations. Cf. Type 314.

Russian: Afanasiev (530B*) *28.*

530B* *The Stolen Brides.* Aided by wonderful horses, the fool steals three brides. All three brothers shoot at their granaries; sound of girls' laughter is heard from the fool's granary. The fool gives a girl to each brother, keeping the youngest for himself.

Lithuanian (*530B) *8.*

531 *Ferdinand the True and Ferdinand the False.* On the advice of a jealous courtier the king assigns the hero difficult tasks, which he performs with the help of grateful animals. Bringing the beautiful bride for the king.

I. *The Hero's Horse and Magic Object.* (a) The hero at his christening is given by a beggar a key, with which he later obtains a horse which speaks and gives advice, or (a^1) the king appears, serves as his godfather, and gives him a ring as a means of recognition: when fifteen years old he sets out to find his godfather; or (a^2) an illegitimate son of the king seeks his father; or (a^3) the hero is on some other quest; or (a^4) the hero, son of a huntsman, goes as hunter unto the king's service. (b) He finds a golden pen (or a golden bird, a spotted animal, a weasel, a diamond, a wild animal covered with glistening diamonds, or an elephant skin) and in spite of the advice of his horse (or his mother or his teacher) picks it up from the ground; he gives this to the king who on the advice of a treacherous courtier sends the hero on dangerous quests. (c) From a thankful fish he receives a fin and from a bird a feather.

II. *The Treacherous Companion.* (a) On the way to the king he is forced to change places with a treacherous companion and to swear silence; together they go into the king's service. (b) At the companion's suggestions he is assigned dangerous quests: (bringing the golden bird, or its cage, or the water of life, etc.), especially the bringing of a golden-haired maiden.

III. *Fetching the Princess.* (a) The hero is to fetch a beautiful princess for the king. (b) On the advice of his horse, he demands as a condition from the king a supply of meat and bread. (c) With these he obtains help from giants, lions, birds, ants who help him perform tasks assigned by the golden-haired maiden. (d) The fish returns his pen which has fallen into the water.

IV. *Beautification by Decapitation.* (a) The princess beheads him and then replaces his head to make him handsomer. (b) The king has the same thing done to him with fatal results. (c) The magic horse changes himself into a prince. — Adapted from BP.

Motifs:

I. N811. Supernatural godfather. H1381.2.2.1. Son seeks unknown father. N826. Help from beggar. D1158. Magic key. B211.1.3. Speaking horse. B133. Truth-speaking horse. B401. Helpful horse. B313. Helpful animal an enchanted person. B350. Grateful animals. B391. Animal grateful for food. B470. Helpful fish. B501. Animal gives part of body as talisman for summoning its aid.

II. K1934. Impostor forces hero (heroine) to change places with him (her). H911. Tasks assigned at suggestion of jealous rivals.

III. T11.4.1. Love through sight of hair of unknown princess. H75.2. Identification by hair dropped by bird. H75.1. Identification by hair found floating on water. H1213.1. Quest for princess caused by sight of one of her hairs dropped by bird (or floating on river). H1381.3.1.1. Quest for bride for king (prince). H951. Countertasks. When a task is assigned, the hero agrees to perform it as soon as the assigner performs a certain other task. N812.0.1. Giant's help secured by feeding him. N812. Giant or ogre as helper. B325.1. Animal bribed with food. H982. Animals help man perform task. B450. Helpful birds. H1132.1.4. Task: recovering pen from sea. B548.2.4. Fish recovers pen from sea.

IV. E15.1. Resuscitation by boiling. E12. Resuscitation by decapitation. D1865.1. Beautification by decapitation and replacement of head. J2411.1. Imitation of magic rejuvenation unsuccessful. D131. Transformation: man to horse. D700. Person disenchanted.

G. Megas *Der Bartlose im neugriechischen Märchen* FFC CLVII 7ff.; *BP III 18 (Grimm No. 126); *Hartmann *Trollvorstellungen* 174f.; *Meyer FFC CLVII; Coffin 2; *Aarne FFC XXIII 125, 126. — Finnish *14;* Finnish-Swedish *1;* Estonian *12;* Livonian *4;* Lithuanian (*531) *76;* Swedish *24* (Uppsala *2,* Göteborg *1,* Lund *6,* Liungman *1,* misc. *14*); Norwegian *29,* Solheim *1;* Danish *49,* Grundtvig No. 10; Icelandic *8;* Scottish *1;* Irish *171,* Beal II 290ff., XI suppl. 50ff.; French *40;* Spanish *2;* Catalan: Amades Nos. 20, 46, 81, 149, cf. 84, 101, 128; German: Ranke *39,* Meckl. No. 69; Austrian: Haiding Nos. 9, 39; Italian *11* (Pentamerone III No. 7, Tuscan [317] c, [320], [888] *3,* Sicilian *5,* Gonzenbach Nos. 30, 83); Rumanian (403D*) *3;* Hungarian *37;* Czech Tille FFC XXXIV 162—177, Soupis II (2) 188—205 *6;* Slovenian *2;* Serbocroatian *8;* Polish *15,* (531A) *1,* (509) *8;* Russian: Andrejev *Ukraine 16,* Afanasiev *30;* Greek *40,* Hahn Nos. 6, 37, Loukatos No. 14; Turkish: Eberhard-Boratav Nos. 81, 207 III, 248, Radloff IV 136f., 373f.; India *3.* — Franco-American *56;* Spanish-American: Rael Nos. 232, 233 (U.S.), Hansen (Argentina) *1,* (Chile) *1,* (Dominican Republic) *4,* (Puerto Rico) *5,* (cf. Puerto Rico 531A) *1;* Portuguese-American (Brazil): Camara Cascudo p. 155; West Indies (Negro) *5;* American Indian (San Carlos Apache): Goddard PaAM XXIV 77.

532 *I Don't Know.* The helpful horse. The hero is driven from home by his stepmother [S31]. He acquires a helpful horse which advises him [B401] to dress in poor clothing [K1816] and to answer all questions with »I don't know» [C495.1]. He takes service as gardener to the king [K1816.1]. He thrice rescues the king (or the princess) from a dragon [R111.5.4.] or other danger [R110] but conceals his identity each time [R222]. The princess notices him, is enamored and marries him [L161]. The hero's name is often »Thirteen» [L10.1.1]. Cf. Type 314.

Finnish *37;* Estonian *1;* Livonian *1;* Lappish *1;* Irish *2;* German *2;* Austrian: Haiding No. 63; Rumanian *1* (also with Type 300 IB); Hungarian *5;* Czech: Tille FFC XXXIV 29—44, Soupis II (2) 261—283 *21;* Serbocroatian *11;* Russian: Andrejev *Ukraine 11*, Afanasiev *31;* Greek *23*, Dawkins *Modern Greek Folktales* No. 39; Turkish: Eberhard-Boratav Nos. 175 III, 247, 257, 258 III *15;* India *1.* — Franco-American *2;* Spanish-American: Hansen (Puerto Rico) *1.*

532* *Son of the Cow (God's godson).* Two oxen plow the copper (iron, stone) field of the king. The hero receives the hand of the princess and the possessions of the kingdom.
Rumanian *15.*

533 *The Speaking Horsehead.* On the journey to her wedding the princess is forced by her waiting-maid to change clothes and places with her. The princess's horse is killed, but through the speaking horsehead which hangs on the wall, the betrayal is revealed. Cf. Types 403, 450. The princess is sometimes blinded and her eyes later bought from the person who has blinded her. She is recognized not only from the speaking horsehead but also by her golden and silver hair, and by a song sung in a stove.

Motifs:

K2252. Treacherous maid-servant. K1911.1.1. False bride takes true bride's place on the way to the wedding. K1934. Impostor forces heroine to change places with her. K1933. Impostor forces oath of secrecy. B401. Helpful horse. B313. Helpful animal an enchanted person. B335. Helpful animal killed by hero's enemy. K1816.5. Disguise as goose-girl (turkey-girl). H151.12. Geese tell of beauty of their mistress and bring about recognition. D1011. Magic animal head. B133.3. Speaking horsehead. The helpful horse is killed. The head is preserved and placed on the wall. It speaks and reveals the treachery practiced against the heroine. S165. Mutilation: putting out eyes. E781.2. Eyes bought back and replaced. H71. Marks of royalty. F545.2.1. Gold star on forehead. H71.2. Gold (silver) hairs as sign of royalty. H12. Recognition by song. H13.2.7. Recognition by overheard conversation with stove. H13.1.2. Recognition by overheard conversation with dog.

**Liungman SSF III 184ff.; *BP II 273 (Grimm No. 89). — Lithuanian *1;* Swedish 6 (Uppsala *1*, Göteborg *1*, Liungman *1*, misc. *3*); Irish *2;* French *2;* Spanish *1;* Catalan: cf. Amades Nos. 27, 191; Flemish: cf 403A; German: Ranke *5;* Italian (Pentamerone cf. IV No. 7, cf.

Tuscan 403a, c, p, [895] a *4*); Hungarian *1;* Polish *6;* Russian: Afanasiev (533A) *5;* Turkish: Eberhard-Boratav No. 75, cf. No. 240 *2;* India *6.* — Franco-American *17;* West Indies (Negro) *2.* — African *3.*

533* *The Snake Helper.* A girl is kind to snake and receives gift of dropping gold from her fingers when she washes her hands. Her father tells the king, who demands to see her. Her wicked godmother and daughter accompany her. En route they take her eyes out and throw her overboard. She is picked up by a kind fisherman. The godmother substitutes the daughter as bride to the king. A fisherman cares for the girl and becomes rich with gold from her hands. The snake seizes the fisherman's boy and commands the fisherman to take the son's eyes and give them to the girl. The girl dresses in beautiful clothes and goes to king's court. She is recognized by king when she washes her hands. He marries her and burns the old woman and her daughter. The snake is the girl's guardian angel and returns to Heaven (cf. Type 506). The fisherman's son recovers sight.

Spanish-American: Hansen (403**D) (Chile) *1,* (Dominican Republic) *1,* (Puerto Rico) *1.*

534 *The Youth Who Tends the Buffalo Herd.* Cf. Types 181, 510C, 511A.

I. *The Youth and the Wild Buffaloes (Cows).* A youth cares for wild buffaloes which he comes upon in the forest and is befriended by them [B395, B396, N832.1, B537]. (a) The youth is lost or abandoned. (b) A tiger carries a youth into the forest, but the youth escapes. (c) A helpful bull (cow) carries the boy into the forest. See 511A. (d) The buffaloes give the youth a horn (flute) with which to call them when he needs help [B501.1] (e) The youth's hair is made golden [F555.1.1, D475.1.10] (he pours milk into a snake hole and the snake is grateful.)

II. *The Abduction of the Youth.* (a) One of the youth's hairs floats down the river (swallowed by a fish) and is found by a princess who falls in love with the youth [T11.4.1.1]. (b) The king sends a parrot (crow) to find the boy (the parrot steals the boy's horn or flute). (c) The boy is brought to the palace.

III. *Conclusions.* (a) The boy calls his buffaloes to the palace. (b) The boy marries the princess.

India *24.*

534* *The Magic Stick, the Golden Feather, and the Speaking Ass* [D1401.1, D1021, B211.1.3.1]. With the aid of the ass the youngest son [L11] heals the horses and can withstand boiling water [D1841.2]. The ass is disenchanted into a princess [D700].

Flemish *1.*

535 *The Boy Adopted by Tigers (Animals).*

I. *A Boy is Adopted by Wild Animals.* (a) The boy is abandoned in the forest, (b) and adopted by tigers. (c) He is given a magic bow and arrow, or (d) magic axe.

II. *The Substitute Bridegroom.* (a) The animals arrange a marriage for him. (b) A monkey or (c) a barber takes his place. (d) The boy goes to live with an old widow who has a lovely daughter. (e) He proves his identity by using his magic objects. (f) He marries the girl to whom he was betrothed and (g) the widow's daughter.

India *7.*

536* *The Diamond Mountain.* A dragon shows the hero a diamond mountain. With the jewels he wins a princess.
Polish (536) *1.*

537 *The Marvelous Eagle Gives the Hero a Box* which he must not open.

I. *The Speaking Eagle.* A man aims to shoot an eagle, when suddenly the bird begins to speak like a human being [B211.3]. The man spares him.

II. *The Grateful Eagle.* The bird has a wing broken. The man cares for it for three years and wastes all his property by feeding the bird. Finally the eagle recovers and will repay the man for his kindness [B380, Q45].

III. *The Journey by Air.* The bird then carries the man on his back across the sea [B552] to his kingdom [B222], and intimidates him three times by nearly dropping him into the sea (the hunter has once aimed three times with his gun at the bird).

IV. *The Secret Box.* The eagle's father (sister) gives him a box [D1174.1] with the warning not to open it before the man reaches home [C321].

V. *The Castle.* Overcome with curiosity, the man, on his way home, opens the box. A castle springs therefrom. For getting the castle back into the box, the man promises his son to the devil [S222].

This is usually an introduction to Type 313B.

**Haavio *Der Etanamythos in Finnland* (FFC CLIV); study in preparation by Isidor Levin (Leningrad); *Anderson FFC XLII 165. — Lithuanian (*320) *22;* Russian: Afanasiev (222*B) *19;* Babylonian Etana myth.

540 (formerly 540*) *The Dog in the Sea.* The dog rescues a man who tries to drown himself [B541.4]. They come to the bottom of the sea, where the man disenchants [D711] the king along with his son (= the dog) and his kingdom.

Finnish *2;* Danish *7,* Grundtvig No. 86; Russian: Andrejev.

541* *Restoring Blind King's Eyes.* The hero receives magic swords from a blind king. He prepares a large wagonload of meat, water, and wine and sets out to recover the king's eyes from a monster. He gives food and drink to the monster and is told where to find the king's eyes. To marry the empress he must pick her from a group of girls identically clad (cf. Type 313 II d). The monster appears as a snake in front of the empress and the hero chooses correctly. Cf. Type 533.

Spanish-American: Hansen (**540) (Dominican Republic) *1.*

545 *The Cat as Helper.* Visit to the castle. Disenchantment.

I. *The Helpful Cat.* (a) A boy or (b) girl inherits nothing but a cat (or fox).

II. *The Cat at the Palace.* (a) The cat takes the girl (boy) to the palace. (b) He tells the king that the boy (girl) is a dispossessed prince. (c) The cat woos the princess for the boy. (d) The boy (girl) always says that he (she) has better things at home.

III. *Visit to the Castle.* (a) The king is to visit the boy's (girl's) castle. (b) The cat goes ahead and has peasants say they are working for his master (mistress). (c) He goes to a giant's castle and through trickery kills the giant and takes possession of the castle for his master (mistress).

IV. *Disenchantment.* (a) The cat's head is cut off and it becomes a prince (or princess).

Motifs:

I. N411.1.1. Cat as sole inheritance. B211.1.8. Speaking cat. B422. Helpful cat. B435.1. Helpful fox.

II. B580. Animal helps man to wealth and greatness. B581. Animal brings wealth to man. B582.1.1. Animal wins wife for his master (Puss in Boots). B582.1.2. Animal wins husband for mistress. K1952.1. Poor boy said by helpful cat to be dispossessed prince. K1952.2. Better things at home. K1954.1. Helpful cat borrows measure for his master's money. K1917.3. Penniless wooer: helpful animal reports master wealthy and thus wins girl for him. K1952.1.1. Poor boy said by helpful animal to be dispossessed prince (wealthy man) who has lost clothes while swimming (in shipwreck).

III. F771.4.1. Castle inhabited by ogres. K722. Giant tricked into becoming mouse.

IV. D711. Disenchantment by decapitation.

Finnish *112;* Estonian *7;* Swedish *51* (Uppsala *13,* Stockholm *5,* Göteborg *11,* Liungman *4,* misc. *18*); Danish *35;* Irish *58,* Beal I 239ff., II 10; Spanish (545C*) *1;* Flemish *5,* Witteryck p. 293 *4;* German: Ranke *4;* Italian (Pentamerone II No. 4); Slovenian *4;* Serbocroatian *1;* Polish *1.* — Franco-American *8;* Spanish-American: Rael Nos. 240, 242 (U.S.), Hansen (Dominican Republic) *5.* — African *10.*

Two forms of the type follows:

545A *The Cat Castle.* The boy inherits a cow, the girl a cat. The cat helps the girl so that she gains the love of a prince and takes possession of the giant's castle for the girl. Cf. Type 505.

See analysis: I b; II a, b, d; III a, b, c; IV a.

Finnish-Swedish *3;* Lappish *1;* Swedish (Lund) *1;* Norwegian *4;* French *16;* Italian (Sicilian *4*); Russian: Andrejev; Turkish: Eberhard-Boratav No. 54 III, IV.

545B *Puss in Boots* (or the helpful fox). The cat coerces the shepherd (and others) to say that they are servants of the hero, and takes possession of the castle of the serpent (or magician).

See analysis: I a; II a, b, c, d; III a, b, c; IV a.

*BP III 487 (Grimm No. 214); Coffin *1.* — Finnish-Swedish *1;* Livonian *1;* Lithuanian *4;* Lappish *8;* Norwegian *29,* Solheim *2;* Italian: D'Aronco *Fiabe 13* (Tuscan 545 a—e *5,* Sicilian *4,* Gonzenbach No. 65); Rumanian *6,* Sainenu 165; Hungarian *5;* Serbocroatian *2;* Russian: Andrejev *Ukraine 11,* Afanasiev *9;* Greek *20,* Hahn II 340ff., Argenti-Rose I 514ff. No. 11, Loukatos No. 15; Turkish: Eberhard-Boratav Nos. 34, 36 IV, 189 III *21;* India *19;* Indonesian: DeVries No. 179. West Indies (Negro) *7.* — African: Frobenius Atlantis III No. 26.

545C* *Boaster Wins the Bride.* (Like Type 545 without animal helper.)
  Italian (Sicilian *545C *1*).

545D* *The Bean King.* Unemployed youth finds a bean on the road. He imagines how rich he could become if he grows beans. He goes to a king and asks for loading places and barrels for his coming crops. The king supposes him wealthy and offers him the princess as wife. When the king wants to see the property of his son-in-law, a grateful ghost whom he has earlier helped furnishes a castle and reports to the king that everything in sight belongs to the youth.
  Hungarian *1*.

545E* *The Cat Leads to Money.* Brother tells his sister to fry fish while he goes to town. A cat steals the fish and the girl follows it. She finds two piles of money. She tells her brother and they take it and become rich.
  Spanish-American: Hansen (545**D) (Dominican Republic) *1*.

546   *The Clever Parrot.*
  I. *The Parrot Wins a Princess for the King.* (a) The king wins the gratitude of a parrot. (b) The parrot takes the king to a princess. (c) The parrot brings a princess to the king.
  II. *Separation.* On the return trip the king and his bride are separated. The parrot reunites them.
  India *9*.

550   *Search for the Golden Bird.* Quest for the wonderful bird. With the help of an animal (wolf, fox) the youngest brother succeeds. On his return he saves his brothers, who betray him.
  See analysis below: I a, b; II; III a, b; IV; V.

ANALYSIS

Types 550 and 551

  I. *Object of the Quest.* (a) A bird which steals golden apples from the king's orchard at night drops a golden feather: the king orders a quest for the bird. (b) A sick (blind) king orders a quest for a magic remedy or (c) for the water of youth.

  II. *The Three Sons.* Three sons of a king go on the quest. The two elder are unkind to animals (old woman, dwarfs) that they meet, and they fail; but the third is kind and receives the help of the animals.

  III. *Success of the Quest.* (a) The hero reaches the tree of the golden bird, but is to receive the bird only after he undertakes further quests. (b) On these he receives a magic horse and a princess, and he takes them, along with the magic bird, home; — or (c) with the help of friendly animals and people the hero reaches a magic garden, where he sees a sleeping princess, lies by her, and on his departure writes his name and leaves it with her. (d) He secures the water of life (youth) and returns home.

  IV. *The Treacherous Brothers.* (a) The hero's elder brothers rob him and throw him into a well or (b) wolf's den. (c) He is helped out and his goods restored by his helpful fox or (b) by the wolf, to which he feeds meat.

V. *Conclusion.* (a) The fox is decapitated and becomes a prince. (b) The princess seeks the father of her child and, in spite of the treachery of the elder brothers, finds and marries the hero.

Motifs:

I. F813.1.1. Golden apple. H1471. Watch for devastating monster. Youngest alone successful. B102.1. Golden bird. Bird with golden feathers. H1210.1. Quest assigned by father. H1331.1. Quest for marvelous bird. H1213. Quest for remarkable bird caused by sight of one of its feathers. H1331.1.2. Quest for three feathers of marvelous bird. H1331.1.3. Quest for golden bird. H1324. Quest for miraculous remedy. H1321.2. Quest for healing water. D1500.1.18. Magic healing water. H1321.3. Quest for water of youth. D1338.1.2. Water of youth.

II. Q2. Kind and unkind. L13. Compassionate youngest son. B313. Helpful animal an enchanted person. B560. Animals advise man. H1233.6. Animals help hero on quest.

III. H1241. Series of quests. One quest can be accomplished when a second is finished, etc. H1239.3. Quest accomplished by means of objects given by helpers. B184.1. Magic horse. D961. Magic garden. N711.3. Hero finds maiden in (magic) garden. T475.2. Hero lies by princess in magic sleep and begets child. H81.1. Hero lies by sleeping girl and leaves identification token with her. H1242. Youngest brother alone succeeds on quest.

IV. K2211. Treacherous brother. W154.12.3. Ungrateful brothers plot against rescuer. K1932. Impostors claim reward (prize) earned by hero. K1931.4. Impostors throw hero into pit. B391. Animal grateful for food. B544. Animal rescues captive. B435.1. Helpful fox. B435.3. Helpful wolf.

V. D711. Disenchantment by decapitation. H1381.2.1. Princess seeks unknown father of her child. L10. Victorious youngest son. L161. Lowly hero marries princess.

**Draak *Onderzoekingen over de Roman van Walewein* (Haarlem, 1939); *BP I 503 (Grimm No. 57), Coffin *3*. — Finnish *55;* Finnish-Swedish *4*, (554*) *1;* Estonian *7;* Livonian *1*, (cf. also 531B*) *1;* Lithuanian *75;* Lappish *2;* Swedish *26* (Uppsala *3*, Göteborg *1*, Lund *4*, Liungman *3*, misc. *15*); Norwegian *16*, Solheim *1;* Danish *9*, Grundtvig No. 13; Irish *225*, Beal XI suppl. 1, 14, XII 86f. No. 3; Basque *2;* French *29;* Catalan: Amades cf. Nos. 113, 114, 143; Flemish *7;* Walloon *1* (cf. 569A); German: Ranke *41*, Meckl. 69, 70; Austrian: Haiding No. 71; Italian *9* (Tuscan 301 l, m, q, u, v, cf. 301 z *6*, Sicilian *2*, Gonzenbach No. 51); Rumanian *13*, Sainenu 540; Hungarian *11*, Dégh (551) No. 23, Honti (320), Berze Nagy (728*) *4;* Czech: Tille FFC XXXIV 177—184, Soupis II (1) 2—18 *4;* Slovenian *16;* Serbocroatian *6;* Polish *25*, (417) *4;* Russian: Andrejev *Ukraine 11*, Afanasiev *12;* Greek *17*, Dawkins *Modern Greek Folktales* No. 2; Turkish: Eberhard-Boratav Nos. 76, 204 III, 206, 257 III *21;* Armenian: Khatchatrianz 105; India *27;* Indonesian:

DeVries No. 181. — Franco-American *51;* Spanish-American: Rael Nos. 199, 200, 201, 235, 238, 239 (U.S.), Hansen (Chile) *1*, Dominican Republic) *5*, (550**A) *6*, (Puerto Rico) *12*, (307**A) *1*, (Cuba) (550**B) *1;* West Indies (Negro) *12*. — African *3*. — Literary Treatments: Chauvin VI 6 f.; Wesselski *Märchen* 217 No. 28.

550A *Only One Brother Grateful.* A magician grants three brothers each a wish [D1761.0.2]. The two elder ones wish for wealth and later show ungratefulness and are punished [Q1.1]. The youngest receives a noble wife and later is hospitable to the disguised magician to the point of sacrificing his child to cure him [S268]. Cf. Type 516.

*Winstedt *FL* LVII 143. — Greek: Dawkins *Modern Greek Folktales* (No. 70) *3* (references to Armenian, Slavic, Berber, Albanian); Turkish: Eberhard-Boratav (No. 110) *1;* Arabic: Basset *1001 Contes* III 302.

551 *The Sons on a Quest for a Wonderful Remedy for their Father.* The youngest succeeds with the help of an eagle (dwarf) and various magic objects. The brothers gain possession of the remedy. The princess searches for the father of her child.

For analysis see Type 550: I b, (c); II; III c, d; IV; V b. Motifs: see Type 550.

Draak *Onderzoekingen over de Roman van Walewein* (Haarlem, 1939); *BP II 394 (Grimm No. 97); Coffin *2*. — Finnish *78;* Finnish-Swedish *12;* Estonian *8;* Lithuanian *13;* Lappish *3;* Swedish *20* (Uppsala *1*, Göteborg *3*, Lund *3*, misc. *13*); Norwegian *4;* Danish *28;* Icelandic *1;* Scottish *4;* Irish *70;* French *13;* Spanish *1;* Flemish *3;* German: Ranke *56;* Austrian: Haiding Nos. 6, 31; Italian (Tuscan 301 d, i, o, p, r *5*, Sicilian *1*, Friuli *3*); Rumanian *2;* Czech: Tille FFC XXXIV 193—200, Soupis II (1) 18—36 *16;* Hungarian *15;* Slovenian *5;* Serbocroatian *5;* Polish *8;* Russian: Andrejev *Ukraine 11*, Afanasiev *27*; Greek *8;* Turkish: Eberhard-Boratav No. 72 V, 81, 206 III, 215 III, IV; India *10*. — Franco-American *37;* Spanish-American: Rael No. 236 (U.S.), Hansen (Argentina) *1*, (Chile, 551+551A) *2*, (Dominican Republic) *6*, (Puerto Rico) *5*, (Uruguay) *1;* West Indies (Negro) *4*. — African *4*.

(*The Man on a Quest for his Lost Wife;* see Type 400.)

551* *A Youth Sets Out to Seek Riches.*
Lappish *2*.

551* *Three Brothers Seek Riches.* Two of them acquire silver and gold. The third receives magic objects from an old man [N821].
Lappish *1;* Slovenian *5*.

552 *The Girls Who Married Animals.*
I. *Marriage to Animals.* (a) A bankrupt man promises his daughters in in marriage in return for safety and money to three animals (bear, eagle, whale); or (b) three girls despairing of marriage say that they will marry any one even if it is an animal (a bear, fox, squirrel, etc.). (c) The animals take the girls as wives.

II. *Visit to Animal Brothers-in-law.* (a) The girls' brother visits them and finds that the animals periodically become men. (b) The brothers-in-law give him parts of their bodies (eagle's feather, etc.) with which their aid may be summoned. — (c) The girls' father visits them and finds food and other things magically provided. (d) The father later tries the same method at home without success.

III. *Help of the Animals.* The brother receives the help of his animal brothers — (a) in saving a princess from a monster (see Type 302 [I c], 518); (b) in recovering a lost castle, wife, and magic objects (see Type 560). Cf. also Types 531, 553.

Motifs:

I. S221.1. Bankrupt father sells his daughters in marriage to animals. B620.1. Daughter promised to animal suitor. C26. Wish for animal husband realized. Girl says she will marry a certain animal. Latter appears and carries her off. B640. Marriage to person in animal form.

II. D620. Periodic transformation. D621.1. Animal by day; man by night. B501. Animal gives part of body as talisman for summoning its aid. B505.1. Magic objects received from animal brother-in-law. D532. Transformation by putting on claw, feather, etc. of helpful animal. D2105. Provisions magically furnished. J2411.3. Unsuccessful imitation of magic production of food.

III. B314. Helpful animal brothers-in-law.

Two forms of the type follow:

552A *Three Animals as Brothers-in-law.* Three princesses are married to animals. The animals help their brother-in-law.

See analysis: I a, c; II a, b; III b.

*BP II 198, III 426ff. (Grimm Nos. 82 a, 104 a). — Finnish *41;* Finnish-Swedish *1;* Estonian *9;* Lithuanian *30;* Lappish *1;* Swedish (misc.) *1;* Norwegian *2;* Danish *5,* Grundtvig No. 7; Irish *8;* German *41;* Austrian: Haiding Nos. 30, 31; Italian *9* (Tuscan 554 b, [314] d, [891 quater], [891 quinquies] *4,* Sicilian *5,* Gonzenbach Nos. 29, 177); Rumanian *6,* Sainenu 459; Hungarian *45;* Czech: Tille Soupis II (2) 3—17, 72—87, FFC XXXIV 101ff., *10;* Slovenian (552) *1;* Serbocroatian (552) *3;* Serbocroatian (552A) *6;* Polish *2;* Russian: Andrejev *Ukraine 8,* Afanasiev *25;* Greek *13,* Hahn No. 25, Dawkins *45 Stories* 157f.; Turkish: Eberhard-Boratav No. 218, cf. 215. — Franco-American *6;* Spanish-American: Rael Nos. 203, 204 (U.S.); Cape Verde Islands: Parsons MAFLS XV (1) 208 n. 1; West Indies (Negro) *2;* American Indian: Thompson *C Coll* II 409ff.

552B *The Animal Sons-in-law and their Magic Food.* The unsuccessful imitation.

See analysis: I b, c; II c, d.

Latvian (*299) *5;* Lithuanian *3;* Swedish *8* (Liungman *5,* misc. *3*); Norwegian (552**) *9,* Solheim *1;* Russian: Afanasiev *3;* India *2.*

553 *The Raven Helper.* A youth shoots a raven; saving of the princess from a sea-monster. Cf. Type 300.

I. *The Raven-feather.* (a) With a feather of the raven the youth gets magic objects and treasure from the raven's sister.

II. *Rescue of Princess.* See Type 300: IV (recue from sea-monster); VI e; VII a, d, (e).

Motifs:

I. H78.1. Youth shoots raven and takes feather to raven's sister as token. B451.5. Helpful raven. B501. Animal gives part of body as talisman for summoning its aid. D532. Transformation by putting on claw, feather, etc. of helpful animal. D1021. Magic feather.

II. H982. Animals help man perform task. B582.2. Animals help hero win princess.

*BP II 22 n. 1 (Grimm No. 62). — Finnish *3;* Finnish-Swedish *1;* Lithuanian *1;* Swedish *9* (Uppsala *1,* Stockholm *1,* misc. *7*); Norwegian *1;* Danish *10,* Grundtvig No. 4; Irish *1;* Catalan: Amades cf. No. 112; German *3;* Hungarian *1;* Slovenian *1;* Russian: Andrejev. — Franco-American *2.*

554 *The Grateful Animals.* A youth earns the thanks of several animals (ants, fish, etc.) and with their help wins the princess by performing three tasks imposed upon him (brings a ring from the bottom of the sea, etc.).

I. *The Animals' Gratitude.* The hero, (a) the youngest of three brothers, (b) rescues from danger or starvation three animals (ants, ducks, bees, raven, fish, fox, etc.).

II. *The Tasks.* With their help (a) he wins a beautiful bride and performs various tasks: (b) sorting out scattered seeds or beads, (c) bringing a ring or key from the bottom of the sea, (d) bringing the water of life and of death (cf. Type 551), (e) building a magic palace, (f) choosing a princess from others identically clad, (cf. Type 313 II d), or (g) hiding from the princess (cf. Type 329). Cf. Types 302, 316, 329, 531, 552, 553, 559. — Adapted from BP.

Motifs:

I. L10. Victorious youngest son. Q2. Kind and unkind. B350. Grateful animals. B391. Animal grateful for food. B360. Animals grateful for rescue from peril of death. B481.1. Helpful ant. B469.4. Helpful duck. B481.3. Helpful bee. B451.5. Helpful raven. B470. Helpful fish. B435.1. Helpful fox. B463.1. Helpful sea-bird.

II. B582. 2. Animals help hero win princess. H982. Animals help man perform task. B571. Animals perform tasks for man. H1091. Task: sorting a large amount of grain (beads, beans, peas) in one night. B548.2.1. Fish recovers ring from sea. B548.2.2. Fish recovers key from sea. H1132.1.1. Task: recovering lost ring from sea. H1132.1.2. Task: recovering lost key from sea. H1321.1. Quest for water of life. H1133.1. Task: building magic castle. H1131.1. Castle produced by magic. H324.

Suitor test: choosing princess from others identically clad. H162. Recognition of disguised princess by bee lighting on her. H321. Suitor test: hiding from princess. She has magic sight.

*BP I 134, II 19, cf. II 451 (Grimm Nos. 17, 62); Coffin 2. — Finnish *11;* Finnish-Swedish *1;* Estonian *60;* Livonian *6;* Lithuanian *48,* (554 A*) *14;* Lappish *1;* Swedish *11* (Uppsala *2,* Göteborg *2,* Liungman *4,* misc. *3);* Danish *15;* Norwegian *2;* Scottish *2;* Irish *55;* French *7;* Spanish *2;* Catalan: Amades Nos. 3, 149, 152, 194; Flemish *10;* Walloon *1* (cf. 514A); German *37;* Italian: D'Aronco *Fiabe 24,* (Tuscan 554 a, c, [878], [889], [916], cf. [308 a] *7,* Friuli *5,* Sicilian *6,* Gonzenbach Nos. 29, 83); Hungarian *16;* Czech: Tille Soupis II (1) 317f., 374—387, II (2) 171ff. FFC XXXIV 207—210, 345f. *16;* Slovenian *18;* Serbocroatian *5;* Polish *24;* Russian: Azadowsky *Russkaya Skazka* No. 5, Andrejev *Ukraine 16,* Afanasiev *24;* Greek *24,* Loukatos No. 16; Turkish: Eberhard-Boratav Nos. 61, 215 III, 253 III *3;* India *15;* Indonesian: DeVries No. 184. — Franco-American *12;* Spanish-American: Hansen (Argentina) *1,* (Puerto Rico) (554**A, 554**B, 554**C) *3,* (Cuba) *1;* West Indies (Negro) *7.*

554* *A Youth Rescues Two Sea Birds* [B360]. They provide him with a knife [D1083] and a ring [D1076]. Wooing a bride.
Lappish *1.*

554A* *King of Fishes Protects Fisher* who puts him back in the water. Calls fish by whistling. Performs king's tasks, etc. Cf. Type 303.
French *1.*

554B* *The Boy in the Eagle's Nest.* Boy is carried off by eagle and raised in nest with eaglets. Eagle helps him woo princess and later rescues her from giant.
Swedish: Liungman (GS 553) *1.*

554C* *Dog Warns Master against Buying a Cow.* Cow soon dies.
Polish (666A) *1.*

555 *The Fisher and his Wife.* The fish fulfills all the wishes of the wife of a poor fisher.

I. *The Wishes Obtained.* (a) A poor fisher catches a fish who is a transformed monster and puts him back in the water; in gratitude the fish grants all the wishes of the wife; — or (b) a poor man goes to heaven on a beanstalk and secures in return for his prayers the granting of his wife's wishes.

II. *The Wishes.* The wife's wishes become more and more extravagant (to be duke, king, pope, God) until she finally loses all.

Motifs:

I. B170. Transformation: man to fish. B375.1. Fish returned to water: grateful. D1761.0.1. Wishes granted without limit. F54.2. Plant grows to sky.

II. C773.1. Tabu: making unreasonable requests. Given power of fulfilling all wishes, person oversteps moderation and is punished. J514.

One should not be too greedy. Q338. Immoderate request punished. L420. Overweening ambition punished.

**M. Rommel *Von dem Fischer un syner Fru* (diss. Karlsruhe, 1935); *M. de Meyer *Vlaamsche Sprookjesthemas* 103ff.; *BP I 138 (Grimm No. 19); Coffin 2. — Finnish *16;* Finnish-Swedish *5;* Estonian *16;* Livonian *1;* Lithuanian *17*, (555A*) *24*, (*774) *4;* Lappish *2;* Swedish *36* (Uppsala *5*, Göteborg *16*, Lund *1*, Liungman *5*, misc. *9*); Norwegian *2;* Danish *1;* Icelandic *1;* Irish *41*, Beal XIV 273ff.; French *32;* Catalan: Amades Nos. 3, 74, 166, 167, 777, cf. 168; Dutch *4;* Flemish *18;* Walloon cf. 779 I, 779 II; German *43;* Austrian: Haiding No. 470; Italian *2* (Tuscan [1354] a, cf. [1354] b *2;* Rumanian *4*, (949B*) *1;* Hungarian *2;* Czech: Tille Soupis II (2) 455 *2;* Slovenian *6;* Polish *12;* Russian: Afanasiev *19;* Greek *1*, Loukatos No. 14; Turkish: Eberhard-Boratav No. 70, cf. 178; Indonesian: DeVries No. 185. — Franco-American *4;* Spanish-American: Hansen (Cuba) *1*, (Puerto Rico) *6;* West Indies (Negro) *6*. — African *11*.

556A* *The Good Stepmother.* The hero weeps on his mother's grave and she appears and imposes tasks. His good stepmother helps him. Grateful animals help him when summoned. The stepmother's sister gives magic objects. With these he performs the tasks, disenchants a princess, returns home and rescues his stepmother from the stake.
Icelandic (556 I*) *1*, (556 IV*) *1*, (556 V*) *1*.

556B* *Curse and Countercurse.* The hero wins a chess game from woman clad in red (blue, green). Curse: No rest for him until he performs tasks — go into woods where birds, dogs, and cattle will seize bear. Countercurse. Good stepmother and grateful animals help. Task: to bring corn (feathers) scattered by the wind, to kill ox. He finds the life-egg of giants and kills them. He flees with imprisoned princess on a flying cloak (transformed eggs) and marries her.
Icelandic (556 II*) *1*.

556C* *Stepmother and Giantess.* Prince hidden in room where his stepmother sleeps. Every night she is visited by a frightful giantess. When the prince is discovered, the giantess lays a curse on him with tasks to perform. These are cumulative. He is helped by persons and animals. He escapes by a magic flight and disenchants his half-giantess stepmother.
Icelandic (556 III*) *8*.

556D* *The Crying Child.* A queen wanting to abandon a child dies instead. The child weeps continually. The king finds a new wife in the house of a large-eyed kindly monster. When the marriage takes place the child stops crying. The new stepmother tells her story. Trolls have abducted her, her sister and her father. The large-eyed monster has saved them. The prince later succeeds with the monster's help.
Icelandic (556 VI*) *2*.

556E* *Kind and Unkind Brothers.* Youngest brother gets help of little men or animals who perform his tasks.
Icelandic (556 VIII*) *1*.

556F* *The Shepherd in the Service of a Witch.* Is to drive the witch's herd (her daughters) to pasture [H1199.12.2]. Grateful animals give help.
Lithuanian (*557) *4*.

559 *Dungbeetle.* The princess made to laugh. Making an absurd parade.

Later forcing the noble suitor out of his bridal bed. Cf. Types 571—574, 621.

I. *Making Princess Laugh.* (a) A princess has been offered to the man who can make her laugh. (b) The hero accomplishes this by means of absurd situations into which he places people (c) with the help of grateful animals or (d) magic objects (a rope that binds and tightens, a magic fiddle, etc.) which he has bought.

II. *Rescue from Imprisonment.* (a) By means of the animals or (b) the objects, he is rescued from a lion's den into which he is thrown.

III. *Driving out the Bridegroom.* (a) In the same manner, when he has been refused the princess in reward, he causes wasps to attack and drive out successive rivals on the bridal night. (b) The princess recognizes his power and marries him.

Motifs:

I. T68. Princess offered as prize. H341. Suitor test: making princess laugh. Sadfaced princess has never laughed. H341.1. Princess brought to laughter by people sticking together. B350. Grateful animals. H982. Animals help man perform task. B571. Animals perform tasks for man. B582.2. Animals help hero win princess. B482.2. Helpful dungbeetle. D1411.1. Magic rope binds person. D1415.2.5. Magic fiddle causes dancing.

II. B544. Animal rescues captive. D1395. Magic object frees person from prison.

III. B481.5. Helpful hornet. B481.4. Helpful wasp. T171. Bridegroom driven from bridal chamber by magic. Usually by hornets or wasps. L161. Lowly hero marries princess.

*BP II 454 n. 1. — Finnish *12;* Estonian *15;* Lithuanian *8;* Norwegian *1;* Danish *5,* Grundtvig No. 20B; Irish *67,* Beal X 3f. No. 26; French *7;* Flemish *5;* German: Ranke *6;* Austrian: Haiding No. 25; Italian *3* (Pentamerone III No. 5, Friuli *2*); Hungarian *1;* Czech: Tille FFC XXXIV 231; Serbocroatian *1;* Russian: Afanasiev *4;* Greek *1;* Turkish: Kunos (1887) No. 28. — Franco-American *16;* West Indies (Negro) *1;* American Indian: Thompson *C Coll* II 411ff. — African *1.*

MAGIC OBJECTS

560—568 The Magic Object is Stolen from the Hero but he Forces its Return

560 *The Magic Ring.* The grateful animals (cat and dog) recover it for him. See analysis below: I a, b; II; III; IV a.

Analysis: Types 560 and 561.

I. *Magic Object Received.* The hero receives a magic ring (stone) which will perform all the wishes of the owner, from (a) a man whose son the hero has saved from death or (b) a cat and dog he has saved or rescued; or (c) he finds it.

II. *Magic Castle.* By means of his wishing ring he builds a magic castle, and marries the king's daughter.

III. *Theft of Magic Object.* The wishing ring is stolen (a) by the wife or (b) by a third person who wants to possess the wife. — (c) The castle and wife are transported to a distant island.

IV. *Recovery of Object.* (a) The hero recovers the missing object with the help of the grateful cat and dog who swim to the island and compel a mouse to steal the ring from the thief's mouth, or (b) with the help of a second magic object which transports the hero to the island. (c) The castle and princess are restored.

Motifs:

I. D810. Magic object a gift. D812. Magic object received from a supernatural being. D1470.1. Magic wishing-object. Object causes wishes to be fulfilled. D1470.1.15. Magic wishing-ring. D817.1. Magic object received from man in return for rescue of child. B360. Animals grateful for rescue from peril of death. B505. Magic object received from animal. B421. Helpful dog. B422. Helpful cat. D840. Magic object found.

II. D1662.1. Magic object works by being stroked. D1131.1. Castle produced by magic. L161. Lowly hero marries princess.

III. D860. Loss of magic object. D861.5. Magic object stolen by hero's wife. K2213. Treacherous wife. D861.4. Magic object stolen by rival for wife. D2136.2. Castle magically transported.

IV. D882. Magic object stolen back. B548.1. Animals recover lost wishing ring. Grateful cat, dog, and snake compel mouse to steal it from thief. K431. Mouse's tail in mouth of sleeping thief causes him to cough up swallowed magic ring. D882.1.1. Stolen magic object stolen back by helpful cat and dog. They steal the ring from the thief's mouth. D881. Magic object recovered by using second magic object.

****Aarne MSFO XXV 3—82; *BP II 541ff.; *Espinosa III 67; Coffin 6. — Italian (Tuscan [870] *1*); Czech: Tille Soupis I 208—212 *5*, FFC XXXIV 268ff.; Slovenian *6;* Serbocroatian *4;* Russian: Afanasiev *45;* Turkish: Eberhard-Boratav No. 58; India *21;* Chinese: Eberhard FFC CXX No. 13.

560A* *Magic Ring and Flying Horse.* Youngest brother with rope and nails scales walls of castle where three princesses are held. He lets them out. His two older brothers pull out nails before he can descend. Youngest princess leaves a wishing ring with hero. He wishes for flying horse and escapes. In disguise he works as servant in palace. His brothers marry the two older princesses. Youngest recognizes hero as servant and tells king she will marry him. King becomes ill from the shock. Older brothers search for lion's milk to cure him. Hero obtains milk with wishing ring and trades it to brothers for gold balls king gave them for wedding presents. Hero puts enemy to flight with the ring. He gives brothers conquered flags for

permission to brand them. King consents to marriage of hero with youngest princess. Finally the hero's brothers' deceits are revealed and balls and brand are shown as evidence. Brothers are turned out. Cf. Types 301, 314, 550.
Spanish-American: Hansen (560 A) (Puerto Rico) *1*.

560B* *Cat and Mice and Magic Box.* Witch follows ox into cave and they fall to island of mice. Man locks cave entrance. Witch arranges with mice to steal magic box from man. Mice steal it but man catches one mouse that promises to lead him to box in return for freedom. Man hides cat in his bosom and when mice threaten him, he lets cat loose. Mice return box on condition that cat does not harm them. Man returns home unharmed.
Spanish-American: Hansen (560**B) (Puerto Rico) *1*.

560C* *Doll Producing Gold Stolen and Recovered.*
French *4*, Antilles *2*.

561 *Aladdin.* The object recovered by means of another magic object. For analysis see Type 560 (I c; II; III; IV b, c).

Motifs:

I. D812.5. Magic object received from genie. D840. Magic object found. D1470.1.5. Magic wishing-ring. D1470.1.16. Magic wishing-lamp. D1421.1.5. Magic lamp summons genie. D1662.2. Magic lamp works by being stroked.

II. D1131.1. Castle produced by magic. L161. Lowly hero marries princess.

III. K2213. Treacherous wife. D860. Loss of magic object. D871.1. Magic object exchanged for worthless. Foolish brother (wife) exchanges old object for new. D2136.2. Castle magically transported.

IV. D881. Magic object recovered by using second magic object.
**Aarne MSFO XXV 3—82; *BP II 547; Coffin *3*. — Finnish *11;* Estonian *5;* Lithuanian *4;* Lappish *2;* Swedish *6* (Uppsala *1*, Lund *1*, Liungman *1*, misc. *3*); Norwegian *2*, Solheim *1;* Danish *9*, Grundtvig No. 6C; Irish *44;* French *11;* Catalan: Amades Nos. 109, 178; Flemish *6;* German: Ranke *16;* Italian: D'Aronco *Fiabe 16* (Tuscan 561 a—c, 675 a, b *5*, Sicilian *2*); Rumanian *1;* Hungarian *4;* Czech: Tille Soupis I 6—30, II (1) 217ff. *14*, FFC XXXIV 256; Slovenian *1;* Serbocroatian *15;* Polish *6;* Russian: Afanasiev *5;* Greek: Dawkins *Modern Greek Folktales* No. 8; Turkish: Eberhard-Boratav No. 180, cf. 173 *15;* India *2*. — Franco-American *8;* Cape Verde Islands: Parsons XV (1) 364 n. 1; West Indies (Negro) *1;* American Indian: Thompson *C Coll* II 397ff., cf. also (Cowichan) Hill-Tout JAI XXXIV 374ff.

562 *The Spirit in the Blue Light* (= Andersen's »Fire-Steel«). Three nights in succession the spirit brings the princess to the hero. In his flight the hero leaves the blue light behind. A comrade brings it to him in prison and it saves him from punishment. The spirit comes in response to a light made by a fire steel or firestone found in an underground room. When the hero is to be executed he asks permission to light his pipe and thus calls the spirit to his rescue.

Motifs:

D1426. Magic object draws woman to man. D845. Magic object found in underground room. D1470.1. Magic wishing-object. Object wishes to be fulfilled. D1421.1.4. Magic light summons genie. N813. Helpful genie. D1421.1.2. Magic fire-steel summons genie. K551. Respite from death until particular act is performed. D1391. Magic object saves person from execution.

**Aarne MSFO XXV 3—83, especially 57; *BP II 535 (Grimm No. 116). — Finnish *43;* Finnish-Swedish *5;* Estonian *15;* Lithuanian *17;* Swedish *6* (Uppsala *3*, Göteborg *1*, misc. *2*); Danish *5*, Grundtvig No. 6A; Irish *30;* French *7;* Catalan: Amades No. 220; Flemish *1;* German: Ranke *33;* Austrian: Haiding No. 469; Hungarian *6;* Czech: Tille Soupis I 27, 606ff. *6*, FFC XXXIV 271; Slovenian *4;* Polish *6;* Russian: Andrejev *2;* Turkish: Eberhard-Boratav cf. No. 219, 291 V; India *1*. — Franco-American *2*.

563 *The Table, the Ass, and the Stick.* The stick compels the treacherous host of the inn to give back the table and the ass.

See analysis below: I a, b, c, d; II a, (b) d.

Analysis: Types 563 and 564.

I. *The Magic Objects.* (a) A poor man receives three magic objects: (b) a table or sack that supplies itself with food, (c) a gold-dropping ass, (d) and a cudgel or (e) a sack containing a mannikin that beats an enemy until called off by its owner.

II. *The Objects Stolen and Recovered.* (a) The first two objects are stolen by the host of an inn, (b) by the hero's brothers (c) or by a neighbor. (d) By means of the cudgel or sack the other objects are recovered.

Motifs:

I. S327. Child cast out because of his stupidity. D1470.1. Magic wishing-object. Object causes wishes to be fulfilled. D1472.1.7. Magic table supplies food and drink. D1472.1.22. Magic sack (purse) supplies food and drink. D1030.1. Food supplied by magic. B103.1.1. Gold-producing ass. Droppings of gold. D1401.2. Magic sack furnishes mannikin who cudgels enemies. D1601.5. Automatic cudgel. D1401.1. Magic club (stick) beats person. D1651.2. Magic cudgel works only for master.

II. D861.1. Magic object stolen by host (at inn). K2241. Treacherous innkeeper. D861.3. Magic object stolen by brothers. D861.2. Magic object stolen by neighbor. J2355.1. Fool loses magic objects by talking about them. D881.2. Recovery of magic object by use of magic cudgel.

**Aarne JSFO XXVII 1—96; *BP I 349 (Grimm No. 36); Coffin *10;* M. de Meyer *Vlaamsche Sprookjesthemas* 112ff. — Finnish *78;* Finnish-Swedish *9;* Estonian *26;* Livonian *2;* Lithuanian *44;* Lappish *1;* Swedish *39* (Uppsala *8*, Stockholm *4*, Göteborg *5*, Lund *2*, Liungman *10*, misc. *10*); Norwegian *20;* Danish *53*, Grundtvig No. 61; Icelandic *2;* Scottish *2;* Irish (*564) *216*, Beal X 3f. No. 26; English *1;* French *77;* Catalan:

Amades No. 36, 86, 167; Dutch *3;* Flemish *16,* Witteryck (p. 300) *16;* German: Henssen *Volk* No. 133, Ranke *54;* Austrian: Haiding No. 40; Italian: D'Aronco *Fiabe 53* (Pentamerone I No. 1, Tuscan 563 a, b, f, l *4,* Friuli *4,* Sicilian *4*); Rumanian *13;* Hungarian *21;* Czech: Tille Soupis I 516—523, 525—530 *20;* Slovenian *8;* Serbocroatian *13,* (563 I) *1;* Polish *27;* Russian: Andrejev *Ukraine 11,* Afanasiev *13;* Greek *19,* Hahn No. 43, Loukatos No. 17; Turkish: Eberhard-Boratav No. 176, 258 III *24;* Berber: Laoust 109; India *20;* Indonesian: DeVries No. 187. — Franco-American *13,* French Antilles *5;* English-American: Nova Scotia: MAFLS XXIV 33f., Baughman *4;* Spanish-American: Rael No. 217—219 (U.S.), Hansen (Chile) *2,* (Dominican Republic) *3,* (Puerto Rico) *8;* Cape Verde Islands: Parsons MAFLS XV (1) 99 n. 1; West Indies (Negro) *18;* American Indian: Thompson *C Coll* II 413f. — African *14.*

564 *The Magic Providing Purse and »Out, Boy, out of the Sack!»* The rich neighbor steals the magic objects. By means of the sack the hero compels the return of the purse.

For analysis see Type 563: I a, b, c, e; II c, d.

**Aarne JSFO XXVII (1909) 48; *Krohn FFC XCVI 48ff. — Finnish *63;* Finnish-Swedish *1;* Estonian *15;* Lithuanian *15;* Swedish *1;* Danish *1,* Grundtvig No. 61; Irish (*563) *216;* Catalan: Amades Nos. 186, 192; Dutch *1;* Flemish *1;* German *1;* Italian (Tuscan 563 c, e, m, p *4,* Sicilian *2*); Czech: Tille Soupis I 523f., 525ff. *10;* Slovenian *1;* Serbocroatian *2;* Polish *14;* Russian: Afanasiev *17;* Turkestan: Radloff VIII No. 24; India *6.* — Franco-American *1;* Spanish-American: Hansen (Dominican Republic) *1,* (Puerto Rico) *1.*

565 *The Magic Mill.* Grinds an enormous amount of meal or salt when the man who has stolen it cannot stop it.

I. *The Magic Mill (Pot).* The hero or heroine receives (a) a magic pot that fills itself with porridge or (b) a mill that grinds meal or salt. (c) Only the owner can command it to stop.

II. *The Mill Keeps Grinding.* (a) In the absence of the heroine her mother commands the pot to work but she cannot stop it and it fills the house with porridge until the owner returns to stop it; or (b) the thief of the object cannot stop it and must give it back to the owner; or (c) a ship-captain steals the mill and takes it aboard ship, where he commands it to grind salt. He cannot stop it and it sinks the ship and keeps grinding. This is why the sea is salt.

Motifs:

I. D1601.10.1. Self-cooking pot. D1472.1.9. Magic pot supplies food and drink. D1601.21.1. Self-grinding salt-mill. D1651. Magic object obeys master alone.

II. D1651.3. Magic cooking-pot obeys only master. C916.3. Magic porridge-pot keeps cooking. Against command, mother of owner bids pot to cook. It fills house with porridge and will not stop until ordered by mistress. A1115.2. Why the sea is salt: magic salt mill.

*BP II 438 (Grimm No. 103); Aarne JSFO XXVII (1909) 67, 80; *Liungman SSF III 205ff.; Krohn FFC XCVI 48. — Finnish *52;* Finnish-Swedish *6;* Estonian *6;* Livonian *1;* Lithuanian *4;* Lappish *1;* Swedish *32* (Uppsala *8,* Stockholm *1,* Göteborg *8,* Lund *2,* Liungman *4,* misc. *9*); Norwegian *8;* Danish *26,* Grundtvig No. 65; Icelandic *3;* Irish *62,* Beal III 53f. No. 3, XIV 215, XVIII 94f.; French *3;* Catalan: Amades No. 57; German: Ranke *15;* Austrian: Haiding No. 4; Czech: Tille Soupis I 530f. *2;* Slovenian *5;* Serbocroatian *3;* Polish *3,* (738) *2;* Russian: Andrejev *1;* Greek *1;* Indonesian: DeVries No. 189; Chinese: Eberhard FFC CXX 107f. No. 63, FFC CXXVIII 81f. No. 38. — Franco-American *3;* Cape Verde Islands: Parsons MAFLS XV (1) 238 n. 2; West Indies (Negro) *2.* — African (Basuto): Jacottet 220 No. 33.

566 *The Three Magic Objects and the Wonderful Fruits (Fortunatus).* The return of the objects is brought about with an apple, the eating of which causes horns to grow.

I. *The Magic Objects.* (a) Three men each receive from a mannikin or from enchanted princess a magic object: (b) a self-filling purse (mantle), (c) a traveling-cap, (d) and a horn (whistle) that furnishes soldiers.

II. *Loss of Objects.* (a) The objects are one by one stolen by a princess with whom the hero plays cards. (b) By means of the traveling-cap they transport the princess to a distant place, but she escapes.

III. *The Magic Apple.* The hero eats an apple that causes horns to grow on his head; later he finds a fruit that removes them.

IV. *Recovery of the Objects.* (a) The hero returns to the court and succeeds in causing the princess to eat an apple; horns grow on her head. (b) In payment for curing her he receives back the magic objects.

Motifs:

I. D812. Magic object received from supernatural being. N821. Help from little man. D5. Enchanted person. D1470.1. Magic wishing-object. Object causes wishes to be fulfilled. D1451. Inexhaustible purse furnishes money. D1455.1. Magic mantle provides treasure. D1520. Magic object affords miraculous transportation. D1520.11. Magic transportation by cap (hat). D1475.1. Magic soldier-producing horn.

II. K2213. Treacherous wife. D861.6. Magic object stolen in card game. R210. Escapes.

III. D992.1. Magic horns (grow on person's forehead). D1375.1. Magic objects (fruit, vegetables, charm, flowers, drink) cause horns to grow on person. D1376.1. Magic objects (fruit, ring) make nose long (restore it). D1375.2. Magic object (fruit, nut, water, flowers) removes horns from person. D881.1. Recovery of magic object by use of magic apples. These apples cause horns to grow. D895. Magic object returned in payment for removal of magic horns.

**Aarne MSFO XXV 85—97; *BP I 470ff., cf. III 3ff. (Grimm No. 122); Coffin 4. — Finnish 80; Finnish-Swedish 3; Estonian 23; Livonian 2; Lithuanian 47; Lappish 1; Swedish 11 (Uppsala 1, Göteborg 2, Liungman 2, misc. 6); Norwegian 7; Danish 25, Grundtvig No. 63; Icelandic 2; Scottish 1; Irish 85, Beal IV 398f., V¹ 280f, IX 102ff.f.; French 27; Catalan: Amades Nos. 29, 52, 77, 136, 146; Dutch 2; Flemish 4; German: Ranke 23; Austrian: Haiding No. 12; Italian 7 (Tuscan 563 g, n, q 3, Sicilian 4, Gonzenbach No. 30); Rumanian 7; Hungarian 8; Czech: Tille Soupis II (1) 283—303 3, FFC XXIV 273; Slovenian 5; Serbocroatian 4; Polish 8, (560A) 2; Russian: Andrejev Ukraine 7, Afanasiev 30; Greek 16, Hahn No. 44; Turkish: Eberhard-Boratav No. 174 III, IV, 175 17; India 4; Indonesian: DeVries No. 189; Chinese: Eberhard FFC CXX 253 No. 196. — Franco-American 8; Spanish-American: Rael No. 244 (U.S.), Hansen (Argentina) 1, (Chile) 1, (Puerto Rico) 1; Cape Verde Islands: Parsons MAFLS XV (1) 238 n. 2; West Indies (Negro) 2; American Indian: Thompson C Coll II 399ff.

567 *The Magic Bird-heart.*

I. *The Bird-heart.* The hero eats the heart of the magic bird and thereby receives the power (a) of spitting gold or (b) of finding each day a coin under his pillow; or (c) he will become king.

II. *The Treacherous Wife.* A woman (or his own wife) causes him to vomit the bird heart and casts him out.

III. *Transformation of the Wife.* He finds a magic herb which transforms one to an ass. He succeeds with this in changing the wife to an ass and avenging himself.

Motifs:

I. D1470.1. Magic wishing-object. Object causes wishes to be fulfilled. B113.1. Treasure-producing bird-heart. Brings riches when eaten. D1561.1.1. Magic bird-heart (when eaten) brings man to knightship. M312.3. Eater of magic bird-heart will become rich (or king).

II. D861.5. Magic object stolen by hero's wife. K2213. Treacherous wife.

III. D965. Magic plant. D983. Magic vegetables. D551.2. Transformation by eating vegetable. D132.1. Transformation: man to ass. D661. Transformation as punishment.

Similar (with the difference in magic object and the vegetable) to Type 566. Often an introduction to Type 303.

**Aarne MSFO XXV 143—200; *BP I 528, *III 3 (Grimm Nos. 60, 122); Coffin 3; *Ranke FFC CXIV 113ff. — Finnish 52; Finnish-Swedish 4; Estonian 15; Livonian 1; Lithuanian 33; Lappish 1; Swedish 6 (Uppsala 1, Göteborg 1, Liungman 1, misc. 3); Norwegian 35; Danish 9; Scottish: Campbell-McKay No. 15; Irish 132, Beal VI 270ff.; French 12; Catalan: Amades No. 61; Dutch 1; Flemish 1; German: Ranke 33; Italian 4 (Tuscan [329], [870], [890] 3, Sicilian 1); Rumanian

9; Hungarian 6; Czech: Tille Soupis I 257, 346f., 548ff.) 8, FFC XXIV 291ff.; Slovenian 1; Serbocroatian 4; Polish 10; Russian: Andrejev *Ukraine 11*, Afanasiev 36; Greek 15, Dawkins *Modern Greek Folktales* No. 22; Turkish: Eberhard-Boratav Nos. 174, 175 III, 220 III 16; Turkestan: Radloff IV 477; Buddhist myth: Malalasekera II 68; India cf. 567A; Indonesian: DeVries No. 190. — Franco-American 10; Spanish-American: Rael No. 243 (U.S.), Hansen (Puerto Rico) 1; West Indies (Negro) 4. — African 1.

567A *The Magic Bird-Heart and the Separated Brothers.*

I. *Two Brothers Wander in the Forest.* (a) They are driven forth when their stepmother claims they have insulted her [K2111], or (b) are driven forth for other reasons [S322.4]. (c) They are spared by the man charged with executing them. He kills an animal and brings its blood, etc., as proof of the death of the brothers [K512]. (d) The queen sees the hen-sparrow feed thorns or fish bones to its stepchildren and asks her husband not to remarry if she should die [J134.1]. He does, however.

II. *The Magic Object.* (a) They discover a magic object (bird, fruit, etc.) which when eaten, will make one king, the other rich, etc. (b) Birds predict that one brother will be made king, the other rich. (c) The magic bird is prepared as a meal for another (by their mother) but the brothers eat it by mistake and flee.

III. *The Adventures of the Elder Brother.* (a) The brothers are separated (b) when one goes to look for water [N311]. (c) In a kingdom where the king has recently died the royal elephant chooses the older brother who is made king [H171.1]. (d) Or the elder brother is chosen a king in some other way.

IV. *The Adventures of the Younger Brother.* (a) The younger brother falls into the hands of a ship-owner and is to be sacrificed so that a becalmed ship may sail [S264.1]. (b) He is carried to a distant land and wins a bride. (c) On the return voyage he is cast overboard (but is helped by his bride). (d) He wins other brides. (e) The younger brother, who magically produces gold, gems, etc., is imprisoned by a strange king, etc., and forced to produce gold, etc.

V. *Reunion.* (a) In the kingdom of his older brother, the younger is recognized by his brother and made prime minister, or (b) The older brother searches for, and finds, his younger brother.

India 17.

569 *The Knapsack, the Hat, and the Horn* [D1472.1.22, D1475.4, D1475.1, D1222]. The youngest of three brothers finds a magic object [D840, D1470.1], exchanges it for another, and by means of the second, secures the first one again [D831]. Objects produce food, soldiers, etc. Makes war against the king. Cf. Type 465A.

*BP I 464 (Grimm No. 54); Coffin 2. — Finnish 12; Estonian 4; Lithuanian 17; Swedish (misc.) 2; Norwegian 1; Danish 14, Grundtvig

No. 61G; Irish *44*, Beal IV 228f. No. 2; French *5;* Catalan: Amades No. 192, cf. 105; Flemish *11;* German *18*, Meckl. Nos. 34, 79; Hungarian *10;* Czech: Tille Soupis I 524f., 532—550, II (1) 294ff., FFC XXXIV 280f. *20;* Slovenian *2;* Russian: Afanasiev *8;* Greek *1*, Hahn No. 15; Turkish: Eberhard-Boratav No. 169 III; India *2;* Indonesian: DeVries No. 191. — Franco-American *8;* English-American: Baughman *2;* Spanish-American: Rael No. 225 (U.S.); West Indies (Negro) *1;* American Indian: Thompson *C Coll* II 404, 406, 408.

570 *The Rabbit-herd.* With the help of his magic pipe he calls the rabbits together. He wins the hand of the princess.

I. *Task: Herding Rabbits.* A king offers the princess as a prize to the man who can herd his rabbits (goats). He has a pipe with which he can call the animals back.

II. *Youngest Brother's Success.* (a) Two elder brothers are unkind to an old woman and fail, but the youngest is kind and receives a pipe with which he can assemble the animals.

III. *Bargains for Magic Pipe.* (a) In the attempt to buy the pipe from him the princess or the queen kisses him, (b) or lies with him; or (c) the king kisses a horse's rump.

IV. *A Sack of Lies.* (a) Before finally granting him the princess, the king orders the boy to tell a sack of lies. (b) He begins to tell until the king (queen) makes him stop and gives him the princess. — Adapted from Christiansen *Norske Eventyr*.

Motifs:

I. T68. Princess offered as prize. H335. Tasks assigned suitors. Bride as prize for accomplishment. H1112. Task: herding rabbits. D1441.1.2. Magic pipe calls animals together.

II. Q2. Kind and unkind. L13. Compassionate youngest son. B845. Wild animals herded. N821. Help from little man. N825. Old person as helper.

III. K1358. Woman kisses (lies with) hero in return for his magic whistle. K1288. King induced to kiss horse's rump: trickster then threatens to tell.

IV. H1045. Task: filling a sack full of lies (truths). K1271.1.1. The bag of lies: threat to tell of queen's adultery. L161. Lowly hero marries princess.

*BP III 267ff. (Grimm No. 165 incident C); DF XLV 134 No. 7; *Arts et Traditions Populaires* I 274; Coffin *2*. — Finnish *79;* Finnish-Swedish *5;* Estonian *8*, (1630* incident IV) *1;* Livonian *1;* Lithuanian *13;* Lappish *1;* Swedish *21* (Uppsala *6*, Göteborg *2*, Lund *1*, misc. *12*); Norwegian *13;* Danish *29*, Grundtvig No. 18B; Icelandic *4;* Irish *17;* French *23;* Spanish *5;* Catalan: Amades Nos. 144, 170, 194; Dutch *1;* German: Ranke *51*, Meckl. No. 74; Austrian: Haiding No. 29; Italian *1* (Tuscan 554C *1*); Hungarian *6;* Czech: Tille Soupis II (1) 279ff.,

303ff., 307ff., 319ff., FFC XXXIV 231ff., 236ff. *15;* Slovenian *3;* Serbo-croatian *15;* Polish *7,* (515) *2;* Russian: Andrejev *2,* (*1630) *2;* Greek *3;* Turkish: Eberhard-Boratav Nos. 58 III, 182 III, IV, 232 IV, V. — Franco-American *14;* English-American: Baughman *3;* Spanish-American: Rael Nos. 3, 7, 9, 316 (U.S.); Portuguese-American (Brazilian): Camara Cascudo p. 139; Cape Verde Islands: Parsons MAFLS XV (1) 251; West Indies (Negro) *3.*

570A *The Princess and the Magic Fish-skin.* She gives herself to a fisherman in exchange for a gold-producing fish-skin. She bears a child and is expelled. With the help of the fish-skin she builds a palace. Her father unwittingly woos her so as to receive the fish-skin. She makes herself known and shames him.

Greek: Dawkins *Modern Greek Folktales* No. 4, Hahn No. 109; Turkish: Eberhard-Boratav No. 71, cf. No. 193 *5;* Arab: Littmann p. 339.

570A* *The Lying Boy.* A boy who always lies is visited by a fairy who tells him not to lie or she will punish him. He lies three times and three noses grow on his face. To remove them he must tell three truths.
Spanish-American: Hansen (836**J) (Puerto Rico) *1.*

570B* *The Sheep and the Magic Flute.* (a) A shepherd rescues a sheep from death, (b) runs away, is lost at sea and rescued by a fish. (c) He receives a magic flute, the sound of which gathers the sheep (cf. Type 570); (d) among them is a queen, enchanted by a shepherd.
Polish (404) *1.*

571—574 *Making the Princess Laugh.* (Often followed by: He to whom the princess turns in bed may have her as reward. — Cf. Type 621).

571 »*All Stick Together.*» All remain hanging to the magic object: bundle of hay, cow, servant boy, preacher, etc.

I. *The Golden Goose.* (a) Of three brothers only the youngest divides food and drink with a hungry man and receives as reward a golden goose; or (b) he gets the magic animal by a lucky bargain (cf. Type 1415).

II. *All Stick Together.* (a) To the magic goose the innkeeper's daughter, who has stolen a golden feather at night, sticks fast, as do also the parson, the sexton, and three peasants.

III. *Making the Princess Laugh.* (a) By means of this strange sight or (b) through three small animals or (c) the foolish acts of the hero or (d) other strange sights, the sad-faced princess is made to laugh. (e) In return for this service the hero is to marry her.

IV. *Tasks.* Before receiving her he is assigned tasks: (a) drinking a cellar full of wine, (b) eating up a mountain of bread, (c) making a land and water ship. He accomplishes these with the aid of his extraordinary companions. See Type 513. — Adapted from BP.

Motifs:

I. Q2. Kind and unkind. L13. Compassionate youngest son. D817.

Magic object received from grateful person. N421. Lucky bargain. N102.1. Golden bird. B172. Magic bird.

II. K422. Thief rendered helpless by magic. D1413. Magic object holds person fast. D2171.3.1. Magic adhesion to goose. D2171.5. Persons magically stick together.

III. H341. Suitor test: making princess laugh. H341.1. Princess brought to laughter by people sticking together (H341.2, by small animals; H341.3, by foolish actions of hero). T68. Princess offered as prize.

IV. H1142.1. Task: drinking wine cellar empty. H1141.1. Task: eating mountain of bread. D1533.1.1. Magic land and water ship. F601.2. Extraordinary companions help hero in suitor tests. L161. Lowly hero marries princess.

*BP II 39 (Grimm No. 64) *Anderson *Novelline* No. 33; Coffin *5;* *Ranke *Schleswig-Holsteinische Volksmärchen* II 300. — Finnish *75;* Finnish-Swedish *12,* (571*) *1;* Estonian *15;* Lithuanian *29;* Lappish (571*) *1;* Swedish *28* (Uppsala *13,* Stockholm *4,* Göteborg *3,* Lund *6,* Liungman *2,* misc. *7*); Norwegian *8;* Danish *37,* Grundtvig No. 20A; Icelandic cf. *2;* Scottish *1;* Irish *182,* Beal IV Supplement 1ff., XI 83f. No. 38, VI 169f. No. 162; English *1;* French *20;* Dutch *4;* Flemish *11;* German *87* (Archive *56,* Ranke (571) *30,* Meckl. No. 72); Austrian: Haiding No. 25; Italian: D'Aronco *Fiabe 9* (Friuli *2,* Tuscan 571 a, b, [2002] a, b *4,* Sicilian *2*); Rumanian *6;* Hungarian *9;* Czech: Tille Soupis I 375ff., II (1) 303ff., 312ff., FFC XXXIV 234 *15;* Slovenian *8;* Serbocroatian *16,* Istrian No. 18; Polish *3;* Russian: Afanasiev *9;* Greek *1,* Hahn No. 110; Turkish: Eberhard-Boratav No. 182, cf. No. 92 *9;* India *2.* — Franco-American *19;* English-American: Baughman *3;* Spanish-American: Rael Nos. 314, 316, 317—320 (U.S.); West Indies (Negro) *1;* American Indian: Thompson *C Coll* II 411ff.

571A *Tale of the Basin.* Lover caught on magic basin and left in an embarrassing position. [K1217].

*BP II 40; *Wesselski *Märchen* 216 No. 27; *Kittredge *Witchcraft* 201 nn. 102, 103; Spanish: Espinosa Nos. 126—132; India: Thompson-Balys. — Spanish-American (Puerto Rico): Mason-Espinosa JAFL XXXIV 174 No. 35.

571B *The Himphamp.* Lover of peasant's (blacksmith's) wife wishes to get rid of the husband. Has nobleman order him to perform impossible tasks [H931, H1010]: finally to make a »Himphamp» (fimfarum, wirrwarr). The husband gets help of the devil [D812.3] (or other supernatural being) and by means of a magic word or object prepares the »Himphamp» on which he binds together [D1413] in obscene situations the wife, the lover, the maid, etc.

*BP II 40ff.; *Ranke *Schleswig-Holsteinische Volksmärchen* II 300. — German: Ranke *11;* Hungarian: Berze Nagy (1752*) *1;* Czech Tille Soupis I 375ff. *2;* Serbocroatian *2.*

571C *The Biting Doll.* A girl is kind to an old lady and receives a magic doll that produces a quantity of money. An envious neighbor borrows the doll and it soils her bed. She throws it out of the house. It bites the king when he passes by. Only the girl is able to make it stop biting. She recovers the doll.

Pentameron V No. 1; Anderson *Novelline* II 37 No. 32, 63 No. 49. — Turkish: Eberhard-Boratav No. 172; Spanish-American: Hansen (**568) (Chile) 2.

572* *The Barking Dog's Head, the Striking Axe, etc.*
Estonian *13*.

572** *Objects Given Away Lose Magic.* A king persuades the hero to give him his magic objects, whereupon these objects lose their qualities. The king gives his daughter to the hero as wife; the objects disappear and he must maintain his son-in-law.
Polish (572) *1*.

573* An orphan girl receives three feathers from an old man; suitors from the courts woo her aggressively; the feathers punish them.
Polish *1*.

574* An old soldier receives a miraculous cane which fulfills his wishes (supplies food, drink, and bedding). A woman steals the cane, neglects herself, and when her daughter has destroyed the cane, falls into misery.
Polish *1*.

575 *The Prince's Wings.* Contest in the preparation of the most wonderful object. Wings. The prince buys the wings from a clever workman. The hero flies to the princess in the tower. They fly away together from the stake where they are to be burned. After they have flown away the father offers half his kingdom as reward to the one will return her. The prince flies back with her and enforces the bargain.

Motifs:

K1346. Hero flies to maiden's room. F1021.1. Flight on artificial wings. R111.3.1. Girl rescued by traveling through air. R215.1. Escape from execution pyre by means of wings. K442.1. Reward offered for stolen object (princess). Q112. Half of kingdom as reward. L161. Lowly hero marries princess.

*BP II 131 (Grimm No. 77 a). — Finnish *26;* Finnish-Swedish *3;* Estonian *10;* Lithuanian *12;* Danish *4;* Flemish *2;* German: Ranke *9;* Austrian: Haiding No. 15; Hungarian *1;* Czech: Tille Soupis II (1) 36ff. *4,* FFC XXXIV 308; Serbocroatian *1;* Polish *1;* Russian: Andrejev *7;* Greek *3;* Turkish: Eberhard-Boratav Nos. 136 III, 175 IV, 291 V; India *7.* — Spanish-American: Rael No. 168 (U.S.).

576 (formerly 576******) *The Magic Knife.* A youth steals the knife from the robbers' castle, kills them with it and wins the preacher's daughter. He conquers his rival by means of the knife.

Motifs:

D838. Magic object acquired by stealing. D1083. Magic knife.

D1400.1.4.3. Magic knife conquers enemy. D1400.1.6. Magic amulet in mouth conquers enemy.
Finnish.

576B* *The Magic Knife* [D1083].
Lappish (576*) *1*.

576C* *The Magic Saber*. The hero with the help of a wizard [D812.6] forges a magic saber [D1082]. With it he equips the king's army and conquers the enemy [D1400.1.4.2].
Finnish-Swedish (576*) *1;* Flemish (576*) *2;* Danish *1*.

576D* *A Man Helps an Old Man* [D817]. Gets from him a magic medicine, the drinking of which renders him invisible [D1361.22]. With its help he becomes rich.
Finnish-Swedish (576***) *1*.

576E* *A Girl Receives Drops from a Witch* which render her invisible [D1361.24]. She escapes from many perils.
Finnish-Swedish (576*****).

577 *The King's Tasks.* The three brothers; the oak in the king's castle yard. The king's daughter is promised to the one who is able to perform certain difficult tasks, usually to cut down a large tree. The three brothers set out, and the youngest is the only one who pays attention to certain things they see on the way, or who shows kindness toward an old woman. Accordingly he receives magic objects. With these and with the information he has he succeeds where the others fail. — Adapted from Christiansen FFC XLVI 25. Cf. Type 550.

Motifs:
H335. Tasks assigned suitors. Bride as prize for accomplishment. T68. Princess offered as prize. H1115.1. Task: cutting down huge tree which magically regrows. D1602.2. Felled tree raises itself again. D950.2. Magic oak tree. H1242. Youngest brother alone succeeds on quest. L13. Compassionate youngest son. Q2. Kind and unkind. H961. Tasks performed by close observation. H971.1. Tasks performed with help of old woman. H821. Magic object received. D1581. Task performed by use of magic object. D1601.14. Self-chopping axe. D1601.18.2. Self-playing violin. D1601.15. Automatic shovel. D1601.16. Self-digging spade. L161. Lowly hero marries princess.

Christiansen "'Displaced' Folktales" *Humaniora* (Taylor Festschrift, Locust Valley, N.Y. 1960) 161—171; Christiansen *Norske Eventyr* 87; Coffin *1*. — Lappish (577*) *1;* Finnish-Swedish (576) *1;* Swedish *4* (Uppsala *2*, misc. *2*); Norwegian (577**) *14*, Solheim *1;* Danish *1;* Irish *4;* Dutch *1;* German: Ranke *1;* Austrian: Haiding No. 67; Italian (Tuscan 554 c *1*); Slovenian *1;* Greek *3*. — Franco-American *2;* Spanish-American: Hansen (Dominican Republic) *2;* West Indies (Negro) *6*.

580 *Beloved of Women.* With the youngest of three brothers all women are in love. At the father's death when the elder brothers wish for riches, etc. the youngest [L10], wishes for [L210] and receives the power to make women love him [D1900]. He secures from the hostess of the inn [D856] three magic objects with which he makes a good living [D1470] (clothes, food, and drink). The king's widow falls in love with him and marries him [L161].

Rittershaus p. 204. — Finnish *24;* Finnish-Swedish *1;* Estonian *7;* Swedish (Liungman) *1;* Norwegian *5,* Solheim *1;* Danish *2,* Grundtvig No. 88; Icelandic *1;* Flemish *1;* Italian (Sicilian): Gonzenbach No. 31; Polish *1;* Russian: Andrejev; Greek *1.* — Franco-American *1.*

580* *The Inexhaustible Purse* [D1451].
Finnish-Swedish *2.*

581 *The Magic Object and the Trolls.* Cf. Types 303, 513.

I. *Magic Objects Acquired.* Two brothers wander immediately after birth [T585] and part at a cross-roads [N772]. The first brother meets three old women with only one eye. He takes it [K333.2] and gives it back in exchange for an all-killing saber [D1082], a recipe for miraculous brewing of beer and a land and water ship [D1533.1.1] which may be carried in the pocket [D631.3.3].

II. *Rescue from the Trolls.* (Cf. Types 300, 303). A princess is to be sacrificed to three trolls [R111.1.3]. Red Knight tries to rescue but climbs a tree in fright. The hero kills the first troll and takes the tongues and departs. Red Knight as impostor [K2265]. Likewise next two days with other two trolls. The impostor is exposed by presentation of the trolls' tongues [H105.1].

III. *Second Rescue.* The hero leaves to free another princess from a troll. By means of his land and water ship he arrives just as this troll is to marry the princess [N681]. By his miraculous brewing the hero kills all the company and rescues the princess. He marries the first princess, his brother the second.

*Ranke *Schleswig-Holsteinische Volksmärchen* II 326; Ranke FFC CXIV 365ff. — German *1.*

581* *The Wishing-Hat.* A boy steals [D838] a wishing-hat [D1470.1.13] from the elves. He provides a bird and a horse for the king.
Lappish *1.*

585 *Spindle, Shuttle, and Needle.* The prince will marry the girl who is at once the poorest and the richest [H1311.2]. She possesses marvelous heirlooms: a spindle that brings the prince to her [D1425.1], a needle that transforms the room [D1337.1.7], a shuttle that makes a magic road [D1484.1, D1485.1].

*BP III 335 (Grimm No. 188). — Irish *1;* German *1;* Hungarian *1;* Russian: Andrejev.

590 *The Prince and the Arm Bands.* The youth whose evil stepmother seeks his life finds two armbands: strong. Adventures. Two lions become his helpers. The stepmother has his eyes put out. He is cured and the stepmother punished. Cf. Type 315.

I. *The Blue Band.* (a) A boy traveling with his mother finds a blue belt (two armbands) which gives him supernatural strength.

II. *The Treacherous Mother*. (a) They find lodgings with a giant who persuades the mother to marry him. (b) They plot to kill the boy. (c) The boy because of his strength defeats the giant. (Cf. Type 650). (d) The mother feigns sickness and sends the boy on a quest for lion's milk; by his great strength he succeeds and later turns the lions on the giant. (e) He is likewise sent for certain magic apples in the garden of the giant's brother; these will cause him to sleep so that the brothers may kill him; the lions protect him.

III. *Rescue of the Princess*. On awakening he rescues a princess from the giants' castle, marries her and lives in the castle, until she leaves to go to her father, king of Arabia.

IV. *Secret of Strength Discovered*. (a) On his return to his mother she gets from him the secret of his strength and steals the belt. (b) The hero is blinded and set adrift in a boat.

V. *Helpful Lions*. Helpful lions rescue him and restore his sight with water which they have seen animal use for that purpose.

IV. *Denouement*. (a) He recovers his belt and avenges himself. (b) He goes to Arabia for his wife and recovers her.

Motifs:

I. D840. Magic object found. D1335.5. Magic ring gives strength. D1335.4. Magic belt gives strength.

II. S12.1. Treacherous mother marries ogre and plots against son. F615. Strong man evades death. Vain attempts to kill him. H931. Tasks assigned in order to get rid of hero. H1211. Quests assigned in order to get rid of hero. H1212. Quests assigned because of feigned illness. H1361. Quest for lion's milk. F615.2.1. Strong man sent to milk lions: brings lions back with him. H1333.3.1.1. Quest for magic apple. D1364.4.1. Apple causes magic sleep. B315. Animal helpful after being conquered. B431.2. Helpful lion. B520. Animals save life. H1333.3.1. Quest for marvelous apple. H1333.3.1.3. Quest for apple of life.

III. R111.1.1. Rescue of princess from ogre. L161. Lowly hero marries princess.

IV. K975. Secret of strength treacherously discovered. S165. Mutilation: putting out eyes. D861. Magic object stolen. S141. Exposure in boat.

V. B512. Medicine shown by animal. It heals another animal with a medicine (herb, water, etc) and thus shows the man the remedy.

VI. D880. Recovery of magic object. Q261. Treachery punished. T96. Lovers reunited after many adventures.

*BP I 551f., III 1ff.; *Ranke *Schleswig-Holsteinische Volksmärchen* II 330; Coffin *1;* *forthcoming study by Luc Lacourcière. — Finnish *2;* Estonian *4;* Lithuanian *34;* Norwegian *3;* Danish *12,* Grundtvig No. 134; Irish *38;* French *14;* German *33* (Archive *32,* Merk. p. 344); Italian (Tuscan [328] *1,* Sicilian *6,* Gonzenbach Nos. 26, 67, 80); Slovenian *6;* Serbocroatian *19,* Istrian No. 19; Polish *17;* Russian: Andrejev, Andrejev Ukraine 2; Greek 3; Dawkins *Modern Greek Folktales* No. 27; Turkish: Eberhard-Boratav No. 108 *13;* South Arabia: Jahn 7; India *3;* Indonesian: DeVries No. 178. — Franco-American *29;* Spanish-American: Hansen (Chile) *1* (Puerto Rico) *1,* cf. (Puerto Rico) (590**A) *1;* West Indies (Negro) *4;* American Indian: Thompson *C Coll* II 391ff.

590A *The Treacherous Wife.* Cf. Types 315, 318.

I. *An Enchanted Castle.* (a) The hero receives three magical objects (a horse, a sword, a shirt) (b) for spending three nights in an enchanted castle or (c) through the gratuitous service of a sorcerer or (d) from an enchanted princess whom he has delivered.

II. *The Treacherous Wife.* (a) Thanks to the magical objects he helps the king in gaining a victory and as a reward he receives the hand of the king's daughter. (b) His wife coaxes out of him the secrets of the magical objects, takes them away, and orders her husband killed; (c) the horse carries back the body cut in pieces to the disenchanted castle, (d) or the hero asks that the cinders of his body be fired from a gun. (e) Resuscitated by the person who gave him the magic objects, he returns to his wife.

III. *The Metamorphosis and the Vengeance.* (a) Recognized and killed he changes in turn into the apple-tree, the bed, the duck; (b) as a duck he takes away the magical objects from the wife's paramour and avenges himself on the wife. (c) He marries the girl who has helped him in the metamorphosis by covering a part of the killed animal in the ground, by picking up the splinter of the felled tree, etc. — Adapted from Krzyzanowski *Polska Bajka Ludowa.*

Motifs:

I. B184.1. Magic horse. D1080. Magic sword. D1056. Magic shirt. D1053. Magic cloak. D1361.14. Magic hat (shirt) renders invisible. D1174. Magic box. D1475. Magic object furnishes soldiers. H1411. Fear test: staying in frightful place. D812.5. Magic object received from genie. D817. Magic object received from grateful person. D700. Disenchantment.

II. D1400. Magic object conquers enemy. T68. Princess offered as prize. K2213. Treacherous wife. K975. Secret of strength treacherously discovered. D861.5. Magic object stolen by hero's wife. E30. Resuscitation by arrangement of members.

III. E610. Reincarnation as animal. E648. Reincarnation: man— object—man. D882. Magic object stolen back.

Polish (568) *7;* Czech: Tille Soupis I 212—219 *6;* Slovenian; Serbocroatian *1.*

590* *The Magical Belt.* The foolish youngest son finds a magical strength-giving belt.
Polish (675) *1.*

591 *The Thieving Pot.* A peasant exchanges his cow [N421, D851] for a magic pot that brings him bread, beer, money, etc. from his rich neighbors [D1605.1, D1412.2].

Finnish-Swedish *1;* Lappish *1;* Swedish *15* (Uppsala *3,* Göteborg *3,* Lund *2,* Liungman *3,* misc. *4*); Norwegian *2;* Danish *22,* Grundtvig No. 62; Irish *1;* Dutch *1;* German *4* (Archive *3,* Henssen Volk No. 134); Slovenian *1;* Russian: Andrejev; Turkish: Eberhard-Boratav No. 73, cf. 94.

591* *Unhappy Lower Class Wife of a King* gets ring from another king, transforms self to bird and flies to him.
Greek (590*) *3.*

592 *The Dance Among Thorns.* Magic fiddle, cards, and gun. The judge is compelled to dance.

I. *The Magic Object and Powers.* (a) A boy, driven from home by an evil stepmother or (b) dismissed from service with a pittance for years of labor, (c) gives his money to a poor man who in return grants the boy's three wishes: (c^1) a magic fiddle that compels people to dance, (c^2) a never failing crossbow, (c^3) the power of having his desires obeyed, or (c^4) other magic objects, or powers.

II. *The Dance in Thorns.* (a) With a Jew (or monk) he shoots a bird on a wager. (b) The loser must go into the thorns naked and get the bird. (c) With the fiddle he makes the loser dance in the thorns. — (d) He defeats a giant by making him dance.

III. *At the Court.* The boy is brought to court for his misdeeds and condemned to be hanged. He gets permission to play his fiddle and compels the judge and whole assembly to dance until he is released. — Often joined with one of the following: Types 303, 314, 325, 326, 330A, B, 475, 502, 569, 570, 571, 650A, 675.

Motifs:

I. S322.4. Evil stepmother casts forth boy. W154.1. Man dismissed after years of service with a pittance. Q42.1. Spendthrift knight. Divides his last penny. He is later helped by the grateful person. D800. Magic object. D1761.0.2. Limited number of wishes granted. D1415.2.5. Magic fiddle causes dancing. D1653.1.4. Unerring bow. D1653.1.7. Infallible gun. D1761.0.1. Wishes granted without limit. D1700. Magic powers.

II. N55. Shooting contest on wager. N55.1. Loser of shooting wager to go naked into thorns for bird. D1415. Magic object compels person to dance.

III. K551.3.1. Respite from death while one plays the fiddle.

*BP II 490 (Grimm No. 110); Coffin *1.* — Finnish *68;* Finnish-Swedish *9;* Estonian *13;* Livonian *6;* Lithuanian *52;* Lappish *1;* Swedish *18* (Uppsala *1,* Stockholm *2,* Göteborg *5,* Lund *2,* Liungman *1*); Norwegian *10,* Solheim *1;* Danish *13,* Grundtvig No. 91; Irish *71,* Beal IX 3f. No. 45; French *34;* Spanish *2;* Catalan: Amades Nos. 52, 152, 1791, cf. 105; Dutch *1;* Flemish *3;* German *48* (Ranke *46,* Meckl.

No. 48, Hennsen Volk No. 135); Rumanian *2;* Hungarian *10;* Czech: Tille Soupis I 502ff. *4;* Slovenian *9;* Serbocroatian *31,* Istrian No. 20; Polish *19;* Russian: Andrejev *4;* Greek *18,* Laographia XI 493; Indonesian: DeVries No. 193. — Franco-American *9;* Spanish-American: Rael Nos. 218, 219 (U.S.), Hansen (Dominican Republic) *1,* (Puerto Rico) *2;* West Indies (Negro) *12.*

593 *Fiddevav.* All who poke in the ashes (the daughter, the woman, the preacher, etc.) must keep saying »Fiddevav», until they are released from the magic [D1413.17]. An old woman [N825.3] gives [D810] the hero a magic stone and advises him to go to the peasant's house at night, to say nothing, but »Thanks» [C495.3] and to lay the stone in the ashes. The stone prevents fire from being made and all who try to make it stick to the poker [D1413, D2172.1]. The hero gets the peasant's daughter in return for release. Cf. Types 330A, 571, 571A, 571B.

Finnish *2;* Norwegian *1,* Solheim *1;* Danish *6,* Grundtvig No. 92; Irish *20;* French *2;* Catalan: Amades No. 2068; German *3* (Archive *2,* Henssen Volk No. 136); Hungarian *3;* Polish *4;* Russian: Andrejev; Greek (594*) *2.* — Franco-American *6;* English-American: Baughman *1;* Spanish-American: Rael Nos. 35—37 (U.S.); West Indies (Negro) *2.*

594* *The Magic Bridle.* A boy, setting out, gets possession of a bridle which tames all kinds of horses [D1442.1], a needle which makes everything fall to pieces [D1562.4], and a gun which always hits what he aims at [D1653.1.7]. He lives as a servant in a castle where he wins a princess for himself [L161].

Swedish (Lund) *1;* Norwegian *1.*

594** *Magic Flute makes Sheep and Men Dance.* Type 592 + Motif Q2 + Type 550 IV + inexhaustible money.

Spanish *1.*

595A* *Cow is Sold for Three Magic Objects:* a bean which makes a tree grow immediately, a singing mouse, a machine binding people [D837]. A peasant's son uses these. The princess is promised to the rescuer from the giant. Help from girl captive of giant. Giant is killed and hero escapes by the use of objects. Cf. Type 313. Impostor. (Heart of giant stolen). Recognition by means of magic mouse. Cf. Types 300, 303.

Icelandic *1.*

595B* *Magic Objects from Dwarf.* A youth fights with dwarf to regain his lost bucket and his wishes are granted. He receives a magic gun, magic slippers, and a magic providing purse. He is carried home by the magic slippers.

Spanish-American: Hansen (**596) (Puerto Rico) *1.*

595C* *The Golden Saber.* A boy, while walking with his widowed mother finds a magic saber; with it he kills the murderer who has attacked his mother. He becomes king and toward the end of his life throws the saber away into a swamp.

Polish (597) *1.*

For this section of the Index, see also:

Type 518. — *Devils (Giants) Fight over Magic Objects.*
Type 513B. — *The Land and Water Ship.*
Type 400. — *The Man on Quest for his Lost Wife.*
Type 403. — *The Black and the White Bride.*

Types 313, 314. — *The Magic Flight.*
Type 707. — *The Three Golden Sons.*
Type 330A. — *The Smith and the Devil.*

610—619 Magic Remedies

(See also Type 551. *The Sons on a Quest for a Wonderful Remedy for their Father.*)

610 *The Healing Fruits.* The sick princess is offered to the man who can cure her [T681, H346]. An old woman [N825.3] gives healing power to the fruits [D1500.1.5] of the youngest brother [Q2, L13]. After the youngest brother has succeeded [L10] he is given tasks: herding rabbits (Type 570); making a land and water ship (Type 513), and fetching a feather from a magic bird (Type 461). He performs the tasks, goes and makes a fortune, returns and humbles the king and marries the princess [L161].

*BP III 267 (Grimm No. 165). — Finnish *2;* Swedish *5* (Uppsala *1,* Göteborg *1,* misc. *3*); Danish *16,* Grundtvig No. 18A; Irish *4;* French *2;* Spanish *1;* Flemish *4;* German *10;* Italian (Sicilian: Gonzenbach No. 22); Hungarian *1;* Czech: cf. Tille FFC XXXIV 236; Polish *1;* Russian: Andrejev *1.* — Franco-American *6.*

611 *The Gifts of the Dwarfs* [F451.5.1]. The son of a merchant is betrothed to the daughter of another merchant. When the boy's father dies the girl's parents regret the arrangement and send him to sea with instructions that he be got rid of. The ship sinks but the boy saves himself on an island. There he receives as reward for the rescue of a child [D817.1] or from a troll or dwarfs, magic objects, among them a magic salve [D1500.1.19]. He heals the sick princess (king) and with his magic sword [D1400.1.4.1] overcomes a hostile army. He returns home as a rich man and marries his first love [T102]. Sometimes mixed with Types 882, 930, or 1650.

Christiansen *Norske Eventyr* p. 90; O'Suilleabhain p. 569 No. 611. — Finnish *13;* Livonian *1;* Swedish (Uppsala) *2;* Norwegian *3,* Solheim *2;* Danish *20,* Grundtvig No. 89; Irish *48;* German: Ranke *5;* Polish *1;* Russian: Andrejev; Greek *3.*

611* *Map Produces Helpful Spirits.* The father of the hero's betrothed finds in the sea a map out of which come the spirits which help him. With the help of these spirits the hero becomes rich, entices his former bride with presents and marries her.
Russian: Andrejev (*611 1) *1.*

612 *The Three Snake-Leaves.* A man has himself shut up in the grave of his dead wife. Example of the snakes.

I. *Death Pact.* (a) The hero promises his bride that if she dies before him he will be buried with her. (b) This happens shortly after the wedding.

II. *Resuscitation.* (a) In the grave he sees a snake revive another with leaves and in this way he resuscitates his wife; or (b) she is restored to life in reply to a prayer, on condition that the husband give up twenty years of his life.

III. *Treacherous Wife.* The wife now falls in love with shipmaster and the two of them throw the husband into the sea.

IV. *Denouement.* (a) A faithful servant resuscitates him with the snake-leaves. (b) The guilty pair are punished. — Adapted from BP.

Parts I and II often appear alone; likewise parts III and IV.

Motifs:

I. M254. Promise to be buried with wife if she dies first. S123.2. Burial of living husband or wife with dead spouse.

II. B512. Medicine shown by animal. It heals another animal with a medicine (herb, water, etc) and thus shows the man the remedy. Sometimes the medicine resuscitates the dead. (The animal is most frequently the serpent.) B491.1. Helpful serpent. D1500.1.4. Magic healing plant. E165. Resuscitation of wife by husband giving up half his remaining life (sometimes vice versa).

III. K2213.5. The faithless resuscitated wife. K2213.2. Faithless wife and paramour throw hero overboard. S142. Person thrown into the water and abandoned.

IV. P361. Faithful servant. E105. Resuscitation by herbs (leaves). Q261. Treachery punished.

*BP I 126 (Grimm No. 16); Wesselski *Märchen* 188; Lingman SSF III 222. — Lithuanian (612A) *2*, (612B) *1;* Swedish *2* (Liungman *1*, misc. *1*); Danish *3;* Basque *1;* French *4;* Spanish *1;* Catalan: Amades cf. No. 193; German *3;* Italian (Sicilian *2*); Rumanian *3;* Hungarian *3;* Czech: Tille Soupis II (2) 212—221 *6;* Slovenian *3;* Serbocroatian *1;* Polish *9;* Russian: Andrejev *7*, Azadowsky *Russkaya Skazka* No. 15; Greek *14;* Turkish: Eberhard-Boratav No. 120 *3;* India *2;* Indonesian: DeVries No. 194. — Franco-American *1;* French Antilles *1;* English-American: Baughman *1;* Spanish-American: Rael Nos 227, 302 (U.S.); Cape Verde Islands: Parsons MAFLS XV (1) 198. — Literary Treatment: Chauvin VIII 119.

612A *The Ungrateful Wife Restored to Life.* See analysis of 612.

II. (c) The wife is bitten by a snake and dies.

III. (a) The man and his wife are separated. (b) The husband becomes an adviser to the king. (c) The wife, who has become a prostitute or dancer, pleases the king and is granted a boon. (d) She demands the death of her husband, whom she recognizes. (e) He tells his story, asking his wife to return what he had given her, and she dies.

India *7.*

612* *The Faithful Lover.* A boy in love with a girl of noble family leaves. The girl promises to wait for him. She dies; the boy in learning this (sometimes by miracle) returns home, vivifies the dead girl, and marries her.

Polish *5.*

613 *The Two Travelers (Truth and Falsehood).* One puts out the other's eyes. The blind man overhears secrets under a tree (gallows) and recovers his sight. The wicked companion has his eyes put out or is killed.

   I. *The Blinded Man.* (a) Two travelers (brothers) dispute as to whether truth or falsehood (or whose religion) is the better and call on others to act as judges; the loser is robbed and (b) blinded; — or (c) a hungry traveler can not receive bread from his evil companion unless he lets his eyes be put out; — or (d) a traveler is robbed and blinded by his covetous companion.

   II. *The Secrets.* (a) The blinded man overhears a meeting of spirits or (b) animals and learns valuable secrets.

   III. *Use of the Secrets.* (a) By means of the secrets he restores his sight, (b) cures a sick king (or princess), (c) opens a dried-up well, (d) brings a withered fruit tree to bearing, (e) unearths a treasure.

   IV. *The Companion Punished.* His victorious companion asks him how he acquired such wealth, attempts in the same way to deceive the spirits (animals), and is torn to pieces by them. — Adapted from BP.

   Motifs:

   I. N61. Wager that falsehood is better than truth. K451.1. Unjust umpire decides a religious dispute. N92. Decision is left to first person to arrive. N2.3.3. Eyes wagered. S165. Mutilation: putting out eyes. M225. Eyes exchanged for food.

   II. F1045. Night spent in tree. Hero goes into tree and spends the night. G661.1. Ogre's secret overheard from tree. N452. Secret remedy overheard in conversation of animals (witches). N451.1. Secrets of animals (demons) accidentally overheard from tree (bridge) hiding place. B253. Secrets discussed in animal meeting.

   III. H963. Tasks performed by means of secrets overheard from tree. D1505.5. Magic water restores sight. D2064.1. Magic sickness because girl has thrown away her consecrated wafer. C940.1. Princess's secret sickness from breaking tabu. V34.2. Princess sick because toad has swallowed her consecrated wafer. H346. Princess given to man who can heal her. H1193. Task: causing dry spring to flow. F933.2. Dry spring restored by removal of certain stone. N452.1. Remedy for lack of water in certain place overheard from conversation of animals (demons). N552.1.1. Reason for withering of tree overheard in conversation of animals (demons). D1563.2.1. Magic chain renders orchard barren. D2101. Treasure magically discovered. H1181. Task: raising a buried treasure.

   IV. N471. Foolish attempt of second man to overhear secrets (from animals, demons, etc.). He is punished.

   **Christiansen *The Two Travellers* (FFC XXIV); *BP II 468 (Grimm No. 107); *Arts et Traditions Populaires* I 274; *Gaster *Studies* II 908ff; *Wesselski *Märchen* 202 No. 14; *Krohn *Neuphilologische Mitteilungen* XXVI (1925) 111ff.; *Eberhard-Boratav *Typen türkischer Volksmärchen*

306; *Liungman SSF III 224ff.; Coffin *12*. — Finnish *87;* Finnish-Swedish *9;* Estonian *22;* Livonian *1;* Lithuanian *40;* Lappish *1;* Swedish *12* (Uppsala *1*, Stockholm *1*, Lund *1*, misc. *9*); Norwegian *8*, Solheim *1;* Danish *37*, Grundtvig No. 70; Icelandic *5;* Irish *2*, Beal II 83, V 218ff., XI suppl. 75ff., XVIII 101; Basque *6;* French *30;* Spanish *1;* Catalan: Amades Nos. 101, 233, 2042, cf. 1414; Dutch *1;* Flemish *10*, Witteryck p. 276, *9;* German: Ranke *54;* Swiss: Haiding Nos. 34, 66; Italian (Pentamerone cf. IV No. 2, Tuscan [304] e, [311] a, c *3*, Sicilian *3*); Rumanian *16;* Hungarian *13;* Czech: Tille FFC XXXIV 341—347, Soupis II (2) 164—173 *13;* Slovenian *14;* Serbocroatian *10;* Polish *25;* Russian: Andrejev Ukraine *16*, Afanasiev *26;* Greek *12;* Turkish: Eberhard-Boratav Nos. 67, 253, 272 IV *21;* India *16;* Chinese: Graham 208 No. 151, 277 No. 394, Eberhard FFC CXX 40ff. No. 28, FFC CXXVIII 49ff. No. 18. — Franco-American *9;* Spanish-American: Rael No. 262 (U.S.), Hansen (Dominican Republic) *2*, (Puerto Rico) *6;* West Indies (Negro) *8*. — African *3*.

613* *Secrets from the Tree.* A boy learns secrets in a tree [N452] and heals the sick princess. He is abandoned on an island and is taken to the king's court by a bird. Cf. Types 301, 506 A.
Lappish *1*. — Spanish-American: Hansen (Dominican Republic) *2*, (Puerto Rico) *5*.

613A* *Witches' Secrets.* The boy overhears the witches' conversation about magic objects, which he gets possession of [D838.9] and which help him win the hand of the princess.
Lithuanian *20*.

613B* *The Frog Princess.* The hero sets out to seek fortune. He overhears witches and learns valuable secrets: how to cure a sick princess with leaves of certain plant (cf. Type 432 III); how to rescue a second princess who will be be exposed to a serpent (with a sword hidden in a certain lake), and how to disenchant a girl bewitched in the form of a frog (killing a lion guarding her and taking water from pond in which frog lives [cf. Type 432 III]). The hero finds the roots of a plant and a magic sword. He cures the sick princess; kills the serpent with the sword, saving the second princess (cf. Type 300 II, IV); and after wounding the lion that guards the enchanted frog, gives it water from the pond, and it becomes a prince. The frog becomes a princess. The hero returns to first princess but she has died; he marries the frog princess.
Spanish-American: Hansen (613**) (Dominican Republic) *1*.

613C* *Brother and Sister Heal the King.* A king with seven sons and seven daughters wants his sons to marry his daughters but the youngest son and daughter do not agree to this plan and leave. They sleep under a tree. The daughter has a dream about an ill king who could be healthy again if he takes a bath in the water coming from that tree. The daughter dresses as a doctor and goes to the ill king's palace with her brother and there they give the king a bath in the special water. The king becomes well again and rewards the brother and sister. They invite the king to a dinner. The daughter dresses like a woman and the king falls in love and marries her.
Hungarian (615*) *1*.

614* *Fatal Climb for Healing Plant.* The son of a sick shepherd climbs on a cliff for the plant which can restore his sick father; he falls into the precipice and perishes.
Polish (614) *1*.

619* *Flight from the Sorcerer.* A young man runs away from a sorcerer, with twelve girls; he rescues a vessel from destruction during the storm, thanks to the cross; he defeats pirates, etc. and marries the queen.
Polish *1*.

620 *The Presents.* The haughty sister misuses her gift and loses it. Of two sisters the haughty one disdains to help an old woman. By means of the old woman's magic wand [D1254.1] she is given a castle and becomes a queen. Because of her haughtiness she is driven forth [Q331]. Her sister receives a present that brings her good fortune [Q2]. Cf. Type 480.
*Köhler-Bolte I 134 (Bladé III 41 No. 5). — Danish *1;* Russian: Andrejev.

621 *The Louse-Skin.* The hero guesses the puzzle and wins the princess. The one she turns to in the night. Cf. Types 425B, 571—574, 559, 850.

I. *The Louse.* (a) The princess has a louse fattened and it becomes as big as a calf. (b) At its death she has a dress made from its skin. (c) She is to marry the man who can guess from what the dress is made. (d) The hero learns by trickery and wins her.

II. *To Whom She Turns* [H315]. Occurs rarely as sequel. See Type 850.

Motifs:

I. B873.1. Giant louse. F983.2. Louse fattened. H511. Princess offered to correct guesser. H522.1.1. Test: guessing nature of certain skin — louse-skin. Louse (flea) is fattened and its skin made into coat (drum, etc.). H573.3. Riddle solved by listening to propounder talk in his sleep. L161. Lowly hero marries princess.

II. H315. Suitor test: to whom the princess turns. Rival suitors sleep with princess. The one she turns to is to have her. They vie in enticements.

**BP III 483 (Grimm No. 212); Coffin *1;* *Anderson *Novelline* No. 92.
— Finnish *90;* Finnish-Swedish *5;* Estonian *7;* Livonian *1;* Lithuanian *6;* Lappish *1;* Swedish *24* (Uppsala *4,* Stockholm *1,* Göteborg *1,* Lund *3,* Liungman *3,* misc. *8*); Norwegian *4;* Danish *13;* Irish *2;* Basque (Delarue) *2;* French *17;* Spanish *4;* Catalan: Amades Nos. 48, 145, 234; Flemish *1;* German *12;* Austrian: Haiding No. 45; Italian *3* (Tuscan [315] a *1,* cf. 1536B b, [850], Sicilian *2,* Gonzenbach No. 22); Rumanian *2;* Hungarian *1;* Czech: Tille Soupis II (1) 323 *2;* Slovenian *1;* Serbocroatian *6;* Polish *2;* Russian: Andrejev *1;* Greek *8,* Dawkins *Modern Greek Folktales* No. 48; Turkish: Eberhard-Boratav Nos. 152 III, 153 III, 212 III *4;* India *3;* Indonesian: DeVries No. 196. — Franco-American *4;* Spanish-American: Rael No. 16 (U.S.), Hansen (Puerto Rico) *3;* Portuguese-American (Brazil): Camara Cascudo p. 139; West Indies (Negro) *2*.

622 *The Talking Bed-Legs.* The king purchases a bed. During the night the legs of the bed speak and warn him of dangers or assist in other ways. [D1154.1.1, D1317.11, D1380.12, D1402.17, D1610.17.1, N454.1].

Cf. Franklin Edgerton *Vikrama's Adventures or the Thirty-Two Tales of The Throne.* Harvard Oriental Series, XXVI (1926). — India *5*.

SUPERNATURAL POWER OR KNOWLEDGE

650A[1] *Strong John.* In the smithy; in the well; in war; at wood-carrying; as great eater; etc. Frequently serves as introduction to Type 301B.

I. *The Strong Youth.* (a) The strong youth is the son of a bear or (b) of a woman of the sea or the woods, or (c) he is born from an egg, or (d) is struck from iron by a smith, or (e) is the son of a man (dream) and a troll-woman. (f) He sucks his mother for many years. (g) He practices his strength by uprooting trees.

II. *His Setting-forth.* (a) On account of his enormous appetite he is sent from home. (b) He works for a smith but drives the anvil into the ground and (c) throws trees on to the roof and breaks it. (d) He has a giant cane made which holds fifty cattle, or (e) he sets forth on adventures.

III. *The Labor Contract.* (a) He makes a contract to work for a man; in payment he is to be allowed to give the man a single blow; the blow sends the man to the sky, or (b) he is to receive in payment all the grain he can carry off (cf. Type 1153); or (c) he makes a bargain that the first to become angry shall have his nose or ears cut off or shall receive a blow (cf. Type 1000); or (d) he serves an ogre as punishment for stealing food.

IV. *The Labors.* (a) Threshing grain: breaks the flail and makes a new one of one of the stable roof-beams (breaks the roof) (Type 1031). (b) Clearing land: breaks tools (Type 1003).

V. *Attempts to Kill the Youth.* (a) Going to the devil's mill: he drives the devil to his master's house. (b) Going for a wild horse (or for the devils in hell): the master throws a millstone on him. He puts it around his neck as a collar (Type 1146) and asks that the chicken stop scratching on him.

Motifs:

I. B631. Human offspring from marriage to animal. F611.1.1. Strong man son of bear who has stolen his mother. F611.1.14. Strong hero son of woman of sea. F611.1.15. Strong hero son of woodspirit. F611.1.11. Strong hero born from egg. F611.1.12. Strong hero struck by smith from iron. F611.1.13. Strong hero son of man and troll-woman. Relations take place in dream. T516. Conception through dream. F611.2.3. Strong hero's long nursing. F611.2.1. Strong hero suckled by animal. F611.3.1. Strong hero practices uprooting trees.

II. L114.3. Unruly hero. F612.1. Strong hero sent from home because of enormous appetite. F612.2. Strong hero kills (overcomes) playmates: sent from home. F614.1. Strong man drives anvil into ground. F614.6. Strong man throws trees on roof and breaks it. F614.2. Strong man uproots tree and uses it as weapon. F612.3.1. Giant cane for strong man. Cane holds fifty cattle. H1221. Quest for adventure.

---

[1] 650A in FFC III, 650 in FFC LXXIV.

III. F613. Strong man makes labor contract. F613.1. Strong man's labor contract: blow at end of year. F613.2. Strong man's labor contract: all grain he can carry. F613.3. Strong man's labor contract: anger bargain. First to become angry shall receive blow. F614.3. Strong man as gardener: destroys plants. F613.4. Strong man serves ogre as punishment for stealing food.

IV. K1422. Threshing grain: granary roof used as threshing flail. K1421. Clearing land: axe broken. K1411. Plowing the field: horse and harness destroyed. F615.3.1. Strong hero attacked with millstone puts it on as collar. F615.3.1.1. Strong hero asks that chickens stop scratching. When his master throws millstone on him he complains that chickens are scratching dirt on him. F615. Strong man evades death. Vain attempts to kill him. H931. Tasks assigned in order to get rid of hero. F615.2.3. Strong man sent for wild horses: brings them back. F615.1. Strong man sent to devil's mill: drives devils to master's house. F80. Journey to lower world. H1272. Quest for devils in hell; hero brings them back with him.

*BP II 285 (Grimm No. 90); *DeVries »Het Sprookje van Sterke Hans in Ostindië» *Nederlandsch Tijdschrift voor Volkskunde* XXIX 97—123; Hartmann *Trollvorstellungen* 105. — Finnish *273;* Finnish-Swedish *26;* Estonian *94;* Livonian *4;* Lithuanian *26;* Lappish *3;* Swedish *71* (Uppsala *7*, Stockholm *4*, Göteborg *12*, Lund *5*, Liungman *3*, misc. *30*); Norwegian *35*, Solheim *3;* Danish *61*, Grundtvig No. 5B; Scottish *2;* Irish *383*, Beal II 148f., IV 228f. No. 3, IV suppl. 1ff., VII 66, 68, 154f. Nos. 3, IX 88, 98; Basque *1;* French *23;* Spanish *2;* Catalan: Amades Nos. 66, 2092; Dutch *1;* Flemish *7;* German *157* (Ranke *154*, Meckl. No. 76 a, b, 78, 79, Henssen Volk No. 137a, 137b); Austrian: Haiding Nos. 41, 48, 65; Italian *1* (Sicilian *1*, Gonzenbach No. 37); Rumanian *3;* Hungarian 20, Dégh No. 25; Czech: Tille Soupis I 171, II (2) 56ff., 87ff. *23;* Slovenian *14;* Serbocroatian *3;* Polish *19;* Russian: Andrejev Ukraine *11*, Afanasiev *27*, cf. (*650 I) *25*, (*650 II) *15*, (*650 III) *3*, (*650 IV) *1;* Greek *15:* Hahn No. 75; Turkish: Eberhard-Boratav Nos. 146 I, 281, Anlage C3 *3;* Indonesian: DeVries No. 197; Chinese: Eberhard FFC CXX 64 No. 38. — Franco-American *16;* Spanish-American Rael No. 340 (U.S.); Cape Verde Islands: Parsons MAFLS XV (1) 343; West Indies (Negro) *9;* American Indian: Thompson *C Coll* II 434ff. — African *3*.

650B[1] *The Quest for a Strong Companion.* The youth seeks a strong adversary to wrestle with. Stays the night in a hut, where two strong men live. Upon seeing them, he takes flight and secretly leaves the house. Meeting a plowman, he begs to be concealed from the strong men pursuing him. The giant plowman hides him in his trousers [F531.5.11], and fights the two men. [J2631].

---

[1] 650B in FFC III, 650B* in FFC LXXIV.

*Anderson in Tauscher *Volksmärchen* 190. — Finnish *17;* Estonian *22;* Lithuanian (*650B) *2;* Catalan: Amades No. 2092; Russian: Andrejev *1;* Turkish: Eberhard-Boratav No. 363 V; Chinese: Eberhard FFC CXX No. 209, FFC CXXVIII No. 129.

650C *The Youth who Bathed himself in the Blood of a Dragon.* (Siegfried of the Nibelungen-Lied). The strong youth slays the dragon and bathes himself in its blood. [D1846.4.] He acquires a horny skin which no weapon can penetrate. He dies from a wound received in the only weak spot on his body — under the armpit — where the dragon's blood has not touched.

Lithuanian (*650A) *6.*

650* *The Strong Youth* [F610] *in Service of the Priest* kills giants [F628.2.39] and steals their catch of fish (a whale).
Lappish *1.*

650** *The Strong Youth* [F610].
Lappish *3.*

650*** *A Man Fishes up a Naked Boy* who grows rapidly [T615]. The boy acquires through his singing [D858] a boat and a sword, and is joined by three companions [F601]. He kills a salmon and makes from its head a fiddle with the playing of which he calls together the animals [D1441.1.3].
Lappish *1.*

650B* changed to 650B.

651* *Devil as Helper with Harvest.* Man does not have big enough sheds to store corn. The devil appears and offers to help with the understanding that the man is not to be sorry later. The devil's helpers aid the man in all his tasks. They cut down all his corn and wheat against his wishes. They eat his food and beat his wife. He cuts off the ear of the helper and receives back his corn and wheat. He rescues a princess by going down to hell and promising his ear to his helper in exchange for the princess. They marry. Cf. Type 301A II, III, IV.
Spanish-American: Hansen (**651): (Puerto Rico) *1.*

652 *The Prince Whose Wishes Always Come True: the Carnation.*

I. *The Godfather.* (a) A king chooses as godfather for his son the first man he meets. (b) The old man chosen as godfather takes the boy secretly to a church, blesses him, and gives him the power to make all wishes come true.

II. *The Treacherous Servant.* (a) A treacherous servant conceals himself and overhears. (b) He steals the boy, smears blood on the queen's mouth, and accuses her of killing and eating the boy. (c) The queen is walled up in a tower.

III. *The Carnation.* (a) The boy is reared by a forester. (b) He falls in love with the forester's daughter who tells him who he is. (c) When the treacherous servant comes for him, the prince transforms him to a dog and his sweetheart to a carnation.

IV. *Denouement.* (a) With the dog and the carnation he takes service in his father's court as huntsman. (b) He gets his food by wishing and transforms the carnation to his sweetheart whenever he desires. (c) The king asks for the carnation, whereupon the boy tells him everything.

(d) The queen is released, the servant imprisoned, and the hero and his sweetheart are married.

Motifs:

I. N811. Supernatural godfather. A king chooses as godfather of his son the first man he meets. The godfather proves to be supernatural. D1761.0.1. Wishes granted without limit.

II. K2250. Treacherous servants and workmen. K2155.1. Blood smeared on innocent person brings accusation of murder. Q455. Walling up as a punishment.

III. R131.8.5. Forester rescues abandoned child. N856.1. Forester as foster father. T52.1. Prince buys twig (flower) (enchanted girl) from her mother. D141. Transformation: man to dog. D212.1. Transformation: man (woman) to carnation.

IV. K1816. Disguise as menial. D2105. Provisions magically furnished. D630. Transformation and disenchantment at will. H151.7. Hero's power to transform girl to carnation brings about recognition. S451. Outcast wife at last united with family. L162. Lowly heroine marries prince (king).

*BP II 121 (Grimm No. 76). — Finnish *6;* Estonian *11;* Lithuanian *20;* Swedish (Lund) *1;* Danish *1;* Irish *1;* French *2;* Dutch *1;* German: Ranke *14;* Czech: Tille Soupis II (2) 118—121 *4;* Slovenian *3;* Serbocroatian *1;* Polish *4;* Russian: Afanasiev *6.* — Franco-American *5;* West Indies (Negro) *1.*

652A *The Myrtle.* A woman gives birth to a myrtle. A prince falls in love with it. From it comes a beautiful fairy. Departing for a journey, he leaves her in the myrtle with a little bell attached. Evil women touch the myrtle, cause the fairy to appear and tear her to pieces. When the prince returns he nearly dies of grief. The fairy is recovered and the evil women punished. Cf. Type 702B*.

BP II 125f.; Köhler-Bolte I 429; *Lo Nigro p. 131; Basile Pentamerone I No. 2 (Penzer I 33). — Italian (Sicilian *651) *1;* Serbocroatian *2;* Greek: Dawkins *Modern Greek Folktales* 137, *45 Stories* 207; Turkish: Eberhard-Boratav 214f.

653 *The Four Skillful Brothers.* The father has them trained. Display of their accomplishments. The bird's nest on the tree. The stolen princess recovered. Cf. Type 513, 514.

I. *The Four Brothers Tested.* (a) Four brothers sent to learn trades return home and are tested. (b) The star-gazer sees how many eggs are in a bird's nest on a tree; the thief steals the eggs; the huntsman shoots them although they are scattered about on a table; the tailor sews them up so that they can be returned. Only a red line is around the neck of the birds when hatched.

II. *Rescue of Princess.* (a) A stolen princess is offered in marriage to her rescuer. (b) The astronomer finds her on a rock in a distant sea; the thief steals her; the huntsman shoots the dragon guardian; the tailor sews together the shattered planks on the boat on which they are returning.

III. *The Reward.* (a) Each claims to be rescuer of the princess and they dispute as to who shall have her. (b) The dispute is still unsettled; or (c) it is proposed that she be divided and thus the true lover is discovered; or (d) they are given half the kingdom instead.

Motifs:

I. P251.6.2. Four brothers. F660.1. Brothers acquire extraordinary skill. Return home and are tested. H504. Test of skill in handiwork. F642. Person of remarkable sight. F642.1. Remarkable star-gazer. Sees birds in nest in distant tree. H1151.12. Task: stealing eggs from under bird. K305.1. Thieving contest: first steals eggs from under bird, etc. F661.4. Skillful marksman shoots eggs scattered over table. F662.1. Skillful tailor sews up broken eggs. F661.1.1. Birds hatched from broken eggs repaired by skillful tailor have red line around neck.

II. R10.1. Princess abducted. T68.1. Princess offered as prize to rescuer. R166. Brothers having extraordinary skill rescue princess. R111.1.3. Rescue of princess from dragon. F662.2. Skillful tailor sews together scattered planks in capsizing boat.

III. H621.2. Girl rescued by skillful companions: to whom does she belong? R111.7. Joint rescuers quarrel over rescued princess. Z16. Tales ending with a question. J1171.2. Solomon's judgment: the divided bride. Q112. Half of kingdom as reward.

*BP III 45 (Grimm No. 129); *Anderson in Tauscher *Volksmärchen* 177; *Basset RTP VII 188; Chauvin VI 133 No. 286, VIII 76 No. 45; *Cosquin *Revue d'Ethnographie et des Traditions Populaires* I 62, II 41; Espinosa III 83 ff.; Liungman SSF III 438; Coffin 2; *Beckwith MAFLS XVII 285. — Finnish *14;* Estonian *8;* Lithuanian *1,* (cf. *467) *3;* Swedish *9* (Liungman *1,* misc. *8*); Norwegian *2;* Danish *18,* Grundtvig No. 9C; Icelandic *4;* Irish *83,* Beal II 191ff.; French *5;* Spanish *3;* Catalan: Amades Nos. 70, 103; Dutch *2;* Flemish *4;* German: Ranke *11,* Meckl. No. 66; Italian *7* (Pentamerone V No. 7, Tuscan 402 r, s, [857] *3,* Friuli *2,* Sicilian *3,* Gonzenbach No. 45); Rumanian (562 II*) *1;* Hungarian *4,* Berze Nagy (614*) *1;* Czech: Tille FFC XXXIV 245, Soupis II (1) 66—68, 162ff. *8;* Slovenian *1;* Serbocroatian *4;* Polish *16;* Russian: Afanasiev *8;* Greek Archive *25,* Dawkins *45 Stories* 103f., *Modern Greek Folktales* No. 48; Turkish: Eberhard-Boratav No. 291 *14;* India *10;* Indonesian: DeVries No. 198; Chinese: Graham No. 142 p. 214; Franco-American *5;* Spanish-American: Rael Nos. 222—224 (U.S.), Hansen (Dominican Republic) *2;* Cape Verde Islands: *Parsons MAFLS XV (1) 106 n. 1; Portuguese-American (Brazil): Camara Cascudo 112; West Indies (Negro) *11;* African *6.*

653A *The Rarest Thing in the World.* A princess is offered to the one bringing the rarest thing in the world [T68.1]. Three brothers set out and acquire magic objects: a telescope which shows all that is happening in the world [D1323.15], a carpet (or the like) which transports one at will [D1520.18], and an apple (or other object) which heals or resuscitates [D1500.1.5.1, E106]. With the telescope it is learned that the princess is dying or dead. With the carpet they go to her immediately and with the apple they cure or restore her to life. Dispute as to who is to marry her [H621.2, Z16].

*Espinosa III 84. — Icelandic (575) *1;* Spanish *1;* Hungarian: Berze Nagy (614*) *1;* Serbocroatian *2;* cf. Polish (462) *1;* Greek: Hahn No. 47. — Spanish-American: Hansen (Dominican Republic) *1,* (Puerto Rico) *1,* (New Mexico) *4,* (Mexico) *1;* Cape Verde Islands: Parsons MAFLS XV (1) 39.

653B *The Suitors Restore the Maiden to Life* [T92.0.1, T92.14].

I. *Resuscitation.* Three (four) suitors woo a girl who dies. They each perform a different task. (a) One watches her grave or funeral pyre. (b) One takes her ashes to the Ganges, etc. (c) One restores her to life by a charm, etc.

II. *Reward.* Query: Which shall have her? (The problem is usually solved in a clever way. Example: the one who brought the girl back to life is like her father; the one who carried her ashes to the Ganges is like her son; the one who watched the funeral pyre is like her husband: therefore she marries him.)

India *8.*

653* *The Four Skillful Brothers.* They catch a wild reindeer and a bear [F660].
Lappish *1.*

654 *The Three Brothers.* The father has them trained.
Trial of their handiwork. The fighting master swings his sword so fast that it does not become wet in a heavy rain; the barber shaves a running hare; the blacksmith shoes a horse while it is galloping.

Motifs:

F660.1. Brothers acquire extraordinary skill. Return home and are tested. H504. Test of skill in handiwork. F667.1. Skillful fencer keeps sword dry in rain. Swings it so fast. F664.1. Skillful flayer skins running rabbit. F665.1. Skillful barber shaves running hare. F663.1. Skillful smith shoes running horse. F673. Man can keep together feathers in great wind.

*BP III 10 (Grimm No. 124). — Finnish *3;* Finnish-Swedish *1;* Estonian *4;* Lithuanian *1;* Swedish (Liungman) *1;* Norwegian *1;* Danish *6;* Irish *39;* French *3;* Catalan: Amades No. 103; Flemish *4;* Witteryck (p. 286) *5;* German *10* (Archive *9,* Henssen Volk No. 138); Hungarian *2;* Czech: Tille FFC XXXIV 246; Russian: Andrejev: Turkish: Eberhard-Boratav Anlage A f. — Spanish-American: Hansen (654**A) (Dominican Republic) *1;* West Indies (Negro) *1.*

654A* *The Three Brothers in the King's Service.* Overnight the cobbler makes boots for the whole army; the tailor, clothes; the fool, a regiment of soldiers.
Lithuanian (*654A) *2*.

654B* *The Merchant's Son* learns to play the violin and skillful games, and to write. With the help of this knowledge he obtains wealth and power.
Russian: Andrejev (*654 I) *1*.

655 *The Wise Brothers.* The king is bastard.
Staying at the king's court they are asked to utter three wise words. As a result of extraordinary powers of deduction, they declare that the king is bastard, the roast is dog meat, etc. All proves to be true.

Motifs:

H505. Test of cleverness: uttering three wise words. Youths called on to do so display in their answers extraordinary powers of deduction. H692. Tasks performed by close observation. J1661.1. Deduction from observation. J1661.1.2. Deduction: king is a bastard. F647.5.1. Marvelous sensitiveness: meat is dog's flesh. Animal has been suckled by a dog. J1661.1.1. Deduction: the one-eyed camel. F647.1. Marvelous sensitiveness: meat (wine) tastes of corpse. J1175.1. The cat in the warehouse.

George A. Megas *Laographia* 1956 p. 1ff.; **Fischer-Bolte; *Anderson in Tauscher *Volksmärchen* 178; Penzer *Ocean of Story* VI 286. — Estonian (925*) *3;* Norwegian (655) *3;* Danish *2*, Kristensen *Jyske Folkeminder* VII 20; French *19;* Catalan: Amades No. 367; Serbocroatian *3;* Polish *1;* Russian: Andrejev (925*); Greek (925, 955*) *18*, Loukatos Nos. 9, 10; Turkish: Eberhard-Boratav Nos. 347 III, 348 *14;* India *12;* Indonesian: DeVries No. 304. — Spanish-American: Hansen (655B) (Argentina) *1*. — African *2*. — Literary Treatment: Chauvin VII 159 No. 438, 162f. No. 439, VIII 92 No. 63.

655A *The Strayed Camel and the Clever Deductions* [J1661.1.1].
Four men see the track of an animal and are able to deduce: (a) It was a camel (or other animal). (b) It was one-eyed (grass is eaten on one side of the road only). (c) It was lame (because of its tracks). (d) It was carrying oil, etc., (drops of oil, etc., are seen on the ground). (e) It had no tail. (f) Other deductions.
They are overheard and charged with having stolen the animal because of their knowledge, but all is explained satisfactorily.
India *6*.

656* *Abused Soldier Receives Help of the Devil* and avenges himself on his captain.
Polish *1*.

660 *The Three Doctors.* The hog's heart, the thief's hand, the cat's eye. The three doctors make a trial of their skill [H504]. One removes one of his eyes, one his heart, and the other a hand [F668.1]. They are to replace them without injury the next morning [E782]. During the night they are eaten and others substituted [X1721.2, E780.2], and one of the doctors thus acquires a cat's eye which sees best at night, one a thief's hand that wants to steal [E781.1.1], and one a hog's heart that makes him want to root in the ground. [E786].

*BP II 552 (Grimm No. 118). — Finnish *50;* Finnish-Swedish *4;* Estonian *1;* Lithuanian *9;* Swedish *13* (Stockholm *2,* Göteborg *2,* Liungman *2,* misc. *7*); Norwegian *2;* Danish *3;* Irish *45;* French *7;* Flemish *3;* German: Ranke *6;* Czech: Tille Soupis II (2) 446f. *6;* Slovenian *3;* Polish *1;* Russian: Andrejev *1.* — Franco-American *4.*

664* *The Soldier Hypnotizes the Innkeeper.*

664A* A soldier in an inn pays with gold and then leaves. The gold pieces turn out to be plain buttons. When the innkeeper calls the soldier into court, the soldier hypnotizes the judge so that he thinks a flood is taking place, and he is forced to go through a series of adventures without leaving the room. Returning to his senses, the judge acquits the soldier.
Russian *5.*

664B* A soldier tells tales and his magic forces an innkeeper to believe that he is a bear and that the soldier is a wolf, that they are being chased by dogs, etc. The innkeeper falls from his plank bed and comes to his senses.
Russian *13.*

665 *The Man Who Flew like a Bird and Swam like a Fish.* In a war gets the sword of the king, who gives him his daughter as wife.

I. *The Hero's Powers.* (a) The power of transforming himself into a bird, a fish, and a hare is given to the hero (b) by an old man with whom he divides his last penny, (c) by a grateful dead man (see Type 505) or (d) by grateful animals (see Type 554).

II. *Fetching the Sword.* (a) When he is serving in war, his hard-pressed king sends him to secure his magic sword, (ring) from the princess. (b) By swimming as a fish, flying as a bird, and running as a hare he reaches the castle and gets the sword. (c) As he leaves the castle, the princess cuts a feather off the bird.

III. *The Impostor.* (a) On his return he is shot as a hare by a man who takes the sword to the king and claims the reward. (b) The hero is restored to life by his helper. (c) He flies as a dove and reaches the castle in time to forestall the wedding. (d) The princess recognizes him by the feather.

Motifs:

I. Q42.1. Spendthrift knight. E341. Grateful dead man. B350. Grateful animals. D630. Transformation and disenchantment at will. D150. Transformation: man to bird. D170. Transformation: man to fish. D117.2. Transformation to hare.

II. D1081. Magic sword. D1470.1.15. Magic wishing-ring. D641. Transformation to reach difficult place.

III. K1931.3. Impostors kill hero. B515. Resuscitation by animals. N681. Husband (lover) arrives home just as wife (mistress) is to marry another. H78.2. Identification by feather taken from hero when he was transformed to bird.

Polívka *Národopisný Věstnik* (Praha, 1919) 199 (Tille FFC XXXIV 370); Peuckert *Deutsche Vierteljahrschrift für Literaturwissenschaft und Geistesgeschichte* XIV (1936) 279 n. 1. — Finnish *18;* Finnish-Swedish *1;* Estonian *11;* Lithuanian *13;* Swedish (Lund) *1;* Danish *3;* Icelandic *1;* Irish *7;* Catalan (665 I): Amades Nos. 154, 169; German *13* (Archive *11*, Meckl. Nos. 81, 82); cf. Italian (Tuscan 313 *1*); Hungarian *3;* Czech: Tille FFC XXXIV 303ff.; Slovenian *3;* Serbocroatian *2;* Polish *2;* Russian: Afanasiev *4.* — Franco-American *6.*
(Cf. Type 302. *The Ogre's Heart in the Egg.*)

666* **Hero and Leander.** Prince swimming to visit mistress is drowned and later brought back to life. [T83].
Polish (667*) *2.*

667 (formerly 667*) **The Wood-Spirit's Foster son.** The boy promised to the wood-spirit [F440] receives from the latter the power to transform himself into various animals [D630.1]. Frees the princess; is thrown into the sea [S142]. Treacherous nobleman claims to be rescuer of the princess [K1932, K1935]. Cf. Types 505, 506, 552.

Finnish-Swedish *1;* Swedish *3* (Uppsala *1*, Lund *1*, Liungman *1*); Danish: *4*, Grundtvig No. 16; Flemish *1;* Russian: Andrejev.

670 **The Animal Languages.** A man learns animal languages. His wife wants to discover his secret. The advice of the cock. Cf. Types 517, 671.

I. *The Gift of the Snake.* A man receives from a grateful snake the power of understanding animal languages. He is not to reveal this secret.

II. *The Curious Wife.* (a) He hears animals talking and laughs. (b) His wife demands that he tell her what he laughed at. (c) She threatens him with death.

III. *The Speech of the Cock.* (a) As he is about to submit to death he hears the cock tell how easily he rules his many wives, while the man cannot rule his one wife. (b) The man keeps his secret and withstands his wife.

Motifs:

I. B350. Grateful animal. B491.1. Helpful serpent. B165.1. Animal languages learned from serpent (not eaten). B216. Knowledge of animal languages. Person understands them. C425. Tabu: revealing knowledge of animal languages.

II. N456. Enigmatic smile (laugh) reveals secret knowledge. T252.3. Wife threatens husband with death if he will not tell secrets. T253.1. Nagging wife drives husband to prepare for suicide. K2213. Treacherous wife.

III. N451. Secrets overheard from animal (demon) conversation. B469.5. Helpful cock. T252.2. Cock shows browbeaten husband how to rule his wife.

**Aarne *Der tiersprachenkundige Mann und seine neugierige Frau* (FFC XV); *BP I 132; Coffin *3;* *Beckwith MAFLS XVII 284. — Finnish *74;* Finnish-Swedish *1;* Estonian *22;* Livonian *3;* Lithuanian *34;* Swedish

2 (Göteborg *1*, misc. *1*); Danish *5;* Irish *39*, Beal IV 314f., V 52f.; French *2;* Catalan: Amades No. 185; Flemish *2;* Walloon *1;* German *7;* Italian (Sicilian 3); Rumanian *7;* Hungarian *6*, Dégh No. 27; Czech: Tille Soupis II (2) 426f. *2;* Slovenian *4;* Serbocroatian *21;* Polish *21;* Russian: Afanasiev *5;* Greek *8*, Loukatos No. 6; Turkish: Eberhard-Boratav No. 56 *9;* India *16;* Indonesian: DeVries No. 200. — Franco-American *1;* English-American: Baughman *2;* Spanish-American: Rael Nos. 268, 269 (U.S.), Hansen (Dominican Republic) *1*, (Puerto Rico) *3;* Cape Verde Islands: *Parsons MAFLS XV (1) 118 n. 1; West Indies (Negro) *4*. — African *17*. — Literary Treatment: Chavannes *500 Contes* I 382 No. 112.

670A *The Woman Who Understood Animal Languages.*
I. *The Ring and the Corpse.* A newly married bride hears jackals, etc., talking and learns that a corpse floating in the river has on its finger a valuable ring [N547]. She pulls the corpse from the river and removes the ring. (a) In order to remove the ring she has to bite off the finger. Her husband sees her, believes her to be a cannibal ogress [N342.6], and decides to return her to her family.

II. *Reconciliation.* En route she overhears animals (birds) telling where a treasure is hidden. Her husband learns the truth and they are reconciled. (a) The husband stays to guard the treasure and the wife returns for her father-in-law. He sees her coming back alone, believes she has killed his son and is returning to kill him, and slays her before she has a chance to speak.

India *8.*

670B* changed to 671B*.

671 *The Three Languages.* The youth learns the languages of dogs, birds, and frogs. Through this knowledge he makes his fortune.

The father drives him out for his stupidity and orders him killed, but a compassionate servant substitutes an animal's heart and lets him escape. By means of his knowledge he cures a sick princess or discovers a treasure (cf. Type 613 III b, c) and marries a princess. Later a bird indicates his election as pope (king).

Often mixed with Type 517.

Motifs:

D217. Animal language learned. B215.2. Dog language. B215.1. Bird language. B215.4. Frog language. L425. Dream (prophecy) of future greatness causes banishment (imprisonment). S11. Cruel father. M373. Expulsion to avoid fulfillment of prophecy. K512.2. Compassionate executioner: substituted heart. B580. Animal helps men to wealth and greatness. H346. Princess given to man who can heal her. D2101. Treasure magically discovered. H41.3. Test of king (pope): his candle lights itself. H171.2. Bird indicates election of king (pope). L161. Lowly hero marries princess.

*BP I 322 (Grimm No. 33). — Finnish-Swedish *1;* Lithuanian *4;* Danish *1;* Icelandic *1;* Irish *5,* Beal XVII 231ff., XVIII 59ff.; French *14;* Flemish *3;* German *4;* Italian (Tuscan [335] *1*); Hungarian: Berze Nagy (762*) *2;* Czech: Tille Soupis I 30 *7;* Slovenian *6;* Serbocroatian *3,* Istrian No. 43; Polish *2;* Russian: Afanasiev *7;* Greek *2.* — Franco-American *7.* — African *9.*

671* *The Father Sends his Son into the Woods to Learn Animal Languages* [B217]. The son saves his father from the hostile army with whom a bridge collapses as they are crossing it.
Livonian (671) *1.*

671B* *The Host Puts the Frog into his Spring* to spend the winter. In gratitude [B165.2] the frog teaches him the language of animals, by means of which the host learns that his people are mistreating the animals.
Livonian (670B) *2.*

671C* *Servant Understanding Language of Birds* learns that lost ring has been swallowed by a duck.
Polish (668) *4.*

671D* *To Die Next Day:* A farmer, who listens to the conversation of the beasts, finds that he is to die the next day. The prediction comes true.
Polish (669) *18.*

671E* *A Magic Boy.* .A boy understands the language of the birds and can interpret dreams. A merchant takes him as if in payment for goods and orders him slaughtered. He orders the heart and liver of this boy served him for dinner in order that he may obtain his wisdom. The boy escapes. The merchant is called to the tsar to interpret a dream. He cannot do this. The boy appears, interprets the dream and exposes the merchant.
Finnish *2;* Russian: Afanasiev (*671 I) *6.*

671F* *The Language of Flowers.* Philosopher in contest with a physician plays dumb and obtains liquid which teaches him the language of flowers. With this knowledge he defeats the physician.
Polish (661) *1.*

671G* *Language of Oxen* learned from fernseed in one's boots.
Slovenian *1.*

672 *The Serpent's Crown* [D1011.3.1, B244.1]. The knowledge of animal languages from the serpent's crown [B165.1.2]. Other powers.
Slovenian *15;* Serbocroatian *3.*

672A *A Man Steals a Serpent's Crown.* He throws a garment behind him when the serpent pursues. The cook cooks the crown and learns, in place of his master, the language of animals, or (and) receives wealth [B112].
BP II 464. — Finnish (672) *9;* Estonian (672*) *36;* Lithuanian *6;* Livonian; Czech: Tille Soupis II (2) 386f. *17;* Serbocroatian *1;* Polish *11;* Russian: Andrejev.

672B *A Little Girl Takes away the Gold Crown* which the serpent has laid down [B765.2]. The serpent dies [E714.2].
*BP II 463. — Swedish (misc.) *1;* Polish *2.*

672C *Serpent at Wedding Leaves Crown.* In return for milk which the maid has fed it [B765.6], a serpent appears at her wedding and leaves a crown of gold and silver [B112]. Cf. Type 285.

*BP II 463. — Serbocroatian *1;* Polish *6.*

672D *The Stone of the Snake.* (a) A peasant falls into a pit and sees a snake, which licks a stone; he imitates and without food remains alive. (b) A comrade who finds that he is imprisoned, is charged with his murder. The peasant gets out from the pit with the help of the snake, and frees the accused.

Estonian (674*) *10;* Czech: Tille Soupis II (2) 379, 387f.; Slovenian *5;* Serbocroatian *1;* Polish (674) *5;* Chinese: Eberhard FFC CXXVIII 142.

672A* *The Snake and the Soldier.* A soldier in his lodgings annoys a snake by giving him salted food. The snake pours water into the mouth of the sleeping soldier and causes his death.

Polish *3.*

672B* *Expelling Snakes.* A sorcerer undertakes to expel snakes from a certain region. He succeeds in decoying the king of the snakes, but dies bitten by the snakes, or falls down with them under the earth.

Polish (672D) *11.*

672C* *Testimony of the Serpent.* A girl possessing a magic serpent is raped by a prince. The serpent appears at the prince's wedding and compels him to marry the girl.

Italian (Sicilian *2,* Gonzenbach No. 46).

672D* *Chernobylnik.* The peasant makes the fish-soup from a snake. The driver tastes it and knows the language of the grass and trees. The master guesses this and forces the driver to name »chernobylnik,» whereupon he loses his knowledge.

Russian: Andrejev (672*B) *1.*

673 *The White Serpent's Flesh.* Contrary to warning, the cook eats the flesh of the white serpent. He learns the speech of animals [B217.1.1].

He hears how two ravens converse: »The house will sink in the earth.» Entreats his master to flee and save himself; or he learns where the queen's necklace has been lost [N451].

BP I 131 (Grimm No. 17); Christiansen FFC CLXXV No. 3030. — Finnish (673) *3;* Estonian (673*) *1;* Swedish *34* (Uppsala *4,* Stockholm *13,* Göteborg *9,* Liungman *1,* misc. *7*); Danish *19;* French *1;* German *2;* Slovenian *1;* Serbocroatian *3;* Polish *2;* Turkish: Eberhard-Boratav No. 57.

674 *Incest Averted — Talking Animals.* A princess, abandoned by or separated from her husband, gives birth to a son. The son is taken from her by trickery and he grows up without knowing who his true mother is. When grown, he sees his mother, falls in love with her [N365.1.1], and goes to her at night hoping to become her lover. On the way he overhears animals (calves) talking [N451] and learns the truth.

India *4.*

675 *The Lazy Boy.* »By the word of the salmon». The princess pregnant. The hero and the princess thrown into the sea in a cask. On the island.

I. *The Hero's Magic Power.* The hero gets the power of making all his wishes come true from a salmon whom he has caught and throws back.
II. *He Tries his Powers.* (a) He makes a saw cut wood of itself; (b) he makes a boat or wagon that will go of itself.
III. *The Princess Laughs.* (a) A princess laughs at him and he wishes her pregnant. (b) She has a child and the child picks him out as father.
IV. *Banishment.* He and the princess are abandoned in a glass box in the sea or a cask in the mountains.
V. *Reinstatement.* (a) By wishing, he makes a castle next the king's and takes his wife into it. (b) He invites and humbles the king.

Motifs:
I. L114.1. Lazy hero. F1761.0.1. Wishes granted without limit. B375.1. Fish returned to water: grateful. B500. Magic power from animals. B474. Helpful salmon.
II. D1601. Object labors automatically. D1523.1. Self-propelling wagon.
III. T513. Conception from wish. H481. Infant picks out his unknown father.
IV. S147. Abandonment on mountain. S301. Children abandoned (exposed). S141. Exposure in boat.
V. D1131.1. Castle produced by magic. L175. Lowly successful hero invites and humbles king.

*BP I 485 (Grimm No. 54A); *Kohler-Bolte I 405, 588; Zs. f. Vksk. VI 174; Wesselski *Hodscha Nasreddin* II 214. — Finnish *143;* Finnish-Swedish *19;* Estonian *37,* (572*) *13;* Lithuanian *20,* (*572) *9;* Lappish *5;* Swedish *41* (Uppsala *8,* Stockholm *1,* Göteborg *1,* Lund *2,* Liungman *3,* misc. *26);* Norwegian *18,* Solheim *3;* Danish *21,* Grundtvig No. 127; Icelandic *4;* Irish *32;* French *13;* German *10* (Archive *9,* Meckl. No. 83); Italian: D'Aronco *Fiabe 15* (Pentamerone I No. 3, Tuscan 571 a, d, 675 a—c *4,* Sicilian *2);* Rumanian *5;* Hungarian *2;* Czech:Tille Soupis II (1) 303—321 *1;* Slovenian *4;* Serbocroatian *8,* Istrian No. 21; Polish *10;* Russian: Azadowsky *Russkaya Skazka* No. 26, Afanasiev *13;* Greek *12,* Loukatos No. 18, Hahn No. 8, Dawkins *Modern Greek Folktales* No. 4; Turkish: Eberhard-Boratav No. 69 *3.* — Franco-American *8;* Spanish-American: Rael No. 271 (U.S.), Hansen (Puerto Rico) *3;* Cape Verde Islands: Parsons MAFLS XV (1) 103; West Indies (Negro) *3;* American Indian: (Ojibwa) Thompson *The Folktale* 68, (Maliseet) Thompson *C Coll* II 413.

675* *Birth of Child from Eating Apple.* Precocious youth as hunter. Grateful old woman gives him luck. Princess is made to laugh at his actions. He sleeps with her and disappears. She bears a child, not knowing the father. The hero escapes the king's attempts against him. Gives riddle in court (Cf. Type 851 IV). Explanation of hero's supernatural birth.
Icelandic (574*) *1.*

676 *Open Sesame.* A poor man observes robbers who enter into a mountain

[F721.4]. Uses, like them [N455.3], the words »Open up» [D1552.2] and gets gold from the mountain [N512]. His rich brother tries to do the same thing but is killed [N471]. The rich brother lends his money scales to the poor brother; a piece of money remains in the scales and thus betrays the secret [N478]. When he is in the mountain he forgets the formula for opening it.

*BP III 137 (Grimm No. 142); Chauvin V 79; *Espinosa III 162; Coffin 6. — Finnish 13; Estonian 5; Livonian 1; Lithuanian 16; Lappish 1; Swedish 2 (Liungman 1, misc. 1); Norwegian 1, Solheim 1; Danish 10, Grundtvig No. 129; Icelandic 1; Irish 57; French 5; Spanish 1; Catalan: Amades Nos. 30, 159, 378; Dutch 5; Flemish 5, Witteryck p. 284 6; German 68 (Archive 65, Merk. p. 61, 326, 337); Austrian: Haiding No. 55 n.; Italian: D'Aronco Fiabe 20, (Friuli 1, Tuscan [311] b, [326] 2, Sicilian 6, Gonzenbach Nos. 79, 197); Hungarian 3; Czech: Tille Soupis I 36ff. 13; Slovenian 4; Serbocroatian 2; Polish 31; Russian: Afanasiev 8; Greek: Loukatos No. 19, Dawkins *Modern Greek Folktales* No. 53; Turkish: Eberhard-Boratav No. 179 4; India 2; Chinese: Eberhard FFC CXX 225 No. 170. — Franco-American 11; Spanish-American: Rael Nos. 343—345 (U.S.), Espinosa (N. Mexico) JAFL XXIV 424, Hansen (Chile) 1, (Dominican Republic) 4, (Puerto Rico) 1, (676**A) (Dominican Republic) 1, (676**B) (Dominican Republic) 1; Cape Verde Islands: Parsons MAFLS XV (1) 1, 8, 13; West Indies (Negro) 44. — African 9.

677 »*Iron Is More Precious than Gold.*» Hero lets himself fall from the ship to the bottom of the sea, where with the help of this charm he acquires much gold [D1273]. Cf. Type 910B.

Finnish 27; Estonian 2; Russian: Andrejev 1.

677* *Below the Sea.* Hero finds himself in a submarine kingdom, entertains the king of the sea, chooses a bride for himself, and returns to earth.

Russian: Afanasiev 677 I.

678 *The King Transfers His Soul to a Parrot.* A king has learned how to transfer his soul [E725] to dead bodies, as has his vizier or another servant. The king transfers his soul to a parrot and the vizier transfers his soul to the king's body. The queen determines the truth (she hears of wise judgments made by the parrot). She tricks the vizier into leaving the body of the king and the king recovers his own body.

*Benfey FFC XCVIII 72—82. — Turkish: Eberhard-Boratav No. 171 1; Turkestan: Radloff IV 445; Mongol: A. Montaert *Folklore Ordos* (Peking, 1947, Catholic University Monumenta Serica Monograph XI) No. 60, pt. 8; India 7.

681 *King in the Bath; Years of Experience in a Moment.* This illusion takes place when the king puts his head under water. [D2012.1].

*Chauvin VI 106 No. 94; Penzer VII 244ff.; Hartland *Science* 225ff.; Turkish: Eberhard-Boratav No. 134 1.

OTHER TALES OF THE SUPERNATURAL

700 *Tom Thumb.* Plowing. The king buys the boy. In thieves' company. In the belly of the cow and of the wolf. Cf. Type 327B.
I. *The Hero's Birth.* A childless couple wish for a child, however small he may be; they have a boy the size of a thumb [F535.1.].
II. *His Adventures.* [F535.1.1] (a) He drives the wagon by sitting in the horse's ear; (b) he lets himself be sold and then runs away; (c) he is carried up the chimney by the steam of food; (d) he teases the tailor's wife; (e^1) he helps thieves rob a treasure-house; (e^2) he betrays the thieves by his cries; (f) he is swallowed by a cow [F911.3.1], makes an outcry [F913], and is rescued when the cow is slaughtered; (g^1) he persuades the fox who has eaten him to go to his father's house and eat chickens, or (g^2) the wolf to go to his father's pantry: he then calls for help and is rescued. — Adapted from BP.
*BP I 389 (Grimm Nos. 37, 45); *M. de Meyer *Vlaamsche Sprookjes- themas* 121ff.; Coffin *1;* Anderson *Novelline* Nos. 34, 35, 93, 94; *Espinosa III 110—116. — Finnish *90;* Finnish-Swedish *5;* Estonian *18;* Livonian *4;* Lithuanian *42;* Swedish *41* (Uppsala *14,* Göteborg *12,* Lund *2,* Liungman *7,* misc. *6*); Norwegian *9,* Solheim *1;* Danish *19,* Grundtvig No. 83; Icelandic *1;* Irish *66,* Beal XII 165; English *1;* Basque *3;* French *59;* Spanish *3;* Catalan: Amades Nos. 54, 92, 190, 232, cf. 135; Dutch *7;* Flemish *12,* Witteryck p. 297 *16;* German *70* (Archive *68,* Merk. 121, Henssen Volk No. 139); Austrian: Haiding No. 68; Italian (Tuscan *3,* Sicilian *1*); Rumanian *12;* Hungarian *5;* Czech: Tille Soupis II (1) 167ff. *6;* Slovenian *25;* Serbocroatian *9;* Polish *11;* Russian: Afanasiev *7;* Greek *14,* Hahn Nos. 55, 99, Argenti-Rose I 536; Turkish: Eberhard-Boratav No. 288 *11;* India *6.* — Franco-American *12;* Spanish-American: Rael No. 342 (U.S.), Hansen (Chile) *3,* (Dominican Republic) *1,* (Puerto Rico) *3;* Cape Verde Islands: *Parsons MAFLS XV (1) 14 n. 2; West Indies (Negro) *3.*

701 (formerly 701*) *The Giant's Toy.* The giant has laborers and horses as dolls. [F531.5.3].
**V. Höttges *Die Sage vom Riesenspielzeug* (Jena 1931). — Livonian (p. 73 No. 225) *2;* Swedish *87;* Lappish (p. 47 No. 73) *1;* Danish *6;* Dutch *1;* Flemish *2;* Slovenian *19;* Polish *7.*

702A* *The Man who Set Out to Go to the Morning Star* [H1282], the moon [H1283], and the sun [H1284].
Flemish (702) *1.*

702B* *The Girl who Originated from a Berry, and the Shepherd boy.* The shepherd boy finds in the forest a berry, which he blows on till a girl transpires from it. He builds her a house in the forest and keeps her there secretly. A wolf devours the girl (cf. Types 123, 327C, 652A). Overcome with grief the boy hangs himself.
Lithuanian *12.*

703* *The Artificial Child.* An aged, childless couple rear a crayfish instead of a child, carve themselves a child from wood, make one from snow, and the like.
Lithuanian (*701) *9;* Russian: Andrejev (703) *4;* Serbian: Vuk No. 24.

704 *Princess on the Pea.* A princess is recognized by her inability to sleep in a bed which has a pea under its dozen mattresses. [H41.1].
 *BP III 330 (Grimm No. 182a); Hdwb. d. Märchens I 575b; Andersen »Prindsessen paa Ærten«; *Fb »seng«; Penzer VI 288ff.; Wirth *American Anthropologist* o.s. VII (1894) 367ff.; Arthur Christensen *Acta Orientalia* XIV 241—257. — Swedish (Lund) *1;* India: Thompson-Balys (H41.1).

705—712 The Banished Wife or Maiden

705 *Born from a Fish.* Cf. Type 303. The king's son finds the speechless maiden in a bird's nest. Marries her. The children are stolen away. She is driven forth by her husband. The riddle.

A man receives a magic fish which he shall feed to his wife. Instead, he eats it himself and becomes pregnant. A girl child is cut of his knee. She is stolen by birds but is found by the prince. The riddle: a fish was my father; a man was my mother.

Motifs:

T511.5.1. Conceptions from eating fish. T578. Pregnant man. T541.2. Birth from wound or abcess. R13.3. Person carried off by bird. C400. Speaking tabu. N711. King (prince) accidentally finds maiden in woods (tree) and marries her. S410. Persecuted wife. H691. Riddle: a fish was my father; a man was my mother.

Christiansen *Norske Eventyr* 96; for the second half cf. Type 450, 451, 700; Dickson *Valentine and Orson* 29 n. 2. — Finnish-Swedish *1;* Swedish *5* (Uppsala *2,* Liungman *1,* misc. 2); Norwegian *1,* Solheim *1;* Danish *10,* Grundtvig No. 45B; Icelandic *1;* Irish *1;* Spanish cf. *1;* German *2;* Polish *2;* Russian: Andrejev; Greek *6,* Dawkins *45 Stories* No. 9. — West Indies (Negro) *1.*

706 *The Maiden Without Hands.* Becomes wife of the king. Is driven forth. Gets her hands back and is received again by her husband.

I. *The Mutilated Heroine.* The heroine has her hands cut off, (a) because she will not marry her father, or (b) because her father has sold her to the devil, or (c) forbids her to pray, or (d) because her sister-in-law has slandered her to her brother.

II. *Marriage to the King.* A king finds her in the woods, (garden, stable, sea) and marries her in spite of her mutilation.

III. *The Calumniated Wife.* For the second time she is cast forth with her newborn children, because (a) the parents-in-law, (b) her father, (c) her mother, (d) her sister-in-law or (e) the devil change a letter to the king.

IV. *The Hands Restored.* (a) By a miracle in the woods she gets her hands back again. (b) She is restored to her husband.

Motifs:

I. S322.1.2. Father casts daughter forth when she will not marry him. Q451.1. Hands cut off as punishment. T411.1. Lecherous father. T327.1. Maiden sends to her lecherous lover (brother) her eyes (hands, breasts) which he has admired. S11.1. Father mutilates children. S211. Child sold to the devil. S12. Cruel mother. S322.2. Jealous mother casts daughter forth. S31. Cruel stepmother. K2212.2. Treacherous sister-in-law. K2110. Slanders.

II. F1033. Person lives without food or drink for a year (or more). N711.3. Hero finds maiden in (magic) garden. N711.1. King (prince) finds maiden in woods (tree) and marries her. L162. Lowly heroine marries prince (king).

III. S51. Cruel mother-in-law. S52. Cruel father-in-law. K2110.1. Calumniated wife. K2117. Calumniated wife: substituted letter (falsified message). K2116.1.1.1. Innocent woman accused of eating her newborn children.

IV. E782.1. Hands restored. H57.5. Recognition by artificial hands. H13. Recognition by overheard conversation (usually with animals or objects). Person not daring to reveal self directly thus attracts attention and recognition. S451. Outcast wife at last united with husband and children.

Däumling *Studie über den Typus des Mädchens ohne Hände* (München, 1912); *BP I 295 (Grimm No. 31); *Knedler »The Girl without Hands: Latin American Variants« *Hispanic Review* X 314ff. (Brazil *1*, Chile *4*, Puerto Rico *2*, New Mexico Spanish *1*, Martinique *2*, Guadeloupe *1*); *Lenz »Un grupo de consejas chilenas« *Revista de Folklore Chileno* III, 1912. — Finnish *24;* Finnish-Swedish *1;* Estonian *9;* Livonian *2;* Lithuanian *33;* Lappish *2;* Swedish *11* (Uppsala *3*, Stockholm *2*, Lund *1*, Liungman *1*, misc. *4*); Danish *11*, Grundtvig No. 46; Icelandic *9;* Scottish *1*, Campbell-McKay No. 20; Irish *98*, Beal III 467f. No. 6, IV 46ff., 168ff., VII 154f. No. 1; French *31;* Spanish *6*, cf. *3;* Catalan: Amades Nos. 96, 361, 1850; Flemish *2;* German *25* (Archive *23*, Merk. p. 52, Meckl. No. 83); Austrian: Haiding No. 47; Italian: D'Aronco *Fiabe 70* (Pentamerone III No. 2, Tuscan *5*, Sicilian *1*, Gonzenbach No. 24); Rumanian *11*, Sainenu 690; Hungarian *10*, Dégh No. 28; Czech: Tille Soupis I 490ff. *9;* Slovenian *8;* Serbocroatian *14;* Polish *18*, (706 A = 706 III) *1;* Russian: Andrejev *Ukraine 22*, Afanasiev *35;* Greek *6;* Turkish: Eberhard-Boratav No. 246 *1;* India *2*. — Franco-American *30;* Spanish-American: Rael Nos. 126, 127, 128 (U.S.), Hansen (Chile) *3*, (Cuba) *2*, (Dominican Republic) *1*, (Puerto Rico) *2*, cf. (706B) (Puerto Rico) *1;* Cape Verde Islands: *Parsons MAFLS XV (1) 180 n. 1; West Indies (Negro) *5*. — African *3*.

706A *Help of the Virgin's Statue.* An infant girl is found and adopted by a priest. When she is grown he wishes to seduce her but she is helped escape by a statue of the Virgin. The girl is found in a house in the woods by a king who marries her. — Priest for revenge kills her two children and she is accused of the murder. Later she is cleared by Virgin.

BP I 18. — Italian (Sicilian 706* *3*, Gonzenbach No. 25).

706B *Present to the Lover.* Maiden sends to her lecherous lover (brother) her eyes (hands, breasts) which he has admired. [T327.1].

****Williamson *Philological Quarterly* XI 149; *BP I 303; *P. Toschi *Fenomenologie del Canto popolare* (Rome, 1947) 226ff., 302; *A. Pallnera »La donzella que se saco los ojos« *Revista de la bibliotica, archivos y museo de ajuntamento de Madrid* VIII (1931) 117ff.; *Crane *Vitry* 158 No. 57; *Penzer III 20f.; Herbert III 72, 611; Hervieux IV No. 120; Alphabet No. 136; *Bin Gorion *Born Judas* IV 175, 283; Pauli (ed. Bolte) Nos. 11, 12; Krappe *Bulletin Hispanique* XXXIX 40; Nouvelles de Sens No. 12. — Spanish Exempla: Keller (T327.1); Italian: Basile *Pentamerone* III No. 2; N. A. Indian: *Thompson *Tales* 273 n. 6. — Africa (Bongola): Weeks 122.

706C *Lecherous Father as Queen's Persecutor.* Children of a queen are killed by her father, who wants to marry her. False murder accusation (knife under pillow, etc.). Queen's husband believes queen has killed children and condemns her. Miracle: children resuscitated. Innocence established. Miraculous palace. Reconciliation.

Greek *10*, Hahn I 70 No. 2, 266 No. 48.

707 *The Three Golden Sons.* The queen bears marvelous children. They are stolen away. The queen is banished. The quest for the speaking bird, the singing tree, and the water of life.

I. *Wishing for a Husband.* (a) Three girls make a boast that if they marry the king they will have triplets with golden hair, a chain around the neck, and a star on the forehead. (b) The king overhears the youngest and marries her.

II. *Calumniated Wife.* (s) The elder sisters substitute a dog for the newborn children and accuse the wife of giving birth to the dog. (b) The children are thrown into a stream but rescued by a miller (or a fisher). (c) The wife is imprisoned.

III. *The Children's Adventures.* (a) After the children have grown up, the eldest son sets out to find his father or (b) to seek the speaking bird, the singing tree, and the water of life. — (c) He and his brother, who goes for him, both fail and are transformed to marble columns. (d) The sister by courtesy and obedience to an old woman succeeds in rescuing them and bringing back the magic objects.

IV. *Restoration of Children.* (a) The attention of the king is drawn to the children and the magic objects. (b) The bird of truth reveals to him the whole history. (c) The children and the wife are restored; the sister-in-law is punished.

Motifs:

I. N201. Wish for exalted husband realized. H71.2. Gold (silver) hairs as sign of royalty. H71.3. Pearls from hair as sign of royalty. H71.7. Child born with chain around neck: sign of royalty. H71.1. Star on forehead as sign of royalty. N455.4. King overhears girl's boast as to what she should do as queen. L50. Victorious youngest daughter. L162. Lowly heroine marries prince (king).

II. K2212. Treacherous sister. K2110.1. Calumniated wife. S410. Persecuted wife. K2115. Animal-birth slander. S430. Disposal of cast-off wife. S301. Children exposed. S142. Person thrown into the water and abandoned. R131.2. Miller rescues abandoned child. R131.4. Fisher rescues abandoned child.

III. H1381.2.2.1. Son seeks unknown father. H1320. Quest for miraculous objects or animals. H1331.1.1. Quest for Bird of Truth. H1333.1.1. Quest for singing tree. H1321.5. Quest for singing water. H1321.4. Quest for dancing water. H1321.1. Quest for Water of Life (water which will resuscitate). D231.2. Transformation: man to marble column. Q2. Kind and unkind. N825.3. Old woman helper. R158. Sister rescues brother(s).

IV. H151.1. Attention drawn by magic objects: recognition follows. K1911.3.1. Substitution of false bride revealed by animal. B131.2. Bird reveals treachery. Q261. Treachery punished. S451. Outcast wife at last united with husband and children.

*BP II 380 (Grimm No. 96); *JAFL XXVII 230; Coffin *7;* Anderson *Novelline* Nos. 9, 50; *Espinosa II 446—460; Straparola IV No. 3. — Finnish *73;* Finnish-Swedish *4;* Estonian *22;* Livonian *3;* Lithuanian *65;* Swedish *28* (Uppsala *11,* Stockholm *2,* Göteborg *4,* Lund *1,* Liungman *2,* misc. *8*); Norwegian *1;* Danish *20,* Grundtvig No. 44; Icelandic *1;* Irish *92,* Beal II 396ff.; Basque *1;* French *29;* Spanish *7;* Catalan: Amades Nos. 98, 153, 177, 180, cf. No. 102; Flemish *3;* German *25* (Archive *23,* Meckl. Nos. 53, 84); Austrian: Haiding No. 27; Italian: D'Aronco *Fiabe 70* (Tuscan 707 a—h, l, m, q, r, t—z, 709 m *18,* Sicilian *7*); Rumanian *22,* Sainenu 391; Hungarian *17,* Berze Nagy 707 I*, 452* *10;* Czech: Tille Soupis I 499ff., II (1) 192ff. *18;* Slovenian *11;* Serbocroatian *6;* Polish *14;* Russian: Azadowsky *Russkaya Skazka* No. 2, Andrejev *Ukraine 11,* Afanasiev *50;* Albanian: Lambertz 156; Greek Archive *40,* Loukatos No. 20, *Laographia* X 381ff., XI 427ff., XVI 199ff.; Turkish: Eberhard-Boratav No. 239, cf. 223, 306 III *55;* India *44.* — Franco-American *14;* Spanish-American: Rael Nos. 123—125 (U.S.), Hansen (Chile) *2,* (Dominican Republic) *4;* Cape Verde Islands: Parsons MAFLS XV (1) 296 n. 1, cf. 289 n. 1; West Indies (Negro) *15;* American Indian: Thompson *C Coll* II 387ff. — African *10.*

707A *Introduction to Three Golden Sons: Ogre Schoolmaster.* One girl does not tell of his eating the children. He leaves her in front of palace. Cf. Type 894.

Greek *4.*

707A* *Virgin to Bear Child.* Girl boasts that if she marries a prince [N455.4] she will bear a child while still a virgin. To test this the prince confines her to a tower. She manages to get a peasant's child as substitute, satisfies the prince and marries him.

Greek (874*) *1*, Hahn No. 112.

707B* *The Wandering Husband.* A prince runs away from home, defeats his rival, and marries a beautiful girl. After having been parted from his wife for a while, he returns home just as she is about to marry another man. While they are parted again, he wants to marry another woman. But then the children of his first wife arrive and tell him about their mother.

Russian: Andrejev *3*.

708 *The Wonder-Child.* Through the magic power of her evil stepmother, a princess gives birth to a monster and is banished. The monster aids her till everything turns out well. The monster is transformed into a prince. Cf. Type 711.

I. *The Monster Child.* (a) Through the enchantments of a witch or (b) the power of a magic apple (or the like) fed her by her stepmother, a maiden gives birth to a monster.

II. *Banishment.* (a) The girl is driven forth into the forest or (b) abandoned in a boat on the sea. (c) The monstrous son shows that he has miraculous powers.

III. *The Son's Help.* (a) The son helps his mother in her work of spinning at a castle. (b) He goes with a prince in search of a bride or on a hunt; they are cast into prison; the boy promises to rescue the prince if the latter will marry his mother. Though the prince imagines the mother must be a monster, he consents.

IV. *Transformation.* (a) The prince marries the mother and rejoices that she is like other people. (b) At the wedding the prince is disenchanted when his mother calls him her son or when his head is cut off.

Motifs:

I. G200. Witch. L112.1. Monster as hero. T511.1.1. Conception from eating apple. T513. Conception by wish. T550. Monstrous births. S31. Cruel stepmother.

II. S410. Persecuted wife. S441. Cast-off wife and child abandoned in forest. S431.1. Cast-off wife and child exposed in boat. D1717.1. Magic power of monster child.

III. H1092. Task: spinning impossible amount in one night. D741. Disenchantment of monster when prince promises to marry the monster's mother. The prince images falsely that the mother is also a monster.

IV. D741.1. Disenchantment of monster when mother acknowledges him as son. D711. Disenchantment by decapitation. L162. Lowly heroine marries prince (king).

*BP II 236. — Finnish-Swedish *1;* Lithuanian *1;* Swedish *9* (Uppsala *3,* Göteborg *1,* Liungman *1,* misc. *4*); Norwegian *9,* Solheim *1;* Danish *21,* Grundtvig No. 32; Irish *14;* French *6;* German *5;* Austrian: Haiding

p. 470; Italian (Tuscan 709i) *1;* Hungarian *6;* Czech: Tille Soupis II (1) 173ff. *6;* Slovenian *1;* Serbocroatian *1;* Polish *3;* Russian: Andrejev. — Franco-American *17.*

708A* *The Rose-girl and the Queen.* Girl from rose replaces queen and banishes her. Queen's son destroys rose-girl by magic and restores his mother. [D431.1.1, E765.1.1].
Coffin *1.* — Spanish (708A*) *2;* Catalan: Amades No. 128.

709 *Snow-White.* The wicked stepmother seeks to kill the maiden. At the dwarfs' (robbers') house, where the prince finds the maiden and marries her.

I. *Snow-White and her Stepmother.* (a) Snow-White has skin like snow, and lips like blood. (b) A magic mirror tells her stepmother that Snow-White is more beautiful than she.

II. *Snow-White's Rescue.* (a) The stepmother orders a hunter to kill her, but he substitutes an animal's heart and saves her, or (b) she sends Snow-White to the house of the dwarfs (or robbers) expecting her to be killed. The dwarfs adopt her as sister.

III. *The Poisoning.* (a) The stepmother now seeks to kill her by means of poisoned lace, (b) a poisoned comb and (c) a poisoned apple.

IV. *Help of the Dwarfs.* (a) The dwarfs succeed in reviving her from the first two poisonings but fail with the third. (b) They lay the maiden in a glass coffin.

V. *Her Revival.* A prince sees her and resuscitates her. The stepmother is made to dance herself to death in red hot shoes.

Motifs:

I. Z65.1. Red as blood, white as snow. L55. Stepdaughter heroine. M312.4. Prophecy: superb beauty for girl. D1311.6.3. Sun answers questions. D1311.2. Mirror answers questions. D1323.1. Magic clairvoyant mirror.

II. S31. Cruel stepmother. K2212. Treacherous sister. S322.2. Jealous mother casts daughter forth. K512.2. Compassionate executioner: substituted heart. F451.5.1.2. Dwarfs adopt girl as sister. N812. Giant or ogre as helper. N831.1. Mysterious housekeeper. Men find their house mysteriously put in order. Discover that it is done by a girl (frequently an animal transformed into a girl).

III. K950. Various kinds of treacherous murder. S111. Murder by poisoning. D1364.16. Hairpin causes magic sleep. D1364.9. Comb causes magic sleep. D1364.4.1. Apple causes magic sleep. S111.1. Murder with poisoned bread. S111.2. Murder with poisoned lace. S111.3. Murder with poisoned comb. S111.4. Murder with poisoned apple.

IV. F852.1. Glass coffin. F852.2. Golden coffin. F852.3. Silver coffin.

V. N711. King (prince) accidentally finds maiden in woods (tree) and marries her. E21.1. Resuscitation by removal of poisoned apple. By shaking loose the apple from the throat of the poisoned girl the prince brings her to life. E21.3. Resuscitation by removal of poisoned comb. Q414.4. Punishment: dancing to death in red-hot shoes.

**Böklen *Sneewittchenstudien* (Leipzig, 1915); *BP I 450 (Grimm No. 53); *Arts et Traditions Populaires* I 281; *Liungman SSF III 242, 439; *Espinosa II 431—441; Coffin *5;* *Dickson *Valentine and Orson* 29 n. 2. — Finnish *20;* Finnish-Swedish *2;* Estonian *8;* Livonian *9;* Lithuanian *29;* Swedish *35* (Uppsala *7,* Stockholm *2,* Göteborg *6,* Lund *2,* Liungman *7,* misc. *11*); Norwegian *7,* Solheim *1;* Danish *13,* Grundtvig No. 120; Icelandic *11;* Irish *55,* Beal VII 154f. No. 2; French *9;* Spanish *3;* Catalan: Amades Nos. 7, 8, 12, 28; Dutch *1;* Flemish *5;* German *11;* Italian: D'Aronco *Fiabe 42* (Pentamerone II No. 8, Tuscan 709 a—h, l, m, o, p, r, s, [316] a, b *16,* Sicilian *6,* Gonzenbach Nos. 2, 3, 4); Rumanian *7;* Hungarian *12,* cf. Berzy Nagy (404*); Czech: Tille Soupis II (2) 103ff. *2;* Slovenian *5;* Serbocroatian *14;* Polish *10;* Russian: Andrejev *Ukraine 16,* Afanasiev *19;* Greek *24, Laographia* XI 449, Hahn No. 103, Dawkins *45 Stories* Nos. 36, 37, *Modern Greek Folktales* No. 20; Turkish: Eberhard-Boratav Nos. 60 IV, 152 IV, 167, Anlage A b, cf. 159. — Franco-American *12,* Louisiana: Claudel *Southern Folklore Quarterly* VI 153ff., French Antilles *1;* Spanish-American: Rael Nos. 121, 122 (U.S.), Hansen (Dominican Republic) *2,* (Puerto Rico) *9;* West Indies (Negro) *14.* — African *5.*

709A *The Stork's Daughter.*

I. *The Abandoned Child.* A baby girl is abandoned [S301] by her parents in the fields or forest [S143] and reared by two storks [S352]. They leave her safely in a tree, but her fire goes out. She goes in search of fire and is given some by an ogress, but she is trailed by the ashes she has left [J1146]. The ogres try to enter, but she is warned by her pets [B521], a dog, a cat, etc.

II. *The Poisoned Nails.* The ogres put poisoned nails by the door. The maiden is scratched by one and falls into a seemingly lifeless swoon [D1364.2]. (a) The storks remove the nails. (b) Her body is put in a glass case [F852].

III. *Resuscitation.* A prince finds her, removes the nail so that she is restored to life [E21], and marries her.

India *9.*

710 *Our Lady's Child.* A girl comes into possession of her foster mother through an unwitting promise to her father. The girl falsely denies having looked into a forbidden room, and becomes dumb. She becomes the wife of the king. The Virgin Mary (a witch, the wicked stepmother) steals away the children. Finally the queen acknowledges her guilt.

Motifs:

S240. Children unwittingly promised (sold). S242. Child unwittingly promised: »what you have at home.» V271. Virgin Mary as foster mother. C611. Forbidden chamber. Person allowed to enter all chambers of house except one. J213. Choice: loss of beauty or speech: latter chosen. Q451.3. Loss of speech as punishment. C944. Dumbness as punishment for breaking tabu. N711.1. King (prince) finds maiden in woods (tree) and marries her. G261. Witch steals children. K2116.1.1. Innocent woman accused of eating her new-born children. H13.2. Recognition by overheard conversation with objects. D2025.1. Speech magically recovered on execution stake. H215. Magic manifestation at execution proves innocence.

**E. K. Seifert *Untersuchung zu Grimms Märchen Das Marienkind* (Diss. München-typescript); Coffin *1;* *BP I 13 (Grimm No. 3); *Espinosa II 345. — Finnish *5;* Finnish-Swedish *6;* Estonian *4;* Lithuanian *21;* Swedish *39* (Uppsala *9,* Lund *1,* Liungman *4,* misc. *25*); Norwegian *8,* Solheim *1;* Danish *12,* Grundtvig No. 45A; Icelandic *1;* Irish *47;* French *4;* Spanish *1;* Flemish *2;* German *21* (Archive *20,* Meckl. No. 85); Austrian: Haiding No. 7; Italian *5* (Pentamerone I No. 8, Tuscan [917] a, b *2,* Sicilian *1,* Gonzenbach No. 20); Rumanian *3;* Hungarian *4;* Czech: Tille Soupis II (1) 65f. *2;* Slovenian *6;* Serbocroatian *1;* Polish *6;* Russian: Andrejev; Greek: Hahn No. 66; Turkish: Eberhard-Boratav No. 154 V. — Franco-American *8;* West Indies (Negro) *2,* (Jamaica): Beckwith MAFLS XVII 131.

711 *The Beautiful and the Ugly Twin.* The deformed maiden disenchanted. A queen is childless and gets from a witch advice how to have a child, but she breaks a condition connected with the advice, and has two girls, a very beautiful one and one deformed (with an animal's head). The ugly sister always assists the handsome one, and is at last to marry a prince. On the wedding day she is transformed and becomes as pretty as her sister. Cf. Types 433B, 708.

Motifs:

T548.2. Magic rites for obtaining child. C152. Tabus during pregnancy. T551.3. Child born with animal head. L145.1. Ugly sister helps pretty one. L162. Lowly heroine marries prince (king). D732. Loathly lady. Man disenchants loathsome woman by embracing her. D1860. Magic beautification.

Christiansen *Norske Eventyr* 99. — Swedish *7* (Uppsala *2,* Liungman *1,* misc. *4*); Norwegian (711**) *6;* Icelandic *7;* Irish *5;* Greek *4;* Turkish: Eberhard-Boratav No. 85 V. — Franco-American *2;* English: Lang FL (1890) *1;* English-American: Baughman *1.*

712 *Crescentia.* The slandered and banished wife is reinstated through her miraculous healing powers. Cf. Type 881.

I. *The Slandered Wife.* (a) She is accused of adultery by her lecherous brother-in-law, with whom she is left by her absent husband. (b) At the home of a robber who has taken her in, her brother-in-law kills her child, smears her mouth with blood, and accuses her so that she is again banished.

II. *Reinstatement.* (a) Through her miraculous power of healing she reaches a high position. (b) Her husband and the various men whose love she has repulsed come to her for healing. (c) Recognition and reconciliation.

Motifs:

I. K2110.1. Calumniated wife. S410. Persecuted wife. K2211.1. Treacherous brother-in-law. K2112. Woman slandered as adulteress (prostitute). N884. Robber as helper. K2155.1. Blood smeared on innocent person brings accusation of murder. K2116.1.1.1. Innocent woman accused of eating her new-born children.

II. D2161. Magic healing power. H151.8. Husband attracted by wife's power of healing: recognition follows. S451. Outcast wife at last united with husband and children.

**A. Wallensköld *Le conte de la femme chaste convoitée par son beau-frère* (Acta Societatis Scientiarum Fennicae XXXIV, Helsingfors 1907); *BP I 18 n. 1; *Köhler-Bolte I 392, 582. — Swedish *2* (Uppsala *1*, misc. *1*); Irish *20*, Beal VIII 3f. No. 3; Dutch *1;* Italian (Tuscan [865] a, b *2*); cf. Rumanian (315C*) *1;* Serbocroatian *3;* Polish (714) *3;* Jewish: Bin Gorion *Born Judas*[2] I 265ff., 270ff., 377. — Franco-American *13;* West Indies (Negro) *12*. — Literary Treatments: Straparola I No. 4; Chauvin VI 159, 323; Ward *Catalogue of Romances* II 680.

713 *The Mother who did not Bear me but Nourished me.* A stepdaughter is accused of bearing her sister's illegitimate child [K2112] and she and the child are expelled [S410]. Wherever they go famine ceases and magic abundance comes [D1652.1, D2081], but famine comes to places they have left [D2157.1]. Eventually by means of apples presented at a banquet the youth reveals the situation [H151.11, cf. H481.1].
**Delarue Fabula II 254ff.

713* *Warrior and Faithful Wife.* A king goes to war. He does not believe accusations charging his wife with unfaithfulness. On his return he finds out that he was right.
Polish (713) *1.*

713A* *Garland (Wreath) of Rue.* An old maid accused of wearing the garland of maidenhood unlawfully places it on a wall to prove her innocence and prays for the garland to stick to the stone. This happens.
Polish (713A) *2.*

715 *Demi-coq.* Is put in with the horses, oxen, etc. The animals taken along (bear, wolf, etc.) help.

I. Two children are left a cock. They cut it in two. Through the help of the boy's fairy godmother the half-cock is made magic.

II. Demi-coq sets out to recover borrowed money. Under his wings he takes with him some robbers, two foxes, and a stream of water. He goes to a castle and asks for money. He is imprisoned with the hens: the foxes eat them up. Likewise in the stable the robbers steal the horses.

When he is to be burned the stream puts out the fire. He is finally given the money. The king eats the cock who crows in his body.

Motifs:

I. F311.1. Fairy godmother. B171.1. Demi-coq. A cock is cut in two and is made magic. Carries robbers, foxes, and stream of water under wings.

II. D915.2. River contained under cock's wings. F601.7. Animals as extraordinary companions. B435.1. Helpful fox. D1382.8. Magic stream quenches fire. K481. Demi-coq by means of his magic animals and magic water collects money. B171.1.1. Demi-coq crows in king's body, when the king eats him.

**Boggs *The Halfchick Tale in Spain and France* (FFC CXI); **R. A. Laval *Revista de Derecho, Historia y Letras* XXXII (1909) 526—538; *BP I 258; D. Bressan RTP XXII 433, Coffin *1*. — Finnish *89;* Finnish-Swedish *4;* Estonian *17;* Livonian *1;* Lithuanian *41;* Swedish *17* (Uppsala *4*, Göteborg *1*, Liungman *2*, misc. *9*); French *72;* Spanish *5;* Catalan: Amades Nos. 41, 108, 352, cf. 135; Flemish *1;* German *5* (Archive *4*, Merk. 313); Italian *2* (Tuscan [208] *1*, Sicilian *1*); Hungarian *6;* Serbocroatian *27;* Polish *6;* Russian: Afanasiev *19;* Albanian: Lambertz 189ff.; Greek *9*, Hahn No. 85; Turkish: Eberhard-Boratav Nos. 33, 54 *8;* India *3*. — Franco-American *5;* French Antilles *1;* Spanish-American: Hansen (Argentina) *1*, (Chile) *1*, (Puerto Rico) *3;* West Indies (Negro) *1*. — African *1*.

715A *The Wonderful Cock.* An old couple have a cock and a hen; the cock flies to the rich man's manor and cries: »Cock-a-doodle-doo, I will eat you!»; the man orders it to be thrown into the stable. It pecks open the horses' heads (eyes): when thrown into the well, it cries, »buttocks, swallow the water!»; finally thrown into the strong-box, bids couple spread a sheet and casts out the money; the hen tries to do likewise but gets dung in place of money.

Lithuanian (715) *41*.

716* *The Value of a Stomach.* The man complains that he is a mere slave of his stomach. When it is taken away from him, he discovers that life has become very dull to him. He recovers his stomach. [J2072.4].

Lithuanian (*716) *8*.

717* *Meat Stolen for Poor Turns to Roses.*

Italian Novella: Rotunda D469.12; Wesselski *Theorie* 163 n. — Catalan: Amades No. 1207; French (713*) *13*.

720 *My Mother Slew Me; My Father Ate Me. The Juniper Tree.* The boy's bones transformed into a bird. The bird lets the millstone fall on the mother. Becomes boy again.

I. *The Murder.* (a) The little boy is slain by his cruel stepmother, who closes the lid of a chest on him. (b) She cooks him and serves him to his father who eats him unwittingly.

II. *The Transformation.* (a) His little stepsister gathers up his bones and puts them under the juniper tree. (b) From the grave a bird comes forth.

III. *The Revenge.* (a) The bird sings of his murder. (b) He brings presents to his father and sister and the millstone for the mother.

IV. *The Second Transformation.* At her death he becomes a boy.

Motifs:

I. Z65.1. Red as blood, white as snow. S31. Cruel stepmother. S121. Murder by slamming down chest lid. G61. Relative's flesh eaten unwittingly. E30. Resuscitation by arrangement of members. Parts of a dismembered corpse are brought together and resuscitation follows. E607.1. Bones of dead collected and buried. Return in another form directly from grave. V63. Bones of dismembered person assembled and buried. E610.1.1. Reincarnation: boy to bird to boy. Boy returns as bird who later becomes the boy. E613.0.1. Reincarnation of murdered child as bird.

III. N271. Murder will out. Q211.4. Murder punished. Q412. Punishment: millstone dropped on guilty person.

IV. E610.1.1. Reincarnation: boy to bird to boy.

*BP I 412 (Grimm No. 47); Coffin *10.* — Finnish *26;* Finnish-Swedish *5;* Estonian *53;* Livonian *1;* Lithuanian *9;* Swedish *15* (Uppsala *6*, Göteborg *2,* Lund *2,* Liungman *1,* misc. *4*); Norwegian *2;* Danish *23,* Grundtvig No. 41; Scottish *2;* Irish *3;* English *3;* French *62;* Spanish *1;* Catalan: Amades No. 35; Dutch *17;* Flemish *21,* Witteryck p. 302: 24; Walloon *1,* (720B) *1;* German Archive *45;* Austrian: Haiding p. 470; Italian *2* (Sicilian *2*); Hungarian *3;* Czech: Tille Soupis I 105 *2;* Slovenian *1;* Serbocroatian *2;* Polish *2;* Russian: Andrejev, Andrejev *Ukraine 3;* Greek *1;* Turkish: Eberhard-Boratav No. 24 III; India *4.* — Franco-American *8;* English-American: Baughman *6,* Lowrimore *California Folklore Quarterly* IV 154; Spanish-American: Hansen (Dominican Republic) *4;* West Indies (Negro) *3;* American Negro (Michigan): *Dorson No. 162.

722* *The Sister in the Underground Kingdom.* A brother wants to marry his sister. She escapes by digging into the earth and comes out in an underground kingdom. After various adventures she marries and then makes peace with her brother.
Russian: Afanasiev 7.

723* *Hero Binds Midnight, Dawn, and Midday* so that it cannot dawn until he frees them.
Hungarian (727) *4.*

725 *The Dream.* The boy refuses to tell his dream to his father, and even to the king. Various adventures. Conquers enemies, wins the princess. Thus the dream is fulfilled. The boy dreams that his parents shall serve him and that the king shall pour water on his hands. (Cf. Type 671). Among his adventures are the solving of riddles and the accomplishment of tasks suggested by a hostile prince.

Motifs: M312. Prophecy of future greatness for youth. M312.0.1.

Dream of future greatness. D1812.3.3. Future revealed in dream. L425. Dream (prophecy) of future greatness causes punishment (imprisonment). S11. Cruel father. M373. Expulsion to avoid fulfillment of prophecy. H911. Tasks assigned at suggestion of jealous rivals. H551. Princess offered to man who can out-riddle her. L161. Lowly hero marries princess.

*BP I 324; Krohn FFC XCVI 95; *Cosquin *Contes indiens* 471ff.; Köhler-Bolte I 430, 432ff. — Finnish *10;* Finnish-Swedish *2;* Estonian *1;* Lithuanian *17;* Swedish (Uppsala) *1;* Danish *5;* French *1;* German *3;* Rumanian *7;* Hungarian *13,* Berze Nagy 932* *3;* Czech: FFC XXXIV 360f., Tille Soupis II (2) 354 *3;* Slovenian (725B) *1;* Slovenian *1;* Serbocroatian *4;* Polish 2 (725A) *6;* Russian: Afanasiev *13;* Greek *11,* Hahn No. 45, Dawkins *Modern Greek Folktales* No. 53; Turkish: Eberhard-Boratav Nos. 125 IV, 197, 258 III *17;* Aramaic: Bergsträsser *15;* India *3.* — Franco-American *2;* West Indies (Negro) *1.*

725* *The Fairy Son.* A poor weaver who does work for a fairy woman refuses to accept a reward; a fairy son is born to his wife; son grows up, dreams two nights of rescuing a girl; a wise man tells him such a girl is a princess in bondage in the Eastern World. He sets off to free her, is kind to a wolf who carries him over a fiery mountain, and to a fox who helps him over hazards, and an old woman who gives him a ball of thread to lead him on. The giant who has the princess in bondage gives him three tasks to do; an old man helps him with these — making crops and trees grow miraculously, changing a lake into wine. The hero gets the giant to enter the lake of wine for a swim, throws in clay which makes the lake become fiery, and the giant is burned to death. The girl the hero has dreamed of comes to him; they marry.
Irish.

725** *The Sleep at the Well.* Youth's favorite horse dies. He falls asleep at a well, a magic sleep, and awakes years later. A magician beside the well gives him a magic horse with which he wins many races and much money in England; he sells the horse to a second man, who also prospers.
Irish.

726 *The Oldest on the Farm.* A wayfarer asks for a night's lodging at a farm. He meets a very old man outside, but he is shown to his father who has to decide, and so on up to the seventh generation [F571.2]. Sometimes mixed up with fairy tradition: the old troll finishes by trying the man's strength. — Adapted from Christiansen *Norske Eventyr* 99.

*Baum JAFL XXX (1917) 379 n. 2; *BP II 400; Hartmann *Trollvorstellungen* 55; Bolte Zs. f. Vksk. VII 205. — Swedish (Göteborg) *2,* (Liungman) *1;* Norwegian (726**) *16,* Solheim *2;* Danish *2;* Scottish: Campbell-McKay (726*) No. 21; Irish *161,* Beal VII 132ff.; Catalan: Amades No. 432; Flemish *1,* Witteryck p. 304 *11;* German *6;* Polish (726A) *1,* (726B) *2;* India *1.* — Franco-American *1;* English-American: Baughman *1;* American Negro (Michigan): *Dorson No. 145. — Literary Treatments: Chauvin VII 61 n. 4 No. 6 A; Clouston *Tales* II 96.

726* *The Dream Vist.* An Irishman goes to Scandinavia and is met successively by a very old man, his still older father and grandfather. A stick is crushed in handshake. He is given soup to drink which gives him power to see all the treasure

the »Danes» have left hidden in Ireland. He comes to Ireland, at old man's request, for a razor hidden in a fairy-fort, guarded by a cat; he brings back the razor; the old men shave and are rejuvenated. He drinks the soup again; sees the hidden treasures and Ireland, and eats some of the soup-flesh. The vision disappears. He is at home as poor as ever.
Irish.

726** *The Prince and his Three Hosts Tell their Adventure.* The powder which causes one to see everything and which makes blind [D1331.3.2]; the man transformed to a dog [D141], the woman to a horse [D131]. The spendthrift.
Flemish *1*.

727* *Invisible Voices.* The youngest of three brothers [L10] serves in a queer place where nobody is seen [D1890]; only a voice gives out the orders. At the end of the year he is bidden to light a big fire [D784]. The enchantment is broken, a castle appears, and the boy is married to the princess [L161].
Norwegian (727**) *2*.

728* changed to 934E.

729 *The Axe Falls into the Stream.* The water-spirit exhibits a golden axe, but the honest man admits that it does not belong to him [Q3.1]. Another man deliberately throws his axe into the water and claims the golden one as his. He gets neither.
Halm Aesop No. 308; Wienert FFC LVI 79. — Lithuanian *8;* French *1;* French Canadian: **JAFL LXVII 211; Polish (742*) *2;* Chinese: Eberhard FFC CXX No. 20; Japanese: Ikeda.

735 *The Rich Man's and the Poor Man's Fortune.* The fortune of the rich brother gives the poor brother the advice to seek his luck under a bush. The poor man goes there and Fortune tells him to become a merchant. He becomes rich. [N181].
Finnish *1;* Estonian (735*) *14;* Lithuanian *21;* Swedish (Uppsala) *1;* Danish *8;* Irish *10;* Serbocroatian *3;* Polish *1;* Russian: Andrejev *Ukraine 11*, Afanasiev *10*. — Franco-American *1*.

735A *Bad Luck Imprisoned* [N112.1]. Bad Luck attaches herself to a poor man and leads him to ruin. He locks up Bad Luck and prospers. An envious brother frees Bad Luck, but she attaches herself to him, not the former poor brother.
BP II 420—422. — Lithuanian (735A) *25;* Hungarian: Berze Nagy (332 I*) *2;* Czech: Tille Soupis I 105 *1;* Russian: Andrejev (735 I*) *4*, Afanasiev *10*.

735* (formerly 935***) One of two brothers always has good luck, the other bad. The latter asks his brother how it happens that everything succeeds for him. The brother says that he plows in the woodshed. The other now does this and finds a buried treasure. [N552].
Finnish-Swedish *1;* Danish (935***) *1*.

735B* *The Couple Persecuted by Adversity.* Wishing to escape the persecution of Adversity, the luckless couple build themselves a new home. Scarcely do they establish themselves in the new home, when Adversity addresses them from the hearth: »I have been waiting for you here for three days.» [N250.2].
Lithuanian *2*.

735C* *The Judge's Bad-luck Boots.* The wealthy merchant becomes a beggar, because of the judge's bad-luck-bringing boots which he acquired through exchange (theft). [N136].
Lithuanian (*2447) *2.*

736 *Luck and Wealth.* The fish with the jewel. Cf. Types 745, 745A. A poor man gets a piece of tin. He gives it to a fisherman under the agreement that the first catch of fish shall be given to him. In the net is a fish with a precious stone in his body. [N421].
Estonian (736*) *1;* Irish *24;* Czech: Tille Soupis I 402ff. *2;* Polish *4,* (736A) *6,* (736B) *1;* Russian: Andrejev *Ukraine 6,* Afanasiev *1;* Turkish: Eberhard-Boratav No. 139. — Franco-American *1;* Spanish-American: Rael No. 93 (U.S.). — Literary Treatments: Chauvin VI 32 No. 202.

736A *The Ring of Polycrates.* A king throws a ring into the sea. It is found next day in a fish brought to him. [N211.1].
*Pauli (ed. Bolte) No. 635; *Wesselski *Mönchslatein* 188 No. 146; *Chauvin V 17 No. 10, 141 No. 68, VI 32 No. 202; *BP IV 332f., 392; Toldo VIII 40; Saintyves »L'Anneau de Polycrate» *Revue de l'histoire des religions* (1912) 1—32; *Loomis *White Magic* 121. — Swedish: Liungman SSF III 271, 441; Irish: *Cross (N211.1); Norwegian: Solheim 20; Italian Novella: Rotunda (N211.1); Serbocroatian (948) *1;* Jewish: *Neuman, *Gaster *Exempla* 210 No. 118, *bin Gorion *Born Judas*[2] II 106, 344, III 51, 55, 300; India (948) *4;* Japanese: Ikeda (N211.1); Korean: Zong in-Sob 29; Philippine: Fansler MAFLS XII 7. — Portuguese-American (Brazil): Camara Cascudo 164. — Africa (Gold Coast): Barker and Sinclair 133.

737 (formerly 737*) *Who Will be her Future Husband?* The general's sword. The girl on the advice of a soothsayer tries to find who will be her future husband [D1825.1.2]. A general appears and forgets his sword. The girl hides the sword. Later, when as the wife of the general she shows him the sword, he strikes her dead.
Estonian *6;* Livonian *2;* Irish *2;* English *5.* — English-American: Baughman *2.*

737A* *Why Have I Nothing?* A luckless man goes to the king to ask him for counsel. The princess: »You should marry.» In punishment for such foolish advice, the king drives her forth and orders her to marry him herself. When they are married, the husband wins an important wager from a merchant, by proving that the object which he has brought for sale really is his wife's property.
Lithuanian *12.*

737B* *The Lucky Wife.* A luckless man becomes successful in all his undertakings when he marries a lucky woman and lives by her luck. [N251.5].
Lithuanian *12;* Serbocroatian *2.*

738* *The Battle of Serpents.* A great serpent takes on its back a man on order to kill another serpent with which it is fighting. After he has brought the man back, it repays him liberally with gold.
Estonian *11;* Livonian (745') *1;* Turkish: Eberhard-Boratav Nos. 57, 66, 80 *3.*

739* *The Luckless Son and His Wizard Father.* Seeing a luck-bringing animal at his

son's house, the father orders it to be destroyed; but the grandchildren eat of its meat and become fortunate. [N251.6].
Lithuanian (738*) *5;* Serbocroatian *1.*

740* *The Expelled Brother.* Two brothers promise each other not to marry. One marries and expels the other. The second brother makes a fortune. The married brother loses all and must beg from the abused brother, who helps him. Recognition.
French Canadian.

740** *The Brother to Hang Himself.* Rich man being asked for help by his poor brother, gives him a rope and advises him to hang himself. The poor brother chooses the tree under which the rich man has buried money. When he tries to hang himself, the tree breaks from the ground and shows the treasure. The rich brother missing the treasure hangs himself. [Cf. J21.15]. Cf. Type 910D.
Polish *5.*

741* *The Rich, the Poor, and the Diamond.* The rich asked for assistance from his poor brother, gives him a dead horse in which a diamond is found.
Polish *1.*

745 *Hatch-penny.* Always returns to its owner. Eaten by cow; owner happens to buy cow and kill her; etc. [D1602.11, N212].
*Chauvin II 129 No. 137; Ward *Catalogue of Romances* II 234, 447. — Livonian *1;* Swedish *5* (Uppsala *1,* misc. *4*); Danish *5;* Irish *1;* Polish *7.*

745A *The Predestined Treasure.* Inside the hollow tree, baked within a loaf of bread, etc. Always comes to the man for whom it was predestined. [N212]. Cf. Types 736, 736A, 947A*.
*Chauvin II 129 No. 137; *Herbert III 234, 377 No. 61, 447; *Oesterley No. 109. — Lithuanian (*934B) *10;* Irish; Russian: Andrejev*834B; West Indies: Flowers 563.

746* *The Flying Stone.* A stepmother decides to enclose her stepdaughter in a large stone and sink it in the sea. The stepsister, seeing that the stone is well furnished and that it can fly, joins the girl. The stone is carried off by a stream and lands near a castle. The girls go out and later meet prince and attendant and marry.
Swedish (GS 746) *3.*

748* *Queen Jealous of Peasant Couple.* A peasant and his wife are given gifts by a dwarf: the cow will always give milk and the brook will have enough fish. — The queen discovers this and goes and pushes woman into the brook. The peasant gives the queen a curse: She must keep saying, »The peasant in the hut slept with me.» The peasant woman is rescued.
Icelandic *1.*

B. RELIGIOUS TALES

750—779 God Repays and Punishes

750A *The Wishes.* Christ and Peter grant a poor peasant who has received them hospitably three good wishes; the rich one, however, they grant three evil wishes. Cf. Type 330A.

I. *Hospitality Rewarded.* (a) Christ and Peter (a god, or other supernatural being) reward hospitality and punish the opposite. (b) A limited number of wishes will be fulfilled.

II. *The Wishes.* (a) The hospitable person uses his three wishes wisely; the inhospitable in his anger makes two foolish wishes (e.g. his horse's neck broken, his wife stuck to the saddle) and must use the third to undo them; or (b) the same with one wish: to keep doing all day what you begin; one gets good linen all day, while the other throws water on the pig; or (c) a husband given three wishes transfers one to his wife who wastes it on a trifle; in his anger he wishes the article in her body and must use the third to get it out.

Motifs:

I. K1811. Gods (saints) in disguise visit mortals. Q1.1. Gods (saints) in disguise reward hospitality and punish inhospitality. D1761:0.2. Limited number of wishes granted.

II. J2071. Three foolish wishes. Three wishes will be granted: used up foolishly. J2073. Same wishes used foolishly and wisely. D2172.2. Magic gift: power to continue all day what one starts. One woman measures linen; another throws water on pig. J2072.3. Short-sighted wish: all he pulls on will follow. J2073.1. Wise and foolish wish: keep doing all day what you begin. J2075. The transferred wish. A husband, given three wishes, transfers one to his wife, who wastes it on a trifle; in his anger he wishes the article in her body and must use the third to get it out.

References for 750 A and B:

Finnish *31;* Finnish-Swedish *9;* Estonian *5;* Livonian (750) *1;* Swedish (Uppsala 750) *3;* Norwegian *1,* Solheim (750) *1;* Irish *94,* Catalan: Amades No. 143; Flemish *16;* German: Henssen Volk No. 171; Indonesian: DeVries No. 213. — Franco-American *12.*

References for 750 A:

*BP II 210 (Grimm No. 87); *Liungman SSF III 440, Coffin *2.*— Lithuanian, *9* (750*A) *14;* Swedish *84* (Uppsala *18,* Stockholm *8,* Göteborg *12,* Lund *6,* Liungman *10,* misc. *30);* Norwegian *4;* Danish 47, Grundtvig No. 128; Icelandic *1,* (750B*) *1;* Irish: Beal III 434; English *2;* French *28,* Spanish *4;* Catalan: Amades Nos. 185, 501, 1962, cf. 200; Dutch *6;* Walloon *4;* German *47* (Archive *46,* Henssen Jül. No. 270); Austrian: Haiding (750 n.) *4;* Italian (Tuscan 555 a—c, 750 b *4);* Rumanian *14;* Hungarian *3,* (750) *5;* Czech: Tille Soupis I 567 *5;* (750) Slovenian *7;* (750) Serbocroatian *3;* Slovenian *7;* Serbocroatian *5;* Russian: Andrejev; India *5;* Indonesian: DeVries No. 213; Chinese: Eberhard FFC CXX 167 No. 111. — English-American: Baughman *1;* Spanish-American: Hansen (Chile) *1,* (Dominican Republic) *1,* (Puerto Rico) *1;* West Indies (Negro) *2;* American Negro (Michigan): Dorson No. 154; American Indian: Thompson *C Coll* II 454.

750B *Hospitality Rewarded.* After a pious beggar has been refused hospitality in a house where a wedding is taking place, he is hospitably received in a poor man's house. The peasant's only cow is killed for him. It comes to life again (or new cows appear) [Q1, Q141].

*BP I 422f.; *Liungman SSF III 440; *Anderson *Novelline* No. 63; Von Sydow »Tors Färd till Utgård» *Danske Studier* (1910) 91ff.; Krohn *Skandinavisk Mytologi* p. 207. — Estonian (750*) *6;* Lithuanian (*750B) *13;* Lappish (750*) *1;* French *4;* Spanish *3;* Catalan: Amades cf. No. 1286; Italian *4* (Tuscan [750] a *1,* Sicilian *3*); Slovenian *18;* Serbocroatian *24;* Russian: Andrejev *1;* Greek *11,* Kretschmer No. 51, Dawkins *Modern Greek in Asia Minor* 523, Loukatos Nos. 4, 11, 17, *Laographia* VI 513 No. 4; India *1.* — Spanish-American: Hansen (Dominican Republic) *2,* (Puerto Rico) *2;* West Indies (Negro) *6.*

750C (formerly 473) *Punishment of a Bad Woman.* The man is kind to the beggar, but the wife is unkind [Q1, Q2]. The beggar invites the man to him and shows him (among other things) that the woman has been turned into a cow [D133.1].

Estonian (473*) *8;* Irish: Beal XXI 330; Italian *2* (Tuscan cf. [333], [753] a *2*).

750D *Three Brothers each Granted a Wish by an Angel Visitor.* They choose (1) plenty of wine, (2) sheep, (3) a good wife). Later as beggar he is refused hospitality by the two elder and he takes their wine and sheep away. The youngest and his wife are rewarded for hospitality. (Sometimes sacrifice of a child is agreed to — cf. Type 516.)

Serbocroatian *13;* Turkish: Eberhard-Boratav No. 110 *1;* Greek: Dawkins *Modern Greek Folktales* No. 70 *3;* Arab: Basset *1001 Contes* III 302.

750* *Hospitality Blessed.* The Savior (or an angel) rewards the hospitable peasant and punishes the inhospitable [Q2].

Finnish *1;* Finnish-Swedish *1;* Swedish (Lund) *1;* Russian: Afanasiev (*751 I) *4.*

750** *The Girls Plucking Berries.* One of them answers an old man in a friendly manner and is rewarded. The other gives a discourteous answer and is punished. [Q2].

Finnish-Swedish 403 II b, c, d.

750** *Young Savior's Miracles.* The Savior when a boy resuscitates a dead boy [E121.1] and makes a plank longer.

Lappish (750**) *1.*

750*** *The Virgin Mary and the Animals.*

Lappish (750***) *1;* Slovenian *7.*

750E* *Hospitality and Sin.* One act of hospitality (to two monks) outweighs a life of sin.

Spanish *1.*

750F* *The Old Man's Blessing.* A poor woman gives children water in which she has washed her hands after making bread for a rich lady. The children are healthy. The old man blesses the woman. Her house becomes finer and filled with money. She borrows scales from the rich lady to weigh money; a piece of money sticks to the scales (cf. Type 676) and the rich lady asks how she received money. The Lord visits the rich lady but is thrown out. She is reduced to poverty.

Spanish-American: Hansen (Argentina) *1,* (Puerto Rico) *6.*

750G* *The Butcher as Devil.* A poor widow begs the godfather of her children, a butcher, for help but he refuses. The woman finds a pot of money in the ground. The

butcher pretends to be the devil and wants the money. The real devil carries him away.
Czech: Tille Soupis I 165—171 *10*.

750H* *The Notary Enters Heaven.* Christ and Apostles are shown hospitality by a woodsman. He is granted a wish [Q451, Q142], and asks that he may always win at cards [N221]. He lives and dies peacefully. On way to Heaven he stops by the house of a wicked, dying notary and wins the notary's soul from the Devil in a card game [E756]. St. Peter does not wish to admit the notary, but the woodsman recalls his hospitality and obtains the notary's entrance.
Spanish (*345) *1*.

751 *The Greedy Peasant Woman.* Christ and Peter ask entertainment from a peasant woman [K1811]. Although the cake magically grows larger [D1652.1.2], she gives them but a morsel. She is punished [Q1.1].
Norwegian *11*, Solheim *5;* Danish *5;* Irish *1;* French *6;* Spanish *1;* Catalan: Amades Nos. 1582, 1585; Italian (Tuscan [751], [752] *2*); Rumanian *11*, Sainenu 841; Hungarian: Berze Nagy (779 VIII) *6;* Slovenian *16*.

751A *The Peasant Woman is Changed into a Woodpecker* [D153.1].
*Dähnhardt II 129ff. — Finnish *18;* Finnish-Swedish *2;* Estonian *3;* Swedish *28* (Uppsala *12*, Göteborg *5*, Liungman *2*, misc. *9*); English *3;* Italian (Tuscan [756] a, b *2*); Czech: Tille Soupis I 573f. *3;* Slovenian *1;* Russian: Andrejev; Turkish: Eberhard-Boratav cf. Anlage A (b); Chinese: Eberhard FFC CXX 123f. No. 83, FFC CXXVIII 91f. No. 49; English-American: Baughman *1*.

751B *The Peasant Woman must Take two Snakes as Foster Children* [Q594].
Finnish *1;* Finnish-Swedish *2;* Estonian *19;* Swedish *4* (Stockholm *1*, misc. *3*); Italian (Tuscan cf. [1440] *1*); Slovenian *2;* Serbocroatian *1*.

751A* *A Man Invites God to his House.* He makes grand preparations for God's reception, yet orders that a beggar, who has come to his doors, be driven away (or the dogs set on him). The beggar, it turns out, was God himself. The conversation at the cross. [K1811.1, Q292.1].
Lithuanian (*770) *24;* Slovenian *1;* Russian: Andrejev (*751 II) *5*.

751B* *The Old Man with the Live Coals.* A poor man goes to seek a light for his fire and comes across an old man seated before a fireplace. The embers he takes home turn to gold. The wealthy man purposely extinguishes his fire at home and requests the old man to give him some coals. »Your house is full of fire.» He finds his homestead in flames. [Q2].
Lithuanian (*771) *15*.

751C* *Wealth Leads to Pride.* Having miraculously become prosperous, the man drives from his home the old beggar (God), his benefactor, and so loses all. [Q292.1].
Lithuanian (*772) *6;* Russian: Andrejev (*796 I) *1*.

751D* *St. Peter Blesses Hospitable Thieves.*
Italian (Sicilian *3*).

752A *Christ and Peter in the Barn.* Threshing with fire [K1811]. The peasant forces them to rise early and thresh in payment for lodging. They separate the grain by means of fire. When the peasant tries to do the same thing the barn burns down. [J2411].

*BP III 452. — Finnish (752) *20;* Finnish-Swedish (752) *1;* Estonian (752) *36;* Livonian (752) *1;* Lithuanian *22;* French *11;* Catalan: Amades No. 2116; Flemish (752) *1;* German *39* (Archive *36,* Merk. 145, Henssen Volk No. 174, Henssen Jül. No. 273; Italian *1* (Sicilian *1*); Rumanian *2;* Hungarian (752) *3;* Czech (752): Tille Soupis I 577ff., II (2) 456—461 (752), 459ff. (752A) *12;* Slovenian (752) *8;* Slovenian *6;* Serbocroatian *8;* Istrian No. 25. — Franco-American *2.*

752B *The Forgotten Wind.* Man allowed to manage the weather forgets to ask the help of the wind. All goes wrong and he must give up management. [J755.1].

Danish *5,* Kristensen *Jyske Folkeminder* VIII No. 656; Livonian (758') *1;* Swedish (Uppsala) *1;* Dutch *1;* German *2;* Italian (Sicilian *1*); Rumanian (752 I*) *2;* Slovenian *3;* Serbocroatian *1;* Russian: Andrejev Ukraine *2.* — Franco-American *3.*

752C *The Prodigious Mower. Saint to mow field in exchange for dinner.* Miraculous speed, miraculous appetite.

**van Gennep *Nouvelle Revue des Traditions Populaires* II 99ff. — French: Perbosc *Gascogne* 254ff.; Italian (Sicilian *1*). — Franco-American *3.*

752C* *The Discourteous Sower.* Tells Christ he is sowing pumpkins (turnips). For his seed maize he harvests only pumpkins. [Cf. A2231.1].
Slovenian *2.*

753 *Christ and the Smith.* Christ takes off the horse's foot in order to shoe him and rejuvenates an old woman by putting her in the fire. The smith tries disastrously to do the same.

Motifs:

K1811. God (Saints) in disguise visit mortals. F663.0.1. Skillful smith calls self master of all masters. E782.4. Horse's leg cut off and replaced. E14. Resuscitation by dismemberment. E15. Resuscitation by burning. E121.2. Resuscitation by Christ. D1886. Rejuvenation by burning. J2411.1. Imitation of magic rejuvenation unsuccessful. A1861.2. Creation of monkeys: old woman thrown into fire. In unsuccessful imitation of Christ, the smith throws an old woman into the fire. She becomes a monkey.

*BP II 198 (Grimm No. 147); Lowes *Romanic Review* V 383; Espinosa III 140—150. — Finnish *59;* Finnish-Swedish *4;* Estonian *22;* Livonian cf. (1694') *1;* Lithuanian *12;* Swedish *13* (Uppsala *6,* Stockholm *1;* Göteborg *2,* Liungman *2,* misc. *2*)*;* Norwegian *2;* Danish *18;* Scottish *1;* Irish *166,* Beal I 66ff., II 346f. No. 1, VII 95ff., VIII 3, X 194ff., XI 59ff., XII 134f. No. 2, XIX 67ff., XVIII 107; French *44;* Spanish *1;* Catalan: Amades cf. No. 1311; Flemish *5;* German *22,* Henssen Jül. No. 272; Italian *3* (Trieste: Pinguentini No. 50, Sicilian *2*); Rumanian *2;* Hungarian *3;* Czech: Tille Soupis I 579f. *1;* Slovenian *11;* Serbocroatian *11;* Istrian Nos. 26, 27; Russian: Andrejev *6;* Greek *1;* Turkish: Kunos (1887—9) No. 50. — Franco-American *8;* Spanish-American:

Hansen (Dominican Republic) *1*, (Puerto Rico) *1*, Rael Nos. 297—299 (U.S.).

753A *Unsuccessful Resuscitation.* Companion tries unsuccessfully to imitate angel who has resuscitated a dead princess. Angel helps him but warns him against trying again.
  Sicilian (*785) *5*.

753* *Jesus Turns a Thief into an Ass.* Later gives him the money he has earned as ass and restores him.
  Italian (Tuscan [753a] *1*, Sicilian *750 *1*); Serbocroatian *15*.

754 *The Happy Friar* becomes unhappier as he receives ever more and more money. He gets rid of his money and becomes happy as before. [J1085.1].
  *Crane 162—3 Nos. 66. — Swedish (Lund) *3;* Irish *1;* Spanish (Espinosa No. 90) *3;* Catalan: Amades Nos. 1273, 1639; Flemish (754*) *1;* German *11;* Czech: cf. Tille Soupis I 78ff. *3;* Slovenian *1;* Greek *1;* Chinese: Eberhard FFC CXX No. 204.

754* *The Virgin's Handkerchief.* A ship-captain answers the three questions of a heathen king and heals the prince with the Virgin Mary's handkerchief [D2161.5.2.2].
  Lappish *1*.

754** *St. Peter and his Wife.* St. Peter is in front of his house in the rain and tells the Lord that the house is full of smoke. The Lord enters. At the rear he finds St. Peter's wife with up-lifted broom-handle. [T251.3].
  Flemish *3*.

754*** (The Wandering Jew) changed to 777.

755 *Sin and Grace.* The rose from the stone table. The preacher's wife magically prevents the birth of her children. Since she throws no shadow, her husband casts her forth as a sinner until a rose shall grow from a stone table. A churchman takes the woman at night into the church. The children appear and forgive their mother. They go back home and the rose springs forth. Cf. Type 765.

  Motifs:
  T572.1. Magic prevention of childbirth. Q251. Punishment for refusal to have children. Q552.9. Punishment: woman who has prevented birth of children casts no shadow. F1038. Person without shadow. Q431.4. Banishment till rose grows from table for preventing childbirth. F971.2. Rose grows from table (stone).
  Cf. Hauffen Zs. f. Vksk. X 436ff.; Bolte Zs. f. Vksk. XIV 114, XVI 311. — Finnish *16;* Finnish-Swedish *5;* Estonian *2;* Lappish *1;* Swedish *58* (Uppsala *8,* Stockholm *4,* Göteborg *32,* Lund *2,* Liungman *2,* misc. *10*); Norwegian *7,* Solheim *1;* Danish *28;* Icelandic *1;* Scottish *1;* French *7;* German Archive *1;* Hungarian *1;* Czech: Tille Soupis II (1) 365ff. *3;* Serbocroatian *4;* Russian: Andrejev (755AB) *2,* Andrejev *Ukraine 2*.

756 *The Three Green Twigs.* The hard penance and the green twigs on the dry branch.
  Slovenian *16;* Serbocroatian *2*.

756A *The Self-righteous Hermit.* A hermit who says of a man being taken to the gallows that he has been punished justly must do penance by wandering as a beggar until three twigs grow on a dry branch. He converts a band of robbers with the story of his misfortunes. The green twigs appear.

Motifs:

Q553.2. Punishment: angel ceases to appear to self-righteous hermit. L435.1. Self-righteous hermit must do penance. Q521.1. Doing penance till green leaves grow on a dry branch. F971.1. Dry rod blossoms.

****Andrejev *Die Legende vom Räuber Madej* (FFC LXIX); *BP III 463 (Grimm No. 206); Köhler-Bolte I 147, 148, *578, 581; *Liungman SSF III 260, 440. — Finnish *1;* Finnish-Swedish *1;* Estonian *3;* Swedish *25* (Uppsala *24,* Göteborg *1);* Danish *10,* Grundtvig No. 58B; Irish (756A, B) *275,* Beal XXI, 307, 317, 331; Spanish *2;* German: Henssen Volk No. 178; Rumanian *6;* Hungarian *1;* Serbocroatian *3;* Russian: Andrejev; Greek *1;* Turkish: Eberhard-Boratav No. 126 IV. — Franco-American *1;* Spanish-American: Rael No. 97 (U.S.).

756B *The Devil's Contract.*

I. *Journey for the Contract.* (a) A boy who has been sold to the devil before birth journeys to hell to get back the contract. (b) A hermit, from whom he has asked the way, directs him to a robber, his brother. (c) The robber takes him to hell.

II. *The Fires of Hell.* (a) In hell the youth obtains his contract and (b) sees the fiery bed or chair prepared for the robber.

III. *The Penance.* (a) Thereupon the robber does penance until his staff puts forth fresh blooms and fruit; assured of forgiveness, he dies happy. Cf. Type 756C.

IV. *The Hermit.* (a) The hermit is astonished but reconciles himself to God's judgment; or (b) blasphemes God and is damned.

Motifs:

I. S211. Child sold (promised) to devil (ogre). S240. Children unwittingly promised (sold). S222. Man promises (sells) child in order to save himself from danger or death. S226. Child promised to devil for directions out of woods when father is lost. S223. Childless couple promises child to the devil if they may only have one. M211. Man sells soul to devil. S224. Child promised to devil for acting as godfather. S225. Child promised to devil for help on road with broken wagon. F81. Descent to hell. F81.2. Journey to hell to recover devil's contract. H1273.1. Quest to devil in hell for return for contract. N843. Hermit as helper. H1235. Succession of helpers on quest. One helper sends to another, who sends to another, etc.

II. Q561. Bed (kettle, seat) heating in hell for certain person. F771.1.9. House of skulls. Murderer's abode. J172. Account of punishments prepared in hell brings about repentance.

III. V29.1. Search for confessor. Great sinner sent from one confessor to another. All say that his sins are too great for forgiveness. Finally he succeeds. V27. Penance magically concluded by confession. Q520.2. Robber does penance. Q521.1.1. Penance: crawling on knees and watering a dry staff until it blooms. Q521.1.2. Penance: carrying water in mouth from a distance and watering dry staff until it blooms. Q172.3. Man admitted to heaven for single act of charity. E756.3. Raven and dove fight over man's soul. E732.1. Soul in form of dove. Q522.3. Penance: creeping naked through thorns. Q544. Penance: being locked in cellar (well) with key thrown into water.

IV. Q312.3. Punishment for finding fault with God's forgiveness of sin.

Andrejev *Die Legende vom Räuber Madej* (FFC LXIX); *BP III 463 (Grimm No. 206); *Liungman SSF III 260, 440. — Lithuanian *48;* Swedish *5* (Göteborg *1*, Lund *2*, misc. *2*); Norwegian (757) *1*; Irish (756A, B) *275*, Beal I 304ff., IV 62f. No. 3, XIV 209ff., XVIII 74ff., 77ff., XXI 310f.; Italian (Tuscan [322] 1); Hungarian: Berze Nagy 756*, 757**, 779 XXVIII* *11;* Czech: Tille Soupis II (2) 230ff. *16;* Serbocroatian *41*, Istrian Nos. 29, 30; Russian: Andrejev *6*.

756C *The Greater Sinner.*

I. *The Crime.* (a) A man seeks to do penance and receive forgiveness for murdering ninety-nine men, (b) for murdering his parents, or (c) for shooting at a consecrated wafer.

II. *The Penance.* (a) After vainly seeking a confessor, he is finally assigned penance: (b) to plant a firebrand and water it with water brought from a distance in his mouth and to plant a garden and offer free hospitality to all; or (c) to carry a bag of stones (one for each murder) on his back or (d) an iron hoop on his head till it falls off; or (e) to pasture black sheep till they become white.

III. *The Second Crime.* (a) After many years of penance the robber intercepts a man who is about to commit a great crime. (b) To prevent the crime the robber kills the man.

IV. *Forgiveness.* (a) The firebrand blooms (the stones or the hoop fall off or the sheep turn white). (b) His confessor tells him that in payment for the last murder all his sins have been forgiven.

Motifs:

I. Q520.1. Murderer does penance. Q211.1. Parricide punished. Q222.1. Punishment for desecration of host. C55.2. Tabu: shooting at consecrated wafer.

II. V29.1. Search for confessor. Great sinner sent from one confessor to another. All say that his sins are too great for forgiveness. Finally he succeeds. Q521.1.1. Penance: crawling on knees and watering a dry staff until it blooms. Q521.1.2. Penance: carrying water in mouth from a distance and watering dry staff until it blooms. Q523.5. Penance: planting garden and offering free hospitality to all. Q521.2. Penance: carrying bag of stones (one for each murder) on the back until it falls off. Q521.3. Penance: carrying iron hoop on head until it falls off. Q521.4. Penance: pasturing black sheep until they become white.

III, IV. Q545. Murderer's penance complete when he kills a greater murderer and prevents a crime.

**Andrejev *Die Legende von den zwei Erzsündern* (FFC LIV). — Irish: Beal XXI 316ff.; Serbocroatian *5;* Russian: Andrejev *4.*

756C* *Receipt from Hell.* Receipt for rent payment is demanded and a poor man must go to hell for it. Brings it back.

Irish: O'Suilleabhainn *Scealta Craibteaca* (1952) No. 58; Kretzenbacher *Der Zeuge aus der Hölle in Alpes Orientales* (Ljubljana, 1959) 33ff. (Slovenian, Swiss, Austrian, French, German, Lithuanian, Estonian).

756D* *More Devout.* Hermit or St. Peter asks Christ if anyone is more devout than he. He is directed to a widow who hides in her house and cares for the murderer of her only son, or to a butcher who shelters murderer of his father. [W15].
Spanish *2.*

756E* *Charity Rewarded* above prayer or hearing of masses [V410.1].
Spanish *1.*

756F* *The Parricide Forgiven.* The man kills his father and mother at the instance of his evil wife. The souls of his parents forgive him, but the parents of his wife fall into hell.
Russian: Andrejev (758) *2.*

757 *The King's Haughtiness Punished* (Roderigo; Jovinian). God sends an angel to take the king's place and form in the bath (or he is deprived of his clothes while hunting). The king is repulsed on all sides until he repents of his haughtiness. [L411].

**H. Varnhagen *Ein indisches Märchen auf seine Wanderung durch die asiatischen und europäischen Litteraturen* (Berlin 1882); *Chauvin II 161 No. 51. — Livonian (757') *1;* Icelandic *1;* Hungarian *1;* Czech: Tille Soupis I 485ff. *1;* Russian: Andrejev *1;* India *3;* Chinese: Chavannes *500 Contes* No. 106. — Spanish-American: Hansen (Dominican Republic) *1;* African *1.*

758 *The Various Children of Eve.* Eve has so many children that she is ashamed when God pays her a visit. She hides some of them and they fail to receive the blessing that God gives those in sight. Thus arises the differences in classes and peoples. [A1650.1].

*BP III 308ff. (Grimm No. 180); *Dähnhardt I 247, II 98f. — Livonian: Loorits FFC LXVI 85 No. 41; Lithuanian (3054); Danish: Thiele II 175; Spanish: Boggs (*758) *1;* Catalan: Amades No. 747; Italian (Sicilian *758) *3;* Serbocroatian *2.*

758A *Origin of Physical Defects.* Wicked people entering heaven on rope fall to earth and are injured. St. Peter misunderstands what God says and lets them fall. [A1338].
Spanish *1.*

759 *God's Justice Vindicated.* (The Angel and the Hermit.) An angel takes a hermit with him and does many seemingly unjust things (repays

hospitality by stealing a cup; inhospitality by giving a cup; hospitality by throwing his host's servant from a bridge and by killing the host's son) [J225]. The angel shows the hermit why each of these was just. Cf. Type 840.

**Schwartzbaum »The Jewish and Moslem Versions of Some Theodicy Legends» Fabula III 119ff.; *Crane *Vitry* 179 No. 109; Ward *Catalogue of Romances* III 8. — Estonian (771*) *1;* Lithuanian *11;* Swedish *1;* Danish *3;* Icelandic 1, (759 I*) *2;* Irish *75,* Beal III 467f. No. 7, X 3f. No. 3, 176ff., XV 287f., XXI 335.; French *2;* Spanish *12;* Catalan: Amades No. 1303; Flemish (771*) *1;* Walloon *1;* German *18* (Archive *16*, Merk. 129, Henssen Jül. No. 269); Italian *3* (Sicilian *3*, Gonzenbach No. 92); Hungarian: (Dégh No. 30, Berze Nagy 758*, Honti 829) *8;* Greek *5*, Dawkins *Modern Greek Folktales* No. 84 *7;* Czech: Tille Soupis I 53ff., 575f. *10;* Slovenian *20;* Serbocroatian *2;* Russian (*759B) *1;* Turkish: Eberhard-Boratav No. 114; India *1.* — Franco-American *3;* Spanish-American: Hansen (Puerto Rico) *1*, (Argentina) *1.*

759A *The Sinful Priest.* People will not take sacrament from him. Another priest (God) shows that even this priest is according to God's will. [V39.3]. Cf. Type 756E*.

Wesselski *Mönchslatein* 98 No. 80; *Alphabet of Tales* No. 687; Irish: Beal XXI 334, 337; Italian (Sicilian 828 [14 e] *1;* Hungarian (828) *1;* Serbocroatian *1.*

759B *Holy Man Has his own Mass.* (Cf. F1011.1, V29.3) When upbraided for not coming to mass, he hangs his coat on a sunbeam. [V43].

*Feilberg *Ordbog* s.v. »solstråle»; *Loomis *White Magic* 29. — Irish: Plummer cxxxix, *Cross (V43), O'Suilleabhain *Handbook* 101, 106, Beal XXI 332ff.; Swiss: Jegerlehner Oberwallis 301 No. 19, 306 No. 19, 309 No. 10, 328 No. 6; Spanish (*1805AB) *2.*

759C *The Widow's Meal.* The king upbraids the wind for blowing away a poor widow's last cup of meal. He finds that the wind has saved a ship full of people by that very act. The king is humbled. [J355.1].

**Schiller *Anthropos* XII—XIII 513. — Finnish *1;* Jewish: Bin Gorion *Born Judas* III 67, *301, *Neuman (J355.1); Indonesian: DeVries FFC LXXIII 324ff.

759* *The Hospitable Widow's Cow Killed.* A poor widow hospitably receives God and St. Peter staying the night. The next day, when God orders the wolf to kill the widow's only cow, St. Peter rebukes God for ingratitude. »She has no need of the cow, for tonight she will be with me.» Or: When the widow suffers her loss without reproach, God rewards her generously.
Lithuanian (*752B) *12.*

760 *The Unquiet Grave.* The man burns his three wives. Finds no rest in the grave. A maiden takes the dead man to a priest and secures his pardon for the murder of his wives.

Motifs:

S62. Cruel husband. Q211.3. Uxoricide punished. E411.1. Murderer cannot rest in grave. E411.0.2. Unquiet dead sinner taken to priest for absolution.

Finnish *26;* Finnish-Swedish *3;* Estonian *10;* Lappish *1;* Danish *17;* Spanish cf. *11;* German: Henssen Jül. No. 228; Serbocroatian *2;* Russian: Afanasiev *1.*

760* *The Condemned Soul.* Miscellaneous motifs.
Lithuanian (3556); Spanish: Boggs (760*A, *B, *C) *6;* Catalan: Amades Nos. 1627, 2122. — Spanish-American: Hansen (*775) (Peru) *32,* (Argentina) *7,* (Puerto Rico) *1,* (760*C) (Chile) *1.*

760A* *The Death of a Miser.* A miser, dying, swallows his money. The devil shakes the money out of him and carries off his body. [Q272.3].
Spanish Exempla: Keller (Q272.3); Russian: Afanasiev (*762) *2.*

761 *The Cruel Rich Man as the Devil's Horse* [Q370]. A peasant is helped against a hard-hearted landlord by magic helper, who performs all tasks. At last he tells master that the horse he has used is an ancestor of the landlord come from hell. [Q584.2].
*Henssen *Mecklenburger Erzählen* No. 88; *Henssen *Volk Erzählt* p. 245. — Finnish *5;* Estonian *11;* Lithuanian (*773) *9;* Spanish (762*) *2;* Catalan: Amades No. 1618; German *15;* Serbocroatian *3;* Russian: Afanesiev *6.*

761* *The Parricide's Fate.* The parricide [Q211.1] through a miracle becomes suspected of theft and comes to the gallows [N271.5].
See Henssen Mecklenburger Erzählen p. 221 No. 88. — Finnish-Swedish *1.*

762 *Woman with Three Hundred Sixty-five Children.* Punished for self-righteous condemnation of unchaste girl. [L435.2.1].
**K. Nyrop *Grevinden med de 365 Børn* (København, 1909); *Taylor *Notes and Queries* No. 251 (Feb., 1923) 96; *Köhler *Lais der Marie de France,* xc; De Cock *Volkssage* 9ff.; Zs. f. Vksk. XIX 469f. — Catalan: Amades No. 1547.

763 *The Treasure Finders who Murder one Another.* Two hunters are shown a treasure. One of them puts poison in the other's wine, but the other kills him, drinks the wine and dies. [K1685].
*BP III 54; *Anderson in Tauscher *Volksmärchen* 181; Basset *1001 Contes* III 181ff.; *Motif K1685. — Livonian (763') *1;* Lithuanian *16;* Lappish *1;* Swedish (Uppsala) *1;* Danish *1;* Irish *1;* Catalan: Amades No. 1691; Czech: Tille Soupis II (1) 238f. *4;* Slovenian *3;* Russian: Andrejev (*937) *3;* India *5;* Chinese: Eberhard FFC CXX 201f. No. 148; Chavannes *500 Contes* I 386 No. 115; Korean Zong in-Sob 186 No. 81. — English-American: Baughman (U.S.) *1;* Brazil: Camara Cascudo p. 78; African *2.* — Literary Treatments: Chaucer's »Pardoner's Tale»; Basset RTP XIV 440; Hart MPh IX 17; Wells MPh XXV 163; Italian Novella: Rotunda; India: Cowell Jātaka I 124.

763* changed to 766.

764 *The Devil's Son as Priest.* A youth (a) encounters the devil or (b) takes liberties with the corpse of a hanged man. With this companion he goes to certain houses, some of which because they are properly ordered the companion may not enter. The Devil (dead man) is able to enter the third house which is occupied by a quarreling, childless or a newly married couple. Prediction: the couple will have a son who is a priest. Since he is the son of the devil those who are sprinkled by him with holy water are damned. — The priest is revealed as the devil's son. Seeks penance and is forgiven.

*S. O'Duilearga »Nera and the Dead Man» *Anniversary Volume for John McNeill* 522—534. — Icelandic: Naumann *Isländische Volksmärchen* (Jena, 1923) 268ff.; Irish *39.*

765 *The Mother who Wants to Kill her Children* [S12]. The father rescues them and keeps them hidden [R153.2.1]. After many years they come forth. The mother dies of fright [Q211.8].

Finnish *4;* Estonian *1;* Lappish *1;* Swedish (Lund) *1;* Irish *1;* Spanish *1;* Catalan: Amades No. 1633; German *2;* Slovenian *1;* Russian: Andrejev. — Franco-American *1.*

765A* *Infanticide Punished.* A girl murders her three illegitimate children. In punishmnet three snakes suck her breast.

Russian (765 I) *1.*

765B* *The Father who Wanted to Kill his Children* [S11, Q211.8].

Lappish *1;* Irish *18* (often combined with Type 326 and with 563—569).

766 (formerly 763*) *The Seven Sleepers.* Magic sleep extending over many years. (Cf. Rip Van Winkle.) [D1960.1].

**Huber *Siebenschläfer;* *Chauvin VII 102 No. 376; *Hartland *Science* 173ff.; *Frazer *Pausanias* II 121; *Loomis *White Magic* 115; Liungman (763*); Coffin *2;* BP III 460 (Grimm No. 202). — Finnish-Swedish: Wessman 18 No. 163; Lappish (763*) *1;* Swedish *8* (Lund *4,* misc. 4); Irish: *Cross; English: Baughman 3; Jewish: Neuman (D1960.1). — English-American: Baughman *3.*

766* *A Boy Refuses to Give the Angels and God Food* [Q286]. God commands Death to take his life.

Lappish *1.*

767 *Food for the Crucifix.* A boy offers bread to a statue of Christ or the Virgin [Q172.1].

**Szövérffy in *Thompson Festschrift* 55ff.; *BP III 474ff.; *Reinhard PMLA XL 93; Irish: O'Suilleabhain 105, Beal XXI 333; Lithuanian: Balys No. 3727; Spanish: Boggs (767*) *1;* Italian (Sicilian *2,* Gonzenbach No. 86); Czech: Tille Soupis II (1) 76ff.; Greek (1322*) *1.*

768 *St. Christopher and the Christ Child.* The saintly ferryman. He carries the child across the stream. The child becomes heavier with each step, but the saint still carries him. The child reveals himself as Christ. [Q25].

*Dähnhardt *Natursagen* II 266; *Schröder Zs. f. Vksk. XXXV—XXXVI 85; *Szövérffy »Zur Entstehungsgeschichte einiger Volkserzählungen« Fabula II 212ff.; *Schwickert Zs. f. Vksk. NF III 14—26; *Loomis *White Magic* 114. — Lithuanian *1;* Swedish *2;* German *1;* Italien *2* (Sicilian *1,* Tuscan *1*); Hungarian: Berze Nagy (779 XX*) *2;* Slovenian *1;* Serbocroatian *3.* — Franco-American *1.* — Literary Treatments: Klapper *Erzählungen des Mittelalters* 111 No. 101; Jacobus de Voragine *Legenda Aurea,* ed. Grässe p. 432.

769 *Dead Child's Friendly Return to Parents.* Frequently to stop weeping. [E324].
*BP II 485; *Feilberg »hånd« I 765a; Dieterich Zs. f. Vksk. XII 147; Irish: O'Suilleabhain 41, Beal XXI 315; English: Child II 238ff., III 244f., 247, V 241, Baughman (E324); U.S.: Baughman (E324); Lithuanian: Balys No. 3525; Spanish Exempla: Keller (E324); Serbocroatian *15;* Chinese: Werner 314; N.A. Indian (Pawnee): Grinnell *Pawnee Hero Stories* (New York, 1889) 145; Eskimo (Greenland): Rink 161.

769* *A Dead Man Released from Purgatory.* A poor woman always prays for souls in purgatory. One day on her way home from church she meets an old man who asks her to deliver a letter to a certain wealthy merchant. The letter, it turns out, is from a dead merchant to his son, asking him to reward the woman for her sincere prayers, owing to which he has been released from purgatory.
Lithuanian *4.*

770 *The Nun who Saw the World.* The nun leaves the convent with her lover. The Virgin takes her place in the convent during the years of her absence. The nun returns repentant. [K1841.1].
**Waterphul *Die Geschichte der Marienlegende von Beatrix der Küstnerin* (Neuwald, 1904); **R. Guiette *La Légende de la sacristine* (1927); *Gröber *Beiträge zur romanischen und englischen Philologie, Festgabe für W. Förster* 421ff.; Toldo Zs. f. Vksk. XV 129ff.; Bolte *ibid* XV 136; Wesselski *Mönchslatein* 46 No. 39; Alphabet No. 468. — French *2;* German *1;* Slovenian *1.* — Franco-American *1.* — Literary Treatment: Maeterlinck »Sœur Beatrice«; Ward *Catalogue of Romances* II 659 No. 27, 723, III 342.

771* See Type 759.

772* *The Flies Instead of Nails on Christ's Heart.* They look like nails and prevent more nails being driven. [A2221.2.1].
Estonian *8.* Cf. Dähnhardt II 214.

773* *The Old Man (God) at St. John's Fire.* Prophesies death for the rich youth on the following day.
Livonian (773') *1.*

773** *God and Devil Dispute over Miser's Soul.* God says Devil may have it if he will fill a cask with money. God knocks bottom out of cask and hangs it in tree over gorge. Devil is unable to fill cask and leaves soul to God.
Spanish: Espinosa II 344f.; Spanish-American: Hansen (*773B) (Puerto Rico) *2.*

774 *Jests about Christ and Peter.* Peter made ridiculous. Cf. Types 785, 791.

774A *Peter Wants to Create a Man.* Puts head on backwards. [E34]. Cf. Type 1169.
Hungarian (Honti 771, Berze Nagy 779 III*) *1.*

774B *Peter Cannot Sell his Ass.*
Wesselski *Hodscha Nasreddin* I 57. — Hungarian (Honti 772, Berze Nagy 779 V*) *3.*

774C *The Legend of the Horseshoe.* Peter unwilling to lean over to pick up a horseshoe, but later does so many times for dropped cherries.
Danish: Zs. f. Vksk. XI 254 (1667); French: RTP X 661; Catalan: Amades Nos. 1294, 2108; Flemish: De Meyere *Vlaamsche Vertelselschat* III 78 No. 4; Czech: Tille Soupis I 581 *2;* Hungarian (Berze Nagy 773*, Honti 773) *4;* Greek: Kretschmer 232 No. 54.

774D *Peter Acts as God for a Day: Tires of Bargain.* A girl takes her goat to pasture and leaves him: »May God care for you!» Peter must run everywhere after the goat. [L423].
*Dähnhardt *Natursagen* II 188. — French: Thuriet *Traditions Populaires de la Haute-Saône* (Paris, 1892) p. 595; German: Henssen Jül. 319 No. 276; Hungarian (Honti 774, Berze Nagy 779 XII*) *2;* Czech: Wenzig *Westslawischer Märchenschatz* p. 89; Slovenian. — Literary Treatment: Hans Sachs Schwänke No. 159.

774E *Peter Gets Permission to Go to Grape-gathering.* Comes into heaven late. Tells that men in prosperity only curse and only in trouble pray.
Köhler *Aufsätze* 75f. — Italian (Tuscan [760] *1*); German: Meier *Volksmärchen aus Schwaben* 137 No. 139; Hungarian (Honti 776*, Berze Nagy 764*) *4;* Slovenian; Serbocroatian *1.*

774F *Peter with the Fiddle.* Peter is punished for going into an inn. Christ enchants him by putting a fiddle on his back. He is laughed at.
*Dähnhardt *Natursagen* II 172; *Henssen Jül. No. 275. — French RTP III 180; Catalan: Amades No. 1307; German *8;* Rumanian: Schullerus *Rumänische Märchen* 410 Nol 210; Hungarian (Honti 777, Berze Nagy 754**) *6;* Slovenian.

774G *Peter's Favorite Fruit.* The Lord asks St. Peter what kind of fruit he likes best. Peter really likes grape and wine best but says he prefers figs. Hence figs bear twice a year.
Spanish (792*) *1.*

774H *Christ Puts Knots in Wood.* Peter, angry at carpenters wants Christ to have iron knots in wood. Christ does make hard knots but not iron. (Cf. A2755.4.) [A2738].
*Dähnhardt *Natursagen* II 164ff. — German: Simrock *Deutsche Märchen* (1864) p. 136; Hungarian (Berze Nagy 779 XXXIII*) *2;* Slovenian.

774J *Why Peter Became Bald.* Did not divide cakes with Jesus. [Cf. A1315.2].
*Bolte Zs. *f. vgl. Litteraturgeschichte* VI 453, XI 69. — Flemish: De

Mont en de Cock *Vlaamsche Vertelsels* 129; Catalan: Amades No. 1295; German (725D') *5;* Hungarian: Berze Nagy (774*) *1.*

774K *Peter Stung by Bees.* Avenges himself on the whole hive. Christ shows the justice in this. [J225.0.2].
Irish: Béal XXI 305; Catalan: Amades No. 1309; Italian (Sicilian *759) *2;* Hungarian: Berze Nagy (779 XIII*) *1;* Serbocroatian *10;* Slovenian (759 e, f) *2.*

774L *Mushrooms from St. Peter's Spittle* [A2613.1].
*Dähnhardt II 107. — Lithuanian (3230); Italian (Sicilian *786) *2;* Hungarian (Berze Nagy 772*) *4.*

774M *Peter as Bad Messenger.* To tell peasants to work from five to seven. Is drunk and says from seven to five.
Hungarian (Honti 775, Berze Nagy 779 XXX*) *2.*

774N *St. Peter's Gluttony.* Jesus keeps asking him questions so that he must continually spit out mouthfuls.
Italian (Sicilian *786 *2*); Slovenian (785C) *1.*

774P *St. Peter and the Nuts.* Complains that large trees have small fruits. Permitted to change this. An immense nut falls on him.
Italian (Sicilian *752D *3*).

775 *Midas' Short-sighted Wish:* everything turns to gold [J2072.1].
*Pauli (ed. Bolte) No. 180. — Lithuanian (*775) *8.*

775* *God and the Emperor of Rome.* It is permitted to the Emperor of Rome to enjoy the companionship of God. Once when the Emperor conceals his wife that she may listen, God ceases coming to him. [C51.4.1].
Estonian *3.*

775A* *A Living Man Wants to See God.* He carries God (old man) on his shoulders to church. [K1811.2].
Lithuanian *3.*

777 (formerly 754***) *The Wandering Jew.* Ceaseless wandering with inability to die, as punishment for blasphemy. [Q502.1, cf. A221.3].
Motif Q502.1; Köhler-Bolte I 406. — Estonian (754) *3;* Livonian (754*) *1;* Lithuanian (778*) *5;* Lappish (754**) *1;* Swedish *36* (Uppsala *21,* Stockholm *5,* Lund *5,* misc. *5*); Norwegian *3;* Danish (754***) *1;* Irish *2;* English *6.* — Franco-American *1;* English-American: Baughman *2.*

778 *To Sacrifice a Giant Candle.* Refusal to make sacrifice after need is past. In distress a person promises a sacrifice to a god (saint) but disregards the promise when the danger passes. [K231.3, K231.3.1].
*Pauli (ed. Bolte) Nos. 304, 305. — Finnish-Swedish (FFC VI p. 35) *2;* Walloon (*1553) *1;* Spanish exempla: Keller (K231.3); German: Merkens I 143 No. 162; Italian Novella: Rotunda (K231.3.1); Hungarian: Berze Nagy (1629*) *1;* Serbocroatian *2;* Gypsy: Krauss *Zigeunerhumor* p. 25; India: Thompson-Balys (K231.3.1); West Indies: Flowers

501. — Literary Treatments: Wienert FFC LVI 78f. (ET 438, 448), 139 (ST 442); Halm Aesop Nos. 49, 58; *Crane Vitry 177 No. 102; Herbert III 8, 36; Scala Celi 56b No. 316.

778* *Two Candles.* An old woman on every occasion lights a candle both to God and the devil, since it is not known where you will wind up on this earth.
Russian: Afanasiev (1625) *1.*

779 *Miscellaneous Divine Rewards and Punishments.*
Slovenian *9.*

779A* *Waiting for a Sign.* Jesus will not permit child to be born until Peter sees favorable sign in heaven.
Hungarian: Berze Nagy (779 IX*) *6.*

779B* *Disrespectful Children Punished.* Children treat their mother badly. She is abducted and the children's home collapses.
Russian: Andrejev (*766A) *1.*

779C* *Hard-hearted Children Punished.* The children refuse to feed their mother and want to sell her, but she becomes rooted to them.
Russian: Andrejev (*766B) *1.*

780—789 Truth Comes to Light

780 *The Singing Bone.* The brother kills his brother (sister) and buries him in the earth. From the bones a shepherd makes a flute which brings the secret to light.

In different versions the murder is revealed in several different ways [N271]: (a) an instrument (harp, flute) is made from the bones [E632] or (b) from a tree growing from the grave [E631].

**Solymossy »Mese a jávorfáról« *Ethnographia* XXXI (1920) 1—25; **Mackensen *Der singende Knochen* (FFC XLIX); *BP I 260 (Grimm No. 28); Coffin *8;* Krohn FFC XCVI 74ff.; *Cocchiara *Genesi di leggendi* (3d ed. Palermo, 1949) 109ff.; Brewster *Maal og Minne* (1953) 49ff.; Espinosa II 326—332; Anderson *Novelline* Nos. 95, 96. — Finnish *1;* Estonian *3;* Lithuanian *35;* Danish *9;* Scottish *1;* Irish *65,* Beal XXI 336; English: Child *English and Scottish Popular Ballads* I 121—135, 494, IV 449; French *36;* Spanish *4;* Catalan: Amades No. 85; Dutch *14;* Flemish *9;* Walloon *9;* German *35* (Archive *34,* Merk. 354); Italian (Tuscan 301b *1,* Sicilian *3,* Gonzenbach No. 51); Rumanian *5;* Hungarian *10;* Czech: Tille Soupis II (2) 181ff. *10;* Slovenian *4;* Serbocroatian *1;* Polish (734) *2;* Russian: Andrejev *Ukraine 15,* Afanasiev *15;* Greek *2;* Turkish: Eberhard-Boratav Nos. 60 IV, 241 *8;* India *7;* Japanese: Ikeda (E632). — Franco-American *15;* English-American: Baughman *1;* Spanish-American: Rael Nos. 91, 92 (U.S.), Hansen (Argentina *3,* Cuba *2,* Dominican Republic *6,* Puerto Rico *6,* Uruguay *1);* Cape Verde Islands: Parsons MAFLS XV (1) 125 n. 1, 136 n. 1; West Indies (Negro) *31.* — African *4.*

780A *The Cannibalistic Brothers.*

I. *The Murder.* Six brothers live with their sister. One day, while cooking, she cuts her finger and blood falls into the food. The older brothers find the food delicious and decide to kill and eat their sister [G36.2]. The youngest refuses, or (a) the other brothers force him to shoot and his arrow kills his sister.

II. *The Speaking Tree.* (a) From her grave a flowering plant grows or a tree [E631]. (b) From the tree a fiddle, flute, etc., is made (c) which, when played, tells of the girl [E632]. (d) From the musical instrument the girl appears (mysterious housekeeper [N831.1]). (e) The girl marries a king or the musician. The brothers come as beggars and are confronted by the girl [L432.1]. (f) They sink into the earth [C984.7, F942], etc., and from their hair grass grows.

India *12.*

780B *The Speaking Hair.* A stepmother buries a girl alive. Her hair grows as wheat or bush and sings her misfortunes [E631]. Thus she is discovered and dug up alive. The stepmother is buried in the same hole [Q581].

Spanish *2,* *Espinosa Cuentos III 89—93 (Spanish *4,* Portuguese *1*); Serbocroatian *1.* — Spanish-American: Hansen (Cuba *3,* Puerto Rico *8*).

780C *The Tell-tale Calf's Head.* In the murderer's hands it turns into the murdered man's head [Q551.3.3].

*BP I 276 n. 2, II 535; *Espinosa II 326. — French *2;* Spanish (780*A) *4;* Catalan: Amades Nos. 1296, 1990. — Spanish-American: Hansen (Puerto Rico) *4.* — North African *4.*

781 *The Princess who Murdered her Child* [Q211.4]. The hero learns the bird language [B131.1, B215]. The bird sings »The bones lie under the tree« [N271.4]. Cf. Type 517.

Finnish *39;* Estonian *3;* Slovenian *2;* Russian: Andrejev *1.* — West Indies (Negro) *3.* — Cf. African *12.*

782 *Midas and the Ass's Ears.* His secret discovered by his barber. Or he whispers the secret to a reed which repeats it.

Motifs:

F511.2.2. Person with ass's ears (Midas). N465. Secret physical peculiarity discovered by barber. D1316.5. Magic reed betrays secret.

*Köhler-Bolte I 383 n. 1, 511, 587; *BP IV 147 n. 7; *Pauli (ed. Bolte) No. 397; Maja Bošković-Stulli (Zagreb) is making a study of the Midas Saga. — French *6;* Rumanian (886 I) *1;* Serbocroatian *126;* Russian: Andrejev (716) *1;* Greek *5,* Schmidt p. 70 No. 4; Turkish: Eberhard-Boratav No. 242 *3;* India *7.* — Spanish-American: Hansen (Chile) *1.*

785 *Who Ate the Lamb's Heart?* Peter and his companions on their travels. The companion eats the heart of the lamb. Denies it. The healing of the princess. When the money is divided, the third part is assigned to the one who has eaten the lamb's heart. The companion declares the lamb had no heart [K402]. When Peter divides the money received for healing the princess the companion confesses in order to get his part [J1141.1.1].

*BP II 149, 153 (Grimm No. 81); Wienert FFC LVI 40, 107; Oesterley *Gesta Romanorum* No. 83; Herbert *Catalogue of Romances* III 205; Pauli (ed. Bolte) No. 57; *Chauvin VIII 101 No. 73; Anderson *Novelline* No. 7. — Finnish *14;* Estonian *12;* Livonian *1;* Lithuanian *51;* Swedish *26* (Uppsala *13,* Göteborg *8,* Lund *1,* Liungman *1*); Danish *1;* Icelandic *1;* Irish *62,* Beal VII 16, XV 287f.; French *7;* Spanish *4;* Catalan: Amades Nos. 1292, 1311; Flemish *10,* (785*) *7;* German *42* (Archive *32,* Hensslen Jül. No. 274, Merk. 126, Meckl. No. 86); Italian *7* (Sicilian *3,* Tuscan 333f., 785 a—c *4*); Rumanian *4;* Hungarian *6;* Czech: Tille Soupis I 600ff. *9;* Slovenian *9;* Serbocroatian *18;* Russian: Andrejev *11,* Andrejev *Ukraine 22;* Greek *1;* India *3;* Indonesian: DeVries No. 214. — Franco-American *7;* Spanish-American: Hansen (Dominican Republic *2,* Chile **1553 *1,* Puerto Rico *4*), Rael Nos. 297—300, 496 (U.S.); West Indies (Negro) *2.*

785A *The Goose with One Leg.* Accused of eating the goose's leg, the thief maintains that it had only one leg, and cleverly enforces his point by showing geese standing on one leg. (Usually the master confounds the rascal by frightening the geese so that they use both legs.) [K402.1].

*Pauli (ed. Bolte) No. 57; *Wesselski *Hodscha Nasreddin* I 229 No. 75; Coffin *3;* Boccaccio Decameron VI No. 4 (*Lee 177). — Lithuanian (*2424) *3;* Flemish: de Meyere *Vlaamsche Vertelselschat* No. 58, (785*) *3;* German: Wossidlo *Aus dem Lande Fritz Reuters* 195; Italian: *Rotunda (K402.1); Hungarian: Berze Nagy (779 VI*) *1;* Czech: Tille Soupis I 572 *3;* India: Thompson-Balys (K402.1); West Indies: Flowers 508.

788 *The Man who was Burned up and Lived Again.* (a) The hero has committed a sin and (b) is therefore burned to death. (c) A part of his body is carried away and (d) from contact with it (or other contact with the hero) a woman conceives and bears a child. (e) The child is the reborn hero.

**Matičetov »Der verbrannte und wiedergeborene Mensch« *Fabula* II 94ff. (Latvian *1;* Lithuanian *4;* Breton *1;* Irish *1;* Hungarian *3;* German *2;* French *3;* Italian *4,* Czech *1;* Slovenian *27;* Serbocroatian *14*); *Köhler-Bolte II 341 No. 36. — Lithuanian (*703) *4;* French *4;* Italian (Sicilian *708) *3.*

790* *St. George Teaches the Poor Man.* »Who steals somewhat and lies somewhat will be rich.« [J556.1].
Livonian (790*) *1;* Lithuanian (*847) *12;* Russian: Andrejev (847*) *6.*

791 *The Savior and Peter in Night-Lodgings.* Peter is twice beaten.
Peter and Christ are sleeping in the same bed. The drunken host returns home and beats Peter. Peter changes places with Christ. The host then comes in to beat the other lodger. Peter again receives the blows. [K1132]. In French often with Type 752A.

*BP III 451 n. 1; Zs. f. Vksk. XXXVII 130, Frobenius *Atlantis* VII 60f.; Fb III 164a »Sankt Peder». — Finnish-Swedish (790*) *1;* Lithuanian *23;* Danish *3;* Icelandic *1;* French *6;* Spanish *1;* Catalan: Amades Nos. 1297, 1302, 2116; Flemish (790*) *9;* German *72* (Archive *70,* Henssen Volk No. 174, Merk. 149); Italian (Sicilian *1*); Hungarian: Honti 778, Berze Nagy 768** *6;* Czech: Tille Soupis I 577ff. *9;* Slovenian *10;* Serbocroatian *15;* Russian: Andrejev *Ukraine 15.* — Franco-American *1.*

791* *The Saint Restored.* Saint torn to pieces, then resuscitated.
Köhler-Bolte II 241. — French (788) *4.*

795 (formerly 795*) *The Punishment of the Angel.* An angel out of pity for a mother who is then suckling two children permits her to remain on earth instead of going to heaven. In punishment the angel must become a sexton. When the child is grown up the angel returns to heaven. [V233.1].

Finnish-Swedish *4;* Estonian (795*) *4;* Livonian *1;* Lithuanian (795*) *4;* Hungarian: Berze Nagy 779 VII* *3;* Czech: Tille Soupis I 56ff. *5;* Slovenian *3;* Serbocroatian *2;* Russian: Andrejev 795A*.

796* *Angels on the Widow's Roof.* The prince sees two angels playing on the roof of a pious widow. He sends her riches. The next year when the prince returns, he sees that, instead of two angels, two devils are playing on the roof. The widow has forgotten God. [Q559.1].
Estonian *3;* Russian (796*).

797* *The Devil Tries to Pass for Jesus.* [K1992]. He forbids the man to cut wood since it is Sunday. Disappears when the man, on the advice of the priest, demands that he show the wounds in his hands and feet.
Estonian *3.*

800—809 The Man in Heaven

800 *The Tailor in Heaven.* In God's absence, Peter lets an unworthy tailor into heaven. The tailor throws God's footstool at an old woman thief on earth. He is expelled from heaven.
Motifs: A661.0.1.2. Saint Peter as porter of heaven. P441.1. Tailor occupies God's throne for a day. F1037.1. Footstool thrown from heaven. L435.3. Self-righteous tailor in heaven expelled.
*BP I 342 (Grimm No. 35). — Estonian *5;* Lithuanian *13;* Scottish *2;* Flemish *2;* German *19* (Archive *17,* Henssen Jül. No. 277, Merk. 103); Hungarian *2;* Czech: Tille Soupis I lf. *2;* Slovenian *1;* Russian: Andrejev *2.* — Buriat: Holmberg Siberian Myth 441.

800A *The Beggar on the Cross in Place of Christ.* Is made to leave the cross for his impatience concerning the sinners. [L435.4].
Lithuanian (800A*) *8.*

801 *Master Pfriem.* The cobbler who was never satisfied is expelled from heaven [Q312.1]. He is admitted by St. Peter, [A661.0.1.2] but warned

against fault-finding [F13]. He sees men carrying a beam crosswise [F171.6.3]. But when he sees the horses hitched in front and behind the wagon [F171.6.4] he cannot keep from complaining. Cf. Types 1180, 1242, 1248.

*BP III 297 (Grimm No. 178). — Finnish *1;* Estonian *3;* German *1;* Russian: Andrejev; Greek: Loukatos No. 6.

802 *The Peasant in Heaven.* On the arrival of the rich man there is song and dance, because of the rarity of such an event. [E758, W245].

*BP III 274 (Grimm No. 167); Hdwb. d. Märchens I 351a s.v. »Burli im Himmel». — Lithuanian *1;* Danish *9;* German *9* (Archive *8,* Henssen Volk No. 261); Slovenian *3;* Russian: Andrejev.

802A* *His Faith into the Balance.* A clerk sees his good and evil deeds being weighed. He asked them to throw his faith in Christ (the Virgin) into the scale. He is saved. [V512.1].

*Herbert III 471; Ward *Catalogue of Romances* II 651 No. 5; Spanish Exempla: Keller (V512.2). — Lithuanian (*802A) *7.*

802B* *Rich Man's Vision.* The rich man soon tires of the things he wanted in heaven, yet when he looks through the keyhole and sees his brother sitting at the throne of God, he spends 200 years gazing at the sight and never tires of it.

Lithuanian (*805) *2.*

802C* *The Rooms in Heaven.* While a good man is yet living on earth, several splendid rooms are prepared for him in heaven. A dead miser asks the living man to give him at least one of them. [Q172.4.1].

Lithuanian (*804A) *4.*

803 *Solomon Binds the Devil in Chains in Hell.* Asks the devil to try on the chains meant for Solomon. Variant: Christ and the Smith in hell. [A1071.1].

**Balys »Lithuanian Legends of the Devil in Chains» (Tautosakos Darbai 321—331); **Krohn, »Der gefangene Unhold» *Finnish-ugrische Forschungen* VII (1907) 129ff.; **F. von d. Leyen *Der gefesselte Unhold* (Prague, 1908). — Finnish (803*) *2;* Estonian (803*) *4;* Lithuanian *23;* Russian: Andrejev Ukraine *15.*

804 *Peter's Mother Falls from Heaven.* It is permitted to the son in heaven [A661.0.1.2] to pull his mother out of hell on a stalk [F51.1.3]. When the other dead catch her feet, she kicks them and falls back into hell [Q291.1].

*BP III 538 (Grimm No. 221); *Anderson *Novelline* No. 16. — Finnish (804**) *2;* Lithuanian *18;* Swedish (misc.) *1;* French *1;* Spanish *3;* Catalan: Amades Nos. 409, 1318; German *9;* Italian *5* (Tuscan *2,* Sicilian *3*); Hungarian: Berze Nagy 779 XXXII* *3;* Slovenian *11;* Serbocroatian *1;* Russian: Andrejev 804*, cf. 460A.

804A *The Bean-stalk to Heaven.* An old couple climb the bean-stalk to heaven. The old woman keeps asking: »Is heaven still far away?» Again falls to earth. Or: the old woman seats herself in God's little carriage, which suddenly drives off with her. Finally both are cast out of heaven.

Lithuanian (*1416A) *43;* Serbocroatian *2;* Russian: Andrejev (*1885) *25,* Afanesiev (*1425) *8.*

804B (formerly 804*) *The Church in Hell.* The man (Solomon) is let out of hell when he threatens to build a church there. [K1781].

Estonian *5;* Livonian *2;* Lithuanian (811A*) *7;* Hungarian: Berze Nagy (462*) *5;* Czech: Tille Soupis 185ff.; Serbocroatian *1;* Russian: Andrejev *2.*

804B* *The Tavern at Heaven's Gate.* Entices so many from heaven that tavern-keeper is let into heaven as preventive.
Slovenian *1.*

805 (formerly 805*) *Joseph and Mary Threaten to Leave Heaven* when the man who has always prayed to them is refused admittance [V254.6].

Estonian *1;* Italian (Sicilian *2*). — Franco-American *2;* Spanish-American: Rael No. 295 (U.S.).

808 (formerly 808*) *The Devil and the Angel Wait for Souls.* By the rich man's deathbed the devil waits for the soul, but by the poor man's child the angel of God waits. [E756.1].

Livonian (808*) *1;* Slovenian *3;* Russian: Andrejev *1.*

808A (formerly 808**) *The Death of the Good and of the Bad Man.* A bee flies out of the man's mouth; a white and black bird fight over the bee until, in the first case, the white gets it, in the second the black.[E756,E734.2].

Coffin *1.* — Estonian (808*) *7;* Lithuanian (*808) *5;* Serbocroatian *1;* Greek *3.*

809* *Rich Man Allowed to Stay in Heaven* for single deed of charity. (Sometimes repaid and sent to hell.)
Finnish *3.*

809** *Old Man Repaid for Good Deeds.* He goes to look at the beggar's house he has helped build and finds himself in paradise.
Russian: Andrejev (*809) *1.*

810—814 The Man Promised to the Devil

810 *The Snares of the Evil One.* The priest permits the man who is promised to the devil to spend the night in the church, and draws a ring around him. The devil cannot tempt him outside the ring.

Motifs: M211. Man sells soul to devil. S211. Child sold (promised) to devil (ogre). K218.1. Devil cheated by having priest draw a sacred circle about the intended victim. D1381.11. Magic circle protects from devil.

*BP II 329ff. (Grimm No. 92). — Finnish (810, 811) *80;* Finnish-Swedish *10;* Estonian *34;* Lithuanian *1;* Lappish *4;* Swedish *56* (Uppsala *20,* Stockholm *6,* Göteborg *11,* Lund *6,* Liungman *6,* misc. *7*); Norwegian *8,* Solheim *3;* Danish: Grundtvig No. 59; Icelandic *3* (cf.

810 I*, 810 VIII* *11*); Scottish *1;* Irish *116*, Beal XXI 309, 316; Flemish *1;* German *20* (Archive *18*, Henssen Volk No. 42, Meckl. No. 89); Italian *1* (Tuscan [1532] *1*); Hungarian (811) *6*, Berze Nagy (810) *5;* Slovenian *2;* Serbocroatian *1;* Russian: Afanasiev. — Franco-American *4;* West Indies (Negro) *1*.

810A *The Devil Does Penance.* The devil takes service with a farmer in return for the bread he stole. Punishes the evil landowner and makes his master prosperous. [G303.9.3.1.1].
  *BP II 294; Wünsche *Teufel* 71f. — Lithuanian (3290, 3292) *6;* Irish: Beal XXI 314; Danish *62;* Slovenian (650) *1;* Serbocroatian *3;* Polish *28*.

810A* *The Priest and the Devil.* The devils demand the priest's daughter. They must build a church overnight. The priest makes the cock crow earlier than usual.
  Russian: Andrejev (*810 I) *1*.

810B* *The Youth Sold to the Devil.* His parents sew him up on three successive nights in a dogskin, a ram's hide and goat's skin. The devil cannot find him.
  Russian: Andrejev (*810 II) *1*.

811 (formerly 811*) *The Man Promised to the Devil Becomes a Priest.* Saves himself. [K218.3]. Cf. Type 756B.
  Finnish-Swedish (811) *5;* Estonian (811) *1;* Danish *1*, Grundtvig No. 58A; Scottish FL XXXIII 388; Irish *107*, Beal X 3—5; German: Henssen Volk No. 177, Plenzat *4;* Hungarian: Berze Nagy 811 *3;* Serbocroatian *2;* Slovenian; Russian: Andrejev.

811A* *The Boy Promised (or destined) to go to the Devil Saves himself by his Good Conduct.*
  *Petit de Julleville *Les Mystères* (Paris, 1880) 228—31; FFC LXIX p. 224. — French *1*, French Canadian *1*.

811B* *Boy by Exceptional Penitence Saves his Mother from Hell.* (Sometimes with Type 471 or 930.)
  French Canadian: Sister Marie-Ursule No. 23.

811C* *Princess Rescued from Devil.* King promises his daughter to devil, who saves him from danger (Type 425 I d 3). Girl saved from devil by peasant boy. Transformation flight (Type 313). Impostor, Recognition.
  Icelandic (814*) *4*.

812 *The Devil's Riddle.* The man is saved by solving the riddle propounded by the devil. The solution discovered in the forest.
  I. *Devil's Contract.* (a) A man (three men) promises himself to the devil at the end of a certain time if he cannot solve three (seven) riddles which the devil propounds [M211].
  II. *The Riddles.* (a) The devil has objects which appear different from what they really are [H523]. Their real nature must be guessed: (a^1) horse — a he-goat, (a^2) cloth — a goat-skin, (a^3) gold cup — cup of pitch; or (a^4) roast meat — dead dog, (a^5) spoon — whale-rib, (a^6) wineglass — horse's hoof, etc.; or (b) he asks seemingly impossible questions: what is sweeter than honey, [H671], softer than swansdown [H672], harder than stone [H673]; or (c) symbolic interpretations (the meanings of the numbers 1 to 7, etc. [H602.1.1]); or (d) he sets impossible tasks [H1010]; see Type 1170ff.

III. *The Solution.* (a) The solution is found by hiding in a tree and overhearing the devil's conversation with a companion [N451.1], or (b) by masking and overhearing [G661.1] or (c) by being hid by the devil's grandmother who gets the secrets from the devil [G530.4], or (d) through the agency of a supernatural helper [N810].

*BP III 12 (Grimm No. 125); Coffin *4;* Dähnhardt I 194ff. — Finnish *12;* Finnish-Swedish *7;* Estonian *27;* Lithuanian *3;* Lappish *1;* Swedish *98* (Uppsala *32,* Stockholm *10,* Göteborg *35,* Lund *8,* Liungman *11,* misc. *28*); Norwegian (813**) *7,* Solheim *2;* Danish *27,* Grundtvig No. 148; Scottish *2;* Irish *14,* English *1;* French *4;* Spanish *1;* Catalan: Amades cf. No. 256; German *38* (Archive *37,* Meckl. No. 89); Italian *3* (Tuscan *2,* Sicilian *1*); Hungarian: Berze Nagy (813*, 814*), Honti (812), Dégh No. 31 *7;* Czech: Tille Soupis I 175, 177ff., 190 *8;* Slovenian *6;* Serbocroatian *4;* Russian: Andrejev (812A) *1;* Greek *9,* Loukatos No. 12, Laographia XV 415. — English-American: Baughman *1.*

812* *The Devil's Riddle Otherwise Solved.*
Lithuanian (*812A) *6;* Rumanian (812A*) *3;* Russian: Andrejev (*812B) *1.*

813 *A Careless Word Summons the Devil* [C12].

813A *The Accursed Daughter.* A man wants to marry a girl although she comes from the devil. He gets the girl, who had been carried off by the devil because of the careless words of the mother (»Go to the devil»).
Russian: Afanasiev (813*A) *19.*

813B *The Accursed Grandson.* An old woman curses a young boy at his wedding; the devil carries him away; his wife goes after him and gets him back from the devil.
Russian: Afanasiev (813*B) *6.*

813C *»May the Devil Skin me* if this is not true.» Devil does.
Serbocroatian *2.*

813* *Bargain with the Devil: Not to Sleep Three Nights.* For a large sum of money, the poor man makes this bargain with the devil. The devil: »Are you asleep?» — »No, I am just thinking». — »What are you thinking of?» — »That on earth there are more crooked trees than straight ones ... more hills than plains ... more water than land» (and the like). The devil goes to ascertain these things. And so for three nights. The man gets the money. The rich man follows the poor man's example but confesses that he has slept, and so the devil wins his soul.
Lithuanian (*813) *10.*

815 *The Deceased Rich Man and the Devils in the Church.* The rich man's money is buried in his skin in the grave. The devil comes to see the money. The cobbler draws a circle about him [D1381.11] to keep the devil off; takes the money and nails the devil fast.

Finnish *35;* Finnish-Swedish *4;* Estonian *3;* Swedish *12* (Uppsala *5,* Stockholm *1,* Göteborg *3,* Liungman *1,* misc. *2*); Irish *1;* English *2;* Hungarian *3;* Serbocroatian *1;* Polish (372*) *4;* Russian: Andrejev.

815* *The Shoemaker who Made Shoes for the Devil.* Saves himself when he does not take all the money he was promised. [K210].
Finnish-Swedish 3.

816* *Devils Tempt the Pope.* From a conversation of the ravens, the priest learns that the devil, in the form of a woman, thinks to tempt the Pope. He ties the devils together with some holy article (rosary or other) and has them carry him on a church door to Rome. Forewarns the Pope. [T332].
**Motif T332. — Lithuanian *12*.

817* *Devil Leaves at Mention of God's Name.* [G303.16.8].
**Motif G303.16.8. — England, Ireland, Wales, U.S.: Baughman; Lithuanian: Balys *Legends* Nos. 651, 774f., 780, 814; Spanish *1*, Keller; Jewish: *Neumann.

818* *The Devil Goes to Confession.* Performs very severe penance, but cannot bear to humble himself and make obeisance before the altar. [V29.8]. Cf. Type 1800.
Lithuanian *6*.

819* *The Devil's Portrait.* A serf painter is ordered by his master to paint a portrait of a devil. The master is found dead.
Russian: Andrejev (*816).

820 *The Devil as Substitute for Day Laborer at Mowing.*

820A *The Devil Mows with a Magic Sickle.* The evil overseer tries to keep up with him and dies of overexertion. [M213]. Cf. Type 1090.
*Deutsches Jahrb. f. Vksk. II 27, 30. — Finnish *19*; Estonian *1*; Swedish (Lund) *1*; Irish *32*; Hungarian: Berze Nagy (819*) *4*; Slovenian *3*; Russian: Andrejev.

820B *The Devil at Haying.* An old woman must have haying done on certain day. A mysterious stranger appears and promises help, comes at the last moment and does the work.
Swedish (GS 819) *4* (Uppsala *1*, Stockholm *2*, Liungman *1*).

821 *The Devil as Advocate.* Cf. Type 1186.

821A *Thief Rescued by the Devil.* A man is accused of theft. The devil carries the judge from the court room and thus repays the hospitality of the accused.
Motifs:
C12.2. Oath: »May the devil take me if...». Devil does. G303.22.11. Devil as advocate of falsely condemned man. Carries off the judge. Q45.2. Hospitality to devil repaid.
Finnish *40*; Estonian *27*; Swedish *4* (Uppsala *2*, Liungman *1*, misc. *1*); Norwegian *1*; Dutch *1*; Czech: Tille Soupis II (2) 368f. *4*; Russian: Andrejev *1*.

821B *Chickens from Boiled Eggs.* Many years after the guest has eaten them, a host demands an enormous sum for twelve boiled eggs, claiming that by this time they have hatched out chickens who have in turn laid eggs, etc. The devil as advocate comes in and demands that the host cook his peas for planting [J1191.2]. »Boiled peas may grow as soon as chickens can be hatched from boiled eggs.» The devil carries off the judge.

*BP II 368 n. 1; *Pauli (ed. Bolte) No. 807. — Finnish *2;* Estonian *3;* Livonian *1;* Lithuanian *11;* Swedish *2* (Uppsala *1,* misc. *1*); Icelandic *2;* Scottish *1;* French *4;* Dutch *1;* German *3;* Italian *3* (Trieste: Pinguentini No. 2, Sicilian *2*); Hungarian *1;* Slovenian *2;* Serbocroatian *3;* Russian: Andrejev, Andrejev *Ukraine 4;* Turkish: Eberhard-Boratav No. 295 *4.* — Spanish-American: Rael No. 34 (U.S.); Cape Verde Islands: *Parsons MAFLS XV (1) 64 n. 2; West Indies (Negro) *14.*

821A* *Devil's Trickery Separates Married Couples and Friends.*
Rumanian (821 I*) *8.*

821B* *Devil as Host at Dinner.* Spoon with handle a fathom long. Beard and moustaches fall out.
Rumanian (821 II*) *3.*

822 *The Lazy Boy and the Industrious Girl.* The Lord and St. Peter come across a very lazy boy and a very industrious girl. Our Lord decrees, much to St. Peter's astonishment, that these two are to be married. [T125].
*Wesselski *Märchen* 214 No. 22; Dähnhardt II 115ff. — Finnish (770*) *1;* Finnish-Swedish (823*) *1;* Estonian (770*) *5;* Lithuanian *10;* Swedish *7* (Stockholm *1,* Göteborg *2,* misc. *4*); Norwegian (822**) *2,* (823*) *4,* Solheim *2;* French *4;* Catalan: Amades No. 1301; German *37* (Archive *33,* Merk. 142, Henssen Jül. No. 271A, Henssen Volk No. 173, Meckl. No. 82); Italian *1* (Sicilian *1*); Hungarian: Berze Nagy (769*) *4;* Czech: Tille Soupis I 574f. *6;* Slovenian *3;* Serbocroatian *23,* Istrian No. 34, Russian: Andrejev (770*) *1.*

822* *The Devil Lends Money to the Man.* When at the end of the term the man comes to pay his debt the people tell him, »The devil has been dead a long time.» The man keeps the money. [K231.4].
Estonian *5;* Livonian *1;* Lithuanian (*1166) *21;* Swedish *6* (Stockholm *2,* Göteborg *1,* misc. *3*); Serbocroatian *1;* Russian: Andrejev.

823* *The Advice of the Devil.* He exhorts the youth to enjoy himself and not to think of God. When the youth has grown old the devil says, »It is now too late to think of God.»
Estonian *1.*

823A* *Mother Dies of Fright when she Learns that she was about to Commit Incest with her Son.* He has disguised himself to test her chastity. [N383.3].
*Krappe Balor 181ff.; Alphabet No. 710 (Secundus). — Hungarian: Berze Nagy *1.*

824 (formerly 824*) *The Devil Lets the Man See his Wife's Unfaithfulness.* Brings him in the form of a he-goat to the wife and her lover. [K1531].
Estonian *2;* Lithuanian (*824) *8;* Russian (*824) *2.*

825 *The Devil in Noah's Ark.* The devil wants to know what Noah is doing when he is building the ark. He persuades Noah's wife to give him a drink. Noah forbids the wife to go into ark until the devil has also been invited. [K485].
I. *Secret Building of Ark and its Destruction by Devil.* (a) God commands Noah to build the ark in secret to escape the deluge [A1015, A1021]. (b) For secrecy the hammer is noiseless or the ax on the stone chopping-

block does not get dull [H1199.13, cf. H1116.1, F837]. (c) The devil seduces Noah's wife and persuades her to give Noah an intoxicating drink [K2213.4.2]. (d) Noah tells his secret and the devil destroys the ark [K2213.4.2, cf. G303.14.1.1, K2213.4]. (e) Noah weeps and angels instruct him how to rebuild ark.

II. *Entrance to Ark.* (a) A gong assembles the animals. (b) Creatures barred or absent from ark.

III. *The Hole in the Ark.* (a) Devil as mouse gnaws a hole in the ark. (d) The serpent rewarded.

**F. L. Utley (Ohio State University) forthcoming study based on 280 versions; *Dähnhardt I 258. — Estonian (825*) *6;* Lithuanian *5;* Irish *4;* Polish (cf. Type 282) *4;* Russian: Andrejev *1.* — Franco-American *4.*

825* changed to Type 470B.

826 (formerly 826*) *Devil Writes down Names of Men on Hide in Church.* Woman laughs when she sees him. [G303.24.1.3].

**Robert Wildhaber *Das Sündenregister auf der Kuhhaut* (FFC CLXIII); *Liungman SSF III 270 No. 826*. — Finnish FFC XXXIII 24 No. 59; Estonian FFC XXV 126 No. 59; Livonian (826') *4;* Lithuanian (*826) *10,* Balys Legends No. 427; Swedish *9* (Uppsala *2,* Göteborg *1,* Liungman *1,* misc. *5*); German (815') *37;* Serbocroatian *2;* Slovenian; Russian: Andrejev (*826) *2.*

827 (formerly 827*) *A Shepherd Knows Nothing of God.* He goes afoot across the water to the priest to ask about God, but returning he sinks to his knees in the water. [V51.1, D2125.1].

**Andrejev »Tri Starca« *Novoje Delo* (Kazan, 1922) (see Anderson Zs. f. Vksk. XXX—XXXII 171); Pauli (ed. Bolte) No. 332. — Estonian: Loorits *Estnische Volkserzählungen* No. 160; Livonian *1;* Lithuanian (*826, *827) *20;* Swedish *8* (Stockholm *2,* Göteborg *2,* Liungman *1,* misc. *3*); Dutch: Sinninghe 139 No. 411 *3;* German: Henssen Meckl. No. 134 d—f; Serbocroatian (827*) *2;* Russian: Andrejev (*827) *3.*

828 *Men and Animals Readjust Span of Life.* At first, thirty years are given to all animals and to man. For the animals it is too long, for man too short. Man is given a portion of animals' lives. Years 1—30 vigorous (man's own); 30—48 burdens and blows (ass's); 48—60 no teeth (dog's); 60—70 foolish (monkey's). [A1321].

*BP III 290 (Grimm No. 176); *Feilberg *Ordbog* II 571b s.v. »menneske«; Halm Aesop No. 173; Wesselski *Bebel* II 135 No. 103. — Lithuanian (3060); Hungarian (827) *1;* India: *Thompson-Balys (A1321).

830 *Refusal to Ask God's Blessing.* Cf. Type 836.

830A *The Boastful Deer-slayer.* The man shoots a stag but denies that God has given it to him and insists that he shot it himself. [J151.4]. The wounded stag jumps up and flees.

Estonian (830*) *16;* Latvian: *Živaya Starina* V 436; Spanish (836*A—G) *22.*

830B »*My Crops will Thrive Here without God's Blessing.*» This is the answer a proud farmer toiling on rich soil, gives to the traveler's (God's) greeting, »God bless you». The only crops he succeeds with grow up where the traveler has left his footmarks. The farmer of the poor soil, because he put his trust in God, is rewarded with good harvest.
Lithuanian (*758) *29;* Hungarian (Honti 753 I, Berze Nagy 766*) *6.*

830C *If God Wills.* Person has successive misfortunes while making plans because he forgets to say, »If God wills.» [N385.1].
Basset *1000 Contes* 421; Coffin *1.* — Lithuanian (*848) *3;* Spanish (836*A) *1;* Italian: Calvino No. 20; Hungarian (753 I) *4.* — Spanish-American: Hansen (836**A) (Dominican Republic) *1*, (Puerto Rico) *1*, Rael No. 493 (U.S.); Portuguese-American (Brazil): Camara Cascudo p. 69.

830C* *Weather Omens.* Christ asks peasant if there will be rain. Two answer that frogs, foxes, etc. predict rain. Third says that he prays to God for rain. Only last blessed with rain.
Slovenian (752a, b).

831 *The Dishonest Priest.* In order to get hold of money found by a poor man, the priest goes with the skin of a he-goat on his back (as Devil) to the man to frighten him [Q551.2]. But when he gets home he cannot get the skin off [Q551.2].
Finnish-Swedish (761**) *2;* Estonian (831*) *11;* Lithuanian *4;* German *2;* Serbocroatian *3;* Russian: Andrejev *Ukraine 10,* Afanasiev *4;* Greek *1*, Megas *Laographia* XV 10, 13.

832 *The Disappointed Fisher.* The fisher, his wife, and his child always get three fishes From greed they kill the child in order to have more fish for themselves. But they catch from then on only two fishes. [Q553.5].
Finnish (832*) *1;* Estonian (832*) *4;* Livonian (832*) *1.*

832* *Asking the Source of Fortune.* Poor couple given abundance by fortune so long as they do not inquire about its source. After many years they become curious and fortune departs.
Catalan: Amades No. 200.

833* *Vanity Punished.* Two beautiful girls go to a magician and ask that they be made even more beautiful. In tar and feathers [Q475.1]. The girls must remain so.
Estonian *1;* Slovenian *1.*

834 (formerly 834*) *The Poor Brother's Treasure.* The poor brother tells his dream to his rich brother: in a certain place lies a gold treasure. [N511]. The rich brother tries to pick it up: dung. When he angrily throws his find into his brother's house, the dung turns to gold. [D1454]. Cf. Types 842, 947A, 1645B.
*Anderson in Tauscher *Volksmärchen* 188. — Finnish *1;* Estonian *1;* Livonian *1;* German: Henssen *Meckl.* No. 118; Hungarian: cf. Berze

Nagy (777*) *5;* Russian: Andrejev (834A) *1;* Greek: Kretschmer No. 36; Turkish: Eberhard-Boratav No. 123 *1;* Chinese: Eberhard FFC CXX No. 176, CXXVIII No. 113. — Spanish-American: Hansen (**824) (Chile) *1.*

834A *The Pot of Gold and the Pot of Scorpions.* (a) A man (and his wife) dream of a pot of gold in a certain place, or (b) a man finds a treasure and leaves it where it is. Thieves overhear, go to the place, dig up the pot, and find it full of scorpions (snakes). As revenge, they pour the contents of the pot into the house of the man. The scorpions (snakes) turn into gold. [N182]. Cf. Type 1645.

Greek (831**) *1;* India *8.*

835* *How the Drunk Man was Cured.* The drunk man lies under the bed. Thinks he is lying in his shroud. [X811].

Estonian *2.*

835A* *Drunk Man in the Mine.* Drunk man taken into mine and made to believe he has been in hell.

Scottish: (information from School of Scottish Studies) *3;* Irish: Beal IV Supplement 18f.

836 *Pride is Punished.* The rich man boasts that God has not the power to make him poor [C454]. While the man is at church, his property burns and he returns home a poor man [L412]. Cf. Types 736A, 830.

Liungman SSF III 271, 441. — Finnish (838) *29;* Estonian (836*) *2;* Lithuanian *9;* Swedish *84* (Uppsala *25,* Stockholm *1,* Göteborg *52,* Liungman *2,* misc. *4);* Irish: Beal XXI 336; Slovenian *1.*

836A* *Tears of Pearl.* Avaricious king is granted request that when newborn daughter cries her tears will become pearls (cf. Type 403 II c). He is cruel to her in order to make her keep on crying. She runs away and goes to live with a poor couple. When their money runs out the girl cries and tells the man to take the pearls to the king. The latter is unhappy. He mourns loss of his daughter and is no longer greedy. The daughter returns home. He requests that gift be taken from her. It is not, but the money from pearls is given to charity.

Spanish-American: Hansen (836**O) (Cuba) *1.*

836B* *Slanderous Lover Punished* by having tongue torn out.

Spanish: Espinosa II 368; Spanish-American: Hansen (836**G) (Colombia) *1.*

836C* *Princess Wants to Marry Man with Green Eyes.* The man she finds is already married. She persuades the king to command the man to kill his wife. The executioner comes to kill the wife, but a bell rings announcing the death of the princess.

Spanish-American: Hansen (836**I) (Puerto Rico) *1.*

836D* *Fighting after Death.* Contentious men become dogs at death and keep up their fighting.

Spanish-American: Hansen (836**K) (Puerto Rico) *4.*

836E* *Miser Lends all his Money to the Devil* for 12½ per cent interest. When he goes to collect he cannot find the Devil.

Spanish-American: Hansen (836**L) (Puerto Rico) *1.*

836F* *The Miser and the Eye Ointment.* A man rubs ointment on left eye and tells a miser he can see treasures of the world. Miser wants to do same. Miser sees mountains

of gold and wants to rub ointment on right eye. Man tells him he will become blind if he does. He rubs it on and immediately is blinded. He becomes a beggar.
Spanish-American: Hansen (836**M) (Puerto Rico) *1*.

837 *How the Wicked Lord was Punished.* He puts poison into the beggar's bread. As the beggar is spending the night at an inn a traveler arrives. Since no other bread is convenient the beggar gives the stranger his bread. The traveler, who is the lord's son, dies of the poison [N332.1].

Estonian (837*) *6;* Lithuanian *15;* Swedish *7* (Göteborg *1*, misc. *6*); Italian *2* (Tuscan *1*, Sicilian *1*); Hungarian: Berze Nagy (786*) *2;* Slovenian (763); Serbocroatian *3;* Russian: Andrejev *Ukraine 2;* Greek *1;* India *2.* — West Indies (Negro) *1*.

838 *The Bad Rearing.* Son on gallows bites his mother's (father's) nose off: punishment for neglect in youth. [Q586]. Cf. Type 756B.

*Chauvin VIII 113 No. 95 n. 1; *Andrejev FFC LXIX 88. — Estonian (838*) *5;* Livonian (838*) *1;* Irish *3;* Dutch *1;* Hungarian: Berze Nagy (779 I*) *1;* India *3.* — Literary Treatments: Aesop (Halm No. 351); Pauli (ed. Bolte) No. 10; Crane Vitry 250 No. 287.

839 *One Vice Carries Others with It.* (The Three Sins of the Hermit). A man is permitted to choose one of the following vices: theft, incontinence, drink. He chooses the last, which seemed to him least harmful. All the other vices follow in the train of the first. [J485].

**Taylor *MPh* XX (1922) 61—94; *Köhler-Bolte I 583. — Estonian (839*) *5;* Lithuanian *2;* Icelandic *1;* Irish *2;* French *4·* Spanish *1;* Catalan: Amades No. 1630, cf. 1718; Russian: Andrejev; India *1.* — Literary Treatments: Pauli (ed. Bolte) No. 243.

839A* *The Hermit and the Devils.* In order to tempt the hermit, the devils wish to rejuvenate him or to get him married. The hermit crosses himself and, instead of a church, they find only a stake.
Russian: Andrejev (839 I*) *1*.

839B* *Thought of the Virgin* saves the wanderer chased by demons.
Russian: Andrejev (839 II*) *1*.

840 *The Punishments of Men.* When a man and his son are passing the night in a house the son is unable to sleep. He sees wonderful things happening all about: a snake creeps from the sleeping man's mouth into the wife's mouth; an axe penetrates the man's head, etc. In the morning the master of the house explains that these are all punishments of mankind [F171.6]. Cf. Type 759.

BP III 302 n. 4. — Finnish (840) *1;* Estonian (840*) *16;* Livonian (840*) *1;* Lithuanian *9;* Slovenian *1;* Serbocroatian *2;* Russian: Andrejev *3*.

840A* *Idam is Given a Vision of the Future,* but he turns away disconsolate because of wars.
Spanish *1*.

840B* *The Judgments in this World.* A virtuous man, a robber, and a thief, want to know their fate. They take three roads and spend their night in various situations:

the first in a good house, the second in a forest during a storm, the third in water. Such will be their fate in this world.
Russian: Andrejev *1*.

841 *One Beggar Trusts God, the Other the King.* The king gives them each a loaf of bread, but the loaf of the second beggar is filled with gold. The beggars not knowing the nature of the loaves exchange them. [N351].
Pauli (ed. Bolte) Nos. 326, 327. — Estonian (841) *4;* Livonian (841*) *1;* Lithuanian *2;* Swedish *8* (Uppsala *1*, Göteborg *1*, misc. *6*); Icelandic *1;* Spanish: Espinosa Jr. No. 185; Russian: Andrejev; Greek *5*, Dawkins *Modern Greek Folktales* No. 81; Turkish: Eberhard-Boratav Nos. 131, 135 *8;* India *5;* Japanese: Ikeda (N351); Chinese: Eberhard FFC CXX 230f. No. 177, Graham (N351); American Indian (Mexican) Pochulata: Boas JAFL XXX 223.

842 *The Man Who Kicked Aside Riches.* A man practices austerities for many years. He asks the god for wealth as a reward and the god signifies that his request is granted. On the way home, the man decides to close his eyes to feel how a blind man feels when he walks. He stumbles against what he thinks is a stone and kicks it aside. It is the pot of gold that the god had placed in his way. [N351.2, Q34]. Cf. Type 947A.
Finnish *1;* India *4*.

842A* *The Beggar Dies in Night Lodgings;* a large sum of money is found sewed up in his coat; on the priest's advice, the money is used towards the purchase and the fattening of pigs; finally all the pigs are slaughtered save one which, when fattened enough, the priest leads to the graveyard, and there it sinks into the dead man's grave. [N524.1].
Lithuanian (*842) *8;* Russian: Andrejev (*842 I) *1*.

842B* *The Serpent at the Wedding.* A prince calls a serpent to witness that he will marry a peasant-girl. As the prince is about to wed another (the daughter of the grand vizir), a serpent twists itself about the bridegroom's neck. It unwinds itself only when the peasant-girl is brought to wed the prince.
Greek *1*.

842C* *Floating Coins.* Coins earned by hard work float on water [J1931] and bring happiness.
*Anderson in Tauscher *Volksmärchen* 173. — Estonian (842*) *1;* Russian (842*) *4*.

843* *The Lazy Weaving-woman.* When she sees how a little bird pecks a hole in a stone, she resumes her work. [J1011].
Estonian *6*.

844 *The Luck-bringing Shirt.* The king becomes lucky when he puts on the shirt of a lucky man. The only man who says he is lucky has no shirt. [N135.3].
**Köhler *Aufsätze* 119ff. — Estonian (844*) *2;* Livonian (844*) *1;* Lithuanian *5;* Swedish (Uppsala) *1;* Irish *22;* Spanish *1;* Catalan: Amades No. 446, 1966; German *1;* Italian *4* (Tuscan *4*); Slovenian *6;* Serbocroatian *2;* Rumanian (949*) *1;* Turkish: Eberhard-Boratav No. 277 III, cf. 277. — English-American: Baughman *1*. — Literary Treatments: H. C. Andersen »Lykkens Galoscher»; Edwin Markham »The Shoes of Happiness».

845 *The Old Man and Death.* Weary old man wishes for death. When Death appears at the summons he asks for help with the load. [C11].
*BP III 294; Halm Aesop No. 90; Jacobs Aesop 216 No. 69; Wienert FFC LVI 81 (ET 468, 469), 109 (ST 212, cf. ST 109, 115, 141, 342). — Italian Novella: *Rotunda (C11); U.S.: Baughman (C11); Slovenian *1;* India: *Thompson-Balys (C11).

845* *People Call on God Only when they Are in Difficulty.*
Slovenian *1.*

846 *Devil Always Blamed.* Devil blamed when cow is in ditch (Who the devil did that?). When she is saved (Thank God!).
*Dähnhardt II 188. — Finnish *3;* Estonian: Aarne FFC XXV 124 No. 49 *5;* Lithuanian (3340); French: Delarue's Collection *5;* German (362*) *1,* (845*) *8,* Henssen Volk 284 No. 175; cf. Slovenian (good and bad vintages) *1.*

846* *The Vengeful Saints.* The man praises one of the saints (on his nameday) and disparages the other. The depreciated saint takes revenge; the praised one helps the man. The man benefits by the conflict. Or: the saints dispute as to which of them the man said »Good-day» to. [Cf. J 1712].
Estonian: Loorits *Estnische Märchen* Nos. 172; Latvian (298 B) *1;* Lithuanian (*846) *5;* Russian: Andrejev (*846) *6.*

847* *Partnership of Honesty and Fraud.* Fraud has cheated his partner, Honesty. They hire a housekeeper. Fraud is to have use of her right side, Honesty of her left. The left side is of little use. Fraud falls in love with her and pays Honesty double all his losses to relinquish his rights.
Spanish (*847) *1.*

848* *The Thief and St. Nicolas.* A thief fleeing, prays to Nicholas and in case of rescue, he promises to light a candle for him. Nicholas hides him in garbage and then explains to him that a candle from a thief would be just as offensive to him as the garbage is to the thief.
Russian: Afanasiev *2.*

849* *The Cross as Security.* A merchant borrows money, leaving a cross or ikon as security; during a storm, fearing a shipwreck, he throws the keg with the money into the water. The keg floats back to the creditor.
Russian: Afanasiev (*849A) *2.*

C. NOVELLE (ROMANTIC TALES)

850—869 The Princess's Hand is Won

850 *The Birthmarks of the Princess.* The pipe and the dancing hogs.
I. *The Markings.* (a) In return for his dancing hogs the princess lets the youth see her naked. (b) With this knowledge he wins the princess.
II. *To Whom She Turns.* (a) As a further test the princess is to be given to the suitor to whom she turns in the night. (b) Rivals sleep with her and contest in enticements: she turns to the hero. Cf. Type 621.

Motifs:

I. H51.1. Recognition by birthmark. H525. Test: guessing princess's birthmarks. K1358. Girl shows herself naked in return for youth's dancing hogs. K443.6. Trickster exacts promise of marriage as price of silence after having seen a princess naked.

II. H315. Suitor test: to whom the princess turns. Rival suitors sleep with princess. The one she turns to is to have her. They vie in enticements.

*BP II 528 (Grimm No. 114); Coffin *3;* Köhler-Bolte I 428f., 464. — Finnish *55;* Finnish-Swedish *4;* Estonian *12;* Lithuanian *5;* Lappish *2;* Swedish *3* (Göteborg *2,* Liungman *1*); Danish *26,* Grundtvig No. 19A; Irish *1;* French *2;* Catalan: Amades cf. No. 395; German *11;* Italian (Tuscan, cf. [856], (850 II): 554 d, 850); Rumanian *6;* Hungarian *8;* Czech: Tille Soupis II (1) 323f. *1;* Slovenian *2;* Serbocroatian *25;* Russian: Afanasiev *11;* Greek *3;* Turkish: Eberhard-Boratav No. 232 III, (850 II) No. 182 V. — Franco-American *24;* Spanish-American: Rael Nos. 7, 8, 10, 358 (U.S.), Hansen (Dominican Republic) *1* (Puerto Rico) *9;* West Indies (Negro) *2.*

850* *Through the Girl's Mistake the Youth Comes to her Room at Night.*
Lappish 2.

850** *A Girl is Carried off to an Island by Robbers.* She kills them with poisoned grass and is taken back home by a young man.
Lappish *1.*

851 *The Princess who Cannot Solve the Riddle.* The prince saved by his true servant in a robber's den. The poisoned raven. The riddle from the hero's own experiences. He wins the princess's hand. Cf. Types 516—518.

I. *The Riddle Contest.* A princess is offered in marriage to the youth who can propose a riddle which she cannot solve.

II. *The Clues.* On the way to the contest the hero is given a clue. He sees a horse poisoned and then eaten by a raven who in turn falls dead. The ravens are then eaten by twelve men who die of the poison.

III. *The Riddle.* (a) The hero propounds the riddle: »One killed none and yet killed twelve» (or (b) the riddle of the unborn, or (c) of the murdered lover.)

IV. *The Princess Won.* (a) The princess tries to find the answer by visiting him at night and learning it from his dreams. He is, however, aware of the visit, keeps a token, and proves that she has visited him; or (b) see Type 853 IV b, c.

Motifs:

I. H342. Suitor test: outwitting princess. H551. Princess offered to man who can out-riddle her.

II. H565. Riddle propounded from chance experience. N332.2. Horse accidentally poisoned instead of master.

III. H802. Riddle: one killed none and yet killed twelve. (Horse is poisoned; raven eats of him and dies; twelve robbers eat raven and die.) H792. Riddle of the unborn. I was unborn; my horse is unborn; I carry my mother on my hands. H805. Riddle of the murdered lover. With what thinks, I drink; what sees, I carry; with what eats I walk.

IV. H81.2. Clandestine visit of princess to hero betrayed by token. H117. Identification by cut garment. Garment is cut and fragment taken as token. K1331. »No!» The princess must answer all questions by »No».

*BP I 188 (Grimm No. 22); Coffin *5;* *Espinosa II 78ff. — Finnish *8;* Finnish-Swedish *2;* Estonian *3;* Lithuanian *9;* Swedish *8* (Uppsala *1,* Lund *2,* misc. *5*); Norwegian *6;* Danish *28,* Grundtvig No. 19N; Icelandic *3;* Scottish *1;* Irish *63;* English *1;* French *4;* Spanish *9;* Catalan: Amades Nos. 389, 425; Flemish *1;* German *19* (Archive *18,* Henssen Volk No. 149); Austrian: Haiding No. 45; Italian *12* (Tuscan 554 a, d, 563 i, [315] e, g *5,* Sicilian 851 + *927 *7*); Rumanian *4;* Hungarian *6;* Czech: Tille FFC XXXIV 220, Soupis II (1) 324ff. *1;* Slovenian *3;* Serbocroatian *2;* Russian: Afanasiev *14;* Greek *6,* Loukatos No. 13, Politis *Laographia* II 381ff.; Turkish: Eberhard-Boratav No. 212 III; India *1;* Indonesian: DeVries No. 215. — Franco-American *17;* English-American: Baughman *2;* Spanish-American: Rael Nos. 3—6 (U.S.), Hansen (Argentina) *6,* (Chile) *5,* (Dominican Republic) *1,* (Puerto Rico) *27;* Cape Verde Islands: Parsons MAFLS XV (1) 256; American Indian: Thompson *C Coll* II 414ff. — African (Gold Coast): Barker and Sinclair 172 No. 34, (Swahili): Werner *African Mythology* 355.

851A *Turandot.* Princess sets riddles for her suitors to be answered on pain of death: riddle of the sun [H762], of the ocean [H734], of the year [H721.1]. Cf. Types 571—574, 621, 725.

*BP I 199; Chauvin V 191 No. 113; RTP XII 603 No. 67; *Kretschmer 329 n. (references to Aramaic, Caucasian, Kirghiz). — Lithuanian (*851A) *1;* Greek *2.*

852 *The Hero Forces the Princess to Say, »That is a Lie.»*
Cf. Types 1875, 1920C, 1960E and G.

I. *The Contest.* (a) A princess is offered to the man who can tell so big a lie that she says, »That is a lie».

II. *The Lies.* The youth tells impossible tales of (a) a great ox; (b) of a tree growing to the skies overnight, of his ascent and descent on a rope of chaff from the sky; or (c) of a man who cuts off his head and replaces it and the like.

III. *The Victory.* The princess (the king) is brought to say the required words when the youth makes up shameful lies about herself.

Motifs:

I. H342.1. Suitor test: forcing princess to say, »That is a lie.»

II. X1237. Lie: remarkable ox or steer. X1036.1. Lie: the great stable. X1201. Lie: the great animal. X920. Lie: the large man. X1424.

The great mushroom. X1423.1. The great cabbage. F54.2. Plant grows to sky. X1547.2. Lie: river of honey. X1757. Rope of sand (chaff). X1726.2. Man cuts off own head, picks it up and replaces it. X1858. Lie: man cuts ice with own hands. X1739.2. Lie: man makes drinking water from his own skull.

III. K1271.1.2. Princess made to speak desired words when hero threatens to report (falsely) her amorous conduct.

*BP II 506 (Grimm No. 112). — Finnish *12;* Finnish-Swedish *1;* Estonian *16;* Lithuanian *13;* Swedish *48* (Uppsala *3,* Stockholm *4,* Göteborg *12,* Lund *5,* Liungman *7,* misc. *17*); Norwegian *12;* Danish *73;* Grundtvig No. 21; Icelandic *5;* Scottish *3;* Irish *228,* Beal IV 151ff.; French *5;* Spanish *1;* Flemish *5;* Dutch *4;* German *31* (Archive *30,* Henssen Volk No. 294); Austrian: Haiding No. 51; Rumanian *2;* Hungarian *6;* Czech: Tille FFC XXXIV 241, Soupis II (1) 241ff. *5;* Slovenian *6;* Serbocroatian *1;* Russian: Andrejev; Greek *1;* India *1;* Indonesian: DeVries No. 217. — Franco-American *8;* Spanish-American: Rael No. 313 (U.S.); Hansen (Dominican Republic) *1.* — African *2.*

853 *The Hero Catches the Princess with her Own Words.* Takes along a dead crow and other objects which he has found.

I. *The Contest.* A princess is offered in marriage to the youth who outwits her in repartee.

II. *The Clues.* On the way to the contest the hero picks up a dead crow, an egg, and other objects.

III. *The Contest.* By producing these objects at the proper time he brings all the princess's words to scorn (often obscene).

IV. *The Princess Caught.* (a) The hero is imprisoned and escapes by means of his magic tablecloth, purse, and fiddle. (b) By his magic fiddle he captures the princess and will release her only if she says »No» to all his questions. (c) By this means he gets her into his bed and marries her.

Motifs:

I. H507.1. Princess offered to man who can defeat her in repartee.

II, III. H507.1.0.1. Princess defeated in repartee by means of objects accidentally picked up.

IV. D1395.2. Escape from prison by use of magic tablecloth. D1395.3. Escape from prison by use of magic purse. D1415.2.5. Magic fiddle causes dancing. K1331. »No!» The princess must answer all questions by »No». L161. Lowly hero marries princess.

Espinosa III 181ff.; Coffin *3.* — Finnish *84;* Finnish-Swedish *9;* Estonian *19;* Livonian *1;* Lithuanian *18;* Lappish *3;* Swedish *52* (Uppsala *6,* Göteborg *12,* Lund *6,* Liungman *10,* misc. *18*); Norwegian *8;* Danish *29;* Irish *11;* English *1;* French *8;* Spanish (853A*) *1;* Catalan: Amades No. 425; Dutch *4;* Flemish *3;* German *27;* Hungarian *2,* Berze Nagy (1565*, 1566*) *2;* Czech: Tille Soupis I 278f., II (1) 321f., FFC XXXIV 237f. *2;* Serbocroatian *1;* Russian: Andrejev *Ukraine 2;* Greek *3.* — Franco-American *7;* Spanish-American: Rael No. 216 (U.S.),

Hansen (Puerto Rico) *1*, (853**B)*1;* Cape Verde Islands: Parson MAFLS XV (1) 139 n. 1; West Indies (Negro) *1.*

853A »*No.*» The princess must answer all questions by »No». By clever framing of his question the hero wins her to his desires. (= 853 IV b, c). [K1331].
*Types 851, 853; *BP I 192; **Kristoffer Nyrop *Nej: et motivs historie* (København, 1891); Dania V 1ff., 164ff.; 166; *Toldo Zs. f. Vksk. XV 69 n. 2. — Italian (Tuscan 563 d, i, o, [315] d *4*).

854 *The Golden Ram.* »Money is all powerful.» The hero boasts that if he had one thing he could marry the princess. The king gives him much gold. He has a golden ram made, is carried in it into the chamber of the princess and wins her [K1341].
H. Hepding »Ein Märchen aus Syra» in *Kyriakides Volume* 267ff.; *BP I 446 n. 2; Köhler-Bolte Zs. f. Vksk. VI 166 (to Gonzenbach No. 68; cf. No. 23); Coffin *5*. — Finnish *127;* Finnish-Swedish *5;* Estonian *2;* Livonian *1;* Lithuanian *2;* Lappish *1;* Danish *13;* Irish *33;* French *2;* Spanish *1;* German Archive *18;* Austrian: Haiding No. 15; Italian *11* (Tuscan 854 a—d, 315f. *5*, Sicilian *6*, Gonzenbach No. 68); Rumanian *3;* Hungarian *5;* Czech: Tille Soupis II (1) 347f, II (2) 612f. *2*, FFC XXXIV 244f.; Serbocroatian *1;* Russian: Andrejev *1;* Greek *6*, Dawkins *45 Stories* No. 14; Turkish: Eberhard-Boratav No. 201; India *2*. — Franco-American *9;* Spanish-American: Rael No. 358, Hansen (Dominican Republic) *1* (Puerto Rico) *1*, (Puerto Rico 854A) *1;* West Indies (Negro) *1;* American Indian: Thompson *C Coll* II 428.

855 *The Substitute Bridegroom.* Cf. Type 870. A handsome youth is hired to take the place of a one-eyed (or crippled) prince (merchant's son) at the latter's wedding. The bride falls in love with the hero and refuses the one-eyed prince. [K19.5.3]. (a) The hero escapes with the bride. (b) The one-eyed prince is tested. He cannot remember the conversation held between the bride and the hero on the preceding night [H17], etc. (c) The bride searches for the hero and eventually finds him. (d) The bride gives alms to all passers-by [H11.1.1]. Eventually she sees the hero. (e) The bride offers a reward to all who tell her a story. The hero appears and tells his story [H11]. (f) The hero has left his name or a verse with the bride. (g) The hero is fated to die at the age of twelve (sixteen) [M341.1] but outwits fate.
India *8.*

856 *The Girl Elopes With the Wrong Man.*
I. *Expulsion.* A youth is driven forth by his father when the youth says he will marry four wives [M373]. (Cf. Type 725).

II. *The Elopement.* (a) While acting as a servant, the hero pretends to be unable to read [K1816.0.3]. He accepts a message and learns that the princess intends to elope with the son of a court official [K1317.9]. (b) He informs the court official, who locks up his son. (c) The hero takes his place and elopes with the princess [K1371.1, N318.2]. When daylight comes the princess realizes she cannot return to her parents.

III. *The Hero Gains Other Wives.* (a) He is bitten by a snake and restored to life [E0] by a girl whom he marries. (b) In the form of a parrot [D658.1, T33] he is bought by a new princess. He marries her. (c) Forced to flee, he hides in the house of a rich merchant and marries his daughter. (d) With his four wives he returns to his father.

India *11.*

858 *When the King Sneezes the Shepherd Refuses to Cry »God Bless You!«* King has him tortured and promises him large gifts if he will say it, but the shepherd refuses until he receives the princess as wife.

Hungarian: Berze Nagy (855*) *2,* Sklarek *Ungarische Märchen* I No. 22; Russian: *Crimson Fairy Book* p. 29.

859 *The Penniless Bridegroom Pretends to Wealth* [K1917]. Cf. Type 545 II b, 1590.

Finnish *15.*

859A *The Penniless Wooer: Patch of Land.* After marriage he takes the bride to look at his land. He puts on soiled clothes. She looks at the land; he points to the patch on his clothes. »That patch is mine.» [K1917.1].
*BP II 203.

859B *The Penniless Wooer: Money in Hand.* An uncle gives the boy a coin and food to hold while he woos for him. He tells the girl's father that the boy has a piece of money in hánd and plenty to eat. Wins the girl. [K1917.2].
*BP II 203.

859C *The Penniless Wooer: »House of my Father with one hundred fifty Lights and Goat Pen.«* When the servant in bed so remarks, the master marries his daughter to him. Arrived at the hut, he explains that the lights are the stars whose beams enter through the cracks in the roof. One goat is tied to the tree. [K1917.4].

Spanish (859*) *1;* German: Henssen Volk 337 No. 280.

859D *»All of These are Mine,»* says wooer as he strokes his whiskers. The girl thinks he is indicating the fields and live stock past which they are riding. [K1917.7].

U.S.: Baughman (K1917.7).

860 *Nuts of »Ay ay ay!«* Princess offered to man who brings a glass of all waters, a bouquet of all flowers and nuts of ay, ay, ay! Hero brings seawater, a beehive and hazelnut with thorns so that the king cries »Ay, ay, ay!» [H1377.1, H1377.2, H1377.3].

Spanish *2;* Jewish: Bin Gorion *Born Judas,* II 114. — West Indies: Flowers 470. — Spanish-American: Hansen (Argentina) *1,* (Puerto Rico) *2.*

860A* *Finding the Hidden Princess.* The king, after hiding his daughter in an iron palace at the bottom of a lake, promises her hand to the man who should find her. [H 322].The youth disguises himself as a bear, and as such, the unsuspicious king takes him to amuse his daughter. Thus he discovers the princess's hiding place.
Lithuanian (*860) *3*.

860B* *The Stolen Woman.* For looking at a beautiful girl (or for taking a picture of her) the hero gives the husband much money. He makes an underground passage into her home, masks as a woman and fools both wife and husband.
Russian: Andrejev (*860) *5*.

861 *Sleeping at the Rendezvous.* A youth having a rendezvous with a princess oversleeps [D1972] and is captured and imprisoned. His sister masks as a man and takes his place in prison. When her sex is discovered all is forgiven and the youth marries the princess.

Greek: Dawkins *Modern Greek in Asia Minor* 432f.; Turkish: Eberhard-Boratav No. 222 *6*.

862 »*He that Asketh Shall Receive.*« The hermit wants to prove the truth of these words of the Gospel. He asks for the hand of the princess. Performs the difficult task imposed upon him. [V316.1].

*BP II 417. — Lithuanian (*779) *2;* Russian: Andrejev (*841 I) *3*.

870—879 The Heroine Marries the Prince

870 *The Princess Confined in the Mound.* She digs herself out: serves at the king's castle. Takes the place of the bride at the wedding. The conversation with the horse, the bridge, the church-door.

I. *Imprisoned Princess.* Because of her faithfulness to her betrothed, a princess along with her maid is confined by her father in an underground prison.

II. *Escape and Service.* (a) After many years she escapes and takes service in the king's castle. (b) The fiancée of her lover, because she wishes to conceal her pregnancy or because of her hideousness, forces the heroine to take her place at the wedding.

III. *The Substituted Bride.* (a) On the way to the church she talks to her horse, to the bridge, and to the church-door and thus reminds the prince of his first love. (b) He gives her a necklace after the wedding.

IV. *Recognition.* (a) When the bride, again in her own clothes, comes to the prince in the evening she cannot recall the conversation on the way to the church and must always consult with the maid. (b) When he wants to see the necklace, the truth comes to light. (c) He drives her away and keeps his faithful sweetheart.

Motifs:

I. S11. Cruel father. R45. Captivity in mound (cave, hollow hill).

II. R211. Escape from prison. K1816.0.2. Girl in menial disguise at lover's court. K1831. Service under a false name. K1843.1. Bride has maid sleep in husband's bed to conceal pregnancy.

III. H13. Recognition by overheard conversation (usually with animals or objects). Person not daring to reveal self directly thus attracts attention and recognition. H13.1. Recognition by overheard conversation with animal. H13.2. Recognition by overheard conversation with objects. H151.5. Attention drawn by magic objects. H92. Identification by necklace.

IV. H15.1. Identity tested by demanding that person say again what he said on former occasion. (Impostor fails). H400. Chastity test. Various means are employed to test a woman's (or man's) chastity. K1911.3. Reinstatement of true bride.

**Liungman *En traditionsstudie över sagan om prinsessan i jordkulan* (Göteborg 1925); *BP III 443 (Grimm No. 198); *Boberg FFC CLI 12.
— Finnish *1;* Finnish-Swedish *6;* Swedish *65* (Uppsala *10,* Göteborg *20,* Lund *1,* Liungman *21,* misc. *13*); Norwegian *22,* Solheim *2;* Danish *40,* Grundtvig No. 48; Icelandic *5;* Irish *2;* French *1;* Spanish (870*B) *1;* Catalan: Amades No. 56; German *3;* Italian (Tuscan (870 III): [304] d, [867] *2*); Russian: Andrejev *1;* Greek: Loukatos Nos. 4, 5; Turkish: (870 II b) Eberhard-Boratav No. 227 *3.*

870A *The Little Goose-Girl* (akin to Type 870). A little girl herding geese tells a prince, who is passing by, that she is going to be married to him [T55]. Attendance at his wedding. Substitute bride. Cf. Type 899 E.

Differs from Type 870 in several important respects: (a) Introduction. (b) The substitution [K1843.1] is in the marriage bed because the prince has a magic stone by his bed that indicates the bride's chastity [H411.1]. (c) The recognition is by ornaments he has given his bed-partner [H90].

Liungman *Två Folkminnesundersökninger* (Göteborg 1925) 1—40. — Swedish *4* (Uppsala *2,* Lund *1,* misc. *1*); Norwegian (871) *4;* Italian (Sicilian *3*); Serbocroatian *2;* Greek *2, Laographia* X 444 No. 30, Dawkins: *Modern Greek Folktales* Nos. 44, 54; West Indies (Negro) *1.*

870A* *The Enclosed Girl Follows her Lover.* A father locks a pretty girl in a glass enclosure so that she will not fall in love. A young man makes love to her. He breaks the glass and they run away. While she is asleep he sails away. Another youth carries her across the sea to the town where her sweetheart lives. He is sick and his mother refuses to let the girl see him. Finally she permits her to visit him. He recovers immediately and they are married.

Spanish-American: Hansen (870**C) (Puerto Rico) *1.*

870B* *Princess Sews for False Bride.* (The False Isolt). A stepmother persecutes a prince or princess. They hide themselves in trees. Another prince woos the princess. The stepmother substitutes her own daughter. The false bride cannot sew, but the princess does it for her. The false bride turns into a monster. All is made clear. Marriage. Punishment.

Icelandic (870B*, 870 I*) *8.*

870C* *Stepmother Makes Love to Stepson,* the king. She imprisons the queen in a mound. The queen finally escapes. Bears son. Recognition by ring. Punishment.

Icelandic *1.*

870D* *Magic Mirror Reflects Blemishes* of character of all women who gaze in it. [H411.15]. King to marry woman without blemishes. Only peasant girl succeeds. Marries king.
    Spanish (*1621) *1*.

871 *Princess and Ogress*. A princess in a forbidden chamber sees a man's picture and falls in love. A magician as bird brings the princess at night to the lover. Once they stay too late. The sun sees them, so that the magician bursts and dies. The girl left alone becomes servant in the palace. There she is threatened by a cannibal princess. She escapes through narrow window and a spring to an otherworld plain. She finds the chiefs of devils boiling brains of the ogress princess. The heroine turns the pot upside down and returns to the well. The ogress is now normal. As reward for good the heroine is sent to her lover's house, where she arrives just as he is to marry another. Recognition and marriage. (Cf. Types 466*, 466**, 475, 475*.)
    Motifs: C611. Forbidden chamber. T11.2. Love from sight of picture. D567. Transformation by sunlight. G11.3. Cannibal witch. F93.0.2.1. Well entrance to lower world. C325. Tabu: looking into pots in hell. D2065.4. Insanity of princess dependent on height of fire. N681.1. Wife finds lost husband just as he is to marry another.
    Greek (871*) *2*.

871A *The Unfaithful Queen*. A girl goes to the king's garden (or underworld) and sees the queen meet a black lover [T232]. She denounces the queen and eventually marries the king. Cf. Type 1511.
    Danish *1;* Italian (Sicilian *871 *1*); Greek: Dawkins *Modern Greek Folktales No.* 41 *5;* India: Thompson-Balys (T232) *5*.

871* *The Princess Who Goes to Seek Trouble* [H1376.5]. At night hides herself up in a tree in the forest; a hunter camps under the tree. His dogs reveal the princess's hiding place, and she is forced to come down. The hunter sleeps by her side, tightly holding her plaits in his hands. By cutting off her hair, the princess unnoticed makes her escape. [K538].
    Lithuanian (*871) *1;* Russian: Andrejev *871 *1*.

872* *Brother and Sister*. The brother is married and his wife [K2212.2] calumniates the sister [K2112], who is chased out into the woods [S143], but thanks to the advice obtained there, she turns back and in time is married to a prince [L162].
    Norwegian (874) *1;* Catalan: Amades No. 80.

873 *The King Discovers his Unknown Son*. Marries the mother.
    A king in disguise leaves a token with a girl to give to their son if one is born [T645]. The boy is twitted with being a bastard and goes on a quest for his unknown father [H1381.2.2.1.1]. The king incognito discovers the boy's liaison with a noble girl and orders his execution. Before the execution the token is discovered and the son acknowledged [N731, H80]. The king marries the boy's mother [L162].
    Danish *13;* Irish *8;* French: Cosquin No. 3; Russian: Andrejev *2,* Azadowsky *Russkaya Skazka* Nos. 34, 35; Greek *8;* India *1*. — Spanish-American: Hansen (Dominican Republic) *1;* West Indies (Negro) *1*.

873* *Love Adventure Told Symbolically.* A girl sleeps unknown with a prince [T475]. Later is recognized by a song telling symbolically what has happened. [Cf. D2006.1, K1557]. Cf. Type 875A.

Greek 2.

874 *The Proud King is Won.* Gifts for the voyage [L221] (as in Type 425C). The youngest daughter sends a message to the king and he replies symbolically showing that he is not interested in her (sends her cloth, rope, and knife). The girl lets herself be sold to the king as a slave. The king becomes enamored and threatens to kill himself. She produces the cloth, rope, and knife. He pretends suicide; she spits on his bier. Reconciliation and marriage.

Italian (Sicilian *872 *1*); Serbocroatian *1;* Turkish: Eberhard-Boratav (No. 188) *18*.

874* *Ariadne-thread Wins the Prince.* The clever maiden who does not lose her way in 1000 rooms. [R121.5.]

Rumanian *1*.

875 *The Clever Peasant Girl.* Through the proof of her cleverness she becomes the king's wife. He becomes angry and banishes her. She takes him home with her as her dearest possession.

I. *The Clever Daughter.* (a) A peasant finds a golden mortar in a field and against the advice of his clever daughter takes it to the king who demands the pestle as well; or (b) two peasants in court must tell the judge what is the most beautiful, the strongest, and the richest thing on earth and one of them answers as his daughter has advised him: spring, the earth, autumn; or (c) the king finds the girl at home and is impressed by her clever remarks.

II. *The Tasks.* The clever girl performs various tasks set by the king: (a) comes neither naked nor clad; (b) answers the question, how much his beard is worth; (c) weaves a cloth with two threads; or (d) quickly hatches out boiled eggs (cf. Type 920A); or (e) carves a fowl so as to give appropriate pieces to all members of the family (Cf. Type 1533).

III. *As King's Wife.* She marries the king and as he decides a dispute over the possession of a colt unjustly, she advises the abused subject how to show the king the absurdity of his decision by an equally foolish act.

IV. *The Dearest Possession.* When the king casts her out and allows her only to take with her the one thing she holds dearest, she takes her sleeping husband along and thus moves him to forgive her. — Adapted from BP and DeVries.

Motifs:

I. J1111.4. Clever peasant daughter. H561.1.2. Found mortar taken to king reveals peasant girl's wisdom. H561.1. Clever peasant girl asked riddles by king. H630—H659 passim. Riddles of the superlative. H641.1. What is most beautiful? The spring. H631.3. What is strongest? Earth. H636. Riddle: what is the richest? Autumn. H632. Riddle: what is the swiftest? Thought. H633. Riddle: what is sweetest? Sleep. H583.8.

Maiden (to king): The house has neither eyes nor ears. (No child at window nor dog in yard to announce king's approach: he therefore finds her not dressed to receive him.) H583.7. King: Where shall I tie my horse? Maiden: Between summer and winter. (Between wagon and sleigh). H583.9. Maiden (to king): Shall I feed you with loss or gain. (A slaughtered hen or milk.)

II. H373. Bride test: performance of tasks. H1050. Paradoxical tasks. H1051. Task: coming neither on nor off the road. H1052. Task: standing neither inside nor outside of gate (forefeet of horse inside, hind feet outside). H1053. Task: coming neither on horse nor on foot (riding nor walking). H1054. Task: coming neither naked nor clad. H1055. Task: coming neither barefoot nor shod. (Comes with one shoe on, one off; or in soleless shoes.) H1057. Task: coming neither by day nor by night. (Comes at twilight.) H1058. Task: standing between summer and winter. (Stands between wagon and sleigh.) H1061. Task: coming neither with nor without a companion. (Comes with an animal.) H1062. Task: coming neither washed nor unwashed. (Comes partly washed.) H1063. Task: coming neither hungry nor satiated. (Eats a thin soup, a leaf, a single grain, or the like.) H1064. Task: coming laughing and crying at once. (Rubs eyes with a twig to simulate crying.) H1065. Task: bringing best friend, worst enemy, best servant, greatest pleasure-giver. H712. Riddle: how much is king's beard worth. H1010. Impossible tasks. H1022.1. Task: weaving cloth from two threads. H1024.1. Task: milking bull. H1024.1.1. Task: making a bull bear a calf. H1021.6.1. Task: weaving a silk shirt from hair; countertask: making a loom from shavings. H1021.1. Task: making a rope of sand. H1023.9. Task: mending a broken jug. H1023.7. Task: sewing together a broken mill-stone. H1023.1. Task: hatching boiled eggs. H951. Countertasks. When a task is assigned, the hero agrees to perform it as soon as the assigner performs a certain other task. J1191.2. Suit for chickens produced from boiled eggs. Countertask: harvesting crop produced from cooked seeds. H1152.1. Task: selling a sheep (goat) and bringing it back along with the money. (Shears and sells wool; brings animal back.) H1185. Task: preparing the food »Oh my». (Needle put in food which causes eater to say »Oh my!») H601. Wise carving of the fowl. Clever person divides it symbolically: head to head of house, neck to wife, etc. L162. Lowly heroine marries prince (king).

III. J1191.1. Reductio ad absurdum: The decision about the colt.

IV. J1545.4. The exiled wife's dearest possession.

DeVries *Das Märchen von Klugen Rätsellösern* (FFC LXXIII); *BP II 349 (Grimm No. 94); *Wesselski *Der Knabenkönig und das Kluge Mädchen* (Prag 1929); *Anderson Hessische Blätter XXVIII 206ff.; *Liungman SSF III 442; *Wisser Zs. f. Vksk. XL 288ff.; *Anderson in Tauscher *Volksmärchen* 188. — Finnish *21;* Finnish-Swedish *5,* (921) *3;* Estonian *5;* Livonian *1;* Lithuanian *41;* Lappish *1;* Swedish *38* (Uppsala *6,* Stockholm *3*, Göteborg *5*, Lund *1*, Liungman *5*, misc. *18*); Danish 32; Scottish *3;* Irish (875 + cf. 875) *454*, Beal I 156f. No. 2, XI 150f. No. 32; French *3;* Spanish *1;* Catalan: Amades No. 401, cf. 1346; Dutch *6;* Flemish *3;* Walloon (923 + *923C) *2;* German *51* (Archive *50*, Merk. 52); Austrian: Haiding No. 44; Italian *10* (Tuscan *7*, Sicilian *1* + 875 II *2;* Rumanian *15;* Hungarian *9;* Czech: Tille (Soupis I 44) *12;* Slovenian *7;* Serbocroatian *15;* Russian: Afanasiev *24*, Andrejev *Ukraine 20;* Greek *20*, Dawkins *Modern Greek Folktales* No. 65, *45 Stories* Nos. 20, 21, Loukatos No. 16, Megas No. 33; Turkish: Eberhard-Boratav Nos. 192 III, 235, 366 IV, cf. 373 *26;* India (875 + 929D) *28;* Chinese: Eberhard FFC CXXVIII S 28 Nos. 2, 10, Ebernard FFC CXX No. 186; Indonesian: DeVries Nos. 234. — Franco-American *2;* English-American: Baughman *2;* Spanish-American: Rael Nos. 1, 2 (U.S.), Hansen (875, 875**A, **924) (Argentina) *1*, (Dominican Republic) *1*, (Puerto Rico) *3;* West Indies (Negro) *6*. — African *3*.

875A *Girl's Riddling Answer Betrays a Theft.* The full moon and the thirtieth of the month. Prince sends servant to clever girl with a round tart, thirty cakes, and a capon, and asks her if it is full moon and the thirtieth of the month and if the cock has crowed in the evening. She replies that it is not full moon, that it is the fifteenth of the month, and that the capon has gone to the mill; but that the prince should spare the pheasant for the partridge's sake. She thus shows him that the servant has stolen half the tart, half of the cakes, and the capon. [H582.1.1]. Cf. Type 873*.

**DeVries FFC LXXIII 347ff.; *BP II 361; Köhler Zs. f. Vksk. VI 59. — Polish (656) *1;* cf. Catalan: Amades Nos. 445, 449; Arab: Azov 401f.; African (Sahel): Frobenius *Atlantis* VI 79—86.

875B *The Clever Girl and the King.* For each impossible task [H1010] she gives countertasks [H951]. Cf. 875 III.
*Lo Nigro 186ff. — Sicilian (875 II) *2*.

875B₁ *Bull's Milk.* A king orders his adviser to bring him bull's milk or to have a bull bear a calf. The daughter of the minister pretends that her father has borne a child. The king thus sees the absurdity of his order. [H1024.1ff.].
DeVries FFC LXIII 43ff.; Fansler MAFLS XII 63; India *7*.

875B₂ *Converting a Moslem into a Hindu.* A Moslem king orders his adviser to turn him into a Hindu. The adviser stands by the road rubbing a donkey. When the king asks why, the adviser says he is trying to change it into a horse (cow). The king sees the absurdity of his order. [J1536.2].
India *5*.

875B₃ *Moving the Well.* A king orders his adviser to move a well. On the advice of his daughter, the adviser tells the king that the king must send his well to help. The king thus sees the absurdity of his order. [H1023.25.1].
India *3*.

875B₄ *Bull's Calves.* The king asks his companion for a tribute of calves born to bulls; the peasant-lad, when questioned, replies: Let me go and ask my father who guards the fields, lest fish come up from the seashore and eat the millet.
   Greek *1*.

875C *The Queen as Gusli-player.* A king goes into a foreign land, where he is thrown in prison. His wife disguises herself as a gusli-player, goes to the hostile king and receives his permission to take with her one of the prisoners. She chooses her husband [J1545.4]. The husband does not recognize her and reproaches his wife for not wanting to help him. The truth is discovered.
   *DeVries FFC LXXIII 275—284; *Bolte-Polivka III 530f. — Russian: Afanasiev (880*B) *1*. — Japanese: Ikeda (J1545.4). — Oceanic: (Philippine): Fansler MAFLS XII 63.

875D *The Clever Girl at the End of the Journey.* She explains enigmatic statements and actions encountered on the way [H586; for details see H586.1.—H586.7]; succeeds in a contest in repartee and in performing impossible tasks.
   I. *The Laughing Fish.* (a) A (dried) fish laughs in the palace [D1318.2.1]. The king orders his wazir to find out why on pain of death. (b) Or a king demands that his wazir or a man solve another problem.
   II. *The Journey.* (a) The wazir or his son sets out on a journey. He meets an old man and makes various enigmatic suggestions; (b) Or two men travel together and one makes enigmatic suggestions: (c) Let us carry one another (meaning tell stories to shorten the way.) (d) Let us get horses in the forest (let us cut walking sticks). (e) Other enigmatic suggestions. (f) Or one man does seemingly absurd things (wears his shoes in the streams, carries them on dry land, etc.). (g) The man's daughter interprets correctly the enigmatic remarks or the seemingly absurd actions. [H586].
   III. *The Wazir's Son marries the Girl.* She answers the original question [H561.1.1.1]. (The fish laughed because there is a man dressed in woman's clothes in the harem.)
   **DeVries FFC LXXIII 42ff.; *Fischer-Bolte 216; *Penzer I 46ff., VII 254, IX, 142. — Icelandic (803*) *6* (merman laughs); India *11*.

875D* *The Prince's Seven Wise Teachers.* The stepmother, rejected by her stepson, the prince, unjustly makes complaint against him to his father [K2111]. On the advice of his tutors, the prince at the gallows proves to his father, that amongst the queen's maids there is a man dressed as a maid — the queen's paramour [K1825.1.1.1]. The queen and her lover are hanged.
   Lithuanian (*656) *2*.

875E *The Unjust Decision: The Oil Press Gives Birth to a Colt* [J1191]. A traveler ties his mare to an oilman's mill. During the night the mare gives birth to a colt. The oilman claims it, saying the mill has given birth to the colt. The judge (a jackal) says he is late because the sea was burning and he

had to put it out with straw, or the like. The absurdity of the oilman's claim is thus made clear.
India 21.

876 *The Clever Maiden and the Suitors.* Answers and understands enigmatic questions. Cf. Type 851A.
Lithuanian (*1465) 11; Rumanian (877) 13.

876A* *Prince and Clever Parson's (Broommaker's) Daughter.* She wins his hand.
Rumanian 4.

877 *The Old Woman who was Skinned.* La Vecchia Scorticata. King marries woman whose finger he has seen and whose voice he has heard. She turns out to be old woman. He has her thrown out. She hangs in a tree. Swan fairies change her into beautiful girl. The king takes her as wife. Her sister tries to imitate, has herself skinned and dies.
*BP IV 203 n. 1. — Catalan: Amades No. 196; Italian 7 (Tuscan [868] a, [886] 3, Pentamerone I No. 10, Sicilian *877 3, Gonzenbach No. 73); Serbocroatian 3; Polish (525) 1; Turkish: Eberhard-Boratav Type 226 19.

877* *Taming the Wild Prince.* Lost in the woods, the little prince grows up among wild animals and lets no one come near him. Only a servant girl succeeds in taming him. [K1399.1].
Lithuanian (*877) 2.

879 *The Basil Maiden (The Sugar Puppet, Viola).*
I. *The Sprinkler of Basil.* A princess before leaving her schoolmistress is used to sprinkling a vase of flowers.
II. *Questions and Counterquestions.* A prince ridicules her with a rhyme but the girl learns from her teacher a rhyme which scorns him in turn. (Question and counterquestion: how many leaves on the plant, how many stars in the sky [H705.3]).
III. *Tricks and Countertricks.* (a) Masking as fisherman the prince receives a kiss from the girl and then reveals the deceit. (b) The girl then induces the prince to kiss his horse's leg and then jeers at him. (c) Hiding under her bed the prince repeatedly sticks the girl with a needle; she complains of the supposed insects biting her. (d) The girl frightens the prince making him believe that Death is coming for him.
IV. *The Sugar Puppet.* The prince takes her as wife but the first night seek to avenge himself by cutting off her head, but she saves herself by putting in her place a puppet of sugar. [K525.1].
*Penzer in Basile I 256; *Espinosa II 61—78, 227—229; *Lo Nigro p. 194; Köhler-Bolte I 374; *Köhler to Gonzenbach No. 35 and Zs. f. Vksk. VI 73. — Icelandic: Rittershaus 205; Spanish (*970) 7; Catalan: Amades No. 383; Italian 8 (Pentamerone II No. 3, III No. 4, Tuscan [920] a—c 3, Sicilian *879 3, Gonzenbach No. 35); Turkish: Eberhard-Boratav No. 192 (a mixture of Types 878 and 878A) 25; Hungarian: Berze Nagy (577**) 9; Greek: Loukatos Nos. 4,5. — Spanish-American: Hansen (**970) (Chile 5, Dominican Republic 1, Puerto Rico 6).

879A *Fisher Husband of the Princess.* He leaves her on the wedding night because she has made fun of his manners. He rises to a high rank but cannot speak. She comes as doctor and tries in vain to cure him [H1194.0.1]. As she is about to be executed he speaks and saves her.
    Italian (Sicilian *902 *1*); Greek (883B*) *7*, Hahn No. 40; Turkish: Eberhard-Boratav (No. 191) *6*.

879A* *A Salesman Receives Kiss* from girl for goods. She disguises as doctor and punishes him.
    Greek *7*.

879A** *Helper Kissed.* Girl is found to give an old man a kiss for helping her with a mealsack. She marries a knight who upbraids her for this kiss. Old man manages for knight to be lost in woods where he must in his turn give her a kiss before he can satisfy his hunger.
    Swedish (GS 902) *3*.

879B* *Dancing Girl's Fortune.* A girl knows how to dance remarkably and thereby makes her fortune.
    Livonian (879') *1*.

879C* *Clever Girl Frees her Brother from Prison* [R158].
    Rumanian (879*) *2*.

879D* *The Clever Sisters.* (Stolen Kettle.)
    Rumanian (879 I*) *1*.

879E* *How will You Keep Yourselves.* (Youngest: »Like beauty and love.«)
    Rumanian (879 II*) *1*.

879F* *How must the Wife Be?* (Beautiful, to please the husband.)
    Rumanian (879 III*) *1*.

880—899 Fidelity and Innocence

880 *The Man Boasts of his Wife.* Is imprisoned in the royal castle. The wife in man's clothing is betrothed to the princess [K1837]. Escapes with her husband [R152.1].
    *BP III 530 note 2 (Grimm No. 218); cf. Beethoven's »Fidelio.« — Finnish *3*; Lithuanian *1*; Irish *2*; Serbocroatian *1*; Russian: Andrejev; Greek *2*, Loukatos No. 1.

880* *The Gambler's Wife.* A serviceman beats his general at gambling, and then marries the general's daughter. Later, he loses all his money at gambling, and returns to his poor parents. His wife, winning back what he has lost, finds her husband.
    Russian: Andrejev (*880 I) *4*.

881 *Oft-proved Fidelity.* A merchant's son marries the king's daughter. An attempt is made to seduce her [K2112]. The man strikes his wife and thinks he has killed her. A physician heals her and wants to secure her for himself [T320.1]. She flees in men's clothes [K1837]. Becomes emperor. Has her picture displayed in a public place [H21]. Is reunited with her husband [R195]. Cf. Type 712.

Finnish *9;* Lithuanian *9;* Danish *1;* Irish *7;* Catalan: Amades No. 372; Italian *5* (Tuscan 709 n—p *3,* Sicilian *2*); Hungarian *5;* Russian: Andrejev *3;* Greek *16,* Loukatos No. 2; Turkish: Eberhard-Boratav Nos. 195, 215 IV, 219 V *18.* — Franco-American *7;* Spanish-American: Hansen (**897A) (Chile) *1.* — Literary Treatments: Cf. Chauvin V 94.

881A *The Abandoned Bride Disguised as a Man.* Cf. Type 884A.

I. *A Prince and his Bride are Separated in a Forest.* (a) She escapes from the would-be seducers [T320.1]. (She shoots an arrow saying she will marry the one who first returns with it and escapes while the men pursue the arrow.)

II. *Experiences Abroad.* The bride, disguised as a man [K521.4.1.1], is chosen king or given other high honors in a strange land. (a) As a servant to the king, she kills or overcomes an ogress. (She hears a cry at night and finds an ogress trying to devour a human corpse. She cuts off the ogress's leg or the like. The king rewards her.) (b) She »marries» a princess, or princesses [K1322].

III. *Reunification.* (a) She displays her picture ((b) an object) in a public place [H21] and posts servants (or stays herself) to overhear comments. (c) She gives alms to all comers. (d) In this way she finds her husband. (e) The would-be seducers are punished.

India *17.*

881* *Woman in Men's Clothes as Physician in Court.* Queen's attempt at seduction repulsed. Queen says doctor has boasted that he could give speech to one born dumb. In court dumb person speaks and tells truth. [K1837, K2111, H916.1.1]. Cf. Types 425K, 434, 514, 514**, 884, 884A.

*Crane *Vitry* 231f. No. 237; *Bolte Zs. f. Vksk. XXVI 89 n. 1; Herbert III 19; Catalan: Amades No. 405; Japanese: Ikeda.

881** *The Poor Girl Pretends to Wealth and Wins the Prince.* Cf. Type 859.

Turkish: Eberhard-Boratav (No. 234) *12.*

882 *The Wager on the Wife's Chastity.* A ship captain marries a poor girl. Makes a wager with a merchant on the chastity of his wife. Through treachery, the merchant secures a token of unfaithfulness (ring). The captain leaves home. The wife follows him in men's clothing. They reach home again and everything is explained. Cf. Type 892.

Motifs:

N15. Chastity wager. K1342. Entrance into woman's (man's) room by hiding in chest. K2112.1. False tokens of woman's unfaithfulness. K1837. Disguise of woman in man's clothes. H94. Identification by ring. K1512.1. Cut-off finger proves wife's chastity.

*BP III 92 n. 1; *Köhler-Bolte I 211—212; Coffin *5; Arts et Traditions Populaires* I 275; Phateine T. Bourboulis *Studies in the History of Modern Greek Story Motifs* (1953) 53ff. — Finnish *28;* Finnish-Swedish *2;* Estonian *4;* Livonian *3;* Lithuanian *14;* Lappish *2;* Swedish (misc.) *4;* Norwegian *3,* Solheim *1;* Danish *29,* Grundtvig No. 131; Irish *81;* Basque *1;* French *6;* Spanish *2;* Catalan: Amades No. 386, 391; German *16;* Austrian:

Haiding p. 471; Italian *10* (Tuscan 892 b—e *4*, Sicilian *6*, Gonzenbach No. *7*); Czech: Tille Soupis II (2) 34—41, 44f. *11;* Serbocroatian *3;* Russian: Andrejev *Ukraine* (882A) *3*, Afanasiev (882A) *14;* Greek *14;* Turkish: Eberhard-Boratav No. 272, 378 *4;* Arab: Littmann 204; India *2;* Indonesian: DeVries No. 311. — Franco-American *25;* Spanish-American: Rael Nos. 130—132 (U.S.), Hansen (Dominican Republic) *1;* Cape Verde Islands: Parsons MAFLS XV (1) 177 n. 1; West Indies (Negro) *1*. — Literary Treatments: Shakespeare's Cymbeline.

882A* *Suitors at the Spinning-wheel.* In the absence of a ship captain his wife annoyed by three suitors. They are all deceived [K1218]. (Locked up and made to spin). Cf. Types 890 IIIb, 1730.
Lappish *1*; Russian: Andrejev (*882B) *1*.

882B* *The Forgiven Skeleton.* The lovers are separated when the man must go away. When he returns he thinks that she has been unfaithful to him. He kills her. He is executed (dies). His skeleton remains at the place of execution (etc.). A servant girl carries the skeleton away. The skeleton is unwilling to let her go back until she succeeds in securing forgiveness for him from his murdered beloved.
Czech: Tille (Soupis I 370—375) *10*.

883A *The Innocent Slandered Maiden.* In the absence of the father, an attempt is made to seduce the daughter. When this attempt fails, she is slandered. The father commands his son to kill his sister. She becomes the wife of a prince. Is trusted to a servant. The latter attempts to seduce her. The girl in men's clothing. All ends happily.

Motifs:

T320.1. Oft-proved fidelity. K2110.1. Calumniated wife. K2112. Woman slandered as adulteress (prostitute). S322.1.3. Father condemns daughter to death because he believes her unchaste. L162. Lowly heroine marries prince (king). K2250.1. Treacherous servant. T320. Escape from undesired lover. K1837. Disguise of woman in man's clothes.

*BP I 305 n. 1; *Anderson in Tauscher *Volksmärchen* 174; Chauvin VI 159f. No 323; Espinosa II 399ff. — Finnish *21;* Finnish-Swedish *1* (883*); Estonian *3;* Lithuanian *8;* Danish *4;* Irish *3;* French *4;* Spanish *1;* German *6* (Archive *5*, Meckl. No. 91); Italian (Tuscan 709 q, cf. 709 n *2*); Rumanian *1;* Hungarian *1*, Dégh No. 3; Czech: Tille Soupis II (2) 41—44, 466f. *3;* Serbocroatian *3;* Russian: Afanasiev *8*, Azadowsky *Russkaya Skazka* Nos. 4, 33; Greek *7*, Dawkins *Modern Greek Folktales* No. 57; Turkish: Eberhard-Boratav Nos. 137 III, 236 V, 245 *4;* Berber: Laoust No. 9; South Arabia: Jahn No. 5; India *2*. — Franco-American *5;* Spanish-American: Rael Nos. 133—135 (U.S.), Hansen (Puerto Rico) (883**C) *1*, (Dominican Republic) (883**B) *1*.

883B *The Punished Seducer.* Two of the three daughters of a merchant are seduced by a prince. The third avoids his seductions and punishes him [L74].

Finnish-Swedish (883*) *1;* Lithuanian *6;* Swedish *12* (Uppsala *1*,

Stockholm 2, Liungman 4, misc. 5); Norwegian (883*) 3; Danish 12; Icelandic 1; French 1; German 1; Italian 5 (Tuscan [919 a—c, e, f] 5); Hungarian (Honti 883B, Berze Nagy 577**) 9; Czech: Tille (Soupis I 377ff.) 3; Serbocroatian 2; Russian: Andrejev (*815 II) 1; Turkish: Eberhard-Boratav No. 192 III.

883C *The Boys with Extraordinary Names.* A maiden expelled from home [S322.1] marries a lowly man and has three sons whom she names »What was I?« »What am I?« and »What will I be?« (or the like) [N271.1]. In this way she attracts the attention of her father and is recognized and reconciled. Cf. Type 960, 1376C*, 1530*.

Greek: Dawkins *Modern Greek in Asia Minor* 284ff., 300ff.; Turkish: Eberhard-Boratav No. 137 *13*.

883C* *The Innocent Slandered Maiden: Alleged Pregnancy.*
Greek 2.

883D* *The Sister Out in the Cold.* She is refused entrance to the house. Makes complaint in song. The brothers bring her clothes. [S357].
Lithuanian (*882C) *1*.

884 *The Forsaken Fiancée: Service as Menial.* A prince forsakes his fiancée in order to pledge himself to another of his father's choice. In men's clothes [K1837], the first fiancée along with her companions goes into the service of the prince. [K1816.0.2]. Test: whether men or maidens [H1578.1]. The prince marries his first fiancée [T102]. Cf. Type 514.

*BP II 56 (Grimm No. 67); Delarue in Boratav *Contes Turcs* 207; Lo Nigro p. 200f. — Livonian *1*; Lithuanian *3*; Icelandic (876*) *3*; Catalan: Amades Nos. 155, 1657, 1995, cf. 405; German *8*; Italian *15* (Pentamerone III No. 6, Tuscan 514 a—f, 707 v, 892 d, cf. 905 *9*, Sicilian *5*, Gonzenbach Nos. 12, 17); Serbocroatian *1*; Greek *6*, Hahn Nos. 10, 101, Dawkins *Modern Greek Folktales* pp. 314ff.; Turkish: Eberhard-Boratav No. 374 *15*. — Franco-American *1*.

884A *A Girl Disguised as a Man* [K1837] *is Wooed by the Queen.* She enters the service of a king who is pleased with the service. The queen makes advances and is repulsed. False accusation [K2111]. The girl's sex is discovered [H1578.1] at the point of execution (or she must interpret the cries of a monster: these tell of her true sex). Cf. Types 514, 881A.

**Fernando de Castro Pires de Lima *A Mulher Vestida de Homem* (Lisbon, 1958); Danish *1*; French (884B) *2*; Basque: Delarue (884B) *1*; Portuguese: Braga No. 14, Coelho No. 19; Pedroso FLS XIII 53; Italian: *Archivo delle trad. pop.* III 372 No. 11, Gonzenbach No. 9; Slovenian *1*; Greek: Dawkins *Modern Greek Folktales* Nos. 17, 47A. — Brazil: Camara Cascudo 155ff.

884B *The Girl as Soldier.* Masks as a man and becomes a successful soldier and officer. Bears child to her lover.
Italian (Sicilian 2).

884A* *The Daughter to Grieve.* A magician (knight, miller) has a daughter (Cekanka,

Milivka). A father makes his daughter promise that after his death she will grieve for him alone in the castle during the spring equinox. The girl is in love with her servant boy. A magician kills the boy and the girl commits suicide. The evil magician becomes insane. The dead girl is changed into a blue flower — the chickory.

Czech: Tille Soupis I 162—5 *6*.

884B* *Girl Dressed as Man Deceives the King.* Vasilisa, the priest's daughter, wears men's clothing and behaves like a man. The tsar finds out about it and calls her to him in order to expose the woman in her. She eludes all of his tricks and leaves him befuddled.

Russian: Afanasiev (884*B) *7*.

885 *The Poor Boy Betrothed to the Maiden.* The bride stolen. The girl's parents coerce her into pledging herself to the preacher. The hero comes in disguise to the wedding. The preacher in jest trusts him with the girl. [K1371.1]. He reveals himself.

Finnish *2;* Finnish-Swedish *4;* Estonian *2;* Livonian *1;* Lithuanian *2;* Lappish *1;* Swedish *6* (Stockholm *3,* Liungman *3*); Danish *6;* English: Child *English-Scottish Ballads* IV 218, 230, V 260f.; German *5* (Archive *4,* Henssen Volk No. 206); Russian: Andrejev. — Franco-American *1;* Spanish-American: Rael Nos. 26, 27 (U.S.). — Literary Treatments: Walter Scott »Lochinvar», Ibsen »Peer Gynt,» Act I.

885A (formerly 885*) *The Seemingly Dead.* The princess, in love with a common lad and compelled to marry one her own station, dies. She is resuscitated by her lover, who then gets her as wife. [K522.0.1].

Chauvin V 134 No. 63; Wesselski *Märchen* No. 8. — Finnish-Swedish *3;* Estonian *2;* Lithuanian (*857) *5;* Italian (Tuscan [873] *1*); Czech: Tille Soupis II (2) 221ff. *8;* Russian: Afanasiev (885*) *2*. — Franco-American *15*.

885** *The Foster Children.* The foster son and his foster sister love each other. The boy goes to sea, returns and marries his boyhood sweetheart. [T127].

Finnish-Swedish (885*) *4*.

886 *The Girl Who Could Not Keep the Secret* that the hero wants to marry her (or that he has seduced her). Hence he seeks another bride. At the betrothal the first fiancée says that she still loves the youth. The new fiancée is thus moved to boast to her husband of her superiority in keeping silent: she has had seven children and has been able to keep this a secret. The youth marries his earlier sweetheart.

Motifs: K1362. Innocent girl sells her »love» and later receives it back. K1275. Girl who cannot keep silent thereby provokes her rival to admit unchastity. J941. Old sweetheart chosen in preference to new.

Finnish *1;* Estonian *1;* Danish *6,* Grundtvig No. 132; Russian: Andrejev. — Literary Treatment: *Von der Hagen *Gesammtabenteuer* No. 21.

887 *Griselda.* The king marries a maiden of the lower class. She promises to be always complacent. The king puts her to the proof by making her believe that he has killed their children and married another wife [H461]. Cf. Types 712, 881, 900.

**Käte Laserstein *Der Griseldisstoff in der Weltlitteratur* (Weimar, 1926); Ilse von Stach, *Griseldis* (1922); **H. Siefkin *Das geduldige Weib in der englischen Literatur bis auf Shakespeare* (Leipzig, 1903); **Cate *Studies in Philology* XXIX 389ff.; *Hibbard *Medieval Romance in England* 289 n. 9; Bolte Zs. f. Vksk. XXXV—XXXVI 290; Hdwb. d. Märchens s.v. »Geduldsprüfung»; Köhler-Bolte II 501, 534; *Philippson FFC L 48ff.
— Finnish *2;* Finnish-Swedish *5;* Lithuanian *5;* Swedish *6* (Uppsala *2,* Liungman *2,* misc. *2);* Norwegian *1;* Danish *11,* Grundtvig No. 36; Icelandic *2;* Irish *2;* Spanish *1;* German *5* (Archive *3,* Merk. 24, Meckl. No. 92); Austrian: Haiding No. 27; Czech: Tille Soupis I 397, 401, 468 *5;* Serbocroatian *1;* Russian: Afanasiev *2;* Greek: Laographia II 479f., Dawkins FL IX 363ff.; Turkish: Eberhard-Boratav No. 306 *3.* — Spanish-American: Hansen (Puerto Rico) *1.*

887A* *The Purchased Wife.* A youth spends all of his hard-earned money to buy a wife. [T52]. The wife teaches him to make precious stone into bricks and to take them to the tsar as a gift. He receives a reward.
Russian (*887 I) *15.*

888 *The Faithful Wife.* The enslaved husband is rescued by his wife disguised as a pilgrim. The white handkerchief.

I. *The Enslaved Husband.* A count is taken into slavery in Turkey [R61].
II. *The Chaste Wife.* (a) He has a shirt (or handkerchief) that remains white as long as his wife at home remains true to him [H431.1]. (b) A messenger of the Sultan's seeks to seduce her, but in vain [T320.1].
III. *The Pilgrim.* (a) Clad as a pilgrim [K1837], she follows the Turk and by means of her harp-playing and her singing wins the Sultan's favor, so that he presents her with three Christian slaves, among them her husband [R152.1].
IV. *Recognition.* When the husband has returned home and is wondering about his long-vanished wife, she arrives in her pilgrim dress and shows herself as his rescuer [H0]. — Adapted from BP.

*BP III 517ff. (Grimm No. 218). — Livonian (890') *1;* Lithuanian *1;* Icelandic *2;* Danish *2;* Irish *2;* French *1;* Catalan: Amades No. 1969; German *10* (Archive *8,* Merk. 150, 185); Czech: Tille Soupis II (1) 251f. *1;* Slovenian *2;* Russian (880B) *1.*

888A *The Wife Who Would Not be Beaten* (Rescues her Husband).

I. *The Husband Threatens to Beat his Wife.* (a) A prince (merchant's son) says he will marry only a girl who will submit to a beating (with a hose) each day [M134]. (b) The prince marries the girl and she refuses to allow him to beat her, saying he does not support her (but her father does).
II. *The Prince Enslaved.* (a) The prince sets out to win his fortune but is enslaved or loses all his fortune and must work at menial tasks. (b) The chess game and the trained cat. See Type 217. (c) The youth in the land of cheaters. See Type 978. (d) The wager on magic objects (the

youth finds a magic object, but when he wagers on it, it will not perform.)

III. *The Rescue.* (a) The wife disguised as a man frees her husband [J1545.6]. (She overcomes the courtesan in a chess game by loosing mice which the trained cat chases [N7], or she tricks the cheaters or wins the wager. (b) She secures tokens from her husband.

IV. *Recognition.* At home when the freed husband falsely boasts of his exploits, the wife displays the tokens [H80]. The husband never beats her.

India *11*.

888* *The Princess Flees to the Forest to Escape Marriage* [T311.1]. She lives in a cave [R315] where a raven serves her [B531]. At last she is discovered through her ring which the raven takes to the king [H94]. Cf. Type 870.
Estonian *1*.

888A* *The Basket-maker.* A man learns a trade (basket-making) so as to win his wife in marriage. She is later taken by a sea-captain; he is cast adrift at sea. Years later, she re-finds her husband on seeing his baskets displayed. Cf. Type 949*.
Irish: O'Suilleabhain p. 625 Nos. 13, 14, 15.

888B* *The Mariner Changed to a Bird.* A boy goes to sea, leaving his fiancée behind; he and other sailors are changed into birds by the captain's adulterous wife [D150]. The bird comes to the girl, tells who he is, bids her pull three feathers from his his tail, which will grant all her wishes [D1021]. She gets work at a king's palace and discomfits three of the servants who want to seduce her. Her fiancée later comes to her disenchanted and they marry.
Irish: MS Iml. a 534 l. a 187—97 in Irish Folklore Commission.

889 *The Faithful Servant.* A lord makes a wager with his neighbor on the fatihfulness of his servant [N25]. The servant is sent to the neighbor's house, where he is made drunk, etc. The neighbor loses the wager. Sometimes joined with Type 930 III a.

*BP IV 181; *Wesselski *Märchen* 200 No. 11; *Arts et Traditions Populaires* I 280 (Frequent in French-Canadian, not in French); Zs. f. Vksk. VI 52; *Espinosa II 242ff. — Lithuanian *3;* Swedish *4* (Uppsala *1*, Lund *3*); Danish *15*, Grundtvig No. 74; Irish *20;* French *4;* Spanish *6;* Catalan: Amades No. 444; Italian *3* (Sicilian *3*, Gonzenbach No. 8); Hungarian *2;* Russian: Andrejev *1;* Greek *1*, Loukatos No. 1. — Franco-American: *5;* Spanish-American: Rael Nos. 40, 41 (U.S.), Hansen (Puerto Rico)*1;* West Indies (Negro) *1*.

890 *A Pound of Flesh.* The wife as judge saves her husband.

I. A merchant buys a bride in Turkey for her weight in gold.

II. He gets the money by giving as security a piece of his own flesh.

III. (a) The husband is abroad and (b) while he is away three merchants fall in love with the young woman. She deceives them all and gets much money in payment for keeping the matter secret (Cf. Types 882A*, 1730). (c) She has decorated the house for her husband's home-coming but he misinterprets her act and casts her into the sea, or (d) sets her on an island whence she is rescued by a ship.

IV. (a) She clothes herself in men's clothing and sets out for Turkey where she finds her husband as prisoner and frees him. (b) His creditor demands the pound of flesh. She appears as judge and frees him. — Adapted from Christiansen *Norske Eventyr*.

Motifs:

I. T52.3. Bride purchased for her weight in gold.

II. M231. Free keep in inn exchanged for good story.

III. K443.2. Clever wife gets money from those who attempt to seduce her. S411. Wife banished. S411.1. Misunderstood wife banished by husband. S141. Exposure in boat. S433. Cast-off wife abandoned on island.

IV. K1837. Disguise of woman in man's clothes. H1385.4. Quest for vanished husband. R152.1. Disguised wife helps husband escape from prison. K1825.2. Woman masks as lawyer (judge) and frees her husband. J1161.2. Pound of flesh (Fleischpfand). Literal pleading frees man from pound of flesh contract.

*Cosquin *Etudes* 456ff.; *BP III 517 (Grimm No. 218); *Köhler-Bolte I 211f.; Wesselski *Märchen* 252 No. 61; *Taylor Hdwb. d. Märchens s.v. »Fleichpfand«. — Swedish *5* (Uppsala *4*, misc. *1*); Norwegian *2*, Solheim *1*; Danish *9*; Icelandic *1*; Irish *37*; Czech: Tille Soupis II (2) 37f. *1*; Greek *1*; Turkish: Eberhard-Boratav No. 297 *2*. — Franco-American *8*; Literary Treatments: Chauvin VIII 200ff. No. 245; Oesterley *Gesta Romanorum* No. 195; Shakespeare's »Merchant of Venice«; Italian Novella: Rotunda (J1161.2).

890* *Rescue by Father.* A youth takes his father's sword and rides against the enemy; he is imprisoned and rescued by his father [R153.3.1].
Lappish *1*.

890A* *The Snake in the Bosom.* A young girl has a snake in her bosom. All relatives refuse help in removing it. Her lover finds the snake, which turns to gold.
English: Child No. 95; Hungarian: Berze Nagy *11*.

891 *The Man Who Deserts His Wife and Sets Her the Task of Bearing Him a Child.*

I. *The Prince Deserts His Wife.* (a) A girl by accident arouses the enmity of a prince, who threatens to make her half a wife, or the like, and marries her, or (b) a prince becomes angry at his wife. (c) The prince deserts his wife, (d) or imprisons her. (e) He sets her the task of bearing him a child whose real father he is and whose real mother she is [H1187]. (f) The girl threatens to force the prince to perform some menial or degrading task.

II. *The Wife Performs the Task.* (a) The wife follows her husband, or (b) escapes from prison. (c) Disguised as a courtesan, she makes love to her husband [K1814], and becomes pregnant. (d) The wife while disguised forces her husband to perform the menial task, or (e) her son forces his father to perform the tasks (as part of type 1525, which see).

III. *Reconciliation.* (a) By tokens which she has secured, the wife is able to prove that she has performed the task.

Frequently mixed with Type 879.

*Penzer in Basile I 256. — Spanish (cf. *445A) *1;* Italian (Sicilian *878 *3,* Gonzenbach No. 36, Pentamerone III No. 4); Serbocroatian *2;* Greek: Dawkins *Modern Greek Folktales* 282ff.; Turkish: Eberhard-Boratav (No. 192 — a mixture of Type 878 and 879) *25;* India *15.*

891A *The Princess from the Tower Recovers her Husband.* (Frequently mixed with 891.)

I. *The Princess in the Tower.* A princess is alone in a tower or gorgeous tent. A prince finds her and they fall in love, but he leaves or the princess's father offers his daughter in marriage to the prince, who refuses.

II. (a) She pursues the prince disguised as a man, succeeds eventually in being recognized as he is about to marry another; or (b) She pursues in a ship, builds a palace opposite the prince and is eventually recognized; or (c) She pursues and as servant-maid wins the prince's love.

Cf. Spanish (*445A) *1;* Greek (*884***) *4,* Dawkins *Modern Greek Folktales* (No. 30) *2;* Turkish: Eberhard-Boratav (Nos. 186, 187, 188) *52.* — Spanish-American: Hansen (**876) (Dominican Republic) *1.*

891A* *The Fourteen Daughters.* A husband leaves his wife who has given birth to fourteen girls. On the seashore, the girls find precious stones. The wife, now prosperous, finds her husband among beggars. [N231].

Lithuanian (*1668) *2.*

891B* *The King's Glove.* The king admires the sleeping wife of a courtier but only leaves his glove on her bed. She is suspected of unfaithfulness. The king invites the courtier and his wife to a banquet. They are to tell adventures. The king and the woman do so in rhyme and the husband sees their innocence.

*Lo Nigro 204. — Italian (Sicilian *891 *1).*

891C* *The Pig Eats the Money.* A wife falsely accused of giving away money says that the pig ate it. The man kills the pig and finds that this is true. Forgiveness.

Spanish (*891) *1.* — Literary Treatment: Libro de los Ejemplos No. 293.

892 *The Children of the King.* While the young prince is traveling, his sister is to govern the country, both their parents being dead. Staying in the service of another king, the boy is told lies about the conduct of his sister by a knight who by treachery has obtained proofs of his reports [K2112.1]. The boy repudiates his sister, but she rights herself, her innocence becomes apparent, and the bad knight is punished [Q261]. Cf. Type 882.

Norwegian (888) *6,* Solheim *2;* Danish *19;* Italian *1* (Tuscan *1);* Greek *Laographia* X 389f.; India *1.* — Franco-American *1.* — Literary Treatment: Shakespeare's »Cymbeline».

893 *The Unreliable Friends* (The Half-Friend). The man kills a hog. He tells his friends that he has killed a man and asks where he can hide the body. All of them drive him away and only his father's half-friend remains true to him in his feigned trouble [H1558.1].

*Basset RTP XXII 10; Crane *Vitry* 185f. No. 120; *Arts et Traditions*

Populaires I 274; *Hdwb. d. Märchens I 94 b; Herbert III 10, 55, 205. — Estonian (893*) *3;* Lithuanian *2;* Icelandic: Sveinsson FFC LXXXIII p. xix, *Boberg *2;* French *11;* Catalan: Amades No. 414; Serbocroatian *3;* Russian: Andrejev; India *2.* — Spanish-American: Rael Nos. 94, 95 (U.S.); Cape Verde Islands: Parsons MAFLS XV (1) 202 n. 2. — African *1.* — Literary Treatments: Penzer Ocean V 87 n. 1; Chauvin IX 15f.; Oesterley *Gesta Romanorum* No. 129; Rotunda (H1558.1); Bin Gorion *Born Judas* IV 32, *274.

894 *The Ghoulish Schoolmaster and the Stone of Pity.* Cf. Type 710.

I. *Ghoulish Schoolmaster.* A princess accidentally sees her schoolmaster eating a corpse (Cf. Type 707A). He lays a curse on her: she is to lie sick for seven years, seven months, and seven days, and then to be transported by a cloud to a mountain.

II. *The Sleeping Prince.* All happens as prophesied. On the mountain in a palace she finds a prince lying as if dead and an inscription saying that he could be awakened if for seven years, seven months and seven days he is rubbed with a certain herb by a maiden who will become his wife.

III. *The Treacherous Slave Girl.* Out of fatigue the princess entrusts her task to a slave. When the prince awakens he marries the slave and the princess becomes her maidservant.

IV. *The Stone of Pity.* She asks from the king's marshall a knife and a stone of patience. The marshall overhears her telling her story to the stone, which swells with pity. The prince listens and sees the stone burst. She is about to kill herself with the knife. The prince interferes. They marry and the slave girl is punished.

Motifs:

I. G11.9. Ogre schoolmaster. Girl sees schoolmaster eat human flesh. Refuses to tell him what she saw. He persecutes her. D2064. Magic sickness. Z72.2. Seven years, seven months, seven days.

II. D1960.3. Sleeping Beauty. Magic sleep for definite period (e.g., a hundred years). D714. Disenchantment by rubbing. D750. Disenchantment by faithfulness of others.

III. K2251.1. Treacherous slave-girl. K1911.1.4. False bride finishes true bride's task and supplants her. The true bride must perform a certain task to win her husband and, being exhausted, commits the task to a slave.

IV. H13.2.2. Recognition by overheard conversation with stone. Q581. Villain nemesis. Person condemned to punishment he has suggested for others.

*BP I 19 nn. 1, 2; *Cosquin *Contes indiens* 112ff.; *Dawkins FL IX 363. — Cf. Irish: O'Suilleabhain Handbook p. 572; Spanish (*445B) *1;* Catalan: Amades No. 173; Italian (Pentamerone II No. 8, Sicilian *894 *2,* Gonzenbach No. 11); Serbocroatian *1;* Slovenian; Greek:

Dawkins *Modern Greek Folktales* Nos. 32, 33 *11*, Hahn No. 66; Albanian: Hahn No. 12; Egyptian: Artin-Pascha Nos. 3, 4; Persian: Lorimer p. 19; Turkish: Eberhard-Boratav (No. 185) *38*.

896 *The Lecherous Holy Man and the Maiden in a Box.*
   I. *The Lecherous Holy Man.* (a) A holy man or (b) another trusted adviser falls in love with a beautiful girl, but she spurns his advances. He convinces the girl's father or husband that the girl is unchaste or that she will bring calamities to the kingdom and that she must be placed in a box and (c) cast into the river or (d) delivered to him. He instructs his followers who are to deliver the box to him (after recovering it from the river) to leave the box in his room, to securely lock the doors, and to ignore any sounds that may come from his room during the night, no matter what they may be [K1333, K1367].
   II. *The Rescue and the Substitution.* (a) A prince or (b) some other helper finds the box before it falls into the hands of the holy man's followers, removes the girl and puts into the box (c) a mad dog or (d) a tiger or other wild animal [K1625, K1674]. The holy man is torn to pieces (Q243.6). (e) The girl weds her rescuer. (f) She is reconciled with her family.
   India *15*.

897 *The Orphan Girl and Her Cruel Sisters-in-Law.*
   I. *The Tasks.* A young girl is left by her seven brothers while they go on a trip in the care of her seven sisters-in-law. They set her tasks [H934.2], hoping she will be unable to perform them so that they can punish her. She is helped by various animals: (a) to bring in from the forest a large load of sticks without using a rope [H1023.19] (a helpful snake winds around the sticks) [B579.5]; (b) to fetch tigress's milk [H1361.1] (the tigress takes pity on her); (c) to fetch water in a sieve (frogs fill the holes in the sieve) [H1023.2.1.2]; (d) to gather seeds scattered in a field (birds help her) [H1091.2]; (e) Other tasks.
   II. *Rescue.* While she is performing the last task, the brothers appear. The sisters-in-law are punished.
   India *13*.

898 *The Daughter of the Sun.* (*The Speechless Maiden; the Puppet Bride.*)
   I. *Virgin in the Tower.* To avoid fulfillment of a prophecy that a princess shall be impregnated by the sun and bear a child, she is confined in a tower. Nevertheless the prophecy is fulfilled. [T381, T521].
   II. *Rescued Child.* The daughter of the sun is exposed [S313] in a garden and is rescued by a prince [R131.1.3].
   III. *The Prince's Wooing.* (a) When she is grown the prince asks her in marriage but she makes a mysterious answer about her origin, — or (b) the girl of mysterious origin is mute and cannot speak until a certain question is asked. (c) Sometimes the girl is really a puppet who only later is vivified.

IV. *The Prince's Marriage.* The prince marries in turn three ladies of royal blood, but they are killed trying to imitate the prodigies of the heroine.

V. *Recognition.* The prince feigns illness and the heroine cares for him and reveals her origin and consents to the marriage.

*Anderson *Novelline* No. 48; *Köhler Zs. f. Vksk. VI 70 No. 28. — Catalan: Amades I 239 No. 100; Italian *13* (Tuscan [308] b, [861] a, b, c, [886] b, c *7*, Sicilian *886A *6*, Gonzenbach No. 28); Greek (402*) *9*, Dawkins *45 Stories* No. 11; Albanian: Hahn No. 108; Turkish: Eberhard-Boratav (No. 91) *13*.

898* *Daughter to be Given to Sun when Twelve.* This is done. Sun learns of her longing to return to her mother and gets helpful hares to take her back. She avoids efforts of a lamia to overpover her and succeeds in returning home.
Greek (810*) *11*, Hahn No. 41.

899 *Alcestis.* Wife sacrifices self for husband when his parents refuse. [T211.1].
Megas *Archiv für Religionswissenschaft* XXX (Sonderabt.) 1—33; *Ruben FFC CXXXIII 230ff. — Hungarian: Berze Nagy (803) *1;* Serbocroatian *1;* Greek *4;* Turkish: Eberhard-Boratav No. 113. — Literary Treatment: Euripides' »Alcestis».

899* *Various Tales of Expelled or Distressed Maidens.*

899A* A princess is expelled by her stepmother. She is adopted by a countess and loved by the countess' son and his friend.
Icelandic (899 I*), Rittershaus 161.

899B* An earl's son woos a princess. He is refused by the empress, her mother. At last the empress has to ask his help against enemies.
Icelandic (899 II*), Rittershaus 238.

899C* A prince not allowed to marry a princess goes to war. She bears a son secretly and leaves it with a faithful court lady. When the princess is to marry a minister's son she flees. All meet at last.
Icelandic (899 III*), Rittershaus 239.

899D* A son of a preacher and his sister who will not marry a certain stranger are set out in rudderless boat; they come to a foreign country where the prince is sick for love of a stranger (i.e., the preacher's daughter).
Icelandic (899 IV*, V*), Rittershaus 248, 250.

899E* A princess escapes from a seducer twice (once with cook-maid as substitute, once has the lover fall into a hole). Good stepmother warns princess he will carry her away; gives her life token. The princess dresses herself beautifully and sits on a golden chair in the prince's (seducer's) way. He takes her to a swineherd. The latter acts as her slave and tells her that the prince is to marry an ugly earl's daughter. The princess again dresses and sits on chair in way of the earl's daughter. She sells to the latter her clothes for one night's sleep by the prince. The earl's daughter must take her place with swineherd. The princess sees by a life token that her stepmother is in danger. She leaves and saves her. The prince discovers everything. Happy marriage. Cf. Types 870, 870A.
Icelandic (899 VI*) *1*.

899F* A wicked peasant girl kills her father, mother, and sister. Another sister escapes and is taken in by a noble lady and learns to be a physician. The wicked sister goes to court, murders the queen, and marries the king. She cuts out tongue of

king's imprisoned father. All is revealed in a trial. The murderess is expelled. The sister (now a doctor) cures the king's father and the king marries her.
  Icelandic (899 VII*) *1*.

900—904 The Shrewish Wife is Reformed

900 *King Thrushbeard.* A princess disdains all her suitors. Names one of them Thrushbeard. Her father marries her to a beggar. Her pride is broken. The beggar reveals himself as King Thrushbeard.

I. *The Suitors.* (a) A king sends abroad invitations for suitors to woo his daughter. (b) A prince sees a picture of the princess (in a forbidden chamber) and falls in love with her.

II. *The Disdaining of the Suitors.* (a) She treats her suitors shamefully and (b) calls them ugly names (Thrushbeard).

III. *The Princess's Wedding.* The princess is married to a beggar because (a) her father in anger makes her marry the first man who comes, or (b) the disguised prince wins her by solving riddles or (c) by gaining admission to her room and winning her love.

IV. *Her Pride Broken.* (a) Her father banishes them. (b) She must endure poverty, (c) menial work, (d) begging, (e) peddling, and finally (f) must take service in the kitchen of the king.

V. *Recognition.* At the wedding of the prince she looks on with full sense of her shame. He reveals himself as the man who has masked as her beggar husband and celebrates the wedding with her.

Motifs:

I. H311. Inspection test for suitors. Suitors for princess's hand must present themselves for public inspection. H311. Suitor contest: bride offered as prize. T11.2. Love through sight of picture.

II. T74.0.1. Suitor ill-treated. T76. Princess calls her suitors ugly names.

III. T62. Princess to marry first man who asks for her. H551. Princess offered to man who can out-riddle her. T45. Lover buys admission to woman's room. K1361. Beggar buys right to sleep before the girl's door, at foot of bed, in the bed. K1341.1. Entrance to woman's room in golden ram. K1816.0.3. Menial disguise of princess's lover. K1817.1. Disguise as beggar. K1817.3. Disguise as harper (minstrel). T72.2.1. Prince marries scornful girl and punishes her.

IV. L113.1.0.1. Heroine endures hardships with menial husband. L431. Arrogant mistress repaid in kind by her lover. H465. Test of wife's endurance. Haughty princess married to beggar and must endure poverty and menial work. Q483. Princess must sell goods on market as punishment.

V. H461. Test of wife's patience. T251.2. Taming of the shrew. H181. Recognition by unmasking.

Philippson *König Drosselbart* (FFC L 1—101); **E. Gigas »Et eventyrs vandring» *Literatur og Historie* 3 saml. (København, 1902); *BP I 443 (Grimm No. 52); *Krohn FFC XCVI 146ff.; Coffin *2;* Krappe *Etudes Italiennes* II 141—153; Espinosa III 187ff.·— Finnish *15;* Finnish-Swedish *7;* Estonian *3;* Lithuanian *14;* Lappish *2;* Swedish *26* (Uppsala *5,* Stockholm *3,* Göteborg *1,* Liungman *3,* misc. *14);* Norwegian *16,* Solheim *1;* Danish *27,* Grundtvig No. 121; Irish *13,* Beal III 274f. No. 2; French *13;* Spanish *4;* Catalan: Amades No. 357; Flemish *2;* German *29* (Archive *28,* Meckl. No. 93); Austrian: Haiding No. 45; Italian *9* (Pentamerone IV No. 10, Tuscan *4,* Sicilian *3,* (*900) *1,* Gonzenbach No. 18); Hungarian *4,* Dégh No. 34; Czech: Tille Soupis I 351ff. *7;* Slovenian *2;* Serbocroatian *1;* Russian: Andrejev *1,* Andrejev Ukraine *6;* Greek Archive *1, Laographia* X 426ff.; Turkish: Eberhard-Boratav No. 190, Anlage A d cf. 224 *33;* India *1.* — Franco-American *2;* English-American: Baughman *1;* Spanish-American: Hansen (Puerto Rico) *3,* cf. (Cuba) (900A) *1;* West Indies (Negro) *4.* — African *1.*

900A *The Goat Face.* A peasant girl marries a king but is ungrateful and discourteous [L113.1.0.1, L431]. A fairy gives her a goat's face [Q281, D682.1]. She is despised and ill-treated [Q482, Q483]. When she humbles herself before her husband she is disenchanted [D700]. Cf. Types 401, 402.

*Basile *Pentamerone* I No. 8. — Italian: Finamore *Tradizioni popolari abruzzesi* No. 1, Gonzenbach No. 53, Nerucci *Sessanta novelle popolari montalesi* Nos. 30, 37, Crane p. 335.

900A* *The Rejected Fiancé.* Two friends have agreed that, if one has a son and the other a daughter they will marry the one to the other; but the father of the girl no longer wants his friend's son as a son-in-law, as he is now poor. The latter having coals that give light at night gives them to the girl on condition that she show him her feet and then lie with him one night. Having in his possession something belonging to the girl (plaits of her hair, etc.), he demands, on the day she is to marry another, that the bargain be respected, and shows the hair, etc., belonging to the girl. The bridegroom abjures the marriage and the girl marries the hero.
Greek *1,* Hahn No. 113.

900B* *Vengeance on Disdainful Girl.* Youth dresses as a bath-house attendant, tricks the girl and then laughs at her.
Russian: Andrejev (*1563 II) *1.*

901 *Taming of the Shrew.* The youngest of three sisters is a shrew. For their disobedience the husband shoots his dog and his horse. Brings his wife to submission. Wager: whose wife is the most obedient. Cf. Type 1370.

Motifs: L50. Victorious youngest daughter. T251.2. Taming of the shrew. H386. Bride test: obedience. N12. Wager on the most obedient wife.

**Philippson *König Drosselbart* (FFC L); Study in preparation by Jan Brunvand (Indiana University); *BP I 443; Bédier *Fabliaux* 464; *Wesselski *Arlotto* II 229 No. 95; Coffin *1;* Köhler-Bolte I 137; *Gigas»Et

eventyrs vandring» *Literatur og Historie* (3e samling) (København, 1902).
— Finnish *39;* Finnish-Swedish *3;* Estonian *10;* Lithuanian *9;* Swedish *5* (Göteborg *2,* Lund *1,* Liungman *2*); Danish *22,* Grundtvig No. 79; Icelandic *1;* Scottish *1, More W. H. Tales* No. 13; Irish *122,* Beal I 345ff., III 257f. No. 2, VIII 3f. No. 4, XII 196ff., XVII 81ff.; French *1;* Spanish *3;* Dutch *1;* German *4;* Austrian: Haiding No. 45; cf. Hungarian: Berze Nagy 1366* *1;* Slovenian *1;* Serbocroatian *2;* Russian: Afanasiev (901A) *9;* India *3.* — Franco-American *5;* English-American; Baughman *2;* Spanish-American: Rael No. 482 (U.S.); American Indian (Zuni): Boas JAFL XXXV 74 No. 3. — Literary Treatments: Rotunda (T251.2); Chauvin II 155 No. 27; Shakespeare »Taming of the Shrew».

901A* *Shrewish Youngest Marries the Prince*, who gets revenge on the wedding night.
Romanian (904*) *1.*

901B* *Who Works Not Eats Not.* The lazy wife punished. Cf. Type 1453.
Russian: Andrejev (901*B) *1;* Greek (903*) *3.*

901C* *Proud Princess Reformed.* Marries fisherman and frees him from gallows.
Rumanian (905*) *2.*

902* *The Lazy Woman is Cured.* Always shows her husband the same spool of thread. The man takes her naked in a bundle of straw to a wedding. [Q495.1]. She becomes industrious. [Q495.] Cf. Types 1374, 1453.
Estonian *3;* Lithuanian (902*) *13;* Slovenian *2;* Serbocroatian *12;* Russian: Andrejev (902*—B*) *2;* Japanese: Ikeda (Q495.1).

902A* *Wife Claims to Live on Steam of Lentils.* Husband takes her into field of lentils. She is hungry. On the ways she mistakes a cricket for olives with feet. [J1771]. (Cf. Type 1458.)
Greek (902*) *2.*

903A* *Quick-tempered Maiden* finds a man equally quick-tempered.
Rumanian (903*) *3.*

903B* *Convivial Fathers-in-law.* The children marry secretly against the will of their parents. Both fathers drive them out and become convivial friends.
Livonian (905') *1.*

903C* *Mother-in-law and Daughter-in-law.* The bad mother-in-law who lets her daughter-in-law be hungry is punished (reformed).
Rumanian (902) *4.*

904* *Ox-tongue for Dinner.* Haughty woman insists on having ox-tongue for dinner every day of the year. Her husband drives 365 oxen to the lawn in front of mansion. He then lets her understand that they must all be destroyed in order to satisfy her. The woman reforms.
Scottish: (School of Scottish Studies Archive) *3.*

905A* *The Wicked Queen Reformed by a Cobbler.* While the wicked queen is asleep, she is made to exchange places with the cobbler's wife. When she wakes up, she thinks herself in hell. The cobbler teaches her to obey and fear her husband. [T251.2.4].
Lithuanian (*904) *2;* Russian (*901 I) *2;* Prussian: Plenzat p. 48.

906* *Vengeance Reversed.* The youth plans vengeance on the girl who refuses to marry him, but he himself is punished by the court.
Livonian (906') *1.*

907* *No Marriage to Hangman.* The girl has a child. She will not marry the hangman and loses her head. [P512].
*Zs. f. Vksk. XXIII 108, XXV 286, XXVII 236. — Livonian (907') *1.*

910—915 The Good Precepts

910 *Precepts Bought or Given Prove Correct* [J163.4, J21].
   *Cosquin *Etudes* 85ff., 100ff.; Wesselski *Märchen* No. 32; Köhler-Bolte II 165—167; Coffin *6;* Clouston FL III 556. — Norwegian: Solheim *1;* Danish *42;* Irish *308;* French *11;* Serbocroatian *2;* Greek: Loukatos Nos. 6, 7. — Franco-American *23;* Spanish-American: Rael Nos. 88—90, 317—320, 492 (U.S.); India (910Z) *11.*

910A *Wise Through Experience.* The precepts. Do not visit your friends often; do not marry a girl from a distance, do not lend your horse, etc. Experience teaches the wisdom of these precepts.
   Motifs: J163.4. Good counsels bought. J21. Counsels proved wise by experience. J21.4. »Do not marry a girl from abroad.« J21.9. »Do not prolong a friendly visit.« Guest stays so long that host gives him black bread instead of white. J21.10. »Do not lend your horse.« L222.1. Modest choice for parting gifts — money or counsels. Counsels chosen. J21.16. »Go to Goosebridge«. Man with disobedient wife finds mules beaten there and made to cross bridge. J21.23. »Rise earlier«. Man seeking explanation for being in debt arises earlier and catches his servants stealing. J21.27. »Do not adopt a child«.
   *Köhler to Gonzenbach No. 81, Zs. f. Vksk. VI 169—71, XIII 108; *Anderson in Tauscher *Volksmärchen* 192; Liungman SSF III 443; Espinosa Nos. 68, 69, 163; *Beckwith MAFLS XVII 155, *284. — Finnish *9;* Estonian *12;* Lithuanian *3,* (*911) *13;* Lappish *1;* Swedish *7* (Göteborg *1,* misc. *6*); Norwegian *2;* Danish: Grundtvig No. 78 A; Icelandic *1;* Spanish *2;* Catalan: Amades No. 403; Flemish *1;* German *4;* Italian (Sicilian *3,* Gonzenbach No. 81); Rumanian *3;* Hungarian *1;* Serbocroatian *2;* Greek *5,* Loukatos No. 6; Turkish: Eberhard-Boratav No. 308 V; Indonesian: DeVries No. 230. — West Indies (Negro) *2.* — African *2.* — Literary Treatment: Chauvin VI 195 No. 367, VIII 138 No. 136.

910B *The Servant's Good Counsels.* Do not leave the highway, etc. The traveler leaves it and falls into the hands of robbers. When you are angry repeat the Lord's Prayer. He is about to kill the man sleeping with his wife: it is his son. Iron is more precious than gold, etc. Cf. Type 677.
   Motifs: J21.7. »Do not cross a bridge without dismounting from your horse«. J21.3. »Do not go where an old man has a young wife.« J21.5. »Do not leave the highway.« J21.11. »Do not walk half a mile with a man without asking his name.« J21.2. »Do not act when angry.« J21.17. »Stay at church till mass is finished«. J163.4. Good counsels bought. — For other good counsels, see the numerous subdivisions of J21.
   *Köhler to Gonzenbach No. 81; Zs. f. Vksk. VI 169; *Anderson in Tauscher *Volksmärchen* 178; BP IV 149; Chauvin VIII 138 No. 136; Basset *1001 Contes* II 391. — Finnish *36;* Finnish-Swedish *1;* Estonian *5;* Livonian *3;* Lithuanian *20;* Swedish (misc.) *1;* Norwegian *3;* Danish:

Grundtvig No. 78B; Icelandic *1;* Scottish *4,* Campbell-McKay No. 6; Irish: Beal II 57ff., VIII 3f. No. 5, X 180ff.; English *1;* Spanish *8;* Catalan: Amades No. 382, cf. 115; Dutch *3;* Flemish *1;* Italian (Tuscan *4,* Sicilian *2,* Gonzenbach No. 81); Rumanian (910 B, 910 E) *14;* Hungarian *3,* Dégh No. 36; Czech: Tille Soupis II (2) 23—28 *7;* Slovenian *3;* Serbocroatian *2;* Russian: Afanasiev *21;* Greek *7,* Dawkins *Modern Greek Folktales* No. 75A, *45 Stories* No. 19, Argenti-Rose I 574ff.; Turkish: Eberhard-Boratav Nos. 204 III, 256 III, 307 IV, 308 *34;* Albanian: Lambertz 175f.; Arab (Egypt) Artin 131f.; India *4;* Indonesian: DeVries No. 229. — Spanish-American: Hansen (Chile) *1,* (Cuba) *1,* (Dominican Republic) *2,* (Puerto Rico) *6;* West Indies (Negro) *7.* — Literary Treatments: Chauvin VIII 138, No. 116.

910C »*Think Carefully Before You Begin a Task.*» The king's throat is to be cut. The barber hired to cut the king's throat sees on the bottom of the basin the words »Whatever you do, do wisely and think of the consequences.» He drops the razor and confesses. [J21.1].

Clouston *Tales* II 317ff. — Finnish *13;* Lithuanian *1;* Swedish *2* (Göteborg *1,* misc. *1*); Icelandic *1;* Russian: Andrejev *1;* Greek *2;* Turkish: Eberhard-Boratav No. 313 *2;* India *8.* — Literary Treatments: Chauvin VIII 140 No. 139.

910D *The Treasure of the Hanging Man.* The dying rich man tells his son to hang himself if he ever loses his property [J21.15]. The son runs through with everything. At last when on the advice of his father he is about to hang himself the roof falls down with money which his father has hidden there. [N526].

*Pauli (ed. Bolte) No. 709; Clouston *Tales* II 53. — Finnish (910D*) *1;* Estonian (910D*) *3;* Lithuanian *7;* Icelandic *2;* Spanish *1;* Dutch *1;* German *3;* Italian: (Pentamerone IV No. 2); Serbocroatian *2;* Turkish: Eberhard-Boratav Nos. 175 III, 215 III, 315, 350 III; India *1;* Japanese: Ikeda. — Literary Treatments: Middle English: »The Heir of Linne»; Chauvin V 133 No 63, *VIII 94 No. 65.

910E *Father's Counsel: Where Treasure Is.* Find treasure within a foot of the ground. (Sons dig everywhere and thus loosen soil of the vineyard, which becomes fruitful.) [H588.7].

Lithuanian (914*) *3;* Catalan: Amades No. 448; India *1;* Slovenian. — Literary Treatments: Aesop (Halm No. 98).

910F *The Quarreling Sons and the Bundle of Twigs.* Peasant puts twigs together and cannot break them. Separately they are easily broken. His sons apply the lesson. [J1021].

*Pauli (ed. Bolte) No. 861. — Serbocroatian *1;* Jewish: *Neuman (J1021); India *1;* Japanese: Ikeda (J1021). — Literary Treatment: Wienert FFC LVI 83 (ET 491), 111 (ST 228); Halm Aesop No. 103; Jacobs Aesop 217 No. 72.

910G *Man Buys a Pennyworth of Wit* [J163.1].
Nouvelles de Sens No. 6; English: Wells 179 (A Peniworþ of Witte). — Catalan: Amades No. 602, cf. 653, 654; Italian (Tuscan 1200, 2); Serbocroatian *1;* Russian: Andrejev (*914) *1;* Turkish: Eberhard-Boratav No. 323 III) *1;* Greek: Hepding *Laographia* VI 310, Argenti-Rose II 600 No. 2; India: Knowles *Kashmir* 39ff., Jacobs *Indian Fairy Tales*. — West Indies: Flowers 474.

910H *Never Travel Without a Companion or Stay Alert.*
I. *Never Travel Without a Companion.* The man can find no other companion, so takes along a crab. (a) He is chosen to become a king or marry a princess. The crab kills the snakes which issue from the nostrils of the queen (princess). See Type 507C. (b) The crab kills a snake and a bird which attack him. See Type 182.
II. *Stay Alert or Awake.* Chosen to become a king or marry a princess, he stays awake and slays the snakes or monster himself. See Type 507C.
India *15.*

910J *Never Plant a Thorn Tree.* A man is advised (by his father): »Never befriend a policeman (soldier) [J21.46]; never plant a thorn tree [H588.30].« Because of a false accusation (made by his wife), the policeman (soldier) whom he has befriended drags him away to court. His turban catches on the thorn tree and is pulled from his head.
India *3.*

910K *The Precepts and the Uriah Letter.* Cf. Type 930.
An exiled king, or the like, becomes an official in another court. He happens to observe an intrigue between the queen and a servant or some other treasonable action, but does not tell the king because he has been advised not to tell slander, or the like. The queen falsely accuses the hero of having attacked her. The king sends him to be beheaded or boiled in oil, having told the executioner to kill the first man who comes to him. Because of another piece of advice, the hero stops in a temple, stops to take a meal, or the like. The queen's lover goes to see if the hero has been executed, arrives before the hero, and is executed [K1612].
Serbocroatian *1;* India *6.*

911* *The Dying Father's Counsel:* »Never say the truth to your wife; never bring up children other than your own; be faithless to your master»; »Do not trust a ruler who rules by reason alone»: counsel proved wise by experience. [J21.27, J21.28].
Lithuanian *13.*

915 *All Depends on How You Take It.* The two stepsisters marry. The daughter of the second wife follows the three precepts of her mother literally; the stepdaughter in conformity with her father's explanations. On their visit the parents find that with the first daughter everything is going wrong; with the second everything is well. [J555.1].
Finnish *3;* Danish *13,* Grundtvig No. 116; Irish *2;* French *4;* Spanish *1;* Russian *1;* Chinese: Eberhard FFC CXX No. 200.

915A *The Misunderstood Precepts.* A dying father gives advice to his son: Always eat bread with honey (working diligently, your bread will be as sweet as honey) [H588.11]; never greet anyone »God bless you in your labours» (start your work earliest, so that not you, but others may greet you thus) [H588.12]; always wear your shoes (walk the fields barefooted, wearing your shoes only when nearing the town) [H588.13]; etc. Following these precepts literally, the son becomes poor, and only later learns their real meaning.
Lithuanian (*915A) *8;* India *3.*

916 *The Brothers Guarding the King's Bedchamber and the Snake.*
I. *The Accusation.* Several brothers are hired by a king to guard his bedchamber. The first brother sees a snake in the bedchamber and kills it, but a drop of its poison falls on the queen. While he is wiping the poison from the queen, she awakes and, believing he is attacking her, accuses him to the king [N342.1] (Cf. Type 516 IV). The other brothers tell, in turn, examples against making a hasty decision. In the morning the truth comes to light.
II. *The Stories:* (a) The Brahman and the Mongoose (Llewellyn and his Dog) (Type 178A), (b) The Faithful Dog as Security for a Debt (Type 178B), (c) The Falcon (Horse) and the Poisoned Water. As a king who is out hunting is about to drink a cup of water, his falcon (horse) knocks the cup from his hand. The enraged king slays the falcon (horse) only to find that the cup was full of poison from a snake [B331.1.1.]. (d) The Parrot and the Fruit of Youth. A parrot brings to a king, his master, some fruit of youth. Unbeknown to the parrot, a snake has dropped poison on the fruit. The king gives one of the fruits to a dog, which dies, and the king slays the parrot. Later the truth comes to light [B331.3].
Turkish: Eberhard-Boratav No. 348 IV; India *15.*

920—929 Clever Acts and Words

920 *The Son of the King (Solomon) and of the Smith.* The children are exchanged. In the children's play Solomon acts as king. Shows his cleverness.
I. *Expulsion of the Prince.* (a) The prince is expelled from home because (a[1]) he reports from his mother's womb her scandalous conduct. (b) He is ordered killed but saved by a compassionate servant and exchanged with the newborn son of a smith.
II. *The Prince Shows his Wisdom.* He is chosen leader of his playmates. While he and the smith's son journey with the king he shows his kingly qualities by the nature of the choices he makes.
III. *Impossible Tasks.* The king gives him or his supposed father impossible tasks: [See Type 875 II for details] coming neither naked nor

clad, bringing best friend and worst enemy, hatching boiled eggs, milking bull or having it bear calf, etc.

IV. *His Cleverness.* (a) He balances a woman's wisdom against dog's dung. (b) He judges the case of the widow's flour which the wind has scattered.

V. *Escape from Father's Pursuit.* He flees and takes service as shepherd. He discomfits with his answers the king's messengers.

VI. *Denouement.* (a) Reconciliation with his father, or (b) he is condemned for seduction but allowed to blow on a horn.

Motifs:

I. T575.1.1.2. Child in mother's womb reveals adultery. T575.1.1.3. Child in mother's womb reveals unjust judgment. S301. Children abandoned (exposed). K512. Compassionate executioner. A servant charged with killing the hero (heroine) arranges the escape of the latter. K1921.1. Son of the king and of the smith exchanged.

II. H41.5. Unknown prince shows his kingly qualities in dealing with his playmates. P35. Unknown prince chosen chief of children in play. J123. Wisdom of child decides lawsuit. King in disguise sees child's game which represents the case. H38.2.5. Substitution of low-caste boy for promised child detected when he prefers long road to short one through jungle (swimming instead of ferry, etc.)

III. H921. King (father) assigns tasks to his unknown son.

IV. J80.1.1. Solomon proves to his mother the inferiority of woman's wisdom. J355.1. The widow's meal. King upbraids wind for blowing away a poor widow's last cup of meal. Finds that the wind has saved a ship full of people by that very act. The king is humbled.

V. K1816.6. Disguise as herdsman.

VI. K551.3. Respite from death until victim has blown on a horn (three times).

**DeVries FFC LXXIII 320ff.; *Wesselski »Der Knabenkönig und das kluge Mädchen« (Sudetendeutsche Zs. f. Vksk. [1930] Beiheft 1) passim; *Chauvin V 86 No. 26 n. 1. — Finnish (920 + 921) *177;* Estonian *39;* Livonian *1;* Lithuanian *4;* Irish *26;* Serbocroatian *2;* Russian: Andrejev *Ukraine 16,* Andrejev (*905) *3,* Afanasiev *9;* Greek *2;* Turkish: Eberhard-Boratav No. 302; India *1;* Indonesian: DeVries FFC LXXIII 323ff. — Franco-American *1.*

920A *The Daughter of the King and the Son of the Peasant.* Suit over boiled eggs. Cf. Type 875.

I. *A King Leaves Home.* If his wife bears girl she is to be beheaded. If a son, she is to reign. She bears a girl and exchanges with peasant woman who has just borne a son. [K1921.1].

II. *The Suit over Eggs.* A merchant buys forty boiled eggs, and sails away without paying. On his return he offers to pay. But demand is made for the value of all chickens and their offspring that would have come from the eggs. [J1191.2]. The case is laid before same king. He considers four years.

III. *The Real Princess and the Real Peasant Son* play at trying the case of the eggs. The princess shows that boiled eggs could not bear chickens. King overhears and decides the case thus. He understands the situation and is satisfied.

Rumanian (921 III*) *2;* Greek (950*) *3,* Kretschmer No. 35.

920B *What Kind of Bird.* Prince of democratic tastes chosen. King asks three sons what kind of bird they would prefer to be. First: an eagle, because it is ruler of birds; second: a falcon, because it is beloved of the nobles; third: a bird which flies with many others, so as to receive advice. King chooses third. [J412.1].

**Taylor (forthcoming study); Pauli (ed. Bolte) No. 677.

920C *Shooting at the Father's Corpse Test of Paternity.* Youngest of supposed sons refuses to shoot and is judged the only genuine son of the dead emperor. [H486.2].

*Herbert III 206; Oesterley No. 45; Scala Celi 98a No. 526; Pauli (ed. Bolte) No. 835; *Nouvelles de Sens* No. 29; Krappe *Bulletin Hispanique* XXXIX 28; L. Schmidt *Oesterr. Zs. f. Vksk.* 1955, 70ff. — Spanish Exempla: Keller (H486.2); Catalan: Amades I 283 No. 367; Italian Novella: *Rotunda (H486.2); *Jewish: bin Gorion *Born Judas* II 123, 345, IV 102, 280, *Neuman (H486.2).

920D (formerly 924**). *The Four Princes.* The one who can name the greatest number of faults of their father is to be king. The youngest prince cannot name a single fault [L22.1]. He becomes king.

Flemish *1;* Slovenian *1.*

920A* *The Inquisitive King.* Solomon wants to know the height of the sky and the depth of the sea. [L414.1].

Lithuanian (*920A) *5;* Hungarian: Berze Nagy (823*) *1;* Serbocroatian *3;* Polish (733) *7.*

920B* *The Lineage of the King's Three Sons.* By their answers to a captive king as to how they will treat him, they show that one is of headsman stock, one of butcher stock, and one of royal family. (Or they are given riddles.)

Greek *3,* Laographia XVI 13 n. 2; Albanian: Lambertz p. 80.

920C* *The Choice of a Wife.* Solomon advises with enigmatic statements.

Greek *2;* Laographia II 361.

921 *The King and the Peasant's Son.* The youth's clever answers to the king's questions (1 ½ men and the horse's head, etc. [H561.4, H583]).

Among the riddles are: (a¹) What do you see? — 1 ½ men and a horse's head (himself, the legs of the king who is horseback in the doorway, and the horse's head [H583.1]) or (a²) Are you alone at home? — Not now; I see the half of two quadrupeds (the king's legs and the forelegs of the horse [H583.1.1]); (b) What are you doing? — I boil those coming and going (beans that keep rising and falling in the water [H583.6]); (c) What is your father doing? — He is in the vineyard and is doing good and bad (prunes vines but sometimes cuts good ones and leaves the bad [H583.2]); (d) What is your mother doing? — At daybreak she baked the bread we ate last week; in the morning she cut off the heads of the well to cure the sick; now she is striking the hungry and compelling the satiated to eat (she bakes bread to repay that borrowed from neighbors last week; she cuts off the chicken's head so as to feed her sick mother; she drives away the hungry hens and stuffs the geese [H583.4]); (e) What is your brother doing? — He hunts; he throws away what he catches, and what he does not catch he carries with him (hunts for lice on his body [H583.3]). (For further details see H583.1—H583.6).

*BP II 359; *DeVries FFC LXXIII 116ff.; Krohn FFC XCVI 154ff.; *Espinosa II 144ff.; Wesselski *Märchen* 227; *Basset *1001 Contes* II 41; Köhler-Bolte I 84, *87, 151ff.; *Anderson FFC XLII 356 n. 2. — Finnish *177;* Finnish-Swedish *10;* Lithuanian *11;* Lappish *2;* Swedish *50* (Uppsala *1,* Stockholm *5,* Göteborg *38,* Lund *2,* misc. *4*); Danish *3;* Irish *228,* Beal III 62 (1); English *1;* French *16;* Spanish *3;* Catalan: Amades No. 401, cf. 370, 388; Dutch *1;* Flemish (922*) *6;* German *56* (Archive *53,* Merk. 48, Henssen Volk Nos. 151—152; Rumanian *2;* Hungarian *9;* Czech: Tille Soupis I 114f. *2;* Slovenian *5;* Serbocroatian *3;* Greek: Loukatos Nos. 15, 16, 17; Russian: Azadowsky *Russkaya Skazka* No. 3, Andrejev cf. 920 II, Afanasiev *9;* India: Thompson-Balys (H585) *1;* Indonesian: DeVries No. 234. — Franco-American *7;* English-American: Baughman *1;* Spanish-American: Rael No. 461 (U.S.), Hansen (Argentina) *1,* (Dominican Republic) *1,* (Puerto Rico) *4;* West Indies (Negro) *4.* — Literary Treatments: Chauvin VI 35 No. 205.

921A *The Four Coins.* (*Focus*). King: What do you do with the four coins you earn? Peasant: First I eat (feed self); second I put out at interest (give my children); third I pay debts (keep my parents); fourth I throw away (give to my wife). [H585.1].

*BP IV 137; *Anderson FFC XLII 356 n. 1; Köhler-Bolte Zs. f. Vksk. VI 161 (to Gonzenbach No. 50). — Livonian (1534*) *1;* Lithuanian (921A*) *12;* German: Wossidlo *Mecklinburgische Volksüberlieferung* (Wismar, 1897) I 249 No. 996; Italian (Sicilian *926) *5;* Hungarian: Berze Nagy (927*, 927**) *5;* Czech: Tille Soupis I 120ff. *4;* Serbocroatian *3;* Russian: Andrejev (921 I*) *12;* India *2.* — African (Swahili): Steere p. 295. — Literary Treatments: *Gesta Romanorum* No. 57.

921B *Best Friend, Worst Enemy.* Task: bringing best friend, worst enemy, best servant, greatest pleasure-giver. (Brings dog, wife, ass, little son respectively.) [H1065].

*Köhler-Bolte I 415, 455; *Pauli (ed. Bolte) No. 423; Herbert III 201; Ward II 231; Oesterley *Gesta Romanorum* No. 124; *Chauvin VIII 199 No. 244; *BP II 365; cf. Type 875; *DeVries FFC LXXIII 220ff.; *Anderson FFC XLII 357 and n. 2; *Wesselski *Märchen* 237 No. 48; Italian Novella: *Rotunda (H1065). — Lithuanian (894*) *6;* Serbocroatian *3;* Russian: Andrejev (*894) *3;* Greek *3.*

921C *Why Hair of Head is Gray before the Beard.* (It is twenty years older.) [H771].
*Wesselski Arlotto II 270 No. 222. — Lithuanian (*921C); German: Merkens No. 93; Czech: (Tille Soupis I 123ff.) 5.

921D *The Fatal Bed.* A sailor says that all his ancestors have drowned. Citizen: »Aren't you afraid of drowning?» Sailor: »How did your ancestors die?» Citizen: »All of them in bed.» Sailor: »Aren't you afraid to go to bed?» [J1474].
*Pauli (ed. Bolte) No. 264. — Finnish.

921E *Never Heard Before.* Task: letting king hear something that neither he nor his subjects have ever heard. (Reads a letter from a foreign king demanding a loan.)
Chauvin VI 39 No. 207. — Finnish *1*.

921B* *Thief, Beggar, Murderer.* Arrested farmer tells who he is: one son is thief (priest), second beggar (teacher), and third murderer (doctor).
Lithuanian (*921B) *5;* Czech: Tille (Soupis I 120—125) *4*.

921C* *Astronomer and Doctor at Farmer's House.* Farmer is the better weather predictor and knows more about choice of wholesome food. (Or the horse's tail surpasses as weather prophet.)
Finnish; Lithuanian (*2448) *4;* Rumanian (921 II*) *3;* Russian: Andrejev (*2132) *1.* Known in United States.

921D* *Witty Answers.* »What is that gentleman?» — »Red.» Or: »Is it a big market to-day?» — »I can't say; I did not measure it» (and the like).
Lithuanian (*921D) *4;* Slovenian.

921E* *The Potter.* Potter amazes the tsar with his clever answers. The tsar orders his nobles to buy pots from the potter. The potter raises the price. A purchasing noble does not want to pay and agrees, instead of payment, to carry the potter into the palace on his shoulders. The tsar makes the potter a noble and the noble a potter.
Russian: Afanasiev (*921 II) *4*.

921F* »*Geese from Rus*» (Old name for Russia). A tsar is talking in riddles with a peasant who has pleased him: The geese from Rus are flying here (that is, the nobles); be able to pluck them. The peasant makes use of this advice with great success.
Russian: Afanasiev (921B) *7*.

921G* *Peasants Need No Spoons.* Get ahead of lords who wait for spoons.
Finnish *14*.

922 *The Shepherd Substituting for the Priest Answers the King's Questions.* (The King and the Abbot):
I. *The Situation.* (a) A king commands a priest to appear before him and answer three questions correctly on pain of death. (b) A shepherd masks as the priest and answers the questions. (c) He is rewarded with the priest's position; or (c¹) replaces the king himself.
II. *The Questions.* Some of the questions asked in the different versions are: (a) How many drops in the sea? (Countertask: first stop all the rivers). (b) How high is heaven? (A half day's journey, for Christ went up at midday; or a fox's tail if it were long enough); (c) How many stars in the heavens? (Grains of sand in sack, leaves on tree, etc.) (d)

How many seconds in eternity? (Bird carries grain of sand from mountain, etc.) (e) How far is one end of the world to the other? (A day's journey, since the sun makes it daily). (f) What is the center of the earth? (Here). (g) How much does the moon weigh? (A pound, since it has four quarters). (h) How much is the king worth? (Twenty-nine pence, since Christ was sold for thirty). (i) Which is the best fowl? (The goose, since it makes the cabbage sweet and the bed soft). (j) What is the swiftest, the sweetest, the most costly? (Cf. Type 875, I b). (k) What am I thinking? (That I am the priest).
Motifs:

I. H512. Guessing with life as wager. H541.1. Riddles propounded on pain of death. K1962. Sham churchman. H561.2. King and abbot. Q113.4. Appointment to priesthood as reward.

II. H696.1. How much water is in the sea? H682. Riddles of heavenly distance. H702. How many stars in the heaven? H703. Riddles: how many hairs are in the head? H705.2. How many leaves are on the tree? H701.1. How many seconds in eternity? A bird carries a grain of sand from a mountain each century; when the whole mountain is gone, the first second of eternity has passed. H681.1. Riddle: how far is it from one end of the earth to the other (east to west)? H681.3.1. Where is the center of the earth? H691.1. Riddle: how much does the moon weigh? H711.1. How much am I (the king) worth? Twenty-nine pieces of silver, for Christ was sold for thirty. H634. Riddle: what is the sweetest song? H638. Riddle: what is the swiftest? H633. Riddle: what is the sweetest? H638. Riddle: what is the costliest? H524.1. »What am I thinking?» »That I am the priest.» So answers youth masking as priest. — For detailed answers see subdivisions of Motif-numbers here given.

**Anderson *Kaiser und Abt* (FFC XLII); FL XLIX 182ff.; *Anderson *Novelline* Nos. 1, 18; *BP III 214 (Grimm No. 152); FL XLIX 182ff.; Loorits Arv VI 117; Espinosa II 101; MAFLS XXIV 53 n. 37; Coffin *6;* Krohn FFC XCVI 162ff. — Finnish *102;* Finnish-Swedish *15;* Estonian *6;* Livonian *2,* (1990') *2;* Lithuanian *17;* Swedish *61* (Uppsala *12,* Stockholm *6,* Göteborg *18,* Lund *8,* Liungman *2,* misc. *15*); Norwegian *9;* Danish *49;* Icelandic *4;* Scottish *5;* Irish *146,* Beal II 196ff., 381ff., VI 169f. No. 163, IX 85, XVI 88; English *4;* French *16;* Spanish *5;* Catalan: Amades Nos. 218, 1346, 1639; Dutch *4;* Flemish *10;* Walloon *4;* German *36* (Archive *34,* Merk. 144, Henssen Volk No. 150); Austrian: Haiding No. 469; Italian *3* (Tuscan [1757] *1,* Sicilian *2*); Rumanian *6,* (216) *1;* Hungarian *2,* Berze Nagy (922 I*—III*) *4;* Czech: Tille Soupis I 117 *6;* Slovenian *14;* Serbocroatian *31,* Istrian No. 42; Russian: Azadowsky *Russkaya Skazka* No. 39, Afanasiev *24;* Greek *3;* Turkish: Eberhard-Boratav No. 235 V; India *6.* — Franco-American *17;* English-American: Baughman *2;* Spanish-American: Rael Nos. 17, 292 (U.S.), Hansen (Argentina) *1;* Cape Verde Islands: Parsons MAFLS XV (1) 94 n. 1.

922A *Achikar.* Falsely accused minister reinstates himself by his cleverness [K2101, P111]. Cf. Type 981.
**Marc »Die Achikarsage» *Studien zur vgl. Literaturgeschichte* II 393ff.; **DeVries FFC LXXIII 365ff., 374; Rumanian (921 I*) *2;* Polish (551*) *2;* Russian (*922 I) *1;* Jewish: *Neuman (K2101); India: Thompson-Balys (P111). — Literary Treatments: Chauvin VI 38, No. 207 n. 5.

922B *The King's Face on the Coin.* A king tells an artisan never to reveal the answer to certain riddle unless he sees the king's face. Defense for disobeying: »I have seen your face a thousand times.» [J1161.7].
Italian (Sicilian *926 *3*); Czech: Tille (Soupis I 120—125) *4;* Greek *3.*

923 *Love Like Salt.* The youngest of three daughters says that she loves her father like salt. The sick father is driven forth, etc. [592.1].
See analysis of Type 510: I c; II a; III c; V.
*BP III 305 (Grimm No. 170), IV 141 (Grimm No. 179); *Anderson in Tauscher *Volksmärchen* 193; *Espinosa No. 107, II 406; *Liungman SSF III 443; Coffin *2.* — Finnish *1;* Lithuanian *3;* Swedish *9;* Danish *1;* French *5;* Spanish *2;* Catalan Amades Nos. 51, 132; Flemish *5;* German *3;* Italian *7* (Tuscan 510 VI a, b, 923 d, s *4,* Sicilian *3*); Rumanian *4;* Hungarian *4;* Czech: Tille Soupis II (1) 276ff. *3;* Serbocroatian *3;* Russian: Andrejev; Greek: Loukatos No. 8; Turkish: Eberhard-Boratav No. 256 III *8;* India *5.*

923A *Like Wind in the Hot Sun.* A wife thus expresses her love for her husband. He is offended but in the hot sun learns the meaning of his wife's saying and returns to her. [H592.1.1].
Swedish *4* (Uppsala *2,* misc. *2*); Norwegian (924**) *7.*

923B *The Princess Who Was Responsible for her Own Fortune* [H592].
I. *Judgment.* When a king asks his daughters who is responsible for their good fortune, or the like, the oldest daughters answer that he is, but the youngest, who says that she alone is, is (a) married to a poor man, a cripple, or the like and forced to live with him in humble circumstances or (b) driven forth [M21]. (c) The story concerns a king and his sons.
II. *Daughter's Success.* (a) Through her wit or her skill she makes the poor man rich and eventually makes him a king or cures him of his disease [N145]. (b) The husband magically changes into a handsome prince [D1866] or (c) She becomes wealthy and later marries a prince.
III. *Reconciliation.* (a) The father visits the new king, recognizes his daughter, and is forced to admit she is responsible for her own fortune. (b) The father has, in the meantime, lost his kingdom and wanders to the palace of his daughter [L419.2].
India *25.*

924 *Discussion By Sign Language* [H607].
*Penzer I 80f. n.; *Pauli (ed., Bolte) No. 32; W. Coland Zs. f. Vksk. XXIV 88; Hertel ibid. XXIV 317; Loewe ibid. XXVIII 126; *Fischer-

Bolte 206. — Lithuanian (922A*) *1;* Swedish (GS 1630) *1;* Irish myth: Cross; Walloon (1613*) *1;* Chinese: Eberhard FFC CXX 194. — Portuguese-American (Brazil): Camara Cascudo pp. 32f.

924A (formerly 923*) *Discussion between Priest and Jew Carried on by Symbols.* E.g., priest raises three fingers (Trinity); Jew raises arm (one God); etc. [H607.1].

*Motif H607.1; *Anderson FFC XLII 354 n. 4; *Köhler-Bolte II 479ff.; *Loewe Zs. f. Vksk. XXVIII 126; Penzer VI 249. — Lithuanian (922*A) *11;* Scottish: Archive *2;* Irish myth: Cross; Spanish Novella: Keller; Italian Novella: *Rotunda; Czech: Tille Soupis II (1) 250 *2;* India: Thompson-Balys; Japanese: Ikeda (H607.1). — Spanish-American: Hansen (**926) (Argentina) *1.*

924B *Sign Language Misunderstood* [J1804]. Two men (a king and a shepherd) are to have a disputation. The king holds up one finger; the shepherd two; the king three, and the like. The king admits he is outdone. The king's one finger was meant to signify »I alone am powerful.» The shepherd thinks the king is asking for one sheep and holds up two fingers, meaning he will give two sheep to the king. The king interprets the two fingers as meaning »God is as powerful as you,» and the like.

Czech: Tille Soupis II (1) 249 *1;* Turkish Eberhard-Boratav No. 312 *4;* India *5.*

925 *Tidings Brought to the King: You Said it, not I.* The messenger arranges it so that the king says the words in the form of a question [J1675.2.1].

*Anderson FFC XLII 362; Icelandic: *Boberg; Spanish (925B) *2;* Catalan: Amades No. 1639; German: Henssen Volk 280 No. 215; Hungarian: Berze Nagy (1567*) *1;* Serbocroatian *1;* Gypsy: Krauss Zigeunermärchen p. 193.

925* *The Most Beautiful.* The three brothers in the garden of the royal palace. The princess asks them what is the most beautiful thing in the garden. He answers »Yourself». [J1472]. He marries the princess.

Estonian: Loorits *Estnische Volksmärchen* No. 73; Flemish *1;* Irish *1.*

926 *Judgment of Solomon.* Two women claim a child. Judge offers to cut it in two. The real mother refuses. [J1171.1].

*Motif J1171.1. — Italian (Sicilian): cf. Gonzenbach No. 56; India *4.* — Spanish-American: Hansen (**656A) (Dominican Republic) *1.*

926A *The Clever Judge and the Demon in the Pot.*

I. *Dispute.* A demon takes on the appearance of a man. The man and the demon dispute as to which is the real husband. (a) A boy (shepherd) who is playing that he is a king or a judge makes wise decisions and is appealed to. Cf. Type 920. (b) A jackal (parrot) is appealed to.

II. *Judgment.* The judge states that whichever can enter a pot or tube is the real husband. As soon as the demon enters the pot, it is covered so that the demon is trapped. Cf. Types 330B, 331. [J1141.1.7].

India *6.*

926B *The Ring to be Cut in Two and Divided Equally between two Quarreling Persons:* real owner laments the loss of the gold. [J1171.1.1].
India *1*.

926C *Cases Solved in a Manner Worthy of Solomon.*
Lithuanian (*920C) *4;* Livonian (926') *1;* Rumanian (961*) *11;* Serbocroatian *1;* India *2*.

926D *The Judge Appropriates the Object of Dispute* [J1171, K452]. Cf. Types, 51***, 518.
Catalan: Amades No. 342; Rumanian (961*) *11*.

926A* »*Purchase not him who Surpasseth thee.*» A widow sends her son to learn a craft, but he learns to play cards and the violin. In order to get back the money she has spent on him she sells her son at the market; he is bought by a dealer in spite of all he tells him: »Purchase not him who surpasseth thee» or »whoever purchaseth me will rue it.» The dealer gives him a letter and sends him to his house as a slave. On the way he saves the ship's master from debt as the latter was losing at cards, and alters the letter to »the dealer's son-in-law» (as in Type 930). By his violin-playing he gains the friendship of the king's son who issues a decree: none shall discharge arms. The dealer arriving by ship discharges a cannon; his son-in-law procures his delivery from the gallows with three empty nutshells.
Greek *9, Laographia* XVI 7 n. 2; Kretschmer No. 32.

926B* *Turning over the Block of Stone* in hope of finding a treasure. In giving back the peasant's horse, he must answer three questions [H703] (how many hairs on my wife's head, etc.).
Flemish (926*) *2*.

926C* *The Betrothed Children.* The children of two merchants have been betrothed from childhood, but they live in different cities. The father sends his son out, giving him allegorical orders (if the duck has fallen into the chaff, carry her, etc.). The bride recognizes her bridegroom by these allegorical expressions.
Finnish *1;* Russian: Afanesiev (926*) *4*.

927 *Out-riddling the Judge.* The accused is set free when the judge cannot solve the riddles propounded to him. The riddles: (a) what has seven tongues in one head? (bird's nest with seven young found in a horse's head); (b) formerly I was a daughter, now I am a mother; (c) or other riddles of peculiar family relationship.

Motifs:
H542. Death sentence escaped by propounding riddle king (judge) cannot solve. R154.2.1. Son frees father by bringing riddle king cannot solve. H79.3. Recognition by voice. H807. Formerly I was daughter, now I am mother; I have a son who was the husband of my mother. (Girl has nursed her imprisoned father through a crack in the prison wall.) H806. Riddle: drink this wine which a bird took to nest. (Stork took bunch of grapes to nest; boy makes wine from them.) H795. Relationship riddles arising from unusual marriage of relatives.

*Kohler-Bolte I 46; Espinosa *Cuentos* II 148—151; Coffin *1;* *Feilberg *Ordbog* I 602 s.v. »hestehoved»; Taylor *RPh* II 297ff. — Finnish (924*) *2;* Finnish-Swedish (921*) *3;* Estonian (924*) *2;* Swedish *89*

(Uppsala *38*, Stockholm *8*, Göteborg *29*, Liungman *5*, misc. *9*); Norwegian (921*) *5*, Solheim *2;* Danish *23;* Irish *9;* English *9;* Spanish (927*A, *B) *2;* Catalan: Amades Nos. 437, 438, 441, 450, 451, cf. 396, 436, 450, 465; Dutch *14;* Flemish (924*) *1;* German *19* (Archive *14*, Henssen Volk Nos. 153—157); Italian *2* (Tuscan cf. [315] c *1*, Sicilian *1*); Serbocroatian *1;* Russian: Andrejev (451) *11;* Greek *3,* (924*) *5.* — Franco-American *3;* English-American: Baughman *15;* Spanish-American: Hansen (927**A, B) (Argentina) *5,* (Chile) *2,* (Puerto Rico) *18;* Portuguese-American: (Brazil) Camara Cascudo p. 123; West Indies (Negro) *8.*

927A *Execution Evaded by Using Three Wishes*. King ordains that the guest who turns his plate shall be executed, but orders that anyone so condemned shall have three wishes granted. One of the wishes: to have all blinded who saw him turn the plate. He is freed. [J1181.1].
*Wesselski *Märchen* 230 No. 40; Herbert III 197; Oesterley *Gesta Romanorum* No. 194; Turkish: Eberhard-Boratav No. 298 *4;* Arabic: Basset *1001 Contes* I 33.

927A* »*Old Saddle*» *Granted by the King*. This is the name of an estate which the king unwittingly gives away. [K193.1].
Lithuanian (925) *4;* Anderson FFC XLII 360.

927B* *The Cock's Ancestry*. Giant cock born from egg rescued from a dead snake's stomach is washed and brooded by a man. Riddle: Born of three mothers, engendered by a father, eaten before birth and washed in a fountain.
Catalan: Amades No. 436.

928 *Planting for the Next Generation*. Man who is planting tree told that it will never mature in his day. He is planting it for the next generation. [J701.1].
*Wesselski *Hodscha Nasreddin* II 235 No. 516; Chauvin II 208 No. 75; Lithuanian (*928) *2;* Italian (Sicilian *752E *1*); Jewish: *Neuman (J701.1).

929 *Clever Defenses*.

929A *Uneducated Father*. Boy defends father: the father was uneducated and the fault was grandfather's.
Greek (927**) *3,* Loukatos No. 7.

930—949 Tales of Fate

930 *The Prophecy*. The poor and the rich man. Cf. Types 461, 1525R*.
I. *The Prophecy*. (a) It is foretold that a poor boy is to become the king's son-in-law.
II. *Sale and Abandonment*. (a) The king buys the boy from his parents. (b) He abandons the boy in a box on a river (or in a forest). (c) He is rescued and adopted by a miller, shepherd, hunter, or merchant.
III. *Uriah Letter*. (a) The king discovers him and sends him with a

letter to the queen with instructions to kill him. (b) On the way robbers change the letter so that the queen is instructed to give the princess to the boy in marriage.

IV. *Sequel.* (a) The king orders his servants to throw the boy into a hot oven but by chance the king's own son is cast in instead; or (b) the youth is sent on dangerous quests. For these see Type 461.

Motifs:

I. M312. Prophecy of future greatness for youth. M312.1. Prophecy: wealthy marriage for poor boy.

II. M370. Vain attempts to escape fulfillment of prophecy. K2015. Child adopted by rich man in order to get rid of him. S210. Children sold or promised. H1510. Tests of power to survive. Vain attempts to kill hero. M371. Exposure of infant to avoid fulfillment of prophecy. S331. Exposure of child in boat (floating chest). S141. Exposure in boat. S143. Abandonment in forest. R131.2. Miller rescues abandoned child. R131.3.1. Shepherd rescues abandoned child. R131.1. Hunter rescues abandoned child. R131.4. Fisher rescues abandoned child. R131.7. Merchant rescues abandoned child.

III. K978. Uriah letter. K511. Uriah letter changed. Falsified order of execution. K1355. Altered letter of execution gives princess to hero.

IV. K955. Murder by burning. K1612. Message of death fatal to sender. H1211. Quests assigned in order to get rid of hero.

Aarne *Der reiche Mann und sein Schwiegersohn* (FFC XXIII 1—115) (Bibliography of studies p. 17); *Anderson in Tauscher *Volksmärchen* 179; *BP I 276 (Grimm No. 29); *Tille Zs. f. Vksk. XXVIII 22. — Finnish *11;* Finnish-Swedish *1;* Estonian *18;* Lithuanian *41;* Lappish *3;* Danish *13,* Grundtvig No. 71; Scottish *1;* Irish *45;* English *1;* French *1;* Spanish *2;* Catalan: Amades No. 1651, (930 III: Amades No. 1640); Flemish *1;* German *13* (Archive *12,* Meckl. No. 94); Austrian: Haiding No. 33 n.; Italian *4* (Tuscan *3,* Sicilian *1*); Rumanian *8,* Sainenu 780; Czech: Tille Soupis I 153ff., II (2) 385 *3,* FFC XXXIV 327; Slovenian *3;* Serbocroatian *17;* Russian: Andrejev *Ukraine 7,* Afanasiev *19;* Greek *13,* Hahn No. 20, Loukatos Nos. 11, 18, Dawkins *Modern Greek Folktales* No. 50; Albanian: Lambertz 100f.; Turkish: Eberhard-Boratav Nos. 125, 126, 128, 214 III, IV *25;* Jewish: Bin Gorion *Born Judas*[2] I 221, 375; India *2.* — Franco-American *10;* Spanish-American: Hansen (Puerto Rico) *1,* (cf. Cuba 930B) *1;* Cape Verde Islands: Parsons MAFLS XV (1) 197; West Indies (Negro) *1.*

930* *Fate Foretold as Punishment.* The same as Type 930 with introduction: A gentleman invites God to his house, yet maltreats an old beggar who comes to ask for night lodgings [K1811.1]; at night hears the birds talk with the old man and learns his fate as punishment. Cf. Type 751A*.

Lithuanian (930*A) *11;* Danish *1;* Greek: Loukatos No. 12.

930A (formerly 930*) *The Predestined Wife.* Unavailing attempt to evade fulfillment of prophecy that prince shall marry peasant girl.

I. *The Prophecy.* A prince (or rich youth) hears a prophecy from an old man (the fates or other supernaturals) that he shall marry a peasant's daughter.

II. *Attempted Evasion.* (a) He stays overnight at the peasant's hut or otherwise obtains control of the lowly girl. (b) He tries to make way with her: (b¹) stabs her, (b²) pierces her forehead, (b³) throws her into bushes, (b⁴) has her hands nailed to tree. (c) He gives money to her parents.

III. *Rescue of the Girl.* (a) She is rescued and (b) healed and (c) becomes beautiful.

IV. *Fulfillment.* (a) The young man is enamored and marries her. (b) He recognizes her by mark on (b¹) forehead or (b²) scarred hands and (c) they live happily; or (d) he makes further attempts to get rid of her (exposing in boat or cask on sea, Uriah letter, demanding return of ring which he throws into the sea). (e) He is reconciled to the workings of fate.

Motifs:

I. T22.2. Predestined wife. M359.2. Prophecy: prince's marriage to common woman. M312.1.1. Prophecy: wealthy marriage for poor girl. M436. Curse: prince to fall in love with witch's daughter. A463.1. The Fates. M301. Prophets.

II. M370. Vain attempts to escape fulfillment of prophecy. S115. Murder by stabbing. S115.2. Murder by sticking needle through head. S143. Abandonment in forest.

III. R130. Rescue of abandoned person. D1860. Magic beautification.

IV. N101. Inexorable fate. H51. Recognition by scar. H56. Recognition by wounds. H1510. Vain attempts to kill hero. S141. Exposure in boat. K511. Uriah letter changed. N211.1. Lost ring found in fish.

**Taylor »The Predestined Wife» Fabula II 45ff.; *BP I 288; *Aarne FFC XXIII 110. — Lithuanian (*934A) *1;* Swedish *6* (Stockholm *1,* Göteborg *1,* Liungman *1,* misc. *3*); Icelandic *1;* Spanish (930*A) *1,* (*932) *1;* Slovenian *4;* Serbocroatian *1;* Russian: Andrejev Ukraine (*934), Andrejev (*934) *1;* Greek *5;* Turkish: Eberhard-Boratav No. 124 *3;* India *3;* Chinese: Eberhard FFC CXX No. 149, CXXVIII No. 95. — Brazil: Camara Cascudo 164ff.

930B *Prophecy: at Sixteen Princess will Fall in Love with Forty Arabs* [M345.1]. She is exposed in crystal pavilion in sea. Forty Arabs come in boat at anchor. She pulls them on rope through window. When she bears a child, she and the nursemaid kill and eat it. — The princess marries a prince. She substitutes nurse in the bridal bed. Princess asks for nursemaid's head [H1843]. Nursemaid reminds her of her devotion and tells story by means of enigmatic statements [H582].

*Taylor Fabula II 58ff.; *Basset *1001 Contes* II 208; Chauvin VIII 104 No. 80. — Greek (933*) *4,* Legrand 257.

930C *Fated Bride Abandoned in Boat.* A king hears a prophecy that he is to marry a poor girl. He gains possession of her and wounds her (usually on the back or hands). He finds her a second time and sets her afloat in a box on a stream. She is rescued and lives in luxury and the king marries her.

*Taylor Fabula II 60ff. (Swedish, Finnish, Danish, Icelandic, Estonian).

930D *Fated Bride's Ring in the Sea.* A prince spends the night in a cottage where a baby is born. He hears a prophecy that he will marry the child. He obtains possession of the child, he puts her in a box and she floats away, is rescued, and reared in luxury. He sees her years later, gives her a ring like his own and says he will not marry her if she loses the ring. He steals the ring and throws it into the sea. It is found in a fish that has been caught. He marries her.

*Taylor Fabula II 64ff. (Modern Greek, English, Scottish Gaelic, Irish, Portuguese [Brazilian], Spanish).

931 *Oedipus.* As foretold by the prophecy, the hero kills his father and marries his mother.

Motifs:

M343. Parricide prophecy. M344. Mother-incest prophecy. M371.2. Exposure of child to prevent fulfillment of parricide prophecy. K512. Compassionate executioner. R131. Exposed or abandoned child rescued. S354. Exposed infant reared at strange king's court (Joseph, Oedipus). N323. Parricide prophecy unwittingly fulfilled. T412. Mother-son incest.

**Constans *La légende d' Œdipe dans l'antiquité, au moyen âge, et dans les temps modernes* (1881); *Megas *Epeteris tou Laographia Archeiou* 1941—2, pp. 3—32, 196—209; *Baum PMLA XXXI; Krappe *Balor* 13 n. 45; Frazer *Pausanias* V 24; Taylor Fabula II 76 n. 66. — Finnish *22;* Lithuanian *1;* Lappish *1;* Irish *61;* Spanish: Espinosa II 145—151; Catalan: Amades No. 366; Italian (Tuscan [852] *1*); Rumanian *3;* Hungarian *2;* Czech: Tille Soupis II (1) 166f. *1;* Russian: Andrejev *2,* Andrejev *Ukraine 14;* Greek *2,* Legrand p. 107; Turkish: Eberhard-Boratav No. 142; Indonesian; DeVries No. 238. — Franco-American *1;* West Indies (Negro) *2;* Spanish American (Hansen *983) (Puerto Rico) *2.*

932* changed to 934.

933 *Gregory on the Stone.* The son of an incestuous union is abandoned and saved by a sailor. He undergoes years of penance and finally becomes pope. The parents come to the pope to be confessed.

Motifs: S312.1. Child of incest exposed. R131.14. Sailor rescues abandoned child. Q541.3. Penance: Gregory on the stone. H151.3. Recognition when parents come to son (priest, pope) to be confessed.

*A. von Löwis of Menar Zs. f. Vksk. XX 45; *Köhler Zs. f. Vksk. VI 173 to Gonzenbach No. 85; *Baum PMLA XXXI 562 n. 59; Krappe *Neuphilologische Mitteilungen* XXXIV (1933) 11—22. — Lithuanian *7;*

Icelandic: Boberg (Q451.3); Irish *12;* French *3;* Spanish (983*) *1;* German *1;* Italian (Tuscan *1,* Sicilian *3,* Gonzenbach No. 85); Hungarian *3;* Czech: Tille Soupis I 396f. *2.* — Franco-American *3;* Spanish-American: Rael No. 103 (U.S.).

934 (formerly 932*) *The Prince and the Storm.* It is prophesied that the prince will perish in a storm. The king confines him in an iron hut underground [M341.2.2]. One day in the absence of the king a storm destroys the hut [M372].

*Köhler in Gonzenbach II 222; *Wesselski *Mönchslatein* 91 No. 77. — Finnish (932*) *1;* Estonian (932*) *8;* Lithuanian (932*) *12;* Swedish (Uppsala) *1;* Irish *116,* Beal VIII 3f. No. 6, X 3f. No. 24; Spanish (449*) *1;* Italian (Tuscan, cf. [337], Pentamerone II No. 3, IV No. 6); Hungarian: Berze Nagy (776*) *2;* Czech: Tille Soupis II (2) 422; Slovenian *6;* Serbocroatian *3;* Russian: Andrejev (932*); India *1.* — Literary Treatment: Chauvin V 253 No. 150, VIII 105 No. 80.

934A *Predestined Death.* The boy (girl) dies at the time and in the manner (by drowning or other) which was predestined at birth by Fate. All efforts to avert the calamity prove futile. [M370.1].

Finnish *1;* Lithuanian (*932A) *14;* Russian (*932 I) *1;* Rumanian (932*) *4;* Hungarian: Berze Nagy (934*) *3;* Serbocroatian 2.

934A[1] *Three-fold Death.* The child to die from hunger, fire, and water. It so happens. [M341.2.4].

*Jackson »The Motive of the Threefold Death in the Story of Suibhne Geilt» *Essays and Studies Presented to Eoin MacNeill* 535—550; Irish myth: *Cross; Estonian: Aarne FFC XXV 136 No. 96; Spanish Exempla: Keller.

934B (formerly 333*) *The Youth to Die on his Wedding Day.* A prince hears a prophecy that on his wedding day [M341.1.1], he is to fall victim to a frightful wolf [M341.2.6]. He tries through various magic means to avoid the enemy [M341.2]. He succeeds in killing the wolf but one of the wolf's claws pierces his breast [M370.1]. By means of life-giving water he is resuscitated [E80].

BP IV 116 No. 10. — Finnish-Swedish (333*) *1;* Estonian FFC XXV 136 No. 94) *2;* Lithuanian (*166) *4;* Swedish *2* (Liungman *1,* misc. *1*); Irish (333*) *53;* Catalan: Amades No. 379; Hungarian: Berze Nagy (368*) *1;* Czech: Tille Soupis II (2) 396f. *4;* Serbocroatian *3;* Greek (934*) *2* (snakebite); India *3.*

934C *Death Forestalls Evil Fates.* A mother is shown what would have been the evil fates of her children if they had not died. [N121.2].

*BP III 472ff.; Irish: Beal XXI 336, O'Suilleabhain 120; Italian (Tuscan) [1442] a, b) *2;* Serbocroatian *1.*

934D (formerly 934*) *Nothing Happens without God.* The only son goes into military service and wants to take vengeance on the recruiting officers.

An old man (God) shows him in spirit a new-born child with a gun and uniform. Now the youth understands that God has determined the fate of everyone. [N121.1.1].

Livonian (934') *1;* Lithuanian (*934C) *8;* Serbocroatian *2;* Russian (cf. 934 I A, 934 I B) *2.*

934D[1] *Outwitting Fate.* A man overhears Fate or a god [K1811.0.2] decreeing that (a) a boy will spend his life in poverty but will always own a bullock or kill a stag a day and (b) that his sister will become a prostitute [N121.3]. When the boy grows up the man advises him to sell his bullock every day so that the god must continually furnish him a new one each day or to wait inside his hut so that the god must bring the stag to him. He advises the girl to demand a handful of pearls for her favors. The god must come in disguise each day because no man can pay such a price. The god soon tires of his duties and agrees to reverse the decrees of fate [K2371.2].

India (936) *6.*

934E (formerly 728*) *The Magic Ball of Thread.* An old woman prophesies [M345] to a queen that her life is bound up with a candle [E765.1.1] and that she shall have a daughter who shall commit murder and incest, and be sentenced to death [M345]. In lighting the candle the princess causes her mother's death. Later on she gets from her stepmother a ball of thread [D1313.1.1] and by following that she succeeds in fulfilling the prophecies and escaping herself. Cf. Type 1184*.

Norwegian (728**) *1;* Serbocroatian *1;* Turkish: Eberhard-Boratav No. 196 *1.*

934* changed to 934D.

934** (formerly 933*) *The Man Scorns the Storm.* Is killed by it [L471].
Finnish (933**) *4;* Swedish (Uppsala) *4.*

934A* *Youth to Drown at a Certain Age.* In spite of all precautions this happens.
Serbocroatian *3.*

934A** *Injured Sorcerer's Prediction* of early death of his injurer comes true.
Polish (341*) *5.*

934B* *The Man Destined for the Jaws of a Wolf* hides himself under a barrel; a girl runs up and implores him to let her hide in the same place; she turns out to be the wolf for whose jaws he was destined.
Estonian (FFC XXV 136 No. 94) *2;* Lithuanian *4.*

934C* *Man will Die if he ever Sees his Daughter's Son.* Many vain efforts to prevent this prophecy. Cf. Type 937A*.
Icelandic (499*) *1.*

934D* *Princess with Unlucky Future Helped by Eagle.* A princess whose unlucky future was foretold at her birth accepts a position as maid-servant; an eagle ravishes a crown which she is preparing for the prince; the king's daughter is thrown into prison; the eagle returns the crown; marriage with the king's son.
Polish (412) *1.*

934E* *False Prophecy* that princess at sixteen shall sit on an ass and ride around the

public square. She is falsely accused of theft and this happens: punishment, riding backwards on an ass.
Greek (933**) *1.*

934E** *Daughter Cursed at Birth.* A childless queen makes a wish for a child red as blood, as white as snow, etc. [Z65.1]. Curse: to bear daughter but to see her only three times and each time to lay a curse on her. This happens. Curses: to slay man, to burn castle, to bear illegitimate child. — A good stepmother helps the girl accomplish all these.
Icelandic *7.*

935 *The Prodigal's Return.* The fortunate marriage and the visit home. The youngest of three brothers [L10] is a prodigal [N172]. He goes abroad as a soldier and swindles his father into sending him money. Through cleverness he makes his fortune and marries the princess [L161]. He visits his parent's home in humble disguise [K1815] and is mistreated by his brothers [K2211]. The princess arrives and the brothers are put to shame.

Finnish *39;* Finnish-Swedish *2;* Estonian *4;* Danish: Grundtvig No. 118; Scottish: Campbell-McKay No. 21; Irish *2;* French *3;* German *22* (Archive *20,* Meckl. Nos. 54, 95); Austrian: Haiding No. 2, n.; Hungarian *1;* Czech: Tille Soupis II (1) 135ff. *11;* Slovenian *1;* Serbocroatian *2;* Russian: Andrejev *1.* — Franco-American *27;* West Indies (Negro) *1;* American Indian (Micmac): Rand 424 No. 80.

935* *The Stepson Mariner.* The merchant's stepson is put out to sea. Makes his fortune. The merchant's own son has bad luck. [N171].
Finnish-Swedish *2.*

935** *The Poor Rope-maker.* Three times he has a large sum of money given to him and the first two times it gets lost. The third time he recovers all the money. [N183].
Finnish *2;* Lithuanian (946*) *8;* Danish *2;* Spanish (945A*) *1;* Greek *6.* — Spanish-American: Hansen (**939) (Cuba) *1.*

955*** changed to 735*.

936* *The Golden Mountain.* A hero hires himself out to a rich man as a worker. The merchant takes him to a golden mountain, drugs him with sleep herbs and sews him up in the skin of an animal. Ravens carry him up on the mountain. The worker digs gold and throws it down to the merchant. The merchant leaves the worker on the mountain. The worker escapes and later tricks the merchant.
Finnish *2;* Russian: Afanasiev (936*) *7.*

937* *Koranski Castle.* The angel prophesies for the widower a happy future. The man finds a deserted robber-castle, marries a widow, and remains in the castle.
Livonian (937') *1.*

937A* *The Hidden Son.* A woman is told that her husband will die when he sees their son. When a son is born she hides him from her husband. The son grows up. The husband gets sick and the son accidentally comes to see him while the wife is away. The husband recognizes the son and dies. The son does his father's work. A thief steals his money and he kills the thief, but he is acquitted when evidence is given that he did it in self-defence. Cf. Type 934 C*.
Spanish-American: Hansen (**937) (Puerto Rico) *1.*

938 *Placidas (Eustacius).* He is converted by a vision. All his goods are destroyed, his wife seized by a ship captain, his young sons carried off by a lion and a bear [N251]. He finally recovers them all [N121].

**Gerould PMLA XIX 335ff.; *Bolte Zs. f. Vksk. XXVIII 154f.; *BP II 264 No. 88; Oesterley *Gesta Romanorum* No. 110; Boccaccio Decameron II Nos. 6, 8 (Lee 34, 39); Loomis *White Magic* 112; Hibbard 3ff.; Herbert III 241; Alphabet No. 311; Dickson 100 n. 7. — Lithuanian *17;* Danish *1;* Irish: *Cross (N251), O'Suilleabhain 42, Beal XXI 315; Italian Novella: *Rotunda (N251); Hungarian (cf. Berze Nagy 881 I*) *3;* Czech: Tille Soupis I 366f. *2;* Serbocroatian *3;* Russian: Andrejev (*931 II) *4;* Greek (888*) *1;* Turkish: Eberhard-Boratav Types 136, 291 *27;* Jewish: *Neuman Bin Gorion *Born Judas*[2] I 374; India *10;* Buddhist myth: Malalasekera II 113, 793. — West Indies: Flowers 564.

938A *Misfortunes in Youth.* A girl decides to have her fortune in old age rather than in youth [J214]. She has a long series of misfortunes (as in Type 938) but finally good luck.

Cosquin *Contes indiennes* 125ff.; *BP II 264. — Italian (Sicilian *735 *2,* Gonzenbach No. 20); Greek (735**) *11, Laographia* XV 20ff.

938B *Better in Youth.* »When do you wish to bear your hardships: in youth or old age?« [J214]. A newly married couple hear this mysterious question, and decide: »better in youth.« The husband is compelled to sell his wife. The gold he receives is carried off by a raven [N527]. Working as a laborer in a foreign land, he discovers the lost gold in a felled tree. He is brought before the sovereign, who recognizes him for her husband.

*Wesselski *Märchen* 236. — Finnish *2;* Lithuanian (*937) *11;* Russian (*931I) *1;* Rumanian (948*) *1.*

938* *Master Discovers that Slave Girl he wants to Marry Is a Near Relative* [T410.1]. Livonian (938') *1.*

938** *King Finds his Wife and Daughter* who have been lost at sea and have had many adventures. [N741.4].
Hungarian: Honti (887 I) *2;* German (887*) *1.*

939 *The Offended Deity.* Cf. Types 757, 947.

I. *A King Offends a Deity* [C50]. He loses his kingdom and his fortune [C930] and is forced to wander in poverty for a term of years. (a) His wife is stolen from him. (b) He must labor at menial tasks. (c) Taken in and helped by a friend, he sees a valuable necklace disappear before his eyes. Knowing he will be suspected of the theft, he is forced to flee. (d) He is bought as a slave and is ordered to throw corpses into a tank and collect a fee. His wife brings the corpse of their son.

II. *Restoration.* The king is eventually restored to his former position. (a) His wife (and child) are restored to him. Cf. Types 757, 947.
India *8.*

939A (formerly 939*) *Killing the Returned Soldier.* The son returns home from military service, brings a large sum of money with him, and is unwittingly killed by his parents.] [N321].

**Maria Kosko »Varia à propos du Malentendu« *Comparative Literature*

X (1958) 367—377; *Köhler-Bolte II 185ff.; John Meier *Deutsche Volkslieder* IV (1959) 298f. — Livonian (939') *1;* Lithuanian *4;* French *6;* Hungarian: Berze Nagy (779*) *1;* Czech: Tille Soupis II (2) 180, 504 *2;* Slovenian; Greek *4,* Hahn I 273 No. 50, **Laographia* I 70. — Franco-American: (as ballad); English-American: Baughman *1* (U.S.).

940 *The Haughty Girl* entices three suitors (unknown to one another) into the churchyard. They revenge themselves by having her marry the hangman thinking he is the governor's son. [K1218.3].

Sébillot RTP IX 344. — Finnish *14;* Finnish-Swedish *5;* Estonian *13;* Lithuanian *12;* Swedish *7* (Uppsala *3,* Göteborg *3,* Liungman *1*); Danish *1;* Irish *6;* French *10;* Spanish *1;* Catalan: Amades No. 533; Dutch *1;* Flemish *2,* Witteryck p. 288: *2;* German *2;* Italian (Tuscan [866] *1*); Hungarian: Berze Nagy 1727B* *1;* Serbocroatian *3;* Russian: Andrejev Ukraine *3.* — Literary Treatment: Pauli No. 185.

940* *The Forgiven Debt.* A peasant finds a sum of money which belongs to several gentlemen. With it he pays off the debt on his land. After ten years he confesses his guilt and wants to surrender his property to them. They let him keep it all. [Q68.2].

Finnish-Swedish (940**); Lithuanian (941*) *2.*

941* *The Princess Disguised as Servant Girl* is mistreated by the son of the mistress of the castle. When he appears as her suitor, she tells him about his actions.

Flemish *1,* Witteryck 298 *1.*

941** *The Rich Man's Courtship.* His wagon falls three times into the mud. At last he arrives at the house, looking like a poor man. He does not marry the haughty daughter of the house but the kitchen maid instead.

Finnish-Swedish (940*) *1;* Danish *1;* Flemish *1.*

944* »*Easy Come, Easy Go!*» The comedian and his little house are carried off by an inundation of the sea. He fiddles the whole time [W25].

Livonian (944') *1;* Serbocroatian *1.*

945 *Luck and Intelligence.* Which is more powerful? Test: peasant who has intelligence in his head is brought to court. Luck saves him.

I. *Introduction.* (a) Intelligence and Luck dispute as to which is the more powerful. (b) As a test a gardener is endowed with intelligence.

II. *The Wooden Doll.* (a) A dumb princess is offered to the man who can make her speak (Cf. Types 571—574). (b) The gardener tells his dog (a picture) in her presence of a woodcarver who made a wooden doll, a tailor who clothed her, and himself who gave her the power of speech: to whom shall she belong? (c) The princess breaks silence. Cf. Type 652.

III. *Saved by Luck.* (a) The king refuses to give the princess to him and condemns him to death. (b) He is saved by Luck.

Motifs:

I. N141. Luck or intelligence?

II. H343. Suitor test: bringing dumb princess to speak. F1023. Creation of person by cooperation of skillful men. D435.1.1. Transformation:

statue comes to life. H621. Skillful companions create woman: to whom does she belong? F954.2.1. Dumb princess is brought to speech by tale ending with a question to be solved. Z16.1. Tales ending with a question.

*BP III 53f.; Basset *1001 Contes* II 312. — Lithuanian *1;* Danish *6;* Irish *1;* Spanish *1;* Rumanian *6;* Hungarian *6;* Czech: Tille Soupis II (1) 101ff. *3,* FFC XXXIV 254; Russian: Andrejev (*559 I) *1;* Greek *2,* Dawkins *Modern Greek Folktales* No. 48; Turkish: Eberhard-Boratav No. 290 *16;* Jewish: Bin Gorion *Born Judas*[2] IV 128, 281; Arab: Basset *1001 Contes* II 65; Berber: Laoust No. 65; India *6;* Indonesian: DeVries II II 396 No. 184. — Spanish-American: Hansen 853**C (Dominican Republic) *1;* West Indies (Negro) *2.* — African: Frobenius *Atlantis* III 100.

945A* *Money and Fortune* test their power on a poor man. Fortune gives him money. He feels secure with money and forgets Fortune. Wasps sting him and he loses the money. Wasps are robbers. Friend gives him a basket of bananas and underneath is the lost money. The man believes in Fortune and becomes wealthy. Where there is no Fortune, money is worth nothing.

Spanish-American: Hansen (945**B) (Dominican Republic) *1.*

946* changed to 982.

946A* *Baldak Borisevich.* A tsar sends the hero to the Turkish sultan to take one of the sultan's horses, to spit in the eye of the sultan himself, etc. The sultan demands the culprit. The daughters of the sultan expose and mark him. The sultan takes him prisoner and orders him hanged. Before the sentence is carried out he sounds his horn. The hero's men hear it and save him.

Russian: Afanesiev *4.*

946B* *Shoes of Poverty.* Poverty attaches itself to the poor man's shoe soles. (Various ways of getting rid of it.)

Rumanian *7.*

946C* *Luck and Blessing Contest.* Luck fails to make man rich with treasure, blessing succeeds with a small gift.

Hungarian (946) *5.*

946D* *Fortune and Coincidence.* A poor man is given money by wealthy men, but owing to unfortunate circumstances he is unable to benefit by it. He finds his fortune in an object (precious stone or the like) which in all appearance seemed to be worthless.

Lithuanian (*946) *8;* Spanish (945*A) *1.*

947 *The Man Followed by Bad Luck.* He escapes from one trouble only to meet with another. Finally, apparently safe, he is killed by a falling stone wall. [N253].

*BP III 289f. (Grimm No. 175a). — Lithuanian *1;* Irish *12;* Czech: Tille II (2) 402 *3;* Greek *3;* Turkish: Eberhard-Boratav cf. No. 131 *4.*

947A *Bad Luck Cannot be Arrested.* Rich man leaves money for poor but latter closes eyes and fails to see it. Cf. Type 842.

Italian (Sicilian *948 *1*); Serbocroatian *2;* Greek: Dawkins *Modern Greek Folktales* No. 79A; Turkish: Eberhard-Boratav No. 131.

947A* *Bad Luck Refuses to Desert a Man.* Cf. Type 745A.

Catalán: Amades No. 188.

947B* *Goddess of Fate Allots Fate to People.* Man spends the night in her house and sees how fate is allotted.
Lithuanian (*936) *8.*

947C* *Quest for Good Luck.* Bad Luck conquered. Cf. Type 460B.
Rumanian (947**) *9.*

949 *The Faithful Servitor.*

I. *The Necessary Sacrifice.* A poor man is befriended by a king. He hears weeping during the night, goes out, and learns from the Fates, a goddess, or a witch that (a) a man must sacrifice himself or (b) a man must sacrifice his sons so that the king can live [S268.1.1].

II. *Denouement.* (a) The man goes to sacrifice himself or himself and his children [H1556.0.2, P361.3] but the goddess, pleased at his faithfulness, sends him away. The king has followed the man, overhears, and rewards him. Or, (b) the man kills himself and/or his sons. The king gains a boon from the goddess and restores them to life.
India *5.*

949* *Young Gentleman Learns Basketwork.* He falls in love with a common girl, who refuses to marry him till he has learned some trade. He learns basketwork and later is obliged to live by this trade. Cf. Type 888A*.
Lithuanian *2.*

949A* *Empress and Shepherdess Change Places.* Latter longs to go back home. [U135].
Rumanian *1.*

950—969 Robbers and Murderers

950 *Rhampsinitus.* The theft in the treasury (bank). The head of one of the thieves cut off. The other thief (brother) sought in vain. The lamentation of the relatives betrays the thief, etc. Cf. Type 1525.

I. *Theft from the Treasury.* (a) The king's treasury is robbed by a former architect who has left a stone loose. (b) The theft is detected by means of a straw fire and the smoke escaping through the holes. (c) The thief is caught in a trap. (d) At his request his brother (son) cuts off his head so that his identity may be concealed.

II. *Finding the Thief.* (a) In order to identify the thief the body is carried through the streets to see if anyone weeps over it. The son has forewarned the family. (b) Though the body is watched by twenty knights in white and twenty in black, the son dresses half white and half black and steals the body.

III. *The Clever Son.* (a) To catch the youth the king gives free access to the princess and has her mark the man who sleeps with her with a black sign: the youth marks all the knights and the king himself. (b) A child will hand a knife to the guilty man; he exchanges a toy with the child and thus deceives the king.

Motifs:

I. K315.1. Thief enters treasury through passage made by him as architect of the building. J1143. Thief detected by building straw fire so that smoke escapes through thief's entrance. K730. Victim trapped. K407.1. Thief has his companion cut off his head so that he may escape detection.

II. J1142.4. Thief's corpse carried through street to see who will weep for him. K407.2.1. Thief's confederate cuts off own arm to furnish alibi for family's grief. K311.0.1. Thief dressed half white, half black.

III. K425. King's daughter put into brothel to catch thief. H58. Telltale hand-mark. Clandestine lover is identified by paint marks left on his skin by his mistress. K415. Marked culprit marks everyone else and escapes detection. H211. Criminal detected by having child hand knife to him. K528. Substitute in ordeal.

Penzer *Poison Damsels* 75ff.; *BP III 395ff.; *Anderson in Tauscher *Volksmärchen* 185; Arts et Traditions Populaires I 279; *Frazer *Pausanias* V 176ff.; Köhler-Bolte I 200; K. Campbell *Seven Sages* pp. lxxxvif.; *Huet RTP XXXIII 1, 109, 253; Coffin *2;* Liungman SSF III 295, 444. — Finnish *25;* Finnish-Swedish *1;* Estonian *8;* Livonian *1;* Lithuanian *11;* Swedish *12* (Uppsala *2,* Stockholm *1,* misc. *9*); Norwegian *4;* Danish *32,* Grundtvig No. 80; Icelandic *9;* Scottish *1;* Irish *208;* French *5;* Catalan: Amades Nos. 412, 1639; German *13* (Archive *10,* Plenzat *1,* Henssen Volk No. 143); Austrian: Haiding No. 74 n.; Italian *6*(Tuscan *4,* Sicilian *2*); Rumanian *3;* Hungarian *2;* Czech: Tille Soupis I 14—19 *5;* Serbocroatian *2;* Russian: Andrejev Ukraine *11,* Afanasiev *16;* Greek *17,* Argenti and Rose I 462ff., Dawkins *Modern Greek Folktales* No. 50 *5;* Turkish: Eberhard-Boratav Nos. 342, 360 III *7;* Caucasian: Dirr No. 74; Turkestan: Radloff IV 193ff.; Berber: Laoust No. 79; India *8.* — Franco-American *14;* French Antilles *4;* Spanish-American: Rael Nos. 352—354 (U.S.), Hansen (Argentina) *2,* (Chile) *2,* (Dominican Republic) *3;* Cape Verde Islands: Parsons MAFLS XV (1) 88; West Indies (Negro) *3.* — Literary Treatments: Chauvin VIII 186; Herodotus, Book II.

951A *The King and the Robber.* The king in disguise joins a bank robber. The robber will not permit him to take more than six shillings, since the king has so many thieves. [K1812.2.1].

*BP III 393 (2). — Finnish *34;* Finnish-Swedish *1;* Estonian *2;* Lappish *2;* Swedish *6* (Uppsala *1,* Stockholm *1,* misc. *4*); Danish *6,* Grundtvig No. 80; German *17* (Archive *16,* Henssen Volk No. 144); Hungarian (Honti 951 A, Berze Nagy 953**) *4;* Czech: Tille Soupis I I 131f. *2;* Russian: Andrejev *1;* Turkish: Eberhard-Boratav No. 344 *3.*

951A* *Three Thieves Rob the Treasury.* Each has his own craft: the first can open doors, the second understands the language of dogs, while the third remembers whomever he sees, be it only once. The king disguises himself as one of their band; his craft is to save a man from the gallows. The third time he sets soldiers to seize them. He reprieves them, when the third thief recognizes him as the king.

Greek *1.*

951B *The Bank Robbery.* The robbers climb with iron nails and discover the conspiracy against the king. [N615].
Finnish *5;* Estonian *1;* Lithuanian *4;* German *1;* Czech: Tille Soupis I 131f. *2;* Russian: Andrejev *3;* Greek *4.*

951C *The Disguised King Joins the Thieves.* The disguised king joins the thieves and listens to their boasts. He boasts he can save them if they are caught. After they rob the palace he informs on them and they are captured. He makes good his boast.
India *4.*

952 *The King and the Soldier.* A soldier prepares to testify before the king against his superior officer. Accompanies the king, whom he does not know, to the robbers' house [K1812.1]. The soldier kills the robbers (or renders them harmless) [N884.1]. The robbers are usually rendered helpless by means of a magic spell [D2072, K422]. The king rewards his companion.
*BP III 450 (Grimm No. 199). — Finnish *42;* Finnish-Swedish *3;* Estonian *5;* Lithuanian *3;* Lappish *2;* Swedish *9* (Uppsala *1,* Stockholm *3,* misc. *5*); Norwegian *4;* Danish *28,* Grundtvig No. 98; Scottish *2;* Irish *17;* French *3;* Catalan: Amades No. 375; Dutch *6;* Flemish *1;* German Archive *27,* Henssen Volk No. 145; Hungarian *1;* Czech: Tille Soupis I 125, 305 *18;* Serbocroatian *5,* Istrian No. 44; Russian: Afanasiev *10.* — Franco-American *4.*

952* *A Sausage and a Revolver.* The man scares a robber with a sausage; later boasts of the event at an inn; the robber hears this; the innkeeper secretly lends the man a firearm, with which the robber is shot down when boldly attempting a second attack.
Finnish *9;* Lithuanian (*970) *2.*

953 *The Old Robber Relates Three Adventures* to free his sons [R153.3.3, J1185]. Each adventure is more frightful than the last [R151.1]. The tales: (1) an adventure with ghostlike cats, (2) Odysseus and Polyphemus (cf. Type 1137), (3) an ogre fooled by the substitution of a corpse for a child who is to be cooked for him [K527], and later by the robber's substituting himself in order to save the child. The rescued child in the last tale is the man's present captor [N763]. The robber is rewarded [Q53].
*BP III 369 (Grimm No. 191a); Liungman SSF III 299, 444; *Wesselski *Märchen* 217 No. 29; Kohler-Bolte I 182. — Swedish (misc.) *7;* Scottish *5;* Irish *203,* Beal III 333ff., IV 182ff., VII 197f. No. 10, X 152ff., XV 237; German Archive *1;* Italian (Sicilian *1*). — Franco-American *2.*

953A* *Father and Son with the Robbers.* While his father sleeps, the son alone kills all the robbers.
Russian: Andrejev (*953).

954 *The Forty Thieves.* The robbers come with seven casks into the house. In one cask is oil, in the others men are hidden. [K312]. The girl kills the robbers.

*Parsons MAFLS XV (1) 1; BP III 142; Basset *1001 Contes* II 302; Coffin *3;* Wesselski *Archiv Orientální* II 432. — Finnish (954*) *1;* Estonian (954*) *1;* Livonian (954*) *1;* Lithuanian *8;* Swedish *1;* Danish *6;* Irish *9;* French *2;* Spanish cf. *1;* Catalan: Amades Nos. 30, 159, 301, 378, 1725; German *8* (Archive 7, Merk. 326); Italian *8* (Tuscan 955 l, [311] b, [326] *3,* Sicilian *5);* Hungarian: Dégh (956B) No. 37; Czech: Tille Soupis I 5; Slovenian 4; Serbocroatian *3;* Greek *11;* Turkish: Eberhard-Boratav No. 153 III, 179 III, 369 III *15.* — India *2;* Franco-American *11;* English-American: Baughman *1;* Spanish-American: Rael No. 344 (U.S.); West Indies (Negro) *1.* — Literary Treatment: Chauvin V 83 n. 3 (1001 Nights).

955 *The Robber Bridegroom* [K1916]. The maiden in the den of robbers. While hidden under the bed she sees another maiden murdered. The severed finger serves her as a token. The girl usually strews her path into the forest with ashes or peas [R145]. When the bridegroom appears, she uses the severed finger of the murdered girl to expose him [H57.2.1]. Cf. Type 311.

*BP I 370 (Grimm No. 40). — Finnish *29;* Finnish-Swedish *12;* Estonian *19;* Livonian *1;* Lithuanian *60;* Lappish (955*) *1;* Swedish *39* (Uppsala *10,* Stockholm *6,* Göteborg *10,* Liungman *8,* misc. *5);* Norwegian *6,* Solheim *1;* Danish *93,* Grundtvig No. 73; Icelandic *2;* Irish *37;* English (955A) *2* (955B) *8;* French *8;* Dutch *4;* Flemish *4,* Witteryck p. 290 *8;* German *73* (Archive *71,* Merk. 325, Henssen Volk No. 146); Austrian: Haiding No. 55; Rumanian *8;* Hungarian *8;* Czech: Tille Soupis II (2) 301—329 *39;* Serbocroatian *6;* Russian: Afanasiev *17;* Greek *2.* — Franco-American *7;* English-American: Baughman (955A) *3,* (955B) *11.*

955A* *The Soldier and the Robber.* A soldier asks to spend the night. The owner takes him in. He turns out to be a robber and orders the soldier to prepare himself for death. The soldier prays. A rattle is heard outside the window. The robber is frightened, the soldier is saved.

Russian: Afanasiev (*965) *2.*

955B* *The Woman among the Robbers.* A woman with her children, having lost her way, finds herself among the robbers who feed her human flesh. They cook her baby in a boiler. She escapes, conceals herself along the road, and reports to authorities.

Russian: Afanaseiv (*955 I) *1.*

956 *Robbers' Heads Cut off One by One as they Enter House* [K912]. Cf. Type 304.

Finnish *6;* Danish *85;* Irish *135,* Beal IV 62f. No. 35; Flemish *1;* Austrian: Haiding No. 55; India *9.*

956A *At the Robber's House.* The man is confined in a hot chamber where many corpses are hanging. As the robbers enter, he cuts off their heads one after the other [K912] and takes their treasure.

Finnish; Danish: See Type 956; Serbocroatian *1;* Russian: Andrejev *3;* Greek *1.* — Franco-American *2.*

956B *The Clever Maiden Alone at Home Kills the Robbers.* A great crowd of robbers come into the house at night. She kills the robbers one by one as they enter [K912]. In revenge one of the robbers appears as suitor for the girl [Q411.1]. The robbers catch the girl in a wood. She flees.
    *BP I 373; Coffin *1;* *Anderson *Novelline* Nos. 36, 51. — Finnish-Swedish (955**) *1;* Estonian (953*) *2,* (955*) *1;* Lithuanian *65;* Icelandic *3;* Scottish *1,* Campbell-McKay No. 13; Spanish *2;* Catalan: Amades Nos. 88, 383; Dutch *7;* German *36* (Archive *35,* Merk. 133); Italian *21* (Tuscan 955a—c, e—n, q, [851], cf. 955d, [850], [863] *16,* Sicilian *5*); Hungarian: Dégh (*954) No. 37; Czech: Tille Soupis II (2) 301—330 *39;* Slovenian *6;* Serbocroatian *6;* Russian: Afanesiev *12;* Greek *10;* Turkish: Eberhard-Boratav Nos. 152 IV, 153, 261 IV, 369 *18;* India *9;* Franco-American *12;* English-American: Baughman *1;* West Indies (Negro) *2.*

956C *Girls in Robbers' Den.* Under pretext of bathing they shut themselves in a room and escape through a window. Sometimes leads to Type 879. Cf. Type 958E*.
    *Espinosa II 61—78, 227—229. — Spanish (*970) *7;* Spanish-American: Hansen (*970) (Chile) *6,* (Dominican Republic) *2,* (Puerto Rico) *7.*

956D (formerly 959*) *How the Girl Saves herself when she Discovers a Robber under her Bed.* She combs her hair at the window and says, »If I am married and my husband comes home drunk and seizes me by the hair, I shall cry, Help! help!» Help comes. [K551.5].
    Estonian *1;* Lithuanian (959B*) *10;* French *2;* Russian (959A*). — India *2.*

956A* *Robber Seized by Beard.* The girl seizes the robber concealed under the bed by the beard [K434.1].
    Lithuanian *5.*

956B* *Robber and Chest Lid.* A girl tells the thief that money is in chest. Slams the lid on him. [K434.3, S121].
    Lithuanian (959C*) *3.*

956C* *The Girl and the Bandits.* A girl who is expelled from her home serves bandits. She blinds one of the bandits, flees and is pursued and escapes by throwing magic objects. She finally settles in a tavern in the woods.
    Polish (356*) *1.*

956D* *Pretended Robber Attack.* The youngest brother extorts from his stingy master, under pretence of a robber attack, money which he divides with his brothers.
    Rumanian (963*) *1.*

956E* *The Girl's Revenge on her Robber.* The robber rapes and kidnaps the girl. She scalds him with boiling water; then he repents and dies.
    Russian: Andrejev (951 I) *1.*

957 *The Bear Chases the Robbers.* The bear-keeper and his bears overnight in the stable when the robbers come. [K335.1.9]. Cf. Types 177, 1161.
    Finnish *13;* Estonian *1;* Lithuanian *4;* Swedish (Lund) *2;* Dutch *1;* Slovenian *1;* Russian: Andrejev *1.*

958 *The Shepherd Youth in the Robbers' Power* calls on his horn for help. The helpers come. [K551.1].

*BP II 501; Wesselski *Märchen* 199; DeVries FFC LXXIII 41ff., 324; Thien Motive 36f.; Child V 483 s.v. »horn«. — Finnish (958*) *2;* Estonian *2* (958*); Swedish *43* (Stockhom *21,* Göteborg *11,* Lund *2,* misc. *9*); Danish *7;* Catalan: Amades No. 1639; German *2;* Hungarian: Berze Nagy (726**) *2;* Serbocroatian *1;* Russian: Andrejev (959*B) *1;* India (K551.3).

958A* *The Thief Tied To a Tree.* Having caught a thief in the act of stealing a horse, the farmer ties him, naked, to a tree and leaves him at the mercy of gnats and ants. After some time, chancing to lose his way, the farmer finds shelter in the very same man's house. He is greatly alarmed. But much to his surprise, the man he has wronged instead of taking vengeance upon him, entertains him generously and even thanks him for the lesson he once received at his hands — it has cured him of the habit of stealing.
Lithuanian (*966) *3.*

958B* *Robbers Frightened by Pretended Cannibalism* [K335.1.10].
Lithuanian (*967) *4.*

958C* *Robber in Shroud.* The station master takes in a stranger with a shroud for the night. In the shroud is hidden another robber [K311.1]. Help summoned by telephone arrives at the last minute.
Livonian (966*) *1.*

958D* *Robber as Beggar.* A woman discovers a thief disguised as a beggar woman and kills him.
Lithuanian (971) *6;* Spanish (973*) *1.*

958E* *Deep Sleep Brought on by a Robber.* A robber, disguised as a beggar, gets night lodging at a farmhouse. Using a candle made of human fat (hand of corpse), he tries to charm the household to deep sleep. One of the members of the household, who has not gone to sleep, sees this and kills the robber. The rest of the family wake up only twenty-four hours later.
Lithuanian (*963) *3.*

958E* *Respite from Death until Toilet is Made* permits escape [K551.4]. Cf. 956C.
Malone PMLA XLIII 410; Breton: Sébillot *Incidents* s.v. »toilette«; Finnish-Swedish *1;* Spanish (970); India: Thompson-Balys (K551.4).

959* changed to 956D.

960 *The Sun Brings All to Light.* The murderer repeats as he sees the ray of the sun the last words of the dying man [D1715]. In this way the crime is brought to light [N271.1]. Or the murder is revealed by the unusual names of boys [N271.2]. Cf. Types 883C, 1376C*, 1530*.

*BP II 531 (Grimm No. 115); Basset *1001 Contes* I 381; *Arts et Traditions Populaires* I 275. — Finnish *1;* Finnish-Swedish *1;* Estonian *5;* Lithuanian *2;* Danish *19;* French *15;* Spanish *2;* Catalan: Amades No. 1100; Dutch *2;* German *31;* Hungarian *2;* Czech: Tille Soupis II (2) 182, 184) *8;* Slovenian *1;* Serbocroatian *3;* Russian: Andrejev *1;* Greek: Dawkins *Modern Greek in Asia Minor* 285; Turkish: Eberhard-Boratav No. 141 *5;* India *1.* — Franco American *1;* Spanish-American: Rael No. 104 (U.S.).

960A *The Cranes of Ibycus.* A murdered man calls on cranes, the only witnesses of the murder, to avenge him. The cranes follow the murderer and point him out. [N271.3].

*BP II 532; *Amalfi Zs. f. Vksk. VI 115ff.; *Zacahariae ibid. IX 336; *Scala Celi* 100b No. 539; Hertz *Abhandlungen* 334; Köhler-Bolte II 563; Chauvin II 123, VII 146; *Krappe *Bulletin Hispanique* XXXIX 27. — England: Baughman (N271.3); Spanish: Espinosa Jr. No. 209; Jewish: *Neuman (N271.3).

960B *Late Revenge.* God avenges murder after thirty years [Q211.0.1]. A poor boy wants to marry the daughter of a rich man. The girl favors him, but she does not like his poverty. The boy murders a merchant and seizes his property. The girl asks him first to find out the nature of the punishment in store for him. The boy spends a night at the murdered man's grave. The dead man rises from his grave, and asks God for justice. A voice comes from heaven saying: »Thirty years from today you will be avenged». [M348]. The girl agrees to marry him. They live happily, and always postpone doing penance. At the appointed time the punishment takes place: the manor sinks and a lake appears [Q552.2.1], leaving only an article (book) of a guest who has accidentally spent the night at the ill-fated house. The guest was forewarned by a mysterious voice, bidding him to flee.

Gesta Romanorum No. 277; *Wesselski *Märchen* p. 27f., 199f.; *BP II 535 n. 1; *A. Senn *Corona*, 1941, p. 8—22; Russian: Andrejev (*751 I); Lithuanian (*787); Serbocroatian (787) *1.*

960B* *Seventh Generation will Pay Penalty.* Man thus warned by heavenly voice. But he is not deterred.
Irish.

961 *Conqueror of Robber Discovers his Money-stick.* Thinking that he has killed the robber, the man takes his stick or knife with big handle. The robber recovers and, disguised as beggar, inquisitively looks at the stick. The man is suspicious and by examining finds much money inside it. [K437.4].

Lithuanian: Balys (962*) *8;* Russian: Andrejev (961 I*) *1.*

961A (formerly 961*) *The Forgotten Cane.* The man believes that he has killed a robber. Forgets his cane in the place where the deed has occurred. Many years later he finds his cane in a house belonging to this robber. [N614].

Estonian (951*) *1;* Lithuanian (*961); Russian (*961).

961B *Money in the Stick.* Before swearing, the cheater hands a stick containing the stolen money to the man he has stolen it from. He then swears that he has repaid it. [J1161.4].

*Köhler-Bolte I 137; *Zachariae Zs. f. Vksk. XXXIII—XXXIV 78; **Lewy *ibid.* XXXVIII 83; Spanish Exempla: Keller (J1161.4); Jewish: *Neuman, *Gaster *Exempla* 210 No. 121a.

962* *Two Men at the Theft of a Hog.* One of them cuts the other one's knee with his axe and thinks he has found the hog.
Estonian (962*) 3.

962** *The Girl Who Played with the Bread.* Tramps on it to keep out of mud. She sinks into the ground.
Lappish (962*) 1; Swedish 26 (Stockholm 3, Göteborg 1, Lund 20, misc. 2); Norwegian 1.

963* *The Dead Man's Bed.* The robbers have a bed that rolls their treasure into the cellar.
Estonian 3.

964 *Thief (Murderer) Deceived into Betraying himself by a Gesture* [J1141.1]. Cf. Type 66A.
Finnish 13; India: Thompson-Balys (J1141.1 and subdivisions).

965* (formerly 965**) *Robbers' Alarm Bell.* The robbers in the wood at Alt-Nabal. Across the road a wire is stretched on which is a bell that will notify the robbers of travelers. [K413].
Livonian 3; Swedish (Stockholm) 1.

966* changed to Type 958C*.

966** changed to Type 970.

967 (formerly 967*) *The Man Saved by a Spider Web.* The web over the hiding place makes the pursuer think the hole is unoccupied. [B523.1].
*Dh II 66f.; Wesselski *Theorie* 42. — Lappish (967) 5; Swedish (967*) 3; English 2; Catalan: Amades No. 983; Dutch 1; Jewish: Neuman, Bin Gorion *Born Judas* III 115ff., Grünbaum *Neue Beiträge zur semitischen Sagenkunde* 195; India 1; Japanese: Ikeda; English-American: Baughman 1; African (Fang): Trilles 139.

967** *Innkeeper Deceived* into going under the floor of the granary; meantime robbed. [K343.0.1].
Livonian (967') 1.

968 *Miscellaneous Robber and Murder Stories.*
Lappish (968*) 1; Lithuanian (*964) 7, (*958) 4; Rumanian (953) 9; Serbocroatian 2; Russian: Andrejev (*966, *967) 2; Turkish: Eberhard-Boratav No. 261 3.

970—999 Other Romantic Tales

970 (formerly 966**) *The Twining Branches.* Two branches grow from the grave of unfortunate lovers and meet above the roof of the church. [E631.0.1].
*Gaidoz *Melusine* IV No. 4; *BP I 262 n. 1; Chauvin V 107 No. 37. — Lappish (966*) 1; Irish 60, Beal II 193f. No. 3, V 212; Catalan: Amades No. 1861; Hungarian: Berze Nagy (721*) 11; Slovenian 5; Turkestan: Radloff IV 340; Japanese: Anesaki 253, 346f.; Chinese: Eberhard FFC CXX 264ff. — English-American: Baughman (966*) 2.

970* *The Stepfather as a Werwolf* [D113.1.1] pursues his stepson [S32] who flees and falls in with robbers. The youth kills the robbers, frees the princess [R111.1.2], and marries her [L161].
    Livonian (970') *1.*

973 (formerly 973*) *Placating the Storm.* A man is thrown overboard from a ship to appease the storm. [S264.1].
    *Child *English and Socottish Ballads* V 496 s. v. »Ships»; Chauvin VII 30 n. 2 No. 212A. — Lappish *1;* Icelandic: *Boberg; Scottish *1* (Baughman); Irish: *Cross; Slovenian *3;* Jewish: Bin Gorion *Born Judas*[2] I 227; Korean: Zong in-Sob 107 No. 57; Buddhist myth: Malalasekera I 1024.

974 (formerly 974*) *The Homecoming Husband.* Husband (lover) arrives home just as wife (mistress) is to marry another. Cf. Types 301, 400, 665. [N681].
    **W. Splettstösser *Der heimkehrende Gatte und sein Weib in der Weltlitteratur* (Berlin, 1899); **Rajna *Romania* VI 359ff.; *BP II 318ff., 335ff., IV 168 n. 6; Bolte Zs. f. Vksk. XII 59, XXVIII 74 n. 2; Huet RTP XXXII 97, 145; Köhler-Bolte I 117, 584. — Lithuanian (509*, 974*) *1;* Lappish (974*) *1;* Norwegian *1;* Icelandic: *Boberg; Catalan: Amades No. 1821; Russian: Andrejev (891*), Andrejev *Ukraine* (891*); Slovenian; Turkish: Eberhard-Boratav (No. 210) *3;* Indonesian: v. Ronkel *Catalogus der Maleische Handschriften* 263. — Franco-American: (974*) *2;* West Indies (Negro): Beckwith MAFLS XVII 278 No. 90. — Literary Treatments: Oesterley *Gesta Romanorum* No. 193.

975* *The Exchanged Children.* Two mothers exchange their children, a boy and a girl [K1921]. The boy becomes a hunter, finds his real mother, and kills his foster-mother.
    Lappish *14.*

975** *Ottokar and Alwine.* The foster daughter of the robber chief of the castle at Mustanum (Melsile) rescues the knight [R162], who returns with an army and marries the maiden.
    Livonian (975') *4.*

976 *Which Was the Noblest Act?* The bridegroom, the robber, and the lover. A bridegroom permits his bride to fulfill a promise to visit her lover on her wedding night. On the way she meets robbers. When he hears her story one of the robbers conducts her to her lover. On hearing her story the lover takes her back to her husband. Query: which was the noblest act? [H1552.1]. (Story sometimes told to discover a thief [J1177].)
    **Bryan and Dempster *Sources and Analogues to Chaucer's Canterbury Tales* 377ff.; Köhler-Bolte I 214—216; Penzer Ocean of Story VII 199; Chauvin VIII 123f. No. 110. — Scottish *1;* Irish *1;* Slovenian *1;* Russian: Andrejev (881 I); Turkish: Eberhard-Boratav No. 348 IV *2;* Jewish: Gaster *Exempla* 206 No. 111, Bin Gorion *Born Judas* II[2] 97, 303. — Spanish-American: Hansen (Argentina) *2,* (Chile) *1.* — Literary Treatmens: Chaucer's »Franklin's Tale».

976A *The Thief Exposed by a Story.* By their father three (four) brothers are left jewels, which one of the brothers steals. They appeal to a wise man to find the thief. The wise man tells the story, »Which was the Noblest Act,» (Type 976). The thief is discovered when he maintains that the thief in the story was the most noble. (a) The thief is discovered in other ways.

India *5*.

977 *The Eloping Couple and the Robbers.* An eloping couple come to the house of a band of thieves who are absent. The mother of the thieves tries to detain the couple, but, unable to keep them until the robbers return, she ties a bag of seeds, or the like, to their horses so that they can be trailed by the fallen seed [R267]. The thieves overtake the eloping couple, but the hero kills all but one who begs to be saved. Watching his opportunity, the spared robber kills the hero. The heroine feigns love for the robber and is able to kill him when his attention is distracted [K872]. The hero is restored to life [E0] by deities who overhear the weeping of the heroine. (a) The heroine later saves the hero who has been transformed into a ram by a witch.

India *8*.

978 *The Youth in the Land of the Cheaters.*
I. *The Cheats.* A youth sets out to trade and comes to a land where cheaters flourish. He loses all his goods. (a) A one-eyed man (woman) states that the youth's father had taken the other eye and demands compensation. (The rescuer demands that the one-eyed man give up his remaining eye so that he can take the eye back and match it with the other [J1512.2].) (b) The same with one-legged man [J1521.6]. (c) A barber agrees to shave the youth for »something» and then demands a huge sum of money, or the like. (The rescuer tricks the barber into accepting »something.» [J1521.5.1].) (d) Other cheating tricks.
II. *The Rescue.* He is rescued by (a) his wife (b) another person who outwits the cheaters and recovers the goods.

India *6*.

980 *Ungrateful Son Reproved by Naive Actions of Own Son:* Preparing for Old Age [J121].
Lithuanian (*996) *4*.

980A *The Half-Carpet.* A man gives his old father half a carpet to keep him warm. The child keeps the other half and tells his father that he is keeping it for him when he grows old. [J121].
*BP II 135 (Grimm No. 78), IV 172 n. 14; *Bédier *Fabliaux* 463f.; Krappe *Bulletin Hispanique* XXXIX 41. — Lithuanian (*996) *4;* Spanish Exempla: Keller; Italian Novella: Rotunda; Hungarian: Berze Nagy (975*) *2;* Slovenian *3;* Russian: Andrejev (982*) *1;* Greek *3;* Japanese: Ikeda; Chinese: Eberhard FFC CXX 256f. No. 201, CXXVIII 102 No. 58. — Portuguese American (Brazilian): Camara Cascudo p. 75. — Literary Treatments: Pauli (ed. Bolte) Nos. 436, 760; Crane *Vitry* 260 No. 288.

980B *Wooden Drinking Cup for Old Man* [J121.1].
    Spanish: Childers; Slovenian *2;* India *1.*
980C *Dragging Old Man only to Threshold* [J121.2].
    Spanish: Childers (J121.2); Hungarian: Berze Nagy (975*) *2.* — Spanish-American: Hansen (Puerto Rico) *1,* Rael No. 489 (U.S.).
980D *Meat Springs as a Toad on the Face of an Ungrateful Son* [D444.2].
    *BP III 162ff.; *Dähnhardt IV 262. — Hungarian: Berze Nagy (779 XXVII*) *1;* Japanese: Ikeda (D444.2).
980* *The Painter and the Architect.* Persuaded by the painter, the king orders his architect to build a tower so that the architect may go through it to heaven to see his father. The architect saves himself through an underground passage [F721.1]. The architect entices the painter to go to heaven. The painter meets his death in the burning tower.
    Estonian *5;* India *12.*

981 (formerly 981*) *Wisdom of Hidden Old Man Saves Kingdom.* In famine all old men are ordered killed. One man hides his father. When all goes wrong in the hands of the young rulers, the old man comes forth, performs assigned tasks, and aids with his wisdom. [J151.1]. Cf. Type 922A.
    **Paudler FFC CXXI; *Anderson in Tauscher *Volksmärchen* 185; Liungman SSF III 302, 444; *Wesselski *Märchen* 237 No. 48; Anderson FFC XLII 182 n. 1; DeVries FFC LXXIII 220ff. — Estonian *4;* Lithuanian (995*) *54;* Swedish *1;* Irish *89,* Beal XII 165, XVIII 114f. No. 4; French *1;* Spanish Exempla: Keller; Italian (Sicilian *1*); Rumanian (910F*) *3;* Slovenian *5;* Serbocroatian *61;* Russian: Afanesiev *1;* Turkish: Eberhard-Boratav cf. No. 197 V; Jewish: Neuman; India *5;* Chinese: Eberhard FFC CXX 115ff. No. 71, CXXVIII 85 No. 41. — Literary Treatments: Pauli (ed. Bolte) No. 446, cf. No. 538; Scala Celi No. 281; Chauvin VIII 199 No. 244; Italian Novella: Rotunda (f151.1).

982 *Supposed Chest of Gold Induces Children to Care for Aged Father.* They think that the chest of stones contains the inheritance. [P236.2, Q281.1].
    *Pauli (ed. Bolte) No. 435; Dunlop-Wilson II 185f.; *BP IV 172; Hdwb. d. Abergl. IV 1290. — Estonian: Loorits *Estnische Märchen* No. 184; Lithuanian (2452) *1;* Spanish (*980A) *1;* Catalan: Amades No. 1480; Flemish (946) *1;* Italian (Sicilian 980 *1*); Slovenian *4;* Greek (1570*) 1; Jewish: Schmidt-Kahle II No. 123; India *4;* Indonesian: Jeynball *Catalogus Maleische en Sundaneesche Hss.* 173.

983 *The Dishes of the Same Flavor.* Man thus shown that one woman is like another and dissuaded from his amorous purpose. [J81].
    *Wesselski *Märchen* 209; Basset *1001 Contes* II 25. — Lithuanian (*981) *1;* Russian: Andrejev (*981 II) *1;* India: Thompson-Balys (J81).

985 *Brother Chosen Rather than Husband or Son.* Only one can be saved; he alone is irreplacable. [P253.3].
    Chauvin II 190 No. 2; Tawney *Journal of Philology* XII 121; Aly *Volksmärchen bei Herodot* 35, 109; Philippine: Fansler MAFLS XII 257 No. 31.

986 *The Lazy Husband.* Forced by his wife to work he joins a caravan and finds in a desert spring a pomegranate and a beautiful girl. He sends the pomegranate to his wife. Out of it fall jewels which make them rich. He returns the stolen girl to her father.

Turkish: Eberhard-Boratav No. 256 *24;* Palestine: Schmidt-Kahle No. 40.

987 *False Magician Exposed by Clever Girl* [K1963.1].

BP III 202 (Grimm No. 149); Lappish: Qvigstad FFC LX 51 No. 99; Estonian: Aarne FFC XXV 137 No. 103; Hungarian: Berze Nagy (594) *1.*

990 *The Seemingly Dead Revives.* The woman gets a ring stuck in her throat. A man enters the grave to steal a ring from the finger of the dead. The woman wakes up and goes home. [K426].

**Bolte Zs. f. Vksk. XX 353, XXX—XXXII 127; **Hertel *ibid.* XXI 282; Coffin *1.* — Finnish (990*) *2;* Estonian (990*) *8;* Lithuanian *3;* Scottish *2;* Irish *77;* English *2;* French *2;* Czech: Tille Soupis I 463ff. *10;* Slovenian *2;* Serbocroatian *1;* Turkish: Eberhard-Boratav cf. Nos. 307, 317 *4.* — Franco-American *3;* English-American: Baughman *2;* Spanish-American: Hansen (Puerto Rico) *2.*

990* *A Merchant's Son Finds the Princess Wounded in a Coffin.* He helps her in her revenge and marries her.

Czech: Tille (Soupis I 2ff.) *3.*

992 *The Eaten Heart.* Adulteress is caused unwittingly to eat her lover's heart. (Sometimes other parts of his body.) [Q478.1].

**Matzke MLN XXVI 1; **K. Nyrop *Sangerens Hjærte* (København, 1908); *Hibbard 253ff.; Hauvette *Romania* XLI (1912) 184ff. *Motif Q478.1. — Catalan: Amades Nos. 1637, 1647, 1812, 1866; Cape Verde Islands: Parsons MAFLS XV (1) 140 n. 1. — Literary Treatments: Boccaccio Decameron IV Nos. 1, 9 (Lee 116, 143).

992A *The Adulteress's Penance.* A husband brings to the table daily a head with a beard as a reminder.

BP I 198; *Pauli (ed. Bolte) No. 223; Chauvin VIII 161. — Turkish: Eberhard-Boratav Nos. 204, 277; Caucasian: Dirr No. 13.

995* *The Recruit Flees from the Suitors.*
Livonian (995') *1.*

D. TALES OF THE STUPID OGRE

1000—1029 L a b o r C o n t r a c t (A n g e r B a r g a i n)

1000 *Bargain Not to Become Angry.* See Type 650A (incident III c. See also Type 1351).

Motifs: K172. Anger bargain. F613.3. Strong man's labor contract: anger bargain. First to become angry shall receive blow.

Note: Type 1000 is usually combined with one or more other types, especially 1000—1029, and also 1060, 1062, 1088, 1115, 1386, 1653, 1725.

*BP II 293 (Grimm No. 90); Köhler-Bolte I 327; Coffin 6. — Finnish 88; Finnish-Swedish 10; Estonian 19; Lithuanian 40, (*762) 42; Lappish 3 (Cf. also 1000*); Swedish 15 (Uppsala 2, Stockholm 2, Göteborg 9, Liungman 1, misc. 1); Danish 37; Norwegian 11, Solheim 2; Icelandic 5; Scottish 1; Irish 159, Beal VI 44ff., X 178ff., XVI 66ff.; French 34; Spanish 5; Catalan: Amades Nos. 2, 402, cf. 75; Dutch 2; German 34 (Archive 31, Meckl. Nos. 77, 99, Henssen Volk No. 170); Austrian: Haiding No. 48; Italian (Tuscan 3); Rumanian 14, Sainenu 807; Hungarian 5; Czech: Tille Soupis II (2) 87—95 15; Slovenian 1; Serbocroatian 13; Russian: Andrejev 7, Andrejev Ukraine 14; Greek 9, Dawkins Modern Greek Folktale No. 69 4; Turkish: Eberhard-Boratav No. 351 IV, 357 18; India (1000 + 1000A) 29; Indonesian: DeVries No. 240. — English-American: Baughman 1; Spanish-American: Rael Nos. 273, 275, 277 (U.S.); Spanish-American: Hansen (Argentina) 3, (Dominican Republic) 11; Cape Verde Islands: Parsons MAFLS XV (1) 113; West Indies (Negro) 5; American Indian: Thompson C Coll II 433f.

1001 *Cutting Wood.* The rascal has a magic cat (snake) in the woodpile. The axe goes into the wood only when the cat gets out. He thus avoids cutting the wood. [D2186].

Finnish 47; Finnish-Swedish 2; Swedish 2 (Uppsala 1, Stockholm 1); Russian: Andrejev.

1002 *Dissipation of the Ogre's Property* through sale, trifling exchange, or giving away [K1400].

Finnish 1; Finnish-Swedish 2; Lithuanian 2; Swedish 4 (Liungman 1, misc. 3); Danish 27; Irish 18; Spanish (1002, 1003*A, 1004*D) 3; Dutch 3; Flemish 1; German 9 (Archive 8, Henssen Volk No. 170); Czech: Tille Soupis II (2) 87—93 10; Serbocroatian 3; Russian: Andrejev; Greek 1; India 1.

1003 *Plowing.* The man is told to come home when the dog does. He beats the dog so that it runs home. Then he destroys the horse and harness and goes home. [K1411]. (Cf. Type 650 incident IVc).

*BP II 285ff., especially 293 (Grimm No. 90); Coffin 2. — Finnish 53; Finnish-Swedish 5; Estonian 6; Lithuanian 17; Swedish 6 (Uppsala 2, Göteborg 1, misc. 3); Norwegian 8; Danish 15; Irish 14; Spanish: Espinosa III Nos. 163—7; German 11 (Archive 10, Henssen Volk No. 170); Hungarian 2; Czech: Tille Soupis II (2) 98ff. 6; Serbocroatian 3; Russian: Andrejev Ukraine 3; Greek 1; India 1. — Spanish-American: Hansen (Argentina) 1, (Dominican Republic) 3, (Puerto Rico) 5; West Indies (Negro) 1.

1003* *Guarding Cattle.* The rascal must stay out until the dog runs home. He binds a cord around the dog's neck and kills him.
Icelandic 2.

1004 *Hogs in the Mud; Sheep in the Air.* The cows driven away, the hogs' tails in the mud, the bell-wether on the tree.

I. *Pigs' Tails.* Left to guard the pigs, the trickster kills and sells them and leaves their tails sticking in the ground. The owner pulls the tails out and is convinced that the pigs have escaped underground. [K404.1].

II. *Sheep in Tree.* Likewise with the sheep whose tails are in the tree: he thinks they have escaped in the air. [K404.3].

III. *Tails in Mouth.* One ox is killed and his tail put in the mouth of another: the owner thinks one has eaten the other [K404.2].

*BP III 392 notes 1, 2 (Grimm No. 192); *Anderson in Tauscher *Volksmärchen* 185; *Jahrbuch für romanische und englische Literatur* VIII 249ff.; Coffin *17;* Espinosa III 130—140. — Finnish *5;* Finnish-Swedish *2;* Estonian *1,* (1525G*) *8;* Lithuanian *1;* Lappish *2;* Swedish *8* (Uppsala *1,* Göteborg *4,* misc. *3*); Norwegian *13;* Danish *9;* Icelandic *1;* Irish *7;* French *6;* Spanish *4;* Catalan: Amades No. 2; Dutch *1;* Flemish *4;* German *17* (Archive *15,* Henssen Volk No. 200, Meckl. No. 99); Austrian: Haiding No. 48; Italian (Sicilian *1,* Gonzenbach No. 37; Czech: Tille Soupis II (2) 88—93 *10;* Slovenian *2;* Serbocroatian *4;* Russian: Andrejev (1525G*) *1;* Turkish: Eberhard-Boratav Nos. 274 V, 352; India *2;* Indonesian: DeVries No. 241. — Spanish-American: Rael No. 284 (U.S.); Spanish-American: Hansen: (Argentina) *1,* (Chile) *1,* (Puerto Rico) *2;* Portuguese American (Brazil): Camera Cascudo 241 No. 1; West Indies (Negro) *4;* African *3;* N. Am. Indian: Thompson *C Coll* II 419ff. No. 19.

1005 *Building a Bridge or Road* with the carcasses of slain cattle. Ordered to build for the ogre's wedding a bridge, not of wood, stone, iron, or earth, he uses cattle. [K1441].

Finnish *114;* Finnish-Swedish *7;* Swedish *29* (Uppsala *12,* Stockholm *2,* Göteborg *1,* Liungman *4,* misc. *10*); Norwegian *6;* Danish *23;* Icelandic *2;* Scottish *2;* Irish *11;* Spanish *1;* Dutch *1;* German *16* (Archive *15,* Henssen Volk No. 201); Hungarian *2;* Czech: Tille Soupis II (1) 87—93 *11;* Serbocroatian *1;* Russian: Andrejev.

1006 *Casting Eyes.* Cf. Type 1685. Ordered to cast eyes on this or that, he kills animals and throws their eyes at the object. [K1442].

Finnish *100;* Finnish-Swedish *7;* Estonian *10;* Livonian *3;* Swedish *32* (Uppsala *19,* Stockholm *1,* Lund *1,* Liungman *5,* misc. *8*); Norwegian *9;* Icelandic *4;* Danish *21;* Scottish *31;* Irish *52;* English *2;* French *6;* Spanish: Espinosa III Nos. 181—186; German *14* (Archive *12,* Henssen Volk No. 191, Henssen Jül. No. 464); Italian (Tuscan 1006 a, b, 1013 b *3*); Slovenian *1;* Serbocroatian *1;* Russian: Andrejev; Greek *1;* India: Thompson-Balys (K1442) *1.*

1006* »*Kill the Sheep that is Looking at You.*» The whole flock is looking, so that the rascal kills them all.

Lithuanian *16;* Russian (*1006).

1007 *Other Means of Killing or Maiming Live Stock* [K1440].
*Anderson in Tauscher *Volksmärchen* 186. — Finnish *13;* Finnish-Swedish *2;* Estonian *9;* Livonian *1;* Lithuanian *16;* Swedish (Uppsala) *2;* Icelandic *1;* Danish *6;* Irish *18,* Beal X 175, 207; French *3;* Spanish *5;* Catalan: Amades No. 2; Dutch *1;* German *15;* Italian *1* (Tuscan 1000 b *1*); Czech: Tille Soupis II (2) 91—94 *8;* Serbocroatian *4;* Russian: Andrejev *2;* Greek *5;* Turkish: Eberhard-Boratav No. 327 III, 330, 357 III; India *1.* — English-American: Baughman *1;* Spanish-American: Hansen (Argentina) *2,* (Puerto Rico) *9;* West Indies (Negro) *1.*

1008 *Lighting the Road,* or painting the house red. The house set on fire. [K1412].
Finnish *51;* Finnish-Swedish *4;* Estonian *3;* Lithuanian *6;* Swedish *4* (Uppsala *2,* Stockholm *1,* Liungman *1*); Danish *20;* Dutch *1;* German *4* (Archive *3,* Henssen Volk No. 201); Hungarian *1;* Czech: Tille Soupis II (2) 89—95 *12;* Slovenian *1;* Serbocroatian *4;* Russian: Andrejev, Andrejev *Ukraine 3;* India *1.*

1009 *Guarding the Store-room Door.* It is lifted off and carried away. [K1413]. Cf. Type 1653A.
Penzer Ocean of Story V 117 n. 1. — Finnish *6;* Finnish-Swedish *3;* Estonian *3;* Livonian *1;* Lithuanian (*1014A) *4;* Swedish *8* (Uppsala *4,* Göteborg *1,* Lund *2,* misc. *1*); Danish *4;* Dutch *3;* German Archive *7;* Italian (Tuscan 1006 a, b, 1013 b *3,* Sicilian *2*); Czech: Tille Soupis II (2) 91 *2;* Slovenian *6;* Serbocroatian *2;* Russian: Afanesiev *6;* Greek *4;* Turkish: Eberhard-Boratav No. 323 IV, 324, 333 III *6;* India *4.* — Spanish-American: Hansen (Argentina) *1,* (Cuba) *1.*

1010 *Repairing the House.* The house or furniture destroyed. [K1415].
Finnish *4;* Finnish-Swedish *1;* Estonian *2;* Swedish *3* (Stockholm *1,* Liungman *2*); Danish *10;* Irish *1;* Spanish *1;* Flemish *1;* German *1;* Hungarian: Berze Nagy (1016**) *1;* Czech: Tille Soupis II (2) 87—95 *15;* Serbocroatian *2;* Russian: Andrejev; Greek *1.*

1011 *Tearing up the Orchard or Vineyard.* Told to cut down wood, the rascal cuts down a neighbor's vineyard. [K1416].
Köhler-Bolte I 327; Espinosa III 130—140. — Spanish *2;* Greek *1;* India *5.* — English-American: Baughman *4;* Spanish-American: Hansen (Argentina) *2,* (Dominican Republic) *2,* (Puerto Rico) *1.*

1011* *Fool to Spin Flax Destroys it.* Given power by fairies to spin and weave all he touches. [D2172.2].
Italian (Sicilian *1011 *1*).

1012 *Cleaning the Child.* Intestines taken out and cleaned. [K1461.1].
*Anderson in Tauscher *Volksmärchen* 187; Köhler-Bolte I 150. — Finnish *83;* Finnish-Swedish *2;* Estonian *27;* Livonian *1;* Lappish *1;* Swedish *12* (Uppsala *2,* Stockholm *3,* Göteborg *2,* Liungman *1,* misc. *4*); Norwegian *6;* Danish *13;* Scottish *1;* German: Archive *6,* Plenzat *2,* Meyer *6;* Hungarian *1;* Czech: Tille Soupis II (2) 88 *1;* Serbocroatian *2;*

Russian: Andrejev *8;* Greek *1;* Turkish: Eberhard-Boratav cf. No. 357 III; India *4;* Indonesia: DeVries No. 241.

1012A *Cleaning the Children.* Rascal impales them. [K1416.3].
Lithuanian (*1013) *8;* Russian: Afanesiev (1012 I) *3.*

1013 *Bathing or Warming Grandmother.* In boiling water or on stove. [K1462].
Finnish-Swedish *1;* Lithuanian *25;* Swedish *10* (Stockhom *3,* Göteborg *2,* Liungman *1,* misc. *4*); Norwegian *3;* Irish *2;* Spanish: Espinosa III Nos. 181—188; Italian (Tuscan 1006 a, b, 1013 b—d *5*); Russian: Andrejev; Turkish: Eberhard-Boratav No. 323, 324 III *13;* India *3.* — Spanish-American: Hansen (Puerto Rico) *1;* West Indies (Negro) *17.* — Oceanic (New Britain): Dixon *Oceanic Mythology* 122.

1014 *Closing the Door Tight.* With iron nails. [K1417].
Estonian (1014*) *1;* German *1.*

1015 *Whetting the Knife.* The whole blade whetted away. [K1418].
Finnish (1054**); Estonian (1015*) *1;* Irish *1.*

1016 *Cleaning the Horse.* Washing in boiling water or currying with a sharp razor. [K1443].
Estonian (1016*) *1,* (1017*) *1;* Livonian (1014') *1;* Lithuanian (*1016A) *2;* Swedish (Uppsala) *3;* Irish *1;* Italian (Tuscan 1006 b *1*); Turkish: Eberhard-Boratav cf. No. 327 III *11.*

1017 *Covering the Whole Wagon with Tar* [K1425].
Livonian (1014**) *1;* Swedish *3* (Stockholm *2,* Lund *1*); Danish *3;* German *3.*

1019* *The Harrow as Hair Brush.* The ogre uses it.
Estonian *1.*

1029 *The Woman as Cuckoo in the Tree.* The anger-bargain is to cease when the cuckoo crows. The ogre's wife climbs into the tree and imitates the cuckoo. She is shot down. [K1691].
Wünsche 29, 33, 36ff., 47, 51ff., 61, 106; Köhler-Bolte I 151; Espinosa III Nos. 163—7. — Finnish *38;* Finnish-Swedish *3;* Estonian *5;* Lithuanian *6,* (cf. *1029A) *2;* Swedish *9* (Uppsala *2,* Stockholm *2,* Göteborg *1,* Lund *1,* misc. *3*); Norwegian *10;* Danish *25;* Irish *24;* French *1;* Spanish *3;* Dutch *1;* German *12* (Archive *11,* Henssen Volk No. 170); Austrian: Haiding No. 48; Italian (Sicilian *1*); Czech: Tille Soupis II (2) 87—93 *10;* Slovenian *1;* Serbocroatian *3;* Russian: Andrejev, Andrejev *Ukraine 5.* — Spanish-American: Hansen (Puerto Rico) *4;* Cape Verde Islands: Parson MAFLS XV (1) 115.

1030—1059 Partnership of the Man and the Ogre

1030 *The Crop Division.* Man and ogre or fox and bear. Of root crops the ogre chooses the tops; of other crops the roots. [K171]. Cf. Types 9B, 1633.

**J. Hackman »Sagan om skördelningen» *Folkloristiska och etnografiska studier* III (1922) 140—170; **Krohn »Bär und Fuchs» JSFO VI 104—111; *BP III 355 (Grimm No. 189); Taylor PMLA XXXVI (1921) 58 n. 34; Wünsche 70—79; Wesselski *Märchen* 254 No. 63; Coffin *12*. — Finnish *8;* Finnish-Swedish *3;* Estonian *25;* Livonian *1;* Lithuanian *23;* Swedish *96* (Uppsala *39*, Stockholm *8*, Göteborg *21*, Lund *13*, Liungman *3*, misc. *12*); Norwegian *3;* Danish *12;* Irish *10;* English *2;* French *55;* Spanish *1*, (*278) *3;* Catalan: Amades No. 1293; Dutch *4;* Flemish *3;* German *24* (Archive *23*, Merk. 308); Italian (Tuscan [1000] *1*); Rumanian *6;* Hungarian *1;* Czech: Tille Soupis I 181f. *3;* Slovenian *8;* Serbocroatian *4;* Russian: Andrejev *Ukraine 12*, Afanesiev *8;* India *6*. — Franco-American (Missouri French): Carrière (K171.1); English-American: Baughman *4;* Spanish-American: Hansen (Argentina) *·3*, (Chile) *1;* West Indies (Negro): Flowers p. 497; American Negro: Parsons JAFL XXX 175; American-Indian: Thompson *C Coll* II 441, 447ff.

1030* *Bargain: Choice of Cows which Go to Old or New Stable.* Only one goes to new stable. (Introduction to Type 1642.)
Greek *12*.

1031 *Granary Roof Used as Threshing Flail* [K1422]. Cf. Type 650A (IV a).
*BP II 285ff., especially 293 (Grimm No. 90). — Finnish *12;* Lappish *1;* Swedish *24* (Uppsala *7*, Stockholm *7*, Göteborg *1*, Liungman *1*, misc. *8*); Norwegian *11;* Danish *13;* Scottish *1;* German *1;* Russian: Andrejev; Indonesian: DeVries No. 242. — American Indian: Thompson *C Coll* II 436 (B).

1035 *Clearing out Manure.* The rascal digs a hole [K1424] or piles manure high [K1424.1].
Finnish *3;* Estonian *8;* Livonian *1;* Swedish *13* (Uppsala *1*, Göteborg *2*, Lund *2*, Liungman *5*, misc. *3*); Russian: Andrejev.

1036 *Hogs with Curly Tails* belong to the man; others to the ogre [K171.4].
Finnish *30;* Finnish-Swedish *1;* Swedish *21* (Uppsala *8*, Göteborg *1*, Stockholm *1*, Lund *5*, Liungman *1*, misc. *5*); English *1;* French *3;* Spanish *1;* German *1;* Hungarian *3;* Slovenian *2;* Serbocroatian *1;* Russian: Andrejev. — English-American: Baughman *5*.

1037 *The Ogre Shears a Pig* instead of sheep [K171.5].
Finnish-Swedish *1;* Estonian *2;* Swedish *11* (Uppsala *9*, Göteborg *2*); Russian: Andrejev.

1045 *Pulling the Lake Together.* The hero threatens to do so with a rope. The ogre is intimidated. [K1744]. Cf. Type 1650.
Finnish *146;* Finnish-Swedish *10;* Estonian *28;* Livonian *4;* Lithuanian *42;* Danish *19;* Irish *92;* French *7;* Spanish: Espinosa Nos. 163—167; German *1;* Hungarian *4;* Czech: Tille Soupis I 192f. *3;* Serbocroatian *1;* Russian: Andrejev *Ukraine 11*, Afanasiev *22;* India *1*. — Franco-American (Missouri French): Carriere (K1744); English-American: Baughman *2;* West Indies (Negro) *1* (1045*).

1045* *Contest in Lifting.* Farmer begins to tie an oak tree to his back, and the devil flees.
Walloon (*1030A) *1.*

1046 *Threat to Haul away the Warehouse.* For this purpose a large rope is made. The ogre is intimidated. [K1745].
Finnish *12;* Finnish-Swedish *1;* Lithuanian *3* (cf. Type 1153); Lappish *3;* Swedish (misc.) *1;* Irish *1;* Hungarian *2;* Serbocroatian *1;* Russian: Andrejev.

1047* *Devil Challenges Farmer to Fight.* Next day, farmer's wife tells the devil the farmer has gone to lead an army of giants; on the next, that he is having his ankles sharpened. Devil flees.
Walloon (*1030B) *1.*

1048 *Buying Wood.* Neither straight nor crooked trees (sawdust). [K186].
Finnish *39;* Finnish-Swedish *1;* Estonian *6;* Russian: Andrejev.

1049 *The Heavy Axe.* The boastful trickster told to cut wood with an axe or get water in a bucket demands one large enough to bring in the whole well (cut the whole forest). The ogre is frightened. [K1741.1, K1741.3].
*BP III 333 (Grimm No. 183). — Finnish *23;* Finnish-Swedish *12;* Estonian *5;* Lithuanian *11;* Lappish *6;* Swedish *27* (Uppsala *4,* Stockholm *4,* Lund *1,* Liungman *2,* misc. *16*); Norwegian (1043) *15,* Solheim *1;* Danish *5;* Icelandic *1;* Scottish *1;* Irish *101,* Beal IV 228f. No. 6, XVII 211ff.; Spanish: Espinosa III Nos. 163—167; Catalan: Amades Nos. 2, 75; German *5;* Austrian: Haiding No. 20; Italian (Tuscan cf. [1005] *1,* Sicilian *1,* Gonzenbach No. 41); Hungarian *8;* Czech: Tille Soupis I 193 *1;* Serbocroatian *6;* Russian: Afanasiev (1049A) *7;* Greek *13,* Loukatos No. 18; Turkish: Eberhard-Boratav No. 162 *15.* — Spanish-American: Hansen (Argentina) *2,* (Chile) *1,* (Dominican Republic) *2,* (Puerto Rico) *6;* French Canadian (1145B).

1050 *Felling Trees.* The ogre and the trickster are to fell a large tree. The trickster purposely dulls his axe on a stone and then asks the ogre to exchange. Rather than work with the dull axe, the ogre does all the work. [K178, K1421]. Cf. Type 650 IV.
*BP II 285ff. — Finnish *59;* Finnish-Swedish *1;* Estonian *2;* Livonian (cf. *1*); Lithuanian *1;* Swedish *10* (Uppsala *4,* Göteborg *2,* Liungman *1,* misc. *3*); Danish *13;* Norwegian *1;* German *4;* Hungarian *1;* Russian: Andrejev *1.*

1051 *Bending a Tręe.* The boastful trickster bends down a tree, but when he pauses to catch his breath the tree shoots him into the sky. [K1112].
*BP III 333 (Grimm No. 183); cf. I 148 (Grimm No. 20). — Finnish *12;* Finnish-Swedish *1;* Livonian cf. (1051) *1;* Lithuanian *3;* Swedish *23* (Uppsala *6;* Stockholm *2,* Göteborg *2,* Lund *1,* Liungman *3,* misc. *9*); Norwegian *14;* Danish *3;* French *1;* Catalan: Amades No. 78; Flemish *1;* German *8;* Austrian: Haiding Nos. 20, 62; Hungarian *4,* Berze Nagy (134*) *2;* Czech: Tille Soupis I 269ff. *6;* Slovenian *5;* Serbocroatian *2;*

Russian: Andrejev *1*, Andrejev *Ukraine 5;* Turkish: Eberhard-Boratav No. 162 III.

1052 *Deceptive Contest in Carrying a Tree—Riding.* The boastful trickster (fox) has the ogre (bear) carry the branches of the tree while he carries the trunk. He rides on the trunk. [K71]. Cf. Type 1640.
  *BP I 149 (Grimm No. 20). — Finnish *251;* Finnish-Swedish *23;* Estonian *25;* Livonian *5;* Lithuanian *8;* Lappish *10;* Swedish *80* (Uppsala *21*, Stockholm *8*, Göteborg *19*, Lund *4*, Liungman *6*, misc. *22*); Norwegian *12;* Danish *22;* Irish *9;* Flemish *1;* German *13;* Russian: Andrejev *3.* — Spanish-American: Rael No. 341 (U.S.).

1053 *Shooting Wild Boars.* Boastful trickster, told to shoot a wild boar or two, asks, »Why not a thousand at one shot?» Frightens ogre. [K1741.2].
  *BP III 333 (Grimm No. 183). — Serbocroatian *1;* Spanish-American: Hansen (Argentina) *1.*

1053A *The Big Rope.* A man makes a big rope in order to be able to capture the whole flock.
  Russian: Afanasiev (*1049B) *3.*

1053* *Harvesting the Hay.* The man calls out, »The wolves are coming!» The ogre is intimidated. [K42.0.1].
  Estonian *4.*

1053** *Putting the Boat into the Water* or pulling it out.
  Lappish (1053*) *1.*

1059* *The Peasant makes the Devil Sit on the Reversed Harrow* [K1117].
  Finnish-Swedish *1;* Swedish *13* (Uppsala *4*, Stockholm *2*, Lund *6*, misc. *1*).

1060—1114 Contest between Man and Ogre

1060 *Squeezing the (Supposed) Stone.* Cheese, egg, etc. Contest in squeezing water out of a stone. The ogre squeezes a stone; the boastful trickster a cheese or egg [K62]. (Sometimes with animal actors.) Cf. Type 1640.
  *BP I 148 (Grimm No. 20); Coffin *3.* — Finnish *144;* Finnish-Swedish *17;* Estonian *14;* Livonian *1;* Lithuanian *33;* Lappish *7;* Swedish *73* (Uppsala *20*, Stockholm *5*, Göteborg *9*, Lund *5*, Liungman *9*, misc. *25*); Norwegian *24*, Solheim *2;* Danish *16;* Scottish *1;* Irish *49*, cf. Beal IV 453; French *2;* Spanish *1;* Catalan: Amades No. 2; Flemish *4;* German *27* (Archive *25*, Henssen Jül. No. 457, Meckl. No. 100); Austrian: Haiding No. 62; Italian (Sicilian *2*, Gonzenbach No. 41); Hungarian *5*, Berze Nagy 133* *2;* Czech: Tille Soupis I 269ff. *12;* Slovenian *11;* Serbocroatian *8;* Russian: Afanasiev *7;* Greek *11*, Hahn No. 18, Loukatos No. 18; India *1.* — English-American: Baughman *1;* Spanish-American: Rael No. 341 (U.S.), Hansen (Argentina) *1*, (Chile) *1*, (Dominican Republic) *1;* Portuguese-American (Cape Verde Islands): Parsons MAFLS XV (1) 114.

1060A (formerly 1060*) *Squeezing the Hand.* The man has an iron glove on. [K73].
  *Liungman SSF III 316. — Estonian *5;* Swedish *41* (Uppsala *15,* Stockholm *8,* Göteborg *1,* Lund *1,* misc. *16);* Danish *3;* Russian: Andrejev *2;* India *1.*
1060A* *Pulling the Finger.* Iron finger. [K74].
  Estonian (1064*) *1;* Danish *1;* Slovenian *1.*
1061 *Biting the Stone* (by ogre); peas, nuts, etc. by man [K63]. Cf. Type 1640.
  *BP I 68 n. 1, II 528 (Grimm No. 114); Espinosa III 130—140. — Finnish *22;* Finnish-Swedish *4;* Estonian *17;* Lithuanian *10;* Swedish *5* (Uppsala *1,* Göteborg *2,* Lund *1,* Liungman *1);* Danish *3;* Irish *2;* French *2;* Spanish *1;* Catalan: Amades No. 75; Dutch *2;* German *15* (Archive *14,* Henssen Volk No. 140); Czech: Tille Soupis I 197 *1;* Russian: Afanasiev *8;* Greek *1;* India *3.* — Spanish-American: Hansen (Dominican Republic) *1.* — African (Ilo of Rodesia): Smith and Dale II 387 No. 13.
1062. *Throwing the Stone.* Bird. In a contest in throwing, the ogre throws a stone, the hero a bird [K18.3]. Cf. Type 1640.
  *BP I 148 (Grimm No. 20); Coffin *1.* — Finnish *26;* Finnish-Swedish *4;* Estonian *15;* Livonian *2;* Lithuanian *31;* Swedish *6* (Uppsala *4;* Lund *1,* Liungman *1);* Norwegian *2;* Danish *2;* Irish *146;* French *8;* Spanish *3;* Catalan: Amades No. 2; Flemish *2;* German *34* (Archive *33,* Meckl. No. 100); Hungarian *5;* Czech: Tille Soupis I 190ff., 269ff. *18;* Slovenian *5;* Serbocroatian *3;* Russian: Andrejev; Greek *2.* — Spanish-American: Rael Nos. 291, 292, 241 (U.S.), Hansen (Argentina) *1;* (Chile) *1;* Cape Verde Islands: Parsons MAFLS XV (1) 114; West Indies (Negro) *2;* American Indian: Thompson *C Coll* II 433. — African *1.*
1063 *Throwing Contest with Golden Club.* The hero shows the ogre the club on a cloud [K18.2]. Cf. Type 1640.
  *Köhler-Bolte I 86; Coffin *6.* — Finnish *248;* Finnish-Swedish *19;* Estonian *31;* Livonian *6;* Lithuanian *30;* Lappish *10;* Swedish *10* (Uppsala *5,* Stockholm *3,* misc. *2);* Norwegian *2;* Danish *9;* Icelandic *1;* Irish *4;* French *4;* Catalan: Amades No. 78, cf. 75; German *10;* Austrian: Haiding No. 65; Italian (Tuscan [1005] *1);* Hungarian *7;* Czech: Tille Soupis I 185ff., 190ff. *8;* Slovenian *2;* Serbocroatian *2;* Russian: Andrejev *Ukraine 13,* Afanasiev *18.* — Franco-American: Barbeau JAFL XXIX 22; Spanish-American: Hansen (Argentina) *1,* (Chile) *1,* (Dominican Republic) *1,* (Puerto Rico) *4* cf. (Puerto Rico **1152) *1;* American Indian: Thompson *C Coll* II 433.
1063A *Throwing Contest: Trickster Shouts.* Is trying to warn people beyond the sea. (Or he warns Angel Gabriel or Saint Peter.) [K18.1, K18.1.1, K18.1.2].
  *Köhler-Bolte I 64. — U.S.: Baughman; American Negro (Michi-

gan): Dorson No. 23; N. A. Indian (Penobscot): Speck JAFL XXVIII 56.

1063B *Throwing Contest: Trickster will Throw Stone* to Constantinople where ogre's sister lives.
Greek *5*, Kretschmer 126 No. 33.

1064 *Making Fire by Stamping on Ground.* Hot ashes prepared beforehand.
Greek *4*, Hahn No. 18.

1064* changed to 1060**.

1065* *Contest in Chopping.*

1065A* Hans chops up the wood with the help of a wedge [K44].
Livonian *1*.

1065B* Hans breaks his axe to pieces; cf. Type 1050.
Livonian (1065') *1*.

1066 *Deceptive Game: Hanging Each Other.* Dupe really hanged. [K852].
*Penzer I 157; *Köhler-Bolte I 210, 585; Icelandic: Boberg; Danish: Christensen DF XLVII 200 No. 36; Estonian: Aarne FFC XXV 122 Nos. 40—42; Swiss: Jegerlehner *Oberwallis* 326 No. 19; Africa (Basuto): Jacottet 30 No. 3.

1070 *Wrestling Contest: Looks Where to Throw him.* The ogre squeezes the man so that his eyes bulge out. The ogre: »Why do you glare so?» »I am looking to see where to throw you.» The ogre flees. [K12.1].
**Hackman *En Finländsk-Svensk Saga av Osteuropeiskt Ursprung* (*Brages Årsskrift* IV, Helsingfors 1910). — Finnish *1*; Danish *1*; Russian: Andrejev; Greek *8*, Hahn No. 18; Albanian: Dozon *Contes albanais* No. 3; Turkish: Radloff VIII No. 6 (= Kunos [1905] No. 8).

1071 *Wrestling Contest (with Old Grandfather).* The man challenged by ogre to wrestling contest persuades the ogre to wrestle his old grandfather, i.e., a bear [K12.2].
**Hackman *En Finländsk-Svensk Saga av Osteuropeiskt Ursprung* (*Brages Årsskrift* IV, Helsingfors 1910); Köhler-Bolte I 477ff. — Finnish *125;* Finnish-Swedish *6;* Estonian *17;* Livonian *1;* Lithuanian *37;* German *5* (Archive *4*, Henssen Volk No. 162); Czech: Tille Soupis I 193f.; Slovenian *1;* Russian: Andrejev *Ukraine 14,* Afanasiev *20.*

1072 *Race with Little Son.* The man challenged by the ogre to running race persuades the ogre to race his little son, i.e., a rabbit [K11.6].
**Hackman *En Finländsk-Svensk Saga av Osteuropeiskt Ursprung* (*Brages Årsskrift* IV, Helsingfors 1910); Köhler-Bolte I 477ff. — Finnish *131;* Finnish-Swedish *5;* Estonian *20;* Lithuanian *41;* Lappish *1;* Swedish (Uppsala) *1;* German *5* (Archive *4*, Henssen Volk No. 162); Hungarian *10;* Czech: Tille Soupis I 185ff., 190ff. *8;* Slovenian *1;* Russian: Andrejev *Ukraine 4,* Afanasiev *23;* Turkish: Eberhard-Boratav cf. No. 162 III.

1073 *Climbing Contest.* The man challenged by the ogre to a climbing contest.

The ogre agrees to contest against man's young one, i.e., a squirrel. [K15.1].

*Hackman *En Finländsk-Svensk Saga av Osteuropeiskt Ursprung* (*Brages Årsskrift* IV, Helsingfors 1910); Köhler-Bolte I 477ff. — Finnish *8;* Finnish-Swedish *2;* Lithuanian *2;* German *4;* Russian: Andrejev.

1074 *Race Won by Deception: Relative Helpers.* The trickster gets others like him to take places in the line of the race. The dupe sees them and thinks the trickster is outrunning him. [K11.1]. (Often told of animals). Cf. Types 275, 275A.

*BP III 343 (Grimm No. 187); Dähnhardt IV 48; Coffin *15.* — Finnish *9;* Finnish-Swedish *1;* Estonian *5;* Lithuanian (*92) *5;* Swedish *56* (Uppsala *6,* Stockholm *3,* Göteborg *31,* Liungman *4,* misc. *12*); Irish *23;* British *2;* Spanish (275*A) *3;* Catalan: Amades No. 305; Flemish *1;* German *1;* Austrian: Haiding No. 62; Russian: Andrejev; Turkish: Eberhard-Boratav No. *42;* India *13.* — Spanish-American: Hansen (275*A) (Argentina) *1,* (Cuba) *2,* (Peru) *2,* (Puerto Rico) *2;* West Indies (Negro) *10;* American Negro (Michigan): Dorson No. 4, (North Carolina): Parsons JAFL XXX 174; American Indian: Thompson *C Coll* II 441, 448. — African *38.*

1075* *Jumping from the Church Tower.* The devil is not allowed to look behind him. The man runs down stairs (or throws his shirt down). [K17.2].
Estonian *2.*

1080* *Laughing Contest.* Dead horse with grinning mouth. The ogre tries to laugh as long as the horse and laughs till he dies. [K87.1; cf. J1169.5].
Rumanian (1332*) *16;* Russian: Andrejev (1080) *1.*

1081 *Contests* in which other animals than those mentioned (bear, rabbit, horse) help the man [K2].

1082 *Carrying the Horse.* The ogre carries the horse on his back and soon has to stop. The man carries it between his legs, *i.e.,* rides. [K72]. Cf. Type 1640.

Köhler-Bolte I 473. — Finnish *14;* Finnish-Swedish *1;* Estonian *8;* Lappish *1;* German *4;* Czech: Tille Soupis I 192f. *3;* Russian: Afanasiev *2.*

1082A *The Soldier Who Rode on Death.* The soldier's bargain with Death: while one carries the other, the one carried is to sing. When it is the soldier's turn to sing, he sings an endless song, so that Death leaves him in peace.

Lithuanian (*1084A) *2;* Serbocroatian *1;* Russian: Andrejev (1084 I) *5;* Rumanian (1615*) *1.*

1083 *Duel with Long Poles or Cudgels.* The rascal with the short pole comes to the ogre and beats him. Then they exchange. The rascal again punishes him. Suggests that he can protect himself by going into the pig-sty. The ogre goes and the rascal beats him through a hole in the wall. [K785].

Lithuanian *19;* French *14;* Italian (Tuscan 1095 b *1*); Hungarian: Honti (1069, 1083) *4;* Slovenian *6;* Serbocroatian *1;* Russian: Andrejev *2.*

1083A *The Duel: Bayonet and Pitchfork.* The man: »You will give me but one wound, with one thrust I shall give you five»; they exchange weapons; the man takes his place behind the fence.
Lithuanian (1083) *19*.

1084 *Contest in Shrieking or Whistling.* The man binds up the ogre's head and then strikes him in the eye. [K84.1].
Bolte Zs. f. Vksk. IX 86. — Finnish *67;* Finnish-Swedish *6;* Estonian *1;* Livonian *2;* Lithuanian *19;* Swedish *3* (Uppsala *2*, misc. *1*); Norwegian *2;* Danish *1;* Catalan: Amades No. 78; German *5;* Austrian: Haiding No. 65; Hungarian *4;* Czech: Tille Soupis I 185ff., 190ff. *8;* Slovenian *1;* Serbocroatian *1;* Russian: Andrejev *Ukraine 17*, Afanasiev *10*.

1085 *Pushing a Hole into a Tree.* Contest with ogre, to push a hole in a tree with his head. The hero has already cut a hole with his axe. [K61]. Cf. Types 1086, 1640.
*BP I 163; Köhler-Bolte I 86; Coffin *5*. — Finnish *108;* Finnish-Swedish *1;* Estonian *9;* Livonian *4;* Lappish *8;* Swedish *9* (Uppsala *1*, Stockholm *2*, Liungman *4*, misc. *2*); Norwegian *1;* Serbocroatian *1;* Russian: Andrejev *1;* India *1*. — Spanish-American: Rael Nos. 291, 292 (U.S.), Hansen (Chile) *1*, (Puerto Rico) *4;* West Indies (Negro) *1;* American Indian: Thompson *C Coll* II 433.

1086 *Jumping into the Ground.* A hole already dug and covered with boughs [K17.1]. Cf. Type 1085.
Finnish *21;* Finnish-Swedish *2;* Estonian *4;* Russian: Andrejev. — Spanish-American: Hansen (Argentina) *1*.

1087 *Rowing Contest.* Boat already sawed through [K14].
Finnish *13;* Russian: Andrejev.

1088 *Eating Contest.* The hero slips his food (or drink) into a bag and makes the ogre believe he is the greater eater. (In many versions the hero cuts open the bag; the ogre imitates and kills himself). [K81.1].
Köhler-Bolte I 186; Espinosa III 130—140, 222—228. — Finnish *38;* Finnish-Swedish *7;* Livonian *1;* Lappish *5;* Swedish *87* (Uppsala *27*, Stockholm *2*, Göteborg *18*, Lund *6*, Liungman *7*, misc. *27*); Norwegian *15*, Solheim *1;* Danish *7;* Scottish *2;* Irish *240*, Beal IV 228f. No. 6, XVII 211ff.; English *4;* French *3;* Spanish *3;* Catalan: Amades Nos. 2, 154; Dutch *4;* Flemish *3;* German *2* (Meckl. No. 100, Henssen Volk No. 169); Austrian: Haiding No. 62; Italian (Sicilian *2*, Gonzenbach No. 41); Hungarian: cf. Tille Soupis II 181ff.; Czech: Tille Soupis I 271ff. *5;* Slovenian *2;* Russian: Andrejev *Ukraine 5;* Greek *3;* Turkish: Eberhard-Boratav cf. No. 162 III, 351 IV; India *1*. — English-American: Baughman *2;* Spanish-American: Hansen (Puerto Rico) *1;* West Indies (Negro) *2;* American Indian: Thompson *C Coll* II 365; 432 (B).

1089 (formerly 1089*) *Threshing Contest* [K42].
Livonian (1089) *1*, Lithuanian *4;* Swedish *4* (Uppsala *1*, Lund *1*,

Liungman *1*, misc. *1*); Irish *1;* German *16;* Hungarian *1;* Russian: Andrejev *1.*

1088* *Deceptive Contest in Drinking Whisky.* The man drinks water, the devil is given vinegar. [K82.3].
Lithuanian (1089*) *4.*

1090 *Mowing Contest.* The man takes the center of the field. The ogre is given a dull sickle and mows around the outside of the field. Tires himself out. [K42.2]. Cf. Type 820.
Estonian *8;* Livonian *1;* Swedish *18* (Uppsala *7*, Stockholm *2*, Göteborg *1*, Liungman *2*, misc. *6*); Danish *11;* Scottish *1,* Irish *37,* English *2,* (*1090A) *3;* German *10.* — West Indies (Negro) *2.*

1091 *Who Can Bring an Unheard-of Riding-Horse.* The man sends his naked wife on all fours in tar and feathers. The devil has never seen such a horse and is defeated [K216.2].
*BP I 411, III 358; MSFO XC 90 No. 42; Dähnhardt I 194. — Finnish *181;* Finnish-Swedish *3;* Estonian *17;* Lithuanian *10;* Lappish *1;* Swedish *18* (Uppsala *3*, Stockholm *2*, Göteborg *7*, Lund *2*, Liungman *1*, misc. *3*); Danish *1;* Irish *5;* Basque *1;* French *14;* Spanish *1;* Catalan: Amades cf. No. 216; Walloon *1;* German *26* (Archive *24*, Meckl. No. 101, Henssen Volk No. 164); Czech: Tille Soupis I 183ff., II (2), cf. 138—141 *32;* Slovenian *1;* Serbocroatian *6;* Russian: Andrejev *2.*

1091A *Guessing the Name of the Devil's Secret Plant* (Tobacco) [H522, K216.2.1].
French *5;* Dutch (1183) *3.*

1092 *Who Can Shoot an Unheard-of Bird* [K31.1]. Similar to Type 1091.
Finnish *73;* Finnish-Swedish *3;* Estonian *4;* Lithuanian *6;* Swedish *9* (Uppsala *1*, Stockholm *2*, Göteborg *3*, Lund *1*, Liungman *1*, misc. *1*); Danish *2;* German *3* (Archive *2*, Meckl. No. 48); Italian (Tuscan *1*); Czech: Tille Soupis I 184 *2;* Serbocroatian *3;* Russian: Andrejev; India *1.* — Spanish-American: Hansen (Argentina) *1,* (Dominican Republic) *1;* West Indies (Negro) *1.*

1093 *Contest in Words. Maxims.* — Usually the devil and the girl [K91]. Cf. Type 875 part II.
Finnish *29;* Swedish *64* (Uppsala *46*, Stockholm *11*, Göteborg *1*, Liungman *3*, misc. *3*); German *1;* Italian (Tuscan 152 a, b *2*); Hungarian *1;* Slovenian *2;* Russian: Andrejev. — Spanish-American: Hansen (Argentina) *1.*

1094 *Contest in Cursing:* arrows sent as curses to ogre [K91].
Hungarian *1;* Russian: Andrejev.

1095 *Contest in Scratching Each Other with the Nails.* The man sends his wife to meet the ogre with whom he is to have the scratching contest. She tells the devil that her husband has gone to have his nails sharpened. She shows him deep wounds her husband has scratched on her body (obscene). The ogre leaves in terror. [K83.1].

*BP III 356, 363; Penzer III 34; Bolte Zs. f. vgl. Litgsch. (n. F.) VII 456. — Finnish *4;* Swedish *3* (Göteborg *1,* Liungman *1,* misc. *1*); Danish *7,* Kristensen *Danske Sagn* I (1892) 454; French *4;* Walloon *1;* German *9;* Italian (Tuscan *2*); Hungarian *1;* Czech: Tille Soupis I 191f., 275f., cf. 190 *4;* Slovenian *2;* Russian: Andrejev *1;* Spanish-American: Hansen (**169) (Puerto Rico) *1.*

1095A *Contest in Scratching Skin off Each Other;* covering self with several ox-hides. [K83.2].
Lithuanian (*1098) *2.*

1096 *The Tailor and the Ogre in a Sewing Contest.* The ogre sews with the whole length of the thread. When he returns from the first stitch, the tailor has his task ready. [K47].

Finnish *16;* Finnish-Swedish *1;* Estonian *2;* Swedish *149* (Uppsala *55,* Stockholm *12,* Göteborg *48,* Lund *13,* Liungman *11,* misc. *10*); Danish *2;* German *13;* Italian (Tuscan *2*); Hungarian *1;* Slovenian *6;* Russian: Andrejev; India *1.*

1097 *The Ice Mill.* Like Type 43 with man and ogre in place of animals. Cf. J741.
French *9;* Russian: Andrejev.

1097* *Contest in Enduring Cold.* The wind overcomes the frost. [H1541.2].
Finnish-Swedish *1.*

1110* *Hans Shows the Devil how Men are Made.* (Obscene).
Livonian *1.*

1115—1129 Attempts to Murder the Hero

1115 *Attempted Murder with Hatchet.* Butter cask (or the like) in the hero's bed so that the ogre coming to murder him stabs the object. [K525.1]. Cf. Type 1640.

*Anderson in Tauscher *Volksmärchen* 191; BP I 148 (Grimm No. 20); Köhler-Bolte Zs. f. Vksk. VI 73 (to Gonz. No. 35); Liungman SSF III 445. — Finnish *195;* Finnish-Swedish *9;* Estonian *19;* Lithuanian *10;* Lappish *11;* Swedish *33* (Uppsala *19,* Stockholm *3,* Göteborg *3,* Lund *1,* Liungman *7*); Norwegian *20;* Danish *47,* Grundtvig Nos. 54, 55; Irish *95;* English *4;* French *1;* Spanish *1;* Catalan: Amades No. 154; Dutch *1;* Flemish *4;* German Archive *23;* Italian (Sicilian *1,* Gonzenbach No. 41); Hungarian *11;* Czech: Tille Soupis I 270ff. *14;* Slovenian *2;* Serbo-croatian *6;* Russian: Andrejev *3;* Greek *9,* Hahn Nos. 16, 231; Turkish: Eberhard-Boratav No. 162; Iran: Christensen p. 9; India *4;* English-American: Baughman *1;* Spanish-American: Hansen (Puerto Rico) *1;* West Indies (Negro) *1.* — African *10.*

1116 *Attempt at Burning.* The hero escapes and after the room he is in is burned he returns and is found sitting on the ashes. »It was a bit hot,» he says. [K1733].

Finnish *137;* Finnish-Swedish *1;* Estonian *5;* Lithuanian *7;* Lappish *4;* Swedish *13* (Uppsala *4*, Stockholm *1*, misc. *8*); Norwegian *2;* Flemish *1;* Hungarian *1;* Serbocroatian *1;* Russian: Andrejev *1;* Greek *3;* Turkish: Eberhard-Boratav No. 162 III.

1116* *Attempt at Drowning.*
Finnish-Swedish *1*.

1117. *The Ogre's Pitfall.* Tricked into falling into it himself [K1601].
Finnish *11;* Lithuanian *1;* Swedish (misc.) *2*. — Spanish-American: Hansen (Puerto Rico) *1*.

1118* *The Abandonement on the Island.* The man conceals himself in the ogre's clothes. [K1616.2].
Finnish; Russian: Andrejev (1118).

1119 *The Ogre Kills his Own Children.* Places changed in bed (night-caps) [K1611]. Cf. Type 327 B.

*BP I 124 note 1 (Grimm No. 15); *Anderson *Novelline* No. 44; Cox *Cinderella* 476, Coffin *13*. — Finnish *41;* Estonian *4;* Lithuanian *1;* Swedish *26* (Uppsala *12*, Stockholm *1*, Liungman *2*, misc. *11*); Danish *1;* Icelandic (cf. Types 328, 471); Scottish *1;* Irish *127;* Flemish *2;* Austrian: Haiding No. 68; Italian (Sicilian: Gonzenbach No. 83); Rumanian *2;* Hungarian *1;* Czech: Tille FFC XXXIV 162; Slovenian *2;* Russian Andrejev; Greek *21;* Turkish: Eberhard-Boratav Nos. 160, 161 *11;* India *5*. — English-American: Baughman *2;* Spanish-American: Hansen (Dominican Republic) *1*, (Puerto Rico) *1;* Cape Verde Islands: Parsons MAFLS XV (1) 73 n. 3; West Indies (Negro) *7;* American Indian: Thompson *C Coll* II 358ff. F. — African *14*.

1120 *The Ogre's Wife Thrown into the Water* [cf. G519.1.4].
Finnish *17;* Estonian *3;* Livonian *4;* Lithuanian *25;* Swedish *8* (Uppsala *1*, Liungman 1, misc. *6*); Danish *1;* Irish *1;* Spanish *1;* German *1;* Hungarian *1;* Berze Nagy (1015**) *1;* Serbocroatian *3;* Russian: Andrejev *Ukraine* 13, Afanasiev *14;* Greek *4;* Turkish: Eberhard-Boratav No. 108 III, 357. — Spanish-American: Hansen (Dominican Republic) *1*.

1121 *Ogre's Wife Burned in his Own Oven* [G512.3.2.1]. Cf. Type 327A.
Cosquin *Etudes* 349ff.; *BP I 115ff. (Grimm No. 15), especially 123; Coffin *2*. — Finnish *133;* Finnish-Swedish *2*, (327) *4;* Estonian (see 327A); Lithuanian (*327C, *327D); Lappish *1;* Swedish *40* (Uppsala *4*, Stockholm *1*, Lund *1*, Göteborg *9*, Liungman *10*, misc. *15*); Danish *1;* Irish *79*, Beal IV 244 No. 6; German *2;* Hungarian *1;* Russian: Andrejev; Greek *7*, Hahn No. 95; Turkish: Eberhard-Boratav No. 161 III; India *17*. — English-American: Baughman *2;* Spanish-American: Hansen (Puerto Rico) *1;* American Indian: Thompson *C Coll* II 358ff. F^1. — African (Angola): Chatelain 113 No. 8.

1122 *Ogre's Wife Killed through Other Tricks* [G519.1].

*BP I 115ff. (Grimm No. 15). — Finnish *12;* Irish *2;* Flemish *1;* Slovenian *2;* Russian: Andrejev; Greek *3;* India *1.* — Spanish-American: Hansen (Dominican Republic) *1.*

1130 *Counting out Pay.* Hole in the hat, and hat over a pit [K275].
*BP III 421 (Grimm No. 195); Coffin 2. — Finnish *200;* Finnish-Swedish *5;* Estonian *45;* Livonian *7;* Lithuanian *38;* Lappish *5;* Swedish *25* (Uppsala *6,* Stockholm *4,* Göteborg *10,* Liungman *2,* misc. *3*); Danish *2;* French *8;* German *26* (Archive *24,* Henssen Jül No. 82, Henssen Volk No. 167); Czech: Tille Soupis 182f. *1;* Slovenian *1;* Serbocroatian *1;* Russian: Andrejev *Ukraine 17,* Afanasiev *16.* — West Indies (Negro) *2.* — Literary Treatments: Baughman 3.

1130* *Two Caskets.* The boy chooses between two caskets (gold and fire). Lappish *1.*

1131 *The Hot Porridge in the Ogre's Throat.* The ogre tricked into burning his throat with hot porridge. [K1033].
Finnish *113;* Finnish-Swedish *6;* Estonian *48;* Lappish *1;* Swedish *220* (Uppsala *168,* Stockholm *21,* Göteborg *1,* Liungman *7,* misc. *23*); Norwegian *20,* Solheim *3;* Danish *1;* Russian: Andrejev.

1132 *Flight of the Ogre with his Goods in the Bag.* The man hides in the bag. [G561]. Cf. Type 311.
*Anderson in Tauscher *Volksmärsehcn* 186; Liungman SSF III 445 No. 1132. — Finnish *84;* Finnish-Swedish *1;* Estonian *23;* Livonian *2;* Lithuanian *8;* Hungarian: Berze Nagy 1014** *2;* Serbocroatian *2;* Russian: Afanasiev *23,* Andrejev *Ukraine 13;* Turkish: Eberhard-Boratav No. 357 *16.* — African (Congo): Weeks 202 No. 1, 212 No. 7. — Literary Treatments: Chauvin VI 30 No. 201.

1133 *Making the Ogre Strong (by Castration).* Same as Type 153 with the ogre in place of the bear.
Motifs: K1012.1. Making the dupe strong — by castration. K241. The castration bargain: wife sent. The trickster castrates the dupe and is to come the next day and be castrated himself. He sends his wife as substitute.
Finnish *14;* Estonian *1;* Lithuanian *8;* Swedish *3* (Uppsala *1,* Stockholm *2*); Danish *13,* Kristensen *Danske Sagn* I (1892) 441, (1928) 276—81; French *3;* Russian: Andrejev *2.*

1134 *Healing the Ogre or Making him Strong* by scalding or injuring otherwise [K1012.2].
Finnish-Swedish *2;* Livonian *1;* Danish *7;* Russian: Andrejev; Greek *5.* — West Indies (Negro) *1.*

1135 *Eye-Remedy.* A glowing mass is put into his eye [K1011]. Cf. Type 1137.
*BP III 375 (incident A). — Finnish *145;* Finnish-Swedish *3;* Estonian *63* (cf. also 1018*, aqua fortis); Livonian *5;* Lithuanian *6;* Lappish *4;* Swedish *21* (Uppsala *2,* Stockholm *3,* Göteborg *5,* Lund *1,* Liungman

2, misc. *8*); Irish *1;* Italian (Tuscan 1139 *1*); Slovenian *5;* Russian: Andrejev.

1136 *Same Episode with Other Deceits of the Ogre* (cobold, water-nix, etc.). [K824.1, K1010].

*BP III 375. — Finnish *35;* Finnish-Swedish *8;* Estonian *1;* Livonian *1;* Norwegian: Solheim *2;* Danish *1;* German *1;* Albanian: Lambertz 9f.

1137 *The Ogre Blinded* (*Polyphemus*). Escape under the ram's belly. Cf. Type 1135.

Motifs: G100. Giant ogre. Polyphemus. K1011. Eye-remedy. Under pretence of curing eyesight the trickster blinds the dupe. (Often with a glowing mass thrust into the eye.) K521.1. Escape by dressing in animal (bird, human) skin. K602. »Noman.» K603. Escape under ram's belly.

**Hackman *Die Polyphemsage in der Volksüberlieferung* (Helsingfors, 1904); *BP III 375ff., incidents A^1, B^1, (Grimm No. 191 a); Coffin *1;* Anderson on Wesselski 46 n.; Delarue: unpublished study. — Finnish *25;* Finnish-Swedish *1;* Estonian *5;* Livonian *1;* Lithuanian *20* (cf. also *1137A) *14;* Lappish *17;* Swedish *19* (Uppsala *2,* Stockholm *3,* Göteborg *5,* Lund *1,* misc. *8*); Norwegian *3;* Icelandic (327A) *8;* Irish *83,* Beal I 9, IV 311, 453; English *2;* French *11;* Spanish *2;* Catalan: Amades Nos. 110, 1462, 1565, 1906; Flemish *2;* German *2;* Italian *5* (Tuscan 1139 *1*, Sicilian *4*); Rumanian *10,* Sainenu 99; Hungarian: Honti 1137, Berze Nagy 1137 + 1141* *6;* Czech: Tille Soupis II (1) 239 *4;* Slovenian *3;* Serbocroatian *6;* Russian: Afanasiev *5;* Greek *9,* Dawkins *More Greek Folktales* No. 4; Turkish: Eberhard-Boratav No. 146 *5;* India *1.*

1138 *Gilding the Beard.* A man named »Such a one» persuades the ogre to have his beard gilded. Covers it with tar, and leaves the ogre caught to the tar-kettle. The ogre with his kettle wanders about and asks everyone »Have you seen such a one?» [K1013.1].

Finnish *40;* Estonian *11;* Lithuanian *18;* Scottish *2;* Italian (Tuscan [1444] a, b *2*); Slovenian *3;* Serbocroatian *1;* Russian: Andrejev *4;* Chinese: Eberhard FFC CXXVIII No. 158. — Spanish-American: Hansen (1940**I) (Puerto Rico) *1,* (1940**J) (Puerto Rico) *1,* (Chile) *1.*

1139 *The Ogre Carries the Sham-Dead Man.* »He smells already» [K522.2].
Finnish *21;* Irish *1;* Russian: Andrejev.

1140 (formerly 1140*) *Sleeping with Open Eyes.* The man claims to do this and deceives the devil into sleeping first [K331.1].
Finnish (1140*) *2;* Slovenian *1;* Russian: Afanasiev.

1141 (formerly 1141*) *Drinking Girl's Reflection.* The ogre attempts to drink the lake dry because he sees in the water the reflection of a girl sitting in the top of a tree [J1791.6.2]. Cf. Types 34, 408.
Estonian (1141*) *41;* India *3;* Japanese: Ikeda (J1791.6.2).

1142 *Hot Tin under the Tail of the Ogre's Horse.* The smith promises to make the horse wild. The ogre on the horse's back. [K1181].

*Wesselski *Hodscha Nasreddin* I 224 No. 64. — Estonian (1142*) *3;* Swedish *9* (Stockholm *3*, Göteborg *1*, misc. *5*); Flemish (1682*) *1*.

1143 *Ogre Otherwise Injured.*

1143A *Ogre's Tongue Cut Off through Hole in Door.* Cannot speak plainly and gets into trouble.
French Canadian *6*.

1143B *Who Has the Longer Nose?* Ogre's nose caught in ventilation hole in roof.
French Canadian *3*.

1143C *Ogre Persuaded to Sit on Pole.* Pierced to death. [K1116].
French Canadian *2*.

1145—1154 The Ogre Frightened or Overawed

[G570, K212, F615.3]. Cf. Type 1070.

1145 *The Ogre Afraid of what Rustles or Rattles.* The man sets juniper on fire [K2345].
Finnish *24;* Livonian *1;* Danish *2;* Russian: Andrejev; Greek *1;* Japanese: Ikeda (K2345).

1146 *Millstones.* Said to be pearls of hero's mother [K1718.2].
Finnish *21;* Swedish *2* (Stockholm *1*, misc. *1*); German *1;* Serbo-croatian *1;* Russian: Andrejev.

1147 *Thunder the Rolling of his Brother's Wagon.* Thus explained by the hero [K718.1].
Finnish *6;* Finnish-Swedish *2;* Swedish *2* (Stockholm *1*, Liungman *1*); Russian: Andrejev; West Indies (Negro) *1*.

1147* *The Friendship between a Man (Carpenter), Thunder-god, and the Devil.* They build themselves a house and plant potatoes (beets). A fairy comes to steal their vegetables. She flogs both Thunder and the devil guarding the vegetables, but she is outwitted by the man in a frightening contest.
Lithuanian (*1147A) *11;* Russian: Andrejev (*176) *2.*

1148 *The Ogre Afraid of the Thunder* (the storm).

1148A *The Ogre Asks the Man to Tell him when it Thunders.* The man deceives him until at last the thunder kills him. [K1177].
Finnish *41;* Estonian *42;* Lappish *1;* Swedish *5* (Stockholm *1*, Liungman *1*, misc. *3*); Danish *1;* Russian: Andrejev (1148).

1148B *The Ogre Steals the Thunder's Instruments (Pipe, Sack, etc.).*
**Loorits *Das Märchen vom gestohlenen Donnerinstrument bei den Esten* (Tartu 1932); Krohn *Skandinavisk Mytologi* 202. — Swedish (Liungman) *1;* Danish *2*.

1149 *Children Desire Ogre's Flesh* (and the like). The man makes the ogre believe that his children eat ogre's flesh. The ogre is frightened away. Cf. Type 125.

Motifs: K1715. Weak animal (man) makes large (ogre) believe that he has eaten many of the large one's companions. K1715.1. Weak animal shows strong his own reflection and frightens him. K1716. Hare as ambassador of the moon. Hare claims to be ambassador of moon. Shows elephant the moon irritated in a spring. Elephant is persuaded that the moon is angry. K1715.2. Bluff: only one tiger; you promised ten. Child (or shepherd) calls out to the small hero (ape, hare) and makes the tiger (ogre) think that he is lucky to escape alive.

*Anderson in Tauscher *Volksmärchen* 171; Aarne FFC XI 154; Brown *American Journal of Philology* XLII 122; *BP I 160 n. 1, III 75 n. 2; Penzer V 49 n. 1; Espinosa III Nos. 255f., 266. — Finnish-Swedish *1;* Lithuanian *3;* Spanish (103*A) *2;* Catalan: Amades, cf. No. 329; Italian (Tuscan [101] *1*); Hungarian *11;* Serbocroatian *2;* Russian: Afanasiev *6;* Turkish: Radloff VIII No. 6 (= Kunos [1905] No. 8), Eberhard-Boratav 162 IV; India *39;* Chinese: Eberhard FFC CXX Nos. M3, M10, FFC CXXVIII Nos. 2, 7, Graham No. 203. — Spanish-American: Hansen (Puerto Rico) *1;* Cape Verde Islands: Parsons MAFLS XV (1) 322; West Indies (Negro) *2.*

1149* »*These Bring the Demons to Life*» (the fire shines). The devil flees away.
Russian: Andrejev (1149 I) *1.*

1150 »*St. George's Dogs.*» (Wolves). Man says, »St. George's dogs are coming!» The ogre flees. [K1725].
*BP III 199. — Estonian *87;* Russian: Andrejev.

1151 *Big Shoes in Front of the Barn.* The man makes giant shoes and places them so that the ogre thinks a giant lives there. [K1717].
Finnish *3;* Swedish (Stockholm) *1;* Russian: Andrejev.

1151* *Boats Said to Be Girl's Shoes,* a bath-house, her cap.
Russian: Andrejev (*1151 I) *1.*

1152 *The Ogre Overawed by Displaying Objects.* See Type 1161A.
A man or men, hiding in a house, try to overawe an ogre by claiming to be even greater ogres. The ogre demands proof. The men poke through the door or window, objects which they have accidentally picked up on their journey and the ogre is intimidated [N691]. A list of the objects used together with the object the ogre mistakes them for follows: (a) A rope is thought to be a hair [K1711.1, K1715.12]. (b) A winnowing fan is thought to be an ear [K1715.12]. (c) Curds or lime, etc., are thought to be spittle [G572.1, K1715.12]. (d) Asked to beat his chest, man beats a drum. (e) Asked to hear his voice, man twists tail of donkey which brays [K2324.1]. (f) A turtle is thought to be a louse from the hero's body. (g) A sword or knife is thought to be his tongue [G572.2], etc. (h) A tree trunk is thought to be his leg. (j) A tub or pot is thought to be his belly, head, etc.
India *13.*

1153 *Wages: as Much as he Can Carry.* To get rid of the boy the master offers him as large wages as he is able to carry himself. The boy says that he will be contented with what the troll can carry. [K1732]. Cf. Type 650.

Lithuanian *3;* Swedish *10* (Uppsala *3,* Stockholm *1,* Lund *1,* Liungman *2,* misc. *3*); Norwegian (1153**) *9;* Danish *8.*

1154 *The Man Who Falls From the Tree and the Demons.* Cf. Types 121, 1653.

I. *Tree Refuge.* Two men take refuge in a tree. Below them (a) demons or (b) tigers assemble. One man, through accident, or overcome by fear, falls from the tree in the midst of the demons or tigers. The man in the tree shouts »Grab the biggest one for me,» or the like, and the demons or tigers flee.

II. *To Bring Demon Skins.* The man (men) first overawes a demon by claiming to have been sent to collect the skins of demons, etc. Cf. Type 1149.

India *12.*

1154* *Devil Afraid of the Hole in which he was held Captive.*
Lithuanian *2.*

1155 *»A Peck of Grain for Each Stack.»* The man makes very small stacks. [K181].
Finnish *43;* Russian: Afanasiev.

1156 *The Ogre Tars the Hero's Boat,* thinking to injure him [J2171.1.2].
Finnish *5;* Russian: Andrejev.

1157 *The Gun as Tobacco Pipe.* The trickster gives the ogre the gun to smoke [K1057]. Cf. Type 1228.

*BP II 530 n. *2;* Feilberg Ordbog III 814 a s.v. »tobak». — Finnish *2;* Estonian *13;* Livonian *2;* Lithuanian *7,* (1860* clarinet) *2;* Swedish *10* (Uppsala *3,* Stockholm *4,* Lund *1,* misc. *2*); Danish *9;* French *1;* Dutch *2;* German *16;* Slovenian *3;* Russian: Andrejev. — English-American: Baughman *2.*

1158 *The Ogre Wants to Look through the Gun Barrel* in the smithy. The smith shoots. [J2131.4.1]. Cf. Type 1228.

Finnish *56;* Lappish *1;* Norwegian *1;* German: Henssen Volk No. 162; Slovenian *2;* Russian: Andrejev.

1159 *The Ogre Wants to Learn to Play.* Finger caught in a cleft of a tree. [K1111.0.1]. Later he is terrified by the man's wife with her legs apart. He thinks he is to be caught again [K1755]. Cf. Types 151, 326, 1095.

*BP I 68 (Grimm No. 8), II 99 n. 1, 421, 530. — Finnish *104;* Finnish-Swedish *4;* Estonian *15;* Lithuanian *6;* Swedish *86* (Uppsala *31,* Stockholm *9,* Göteborg *9,* Lund *11,* Liungman *10,* misc. *16*); Scottish *1;* Catalan: Amades cf. No. 154; Flemish *1;* German *26;* Italian (Tuscan [1005] *1;* Hungarian *3,* Berze Nagy (1160*) *2;* Czech: Tille Soupis I 197, 200f., II (2) 389f. *13;* Slovenian *2;* Serbocroatian *1;* Russian: Afanasiev *6;* Greek *1.*

1160 *The Ogre in the Haunted Castle.* Beard caught fast. Cf. Type 326.
Motifs: E282. Ghosts haunt castle. K1111.1. Ogre's (dwarf) beard caught fast.
*BP III 259. — Finnish *108;* Finnish-Swedish *1;* Estonian *2;* Lappish *1;* Swedish *98* (Uppsala *6,* Stockholm *9,* Göteborg *46,* Lund *11,* Liungman *10,* misc. *16*); Norwegian *1;* Danish *1;* Flemish *1;* Hungarian *1;* Russian: Andrejev.

1161 *The Bear Trainer and his Bear.* The bear drives the ogre from the room. »Is the big cat still living?» Cf. Type 957. A man with a bear passes the night in a place frequented by ogres. The ogres come, discover the bear, think it is a cat, and try to feed it. The bear chases them all out. Later they ask whether the man still has the big white cat. The man answers that it now has many kittens, and the ogres promise never to come again. [K1728].
**Taylor MPh XVII 305—24; **Christiansen »Kjætten paa Dovre» *Videnskapsselskapets Skrifter* 2. kl. (1922) No. 6; Liestøl »Kjetta på Dovre» *Maal og Minne* 1933 pp. 24ff.; BP IV 173; Schier *Mitteldeutsche Blätter für Volkskunde* X (1935) 164ff.; Christiansen FFC CLXXV No. 6015; *Bolte Zs. f. Vksk. XXXIII—XXXIV 33—38, XLI 282f.; Hartmann *Trollvorstellungen* 19, 54. — Finnish *42;* Finnish-Swedish *2;* Estonian *19;* Lithuanian *26;* Swedish *42* (Uppsala *14,* Stockholm *4,* Göteborg *8,* Lund *5,* Liungman *3,* misc. *8*); Norwegian *32,* Solheim *5;* Danish *20,* Kristensen *Danske Sagn* I (1892) 434ff., (1928) 291f.; German *15* (Archive *14,* Meckl. No. 102); Czech: Tille Soupis II (2) 390f. *6;* Slovenian *10;* Russian: Andrejev *1.*

1161A *The Fatted Cow.* The devil gives the man a cow to be pastured for an indefinite length of time. After waiting in vain for the devil to claim his cow, the man sells it. When at last the devil does come for his cow, the man makes gifts of: his father's comb for combing whiskers (harrow), a whip (flail), a sugar-basin (large wooden mortar), a tobacco-box (trap). Instead of the cow, the man shows him a bear. The devil rides it and says: »How you have fattened my cow!»
Lithuanian (*1146A) *6;* Russian: Andrejev (*1161 I) *1.*

1162 *The Iron Man and the Ogre.* In order to save the king's daughter from the ogre an iron man is forged. The ogre is driven away. [K1756].
Estonian *3;* Lithuanian *4;* Swedish *2* (Göteborg *1,* Liungman *1*); Russian: Andrejev *5.*

1162* *The Devil and Children.* Devil does not go to picnic when he hears that there are many young children there. Nothing for him to do where there are young children.
Spanish (1149*A) *1.*

1163 *The Ogre Teaches the Smith how to Use Sand in Forging Iron.* The ogre blames the smith for his stupidity. Since then smiths have used sand. [G651].
Finnish *40;* Finnish-Swedish *2;* Estonian *15;* Lithuanian: Balys Le-

gends No. 753; Swedish (Uppsala) *4;* Danish *4;* German *5* (Archive *4,* Henssen Volk No. 104); Russian: Andrejev *1.*

1163* *The Devil and the Blacksmith.* Devil challenges smith to finish work in a limited time. Smith stops, hides the work, and claims that it is long since done.
Walloon *1.*

1164 *The Evil Woman Thrown into the Pit.* Belfagor. The ogre comes out, since he cannot remain below with her. [K2325, T251.1.4].
*BP I 382, 388, IV 176 n. 1; S. Prato RTP IV 174; *Laographia* XVII 137ff. — Finnish *39;* Estonian *17;* Lithuanian *19;* Lappish *2;* Swedish *6* (Uppsala *2,* Stockholm *1,* Lund *1,* misc. *2*); Danish *1;* Spanish (*340) *4;* Catalan: Amades No. 220; German *1;* Italian (Sicilian *1*); Rumanian *3;* Hungarian *2;* Czech: Tille Soupis I 87 *19;* Serbocroatian *2;* Russian: Andrejev *Ukraine 9,* Afanasiev *17;* Greek *5;* Turkish: Eberhard-Boratav No. 377 *4;* India *1.* — Portuguese American (Brazil): Camara Cascudo p. 40.

1164A *Devil Frightened by Threatening to Bring Mother-in-law* [K2325].
Lithuanian (*1164A) *24;* Spanish (*340) *3;* Serbocroatian *1.*

1164B *Even the Devil Cannot Live with a Widow.* The man, finding himself in hell, gladly declares that life there is much better for him, compared to the life he spent on earth with his wife. He makes a bargain with the devil: should the latter endure life with his wife for three years, the former would be set free from hell. The devil is the loser. [T251.1.2.2].
Lithuanian (*1164B) *11.*

1164C *Devil Baked inside a Loaf of Bread.* Is afraid of the woman.
Lithuanian (*1164C) *4.*

1164D *The Demon and the Man Join Forces.* Cf. Types 332, 1862B.
I. *The Cowed Demon.* (a) A woman drives off with a broom both her husband and a demon who lives nearby, or the woman frightens a demon in some other way. (b) A man sings so poorly that his relatives force him to sing under a tree in a field and hire a poor man to be his audience. A demon in the tree, tormented by the singing, and pitying the poor man, agrees to help the poor man.
II. *The Demon Possesses the Princess* [K1955.6]. The demon enters the body of the princess, queen, etc. The man, his confederate, exorcises the demon and is richly rewarded. The demon warns the man to exorcise the demon again.
III. *The Demon Frightened.* The demon enters another princess, and the man is ordered, on pain of death, to drive out the demon. When he comes to the princess, he tells the demon that (a) his wife (b) the singer is outside [T251.1.1]. The demon leaves.
India *9.*

1165 *The Troll and the Christening.* A farmer is on friendly terms with a troll whom he does not wish to invite to his child's christening, knowing the troll's appetite. Not wishing to offend him, he sends to invite him; but he is to say that among the guests will be found the Virgin Mary, Thor the Thunderer, etc. The troll thinks he had better stay away, but he will give the finest present. [K1736].

*Hartmann *Trollvorstellungen* 50; *Balys *Tautosakos Darbai* VI 137—161. — Lithuanian *18;* Swedish *160* (Uppsala *51,* Stockholm *19,* Lund *5,* Göteborg *60,* Liungman 6, misc. *19*); Norwegian (1165**) *17,* Solheim *2;* Danish *55,* Kristensen *Jyske Folkeminder* IV 282 No. 401.

1165* *The Blind Giant* (Stallo) is killed or frozen [G121].
Lappish *9;* Swedish (Uppsala) *2.*

1166* *The Devil Keeps Guard in Place of the Soldier.* Cannot endure it that the straps of his knapsack cross each other [G303.16.3.2]. Is punished.
Estonian *12;* Lithuanian (1168*) *2;* Hungarian: Berze Nagy 655 *1;* Serbocroatian *1;* Russian: Afanesiev *1.*

1166** *A Shoemaker Frightens the Devils* and gets gold [K335].
Lappish (1166*) *1.*

1167* *The Youth Imprisons the Devil* in his own iron house [G513]. Cf. Type 328.
Lappish *1.*

1168 *Various Ways of Expelling Devils* [D2176].
Lithuanian (*1179) *8;* Serbocroatian *1.*

1168A *The Demon and the Mirror.* Cf. Types 92, 1336A.
The man has a mirror in his bag. He tells (a) the demon (or (b) the tiger) that he has captured other demons (tigers) and shows him the bag, whereupon he sees his reflection and, mistaking it for another demon, (tiger), flees. [J1795.1, K1715.1, K1883.7].

*Penzer V 49 n. 1; Chauvin II 88 No. 25. — India *12.* — American Negro (Georgia): Harris *Friends* 134 No. 18, (Virginia): Parsons JAFL XXXV 264 No. 12.

1168B *The Tree-Demon Pays the Man to Save the Tree* [N699.5]. A man goes to cut a tree. The demon who lives in the tree promises to bring the man a large amount of rice each year if the man will desist. Later the demons who must collect the rice tire of the bargain. One goes to devour the man and tries to enter his house through a drain hole. The man hears a noise in the hole, believes it is a neighbor's cat, and hits the demon on the head with a mallet. The demon pretends he has come to ask whether the man wants his rice husked or not. (a) The demon is frightened in some other way.
India *9.*

1168C *The Virgin Mary Saves a Woman Sold to the Devils.* A man sells his wife to the devils. The woman first goes to church to pray to Mary. The Virgin Mary appears in the form of the woman. The devils: »We do not need her». [K1841.3].
Lithuanian (*1167) *9;* Rumanian (827*) *2;* Serbocroatian *1.*

1169 *Changing Heads with the Devil.* St. Peter accidentally strikes off heads of the devil and an old man. Trying to undo the damage he places heads back on wrong bodies. Cf. Type 774A. [A1371.1, E34].

Lithuanian (3047) *14;* Swedish (GS 1169) *3;* Flemish: De Meyer FFC XXXVII 83 No. 11b *5;* Slovenian *2.*

1170—1199 A Man Sells his Soul to the Devil

Saves it through deceit, usually by imposing an impossible task on the devil [M211, G303.16.19.3].

1170 *The Evil Woman in the Glass Case as Last Commodity.* The man is to belong to the ogre as soon as he has sold his goods. If he has any goods that no one will buy, he is to be free. The man puts an evil old woman in a glass case. When the devil sees her he recognizes her: »Whoever knows her will refuse to buy her.» The man goes free. [K216.1].

Boggs *Studies in Philology* 1934 pp. 32ff. — Finnish *45;* Finnish-Swedish *7;* Swedish *57* (Uppsala *6,* Stockholm *3,* Göteborg *33,* Lund *2,* Liungman *3,* misc. *10*); Danish *2;* Irish *1;* Flemish *1;* German Archive *1;* Slovenian *1.*

1170A *Task: Selling Three Old Women.* (Devil finds that no one wants them.) [H1153].

*BP III 16.

1171 *A Rabbit in Each Net.* The man is to belong to the devil if the latter can catch a rabbit in each of hundred nets set in high trees. [H1024.3].

BP III 16 (Grimm No. 125); Dähnhardt III 23. — Finnish *57;* Swedish (Uppsala) *2;* Danish *5;* Russian: Andrejev.

1172 *All Stones from the Brook or the Field* [H1124].

Finnish *2;* Swedish *5* (Uppsala *1,* Stockholm *2,* Liungman *1,* misc. *1*); Danish *20;* German *2;* Serbocroatian *1;* Russian: Andrejev.

1172* *Devil to Count Stars,* grass, sands of sea, etc.

Walloon (*1172A) *1.*

1173 *Knots from the Drops of Spilled Brandy* [H1021.4].

Finnish *1;* Russian: Andrejev.

1173A (formerly 1173*) *The Devil is to Fulfill Three Wishes* of the peasant. The peasant wishes for all the tobacco and brandy in the world and then some more brandy in addition. The devil cannot fulfill the wish. [K175].

Finnish-Swedish *1;* Swedish *4* (Uppsala *3,* Stockholm *1*).

1174 *Making a Rope of Sand* [H1021.1].

*BP II 513, III 16 (Grimm Nos. 112, 125); *DeVries FFC LXXIII 155 n. 1; Feilberg *Ordbog* III 25b s.v. »reb»; Hdwb. d. Märchens I 431b n. 45. — Finnish *4;* Estonian *11;* Lithuanian *1;* Swedish *24* (Uppsala *6,* Stockholm *4,* Göteborg *8,* Liungman *1,* misc. *5*); Icelandic *1;* Scottish *4;* Irish *3,* Jackson FL XLVII 290; English *2;* Rumanian *2;* Russian: Andrejev.

1175 *Straightening Curly Hair* [H1023.4].
 *BP III 15 (Grimm No. 125). — Finnish *45;* Finnish-Swedish *2;* Estonian *8;* Livonian *2;* Lithuanian *4;* Swedish *47* (Uppsala *15*, Stockholm *7*, Göteborg *18*, Lund *1*, Liungman *2*, misc. *4*); Danish *10;* Irish: Jackson FL XLVII 290; French *3;* Walloon *1;* German *12* (Archive *11*, Henssen Volk No. 163); Italian (Sicilian *1*); Czech: Tille Soupis I cf. 177ff. *5;* Serbocroatian *2;* Russian: Andrejev *1;* Greek *1;* India *3*. — Spanish-American: Hansen (Puerto Rico) *1*.

1176 *Catching a Man's Broken Wind* or making a knot of it [H1023.13].
 *BP III 16 (Grimm No. 125). — Finnish *30;* Finnish-Swedish *2;* Estonian *1;* Lithuanian *5;* Swedish *61* (Uppsala *17*, Stockholm *11*, Göteborg *25*, Liungman *2*, misc. *6*); Danish *8;* Irish *4;* French *1;* Dutch *2;* Flemish *1;* German *44* (Archive *42*, Meckl. No. 103, Henssen Volk No. 165); Italian (Tuscan [1004] *1*); Hungarian: Berze Nagy (1177*)*2;* Serbocroatian *1;* Russian: Andrejev *2*.

1177* *Catching a Noise* [H1023.12].
 Swedish *2* (Göteborg *1*, Lund *1*); Danish *2;* Irish *1;* Flemish *1*.

1177** *Bringing the Women's Grindstone* [H1014].
 BP III 16 (Grimm No. 125). — Estonian (1177) *6*.

1178 *The Devil Outriddled.* Boy promised to the devil saves himself by giving riddles or enigmatic tasks that the devil cannot solve or perform. [G303.16.19.3].
 **Wesselski *Niederdeutsche Zs. f. Vksk.* X 1ff.; Fb I 267 a. — Icelandic (813 I*) *3*, (813 II*) *1;* England: *Baughman (G303.16.19.3); India: Thompson-Balys (G303.16.19.3) *3*.

1178* *Unraveling a Net* [H1094.1].
 Livonian (1178') *4;* Swedish *13* (Uppsala *1*, Stockholm *4*, Göteborg *6*, Liungman *1*, misc. *1*).

1178** *The Devil at the Grindstone.*
 Finnish-Swedish (1178*) *3;* Swedish *23* (Uppsala *17*, Stockholm *4*, Lund *1*, Liungman *1*).

1179 *The Ogre on the Ship.* Must pump out the water (the whole sea). [H1023.5].
 *BP III 16 (Grimm No. 125). — Finnish *4;* Finnish-Swedish *6;* Estonian *1;* Livonian *4;* Swedish *38* (Uppsala *4*, Stockholm *1*, Göteborg *27*, Lund *1*, Liungman *1*, misc. *4*); Norwegian (1179**) *1;* Danish *2;* German *2;* Russian: Andrejev.

1179* *The Devil Holds the Ship Fast* on the anchor chain.
 Estonian *1;* Swedish *2* (Uppsala *1*, Liungman *1*).

1180 *Catching Water in a Sieve.* The ogre and the girl [H1023.2]. Cf. Type 480.
 *BP III 16 (Grimm No. 125), cf. III 477 n. 1. — Finnish *13;* Estonian *1;* Livonian *1;* Lithuanian: Balys *Legends* No. 354; Swedish *4* (Göteborg *1*, Liungman *1*, misc. *2*); Danish *16;* Icelandic *2;* Irish *27;* English *1;* Spanish *1;* Catalan: Amades No. 215; German *2;* Czech: Tille Soupis I 182f. *2;* Serbocroatian *1;* Russian: Andrejev; Greek *2;* India *5;* Japa-

nese: Ikeda (H1023.2). — Spanish-American: Hansen (**1191) (Argentina) *2;* West Indies (Negro) *1.*

1180* *Sweeping and Winnowing Peas on Ice.* Sliding on the ice, the devil hurts himself.
Lithuanian (*1177) *2.*

1181 *Stick from the Body.* The ogre will help the man only in exchange for a part of the man's body. The man gives him a paring from his finger nail. [H1021.7].
*BP III 200. — Danish *3;* German: von Alpenburg *Mythen und Sagen Tirols* (Zürich 1857) 282f.; Russian: Andrejev.

1182 *The Level Bushel.* The student is to come into the devil's power if at the end of a year he does not at least return for the heaping bushel of gold a level one. The student forthwith hands back the level bushel and keeps the surplus. [K223].
*BP III 14 n. 3, 364, (Grimm Nos. 125, 189). — Finnish *1;* Finnish-Swedish *3;* Swedish *9* (Uppsala *3,* Stockholm *1,* Göteborg *4,* misc. *1*); Danish *12;* Dutch *3;* German *9* (Archive *7,* Henssen Jül No. 83, Henssen Volk No. 168); Russian: Andrejev.

1182A (formerly 1182*) *The Copper Coin.* Every time it is paid out the devil must make a new one. The man buys an expensive property and pays with a great many copper coins. He threatens to buy another and the devil goes back on contract. [K183].
Finnish-Swedish *1;* Swedish *10* (Uppsala *3,* Stockholm *4,* Lund *1,* Liungman *2*); Danish *1.*

1183 *Washing Black Cloth White: Task for Devil.* Sometimes cattle, wool, black man. [H1023.6]. Cf. Types 480, 1312.
*Roberts Type 480 p. 165; *Feilberg *Ordbog* I 406b s.v. »får», I 700b s.v. »hvid,» III 268a s.v. »skjorte», III 467b s.v. »sort». — Swiss: Jegerlehner Oberwallis 314 No. 113, 328 No. 10; Spanish-American: Hansen (**1191) (Argentina) *3.* Cf. Lithuanian (1187*) *4.*

1183* *Saying within Gunshot what Wild Game is Before one.* The woman covered with feathers. [K216.2]. Cf. Types 1091, 1092.
Flemish *4.*

1183** *Filling the Yard with Manure* [H1129.1].
Livonian (1183') *1;* Swedish (Uppsala) *2.*

1184 *The Last Leaf.* The man is to pay the devil when the last leaf falls from the oak tree. It never falls. [K222, cf. K221].
*BP III 14, 200; *Krappe Balor 154ff.; *Feilberg *Ordbog* I 189a s.v. »djævel», II 518 s.v. »lov»; Dähnhardt Natursagen I 179. — Estonian: Aarne FFC XXV 152 No. 79; Lithuanian *7;* Swedish *4* (Stockholm *2,* Lund *1,* misc. *1*); Danish *11;* Scottish (Lowland Scotland): Baughman *1;* Irish *1,* Beal XXI 313; German *15* (Archive *14,* Henssen Volk No. 103); Czech: Tille Soupis I 184 *1;* Slovenian *2;* Serbocroatian *1.*

1184* changed to 1187.

1185 *The First Crop.* The man to pay the devil when he harvests his first crop. He plants acorns. [K221].
*BP III 364. — Swedish *16* (Lund *14*, misc. *2*); Danish *10*.

1185* *When Pigs Walk.* The debt will be returned to the devil when the pigs walk instead of run home. [K226].
Lithuanian (1183A*) *1*.

1186 *With his Whole Heart.* The judge carried off. (The Devil and the Advocate.)
The devil refuses to take things not offered him with the whole heart. He hears the judge (advocate) cursed for fraud with such sincerity that he carries him off. [M215].
Taylor PMLA XXXVI 35ff., also in Bryan and Dempster 269—74; **Christensen *Festskrift til A. Kjær;* Feilberg *Ordbog* s.v. »Lade foged, ride foged»; Ward *Catalogue of Romances* III 592. — Finnish (821C) *3;* Swedish *5* (Uppsala *3*, misc. *2*); Danish *12;* Norwegian (1183) *2;* Irish *3;* French *1;* Dutch *1;* German Archive *15;* Russian: Andrejev *Ukraine* (821C*). — Literary Treatments: Pauli (ed. Bolte) Nos. 81, 107; Chaucer's »Frair's Tale».

1187 (formerly 1184*) *Meleager.* Permission to live as long as candle lasts. Cf. Type 934E.
E765.1.1. Life bound up with candle. When the candle goes out person dies. K551.9. Let me live as long as this candle lasts.
*Krappe in Penzer *Ocean of Story* VIII 107; *Anderson *Die Meleagrossage bei den Letten* (Philologus N. F. XXXIII [1923]). — French (1184*) *3;* Flemish (1184*) *1;* Irish (1184*) *20.* — Franco-American (1184*) *1.*
— Literary Treatments: Greek myth: Meleager.

1187* *Unfinished Work.* Man to belong to the devil when work is finished. It is never finished.
Italian (Sicilian *1187 *1*).

1188 »*Come Tomorrow*». The devil keeps calling daily until the gate with the inscription rots. He then claims his debtor. [K231.12.1]. Cf. Type 332D*.
Finnish *3;* Lithuanian (*1183) *2;* German: Plenzat p. 47 *1;* Hungarian: Berze Nagy (334*) *1;* Serbocroatian *1;* Russian: Andrejev (*1183) *1.*

1190* *The Man Thought Hanged.* The man promises himself to the devil if he receives money. He stuffs his clothes with straw and hangs them up. The devil thinks the man has hanged himself and is satisfied. [K215].
Estonian *5;* Greek *1, Laographia* XVII 140.

1191 *The Dog on the Bridge.* Unwitting bargain with devil evaded by driving dog over bridge first. The child has been unwittingly promised (the first thing that goes over the bridge). [S241.1].
Kittredge *Witchcraft* 206, *518 n. 19; Hazlitt *Shakespeare Jest Books* I 86f. No. 67; *Mensa Philosophica* No. 11. — Italian (Tuscan [776] a, b, *2*).

1192* *The Mouse as the Devil's Bride.*
Estonian *1.*

1193* *Freeing Oneself from Devil by Singing Hymn.*
Lithuanian (*1190) *6.*

1194* *The Devil is Ordered to Make Needles.* He is unsuccessful in the task.
Lithuanian (*1188) *1.*

1199 *The Lord's Prayer.* The man about to be taken by the Devil or Death begs respite long enough to repeat the Lord's Prayer for the last time. The Devil must wait. [K551.1]. Cf. Types 122A, 227, 332, 955.
*BP I 381, 404ff., II 164. — Finnish *1;* Swedish *11* (Uppsala *10,* Lund *1*); Danish *20;* Irish *7;* French *1;* Catalan: Amades No. 203; German *1;* Italian (Tuscan 333 b *1*); Hungarian (1199A*) *1.*

1199A *Preparation of Bread.* Respite from death gained by tale of the preparation of bread (flax) [K555.1.1, K555.1.2].
BP I 222, 331; Lithuanian (365A, 164*) *25;* Rumanian (1199˙I*) *9;* Hungarian: Berze Nagy (346*) *3.*

1199B *The Long Song.* Respite from death gained by long-drawn-out song [K555.2, K555.2.2].
Lithuanian (1084A*) *2;* Russian: Andrejev (*1084 I) *5;* Indonesian: DeVries No. 113.

III JOKES AND ANECDOTES

NUMSKULL STORIES

1200 *The Sowing of Salt.* The numskull sows it like grain and expects it to produce salt [J1932.3], or plants a cow's tail to produce calves [J1932.4.1].
*Wesselski *Hodscha Nasreddin* II 209 No. 423; *Christensen DF XLVII 206, 231 No. 57. — Finnish *14;* Finnish-Swedish *4;* Estonian *2;* Livonian *1;* Lithuanian *1;* Swedish *25* (Uppsala *7,* Lund *1,* Liungman *5,* misc. *12*); French *5;* Walloon *2;* German *8;* Italian (Tuscan, cf. 1206 *1*); Rumanian *1,* Sainenu 911, 934; Hungarian *4;* Slovenian *2;* Serbocroatian *6;* (1200b) Serbocroatian *1;* Russian: Andrejev; Greek *4,* Argenti-Rose (Chios), Loukatos No. 15; Turkish: Eberhard-Boratav cf. No. 327 V; India *2.* — Spanish-American: Rael No. 60 (U.S.). — African *1.*

1200A *Sowing all Seed in one Place.*
Greek *2.*

1201 *The Plowing.* Four men carry the horse in order not to tramp up the field [J2163].
*Wesselski *Bebel* I 138 No. 43. — Finnish *11;* Finnish-Swedish *3;* Estonian *2;* Livonian *1;* Swedish *3* (Uppsala *1,* misc. *2*); Walloon *1;* German *15;* Hungarian *3;* Slovenian *3;* Russian: Andrejev. — English-American *1.*

1202 *The Grain Harvesting.* The grain is shot down with guns. When the unknown sickle is bought and tried, one man is cut with it. As punishment it is drowned. Cf. Type 1650.
Motifs: J2196. Grain shot down with guns. People unacquainted with the sickle. N411.2. Sickle sold for fortune in land without sickles. J1865. Sickle punished by drowning. J2514. Sickle bought at great cost given back.
*BP II 72 note 1 (Grimm No. 70). — Finnish *20;* Finnish-Swedish *1;* Estonian *1;* Livonian *1,* (1204') *1;* Catalan: Amades Nos. 410, 557, 1259; German *4;* Russian: Afanesiev *4.* — Spanish-American: Hansen (Puerto Rico) *1.*

1203 *The Scythe Cuts one Man's Head off.* All have theirs cut off. [J2422].
Finnish *13;* Finnish-Swedish *1;* Estonian *1;* Lithuanian *5;* Lappish *1;*

Swedish *24* (Stockholm *2*, Göteborg *10*, Lund *1*, misc. *11*); Catalan: Amades No. 410; German *1*, Henssen Volk No. 222; Hungarian: Berze Nagy (1340*) *1;* Russian: Andrejev *1*.

1203A *The Scythe Thought to be Serpent.* The numskulls find a scythe and take it for a serpent; they strike it, it jumps up and catches on the neck of one of them; pulling the »serpent», they cut off the man's head.
Lithuanian (1203) *5;* cf. Type 1315.

1203* *Mowing the Grass.* The boy is to mow grass. He mows the grass-field down [K1423].
Finnish *1;* Finnish-Swedish *2;* Swedish (Stockholm) *1*.

1204 *Fool Keeps Repeating his Instructions* so as to remember them. He usually forgets them [J2671.2]. Cf. Type 1687.
Clouston *Noodles* 133; German Archive (1204*) *18*, Henssen Volk 387 No. 233 (7).

1204* *The Run-away Crop.* Corn cut down so that it will not be blown away by wind. Cf. Types 1279A, 1290*, 1290A*.
Hungarian: Berze Nagy *4*.

1204** *Milking a Hen.* Old woman tries to milk a hen; insults her because she does not feed her chicks with milk.
Russian *2*.

1208* *The Belled Salmon.* Bell is tied on salmon (eel) so that it can be found later.
Walloon *3*.

1209* *Hatching Fish from Cheese.* Numskull is persuaded that fish can be hatched from white cheese. When his body heat produces maggots in the cheese, he thinks they are fish.
Walloon *1*.

1210 *The Cow is Taken to the Roof to Graze* [J1904.1]. Cf. Type 1408. Usual combinations: Types 1286, 1384, 1540, 1653A.
*Köhler-Bolte I 66, 135; Christensen DF XLVII 219 No. 81; Clouston *Noodles* 55; Coffin *6;* Espinosa III 147 Nos. 181—188. — Finnish *23;* Estonian *8;* Lithuanian *13;* Swedish *15* (Uppsala *2*, Stockholm *1*, Liungman *1*, misc. *11*); Scottish *1;* Irish *178*, Beal II 24, Jackson FL XLVII 290; English *3;* French *12;* Catalan: Amades Nos. 623, 652, 1667; Dutch *3;* Flemish *10;* Walloon *1;* German *28* (Archive *27*, Henssen Volk No. 230); Swiss: Jegerlehner *Oberwallis* 295 No. 15; Italian *3* (Tuscan 1200, 1210b *2*, Trieste: Pinguentini No. 77); Hungarian *14*, Dégh No. 40, cf. Berze Nagy (1232*); Slovenian *4;* Serbocroatian *5;* Istrian No. 46; Czech: Tille Soupis I 409, 411 *2;* Russian: Andrejev *Ukraine 11*, Afanesiev *10;* Turkish: Eberhard-Boratav No. 331 III. — English-American: Baughman *3;* Spanish-American: Hansen (Puerto Rico) *2*.

1210* *Ass Hoisted up to Tower* but hanged in the process.
Spanish *2*.

1211 *The Peasant Woman Thinks the Cow Chewing her Cud is Mimicking Her.* Kills the cow. [J1835].

Finnish *15;* Finnish-Swedish *4;* Estonian *4;* Lithuanian *2;* Swedish (Uppsala) *1;* Irish *1;* German *2;* Hungarian *1;* Slovenian *1;* Serbocroatian *1;* Russian: Andrejev; Greek *1;* Turkish: Eberhard-Boratav cf. No. 323 III, 327 III *3;* India 6.

1211* *Water on Calf's Back.* When the calf will not drink, the peasant woman throws the water on its back [J1903.1].
Finnish (1211**) *2.*

1212 *The Horse is Drawn across the Ice.* Its skin is rubbed off [J1972].
Finnish *14;* Serbocroatian *1;* Russian: Andrejev.

1212* *Pig Blindfolded* when it refuses to take the right fork of road.
Walloon (*1229) *1.*

1213 *The Pent Cuckoo.* Fools build an enclosure to keep in the cuckoo. She flies over the hedge. They say that they have not built the hedge high enough. [J1904.2].
**Field *Pent Cuckoo;* Clouston *Noodles* 27. — Walloon *1;* England: Baughman *1.*

1213* *The Attentive Donkey.* The villager believes that the donkey who is moving his ears listens to what he tells him.
Greek *1.*

1214 *The Persuasive Auctioneer.* The auctioneer praises the man's worthless cow so much in his speech that the man takes her back himself. [J2087].
Wesselski *Hodscha Nasreddin* I 276 No. 309; Clouston *Noodles* 72. — Serbocroatian *1.* — U.S.: Baughman (J2087) *1.*

1214* *Driving a Horse into his Collar* instead of putting it on him.
Russian *6.*

1215 *The Miller, his Son, and the Ass: Trying to Please Everyone.* Asinus Vulgi. Miller blamed when he follows his son on foot; when he takes the son's place on the ass; when he takes the son behind him; and when he puts the son in front of him. [J1041.2].
*Chauvin II 148 No. 2, III 70, 145, VIII 140; *Wesselski *Hodscha Nasreddin* II 244 No. 541; Herbert III 420; *Pauli (ed. Bolte) No. 577; Scala Celi 135a No. 745; Alphabet No. 765. — Norwegian: *Norske Folkekultur* XI 79; England: Baughman; Spanish Exempla: Keller (J1041.2); Catalan: Amades No. 527; German: Zender *Aus Eifel und Ardennen* 100 No. 52; Italian (Tuscan [1561] *1*); Rumanian 1331—46 (13) *1;* Hungarian: Berze Nagy (1687*) *1;* Slovenian; Serbocroatian *1;* Turkish: Eberhard-Boratav No. 336 *1;* India *1.* — Spanish-American: Hansen (**1341) (Puerto Rico) *1.* — Literary Treatment: Italian Novella: *Rotunda.

1216* *Prescription washed off by Rain.* Written in chalk on door.
Walloon *1.*

1218 *Numskull Sits on Eggs to Finish the Hatching.* Cautions people to be quiet and not frighten the eggs. (Sometimes puts on honey and feathers before sitting on the eggs.) [J1902.1]. Cf. Type 1677.

*BP I 316; *Wesselski *Hodscha Nasreddin* II 212 No. 433; *Wesselski *Bebel* II 146 No. 148; Christensen DF XLVII 210 No. 63; Breton: Sébillot Incidents s.v. »oeuf»; Spanish: Espinosa III 147 Nos. 181—188; French *1;* Italian (Pentamerone I No. 4, Sicilian (*1016) *2,* Gonzenbach No. 37).

1218* *Heartless cow.* Butcher promises farmer the heart when cow is slaughtered. He sells it and reports cow had no heart. The farmer is not surprised: the cow was unsentimental.
Walloon *1.*

1219* *Light for the Cat.* Housewife installs cat in the cupboard; lights a lamp so it can see mice.
Walloon *1.*

1220 *The Fish-net is Stretched out on the Heath* [J1973]. Cf. Type 1290.
Finnish *5;* German *1;* Russian: Andrejev.

1221A* *Fish too Large for Pan Discarded.*
Walloon *1.*

1221B* *Pan too Small for Planned Cake.*
Walloon *1.*

1224* *The Finder's Right.* A man stoops for coin and drops the statue of the Virgin. He thinks she saw the coin first and puts the coin on the altar.
Walloon *1.*

1225 *The Man Without a Head in the Bear's Den.* A man's head is snatched off by accident and his companions do not see what has happened. Debate: did he ever have a head? [J2381].
**Wesselski *Hodscha Nasreddin* II 192 No. 374; *Bolte *Frey* 220 No. 12; Christensen DF XLVII 192—93 No. 19. — Finnish *15;* Lappish *4;* Swedish *16* (Uppsala *6,* Stockholm *3,* Lund *1,* misc. *6*); Irish *2* (with 1210 and 1540); Dutch *1;* Rumanian *2;* Slovenian *1;* Serbocroatian *8;* Russian: Andrejev *3;* Greek *1,* Loukatos No. 24; Turkish: Eberhard-Boratav No. 331 III; Arab (lower Euphrates): C. G. Campbell p. 19; India: Thompson-Balys (J2381) *1.*

1225A *How did the Cow Get on the Pole?* A fool hides his purse on a pole on a cliff. A rascal substitutes cow-dung for the money. The fool is interested only in how the cow could have reached the purse. [J2382].
*Wesselski *Hodscha Nasreddin* I 236 No. 110; Köhler-Bolte I 497; Anderson Hessische Blätter XLVI 170. — French: RTP II 107ff., IV 482ff., XI 646; Walloon (1221, 1221B) *2;* Rumanian: Schullerus FFC LXXVIII 69 No. 8 *5;* Italian (Trieste: Pinguentini No. 3); Greek (1677**) *3.* — Cf. Hungarian: Berze Nagy (1789*) — milk on statue's lips *3;* cf. Polish (662) *1.*

1225* *Ass Rescued from Well.* Fool worried lest ass's tail drop water and dirty well.
Greek *1.*

1226 *The Rabbit Catch.* The trap on the stable roof. Cf. Type 1171.
Finnish *1;* Russian: Andrejev.

1227 *One Woman to Catch the Squirrel; Other to Get the Cooking Pot.* One falls from the tree and kills herself; the other breaks the pot. [J2661.3].

Finnish *75;* Finnish-Swedish *4;* Estonian *4;* Lithuanian *1;* Lappish *1;* Swedish *20* (Uppsala *14,* Stockholm *4,* Göteborg *1;* Liungman *1*); Norwegian *3;* German *1;* Slovenian *3;* Serbocroatian *1;* Russian: Andrejev; Greek *1.*

1228 *Shooting with the Gun.* A man looks down the gun-barrel as it is shot [J2131.4.1]. Cf. Type 1158.

Finnish *22;* Finnish-Swedish *1;* Estonian *7;* Livonian *1;* German: Henssen Volk No. 225; Lithuanian *2;* Hungarian *2;* Russian: Afanasiev *3;* Greek: Loukatos No. 15.

1228A *Fools Shoot from Wooden Gun* which explodes and kills several. They rejoice that the enemy has had even more loss.

Serbocroatian *2.*

1229 *If the Wolf's Tail Breaks.* Trickster and companion are wolf hunting. The companion goes into the wolf hole. The wolf comes out. The other catches the wolf by the tail and the wolf scratches dust into the companion's eyes. »What a dust.» — »If the wolf's tail breaks, you will see another kind of dust!» [X1133.3.2]. Cf. Types 1694*, 1875, 1896.

Wesselski *Hodscha Nasreddin* I 216 No. 48. — Swedish (GS 1229) *4,* (Uppsala *1,* misc. *3*). — West Indies (Negro): Flowers 585.

1229* *Shoveling Nuts with a Hayfork.*
Hungarian: Berze Nagy *3.*

1230* *The Pilgrimage Vow.* Woman on a pilgrimage accidentally disarranges her skirt. Her husband does not tell her since he thinks she has vowed to take pilgrimage thus.
Walloon *1.*

1231 *The Attack on the Hare (Crayfish).* Seven men make strenuous plans for the attack on the fierce animal. One screams with fright and the animal runs away. [J2612]. Cf. Type 103.

*BP II 556, III 286; Christensen DF XLVII 220 No. 82; Swiss: Jegerlehner 307 No. 34.

1231* *Manuring the Soil with Lard.* Cf. Type 1291B.
Hungarian: Berze Nagy *2.*

1238 *The Roof in Good and Bad Weather.* The man does not need a roof when it is fair; cannot put it on when it rains. [J2171.2.1]. Cf. Types 43, 81.

*Pauli (ed. Bolte) No. 599; Wienert FFC LVI (ET ⁓69), 134 (ST 402); Halm Aesop No. 222; Japanese: Ikeda. Cf. Russian: Andrejev No. 72.

1240 *Man Sitting on Branch of Tree Cuts it off* [J2133.4].

*Delarue in Millien et Delarue *Nivernais* 293f.; Wesselski *Hodscha Nasreddin* I 216f. No. 49; Köhler-Bolte I 51, 135, 486—490; Clouston *Noodles* 158; Coffin *3;* Christensen DF XLVII 229. — Finnish *4;* Estonian *10;* Livonian *3;* Lithuanian *9;* Irish *2;* French *13;* Spanish *1;*

Flemish *4;* Walloon *1;* German: Henssen Jül. No. 463; Swiss: Jegerlehner 293 No. 2; Italian *5* (Tuscan 1642 *1;* Sicilian *4*);Hungarian: Berze Nagy (1654*) *2;* Czech: Tille Soupis I 418f. *2;* Slovenian *3;* Serbocroatian *6;* Russian: Andrejev; Greek *1*, Loukatos No. 22; India *9*. — English-American: Baughman *5;* Spanish-American: Hansen (Puerto Rico) *3;* West Indies (Negro) *1*. — Literary Treatment: Chauvin II 201 No. 47.

1240A *Man Jumps on Dead Branch of Tree.* It breaks.
Greek (1240*) *1*.

1241 *The Tree is to be Pulled Down* in order to give it water to drink [J1973]. A man sticks his head in the branches [J2131.5.3].
*Christensen DF XLVII 179, 192ff. — Finnish *19;* Finnish-Swedish *6;* Swedish *11* (Uppsala *8*, Stockholm *1*, Lund *1*, Liungman *1*); Dutch *1;* German *1;* Serbocroatian *2;* Russian: Andrejev *1;* Greek: Loukatos No. 22; Spanish-American: Hansen (Puerto Rico) *1*.

1241A *Pulling out the Tree.* Fools try to save tree on cliff. All on rope pull out tree. It pulls them down into pit.
Greek (1241*) *1*.

1242 *Loading the Wood.* »If the horse can pull one load, he can pull two» [J2213.4].
*Christensen DF XLVII 224 No. 86. — Finnish *1;* Finnish-Swedish *2;* Estonian *1;* Swedish *18* (Uppsala *12*, Stockholm *3*, Lund *2;* Liungman *1*); Russian: Andrejev.

1242A *Carrying Part of the Load.* A rider takes the meal-sack on his shoulder to relieve the ass of his burden [J1874.1].
*Wesselski *Hodscha Nasreddin* II 229 No. 490; *Fb III 720b s.v. »sæk»; *Clouston Noodles 19; Field Pent Cuckoo 3. — England, U.S.: Baughman (J1874.1); French: Sébillot *Litterature orale de la Haute Bretagne* 387; Dutch (1212*) *1;* Italian Novella: Rotunda (J1874.1); Rumanian: Schullerus (FFC LXXVIII 98 [9 No. 5]) *1;* Hungarian: Berze Nagy (1349 XII*) *1;* Slovenian; Russian: Afanasiev (*1213) *1*. — Spanish-American: Hansen (Puerto Rico) *2*.

1242B *Balancing the Mealsack.* Man puts sack of meal on one side of saddle, balances it on the other side with a rock. [J1874.2].
Walloon (*1205) *1;* U.S.: Baughman (J1874.2).

1242* *Felling the Tree.* The fool cuts so that the whole tree will fall on the wagon. Breaks the wagon and kills the horses.
Greek (1242**) *1*.

1243 *The Wood is Carried Down the Hill.* Then carried back up in order to roll it down [J2165].
Clouston *Noodles* 59. — Finnish *22;* Lappish *1;* Swedish *7* (Uppsala *3*, Stockholm *1*, misc. *3*); German *1;* Russian: Andrejev.

1244 *Trying to Stretch the Beam* [J1964.1].

Finnish *9;* Estonian *4;* Lithuanian *1;* Lappish *1;* French *1;* Catalan: Amades No. 557; Dutch *4;* Flemish *3;* German *17* (Archive *16,* Henssen Volk No. 221); Hungarian *6;* Serbocroatian *1;* Russian: Afanesiev *4.*

1245 *Sunlight Carried in a Bag into the Windowless House.* When this plan does not succeed they gradually pull down the house in order to get light. [J2123].

Coffin 6. — Finnish *57;* Finnish-Swedish *5;* Estonian *1;* Livonian *1;* Lithuanian *11;* Lappish *1;* Swedish *39* (Uppsala *15,* Stockholm *5,* Liungman *7,* misc. *12);* Norwegian *1;* Icelandic *1;* Irish *19;* English *1;* French *7;* Catalan: Amades No. 398; Dutch *3;* Walloon (*1245A) *1;* German *17* (Archive *16,* Henssen Volk No. 232); Italian (Tuscan 1200 *1);* Hungarian *5,* Dégh No. 41; Czech: Tille Soupis I 408 *1;* Slovenian *2;* Serbocroatian *1;* Russian: Andrejev; Turkish: Eberhard-Boratav No. 331 III *3.* — English-American: Baughman *5.*

1245* *White Sheep-skin as Source of Light* [J1961].
Livonian (1245) *1.*

1245** *Trying to Catch Light in a Mouse-trap* [J1961.1].
Flemish *1.*

1245A* *Carrying out the Smoke in a Sieve.*
Russian: Andrejev (1245 I) *1.*

1246 *The Axes Thrown Away.* The first lets his axe fall. The others throw theirs into the same place [J2171.4].

Feilberg *Ordbog* IV 199a s.v. »hammer»; Christensen DF XLVII 194. — Finnish *10;* Finnish-Swedish *4;* Swedish *26* (Uppsala *11,* Stockholm *3,* Lund *1,* Liungman *3,* misc. *8);* Irish *1;* Flemish *3;* German: Henssen Volk No. 234; Russian: Andrejev.

1246* *Building the Church.* For amusement they throw away the beams from the scaffolding until it all falls down. [J2171.3].
Finnish-Swedish (1245*) *1.*

1247 *The Man Sticks his Head into the Hole of the Millstone.* It rolls into the lake. [J2131.5.4]. Cf. Type 1241.

Finnish *24;* Livonian *3;* Icelandic *1;* German *4* (Archive *3,* Henssen Volk No. 223); Serbocroatian *4;* Russian: Andrejev.

1248 *Tree-trunks Laid Crosswise of the Sledge* [J1964]. Cf. Type 801.

BP III 302. — Finnish-Swedish (1242) *1,* (1242**) *1;* Swedish *25* (Uppsala *19,* Stockholm *3,* Liungman *1,* misc. *2);* English *1;* German *9,* (Archive *8,* Meckl. No. 104); Chinese: Eberhard FFC CXX 274 No. 1 VIII, FFC CXXVIII 231 No. 138.

1249 *Oxen Hitched Before and Behind Wagon* [F171.6.4]. Cf. Type 801.
Slovenian *1.*

1250 *Bringing Water from the Well.* A log is laid across the top of the well. One man holds to the log with his hands, the next climbs down and holds to his feet, and so on; the uppermost man becomes tired and lets go to spit on his hands. [J2133.5]. Cf. Type 121.

*Penzer Ocean V 170 n. 1; Delarue in Perbosc *Gascogne* 291f.; Köhler-Bolte I 51, 135, 486ff.; Wesselski *Hodscha Nasreddin* I 216f. No. 49; *Schweizerisches Archiv für Volkskunde* XXIII 36; Christensen DF XLVII 229; Clouston *Noodles* 158; Coffin *8;* Feilberg *Ordbog* III 967 s.v. »træ«. — Finnish-Swedish (1247*) *1;* Swedish *19* (Uppsala *9,* Stockholm *4,* Lund *2,* misc. *4*); Irish *3;* English *4;* French *16,* Spanish: cf. *1;* Dutch *5,* Flemish (1247*) *2;* Walloon (*1250B) *1;* German *25* (Archive *23,* Henssen Volk No. 227, Henssen Jül No. 463); Rumanian: FFC LXXVIII 69 No. 10 *2;* Hungarian (Berze Nagy 1334*) *4;* Slovenian *3;* Serbocroatian *1;* Greek *3;* India *3;* Chinese: Chavannes II 324; English-American: Baughman *5;* Spanish-American: Hansen (Cuba) *1,* (Puerto Rico) *1;* American Negro: Parsons JAFL XXXV 302; American Indian: (Muskhogean) Swanton JAFL XXVI 218, (Zuni) Cushing, *Zuni Folk Tales* 229. — Literary Treatments: Chauvin II 201 No. 47.

1250A *Hampers Piled up to Measure Tower* (Climb Tree). Bottom removed and all fall. Cf. Type 121. [J2133.6.1].

Espinosa III 147. — French (1250B*) *7;* Spanish (1703*) *1;* Greek (1240**) *3;* Spanish-American: Hansen (Dominican Republic) *1,* (Puerto Rico) *2.* — African (Ashanti): Werner *African Mythology* 125.

1250B *The Fool Dangling from the Elephant's Tail* [J2133.5.2]. A supernatural elephant (cow) descends from the sky and tramples a man's field. The next night he hides, seizes the elephant's tail, and is carried to the sky. He returns and tells his friends who also want to visit the sky. They form a human chain with the first man hanging on to the tail of the elephant. When they are in the air, the others ask the first man a question. He lets go to gesticulate with his hands while answering, or the like.

India *7.*

1255 *A Hole to Throw the Earth in.* Numskull plans to dig a hole so as to have a place to throw the earth from his excavations. [J1934].

*Wesselski *Hodscha Nasreddin* II 227 No. 480. — Swedish: Christensen DF XLVII 201 No. 37; Danish: Christensen DF XLVII 134 No. 37; Catalan: Amades pp. 1204ff. No. 1638; Dutch: Cornelissen *Nederl. Volkshumor* I 225; German: Merkens II 18 No. 23; Hungarian: Berze Nagy (1332*) *2;* Jewish: Neuman (J1934).

1260 *The Porridge in the Ice Hole.* They put meal into the ice hole and then, one after another, all jump in to taste the porridge. [J1938].

**Ranke FFC CLIX; Coffin *1.* — Finnish *60;* Finnish-Swedish *4;* Estonian *1;* Lappish *7;* Swedish *47* (Uppsala *17,* Stockholm *7,* Göteborg *1,* Lund *7,* Liungman *4,* misc. *11*); Norwegian *1;* English *2;* French *1;* Serbocroatian *1;* Turkish: Eberhard-Boratav No. 333 III *2.*

1260A *Hare Soup.* Hare (crab) escapes from water heating to make soup. Later numskulls drink and think they have good soup.

**Ranke FFC CLIX; *Wesselski *Hodscha Nasreddin* I 21 No. 40. — German (1205*) *2.*

1260* *The Fool Puts One Stick of wood in the Stove.* »Several others are burned up.» [J1963].
Finnish (1260**) *1*.

1260** *Jumping into the Sea for Fish.*
Lappish (1260*) *2;* Swedish *9* (Uppsala *1*, Liungman *5*, misc. *3*).

1260A* *Flour in River.* Woman to mix flour for bread puts it in river and loses it all.
French Canadian (1386*).

1260B* *Numskull Strikes all Matches in Order to Try them* [J1849.3].
Christensen DF XLVII 207 No. 60. — Finnish *5*.

1261 *The Slaughter of the Ox.* In preparation, the feet are cut off the evening before. [J2168].
Finnish *1;* Russian: Andrejev.

1261* *The Old Woman Throws the Yeast into the Stove,* since she has forgotten to knead it into the dough [J1962].
Finnish (1261**) *1;* Swedish *2* (Uppsala *1*, Stockholm *1*).

1262 *Roasting the Meat.* The fire on one shore of the lake, the meat on the other. [J1945, J1191.7]. Cf. Type 1804B.
*Anderson in Tauscher *Volksmärchen* 180; *Christensen DF XLVII No. 13; *Wesselski *Hodscha Nasreddin* II 212 No. 434. — Finnish *4;* Catalan: Amades No. 487; French *8;* Walloon (*1262A) *1;* Italian (Sicilian *1262 1*); Serbocroatian (fish) *2;* Slovenian *2;* Russian: Andrejev; Iraq: Meissner *Neuarabische Märchen aus Iraq* (1903) 77; India *5*. — Spanish-American: Rael No. 438 (U.S.). — African (Swahili): Büttner *Anthologie der Suaheli-Litteratur* (1894) II 90 No. 5, Velten *Märchen und Erzählungen der Suaheli* (1898) 27, (Abyssinia): Littmann *Publications of the Princeton Expedition to Abyssinia* II 34 No. 25, Courlander-Leslau *The Fire on the Mountain* 7.

1262* *The Fool Spits into the Hot Porridge.* He has seen the smith spit on the hot iron. [J2421].
Finnish (1262**) *2;* Swedish (Uppsala) *1;* Serbocroatian *2*.

1263 *The Porridge Eaten in Different Rooms.* The porridge in one, the milk in another [J2167].
Finnish *7;* Estonian *9;* Lithuanian *9;* Italian (Tuscan *1*); Russian: Afanasiev *2*. — African *1*.

1264* *The Boiling of the Porridge Pot.* The woman thinks the pot is complaining to her. [J1875.2]. Cf. Type 1318**.
Estonian: FFC XXV 137 No. 101; Russian: Andrejev (*1264).

1265* *Two for the Price of One.* The fool sells two fox-skins pulled into each other [J2083.2], (or mixes other skins with them).
Finnish *1;* cf. Finnish-Swedish (1300*); Estonian *2*.

1266* *A Third for one-fourth.* In the grain-sale the fool sells a third of a cask for the price of a fourth. [J2083.1].
Estonian *2*.

1266A* *Numskulls Buy a Church in Common:* each pays the full price [J2037.1].
Lithuanian (*1336) *2*.

1268* *Electing a Mayor: Inspection from Rear.* A man is chosen whose wife can recognize him among others from the rear. Prearranged signal (soup on shoes, or hole in trousers).
French: Delarue *9*, *Mélusine* II 422; German (1264*) *3*.

1270 *The Drying of the Candle.* The candle is laid in the stove to dry; melts [J2122].
Finnish *3;* Catalan: Amades No. 583; Italian (Tuscan *1*); Russian: Andrejev. — English-American: Baughman *1.*

1271* *Wearing out the Window.* Children are forbidden to look through the window glass lest they wear it out too soon.
Slovenian *1.*

1271A* *Warming the Stove with Wool* [J1873.3].
Livonian (1271A') *1;* Swedish (Uppsala) *1.* Cf. J1942.

1271B* *Tying Yarn around the Stove* so that the heat will not escape [J1942].
Livonian (1271B') *1.*

1271C* *Cloak Given to Stone* to keep it warm [J1873.2].
*Köhler-Bolte I 71. — Norwegian (1651) *1;* Japanese: Ikeda [J1873.2].

1272* *Drying Snow on the Stove* [J2121].
Livonian (1272') *2.*

1273A* *Numskull Bales Out the Stream.* He comes to a stream but not wishing to get his feet wet he sits to wait for the stream to run down. He helps to bale the stream out with a hazelnut shell and keeps it up for months. [J1967].
Italian: Gonzenbach No. 17, Italian Novella: Rotunda [J1967].

1273B* *Greasing Wheel after Journey is Over.*
Swedish (Uppsala) *2.*

1273C* *Numskulls Wash their Pie as they would Cloth.*
Hungarian: Berze Nagy (1349*) *2.*

1274* *The Devils Build a Ship with a Wooden Saw.* The ship has no bottom and is so narrow nothing can get into it. [J2171.1.1].
Livonian (1274') *1.*

1275 *The Sledges Turned* in the direction of the journey. At night turned around by a joker. [J2333].
Finnish *6;* Slovenian *3;* Russian: Andrejev.

1275* *Travelers Lose Way and Get Turned Around.* Find themselves back home.
Walloon *1.*

1276 *Rowing without Going Forward.* One woman rows in one direction, another in the opposite; or rowing in a boat which is tied up. [J2164.1, J2164.2].
Finnish *39;* Finnish-Swedish *2;* Lappish *1;* Swedish *10* (Uppsala *6,* misc. *4*); Norwegian *4;* Rumanian *1;* Serbocroatian *2,* Istrian No. 47; Russian: Andrejev; Indonesian: De Vries No. 248.

1276* *Prayer for Change of Wind.* An old woman rowing against the wind prays to have it change. It does and she must row against it on the return.
Finnish *15.*

1277 *The Boat Gets Tired.* The woman tries to tire out her rival's boat so as to win the race, but only tires herself. [J1884].
*Christensen DF XLVII 190. — Finnish *5;* Swedish *3* (Uppsala *2,* misc. *1*); Russian: Andrejev.

1277* »*The Reef is Old, the Ship New.*» They think that the vessel will endure the shocks better than the reef [J2212.4].
Finnish-Swedish *1.*

1277** *The Anchor Large Enough.* The fool thinks that the wooden anchor would hold if it were only large enough [J2212.3].
Finnish *2*.

1278 *Marking the Place on the Boat.* An object falls into the sea from a boat. Numskulls mark the place on the boat-rail to indicate where it fell. [J1922.1].
*Clouston *Noodles* 99; Penzer V 92 n. 2; Coffin *3;* Feilberg *Ordbog* IV 81a s.v. »båd.» — Finnish *9;* Finnish-Swedish *4;* Livonian *2;* Swedish *3* (Uppsala *1*, Lund *2*); Irish *1;* English (1278 C) *2;* German *8;* Slovenian *2;* Serbocroatian *2;* Russian: Andrejev; Indonesian: De Vries No. 250; India *1;* Japanese: Ikeda (J1922.1). — English-American (1278 B) *5*.

1278* *Under the Cloud.* The fool seeks the ears of grain in the direction of the cloud toward which he had sowed the grain [J1922.2.1].
Finnish *1;* Estonian *1;* Latvian (**228) *3*.

1279 *Protected by the Needle.* In a storm on the ice, fools stick needles into the ice to keep from blowing away. [J1965].
Finnish *4;* Slovenian *2;* Russian: Andrejev.

1279A *Holding Down the Horse.* Fearing that the wind will carry away the horse fools weight him down with great stones. Cf. Type 1204*.
Icelandic (1349 I*) *3*.

1280 *The Needle (or the like) Falls into the Sea.* The man hunts it the next summer. [J1921].
Finnish *3;* Russian: Andrejev.

1281 *Getting Rid of the Unknown Animal.* The cat (owl) is bought. Eats many mice. To kill it they set the house on fire. [J2101]. Cf. Type 1651.
*BP II 72 n. 1, III 286 (Grimm Nos. 70, 174). — Finnish *35;* Estonian *1;* Swedish *8* (Uppsala *2*, Lund *3*, Liungman *1*, misc. *2*); Icelandic *1;* Dutch *1;* Flemish *1;* German *14* (Archive *13*, Henssen Volk No. 235); Hungarian *1;* Slovenian *1;* Russian: Andrejev; Turkish: Eberhard-Boratav No. 45, cf. 274 IV, 329 V *3;* Chinese: Eberhard FFC CXX p. 298.

1281A (formerly 1281*) *Getting Rid of the Man-eating Calf.* A fool, liking the shoes on the feet of a man hanged on a gallows, cuts off the swollen feet in order to carry off the shoes. In the room in which he sleeps that night is a newborn calf. The next morning the man takes the shoes but leaves the feet. Peasants agree that the calf has eaten the man all but the feet. They burn the house to destroy the calf. [J1815].
*Wesselski *Bebel* I 231 No. 144; *Köhler-Bolte I 68f. — Finnish-Swedish (1281*) *4;* Swedish (1281*) *9* (Uppsala *3*, Lund *3*, Liungman *3*); Danish DF L 65, Nyrop Dania I (1890) 283ff., cf. II 68ff.; Slovenian; Spanish-American Rael No. 327 (U.S.).

1282 *House Burned Down to Rid it of Insects* [J2102.4].
*Pauli (ed. Bolte) No. 37; *BP III 288; Wesselski *Hodscha Nasreddin* I 244 No. 137; Christensen DF XLVII 219ff. No. 82; India *1;* Indonesia: De Vries No. 267.

1282* *Garden Paved to Keep out Moles.*
Danish *2;* Walloon (*1214A) *1.*

1284 *Person Does Not Know Himself.* In new clothes, with beard cut off, etc. [J2012]. Cf. Type 1383 (The Woman Does not Know Herself).
*L. Schmidt *Oesterreiche Zs. f. Vksk.* 1954, 129ff.; Wesselski *Hodscha Nasreddin* I 274 No. 298, I 214 No. 43; Wesselski *Mönchslatein* 193 No. 152; Christensen DF XLVII 27, 221 No. 83; Feilberg *Ordbog* s.v. »selv».
— Walloon (*1383B) *1;* Hungarian: Berze Nagy (1409*) *7;* India *2.*

1284A *White Man Made to Believe he is a Negro* [K2013.1].
Clouston *Noodles* 7; L. Schmidt *Oesterreiche Zs. f. Vksk.* 1954 p. 130.
— Walloon (*1380A) *1;* France *2,* England, U.S.: Baughman (J2013.1).

1284* *Forcing the Hen* to brood her chickens.
Estonian: Loorits *Estnische Märchen* No. 143; Hungarian: Berze Nagy (1284*) *2.*

1285 *Pulling on the Shirt.* The shirt is sewed together at the neck. The man's head is cut off so that the shirt can be put on him. [J2161.2].
Finnish *18;* Finnish-Swedish *5;* Lithuanian *3;* Swedish *36* (Uppsala *13,* Stockholm *4,* Lund *1,* Liungman *7,* misc. *11*); Icelandic *1;* Irish *3;* Dutch *2;* Russian: Andrejev.

1286 *Jumping into the Breeches.* The woman tries to pull on her husband's breeches for him on both legs at once. [J2162].
Köhler-Bolte I 82; Clouston *Noodles* 201; Coffin 7. — Finnish *5;* Finnish-Swedish *2;* Estonian *3;* Lithuanian *2;* Swedish *9* (Uppsala *4,* Stockholm *2,* Liungman *1,* misc. *2*); Scottish *1;* Irish *25,* Beal II 24, Jackson FL XLVII 290; English *2;* Catalan: Amades No. 398; Dutch *2;* Walloon *1;* German *13;* Italian *3* (Tuscan 1450a—c *3*); Slovenian *2;* Serbocroatian *2;* Russian: Andrejev *2;* Turkish: Eberhard-Boratav No. 331 III. — English-American: Baughman *3;* Spanish-American: Hansen (Puerto Rico) *1.*

1287 *Numskulls unable to Count their own Number.*
Motifs: J2031. Counting wrong by not counting oneself. Numskulls conclude that one of their number is drowned. J2031.1. Numskulls count selves by sticking their noses in the sand. They then count the holes.
*BP III 149 (Grimm No. 143) n. 1; Wesselski *Hodscha Nasreddin* I 267 No. 261; Clouston *Noodles* 28ff.; Field *Pent Cuckoo* 8; Coffin *5;* Köhler-Bolte I 112; Christensen DF XLVII 181ff. — Finnish *23;* Finnish-Swedish *4;* Lithuanian *1;* Swedish *52* (Uppsala *22,* Stockholm *9,* Göteborg *2,* Lund *3,* Liungman *3,* misc. *13*); Norwegian *1;* Irish *36;* English *3;* French *19;* Catalan: Amades No. 603, cf. 509; Dutch *2;* Flemish *8;* Walloon *1;* German *6;* Swiss: Jegerlehner *Oberwallis* 317 No. 153; Hungarian *1;* Slovenian *3;* Serbocroatian *4;* Russian: Afanasiev (1287A B) *1;* India *13;* Indonesian: Coster-Wijsman 66 No. 111. — English-American: Baughman *1.*

1287* *Detecting Poisonous Mushrooms.* A peasant is told that a ten-sou piece (silver) will

darken mushrooms if they are poisonous. Since he has only nine sous, he removes one-tenth of the mushrooms.
Walloon (*1207) *1*.

1288 *Numskulls Cannot Find their Own Legs.* A stranger helps them with a switch. [J2021].
*BP III 150 (Grimm No. 143); Fb IV 32b s.v. »ben». — Finnish *17;* Estonian *1;* Swedish *10* (Uppsala *2*, Stockholm *4*, Göteborg *1*, Lund *1*, Liungman *1*, misc. *1*); Icelandic *1;* French *10;* Catalan: Amades Nos. 398, 557; Dutch *2;* Italian (Tuscan 1200, 1288b, 1450a *3;* Hungarian: Dégh No. 41; Slovenian *1;* Serbocroatian *1;* Russian: Andrejev *1;* Greek Archive *1*, Hepding *Laographia* VI 309, Argenti-Rose (Chios) II 597, Loukatos No. 20; Turkish: Eberhard-Boratav No. 331 III *2*. — English-American: Baughman *1*.

1288* »*These Are Not my Feet*,» says a peasant, whose boots have been stolen while he was in a drunken sleep; »My feet had boots on them.»
Finnish *1;* Russian: Andrejev (*2063) *1*.

1288A *Numskull cannot Find Ass he is Sitting on* [J2022].
*BP III 150 (Grimm No. 143). — Catalan: Amades No. 509; German *8;* Italian *3* (Trieste: Pinguentini No. 94, Sicilian *2*); Hungarian: Berze Nagy (1349 II*) *1;* Serbocroatian *4*. — Spanish-American: Hansen (Puerto Rico) *1*.

1289 *Each Wants to Sleep in the Middle* [J2213.1].
Finnish *4;* Hungarian *2;* Greek *1;* Russian: Andrejev *1*. — African (Ila, Rhodesia): Smith and Dale II 416 No. 15.

1290 *Swimming in the Flax-field.* Peasants go to visit the sea. They see a waving flax-field, and thinking it is the sea, jump in for a swim. [J1821].
*BP III 205; Köhler-Bolte I 112; Coffin *2;* Christensen DF XLVII 195 No. 20. — Finnish *13;* Finnish-Swedish *4;* Swedish *40* (Uppsala *15*, Stockholm *7*, Göteborg *1*, Lund *4*, Liungman *1*, misc. *12*); French *13;* Walloon *1;* Hungarian *5;* Slovenian *1;* Serbocroatian *1;* Russian: Andrejev; India *6*.

1290A* *Man Thinks Undulating Wheat Fields are Marching.* He opens city gates to welcome the wheat. It does not arrive and he assumes it was moved en route.
Walloon (*1715) *1;* Hungarian: Berze Nagy (1229*) *3*.

1290B* *Sleeping on a Feather.* Numskull, finding that one feather makes a hard pillow, thinks a sackful would be unbearable. [J2213.9].
*BP III 239; Hdwb. d. Märchens I 15. — Canada: Baughman (J2213.9); German (well known).

1291 *One Cheese Sent to Bring Back Another.* One cheese falls and rolls down the hill. She sends the second to bring back the first. [J1881.1.2].
*BP I 521 (Grimm No. 59); Coffin *4*. — Finnish *3;* Finnish-Swedish *1;* Livonian (1291) *2;* Icelandic (1431*) *1;* Irish *2;* English (1291*) *2;* Dutch *2;* Walloon *1;* German *4;* Hungarian: Dégh No. 39; Russian: Andrejev. — Spanish-American: Hansen (Puerto Rico) *1;* West Indies (Negro) *2*.

1291A *Three-legged Pot Sent to Walk Home* [J1881.1.3].
Clouston *Noodles* 36; Field *Pent Cuckoo* 5; BP I 521 n. 1. — England: Baughman (J1881.1.3); Spanish: Espinosa III 147; North American Indian: Thompson *C Coll* II 417f.

1291B *Filling Cracks with Butter.* Numskull sees cracks in the ground and feels so sorry for them that he greases them with the butter he is taking home. [J1871].
*BP I 521; Wesselski *Hodscha Nasreddin* I 250 No. 165; Hungarian (1231*); Missouri French: Carrière. Cf. Type 1386.

1291C (formerly 1291*) *The Table is Thrown out of the Sledge.* It is to go along by itself. [J1881.14]. The freezing street fence.
Finnish-Swedish *1*.

1291D *Other Objects Sent to Go by Themselves* [J1881.1].
Wesselski *Hodscha Nasreddin* I 272 No. 281; Missouri French: Carrière; Spanish: Espinosa III 147; Indonesian: Coster-Wijsman 72 No. 130. — Icelandic (1349 X*) *1*.

1291* changed to Type 1291C.

1291** *Fools Let Horse Loose to Find Road Home.*
Icelandic (1349X*) *1*.

1292* *Etiquette of a Guest.* A married daughter visiting her mother will not drive away a hog rooting in the garden since she is guest in the house.
Lithuanian (*1292) *2*.

1293 *Numskull Stays until he has Finished.* As he is making water he hears a brook flowing and mistakes what it is. He waits for a day and a half. [J1814].
*Köhler-Bolte I 485 No. 23; *Wesselski *Bebel* II 150ff., *Wesselski *Hodscha Nasreddin* I 210 No. 23; French: Fleury *Litterature orale de la Basse Normandie* 204; German: Merkens I 162 No. 193 g.; U.S.: Baughman (J1814); Hungarian: Berze Nagy (1349 XXXI*) *1*.

1293* *Learn to Swim.* The fool almost drowns when swimming. The others blame him: »Learn to swim on dry ground before you go into the water.« [J2226].
Estonian (1292*) *1;* Russian (1292*).

1293** *Keeping Life In.* The man binds a belt around his wife's neck so that life will not escape from her. She chokes to death.
Estonian (1293*) *2*.

1293A* *Woman Breaks all her Dishes* to make place for a pot.
Hungarian (Honti 1293, Berze Nagy 1388*) *3*.

1293B* *Head in the Water.* Peasant on floating log head downward in water allowed to drown: »He is drying his leggings.«
Russian: Andrejev (*1292 I).

1294 *Getting the Calf's Head out of the Pot.* A calf gets its head caught in the pot. A fool cuts off the calf's head and then breaks the pot to get it out. [J2113].
Clouston *Noodles* 89; Greek *2*, Dawkins *Modern Greek in Asia Minor* 503 No. 10; India *4*.

1294A* *Child with Head Caught in Jar.* People to cut off the head. Stranger advises to break the jar.
Rumanian (1285A) *1*.

1294B* *Ass Laden with Hay Caught between Bushes.* Fool sets fire to bushes to free him.
Greek *1*.

1295 *The Seventh Cake Satisfies.* Fool regrets that he had not eaten number seven first since that was the one that brought satisfaction. [J2213.3].
*Von der Leyen *Das Märchen* 78 and Herrigs Archiv CXIV 20 n. 2. — German: Merkens No. 89; Russian: Afanasief (*2076) *1*.

1295A *Fasting the First Month.* Numskull having enough food to last him eleven out of the twelve months fasts the entire first month so as to get the ordeal over. He starves with eleven month's supply on hand. [J2135.1].
Clouston *Noodles* 89; India *1*.

1295B *The Seventh Cucumber.* The thief, picking the seventh cucumber, remembers the Seventh Commandment; starts again from number one. Catching the thief, the owner beats him, counting from one to five (the Fifth Commandment) and then begins anew.
Lithuanian (*2426) *2*.

1295A* *Tall Bridegroom Cannot Get into Church.* Is hit on back and thus falls down and can enter.
Danish *2;* Greek *4,* Kretschmer No. 20.

1295B* *Man on Camel has Doorway Broken Down so that he can Ride in.* It does not occur to him to dismount. [J2171.6, cf. J2199.3.]
India: Thompson-Balys.

1296 *Fool's Errand.* People sent to get imaginary things. (Left-handed monkey wrench and the like.) [J2346].
*Hepding *Hessische Blätter* XVIII 110ff.; *Arts et Traditions Populaires* I (1953) 5; *Folkminnen och Folktankar* XVIII (1931) 18. — Swedish (Uppsala) *7;* Canada, England, United States: Baughman (J2346).

1296A *Fools go to Buy Good Weather* (Storm, spring). Bring back swarm of bees (butterfly) in sack. [J2327]. Cf. Type 910 G.
*Köhler-Bolte I 324f. — Catalan: Amades No. 602; French *4;* Italian: Widter-Wolf *Volksmärchen aus Venetien* No. 19; Hungarian: Berze Nagy (1292*) *1;* Swiss: Jegerlehner 150 No. 10; Greek: Hepding *Laographia* VI 310; Merkens I 36 No. 46, 52 No. 68.

1296B *Doves in the Letter.* A fool is to take two doves (eels) in a basket to a peasant, along with an explanatory letter. On the way the doves escape. The peasant reads the letter. »Where are the two doves that are in the letter?« »They escaped from the basket. It's lucky they are in the letter.«
*Christensen DF XLVII 139 No. 48. — German: Merkens III 219 No. 209.

1296* *The Unbalanced Field.* Villagers are unwilling to plow one end of the field lest the other became unbalanced.
Hungarian: Berze Nagy (1296*) *2*.

1297* *Jumping into the River after their Comrade.* Through misunderstanding one of the men jumps into the river. He calls out; the others think that he wants them to follow, and all jump in and are drowned. [J1832].
*BP II 556 n. 1; Japanese: Ikeda.

1300* changed to Type 1265*.

1301* *Prayer in Latrine.* A man having forgotten his prayers falls into a latrine. The only prayer he can remember is »God, give us this day our daily bread.»
French-Canadian.

1302* *Animal Troops.* A peasant plans to send cows and bees against an invading army [K2351.2].
Greek *1*.

1305 *The Miser and his Gold* [W153].

1305A *Workman Looks at Miser's Gold.* It will do him as much good as it does the miser.
Irish.

1305B *Miser's Treasure Stolen.* He should imagine the treasure still there: he will be as well off as before. [J1061.4].
*Wesselski *Hodscha Nasreddin* I 259 No. 201; Halm Aesop No. 412. — Irish; India: Thompson-Balys (J1061.4) *1*.

1305C *Miser Would Drink Molten Gold.* Given melted butter instead. Thinks he is taking his gold with him to the grave.
Irish.

1309 *Choosing the Clean Figs.* From figs which have been urinated on he is to choose only clean ones. In testing he eats them all.
Rumanian FFC LXXVIII 95 *1;* Hungarian: Berze Nagy (1319 XXIX*) *1*, Kirchhof *Wendunmuth* (1869) No. 123; Serbocroatian *2*.

1310 *Drowning the Crayfish as Punishment.* Eel, crab, turtle, etc. express fear of water and are thrown in. [K581.1].
*Dähnhardt *Natursagen* IV 43; Köhler-Bolte I 266. — Finnish *12;* Finnish-Swedish *3,* (222*) *5;* Livonian *1;* Estonian *1;* Lithuanian *3;* Swedish *10* (Uppsala *3,* Stockholm *1,* Göteborg *1,* Lund *1,* misc. *4*); Danish *9;* English: Baughman *2;* French *10;* German *12* (Archive *11,* Henssen Volk No. 229); Hungarian: Berze Nagy (1349 XIII*) *1;* Slovenian *2;* Russian: Andrejev; India *4;* Indonesian: Dixon 195, 196, n. 32, *De Vries *Volksverhalen* II No. 107. — Spanish-American: Hansen (Argentina) *1,* (Cuba) *1,* (Dominican Republic) *4,* (Puerto Rico) *2;* West Indies (Negro) *3;* American Indian: *Thompson *Tales* 302 n. 108. — Africa *22;* Oceanic (Philippine): Fansler MAFSL XII 443, (Tinguian): Cole 196, 197 n. 1.

1310A *Briar-patch Punishment for Rabbit.* By expressing fear of being thrown into the briar-patch he induces his captor to do so. He runs off. [K581.2]. Often a sequel to Type 175.
**Ruth I. Cline *American Literature* II 72ff.; **Espinosa JAFL XLIII 129ff.; *Dähnhardt IV 26; Köhler-Bolte I 266; *Parsons FL XXX 227.

— Missouri French: Carrière; Louisiana Creole: Fortier MAFLS II 108; Indonesia: De Vries *Volksverhalen* II 381 f. No. 147 (duck); Oceanic: Meyer *Mythen und Erzählungen der Küstbewohner der Gezellehalbinsel* 49, 187; N. A. Indian: *Thompson *C Coll* II 446; Africa (Ila, Rhodesia): Smith and Dale II 395, (Zanzibar): Bateman 38 No. 2; American Negro (Georgia): Harris *Remus* 16 No. 4; Barbadoes: Parsons JAFL XXXVIII 270; Jamaica: *Beckwith MAFLS XVII 244; West Indies: Flowers 516.

1310B *Burying the Mole as Punishment* [K581.3].
*Feilberg *Ordbog* III 1190b s.v. »ål». — Flemish (1317*) *2;* Walloon (*1214) *1;* French: RTP V 305, XI 646, XVII 547.

1310C *Throwing the Bird from a Cliff as Punishment* [K581.4].
Finnish-Swedish (222*) *5;* English: Baughman *2.* — African (Ekoi): Talbot 397.

1310* *The Crab is Thought to be the Devil.* Becomes red [J1781].
Finnish (1310**)*1.*

1311 *The Wolf Taken for a Colt.* In the man's absence eats the mare [J1752].
Finnish *7;* Estonian *1;* Swedish (Lund) *1;* Russian: Andrejev.

1312 (formerly 1312*). *The Bear Taken for a Dog* [J1753].
Finnish (1312) *4;* Russian: Andrejev. — Spanish-American: cf. Hansen (Dominican Republic) *1.*

1312* *Trying to Wash Black Animal White* [J1909.6]. Cf. Type 1183.
Wesselski *Hodscha Nasreddin* I 246. No. 142. — Slovenian.

1313 *The Man who Thought Himself Dead.* Has the corpse eat bread. (Usually has eaten from a pot of preserves said to be poisoned.)
Motifs: J2311.2. The »poisoned» pot. The wife tells the husband that a certain pot of preserves is poisoned. He decides to kill himself and eats the preserves. He believes that he is poisoned and lies down for dead.
*BP III 337; Wesselski *Hodscha Nasreddin* II 237 No. 522; Wesselski *Morlini* 49; Bolte *Frey* 214; Coffin *2;* Clouston *Noodles* 122; cf. also Motif-Index J2311—J2311.12. — Finnish *4;* Estonian *16;* Danish *3;* Dutch *2;* Flemish *4;* German *3;* Italian *2* (Pentamerone I No. 4, Tuscan 1642 *1*); Rumanian *8;* Slovenian *2;* Russian: Andrejew *4;* Turkish: Eberhard-Boratav No. 361 *1.* — Spanish-American: Hansen (Puerto Rico) *3;* West Indies (Negro) *1.*

1313A *The Man Takes Seriously the Prediction of Death* [J2311.1, J2311.1.1, J2311.4].
I. *The Fool and the Prophet.* (a) A passerby tells a fool who is sitting on a tree limb and sawing the limb that he will fall. When the fool falls, he believes the passerby to be a prophet. See Type 1240. (b) The fool demands that the »prophet» or a fortuneteller tell him when he will die.
II. *The Death Prophecy.* He is told he will die (a) when a red thread or

the like comes from his body, (b) when his hands and feet become cold, (c) when a drop of water falls on his head, or (d) other signs.

III. *The »Dead» Man.* The prophesied event occurs and the fool thinks he is dead. (a) When his pall-bearers or passersby argue over which road to take, the fool sits up and advises them: »When I was alive, I took such a one.» (b) He is beaten by the soldiers, etc., and returns home to warn his friends to avoid soldiers in the afterworld, etc.

*Wesselski *Hodscha Nasreddin* I 216f. No. 49; *Köhler-Bolte I 135, 486, 505; Pauli (ed. Bolte) No. 860. — Lithuanian (*1240A) *7;* French: Millien et Delarue 293 n. 24; French-Canadian; Walloon; Italian Novella: Rotunda (J2311.4); Hungarian: Berze Nagy (1694*) *2;* Serbocroatian *5;* Slovenian *1;* India *15.*

1313B »*When Shall I Die?*» — »When the buttocks turn cold». Is saved from death by a whipping.
Lithuanian (*1240A) *7;* Serbocroatian *1.*

1313C *Dead Man Speaks up.* A numskull who has lain down thinking he is dead is carried off in a bier. The carriers lose their way. He speaks up, »I always went that way when I was alive.» [J2311.4].
Wesselski *Hodscha Nasreddin* I 216f. No. 49; Walloon *1;* Italian Novella: *Rotunda; Serbocroatian *5;* India (1313A III) *12.* Cf. Pauli (ed. Bolte) No. 860.

1313A* *In the Open Grave.* A drunk man falls in and thinks he is dead when he wakes up. [J2311]. Cf. Type 1531.
*Wesselski *Hodscha Nasreddin* Nos. 6, 46, 49, 121. — Finnish *7.*

1314 *The Buttercask Taken for a Dead Man.* Fools knock it in two. [J1783.1].
Finnish *9;* Russian: Andrejev; Greek: Loukatos No. 9.

1315 *The Big Tree Taken for a Snake.* Killed with guns and spears. [J1771.1].
Finnish *3;* Danish *2;* German: Meckl. No. 104; Russian: Andrejev; India *1.*

1315* *The Steamship Thought to be the Devil* [J1781.1].
Finnish-Swedish (1315**) *2;* Slovenian (train, bicycle) *1.*

1315** *A White Mare Thought to be a Church* [J1761.2].
Finnish-Swedish (1315***) *2;* Swedish *9* (Uppsala *3,* Stockholm *2,* Lund *1,* misc. *3*); Danish *1;* Serbocroatian *1.*

1315A* *The Mill Taken for a Church.* The husband who is not a churchgoer is sent by his wife to church with an offering of a fowl. He takes a mill for a church and its grindstone for saints and leaves the offering at the mill.
Lithuanian (*1751) *3.*

1316 *Rabbit Thought to be a Cow.* Servant sent to bring in cows is found chasing rabbits. [J1757]. Cf. Type 570.
*BP III 260 (Grimm No. 162). — U.S.: Baughman (J1757) *3.*

1316* changed to Type 1339A.
1316** changed to Type 1339B.
1316*** *The Earthworm Thought to be a Snake or other Monster* [J1755].
Swedish (Lund) *2;* Flemish *5;* India *1.*

1316**** *The Ass Thought to be a Hare* [J1754].
Flemish *1;* Walloon (*1317) *1.*

1317 *Blind Men and Elephant.* Four blind men feel an elephant's leg, tail, ear, and body respectively, and conclude it is like a log, a rope, a fan, and something without beginning or end. [J1761.10].
*Taylor *English Riddles in Oral Tradition* (Berkeley, 1951) 582; Chavannes I 336 No. 86; Rhys David »Does Al-Ghazzali Use an Indian Metaphor?» *Journal of the Royal Asiatic Society* 1911. — India *2.*

1317* *The Dungbeetle is Mistaken for a Bee* [J1751]. »I know you well enough; you have put on a blue coat.»
Finnish *2;* Estonian *4;* Swedish *9* (Uppsala *1,* Stockholm *1,* Lund *1,* misc. *6);* Danish *10;* India *2.*

1318 *Objects Thought to be Ghosts* [J1782].

1318A (formerly 1318*) *Robber or Animal in the Church Thought to be a Ghost* [J1782.1].
Swedish (Uppsala) *1;* Flemish *5.* — Franco-American; English-American: Baughman (J1782.2) *1.*

1318B *Dropping Dough Thought to be Ghosts.*
Finnish (FFC XXXIII 47 No. 101) *2;* Lithuanian (1264) *1;* Estonian (FFC XXV 137 No. 101) *2;* Swedish (GS 1337) *15,* Russian: Andrejev (1264 I).

1318C *Person in Haunted House Shoots off all his Toes* thinking they are ghosts [J1782.8]. (Cf. J1838.)
Finnish *1;* U.S.: Baughman (J1838).

1319 *Pumpkin Sold as an Ass's Egg* [J1772.1]. Thrown into a bush. The numskull thinks the rabbit which runs out is a colt.
*BP I 317f.; Hepding *Hessische Blätter* XVIII 108, *Laographia* VII 308; *California Folklore Quarterly* II 29; Frey *Gartengesellschaft* 214; Köhler-Bolte I 50, 135, 323, 506; Clouston *Noodles* 38; Fb III 1142a s.v. »æg»; Wesselski *Hodscha Nasreddin* I 249 No. 163; Coffin *8;* Christensen DF XLVII 208 No. 63. — Estonian (1676*) *4;* Lithuanian *21;* Swedish *14* (Uppsala *3,* Stockholm *3,* Göteborg *1,* Lund *2,* misc. *5);* Danish *1;* Scottish *1;* Irish *34;* French *39;* Catalan: Amades No. 363; Flemish (1319*) *4,* (1676*) *4;* Walloon (1319 A*) *1;* German *29* (Archive *28,* Henssen Volk No. 224); Swiss: Jegerlehner Oberwallis 324 No. 157; Hungarian: Berze Nagy (1336*) *10;* Italian (Sicilian *2);* Slovenian *5;* Serbocroatian *5;* Russian: Andrejev (1676*) *2;* Greek *1;* India *7;* Chinese: Eberhard FFC CXX p. 275, CXXVIII Nos. 139, 233, Graham No. 205 p. 224. — English-American: Baughman *10;* Spanish-American: Hansen (Argentina) *1,* (Chile) *1;* West Indies (Negro) *1;* American Negro: (Michigan) Dorson No. 147; North American Indian (Wyandot): Barbeau GS Can XI No. 78. Literary Treatment: Pauli (ed. Bolte) II 437 No. 841.

1319* *Other Mistaken Identities.*

1319A* (formerly 1321*). *The Watch Mistaken for the Devil's Eye.* Knocked to pieces. [J1781.2].
: Finnish *1;* Estonian *6;* Lithuanian (*1679); Rumanian 1331—1346 (3) *2;* Flemish *4;* Hungarian: Berze Nagy (1344*) *6;* Greek *1.* — American Negro (Michigan): Dorson No. 48.

1319B* *Frog Thought to be Fig.* Fool asks if it has wept.
: Danish *4;* Greek (1319*) *1.*

1319C* *The Drowned Fish.* Fish jumps from river. Fools think it is drowned and bury it.
: Greek (1318**) *2,* Kretschmer No. 20.

1319D* *Mistaken Identities:* wolf as shepherd dog; snow on mountain for hairs of mountain; vultures for angels; snow for cheese; snow for white earth.
: Greek (1318**) *3.*

1319E* *Fox Mistaken for Rabbit and Cooked.* Fools wonder why it will not boil.
: Greek (1316*) *1.*

1319F* *Bear Mistaken for a Foreigner* [J1762.8].
: Lithuanian (*1283) *2.*

1319G* *Boot Mistaken for an Axe-sheath.*
: Lithuanian (*1282) *2.*

1319H* *Boat Believed to have had a Colt.*
: Swedish (Uppsala) *3.*

1319J* *Fool Eats Beetle Thinking it Is Blueberry with Wings.*
: Finnish *2;* Swedish (Uppsala) *3.*

1319K* *Fools take Moon to be Warship.* Lock themselves in and become hungry.
: Icelandic (1349 VII*) *1.*

1319L* *Moonlight Thought to be Milk.*
: Hungarian: Berze Nagy (1321*) *4.*

1319M* *Storks Thought to be Cows.*
: Hungarian: Berze Nagy (1349 I*) *4.*

1320 *Breath in the Cold Air Taken for Tobacco Smoke* [J1801].
Finnish *4;* Russian: Andrejev.

1320* *Fish-eating Ikon.* Fool thinks ikon in bag has eaten fish he carried with it. Breaks ikon.
: Greek (1322**) *2.*

1321 *Fools Frightened.* Cf. Type 1677.
: Danish *4.*

1321A *Fright at the Creaking of a Wheelbarrow (Mill)* [J2615].
: Flemish (1321*) *5;* India: Thompson-Balys (J2615). — U.S.(North Carolina): Brown Collection I 697.

1321B *Fools Afraid of their own Shadow.*
: Icelandic (1349 II*) *1.*

1321C *Fools are Frightened at the Humming of Bees.* Thinks it is a drum. [J2614.1].
: *BP II 555; Christensen DF XLVII 194ff. No. 20.

1321* changed to Type 1319A*.

1321D* (formerly 1323*) *The Ticking of Clock Thought to be the Gnawing of Mice* [J1789.2].
: Christensen DF XLVII 187. — Swedish *4* (Stockholm *2,* Lund *1,* misc. *1*); Danish *2;* French *2;* Flemish *1.*

1322 (formerly 1322*) *Words in a Foreign Language Thought to be Insults* [J1802]. Cf. Type 1699.
*BP III 149; Hepding *Laographia* VI 314. — Swedish (Uppsala) *1;* Flemish *5.* — Franco-American.

1322A* *Grunting Pig.* Numskull thinks that grunting pig is calling his name.
Hungarian: Berze Nagy (1337*) *2.*

1323 (formerly 1322**) *The Windmill Thought to be a Holy Cross* [J1789.1].
Christensen DF XLVII 212 No. 68. — Finnish *4;* Finnish-Swedish (1315*) *5;* Danish *2;* Irish *7;* Serbocroatian *2;* Russian: Andrejev *2;* India *2.*

1323* changed to Type 1321D*.

1324* *The Man behind the Crucifix* says »good evening» to the drunken man, who thinks Christ is speaking to him [K1971.7]. Cf. Type 1380.
Swedish *9* (Uppsala *8,* Stockholm *1*); Flemish *2.*

1324A* *Crucifix Punished* for permitting a hail storm [V123].
Hungarian: Berze Nagy (1346*) *3.*

1325 *Moving Away from Trouble.*

1325A (formerly 1325*) *The Fireplace Gives too Much Heat.* Instead of putting out the fire fools decide to move the fireplace. [J2104].
Flemish (1325*) *4;* German: Henssen Volk No. 226.

1325B *Moving the Church away from the Dung.*
Irish.

1325C *Moving a House to Prevent Wind from Blowing through the Door.*
Irish.

1325D *Moving a House away from Nettles.*
Irish.

1325* *Bird's Dung Falls on Record Books:* decision to exile all sparrows.
Greek (1300*) *1.*

1326 *Moving the Church.* The stolen coat. To see whether the church is moving someone lays down his coat in front of it. It is stolen. They think the church has passed over it. [J2328].
Köhler-Bolte I 135, 324; Hepding *Hessische Blätter* XVIII 106; Coffin *2;* Christensen DF L 218 No. 79. — Danish *2;* Irish *12;* French *18;* Catalan: Amades Nos. 557, 586, 606, 620, 656; Dutch *3;* Flemish (1326*) *3;* Walloon *1;* German *20* (Archive *19,* Henssen Volk No. 231); Italian (Tuscan 1200 *1*); Hungarian (Berze Nagy 1299*) *7;* Slovenian *2;* Serbocroatian *6;* Istrian No. 48; English-American: Baughman *1.*

1326A *Straightening the Bridge.* A man slips on cow-dung; thinks the bridge has collapsed.
Walloon *1.*

1326B *Moving the Large Stone.* Rope stretches and peasants think stone is moving. Rope breaks and all fall into water.
Walloon *2.*

1327 *Emptying the Meal Sack.* To convince arguers of the emptiness of their quarrel he empties sack of meal (pot of oil). [J2062.1].

Clouston *Noodles* 26, Field *Pent Cuckoo* 2; England: Baughman (J2062.1); Serbocroatian *1;* Greek (1284*) *1.*

1327A *Fool Reenacts Case in Court.* Shows how the pig was kicked to death, the judge to act as the pig.

Hungarian: Berze Nagy (1294*) *3.*

1327* *The Cup with Two and Three Handles.* When the servant girl presents the cup to her host (the emperor) she holds the handle herself. When there are three she holds the third one toward her. [J2665.1].

Flemish *3.*

1328* *Letting the Boiling Milk Run over,* thinking that it is overflowing [J1813.2].

Flemish *1;* India *1.*

1328A* *Oversalting the Soup.* Each member of the family remembers to put in salt.

Finnish *13.*

1329* *To Keep the Croaking Frogs from Disturbing the Prince's Slumber* they shoot at them all night [J2105].

Flemish *1.*

1330 *Quenching the Burning Boat.* People row to land and fetch water from a spring to put out the fire. [J2162.3].

Finnish *2;* Finnish-Swedish *3;* Japanese: Ikeda (J2162.3). — Slovenian *1;* Russian: Andrejev; Greek: Loukatos No. 16.

1330* *Salt for Salt-carriers.* Fools carrying loads of salt send for salt for their food.

Greek *1.*

1331 *The Covetous and the Envious.* Of two envious men one is given the power of fulfilling any wish, on condition that the other shall receive double. He wishes that he may lose an eye. [J2074]. Cf. Type 750.

*BP II 219 note 1; Crane *Vitry* 212 No. 126; Pauli (ed. Bolte) No. 647; Reinhard JAFL XXXVI 383 n. 1; Krappe *Bulletin Hispanique* XXXIX 31. — Lithuanian *1;* Catalan: Amades No. 507; Flemish (1331*) *1;* Hungarian: Berze Nagy (1349 XXX*) *1;* Greek (1610*) *1,* (Chios): Argenti-Rose II 610 No. 3; India *4.* — Literary Treatments: Bédier *Fabliaux* 457; Aesop: Wienert FFC LVI 79 (ET 446), 132 (ST 387); *Scala Celi* 106b No. 589; Italian Novella: Rotunda. (J2074); Spanish Exempla: Keller.

1331* *Learning to Read.*

1331A* *Buying Spectacles.* Ignorant man thinks he can thereby immediately read.

Walloon (*1233) *1.*

1331B* *Letters too Small.* Boy cannot read because letters are smaller than in his schoolbook. [J2258].

India (J2258) *1.*

1331C* *Writing Letters Slowly:* recepient cannot read fast.

United States: Baughman (J2422.2).

1331D* *Teaching Latin.* Fool cuts off tip of pupil's tongue and orders him to lick cold iron. Pupil injures himself. [K1068.2].

Lithuanian (*2444) *1.*

1332 *Which is the Greatest Fool* [J1712]. Cf. Types 1384, 1685A.

A passerby salaams to or tosses a coin to three (four) men. They ask him for whom it was intended. He says he meant it for the greatest fool [J1712]. Each tells a story to prove he is the greatest:

(a) *Who Will Speak First.* Type 1351.

(b) *The Hungry Fool at his In-Laws — Cheeks Cut.* The fool goes to visit his parents-in-law and, being bashful, refuses to eat. Later he stuffs eggs, etc., into his mouth only to be discovered by his mother-in-law who calls a surgeon. The surgeon believes the fool's cheeks are abcessed and cuts them open [X372.4.1].

(c) *The Fool at his In-Laws — Falls into Well.* The bashful fool dresses as a beggar to visit his parents-in-law. When his mother-in-law comes out of the house to give him food, he backs away and tumbles into a well, etc.

(d) *The Hungry Fool at his In-Laws — the Priest Beaten.* Type 1685A.

(e) *Other tales about fools.*

Wesselski *Hodscha Nasreddin* I 263 No. 237; Christensen DF L 91. — India *10*. — West Indies: Flowers 484.

1332* *Forgetfulness Causes Useless Journey* [cf. J2241].

1332A* *Fools Forget to Borrow Horse* until journey is almost over: return for him.
Icelandic (1349 III*) *1*.

1332B* *Fools Forget to Greet Hostess* of the inn. Return.
Icelandic (1349 IV*) *2*.

1332C* *Doctor no Longer Needed.* As the fool starts for the doctor the wife changes her mind. He continues to the doctor so as to tell him about it and to say that now he need not come. [J2241].
*Wesselski *Hodscha Nasreddin* II 233 No. 456.

1333 *The Shepherd who Cried »Wolf!« too often.* When the wolf really comes no one believes him [J2172.1].

Aesop (Halm No. 353, Jacobs No. 43); India *4*. — West Indies: Flowers 489.

1334 *The Local Moon.* A numskull greets the old moon as if it were new. »I haven't seen it before, for I have just come to the city.« (Each town thought to have a different moon.) [J2271.1].

*Wesselski *Hodscha Nasreddin* I 218 No. 52. — Walloon (*1334) *1;* Italian (Tuscan [1212] *1*); Serbocroatian *1;* Russian: Afanasiev (*2060) *1;* Greek (1324*) *1;* India *2*.

1335 *The Eaten Moon.* The numskull sees a cow drink from a pool where the moon is reflected. The moon goes under a cloud. He thinks the cow has eaten the moon and slaughters her to recover it. [J1791.1].

Wesselski *Hodscha Nasreddin* I 241 No. 124; Köhler-Bolte I 90, 498; Christensen DF XLVII 181. — French *4;* Walloon (*1335A) *1;* German *9* (Archive *8*, Henssen Jül. No. 462); Italian (Sicilian *3*); Hungarian: Dégh No. 41; Slovenian *1;* Greek: Hepding *Laographia* VI 308f.

1335A *Rescuing the Moon.* A numskull sees the moon in the water and throws a rope in to rescue it, but falls in himself. He sees the moon in the sky. At least the moon was saved! [J1791.2].
  *Wesselski *Hodscha Nasreddin* I 241 No. 124; Christensen DF XLVII 217—18 no. 78. — French *9;* Catalan: Amades cf. Nos. 604, 607; Greek (1325*) *3;* Walloon (1335B) *1;* Spanish-American: Hansen (Puerto Rico) *1;* American Negro: Harris *Nights* 100 No. 19.

1335* *Setting Sun (Rising Moon) Mistaken for Fire* [J1806].
  Christensen DF XLVII 176, 196; American Negro: Harris *Nights* 230 No. 39, Work JAFL XXXII 403, Parsons MAFLS XVI 32. — Finnish *2.*

1336 *Diving for Cheese.* Man (animal) sees moon reflected in water and, thinking it a cheese, dives in for it. [J1791.3]. This is Type 34 with human actors.
  *Dähnhardt *Natursagen* IV 230f.; *Clouston *Noodles* 44; Field *Pent Cuckoo* 18; Köhler-Bolte I 107; Christensen DF XLVII 217—18 No. 78. — Flemish: De Meyere *Vlaamsche Vertelselschat* II 68 No. 8; French: Gaidoz et Sébillot *Blason Populaire de France* 112; Spanish: Espinosa III Nos. 206f.; Hungarian: Berze Nagy (1325) *1;* Greek (1325**) *1;* India *1.* — N. A. Indian: Thompson *Tales* 295 n. 81. — African (Zulu): Callaway 357 (cf. J1791.4).

1336A *Man does not Recognize his own Reflection in the Water (Mirror)* [J1791.7]. Cf. Types 92, 1168A, 1383.
  *Wesselski *Hodscha Nasreddin* I 276 No. 311; Penzer VI 86f. — Finnish *2;* Greek (1326*, 1326**) *3;* Turkish: Eberhard-Boratav No. 329 *1;* India *1;* Indonesian: DeVries No. 17; Hawaii: Beckwith *Myth* 441; Chinese: Eberhard FFC CXX 298 No. 7 III; Korean: Eckart *Koreanische Märchen* (1920) 31ff. — English-American (U.S.): Randolph *Talking Turtle* p. 62; American Negro: Harris *Remus* 68 No. 14.

1337 *Peasant Visits the City* [J1742]. (Cf. Type 1339D.)

1337A *Other Side of the Street.* Peasants seeking an inn in the city, cross and recross street seeking »the other side».
  Walloon (*1275B) *1.*

1337B *Garbage for Sale.* Country woman seeing garbage wagon in city thinks garbage is for sale [J1742].
  Greek (1340*) *1.*

1337C *The Long Night.* A group of peasants stop at an inn, taking the one room available. The night seems interminable; finally it develops that they have been inside a cupboard for 24 hours. Cf. Type 1684A*.
  Pauli (ed. Bolte) No. 263. — Finnish *21;* Spanish (1684) *2;* Walloon (*1223) *2.*

1338 *City Strangers Visit the Country.*

1338A (formerly 2010*) The girl who had lived in the city: »Do turnips grow on the ground or on a tree?» [J1731].
  Estonian (2010) *7.*

1339 *Strange Foods.*
Serbocroatian *1.*

1339A *The Fool is Unacquainted with Sausages.* He squeezes the inside out and takes the covering for a sack [J1732.1].
Estonian *1.*

1339B *Fool is Unacquainted with Bananas.* Throws away the fruit, finds the rest bitter. (Similar for watermelon, plums.) [J1732.2].
England, Canada, United States: Baughman.

1339C *Woman Unacquainted with Tea* serves the boiled leaves with butter (or boils unground coffee beans). [J1732.3]. Cf. Type 1691B.
Finnish *20;* Scotland: Baughman; German: Knoop *Sagen und Erzählungen aus der Provinz Posen* 211 No. 6, Jungbauer *Volk Erzählt* p. 309.

1339D *Peasants in a City Order a Whole Portion of Mustard.* Burn themselves. [J1742.3].
Pauli (ed. Bolte) No. 672; Köhler-Bolte I 498. — Finnish (pepper); Livonian (1316) *1;* Swedish (1316**) *3.*

1339E *All Cooked for One Meal* (beans, rice, tea, bacon). [J1813.7, J1813.9, J1813.9.1.]
Lithuanian (*2439) *1;* Russian (!710*) *1;* U.S.: Baughman (J1813.9).

1341 *Fools Warn Thief what Not to Steal.* Explain where everything is and where the key is kept. [J2091, J2091.1]. Cf. Types 1525P, 1577*.
*Bolte Zs. f. Vksk. IX 87; *Pauli (ed. Bolte) No. 74. — Icelandic (1431*) *2;* Hungarian: Berze Nagy (1688*) *1.*

1341A *The Fool and the Robbers.* Fool's talking causes himself and companion to be robbed. Thieves stumble over him as he lies on the ground. »What is this, a log?» The fool: »Does a log have five annas in its pocket?» When they have robbed him he says, »Ask the merchant in the tree if my money is good.» They rob the merchant. [J2356; cf. N455.1]. Cf. Type 1577*.
Clouston *Noodles* 100. — Spanish (*1654) *1;* Hungarian: Berze Nagy (1688**) *3;* Spanish-American: Hansen (**1676) (Puerto Rico) *2.*

1341B *The Lord has Risen.* A parson hides his money in a holy place and leaves a sign. »The Lord is in this Place.» A thief takes the money and leaves a sign, »He is risen and is no longer here.» [J1399.1].
*Pauli (ed. Bolte) No. 74. — Flemish: De Meyere *Vlaamsche Vertelselschat* III 146 No. 242; Greek (1736*) *1;* Chinese: Eberhard FFC CXX p. 271 No. 1, IV, 2.

1341C *Robbers Commiserated.* A buffoon says to robbers in his house, »You can't find anything here in the dark, for I can find nothing in broad daylight.» [J1392.2].
*Wesselski *Bebel* I 132 No. 32; Scala Celi 104b No. 567; Mensa Philosophica No. 62. — Finnish *6.*

1341A* *Thief as Dog.* Thief enters house to steal but stumbles over chair. The husband wonders what the noise is. The wife says that it is probably the dog. The thief stumbles over box. The husband gets up and asks who is making noise. The thief crouches like a dog and says, »It is I, the dog.» Cf. Type 1363*.
Serbocroatian *1*. — Spanish-American: Hansen (Dominican Republic) *1*.

1341B* *Escaped Slave's Talkativeness* brings about his recapture.
Spanish-American: Hansen (**1709A) (Cuba) *1*.

1342 *Warming Hands and Cooling Soup with Same Breath.*
Halm Aesop No. 64. — Catalan: Amades No. 1665; Hungarian: Berze Nagy (1349 XXVI*) *2*.

1343 *Hanging Game.* Comrade to rescue fool when he whistles. Hangs himself. [N334.2].
Christensen DF XLVII 200 No. 36; Feilberg *Ordbog* I 731b s.v. »hænge». — Estonian FFC XXV 122 Nos. 40, 41; Lithuanian (3309) *2*; Swedish (GS 1339) *7*; Danish *8*; Icelandic: Boberg (N334.2).

1344 *Lighting a Fire from the Sparks from a Box on the Ear.* Cf. Type 1372.
Swedish (GS 1343) *15* (Uppsala *6*, Stockholm *1*, Göteborg *1*, Liungman *2*, misc. *5*).

1345* *Stupid Stories Depending on Puns.*
Greek *3*.

1346* *Easy Problem Made Hard.*

1346A* *Guess how Many Eggs I Have and you shall Get all Seven* [J2712.2].
Christensen DF XLVII 214 No. 73. — Swedish (Uppsala) *3*; Greek (1699) *2*.

1347 *Living Crucifix Chosen.* Peasants take their old crucifix to an artist for a new one. The artist asks them whether they want a living or dead crucifix. Argument: living God takes less for upkeep and he can be killed later. [J1738.2].
*Pauli (ed. Bolte) No. 409; Italian Novella: Rotunda (J1738.2); French *9;* Walloon (1869*) *2*; Hungarian: Berze Nagy (1335**) *4*.

1347* *The Statue's Father.* A vigilant at image of St. Joseph's believes he has been told to rest for fifteen days. Returns to find old image gone and a new one in its place. He thanks the statue for the favor done him by its father.
Walloon (*1677) *1*.

1348 (formerly 2009*) *The Imaginative Boy.* »I surely saw a hundred wolves.» — »There weren't so many as that.» — »Well, what made the noise in the bushes?» [W211.2].
Estonian *4;* Lithuanian (*1863) *2;* Flemish: De Meyere *Vlaamsche Vertelselschat* III 66 No. 200; German (well known); Italian (Tuscan 1875) *1;* Serbian: Krauss *Sagen und Märchen der Südslaven* II 169 No. 120; Serbocroatian *1;* Russian: Afanasiev *1;* Gypsy: Kraus *Zigeunerhumor* p. 161; India *2*.

1349* *Miscellaneous Numskull Tales.*

1349A* *Covering the Cow.* Fools lay themselves on her back.
Icelandic (1349 VI*) *1*.

1349B* *Fools Leave Old Woman Behind on Beach.* Drowned at high tide.
Icelandic (1349 VIII*) *2*.

1349C* *Fools Buy Iron to Make a Boat.* Try it on way home. Iron sinks.
Icelandic (1349 IX*) *1*.

1349D* *What Is the Joke?* Nobleman asks peasant to hit his hand. Withdraws it so that peasant hits the wall. Later peasant tries this on a friend — but friend is to hit peasant's face.
Hungarian: Berze Nagy (1331*) *3*.

1349E* *To Prevent Straying.* Remedy for keeping animals from straying from home used to keep person from going off with Gypsy.
Swedish (GS 1344) *61* (Stockholm *50*, Göteborg *1*, misc. *10*).

1349F* *To Save the Honor of his Village*, a peasant climbs a tree to answer the cuckoo from the next village. While he is doing so, a bird eats his horse.
Hungarian: Berze Nagy (1341*) *2*.

1349G* *Cold Spell has Broken.* Mother concerned about her son outside in the cold sits by the stove and says »It seems to me the cold spell has broken.»
Rumanian (1481*) *1*.

1349H* *Castrating a Dead Horse.*
Hungarian: Berze Nagy (1349 XVII*) *2*.

1349J* *Fur Coat Stroked with Whetstone* in order to clean it.
Hungarian: Berze Nagy (1349 VII*) *3*.

1349K* *Numskulls Try to Push the Fog Away.*
Hungarian: Berze Nagy (1349 XXVIII*) *6*.

1349L* *Curing Fever by Dipping into Well.* When his mother, wife, etc., is ill with a fever, the fool dips her into a well, because he remembers seeing an iron sickle cooled in that way. [J2214.9, J2412.6].
India (1338*) *4*.

1349M* *The Answered Prayer.* Man without food calls on God and accidentally gets food. Thinks God has answered prayer.
Danish *1*; German (1388*), Henssen *Volk Erzählt* No. 286.

1349N* *Leeches Prescribed by Doctor Eaten by Patient.*
*Christensen DF XLVII 139 No. 47; French: RTP XI 519; German: Merkens II 109 No. 131.

STORIES ABOUT MARRIED COUPLES

1350 *The Loving Wife.* The man feigns death. The wife is immediately ready to take as husband the man who brings her the news. Cf. Type 1510.

Motifs: K2213. Treacherous wife. H466. Feigned death to test wife's faithfulness. T231.3. Faithless widow ready to marry messenger who brings news of husband's death.

Jackson FL XLVII 290 (3); Espinosa II 355ff. — Finnish *8;* Swedish *4* (Uppsala *2*, Stockholm *1*, misc. *1*); Norwegian *1;* Danish *2*, Grundtvig No. 102; Scottish *2;* Irish *85*, Beal II 53f., III 257f. No. 4, VII 71; Spanish *2;* Rumanian *3;* Hungarian: Dégh No. 30, Berze Nagy (1459*) *1;* Russian: Andrejev *1;* India *1.* — Spanish-American: Hansen (Argentina) *1;* West Indies (Negro) *1.* — African *1.*

1351 *The Silence Wager.* A man and his wife make a wager as to who shall speak first (close the door). The man (woman) becomes jealous and scolds; loses the wager. [J2511].

**W. N. Brown »The Silence Wager Stories: their Origin and their Diffusion» *American Journal of Philology* XLIII (1922) 289—317; *Anderson in Tauscher *Volksmärchen* 189; Bolte Zs. f. Vksk. XXVIII 135 n. 1; Köhler-Bolte II 578; Liungman SSF III 447; Wesselski *Hodscha Nasreddin* I 263ff.; Clouston *Tales* II 15ff.; Coffin *2;* Basset *1001 Contes* II 401. — Finnish *2;* Lithuanian *1;* Swedish (Uppsala) *1;* Norwegian *1;* Danish *8;* Scottish *1;* Irish *11;* English *1;* French *7;* Catalan: Amades No. 371; Dutch *1;* Flemish *3,* [1315*] *3;* Walloon *2;* Italian *4* (Tuscan [1365] *1,* Sicilian *3*); Hungarian *2;* Czech: Tille Soupis II (2) 396 *4;* Slovenian *8;* Russian: Andrejev *1;* Greek *2,* Loukatos No. 23; Turkish: Eberhard-Boratav No. 334 *2;* Iran: Christensen No. 27; Palestine: Smith-Kahle No. 30; India (1351 + 1351A Ind) *15;* Chinese: Eberhard FFC CXX 276 No. 1 (XV), FFC CXXVIII 235f. No. 142. — Spanish-American: Hansen (Argentina) *1,* (Puerto Rico) *1;* Portuguese-American (Brazilian): Camara Cascudo p. 48; West Indies (Negro) *1;* French-Canadian *1.*

1351A *God Help You!* Husband and wife quarrel and place a plank between them in bed. During the night the husband sneezes. »God help you,» says the wife. »Do you really mean that?» he asks. »Yes!» »Then away with the plank!» Cf. Type 1443*.

*Ranke in *Peuckert Festschrift* 45 n. 14; Zs. f. Vksk. XVI 293. — Spanish (*1355) *1.*

1351A* *Lost Tongue.* When man reproves wife for verbosity, she becomes silent. After two days, he begins extensive search until wife asks »What are you hunting for?» — »Your tongue.»

Walloon *1;* Hungarian: Berze Nagy (1371*) *2.*

1351B* *Guilty to Speak First.* Shopkeepers are arrested for quarreling. Judge tells the one who was wrong to speak first. Both remain silent.
Walloon *1.*

1351C* *Obstinate Wife Protests* when she thinks her husband is about to be castrated.
Finnish *7.*

1352 *The Devil Guards the Wife's Chastity.* A man leaving home commends his wife to the devil [C12.4]. The devil carries off all lovers and guards her. He says that he had rather guard wild horses. Cf. Type 1164.

*Wesselski *Märchen* 193; **W. D. Paden JAFL LVIII (1945) 35ff.; Coffin *1.* — German *1.*

1352A *Seventy Tales of a Parrot Prevent a Wife's Adultery.* The parrot keeps her interested until her husband's return. [K1591]. Cf. Types 435*, 1422. Introduction to *Seventy Tales of a Parrot.*

*Schmidt *Çukasaptati* (Kiel, 1894, Stuttgart, 1896); Köhler-Bolte I 47, 336, 513; Clouston *Tales* II 196ff.; Spanish (*435) *2;* Italian (Tuscan [853], [923] *2,* Sicilian *1352 2*); Serbocroatian *2;* Turkish: Eberhard-Boratav No. 52 *1.*

1352* *The Woman's Coarse Act.* The widow mourns for her husband. When the new suitor tells her to knock out the teeth of the deceased with a stone and she obeys him, he leaves her. [T231.4].
    Estonian 2. Cf. Type 1510.

1353 *The Old Woman as Trouble Maker.* Beats the devil [G303.10.5]. She advises a loving wife to cut hairs from her husband's beard as a means of increasing his love. She tells the man that his wife is untrue and will try to cut his throat. He kills his wife. [K1085]. Cf. Type 1573*.
    O. Gjerdman *Saga och Sed* (1941) 1ff.; Wesselski *Märchen* 194; Prato Zs. f. Vksk. IX 189ff., 311ff. — Finnish-Swedish (FFC VI 15) *2;* Estonian (1165*) *1;* Lithuanian *21;* Swedish *48* (Uppsala *6,* Stockholm *3,* Göteborg *23,* Lund *4,* Liungman *2,* misc. *10*); Norwegian *4,* Solheim No. 823 *1;* Danish: MS. DFS (E. T. Kr. 1051); Icelandic (823) *3;* Scottish *1;* Irish *53,* Beal II 206, IX 66f. No. 2, XVIII 144f. No. 1; French *3;* Dutch *1;* German *10* (Archive *8,* Henssen Jül. No. 471, Henssen Volk No. 242); Hungarian: Berze Nagy (369*) *1;* Czech: Tille Soupis I 81 *3;* Slovenian *1;* Serbocroatian *5;* Russian: Andrejev (1165) *1;* India *3.* — Literary Treatment: Chauvin II 158 No. 48, 195 No. 20.

1354 *Death for the Old Couple.* Woman with sick husband: »Would that Death might take me in his stead.» When Death comes she points to her husband. [J217.0.1, K2065.1].
    Lithuanian (1355) *2;* German: Peuckert *Schlesische Märchen* No. 229; Italian Novella: Rotunda (K2065.1); Serbocroatian *4;* India: Ruben FFC CXXXIII 118; U.S.: Baughman (J217.0.1.1).

1354A* *Widower's Relief.* Old man of dead wife: You have caused me much trouble, but now you will not do so again.
    Greek (1294*) *1.*

1354B* *Widower's Good Day.* A mourning widower is taken to a cabaret by his friends. Enjoying himself, he concludes that it has been a good day.
    Walloon (1359*) *1.*

1355 *The Man Hidden under the Bed.*

1355A *The Lord Above; the Lord Below.* A husband returning home surprises a woman and her paramour and a numskull who has blundered in. The woman hides the numskull in the bed and the paramour under it. The husband, who is leaving on a journey, lifts his hands to heaven and says, »I commend you to the Lord above.» — The numskull: »Commend her rather to the lord below!» [K1525].
    *Wesselski *Hodscha Nasreddin* I 271 n. 1, *Bebel* II 99 No. 2; Köhler-Bolte III 167; *Morlini* 286 No. 30; Bédier *Fabliaux* 453; Lithuanian (2912*) *3;* German: Blumml *Beiträge zur deutschen Volksdichtung* (1908) 129 No. 1; Rumanian (1380 II) *1,* (1654*) *1;* Serbocroatian *1.* — Portuguese-American (Brazil): Camara Cascudo p. 46.

1355B *Adulteress Tells her Lover,* »*I Can See the Whole World.*» Hidden shepherd asks, »Can you see my lost calves (ass)?» [K1271.4].
    Lithuanian (*2905) *5;* Hungarian: Berze Nagy (1654*) *3;* India *1;*

French-Canadian. — Literary Treatment: Italian Novella: Rotunda (K1532.3); *Cent Nouvelles Nouvelles* No. 12.

1355C *The Lord Above Will Provide.* A youth and a maid come under a tree. »Who shall provide for our child?» »He above (God) will take care of it.» The man in the tree: »I will do nothing of the kind!» [K1271.5].

*BP I 50; Wesselski *Hodscha Nasreddin* I 271. — Finnish *55;* Lithuanian (2912*) *3;* Rumanian: Schullerus (1654*) *1,* Hungarian: Berze Nagy (1655**) *2.*

1355* (Obscene).
Livonian (1356') *1.*

1355A* *Unfaithful Wife as Judge.* A miller tells the husband about his unfaithful wife and they find a lover with her. She plays the role of a judge and sentences all three men to be punished.
Russian: Andrejev (*1355) *2.*

1356* (Obscene.)
Livonian (1356') *1.*

1357* *Wife's Duty to Have Lovers.* The husband: »Every wife should have lovers, otherwise a husband has no respect for her.» The wife confesses.
Russian: Andrejev *3.*

1358 *Trickster Surprises Adulteress and Lover.* Cf. Types 1535 III a, b, c, 1725.

1358A *Hidden Paramour Buys Freedom from Discoverer.* Naked and blackened he flees and is taken for the devil. [K443.1, K1555.2, K1554.1]. (= Type 1535 III c, cf. Type 1406*.)

*BP II 1ff. — Lithuanian *22,* (*1360A) *30;* Russian: Afanasiev (*1360 I) *13;* Japanese: Ikeda (Type 1535); England: Baughman (K1554.1*) *1;* U.S.: Baughman (K1554.1*) *2.*

1358B *Husband Carries Off Box Containing Hidden Paramour* [K1555]. (= Type 1535 III b.)

**A. Stepphun *Das Fabel vom Prestre comporté und seine Versionen* (Königsberg, 1913); *BP II 18; *Basset *1001 Contes* II 45; *Toldo Zs. f. Vksk. XIII 412, 420; *Wesselski *Mönchslatein* 10 No. 5; *Cent Nouvelles Nouvelles* No. 73; Italian Novella: Rotunda; India: Thompson-Balys (K1555) *2;* Japanese: Ikeda (K1555).

1358C *Trickster Discovers Adultery: Food Goes to Husband Instead of Paramour.* [K1571]. (Cf. Types 1535 III, 1725).

*BP II 18; von der Hagen *Gesammtabenteuer* III *xxix; Wesselski *Märchen* 216 No. 27. — Lithuanian (1360A*) *1,* (2901*) *1,* (2902*) *1;* Rumanian: Schullerus (1380 VIII*) *6;* India: Thompson-Balys (K1571) *3.*

1358* *Child Unwittingly Betrays his Mother's Adultery.* Tells father not to step across chalk line drawn around secretary; if he does secretary may do to him what he did to Mother the other day. [J125.2.1].
Cent Nouvelles Nouvelles No. 23. — Finnish *7.*

1359 *The Husband Outwits Adulteress and Paramour.* (Cf. Type 1380.)

1359A (formerly 1406*) *Hiding the Lover.* The wife hides her lover three times

from her husband. Finally the man sets the house on fire. The wife rescues her lover. [K1554]. Cf. Type 1730.
   *von der Hagen *Gesammtabenteuer* II xxxvi No. 41. — Finnish-Swedish (1406*) *3*.

1359B *The Husband Meets the Paramour in the Wife's Place.* Beats him (or cuts off privates). [K1561].
   *Wesselski *Bebel* II 149 No. 161; *Nouvelles Recreations* No. 60; N. A. Indian (Malecite): Mechling GSCan VI 83 No. 21, (Fox): Jones PAES I 145.

1359C *Husband Prepares to Castrate the Crucifix.* The artist's wife's paramour poses as a crucifix when caught. When he sees the husband's preparations, he flees naked. [K1558].
   Köhler-Bolte II 469; Flemish (1827); Spanish: Espinosa II No. 42. — Lithuanian (*1730A, B) *14;* Russian: Azadowsky *Russkaya Skazka* No. 20, Andrejev (1730 II) *4;* India: *Thompson-Balys. — Literary Treatments: Rotunda Novella (K1558).

1359* *Adulteress's Spoiled Food.* Woman saving food for her lover persuaded that her food is spoiled (lost).
   Greek (1409*) *4.*

1360 *The Man Hidden in the Roof.* Cf. Type 1776.

1360A *Flight of the Man from his own House.* Abed with his wife, is frightened away by intruder, who then steals his clothes. [K1272].
   Finnish *41;* Finnish-Swedish *2;* Swedish (Uppsala) *11;* Danish: MS. DFS; Hungarian *1;* Russian: Andrejev; Turkish: Everhard-Boratav cf. No. 318, Anlage C *10.*

1360B *Flight of the Woman and her Lover from the Stable.* The man who has seen them comes into the woman's house. Meal at which the situation is related in the form of a tale. The woman gives him money to cease. [K1271.1.4.1]. Cf. Type 570 IV.
   *BP II 18 n. 1. — Finnish *52;* Livonian *1;* Norwegian *2;* Danish *7;* Irish: Jackson FL XLVII 291, Beal XI 191, XVII 83f.; Dutch *3;* Russian: Andrejev; Greek: Loukatos No. 19; Turkish: Eberhard-Boratav No. 274 *10.*

1360C *Old Hildebrand.* The concealed husband tells what he sees. The husband has left home. Suspecting his wife, he has himself carried back in a basket and finds his wife entertaining the priest. They make rhymes about the husband's absence and their own good times. From his hiding place he answers in rhymes. [K1556]. Cf. Type 1535 III b, c.
   **Walter Anderson *Der Schwank vom alten Hildebrand* (Dorpat, 1931); *L. Schmidt in *Festschrift für Eduard Castle* (Vienna 1955) 13ff.; *BP II 373 (Grimm No. 95); Coffin *5.* — Estonian *10;* Livonian *2;* Swedish (Uppsala *3,* Lund *2,* Liungman *1,* misc. *4*); Danish *14;* Irish *148,* Beal VII 71; French *12;* Spanish *3;* German *5* (Archive *3,* Merk. 263, Hens-

sen Jül. No. 472); Italian (Pentamerone cf. II No. 10, Sicilian *3*); Rumanian (1380 III*) *2;* Hungarian: Berze Nagy (1751*) *1;* Czech: Tille Soupis II (2) 391f. *4;* Serbocroatian *22;* Russian: Afanasiev (*1361 I) *15;* Turkish: Eberhard-Boratav No. 273 *2;* India *1.* — English-American: Carter JAFL XXXVIII 366 No. 14, Halpert JAFL LV 134; Spanish-American: Hansen (Cuba) *1;* West Indies (Negro) *4.*

1361 *The Flood.* A priest persuades the man to sleep in a hanging tub to escape the coming flood [K1522]. Meantime he dallies with the man's wife. Another lover comes to the window. The priest presents his rump to be kissed [K1522]. The other lover the second time burns the priest with a hot iron [K1577]. The priest yells: »Water!» The husband thinks the flood has come, cuts the tub ropes, and falls.

**Thompson »The Miller's Tale» in Bryant and Dempster 106ff.; *Hammond *Chaucer: A Bibliographical Manual* 275; *Barnouw »The Miller's Tale van Chaucer» *Handlingen van het 6. nederlandsche Philologencongres,* 1910; Coffin *1;* Chaucer's »Miller's Tale.» — Livonian (1361') *1;* Lithuanian *11;* Swedish *6* (Stockholm *4,* misc. *2);* Danish *14;* Irish *26;* Dutch *1;* German *1;* Serbocroatian *2;* Russian: Andrejev (1730 III*); Turkish: Eberhard-Boratav No. 355 *2.* — English-American: Baughman *1;* Spanish-American: Rael No. 45 (U.S.); West Indies (Negro) *1.*

1362 *The Snow-Child.* (Modus Liebinc.) A sailor's wife bears a son in his absence and says that it came from eating snow. Later the husband makes away with the boy, who, he says, melted in the sun. [J1532.1].

*BP IV 130; *Christiansen *Maal og Minne* (1954) 48f.; Bédier *Fabliaux* 460; Penzer Ocean V 64; K. Breul *The Cambridge Songs* (1915) pp. 81ff. No. 22. — Norwegian (1361**) *1;* Danish *1;* Icelandic *3;* French *1.* — Literary Treatments: Pauli (ed. Bolte) No. 208; Italian Novella: Rotunda (J1532.1).

1362A* *The Three Months' Child.* The wife calculates: he is married three months, I for three and both of us for three — nine in all. [J2342].

Finnish *6;* Swiss: Tobler *Appenzeller Witz* (1902) 121; German: Merkens No. 171; Rumanian (1350 V*) *1;* Greek (1460*) *1.*

1362B* *Marrying Man of Forty.* A husband on his deathbed advises his wife to marry a man of forty. She prefers two of twenty each. It all comes to the same. [J2212.1.1]. Rumanian (1389*) *2.*

1363 *Tale of the Cradle.* Two youths pass the night with a family where all sleep in a common room, with a cradle at the foot of one of the beds. The moving of the cradle in the night confuses those walking about so that the strangers sleep with the wife and the daughter. [K1345]. (Appears frequently with Type 1544.)

**Varnhagen »Die Erzählung von der Wiege» *Englische Studien* IX 240; **Hart »The Reeve's Tale» in Bryan and Dempster 124ff.; Coffin *3.* — Danish *9;* Scottish *1;* Irish *123;* Spanish cf. *1.* — Spanish-American: Hansen (1363*A) *1,* cf. (Dominican Republic) *3,* (Puerto Rico) *3.*

1363* *The Second Cat.* Two boys spend the night in a girl's house because of bad weather.

The father hears one boy abed with girl. »Who is there?» – The boy meows like cat and the father is satisfied. The second boy has same experience. »Who is there?» »This is the second cat.» Cf. Type 1341A*.
French-Canadian.

1364 *The Blood-brother's Wife.* The story told as a dream.

I. *The Divided Gifts.* Two knights swear blood-brotherhood and agree to divide all winnings. The wife of the first is enamored of the second, who, not knowing who she is, acquiesces and receives rich gifts from her. He divides with the husband, who recognizes the gifts and discovers the facts.

II. *The Hidden Lover.* The husband tries in vain to surprise his wife and lover. See Types 1419B, 1419C.

III. *The Adventure as a Dream.* The husband gives a banquet and hides his wife behind a screen in the same room. He calls upon the lover to tell the revelers his love adventure [K1564]. The lover does so but just before the end of his narration sees the woman behind the screen and recognizes her. »Just then I woke up,» he says, and no one believes his tale. [J1155].

*Wesselski *Märchen* 187 No. 2; Toldo Zs. f. Vksk. XV 60; Hilka and Soederhjelm *Neuphilologische Mitteilungen* (Helsingfors, 1913) 15ff. — Irish *1;* Icelandic *2;* French *1;* Spanish cf. *1;* Turkish: Eberhard-Boratav No. 266, cf. 194 *6;* Arab: Littmann 384ff. — Spanish-American: Hansen (Argentina) *1.*

1365 *The Obstinate Wife.*

Swedish *33* (Uppsala *2,* Göteborg *31*); Irish *49;* Catalan: Amades cf. No. 400; Walloon *1;* Hungarian *4;* Slovenian *3;* Serbocroatian *3;* Japanese: Ikeda. — West Indies (Negro) *5.*

1365A *Wife Falls into a Stream.* The husband searches for his drowned wife upstream. She is too obstinate to go with the current. [T255.2].

*Pauli (ed. Bolte) No. 142; Crane *Vitry* 225f. No. 227; Köhler-Bolte I 506 note 1; Wesselski *Hodscha Nasreddin* I 270 No. 276; Moltke Moe *Samlede Skrifter* I 209; Coffin *1.* — Finnish *68;* Finnish-Swedish *3;* Estonian *2;* Lithuanian *5;* Swedish *14* (Uppsala *3,* Stockholm *3,* Göteborg *1,* Lund *2,* Liungman *4*); Norwegian *4;* English *2;* French *1;* Spanish *1;* Walloon *1;* German *2;* Slovenian *2;* Russian: Afanasiev *6;* India *1.* — English-American: Baughman *2;* Spanish-American: Rael No. 78 (U.S.). — Literary Treatment: Italian Novella: Rotunda (T255.2).

1365B *Cutting with the Knife or the Scissors.* At the end of the argument the man throws his wife into the water. With her finger she makes the motion of shearing with the scissors. [T255.1].

Halpert SFLQ VII (1943); FL L (1939) 73; JAFL XLVII (1934) 306; Köhler-Bolte I 136; Taylor *Washington Univ. Studies* IV (1917) 181 n. 28; Bédier *Fabliaux* 468; Pauli (ed. Bolte) No. 595; Moe *Samlede Skrifter* I 209ff.; Coffin *1.* — Finnish *1;* Finnish-Swedish *2;* Swedish *44* (Uppsala *27,* Stockholm *4,* Lund *5,* Liungman *2,* misc. *6*); Icelandic *1;* Irish: Beal

XI 150f. No. 35; English *2;* French *1;* Spanish *1;* Dutch *1;* Flemish *1;* Italian (Tuscan 1365C *1,* Sicilian *2*); Rumanian *2;* Slovenian *5;* Serbocroatian *3;* Russian: Afanesiev *1;* Greek: Loukatos No. 38, *Laographia* VI 649. — English-American: Baughman *8.* — Literary Treatments: Crane *Vitry* No. 222.

1365C *The Wife Insults the Husband as Lousy-head.* (Introduction like B.) She makes sign of cracking a louse as she sinks. [T255.3].
Pauli (ed. Bolte) No. 872; Coffin *1.* — Swedish *12* (Uppsala *1,* Stockholm *2,* Lund *4,* Liungman *1,* misc. *4*); Norwegian *1;* French *9;* Spanish *1;* Flemish *1;* Walloon *1;* German *6* (Archive *5,* Henssen Volk No. 237); Italian (Trieste): Pinguentini No. 9; Russian: Andrejev *1.* — Literary Treatments: Crane *Vitry* No. 221.

1365D* *Which Shall Eat the Third Egg* [T255.4].
Coffin *1.* — Spanish *2;* Catalan: Amades No. 400. — Spanish-American: Hansen (Dominican Republic) *1,* (Puerto Rico) *6,* (Cuba) *1.*

1365E* *Whose Hair is in the Soup?*
Spanish *1.* — Spanish-American: Hansen (Puerto Rico) *1.*

1365F* *The Buried Wife.* Quarreling with her husband about some trifle, the wife lets herself be buried but still does not agree with him.
Russian: Afanasiev (1365*D) *3.*

1365G* *Rats or Mink.* Husband and wife argue: were holes in floor made by rats or mink?
French Canadian.

1365H* *Big Bird or Little Bird:* husband and wife argue.
Greek (1365B*) *1.*

1365J* *Asking by Opposites.* Always asking obstinate wife opposite of what is desired.
Rumanian (1365D*) *1.*

1365K* *The Obstinate Husband* (father).
French-Canadian.

1366* *The Slippered Husband.* The wife beats the husband. The man under the table: »The man always has a man's heart.» [T251.6].
Finnish *2;* Estonian *1.*

1366A* *Search for Husband in Command.* Man has hundred hens and three horses. He is to give hen where woman is chief of the house, a horse where the man is. He fails to give away any horses since the wife tells the man which to choose. Cf. Type 1375.
Finnish *3.*

1367 *Trickster Shifts Married Couples in Bed.* Old man married to young woman and young man married to old woman. The shift is satisfactory to the young couple. [K1318].
*BP III 394 (3); Anderson FFC XLII 364; Köhler-Bolte II 305ff.

1367* *To Live with Evil Woman.* Hanging chosen instead. Cf. Types 1164, 1170.
Rumanian (1366*) *2.*

1370 (formerly 1370*) *The Lazy Wife.* The cat beaten for not working. The wife must hold the cat and is scratched. [W111.3.2]. Cf. Type 901.
Finnish *2;* Finnish-Swedish *1;* Estonian *5;* Swedish (Liungman) *1;* Danish: Kristensen *Jyske Folkeminder* XII 255 No. 284; German: Fröhle

Kinder- und Hausmärchen (1853) No. 253; English: Child No. 277; Rumanian (1370*) *5;* Hungarian *3;* Serbocroatian *12;* Slovenian *1;* Russian: Andrejev *2;* Greek *1.*

1370A* »*He Who Will not Work, Shall not Eat*». An idle daughter-in-law learns to work.
Lithuanian *5.*

1370B* *Wife too Lazy to Spin.* Supposed dead husband comes back to life and gives his wife a beating, because there was no shirt even in the event of death. Cf. Type 1350. [W111.3.5].
Lithuanian *1;* Serbocroatian *1;* Russian (*1370 I) *2.*

1370C* *Stopping the Milk Pail.* The lazy woman stops the milk pail so that the milk will not flow.
Russian: Andrejev (*1370 II) *1.*

1371* *The Woman is to Pile up the Pottery.* She breaks the pots into pieces and piles up the fragments. [J2465.2].
Flemish *1;* Hungarian (12°3) *1.*

1371** *The Lazy Wife.* She has on a soiled dress. She sees her husband returning from market and thinks that he is bringing her a new dress, but he is bringing a goose. [W111.3.1].
Livonian (1371') *1;* Italian (cf. Tuscan [1359] *1*).

1371A* *Darkening the Flour.* The husband steals some white flour and fears that the theft will be discovered. The wife: »I'll bake some loaves with the white flour which will be darker than rye; they won't find out».
Russian: Afanasiev (*1371) *2.*

1372 *The Box on the Ears.* The man gets a box on the ears in the pharmacy. Cures his wife with this remedy. [J2494]. Cf. Type 1344.
Feilberg *Ordbog* III 1182 s.v. »ørefigen»; Christiansen DF XLVII 208 No. 62. — Finnish *2;* Finnish-Swedish (1370*) *6;* Livonian (1370*) *1;* Swedish *8* (Uppsala *4,* Stockholm *1,* misc. *3*); Flemish (1370*) *2;* German *3* (Archive *2,* Henssen Volk No. 239); Rumanian (1700*) *3;* Slovenian *1.*

1372* *The Wife's Disease.* The woman feigns periodic attacks of a sickness that can only be cured by eating a great number of delicacies. Her husband feigns the same disease. [J1511.3].
Flemish *1;* West Indies (Negro) *3.*

1373 *The Weighed Cat.* A man buys three pounds of meat. His wife eats it and says that the cat ate it. The man weighs the cat and finds that it does not weigh three pounds. [J1611].
*Wesselski *Hodscha Nasreddin* II 185 No. 348. — Spanish *1;* Italian (Sicilian *1374 *2*).

1373A *Wife Eats so Little.* Eats in husband's absence. Discovered. [K1984.2, S411.4]. Cf. Types 1407, 1458.
*Espinosa *Cuentos* II 238ff. — Spanish (*1374) *1;* India (S411.4) *1.* — Spanish-American: Hansen (Puerto Rico) *1.*

1373A* *Wife Says Cat Ate the Meat.* Magic beans declare truth. [D1619.1].
Spanish *1.*

1373B* *Girl Eats Chicken.* Gives father flesh from own buttock. [K492].
Spanish *1;* Spanish-American: Hansen (Puerto Rico) *3.*

1374* *Woman who Doesn't Know how to Bake Bread.*
Rumanian *1.*

1375 (formerly 1375*) *Who can Rule his Wife?* The husband leaves his wife and goes on the advice of his father-in-law with an egg basket to seek through the wide world for a man who can manage his wife. But after a year he returns to his wife without having found such a man. [T252.1]. Cf. Type 1366A*.
*Liungman SSF III 349. — Livonian (1375') *1;* Swedish (Stockholm *1); Dutch (905*) *2;* Italian (Tuscan [1358] *1*). — Brazil: Camara Cascudo p. 40ff.

1376A* *Story-teller Interrupted by Woman.* A husband warns his wife against listening to stories. She allows travelers to spend the night in payment for stories, not taking money. This is ruinous to the husband. One traveler agrees to tell stories all night, if they do not interrupt him. Instead of stories he repeats the same one. The wife interrupts him, the husband beats her thoroughly.
Russian *3.*

1376B* *Story-teller Interrupted — All Must Tell.* A soldier tells tales. He repeats the same one. When they interrupt him, he forces the master of the house to tell tales, the master forces the mistress, the mistress the workers, etc.
Russian *3.*

1376C* *Combined Names.* Two brothers have names that taken together mean something else. Mother calls them together, absurd results. Cf. Types 883C, 960, 1461, 1530*.
French-Canadian (1541*).

1377 *The Husband Locked out.* Puteus. An adulteress returns home late at night and her husband refuses to admit her. She threatens to throw herself into the well. The husband goes after her. She enters the house and bars him out. [K1511].
Basset *1001 Contes* II 128; Wesselski *Hodscha Nasreddin* II 185 No. 350; Campbell *Sages* xc (Puteus); Rotunda (K1511). — Swedish (misc.) *1;* French *2;* Dutch *3;* India *1.* — African *1.* — Literary Treatments: Chauvin VIII 184 No. 224, IX 23; Alphabet No. 538; Boccaccio Decameron VII No. 4; Spanish Exempla: Keller; Dunlop-Wilson II 111f.

1378 *The Marked Coat in the Wife's Room.* A procuress obtains a woman for her client by leaving a marked coat in her room. The husband drives the wife away and she joins her lover. The procuress then goes to the husband and alleges that she lost a coat with certain marks. The husband is deceived and takes the wife back. [K1543].
*Bédier *Fabliaux* 443; **Eberling *Auberée, altfranzösische fabel,* etc. (Berlin, 1891); Spanish Exempla: Keller (K1543).

1378A* *The Husband in the Tavern.* A wife is looking for her husband in a tavern. Having found out that he always spends five kopeks for drink, she demands ten kopeks for herself.
Russian: Afanasief (*1375 I) *1.*

1378B* *Wife's Temporary Success.* A wife wants to get the upperhand of her husband. The husband for a while gives her this opportunity; and then beats her.
Finnish *1;* Russian: Afanasiev (*1375) *3.*

1379 *Wife Deceives Husband with Substituted Bedmate* [K1843].
Finnish 7; Icelandic: Boberg (K1843); Jewish: *Neuman (K1843); India: *Thompson-Balys (K1843).

1379* *False Members.* On wedding night older couple get ready for bed. To husband's astonishment wife removes false breasts, teeth and glass eye. Husband finally says, »Throw me a buttock for a pillow.»
Spanish-American: Hansen (Cuba) *1*.

1380—1404 The Foolish Wife and her Husband

1380 *The Faithless Wife.* Asks God how she can fool her husband. The husband from the tree (or rafters) tells her that she can make him blind by feeding him milk-toast. The husband feigns blindness and slays the lover. The body is thrown into the river. Cf. Types 1324*, 1375, 1388*, 1405, 1461*, 1476, 1536 C, 1575*, 1829.

Motifs: K1971. Man behind statue (tree) speaks and pretends to be God (spirit). K1971.1. Husband answers behind the statue when wife wants to know how to fool him. K1553. Husband feigns blindness and avenges himself on his wife and her paramour.

*BP III 124; *Anderson in Tauscher *Volksmärchen* 177; Taylor MPh XV (1917) 227 n. 1; Coffin *2*; Stiefel Zs. f. Vksk. VIII 74, XXXIX 215. — Finnish *103*; Finnish-Swedish *4*; Estonian *7*; Lithuanian *14*; Swedish *5* (Uppsala *2*, Stockholm *1*, misc. *2*); Icelandic *1*; Irish *1*; French *1*; Spanish *2*, Espinosa Nos. 33, 34; Catalan: Amades No. 537; Dutch *4*; German *6* (Archive *5*, Henssen Volk No. 141) ; Italian (Tuscan [1368] *1*, Sicilian *1*); Rumanian *3*; Hungarian *1*; Czech: Tille Soupis II (2) 394 *3*; Serbocroatian *8*; Russian: Afanasiev *20*; Greek *9*; Turkish. Eberhard-Boratav No. 263 *3*; India *6*; Indonesian: De Vries No. 272. — American Negro (Michigan): Dorson No. 35; West Indies (Negro) *2*. — Literary Treatments: *Panchatantra* (tr. Ryder) III 18.

1380* *The Man as God on a Tree.* He forces his wife to confess adultery. [K1971.5].
Finnish (1575*); Estonian *1*; Lithuanian (*1380A) *2*; Russian *1*.

1380** *Same.* He says that the girl has had a child by such and such a man. [K1971.5.1]. Marriage.
Estonian *2*; Russian (1380**) *1*.

1380A* *Wife to Spin.* Husband behind saint's statue advises wife to spin [K1971.4]. Cf. Type 1405.
Spanish (1375*) *6*; Serbocroatian *1*.

1381 *The Talkative Wife and the Discovered Treasure.* The wood-cock in the fish-net and the fish in the bird-trap. The woman under the bath tub (for fear of rumored war). The woman is considered mad and the man can keep his treasure. The husband has foolishly told his talkative wife of discovered treasure. To discredit her talk he tells her of impossible things, which she repeats, and frightens her with reports of a war of animals or the end of the world, so that she hides. [J1151.1.1].

*BP I 527; Bédier *Fabliaux* 196, 466. — Finnish *117;* Finnish-Swedish *4;* Estonian *31;* Livonian *3;* Lithuanian *31;* Lappish *3;* Swedish *5* (Uppsala *1*, Stockholm *2*, misc. *2*); Norwegian *2;* Icelandic *1;* Irish *2;* French *7;* Spanish cf. *2;* Catalan: Amades No. 431; Dutch *1;* Flemish *4;* German *12;* Rumanian *10;* Italian (Sicilian 2, Gonzenbach No. 37); Czech: Tille Soupis I 411ff. *3;* Hungarian *5;* Serbocroatian *6;* Russian: Afanasiev *17*, Andrejev *Ukraine 16;* Greek *6*, Loukatos No. 29; Turkish: Eberhard-Boratav No. 333, cf. 133 V, 372 *20;* India *11.* — Spanish-American: Rael No. 331 (U.S.).

1381A *Husband Discredited by Absurd Truth.* Wife puts fish in furrow where husband plows them up (or like absurdity). At mealtime the husband says, »Where are the fish?» — »What fish?» — »Those I plowed up.» He is laughed to scorn. [J1151.1.2].

*Bédier *Fabliaux* 196, 436; India *1.*

1381B *The Sausage Rain.* (Or rain of figs, fishes, or milk.) A mother in order to discredit testimony of her foolish son who has killed a man makes him believe that it has rained sausages. When he says that he killed the man on the night it rained sausages his testimony is discredited. [J1151.1.3].

*Wesselski *Hodscha Nasreddin* II 184, 195, 204 Nos. 347, 383, 407; *BP I 527; Italian (Pentamerone I No. 4, Gonzenbach No. 37); Spanish (1696A*) *2;* India *10.* — Literary Treatment: Chauvin VI 126, VIII 35, 69.

1381C *The Buried Sheep's Head:* test of wife's ability to keep secret. Husband tells her that he is burying head of murdered man. She is to keep secret. She tells. When head is dug up it is sheep's head. [H472.1].

*T. Zachariae Zs. f. Vksk. XXXII—XXXIV 77; *DeVries FFC LXXIII 220ff., 224 n. 1. — French: Sébillot *Haute-Bretagne* II No. 49, Cosquin *Lorraine* No. 77; German: Curtze *Volkstümliches aus Waldeck* 167 No. 25, Zender 73 No. 63; Rumanian (1381 I*) *3;* Slovenian; Jewish: Bin Gorion *Born Judas* IV 25, 275; India *4.*

1381D *The Wife Multiplies the Secret.* To prove that a woman cannot keep a secret the man tells his wife that a crow has flown out of his belly (or that he has laid an egg). She tells her neighbor that two crows have flown. Soon he hears from his neighbors that there were fifty crows. [J2353].

*Pauli (ed. Bolte) No. 395; Wesselski *Hodscha Nasreddin* II 244 No. 542; Chauvin VIII 168, 197; Spanish (1381*A) *2*, Espinosa II Nos. 68—69; Italian Novella: Rotunda; Hungarian: Berze Nagy (1631*) *4;* Serbocroatian *1;* Jewish: Gaster Exempla 196 No. 56; India *4.*

1381E *Old Man Sent to School* finds money the first day he goes. When questioned about it, says he found it the first day he went to school; questioner thinks this long ago. (Sometimes used as introduction to Type 1600.) Cf. Type 1644.

Irish: O'Suilleabhain *Handbook* 647 No. 100; Catalan: Amades No. 427; Hungarian: Berze Nagy (1645**) *5*. Also well known in Russia (W. Anderson).

1381* *Selling the Old Donkey.* Man tells wife he is going to sell the old donkey at fair for a great amount of money, but warns her not to tell neighbor's wife. She finally tells. Neighbor exchanges his young donkey for man's old one and goes to fair. Neighbor cannot sell old donkey.

Spanish-American: Hansen (**1392) (Puerto Rico) *1*.

1382 *The Peasant Woman at Market.* The sale of the cow. The woman made drunk or is to give a pawn; cf. Type 1385. Doesn't know herself any more; cf. Type 1383. The husband fishes in the street and thus discovers the buyer of the cow. [J1149.2].

Finnish *79;* Finnish-Swedish *9;* Estonian *4;* Lappish *1;* Swedish *11* (Uppsala *7*, (1382 and 1383) *3*, Lund *1*); Danish: Grundtvig No. 107; Russian: Andrejev, Andrejev *Ukraine 6*.

1382* (formerly 2007*). *Horse for Bones.* The woman exchanges her horse for a sack full of bones which she has been told are filled with gold. When she reaches home, she discovers that she has been betrayed. [J2099.1].

Estonian (2007*) *2*.

1383 *The Woman Does not Know Herself* in tar and feathers or with garments cut off. The dog does not recognize her [J2012.2, J2012.3]. Cf. Types 1284, 1336A, 1382, 1531A, 1681.

*BP I 335, especially 341 (Grimm Nos. 34, 59). — Finnish *33;* Finnish-Swedish *2;* Estonian *4*, (1409*) *2;* Lithuanian *8;* Swedish *9* (Uppsala *8*, Lund *1*); Irish *3;* English *1;* Dutch *4;* Flemish *3;* German *5;* Hungarian *1*, Dégh No. 39; Czech: Tille Soupis I 413f. *2;* Russian: Andrejev *Ukraine 11*, Afanasiev *14*. — English-American: Baughman *1*.

1384 *The Husband Hunts Three Persons as Stupid as his Wife.* Cf. Types 1450, Clever Elsie; 1385, The Foolish Wife's Pawn. The man finds three as foolish [H1312.1]. Cf. Type 1540, The Student from Paradise. This type combines with many others, particularly 1310, 1245, 1265, 1286, 1326, 1371*, 1385, 1386, 1387 and 1450, 1540, 1653, 2022B.

*BP I 335, II 440 (Grimm Nos. 34, 104); Jackson FL XLVII 291; Coffin *9*. — Finnish *30;* Finnish-Swedish *6;* Estonian *16;* Livonian *1;* Lithuanian *24;* Lappish *1;* Swedish *61* (Uppsala *6*, (1384) *12*, Stockholm *5*, Göteborg *4*, Lund *5*, Liungman *9*, misc. *20*); Norwegian *12;* Danish: Grundtvig No. 107; Icelandic *2;* Scottish *1;* Irish *95*, Beal II 24, IV suppl. 1ff., XIII 272ff., XX 3f. No. 5; English *3;* French *11;* Catalan: Amades cf. No. 398; Dutch *6;* German *23* (Archive *22*, Merk. 32): Austrian: Haiding No. 40; Italian (Tuscan 1450a—c *3*, Sicilian *2*); Rumanian *4;* Hungarian *5*, Dégh No. 41; Czech: Tille Soupis I 404ff. *17;* Slovenian *3;* Serbocroatian *8;* Russian: Andrejev *Ukraine 16*, Afanasiev *12;* Greek *5*, Loukatos No. 20; Turkish: Eberhard-Boratav No. 331 *9*. — Franco-American; English-American: Baughman *10;* Spanish-American: Hansen (Puerto Rico) *1;* West Indies (Negro) *1*. — African *2*.

1385 *The Foolish Wife's Pawn.* The wife sells cows. Gets one of them back as pledge for the unpaid purchase price [J2086]. Cf. Types 1382, 1384.

*BP II 440 (Grimm No. 104); Christensen DF L 35; Finnish *33*; Finnish-Swedish *1*; Estonian *4*; Lappish *1*; Irish *1*; Dutch *2*; German *12*; Russian: Andrejev; Greek *2*.

1385* *Learning about Money.* The stupid wife does not know about money. Her husband gives money a nonsense name. She exchanges it for worthless articles.
French-Canadian.

1386 *Meat as Food for Cabbage.* The wife places pieces of meat on a growing cabbage. [J1856.1]. Cf. Type 1642.

*BP I 520 (Grimm No. 59). — Finnish *23*; Finnish:Swedish *2*; Estonian *17*; Livonian *2*; Lithuanian *4*; Swedish *3* (Uppsala *1*, Stockholm *2*); Norwegian *2*; Scottish *2*, Campbell-McKay No. 19; Irish *190*, Beal VIII 3f. No. 8; Flemish *4*; German *14*; Hungarian *1*; Czech: Tille Soupis I 414 *2*; Slovenian *7*; Serbocroatian *8*; Russian: Andrejev; Indonesian: Coster-Wijsman 60 No. 92. — English-American: Baughman *2*.

1387 *The Woman Goes to get Beer.* While she chases the dog the beer runs into the cellar; she scatters meal over it. Cf. Types 1408, The Man who Does his Wife's Work; 1450, Clever Elsie; 1653A, Guarding the Door. [J2176, J2176.1].

*BP I 316, 521ff. (Grimm Nos. 32, 59); *Anderson *Novelline* No. 59; Jackson FL XLVII 291; Christensen DF L 49. — Finnish *7*; Finnish-Swedish *1*; Estonian *24*; Livonian *2*; Lithuanian *8*; Swedish *16* (Uppsala *3*, Stockholm *1*, misc. *12*); Irish 54, Beal II 24; German *11*; Italian *3* (Pentamerone I No. 4, Tuscan [1219], [1220] *2*, Sicilian *1*); Hungarian *3*, cf. Berze Nagy (1412*) *5*; Czech: Tille Soupis I 414 *2*; Serbocroatian *2*; Russian: Andrejev; Greek *6*. — Spanish-American: Hansen (Argentina 1631**A) *1*.

1387A *The Lazy Wife Throws Bread Out of Window* instead of putting it back into oven. [W111.3.3]. (Often combined with 1387.)
Spanish (1389*) *2*; Greek (1387*) *4*, *Laographia* XVI 543.

1387* *Woman must do Everything like her Neighbors.* Absurd results. (Cf. Type 1696.)
Rumanian (1387 I*) *4*.

1388 (formerly 1388*) *The Servant Girl Hides behind the Statue of the Virgin Mary.* Maid behind the statue of Virgin advises the mistress to give the servants better food. [K1971.3.1]. Cf. Types 1380, 1461.

Flemish *3*; German: Zender 91 No. 95; Slovenian *1*; Japanese: Ikeda (K1971.3.1).

1388A* *Choose what Food you will Have.* — All.
Serbocroatian *3*.

1389* *The Stingy Peasant Woman Gives her Servant some Little and some Big Lumps of Sugar.* She says the little ones are the sweeter. The servant says he doesn't like sweets, and takes the larger lumps. [J1341.8].
Flemish *2*.

1390* *The Dish Which the Husband Hates and Which the Wife Keeps Serving him.* The husband says that it will make him happy and thus gets rid of it. [T255.5].
Flemish *4*.

1391 *Every Hole to Tell the Truth* (Les bijoux indiscrets). A man receives magic power to make every hole speak the truth. Thus learns from his wife's speaking private parts of her adultery. [D1610.6.1, H451, cf. K1569.7]. Cf. Type 1539**.
*Taylor MLN XXXI (1916) 249 n. 2; von der Hagen *Gesammtabenteuer* III*v, 17; Chauvin VIII 88; Italian Novella (D1610.6.1). — Swedish: *Kryptadia* II 171; Hungarian: Berze Nagy (678*) *1;* Serbocroatian *1;* Turkish: Eberhard-Boratav (No. 122) *5*.

1392* *Old Widow with Young Man as Suitor.* He carries away all her house furnishings and leaves her in the woods.
Rumanian (1388*) *4*.

1393 *The Single Blanket.* Quarreling women left by their husbands in very cold room with a single blanket use it together and are reconciled. — Finnish *29*.

1395* *Unused Sex-Organs.*
Livonian (1395') *1*.

1405—1429 The Foolish Man and his Wife

1405 *The Lazy Spinning Woman.* The woman hidden in the bushes calls out to her husband, who is cutting wood: »Whoever cuts wood for a spinning wheel will die; whoever uses the wheel will be destroyed.« The man becomes worried and no longer keeps her at the reel [K1971.4.1]. When they boil the yarn, she places tow in the kettle and makes the husband believe that through his carelessness the yarn has turned into tow [J2325]. He speaks to her no more of spinning. Cf. Type 501 III.
*BP III 44 (Grimm No. 128); *Hdwb. d. Märchens II 148 a nn. 381—391. — Finnish *11;* Finnish-Swedish *5;* Estonian *6;* Lithuanian *9;* Swedish *3* (Lund *1*, misc. *2*); Irish *1;* German *5* (Archive *4*, Merk 49); Rumanian *4;* Slovenian *1;* Serbocroatian *14*, Istrian No. 50; Russian: Andrejev; Greek *2*.

1405* *Woman will keep All Days Holiday* in honor of saint.
Greek *1*.

1406 *The Merry Wives Wager* which can best fool her husband. One makes her husband think that he is dead. Another makes her husband believe that she spins, weaves, and sews clothes so fine that they cannot be seen; a third makes hers believe that he is a dog and so he barks at people who pass. Cf. Types 1313, 1620.
Motifs: J2301. Gullible husbands. K1545. Wives wager as to who can best fool her husband. J2311.0.1. Wife makes her husband believe that he is dead. J2312. Naked person made to believe that he is clothed.

J2013.2. Man made to believe that he is a dog. He barks at people. J2314. Layman made to believe that he is a monk. J2315. Wife persuades husband that she has returned immediately. She goes to a neighbor's to cook fish. She is gone for a week. She gets a new fish and cooks it and returns home with the hot fish. She convinces her husband of her short absence. J2316. Husband made to believe that his house has moved during his absence. The wife and her confederates transform the house into an inn with tables, signs, drinkers, etc. The husband cannot find his house. J2324. Wife persuades her husband to have a good tooth pulled.

*Crane *Vitry* No. 231, cf. 248; Pauli (ed. Bolte) No. 866; *Clouston *Noodles* 163, 166; Liebrecht *Zur Volkskunde* 124; Christensen DF XLVII 229, DF L 59, 64; Wesselski *Hodscha Nasreddin* I 274 No. 298. — Estonian (1409*) *2;* Lithuanian *7;* Swedish *9* (Uppsala *2,* Stockholm *1,* Liungman *2,* [GS 1340] *4*); Norwegian *6;* Danish: Grundtvig No. 103; Icelandic *3;* Irish *70,* Jackson FL XLVII 291, Beal XVII 85ff.; French *5;* Spanish (1424*) *1;* Catalan: Amades No. 676; Italian (Sicilian *2*); Hungarian: Honti (1413) *2,* Berze Nagy (1409*) *7;* Czech: Tille Soupis II (2) 134ff., 357ff. *4;* Serbocroatian *1;* Russian: Andrejev *Ukraine 10;* Greek *3,* Loukatos No. 29; Turkish: Eberhard-Boratav No. 271; Arab: Littmann 378, (Egypt) Artin 25f. — English-American: Baughman *1.* — Literary Treatments: Bédier *Fabliaux* 265—267, 458—468; Italian Novella: Rotunda (J2312, J2314).

1406* changed to Type 1359B.

1407 *The Miser.* Gives his wife too little to eat. On the advice of the servant boy, he spies on her from inside the chimney, under the bolster, etc. Gets burned in the chimney, beaten in the bed. [W153.2]. Cf. Types 1373, 1458.

Finnish *1;* Finnish-Swedish *1;* Swedish *8* (Uppsala *4,* Liungman *2,* misc. *2*); Danish: Grundtvig No. 101; Irish *20,* Beal IV 62f. No. 1; German *1;* Russian: Andrejev; Spanish-American: Hansen (Puerto Rico) *1;* West Indies (Negro) *1.*

1407A *Everything!* Greedy and sick old man or woman sees servant girl eating a great deal. Complains that she is eating up everything from her employers. Girl hears only »everything« and takes this as a testament. [Cf. J1521.2].

Swedish (GS 1409) *2* (Liungman *2*); Italian (Sicilian *1407) *2;* Rumanian (1407 I*) *2;* Czech: Tille Soupis II (2) 425f. *5;* Turkish: Eberhard-Boratav Nos. 367, 368 III *9.*

1408 *The Man who Does his Wife's Work.* Does everything wrong [J2431]. Lets cow graze on the roof; cf. Type 1210. Ties the rope's end to his foot [J2132.2]. Lets the beer run out; cf. Type 1387. In the chimney.

*BP I 321; Bolte *Frey* 222 No. 20; Coffin *1;* Feilberg *Ordbog* III 1175a s.v. »øl«. — Finnish *99;* Finnish-Swedish *9;* Estonian *8;* Livonian *1;*

Lithuanian *11;* Swedish *46* (Uppsala *20,* Stockholm *1,* Lund *1,* Liugman *2,* misc. *22*); Norwegian *12,* Solheim *1;* Icelandic *1;* Irish *45,* Jackson XLVII 291; French *9;* Catalan: Amades No. 377, cf. 440; Flemish *3;* German *12;* Italian (Tuscan [1219] *1*); Hungarian: Berze Nagy *5,* (1412*) *5,* Dégh No. 40; Czech: Tille Soupis I 427ff. *8;* Serbocroatian *16,* Istrian No. 51; Russian: Afanasiev *4;* Greek *4,* (Chios): Argenti-Rose I 510f. — English-American: Baughman *1.*

1408A *Old Man has Churn on his Back* as he bows over after water in the spring. Swedish (GS 1388) *7* (Uppsala *1,* Stockholm *1,* Liungman *1,* misc. *4*).

1408B *Fault-finding Husband Nonplussed.* The wife has cooked so many dishes that when he complains, she can always supply another. Finally he says, »I had rather eat dung.« She produces some. [J1545.3].
*Wesselski *Theorie* 175; Plattdeutsch: Wisser *Plattdeutsche Volksmärchen* (Jena 1922, 1927) II 98; India (Kashmir): Knowles 245.

1409 *The Obedient Husband.*

1409A *Obedient Husband Hangs his Wife.* Wife had wished only to test her husband's love for her. [J2523.1].
Lithuanian (*1378) *1.*

1409B *Leave of Absence.* His wife says, »You may go away for a little while.« He stays away for days and then sends a messenger to his wife asking if he has been away long enough. [J2523].
*Wesselski *Hodscha Nasreddin* I 232 No. 84; Serbocroatian *1;* India *1.*

1409C *Obedient Husband Walks Slowly.* Arrives home after dawn when wife's lover has gone. [J2523.2].
India *1.*

1409* *The Woman Cooks Dog for Dinner.* The deceived husband calls the dog to feed him the bones.
Serbocroatian *3.*

1410 *Four Men's Mistress.* A husband disguises as a priest to hear his wife's confession. She says that she has been the mistress of a servant, a knight, a fool, and a priest; i.e., her husband when he was her servant, and later her knight. He had then been a fool for demanding her confession, and was a priest because he had heard it. [J1545.2].
*Pauli (ed. Bolte) No. 793; Wesselski *Mönchslatein* 109 No. 93; Boccaccio Decameron VII No. 5 (Lee 198); *Scala Celi* 49a No. 275; *Hibbard 41 n. 12; *Cent Nouvelles Nouvelles* No. 78. — Catalan: Amades No. 1840; Italian Novella: Rotunda (J1545.2).

1411* *The Raven Child.* A childless woman is blamed by her husband. She catches a raven and dresses it as child. The man is happy. The raven flies away. The man: »Grow up and live in heaven!«
Icelandic (1410*) *2.*

1415 *Lucky Hans.* Foolish bargains. He trades his horse for a cow, the cow for

a hog, the latter for a goose, until finally he has nothing left [J2081.1]. Wins the wager when his wife does not get angry [N11].
*BP II 199 (Grimm No. 83); *R. Th. Christiansen Beal III 107ff.; *Hdwb. d. Märchens I 187 n. 131; Coffin 2. — Finnish 23; Finnish-Swedish 8; Estonian 1; Livonian 1; Lithuanian 8; Swedish 15 (Uppsala 3, Stockholm 1, Lund 1, Liungman 2, misc. 8); Norwegian 4; Icelandic 2; Irish 21, Jackson FL XLVII 291, Beal IX 113ff., X 3f. No. 42; English: Wells 118 (Octovian); French 7; Spanish 2; Catalan: Amades No. 399; Dutch 1; Flemish 8; Walloon (1415A—D) 4; German 9 (Archive 8, Merk. 98); Rumanian 3; Hungarian 3; Slovenian 3; Serbocroatian 2; Russian: Afanasiev 6; Greek 2; Turkish: Eberhard-Boratav Anlage C9; India (1415 Ind) 8; Indonesian: Coster-Wijsman 57 No. 84. — English-American: Baughman 3; Spanish-American: Rael No. 55(U.S.), Hansen (Puerto Rico) 2; West Indies (Negro) 1; American Indian (Zuni): Boas JAFL XXXV 74 No. 3. — African (Ibo, Nigeria): Thomas 128.

1416 *The Mouse in the Silver Jug.* The New Eve. A poor woman laments at Eve's curiosity and says women are no longer so. The king lets them enjoy themselves in castle, but they must not open a certain silver jug [C324]. The woman can not let it alone. There is a mouse in the jug. [H1554.1]. The king sends them home.
*BP III 543 n. 1; *Krappe *Bulletin Hispanique* XXXIX 44; Coffin 1; Feilberg Ordbog IV 3b s.v. »Adam»; Pauli (ed. Bolte) No. 398; Crane *Vitry* 139 No. 13; *Arts et Trad. Pop.* I 275. — Lithuanian 13; Lappish 5 (1416*); Swedish 10 (Uppsala 4, Stockholm 1, Göteborg 2, Liungman 1, misc. 2); Norwegian (1416**) 2; Irish 23, Jackson FL XLVII 291, Beal III 4; English 1; French 12; Catalan: Amades No. 2075; German 6 (Archive 5, Henssen Volk No. 238); Serbocroatian 1; Russian: Andrejev (790*) 1; Jewish: Neuman (C324). — Spanish-American: Rael No. 64 (U.S.).

1417 *The Cut-off Nose (Hair).* Lai of the Tresses. A woman leaves her husband's bed and has another woman take her place. The husband addresses her, gets no answer, and cuts off her nose (hair). In the morning the wife still has her nose (hair). The husband is made to believe that it has grown back by a miracle (or that he was dreaming) [K1512].
*Bédier *Fabliaux* 228ff.; Penzer V 47 n. 3, 223ff., VI 271. — English 1; Czech: Tille II (2) 400 3; India 4. — Literary Treatments: Chauvin II 66, VI 100 No. 267; Boccaccio Decameron VIII No. 8 (Lee 222); Bødker Exempler 280 No. 24; Italian Novella: Rotunda (K1512).

1418 *The Equivocal Oath.* A husband insists that his wife take oath that she has been intimate with no one but himself. The paramour masks as ass-driver. She hires an ass from him, falls down, and lets him pick her up. She swears no one has touched her except the husband and the ass-driver. [K1513].
**Meyer *Isoldes Gottesurteil in seiner erotischen Beziehung* (Berlin, 1914);

*BP IV 154, 387f.; *Pauli (ed. Bolte) No. 206; *Hertel Zs. f. Vksk. XVIII 385; *Basset *1001 Contes* II 4; *Schoepperle I 225f. — Icelandic *1;* India *5;* Chinese: Chavannes *500 Contes* I 387 No. 116; Spanish-American: Rael No. 487 (U.S.). — Literary Treatments: Rohde *Der griechische Roman* 484; Italian Novella: Rotunda (K1513).

1418* *The Father Overhears.* A bride in bed confesses to her husband that she has had a man once. He leaves. The mother under the bed asks the daughter why she has confessed. The mother says, »I have had many men but never confessed to your father.» The hidden father overhears and leaves to join his son-in-law.

French Canadian; U.S. (Ozarks): Randolph *Devil's Pretty Daughter* p. 61. Said to be current in Germany.

1419 *The Returning Husband Hoodwinked* [K1510].

Irish *2;* India *6.* — English-American: Baughman (1419E) *2*, Hansen (Puerto Rico) *2*, (Cuba) *5;* West Indies (Negro) *1.* — African *2.*

1419A *The Husband in the Chicken House.* The husband returns unexpectedly and surprises his wife with her lover. She makes the husband believe he is pursued and hides him in the chicken house. [K1514.1].

Schofield *Sources and History of the Seventh Novel of the Seventh Day in the Decameron* (Harvard Studies and Notes II, 1893); *Bédier *Fabliaux* 450. — Finnish-Swedish (1406) *2;* India *2.* — Literary Treatments: Boccaccio *Decameron* VII No. 7 (Lee 213); *Italian Novella: Rotunda (K1514.1); *Cent Nouvelles Nouvelles* No. 88.

1419B *The Animal in the Chest.* Substituted for the lover. The husband has locked the surprised paramour in a chest while he fetches his family as witness of his wife's unfaithfulness. She frees the lover, substitutes an animal, and discountenances the husband. [K1515].

*Wesselski *Hodscha Nasreddin* II 187 No. 363; *Schweizerisches Archiv für Volkskunde* XX 43; *Rotunda Novella (K1515). — Literary Treatment: *Cent Nouvelles Nouvelles* No. 61.

1419C *The Husband's One Good Eye Covered (Treated).* The wife holds a cloth in front of his eye (K1516) or pretends to treat it [K1516.1] so that he cannot see the paramour.

*Chauvin IX 20 Nos. 7, 8; Bédier *Fabliaux* 119, 466; Wesselski *Märcen* 187 No. 2; Jellinek *Euphorion* IX 162f.; Hdwb. d. Märchens I 94b; Krappe *Bulletin Hispanique* XXXIX 27. — Spanish *2;* India *2.* — Literary Treatments: Chauvin IX 20 Nos. 7, 8; Italian Novella: Rotunda (K1516); *Alphabet of Tales* No. 535; *Scala Celi* No. 504; *Gesta Romanorum* (ed. Oesterley) No. 122.

1419D *The Lovers as Pursuer and Fugitive.* The wife is visited by two gallants. When the husband approaches, one goes out with drawn sword; the other hides in the house. She convinces her husband that she has given refuge to a fugitive. [K1517.1, cf. K1517—K1517.12].

*Basset *1001 Contes* II 143; *Wesselski *Hodscha Nasreddin* II 186 No. 351; Bédier *Fabliaux* 229ff.; Chauvin VIII 39 No. 7, IX 21 No. 8; Hdwb. d.

Märchens I 99b. — Swedish (misc.) *2;* India *2.* — Portuguese American (Brazil): Camara Cascudo p. 52. — Literary Treatments: Chauvin VIII 39 No. 7, IX 21 No. 8; Boccaccio Decameron VII No. 6 (Lee 203); von der Hagen *Gesammtabenteuer* II xxxii ff.; Dunlop-Wilson II 114ff.; Italian Novella: Rotunda (K1517.1).

1419E *Underground Passage to Paramour's House* (Inclusa). Woman goes from one to the other. Her husband is made to believe that the woman next door is her sister. [K1523].
  *BP I 46 n.; *Fischer-Bolte 219; Wesselski *Märchen* 188 No. 2; Chauvin V 213 No. 121, VIII 96 No. 67; Köhler-Bolte I 393; Searles MLN XVII 165ff.; Campbell *Sages* cx.; Krappe *Archivum Romanicum* XIX (1935) 213—226; *Cent Nouvelles Nouvelles* No. 1; Icelandic: *Boberg (K1523); Italian Novella: *Rotunda (K1523), Italian (Sicilian *874 *5*, 1406 *2*, Gonzenbach No. 56); Hungarian: Berze Nagy (891*) *1;* Greek (1406**) *9*, Dawkins *Modern Greek Folktales* No. 60 *7*, Hahn No. 29; Turkish: Eberhard-Boratav No. 267 *6;* India *1*.

1419F *Husband Frightened by Wife's Paramour in Hog Pen.* The husband sees the paramour who has hidden in the pen and says, »Who are you?» »I am a miserable hog.» The husband thinks that his hogs are possessed. [K1542]. (Cf. K1515, K1555, K1566, K1574.)
  Wesselski *Bebel* I 206 No. 92; Spanish: Espinosa III No. 193.

1419G *The Priest's Breeches.* Husband returns unexpectedly to get his heavy breeches. The wife by mistake throws him the priest's breeches. Later claims to belong to an order using such breeches.
  Italian (Tuscan [1779] *3); Serbocroatian 2.

1419H *Woman Warns Lover of Husband by Singing Song* (or parody incantation) [K1546, K1546.1].
  Finnish *51;* Italian Novella: Rotunda (K1546), Boccaccio Decameron VII No. 1; U. S.: *Baughman (K1546.1).

1419E* *Husband Cannot Recognize Himself* and does not know what to do. (Cf. Type 1383.) Often with Type 1419 E.
  Greek *9*.

1419J* *Husband Sent for Water.* The husband returns home when a lover is with his wife. Under the pretext of his wife's illness they send him to fetch water. Meanwhile, her lover escapes.
  Russian: Andrejev (1406*B) *1*.

1419K* *Lover Hidden in Chest,* etc. A wife hides her lover in a feather bed, in a wardrobe, in a chest. He escapes.
  Russian: Andrejev (1406*C) *1*.

1419L* *Wife Disguised as Bishop,* the lover as friend. Husband punished.
  Russian: Andrejev (1406*D) *2*.

1420 *The Lover's Gift Regained* [K1581].

1420A *The Broken (Removed) Article.* The lover breaks (or removes) an article

of housefold equipment, and convinces the husband that for that reason the wife has confiscated that which he gave her as a present.
**Spargo FFC XCI; cf. Type 1420B.

1420B *Horse and Wagon as Gift.* The lover regains the gift of horse and wagon by pretending to the husband that the wife has confiscated them because he brought wood of uneven quality.
**Erk-Böhme *Deutscher Liederhort* (Leipzig 1893—94) I, 40ff.; **Spargo FFC XCI. Cf. Walloon (*1357) *1*.

1420C *Borrowing from the Husband and Returning to the Wife.* The lover borrows money from the husband with which to corrupt the wife, later telling the husband that the money was returned to the wife during the husband's absence.
**Lee *Decameron*, 247ff.; **Spargo FFC XCI; Chaucer's Shipman's Tale.

1420D *Accidental Discovery of Identity.* The lover, ignorant of the identity of the husband, tells him of his experience with the wife. The husband persuades the lover to lead him to the scene, where the wife is compelled to restore all but a small part of the money.
**Euling *Studien über Heinrich Kaufringer* (Breslau, 1900) 65ff.; **Spargo FFC XCI.

1420E *Piece of Cloth as Gift.* The lover regains by a ruse and thievery the borrowed piece of cloth which he has presented to his mistress.
**Spargo FFC XCI.

1420F *Jewelry as Gift.* The lover presents the wife with a valuable piece of jewelry, which he regains by pretending to the husband that he has left it as a pledge.
**Wesselski *Bebel* ch. 49; **Bolte *Frey's Gartengesellschaft* No. 76; **Spargo FFC XCI.

1420G *Anser Venalis. (Goose as Gift).* The lover regains his gift by a ruse (obscene).
**Semerau, *Die Schwänke und Schnurren des Poggio* (Leipzig, 1905) No. 69; **Spargo FFC XCI.

1422 *Parrot Unable to Tell Husband Details of Wife's Infidelity.* Wife has the parrot describe a storm realistically. Husband observes contrast in the two tales. [J1154.1]. Cf. Types 243, 1381.
French *2;* Turkish: Eberhard-Boratav No. 53 *4;* India *1.* — Literary Treatments: Chauvin VIII 35f. No. 3; Bødker Exempler 286 No. 35; Spanish Exempla: Keller; Italian Novella: *Rotunda (J1154.1).

1423 *The Enchanted Pear Tree.* The wife makes the husband, who has seen her adultery from the tree, believe that the tree is magic (or that he has seen double) [K1518].
Robinson *Complete Works of Geoffrey Chaucer* (Boston, 1933) 817 (Mer-

chant's Tale); *Basset *1001 Contes* 150ff.; *Bédier *Fabliaux* 468; *Stiefel Zs. f. Vksk. VIII 79; *Wesselski *Mönchslatein* 121 No. 103; *Wesselski *Märchen* 214f. No. 23; Coffin *2;* Hdwb. d. Märchens I 95f. — Finnish *3;* Scottish *1;* Irish *20;* French *1;* Spanish *1;* Dutch *1;* cf. Hungarian: Berze Nagy (1410*) *1;* cf. Russian: Afanasief (*1563 III) *2;* Turkish: Eberhard-Boratav No. 271. — English-American: Baughman *2;* Spanish-American: Hansen (**1425) (Puerto Rico) *1.* — Literary Treatments: Chauvin VIII 98 No. 69, IX 39 No. 34; Crane *Vitry* 240 No. 251; Boccaccio Decameron VII No. 9 (Lee 231); *Mensa Philosophica* No. 76; Dunlop-Wilson II 120f.; Italian Novella: Rotunda (K1518).

1424 *Friar Adds Missing Nose* (fingers) to unborn child: foetus is imperfect and he will substitute for absent husband. Is praised by the latter on his return. [K1363.2].
Nouvelles Récréations No. 9; Italian Novella: Rotunda (K1363.2); West Indies: Flowers 538.

1424* *Wife Recovers What her Husband first Found and then Lost.* Man finds money, which he gives to beggar. Clever wife goes in pursuit of beggar and spends the night with him at an inn. She assumes a vulgar name and fools beggar out of his money.
Lithuanian (*1424) *14.*

1425 *Putting the Devil into Hell.* Obscene trick used to seduce woman. [K1363.1].
French *2;* French Michigan *1;* Italian Novella: Rotunda (K1363.1).

1425A* *Returning Red-Haired Boy.* A dying wife asks her husband to return a borrowed kettle to a neighbor man. He promises. »Then when you take the kettle with you, also take the little boy with the red hair.«
French-Canadian.

1425B* *Why Seventh has Red Hair.* Dying husband asks wife why six children have hair alike, only seventh has red hair. Is the seventh's father someone else? No, only seventh is yours.
French-Canadian.

1426 *The Wife Kept in a Box* [T382, F1034.2.1, J882.2]. A man, disgusted by the infidelity of his wife, wanders off and watches while a fakir (demon, etc.) takes his wife from a box, where he keeps her thinking to keep her chaste. The man sees that the woman has a man with her in the box, or has tricked her husband in other ways.
*Hertel Zs. f. Vksk. XIX 83ff.; *Littmann *1001 Nächten* I 20—22; Wesselski *Märchen* 185. — Russian: Andrejev (*895) *1;* Turkish: Eberhard-Boratav No. 275 *1;* Turkestan: Jarring *Materials to the Knowledge of Eastern Turki* III (Lund, 1951) 65—75; Jewish: *Neuman (T382); Buddhist myth: Malalasekera II 1053; India *3;* Japanese: Ikeda (T382); Chinese: Eberhard FFC CXXVIII 297 No. 189, Chavannes *500 Contes* No. 109.

1426* *Man with Unfaithful Wife Comforted* when he sees jealous husband who carefully guards wife cuckolded. [J882.2].
*Wesselski *Märchen* 185 No. 1; Köhler-Bolte II 625; Italian Novella: Rotunda (J882.2); Hungarian: Berze Nagy (977*) *1;* India: Thompson-Balys (J882.2).

1429* *Water of Slander.* To an old woman who quarrels with her husband, a hermit gives a »water of slander». The quarrels stop when she takes this water into her mouth.
Russian: Andrejev *1*.

1430—1439 The Foolish Couple

1430 *The Man and his Wife Build Air Castles.* They make great plans for success but disagree over the conclusion. They quarrel over details and lose everything. Cf. Type 1681*.

Motifs: J2060. Absurd plans. Air-castles. J2060.1. Quarrel and fight over details of air-castles. J2061. Air-castle shattered by lack of forethought. J2061.1. Air-castle: the jar of honey to be sold. In his excitement he breaks the jar. J2061.1.1. Air-castle: basket of glassware to be sold. In his excitement he breaks the glassware. J2061.1.2. Air-castle: basket of eggs to be sold. In her excitement she breaks all the eggs. J2061.2. Air-castle: pail of milk to be sold. Proud milkmaid tosses her head (or kicks the pail in her sleep) and spills the milk.

*BP III 261f., 264f., *Anderson in Tauscher *Volksmärchen* 176, 275; *Gerould MLN XIX 225, 226, 228, 229; Wesselski *Hodscha Nasreddin* I 249 No. 163; Pauli (ed. Bolte) No. 520. — Finnish *25;* Estonian *22;* Lithuanian *10;* Swedish (Uppsala) *1;* Icelandic (1431*) *2;* Irish *13,* Jackson FL XLVII 291; Spanish *11;* Dutch *2;* Flemish *1,* (161*) *1;* German *4;* Italian (Tuscan *2,* Sicilian *1*); Rumanian *1;* Hungarian *5;* Slovenian *5;* Serbocroatian *1;* Russian: Afanasiev (1430*) *4;* Greek *2;* Jewish: Bin Gorion *Born Judas* IV 55, 277; India 2 (1430A) *10;* Indonesian: DeVries No. 269, Coster-Wijsman 65f. Nos. 107—110; Chinese: Eberhard FFC CXX 279 No. 4, FFC CXXVIII 237 No. 144. — Spanish-American: Hansen (Dominican Republic) *1,* (Puerto Rico) *1.* — Literary Treatments: Chauvin II 100f., 118f. No. 3, V 161—163, 296 No. 85, VIII 173 No. 196; Crane *Vitry* 154f. No. 51; Aesop (Jacobs) No. 77; Bødker *Exempler* 300 No. 65; Spanish Exempla: Keller; *Nouvelles Récréations* No. 12.

1430A *Foolish Plans for the Unborn Child.* [J2060.1.]. Cf. Type 1450.
*BP III 275 (Grimm No. 168); *Anderson in Tauscher *Volksmärchen* 176; Chauvin VIII 178 No. 209. — German: Plenzat (1430) *3;* Rumanian (1430) *1;* Russian: Afanasiev (1430B) *1.*

1431 *The Contagious Yawns.* A husband planning to punish his wife, who has yawned in church at the same time as a man, sees his error when his wife in the woods calls out, »The squirrels hop from bough to bough as the yawns from mouth to mouth.» [J1448].

Finnish *10,* Aarne FFC VIII 6 No. 23, XXXIII 52 No. 23; Estonian: Aarne FFC XXV 141 No. 12; Livonian: Loorits FFC LXVI 84 No. 35; Swedish (Uppsala) *6;* Serbocroatian *1.*

1433* *Man and Wife Leave Food to get Wine.* It is stolen. They think flies have eaten it. (With Type 1586.)
　　Greek (1431*) *2*.

1434* *The Egg-Excreter.* A gullible wife is made to believe that her husband can excrete eggs. Planning to make money thus, she invites to an exhibition. She gives a purgative and holds an apron to catch the eggs. To husband, »Don't go so fast, you are breaking them all.»
　　French Canadian.

1435* *The Hidden Girl.* The daughter is hidden from the suitor but he is told where she is. (Sometimes by parents and sometimes by girl.) [W136.1, V465.1.2.1].
　　Pauli (ed. Bolte) No. 13. — Icelandic *1*.

1437 *A Sweet Word.* A quarrelsome husband asked by his dying wife for a sweet word answers, »Honey is sweet or throws a Bible at her.» [J1541.1, J2497]. Cf. Type 1696B*.
　　*Köhler-Bolte I 3; *BP III 278. — Finnish *5*.

STORIES ABOUT A WOMAN (GIRL)

1440 *The Tenant Promises his Daughter to his Master* against her will. The master sends for »that which was promised him». The daughter sends a horse and it is taken into the master's chamber. [J1615].
　　Finnish *12*; Estonian cf. 1191*; Norwegian *1*; Russian: Andrejev *1*.

1441 *Respite from Wooer while he Brings Clothes all Night.* The girl wastes time trying them on. [K1227.3]. Cf. Types 311, 312, 955.
　　*BP I 221; Roberts 175; Estonian: Aarne FFC XXV 120 No. 31; Lithuanian: Balys *Legends* Nos. 345f., 363, 398.

1441* *Old Woman Substitute.* The master wants to come at night to a young girl. She substitutes an old woman. [K1223].
　　Toldo Zs. f. Vksk. XIV 47. — Finnish; Estonian *1*; Livonian *1*; Swedish (Stockholm) *2*; Danish: MS DFS; Russian: Afanasiev. — Literary Treatment: Rotunda Novella (K1223).

1441A* *The Inked Girl.* A girl is brought to her master. At night she smears herself with ink in place of spirits and is taken for the devil.
　　Russian: Andrejev (*1440 I).

1441B* *God-father and God-mother.* The god-mother calls the god-father into a sheepcot, then into a cowhouse, then into a room. But instead of herself, she sends her husband.
　　Russian: Andrejev (*1441 I) *1*.

1441C* *Father-in-law and Daughter-in-law.* The youngest of the three daughters-in-law sings a song in favor of her father-in-law, and goes to meet his amorous wish.
　　Russian: Andrejev (*1442) *1*.

1442* *Stupid Queen's Unsuccessful Imitation of Magic* performed by husband's mistress: (1) resuscitation, (2) quenching fire, (3) sailing on magic bed cover. Cf. Type 531.
　　Icelandic *1*.

1443* *The Pillow too High.* An unmarried man and woman traveling sleep overnight with pillow between them. Next day her hat blows off and a fence must be

climbed to retrieve it. He offers to get it. »No, you couldn't climb a fence, for you couldn't climb over a pillow last night.« Cf. Type 1351*.
*Ranke in *Peuckert Festschrift* 46 n. 15 (Germany 1954). Heard by me in Kentucky about 1906 (told of a local character).

1445* *Till the Front Sweats.* The mother orders her daughter to knead the dough until the front (Stirn) of the oven sweats. The girl's forehead (Stirn). [J2499.1].
Estonian *3*.

1446 (formerly 1446*) *Let them Eat Cake.* The queen has been told that the peasants have no bread. [J2227].
Bolte *Montanus* 601 No. 48. — Estonian (1446) *1;* German: Beng *Der Hazeltrog* (1952) 124; cf. Russian: Afanasiev (*2065) *1;* India *2*.

1447 *Drinking only after a Bargain.* A woman having thus sworn keeps buying and selling the same mule many times a day. [K236.2].
*Pauli (ed. Bolte) No. 306; *Scala Celi* 81a No. 463; *Crane *Vitry* 255 No. 277; Herbert III 24. — Danish: Christensen DF XLVII No. 18; Arab: Campbell *Tales from the Arab Tribes* (1949) 56.

1447* *The Dirty Woman.* After three washings and the use of three pounds of soap she becomes clean and fair. [W115.2].
Livonian (1447') *1;* Greek *1*.

1447A* *Selling Wine to Each Other.* The married couple clever in business. Sell each other gradually the wine they have bought at the bargain.
Rumanian (1433*) *1;* Slovenian.

1448* *Burned and Underbaked Bread.* Wishing to rid herself of her father-in-law, the daughter-in-law starts to feed him burned bread; but the old man begins to thrive on it. When she tries underbaked bread, the old man dies very soon.
Lithuanian (*2427) *2*.

1449* *The Stingy Hostess at the Inn.* She should be glad to give something to eat, but she has no spoons. A practical joker brings along the necessary spoons. [J1561.4.1].
Livonian (1449') *1*.

1449** *Stingy Dead Woman Raises her Head* to correct laundress's account when latter attempts to cheat dead woman's daughter. [W152.3].
Spanish (*1482) *1*.

1450—1474 Looking for a Wife

1450 *Clever Elsie.* The girl is to get beer from the cellar. Falls into a study as to what her first child's name shall be. Likewise the girl's father and mother. The suitor departs. [J2063]. Cf. Types 1384, 1387, 1430A.
*BP I 335 (Grimm No. 34); Clouston *Noodles* 191; Christensen DF L 35; Coffin *8*. — Finnish *27;* Finnish-Swedish *4;* Estonian *6;* Lithuanian *4;* Lappish *1;* Swedish *19* (Uppsala *6*, Stockholm *2*, Lund *2*, Liungman *2*, misc. *7*); Norwegian *3;* Danish: Grundtvig No. 125; Irish *54;* French *30;* Walloon *1;* German Archive *3;* Italian (Tuscan *1*); Rumanian *1;* Hungarian *5*, Dégh No. 41; Czech: Tille Soupis I 404ff. *7;* Slovenian *1;* Serbocroatian *5;* Russian: Andrejev *Ukraine 11*, Afanasiev *10;* Greek *6*, (1450*) *4;* Kretschmer No. 20; Turkish: Eberhard-Boratav No. 331 III

4; Jewish: Bin Gorion *Born Judas* IV 55, 277; India *1.* — English-American: Baughman *6;* Spanish-American: Hansen (Puerto Rico) *1;* West Indies (Negro) *5.*

1451 *The Thrifty Girl.* The thrifty girl makes herself a dress from the flax the lazy fiancée has thrown on the floor. The young man chooses the thrifty girl. [H381.1].
BP III 239 (Grimm No. 156). — Irish: Jackson FL XLVII 291; Russian: Andrejev.

1452 *Bride Test: Thrifty Cutting of Cheese.* Three girls tested. First eats rind and all, second cuts away good cheese, third cuts away just enough. [H381.2].
*BP III 236 (Grimm No. 155). — Swedish *9* (Uppsala *2,* Stockholm *2,* Lund *5*); Norwegian: Solheim *1;* French *2;* Flemish (1452*) *1;* Walloon (1452A*) *1;* Hungarian *1;* Russian: Andrejev. — English-American (North Carolina): Brown Collection I 702.

1453 *Bride Test: Key in Flax Reveals Laziness.* Suitor hides key in flax on spinning wheel. Finds it there next day. [H382.1].
*BP III 236 (Grimm No. 155). — Finnish *30;* Finnish-Swedish *4;* Estonian *12;* Livonian *1;* Lithuanian *2;* Lappish *3;* Swedish *47* (Uppsala *22,* Stockholm *7,* Göteborg *1,* Lund *7,* Liungman *4,* misc. *6*); Norwegian *10,* Solheim *2;* Hungarian *2;* Serbocroatian *1;* Russian: Andrejev.

1453A *The Fast Weaver.* Girl keeps dropping shuttle on floor.
Finnish *19.*

1453* *The Lazy Girl doesn't Know where the Spring Is* [W111.5.2].
Livonian *1;* Lappish *1.*

1453** *The Slovenly Fiancée* [W115.1].
Finnish *4;* Finnish-Swedish *2;* Swedish (Lund) *1;* Catalan: Amades No. 435.

1453*** *Three-weeks-old Dough.* The girl still after three weeks has dough under her finger nails [H383.1.1]. Cf. Type 1462*.
Finnish *2;* Estonian *13;* Lithuanian (1454*) *5;* Swedish *4* (Lund *2,* Stockholm *2*); Russian: Andrejev (1453*) *1.*

1453**** *Puella pedens.*
Finnish-Swedish *1;* Estonian (1459*) *3;* Swedish (Uppsala) *4;* Hungarian: Berze Nagy (1479*) *1.* — Spanish-American: Hansen (**1459, **1460) (Dominican Republic) *1,* (Cuba) *1.*

1453A* *The Untidy Bride.* »I haven't put my hand in the pot since my father bought it.»
Rumanian (1459*, 1374 I*) *4.*

1454* *The Greedy Fiancée.* The suitor on a visit. The porridge. The girl lays a bowl of porridge in the place of the basket of wool under the bed. Says she can finish six of them in one day. The suitor sees the deceit and leaves [H385].
Finnish *3;* Norwegian (1462*) *1;* German: Selk *Volksschwänke aus Angeln* p. 15; Greek: Loukatos No. 21.

1455 *The Hard-hearted Fiancée.* The father-in-law disguised as a beggar [H384.1].
Finnish *17;* Estonian *4;* Lithuanian *1;* Swedish *4* (Liungman *1,* misc. *3*); Irish *251;* Russian: Andrejev.

1455* *The Stingy Bride.* Her bridegroom comes to visit her and discovers her stinginess.
Russian: Andrejev (1454).

1456 *The Blind Fiancée.* The search for the needle. The girl mistakes the dish for a cat. The blindness is thus discovered. [K1984.5].

*BP III 237. — Finnish *65;* Estonian *17;* Lithuanian *6;* Swedish *46* (Uppsala *28*, Stockholm *6*, Lund *3*, Liungman *4*, misc. *5*); Norwegian *11*, Solheim *1;* Danish: Grundtvig No. 164; Irish *7;* Dutch *1;* German *5;* Rumanian *1;* Slovenian *2;* Serbocroatian *1;* Russian: Andrejev *2;* India *4*. — English-American: Baughman *1;* American Negro (Michigan): Dorson No. 155.

1456* *The Blind Girl and her Fiancé.* Her fiancé leads her about the room and steals her property.
Russian: Andrejev (*1480) *2*.

1457 *The Lisping Maiden.* The suitor on a visit. The impediment in speech discovered. The girls have been warned against talking but forget and speak out. [K1984.1]. (Sometimes other impediments or deformities.)

*BP III 237; Bolte Zs. f. Vksk. III 58, VII 320; Coffin *4*. — Finnish *57;* Estonian *9;* Livonian *2;* Lithuanian *6;* Swedish *36* (Uppsala *15*, Stockholm *6*, Göteborg *1*, Lund *6*, Liungman *2*, misc. *6*); Norwegian *3;* French *1;* Catalan: Amades No. 2034; German *20* (Archive *19*, Henssen Volk No. 244); Italian (Tuscan [1453] *1*, Trieste: Pinguentini No. 8); Hungarian *9;* Serbocroatian *2;* Russian: Andrejev *4;* Greek: Argenti-Rose II 604f., Loukatos No. 22; Turkish: Eberhard-Boratav No. 338; Japanese: Ikeda. — Spanish-American: Rael No. 74 (U.S.), Hansen (Chile) *1*, (Puerto Rico) *2*.

1457* *Man with Stammer Goes Matchmaking* and is advised not to speak at all. He sees potatoes for a meal being left too long on the fire and blurts out many stammers. Match not made.
Irish.

1458 *The Girl who Ate so Little.* The girl eats lightly and the mother declares this is always so. Next day the suitor sees her baking and discovers that she can eat. [K1984.2]. Cf. Types 1373, 1407.

Lappish (1458*) *1;* Swedish (Uppsala) *2;* Norwegian (1458**) *9;* Solheim *1;* Irish *38*, Beal IV 312f.; German: Merk. 48; Slovenian *2;* Turkish: Eberhard-Boratav No. 319.

1458* *The Bride Cooks Porridge full of Lumps.* The step-mother says, »Good porridge for it has many lumps in it.« The bride: »I have already taken a stockingful out«.
Finnish *2;* Estonian *1*.

1459* *The Suitor Takes Offense at a Word* used by the girl.
Lappish *1*.

1459** *Keeping up Appearances.* The suitor comes to a very poor farm where the people make desperate efforts to appear rich. [K1984].
Finnish *9;* Norwegian *2;* Swedish *4* (Stockholm *3*, Lund *1*).

1460* *Mutual Mockeries of Girl and Suitor.* The girl laughs at his attempt to mount his horse. He repays by spying on her attempt to beautify herself.
Livonian (1549') *1;* Russian: Andrejev (*1460) *1*.

1461 *The Girl with the Ugly Name.* Her mother gives her a new one. The girl does not recognize it when she is called in, and her mother must use the old one. [K1984.3].
Herbert *Catalogue of Romances* III 174 No. 87, 421 No. 83. — Lithuanian *3;* Norwegian (1460**) *2,* Solheim *1.* — English-American: Baughman (1461*) *2.*

1462 (formerly 1461*) *The Unwilling Suitor Advised from the Tree.* Girl hidden in tree makes suitor think he is being advised by angels to marry her. He does so. [K1971.6]. Cf. Types 1380, 1476.
Norwegian (1561**) *4;* India *1.*

1462* *Clean and Tidy.* A suitor mentions casually that it is difficult to get seven-year old porridge, which he is to use as medicine. In the pots and pans of the house there is enough to be found, says the mother of the girl. Cf. Type 1453***.
Swedish *4;* Norwegian *1.*

1463 *Finger-drying Contest Won by Deception.* Three daughters are to wet hands; the first to have hands dry is to be the first to marry. The youngest waves her hand, exclaiming, »I don't want a man!» She wins. [K95].
*Pauli (ed. Bolte) No. 14. — Finnish *9;* U.S.: Baughman (K95); North Carolina: Brown Collection I 701; Italian Novella: Rotunda (K95).

1463A* *Foolish Bride Gives away Dowry.* While her parents are away from home matchmaker and a suitor come to the foolish girl. By following her mother's advice literally, she gives away her dowry to the tricksters. [J2463.1].
Lithuanian *11.*

1463B* *Secret Instructions in Weaving.* A youth is looking for a wife. The girl has not learned to weave, but she understands how to interpret instructions of the youth given in riddles.
Swedish (GS 1463) *5* (Uppsala *2,* Liungman *1,* misc. *2*).

1464A* *Bachelor will only Marry Girl who can Lay Eggs.* Mother has girl sit on eggs and makes him believe she can lay eggs. They marry. Mother advises girl to excuse herself on wedding night for a moment. She falls downstairs and cries that she has broken her egg-making organ.
French-Canadian.

1464B* *Girl Resents Name of* »*Sow*». A girl eloping hears her fiancé refer to her as »the sow». She returns to her room on a pretext and refers him to the »sow in the stable».
Walloon (*1464) *1.*

1464C* *Good Housekeeping.* A suitor comes when the room is not in order. The first two sisters apologize for it, but third puts it in order — wins suitor.
Swedish (GS 1464) *14* (Uppsala *6,* Stockholm *1,* Liungman *3,* misc. *4*).

1464D* *Nothing to Cook.* The bride says she can not cook. The groom: it doesn't matter since I have nothing to cook.
Finnish *6.*

1465* *The Root, not the Branch.* The youth asks for the youngest daughter (the branch of the tree) in marriage. But he is promised the eldest (the root of the tree). [H611].
Livonian *1.*

1465A* *The Concentrated Washer.* A mother seeking a wife for son takes the one who does not busy herself with anything else while she is doing the washing.
Swedish *8* (Uppsala *6,* Lund *1,* misc. *1*).

1468* *Marrying a Stranger.* The girl shortly to be married complains, »It was all very well for you, mother, to marry father, but I am to marry a complete stranger. [J2463.2].
Finnish *3;* Lithuanian *1;* Russian: Andrejev (*2078A).

1470* (Obscene.)
Livonian *1.*

1475—1499 Jokes about Old Maids

1475 *Marriage Forbidden Outside the Parish.* An order is read in church forbidding the young people to marry girls from other parishes. [X751].
Finnish *15;* Finnish-Swedish *1;* Estonian *5;* Livonian *1;* Irish *1;* Russian: Andrejev; Portuguese-American (Brazil): Camara Cascudo Estorias p. 50.

1476 *The Prayer for a Husband.* The old maid prays in church that she may get a husband [X761]. The (supposed) advice of God (the church janitor) [K1971.9]. She must raise her foot to her neck (or other disgraceful act). Cf. Type 1462.
BP III 120 (Grimm No. 139); *Toldo Zs. f. Vksk. XIII 422 n. 1; Coffin *1.* — Finnish *8;* Estonian *6;* Livonian *1;* Norwegian: Solheim *1;* Irish *1;* English *2;* French *12;* Spanish *3;* Dutch *3;* Flemish *11;* Walloon (1476A) *1;* German *36* (Archive *33,* Henssen Jül. No. 474, Henssen Volk No. 285; Meckl. No. 128); Hungarian: Berze Nagy (1476**) *1;* Serbocroatian *1;* Slovenian; Russian: Andrejev *1,* Andrejev *Ukraine 5;* India *2.* — English-American: Baughman *2;* Spanish-American: Hansen cf. (Cuba) *2.*

1476A *Prayer to Christ Child's Mother.* Sexton behind crucifix tells old maid she will have no husband. She tells Christ child he knows nothing about it. She is praying to his mother.
BP III 120. — Serbocroatian *1.*

1476B *Girl Married to a Devil.* Despairing of ever finding herself a husband, the old maid exclaims: »I would marry even the devil, were he to marry me.» The devil takes her at her word. [G303.13.5.1].
Lithuanian: Balys No. 3253, Legends Nos. 367ff.; Serbocroatian *2.*

1476C *Old Maid Asks for Death.* A rascal steals into her bed at night. — »Oh sweet death, keep killing me.»
Finnish *27;* Icelandic (1541 I*) *1.*

1477 *The Wolf Steals the Old Maid.* She keeps him for a husband [X755].
Finnish *20;* Estonian *1;* Russian: Andrejev; Greek *2;* Turkish: Eberhard-Boratav No. 322 *2.*

1477* *Old Maid Tells the Wolf to Come to Bed.* Boys have brought the wolf into her room. She thinks it is a young man.
Finnish *6.*

1478 *The Meal of Beans.* One of the old maid's three teeth breaks off [X754].
Finnish *2;* Estonian *6;* Russian: Andrejev.

1479* *The Youth Promises to Marry the Old Maid* if she will sit all night on the roof. She falls down. [X753].
Coffin *1.* — Finnish *1;* Estonian *2;* Russian: Andrejev. — American Negro (Michigan): Dorson No. 156.

1479** *Statue Avenged.* The woman whose prayer St. Anthony has not granted avenges herself on his statue. [V123].
Flemish (1479*) *3;* Serbocroatian *2.* — English-American: Baughman (1479*) *1.*

1480* *The Old Maid in Bed.* On one side is a bundle of straw (her husband) and the other a dog (her child). She gives the straw bundle a push and thereupon falls on the floor herself. [X752].
Estonian *2;* cf. Livonian.

1485* *Pretty Lips.* The mother tells the old maid to say »Tirlipp» in church so that her lips shall remain pretty [X756].
Estonian *1;* Meyer *Plattdeutsche Volksmärchen* 284 No. 102.

1485A* *Old Maid Wants to Attract Attention.* Wears a horse collar about her neck to church.
Finnish *25.*

1486* *The Daughter Talks too Loud.* The mother bids her hold half of her mouth closed. She holds it and then shrieks louder. [X756].
Livonian *1.*

1487* *Guarding Against Neglect.* The old maid has eleven cocks and one hen, so that hen will not be neglected as she has been.
French-Canadian.

1490* *The Contract to be Burned.* A girl asks her father how it feels to be married. He tells her that it means beatings. She has the bridegroom sign a contract to touch her only once a year. After the first night she burns the contract.
Finnish *9.*

1498* *Boys Seduce Girl Sleeping in Barn.*
Livonian *1.*

1499* *Catching Rams.* On St. Sylvester's Night the girls catch rams in the sheep stall. One of the girls catches a one-eyed ram.
Livonian *1.*

1500—1524 Other Anecdotes of Women

1501 *Aristotle and Phyllis.* The philosopher warns the king against uxoriousness. In revenge the queen beguiles the philosopher into letting her ride him on all-fours. The king comes and sees. [K1215].
**Moth *Aristotelessagnet;* **Borgeld *Aristoteles en Phyllis* (Groningen 1902); *Basset *1001 Contes* II 140; *G. Paris Romania XI 138; Wesselski *Hodscha Nasreddin* II 203 No. 402; *Bédier *Fabliaux* 204, 387, 446; *Herbert *Catalogue* III 87; RTP XV 110; von der Hagen *Gesammtabenteuer* I xxv 17. — Indonesian: Voorhoeve 164 No. 170, Bezemer *Javaansche en Malaische Legenden* 170f.; Chinese: Chavannes III 236. — Literary Treatments: *Scala Celi* No. 501; Italian Novella: Rotunda (K1215).

1503* *The Daughter-in-law and the Real Daughter.* The mother-in-law always favors the daughter, with absurd results.
Finnish *50.*

1510 *The Matron of Ephesus (Vidua).* A woman mourns day and night by her husband's grave. A knight guarding a hanged man is about to lose his life because the corpse has been stolen from the gallows. The matron offers him her love and substitutes her husband's corpse on the gallows so that the knight can escape. [K2213.1]. Cf. Type 1752*.
****Grisebach *Die Wanderung der Novelle von der treulosen Witwe durch die Weltlitteratur;* **forthcoming study by Elizabeth Brandon (University of Houston); Pauli (ed. Bolte) No. 752; Ranke *Rheinische Jahrb. f. Vksk.* IV 90ff.; Chauvin VIII 210 No. 254; K. Campbell *Seven Sages* pp. cii. — Lithuanian *1;* Swedish (misc.) *4;* Icelandic *2;* Irish *5,* Beal III 501 No. 11; Spanish: Espinosa II No. 93; German *1;* Hungarian: Berze Nagy (1459*) *1;* Slovenian *1;* Russian: Andrejev (1352*) *1;* Turkish: Eberhard-Boratav No. 278; Jewish: Bin Gorion *Born Judas* III 240ff., 315; Caucasus: Dirr No. 70; Berber: Laoust No. 33. — Literary Treatments: Crane *Vitry* No. 232; Italian Novella: Rotunda (K2213.1).

1511 *The Faithless Queen.* Cf. Type 871A.
   I. *The Queen and the Loathsome Paramour* [T232]. (a) A king follows his queen as she slips out of their bedchamber. (b) The queen goes to her lover, a loathsome cripple, beggar, etc., (c) who beats her for coming late to their rendezvous. (d) The king's friend or a third person follows the wife and sees all.
   II. *The Queen Murders her Husband.* (a) At the order of her lover, the queen murders her husband. (b) When she returns to her lover, he spurns her, saying she would also murder him when she is tired of him [K2213.2].
India *13.*

1511* *Advice of the Bells.* A woman asks the priest about marrying a servant, and is told to listen to the advice of the bells. She hears them, receives a positive answer, and marries; the man turns out to be a drunkard, and the bells change their advice, but too late.
Walloon *1.*

1515 *The Weeping Bitch.* (Catala.) The procuress persuades the woman. She throws pepper into the eyes of a bitch so that it weeps. She pretends to the virtuous woman that the weeping bitch is a woman transformed because of her failure to respond to her lover. The woman is persuaded. [K1351].
****Penzer I 169; *Pauli (ed. Bolte) No. 873; *Krappe *Bulletin Hispanique* XXXIX 38. — Swedish (misc.) *1;* Icelandic *1;* Spanish *1.* — Literary Treatments: Chauvin VIII 45 No. 13; Crane *Vitry* 239 No. 251; Oesterley No. 28; von der Hagen *Gesammtabenteuer* I cxii; *Scala Celi* No. 510.

1516* *Pleasant Purgatory.* Husband had rather spend eternity in purgatory than be returned to his wife [T251.1.2].
Spanish *1.*

1516A* *Christ not being Married Knew Nothing of Suffering* [T251.0.2].
Spanish *1*.

1516B* *Long Marriage is Purgatory.* St. Peter admits a husband of many years to heaven: his purgatory is already served. A husband of two days is, however, turned away. Cf. Type 1410*.
Walloon (*1518, *1518A) *2*.

1516C* *Twice a Fool.* Man ejected from heaven for folly of marrying twice [T251.0.1].
Finnish *4;* French *4;* Spanish (*1410) *1;* Catalan: Amades No. 1315.

1516D* *The Marriage Fee.* When the priest demands promised payment for marrying him, the unhappy husband suggests that the priest un-marry him instead. [Cf. K1362, J1174.2].
Walloon.

STORIES ABOUT A MAN (BOY)

THE CLEVER MAN

1525 *The Master Thief.* [K301].
Note: references given here usually refer to 1525 with several of its subdivisions, especially 1525A—1525D.
*BP III 379; *Liungman SSF III 449; *Frazer *Pausanias* IV 192; Coffin *10;* Wesselski *Theorie* 17f. — Swedish *44* (Uppsala *1*, Stockholm *7*, Göteborg *4*, Lund *1*, Liungman *8*, misc. *23*); Norwegian *23*, Solheim *2;* Scottish *6*, Campbell-McKay No. 11; Irish *479*, Beal III 364f. No. 2, IV 431ff., V 75ff., VII 72ff., VIII 211ff., X 165ff., XVII 97; Dutch *5;* German *41;* Austrian: Haiding No. 74; Italian (Pentamerone III No. 7, Tuscan 950a, 1525A a—g *8*); Rumanian *8;* Slovenian *14;* Serbocroatian *10;* India *8;* Chinese: Eberhard FFC CXX 354 No. 21f., CXXVIII No. 182. — Franco-American (Missouri): Carrière (K301, K362.2); Spanish-American: Rael Nos. 292, 364, 347, 349—353, 355 (U.S.); West Indies (Negro) *21*. — Literary Treatments: Italian Novella: Rotunda (K301).

1525A *Theft of Dog, Horse, Sheet or Ring;* finally the priest (in the sack to heaven); cf. Type 1737.
I. *Theft as a Task.* (a) A good-for-nothing who has run away from home returns as a great man, boasts of his skill as a thief [K301.1], or (b) brothers learn trades and return home and boast; thus the earl hears of the trained thief [F660.1, H915]. (c) The earl puts the youth to tests [H1151].

II. *Theft of Horse.* (a) He steals the earl's horse [H1151.2] by dressing as an old woman and making the stable boys drunk [K332]; or (b) horses or cattle from drivers by chasing a rabbit so that the drivers join the chase [K341.5.1].

III. *Theft of Sheet and Ring.* He steals the countess's sheet and ring [H1151.3, H1151.4] while he deceives the count into shooting and burying a dead man [K362.2].

IV. *Places Exchanged in Sack.* He lures the parson and the sexton into a sack by telling them that he is Peter and that as the Day of Judgment has come he will take them to heaven [K842]. Cf. Types 1535 V, 1737.

*BP III 33ff., 379, 390 n. 2, 391, 393 (Grimm No. 192); Pauli (ed. Bolte) No. 850. — Finnish *235;* Finnish-Swedish *10;* Estonian *39;* Livonian *1;* Lithuanian *97;* Lappish *2;* Swedish *9* (Lund *4,* misc. *4,* [1525 AB] *1*); Icelandic *6;* Irish (see 1525), Beal II 358, V 78, VII 72, X 200, Jackson FL XLVII 291; French: Cosquin No. 70; Spanish *1,* Espinosa Cuentos III 229ff.; Catalan: Amades Nos. 374, 409; Flemish *9,* Witteryck p. 286 *10;* German *29* (Archive *28,* Henssen Volk No. 142); Hungarian *12;* Czech: Tille Soupis II (2) 283—296 *21;* Slovenian *3;* Serbocroatian *25,* Istrian No. 53; Russian: Andrejev *Ukraine 28,* Afanasiev *39;* Greek *11;* Turkish: Eberhard-Boratav No. 346, cf. 160 III *3;* India: Thompson-Balys *2;* Indonesian: DeVries No. 157; Japanese: Ikeda. — English-American: Baughman *2;* Spanish-American: Hansen (Argentina) *2,* (Chile) *1,* (Dominican Republic) *2,* (Cuba 1525**J) *1.* — Oceanic (Philippine): Fansler MAFLS XII 71f. — Literary Treatments: Chauvin VIII 136.

1525B *The Horse Stolen.* The man pretends to show how the horse can be stolen. Really leads it away. [K341.8]. Cf. Types 1540, 1542.

Finnish *3;* Swedish *2* (Lund *1,* misc. *1*); German *2;* Hungarian *1;* Russian: Afanasiev (*1528) *7;* Greek (1525B*) *1;* Turkish: Eberhard-Boratav No. 346 *3;* Japanese: Ikeda. — English-American: Baughman (K341.8); Spanish-American: Hansen (Dominican Republic) *1,* (Puerto Rico) *1;* American Indian: Thompson *C Coll* II 426ff.

1525C *The Traveler Watches the Man Fishing in the Street.* Meanwhile the latter's confederates rob the traveler's wagon. [K341.11].

Finnish *5;* Estonian *1;* Swedish (Lund) *1;* Spanish *1;* Walloon *1;* Russian: Andrejev *1.*

1525D *Theft by Distracting Attention.* The ram is stolen when the thief distracts attention from himself (a) by laying out shoes separately (saber and sheath, knife and fork); the owner finds one and then searches for the other [K341.6], or (b) by apparently hanging himself in the woods [K341.3], or (c) by imitating the bellowing of cattle [K341.7] (d) The clothes are stolen (the man beguiled into bathing). (For continuation see 1525J$_1$.)

*BP III 390 n. 2, 391 nn. 1, 2, 4; Anderson *Novelline* No. 37; *Parsons MAFLS XV (1) 85. — Finnish *114;* Estonian *29;* Lithuanian *30,* (1525H*) *2,* (*2425) *4,* (*2426) *2;* Lappish *2;* Swedish *4* (Uppsala *1,* Lund *3*); Irish: Jackson FL XLVII 291; English *1;* French *3;* Catalan: Amades No. 392, cf. 412; Flemish *2;* German *2* (Archive *1,* Henssen Volk No. 143); Italian (Sicilian *2,* **1525H *2,* Gonzenbach No. 37); Rumanian *3;* Hungarian: Berze Nagy (1727A*) *3;* Czech: Tille Soupis II (2) 287—296 *17;* Serbocroatian *20;* Russian: Afanasiev *16;* Greek *9,*

(1525C* 5, 1525D* 4); Turkish: Eberhard-Boratav No. 341 6; India 4.
— English-American: Baughman 5; Spanish-American: Hansen (Argentina) 1, (Chile) 1, (Dominican Republic) 1; (Puerto Rico) 1.

1525E *The Thieves and their Pupil.* They take turns in stealing from each other [K306]. In this way the pupil becomes the final winner [L142.1].
*BP III 393 n. 1; *Gering *Islendzk Aeventyri* (Halle, 1882—83) II 210ff. — Lithuanian 4; Danish: Grundtvig No. 111; Icelandic 3; Italian 5 (Tuscan 1563 a—c 3, Sicilian *1525E 2); Hungarian: Dégh No. 43; Czech: Tille Soupis I 131; Russian: Andrejev 4; Turkish: Eberhard-Boratav No. 343, 360, cf. 340 11.

1525F *The Youth Steals Horses from two Preachers* and money from the preacher's wife. As gravedigger. In the sack in the river [K842]; cf. Types 1535, 1737.
Köhler-Bolte I 210, 348; Pauli (ed. Bolte) 82. — Finnish 6; Finnish-Swedish 1; Estonian 1; French 6, Cosquin No. 81; Russian: Andrejev.

1525G *The Thief Assumes Disguises* [K311].
I. *Theft as Task.* To test his ability, the king, his parents, or the thief's teacher sets him a task to steal some inaccessible object, etc. He succeeds in stealing it. Cf. 1525A I.
II. *The Cast-Out Queen.* A king casts out his queen. When she bears a son, she rears him as a thief. By a series of clever thefts, he attracts the attention of the king and brings about a reconciliation between his parents.
III. *Entering the City.* The thief succeeds in entering a heavily guarded city (even though the king has been warned of his approach).
IV. *Theft by Disguising.* The thief (thieves) steals from and escapes from or entraps the king, the police chief, the adviser, etc., by assuming various disguises, usually female. (a) The thief disguises as Siva riding on a bull and offers to take the king, etc., to heaven. Cf. 1525A IV. (b) The thief disguises as the police chief's son-in-law and steals the daughter's jewel. (c) The thief disguises as an old woman grinding corn and gets the adviser to take his place. (d) The thief disguises as a fakir and gets the king to take his place.
Slovenian; India 15.

1525H *Thieves Steal from each other* [K306].
India: *Thompson-Balys; Hawaii: Beckwith Myth 446.

1525H$_1$ *One Thief Steals Egg from Bird's Nest.* Second steals it from first's breast.
*BP III 393 n. 1. — Greek 2; Spanish American: Hansen (1525A I**d) (Argentina) 1, (Dominican Republic) 1.

1525H$_2$ *The Stolen and Restolen Ham.* Two thieves steal a ham from a former companion who has married, have it stolen back, and resteal it. (Cf. K341.7.1, K362.4). [K306.1].

*Gering *Islendzk Aeventyri* (Halle, 1883) II 210ff.; *DeVries *Tijdschrift voor Nederlandsche Taal- en Letterkunde* XLV 213ff.

1525H₃ *Two Boys Steal Roast Pig from Grandparents* by asking grandmother in her sleep where it is hidden. Grandfather recovers pig. First boy dresses in grandmother's clothes and secures pig from grandfather.
Spanish-American: Hansen (1525**H) (Chile) *1*.

1525H₄ *The Youth in the Bee Hive*. Thieves stealing a large beehive take it away and make a fire under it. Flee when they hear an earlier thief screaming in the hive. [K335.1.6.3].
Lithuanian (*1887) *4;* Swiss: Jegerlehner 287 No. 60; French: Delarue *Arts et Traditions Populaires* XI (1953) 39, 50; German: Henssen *Ueberlieferung und Persönlichkeit* (Münster, 1951) 131 No. 54; Serbocroatian *3;* Greek (1528*) *1;* Chinese and Persian: Eberhard FFC CXX 354 No. 22.

1525J *Thieves Cheated of their Booty*. Trickster steals the goods. [K335.1].
Wesselski *Hodscha Nasreddin* II 211 No. 428, 215 No. 446; Missouri French: Carrière; Italian Novella: Rotunda (K335.1); India: Thompson-Balys.

1525J₁ (formerly 1525D [e]) »*Those Others Did it.*« Rascal hits ox he has killed and cries out. The thieves flee leaving their treasure. [K335.1.3]. Cf. Types 130, 1522, 1650, 1653, 1654**, 1875.
Serbocroatian *20;* India (K335.1.3).

1525J₂ *Thief Sent into Well by Trickster*. A weeping boy tells a passing thief that he has lost a silver cup in a well. The thief takes off his clothes and goes after the cup, intending to keep it. He finds nothing. When he comes up, his clothes have been stolen. [K345.2].
Hdwb. d. Märchens I 346a n. 126; BP III 392f.; Wienert FFC LVI 84 (ET 502), 106 (ST 183); Greek (1525 D*) *4;* India *1*.

1525K *Ubiquitous beggar*. In disguise obtains alms three times from the same person. [K1982].
Herbert *Catalogue of Romances* III 282; Spanish: Espinosa Jr. Nos. 210f. Cf. North American Indian: Thompson *Tales* 310 n. 117d.

1525L *Creditor Falsely Reported Insane when he Demands Money* [K242].
*Wesselski *Arlotto* II 225 No. 92, *Gonnella* 98 No. 2. — Lithuanian *9;* Spanish (*1848) *1*. — Literary: Italian Novella: Rotunda.

1525M *Mak and the Sheep*. Stolen sheep dressed as baby in cradle, so that thief may escape detection. [K406.2].
**Whiting *Speculum* VII 552; Feilberg *Ordbog* II 370a s.v. »lam», IV 228a s.v. »hundehvalp»; *Baugh MPh XV 729; *Smyser JAFL XLVII 378; *Stroup JAFL XLVII 380; *Southern Folklore Quarterly* III 5f.; Middle English: Second Shepherd's Play; Irish myth: Cross (K521.1.3.). — Spanish (1735*B) *1;* German (well known). — American Negro (Michigan): Dorson Nos. 24, 25.

1525N *The Two Thieves Trick Each Other.* Cf. 1525E, 1532.

I. *The Exchange of Spurious Articles.* (Example: one man has a pot of sand covered with ghi, the other a brass ring covered with gold. They exchange.) [J1516].

II. *The Jobs Exchanged.* One has to tend an unmanageable cow, the other to carry water in a leaky vessel, etc. At the end of the first day each tells the other how pleasant his job has been. They exchange jobs on the second day. [J2431.1, K1687].

III. *Wealth Exchanged.* They steal (find) wealth and each tries to trick the other out of his share. (a) The »wealth» turns out to be a box of stones, etc.

IV. *Carrying in Box.* One hides in a box and is carried by the other, who thinks he is carrying the money [K307.1].

India *13*.

1525P (formerly 1525G*) *The Theft of an Ox.* The tail of the larger ox in the mouth of the smaller, as if the latter has eaten up the greater. [K404.2]. Cf. Type 1004.

*BP III 292 n. 2. — Estonian *7*; Lithuanian *14*; Russian: Andrejev (1525G*) *1*.

1525Q *The Two Thieves Married to the Same Woman.* Two thieves are married to (are courting) the same woman. She promises to be the wife of the one who is the cleverest thief. Contest in thievery.

India *3*.

1525R (formerly 1525*) *The Robber Brothers.* The youngest plays various tricks on the others and gets more booty than they. [K308, L142.1].

Finnish-Swedish *2*; Swedish *10* (Uppsala *1*, misc. *9*); Norwegian (1654) *22*; Serbocroatian *1*; Greek *1*.

1525H* *The Theft of a Sheep.* The sheep sits at the helm of the boat dressed in a coat [K406.1].

*Anderson *Novelline* No. 11. — Finnish (1525H**) *1*; Russian: Andrejev *1*.

1525J* *Thief Leaves Food Untouched when Owner Pretends to be Poisoned by it.* (Playing poison.) [K439.5].

American Negro (Georgia): Harris *Friends* 54 No. 7, *Nights* 297 No. 50; Bahama: *Parsons MAFLS XIII 122; West Indies: Flowers 511.

1525K* *Umpire Awards his own Stolen Coat to Thief* [K419.3].

Lithuanian *14*; Russian: Afanasiev (*1525 I) *12*.

1525L* *Theft Committed While Tale is Told.* One party steals while the other relates the situation, in the form of a tale, to the gentleman who is being robbed. [K341.20].

Lithuanian (*1525 J) *6*; Serbocroatian *1*; Russian: Afanasiev (*1525 II) *7*; India (K341.20).

1525M* *Does he Need Suet?* A soldier, who is stealing suet, asks the owner, who is coming in on account of the noise, whether he needs some suet.

Russian: Afanasiev (1525*J) *2*.

1525N* *Theft of Butter by Confederate* while clothes are being measured [K365].

Russian: Afanasiev (*1525 III A, B *2*).

1525P* *Thief Pretends to Be Religious* and warns peasant to hide his money. Peasant tells him where money is hidden. Cf. Types 1341, 1577*.
Spanish (*1525G) *1*.

1525Q* *The Thief's Dance.* While singing and dancing in the farmer's house, the thief gives hints to his friend in the loft, how to steal the bacon. [K341.21].
Lithuanian (*1630) *3;* Russian (1525 II) *7*.

1525R* *To Detain Bearer.* Trickster sends letter ordering bearer detained and meanwhile steals bearer's wife [K1388]. Cf. Type 930.
Spanish (*1850) *1*.

1526 *The Old Beggar and the Robbers.* The robbers dress an old beggar up in fine clothes. They take him in front of the shopkeeper's house. Get many goods on the credit of the fine gentleman. Disappear with the goods and leave the old man behind. [K455.3]. Cf. Types 1531, 1920E.
**Ranke »Der Bettler als Pfand» *Philologie* LXXVI 149ff.; *BP III 394 (4). — Finnish *13;* Estonian *3;* Lithuanian *3;* French *4;* Flemish *1;* German *2* (Archive *1*, Henssen Volk No. 147); Hungarian *2*.

1526A *Supper Won by a Trick:* another person to pay [K455.1, K455.2, K455.4, K455.5]. Cf. Type 1920E.
*Chauvin VI 132 No. *285;* *Bédier *Fabliaux* 447; *Wesselski *Bebel* II 136 No. 111; *Pauli (ed. Bolte) No. 646. — Finnish *26;* Lithuanian (*1547) *3;* Spanish (1848) *1;* French *8;* Czech: Tille Soupis II (2) 447f. *3;* Serbocroatian *1;* Greek (1526*) *1*.

1526A* *Swindlers Dressed as Police.* Doing the search, they rob a rich master.
Russian: Andrejev (*1526 I) *1*.

1526B* *The Thief and the Parrot.* A soldier, formerly working as a man-servant for his master, breaks into his home, learns from the parrot where the money is and steals it. The parrot cannot recognize the thief among the soldiers.
Russian: Andrejev (*1526 II) *1*.

1527 *The Robbers are Betrayed.* The master and servant exchange places for a day. The servant in tar and feathers. Has his former master take him to the robbers' house. They flee in terror and leave their treasure behind. Cf. Types 1525H, 1650, 1653, 1654**. [K335.1, K335.1.8].
Finnish *12;* Livonian *1;* Irish *1;* Flemish *1;* German *1;* Hungarian *2;* Russian: Azadowski *Russkaya Skazka* Nos. 7, 25; Greek: Loukatos No. 25.

1527A (formerly 1528*) *Robber Induced to Waste his Ammunition,* then seized [K631.2, K724].
*BP III 455; Wesselski *Märchen* No. 36. — Lithuanian (*1525M) *2;* Flemish (1528**) *2;* Dutch (1528**) *1;* German (well known); Russian (1528*) *10;* Korean: Zs. f. Vksk. XXII 78. — U.S., Scotland: Baughman (K631.2); Spanish-American (U.S.): Rael No. 462.

1527* *The Three Wanderers Seek Night Lodgings.* Two go into the house; the third climbs on the roof and stops up the chimney with his coat. The room is filled with smoke; those who dwell in the house are frightened and grant free night lodgings. [K330].
Finnish; Finnish-Swedish *1;* Swedish *5* (Uppsala *3*, Stockholm *2*).

1528 *Holding Down the Hat.* A rascal stands by the side of a road near his hat

under which he has hidden dung. When the dupe arrives he offers to pursue the rascal with the dupe's horse if the latter will guard his hat under which is a beautiful bird. He escapes with the horse. [K1252]. Cf. Types 1540 (II a), 1731.
*Aarne FFC XXII 86, 96; *Parsons MAFLS XV (1) 54; Coffin *11*. — Lithuanian *12;* Swedish *55* (Stockholm *50,* Liungman *2,* misc. *3*); Scottish *1;* Irish *1;* French *2;* Dutch *1;* Flemish (1529**) *1;* Walloon (*1528A) *1;* German *1;* Slovenian *1;* Serbocroatian *1;* Czech: Tille Soupis I 404ff. *16;* Russian: Afanasiev *15;* Indonesian: DeVries No. 185B. — English-American: Baughman *2,* (1528*) *1;* Spanish-American: Rael No. 286 (U.S.), Hansen (Argentina) *1,* (Chile) *1,* (Dominican Republic) *2,* (Puerto Rico) *4;* Cape Verde Islands: Parsons MAFLS XV (1) 54; American Indian: Thompson *C Coll* II 420, 426. See also Estonian and Finnish under 1731.

1528* changed to Type 1527A.

1529 *Thief Claims to have been Transformed into a Horse.* While the owner sleeps, the peasant steals his horse. He hitches himself to the owner's wagon and says that he is a horse transformed to a man. [K403].
*BP III 9, 391 n. 3; Chauvin VII 137; *Wesselski *Hodscha Nasreddin* II 229 No. 487; *Basset *1001 Contes* I 492. — Estonian *2* (1529*); Lithuanian *11;* French *14;* Spanish: Boggs (1852*) *1;* Catalan: Amades No. 505; Dutch *2;* Flemish (1529*) *2;* German: Henssen Jül No. 479, Meckl. No. 113; Italian (Sicilian *1*); Czech: Tille Soupis I 251ff. *5;* Hungarian: Berze Nagy (1543*) *2;* Slovenian *2;* Serbocroatian *4;* Russian: Andrejev *Ukraine 8,* Afanasiev *1;* Turkish: Eberhard-Boratav No. 341 III. — Spanish-American: Hansen (*1852) (Chile) *1.* — Oceanic (Philippine): Fansler MAFLS XII 437.

1529A* *The Exchange of Horses.* Gentleman agrees to exchange good horse for the peasant's jade, provided the peasant will eat its excrements. Peasant finds no difficulty in the task, whereas the gentleman, put to the same condition when he wants to get back his horse, finds it impossible.
Lithuanian (*1533) *2;* Russian: Andrejev (*1529 I) *1.*

1529B* *Wolf-hunting Sheep.* A peasant sells a master a sheep which supposedly hunts the wolves. The wolves devour the sheep.
Russian: Andrejev (*1529 II) *1.*

1530 *Holding up the Rock.* The rascal puts his shoulder under a great rock and pretends to hold it up. He persuades a man to take his place and then runs away with the dupe's goods. [K125.1]. Cf. Types 9A, 1731.
*Parsons JAFL XXX 237, XXXI 229, MAFLS XV (1) 59; Coffin *25.* — Rumanian (1332*); Hungarian: Dégh No. 46; Turkish: Eberhard-Boratav No. 351 III, 352. — Spanish-American: Rael Nos. 373, 376 (U.S.), Hansen (Argentina) *1,* (Chile) *1,* (Dominican Republic) *1,* (Puerto Rico) *3* (**74U animals) *4;* American Indian (Mexican): Boas JAFL XXV 206, 237; Cape Verde Islands: Parsons JAFL XXX 235. — African *11.*

1530* *The Man and his Two Dogs.* The names of the dogs are »The Shepherd» and »Get the Stick.» When the man calls his dogs to dinner the thief thinks he is telling the shepherd to get a stick. [J2493]. Cf. Types 883C, 960.

Finnish *1;* Estonian *4;* Spanish (1940*D) *1,* Espinosa Cuentos II 253f.; Slovenian *2;* Russian: Andrejev; Greek *1,* (1660*) *1.* — Spanish-American: Hansen (1940*D) (Argentina) *1.*

1531 *The Man Thinks he has Been in Heaven.* The rich lord puts fine clothes on a drunken peasant and gives him good food and drink. [J2322]. Cf. Types 1313A*, 1526.

*Chauvin V 274 No. 155; Köhler-Bolte I 68, 580f.; Wesselski *Archiv Orientální* I (1929) 80f. — Estonian (1531*) *2;* Lithuanian *3;* Irish *3;* Dutch *1;* Walloon (*1531A); Hungarian: Berze Nagy (1614*) *1,* Honti (917) *2;* Serbocroatian *3;* Turkish: Kunos (1887—9) No. 39 = Kunos (1905) No. 25. — Literary Treatments: Shakespeare's Induction to »The Taming of the Shrew»; Italian Novella: Rotunda (J2322).

1531A *Man Shaved and with Hair Cut does not Recognize Self* [J2012.1]. Cf. Types 1382, 1383.

Spanish (*1683) *1;* Serbocroatian *5.*

1531B *Man Needs Patch on Pants to Recognize Himself.* Sees another with one exactly like his. [J2012.5].

Spanish (*1683B) *1.*

1532 *The Voice from the Grave.* Cf. Types 1380, 1476, 1676. (a) Two rascals hear of a wealthy man who has recently died. One digs a hole near the grave with a speaking tube leading out or hides near the grave. The other goes to the relatives of the dead man claiming that the dead man before his death had borrowed a large sum of money from him and demanding that the relatives come to the grave and ask the dead man about the debt. The confederate from his place of concealment answers that the debt must be paid. [K451.5, K1974]. (b) The rascal who receives the money escapes, leaving his confederate still buried in the ground.

India *11.*

1532* *Seasickness Cured.* The clever sailor boy sells a piece of coal as a remedy for seasickness. He calls the coal »Babylon stones». [K115.2].

Livonian *1.*

1533 *The Wise Carving of the Fowl.* A clever person divides it symbolically: head to head of house, neck to wife, wings to daughters, legs to sons; keeps rest for himself. (Cf. Type 875 II e.) [H601].

*BP II 360; *Taylor JAFL XXXI 555; *Köhler-Bolte I 428, 499, 582, II 645ff.; *Pauli (ed. Bolte) No. 58. — Livonian (1533*) *1;* Lithuanian (1580*) *4;* Swedish *2* (Uppsala *1,* misc. *1*); Catalan: Amades No. 370; German: Peuckert *Schlesische Märchen* No. 263; Hungarian: Berze Nagy (1542*) *1;* Russian: Afanasiev (*1580) *12;* Greek: Hallgarten *Rhodos* (1929) 222; Jewish: Neuman (H601); India *2.* — Oceanic (Philippine): Fansler MAFLS XII 63, 253, 351. — Literary Treatments: Italian

Novella: Rotunda (H601); Wesselski *Hodscha Nasreddin* No. 399, Wesselski *Märchen* No. 40; *Scala Celi* No. 205.

1533A *Hog's Head Divided According to Scripture.* To be divided among three students according to their skill in quoting. First: »And they cut one ear off» (takes ear). Second: »And they gave him a box on the ear» (takes other ear). Third: »And they took him away secretly» (takes whole hog away). [J1242.1]. (Variants: other foods.)
*BP II 361. — French *20;* Serbocroatian *3.*

1534 *Series of Clever Unjust Decisions*: plaintiff voluntarily withdraws. (1) Man pulls off borrowed horse's tail: he shall keep horse till tail grows on. (2) Man falls out of bed and kills a baby (or causes a miscarriage): he shall beget a new baby for the mother. (3) Man falls from a bridge and kills boatsman's son: shall allow boatsman to fall from bridge and kill him. [J1173].
*Wesselski *Hodscha Nasreddin* II 234 No. 515; *Köhler-Bolte II 578; Penzer VI 83f.; *Feilberg Danske Studier (1920) 2ff.; Spanish (1535*A) *1;* Dutch (891*A) *2;* Italian (Sicilian *947 *1*); Serbocroatian *12;* Russian: Andrejev (1660) *5;* Greek (1535A*) *3,* (927*) *2,* Kretschmer No. 10; Turkish: Eberhard-Boratav No. 296 *2;* India *13.* — Spanish-American: Hansen (1535*A) (Argentina) *2,* (Dominican Republic) *1.* — Literary Treatments: Italian Novella: Rotunda (J1173).

1534A *The Innocent Man Chosen to Fit the Stake (Noose).*
I. *The Holy Man and His Disciple.* A holy man and his disciple come to a city where the king and all his ministers are fools, and where all items of food sell for the same price [J342.1.1, X1503.3]. The holy man leaves at once, but the disciple stays despite the warnings of the holy man [N347.7].
II. *The Crime.* (a) The Collapsed Wall. A burglar tries to break into a house but is killed when the wall collapses. The householder is called before the king and sentenced to death. The householder, however, blames the mason who built the wall who, in turn, blames the man who supplied the mortar, etc., until finally one man is found who is too stupid to offer an alibi. He is condemned to death [J2233]. See 2031A*. (b) A man is condemned to death for some other reason.
III. *The Man Chosen to Fit the Stake (Noose).* (a) It is found that the condemned man is too thin to fit the stake (noose). The disciple is chosen to be impaled (hanged) in his place. [J2233.1.1, N178.2]. (b) The holy man reappears and announces that he has discovered that the next man to be executed will go directly to heaven [K841.1, J1189.3]. The king leaps upon the stake himself [K842.4, K843].
India *21.*

1534* changed to 921A.

1534A* *Barber Substituted for Smith at Execution.* Village has too many barbers and too few smiths. [J2233.1].
Hungarian: Berze Nagy (1347*) *3.*

1534B* *Maimed Cattle to Recover.* A poor man maims the rich man's cattle. The judge decides that they shall belong to the poor man until they get well.
Hungarian (926*) *1;* Serbocroatian *3.*

1534C* *Judge Persuaded by Highflown Speech* which he does not understand. Unjust decision.
Catalan: Amades No. 416.

1534D* *Sham Dumb Man Wins Suit.* The trickster meets a man in a narrow place in the road and calls out to him to make room. The man refuses and the trickster turns over the cart. In court the trickster plays dumb. The plaintiff says, »He is not dumb; he called to me several times to get out of the way.« Damages are assessed against the *plaintiff* for negligence. [K1656].
*Wesselski *Hodscha Nasreddin* II 210 No. 425. — Spanish (*1587) *1.*

1535 *The Rich and the Poor Peasant.* (Unibos.) The rich peasant kills the poor one's horse. The clairvoyant horse-skin and the adulterous priest. The rich peasant kills his horse and his wife. Diving for sheep.

I. *The Watcher Penalized.* Money is exacted from a watcher who permits the theft of (a) a chest falsely said to be full of money [K443.3.1] or (b) a wooden cow supposed to be a real cow [K443.4].

II. *False Money.* Lime (or ashes) said to be gold is sold or exchanged. [K121].

III. *Magic Cow-hide.* (a) The pseudo-magic cow-hide [K114] (horse-hide, bird-skin) is sold to the adulteress or her husband [K1571.1], or (b) it is exchanged for the chest in which the paramour is hidden [K1574]. Cf. Type 1358B. (c) The paramour pays to be freed [K443.1]. Cf. Type 1358A. (d) Money is otherwise found.

IV. *Fatal Imitation.* (a) When the trickster reports the price his cow-hide has brought him, his enemy kills all his cows to sell their hides [K941.1] or burns his house to get high price for ashes [K941.2]. (b) The trickster by means of a flute (fiddle, knife, staff) resuscitates an apparently dead woman: his enemy buys the object and tries it disastrously [K913].

V. *Fatal Deception.* (a) The trickster escapes from a sack (chest) through exchange with a shepherd [K842]; see Type 1737. (b) His enemy wants to get sheep in the same manner and dives to the bottom of the sea for the sheep; cf. Type 1525.

Note. Tales containing only part Va are listed under Type 1737, which is identical.

**Josef Müller *Das Märchen vom Unibos* (Jena 1934); *Anderson *Hessische Blätter f. Vksk.* XXXIV 156; *Anderson in Tauscher *Volksmärchen* 172; De Meyer *Vlaamsche Sprookjethemas* pp. 133ff.; *BP II 1ff., III 188, 192, 393; *Parsons MAFLS XV (1) 51; Köhler-Bolte I 91, 190. — Finnish *172,* Finnish:Swedish *27;* Estonian *57;* Livonian *9;* Lithuanian *106,* (*1535A) *4;* Lappish *7* (see also Type 1737); Swedish *53* (Uppsala *14,* Stockholm *4,* Göteborg *2,* Lund *7,* Liungman *3,* misc. *23);* Norwegian *27,* Solheim *1;* Danish: Grundtvig Nos. 99, 112; Icelandic *9;* Scottish *3;* Irish *401,* Beal IV 228f. No. 4, VIII 3f. No. 7, XVIII 95ff., 101ff., XIV 256ff.; French *92;* Spanish *9,* Espinosa Jr. No. 26; Catalan: Amades Nos. 356, 364, cf. Nos. 408, 410; Dutch *11;* Flemish *13,* Witteryck p. 278 *16;* German *89* (Archive *83,* Merk. 178, Plenzat *3,* Henssen Jül. No. 459, Henssen Volk No. 205); Italian *3* (Tuscan 1539 b, cf. 1360C *2,* Sicilian *1535 *1*); Rumanian (1380 VIII*) *4;* Hungarian *12;* Czech: Tille Soupis II (2) 144—154 *15;* Slovenian *18;* Serbocroatian *25;* Russian: Azadowsky *Russkaya Skazka* No. 16, Andrejev (1535A) *Ukraine 11*, Afanasiev (1535A) *21*, (1535*B) *24;* Greek *2,* Loukatos No. 57; Turkish: Eberhard-Boratav Nos. 273, 274, 275, 276, 351 III *40;* Indonesian: Coster-Wijsman 26 No. 5; India *49;* Japanese. — English-American: Baughman *7;* Spanish-American: Rael Nos. 279, (302), 304—307, 355 (U.S.), Hansen (Argentina) *2;* (Chile) *2,* (Dominican Republic) *12,* (Puerto Rico) *22;* Portuguese-American (Brazil): Camara Cascudo p. 243; West Indies (Negro) *20;* American Indian: Thompson *C Coll* II 419ff., (Micmac): Parsons JAFL XXXVIII 125 No. 43. — African *2.*

1536 *Disposing of the Corpse* [K2151].

1536A *The Woman in the Chest.* The servant boy has determined to steal. A woman lies down in a chest to spy on him. The boy kills her. He makes the preacher (rich man) believe that she has died, and at the latter's request he undertakes to bury her. Puts the corpse in the corn loft, in the stall, in the trunk of the traveling merchant, on a horse. All believe that she has returned from the dead. [K2321, K2151]. Cf. Type 1537.

*Taylor *MPh* XV (1917) 225 n. 1; Parsons MAFLS XV (1) 73, 360; Köhler-Bolte I 190; *Archiv f. slav. Phil.* XVII 581, XIX 267; Coffin *2;* Espinosa *Cuentos* III 166—180. — Finnish *130;* Finnish-Swedish *1* (1537**); Estonian *32;* Lithuanian *31;* Lappish *1;* Swedish *13* (Uppsala *2,* Göteborg *1,* Lund *2,* misc. *8*); Norwegian *9;* Danish: Grundtvig No. 110B; Icelandic *3;* Scottish *1;* Irish *245,* Beal II 363f. No. 2, III 257f. No. 1, IV 228f. No. 5, XX 3f., No. 6; French *10;* Spanish *1;* Catalan: Amades No. 368; Flemish *2;* German *10* (Archive *9,* Meckl. No. 115); Hungarian *1;* Czech: Tille Soupis II (1) 437ff. *5;* Slovenian; Serbocroatian *2,* Istrian No. 60; Russian: Andrejev (1536) *2,* Andrejev *Ukraine 11;* India (K2152); Korean: Zong in-Sob 197 No. 96. — Spanish-American: Rael Nos. 308—311 (U.S.), Hansen (Argentina) *1,* (Puerto Rico) *1;* West Indies (Negro) *1.* — Literary Treatments: Clouston *Tales* II 242.

1536B *The Three Hunchback Brothers Drowned.* The three hunchback brothers are killed. A drunken man is employed by the woman who has accidentally slain them to throw one into the river. He does so. Then she puts another one out and finally the third [K2322]. The man thinks they keep coming to life. Finally he sees the hunchback husband and drowns him.

**Pillet *Das Fabliau von les trois bossus menestrels* (1901); *BP III 485 (Grimm No. 212); Bédier *Fabliaux* 236; Taylor *MPh* XV (1917) 223 n.

3; Coffin *6;* *Espinosa II Nos. 31f. — Finnish-Swedish (1537*) *5;* Livonian (1601') *1;* Lithuanian *12;* Swedish *10* (Uppsala *1,* misc. *9);* Icelandic *1;* Irish: Beal III 355; Spanish *3;* Catalan: Amades No. 431; Dutch *1;* Flemish (1537*) *2;* Walloon *1;* Italian *3* (Tuscan *2*,Sicilian*1*); Hungarian: Berze Nagy (1726A*) *4;* Czech: Tille Soupis II (1) 440ff. *4;* Serbocroatian *5;* Slovenian; Russian: Andrejev (*1730 I) *1;* Turkish: Eberhard-Boratav No. 264 *6;* Arab: Littmann 373ff.; India *2;* Chinese: Eberhard FFC CXX 337 No. 12, FFC CXXVIII 276 No. 175. — Franco-American (French Canadian): Barbeau JAFL XXXII 161 No. 88; Spanish-American: Rael No. 488 (U.S.), Hansen (Chile) *1,* (Puerto Rico) *4,* (1536*D) (Puerto Rico) *1;* West Indies (Negro) *4.* — Literary Treatments: Chauvin VIII 72; Italian Novella: Rotunda (K2322).

1536C *The Murdered Lover.* His corpse carried about. A combination of Types 1380 and 1537.
*Taylor MPh XV (1917) 226 n. 1. — Lithuanian *1;* Greek *3;* India *3.* — West Indies (Negro) *1.*

1536* *Fool Accuses Doctor of Killing Priest* and demands money to keep quiet. Fool kills another man and hides. He accuses policeman, who gives him money.
Spanish-American: Hansen (**1534) (Puerto Rico) *1.*

1537 *The Corpse Killed Five Times.* The corpse on the horse, in the sleigh, in the boat [K2151, K2152]. Cf. Type 1536A.
Suchier *Der Schwank von der viermal getöteten Leiche* (Halle a. S., 1922); *BP II 10 (G²); Taylor *MPh* XV (1917) 221—226; Köhler-Bolte I 65; Espinosa III Nos. 176, 189; Coffin *12;* *Espinosa JAFL XLIX 181—193. — Finnish *45;* Finnish-Swedish *8;* Estonian *6;* Lappish *1;* Swedish *6* (Uppsala *2,* Göteborg *1,* misc. *3);* Norwegian *2,* Solheim *1;* Danish: MS DFS; Icelandic *3;* French *12;* Spanish *2,* (1537*A) *1,* (1537*B) *1;* Dutch *4;* Flemish: Köhler-Bolte I 65, Witteryck p. 278 *8;* Walloon (*1537C) *1;* German *8* (Archive *7,* Henssen Volk No. 263); Italian (Sicilian *2*); Rumanian *3;* Hungarian: Dégh No. 44 *5;* Slovenian *3;* Serbocroatian *5;* Russian: Afanasiev *21;* Greek *1;* Turkish: Eberhard-Boratav No. 351 III, 359 III, 368; India (1537 + 1537A) *19;* Indonesian: DeVries No. 278. — Franco-American: Baughman *1;* English-American: Baughman *4;* Spanish-American: Rael Nos. 273, (277), 279, 280 (U.S.), Hansen (1537C—**J) (Cuba) *3,* (Dominican Republic) *7,* (Puerto Rico) *2;* Cape Verde Islands: Parsons MAFLS XV (1) 73 n. 3; West Indies (Negro) *3;* American Indian: Thompson *C Coll* II 420ff. (F). — Literary Treatments: Montaiglon-Raynaud V 115, 215, VI 117; Pauli (ed. Bolte) No. 598; Bédier *Fabliaux* 469; Italian Novella: Rotunda (K2151).

1537* *Corpse's Legs Left.* A soldier cuts off the legs of a corpse. Later he gets night-lodgings in a rich farmer's house, which he leaves secretly at night. The soldier's confederate accuses the farmer of murder and blackmails him. [K2152.2].
Lithuanian (*1537A) *2;* Russian: Afanasiev (*1537 I) *5.*

1538 *The Youth Cheated in Selling Oxen.* Avenges himself. As carpenter and as doctor in the purchaser's house he punishes the latter [K1825.1.3]. Brings it about that the miller is hanged in his place [K841].

*BP III 394 (5); Espinosa III 207—212; Coffin *1*. — Finnish *19;* Finnish-Swedish *1;* Estonian *3;* Lithuanian *15;* Norwegian *7*, Solheim *1;* French *14;* Spanish *2;* Catalan: Amades Nos. 423, 2089; Italian *7* (Tuscan [1771], [1772], cf. [1619] *3*, Sicilian *4*, Gonzenbach No. 82); Hungarian *2;* Serbocroatian *2;* Russian: Afanasiev *5;* Greek *1;* Turkish: Eberhard-Boratav No. 360 III. — English-American: Baughman *1;* Spanish-American: Rael Nos. 356, 357 (U.S.), Hansen (Chile) *2*, (Dominican Republic) *1*, (Puerto Rico) *4*.

1538* *The Jester-bride.* A jester dresses himself in his sister's clothes and lives with a priest as a worker. Young men court the supposed girl. On the wedding night he ties a goat in his place and then demands indemnities for his ruined sister supposedly changed into a goat.
Russian: Afanasiev (*1538 I) *12*.

1539 *Cleverness and Gullibility.* The youth sells pseudo-magic objects and animals. The wolf is sold as a goat [K132]. The rabbit as letter carrier [K131.1]; the hat that »pays everything» [K111.2]; the wand that revives the dead [K113.4]. The teaching of languages or the self-cooking pot [K112.1]. The gold-dropping horse [K111.1]. The youth has himself buried alive and stabs his enemy from out of the ground with a knife [K911.1]. (Sometimes: substitute in sack to go to heaven, or to marry the princess. See Types 1737 and 1535 V.)

*BP II 10 (Grimm No. 61); Delarue in Perbosc 284f.; Wesselski *Hodscha Nasreddin* II 198 No. 391 (for the last incident). — Finnish *253;* Finnish-Swedish *17*, (1539*) *4;* Estonian *32;* Livonian *1;* Lithuanian *60;* Lappish *2;* Swedish *18* (Uppsala *2*, Lund *1*, Liungman *5*, misc. *10*); Norwegian *9*, Solheim *1;* Danish: Grundtvig No. 108; Scottish *2;* Irish *154;* English *1*, (1539A) *1*, (1539B) *2;* Catalan: Amades Nos. 364, 407; Dutch *8;* Flemish *7*, (1591*) *1*, (1592*) *1;* German *29* (Archive 26, Henssen Jül. No. 458, Henssen Volk No. 204, Merk. 181); Italian *17* (Tuscan 1539 a, c—i; cf. [1618] *8*, Sicilian *9*, Gonzenbach Nos. 70, 71); Rumanian *8;* Hungarian *6;* Czech: Tille Soupis II (2) 154ff. *7;* Slovenian *5;* Serbocroatian *13;* Russian: Andrejev *Ukraine 24*, Afanasiev *41;* Greek *29*, Hahn No. 42; Turkish: Eberhard-Boratav Nos. 176 IV, 351 *35;* India *32;* Indonesian: DeVries No. 279; Chinese:Eberhard FFC CXX 245 No. 191, CXXVIII 209ff. No. 121. — English-American: Baughman *1;* Spanish-American: Rael Nos. 293, 360 (U.S.), Hansen (Argentina) *6*, (Chile) *4*, (Cuba) *1*, (Puerto Rico) *16;* West Indies (Negro) *5;* American Indian: Thompson *C Coll* II 419ff. (A), 413 (B). — African *2*.

1539* *The Soldier, the Peasant, and the Statue.*
Finnish-Swedish *1*.

1539** *Truth-telling Member.* Returning husband makes wife believe her vagina has told him of priest's presence [D1610.6.1, H451]. Cf. Type 1391.
French-Canadian.

1540 *The Student from Paradise (Paris).* The woman sends money or clothes to paradise for her deceased husband. The horse is stolen.

I. *Goods Sent to Paradise.* A student tells a woman that he comes from Paris. She understands him to say paradise and gives him money and goods to take to her husband [J2326].

II. *The Stolen Horse.* When the woman's son (second husband) tries to overtake the student and recover the goods, the student tells him, (a) that the thief has escaped through the woods: the man leaves his horse, and the student rides it away [K346.1]; or (b) that the thief has gone to heaven by way of a tree: while the man lies on his back to look, the student steals the horse [K341.9].

**Aarne *Der Mann aus dem Paradiese* (FFC XXII 3—109); *BP II 440; *Wesselski *Märchen* 305; *Krohn FFC XCVI 155; *Clouston *Noodles* 204—217 passim; *Pauli (ed. Bolte) No. 463; *Christensen DF L 35. — Finnish *139;* Finnish-Swedish *6;* Estonian *32;* Livonian *3;* Lithuanian *30;* Swedish *170* (Uppsala *149,* Stockholm *2,* Lund *1,* Liungman *5,* misc. *16*); Norwegian (1384) *2;* Danish: Grundtvig No. 107; Icelandic *1;* Irish *163,* Beal III 240f. No. 2, IV suppl. 1ff.; English *1;* French *14;* Dutch *6;* German *25;* Rumanian *2,* Hungarian *3;* Czech: Tille Soupis I 404ff.; Slovenian *6;* Serbocroatian *11;* Russian: Andrejev *Ukraine 16,* Afanasiev *16;* Greek *8,* Loukatos No. 24; Turkish: Eberhard-Boratav No. 331 III, V, 339 *6;* Palestine: Schmidt-Kahle No. 97; India (J2326, K346.1); Indonesian: DeVries No. 284; Coster-Wijsman 73 No. IV, Jackson FL XLVII 291. — Spanish-American: Hansen (Argentina) *1,* (Chile) *1;* West Indies (Negro) *2.* — Literary Treatments: Wesselski *Bebel* No. 50; Wesselski *Hodscha Nasreddin* I 275 No. 305.

1540* *The Clever Youth Cheats the King* (parson).
Lappish *6.*

1540A* *Lady Sends Pig as Wedding Hostess.* A peasant, doffing his cap, bows to the pig and invites it to be his wedding hostess. The foolish lady gives the peasant not only the pig, but also a carriage to take the »hostess» to the wedding. Her husband goes in pursuit of the rogue, and is himself deceived by the latter.
Lithuanian (*1384A) *9;* Russian: Andrejev (*1541 I) *11.*

1541 *For the Long Winter.* The numskull has been told to keep the sausage »for the long winter». When the trickster hears this, he claims to be Long Winter and receives the sausage. [K362.1, cf. also J2355, K1821.1].

*BP I 521, 526; *Christensen DF L 46; *Parsons MAFLS XV (1) 194 n. 3; *Köhler-Bolte I 341f.; Coffin *5;* *Zs. f. Vksk. XV 71. — Finnish *52;* Finnish-Swedish *3;* Estonian *6;* Lithuanian *18;* Lappish *1;* Swedish *25* (Uppsala *11,* Stockholm *2,* Göteborg *1,* Lund *8,* Liungman *1,* misc. *2*); Norwegian *4;* Danish: Grundtvig No. 107; Icelandic *2;* Scottish *2;* Irish *131,* Beal XV 237f. No. 3, VII 197f. No. 2, VIII 87, XIII 272ff., Jackson FL XLVII 292; French *14;* Spanish *1;* Dutch *6;* Flemish *8;* Walloon *1,* (*1541A) *1;* German *20* (Archive *19,* Meckl. No. 107); Austrian: Haiding No. 40; Italian (Sicilian *2,* *1541 *2*); Hungarian *1;* Czech: Tille Soupis I 404—412; Slovenian *9;* Russian: Afanasiev *8;* Turkish:

Eberhard-Boratav Nos. 332 III, 333 III; India 9. — English-American: Baughman 2; West Indies (Negro) 5; American Indian: Thompson *C Coll* II 417f. (A). — Literary Treatments: Sercambi *Novelle* No. 63.

1541* changed to Type 1545.

1541** *The Student Betrays the Shoemaker.* Gets his shoes without paying for them.
Finnish-Swedish *1*.

1541*** »*Today for Money, Tomorrow for Money*».
Finnish-Swedish *1*.

1541**** changed to Type 1546.

1542 *The Clever Boy.* Peik with his fooling-sticks.

I. *Deceptions as a Trade.* Brother and sister live together but are poor and Peik goes out to make a living by fooling people [K301]. See Type 1525A.

II. *Animal Bargains.* (a) He gets the king's horse by borrowing it to ride home for his fooling-sticks; see Type 1525B [K341.8.1]; (b) he sells the king a wolf to guard the fowls [K133.1] and a bear to guard the cows [K133.2]. Cf. Type 1539.

III. *Pseudo-Magic Objects.* The king is fooled into buying a self-cooking kettle and the staff it hangs on. Cf. Type 1539. [K112.1].

IV. *Sham Murder.* The boy feigns killing and resuscitating his sister with a magic pipe [K113]; the king tries it with fatal results [J2401]. Cf. Type 1535 IV b.

V. *Companion to the Princess.* Peik in his sister's clothing is taken to the palace as companion to the princess. A prince comes as a suitor to Peik, who escapes. The princess is with child. [K1321.1].

VI. *Substitute Receives Punishment.* (a) Peik is caught, put in a cask, and exchanges place with a shepherd [K842]; cf. Types 1535 V a, 1737; (b) Peik is to be hanged but changes with a miller [K841]; cf. Type 1538. (c) The king forgives Peik and takes him as son-in-law [L161]. — Adapted from Christiansen *Norske Eventyr*.

Swedish *13* (Uppsala *1*, Lund *2*, Liungman *1*, misc. *9*); Norwegian (1542**) *15*, Solheim *1;* Icelandic *3;* Irish *127;* Walloon *1;* German *1;* Serbocroatian *3;* Russian: Andrejev; Turkish: Eberhard-Boratav No. 364 *2;* American Indian: Thompson *C Coll* II 419ff.

1542A *Return for Tools.* Trickster pretends to ride home for tools to perform his tricks; steals horse. (1542 IIa alone.) [K341.8.1].
Estonian (1525*) *6;* Lithuanian (*1532); Rumanian (1332*).

1542* *Sailor Substitute.* The sailor takes the lover's place with a girl.
Finnish-Swedish *1*.

1542** (formerly 1542*) *The Maiden's Honor.* The mother tells the girl to guard her honor. The tailor promises to sew up her »Honor». [K1363].
Finnish *4;* Estonian (1542*) *1;* Flemish *6;* Livonian *1;* Russian: Andrejev. Cf. Rotunda Novella [K1363.1].

1542B* *Trouble-maker in Night-lodgings.* Comes riding a wolf and asks for hospitality.

Wolf kills sheep; beehive in bed; bees sting family and cause father to kill son. [K2138].
Lithuanian (*1878) 7.

1543 (formerly 1543*) *Not One Penny Less.* Eavesdropping sexton duped into giving suppliant money. The trickster prays to the Virgin for a certain sum of money and not one penny less and promises repayment of double at the end of the month. The sexton throws the money to him, but never receives it back. [J1473.1, K464].

*Wesselski *Hodscha Nasreddin* I 220ff. No. 54; BP I 67. — Flemish (1543*) *3;* Hungarian (1728*) *2;* Czech: Tille Soupis II (2) 422f. *3;* Russian: Andrejev (*1609); Greek (1587*) *1.* — Spanish-American: Hansen (**1618) (Puerto Rico) *1.*

1543* *The Man Without a Member:* foolish wife gives her husband money to buy himself one. [J1919.8].
Finnish *3;* Estonian *6;* Livonian *1;* Flemish *3;* Lithuanian (*2911) *4;* Czech: Tille Soupis II (2) 422f.

1543A* *A Combing-machine.* A worker buys a combing-machine for a girl. She becomes pregnant. They drive the worker away, but the girl still wants his combing-machine.
Russian: Andrejev (1543*) *1.*

1543B* *No Invitation Needed.* The rascal acts as if he did not understand hints of the peasant and eats the dinner without invitation. Cf. Type 1544.
Russian: Andrejev (1570B*) *2.*

1543C* *The Clever Doctor.* The patient: »I have a bad memory, no sense of smell, and never tell the truth to anyone». The doctor cures him by putting dung into his mouth.
Lithuanian (*1543) *2.*

1543D* *Stone as Witness.* A farmer will not pay his servant the wages due. Closing his bargain with the servant he had said: »May this stone be witness.» Judge orders the stone brought to court. The farmer: »Oh, but the stone is too big (or very far away)».
Lithuanian (*1549) *4.*

1544 *The Man who Got a Night's Lodging.* The rascal feigns deafness and eats the best food. He accepts the hospitality before it is offered [K1981.1]. He takes the man's horse out of the stable and puts his own in. He is to pay for his lodging with a goat skin; he takes one of the man's own goats [K258]. At table they put poor food before him but he continues to get the best. At night he manages to sleep with the wife or daughter. When the woman puts out food for her husband in the night he gets it himself. He makes the women believe that the man knows all about them and they confess [K1572]. The man becomes angry and is going to kill the rascal's horse; he kills his own instead [K942].

Aarne FFC XX 79 (No. 24). — Finnish (1570) *2;* Estonian (1570*) *3;* Swedish *2* (Göteborg *1,* misc. *1*); Norwegian (1544**) *9;* Scottish *8;* Irish *157,* Beal XV 237f. No. 2, XVII 75; Spanish *1;* Serbocroatian *3;* Russian: Andrejev (1570*A); Turkish: Eberhard-Boratav No. 356 *6;* India *3.* — West Indies (Negro) *1.*

1544* changed to Type 1545B.

1544A* *A Soldier's Riddle.* After having asked to stay over the night with an old woman, a soldier notices a roasted cock in the oven and places it in his bag. Punning conversation with old woman.
Finnish *7;* Russian: Afanasiev (*1545) *6.*

1545 (formerly 1541*, 1732*) *The Boy with Many Names.* By use of many fanciful names he cheats and seduces. [K602].
Liungman SSF III 370, 450, (1541). — Finnish *6;* Finnish-Swedish *3;* Estonian (1732*) *5;* Swedish *9;* Norwegian (1732) *6;* Irish *6;* Spanish (1940*B) *2;* Flemish *2,* cf. 1541*; Hungarian: Berze Nagy (1566*) *1;* Czech: Tille Soupis II (2) 121ff. *4;* Serbocroatian *1;* Russian (*1701) *1.* — Franco-American (Canadian) *5;* Spanish-American: Hansen (1940**B) (Chile) *1.*

1545A *Learning to Sleep in Bed.* A man gets lodging in a beautiful woman's house. He pretends not to know how to sleep in bed; she must go with him.
Greek (1544**) *1,* Hahn No. 44, Kretschmer No. 65; Turkish: Eberhard-Boratav No. 199 *7;* Arab: Campbell *Tales from the Arab Tribes* (1949) p. 43.

1545B (formerly 1544*) *The Boy who Knew Nothing of Women.* Cautious farmer seeks laborer who knows nothing about sex. Trickster makes silly explanation of copulation of animals. When admitted into service, seduces both farmer's wife and daughter. [K1327].
Finnish *1;* Estonian *5;* Lithuanian (*2907) *5;* Swedish *5* (Stockholm *2,* misc. *3*); Flemish *2;* Czech: Tille Soupis II (2) 395f. *1;* Russian: Andrejev (1544A*) *1,* (cf. 1544B*) *1.* — Spanish American: Hansen (**1564) (Dominican Republic) *1.*

1545* *Keeping Warm in Bed.* The girl has learned from the youth. Offers to get her chilled father warm.
Livonian *1.*

1545A* *It's a Man.* A man enters a girl's room disguised as a woman. She cries out in alarm. »It's a man!» Her blind father thinks that someone is announcing the birth of a male child.
Italian (Sicilian *1545 *2*).

1546 (formerly 1541****) *The Lump of Gold.* A man asks a goldsmith what he would pay for a lump of gold of a certain size. In the belief that the man has found such a lump of gold the goldsmith pays him a large sum. [K261, K461.2.1].
*Wesselski *Bebel* I 230 No. 141. — Finnish-Swedish *3;* French *7;* Flemish *1.* — French-Canadian *1;* Spanish-American: Hansen (1540**D, Argentina) *1,* (1550**F, Cuba, Puerto Rico) *2,*(1550**G, Cuba) *1,* Rael Nos. 447, 448 (U.S.).

1546* (Obscene.)
Livonian *1.*

1547* *The Trickster with Painted Member.* The father wants his daughter's child to be a bishop. [K1398].
Livonian *1;* Lithuanian (*2914).

1548 *The Soup-stone* needs only the addition of a few vegetables and a bit of meat [K112.2].
   *Prato RTP IV 168. — Lithuanian *2;* Swedish *10* (Uppsala *4,* Stockholm *1,* misc. *5*); Norwegian: Solheim *1;* French *2;* Slovenian *2;* Serbocroatian *1;* Russian: Afanasiev *8.* — English-American: Baughman *4.*

1548* *The Gift of the Fool.* Of three brothers the shoemaker makes shoes for the queen and the princess; the tailor, clothes; the fool — children. [J1272].
   Livonian *1;* Lithuanian (*654A) *2.*

1549* (Obscene.)
   Livonian *1.*

1550* *The Soldier and the Merchant.* A soldier furnished with a room at the merchant's house is abused and ridiculed. The soldier informs the tsar, and then marries the merchant's daughter.
   Russian: Andrejev (1550) *1.*

1551 *The Wager that Sheep are Hogs.* A trickster wagers with a sheep driver that the sheep he is driving are hogs. The next man to overtake them will act as umpire. The trickster's confederate now arrives and declares that they are hogs. [K451.2].
   *Clouston *Tales* II 27; *Pauli (ed. Bolte) No. 632; **Camara Cascudo »Tradicion de un Cuento Brasileno» (Separata de *Archivos Venezolanos de Folklore* I (1952) No. 2; *Penzer V 104; *Wesselski *Hodscha Nasreddin* II 213 No. 437. — Catalan: Amades No. 423; Dutch *1;* German *2* (Archive *1,* Henssen Jül. No. 458); Italian (Tuscan [1771] *1*); Serbocroatian *1;* India *4.* — Franco-American (Missouri French): Carrière; English-American: Baughman *1;* Spanish-American: Rael No. 360 (U.S.); Portuguese-American (Brazil): Camara Cascudo p. 25. — Literary Treatments: Chauvin II 96 No. 51, VII 150 No. 430; Oesterley *Gesta Romanorum* No. 132; Crane *Vitry* 141 No. 20; Hazlitt *Shakespeare Jestbooks* II 176; Bødker *Exempler* 295 No. 56.

1551* *How Much the Ass Cost.* As the fool brings the new ass home everyone wants to know how much it cost. He has all publicly assemble and announces just what it cost. [J1601].
   Spanish (1550C*) *1,* Espinosa No. 54. — Spanish-American: Hansen (Puerto Rico) *1.*

1552* *The Hare at Third Remove.* A man receives a present of a hare. Later a crowd comes to him for entertainment saying that they are friends of the man who presented the hare. This happens a second time. He serves them clear water. »It is the soup from the soup of the hare.» [J1551.6].
   Wesselski *Hodscha Nasreddin* I 234 No. 97; Walloon (1781*) *1.*

1553 *An Ox for Five Pennies.* A woman who has been left the ox on condition that she give the proceeds to the poor offers it for five pennies, but it must be bought along with a cock at twelve florins. She gives the five pennies to the poor and keeps the twelve florins. [K182].
   *Pauli (ed. Bolte) No. 462; *Wesselski *Hodscha Nasreddin* II 188 No. 370. — Lithuanian (*2449) *1;* French *8;* German: Merkens II 163 No. 196; Slovenian; India (Thompson-Balys K182.1) *1;* Arabic: RTP XVI 158.

1553A* *The Sailor's Promise.* A sailor makes elaborate promises to the saints while in danger; will say no more about them when at home. [K231.²¹]
Walloon *1*.

1553B* *Pleasing the Captain.* Ship's captain agrees to let Galician ride free if he can sing a song which pleases the captain. He sings that he should pay captain. This pleases captain and Galician rides free.
Spanish (*1546) *1*.

1553C* *The Chapter.* A man, desiring a benefice from the church, finds each monk charming in private but cannot stand them as a group. He invites them to a meal of fine foods revoltingly mixed in one dish. [Cf. J81].
Walloon (1554*) *1*.

1555 *Milk in the Cask.* Order to put a small vessel of milk into huge container. Of a small shrewd group each by himself pours water thinking this will not be detected if the others pour milk. [K231.6.1.1]. (Sometimes told of wine.)

Catalan: Amades No. 320; Walloon (*1557) *1*; India *1*; cf. Pauli (ed. Bolte) No. 644.

1555A *Paying for Bread with Beer.* A man orders a bottle of beer, then returns it and takes a loaf of bread instead. He refuses to pay for the bread because he has returned the beer undrunk. He refuses to pay for the beer because he has not drunk it. [K233.4].

U.S.: Baughman (K233.4); French Canadian; Walloon (*1385A) *1*.

1555B *The Rum and Wäter Trade.* A trickster fills his gallon jug half full of water, then has it filled with rum at liquor shop. When the seller refuses credit, he pours back half of the liquid — now half rum and half water. (Sometimes the trickster repeats the operation, getting richer mixture with each transaction.) [K231.6.2.2].

U.S.: Baughman (K231.6.2.2); Serbocroatian *7*.

1556 *The Double Pension (Burial Money).* A husband and wife are jointly under a pension from the king. She reports her husband dead and gets the whole pension. He likewise reports her dead and gets the whole money. [K441.1]. (Sometimes concerned with money for the burial.) [K482.1].

*Chauvin V 274 No. 155 n. 1. — Scotland *4*; Hungarian: Berze Nagy (1614*) *1*; India *1*; Philippine: Fansler MAFLS XII 154. — African (Somali): Reinisch *Somali-Sprache* No. 48.

1557 *Box on the Ear Returned.* At table each gives his neighbor a box on the ears. The soldier is to give it to the king, but he returns it to the courtier from whom he has received it. [K2376].

Anderson FFC XLII 360; Hdwb. d. Märchens II 234. — Finnish; Lithuanian: Balys (*924B) *5*; Swedish (GS 1543) *35* (Uppsala *2*, Stockholm *29*, misc. *3*); Catalan: Amades No. 1385; Wend: Schulenberg *Wendische Volkstum* 8; Russian: Andrejev (1637*) *1*.

1558 *Welcome to the Clothes.* A man at a banquet is neglected because of his poor clothes. He changes clothes, returns, and is honored. »Feed my clothes,» he says, »for it is they that are welcomed.» [J1561.3].

*Pauli (ed. Bolte) No. 416; Wesselski *Hodscha Nasreddin* I 222 No. 55; *Prato RTP IV 167. — Italian (Sicilian *1564 *2*, Gonzenbach No. 37); Hungarian: Berze Nagy (1349 XXXII*) *1;* India *5.* — Literary Treatments: Rotunda Novella (J1561.3).

1559A* *Deceptive Wager: Human or Animal Hunger.* Wager: whose hunger is it more difficult to appease — that of man or that of beast? When nuts are strewn before master's well-fed guests, they snatch and eat them. Herdsman wins wager. [N73]. Cf. Type 1621A*.
Lithuanian (1545*) *1.*

1559B* *The Uglier Foot.* A traveling man comes to a house and gets meal; talks, shows his foot to the owner and lays a wager that there is a foot uglier than it in the house; owner wagers that there is not. Traveler then lays bare his other foot, which is much uglier than the first. Wins.
Irish.

1559C* *Some Things Not for Sale.* Man enters a huge shop where everything is said to be available. He bets with the owner that there are some things he cannot supply. The bet is accepted; the man then asks for six pairs of spectacles for his geese, a saddle for a frog, three sailfuls of wind to drive his sailing boat home, etc. etc. Wins the bet.
Irish.

1560 *Make-believe Eating; Make-believe Work.* At the table the peasant says, »We will only act as if we were eating.» At work the servant: »We will only act as if we were working.» [J1511.1].
Coffin *2.* — Finnish *16;* Finnish-Swedish *5;* Estonian *9;* Livonian *1;* Swedish *2* (Stockholm *1,* misc. *1*); Norwegian *2;* French *4;* German *3;* Slovenian *6;* Serbocroatian *1;* Russian: Andrejev. — Spanish-American: Hansen (Puerto Rico) *1.*

1560* *The Youth Eats up the Stingy Peasant's Butter.* He says that he is getting from his master »that which was promised him.»
Finnish; Finnish-Swedish *3;* Swedish *10* (Uppsala *8*, Stockholm *2*).

1560** *The Peasant and his Servant Driven by Rain into the Hay Barn.* To the peasant's question as to whether it is still raining the boy always answers in the affirmative, though the weather has really cleared. [W111.2.7].
Finnish *2;* Finnish-Swedish (1561*) *2.*

1561 *The Lazy Boy Eats Breakfast, Dinner, and Supper One after the Other* without working. Then he lies down to sleep. [W111.2.6].
Coffin *1.* — Finnish *8;* Finnish-Swedish *1;* Estonian *9;* Lithuanian *6;* Swedish *5* (Uppsala *3*, Lund *1*, misc. *1*); Irish *20;* English *1;* Dutch *3;* Flemish *3;* Walloon (1561A) *1;* Rumanian *2;* Hungarian *1;* Slovenian *5;* Serbocroatian *1;* Russian: Andrejev *2,* (*1561 I) *1,* Andrejev *Ukraine 11.* — English-American: Baughman *2.*

1561* *The Boy »Loses his Sight».* No butter on the bread. [J1561.4.2].
Finnish-Swedish (1561**) *2;* Swedish *24* (Uppsala *18*, Stockholm *4*, Lund *1*, misc. *1*).

1561** *Servant Gives all Heavy Work to Others;* takes largest portions at dinner. [J1561.4].
Finnish *84;* Finnish-Swedish (1561***) *4;* Spanish: Espinosa *Cuentos* III 130—140; Serbocroatian *2.*

1562 »*Think Thrice before you Speak.*» The youth obeys literally the precept even when he sees the master's coat on fire. [J2516.1, cf. J571.1].
   Pauli (ed. Bolte) No. 387; Chauvin VIII 170 No. 187. — Finnish *4;* Finnish-Swedish *1;* Swedish *3* (Stockholm *2,* Lund *1*); Irish *1;* English *1;* Flemish *1;* India *1.*

1562A *The Barn is Burning.* The master has taught the servant to give peculiar names to everything. When the cat sets the barn afire the servant uses those extraordinary names and is so delayed that the fire is out of control. [J1269.12]. Cf. Type 1940.
   *Zs. f. Vksk. XXVI 8, 370, XXVII 135, XXVIII 135; *Jackson FL XLVII 190—202, 280 (English *12,* Scottish *2,* Irish *5,* Welsh *4,* U.S.A. *2*), Baughman (same references); Espinosa II 260—264. — Cf. Lithuanian (*2421) *3;* Spanish (1940A*) *7;* Catalan: Amades No. 1323; Italian (Tuscan [1736] *2,* Sicilian *1699 *3*); Czech: Tille Soupis 448f. *5;* Russian: Andrejev (1940) *6.* — Spanish-American: Hansen (1940*A) (Chile) *1,* (Dominican Republic) *1,* (Cuba) *1,* (Puerto Rico) *1;* American Negro (Michigan): *Dorson No. 42. — Literary Treatments: *Nouvelles Récréations* No. 21.

1562B *Wife Follows Written Instructions.* She is to follow instructions which the husband has written down on a card. He falls into a brook and is about to drown. She goes home to see what his instructions on this point are. [J2516.3.1].
   *BP III 151; *Pauli (ed. Bolte) No. 139; Christensen DF XLVII 226 No. 92.

1562A* *Deceptive Bargain: Fasting Together.* The servant girl eats secretly; the miser starves. [K177].
   Danish: Kristensen *Jyske Folkeminder* VII No. 30. — Lithuanian (*1568A) *4.*

1562B* *Dog's Bread Stolen.* The miserly master and the clever workman. A master gives a workman one loaf of bread per day with which to feed the dog. So that he himself may be full and the loaf still appear to be whole, the worker takes the soft part out of the loaf.
   Russian: Afanasiev (*1567 I) *3.*

1562C* *Miser Eats at Night.* An old man gives his daughters-in-law nothing to eat, but he eats at night. They complain to their father, who comes, discovers the trickery of the old man and breaks him of his miserliness.
   Russian: Afanasiev (*1567 II) *1.*

1562D* *The Boy Goes to Sleep on his Job* but the master does not dare punish him.
   Spanish (1019*) *3.*

1562E* *Why doesn't Servant Boy Eat the Herring?* — »I have sent it to bring the butter.»
   Finnish *10;* Swedish (1561****) *8* (Stockholm *1,* Uppsala *7*).

1562F* *Boy Puts both Hands into the Soup Bowl* trying to get the only pea. (Or manages to get more peas in the soup.)
   Finnish *24;* Swedish (1561***) *15* (Stockholm *1,* Uppsala *14*).

1562G* *Strange Names.* An old woman and her son, staying overnight call themselves by strange names. Misunderstandings occur at night. Cf. Types 1461, 1545.
   Russian: Andrejev (*1530 I) *2.*

1563 »*Both?*« asks the boy sent to get two articles. »Yes, I said both.« He has his will of the master's (ogre's) two daughters. [K1354.1, cf. K1354.2.1].
Köhler-Bolte I 150, 291; Bolte *Montanus Gartengesellschaft* 611 No. 73; Coffin *5*. — Finnish *41;* Finnish-Swedish *5;* Estonian *5;* Lithuanian *21;* Swedish *2* (Stockholm *1*, misc. *1*); Norwegian *2;* Icelandic *4;* Irish *11;* French *3;* Dutch *2;* Walloon *1;* German: Henssen Volk No. 199; Hungarian *1;* Serbocroatian *4;* Russian: Andrejev. — English-American: Baughman *1;* Spanish-American: Hansen (Chile) *1*, (Puerto Rico) *2;* Cape Verde Islands: Parsons MAFLS XV (1) 115; American Indian: Thompson *C Coll* II 420ff. — Literary Treatments: Chauvin VI 180 No. 342.

1563* *Sham Threat: either . . . or.* »Either you give the road or I (will give it to you, or the like).« [K1771.2].
*Wesselski *Hodscha Nasreddin* II 21ff. No. 450. — Finnish *1;* Lithuanian (*1564) *3*.

1564* *The Clever Granary Watcher.* He steals his master's grain. The wagon falls into a ditch. As the master by chance comes to the place the watcher explains that the grain is his own. The master thereupon orders the other servants to help the watcher. [K405.1].
Estonian *1*.

1564** The same. He says that he is bringing some of his grain to the master, whereupon the master rightly grows suspicious. [K439.2].
Estonian (1565*) *3*.

1564A* *The Crooked Handle.* Servant says he is skilled in using the crooked handle. But he means not the scythe but the spoon.
Finnish *12*.

1565 *Agreement Not to Scratch.* In talking, the trickster makes gestures and scratches without detection. [K263].
*Bolte Zs. f. Vksk. XIX 310 n. 2. — German: Knoop *Sagen und Erzählungen aus der Provinz Posen* (Posen, 1893) 216 No. 11; Turkish: Eberhard-Boratav No. 321 *1;* India *1;* Chinese: Eberhard FFC CXX p. 310 No. 10; Korean: Eckart *Koreanische Märchen* (1929) 74 No. 23. — French Canadian (K263); Spanish-American: Rael No. 66 (U.S.); North Carolina: Brown Collection I 701; American Negro (Georgia): Harris *Nights* 214 No. 37, (South Carolina): Parsons JAFL XXXVIII 218; Jamaica: Beckwith MAFLS XVII 36 No. 29; West Indies: Flowers 502. — African: Bleek *Reineke Fuchs in Africa* (1870) 143.

1565* *The Big Cake.* During Lent the peasants are not to eat more than a single cake. They make one as big as a cart wheel. [K2311]. (Or they go to sea on Friday so as to eat flesh without sin.)
Flemish (1564*) *1;* Serbocroatian *1*.

1565** *Turnips as Bacon.* The peasant compels his servant to call turnips, bacon. The circumstances favoring, the servant compels the master to call a cat a rabbit. [K1511.2].
Finnish (herring, salmon); Flemish (1565*) *2*.

1565A* *The Saint's Encouraging Smile.* Praying at a saint's image, a peasant steals a coin from the altar. Since he believes the image is smiling he steals another.
Walloon (*1565) *1*.

1566* changed to Type 1567A.

1566** *Butter vs. Bread.* The peasant weighs the butter which he is selling to the baker against the bread which he has bought from him [K478].
Flemish (1566*) *1*.

1566A* *Maids must Rise even Earlier.* They have killed the cock for waking them too early, but their mistress punishes them. [K1636].
Wienert FFC LVI 64 (ET 279), 116 (ST 262); Halm Aesop No. 10. — Russian: Andrejev (*1566 I) *1*.

1567 *Hungry Servant Reproaches Stingy Master.* Cf. Type 1389*.

1567A (formerly 1566*) *Stingy Innkeeper Cured of Serving Weak Beer.* She always gives the servants a pitcher of weak beer before meals so as to fill them up. One of them: »I wash out my insides so as to have more room for food.» She changes her practice. [J1341.7].
Finnish; Estonian *3;* cf. Livonian *1*.

1567B (formerly 1567**) *Softening Bread-crusts.* An avaricious master feeds bread-crusts to his servants. »The crusts are already getting soft.» [J1341.1].
Estonian *3*.

1567C *Asking the Large Fish.* Parents serve boy a small fish and keep back a large one for themselves. Knowing this, the boy puts the fish to his ear. He says that he has asked the fish a question; the fish cannot answer but tells him to ask the large fish under the bed. [J1341.2].
*Wesselski *Hodscha Nasreddin* I 247 No. 158; *Pauli (ed. Bolte) No. 700; L. Schmidt Oesterr. Zs. f. Vksk. 1954, 134. — Finnish *4;* Lithuanian (*1565) *2;* Italian Novella: Rotunda (J1341.3).

1567D *Two Eggs.* Widow serves tailor one egg. He sings, »One egg, one egg.» She decides one egg is not enough and serves him two next time. He then sings »Two eggs are two eggs.» He is next given two eggs and a sausage, etc. [J1341.4].
Spanish (*1715) *1*.

1567E *Hungry Apprentice's Lies Attract Master's Attention.* [J1341.5].
Spanish (*1718) *1*.

1567F *Hungry Shepherd Attracts Attention.* He tells of a cow with four teats who bore five calves. They ask what the fifth calf does while the other four are nursing. »It just looks on as I am doing now.» [J1341.6].
Spanish (1555) *1;* French: Delarue in *Bulletin Folklorique d'Ile-de-France* XII (1950) 130f.; German: Meyer *Plattdeutsche Volksmärchen* No. 198. — Spanish American (U.S.): Rael Nos. 420, 421.

1567G *Good Food Changes Song.* Hired men sing of displeasure with food; change song when food is improved (cante fable) [J1341.11].
Finnish *5;* England: Baughman *3;* U.S.: Baughman *6*.

1567* *Boys Give the Herring Matches for Feet*, and make a dummy butter-merchant. Thereafter they get butter with their bread.
Finnish *1;* Serbocroatian *1*.

1567** changed to Type 1567B.

1567*** changed to Type 1574C.

1568* *The Master and the Servant at the Table.* The master turns the plate around. »This plate costs three marks.» The servant turns it back: »Indeed, it is worth that much.» [J1562.1].
*Wesselski *Arlotto* II No. 89. — Finnish *3;* Estonian *7;* Livonian *1;* Lithuanian *2;* German: Meyer *Plattdeutsche Volksmärchen* No. 88; Gypsy: Krauss *Zigeunerhumor* 140; Slovenian *1.* — Spanish-American: Hansen (**1568AB) (Cuba) *2.*

1568** *The Master and the Pupil Quarrel.* »What God has joined together let no man put asunder.»
Finnish *2;* German: Meyer *Plattdeutsche Volksmärchen* (Neumünster, 1925) No. 194.

1568*** *The Rich Son-in-law.* The burgomaster will marry his daughter only to a rich man. The poor youth and his ingenious friend.
Flemish (1568*) *2.*

1568A* *The Farmer's Leg Never Falls.* He always sleeps after dinner in the field arranging that one foot will fall to the ground and wake him so that he can start the servant's to work. They arrange to keep the foot from falling and he sleeps till evening.
Finnish *15.*

1569* *How the Servant Boy Reformed his Master.* He tells the master: »I had a dream that I should find a large treasure if I should take the most honest man with me.» He goes with his master three nights to seek the treasure. Finally, when they were lost, he says: »You shall die of hunger unless you reform.» The master promises. Cf. Type 1572E*.
Estonian *2.*

1569** *Clothing the Servant.* The master is to clothe his servant (at his expense). The servant insists that the conditions be fulfilled literally, that the master shall put on his clothes for him. [J2491].
Flemish (1569*) *1.*

1570* »*Gorge silently*». A soldier, who is spending the night, eats up a whole dish of dumplings. He asks what this food is called. The lady of the house answers: »Gorge silently». The soldier: »Please give me some more of this gorgesilently.»
Russian: Afanasiev (*1570 I) *1.*

1571* *The Servants Punish their Master.* The master, suspecting his servants of stealing, spies on them. The servants think he is a thief and give him a whipping. »I am the master of the house.»
Estonian *18.*

1572* *The Master's Privilege.* The lazy servant and the master both have their faults. After dinner the servant takes a fit and goes to sleep. In the same way, the master: he beats the boy. The boy is cured of his laziness. [J1511.4].
Finnish *5;* Estonian *6;* cf. Livonian *2;* Swedish *3;* German: Dähnhardt *Schwänke* (1908) No. 82; Russian: Andrejev (1572A*).

1572A* *The Saints Ate the Cream.* The servant eats his master's cream, then having smeared the remainder of it on the lips of the effigies of the saints, puts all the blame on them.
Lithuanian (*2440) *8.*

1572B* *What God Gave Him.* The guest pulls all of the meat out of the soup: »What I hooked, that is what God gave me.» After dinner the host with these same words pulls the guest by the hair.
Russian: Afanasiev *1.*

1572C* *No Forced Gift.* The host reproaches the guest for refusing a treat: »Don't disobey!» The guest: »Don't order!»
Russian: Afanasiev 2.

1572D* *Gifts Literally Accepted.* The host dislikes for anyone to refuse him. Taking advantage of this, a sly guest literally accepts the proposal of the host and takes off his horse and other things.
Russian: Afanasiev (*1572 I) *1*.

1572E* *The Clever Coachman and Hungry Master.* Purposely loses his master in the forest, who, when he went on a journey, always omitted to order him his share of food. Cf. Type 1569*.
Lithuanian (*2430) *3*.

1572F* *Turning the Shovel Backwards.* The servant eats with his spoon turned backwards; the master unloads his wages (grain) with the shovel also turned backwards.
Lithuanian (*2426B) *2*.

1572G* *The Travelers and the Miser.* Naming a variety of dishes to the hungry travelers, the miser keeps asking: »Would you eat of them?» — »We would» — »Yes, if they were here to eat» ... After being shown their way, the travelers beat the miser, and ask him: »Would your brother defend you?» — »Surely, he would.» — »Yes, if he were here».
Lithuanian (*2426A) *2*.

1572H* *»That Is All».* The farmer assigns numerous tasks, each time with »That is all.» The servant quits with the same words.
Walloon (*1636) *1*.

1573* *The Clever Servant as Trouble Maker.* He lays the skin of a dead dog in the bed of of his master and mistress in order to make trouble beween them. Likewise he breeds enmity between the daughters. [K2134]. Cf. Type 1453.
Estonian *4*; Lithuanian (*2431) *2*; Russian: Andrejev (1573*) *4*.

1573** *Inspecting the Daughter.* The boy makes an axe-handle without sighting. One of the daughters is promised him. »Will I get that daughter?» He looks carefully enough.
Finnish *3*.

1574 *The Tailor's Dream.* A tailor dreams that at Judgment Day he sees a flag made up of all the pieces of cloth he has stolen. Upon waking he asks his servants to warn him if they ever see him tempted to steal again. This happens. He replies, »The piece I am about to steal does not fit into the flag.» [J1401].
*BP I 343; *Wesselski *Hodscha Nasreddin* I 256 No. 190.

1574A (formerly 2005*). *The Oversight of the Thievish Tailor.* He sews the stolen piece of cloth on the outside of his coat thinking it is on the inside. [X221].
Estonian (2005*) *1*; Finnish (2005*) *1*.

1574B (formerly 2005**). *The Tailor Cuts the Piece out of his Own Coat* [X221.1].
Swedish (2005*) *6* (Göteborg *1*, misc. *5*).

1574C (formerly 1567***). *The Devil's Share.* The stingy woman has the tailor come to her house to cut cloth. He throws a piece out of the window, »the devil's share.» While the woman has gone after it he cuts off a piece for himself. [K341.13].
Finnish *2*; Swedish (Uppsala) *3*; Flemish (1567*) *1*; India *1*.

1574* *The Flattering Foreman.* Always answers his master's questions: »I have thought of the same thing too.» He falls into a trap when in the same way he answers his master's words, »I am going to sow salt.» [K1637].
Estonian (1574) *4;* Irish *1;* American Negro (Michigan): Dorson No. 32.

1575* *The Clever Shepherd.* A man will not pay back money borrowed from the shepherd. The latter climbs a tree and from there calls out threats. The man thinks God is calling and repays the loan [K1971.2]. Cf. Type 1380.
Wesselski *Hodscha Nasreddin* II 203 No. 403. — Finnish *1;* Estonian *3;* Russian: Andrejev *1.*

1575** The same. Bad food at the house. The boy on the tree. [K1971.3]. Cf. Type 1380.
Finnish *2.*

1576* *The Inventive Coachman.* Makes the horse run by binding a bundle of hay to the shaft. [J1671].
Estonian *1.*

1577 *Blind Men Duped into Fighting: Money to be Divided.* Trickster says that he is giving one of them money to be divided with the others. Gives it to none. They quarrel and fight. [K1081.1]. (Cf. K1883.6.)
*Wesselski *Gonnella* 126 No. 21; *Bédier *Fabliaux* 447; Lithuanian (1577*) *1;* Estonian (1577*) *3;* Russian (*1577 I) *2;* Italian Novella: Rotunda (K1081.1). — Brazil: Camara Cascudo 43; Spanish-American (U.S.): Rael No. 464.

1577* *Blind Robber Paid Back.* The blind beggar steals 100 marks from the man. The latter steals into the blind man's house and overhears that he has 1000 marks hidden and steals them [N455.1]. Cf. Types 1341, 1525P*.
Estonian *3;* Slovenian *1;* Turkish:Eberhard-Boratav No. 345 *3.*

1578* *The Inventive Beggar.* He gives the woman a knife to cut him a slice of white bread. He gets the whole loaf when he says that he has just cut a dog with the same knife. [K344.1].
Estonian *1.*

1578A* *The Drinking Cup.* A thirsty man stops at a house and asks for water. He is offered water in a cup. After he drinks the water, he asks the boy if his mother will care if he drinks more. The boy answers no, because there is a dead rat or worms in the water. The man tries to break the container on the boy's head. The boy tells him not to, because his mother uses it as a urinal, or it is used to feed the dog.
Spanish-American: Hansen (**1554) (Cuba) *1,* (Dominican Republic) *2.*

1578B* *How a Woman Came to Loathe Tripe.* Is shown the unappetizing manner of its preparation.
Lithuanian (*2442) *3.*

1579 *Carrying Wolf, Goat, and Cabbage across Stream.* A man is to set across a stream, in a boat that will hold himself and only one other object, a wolf, a goat, and a cabbage. He must do this so that the wolf doesn't eat the goat, nor the goat the cabbage. Two solutions: (1) (a) take goat over, (b) take wolf over and goat back, (c) take cabbage over, (d) take goat over; (2) (a) take goat over, (b) take cabbage over and goat back, (c) take wolf over, (d) take goat over. [H506.3]. Cf. Type 212*.
*Bolte Zs. f. Vksk XXXIII—XXXIV 38; Feilberg *Ordbog* III 970a s.v. »ulv», II 354f. s.v. »kål». — Catalan: Amades No. 471, cf. 472;

Africa: Atlantis I 246 No. 45; Littmann *Princeton Expedition to Abyssinia* II 40 No. 29.

1579* *Reverse Merit.* The tricky inn-keeper praises the forest guards before the baron in exactly the reverse of their merit, so that the pursuer of the thief of wood loses his place and the other, who permits the wood to be stolen, receives a reward. [K2136].
Livonian *2*.

1580* (Obscene.)
Livonian *1*.

1580A* *Fool Overmounts.* Failing to mount his horse, fool makes such extra effort that he falls on the other side. (Thanks to St. Anthony!)
Italian (Tuscan 1580 a, b *2*); Slovenian *1;* Serbocroatian *4*.

1581* *Shoemaker Makes Shoes Without Measuring.* Scatters ashes and measures the tracks. [J1146].
Slovenian *2*.

1584* *Cunning Monks Appropriate Field* which they helped to mow.
Lithuanian *2*.

1585 *The Lawyer's Mad Client* (Patelin says »Baa«!) The man sells the same oxen to several people. On the advice of the judge (lawyer) he feigns insanity when brought to court. When his fee is demanded he still feigns insanity. [K1655].

**Oliver JAFL XXII 395; Anderson *Novelline* No. 11; *Prato RTP IX 537; *Dubsky RTP XXIII 427; *Bolte *Wickrams Rollwagenbüchlein* 371 No. 36; Coffin *5*. — Finnish *15;* Lithuanian *3;* Scottish *3;* Irish *59*, Jackson FL XLVII 292; French *3;* Catalan: Amades cf. No. 525; Dutch *3;* Flemish *5*, (1585*) *1;* German: Archive *13;* Italian (Tuscan *1*); Czech: Tille Soupis II (2) 106—108 *6;* Slovenian *1;* Serbocroatian *3;* Russian: Andrejev; Greek *2;* India *2*. — English-American: Baughman *2;* Spanish-American: Rael No. 449 (U.S.), Hansen (Dominican Republic) *2*, (Puerto Rico) *2;* West Indies (Negro) *2*. — African *1*. — Literary Treatments: Rotunda Novella (K1655).

1585* *The Peasant's Promise.* Consulting an attorney, a peasant promises a rabbit as payment. His defense for non-payment: has directed the rabbit to go to his attorney's house, but was mistaken in the address. [Cf. J1881.2.2].
Walloon (*1588) *1*.

1586 *The Man in Court for Killing a Fly.* Told by the judge he should kill a fly wherever he sees it. Kills the fly on the judge's nose. [J1193.1].

*BP I 519; Pauli (ed. Bolte) No. 673; *Anderson *Novelline* Nos. 54, 55, 100—102; *Espinosa Cuentos III 191ff. — Finnish *4;* Danish (Type 192) *1;* French *8;* German *2;* Italian *9* (Tuscan 2016 a—f *6*, Sicilian *3*); Rumanian (1331—46 [4] *2;* Hungarian *4;* Slovenian *3;* Serbocroatian *2;* Russian: Andrejev *1;* Greek: Argenti-Rose III 625; Indonesian: DeVries No. 285; Japanese: Ikeda (N333.1). — Spanish-American: Rael No. 326 (U.S.), Hansen (Puerto Rico) *12;* Cape Verde Islands: Parsons MAFLS XV (1) 289; West Indies (Negro) *4*.

1586A *Fatal Killing of the Insect.* (a) A fool sees a fly light on his mother's (companion's) head and hits it with an axe, etc., killing his mother [J1833.1, N333.1]. (b) When a grasshopper (fly) lights on a hunter's shoulder, his companion shoots it, killing the hunter. (c) A tame bear sees a bee light on his sleeping master's mouth and drops a heavy stone on the bee, killing his master [N333.2]. Cf. Type 163A*

Latvian (**248) *1;* Italian (Tuscan [1206] *1*); Serbocroatian *3;* Greek (1228*) *4.* — India *9.*

1587 *Man Allowed to pick out Tree to be Hanged on.* Cannot find one. [K558].

*Crane *Vitry* 161 No. 62; *Pauli (ed. Bolte) No. 283; Krappe *Bulletin Hispanique* XXXIX 25; U.S., England: Baughman; Swiss: Jegerlehner 324 No. 161; Spanish Exempla: Keller.

1587* *Dog as Weapon.* »Whoever wants to strike someone will find a weapon.« The accused strikes the judge with a dog.

Finnish (1587**) *2.*

1587** *Accuser is a Madman.* The robber who makes people believe his accuser is mad [K1265]. Cf. Type 1525L.

Flemish (1587*) *3.*

1588* *The Unseen.* The judge asks the witness, »Did you see it?« The witness does something that is heard but not seen and then asks the judge, »Did you see it?«

Flemish *2.*

1588** *Cheater Caught by Seizing on his own Words.* Taking advantage of the careless remark made by the hungry son of a merchant (»each spoon of this food is worth a hundred rubles«), the innkeeper demands a large sum of money for the dinner. A clever man saves the situation by catching on the innkeeper's own words and compelling him to return the money.

Lithuanian (*1588) *4;* Russian (*1588) *1.*

1589 *The Lawyer's Dog Steals Meat.* The lawyer tells the butcher that the dog's owner (himself) is liable for damages. He asks double the amount of the damages as fee. [K488].

Irish *2;* English *3;* Flemish (1589*) *1;* Walloon *1.*

1590 *The Tresspasser's Defense.* With earth from his own property in his shoes, the man swears, when he is on his neighbor's land, that he is on his own. [J1161.3, K1917.1]. Cf. Types 859A, B, C, D.

*BP II 203 (Grimm No. 84); Archiv f. d. neueren Sprachen CXXVII 281 n. 1; Wesselski *Gonnella* 97; *Anderson FFC XLII 362 n. 1; Feilberg *Ordbog* I 234 s.v. »ed«, II 45b s.v. »jord«; W. Uhl *Murners Gäuchmatt* 268; Bobertag in Kürschners *Deutsche Nationalliteratur* XXV 9. — Swedish *17* (Uppsala *11,* Stockholm *5,* misc. *1*); Danish: Kristensen *Danske Sagn* V (1897) 443ff., (1934) 324ff.; Icelandic *2;* Irish *4;* English *1;* Dutch *6;* Flemish (1590*) *2;* German: Henssen Volk No. 58 a; Italian (Sicilian *1*); Slovenian *2;* Russian: Andrejev (*1636) *1.* — Spanish-American: Rael No. 291 (U.S.); West Indies (Negro) *2;* American Indian: Thompson *C Coll* II 428.

1591 *The Three Joint Depositors.* Money is left with a banker by three joint depositors. The money is to be delivered only on demand from all three.

One of the men steals the money. The others sue the banker for the money. He agrees to deliver it when all three jointly demand it. [J1161].

*Clouston *Tales* II 1 ff.; *Wesselski *Arlotto* I 205 No. 41; *Chauvin VIII 63 No. 28; *Burton *1001 Nights* VI 210 f.; Penzer *Ocean of Story* I 186; Baumgarten *Arch. f. Rel. wiss.* XXIV (1927) 27 n. 1; Pauli (ed. Bolte) No. 113; Krappe *Bulletin Hispanique* XXXIX 21 No. 77. — Swedish 2 (Lund *1*, misc. *1*); English *1;* Slovenian *1;* India *3.*

1592 *The Iron-eating Mice.* The trustee claims that mice have eaten the iron scales confided to him. The host abducts the trustee's son and says that a falcon has carried him off. [J1531.2].

*BP II 372; Chauvin II 92 No. 37; Bødker Exempler; Spanish Exempla: Keller; Italian Novella: Rotunda; India *8,* Penzer *Ocean of Story* III 250, V 62, *64; Indonesian: DeVries No. 299.

1592A *The Transformed Golden Pumpkin.* The borrower of golden pumpkin returns a brass pumpkin and claims that the gold has turned to brass. The lender takes the borrower's son and returns with an ape. He claims that the boy has turned into an ape. [J1531.1].

Köhler-Bolte I 533; India *1.*

1592B *The Pot Has a Child and Dies.* A borrower returns a pot along with a small one saying that the pot has had a young one. The pots are accepted. He borrows the pot a second time and keeps it. He sends word that the pot has died. [J1531.3].

*BP II 372 n. 2; *Wesselski *Hodscha Nasreddin* I 213 No. 35; DeVries FFC LXXIII 273 n. 1. — Rumanian (1705*) *2;* Serbocroatian *2;*India: Thompson-Balys (J1531.3); Indonesia: DeVries FFC LXXIII 273 n. 1.

1592A* *Counterfeit Money Burned up.* A priest who has lent money to a Jew, but will not lend to a farmer, on being reproached by the latter, says that the money he lent the Jew was »false«. When the Jew gets to know this, he claims that as soon as he heard the money was false he burned it up. [J1511.10].
Lithuanian (1772*) *3.*

1592B* *The Deceived Merchant.* While he is making calculations, he asks the age of his youngest daughter, the elder daughter, and the mother, and always adds this to the number that he has recorded. [J2035].
Flemish *1;* Swedish (Stockholm) *1.*

1600 *The Fool as Murderer.* The brothers put a he-goat in place of the body and thus save their brother. [H472.1, K661.1]. Cf. Type 1381B, C, E.

Delarue in notes to Boratav *Contes Turques* 215. — Finnish *18;* Estonian *19;* Lithuanian *42;* Swedish *5* (Uppsala *2*, Liungman *1*, misc. *2*); Norwegian *1;* Scottish *3;* Irish *155;* French *4;* German: Henssen Jül. No. 468; Italian (Sicilian *5*, Gonzenbach No. 37); Slovenian *2;* Serbocroatian *2;* Russian: Afanasiev (1600A) *15;* Greek *5;* Turkish: Eberhard-Boratav No. 323 *18;* India *8;* Indonesian: DeVries No. 308, Coster-Wijsman 53 No. 78. — Literary Treatments: Chauvin VI 126 No. 280; Wesselski *Hodscha Nasreddin* II 183 No. 347.

1605* *The Tax-Exempter.* The stallion serves the officer's mare and he is content.
Finnish (1605) *10.*

1610 *To Divide Presents and Strokes.* The boy (peasant) promises the soldier what the king has promised to give him. The soldier receives a beating in place of the boy. [K187]. Cf. Types 1642, 1689.
**Reinhard »Strokes Shared» JAFL XXXVI 380—400; *BP I 62ff. (Grimm No. 7); Pauli (ed. Bolte) No. 614; Basset *1001 Contes* I 321; Köhler-Bolte I 495; Zachariae Zs. f. Vksk. XXXIII—XXXIV 71; Toldo Zs. f. Vksk. XIV 61 n. 2; Coffin *1.* — Finnish *21;* Finnish-Swedish *1;* Estonian *5;* Lithuanian *13;* Swedish *16* (Uppsala *1,* Stockholm *10,* Lund *1,* Liungman *1,* misc. *3*); Danish: MS. DFS; Irish *4;* Spanish *1;* Dutch *1;* Flemish *2;* German *10* (Archive *9,* Henssen Volk No. 213); Italian *4* (Tuscan 1650 *1,* Sicilian *3,* Gonzenbach No. 75); Hungarian *3;* Czech: Tille Soupis II (2) 417ff. *11;* Slovenian *5;* Serbocroatian *2;* Russian: Andrejev *Ukraine 11,* Afanasiev *3,* Andrejev (*1610 II) *1;* Greek *2;* India *4.* — Spanish-American: Rael No. 314 (U.S.). — African *2.*

1611 *Contest in Climbing the Mast.* The boy falls from the mast and lodges in the rigging: »You do the same thing!» The sailors are persuaded that he is an expert sailor. [K1762].
Coffin *1.* — Finnish *5;* Finnish-Swedish *1;* Swedish *2* (Lund *1,* misc. *1*); Danish: MS. DFS; Russian: Andrejev; Cape Verde Islands: Parsons MAFLS XV (1) 190; American Indian: Thompson *C Coll* II 433.

1612 *The Contest in Swimming.* The swimmer takes a knapsack of provisions on his back. His rival is afraid and gives up. [K1761].
Coffin *1.* — Finnish *21;* Finnish-Swedish *3;* Swedish *2* (Lund *1,* misc. *1*); Danish: MS. DFS; Irish *13;* Russian: Andrejev; India *1;* Cape Verde Islands: Parsons MAFLS XV (1) 190; American Indian: Speck JAFL XXX (1917) 482 No. 7; American Negro (Michigan): Dorson No. 22.

1613 »*Playing-Cards Are my Calendar and Prayerbook.*» A soldier reproved for playing cards during church service answers thus and shows so cleverly the symbolic meanings of each of the cards that he receives a reward. [H603].
**Bolte Zs. f. Vksk. XI 376ff.; *Wilson FL L 263ff — Finnish *7;* Finnish-Swedish *1;* Swedish *8* (Uppsala *3,* Lund *2,* Liungman *1,* misc. *2*); Danish: MS. DFS; Icelandic *1;* Scottish *1;* Irish *17,* Beal XV 261ff.; English *4;* French *3;* Catalan: Amades No. 1389; Walloon *1;* German *4;* Russian: Andrejev; English-American: Baughman *1;* Spanish-American: Hansen (Argentina) *1.*

1614* *A Clever Device.* The well the man has dug falls in. He throws his clothes into the hole and hides. People going to church think that the man is drowned and dig the well out. [K474].
Estonian *1;* Irish *2.*

1614** *The Man who Bought himself the Itch.*
Lappish (1614*) *1.*

1615 *The Heller Thrown into Other's Money.* A rascal sees robbers dividing their booty. He puts a red string through his only coin (a heller) and slips it into the others' money. He claims the money as his, and says he has marked it with a heller having a red string through it. The robbers divide. [K446].
  *Wesselski *Hodscha Nasreddin* II 197 No. 387; *Pauli (ed. Bolte) No. 566. — India *2.* — Literary Treatments: Chauvin V 254 No. 151 n. 2, VII 153.

1617 *Unjust Banker Deceived into Delivering Deposits* by making him expect even larger. In order to make the impression of honesty he delivers the one chest of money. The ten chests which he then receives are filled with stones. [K1667].
  *Penzer III 118ff.; *Chauvin IX 24 No. 13; *Krappe Bulletin Hispanique XXXIX 27; Boccaccio Decameron VIII No. 10 (Lee 266). — Spanish *1;* Jewish: Neuman (K1667); India *4.* — Literary Treatments: Rotunda (K1667).

1620 *The King's New Clothes.* An impostor pretends to make clothes for the king and says that they are visible only to those of legitimate birth. The king and courtiers are all afraid to admit that they cannot see the clothes. Finally a child seeing the naked king reveals the imposture. [K445].
  **Taylor MPh XXV 17; *Wesselski *Gonnella* 133 No. 33. — Lithuanian *5;* Swedish *5* (Uppsala *1,* Stockholm *1,* misc. *3*); English *1;* Spanish *1;* German *2* (Archive *1,* Henssen Volk No. 188); Italian (Tuscan [1739] *1*); Slovenian *1;* India: Thompson-Balys (K445). — Literary Treatments: Chauvin II 156 No. 32, VIII 130 No. 120; Rotunda (K445).

1620* *The Conversation of the One-eyed Man and the Hunchback.* »What kind of burden are you carrying?» — The hunchback: »Why can't you carry two windows?» (Sometimes bald-headed and red-headed men, or people with deformities carry on repartee.)
  Finnish *2;* Estonian *1;* Flemish *1;* German: Jungbauer *Volk Erzählt* 380.

1621* *The Horse is Cleverer than the Priest.* The peasant: The horse does not step twice into the same hole, but the priest has two children by the same girl.
  Anderson FFC XLII 359 n. 2. — Estonian *1;* Danish: Kristensen *Kirketjenste* 212ff. Nos. 545ff.; Hungarian: Berze Nagy (928*) *2.*

1621A* *Ass Refuses to Drink after it has had Enough.* Thus teaches lesson to master. [J133.2].
  Pauli (ed. Bolte) No. 239. — Slovenian *3.*

1623* *An Old »Hen» instead of a Young One.* Instead of a young girl, the servant brings his master an old woman. Cleverly explains to his mistress why his master dismissed him — is taken back into service.
  Lithuanian (*1621) *4.*

1624 *Thief's Excuse: the Big Wind.* A vegetable thief is caught in a garden. Owner: How did you get into the garden? A wind blew me in. How were the vegetables uprooted? If the wind is strong enough to blow me in, it can uproot them. How did they get into your bag? That is what I was just wondering. [J1391.1].
  *Wesselski *Hodscha Nasreddin* I 207 No. 7, cf. II 214 No. 441. —

German: Haltrich *Zur Volkskunde der Siebenbürger Sachsen* (1885) 114; Rumanian: Schullerus FFC LXXVIII 96 *1;* Hungarian: Berze Nagy (1624*) *1;* Serbocroatian *2;* Gypsy: Krauss *Zigeunerhumor* 87.

1624A**Shortest Road.* Gypsy intending to steal bacon falls through hole in ceiling. Says he was taking the shortest road.
Hungarian *1;* Serbocroatian *2.*

1624B* *The Theft of Bacon.* Making off with the bacon, the Gypsy accidentally enters the farmer's living-room. Boldly says: »Master, the devil from hell sends you bacon». The farmer: »Take yourself off to hell with the bacon».
Lithuanian (*1627) *7;* Russian: Andrejev 1525*J *1.*

1624C* *The Horse's Fault.* The horse had stood across the road. The thief had wanted to jump over it, and, in doing so, found himself on its back.
Lithuanian (*1627C) *4.*

1624D* *Toothache Given as Reason for Theft.*
Lithuanian (*1627D) *1.*

1624E* *Need to Whet Knife.* A servant sees a student steal a ham. He substitutes a rock. The student borrows a knife. When he finds the rock he says that he wanted to whet the knife on the stone.
Catalan: Amades No. 418.

1626 *Dream Bread.* The most wonderful dream. Three pilgrims agree that the one who has the most wonderful dream shall eat the last loaf. One eats it. He declares he dreamed the others were dead and would not need it. [K444].

**Baum JAFL XXX 378; *BP IV 139; *Wesselski *Hodscha Nasreddin* II 243 No. 540; *Ward *Catalogue of Romances* II 240, III 246; *Krappe Bulletin Hispanique XXXIX 22 No. 98; Coffin *9;* L. Schmidt Oesterr. Zs. f. Vksk. 1954, 135. — Lithuanian *8;* Icelandic (1626*) *1;* Irish *42;* French *2;* Spanish *1;* Dutch *1;* German *1;* Italian *3* (Tuscan *1,* Sicilian *2*); Hungarian: Berze Nagy (1792*) *1;* Czech: Tille Soupis II (2) 382 *6;* Slovenian *3;* Serbocroatian *2;* Russian: Andrejev (2100*) *4,* Andrejev *Ukraine* (2100*) *1;* Greek (1920E*) *10, Laographia* XVII 137, 176ff.; Jewish: Neuman (K444); India: Thompson-Balys (K444); Japanese. — Franco-American: Barbeau JAFL XXIX 12; English-American: Baughman *4;* Spanish-American: Rael No. 87 (U.S.), Hansen (Puerto Rico) *10,* cf. *1942 *1;* Portuguese-American (Brazil): Camara Cascudo p. 30. — Literary Treatment: Dunlop-Wilson II 201, *Gesta Romanorum* (Oesterley No. 106); *Scala Celi* No. 415; Rotunda (K444).

1627* *Students and the Eclipse of the Moon.* Knowing about the eclipse they make peasants believe that they tar the moon black and then wipe it clean again.
Swedish (GS 1627) *6.*

1628 *The Learned Son and the Forgotten Language.* Having left the seminary, a son speaks only Latin, pretending to have forgotten his own language. When a rake strikes him in the forehead, he screams in his own tongue »Devilish rake!» [J1511.11]. Cf. Type 1641 C.

*Zs. f. österreichische Vksk. XI 118; *Zs. f. Vksk. XVI 25, 298, 449; *Pauli (ed. Bolte) II 283; BP II 413. — Lithuanian (*2423) *2;* Swedish

(GS 903, 1628) *8* (Stockholm *1*, Liungman *1*, misc. *2*, Uppsala *4*); French *1;* German: Meyer *Plattdeutsche Volksmärchen* No. 191, Zender *Volksmärchen aus der Westeifel* 123 No. 155; Italian (Tuscan cf. 1213 *1*); Hungarian: Berze Nagy (1686*) *4;* Slovenian *2*, Serbocroatian *1;* Russian: Andrejev (*2082) *1;* French Canadian.

1628* *So They Speak Latin.* Lazy boy makes his father believe he has finished school and can speak Latin.
Liungman SSF III 451 (GS 1628). — Swedish (GS 1628) *3*.

1629* *The Supposed Magic Spell.* The thief orders the farmer to crawl into a tub and to sit there quietly and not look about, while he makes a magic spell (cures him of childlessness). Meanwhile, he steals all the farmer's property. [K341.22].
Lithuanian (1629) *8;* Italian Novella: Rotunda [K341.22]; India: Thompson-Balys.

1630A* *Has Beaten Father's Cap.* Son confesses — but father's head was inside. (Sometimes mother's jacket.) Cf. Type 1800.
Rumanian: Schullerus FFC LXXVIII 97 Nos. 5, 7—10 *5;* Hungarian: Berze Nagy *2*.

1630B* *The Bear Thought to be a Log* [J1761.9]. A man, thinking he sees a log (blanket) in the river, swims out and seizes it. It is a bear which seizes him. Friends on shore shout »Let go of the log.» He answers »The log won't let go of me.»
India *3*.

1631 *Horse which will not Go over Trees.* A salesman tells the buyer that he is selling the horse because it eats too much and will not climb trees. On the way home the horse bites everyone and refuses to cross a bridge. Seller is literally correct. [K134.1].
*Wesselski *Bebel* I 133 No. 33; *Pauli (ed. Bolte) No. 112. — Cf. Finnish *7;* Lithuanian (*1631) *5;* cf. Hungarian: Berze Nagy (1625*) *1;* England: Baughman.

1631A *Mule Painted and Sold Back to Owner.* Trickster grooms master's old mule and then sells him back without detection at huge profit. [K134.3].
*Anderson *Novelline* No. 38; *Nouvelles Recreations* No. 25. — Catalan: Amades No. 415; Czech: Tille Soupis II (2) 423 (ox). — Spanish-American: Hansen (**1549) (Chile) *1*, (Puerto Rico) *1*.

1631* *The Tailor and the Smith as Rivals.* The tailor declares that the smith is blind. Keeps striking on the iron. [T92.12.1].
Estonian *3;* Lithuanian (*1693A) *5*.

1632* *The Gypsy and the Jew Traveling together.* The Jew complains to his companion that, excepting themselves, there are no honorable people living. The Gypsy cheats the Jew of his horse. »Since there is no honor anywhere, let there be none between us».
Lithuanian (*1632) *6*.

1633 *Joint Ownership of the Cow* [J242.9, J1241]. Cf. Types 9B, 1030. A man dies, leaving property to be shared between his two sons. (a) The older brother claims the back half of the cow and gives the younger the front half. The older brother gets the milk and the younger must feed the cow. Or (b) similar deceitful sharing. A friend or relative advises the younger brother how to trick the older and gain his fair share.
India *9*.

1634* *Various Tricks Played by Gypsies.*
Lithuanian (*1639) *3.*

1634A* *Fish Promised in Return for Bacon.* »Drink up the river, you shall then have fish. All the fishes there are mine.» [K231.11].
Lithuanian (*1634) *4;* Russian: Andrejev (*2104).

1634B* *Skin-dressing Liquid in place of Cider.* A Gypsy, who has been entertained with this liquid, says to his hostess: »I can tell you why you have no children — this acid has burned them all».
Lithuanian (*1636) *4.*

1634C* *Eating against his Will.* Gypsy wanting cheese pretends to be unwilling to eat it. Owner forces it on him.
Hungarian (1620*) *1.*

1634D* *How to Beat a Gypsy.* Gypsy thief being beaten tells captor that he does not know how to beat a Gypsy. In the discussion Gypsy escapes.
Hungarian (1621*) *1.*

1634E* *Throwing the Thief over the Fence.* Thief, surprised at theft says: »Do your worst, only don't throw me over the fence.» When thrown over, he escapes. [K584]. Cf. Type 1310.
Lithuanian (*1627) *9.*

1635* *Eulenspiegel's Tricks* [K300]. See also Types 921, 922, 1542, 1590, 1620, 1685, 1835.
Livonian *1;* Swedish *6* (Uppsala *2,* Lund *4*).

1636 *The Repentant Thief* pretends to have found stolen cow. He upbraids the owner for not guarding her better. [K416].
*Wesselski *Mönchslatein* 119 No. C; *Mensa Philosophica* No. 52. — Finnish *7;* Lithuanian (*1635) *8;* Russian: Afanasiev (*1545) *6.*

1638* *Why It Is not a Sin for a Gypsy to Steal.* Helpful at crucifixion. [A1674.1].
Lithuanian *1.*

1639* *King Enriches Clothier.* He prescribes certain clothing for an occasion: thus enriches friendly clothier.
Finnish *9.*

LUCKY ACCIDENTS

1640 *The Brave Tailor.* Seven with one stroke. While fleeing defeats the enemy (the sign-post on his arm). Kills wild-boar. Also incidents belonging to the stupid ogre and the clever man; cf. Types 1000ff.

I. *Boastful Fly-Killer.* The tailor kills seven flies and puts an inscription on his girdle, »Seven with one stroke».

II. *Lucky Successes.* He is put to various tests of his prowess: squeezing the stone, etc. See Types 1051, 1052, 1060, 1061, 1062, 1063, 1082, 1085, 1115.

III. *Lucky Hunter.* At the order of the king (a) he kills two giants by striking one from ambush and thus bringing about a fight in which they slay one another; (b) he tricks a unicorn into running his horn into a tree; (c) he drives a wild boar into a church and captures him.

IV. *The Wedding.* (a) He is married to the princess but soon betrays his calling by asking for thread. (b) Soldiers are sent to take him but he intimidates them with his boasting.

V. *At War.* In war when his horse runs away he grasps a cross from the graveyard (a tree) and waves it so that the enemy flee in terror.

Motifs:

I. J115.4. Clever tailor. K1951.1. Boastful fly-killer: »seven at a blow». A tailor who has killed seven flies writes on a placard: »Seven at a blow.» He is received as a great warrior.

II. K1112. Bending the tree. Hero bends tree over but when he catches breath the tree shoots him to the sky. K71. Deceptive contest in carrying a tree: riding. K62. Contest in squeezing water from a stone. K63. Contest in biting a stone. The ogre bites a stone; the man a nut. K18.3. Throwing contest: bird substituted for stone. The ogre throws a stone; the hero a bird which flies out of sight. K18.2. Throwing contest: golden club on the cloud. Trickster shows the ogre the club he has thrown. (Really only a bright spot on the cloud.) K72. Deceptive contest in carrying a horse. The ogre carries it on his back and soon tires; the man carries it between his legs (rides). K61. Contest in pushing hole in tree: hole prepared beforehand. K525.1. Substituted object left in bed while intended victim escapes.

III. K1082. Ogres (large animals, sharp-elbowed women) duped into fighting each other. K771. Unicorn tricked into running horn into tree. K731. Wildboar captured in church.

IV. H38.2.1. Tailor married to princess betrays self by calling for needle and thread. K1951.3. Sham-warrior intimidates soldiers with his boasting.

V. K1951.2. Runaway cavalry-hero.

*BP I 148ff. (Grimm No. 20); **Bødker »The Brave Tailor in Danish Tradition» *Thompson Festschrift* 1 ff.; *Wisser Zs. f. Vksk. XXII 166ff.; *Anderson *Novelline* No. 56; Coffin *9;* Espinosa III 222ff. — Finnish *60;* Finnish-Swedish *2;* Estonian *13;* Livonian *1;* Lithuanian *54;* Lappish *1;* Swedish *23* (Uppsala *6,* Liungman *2,* misc. *15*); Norwegian *9,* Solheim *1;* Danish: Grundtvig No. 94; Icelandic *8;* Irish *277,* Jackson FL XLVII 292, Beal X 3f. No. 44; English *1;* French *19;* Spanish *1;* Dutch *2;* Flemish *11,* Witteryck p. 281 *12;* German *40* (Archive *37,* Merk. 104; Henssen Jül. No. 457, Henssen Volk No. 246); Austrian: Haiding No. 62; Italian *5* (Tuscan 1640 a, b, [303] *3,* Trieste: Pinguentini No. 10, Sicilian *1,* Gonzenbach No. 41); Rumanian *2;* Hungarian *8;* Czech: Tille Soupis I 268ff. *17;* Slovenian *11;* Serbocroatian *23;* Russian: Andrejev *Ukraine* 11, Afanasiev *20;* Greek *12,* Hahn Nos. 16, 18; Turkish: Eberhard-Boratav No. 162, 199 IV, 351 IV, 365, cf. 317 *44;* Berber: Laoust No. 82; Iran: Christensen *Iran* No. 8; India *25;* Indonesian: DeVries No. 301. — English-American: Baughman *4;* Spanish-American: Rael Nos. 337, 338, 341 (U.S.), Hansen (Chile) *1,* (Dominican Republic) *3*, (Puerto Rico) *2;* Cape Verde Islands: Parsons MAFLS XV (1) 117; West Indies (Negro) *14;* American Indian: Thompson C Coll II 430 ff. — African *1*, *Atlantis* III 25.

1641 *Doctor Know-All.* The stolen horse. The stolen money (»That is one of them»). The covered dish (»Ah, poor crab that I am»). Often joined with the story of the sawed pulpit; cf. Types 1810C*, 1825C.

I. *The Sham-Doctor.* A peasant named Crab (Cricket, Rat) buys the clothes of a doctor and calls himself Doctor Know-All.

II. *Betrayal of the Theft.* He is employed to detect a theft and is first feasted. At the entrance of the first servant (or at the end of the first day) he remarks, »That is the first one (second, third)». The servants confess.

III. *The Covered Dish.* As a test of his powers he is to tell what is in a covered dish (crabs): in despair he says, »Poor Crab!»

IV. *The Stolen Horse.* (a) By giving a purgative he unwittingly assists in the discovery of a stolen horse or (b) takes the owner to the horse that he has previously hidden.

Motifs:

I. K1956. Sham wise man.

II. N611.1. Criminal accidentally detected: »that is the first» — sham wise man. N611.2. Criminal accidentally detected: »That is the first» — sleepy woman counting her yawns. Robber hearing her flees.

III. N688. What is in the dish: »Poor Crab».

IV. K1956.1. Sham wise man gives a purgative and helps find a lost horse. K1956.2. Sham wise man hides something and is rewarded for finding it.

*BP II 412—413; *Anderson in Taucsher *Volksmärchen* 181; Pauli (ed. Bolte) Nos. 791, 818; Coffin *8*. — Finnish *97;* Finnish-Swedish *18;* Estonian *9;* Livonian *2;* Lithuanian *73;* Lappish *3;* Swedish *26* (Uppsala *6*, Stockholm *1*, Göteborg *1*, Liungman *1*, misc. *17*); Norwegian *15*, Solheim *1;* Icelandic *5;* Irish *86*, Jackson XLVII 292, Beal V 222, X 182ff., XVIII 89ff.; French *28;* Spanish *1;* Catalan: cf. Amades No. 365; Dutch *2;* Flemish *9*, Witteryck p. 303 *11;* Walloon (*1641A, cf. *1641B) *2;* German *23* (Archive *22*, Henssen Volk No. 245); Italian *3* (Tuscan [904] *1*, Sicilian *2*); Hungarian *5*, Dégh No. 46, Berze Nagy (1641 I*) *2;* Czech: Tille Soupis I 259, 266 *11;* Slovenian *6;* Serbocroatian *5;* Russian: Andrejev *Ukraine 11*, Afanasiev *28;* Greek *6*, Loukatos No. 26; Turkish: Eberhard-Boratav No. 311 *19;* Berber: Laoust No. 78; India *30;* Indonesian: Coster-Wijsman 29ff. Nos. 6, 7, DeVries No. 302; Chinese: Eberhard FFC CXX 243ff. No. 190, FFC CXXVIII 206ff. No. 120. — English-American: Baughman *1;* Spanish-American: Rael Nos. 13—15, (302) (U.S.), Hansen (Argentina) *1*, (Dominican Republic) *4*, (Puerto Rico) *1;* West Indies (Negro) *20;* American Negro (Michigan): *Dorson No. 20, Harris *Friends* 24 No. 3.

1641A *Sham Physician Pretends to Diagnose Entirely from Urinanalysis.* Really from observation and inference from trifles [K1955.2]. Cf. Type 1739.
 *Chauvin VIII 106 No. 81; *Pierre Faifeu* No. 20; *Nouvelles Récréations* No. 59; *Cent Nouvelles Nouvelles* Nos. 20, 21.

1641B *Physician in Spite of Himslef.* Because of wife's foolish report that her husband is a famous doctor he is commanded to cure the queen [H916.1.1]. She laughs at his foolishness and dislodges the fish bone (breaks the abscess) [N641].
 *Bolte Zs. f. Vksk. XXVI 89 n. 1; Wesselski *Mönchslatein* 19 No. 13, *Theorie* 163; Crane *Vitry* 231f. No. 237; Herbert III 19. — French *5;* Walloon (1552*) *1;* Italian: (Tuscan [319] *1*); Japanese: Ikeda (H916.1.1).

1641C *Charcoal-burner Latin.* Peasant accidentally pronounces some words sounding like Latin. He thus gets a reputation for learning. Becomes priest (or wins princess). [K1961.1.2]. Cf. Types 1628, 1825B.
 *BP III 116. — Swedish (GS 1629) *7;* Catalan: Amades No. 2041.

1641A* *The X-Ray Machine.* A doctor takes an X-ray machine to a new town and promises to diagnose everything. Magistrate's wife comes for examination. He tells her she is going to have a baby. She and her husband argue about whether child will be boy or girl. She returns to doctor who, after putting her under X-Ray, says child's legs are crossed, thus making it impossible to determine the sex.
 Spanish-American: Hansen (Cuba) *1.*

1641B* *Who Stole from the Church?* — Thieves.
 Spanish (1550*B) *1;* Spanish-American: Hansen (1550E) (Argentina) *1.*

1641C* *Do Not Postpone till Tomorrow what You Can Do Today.* Farmer follows lawyer's advice and saves hay. Lawyer credited with great wisdom.
 Walloon (*1594) *1.*

1642 *The Good Bargain.* The fool throws money to the frogs. Sells butter to sign-post and meat to the dogs. Makes the princess laugh.
 I. *Money to the Frogs.* The numskull throws money to the frogs so that they can count it.
 II. *Selling to Dogs.* (a) He sells meat to dogs, (b) butter to a sign-post.
 III. *Making the Princess Laugh.* He complains of his losses to the king and makes the princess laugh. She is offered him as a wife. Cf. Types 571—574.
 IV. *Strokes Shared.* When he does not want to marry the princess, the king tells him to return later for his reward; see Type 1610.
 V. *The Borrowed Coat.* When, on the Jew's complaint, the hero is summoned before the king, he borrows the Jew's coat and then discredits the Jew's testimony when the latter says that the hero is wearing his coat.
 Motifs:
 I. J1851.1.1. Numskull throws money to frogs so that they can count it. J1851.1.2. Oil sold to iguana. Treasure found.
 II. J1852. Goods sold to animals. J1853. Goods sold to object. J1853.1. Fool sells goods to a statue. He is told not to sell to talkative people. The statue is the only one he can find who is not talkative.

III. H341. Suitor test: Making princess laugh. Sadfaced princess has never laughed.
IV. K187. The boy promises the soldier what the king has promised to give him. The soldier receives a beating in place of the boy.
V. J1151.2. Witness claims the borrowed coat: discredited.
*BP I 59 (Grimm No. 7); Espinosa Cuentos III 147, 191ff., 253ff.; Wesselski *Hodscha Nasreddin* II 211, No. 426; Coffin *5*. — Finnish *82;* Finnish-Swedish *4;* Estonian *23;* Livonian *3;* Lithuanian *12;* Swedish *23* (Uppsala *5*, Stockholm *1*, Lund *1*, Liungman *4*, misc. *12*); Irish *2;* Spanish *2*, (*1693) *1;* Walloon *1;* German *19;* Austrian: Haiding No. 25; Italian *6* (Pentamerone I No. 4, Tuscan 1642, cf. 1006b, 1013b *3*, Trieste: Pinguentini No. 15, Sicilian *1*); Hungarian *6;* Rumanian *5;* Czech: Tille Soupis I 423ff., II (2) 422—424 (Part 7) *8;* Slovenian *1;* Serbocroatian *4;* Russian: Andrejev (1789*) *5;* Greek *20;* Turkish: Eberhard-Boratav 333 III, cf. 327 *23;* Chinese: Eberhard FFC CXX 272, FFC CXXVIII 227f. No. 135. — Spanish-American: Rael Nos. 358, 359 (U.S.), Hansen (Puerto Rico) *12;* West Indies (Negro) *2*. — Oceanic (Philippine): Fansler MAFLS XII 352.

1642A *The Borrowed Coat.* (1642 V without the rest of 1642.) [J1151.2].
*BP I 65. — Estonian (*1789) *3;* Lithuanian (*1642A) *12;* Russian: Andrejev (*847) *4*. — Literary Treatments: Chauvin VI 126 No. 280; Rotunda (J1151.2); India (J1151.2).

1643 *The Broken Image.* The fool sells his cow to a crucifix [J1853.1.1]. He knocks it to pieces because it will not pay him. He finds a treasure inside [N510].
*Anderson in Tauscher *Volksmärchen* 187; *BP I 60f. (Grimm No. 7); *Chauvin VIII 94; Espinosa *Cuentos* III 191ff.; Wesselski *Hodscha Nasreddin* II 211 No. 426; Liungman SSF III 451; Anderson *Novelline* No. 39. — Livonian (1642) *3;* Swedish (Uppsala) *4;* Irish *8;* French *15;* Spanish *1;* Dutch *1;* Flemish (1642*) *2;* Walloon (*1696B) *1;* German *11* (Archive *8*, Henssen Volk No. 250, Plenzat (1642) *2*); Italian (Tuscan 1006 b, [1222] *2*, Sicilian *3*, Gonzenbach No. 37); Hungarian: Berze Nagy (1646*) *4;* Slovenian *5;* Serbocroatian *8;* Czech: Tille Soupis I 414ff. *37;* Russian: Afanasiev *11;* Turkish: Eberhard-Boratav No. 323 *18;* India (1643A Ind) *5*. — Spanish-American: Hansen (Puerto Rico) *1*. — For Finnish, Finnish-Swedish and Estonian see Type 1642. — Literary Treatments: Cf. Wienert FFC LVI 80 (ET 459), 138 (ST 430).

1643* *Pot Full of Meat Set Out.* Bird with jewel in mouth lets the jewel fall down by the pot.
Rumanian (1706*) *1*.

1644 (formerly 1645*) *The Early Pupil.* The innkeeper hears from the baron that education makes one rich, and he immediately goes to school. The teacher tells him that he has come too late. The innkeeper comes a little earlier each day until one morning in the twilight he finds a purse full of gold. [N633]. Cf. Type 1381E.

Livonian (1645') *3;* Lithuanian (1665*) *3;* German: Wisser *Plattdeutsche Märchen* II 800; Hungarian: Berze Nagy (1645**) *5;* Slovenian *1;* Serbocroatian *2;* Russian: Andrejev (1665*) *1.* — French Canadian.

1645 *The Treasure at Home.* A man dreams that if he goes to a distant city he will find treasure on a certain bridge. Finding no treasure, he tells his dream to a man who says that he too has dreamed of treasure at certain place. He describes the place, which is the first man's home. When the latter returns home he finds the treasure. [N531.1]. Cf. Type 834.

**Bolte Zs. f. Vksk. XIX (1909) 290—98; *Wesselski *Mönchslatein* 120 No. 101; *Hauffen Zs. f. Vksk. X 432; Feilberg *Ordbog* III 235a, IV 62b s.v. »bro»; *DeCock RTP XV 294; Coffin *1.* — Lithuanian (3636); Swedish *2* (Uppsala *1,* misc. *1*); Icelandic *1;* Scottish *7;* Irish *309,* Beal VII 75, XVII 222; Welsh: T. Gwynn Jones *Welsh Folklore and Folk Customs* (1929) 92; English *3;* French *5;* Spanish *1;* Dutch *3;* German *7;* Czech: Tille Soupis II (1) 234—238 *9;* Hungarian: Berze Nagy (557*) *1;* Greek (1645*) *1;* Turkish: Eberhard-Boratav No. 133 *2;* Japanese: Ikeda. — Literary Treatments: Chauvin VI 94 No. 258; Basset RTP XXV 86.

1645A *Dream of Treasure Bought.* Treasure has been seen by man's soul absent in sleep in form of a fly (or bubble). The purchaser of the dream finds the treasure. [N531.3]. Cf. Type 840.

Lithuanian: Balys No. 3520; Persian: Lorimer *Persian Tales* 311 No. 49; Japanese: Ikeda (840A). Cf. Spanish-American: Hansen (1648**B) (Chile) *1.*

1645B *Dream of Marking the Treasure.* A man dreams that he finds treasure and that he marks the spot with his excrements. Only the latter part of the dream is true. [X31].

*Wesselski *Arlotto* II 267 No. 216, *Hodscha Nasreddin* I 278 No. 314; Pauli (ed. Bolte) Nos. 789, 846. — Lithuanian: Balys *Legends* No. 788f.; Czech: Tille Soupis II (2) 427 *3;* Greek: (816*) *2;* Palestine: Schmidt-Kahle II No. 105. — Brazil: Camara Cascudo p. 56. — Literary Treatments: Rotunda (X31).

1645* changed to 1644.

1645A* *Priest Points out Treasure.* The owner of store finds clerk lying unconscious one morning. When he is revived he tells of having seen a priest who told him about treasure buried beneath orange tree. The owner dismisses the clerk and digs around the tree. He finds treasure. (Sometimes priest is phantom.)
Spanish-American: Hansen (**1648AC) (Chile) *2.*

1645B* *God will Care for all.* A peasant imitates the idle rich and says, »God will care for all.» His neighbor borrows his ass and accidentally finds hidden money but is caught in the pit. The ass carries the gold to his master.
Greek *3,* Kretschmer No. 36.

1646 *The Lucky Blow.* (a) A man in anger or by accident knocks off the king's crown or turban. A poison snake is found in the crown and the king thinks the man has saved him. [N656]. (b) A man is angered by the

king, pushes the king or drags him out of the palace into the courtyard to beat him. The roof of the palace collapses onto the spot where the king was standing and the king thinks the man has saved him. [N688.1].
India 6.

1650 *The Three Lucky Brothers.* Their inheritances: a cock, a scythe, a cat. The fortunate sales.

I. *The Inheritances.* (a) The eldest brother inherits a cock, the second a scythe (see Type 1202), the youngest a cat (see Type 1651); or (b) they inherit a millstone, a musical instrument, and a reel.

II. *Luck.* (a) They reach countries where these objects or animals are unknown, and sell them for a fortune [N411]; or (b) the eldest brother lets the millstone fall on robbers who are counting their money (see Type 1653); (c) the second brother calls together wolves with his musical instrument (see Type 1652); (d) the third threatens to draw the lake together with his reel (see Type 1045).

*BP II 69 (Grimm No. 70) for I a; II a; *Delarue-Félice *Haute-Bretagne* 270ff. — Finnish *140;* Finnish-Swedish *6;* Estonian *3;* Livonian *2;* Lithuanian *19;* Irish *28*, Beal III 445f.; French *26;* Catalan: Amades Nos. 373, 410; Flemish *7;* German *3;* Hungarian *1;* Czech: Tille Soupis I 489f. *4;* Slovenian *8;* Serbocroatian *2;* Russian: Andrejev *1;* Greek *3*, Dawkins *Kyriakides Volume* 150f., Loukatos No. 28; India *9*. — Franco-American (Canada) *3;* Spanish-American: Hansen (Dominican Republic) *1;* West Indies (Negro) *1*.

1651 *Whittington's Cat.* In a land where cats are unknown, he sells it for a fortune. Cf. Types 1281, 1650.

I. *He Gets the Cat.* (a) The hero is left a cat as his only inheritance [N411.1.1] (see Type 1650); or (b) he earns or finds four coins which he tests by throwing them into a stream: only one floats; the rest are counterfeit [J1931]. With this he buys a cat.

II. *Sale of the Cat.* He takes his cat to a mouse-infested land where cats are unknown [F708.1] and sells it for a fortune [N411.1].

*Anderson in Tauscher *Volksmärchen* 173; *BP II 69ff. (Grimm No. 70). — Finnish *61;* Finnish-Swedish *4;* Estonian *6;* Livonian *1* (cf. 1281); Lithuanian *10;* Swedish *6* (Uppsala *2*, misc. *4*); Norwegian *6;* Icelandic *1;* Scottish *5*, Campbell-McKay No. 23, (Cape Breton): Leach in *Thompson Festschrift* 51 No. 9; Irish *20*, Beal X 3f. No. 6, XV 165ff.; English *2;* Catalan: Amades No. 373; Dutch *1;* German *2* (Archive *1*, Henssen Volk No. 247); Italian: Calvino No. 173, Sicilian *2*, Gonzenbach No. 76; Hungarian *3;* Serbocroatian *2;* Russian: Afanasiev *3;* Greek *4*, Loukatos No. 28; Turkish: Eberhard-Boratav No. 45, 256 IV, 295 IV *4;* India *1;* Indonesian: DeVries No. 305. — Franco-American (Canada) *3;* Spanish-American: Hansen (Dominican Republic) *1;* West Indies (Negro) *1*.

1651A *Fortune in Salt.* A merchant's son sells salt in a saltless land for a fortune [N411.4].

Estonian (1651*) *2;* Russian: Afanasiev (1651*) *7;* Greek (1651* with Type 611) *3;* India *1.*

1652 *The Wolves in the Stable.* The youth plays music, entices them out, and gets them to dancing. Receives much money from the man who has let them out. [K443.5]. Cf. Type 1650.

Finnish *34;* Estonian *1,* (cf. also 2002*) *5;* Russian: Andrejev *Ukraine 3;* Greek *1.*

1653 *The Robbers under the Tree.* Object falls on robbers from a tree. They flee and leave money. [K335.1.1]. Cf. Types 1650, 1875.

*Anderson in Tauscher *Volksmärchen* 173; *Anderson *Novelline* Nos. 39, 103, 104; *BP I 520 (Grimm No. 59); Espinosa III 191ff.; Coffin *12.* — Finnish *69;* Estonian *22;* Lappish *4;* Swedish *12* (Uppsala *3,* Liungman *4,* misc. *5);* Norwegian: Solheim *1;* Danish: Grundtvig No. 105; Irish *259,* Beal VII 197f. No. 2, X 175; English *4;* French *29;* Spanish *1,* Espinosa III 19f. No. 84; Catalan: Amades No. 364; Flemish *16;* Walloon *1;* German: Archive *18,* Plenzat *1;* Sorb: Nedo No. 32 b; Czech: Tille Soupis I 413, 421ff.; Slovenian *7;* Serbocroatian *13;* Turkish: Eberhard-Boratav No. 351 III, 357 IV; India *9;* Indonesian: DeVries No. 306; Japanese *1.* — Franco-American *19* (Canada *15,* Louisiana *3,* Missouri *1*); English-American: Baughman *3;* Spanish-American: Hansen (Cuba) *3,* (Dominican Republic) *2,* (Puerto Rico) *6;* Cape Verde Islands: Parsons MAFLS XV (1) 194; West Indies (Negro) *11.*

1653A *Guarding the Door.* [K1413]. Man and wife in the tree. They let the door fall. The frightened robbers flee and leave their treasure. [K335.1.1.1]. Cf. Type 1009.

*Anderson *Novelline* Nos. 103, 116. — Finnish-Swedish *2* (also 1653*); Livonian *1;* Lithuanian *4;* Swedish (Lund) *1;* Scottish *2, More W. H. Tales* No. 9; Spanish *1;* Catalan: Amades No. 456; Dutch *9;* Walloon (*1696B, *1703A) *2;* German *8;* Hungarian *7,* Dégh No. 39; Czech: Tille Soupis I 413 *1;* Slovenian *3;* Russian: Andrejev; Turkish: Eberhard-Boratav Nos. 323 IV, 324, 333 III, 351 III, 351 IV *13.*

1653B *The Brothers in the Tree.* The foolish brother lets the door (or corpse) fall. [K335.1.1.1, K335.1.2.1]. Cf. Type 326B*.

*Anderson *Novelline* Nos. 39, 104. — Finnish-Swedish *12;* Livonian *2;* Lithuanian *60;* Swedish (Uppsala) *4;* Norwegian (1654) *2,* Solheim *1;* Spanish *1;* German *7;* Italian (Tuscan 1006 a, b, 1013 b, c, 1539 b *5);* Czech: Tille Soupis I 421ff. *16;* Slovenian *1;* Serbocroatian *10;* Russian: Andrejev *3,* Andrejev *Ukraine 11;* Greek *14, Laographia* VI 492, Argenti-Rose I 532, Megas *Paramythia* No. 40, Hahn No. 34; Turkish: Eberhard-Boratav Nos. 323 IV, 324. — West Indies (Negro) Jamaica: Beckwith MAFLS XVII 283; American Indian: Thompson *C Coll* II 396, 407, 420ff.

1653C *Robbers Scared by a Millstone.* As the wronged robber exclaims to his fellows, »Thunder upon you», the fool drops the millstone.

Lithuanian *3;* Slovenian *3.*

1653D *The Hide Dropped from the Tree.* Cowhide dropped from the tree frightens away robbers who leave their wealth. [K335.1.1.2]. Cf. 1535 III e, 1650.
India *11.*

1653E *The Entrails Dropped from the Tree.* A fool carries animal entrails up into the tree. Below him rests a prince and his entourage. The fool drops the entrails on the prince, who flees with his followers, leaving behind all his goods, which the fool appropriates.
India *5.*

1653F *Numskull Talks to Himself and Frightens Robbers Away* [N612].
*Wesselski *Hodscha Nasreddin* II 211 No. 428, *215 No. 446; Italian (Sicilian *1541 *2*, *1653C *3*); Serbocroatian *3;* India: *Thompson-Balys (N612).

1653* (See Type 1654.)

1653A* *Pretended Corpse at Practice Funeral.* The priest sees the pretense and kills the pretender.
Greek (1844*) *3.*

1654 (formerly 1653*, 1654**) *The Robbers in the Death Chamber.* When a man comes to another to demand payment of a debt, the latter feigns death. The creditor keeps watch over the corpse. Robbers come to divide their money. The creditor and the feigned dead man divide the robber's money between them. [K335.1.2.2].
Wesselski *Märchen* 429. — Finnish-Swedish (1653*) *1;* Estonian *15* (1654*); Lithuanian (1654*, *1654A) *41;* Spanish (1532) *1,* (1654*) *1,* (1716*) *3;* Italian (Sicilian *1653 *1,* 1654 *2,* Gonzenbach No. 37); Hungarian: Berze Nagy 1643* *8;* Czech: Tille (Soupis I 358ff.) *7;* Slovenian *1;* Serbocroatian *24,* Istrian No. 61; Russian: Afanasiev (1654*) *9;* Greek (1527*) *5;* Turkish: Eberhard-Boratav No. 353 *9;* Palestine: Schmidt-Kahle No. 28; Aramaic: Bergsträsser No. 8; India *6.* — Spanish-American (U.S.): Rael No. 312.

1654* *Precious Cod.* Two brothers catch a cod out of whose mouth silver and gold runs.
Lappish *1;* Slovenian *1.*

1654** changed to 1654.

1655 *The Profitable Exchange.* The eaten grain and the cock as damages. Cf. Type 170.
  I. *Profitable Exchanges.* (a) The hero has only a grain of corn; this is eaten by a cock and he gets the cock as damages [K251.1]. (b) Likewise when the hog eats the cock, and (c) the ox eats the hog.
  II. *The Princess Won.* (a) He exchanges his ox for an old woman's corpse (see Types 1536, 1537) and makes it appear that the princess has murdered her. (b) She marries him in order to avoid scandal [K1383].
  III. *Denouement.* (a) He has a son by her who surpasses him in cunning, or (b) the princess is stolen from him and a dog substituted [K1223.1].
  R. Th. Christiansen Beal III 108ff., IV 96; *BP II 201; *Anderson *Novelline* Nos. 105—107; Coffin *1.* — Lithuanian *10;* Norwegian (1655)

4; Irish *11,* Jackson FL XLVII 292, Beal IV cf. 96; French *35;* Spanish *1;* Catalan: Amades No. 384; Dutch *1;* Walloon (1655A) *1;* Italian *8* (Tuscan *4,* Sicilian *4*); Hungarian *1,* Berze Nagy (1647*) *4;* Serbocroatian *2;* Turkish: Eberhard-Boratav No. 19, cf. No. 35 *14;* India *3;* Chinese: Eberhard FFC CXX No. 30, CXXVIII No. 19. — Franco-American (Canada) *12,* (Missouri) *2;* Spanish-American: Rael No. 47 (U.S.), Hansen (Chile) *1,* (Cuba) *1;* West Indies (Negro) *6,* *Jamaica: Beckwith MAFLS XVII 262 No. 63; American Indian (Zuni): Boas JAFL XXXV 76 ff. No. 4. — African *12.*

1656 (formerly 2403) *How the Jews Were Drawn from Heaven.* Someone cries: »Clothes are being auctioned off in hell.» [X611].

Finnish (2003* *2;* Estonian (2003*) *4;* Livonian (2003*) *1;* Lithuanian (1868*) *2;* Swedish (Stockholm) *3;* English *1;* Dutch *3;* Slovenian *2;* Russian: Andrejev (2003*). — English-American: Baughman *2.*

1660 *The Poor Man in Court.* He has a stone in his purse to throw at the judge if he is sentenced. The judge thinks that he has money to use as a bribe and acquits him. [K1705].

*Wesselski *Hodscha Nasreddin* I 253 No. 171. — Estonian (1660*) *1;* Livonian (1660*) *1;* Lithuanian *4;* Catalan: Amades No. 1639; Hungarian: Berze Nagy (926*) *1;* Czech: Tille Soupis II (2) 438f. *1;* Serbocroatian *1,* Istrian No. 66; Russian: Azadowsky *Russkaya Skazka* No. 30, Afanasiev *11;* Turkish: Eberhard-Boratav No. 296.

1661 *The Triple Tax.* A poet is given by the king the right to demand a coin from the first hunchback he meets, from the first man of a certain name, and the first man of a certain city. He sees a hunchback and demands the coin. A quarrel arises in which it appears that the hunchback also has the required name and residence. With each revelation the poet demands a new coin. [N635].

*Pauli (ed. Bolte) No. 285; *Wesselski *Hodscha Nasreddin* II 194 No. 382; *Basset *1001 Contes* I 521. — Icelandic *1.* — Literary Treatments: Chauvin IX 19 No. 5.

1663 *Dividing Five Eggs Equally between Two Men and one Woman.* Three to the woman and one to each of the men. Men already have two (testicles). [J1249.1].

*Fischer-Bolte 207. — German: Bolte *Montanus* No. 14, p. 595; Palestine: Schmidt-Kahle II 155; Ukraine: Hnatjuk II 407; cf. Serbocroatian *2.*

1666* *The Fool's Prayer.* The clever brothers work, the foolish brother only prays; finally he acquires all the property.
Lithuanian *2.*

1670* *How the Soldier became General.* When he is to keep guard he goes to bathe. The king comes and the soldier takes his place naked. The king invites him to come

naked to the castle. He asks which of the women want him for a husband. A general's daughter. The soldier is promoted to be general. [N625].
Estonian 2; Russian: Andrejev.

1671* *To Buy an Island.* A drunk man goes to the king and wants to buy an island (city) [X812].
Livonian 1; Serbocroatian 2.

1672* changed to 1699.

1673* *The Blind, the Lame, and the Deaf as Witnesses in Court* [X141]. Cf. Type 1698.
Livonian 1; Serbocroatian 2.

1674* *Anticipatory whipping.* A schoolmaster whips his pupils to keep them from wrongdoing. He does not wait until after the deed is done. [J2175.1].
*Wesselski *Hodscha Nasreddin* II 231 No. 499. — Serbocroatian 2.

THE STUPID MAN

1675 *The Ox (Ass) as Mayor.* The peasant has his ox study. The man who is to teach the ox [K491] slaughters it and tells the peasant that it has gone to the city and become a merchant (mayor). The peasant goes to visit him, meets a man who is named Peter Ox (or the like) and greets him. He acknowledges the acquaintance and inherits money. [J1882.2].
*BP I 59; *Bolte Zs. f. Vksk. VII 93ff.; Köhler-Bolte I 491. — Finnish *11*; Finnish-Swedish *1*; Estonian *7*; Lithuanian *9*; Swedish *7* (Uppsala *2*, Stockholm *2*, Lund *1*, misc. *2*); Norwegian *3*; Danish: MS DFS; Irish *2*; Dutch *1*; Flemish *2*; German *15* (Archive 13, Meckl. No. 117, Henssen Volk No. 248); Hungarian: Dégh No. 47; Slovenian *1*; Serbocroatian *7*; Russian: Andrejev *1*; Greek *1*; India *4*.—Franco-American (Canada) *6*. — Literary Treatment: Chauvin VII 170.

1675* *A Mayor Chosen by a Footrace.* Contestants must make their way across a marsh. A calf walks across and is the victor.
Walloon (*1675A) 2.

1676 *Joker Posing as Ghost Punished by Victim.* Supposed ghost betrays himself by speaking or whistling. [N384.10, N384.11]. Cf. Type 1532.
Estonian (FFC XXV 115 No. 14) *7*; Finnish-Swedish (FFC VI 35) *1*; Lithuanian (3443) *7*, (3443A) *6*; French (942*) *11*; Dutch (924*B) *4*, (cf. 942*A) *6*; Walloon (*1711) *1*; German: Henssen *Volk Erzählt* 90 No. 64. — U.S.: Randolph *Talking Turtle* p. 32; Franco-American *8*.

1676A »*Big 'Fraid and Little 'Fraid.*» A man decides to frighten another (or his son or servant). He dresses in a sheet; his pet monkey puts on a sheet and follows him. The person who is doing the scaring hears his intendad victim say, »Run Big 'Fraid, run; Little 'Fraid'll get you.» The scarer sees the monkey in the sheet, runs home. [K1682.1]. Cf. Type 1791.
Canada, England, U.S., Wales: *Baughman (K1682.1) *10*. — American Negro (Michigan): Dorson No. 151. — Cf. Spanish-American: Hansen (**367) (Puerto Rico) *1*.

1676B *Clothing Caught in Graveyard.* Man thinks that something terrifying is holding him and dies of fright. [J2625, N384.2; cf. N384 and its subdivisions.]

Cf. Finnish *6;* Swedish (Uppsala *6*); Dutch (943*) *2;* Catalan: Amades Nos. 516, 2102; Slovenian *1;* Irish, English, Anglo-American: Baughman (N384.2) *11.* — Spanish-American: Hansen (**1677) (Puerto Rico) *1.* — Italian Novella: Rotunda (J2625).

1676C *Voices from Graveyard.* People mistake them for ghosts and flee in terror. Cf. Type 1532.
Finnish *20.*

1676* *The Foolish Peasant Studies Medicine.* The doctor has him eat his excrements.
Flemish *4;* Hungarian: Berze Nagy (1693*) *2.* — French-Canadian (1676**) *2;* Spanish-American: Hansen (**1709B) (Chile) *1.*

1677 (formerly 1677*) *The General Hatches out an Egg.* The page induces the general to take his place in sitting on the eggs. Then he calls the king to look. [K1253]. Cf. Types 1218, 1319.
Anderson *Novelline* Nos. 59, 108. — Estonian *2;* Catalan: Amades No. 377; Italian (Tuscan 1642, [1226] *2*); Hungarian: Berze Nagy (1411*) *3;* Serbocroatian *1;* Greek *4.*

1678 *The Boy who had Never Seen a Woman.* When he sees a girl and asks his father what it is, the father tells him it is Satan. Asked what he most likes, he says »The Satans». [T371].
*BP IV 358, 381, V 250; *Christiansen *Maal og Minne* (1954) 45ff.; *Liebrecht *Zur Volkskunde* 441; DeCock *Studien* 76; Coffin *1.* — Livonian (1676*) *1;* Lithuanian *5;* Swedish *2;* Norwegian (1676**) *1;* Irish *28,* Jackson FL XLVII 292; French *6;* Flemish (1614*) *2;* Slovenian *1;* Serbocroatian *1;* Greek *1;* Japanese *1.* — Franco-American *6* (Canada *4,* Louisiana *2*); English-American: Baughman *3;* American Negro (Michigan): Dorson No. 157. — Literary Treatments: Chauvin III 105 No. 16; Crane *Vitry* 169 No. 82.

1678* *In Passion Play the Christ Says,* »*I Am Thirsty*»; the thief on the left speaks up, »I too.» [J2041.1].
Pauli (ed. Bolte) No. 864. — Hungarian: Berze Nagy (1626**) *1.*

1679* *Conscript cannot Tell Left from right:* sergeant renames his feet »Bread» and »Meat».
Walloon *1.*

1680 *The Man Seeking a Midwife* accidentally kills the dog, drowns the midwife, and kills the child [J2661.2].
Finnish *48;* Estonian *4;* Lithuanian *2;* German *1;* Russian: Andrejev *1;* Greek *1.*

1681 *The Boy's Disasters.* Foolishly kills his horse, throws his axe into the lake to kill a duck. Undresses to recover axe. Clothes stolen. Goes into barrel of tar to hide. In tar and feathers. [J2661.4]. Cf. Types 1383, 1690*.
Estonian *8;* Livonian *1;* Lithuanian *12;* Rumanian (1660) *1;* Serbo-

croatian *13;* Russian: Andrejev *1;* Greek *2.* — Franco-American *2* (Canada *1,* Louisiana *1*); Spanish-American: Hansen (Argentina) *1.*

1681A *Fool Prepares for the Wedding (Funeral).* On the way back from city he gives the meat to dogs, puts the pots on the stumps so that they will not freeze, spreads butter on the road so that it will be easier for the horses, puts salt in the river so that the horse will drink better, etc. [J1850]. When the horse does not drink he kills it, throws cups and spoons on the road so that they will clatter, etc. He arrives home with nothing. Cf. Types 1291B, 1386, 1642.

Lithuanian (*1677) *27;* Spanish (1693*) *1;* Hungarian: Berze Nagy (1689*) *1;* Russian: Afanasiev (*1681 I, II) *15.*

1681B *Fool as Custodian of Home and Animals.* Bathes grandmother in boiling water; kills baby, etc. (Same as Types 1012, 1013 but with stupid boy instead of rascal.)

Motifs: J2125. Guarding the chickens from the fox. Numskull ties their beaks and weighs them down in the river with stones. J2465.3. Feeding the child. Fool feeds it steaming food and kills it. J2173.5. Fool kills chickens by throwing them off a balcony against a stone. Kites carry them off. K1461. Caring for the child: child killed. K1462. Washing the grandmother — in boiling water.

*BP III 337ff.; *Wesselski *Hodscha Nasreddin* II 212 No. 431; *Espinosa III 67—70. — Greek: Hahn I 219 No. 34, Dawkins *Modern Greek in Asia Minor* 405; Rumanian *5;* Serbocroatian *6;* India *8.* — Spanish-American: Hansen (**1704) (Cuba) *1,* (Puerto Rico) *23,* (1706) (Dominican Republic) *4,* (Puerto Rico) *3,* (*1692) (Puerto Rico) *5,* (*1693) (Argentina) *1,* (Chile) *1,* (Puerto Rico) *2.*

1681* *Foolish Man Builds Aircastles.* (Cf. Type 1430.)
Finnish *2;* Greek *2.*

1681A* *Take Care of the Stopper.* The tar-maker bids his son to take care of the stopper, i.e., to see that it does not get loose from the barrel. The son puts the stopper into his pocket, and all the tar runs out. [K1414]. Cf. Types 1387, 1653A, 1696.
Lithuanian (*1706) *2.*

1682 *The Groom Teaches his Horse to Live without Food.* It dies. [J1914].
Estonian (1682*) *3;* Livonian (1682*) *1;* Lithuanian *2;* Swedish *6* (Uppsala *2,* Stockholm *1,* misc. *3*); English *1;* Spanish (836*C, hen leaves home) *2;* Catalan: Amades No. 2035; Walloon *1;* German *2;* Italian *2* (Tuscan *1,* Trieste: Pinguentini No. 110); Slovenian *4;* Serbocroatian *1;* Russian: Andrejev; Greek *1.* — Spanish-American: Rael No. 417 (U.S.). — Literary Treatments: Aesop: Halm No. 176.

1682* *Pitch on Tail of Ass* to hasten its pace, and on its master to enable him to keep up.
Walloon (*1686A) *1.*

1683* *A Peasant Counts Pebbles.* A soldier extorts a fine from him according to a number of pebbles he has; the peasant calls out fewer than he counts and makes merry, thinking that he had fooled the soldier.
Russian: Afanasiev *2.*

1684A* *The Long Night.* Fool locked in dark room made to believe that it is continuous night [J2332]. Cf. Type 1337C.
Spanish (*1684) *2;* Italian Novella: Rotunda (J2332).

1684B* *The Fool's Wedding.* Fool repeats questions of wedding ceremony, with absurd results. Cf. Type 1820.
Danish (1684*) *3.*

1685 *The Foolish Bridegroom.* Dog »Parsley» in the soup [J2462.1]. Clearing out the room (throws out the stove) [J2465.5]. To »throw good eyes» at the bride (throws ox-eyes and sheep-eyes on the plate) [J2462.2]. Cf. Type 1006. She flees. The he-goat in the bride's place in bed [K1223.1].

*BP I 311 (Grimm No. 32); Pauli (ed. Bolte) No. 762; *Anderson *Novelline* Nos. 109,110; Köhler-Bolte I 65; Espinosa Cuentos III 190ff. — Finnish *43;* Finnish-Swedish *11;* Estonian *69;* Livonian *2;* Lithuanian *5,* (*1006A) *6,* (*1686) *4;* Lappish (1685*) *2;* Swedish *72* (Uppsala *35,* Stockholm *15,* Göteborg *1,* Lund *5,* Liungman *5,* misc. *11);* Norwegian *21,* Solheim *5;* Irish *49,* Beal VI 94ff.; French *7;* Spanish *1;* Catalan: Amades cf. Nos. 440, 1339; Flemish *3;* German *17* (Archive *13,* Henssen Jül. Nos. 464, 467, Volk No. 191, Meckl. No. 106); Italian *2* (Tuscan 1013 b *1,* Trieste: Pinguentini No. 26); Hungarian *9,* Berze Nagy (1018**) *1;* Czech: Tille Soupis I 420ff., cf. II (2) 87ff. *4;* Slovenian *5;* Serbocroatian *12;* Russian: Andrejev (*1012 II) *5,* (*1538 I) *10,* Afanasiev (1685A) *8,* (1685B) *8;* Greek *1;* India *5.* — Franco-American (Canada) *6,* (Louisiana) *3;* Spanish-American: Hansen (Puerto Rico) *2,* (*1686 A B C) (Dominican Republic) *2,* (Argentina) *1.*

1685A *The Stupid Son-in-Law.* Cf. 1000—1000 A Ind (j), 1332, 1691.

I. *The »Night-Blind» Fool.* (a) As night approaches, he grabs the tail of a bull so that it will lead him home. He is dragged through the mire and brambles. (b) He thinks a cat is eating from his plate and strikes at it. It is his mother-in-law serving him food. Cf. Type 1456. (c) He stumbles into mother-in-law's bed; pretends he has come to beg her pardon. (d) Devises tricks so in-laws will lead him to house.

II. *Foraging for Food.* (a) Being hungry during the night, he is let down into the house by a companion (Cf. Type 1775). He is mistaken for a spirit. The priest is called, but the fool pours flour on the priest. The priest runs out of the house and is beaten by the watchers who think the priest a spirit. [J1786.4]. (b) The fool gets covered with honey and wool and thinks he has become a sheep [J2012]. He hides in a sheepfold and is taken by sheep thieves, or he comes out and frightens them away.
India *14.*

1685A* *Fool Sets up a Trap Beside his own House.* An old woman or his own mother falls into it. (Sequel: Type 1537.)
Russian: Afanasiev (1685 I*) *7;* Serbocroatian.

1686* *The Price of Wood.* Foolish boy to receive »sleeping together» from girl as price of wood. She serves him coffee and he thinks he has received his pay.
Finnish *2;* Estonian *1;* Swedish (Stockholm) *1.* — French-Canadian.

1686** *Numskull Believes he is Married to a Man.* In the bride's bed lies a man while the

bride lies under the bed. When bridegroom enters he thinks the bride has been transformed.
Swedish (GS 1686) *9* (Uppsala *1*, Lund *6*, Liungman *1*); Danish: *Danske Studier* (1912) p. 186.

1687 (formerly 1687*) *The Forgotten Word.* The fool as he falls into hole forgets the word which he is to remember [D2004.5]. Through the advice of a passer-by he recalls it. Cf. Type 1240.
Coffin *2.* — Finnish *2;* Estonian *2;* Livonian *1;* Lithuanian *4;* Swedish *5* (Uppsala *1*, Liungman *2*, misc. *2*); Flemish *7;* German: Jahn *Volkssagen aus Pommern und Rügen* No. 649, Merkens *Was sich das Volk Erzählt* I 124; Hungarian: Berze Nagy (1206*) *1;* Russian: Andrejev *3;* India *6;* Japanese (frequent). — French-Canadian *2;* Spanish-American: Hansen (**1691AB) (Cuba) *1* (Puero Rico) *1*.

1688 *The Servant to Improve on the Master's Statements.* The wooer makes boasts to the girl and the servant always doubles the master's boast. Finally the master says, »I have poor eyesight.» — The servant, »You don't see at all.» (Or the master coughs and apologizes; the servant says that he coughs all night.) [J2464].
*Pauli (ed. Bolte) No. 221; *Bolte Zs. f. Vksk. IX 88 No. 46. — Finnish *1;* Finnish-Swedish (1685*) *1;* Estonian (1688*) *2;* Lithuanian *3;* Swedish *5* (Stockholm *1*, misc. *4*); Norwegian (1677**) *5;* French *3;* Spanish (*1688A) *1;* German Archive *4;* Rumanian: Schullerus FFC LXXVIII 97 No. 7; Serbocroatian *9*, Istrian No. 64; Greek *2.* — Franco-American (Canada) *1;* Spanish-American: Rael Nos. 67, 427, 428 (U.S.), Hansen (**1688 A—G) (Puerto Rico) *2*, (Dominican Republic) *1*, (Argentina) *1*, (Cuba) *3*. — Literary Treatment: *Scala Celi* No. 688.

1688A* *Jealous Suitors.* Two suitors go courting the same girl; maim each other's horses.
Lithuanian (*1693) *5*.

1688B* *Two Match-Makers.* Both spend the night at the girl's home. The poor suitor effects the disgrace of his rich rival. Or: the match-maker, taking fancy to the girl, brings about the downfall of the suitor he is sponsoring, and himself woos the girl.
Lithuanian (*1692) *5*.

1688C* *Prince Plans to go Courting.* Leaves orders to be wakened early. Overconscientious servant.
Spanish (1707*) *1*.

1689 »*Thank God they Weren't Peaches.*» The man plans to take peaches as a present to the king. He is persuaded rather to take figs. They are green and the king has them thrown in his face. He is thankful that they weren't peaches. [J2563].
*Wesselski *Hodscha Nasreddin* I 227 No. 71; Clouston *Tales* II 407ff. — Swedish *8* (Uppsala *3*, misc. *5*); Catalan: Amades No. 583; Hungarian (Honti 1535 I) *4.* — English-American: Baughman *1;* Spanish-American: Hansen (1535) (Puerto Rico) *1;* Portuguese-American (Brazil): Camara Cascudo p. 45; West Indies (Negro) *1.* — Literary Treatments: Rotunda (J2563).

1689A *Two Presents to the King:* the beet and the horse. Raparius. A farmer takes an extraordinary beet as present to the king and receives a large reward. His companion is eager for a reward and leads a handsome steed to the palace. The king rewards him with the beet. [J2415.1]. Cf. Type 1610.

*Pauli (ed. Bolte) No. 798; BP III 188ff.; *Gaster Exempla 190 No. 25; Köhler-Bolte I 136. — Finnish *1;* England: Baughman (J2415.1); Italian Novella: Rotunda (J2415.1), (Tuscan 555C *1*); Hungarian: Honti (1535 I), Berze Nagy (905) *5;* Greek (928**) *1;* India *1*. — Spanish-American: Hansen (836**N) (Puerto Rico) *1;* West Indies: Flowers 490.

1684B *The Recipe is Saved.* A hawk steals the fool's meat; he is grateful that the recipe remains. [J2562].

*Wesselski *Hodscha Nasreddin* II 231 No. 498. — French: RTP IV 484f.; German: Zender 103 No. 121; Greek: Hallegarten *Rhodos* p. 218; Arab: Littmann (1955) No. 33; Chinese: Eberhard FFC CXX 275 No. 1 (XII).

1689* *Fool Appointed to Fictitious Office Boasts of it.* »Administrador de la yesca.» [J2331.2].
Spanish *1;* Greek (1705*) *1*.

1690* *The Fool Gets Everything Backward* and loses everything [J2650].
Livonian *2;* Serbocroatian *1;* Russian (*1696B) *2,* (1720*) *9*.

1691 »*Don't Eat too Greedily.*» The fool starves himself at table since a cat steps on his foot and he thinks his companion is giving him hint to stop eating. He later hunts food in house and gets into trouble. [J2541]. Cf. Type 1775.

Lithuanian (*1691, *1691A) *19;* Spanish (1363*A) *1;* Walloon: Marischal *Volkserzählgut in der Gegend von Malmedy* (1942) 127; German (well known); Italian (Tuscan [1220] *1*); Hungarian: Honti (1410), Berze Nagy (1616*) *5;* Serbocroatian *1;* Chinese: Eberhard FFC CXX 286; India *4;* English-American (Ozarks): Randolph *Who Blowed up the Church House* 16, 185; Spanish-American: Hansen (1363*A) (Dominican Republic) *3,* (Puerto Rico) *3.*

1691A *Hungry Suitor Brings Food from Home* so as not to eat too greedily.
Lithuanian *8;* Greek (1696**) *2.*

1691B *The Suitor who Does not Know how to Behave at Table.* Skins the peas, etc.
Lithuanian (*1696A) *8;* Russian: Andrejev (1696*B) *2.* Cf. Type 1339C.

1691A* *One Preacher Enough.* A fool starts to preach while the preacher is delivering his sermon: beaten [J2131.1.1].
Spanish (*1690) *1.*

1691B* *Too Much Truth.* A man asked to tell the truth says that his host, his hostess, and the cat have but three eyes between them. He is driven off for his truth telling. [J551.4].
Pauli (ed. Bolte) No. 3. — German (well known); Ukraine: Zs. f. Vksk. IX 408.

1692 *The Stupid Thief.* Cf. Type 177. A fool accompanies a group of thieves, who send him into the house while they wait outside.
　I. *Following Directions Literally.* (a) Told to bring out something »heavy» (i.e., valuable), he brings out a heavy mortar, or the like [J2461.1.7]. (b) Told to bring out something shining (i.e., gold, etc.), he brings out a mirror, or the like [J2461.1.7.1].
　II. *Awakening the Inhabitants.* (a) Being unable to carry his load of loot outside, he awakens one of the men of the house to help him [J2136.5.6]. (b) Seeing a drum or musical instrument in the house, he plays upon it loudly [J2136.5.7]. (c) He decides to cook himself some food while in the house. One of the sleeping inhabitants groans in his sleep [J2136.5.5]. The fool thinks he is asking for food and pours boiling hot food on his hand or in his mouth.
　India *18.*

1692A* *Drunkard's Pig is Stolen* and a dog put in its place. Drunkard tells it not to pretend to be a dog.
　Walloon (*1691) *2.*

1693 *The Literal Fool — the Burning of Lanka. Pots broken; fire set.*
　A fool (or trickster) follows instructions literally and disastrously. He is taken before a judge or rajah, but is freed. (a) An oil seller tells a fool (or a trickster), who has spilled a little oil, that spilt oil brings good luck. The fool breaks all the oil seller's pots, allowing the oil to run out [J2214.7]. (b) An oil seller tells the fool, »Show me something I never saw.» The fool breaks all the oil pots. (c) A woman asks, »What was the burning of Lanka like?» He sets fire to her house to demonstrate [J2062.3]. (d) A betel seller refuses to give him any betel, saying »Rub your lips against those of the next person you see.» He kisses his daughter.
　India *8.*

1694 *The Company to Sing like the Leader.* When his foot is caught in a wheel, his companions keep repeating his call for help as a song. [J2417.1]. Cf. Type 1832M*.
　*Christensen DF XLVII 189 No. 14, 194 No. 19. — Lithuanian (*1694) *3;* French *8;* Russian: Andrejev (1825*D) *2;* India *1;* Chinese: Eberhard FFC CXX 285 No. 64, FFC CXXVIII 244f. No. 148.

1695 *The Fool Spoils the Work of the Shoemaker, the Tailor, and the Smith.* Makes shoes for animals as well for men since he expects a cold winter. [J1873.1, W111.5.9].
　Finnish *18;* Estonian *13;* Livonian (1694') *1;* Lithuanian *1,* (*2446) *8;* Greek *1;* German: Henssen Volk No. 186; Serbocroatian *1.*

1696 »*What Should I have Said (Done)?*» The mother teaches the boy (the man his wife) what he should say (do) in this or that circumstance. He uses the words in the most impossible cases and is always punished. [J2461]. Cf. Types 1681A, 1681B.
　Motifs: J2461. What should I have done (said)? J2461.1.1. Literal

numskull drags jar (bacon) on string. He has sent a pig home alone. Told that he should have led it by a string. J2461.1.2. Literal numskull is gay at a fire. He has wept at a wedding and been told to be gay. J2461.1.3. Literal numskull throws water on roasting pig. Told that he should have thrown water in the fire when the house was burnt. J2461.1.5. Literal fool strangles the hawk. On last trip he has lost the gloves and has been told that he should have put them in his bosom. He puts the hawk inside his shirt. J2461.1.6. Literal fool carries the harrow in his hand. He has killed a sparrow by his stupidity and has been told that he should have carried it in his hand. J2461.2. Literal following of instructions about greetings. Numskull gives wrong greeting and is told how to give the correct one. When he tries it, however, the conditions are wrong. J2461.2.1. Literal numskull kisses a pig. Told that he should have kissed the old woman. J2129.4. Fool sticks needle in haywagon. He has been told to stick it in his sleeve. It is lost.

*BP I 315, 524f., III 145; *M. de Meyer *Vlaamsche Sprookjesthemas* 164ff., 172ff.; *Taylor JAFL XLVI 78 No. 1696; **Haavio FFC LXXXVIII 94ff.; *Wesselski *Hodscha Nasreddin* I 251f. No. 169; Pauli (ed. Bolte) No. 762; Coffin *4*. — Finnish *106;* Finnish-Swedish *10;* Estonian *30;* Livonian (1696) *1;* Lithuanian *34;* Lappish *1;* Swedish *57* (Uppsala *14*, Stockholm *3*, Göteborg *3*, Lund *7*, Liungman *6*, misc. *25*); Danish: Grundtvig No. 109A; Icelandic *4;* Irish *115*, Jackson FL XLVII 292, Beal III 44ff.; English *1;* French *59;* Spanish *3*, (1703*, 1705*) *2*, Espinosa Cuentos III 147, 191ff.; Catalan: Amades Nos. 376, 411; Dutch (1696B) *2;* Flemish A *26*, B *13*, Witteryck p. 293 *7*, 296 *9;* Walloon *1;* German *19* (Archive *15*, Merk. 97, 132; Henssen Jül. No. 469; Henssen Volk No. 249); Italian *3* (Tuscan [1227], [1228] *2*, Sicilian *1*); Rumanian *7;* Hungarian *10*, Berze Nagy *4*, (1684*) *9;* Czech: Tille Soupis I 414ff. *30;* Slovenian *12;* Serbocroatian *14;* Russian: Andrejev (1696A) *8;* Greek *8*, Argenti-Rose II 597ff., Hahn No. 3, Loukatos No. 29; Turkish: Eberhard-Boratav No. 328 *16;* Tatar: Radloff VII 1ff. No. 1; India *7;* Indonesian: Coster-Wijsman 54ff., Nos. 79—82; Japanese *20;* Chinese: Eberhard FFC CXX 290f. No. 6 (III), FFC CXXVIII 278f. No. 152. — Franco-American (Canada) *16*, (Missouri) *1*; (Louisiana) *2;* English-American: Baughman *3;* Spanish-American: Hansen (Argentina) *1*, (Chile) *1*, (Puerto Rico) *2*, (*1690): (Puerto Rico) *3*, (*1703 A—D): (Puerto Rico) *3*, (*1703 A—D): (Argentina) *2;* West Indies (Negro) *8;* American Indian: Thompson *C Coll* II 417ff., (Wyandot): Barbeau GS Can XI 224 No. 68. — African *3*.

1696A* *Bread for Stone.* Priest tells villagers that if anyone throws a stone at them they should throw bread back. When an old woman throws a small piece of stone at her son, he throws a large loaf of bread at her and almost kills her. [J2461].
    Hungarian: Berze Nagy (1698*) *1;* cf. India (J2461.9).

1696B* *Say Only Round* (= *good*) *Words.* Fool names only round objects. [J2489]. Cf. Type 1437.
    Greek (1696*) *5*.

1697 »*We Three; For Money.*» Three travelers in a foreign land know only three expressions in the foreign language. By the use of these they get themselves accused of murder. [C495.2.2]. Cf. Type 360.
*BP II 561 (Grimm No. 120); *Wesselski *Mönchslatein* 37; Coffin *3*. — Finnish *14;* Finnish-Swedish *3;* Estonian *2;* Lithuanian *6;* Irish *86,* Beal I 298ff.; English *1;* French *21;* Spanish: Espinosa Cuentos I No. 29; Dutch *8;* Flemish *8,* Witteryck p. 289 *7;* German *3* (Archive *2,* Henssen Volk No. 128); Austrian: Haiding No. 469; Italian (Tuscan 360 *1*); Rumanian *2;* Czech: Tille Soupis II (2) 445f. *3;* Slovenian *1;* Serbo-croatian *2;* Russian: Andrejev *1,* Andrejev *Ukraine 5;* India *3*. — Franco-American (Canada) *3,* (Louisiana) *3;* English-American: Baughman *1;* Spanish-American: Rael No. 69 (U.S.), Hansen (Dominican Republic) *1,* (Puerto Rico) *1;* West Indies (Negro) *1;* American Negro (Michigan): *Dorson No. 150.

1698 *Deaf Persons and their Foolish Answers* [X111].
**Aarne *Schwänke über schwerhörige Menschen* (FFC XX). — Finnish (2008*) *10;* Estonian (2008*) *10;* Swedish *15* (Uppsala *13,* Lund *1,* misc. *1*); Danish; Icelandic *5;* Irish *56,* Beal VII 93; English (1698B) *1;* French *11;* Spanish *2;* Catalan: Amades No. 447; Flemish (1931*) *1,* (2007*) *1;* German *34* (Archive *31,* Meckl. No. 119, Henssen Volk Nos. 253, 254); Italian (Trieste: Pinguentini No. 90); Rumanian (1701*) *3;* Slovenian *5;* Russian: Andrejev (2008*) *1;* Greek: Weinreich *Kyriakides Volume* 692ff. — Franco-American (Canada) *20,* (Louisiana) *1;* English-American *6;* Spanish-American: Rael No. 72 (U.S.); Portuguese-American (Brazil): Camara Cascudo *Revista de Dialectologia y Tradiciones Populares* IX (1953) 251ff. — African *1*.

1698A *Search for the Lost Animal.* A inquires for his lost animal. — B talks about his work and makes a gesture. — A follows the directions of the gesture and happens to find the animals. He returns and offers an injured animal to B in thanks. B thinks he is blamed for injuring the animals. Dispute. Taken to deaf judge. [X111.1].
Aarne FFC XX 16ff. — Lappish (1980) *3;* Greek: Kretschmer No. 17; Turkish: Eberhard-Boratav No. 320 *2;* Berber: Laoust No. 35; Palestine: Schmidt-Kahle 95; India *2*.

1698B *Travelers Ask the Way.* Travelers ask their direction. Peasant thinks they want to buy oxen. — Peasant's wife arrives; thinks they say her food is too salty. — Daughter-in-law and father-in-law misunderstand each others. [X111.2].
Aarne *ibid* 28ff. — India *4*.

1698C *Two Persons Believe Each Other Deaf.* A trickster tells each of two persons before they meet that the other is deaf and must be shouted at. A great shouting takes place, and each thinks the other out of his wits. [X111.3].
Aarne *ibid.* 29ff.; Wesselski *Gonnella* 118 No. 16. — Lithuanian *2;*

Swedish (Stockholm) *8;* English *1;* Italian (Sicilian *3,* Gonzenbach No. 75); Serbocroatian *2;* Greek (2008B*); India: Dracott *Simla Village Tales* p. 166.

1698D *The Wedding Invitation.* Lord: Good Morning, Peter. — Peasant: I come from Bingen. — L. What is the hog worth? — P. Two weeks from next Sunday (the wedding). — L. Shall I come to the wedding? — P. Three and a half gulden. [X111.4].
Aarne *ibid.* 35ff.; Pauli (ed. Bolte) No. 719. — Lithuanian *4;* Swedish (Uppsala) *3;* India (X111.7); Indonesian: DeVries No. 296. — Spanish-American: Hansen (Cuba) *4*, (Puerto Rico) *2*, (Chile) *1*.

1698E *The Old Man on the Bridge.* Lord: Good day, Caspar. — Caspar: I am making a reel. — L. Good day, Caspar. — C. It is worth four pence. — L. Good day, Caspar. — C. Yes, my Lord, whenever you wish. [X111.5].
Aarne *ibid.* 38ff.; Pauli (ed. Bolte) No. 719. — English-American: Baughman *1*.

1698F *The Deaf Man and the Proud Nobleman.* The nobleman amuses himself at the expense of the deaf man. Finally — Nobleman: I wish you a thousand gallows and ropes around your neck. — Peasant: My Lord, I wish you twice as many. [X111.6].
Aarne *ibid.* 39ff.

1698G *Misunderstood Words Lead to Comic Results.* In some the people are not really deaf but fail to catch a word (Aarne *ibid.* 40ff.), in some they are deaf (Aarne *ibid.* 76).
Danish: MS. DFS.

1698H *The Man with the Bird in the Tree.* A traveler asks the way and the man in the tree keeps telling him about the bird he has caught. (The questions and answers often rhyme.) [X111.8].
Aarne *ibid.* 41ff.

1698I *Visiting the Sick.* A deaf man plans a conversation with expected answers as he goes to visit the sick. The answers turn out otherwise. — A. How are you? — B. I am dead. — A. Thank God! What have you eaten? — B. Poison, I think. — A. I hope it agrees with you. [X111.9].
Aarne *ibid.* 50ff.; India *1*.

1698J »*Good Day,*» — »*A Woodchopper.*» The workman answers the traveler's courtesies with remarks about his work [X111.10]. Cf. Type 1698H.
Aarne FFC XX 51ff., cf. 67ff., 72, 75 (Types 12, 13, 16, 18). — Swedish *22* (Uppsala *9*, Stockholm *1*, Göteborg *1*, Lund *1*); Norwegian: Solheim *2;* Spanish *1*. — Spanish-American: Hansen (Cuba) *3*.

1698K *The Buyer and the Deaf Seller* [X111.11].
Aarne FFC XX 60ff., 69ff. (Types 11, 14, 15). — Swedish *7* (Uppsala *5*, Stockholm *1*, Lund *1*); English *1*.

1698L *The Deaf Parson.* The youth answers unintelligibly but is praised nevertheless [X111.12].
Finnish (1742**) *4.*

1698M *The Deaf Bishop.* The drunken priest says, »In the morning I take a drink of rum and afterwards four or five little drinks.» [X111.13].
Finnish (1846*) *2;* Estonian (1846*) *1;* Lappish (1980) *3.*

1698N *Pretended Deafness.* People pretend deafness, but when proper question is asked they betray themselves. (Or playing deaf when a service is asked.) Cf. Motif K231.15.
French *4;* French Canadian (1702*).

1698A* *To Strike Finger.* The master orders his servant boy to strike off his finger that has become dirty. He sticks his finger through a hole. The boy strikes with a burning piece of wood. The master sticks the finger into his mouth.
Finnish *1;* Estonian *5;* Livonian *2;* Swedish *30* (Uppsala *2,* Stockholm *27,* Lund *1).*

1698B* *Refusal to Eat.* The servant thinks to deceive his master by refusing to eat [J2064].
Flemish (1698*) *1.*

1698C* *Serfs Congratulate their Master.* The delegate, coming into the room, slips and falls: »The devil take you!» The serfs waiting outside the door think he is congratulating. All cry in one voice: »You and your family». [J1845].
Lithuanian (*1708) *3;* Rumanian: Schullerus FFC LXXVIII 98 No. 14; Hungarian: Berze Nagy (1295*) *4.*

1699 *Misunderstanding Because of Ignorance of a Foreign Language* [J2496.2]. Cf. Type 1322.
Livonian (1672') *1;* German: Zs. f. Vksk. XLI 173ff.; French: Zs. f. Vksk. XLI 173ff.; Hungarian: Berze Nagy (1333*) *1;* Slovenian *1;* Serbocroatian *1;* Russian: Andrejev (*2008 II) *5;* India *1.* — Spanish-American: Hansen (**1687 A—C) (Puerto Rico) *6,* (Chile) *1.* — U.S. Negro (Michigan): Dorson p. 79. — Africa (Gold Coast): Barker and Sinclair No. 18.

1699A *Criminal Confesses because of Misunderstanding of a Dialect* [N275.2].
BP II 412, 534. — Slovenian.

1699B *The Changed Order.* New recruits learn answers to questions in foreign language. Order changed in asking brings confusion. [J1741.3.1].
Cf. Lithuanian (*2420) *2;* Spanish (*1697A) *1;* England: Baughman (J1741.3.1); Russian: Afanasiev (*2140) *1.*

1699* *The Coffin-Maker.* Since the coffin is too short, the corpse's feet are cut off. The priest: »On the last day he will rise». One of the coffin-makers: »Did I say that?» [X422].
Estonian *3.*

1700 »*I don't Know.*» The man thinks that »I don't know» is a person's name [J2496].
Finnish *3;* Estonian *2;* Serbocroatian *1;* Greek *1.* — American Negro (Michigan): *Dorson No. 47. — African (Gold Coast): Barker and Sinclair 95 No. 18.

1701 *Echo Answers.* Only end of question comes back. Misunderstanding. [K1887.1].
    Finnish *3;* Swedish (GS 1336) *17* (Uppsala *8*, Stockholm *1*, misc. *8*); Spanish: Espinosa Jr. No. 172; Chinese: Graham (K1887.1).

1702 *Anecdotes about Stutterers.* One stutterer thinks the other is imitating him.
    Slovenian; Russian: Andrejev (*2008 I) *1.*

1702A* *A Laconic Conversation.* Two taciturn peasants understand each other through half words.
    Russian: Afanasiev (*2050) *1.*

1702B* *Bridal Couple will not Talk to Each Other,* each trying to hide his stuttering.
    Serbocroatian *1.*

1702C* *Dialogue of the Simpleton and the Jester.* »Is the fair large?» »I did not measure it.» »Is it strong?» »I did not test it,» etc. One of the speakers confuses the other, saying that he saw a gray bear, hare in a tree, etc.
    Russian: Afanasiev (*2014 II) *6.*

1704 *Anecdotes about Absurdly Stingy Persons.*
    Finnish *17.*

1704* *Soldier Eats with his Saber.* Peasant brings him the manure shovel.
    Rumanian *1.*

1705 *Talking Horse and Dog.* A person is frightened by animals successively replying to his remarks. Example: The man riding the horse and followed by the dog tells the horse to jump over a hole. Horse says, »I will not.» Man turns to dog and says, »Isn't that strange, a horse talking!» The dog says, »Yes, isn't it.» Often the man runs, meeting other animals which answer him, until he falls exhausted. [B210.1, B211.1.1.1*].
    U.S.: Baughman *7.*

1705A* *Drunk Man at the Wedding.* Goes to sleep and never reaches it, though at home he praises the wedding. [X813].
    Livonian *1.*

1705B* *The Bear Taken for St. Martin.* On St. Martin's day the master compels his men to go to the woods to work. They return and tell him that St. Martin is greatly offended at such an outrage and will not permit them to do the work. He goes himself to remonstrate with the saint. Encounters a bear (St. Martin) [J1762.2.1], promises to observe St. Martin's day.
    Lithuanian (*1705) *5;* Russian: Andrejev (*2103B) *1.*

1706* *Thief Frightened by Bagpipe.* [K335.1.5].
    Livonian *2.*

1707 *The Noseless Man.* A man who has lost his nose persuades others that they, too, can see God if they will cut their noses off. They do so, whereupon he scoffs at them. [J758.1.1]. Cf. Types 64, 1203.
    India *5.*

1707* *The Gypsy Boy Receives the Beating* in place of the peasant lad.
    Livonian *1.*

1708* *The Baron Shoots the Pipe out of the Jew's Mouth* [F661.2].
    Livonian *1;* Swedish (Stockholm) *1.*

1709* *The Jews Fear the Sign of the Cross* and are betrayed [V342].
Livonian *1*.

1710 (formerly 1710*) *Boots Sent by Telegraph.* A peasant hangs boots and an accompanying letter on a telegraph wire, expecting them to reach the city. [J1935.1]. (Sometimes the peasant thinks the wrong address has been used.)
*Anderson *Zu Wesselski* 40; Christensen DF XLVII 204 No. 50. — Livonian (1710') *1;* Swedish *3* (Stockholm *1*, Lund *2*); French: well known (Delarue); German: well known (Ranke); Italian (Tuscan [1355] *1*); Slovenian; Greek: Hepding *Laographia* VI 307, Argenti-Rose II 600. — English-American: Baughman (1710*) *1*, (Ozarks): *Randolph *Devil's Pretty Daughter* 195; Spanish-American: Hansen (**1701) (Cuba) *1*, (Puerto Rico) *1*.

1710* changed to 1710.

1711* *A Wood-cutter does not Fear the Dead.* Tricksters leave him with a mock corpse, who begins to breathe. He says that the dead do not breathe, and strikes the man on the head with a hammer. [J2311.12].
Walloon *1*.

1715 *Sleeping Juror Votes on the Wrong Case.* (Various absurd situations.) Cf. Type 1828.
Finnish *98*.

1716* *The Adventures of the Three Brothers.* Two of the brothers are foolish, the third stupid; when they go duck-shooting two miss the birds, the third makes a bad shot; they find three boats, two of which are leaky, the third bottomless; two of the brothers are drowned, the third sinks to the bottom.
Lithuanian (*1700) *9*.

1717* *The Fancy Ailment.* A fine lady explains her ailment in complicated poetic paraphrase. The lady's servant explains briefly in vulgar language.
Spanish (1940*H) *2;* Spanish-American: Hansen (1940*H) *1*.

1718* *God Can't Take a Joke.* A drowning man calls on God for help and as he is apparently escaping denies he was helped. But he falls again: »God, can't you take a joke?«
Finnish *37*.

1720* *The Devil's Son is with his Mother at Night* in his father's place [G303.11.1.1].
Livonian *1*.

JOKES ABOUT PARSONS AND RELIGIOUS ORDERS

Note: Types in the following division (1725—1874) often refer to others than a parson. For a good introduction to jokes on parsons [X410], see Kristensen *Kirketjeneste* and Wesselski *Arlotto*.

1725—1774 The Parson Is Betrayed

1725 *The Foolish Parson in the Trunk.* The clever rascal gets ready to throw the trunk into the water; see Type 1535, incidents III b, c, 1358.

Motifs:

K1574. Trickster as sham magician buys chest containing hidden paramour. K1571. Trickster discovers adultery: food goes to husband instead of to paramour. K1573. Trickster sends his master running after the paramour. K1572. Trickster makes woman believe that her husband is coming to punish her adultery. She confesses.

*BP II 18, 131, III 401 n. 1; Chauvin VI 178. — Finnish *55;* Finnish-Swedish *7;* Estonian *16;* Livonian *1;* Lithuanian *2;* Swedish *28* (Uppsala *10*, Stockholm *3*, Liungman *1*, misc. *4*); Norwegian (1543**) *13*, Solheim *1;* Danish: Grundtvig No. 99; Scottish *1;* Irish *27;* French *1;* Spanish *1;* Dutch *2;* Flemish *2;* German *14;* Italian (Tuscan [1367] *1*, Sicilian *1380 *2*); Rumanian (1380 VII) *6;* Hungarian *4;* Czech: Tille Soupis II (2) 395 *4;* Serbocroatian *3;* Russian (*1360 I) *13*, Azadovsky *Russkaya Skazka* No. 27, Andrejev *Ukraine 21;* Greek *7;* Turkish: Eberhard-Boratav No. 359 *8;* India *3*. — Franco-American (Missouri).

1726* *The Parson Seduces the Servant's Wife.* The latter out of revenge fishes up a golden ring. (Obscene).
Finnish (1726**) *3*.

1726A* *Earrings for Silence.* After seducing priest's wife, peasant demands earrings as price of silence. [K1582.1].
Russian: Andrejev (1726**) *1*.

1727* *Students and Later the Parson with the Amorous Princess.* The Jew under the bed.
Livonian *1*.

1728* *The Parson and his Wife Naked in the Woods.* (Obscene.)
Livonian *1*.

1729A* *The Priest is Invited by the Teacher*, but the teacher's wife and lover have eaten the roast goose.
Rumanian (1778*) *1*.

1730 *The Entrapped Suitors.* (Lai l'épervier). The parson, the sexton, and the churchwarden visit the beautiful woman. The three undressed men are hidden when the husband comes home. The woman invites guests. The three chased off [K1218.1]. Cf. Types 882A*, 1359.

*Bédier *Fabliaux* 454ff., *Wesselski *Morlini* 315 No. 73; *Cosquin *Etudes* 457ff.; Clouston *Tales* II 289ff. — Finnish *111;* Finnish-Swedish *1;* Estonian *18;* Lappish *1;* Swedish *12* (Uppsala *5*, Stockholm *2*, Göteborg *1*, Lund *2*, Liungman *1*, misc. *1*); Scottish *4;* Irish *22*, Beal III 355; French *2;* Spanish *2;* Dutch *1;* Flemish *1;* German *15* (Archive *14*, Henssen Volk No. 262); Rumanian *5;* Hungarian: Honti (1730), Berze Nagy (1726A*B*, 1727A*) *15;* Czech: Tille Soupis II (2) 259ff. *4;* Serbocroatian *5;* Russian: Azadovsky *Russkaya Skazka* Nos. 32, 33, Andrejev (1730 II*) *12;* Greek *10;* Turkish: Eberhard-Boratav No. 249, 268 *4;* India *8*. — Franco-American (Canadian) *1;* Spanish-American: Rael No. 42 (U.S.). — African *3*. — Literary Treatments: Penzer *Ocean* I 33ff., 42ff., 160ff.; Chauvin VI 12 No. 185; von der Hagen *Gesammtabenteuer* III *xxix.

1730A* *Seducer Led into Pigsty.* A gentleman lays snares for a maiden. She entices him into a pigsty and locks him up. [K1218.2].
Finnish-Swedish *1.*

1730B* *Lover Left Outside Naked.*
Greek *2.*

1731 *The Youth and the Pretty Shoes.* By playing upon their desire for the pretty shoes he has stolen [T455.3.2], he betrays the wife, the daughter, and the servant girl of the parson [K1357] and finally the parson himself, who is standing by his side. Healing of the scab; holding the bung of the wine-cask. (Obscene.)

**Spargo FFC XCI 49—53. — Finnish *76;* Finnish-Swedish *1;* Estonian *25;* Livonian *1;* Lithuanian *3;* Danish *2;* English *1;* Flemish *1;* German Archive *6;* Russian: Andrejev (1731, *1731 I) *3.* — U.S. (North Carolina): Boggs JAFL XLVII 309.

1732* changed to 1545.

1733A* *The Servant Ties a Man with his Wife and Daughter in a Field.* (Obscene.)
Finnish (1733**) *3.*

1733B* *Blacksmith Ties Wife and Lover Together* and takes them to the king.
Hungarian (1752*) *1.*

1734* *Whose Cow was Gored.* Eye for eye. A bell-ringer hears a priest preach an eye for an eye, etc. When the priest's cow gores the bell-ringer's cow to death the latter demands the priest's cow in exchange. The priest refuses. But it would have been different if it had been the priest's which was gored.
Swedish (GS 1734) *5* (Göteborg *2,* Liungman *1,* misc. *2*).

1735 »*Who Gives his Own Goods shall Receive it Back Tenfold.*» The parson preaches from this text, and a peasant tests it by giving the parson a cow, which brings all the parson's cows back home with her [K366.1.1]. A quarrel arises over the cows and it is agreed that the man who can say »good morning» to the other first shall keep the cows [K176]. The peasant is the first on the spot and becomes witness to a scene between the parson and his housekeeper. When the parson notices what has happened he lets the peasant keep the cows. — Adapted from Christiansen *Norske Eventyr.*

*BP I 292; *Bédier *Fabliaux*[2] 451f.; *Pauli (ed. Bolte) No. 324. — Finnish *123;* Finnish-Swedish *8;* Estonian *6;* Lithuanian *12;* Lappish *1;* Swedish *40* (Uppsala *15,* Stockholm *5,* Göteborg *2,* Lund *3,* Liungman *2,* misc. *13*); Norwegian *5;* Danish: Kristensen *Kirketjeneste* pp. 169ff.; Icelandic *2;* Irish: Jackson FL XLVII 292; French *4;* Dutch *3;* Flemish *3;* German *29;* Hungarian *3,* (cf. 1690*) *1;* Czech: Tille Soupis II (2) 366f. *6;* Slovenian *2;* Serbocroatian *3;* Russian: Andrejev. — Franco-American: (Canadian) *3,* (Louisiana) *1;* Spanish-American: Rael No. 463 (U.S.).

1735A *The Bribed Boy Sings the Wrong Song.* The sexton steals the priest's cow. The next day the sexton's son sings, »My father stole the priest's cow.» The priest pays the boy to sing in church. But the sexton teaches the boy a new song, »The priest has lain with my mother,» and this is sung in church. [K1631].

Coffin *3.* — Danish: Kristensen *Kirketjeneste* 88ff.; England, U.S.: Baughman (K1631); Spanish: Boggs (*1735A) *1;* Italian (Tuscan [1741ab] *2*); Serbocroatian *1;* West Indies (Negro): Flowers 541f.

1735B *The Recovered Coin.* Man retrieves his coin from offering box with a thread. Curé says »May God repay you!» — »It has returned already.» Irish *2;* English *1;* Walloon (*1735C) *1.*

1736 *The Stingy Parson.* The boys do no mowing the whole day. »May the grass grow up again! May the gold in the purse turn to wasps!» A parson is known for being unusually stingy. He sends his boys to the meadow to mow, and they do nothing. On the way home one of them takes a wallet and puts a wasp-nest in it. He tells the parson that he has found a bag (wallet) with money, and the parson immediately claims it. Finally the boy lets him have it but makes a wish that the money may turn to wasps, and that the hay on the meadow may rise up again. Both things happen. [K1975, K1975.1]. — Adapted from Christiansen *Norske Eventyr.*

Finnish *39;* Finnish-Swedish *5;* Estonian *2;* Lithuanian *5,* (*1633) *3;* Swedish *19* (Uppsala *5,* Stockholm *1,* Göteborg *1,* Lund *7,* misc. *5*); Norwegian: Solheim *8;* Danish: Grundtvig No. 100A; Catalan: Amades No. 406; Dutch *2;* Flemish *3;* German *5;* Rumanian (1736 I) *2;* Russian: Andrejev *3;* India *1;* Japanese: cf. Ikeda *19.* — Franco-American (Canadian) *2.*

1736A *Sword Turns to Wood.* Man to be executed is said to be guilty unless his sword turns to wood. This happens and he is freed. (He has substituted a wooden sword.)

Hdwb. d. Märchens I 114, II 242ff.; Wesselski *Erlesenes* pp. 115ff. — Finnish *4;* German: Zender; Italian (Sicilian 1661 *2*); Czech: Tille Soupis I 129ff. *3;* Greek: Hallgarten *Rhodos* 172; Turkish: Eberhard-Boratav No. 309 *4.*

1737 *The Parson in the Sack to Heaven.* The youth claims to be the Angel Gabriel [K842]. (Dupe not always a parson; sometimes told of animals.) Cf. Types 1525A, 1535 (IV).

*BP II 10ff., 18, III 188, 192, 379, 393; *Anderson *Novelline* No. 111; *Cosquin *Etudes* 392. — Finnish *26;* Estonian *11;* Livonian *3;* Lithuanian (*1535 A) *21;* Lappish *1,* (1737*) *2;* Swedish *6* (Liungman *3,* misc. *3*); Norwegian: Solheim *1;* Irish *6;* French *2;* Spanish *7;* Catalan: Amades No. 374; Dutch *1;* German *3;* Austrian: Haiding No. 74; Italian (Tuscan 950 a, 1525A c—e, g, 1737 a, b *7*); Rumanian *3;* Czech: Tille Soupis II (2) 283ff. *10;* Russian: Afanasiev *5;* Cheremis: Sebeok-Nyerges (K714.2.1); Serbocroatian *2;* Greek *10,* (1737*) *2;* Turkish: Eberhard-Boratav Nos. 314, 344 II, 346, 360, cf. 368 *3;* India (K842); Indonesian: Dixon 191 n. 14, DeVries No. 276, Coster-Wijsman 26 No. 5; Japanese: Ikeda (cf. Type 1535 IV); Korean: Zong in-

Sob 104 No. 56. — Franco-American (Canadian) *1*, (Missouri) *1;* Spanish-American: Rael Nos. 278, 355A (U.S.), Espinosa JAFL XXIV 419ff. (New Mexico), Hansen (**74K) (Chile) *2*, (Cuba) *1*, (Peru) *1*, (Puerto Rico) *4;* West Indies (Negro) *15;* American Negro: Harris *Remus* 111 No. 23, 140 No. 29, *Nights* 177 No. 31, 185 No. 32, (Alabama): Work JAFL XXXII 400; American Indian: Thompson *C Coll* II 419ff. — African: Frobenius *Atlantis* II 220ff., VIII 54f., 175ff. — Philippine: Fansler MAFLS XII 196, 438, 444. — Literary Treatments: Chauvin V 247, No. 147 n. 1.

1738 *The Dream: All Parsons in Hell.* The smith, who is sick, sends for the parson, who at first refuses to come on account of bad weather. When he arrives the smith says that he has dreamed that he went to heaven, where St. Peter would not admit him before he saw a priest. There were no priests in heaven, but all in hell. [X438]. Cf. Type 1860A.

Finnish *11;* Finnish-Swedish *4;* Estonian *3;* Lithuanian (cf. *1847); Swedish *4* (Uppsala *1*, Lund *1*, misc. *2*); Danish: MS DFS; Dutch *1;* German *31* (Archive *29*, Henssen Volk No. 270, Henssen Jül. No. 475; Slovenian *1;* Russian: Andrejev; Greek: Loukatos No. 58. — Franco-American (Canadian) *3;* American Negro (Michigan): Dorson No. 45.

1738A* *What does God Do?* — He sits and wonders why there are no parsons in heaven. [X438, cf. H797.2]. Cf. Types 922, 1833C.
Finnish *4*.

1738B* *The Parson's Dream.* All his parishioners in hell or in a disagreeable position [X438.1].
Lithuanian (*1847) *3;* Flemish (1738**) *4;* French-Canadian *4*.

1738C* *Chalk Marks on Heaven's Stairs.* The parson and sexton may enter heaven if they mark each sin with chalk on the stairs. The parson must return for more chalk. Cf. Type 1848.
Finnish *2*.

1739 *The Parson and the Calf.* A sick parson is made to believe that he will bear a calf. In having his urine examined by a doctor, a cow's is substituted by mistake. (Or he dreams that he has borne a calf.) When a calf comes into the house he thinks that he has borne it. [J2321.1].

*BP I 317 n. 1; Feilberg *Ordbog* s.v. »kalv»; *Wesselski *Bebel* I 232 No. 148; Coffin *1;* Christensen DF L 72ff. — Finnish *64;* Finnish-Swedish *4;* Estonian *16;* Livonian *2;* Lithuanian *13;* Swedish *33* (Uppsala *16*, Stockholm *7*, Lund *3*, Liungman *4*, misc. *3*); Norwegian *6;* Danish: Grundtvig No. 113; Icelandic *1;* Scottish *3;* Irish *9;* English *1;* French *5;* Flemish *1;* German *16;* Italian *3* (Tuscan *2*, Sicilian *1739 *1*); Czech: Tille Soupis II (2) 444f. *5;* Serbocroatian *4;* Russian: Andrejev *6*, Andrejev *Ukraine 11;* Turkish: Eberhard-Boratav No. 367 V *1*. — Franco-American (Canada) *4;* Spanish-American: Rael No. 327 (U.S.). — Literary Treatments: See Motif J2321 with literary references.

1739A* *Man Thinks he has Given Birth to a Child by Letting Wind* [J2321.2].
Italian (Pentamerone II No. 3, Sicilian *1739 *1*); Christensen DF XLVII 228 No. 93.

1739B* *Cat Has Kittens on Bed of a Sick Man.* He thinks his suffering is not in vain, as he has borne kittens.
Walloon *1.*

1740 *Candles on the Crayfish.* The rascal puts burning candles on the backs of the crayfish. The parson and sexton think them the souls of the dead. He robs them meanwhile. [K335.0.5.1].
BP III 388. — Estonian (1740) *6;* Livonian (1740*) *3;* Swedish *5* (Liungman *1,* misc. *4*); English *1;* Austrian: Haiding No. 74; Serbocroatian *2;* Russian: Andrejev; Greek *6.*

1740A *Candles on Goat's Horns.* A goat goes into a church. The villagers think she is sent by saint and light candles on her horns. She sets fire to farms.
Greek (1316*, 1740*) *34.*

1740B *Thieves as Ghosts.* Rascals dress in white and make owner of figtree from which they are stealing believe they are ghosts. He flees.
Spanish (*1532) *1;* Spanish-American: Hansen (1532**A) (Argentina) *1.*

1740* *The Parson's Tithes.* The parson does not demand his tithes but his share of a sum of money that has been found.
Finnish-Swedish *3;* Swedish (Uppsala) *5.*

1741 *The Priest's Guest and the Eaten Chickens.* The servant who has eaten the chickens tells the guest to flee because the priest is going to cut off his ears, and he tells the priest the guest has stolen two chickens [K2137]. The priest runs after him crying, »Give me at least one of them.»
*BP II 129 (Grimm No. 77); *Western Folklore* XIV 162f.; Pauli (ed. Bolte) No. 364; Feilberg *Ordbog* III 118a s.v. »Øre»; Coffin *2;* Wesselski *Hodscha Nasreddin* II 245 No. 543. — Swedish *7* (Stockholm *1,* Göteborg *1,* Lund *3,* Liungman *1,* misc. *1*); Danish: Kristensen *Kirketjeneste* pp. 195ff.; Icelandic *4;* Scottish *1;* Irish *21;* French *10;* Catalan: Amades No. 1336; Dutch *1;* Flemish (1740*) *3;* Italian (Sicilian *1*); Hungarian: Berze Nagy (1389*) *2;* Czech: Tille Soupis II (2) 399f. *3;* Turkish: Eberhard-Boratav No. 359 *8;* India (1741A Ind) *3.* — Literary Treatments: Chauvin VI 179 No. 341.

1741* *The Parson is Dissatisfied with his Share* of the sausage from a horse's intestine.
Finnish *2;* Estonian *4;* Swedish *7* (Uppsala *2,* Liungman *1,* misc. *4*).

1743* *The Promised Gift.* During the sermon the priest demands the gift promised him by a woman at confession; the woman answers that the priest himself admitted often committing such sins.
Lithuanian *1;* Serbocroatian *1;* Russian: Andrejev *1.*

1745 *Three Words at the Grave.* The priest made sick of his bargain. A poor man in return for a steer gets permission from the priest to speak three words at the burial of his enemy, the rich man. Priest: »From the earth are you come.» Man: »Now the steer is dead.» Priest: »In the earth shall you remain.» Man: »Father, do you want the meat?» Priest: »I wish you were in hell!» [K262].
Danish: Kristensen *Kirketjeneste* 139ff., 152ff.

1745* *Parson Sees the Devil.* The parson denies the existence of the devil. The bear-showman lets the bear climb up the pulpit. The parson thinks the bear is the devil. [X425].
Livonian *1;* Russian: Andrejev (*1737 I) *1.*

1746* *Priest Must Bail Out the Boat.* How can boatman return alone with no helper? Boatman: I will put the plug back into the hole.
Finnish *8.*

1750 *The Parson's Stupid Wife.* A mercenary lover makes the parson's wife believe that chickens can be taught to talk [J1882.1]. At her request, he undertakes to hatch out hen's eggs and receives large amounts of corn to feed them. When the chickens hatch, he declares that they sing »The peasant has slept with the parson's wife.» He is allowed to keep the corn [K1271.1.3].
Pauli (ed. Bolte) No. 843. — Finnish-Swedish *1;* Estonian *7;* Swedish (misc.) *1;* Danish: MS. DFS; German *3,* (1778**) *20;* Czech: Tille Soupis II (2) 450 *4;* Russian: Andrejev; Turkish: Eberhard-Boratav No. 368 *10.* — English-American: Baughman *2.*

1750A *Sending a Dog to be Educated.* The servant fools the priest out of a large sum of money for the supposed education of a dog. Later on tells him that he has slain the dog because it enquired: »Does our Rector still keep relations with Barbara?» — »It is well you have slain him — a dog remains a dog». Cf. Type 1675.
*Pauli (ed. Bolte) No. 843. — Lithuanian (*1676) *2;* Danish: Kristensen *Danske Skæmtesagn* (1901) 15; German (well known); Serbocroatian *1.*

1761* *Impostor Hiding in Holy Image Beaten.* [K1971.12].
Penzer V 59 n. 2; Italian (Tuscan [1761] *1*); Italian Novella: Rotunda (K1917.12); Serbocroatian *2;* Jewish: bin Gorion *Born Judas* IV 61, 277; India: *Thompson-Balys (K1917.12).

1775—1799 Parson and Sexton

1775 *The Hungry Parson.* On the hunting trip. Overnight at the peasant's house. In the night the parson hunts the porridge to satisfy his hunger. (The sexton has given him the end of a rope to guide him) [X431]. Cf. Type 1691.
Feilberg *Ordbog* III 187a s.v. »seng». — Finnish *185;* Finnish-Swedish *9;* Estonian *39;* Livonian *6;* Lappish *2;* Swedish *32* (Uppsala *13,* Stockholm *5,* Göteborg *1,* Lund *4,* Liungman *3,* misc. *6*); Norwegian *8;* Danish: Grundtvig No. 100B; Icelandic *5;* French *20;* Spanish *1;* German *15* (Archive *14,* Henssen Volk No. 269); Italian *5* (Tuscan 1000 a, [1220], [1762], [1763] *4,* Sicilian *1*); Hungarian: Honti (1775), Berze Nagy (1616*) *5;* Czech: Tille Soupis I 420ff. *18;* Serbocroatian *3;* Istrian No. 4; Russian: Azadovsky *Russkaya Skazka* No. 12, Andrejev *12;* Greek *3;* Chinese: Graham No. 602 p. 224. — English-American: Baughman *1;* Spanish-American: Rael No. 289 (U.S.); American

Indian: (Micmac) Rand Nos. 57, 69, (Ojibwa): Laidlaw *Ontario Archeological Report*, Reprint (1918).

1775A* *The Parson's Dreams*. An unmarried parson staying overnight wants to visit the peasant's daughter. Has realistic dreams and wanders about in his sleep and gets into embarrassing position.
Icelandic (1729*) *2*.

1776 *The Sexton Falls into the Brewing-Vat*. The parson has illicit relations with the maid. The sexton falls from his hiding place into the brewing-vat. The parson and maid think it is the devil and flee [K1271.1.4]. The sexton gets the beer [K335]. Cf. Type 1360.
Finnish *20;* Finnish-Swedish *5;* Swedish *9* (Uppsala *7*, Stockholm *1*, misc. *1*); Norwegian *2;* Danish: MS. DFS. (E. T. Kr. 1496); Spanish *1;* German *21;* Hungarian *1;* Russian: Andrejev. — Literary Treatment: Rotunda [K1271.1.4.2].

1776* *The Parson, the Sexton, and the Eel*.
Finnish-Swedish *5*.

1776A* *The Tell-tale Lobsters*. A friend brings lobsters to a priest. They are said to turn black if cooked by a maiden, otherwise red. They turn red, and the servant girl charges him with having revealed their affair.
Walloon (*1874) *2*.

1777A* *»I Can't Hear You»*. The rector confesses his sacristan: both are guilty of sins which neither wishes to acknowledge to the other. [X441.1].
Lithuanian (*2451) *1;* Rumanian *1;* Serbocroatian *3*.

1779A* *A Good Rat Poison*. Precentor tells parson he has a good rat poison — poverty and an empty storehouse.
Finnish *4*.

1781 *Sexton's Own Wife Brings her Offering*. The priest grants to the sexton the offerings brought by all women whom the priest has loved. The priest always calls out »Take» when these women offer. The sexton's own wife comes. The priest calls out »Take!» (Cf. Q384.) [K1541].
Wesselski *Bebel* I 185 No. 40. — Finnish *13*.

1785 *The Parson Put to Flight During his Sermon* [X411].
Swedish (Uppsala) *1;* Irish *2;* German *1*. — West Indies (Negro) *2*.

1785A *The Sexton's Dog Steals the Sausage from the Parson's Pocket* [X411.1].
Finnish *60;* Finnish-Swedish *1;* Swedish *11* (Uppsala *2*, Stockholm *3*, Lund *1*, Liungman *2*, misc. *3*); Danish: Kristensen *Kirketjeneste* p. 164; Russian: Andrejev.

1785B *The Sexton Puts a Needle in the Sacramental Bread*. The parson strikes on it with his hands [X411.2]. Cf. Type 1836*.
Finnish *1;* Finnish-Swedish *3;* Estonian *5;* Livonian *1;* Lithuanian *3;* Swedish (Uppsala) *2;* Danish: Kristensen *Kirketjeneste* p. 112; Flemish *1;* German *3*, Henssen Volk No. 282; Russian: Andrejev.

1785C *The Sexton's Wasp-nest*. The parson sits on it and the wasps chase him [X411.3]. Cf. Type 49.

Finnish *3;* Finnish-Swedish (1825**) *1;* Estonian *4;* Swedish *3* (Uppsala *2,* Lund *1*); German: Henssen Volk No. 283; Russian: Andrejev; West Indies (Negro) *1.*

1785* changed to 1804*.

1785** *The Parson is to Command the Ship without Cursing.*
Finnish-Swedish *1.* Cf. Italian (Tuscan [1767] a, b *2).*

1786 *The Parson in the Church on the Ox.* Wants to show how Christ rode to Jerusalem. Rides into the church on an ox. The sexton sticks the ox with a needle. [X414].

Finnish *18;* Finnish-Swedish *1;* Swedish (Uppsala) *2;* German *1;* Russian: Andrejev.

1789* *The Sexton Steals the Parson's Money.* The parson lends him a fur coat when he is summoned to court, but he also keeps this.
Estonian *3* (Cf. Type 1642).

1790 *The Parson and Sexton Steal a Cow.* Dispute over the booty. Summoned to court. In return for the cow and money, the sexton agrees to get them free. Tells the whole story. Then says, »Just then I waked up» [J1155]. They are freed. Cf. Type 1364.

Finnish *48;* Finnish-Swedish *3;* Estonian *7;* Lithuanian *10;* Swedish *2* (Lund *1,* misc. *1*); Danish: Kristensen *Kirketjeneste* pp. 183ff.; German *1;* Hungarian *2;* Serbocroatian *2;* Russian: Andrejev *Ukraine 4.*

1791 *The Sexton Carries the Parson.* Thieves steal a sheep or turnips. The lame parson has himself carried by the sexton. The sexton hears the thieves in the cemetery cracking nuts and thinks it is the devil cracking bones. With the gouty parson on his back he comes upon the thieves who, thinking it is their companion with a sheep, call out, »Is he fat?» The sexton: »Fat or lean, here he is.» [X424].

*BP III 395 (6); Pauli (ed. Bolte) No. 82; Coffin *12.* — Finnish *131;* Finnish-Swedish *7;* Estonian *24;* Lithuanian *3;* Swedish *48* (Uppsala *24,* Stockholm *8,* Göteborg *2,* Lund *7,* Liungman *2,* misc. *5*); Norwegian *3,* Solheim *2;* Danish: Grundtvig No. 167; Scottish *6;* Irish *207;* Beal XVIII 45f. No. 4, 114 No. 10; English *4;* French *12;* Spanish *2;* Dutch *2;* Flemish *6;* German *32* (Archive *30,* Henssen Jül. No. 480, Henssen Volk No. 148); Rumanian *1;* Hungarian *4;* Czech: Tille Soupis II (2) 454f. *4;* Slovenian *4;* Serbocroatian *1;* Russian: Andrejev *1;* India: Thompson-Balys. — Franco-American: Baughman *4;* English-American: Baughman *19;* Spanish-American: Rael No. 65 (U.S.); West Indies (Negro) *3;* American Negro (Michigan): Dorson No. 38. — Literary Treatments: *Scala Celi* No. 547; *Alphabet of Tales* No. 333.

1792 *The Stingy Parson and the Slaughtered Pig.* The stingy parson does not want to give anyone a part of his pig, which he has just slaughtered. The sexton advises him to hang the pig up in the garden overnight so as to make everyone think it has been stolen. The sexton steals it himself. [K343.2.1]. Cf. Type 1831.

Pauli (ed. Bolte) No. 790; Coffin *1;* Taylor MPh XV 226. — Swedish (Uppsala) *2;* Danish: Kristensen *Fra Bindestue og Kolle* II No. 25, *Kirketjeneste* pp. 180ff.; Irish *2;* French *8;* Catalan: Amades No. 1367a; Dutch *1;* Flemish (1792*) *2;* German *32* (Archive *31,* Henssen Volk No. 264); Italian (Tuscan [1566] *1*); Serbocroatian *1.* — English-American: Baughman *4;* Spanish-American: Rael No. 54 (U.S.). — Literary Treatment: A. C. Lee *Decameron* 257—258.

1792A *The Priest's Pig.* A man going on a journey changes clothes on the way with another man. Latter is found drowned, and is buried as the first man. The first man's wife is to be re-married by the priest and is to give the priest a pig as payment. The priest sends his servant at night for the pig, but is attacked in the pigsty by the first husband, who has returned home and been refused admittance by his wife who thinks him a ghost.. Next day all run from him on the way to church, until the priest finally finds out the truth.

Irish.

1800—1849 Other Jokes about Clergy or Religious Orders

1800—1809 Jokes about the Confessional. Cf. Type 818*

1800 *Stealing Only a Small Amount.* Man promises in confession to steal only a small amount. Steals rope with mare on end of it. [K188]. Cf. Type 1630A*.

Coffin *1.* — Finnish *6;* Spanish (1800*A) *2;* French *1;* Spanish-American: Hansen (**1878) (Puerto Rico) *1;* West Indies (Negro): Flowers p. 498.

1804 *Imagined Penance for Imagined Sin.* A penitent confesses that a plan to sin has entered his mind. Priest tells him that the thought is as good as the deed. Assesses four florins as penance. Penitent says that he had only had it in his mind to give the florins; he must take the thought for the deed. [J1551.2].

Monograph in preparation by Fritz Harkort (Kiel); *Pauli (ed. Bolte) No. 298; *Wesselski *Gonnella* 110 No. 10; *Fischer-Bolte 210; French *5;* Italian (Tuscan [1743] a, b *2*); Czech: Tille Soupis II (2) 384f. *2;* Serbocroatian *2.* — Spanish-American: Hansen (1800E) (Cuba) *1.*

1804A *The Priest Administers to a Man Sick with Infectious Disease.* Shows him the Host through the window, and says: »Have hope and imagine you receive it.« The man shows the priest a coin through the window, and repeats the same phrase.

Lithuanian (*1844) *1.*

1804B *Payment With the Clink of Money* [J1172.2]. Cf. Type 1262.
**Harkort (see Type 1804); *Pauli (ed. Bolte) No. 48; *Nouvelles de Sens* No. 9. — Finnish *17;* French (1844*) *3;* Italian Novella: Rotunda (J1172.2); Serbocroatian *1;* India *1;* Indonesian: DeVries's list No. 297.

1804* (formerly 1785*) *The Eel Filled with Sand.* A man receives absolution but must promise the priest a certain weight in eels. They are filled with sand.
Finnish-Sweden (1785*) *3;* Swedish (1785*) *6* (Stockholm *2,* Lund *1,* misc. *3*).

1805 *Confessions of a Pious Woman.* Allegorically tells her sin; repeatedly confesses the sin she committed in her youth, as its remembrance gives her delight (and the like). Cf. Type 1851.
Lithuanian (*1848) *4.*

1805* *The Priest's Children.* After confessional: »All children with curly (red) hair are priest's».
Rumanian (1839*) *2.*

1806 *Will Lunch with Christ.* Priest tells condemned man after confession that he will dine with Christ that evening. The mule that carries him to the scaffold goes very fast and the criminal says, »At this rate I shall lunch with Christ.» [J1261.3].
Spanish (1855*) *1;* Serbocroatian *1.*

1806A* *Priest as Prosecutor.* Two peasants go to confession. Priest questions the first about the death of Christ. He tells his companion that the priest sounds like a lawyer investigating a murder case. They flee for fear of being accused.
Spanish-American: Hansen (**1806) (Puerto Rico) *1.*

1806B* *To Change Places with Priest.* A man condemned to die is not a Catholic and does not want to confess. Several priests talk to him but in vain. Finally a clever priest succeeds in explaining the advantages of dying, hoping to get him to accept religion. The man reflects for moment and says, »Do you want me to change places with you?»
Spanish-American: Hansen (**1858) (Cuba) *1.*

1807 *The Equivocal Confession.* A man makes an equivocal confession to the priest he has robbed, e.g., says that he has saved a man from a bear, (meaning that he stole the priest's furs); asks his confessor for guidance. The priest, misunderstanding the confession, even praises the man for having performed a good deed.
Lithuanian (*1628) *15;* Czech: Tille Soupis II (2) 383; Slovenian; Serbocroatian *3;* Greek (1807*) *1.*

1807A »*Owner has Refused to Accept it.*» A rascal steals a priest's watch. He tells the priest that he has stolen a watch and offers it to him as a payment for a past favor. The priest refuses to accept stolen goods. Commands the thief to return the watch to the owner. »But the owner has refused to accept it.» »Then you may keep it.» [K373].
Finnish *1;* Danish: Kristensen *Kirketjeneste* 126; Czech: Tille Soupis II (2) 383; Maltese: Ilg *Maltesische Märchen* (Leipzig, 1906—07) No. 135; Arab: Littmann 112 No. 6; Spanish-American (U.S.): Rael No. 466.

1807B *Sleeping with God's Daughters.* Literal penance: the boy outwits the pope.

For three years not to drink wine, not to lie in bed, nor sleep with a prostitute. He goes to a convent, sleeps on eiderdown, and sleeps with the nuns (God's daughters). When the pope condemns him he says he will go to his brother-in-law (Christ: he has wedded God's daughters). [J1161.5, cf. J1764.5].

*Feilberg *Ordbog* II 693 s.v. »nonne». — Danish: Kristensen *Jyske Folkeminder* VII No. 36; Serbocroatian *1*.

1807A* *Who has Lost This?* A rascal finds a bag of money. The priest advises him to carry it through the streets asking if anyone lost it. He puts it in large horn so that people cannot see it. They think he is asking about the horn and no one claims it. When he tells the priest he has complied, the priest tells him to keep money.

Spanish-American: Hansen (556**A) (Puerto Rico) *1*.

1810 *Jokes about Catechism.* Cf. 1832D*, 1832G*, 1832K*, 1833D.

Finnish *286;* Spanish-American: Hansen (1842**D) (Puerto Rico) *1*.

1810A* (formerly 1846*) *How Many Gods Are There?*
Irish *26;* Flemish (1846*) *8;* Serbocroatian *1*.

1810B* *Ignorant Priest at Catechism.* Punishment of young student.
Greek (1846**) *6*.

1810C* *The Big Fish.* Ignorant boy has a fish with him at catechism. In confusion he mutters »The fish.» This is the correct answer about St. Peter. [Cf. N688]. Cf. Type 1641 III.
Finnish *21*.

1811 *Jokes about Religious Vows.*
Slovenian.

1811A *Vow not to Drink from St. George (April 23) to St. Demitry (October 26).* Understood as from one church to other.

Rumanian (1849*) *1*. There is a story of Yale students who say they have been to Chapel and Church (a busy street corner).

1811B *The Patience of Job.* Man breaks resolution and swears when he is caught in a fox trap (or when his wife spills the beer).
Finnish *22*.

1812 *Wager: to Dance with Nun.* Man tells nun she must undress. Nun outraged refuses. Then you must dance a few steps with me. Nun prefers this and does. Man wins wager. (Nun's song while dancing a part of tale).
French-Canadian.

1820 *Bride and Groom at Wedding Ceremony.* They make unusual or absurd answers. Cf. Type 1684B*.
Finnish *13*.

1821 *Naming the Child (Christening).*

1821A *Child Named »Somebody.»* God-parents who have not decided on a name: »Call him somebody.»
Finnish *19;* Spanish (*1843) *1*.

1822 *Equivocal Blessings.*

1822A *As Full as the Nut.* May this house be as full as this nut in my hand. (Nut is hollow).
Serbocroatian *2.*

1823 *Jokes about Baptism.*
Finnish *20.*

1824 *Parody Sermon.* [K1961.1.2.1].
*BP III 116; Feilberg *Ordbog* II 582a s.v. »messe»; Bolte Zs. f. Vksk. XIX 182; Boccaccio Decameron VI No. 10 (Lee 179); Wesselski *Arlotto* I 174ff. No. 3. — Finnish *5;* Lithuanian (1835*) *7;* French *6;* Italian Novella: Rotunda (K1961.1.2.1); Serbocroatian *1;* West Indies: Flowers 549.

1825 *The Peasant as Parson* [K1961.1].
*BP II 413. — Irish *5;* French *13;* Rumanian *4;* Spanish-American: Rael No. 30 (U.S.), Hansen (1825G) (Cuba) *1.*

1825A *The Parson Drunk.* Love affair of the bishop and the parson's wife. When the bishop comes in response to complaints, the parson preaches about the love affair [J1211.1]. The troubles of laymen made plain. [K1961.1.1].
*Pauli (ed. Bolte) No. 711. — Finnish *45;* Swedish *20* (Uppsala *7,* Stockholm *3,* Göteborg *3,* Lund *2,* misc. *5*); Norwegian *1;* German *1;* Serbocroatian *2;* Russian: Andrejev *2.* — Literary Treatments: Rotunda (J1211.1.1).

1825B »*I Preach God's Word.*» The parson keeps repeating this expression or »God made the world from nothing» or a few Latin words instead of preaching [K1961.1.2.7]. The troubles of laymen [K1961.1.1].
*BP II 413, III 116. — Finnish *2;* Finnish-Swedish *3,* (1825*) *5;* Swedish *12* (Uppsala *5,* Stockholm *3,* Göteborg *1,* Liungman *1,* misc. *2*); Norwegian *1;* Danish: Grundtvig No. 114; Spanish *2;* Catalan: Amades No. 1321; Flemish *1,* (1826*) *4;* Hungarian *2;* Slovenian *1;* Serbocroatian *4;* Russian: Andrejev *2;* Greek: Loukatos No. 37. — Spanish-American: Hansen (1825) (Puerto Rico) *1,* (1825**F) (Puerto Rico) *1.*

1825C *The Sawed Pulpit.* The ignorant parson is to preach. Beforehand he saws the pulpit almost through. Predicts that a miracle will happen. The pulpit falls down. [K1961.1.3]. Cf. Type 1641.
*BP II 413. — Finnish *1;* Finnish-Swedish *7;* Estonian *1;* Lithuanian *3;* Lappish *1;* Swedish *5* (Uppsala *1,* Lund *1,* Liungman *1,* misc. *2*); Norwegian *15,* Solheim *1;* Icelandic *1;* Dutch *1;* Flemish *3;* German *3;* Italian (Tuscan *3*); Czech: Tille Soupis II (2) 393f., 448f. *10;* Slovenian *1;* Russian: Andrejev; Greek: Loukatos No. 36. — West Indies (Negro) *1.*

1825* changed to 1785C*.

1825D* *Fire in the Boots.* The peasant as priest asks his parishioners to do what he does.

The fire falls from the censer into his boots. He stamps his feet, then lies down on the floor and kicks. The parishioners imitate him. Cf. Type 1694.
Russian: Andrejev 2.

1826 *The Parson has no Need to Preach.* Those who know may teach those who don't know. [X452]. (Or no need give sermon about saint since he has performed no miracles since last year [X425.1]). Cf. Type 1833F.
Wesselski *Arlotto* I 188 No. 8. — Finnish *1;* Estonian (1826*) *1;* German *1;* Rumanian *2;* Czech: Tille Soupis II (2) cf. 393f. *3;* Serbocroatian *1;* Russian: Afanasiev *6;* — Literary Treatments: Rotunda (X452.1).

1826* *The Ungrateful Beggar and the Parson.*
Lappish *1.*

1826A* *The Escaped Saint.* A gypsy has taken a saint's picture from the church. Priest thinks that the saint has escaped from him because he was not a good priest.
Anderson FFC XLII 349; French: Tegethoff II 122; Hungarian: Berze Nagy *1.*

1827 *You Shall See me a Little While Longer.* The parson takes a drink of liquor during the sermon. [X445.1]. Cf. Type 1698M.
Finnish (1827*) *6;* Estonian (1827*) *2;* Lappish *1;* Swedish *5* (Uppsala *3,* Liungman *1,* misc. *1*); Danish: Kristensen *Kirketjeneste* p. 98.

1827A *Cards (Liquor Bottle) Fall from the Sleeve of the Preacher.* He saves the situation by making suitable comparisons to the congregation: »So shall you fall to hell« (and the like).
Finnish *55;* Lithuanian (*1785E) *2.*

1827* *The Old Man as Neighbor of the Parson.* Accuses the bailiff and the parson of theft. They are hanged. He marries the parson's widow to a young man. She is rejuvenated.
Lappish *1.*

1827** See Type 1829.

1828 *The Cock at Church Crows,* and the sexton awakes and begins to sing [X451].
Finnish; Finnish-Swedish (1831*) *1;* Swedish *3* (Liungman *1,* misc. *2*); Danish: Kristensen *Kirketjenste* pp. 71ff., 91ff.; Catalan: Amades cf. 1341.

1828* *Weeping and Laughing.* The parson preaches so that half the congregation weeps and the other half laughs. Without breeches. [X416].
Anderson FFC XLII 357; Wesselski *Morlini* 297 No. 44. — Finnish *3;* Estonian *3.* — Spanish-American: Hansen (1835D) (Cuba) *1,* (1835C) (Cuba) *1.*

1829 (formerly 1827**) *Living Person Acts as Image of Saint* [K1842]. Cf. Type 1380.
Anderson FFC XLII 359; Lithuanian (1730B*); Swedish (Uppsala) *1;* Danish: *Skattegraveren* X (1888) 165; French *20;* Spanish (*1787A, C) *2,* Espinosa II No. 42; Flemish (1827*) *5;* German (well known); Italian (Tuscan [1369], [1784] *2*); Slovenian *1;* Serbocroatian *4,* Istrian No. 62; India *1;* West Indies: Flowers 546f.

1829* changed to 1831B.

1829A* *Saint's Image Smeared with Milk* so as to divert suspicion of milk theft.
Hungarian: Berze Nagy (1789*) *3.*

1829B* *Man Acts as Statue of Saint in Order to Enter Convent* [K1842.1].
Spanish *1.*

1830 *In Trial Sermon the Parson Promises the Laymen the Kind of Weather they Want.* They cannot agree. »Then you may have it as it was before.» [J1041.1].
Wesselski *Hodscha Nasreddin* I 218 No. 51. — Finnish *13;* Swedish *2* (Uppsala *1,* Stockholm *1*); Irish *2;* French *1;* Catalan: Amades Nos. 1310, 1372; Flemish *1;* German *2;* Rumanian *1;* Hungarian *2;* Slovenian *4;* Serbocroatian *1;* Russian: Andrejev. — Literary Treatment: Aesop (Halm No. 166).

1831 *The Parson and Sexton at Mass.* The Sexton has been sent to steal the lamb. At mass the priest and sexton discuss the theft in antiphony: »Did you get the lamb-a-a-a-a?» »I didn't get it; I got a hell of a beating a-a-a-a. [X441]. (In Catholic stories the antiphonies are made to sound like Latin.) Cf. Type 1792.
Finnish *45;* Estonian *9;* Lithuanian *3;* Swedish (Uppsala) *1,* cf. 1833**; Irish *1;* French *3;* Spanish *6;* Catalan: Amades cf. No. 1334; Dutch *2;* German *14* (Archive *13,* Henssen Volk No. 273); Italian (Tuscan 1831, cf. [1731] *2*); Rumanian *3;* Hungarian *1;* Serbocroatian *3;* Russian: Andrejev *2.* — Spanish-American: Hansen (1831**D) (Cuba) *1;* American Negro (Michigan): Dorson No. 129.

1831A *The Parson as Shopkeeper.* »In the name of the Father and the Son and the Holy Ghost the price of sugar has risen».
Finnish *6.*

1831B (formerly 1829*) *The Parson's Share and the Sexton's.* During the sermon the parson bids the sexton see if anyone is coming. The sexton: »A man is coming with a wheel on his shoulders.» The parson: »God gives it to you.» The sexton: »Now a man is coming with half a hog on his shoulder.» The parson: »God gives it to me.» [J1269.1].
Estonian (1829*) *1;* Swedish *5* (Uppsala *4,* Lund *1*); Russian: Andrejev (1829*) *1.*

1831A* *Inappropriate Actions in Church: various.*
Finnish *48.*

1832 *The Sermon about the Rich Man.* A boy rides with a rich man. Goes into church and leaves his coat lying in the sled. Hears the parson preach about the rich man who went to hell. The boy calls out, »Then he took my coat along» [X435.5].
Finnish *24;* Finnish-Swedish *1;* Norwegian *1;* German *1;* Russian: Andrejev.

1832* *Boy Answers the Priest.* Cf. Type 1810.
Finland *21.*

1832A* *The Seven Deadly Sins.* Poor boy says eight: eighth is the scorn of the poor. Priest

gives boy new clothes. Next day boy says there are only 7. Priest has erased the eighth.
French-Canadian.

1832B* *What Kind of Dung.* A boy on road is looking at something. Priest: What are you looking at? Boy: I don't know. Priest: It is horse's dung. Boy: I was wondering whether it was the dung of a horse or a mare. Cf. Type 1225A.
French-Canadian.

1832C* *How Many Turkeys.* A boy is sitting on a fence. The priest asks him: How many turkeys will it take to cover the fence? Boy: If they are all as big as you, only one.
French-Canadian.

1832D* *How Many Sacraments are there?* — Boy: I don't know. How many poles are there in my father's fence? — Priest: I wasn't there when the fence was made. — Boy: And I was not there when the sacraments were made.
French-Canadian.

1832E* *Good Manners.* A boy takes game (rabbit) to priest from his mother. He throws it at priest. The priest wants to teach the boy good manners and exchanges places. The priest knocks and says to boy »My mother sends you this rabbit.» The boy reaches in pocket: »Here is money for you.»
French-Canadian.

1832F* *Boy Invited to Dinner by Priest.* Boy told to help himself to turkey and that whatever he does to turkey priest will do to him. He draws out the stuffing from rear with his finger.
French-Canadian.

1832G* *Four Persons of Trinity.* Father, Son, Holy Ghost, and *Amen.* (Cf. Type 1833D).
French-Canadian.

1832G** *The Holy Spirit.* Boy preparing to go to early mass loses shoes. Father: Pray to Holy Spirit to enlighten you. Boy: I have a lantern and don't need the Holy Spirit.
French-Canadian.

1832H* *No Objections.* A priest publishes bans of marriage. He explains to the boy that it is to see if there are any objections. Boy imitates by announcing that he is to take fruit from basket and hears no objections.
French-Canadian.

1832J* *Choice of Apples.* Priest: Here are three apples. One is with 25 cents (heaven), one with 50 cents (purgatory), and one, one dollar (hell). Choose. Boy: I take them all and then I can go where I please.
French-Canadian.

1832K* *God's Omnipotence.* Priest to boy: Name one thing that God cannot do. Boy: Make your mouth larger without moving back your ears.
French-Canadian.

1832L* *A Woman Orders Mass to be Said for her Stolen Ox.* During Mass the priest sings; the woman thinks she is being asked questions about her ox, and answers him.
Lithuanian (*1393) *3.*

1832M* *Priest's Words Repeated.* Man sent to priest for religious service to repeat priest's words. Keeps repeating »Who are you?» »Where do you come from?» [J2498.2]. [Or choir keeps repeating priest's apology. Cf. Type 1694.]
Field *Pent Cuckoo* 8. — Finnish *18;* India: Thompson-Balys (J2498.2) *1.* — England, U.S.: Baughman (J2498, J2498.1).

1832N* *Lamb of God Becomes Sheep of God.* Has grown up since youth learned about it. [J2212.6].
Wesselski *Hodscha Nasreddin* I 235 No. 105. — Finnish *2.*

1832P* *The Devil!* Boy in rear of confirmation class is struck by another boy and cries out »The devil!» This is the correct answer.
   Finnish *43*.

1833 *Application of the Sermon* [X435].
   Coffin *2*. — Finnish *51;* Finnish-Swedish *3;* Estonian *11;* Livonian *1;* Irish *76;* English (1833 E) *11;* Spanish *1*, (1842A, B, C) *3;* German *2* (Archive *1*, Henssen Volk No. 276); Italian (Tuscan *1*); Serbocroatian *1;* Russian: Andrejev; Hungarian *1*. — English-American: Baughman (1833E) *1;* West Indies (Negro) *1*.

1833A »*What Says David?*» The boy: »Pay your old debt.»
   Variants: (a) »What evil did Adam do?» — »He (shoemaker) made my shoes too little.» (b) »What kind of man was Moses?» — He was a day laborer.» [X435.1].
   Wesselski *Arlotto* II 233 No. 113. — Finnish (1842**) *4;* Estonian *11;* Swedish *20* (Uppsala *10*, Stockholm *4*, Göteborg *1*, Lund *3*, Liungman *1*, misc. *1*); Danish: Kristensen *Kirketjenste* p. 42; Scottish *1;* English *5;* Dutch *1;* Flemish (1833*) *3;* Walloon *1*. — English-American: Baughman *6;* American Negro (Michigan): Dorson No. 128.

1833B The parson: »*Where did the Father Stay?*» »He stayed to hold the oxen.» [X435.2].
   Finnish (1844**) *6;* Swedish *6* (Lund *3*, Liungman *1*, misc. *2*); Hungarian: Berze Nagy (1699*) *1*.

1833C The parson: »*Where Was Christ when he Was neither in Heaven nor on Earth?*» — »He was in the willow grove looking for a stick to beat those who ask foolish questions». [X435.3]. (Variant: What does God do? Cf. Types 922, 1738A*.)
   Finnish (1843**) *5;* Russian: Andrejev (1843**) *1*.

1833D *The Names of the Persons of the Holy Trinity.* The priest's example: the three cows. »The Holy Ghost has just had a calf». [X435.4].
   RTP XV 503. — Swedish (Stockholm) *4;* English *1;* French *3;* Flemish (1844**) *12*. — West Indies (Negro) *1*.

1833E *God Died for You.* Old woman: »Heavens, is the old man dead? We never get any news out here in the country.» (Variants: Christ, when there is a man in the village named Christ). [J1788.4].
   *Ranke in *Peuckert Festschrift* (1955) 42; *Peuckert *Deutsches Volkstum in Märchen und Sage* (1938) 164 n. 1; Christensen DF XLVII 205 No. 55 B. — Finnish *2;* Swiss: *Appenzeller Witz* (1902) 45; French: Sébillot *Les joyeuses histoires de Bretagne* (1910) 294f.; U.S.: Baughman (J1788.4).

1833F *The Same Old Story.* Complaint that on Good Friday they are still telling the same story as years ago. Cf. Type 1826.
   Finnish *11*.

1833G *Old Woman Prefers Hell* if it is only warm.
   Finnish *28*.

1833H (formerly 1834*) *The Large Loaves.* The parson preaches that the loaves with which Jesus fed the people in the wilderness were as big as the Ural Mountains. The mason asks what kind of oven they were baked in. [X434.1].

Cf. Finnish *4;* Livonian *1;* Catalan: Amades cf. No. 1349; Rumanian (1832 II*) *1.*

1833* *The Poor Parson's Sermon.*
Finnish-Swedish *5;* Serbocroatian *1.*

1833** *Other Anecdotes of Sermons.*
Finnish-Swedish *20* (Uppsala *17,* Lund *2,* Liungman *1*); Spanish-American: Hansen (1833**E) (Cuba) *1;* West Indies (Negro) *1.*

1833A* *A Mighty Fortress.* Two hoboes afraid of a burning wheel (or the like) sing »A Mighty Fortress is our God». One decides to run away no matter how mighty the fortress is.
Swedish (GS 1342) *10* (Uppsala *3,* Stockholm *3,* Göteborg *1,* Lund *1,* misc. *2*); Danish (1342*) *12.*

1834 *The Clergyman with the Fine Voice.* When officiating he sees an old woman weeping and believes her to be touched by his singing. Feeling flattered, he asks her why she weeps, but she answers that she had been reminded of her old goat that had been taken by the wolf [X436]. (Variant: she is afflicted by the thought that her son is studying to be a parson.) [X426].

Pauli (ed. Bolte) No. 576; Wesselski *Hodscha Nasreddin* II 243 No. 539; Christiansen *Maal og Minne* (1954) 49ff.; *Crane *Vitry* 157 No. 56; Feilberg *Ordbog* II 882 s.v. »prædiken»; *Scala Celi* 25a No. 164. — Finnish; Swedish *4* (Uppsala *2,* Liungman *1,* misc. *1*); Norwegian (1834**) *2;* French *8;* Spanish *1;* Walloon (1834A) *1;* German *3* (Archive *1,* Henssen Volk Nos. 284 a, 284 b); Italian (Trieste: Pinguentini No. 97); India *3.* — West Indies (Negro) *2.* — Literary Treatments: Rotunda (X436).

1834A* (formerly 1865*) *A Fool's Vocation.* The innkeeper explains to the priest that he would let his son study for the priesthood if the boy were a fool [X420].
Livonian *2;* Finnish *1.*

1834B* (formerly Type 1860') *The Parson Wants No one Except a Parson as a Son-in-law.* But he gets a lawyer whom he sends to preach.
Livonian *1.*

1835* *Not to Turn Around.* The parson forbids people to look behind them at church, and calls out during the sermon the names of those who enter.
Livonian *1.*

1835A* *Gun Accidentally Discharged in Church.* The priest's explanation.
**Ranke *Die Heimat* (Neumünster) LXI (1954) 9, 295ff. — Finnish *2.*

1835B* *The Pasted Bible Leaves.* The parson reads Genesis and constructs Eve according to the dimensions of Noah's Ark. (Rascals have pasted the leaves together.)
Finnish *4.* Common in America.

1835C* *Minister Cannot Answer.* The minister lets the parishioners ask questions. He cannot answer them.
Finnish *22.*

1835D* *Wager: Parson to Read Prayer Without Thinking of Anything Else.* Interrupts reading

to ask more about what he will win. (Has been promised a horse. — Will he get harness too?).
Finnish 2.

1835E* *Ignorant Priest Forces Rolls of Cloth Instead of Bread down a Dying Man's Throat.* [J1738.1].
Wesselski *Bebel* I 222 No. 116. — Finnish 5.

1835F* *All Red Beards Go to Hell.* Red-bearded parson: »Not quite all.»
Finnish 10.

1836 *The Drunken Parson.*
Finnish 6.

1836A *The Drunken Parson: »Do not Live as I Live,* but as I preach».
Finnish 5.

1836B *Law Carries the Gospel.* Lawyer carries drunken parson home.
Finnish 5.

1836* *Rascals Spread Butter over the Altar-bread.* The parson preaches, »What is the life of man?» and therewith brings his hand down on the altar-bread: »Pure butter!» [X417]. Cf. Type 1785B.
Livonian 1.

1837 *The Parson to Let a Dove Fly in the Church.* It dies in his pocket (or has other accident). [X418].
Finnish 28; Finnish-Swedish 1; Estonian 2; Swedish 5 (Stockholm 3, Lund 1, Liungman 1); Danish: Kristensen *Kirketjenste* pp. 45ff.; Irish 3; French 3; Catalan: Amades No. 1355; Dutch 2; German 18 (Archive 16, Henssen Jül. No. 477, Henssen Volk No. 271); Hungarian 1; Slovenian 2; Serbocroatian 1; Russian: Andrejev; Greek: Loukatos No. 36.

1837* *A Pet Dove Drops Excrement in the Priest's Soup,* and is forgiven. A servant complains that if it were he who had done it, he would be disciplined.
Walloon 2.

1838 *The Hog in Church.* The hog has been locked by mistake in the church all week. When the congregation comes the hog runs between the parson's legs and carries him out. [X415].
*Feilberg' *Ordbog* s.v. »svin». — Finnish 12; Finnish-Swedish 4; Estonian 6; Swedish 22 (Uppsala 10, Stockholm 1, Lund 3, Liungman 2, misc. 6); French 9; Spanish 1; German 14 (Archive 13, Henssen Volk No. 267); Rumanian 1; Hungarian 1; Serbocroatian 1; Russian: Andrejev.

1839 *The Card-playing Parson.*

1839A *Parson Calls out Cards.* The parson plays cards all Saturday **night**. He goes to sleep at church and calls out the names of the cards. [N5].
Livonian (1839A') 1; Lithuanian (*1785E) 2; Irish 11; German 5; West Indies (Negro) 1.

1839B *Sermon Illustrated.* The parson wagers with the students that he will begin his semon with an illustration from card-playing [N71].

Finnish *2*, cf. also 1827A; Livonian *1* (1839B'); Swedish *5* (Göteborg *1*, Lund *3*, Liungman *1*); Danish: Kristensen *Kirketjeneste* pp. 33ff.

1839* *Making Thunder.* The priest's servant girl is to make thunder. She falls through the church ceiling.
Flemish *1*.

1840 *At the Blessing of the Grave the Parson's Ox Breaks Loose.* »Now the devil has him.» [X421].
*Feilberg Ordbog III 908b s.v. »tyr». — Finnish *56;* Finnish-Swedish *1;* Swedish cf. (1833**) *3* (Uppsala *2*, Lund *1*); Irish *1;* Russian: Andrejev. — Spanish-American: Rael (U.S.) No. 472.

1840A *The Parson's Ox.* (Other jests about an ox or cow due the parson for funeral.)
Finnish *29*.

1840B *The Stolen Ham (Goat).* The priest steals a ham but promises to pray for the man he has stolen it from. Priest: O God curse the man who lost the ham and bless him who stole it.
Finnish-Swedish: *Finlands svenska Folkdiktning* I B 2 p. 238; Swedish (GS 1842) *8* (Uppsala *5*, Stockholm *1*, Lund *1*, misc. *1*).

1841 *Grace before Meat.* The parson asks the boy: »What does your father say when you begin to eat?» »You young devil, etc.» [X435.2].
Finnish (1841*) *1;* Estonian (1841*) *3;* Livonian (1841*) *1;* Swedish cf. (1833**) *2* (Stockholm); Irish *3;* Walloon *1;* Serbocroatian *2;* English-American: Baughman *1*.

1841* *Where did Nicodemus Go!* To his wife.
Livonian *1*.

1842 *The Testament of the Dog.* The owner of a dog has him given Christian burial. The bishop thereupon pretends that the dog has left the church a large legacy. [J1607].
**Feilberg »Hundens Testament» *Festskrift til E. T. Kristensen* 11ff.; *Anderson FFC XLII 359 n. 3; Pauli (ed. Bolte) No. 72; Italian Novella: Rotunda (J1607); *Cent Nouvelles Nouvelles* No. 96. — Catalan: Amades No. 1345; Czech: Tille Soupis II (2) 367; Russian: Fabula I 238, Ukraine: *ibid* 239; Persian: *Märchen aus Iran* 187.

1842A* *The Avaricious Priest,* who hoped to earn much for church services, is outwitted.
Lithuanian *3;* Rumanian (1846*) *6;* Serbocroatian *1*.

1842B* *Cheeses Due to the Minister.* Woman makes them so disgusting that minister refuses them.
Finnish *38*.

1842C* *The Rector's Nights.* The rector's friend proves that the former is in the habit of spending the night with his housekeeper (the incident of the stolen spoons).
Lithuanian (*1843) *2*.

1843 *Parson Visits the Dying.* (Various anecdotes).
Finnish *19*.

1844 *The Parson Visits the Sick.* Cf. Type 1698 I.

1844A *No Time for Sickness.* Mother busy with her children has no time to be sick. Finnish *11*.

1844* *Priest Pretends a Dream* and injures flageolet player of whom he is jealous. Spanish *1*.

1845 *The Student as Healer* has sign hung around the neck of a sick calf on which is written: »If he does not live, let him die.» Later, as parson, he is sick. They propose to heal him with the same remedy. [J1513.1]. (Or the priest sponsors a sham doctor with the same result).

Hepding Hessische Blätter XXXVIII 78ff. — Finnish *11;* Livonian cf. (1845) *2;* Swedish *21* (Uppsala *10*, Stockholm *1*, Lund *2*, misc. *8*); Norwegian *3;* Scottish *1;* Catalan: Amades cf. No. 2043; German *6* (Archive *5*, Henssen Volk No. 307); Czech: Tille Soupis II (2) 453f. *2;* Russian: Andrejev *Ukraine 3.*

1846* changed to 1810A*.

1847* *Biblical Repartee.* The gentleman and the priest quarrel. The gentleman strikes the priest with a cane: »This is Moses' staff.» The priest shoots with a pistol: »This is Aaron's holy censer.» [J1446]. — Or: »Whoever shall smite thee on the right cheek, turn to him the other also.» — »For with what measure you mete, it shall be measured to you again». Estonian *2;* Finnish *6.*

1848 (formerly 1848*) *A Pebble for each Sin.* The man who cannot remember the number of his sins. The priest has him put a pebble in a sack for each sin. The man comes to confession with three large sacks of pebbles. [J2466.1]. Cf. Type 1738C*.

*Wesselski *Hodscha Nasreddin* I 207 No. 9. — Irish *2;* English *2;* French *1;* Flemish (1848*) *1;* German: Dittmaier No. 468; English-American: Baughman *1.*

1848A *The Pastor's Calendar.* Recognizes Easter when he sees colored egg shells. On Ash Wednesday has put into a bottle forty-eight pumpkin seeds to chew for each feast day.

*Köhler-Bolte I 484; Wesselski *Hodscha Nasreddin* I 207 No. 9. — Rumanian (1825E) *2.*

1848B *Beans in Pocket.* Ignorant priest keeps account of Lent by counting beans in pocket. Woman mixes them up. [J2466.2].
Greek (1841*) *5.*

1848C *Saint's Account Book.* Priest paid for number of times he mentions saint in sermon keeps account on notched stick. Must get second stick.
Spanish (1836*) *1.*

1848D *Priest Confuses Easter and Christmas.*
Russian: Andrejev (*1850) *2.*

1849* *The Priest on the Cow's Tail.* When the cow is being milked, the priest ties her tail to a button on his coat. The wasps sting her and she runs away with the priest. [J2132.3].
Estonian 5.

ANECDOTES ABOUT OTHER GROUPS OF PEOPLE

1851 *Jokes about Devout Women.* Cf. Type 1805.
Lithuanian (*1835, *1846, *1847, *1849) *20*.

1853 *Jokes on Millers.*

1853A* *The Double-cheating Miller.* He confesses that he has an oversized measure and agrees to get a smaller one. He measures back the grain in the smaller one. [K486].
Spanish (1800*B) *1*.

1853B* *Dishonest Miller Unmasked* at funeral given celebrating his honesty.
Spanish (1864*) *1*.

1854* *Tales of Cowardly Tailors.* Cf. Type 1640.
Motifs: J2623. Tailor puts on thimble as protection from slug. K1837.1. Boasting coward exposed by wife who masks as highwayman and robs him.
Spanish *2*.

1855 *Jokes about Jews* [X610]. Cf. Type 1656.
Lithuanian (*1854—*1869) *121;* Serbocroatian *1*.

1855A *Jewess makes Parents Believe that she is to Give Birth to the Messiah.* She bears a girl. [J2336].
*Wesselski *Mönchslatein* 65 No. 53; *Wesselski *Bebel* I 213 No. 104; Italian Novella: Rotunda (J2336). — Lithuanian (*1864) *4;* German (well known).

1860 *Jokes on Lawyers.*

1860A *Lawyers in Hell.* Beggar frightens lawyer into giving by telling him of all the lawyers in hell. [X312]. Cf. Type 1738.
Spanish (819*); German: Zender No. 28; Serbocroatian *2*. Cf. U.S.: Baughman (X312).

1860B *Dying like Christ — between Two Thieves.* The dying man has the lawyer and the notary stand on either side of him. [X313].
Spanish (1583*); Finnish (1843A*) *1;* German: Merkens No. 187. — U.S.: Baughman (X313).

1860C *Doubts his own Guilt.* Eloquent lawyer makes obviously guilty client doubt his own guilt. [X319.1].
Canada, U.S.: Baughman (X319.1).

1860' changed to 1834B*.

1860A* *The Thick Forest.* So thick that the lawyer can hardly get through. Says he saw moose with enormous antlers there. How?
French-Canadian.

1861 *Jokes on Judges.*

1861A *The Greater Bribe.* Judge awards decision to the greater bribe [J1192.1].
*DeVries FFC LXXIII 263; Pauli (ed. Bolte) Nos. 125, 128, 852, 853; *Scala Celi* 20a No. 122. — Finnish *6;* England: Baughman (J1192.1); Italian Novella: *Rotunda (J1192.1); Jewish: Neuman (J1192.1); India: *Thompson-Balys (J1192.1).

1861* *Keep your Seats!* A proud woman enters the church just as the congregation is rising for prayer. She thinks they are rising for her and bids them be seated.
Finnish *6.*

1862 *Jokes on Doctors (Physicians)* [K1955, X372]. Cf. Types 660, 1641, 1739, 1845.
Serbocroatian *1.*

1862A *Sham Physician: Usiing the Flea Powder.* Catch the flea, open its mouth, and place the powder inside. [K1955.4].
Pierre Faifeu No. 18; Spanish (1550A*) *1;* German: Wossidlo *Aus dem Lande Fritz Reuters* 143; Italian Novella: Rotunda (K1955.4).

1862B *The Sham Physician and the Devil in Partnership.* The devil is to enter the girl and the physician will collect reward for driving the devil out. [K1955.6].
Spanish (340*) *4;* India (1164D) *9;* Cape Verde Islands: *Parsons MAFLS XV (1) 193 n. 1.

1862C *Imitation of Diagnosis by Observation: Ass's Flesh.* A doctor tells his patient that he has eaten too much chicken, and this the patient confesses. The doctor's son wants to know how the diagnosis was made. The doctor says that as he rode up he observed chicken feathers and made his conclusions. The son imitates. He sees an ass's saddle. Diagnosis: you have eaten too much ass's flesh. [J2412.4].
*Wesselski *Hodscha Nasreddin* I 250 No. 167; *Pauli (ed. Bolte) No. 792; Italian Novella: Rotunda (J2412.4); German: Merkens III 127 No. 103; Greek (Lesbos): Georgeakis et Pineau 131. — India *3.* — Spanish-American: Hansen (Puerto Rico) *1.*

1865 *Jokes about Foreigners.*
Lithuanian (*1870) *18;* Slovenian *2;* Serbocroatian *13.*

1865* changed to 1834A*.

1867 *Jokes about the Gentry.*
Lithuanian (*1871) *2;* Russian: Andrejev (2054*, 2067*) *2.*

1870 *Jokes on Various Religions and Sects.*
Lithuanian (*1872, *1873) *15;* Slovenian.

TALES OF LYING
[X900—X1899]

1875 *The Boy on the Wolf's Tail.* He hides himself in the mill and frightens the robbers from their treasure; cf. Type 1653. Is hidden in a barrel. Holds fast to the wolf's tail through a hole in the barrel. [X1133.3]. Cf. Types 169H*, 1229, 1900.

*BP I 410; Feilberg *Ordbog* III 935a s.v. »tønde«, III 114a s.v. »ræv«.
— Finnish *120;* Finnish-Swedish *3;* Estonian *15;* Lithuanian *42;* Swedish *5* (Stockholm *2*, misc. *3*); Danish: Grundtvig No. 95; Irish *2;* French *29;* Catalan: Amades No. 530; Dutch *6;* Flemish *7;* German *25* (Archive *21*, Merk. 308, Henssen Jül. No. 482 a, b, Henssen Volk No. 295, Meckl. No. 121); Rumanian *3;* Hungarian *6;* Czech: Tille FFC XXXIV 311; Russian: Andrejev *Ukraine 11*, Afanasiev *5*. — English-American: Baughman *3*. — Literary Treatments: John Fraser *A Tale of the Sea and other Poems* (Montreal, 1870).

1876 *The Geese on the Line.* The hawk flies away with them on it. The geese have been bound together as protection from the hawk. [X1267.1].

Cf. BP III 337 (Grimm No. 185) ; *Anderson *Novelline* No. 14. — Finnish *55;* Finnish-Swedish *1;* Estonian *6;* German *5;* Italian (Tuscan [1224] ·*1*); Slovenian *4;* Serbocroatian *3;* Russian: Andrejev.

1876* *Releasing the Rabbit.* A hunter shoots at captured rabbit tied to a pole. He hits the string and breaks it; the rabbit escapes.

Italian (Tuscan [1876] *1*); Serbocroatian *1*.

1877* *The Boy in the Hollow Tree.* The woodcutter chops on the tree. Frightened, he leaves his horse behind. [X1854.1].

Finnish (1877) *39;* Estonian (1877) *4;* Russian: Andrejev (1877*A) *5*.

1878* *Cat Stew.* A traveler is fed a stew and eats much. Told it is cat he has eaten, he throws up the cat and four kittens.

French-Canadian.

1880 *The Boy has a Hat of Butter*, clothes of paper. Is shot from a cannon [X1853, X1852], etc. (an end-formula).

Feilberg *Ordbog* II 87 s.v. »kanon«. — Finnish *46;* Finnish-Swedish *1;* Livonian *12;* Lithuanian *8;* French *3;* Dutch *1;* Russian: Afanasiev *7*. — Literary Treatments: Münchhausen, ch. 13.

1881 *The Man Carried through the Air by Geese* [X1258.1].

Coffin *2*. — Lithuanian *5;* Irish *2;* Dutch *1;* Flemish (1881*) *2;* German *3;* Serbocroatian *1;* Russian: Afanasiev (1876B*) *5;* Japanese: Ikeda; English-American: Baughman *12*. — Literary Treatments: Münchhausen, ch. 2.

1881* *Parrots Fly Away with Tree.*

Spanish-American: Hansen (1889**M) (Argentina) *2*.

1882 *The Man who Fell out of a Balloon.* Buried in the earth, he goes to get a spade to dig himself out. [X1731.2.1]. (First ed. X917.)

Gardner JAFL XXVII 305; Köhler-Bolte I 323. — French *6;* Dutch *1;* Flemish (1896*) *3;* German: Merk. 242; Hungarian *2;* Russian: Afanasiev (1877B*) *7.* — English-American: Baughman *10.*

1882A *Man Caught in Log (cleft tree) Goes Home to Get Axe* to cut himself out.
Hungarian: Berze Nagy (1961**A) *17,* Honti *2;* Russian: Afanasiev (1877*B) *8.*

1886 *Man Drinks from own Skull.* The skull falls into the water and a duck makes a nest in it.
*BP II 514 No. 112. — Russian (*1886) *4.*

1886* *Fighting Sheep Butt Each Other* hundreds of miles.
Spanish-American: Hansen (1889**D) (Argentina) *1.*

1887* *Cattle Merchant's Voyage Across the Sea.* A man floats across the sea on a mat. On the other shore are many cattle. One after the other he carries the herd of bulls over to his native shore. With the last one he himself flies over, having seized hold of its tail.
Russian: Afanasiev *8.*

1888* *Men or Animals Thrown to Sky* (heaven).
Spanish-American: Hansen (1889**A) (Argentina) *1,* (1889**C) (Argentina) *1,* (1889**J) (Argentina) *1.*

1889 *Münchhausen Tales* [X900]. The following types appearing elsewhere in this work belong to the Münchhausen canon: 513 A, Six Go Through the Whole World; 1880, Boy Shot from a Cannon; 1881, The Man Carried through the Air by Geese; 1890, The Lucky Shot; 1894, The Man Shoots a Ramrod Full of Ducks; 1896, The Man Nails the Tail of the Wolf to the Tree; 1910, The Wolf Harnessed; 1930, Schlaraffenland.

**Vidossi *In Margine ad alcune Avventure di Münchhausen* (FFC CLXII); Münchhausen *Wunderbare Reisen* (references by chapter). — Finnish-Swedish (1880*) *6;* Lappish (1890*) *3;* Swedish *12* (Uppsala *5,* Lund *5,* misc. *2*); Irish *8;* French *12;* German *6.* — West Indies (Negro) *13.*

1889A *Shooting off the Leader's Tail.* An old blind bear is being led by a young bear, whose tail the old bear has in his mouth. The hunter shoots off the young bear's tail and seizes it. Thus leads the old bear home. [X1124.1].
Pauli (ed. Bolte) No. 748; Münchhausen, ch. 2. — German: Dittmaier 185 No. 156; Slovenian. — U.S.: Baughman *3.*

1889B *Hunter Turns Animal Inside Out.* He reaches down animal's throat, grasps his tail, and turns him inside out. [X1124.2].
Wesselski *Bebel* II 137 No. 115; Münchhausen, ch. 2; Finnish *2;* Catalan Nos. 285, 2051; Serbocroatian *1.* — U.S.: Baughman *5;* French Canadian.

1889C *Fruit Tree Grows from Head of Deer* shot with fruit pits. [X1130.2].
Münchhausen, ch. 2. — German: Merk. II 182; India *1;* Canada, U.S.: Baughman *13;* Spanish-American: Hansen (1889**G, **O) (Argentina) *2.*

1889D *Tree Grows out of Horse and Gives Rider Shade* [X1130.2.1]. (First ed. X923.)
  Feilberg *Ordbog* III 868 s.v. »træ.»

1889E *Descent from Sky on Rope of Sand (chaff)*. [X1757]. Cf. Type 582.
  BP II 513; Münchhausen, ch. 5; Icelandic (1883) *3;* Missouri-French: Carrière.

1889F *Frozen Words (Music) Thaw* [X1623.2.1].
  Münchhausen, ch. 5. — Finnish *4;* Catalan: Amades Nos. 420, 477. — Canada, U.S.: Baughman (X1623.5.2) *8;* U.S. Negro (Michigan): Dorson No. 141.

1889G *Man Swallowed by Fish.* Ships and many people inside. Rescued. [F911.6, F913, X1723.1].
  Münchhausen, ch. 8. — English-American: Baughman (X1723.1) *10.* — African *19.*

1889H *Submarine Otherworld.* Marine counterpart to land. [F133].
  Münchhausen, ch. 13; Patch PMLA XXXIII 627 n. 92, *Other World* *380 s.v. »Land-beneath-the-waves»; Wimberly 134; Ward II 525; Penzer VI 280; Smith Dragon 109. — Irish myth: Cross; Scotch: Campbell *Tales* III 420; Welsh: MacCulloch Celtic 122f.; North Carolina: *Brown Collection* I 636; *Breton: Le Braz II 37ff.; Spanish Exempla: Keller; Slavic: Máchal 270; Japanese: Ikeda; Hawaiian: Beckwith Myth 69; Maori: Clark 111; American Indian: (Klikitat): Jacobs U. Wash II 7; African *6.* — Literary: Chauvin V 151 No. 73.

1889J *Jumper over Water Turns Around Midway of Jump and Returns* [X1741.2].
  Münchhausen, ch. 4. — U.S.: Baughman (X1741.4.1) *6.*

1889K *A Cord Made of Chaff.* A man climbs up to the sky on a tree and descends on leather belts. Since the belts are not long enough, he makes a cord out of chaff and falls.
  *BP II 513 No. 112; Münchhausen, ch. *5;* Russian: Afanasiev (*1885) *23.*

1889L *Lie: the Split Dog.* Put back together but back legs point upwards. [X1215.11].
  Münchhausen, ch. 2. — England, Canada, U.S.: Baughman *16;* Spanish-American: Hansen (1889**J, K, L) (Argentina) *3.*

1889L* *Double Pig.* A pig is eating potatoes in a garden. The owner cuts the pig in two with an axe. The two parts of the pig continue to eat two rows instead of one.
  French-Canadian.

1889L** *Mittens Chase Deer.* Hunter has mittens made of skin of favorite dead dog. Sees deer in forest. »If I only had my dog!» The two mittens chase the deer. French-Canadian *1.*

1889M *Snakebite Causes Object to Swell* (hornet, bee sting) [X1205, X1205.1].
  Münchhausen, ch. 2. — U.S.: Baughman [X1205] *37.*

1889N *The Long Hunt.* Dog points birds (chases game) for many days (months). [X1215.9]. Cf. Type 1920F*.
Münchhausen, ch. 3. — U.S.: Baughman (X1215.9) *4;* Spanish-American: Hansen (1889**E) (Argentina) *2.*

1889P *Horse Repaired.* Man accidentally cuts his horse in two and rides off on the front part; later returns and sews the front part to the back part.
Münchhausen, ch. 4. — German: *Blätter für pommersche Volkskunde* III 140; Russian: Afanasiev (*1912) *7.*

1890—1909 Hunting Tales [X1110]

1890 *The Lucky Shot.* Discharge of gun kills the heath-cock, which falls on the sprouts on the tree, which kills the bear, etc. [X1124.3].
Münchhausen, ch. 2. — Finnish *44;* Estonian *3;* Lithuanian *1;* Swedish *5* (Uppsala *1,* Stockholm *1,* Lund *1,* misc. *2*); Irish *4;* English: Baughman (1890A) *2;* Russian: Afanasiev *1.* — Franco-American *2;* English-American: Baughman (1890A) *9;* American Negro (Michigan): Dorson No. 138.

1890A *Shot Splits Tree Limb.* Bird's feet caught in the crack, and other lucky accidents bring much game. [X1124.3.1].
English-American: Baughman (1890B, C) *13;* Franco-American *1.*

1890B *Bursting Gun and Series of Lucky Accidents.*
English-American: Baughman (1890D) *7.*

1890C *Two Bullets with one Charge* plus series of lucky accidents.
English-American: Baughman (1890E) *3.*

1890D *Ramrod Shot* plus series of lucky accidents. Cf. Type 1894.
English-American: Baughman (1890F) *8.*

1890E *Gun Barrel Bent* to make spectacular shot. [X1122.3].
Canada, U.S.: Baughman (X1122.3.1) *8.*

1890F *Lucky Shot: Miscellaneous Forms.*
French-Canadian *1;* English-American: Baughman (1890G) *5;* Serbocroatian *1.*

1890A* *Planting Pole to Catch a Bear.* Climbing to top of pole, and then beating bear with other end.
French-Canadian.

1890B* (formerly 2006*) *Fatal Bread.* The boy lets a piece of bread fall from the tree on to the bear's nose. The bear dies. [N331.2].
Estonian (2006*) *3.*

1891 *The Great Rabbit-Catch.* The rabbits freeze their feet fast to the ice at night [X1115.1].
Finnish *42;* Irish *1;* German *3;* Russian: Andrejev. — English-American: Baughman *4.*

1891A* *Lighted Candle* attracts rabbits so that they are caught.
   Finnish 3.

1891B* *Rabbits (hares) Caught by making them Sneeze.*
   Finnish 3.

1892 *The Trained Horse Rolls in the Field.* Oats grow in his flanks. The man ties a club to the horse's tail and thus kills many moor-hens. [X1241.2.2].
   Finnish 31; Finnish-Swedish 1; Estonian 1; Lithuanian 1; Austrian: Haiding No. 57; Russian: Andrejev. — Spanish-American: Hansen (1889**D) (Argentina) 1.

1892* *Wolf Made into Cheese.* A wolf falls into a wooden trench bringing milk from mountain to village, and is worked up into cheese. Later he carves out a scythe and escapes, and with the scythe mows the meadows.
   Serbocroatian 1.

1893 *The Man Lays a Bag by the Fence-hole* and all the hares run into the bag [X1114].
   Estonian (1893*) 1. — English-American: Baughman 1; West Indies (Negro) 1.

1893A* (formerly 1895*) *Two Hares Run into Each Other* and are caught [X1114.1].
   Irish 1; English 2; Flemish 2.

1894 *The Man Shoots a Ramrod Full of Ducks* [X1111].
   Münchhausen, ch. 2. — Finnish (1894**) 1; Swedish 6 (Uppsala 3, Lund 2, misc. 1); Irish 6; German 4; Franco-American: (Canada) 4, (Louisiana) 4.

1895 *A Man Wading in Water Catches Many Fish in his Boots* [X1112].
   Finnish 6; Flemish 3; German 2 (with 1890); Russian: Andrejev 1; English-American: Baughman 3.

1895* changed to 1893A*.

1895A* *Larger and Larger Fish.* A man catches a small trout; with this larger and then larger, each as bait for other.
   French-Canadian.

1895B* *The Fish-Soup in the Sea.* The sun settles in the sea, and from it the water warms; and the fish-soup is cooked.
   Russian: Andrejev (*1895 I) 1.

1895C* *A Horse Climbs through his Collar.* A horse bends over the water to drink; the collar slips from him together with the cart; he unharnesses himself and goes away.
   Russian: Afanasiev (*1896 I) 1.

1896 *The Man Nails the Tail of the Wolf to the Tree* and beats him. The wolf runs away and leaves his skin hanging. [X1132.1]. Cf. Type 1229.
   Münchhausen, ch. 2: Coffin 1. — Finnish (1896*) 1; Estonian (1896*) 8; Swedish (Lund) 1; Norwegian 1; German 3 (Archive 2, Henssen Volk No. 297 1); Russian: Andrejev 1. — Franco-American (Canada) 1; English-American: Baughman 4; West Indies (Negro) 1.

1896* *Hunting the Wolves with Rod and Line* [X1124.4].
   Norwegian 1.

1898* *Adventures as a Dog.* A man tells of his adventures while he was in shape of a dog. Hungarian: Honti *2*.

1900 *How the Man Came out of a Tree Stump (Marsh):* the bee's nest. When the bear comes, the man grasps his tail and the bear thus pulls him out. [X1133.4]. Cf. Type 1875.
   Coffin *2*. — Estonian (1900*) *3;* Slovenian *1;* Russian: Afanasiev (1900*B) *18*. — English-American: Baughman *8*.

1910 *The Bear (Wolf) Harnessed.* Eats the horses, is harnessed and runs in harness [X1216.1].
   **Vidossi FFC CLXII 3ff.; Aesop Halm No. 70, Münchhausen, ch. 1; Coffin *1*. — Finnish (1910*) *1;* Estonian (1910*) *5;* Lithuanian *1;* French *1;* Russian: Andrejev *Ukraine* 1, Afanasiev *5*. — Franco-American *1;* English-American: Baughman *2*.

1911 *Cart as Legs.* Small cart serves as back legs for crippled sow. Pigs have also these carts. (Similar stories about other animals.) [X1202.1].
   U.S.: Baughman (X1202 a—g) *10*.

1911A (formerly 1911**) *Horse's New Backbone.* The man makes a new backbone for his horse out of a stick when the old one breaks in two [X1721.1]. Or a flayed horse is covered with sheepskin and produces excellent wool.
   Coffin *1*. — Finnish *1;* Swedish *5* (Uppsala *1*, Liungman *1*, misc. *3*); Irish *3;* English-American: Baughman *1*.

1912 *Crippled Cat Uses Wooden Leg to Kill Mice.* [X1211.2].
   U.S.: Baughman (X1211.2) *7*.

1913 *The Side-hill Beast.* Animal with two short legs on one side for convenience in living on hillsides. It can walk around the hill in only one direction. [X1381].
   U.S.: Baughman *15;* North Carolina: *Brown Collection* I 703 *1*.

1916 *The Breathing Tree.* A hunter cuts down a tree packed so full of animals that a crack opens as the animals inhale, closes when they exhale. [X1116].
   U.S.: Baughman *9*.

1917 *The Stretching and Shrinking Harness.* A man driving a team with a wagon in the rain finds on arrival at the top of the hill that the tugs of rawhide have stretched and that the loaded wagon is still at the bottom. He unhitches the horses and throws the harness across a stump. Later when the sun comes out and shrinks the tugs they draw the load to the top of the hill. [X1785.1].
   U.S.: Baughman *19;* American Negro (Michigan): *Dorson 138.

1920 *Contest in Lying.*
   *Köhler-Bolte I 322; *BP II 514. — Finnish *3;* Swedish *7* (Lund *2*, Liungman *1*, misc. *4*); Irish *35*, Jackson FL XLVII 292; French *12;* German *3;* Austrian: Haiding No. 51; Slovenian *11;* Serbocroatian *5*.

— Franco-American (Canada) *5;* Spanish-American: Hansen (1889**F) *1;* West Indies (Negro) *1.*

1920A The First: »*The Sea Burns*». The other »Many fried fish» [X908]. Variant: The first tells of the great cabbage (cf. Type 1960D), the other of the great kettle (cf. Type 1960 I) to cook it in [X1423.1].

Finnish *110;* Finnish-Swedish *4;* Danish: Grundtvig No. 95; Irish: Beal I 197; Catalan: Amades No. 76; Walloon *1;* German *1;* Rumanian *7;* Hungarian *2;* Russian: Andrejev *3;* Greek *3,* Loukatos No. 20. — English-American: Baughman *9.*

1920B The one says, »*I Have not Time to Lie*» and yet lies [X905.4]. The great catch of fish [X1150.1]. Cf. Type 1960 C.

Coffin *1.* — Finnish *1;* Estonian *9;* Lithuanian *1;* Irish: O'Suilleabhain Handbook 620f. Nos. 42—45; German *3;* Russian: Andrejev *1;* Chinese: Eberhard FFC CXX 308ff. No. 18, FFC CXXVIII 260ff. No. 160; English-American: Baughman *11.*

1920C *The Master and the Peasant: the Great Ox.* The master brought to say »You lie» [X905.1].

*BP II 508ff. — Finnish *1;* Estonian: Aarne FFC XXV 119 No. 27; Livonian: Loorits FFC LXVI 51 No. 89; Lithuanian *21,* (1920D*) *20;* Swedish *3* (Uppsala *1,* Lund *2*); German *10;* Serbocroatian *1;* Russian: Andrejev *Ukraine* (1920*D) *13*,[1] Afanasiev *4;* Greek (1930D*) *13,* Dawkins *Modern Greek in Asia Minor* 408, Hahn I 313 No. 59, *Laographia* II 197; Turkish: Eberhardt-Boratav Nos. 358, 363 *15.*

(*The Hero Forces the Princess to Say* »*That is a Lie.*» See Type 852.)
(*Bargain Not to Become Angry.* See Type 1000.)

1920D *The Liar Reduces the Size of his Lie* when his brother steps on toes to remind him of his lying habits, or when challenged. [X904.1, X904.2].

*Wesselski *Märchen* No. 38. — Finnish *5;* German: Wisser *Plattdeutsche Volksmärchen* II 186. — U.S.: Baughman *3.*

1920E *Greatest Liar Gets his Supper Free.* Wager. Each lie is corroborated by a confederate, who poses as a newly arrived stranger. [K455.7]. Cf. Type 1526A.

*BP II 509. — Serbocroatian *8.*

1920F *He Who Says* »*That's a Lie*» *Must Pay a Fine.* Men wager that the first to say »That's a lie» will pay a fine. One tells a story showing that the second man owes him a sum of money equal to the agreed on fine. Cf. Types 920C, 852.

Slovenian *8;* India *4.*

1920G *The Great Bee and Small Beehive.* Lie: the great bee. Liar says that in a certain place bees are as big as sheep. — And the beehives? — The same as ours. — How do the bees get in? (Various answers.) [X1282.1].

*BP II 515; *Wesselski *Hodscha Nasreddin* II 219. — German: Müller-

Fraureuth *Deutsche Lügendichtungen* (1881) 58ff., 72, 127, 137; Slovenian *2;* Serbocroatian *1;* Gypsy: Krauss *Zigeunerhumor* p. 160.

1920H *Buying Fire by Story-telling.* Three Brothers go to an old man's camp for fire. The old man agrees to give them fire for a story. Two brothers cannot tell stories; the third does on the condition that the old man will not interrupt him. He tells tall tales; finally the old man interrupts him with the word »lie». In accordance with the agreement, the hero cuts three belts out of the old man's back. Cf. Types 1920C, 1920F, 852.

Russian: Afanasiev (1920*D) *21;* Greek: Dawkins *Modern Greek Folktales* No. 68 *6;* Turkish: Eberhard-Boratav No. 358 *15.*

1920A* *Tall Corn.* One tells of his corn which grow ten feet high, the other tells of his which grows to eaves of two-story house. The first asks how he harvested it. The second: »From the upstairs windows.»
U.S.: Baughman (1920E*) *1.*

1920B* *Big Strawberries.* One tells of his big strawberries; four berries fill a half-pint measure. The second remarks that none of his would go through opening of a half-pint measure.
U.S.: Baughman (1920E*) *1.*

1920C* *Speed in Skills.* Each tells of remarkable skill which he has acquired. See F660ff.
English-American: Baughman (1920 I*) *4.*

1920D* *Climbing to Heaven.* First brother tells about plant that grew to Heaven (cf. Type 1960G). Second tells about thread that reached Heaven. Third tells about lighting cigarette on moon. When third is asked how he did it, he exclaims, »I climbed up on the thread and down on the plant.» He wins father's inheritance.
Spanish-American: Hansen (1920**D) (Chile) *1.*

1920E* *Lie: Seeing (Hearing) Enormous Distance.*
Finnish *5;* Swedish (GS 1962) *2;* Spanish-American: Hansen (1920**E) (Puerto Rico) *1.*

1920F* *Skillful Hounds.* The first tells of a hound which keeps a raccoon treed until the hound starves; the second tells of a hound which trails a deer back to its birthplace. [X1439.2, X1440.2, X1215.9]. Cf. Type 1889N.
Münchhausen, ch. 3. — U.S.: Baughman (1920F*) *1.*

1920G* *Rabbits Baste Themselves.* Fat rabbits baste themselves in baking; bottle made from skin of greyhound leaps from man's girdle, catching hare [X1442.2].
English-American: Baughman (1920G*) *1.* Cf. Type 1930.

1920H* *Will Blow Out Lantern.* The first tells of catching large fish; the second of catching a lantern which is still burning. The first teller remonstrates; the second agrees that if the first will take twenty pounds off his fish he will blow out the light in his lantern.
English-American: Baughman (1920H*) *2.*

1922* (formerly 1991') *Hare with Rotted Ears.* The plowman found in a beautiful chest a hare with rotted ears. Whoever hears that will have his ears rot. [X942].
Livonian (1991') *1.*

1925 *Wishing Contests* [J1106].
Finnish-Swedish (1925*) *2;* Swedish (Uppsala) *1;* Slovenian *2.*

1925*(formerly 1951*) *Three Competing Wishes.* The first of three brothers wishes for himself a church full of needles, and the third wishes for all that the other brothers have wished for. [H507.3.1].
Finnish (1951**) *1;* cf. Type 750.

1927 *The Cold May Night.* A very cold night comes in May. Hearing of a much colder night long ago, a man sets out to find about it. In his travels he comes to (a) an otter lying in a deep hole on top of a rock: he has been so long lying there that the rock has been worn merely by his body; the otter had not experienced the cold night of long ago, but had heard of it, and sends the man to (b) an old eagle or hawk which is perched on an anvil and has worn the anvil almost through by the touch of its beak after eating; so on to the third, a salmon (c) which has only one eye: the salmon had been alive on the cold night long ago and had lost its eye then; it has leaped out of the water after a fly, and so suddenly did it freeze that when the salmon fell back to the water, the water was frozen hard; the salmon lay on the ice, and a bird had picked out its·eye; the blood from the eye finally melted the ice, and the salmon got back to the pool. [B841, B124.1, X1620]. Cf. Type 244**.
Irish.

1930 *Schlaraffenland.* (Land of Cokaygne.) Land in which impossible things happen: doves fleece a wolf, roast fowls fly, etc. [X950].
Motifs: X1503. Schlaraffenland. X1712. Schlaraffenland lies three miles beyond Christmas. X1503.4. Mountain of grain to be eaten through on way to Schlaraffenland. X1156.1. Fish caught with another's cries. X1208.2. Roast hens fly, heads to sky, tails to ground. X1211.1. Cat scratches out bear's tongue. X1215.12. Greyhounds drag mill out of water. X1226.1. Mice consecrate bishop. X1235.4. Cow climbs to roof. X1235.5. Cow puts bread in oven. X1241.2.3. Horses knead dough. X1242.0.1.1. Ass with silver nose hunts hares. X1244.1. Goat carries one hundred cartloads of grease. X1244.2. Goats heat oven. X1252.1. Crows mow meadow. X1855. Plow without horse or wheels. X1256.1. Doves tear up wolf. X1267.2. Hawk swims. X1294.1. Flies build bridge. X1342.3. Frog eats plowshare. X1344.1. Crab hunts hare. X1345.1. Snail kills lion. X1472.1. Pancakes growing on lime-tree. X1528.1. Mountain of cheese. F771.1.10. Gingerbread house. X1547.2.1. Honey flows up high mountain. X1561. Rome hanging by thread. X1727.1. Barber shaves wife's beard. X1741.4. Anvil swims river. X1791. Deaf, dumb, blind, and lame men catch hare. X1796.1. Footless man outruns swift horse. X1817.1. Razor-sharp sword as footbridge. X1856. Suckling children rock mother in cradle. X1856.1. Child throws down a kid. X1856.2. Child throws down mill-wheels from one town to another. X1857. Man drowned on mountain.

*BP III 244ff. (Grimm Nos. 158, 159). — Finnish *5;* Lithuanian *1;* Lappish *1;* Swedish *18* (Uppsala *5,* Stockholm *1,* Lund *12*); Irish *1,* English *2;* French *1;* Spanish *1;* Slovenian *5;* Russian: Afanasiev *6;* — English-American: Baughman *2;* Spanish-American: Hansen (1930**A) (Puerto Rico) *1.* — African *3.* — Literary Treatments: Herodotus III 17, 18; Münchhausen, ch. 17; Boccaccio *Decameron* VIII No. 3.

1930A* *The Wealth of the Poor:* instead of horses — cats, instead of cows — chickens, the harvest — one stack, etc.
Russian: Afanasiev (*1930 I) *8.*

1930B* *Boasting of a Dowry.* The girl boasts of a worn-out, ragged dowry; because of the worn and ragged outfit of the young man, etc. They marry.
Russian: Afanasiev (*1930 II) *3.*

1930C* *The Sea Burns, a Boat Sails on the Field,* a bear flies high in the sky, etc.
Russian: Afanasiev (*1931B) *3.*

1931 *The Woman Who Asked for News from Home.* Gets many impossible answers, which she believes. »The cock has become sexton.» — »That is why he sang so well in the morning» [J2349.4]. Cf. Type 1920A.
Finnish *33;* Estonian *2;* Lithuanian *5;* Swedish *4* (Uppsala *1,* Lund *2,* misc. *1*); Italian (Tuscan [1783] a, b *2*); Russian: Afanasiev (1931A) *2.*

1932 *Church Built of Cheese,* roofed with pancakes and the door locked with a sausage [F771.1.10, X1863]. Cf. Type 327A.
Bolte Zs. f. Vksk. IX 85. — Lithuanian (*1883) *34.*

1935 *Topsy-Turvy Land.* Land where all is opposite from the usual. [X1505].
*BP III 244ff., *254ff.; Wienert FFC LVI 44ff. — Russian: Afanasiev (*1931C) *8.*

1940 *The Extraordinary Names.* The place where animals and things have extraordinary names [F703, X1506]. Cf. Type 1562A.
*BP III 129 (Grimm No. 140), IV 183; Basset *Contes berbères* 350 No. 209; Bolte Zs. f. Vksk. XXVI 8, 370; Delarue *Arts et Traditions Populaires* I 275; Köhler-Bolte I 421; *Anderson *Novelline* No. 8. — Finnish *5;* Estonian *2;* Danish: Grundtvig No. 13; Irish *39,* Beal II 94, 221f. No. 7, Jackson FL XLVII 292; French *6;* Spanish (1940*C, *E, *F, *G) *5,* Espinosa II 160; Dutch *1;* Flemish *11,* Witteryck p. 274 *19;* German *4;* Russian: Afanasiev *11.—* Spanish-American: Rael No. 288 (U.S.); West Indies (Negro): Flowers 585.

1948 *Too Much Talk.* Three men vowed to silence go to a glen away from the world. At the end of seven years one speaks: I heard a cow lowing. Others are angry but silent. At the end of seven years more, second one says: 'Twas not a cow but a bull! The third is very angry but still silent. At the end of seven years more, the third one says: I'm leaving this place. The glen is bothered by you! (too much talk). (This tale is told with many variations.)
Finnish *70;* *Norwegian: Christiansen *Maal og Minne* (1954) 44; Irish: Beal I 306, XII 138, O'Duilearga *Leabhar Sheain I Chonaill* (1948) 196. Cf. Ranke in *Peuckert Festschrift* (1955) 51f.

1950 *The Three Lazy Ones.* Who is the laziest. Each recounts a proof of his laziness. [W111.1].
*BP III 207 (Grimm No. 151); Wesselski *Märchen* 213 No. 21. — Finnish *23;* Finnish-Swedish *1;* Estonian *3;* Lithuanian *4;* Lappish *1;* Swedish *4* (Lund *3,* misc. *1*); Icelandic *1,* Irish *85,* Beal II 218, Jackson

FL XLVII 292; English *1;* French *2;* Spanish *1;* Catalan: Amades No. 362; Flemish *5;* German *4* (Archive *3*, Henssen Volk No. 288); Italian (Trieste: Pinguentini cf. No. 30, Sicilian *2*); Rumanian *2*, (1698*) *4;* Hungarian *1;* Slovenian *8;* Serbocroatian *2;* Russian: Andrejev *1;* Turkish: Eberhard-Boratav No. 335 *1;* India *6*. — English-American: Baughman *1;* Spanish-American: Hansen (**823AB) (Puerto Rico) *3*, (Dominican Republic) *1*.

1950A *Help in Idleness.* Second idle worker tells the overseer he is helping the first.

Dutch: Cohen *Nederlandsche Sagen und Legenden* II 377; Walloon (1950C*) *1;* German: Meyer *Plattdeutsche Volksmärchen* 283 No. 200; Italian (Trieste: Pinguentini No. 91).

1951 *Is Wood Split?* A lazy man asks if wood is split before he accepts it as a gift [W111.5.12]. Sometimes, if rice is cooked.

U.S.: Baughman (W111.5.12) *9;* American Negro (Michigan): *Dorson No. 142; Spanish-American: Hansen (**823C) (Dominican Republic) *1*.

1951* changed to 1925*.

1960 *The Great Animal or Great Object.*

Lithuanian *13;* Swedish *30* (Uppsala *3*, Stockholm *11*, Lund *7*, Liungman *2*, misc. *7*); Norwegian *7;* Irish *57;* French *6;* German *44* (Archive *43*, Henssen Jül. No. 481); Austrian: Haiding Nos. 51, 57; Hungarian *5*.

1960A *The Great Ox* (horse, sheep, etc.) [X1201, X1223.1, X1233.1.1, X1235.1, B871.1.1.1].

*BP II 515 (Grimm No. 112). — Finnish *41;* Estonian *2;* Lithuanian (*1879) *5;* Swedish (Uppsala) *5;* Norwegian: Solheim *1;* Catalan: Amades No. 439; German *18* (Archive *17*, Meckl. No. 122); Rumanian *2;* Hungarian *1;* Slovenian *1;* Greek *6*. — West Indies (Negro) *1*.

1960B *The Great Fish* [X1301].

Finnish *162;* Finnish-Swedish *3;* Swedish *15* (Uppsala *11*, Lund *4*); Dutch *4;* Greek *1*. — West Indies (Negro) *1*.

1960C *The Great Catch of Fish* [X1150.1]. Cf. Type 1920B.

Finnish; Swedish (Uppsala) *3;* Serbocroatian *1*.

1960D *The Great Vegetable* (cabbage, potato, etc.) [X1401]. Cf. Type 1920A.

*BP III 169, *II 515 (Grimm No. 146). — Finnish *149;* Finnish-Swedish *2;* Estonian *7;* Swedish (Uppsala) *3;* Norwegian *1;* Spanish *1;* Flemish *1;* German *14;* Italian (Sicilian *2*); Rumanian (1960H) *2;* Hungarian *1;* Slovenian *3;* Serbocroatian *3;* Russian: Afanasiev (1960*D I, turnip) *1;* Greek *11;* Turkish: Eberhard-Boratav No. 358, 363 *18;* India *3*. — Spanish-American: Hansen (1889**N) (Argentina, melon) *1;* West Indies (Negro) *1*.

1960E *The Great Farmhouse* (stable, cowshed, mill, etc.) [X1030.1, X1036.1].

Finnish *70;* Estonian *1;* Lappish *1;* Swedish *6* (Uppsala *5*, Lund *1*); German *4;* Turkish: Eberhard-Boratav No. 358 III *15.*

1960F *The Great Kettle* [X1030.1.1]. Cf. Type 1920A.
Finnish *76;* Finnish-Swedish *1;* Walloon *1;* German *5;* Italian (Sicilian *2*); Slovenian *2.*

1960G *The Great Tree* (plants growing to heaven, etc.) [F54]. Cf. Types 328, 555.
*BP II 511 (Grimm No. 112). — Finnish *56;* Finnish-Swedish *1;* Estonian *43;* Livonian *1;* Lappish *1;* Swedish (Uppsala) *7;* Norwegian: Solheim *1;* Catalan: Amades Nos. 74, 86, 167, cf. 201; Dutch *3;* Flemish *6;* German *24* (Archive *21*, Meckl. No. 122, Henssen Volk Nos. 293, 294); Italian (Tuscan 563 a, l, 707 u, [1354] a *4*); Hungarian *1;* Slovenian *51;* Russian: Afanasiev *6*, (1960*G I, sweetpea to sky) *10;* Greek (1920D*) *31;* Turkish: Eberhard-Boratav No. 173 V.

1960H *The Great Ship* [X1061.1].
BP II 516. — Finnish-Swedish (1960) *3;* Swedish *4* (Uppsala *3*, Lund *1*); Norwegian: Solheim *1;* Dutch *6;* German *1.*

1960J *The Great Bird* [B31.1].
Flemish *1;* German *1;* Rumanian *1;* Slovenian *3;* Russian: Afanasiev (*1960C I The fruitful duck lays boatload of eggs) *1.* — West Indies (Negro) *2.*

1960K *The Great Loaf of Bread; the Great Cake, etc.* [X1811.1].
Swedish (Uppsala) *2;* Flemish (1920*) *6;* German *4.*

1960L *The Great Egg* [X1813].
*Feilberg *Ordbog* III 1142a s.v. »æg»; U.S.: Baughman (X1813); India: Thompson-Balys. — Spanish-American: Hansen (1960Z) *1.*

1960M *The Great Insect.*

1960M₁. *Large Mosquitoes Fly off with Kettle.* They have drilled through kettle. Their bills are clinched inside like nails. [X1286.1.4].
U.S.: Baughman (X1286.1.5) *24.*

1960M₂. *Large Mosquitoes Carry off Men or Animals* [X1286.1.5].
English-American: Baughman (X1286.1.6) *12.*

1960M₃. *Large Bumblebee.* Battles with bear.
Russian: Afanasiev (1960*A I) *1.*

1960Z *Other Stories of Great Objects and the Like* [X1049].
Finnish-Swedish (1960**) *4;* Swedish *3* (Uppsala *2*, Lund *1*); Danish: MS. DFS.

1961 *The Big Wedding.* Giant with sixty daughters [X1071].
Norwegian: Solheim *2*, (1961**) *2.*

1961A* *Rivers in a Bag.* Man carries three rivers in bag, drops bag and lets rivers out. They carry him to destination.
Hungarian: Berze Nagy (1961**B) *32.*

1961B* *Boat from Walnut.* Man shakes walnut tree and makes a boat from a walnut.
Hungarian: Berze Nagy (1961**C) *15.*

1961C* *The Four-horse Coach.* Man takes four horses, two in front of the coach and two after it. On the road they lose a wheel: takes a horse to go back and find it. He tries to put the wheel around the horse's neck, and the horse breaks his leg. Cf. Bolte-Polivka III 298—299; Hungarian: Berze Nagy (1961**D) *2.*

1961D* *Which Pig Belongs to Which Sow?* Pretended wise man cannot tell.
Hungarian: Berze Nagy (1961**E) *2.*

1962 *My Father's Baptism (Wedding).* (Lying-tale with many episodes.)
Hungarian: Honti *18*, Berze Nagy (1961A**, B**, C**) *53.*

1962A *The Great Wrestlers.* Cf. Types 650B*, 1960. [F531.6.8.3.3, H1225]. (a) A prodigious wrestler (eater) sets out to challenge another. (The daughter of the second picks up an elephant and carries it about, or calls it a mouse.) [X941.3]. (b) They meet an old woman who says they may wrestle on her arm [X941.2], handkerchief, etc. (c) A great bird picks them (and many animals) up and flies off with them. (d) The bird drops them into the eye of a princess, who says a speck of dust has fallen into her eye, or the like [X941.4].
India *11.*

1963 *Lie: Boat without Bottom Sails Sea.*
BP III 118. — German (1963) *17*, Henssen *Volk Erzählt* No. 293.

1965 *Knoist and his Three Sons.* Blind, lame, naked go on hunt. [X1791].
Boratav »Les trois compagnons infirmes» *Fabula* II 231ff.; Honti *Hdwb. d. Märchens* II 597; *BP III 116 (Grimm No. 138); *Anderson *Novelline* No. 112; *Spiess *Orientalische Stoffe in den Kinder- und Hausmärchen der Brüder Grimm*, p. 30. — German (1962*) *15*, Henssen *Volk Erzählt* No. 293; Hungarian: Berze Nagy (1961F) *1;* Walloon (1884*) *1.* — Spanish American: Hansen (1920**F), (Puerto Rico) *1.*

1991' changed to 1922*.

IV FORMULA TALES

CUMULATIVE TALES

The following, belonging elsewhere, have been assigned new numbers as indicated

2005* changed to 1574A.
2005** changed to 1574B.
2006* changed to 1890B*.
2007* changed to 1382*.
2009* changed to 1348.
2010* changed to 1338A.

2000—2013 Chains based on numbers or objects

2009 *Origin of Chess.* Inventor asks one wheat-grain for the first square, two for the second, four for the third, eight for the fourth, etc. The king cannot pay. [Z21.1].
**Taylor JAFL XLVI 79 No. 2009; *Livingston *Modern Language Notes* XLV 246—51; Murray *History of Chess* (Oxford, 1913) 207—9, 755.

2010 *Ehod mi yodea (One; who knows?).* Le dodici parole della verità. Las doce palabras retorneadas. The numbers from one to twelve are brought into relation with various objects, often of religious significance. [Z22].
**Espinosa *Revista de Filologia Espanola* XVII 390ff.; *Taylor JAFL XLVI 79 No. 2010; *BP III 15 n.; *Greenleaf *Ballads and Sea-songs of Newfoundland* (Cambridge, Mass., 1933) 93 No. 41; **Hdwb. d. Märchens II 171ff.; *Newell »The Carol of the Twelve Numbers« JAFL IV (1891) 215—220; Di Carlo *Il Folklore Italiano* I 186; Cheroni *ibid.* IV 178; Corso *ibid* VII 92; Caputo *ibid.* VII 298; Köhler-Bolte III 370 n. 2. — Lithuanian *12;* Swedish (GS 2036) *9* (Uppsala *2,* Stockholm *2,* Liungman *1,* misc. *4);* French *25,* (2045*) *1;* Spanish: Espinosa II 111— 143, (2045*) *1;* Russian: Andrejev No. 812B*; Jewish: *Neuman (Z22). — Spanish-American: Hansen (*2045) (Argentina) *4,* (Chile) *6,* (Puerto Rico) *3;* West Indies (Negro) *1.*

2010A *The Twelve Days (Gifts) of Christmas:* 1 partridge, 2 turtle-doves, 3

French hens, 4 colly birds, 5 gold rings, 6 geese, 7 swans, 8 maids, 9 drummers, 10 pipers, 11 ladies, 12 lords. [Z22.1].
**Taylor JAFL XLVI 79 No. 2010A, Hdwb. d. Märchens II 172b; Kristensen *Danske Dyrefabler* 146—60 Nos. 337—348; Feilberg *Ordbog* I 54, IV 248 s.v. »Juledagsgave»; Norlind *Svenska Allmogens Liv* 612. — Swedish (GS 2041) *30*.

2010B *The Twelve kinds of Food:* 1 partridge, 2 turtle-doves, 3 wood-pigeons, 4 ducks, 5 rabbits, 6 hares, 7 hounds, 8 sheep, 9 oxen, 10 turkeys, 11 hams, 12 cheese. [Z22.2].
**Taylor JAFL XLVI 80 No. 2010B, Hdwb. d. Märchens II 172b; Kristensen *Danske Dyrefabler* 150—54 Nos. 351—370.

2010 I *How the Rich Man Paid his Servant* (Lönen hos den rike man). A farmer pays his servant in the first year a hen, in the second a cock, goose, goat cow, horse, . . . girl, farmstead. [Z23].
**Taylor JAFL XLVI 80 No. 2010 I; Kristensen *Danske Dyrefabler* 168—78 Nos. 392—418; Norlind *Svenska Allmogens Liv* 612. — Lithuanian *3*.

2010 I A. *The Animals with Queer Names:* as hen (henny-penny), cock (cocky-locky), goose (goosey-poosey). [Z53]. Cf. Types 1940, 2033.
*Wesselski Hessische Blätter XXXII 55; *Taylor JAFL XLVI 80 No. 2010 IA; Jacobs *English Fairy Tales* 118; *Norlind *Svenska Allmogens Liv* 612; Kristensen *Danske Dyrefabler* 182 Nos. 431—32. — Spanish-American: Hansen (*2052) (Cuba) *1;* Antigua (British West Indies): Johnson JAFL XXXIV 68 No. 24.

2011 *Where have you Been, Goose?* — In the fields. — What have you in your beak? — A knife. — etc. (Tile, water, ox, firewood, old woman, friars, mass, shirts.) [Z39.4].
*Taylor JAFL XLVI 80 No. 2011, Hdwb. d. Märchens II 174a; Spanish (2018*A). — Cheremis: Sebeok-Nyerges (Z39.4.1, Z39.4.2).

2012 *The Forgetful Man Counts the Days of the Week.* On Monday they go to mill, etc. — He thus discovers that it is Sunday. [Z24].
Finnish (2012*) *8;* Estonian (2012*) *1;* French *5;* Russian: Andrejev *Ukraine 4*.

2012A *Widower Tells of his Courtship, his Marriage, and the Death of his Wife*, all in a week [Z24.1].
*Taylor JAFL XLVI 80 No. 2012A; cf. Bolte *Archiv f. neueren Sprachen* XCVIII 87ff., 281ff., XCIX 9ff., C 149ff., 298f. — Spanish *1;* German: Zender No. 88.

2012B *Life Story in Ten Hours:* »At one I was born . . . at ten my child's soul was crowned in heaven.» [Z24.1.1].
*Taylor JAFL XLVI 80 No. 2012B. — Spanish *1.*

2012C *Bird Advises Man to Treat his Lazy Children as she does her Young:* »In

March I make my nest ... in August I have nothing more to do with my young.» [Z24.1.2].
*Taylor JAFL XLVI 80 No. 2012C. — Spanish *1*.

2012D »*Solomon Grundy, born on Monday ... buried on Sunday.*» [Z24.1.3].
*Taylor JAFL XLVI 80 No. 2012D; Halliwell *Nursery Rhymes of England* 33 No. 49.

2013 *There Was Once a Woman; the Woman had a Son;* the son had breeches; the breeches had black buttons, etc. At last, »Shall I tell it all again?» [Z49.4]. Cf. Types 2300, 2320.
Finnish (2013*) *3;* Estonian (2013*) *5;* cf. Hungarian: Berze Nagy (1962E*) *14*.

2013* *Fly Forgets her Name;* asks woodcutter, axe, tree, etc., in vain. Finally foal in mare's belly says her name is »fly». [Z25].
India *1*.

2014 *Chains Involving Contradictions or Extremes* [Z51.1]. Cf. Type 2335.
Taylor JAFL XLVI 81 No. 2014, Hdwb. d. Märchens II 175b. — Estonian (2014) *7;* Swedish *10* (Uppsala *4,* Liungman *1,* misc. *5*); French *5;* Spanish *2,* (*2225, *2226, *2227, *2228) *4;* Dutch *1;* Walloon *1;* Rumanian (1961*) *2;* Slovenian *1;* Serbocroatian *1;* Russian: Afanasiev *8*. — English-American: Baughman *3*.

2014A (formerly 2014) *The House is Burned Down.* — That is too bad. — That is not bad at all, my wife burned it down. — That is good. — That is not good, etc. [Z23].
Estonian (2014*) *7;* Rumanian (1331—41 [11]) *2*.

2015 *The Goat who Would not Go Home.* One animal after another tries in vain to persuade the goat to go home. Finally a wolf (bee) bites him and drives him home. [Z39.1]. Variants: a hog, wolf, cat or the like [Z39.1]. Often mixed with Type 2030. Cf. Type 212.
*BP I 348 n. 1, cf. II 100; **Haavio FFC LXXXVIII; Coffin *1*. — Finnish (2015**) *3;* Swedish *68* (Uppsala *30,* Stockholm *7,* Göteborg *2,* Liungman *8,* Lund *1,* misc. *20*); Norwegian: Solheim *5,* (Christensen *Norske Eventyr* 147, FFC XLVI 40); French *24;* Catalan: Amades No. 246; Dutch *7,* (2015 var.) *9;* Flemish (FFC XXXVII 81 B) *17;* Italian *2* (Sicilian *2*); Hungarian: Berze Nagy (286*A) *21;* Slovenian; Serbocroatian *5;* Russian: Afanasiev *14;* Turkish: Eberhard-Boratav cf. Nos. 24, 27 *3*. — Spanish-American: Rael Nos. 403, 404 (U.S.), Hansen (Puerto Rico) *4*.

2015* *The Goat who would not Leave the Hazel Bush.* Final formula: The devil goes to strangle the Jew, the Jew to kill the ox, the ox to drink the water, the water to quench the fire, the fire to burn the stone, the stone to blunt the axe, the axe to cut the rope, the rope to tie the hunter, the hunter to shoot the goat — the goat leaves the hazel bush, the wee goat leaves the hazel bush. [Z39.1.1].
Lithuanian (2030).

2016 »*There Was a Wee Wee Woman,* who had a wee wee cow» [Z39.2].

*Taylor JAFL XLVI 81 No. 2016, Hdwb. d. Märchens II 176a; Jacobs *English Fairy Tales* 57. — Finnish (2016**) *1;* Swedish *13* (Uppsala *3,* Göteborg *1,* Liungman *1,* misc. *8*); Danish *8* (Kristensen *Danske Dyrefabler* 122 ff. Nos. 230—37; English *1;* French *1;* Catalan: Amades Nos. 465b, 466, 467, 468, 469, 470; Italian (Tuscan 2016 b, f *2*); Russian: Andrejev 2, Andrejev *Ukraine* (2015 I*).

2016* »*Where to Put Old Woman?*» A peasant asks the tar-boiler for tar with which to tar his boat; the boat is needed to catch fish, the fish to feed the children, etc.
Hungarian: Berze Nagy (286*D) *20;* Russian: Andrejev (*2015 II) *1.*

2017 *The Crow on the Tarred Bridge.* His beak and his tail alternately stick. [Z39.3]. (Endless). Cf. Type 2300.
*Taylor JAFL XLVI 81 No. 2017, Hdwb. d. Märchens II 190a. — Finnish (2017**) *11;* Lithuanian *3;* cf. Hungarian: Berze Nagy (1962C*) *15.*

2018 »*Where is the Warehouse?*» — »The fire burned it down.» — »Where is the fire?» — »The water quenched it.» [Z49.5].
Finnish (2014**) *1;* Estonian (2014*) *7;* Lithuanian *6;* English *1;* Spanish (2018*A) *2,* Espinosa Cuentos III 463—473; Catalan: Amades cf. No. 236; Hungarian: Berze Nagy (286C*) *2;* Slovenian *2;* Russian: Andrejev (*2015 I) *2,* Andrejev *2.* — Spanish-American: Hansen (2018*A) (Argentina) *4,* (Puerto Rico) *2.*

2018* *From Iron a Hatchet,* from hatchet cut trees, from trees build house, in house have wife and children.
Hungarian: Berze Nagy (286D*) *20.*

2019—2020 Chains involving a wedding

See in general Taylor Handwb. d. Märchens s.v. »Formelmärchen» No. 11. Cf. Types 65, 2023.

2019 *Pif Paf Poltrie.* Each member of a family is assigned a characteristic function; various wooers appear and are rejected until the one which is apparently the most unpromising is chosen. [Z31.1].
*BP III 71—74 (Grimm No. 131); *Taylor JAFL XLVI 81 No. 2019; Greek: Loukatos Nos. 31, 32, 33; India: Thompson-Balys.

2019* *Louse and Flea wish to Marry.* Mosquito, toad, ant, etc. volunteer to supply the wedding feast [Z31.2].
Spanish (2020*); Spanish-American: Hansen (Argentina) *1,* (Chile) *1.*

2021—2024 Chains involving a death — animal actors [Z32]

2021 *The Cock and the Hen.* The hen chokes to death on a grain. Various animals join the funeral procession. The funeral carriage breaks down or the procession drowns. [Z32.1].

*BP II 147 n. 1; *Wesselski Hessische Blätter XXXII 2ff.; *Taylor JAFL XLVI 82 No. 2021; H. Haavio FFC XCIX. — Swedish *22* (Uppsala *5*, Stockholm *2*, Lund *1*, Liungman *5*, misc. *9*); Norwegian *7;* Irish *28;* German *5* (Archive *3*, Merk. 314, Meckl. No. 27); India: Thompson-Balys.

2021A *The Death of the Cock.* (Der Tod des Hühnchens.) The cock chokes and the hen seeks aid of objects and persons (stream, tree, pig, miller, baker, etc.). [Z32.1.1].
**Haavio FFC XCIX; *BP II 146; *Taylor JAFL XLVI 82 No. 2021A; *Wesselski Hessische Blätter XXXII 2ff. — Latvian (*241A) *19;* Hungarian: Berze Nagy (286*) *17;* Russian: Afanasiev (*241 I) *9*.

2021B (formerly 241*) *The Cock Strikes out the Hen's Eye with a Nut.* The cock blames the hazel bush for tearing its knickers, the hazel bush the goat for gnawing at it, the goat the shepherd-boy for not tending it, the boy his mistress for not baking him a bun, the mistress the pig for eating up the dough, the pig the wolf for killing its young. [Z43.2].
BP II 149 No. 80. — Livonian (241) *1;* Latvian (241*) *48;* Lithuanian (*2031G) *19;* Russian: Afanasiev (*241 II) *1;* Turkish: Eberhard-Boratav Nos. 25, 26, 28 *3*.

2021* *The Louse Mourns her Spouse, the Flea.* The dog bays, the cart runs away, hits a tree, the bird moults, the child breaks the pots. The father punishes the child, who throws a stone at the bird which pecks the tree, which pushes back the cart, which crushes the dog's paw and kills the flea. The louse sees that the flea is dead, and eats the soup.
Walloon (*2036) *1*.

2022 *The Death of the Little Hen* is characteristically mourned by objects and animals: e.g. flea, door, broom, cart, ashes, tree, girl. [Z32.2].
*BP I 293 (Grimm No. 30); *Anderson *Novelline* Nos. 68, 79; *Taylor FFC XLVI 82 No. 2022; Coffin *2*. — Latvian (**241) *27;* Swedish (Lund) *1;* Norwegian: Solheim *1;* Danish: MS. DFS.; Irish *7;* French *26;* Spanish (2023*); Catalan: Amades Nos. 239, 240, 241, 247; Flemish *5* (FFC XXXVII 81A); Italian *10* (Tuscan *5*, Sicilian *5*); Hungarian: Berze Nagy (*286B) *2;* Russian: Andrejev (*241 II); Turkish: Eberhard-Boratav No. 30 *5;* India *2*. — Franco-American (Missouri): Carrière; Spanish-American: Rael No. 393 (U.S.); Cape Verde Islands: Parsons JAFL XXXIII 37.

2022A *The Death of the Little Hen Described with Unusual Words.* Each act of mourning described by a neologism: the table untables itself. [Z32.2.1].
*Taylor JAFL XLVI 82 No. 2022A, Hdwb. d. Märchens II 177a; Tegethoff *Französische Märchen* II 78 No. 18; Rolland *Rimes et jeux d'enfance* (1881) 119f. — Danish: Kristensen *Danske Dyrefabler* 98ff. No. 171ff.; Hungarian: Berze Nagy (*286*B) *2*.

2022B *The Hen Lays an Egg, the Mouse Breaks it.* Sorrowing over this mishap all show extraordinary behavior; the master puts an end to it. Final formula: hen strips off feathers, rubbish heap catches fire, oak falls to ground, hare drowns self, magpie twists leg, ox breaks horns, river flows blood, maid breaks pails, housewife scatters dough. Master locks up wife and maid, goes to seek people more foolish. [Z39.5]. Cf. Type 1384.

BP II 105f. — Lithuanian (2022) *18;* Russian: Afanasiev (*241 III) *5;* Rumanian (1963*) *4.*

2023 *Little Ant Finds a Penny, Buys New Clothes with it, and Sits in her Dooeway.* Various animals pass by and propose marriage. She asks what they do at night. Each replies with its characteristic sound, but none pleases her but the little quiet mouse, whom she marries. She leaves him to tend the stew, and he falls in and drowns. She weeps and, on learning the reason, bird cuts off its beak, dove cuts off its tail, etc. [Z32.3].

*Taylor JAFL XLVI 82 No. 2023; Coffin *1.* — French *1;* Spanish (*2023) *7,* Espinosa III 445—450; Catalan: Amades No. 345; Italian: Crane *Italian Popular Tales* (1885) 376f,; Turkish: Eberhard-Boratav No. 21 *15.* — Spanish-American: Hansen (Cuba) *2,* (Puerto Rico) *7.*

2023* *Mourning about the Dead Ass (Tulsi Das):* from washerman to the queen. »But who is Tulsi Das?« The report is traced back to the washerman, who says: »He was my ass.» [Z32.5].
India *3.*

2024* *Rabbit Borrows Money* from beetle, chicken, fox, dog, tiger, and hunter. When beetle comes to collect, rabbit tells him to go behind board while he counts the money. Instead, he calls chicken to eat beetle, fox to eat chicken, etc.
Spanish-American: Hansen (**2024) (Venezuela) *1.*

2025—2028 Chains involving the eating of an object; members of chain are not interrelated

Taylor *Handwb. d. Märchens* s.v. »Formelmärchen« No. 14.

2025 *The Fleeing Pancake.* A woman makes a pancake which flees. Various animals try in vain to stop it. Finally the fox eats it up. [Z33.1].

*Zs. f. Vksk. XVII 133—141; Coffin *3;* *Dähnhardt III 272.— Lithuanian *54;* Latvian (*296) *13;* Swedish (Uppsala) *2;* Norwegian: Christiansen *Norske Eventyr* 148 *4;* Danish: Kristensen *Danske Dyrefabler* 58; Scottish *1;* Irish *36;* Dutch *6;* German Archive *1;* Slovenian *1;* Serbocroatian *1;* Russian: Afanasiev (296*) *9;* English-American: Baughman *4.*

2026* *Man Wheedles Horn from Goat* and exchanges it for fish from sea. He coaxes first smith to give him fire to cook fish, but he burns his arm. Second smith removes fire from his arm and gives him a hammer in exchange. Third smith takes hammer away and gives him an axe. Man chops down tree with axe but it falls on him and kills him.
Spanish-American: Hansen (**2026) (Cuba) *1.*

2027 *The Fat Cat.* While the mistress is away the cat eats the porridge, the bowl, and the ladle. When the mistress return she says »How fat you are!» The cat: »I ate the porridge, the bowl, and the ladle and I will eat you.» The cat meets other animals and eats them after the same conversation. Finally eats too many. [Z33.2]. Cf. Types 333, 1631.

*Feilberg *Ordbog* III 108b s.v. »kat». — Swedish *63* (Uppsala *20*, Stockholm *5*, Göteborg *5*, Lund *1*, Liungman *12*, misc. *20*); Danish: Kristensen *Dyrefabler* 59ff., Nos. 119—130 *12;* India *5*. — American Negro (Michigan): Dorson No. 164.

2027A *Woman Meets a Pig.* »Good morning.» »Why are you up so early?» »I am not up so early. I have drunk seven vats of milk and eaten seven plates of porridge and I shall eat you.» She eats the pig. [Z33.3].

*Taylor *JAFL* 83 No. 2027A; Swedish: Norlander »Barnvisor och barnrim» *Svenska Landsmålen* V No. 5 n. 265.

2027* »*Get into my Belly.*» The wee cock, lost in the woods, orders the fox, the bear, and the wolf, to get into his belly. Overawed, the beasts make their apologies, promising never to annoy him again. The bear even carries the cock home. [K547.1]. Cf. Type 715.

Lithuanian (*2007) *1*.

2028 *The Troll (Wolf) who was Cut Open.* A troll eats the watcher's five horses and finally the watcher himself. The master goes to investigate. The troll: »I ate the five horses, I ate the watcher, and I will eat you.» Does so. Likewise with wife, servant, daughter, son, and dog. The cat scratches the troll open and rescues all. [Z33.4]. Cf. Type 333.

*Feilberg *Ordbog* II 108b s.v. »kat», III 1139 s.v. »æde», IV 43 s.v. »bjørn». — Danish: Kristensen *Dyrefabler* 68ff., Nos. 131—144 *13;* Icelandic *1;* French *1;* Russian: Andrejev (333B*) *18*. — English-American: Baughman *1*.

2028A* *Louse and Crow Make Covenant of Friendship.* Louse eats crow despite crow saying, »If I strike you once with my beak you will disappear; how then can you talk of eating me?» Likewise louse eats loaf of bread, she-goat, cow, buffalo, five sepoys, wedding procession with one lakh of people, elephant, tank of water. A sepoy cuts louse in two with his sword and rescues all. [Z33.4.1].

India: Thompson-Balys (Z33.4.1) *1*.

2029 *Chains Involving other Events without Interrelation of Members* [Z39].

Taylor *JAFL* XLVI 84 No. 2029.

2029A* *Girl Left in Tree by Sisters:* asks monkey, ape, bear, and tiger to put her down or else bite her. All refuse. Panther comes and devours her. [Z39.7].

India *1*.

2029B* *Small Grain-measure Runs Away* when her husband beats her: succession of suitors. [Z39.8].

India *1*.

2029C* *Series of Things Acquired by Mouse* — »You cannot have this but you may have that instead,» etc. Clod—fish—cakes—kid—goat—drum—girl. Girl kills mouse accidentally. [Z39.9].

India (170A III) *12*.

2029D* *A Widow with Many Children* is being courted. One day she is asked if she wishes to marry, another day if she has a house, a garden, cows, etc. She replies affirmatively. When she wishes for children, the suitor returns no more.
Walloon *1*.

2030 *The Old Woman and her Pig.* Her pig will not jump over the stile so that she can go home. She appeals in vain for help until the cow gives her milk. The final formula is: cow give milk for the cat, cat kill rat, rat gnaw rope, rope hang butcher, butcher kill ox, ox drink water, water quench fire, fire burn stick, stick beat dog, dog bite pig, pig jump over stile. [Z41].

Goebel Hdwb. d. Märchens I 256ff. s.v. »Birnli»; *BP II 104, 108; *Taylor's analysis; Köhler-Bolte I 136; Coffin *8;* Feilberg *Ordbog* IV 12 s.v. »and». — Lithuanian *10;* Swedish *22* (Uppsala *1*, Stockholm *4*, Göteborg *1*, Lund *3*, Liungman *5*, misc. *8*); Scottish *8;* Irish *95;* Beal IV 298ff., X 298f., Jackson FL XLVII 292; English *2;* Spanish *1* (A), *2* (B), *2* (C); Catalan: Amades Nos. 254, 589; Italian *6* (Tuscan *4*, Sicilian *2*); Hungarian: Berze Nagy (286*) *17;* Slovenian *1;* Turkish: Eberhard-Boratav No. 31 *3;* India: *Emeneau JAFL LVI 272, *Thompson-Balys (Z41) *3;* Indonesian: DeVries No. 21. — Franco-American (Missouri): Carrière; English-American: Baughman *6;* Spanish-American: Hansen (Dominican Republic) *1*, (Puerto Rico) *1*, (Argentina, 2030F) *1;* West Indies (Negro) *7*. — African (Benga): Nassau 200 No. 30, (Hottentot): Bleek 33 No. 17, (Gold Coast): Barker and Sinclair 177 No. 35, (Ila, Rhodesia): Smith and Dale II 392 No. 17, (Thonga): Junod 223; Jamaica: Beckwith MAFLS XVII 286 No. 138.

2030A *Ant Plants Chickpeas;* becomes impatient because they do not begin to sprout the next day; and asks gardener to remove tree under which she planted them. He refuses. She makes vain appeals until finally butcher threatens to kill ox, ox to drink water, water to put out candle, candle to burn stick, stick to beat cat, cat to eat mouse, queen, king, justice, gardener's wife who persuades her husband to remove the tree.
Spanish *1*. — Spanish-American: Hansen (Cuba) *1*.

2030B *Crow must Wash his Bill in Order to Eat with Other Birds.* Asks water; water must first have horn from stag, who must first have milk from cow, etc. [Z41.2].

*Wesselski Hessische Blätter XXXII 33. — Spanish: Espinosa *Cuentos* III 450—458; India *7*. — Spanish-American: Hansen (Chile) *1*.

2030C *Mouse Eats Old Couple's Cheese.* Cat kills mouse for eating cheese. Dog kills cat for eating mouse. [Z41.1].

*Wesselski Hessische Blätter XXXII 25. — Spanish (2030*C) *2*.

2030D *The Pear will not Fall.*
**Goebel Hdwb. d. Märchens I 256ff. s.v. »Birnli»; *BP II 100f.

2030E *Der Bauer schickt den Jockel aus.*
*BP II 102f.

2030F *Jukel Fetches Wine.* (A special Bohemian form.)
*BP II 103.

2030G *A Goat is Driven away from Nuts or Cabbage.*
*BP II 104f.

2030H *La Chanson de Bricon (a cock).*
*RTP XIV 47, XV 220.

2030J *A Disobedient Boy.*
Swedish: Norlind *Svenska Allmogens Liv* 613.

2030A* *Conflict between Fowl and Thistle.* Wind obeys and breaks the chain. [Z41.3].
India: Thompson-Balys (Z41.3) 2.

2030B* *Pulling the Needle out of the Seamstress's Hand.* Final formula: That was just what the cat was waiting for — it sprang to devour the mouse, the mouse to tear the spider's web, the spider to entangle the dog, the dog to eat the goat, the goat to gnaw the rushes, the rushes to grow in the stream, the stream to quench the fire, the fire to burn the stone, the stone to beat the axe. The axe soon pulled out the needle that was stuck in the seamstress's hand. [Z41.8].
Lithuanian (2005*) *1.*

2030C* *The Lazy Servant and the Grain.* »Lentils, lentils, get into my sack!» Final formula: the hungry hawk attacks the hens, the hens the worms, the worms the stick, the stick the ox, the ox runs to the water, the water attacks the fire, the fire the hunters, the hunters the wolf, the wolf the goat, the goat the willow, the willow the cat, the cat the mice, the mice the lentils, the lentils go whoosh whoosh into the sack. [Z41.9].
Lithuanian (2011*) *1.*

2030D* *Lady Owns a Goat which Eats her Tree.* She asks for help. Final formula: Lady, give me wood; wood is not mine, it belongs to woodcutter. Woodcutter broke my axe; axe is not mine, it belongs to the oven. The oven burned my fish; it is not mine, it belongs to the river. The river carried away my horn; the horn is not mine, it belongs to the goat. The goat ate the tree; the tree is not mine, it belongs to the man.
Spanish-American: Hansen (2030**E) (Puerto Rico) *1.*

2030E* *Fox and Cat Engage in Jumping Contest,* winner to cut off loser's tail. Cat wins and fox wants tail returned. Cat will return it for milk. Fox asks cow for milk. Cow does not wish to give milk unless it is given grass; meadow, water; river, kettle; kettlemaker, meat. Butcher gives meat to fox but fox says he will not repay him. Butcher turns dogs loose and fox is killed.
Spanish-American: Hansen (2030**F) (Argentina) *1.*

2031 *Stronger and Strongest.* The frost-bitten foot. Mouse perforates wall, wall resists wind, wind dissolves cloud, cloud covers sun, sun thaws frost, frost breaks foot. [Z42].
**DeCock *Volkssage* 22—36; *BP I 148 n. 2, IV 335 No. 28; Clouston *Tales* I 309; *Taylor JAFL XLVI 84 No. 2031, Hdwb. d. Märchens II 182ff.; Haavio FFC LXXXVIII 20; Köhler-Bolte II 47; Stiefel Zs. f. Vksk. V 448—50. — French *10;* Spanish *1;* Catalan: Amades No. 253; Greek *1;* Turkish: Eberhard-Boratav Nos. 24, 27 *4;* India *5;* Indonesian: DeVries No. 1, Voorhoeve 166 No. 176. — Spanish-American: Hansen (Chile) *1,* (Puerto Rico) *4,* (California): Espinosa JAFL XXVII 222; American Indian (Tehuano): Boas JAFL XXV 219. — African (Ekoi):

Talbot 384, (Zanzibar): Bateman 67 No. 5. — Literary Treatment: Benfey Panchatantra I 373—78, II 264; Chauvin II 97f.

2031A *The Esdras Chain: Stronger and Strongest*, wine, king, woman, truth [Z42.1].
*Taylor JAFL XLVI 85 No. 2031A, Hdwb. d. Märchens II 184b; DeCock *Volkssage* 35f. — Jewish: Neuman (Z42.1). — Literary Treatments: Oesterley *Gesta Romanorum* No. 258.

2031B *Abraham Learns to Worship God*. At nightfall Abraham worships a star, then the moon, then the sun, and finally gives up idolatry. [Z42.2].
*Taylor JAFL XLVI 85 No. 2031B; Hdwb. d. Märchens II 184b; Köhler-Bolte I 578; Basset RTP VII 397; — Jewish: Neuman (Z42.2). — Literary Treatment: Koran, Surah 6, 75—78.

2031C *The Man Seeks the Greatest Being as a Husband for his Daughter*. (a) A man catches a mouse or rat which changes into a girl. He treats her as his daughter. (b) A man wants to wed his daughter to the greatest being in the world. Typical formula: man goes to sun; cloud covers sun, wind moves clouds, mountains stop wind, rats dig holes in mountain.
India *5*.

2031A* *Wall in Construction Collapses*. Finally the king finds out that the sea is guilty. (The chain: mason—cement mixer—beautiful singing woman—pearl necklace —jeweller—diver—sea.) [Z49.11.1].
India *11*.

2031B* *The Most Powerful Idol*. A brahmin worships idol and sets sacrifices before it daily. Rat devours offerings and he sets it up as his idol as a being more powerful than his idol. When cat devours rat, he worships it instead. His wife accidentally kills the cat, so he sets her up to worship. He happens to slap her and she loses consciousness. Thereafter he worships himself as most powerful after all. [Z42.3].
India *1*.

2032 *The Cock's Whiskers*. A mouse throws a nut down from a tree and hits a cock on the head. He also steals the cock's whiskers. The cock goes to get an old woman to cure him. The final formula is: Fountain give up water for forest, forest give up wood for baker, baker give up bread for dog, dog give up hairs to cure the cock. [Z43]. (Variant: mouse loses tail.)
*BP II 107 (Grimm No. 72 a); Haavio FFC XCIX 136; RTP XV 220. — Swedish: Norlind *Svenska Allmogens Liv* 613 »Tupen och hänen», Lund *1;* Irish: Beal I 61, Jackson FL XLVII 292; French *23;* Catalan: Amades Nos. 235, 237, 238, 242, 243, 244, 245, 248, 249, 250, 251, 252; German Archive *4;* Italian *10* (Tuscan [2000], [2001], [2003] a, b, [2004] *5*, Sicilian *5*); Rumanian (1962) *8;* Hungarian: Berze Nagy (286*A) *20;* Serbocroatian *1;* Russian: Andrejev (241 I*) *7;* Turkish: Eberhard-Boratav No. 29 *4;* Armenian: Khatchatrianz 137ff. — Franco-American (Missouri) *1*, (New Eng.) *1;* West Indies (Negro) *4;* American Indian (Zuñi): Cushing *Zuñi Folk Tales* 411.

2032A *Toad asks Magpie in Tree to Throw down a Chestnut*. Magpie refuses, saying it might break its beak. Toad promises, if that happens, to get a horsehair to tie it up again. Magpie throws chestnut and breaks beak. Toad asks ass for hair, but ass first demands grass; mower demands sheep; shepherd, pup; mother dog, bread; baker, stumps. Toad cuts the stumps and gets the hair. [Z43.1].

*Wesselski Hessische Blätter XXXII 24; Latvian (*241B) *1;* Spanish (2032*A) *1.* — Spanish American: Hansen (Cuba) *1.*

2033 *A Nut Hits the Cock's Head* and he thinks the world has come to an end. He sends the hen to tell the duck. The duck tells the goose, the goose the hare, the hare the fox, the fox the wolf. Final formula: »Fox who told you?» — »Hare». — »Hare, who told you?» — »Goose», etc. [Z43.3]. For sequel see Type 20C. Sometimes animals have queer names (Cf. Type 2010 I A).

Feilberg *Ordbog* I 750 s.v. »høne»; Taylor JAFL XLVI 85 No. 2033, Hdwb. d. Märchens II 185 a; Wesselski Hessische Blätter XXXII 19. — Lithuanian *3;* Swedish (misc.) *1;* Danish: Kristensen *Dyrefabler* 103 No. 177; Scottish: Campbell-McKay No. 4; Irish *26;* French *1;* German *1;* Turkish: Eberhard-Boratav No. 20. — Spanish-American: Hansen (Cuba) *2,* (Puerto Rico) *1;* American Negro (Georgia): Harris *Nights* 108 No. 20. — African *3.*

2034 *The Mouse Regains its Tail.* The cat bites off the mouse's tail and will return it in exchange for milk. The mouse goes to the cow for milk, the farmer for hay, the butcher for meat, the baker for bread. Other persons mentioned are the locksmith and the miner. [Z41.4].

*Taylor JAFL XLVI 86 No. 2034, Hdwb. d. Märchens II 185b; Wesselski Hessische Blätter XXXII 28; *Newell JAFL XVIII (1905) 34 n. 1; BP II 107—8; Basset *Contes berbères* No. 45, *Nouveaux contes berbères* No. 168; Coffin *2.* — England, U.S.: *Baughman (Z41.4). — African (2034C*) *23.*

2034A *Mouse Bursts Open when Crossing a Stream.* Series of helpers similar to Type 2034. [Z41.4.1].

*Taylor JAFL XLVI 86 No. 2034A; *Wesselski Hessische Blätter XXXII 28; BP II 107—8. — Slovenian (letter from I. Grafenauer) *4.*

2034B *My Dog Picked up a String,* but did not wish to give it to me unless I gave her bread. Cupboard did not wish to give bread unless I gave it a key; smith, charcoal; charcoal-burner, calf's legbone; butcher, milk; cow, grass; meadow, water; clouds, dove's feather. Dove gave me a feather which I gave to clouds, etc. [Z41.4.2].

*Taylor JAFL XLVI 86 No. 2034B; Spanish (2030D) *2.*

2034C *Lending and Repaying: Progressively Worse (or better) Bargain.* Cf. Type 1415 [J2081.1, Z41.5].

Lithuanian (2009*); Swedish (GS 2043) *8;* African (Tonga): Torrend *Specimens of Bantu Folklore* (New York, 1921) 169ff., (Ila): Smith and

Dale II 392ff. No. 17, (Pende): Frobenius *Atlantis* XI 265 No. 4, (Bassari): *ibid.* 97ff. No. 12, (Ashanti): Rattray 268 No. 73.

2034D *Bird's Pea gets Stuck in Socket of Mill-handle.* She goes to carpenter, king, queen, who refuse to help. She asks snake to bite the queen, stick to beat snake, fire to burn stick, etc. Final formula: cat eats mouse, mouse cuts plant creeper, creeper snares elephant, elephant drinks up sea, sea quenches fire, fire burns stick, stick beats snake, snake bites queen, queen speaks to king, king chides carpenter, carpenter cuts mill handle, and pea is extracted. Questions in rhyme. [Z41.6, Z41.6.1].

India *12*.

2034E *The Bird Seeks a Mason to Free its Young* [Z49.7]. The bird lays an egg in a crack in a rock or its young are trapped in a rock (tree). The bird goes for a mason (carpenter) for help. Typical final formula: Jackal eats hen, hen pecks at lizard, lizard crawls up elephant's trunk, elephant attacks hunter, hunter shoots wild boar, wild boar attacks king, king forces mason to cut open stone.

India *3*.

2034A* *The Wormwood does not want to Rock the Sparrow.* Final formula: the worms begin to gnaw the rods, the rods to beat the oxen, the oxen to drink the water, the water to quench the fire, the fire to burn the hunters, the hunters to shoot the wolves, the wolves to kill the goats, the goats to gnaw the wormwood, the wormwood to rock me — it rocked and rocked me to sleep. [Z41.7].

Lithuanian (2003*).

2035 *House that Jack Built.* Final formula: This is the farmer that sowed the corn that fed the cock that crowed in the morn, that waked the priest all shaven and shorn, that married the man all tattered and torn, that kissed the maiden all forlorn, that milked the cow with a crumpled horn, that tossed the dog, that worried the cat, that caught the rat, that ate the malt that lay in the house that Jack built. [Z44].

*BP II 108; Köhler-Bolte I 517f.; Feilberg *Ordbog* I 687a, IV 229 s.v. »hus»; Haavio FFC LXXXVIII 88 n. 2; Coffin *1*. — Swedish (Stockholm) *25;* Danish: Kristensen *Danske Dyrefabler* 132ff. Nos. 272, 295; Irish *6;* French *6;* Catalan: Amades cf. No. 255; India: Thompson-Balys (Z44) *1*. — African *3*.

2035A *The House the Old Man was to Build.* The woman for whom he is to build the house has some beans for him. The goat eats these up. Cumulative search. Final formula: Smith give me my iron, iron which belongs to the man, man who ate up my fish, fish which belongs to the sea ... sea — shirt — washerwoman — soap — woman — wood — press — grease — herder — cheese-frame — fig-tree — horn — goat — beans. [Z44.1].

*Parsons JAFL XXV 219, XXVII 222, XXXIII 40, MAFLS XV (1) 207 n. 1.

2036 *Drop of Honey Causes Chain of Accidents.* Hunter drops honey in a grocery;

weasel eats honey; cat chases weasel; dog chases cat; grocer kills dog: all the cause of a bloody feud between villages. [N381].
*Taylor JAFL XLVI 87 No. 2036; *BP II 104 n. 2; *Wesselski Hessische Blätter XXXII 21; Chauvin VIII 41 No. 9; Spanish Exempla: Keller (N381).

2037 »*I Killed my Grandmother because she Refused to Cook a Hare.* I killed a priest because he said my crime was bad. A friar absolved me to avoid being killed.» [Z49.1].
*Taylor JAFL XLVI 87 No. 2037; Spanish (*2026).

2037A* *Series of Trick Exchanges: razor—pot—bride—drum by tricky fox.* Fox sings formula of exchanges. [Z47.1].
India: *Thompson-Balys (Z47.1) 9.

2038 *Cumulative Pursuit.* Boys get help. One of them injures the helper. Pursued. Ridden by kind hen. One injures the hen. Hen pursues, etc. [Z49.2].
*Taylor JAFL XLVI 87 No. 2038; Jamaica: Beckwith MAFLS XVII 264f. No. 70.

2038* *Going out to Earn Wages.* Acquires various things (house, animals, etc.) all with peculiar names. (Or animals are described by their cries.) Cf. Type 2010 I A. Cf. *BP III 129.
Swedish *16* (Uppsala *5*, Stockholm *4*, Liungman *2*, misc. *5*.

2039 *The Horseshoe Nail.* For want of a nail the shoe was lost, for want of a shoe the horse was lost, for the want of a horse the rider was lost . . . and all for the want of a horseshoe nail. [Z45].
*BP III 335—37. — French *1*.

2039* *This is the Key to the Lady's Chest.* Series: smith, axe, stick, cat, rat, strap, key.
Swedish (GS 2039) *35* (Stockholm *30*, Liungman *1*, misc. *4*).

2040 *The Climax of Horrors.* The magpie is dead. Overate on horseflesh. — Horse dead? — Overworked at fire — Horse burned down? etc. [Z46].
**Zachariae *Kleine Schriften zur indischen Philologie* 191ff. s.v. »Botenart»; *Taylor JAFL XLVI 87 No. 2040; *Bolte Zs. f. Vksk. VII 99 n. 5; Wesselski *Hodscha Nasreddin* II 203; Wesselski *Mönchslatein* 25 No. 20; *Crane *Vitry* 216ff. No. 205. — Lithuanian (*2040) *2*; English *1*; Spanish (*925A) *2*; Hungarian *36*; Serbocroatian *1*; Russian: Afanasiev (*2014 I) *4*; India *3*. — English-American: Baughman *4*.

2041 *The Bird Indifferent to Pain.* A man catches a mango-bird eating mangoes and strikes it against the roots of a mango-tree. The bird cannot be made to say it suffers from the blow. In turn, he puts it in water, strikes it on the ground, a stile, a door-frame, singes its feathers, cuts it up, cooks it, and eats it. The bird always expresses indifference in a cumulative rhyme. At last bird asks him to look out of the window, whereupon it flies out of his nose and the man dies. [Z49.3].
*Taylor JAFL XLVI 87 No. 2041. — India *2*.

2041* *There Is a Mountain, on the Mountain a Tree.* Series: spot, louse, feather, bird, egg, tree, mountain.
Swedish (GS 2042) *17*.

2042 *Chain of Accidents: the Ant (Crab) Bite and its Consequences* [Z49.6ff.]. An ant (crab) bites a wild boar or another animal. The wild boar runs headlong into a tree. A bird nesting in the tree flies off in fright, alarming an elephant, which tramples on another animal, etc.
India *10.*

2042A* *Trial Among the Animals.* Deer steps on kitten: cat investigates. Deer has been frightened by bird, this bird by another bird ... by crab's pointed claw, crab by mouse in his hole. Cat eats mouse. (Frog croaks because turtle carries his house on his head; turtle carries house because firefly is bringing fire; firefly brings the fire because mosquito tries to bite him, etc.) [Z49.6].
India: Thompson-Balys (Z49.6) *5;* Indonesia, Malaya: Dixon 202; Philippine: Fansler MAFLS XII 390.

2042B* *Birds Fight and Cause Series of Accidents to other Animals and People* [Z49.6.1]:
India: Thompson-Balys *1.*

2042C* *Bite (prick) Causes Series of Accidents* [Z49.6.2].
India: *Thompson-Balys *3.*

2042D* *Man Sharpening his Dao is Bitten by a Prawn.* He cuts down a big bamboo; a fruit falls from bamboo and strikes a bird on the nape of the neck; the bird scratches up an ant's nest with his feet; the ant bites a wild boar in the eye; and the boar bears down upon a plantain tree where a bat dwells under a leaf; the bat seeks refuge in the ear of an elephant, and the elephant kicks down the house on an old woman. She rushes out and falls into a well. [Z49.6.3].
India: *Thompson-Balys *2.*

2044 *Pulling up the Turnip.* Final formula: The mouse holds onto the cat, the cat holds onto Mary, Mary holds onto Annie, Annie holds onto grandmother, grandmother holds onto grandfather, grandfather holds onto the turnip — they all pull and pull it out. [Z49.9].
Lithuanian (2008*) *6;* Swedish *11* (Uppsala *1,* Stockholm *3,* Liungman *2,* misc. *5*); Catalan: Amades No. 254; Russian: Andrejev (1960 G*) *7.*

2044A* *Biting a Grain in Half.* Final formula: Forester attacks bear, the bear the wolf, the wolf the dog, the dog the cat, the cat the mouse, the mouse the grain — the grain is bitten in two. [Z49.8].
Lithuanian (2006*) *1.*

2045A* *Hermit must get Cat to Kill Rats* in hunt, cow to give cat milk, etc. [Z49.12].
India *1.*

2045B* *Chain of Killings:* bulbul destroys flower and is killed by cat; cat shaken by dog; dog killed by boy; boy sentenced to death by king. [Z49.13].
India *1.*

2046* *Cyclone Destroys Old Couple's House.* Various animals including horse, elephant, donkey, cow, ox, goat, monkey, and cat all offer to help rebuild it, but in vain. Finally dog coordinates their efforts and they succeed in restoring house.
Spanish-American: Hansen (**2050) (Cuba) *1.*

2047* »*Why doesn't the Plant Grow (Blossom)?*» The gardener asks the plant why it doesn't grow (blossom). »Because the cow eats me.» Cow complains that the herdboy doesn't take it to the river. The boy complains that the cook doesn't feed him, etc.
India *4.*

2075 *Tales in which Animals Talk.* Their talk is in imitation of their real sound. E.g. bull, cow, calf talk about going to the next pasture, etc. Bull with bass voice, calf with very small and cow with medium. Cf. Types 206, 236.
French-Canadian *6.*

CATCH TALES

2200 *Catch-tales.* The manner of telling forces the hearer to ask a particular question, to which the teller returns a ridiculous answer. [X13].
Finnish *10;* Irish *6;* English *1;* French *12;* Catalan: Amades No. 465; Dutch *8;* Flemish (FFC XXXVII 82) *5;* Italian (Sicilian *2*); Hungarian: (Berze Nagy 1962 I**, H**) *12;* Serbocroatian *1.* — English-American: Baughman *8.*

2201 *Death to Listener.* At the end of the story, the story-teller uses a fearful voice and points at one of his audience: »You'll be the hundredth one to die.»
Hungarian: Berze Nagy (1964) *5.*

2202 *Teller is Killed in his own Story* (Catch tale). [Z13.2].
Canada, U.S.: Baughman (Z13.2) *3.*

2204 *The Dog's Cigar.* Man is smoking a cigar (pipe) in train; it falls out of the train; a dog jumps out after it; the dog arrives at the station later . . . »What do you think he had in his mouth?» »The cigar (pipe)?» »No, his tongue!» [Z13.4].
Irish. Also reported from Germany (Walter Anderson). — U.S.: Baughman (Z13.4) *2.*

2205 *Come here, Lean!* Girl finds 3 coins and buys 3 pigs: (1) the lean, (2) the fat, (3) the tail. »Come here, Lean.» »I can't, I am too lean.» »Come here Fat.» »I can't, because I am too fat» — »And the other, what was it named?» »The tail.» — »Lift the tail, etc.»
*Anderson »Ein Vexiermärchen aus San Marino» Zs. f. Vksk. XLVI 15. — Irish (boys named Pepper, Salt, Be Silent); Italian (San Marino) *23;* Hungarian: Berze Nagy (1962F**) *9.*

2250—2299 Unfinished tales

2250 *Unfinished Tales.* Just as interest is aroused the narrator quits. »If the bowl had been stronger my tale had been longer». [Z12].
*BP II 210, III 455; Köhler-Bolte I 269; Taylor Hdwb. d. Märchens II 189b. — Swedish *10* (Stockholm *9,* Liungman *1*); Norwegian: Solheim *1;* Dutch *3;* Flemish: de Meyer FFC XXXVII 82; Serbocroatian *1,* Istrian No. 67a; Russian: Andrejev (2020*). — English-American: Baughman *1.*

2251 *The Rabbit's Tail.* The old king left a big mountain for his three sons. They dug in the mountain and found a big iron box and a little rabbit in it. If that rabbit's tail was longer my story would be longer too.
Hungarian: Berze Nagy (1962*A) *14;* Serbocroatian *4.*

2260 *The Golden Key.*
*BP III 455f. (Grimm No. 200).

2271 *Mock Stories for Children.* When children, by persistently demanding a story, become a nuisance to their elders, the latter get rid of them by telling brief »mock stories», e.g. the dog's name was »Enough.»
Lithuanian (*2301) *3;* Slovenian.

2275 *I Give you the Story of the Green Pig — I don't mean that.*
Hungarian: Berze Nagy (1962*G) *6.*

2280 *Old Woman's Dogs Run Away* one at a time and leave her alone. She starts to weep — and she is still weeping.
Catalan: Amades No. 433.

OTHER FORMULA TALES

2300 *Endless Tales.* Hundreds of sheep to be carried over stream one at a time, endless quacking of geese, etc. The wording of the tale so arranged as to continue indefinitely. [Z11]. Cf. Types 2013, 2017.
*BP II 209; Taylor Hdwb. d. Märchens II 190a; Zs. f. Vksk. n. f. VIII (1938) 19; Coffin *1.* — Lithuanian *112;* Icelandic *1;* Scottish *1;* Irish: Beal VII 76; English *1;* French *6;* Catalan: Amades No. 258; Dutch *7;* Flemish (FFC XXXVII 82) *12;* Italian (Sicilian *1*); Hungarian: Berze Nagy (1962*B) *9;* Russian: Andrejev (2020*); India 3; Chinese: Eberhard FFC CXX 304f. No. 6f., CXXVIII 258ff. No. 159. — Franco-American: Baughman *1;* English-American: Baughman *6;* Spanish-American: Rael No. 73 (U.S.), Hansen (Puerto Rico) *2;* Portuguese-American (Brazil): Camara Cascudo Estorias p. 61. — Literary Treatments: Rotunda (Z11); Spanish Exempla: Keller (Z11).

2301 *Corn Carried away Grain at a Time* (endless tale). [Z11.1].
Serbocroatian *1;* Canada, U.S.: Baughman (Z11.1).

2301A *Making the King Lose Patience.* King to give his daughter in marriage to whoever will make him lose patience. Rascal starts telling how an ant came to a huge heap of grain and took a grain home with him; next day he came again and took another grain home; and so on. The king loses patience, and gives him his daughter. (Often a part of Type 852.)
Irish.

2301B *The Fianna Went over the Hill.* A storyteller starts off a tale about the Fianna by saying: One day the Fianna went west over the hill and then they came back east over the hill and then they went west over the hill.

... A listener loses patience and says: »In God's name, get them out of the hill!»
Irish.

2320 *Rounds.* Stories which begin over and over again and repeat. [Z17]. Cf. Type 2013.
*BP II 209f. No. 86, III No. 200; Taylor JAFL XLVI 88, Hdwb. d. Märchens II 190. — Lithuanian (2300) *112;* Irish; Russian: Afanasiev (*2020) *9;* India: Thompson-Balys *1;* U.S.: Baughman (Z17).

2322 *Tale Avoiding all Pronouns* [Z15].
Lang *English Fairy Tales* 118.

2330 *Game-tales.* (Used as game.) Z19.1.
*BP II 210.

2335 *Tales Filled with Contradictions* [Z19.2]. Cf. Type 2014.
West Indies: Flowers 587.

2340 *Tales Illustrated by Game of Cards.*
Catalan: Amades Nos. 64, 394, 473, 474, 475, 476.

V UNCLASSIFIED TALES

UNCLASSIFIED TALES

2400 *The Ground is Measured with a Horse's Skin (ox-hide)* [K185.1].
*Basset *Rev. d'ethnographie et des trad. pop.* IV 97; Coffin *1*. — Finnish (2000*) *1;* Estonian (2000*) *2;* Icelandic *2;* Catalan: Amades Nos. 1763, 1825; Czech: Tille Soupis II (1) 373 *2;* Serbocroatian *1;* Russian: Andrejev (2000*) *2.* — English-American: Baughman *2.*

2401 *The Children Play at Hog-killing.* One of the children's throat cut. [N334.1].
BP I 202 (Grimm No. 22a). — Estonian (2001) *1;* English *1;* German *1.*

2403 changed to 1656.

2404 *The Boastful Servant.* Boasts that he has scolded his master. But he does it so that the master does not hear. [K1776].
Finnish (2004*) *3;* Estonian (2004*) *2.*

2411 *The Boy with Active Imagination.* »If I had one and then got two more, I should have three.» [W211.1].
Finnish (2011*) *2;* Estonian (2011*) *1;* Danish: MS. DFS; Serbocroatian *1.*

CHANGES IN NUMBERS

The following types proposed in various regional surveys or archives appear in this work under numbers different from those suggested.

Finnish:[1] 73*: 76; 770*: 822; 811: 810; 924*: 927; 932*: 934; 933**: 934*; 1054**: 1015; 1570*: 1544; 1742**: 1698L; 1842**: 1833A; 1844*: 1833B; 1846*: 1698M; 1951**: 1925*; 2000*: 2400; 2003*: 1656; 2004*: 2404; 2005*: 1574A; 2008*: 1698; 2011*: 2411; 2014**: 2018.

Finnish-Swedish: 222*: 1310C; 333*: 934B; 761**: 831; 823*: 822; 838*: 836; 921**: 875; 935***: 735*; 940*: 941**; 955*: 312; 955**: 956B; 1097*: 298; 1242* and 1242**: 1248; 1245*: 1246*; 1315*: 1323; 1370*: 1372; 1406*: 1359A; 1406**: 1418A; 1532*: 1536B; 1532**: 1536A; 1561*: 1560**; 1653*: 1654; 1685*: 1688; 1825**: 1785C; 1831*: 1828; 1880*: 1889.

Estonian: 74*: 156; 75*: 77; 126*: 125A; 233*: 247A*; 332*: 335; 408*: 409; 471*: 470B; 472*: 470A; 473*: 750C; 754*: 777; 770*: 822; 771*: 759; 924*: 927; 925*: 655; 932*: 934; 951*: 961A; 953*: 956B; 955*: 956B; 962*: 952*; 963*: 953A*; 1017*: 1016; 1064*: 1060**; 1068*: 1135; 1165*: 1353; 1191*: 1440; 1292*: 1293*; 1409*: 1383; 1459*: 1453****; 1525G*: 1004; 1528*: 1542A; 1565*: 1564**; 1676*: 1319; 1732*: 1545; 1789*: 1642A; 1846*: 1698M; 2000*: 2400; 2001*: 2401; 2003*: 1656; 2004*: 2404; 2005*: 1574A; 2008*: 1698; 2011*: 2411.

Livonian: 99': 222B*; 201': 34A; 241*: 2021B; 241': 2032B; 408*: 419; 531B': 301; 670B: 671B*; 670B*: 150A*, 278C; 745': 738*; 754*: 777; 758': 752B; 890': 888; 905': 903B*; 964: 312; 966*: 958C*; 1014**: 1017; 1204': 1202; 1316*: 1339D; 1370*: 1372; 1549': 1460*; 1601': 1536B; 1642: 1643; 1645': 1644; 1672': 1699; 1676*: 1678; 1684': 1681A; 1694': 753, 1695; 2003*: 1656; 2015': 36.

Latvian: 50A***: 53; 51*: 50C; 64*: 68B; 64****: 59; 82*: 87B; 86*: 80A*; 113*: 93; 122D*: 6; 125*: 219C*; 127*: 132; 128*: 111A; 162*: 163; 166A*: 123B; 167*: 169; 168*: 169; 168A*: 179A*; 168C*: 166B$_4$*; 168E*: 171A*; 168F*: 171B*; 168***: 167A; 179B: 152A*; 208: 207A*; 213*: 219A*; 217*: 219G*; 218*: 219E*; 219B*: 218B*; 226*: 232D*; 238*: 240*; 241*: 2021B; 241**: 2022; 241A*: 2021A; 241B*: 2032A; 248**: 1586A; 249*: 289; 251A*: 255*; 276AB*: 288B*; 277*: 278; 279*: 278B; 279**: 278A; 280B*: 278D*; 281*: 298G*; 284A*: 56C*; 285A**: 283E*; 285B**: 283D*; 286*: 283F*; 287*: 293F*; 288*: 293E*; 289*: 293D*; 291**: 293B*; 292*: 293A*; 296*: 2025; 298B: 846*; 299*: 552B; 299A—D**: 294.

Lithuanian: 66*: 68B; 92*: 1074; 106*: 47D; 106*: 117*; 122E: 126C*; 133*: 61B; 140*: 157B*; 161: 159B; 162: 163;

---

[1] For full titles of works referred to, see pp. 10—12 above. If the change is only within a single number (e. g. 72* to 72A*) it is disregarded.

162*: 163;   164*: 1199A;   166*: 934B;
167*: 169G*;   202*: 200A, 200B;   215*:
219D*;   223*: 244A*;   239*: 6;   239*:
227*;   278*: 293G*;   286*: 150A*;   286*:
278C*;   290*: 293C*;   314C*: 480A*;
365A*: 1199A;   368*: 407B;   422*: 401A;
422A*: 437;   422B*: 401A*;   446*: 437;
452*: 451A;   453 . 452C;   467*: 653;
472*: 471;   481*: 511;   482*: 480; 530A*:
314A;   552*: 566F;   651*: 300A;   656*:
875D*;   703*: 788;   730*: 480C*;   738*:
739*;   758*: 830B;   761*: 958D*;   762*:
1000;   770*: 751*;   771*: 751B*;   772*:
751C*;   774*: 555;   778*: 777;   779*: 862;
782*: 465A*;   787*: 960B;   806*: 471;
811A: 804B;   847*: 780*;   848*: 93;   848*:
830C;   882C*: 883D*;   894*: 875F;   894*:
921B;   904*: 901A*;   904*: 905A*;   911*:
910A;   914*: 910E;   922A*: 924A;   924B*:
1557;   925*: 927A*;   934A*: 930A;
934B*: 745A; 936*: 947B*; 937**: 938B;
941*: 940*;   946*: 935**;   958*: 969;
959B*: 956D;   959C*: 956B;   963*:
954A*;   963*: 958E*;   964*: 969;   966*:
958A*;   967*: 958B*;   970*: 952**;
981*: 983;   995*: 981;   996*: 980; 1006A:
1685;   1013*: 1012A;   1014A*: 1009;
1084A*: 1199B; 1084A*: 1082A; 1089*:
1088*;   1098*: 1095A;   1146A*: 1661A*;
1166*: 822*;   1167*: 1168C;   1168*:
1166*;   1177*: 1180*;   1179*: 1168;
1183*: 1188;   1183A*: 1185;   1190*:
1193*; 1240A*: 1313A; 1282*: 1319G*;
1283*: 1319F*;   1336*: 1266A;   1360A*:
1358C;   1370*: 1372;   1378*: 1409A;
1384A*: 1540A;   1416A*: 804A;   1425*:
1424*;   1465*: 875**;   1525M*: 1527A;
1533*: 1529A;   1535A*: 1737;   1545*:
1559A*: 1547*: 1526A; 1549*: 1543D*;
1565*: 1567C;   1568A*: 1562A*;   1580*:
1533;   1621*: 1623*;   1627*: 1624B*,
1634E*;   1627C*: 1624C*;   1627D*:
1624D*;   1630*: 1525Q*;   1631*: 1625;
1635*: 1636;   1636*: 1634B*;   1639*:
1634;   1665*: 1644;   1668*: 891A*;
1669,   1670: omitted;   1676*: 1750A;

1677*: 1681A;   1679*: 1319A;   1686*:
1685;   1692*: 1688B*;   1693*: 1698A*;
1700*: 1716*;   1708*: 1698C*;   1730A*,
1730B*: 1359D;   1730B*: 1829;   1751*:
1315A*;   1772*: 1592A*;   1785E*:
1827A;   1784E* : 1839A;   1835*, 1846*,
1847*,   1849*: 1851;   1835*: 1824;
1843*: 1842C*;   1844*: 1804A;   1847* :
1738;   1848*: 1804;   1860*: 1157;
1863*: 1348;   1870*: 1865;   1871* :
1867;   1872*,   1873*: 1870;   1878* :
1542B*;   1879*: 1960A;   1883*: 1932;
1887*: 1525A$_4$; 2007*: 2027*; 2008*:
2044;   2009*: 2034C;   2031G*: 2021B,
2032B;   2300*: 2320;   2301*: 2271;
2420*: 1699B;   2423*: 1628;   2424*:
785A;   2425*: 1525D;   2426*: 1295B;
2426* : 1525D;   2426A*: 1572G*;
2426B*: 1572F*;   2430*: 1572E*;
2431*: 1573;   2439*: 1339E;   2440*:
1572A*;   2442*: 1578B*;   2444*:
1331D;   2446*: 1695;   2447*: 735C*;
2448*: 921C*;   2449*: 1553;   2452*:
982;   2521*: 1777A*;   2901*: 1358C;
2902*: 1358C;   2905*: 1355B;   2911*:
1543;   2912*: 1355A, 1355C;   3047*:
1169; 3054*: 758; 3230*: 774L; 3290*,
3292*: 810A;   3309*: 1343;   3340*:
846;   3443*,   3443A*: 1676;   3520*:
1645A;   3636*: 1645;   3655*: 449;
3727*: 767.

Lappish: 5*: 154;   133*: 61B;   287*:
283G*;   754**: 777;   963*, 964*, 965 :
omitted;   966*: 970;   1460 : omitted;
1980 : 1698M; 1880* : 1889.

Swedish: 72 : 81; GS131 : 132; GS902 :
879A*;   GS903 : 1628;   1316**: 1339D;
GS1334 : 1349; GS1336 : 1701; GS1339 :
1343; GS1340 : 1406; GS1342 : 1833A*;
GS1343 : 1344;   1541*: 1545;   GS1630 :
924; 2005* : 1574B; GS2042 : 2041*.

Norwegian: 18**: 48*;   123*: 122;
728*: 934D;   757**: 756B;   813**: 812;
823*: 822;   871**: 870A;   874 : 872*;
888 : 892;   924**: 923A;   926*: 927;
969*, 970*, 972* : omitted; 1043 : 1049;

1183 : 1186; 1561** : 1462; 1654 : 1525R; 1654 : 1653B; 1676* : 1678; 1677** : 1688.

Danish: 56C* : 56E*; 150B : 161; 754** : 777; 1342* : 1833A*.

Icelandic: 302I* : 302B*; 302I* : 511A; 327A : 1137; 378, 471 : 1119; 499A* : 934C*; 556I*, IV*, V* : 556A*; 556II* : 556B*; 556III* : 556C*; 556VI* : 556D*; 556VIII* : 556E*; 575 : 653A; 595* : 595A*; 728* : 934D*; 728* : 934E**; 813I*, II* : 1178; 814* : 811C*; 876* : 884; 1349* : 1291D; 1349I* : 1279A; 1349II* : 1321B*; 1321III* : 1332A*; 1321IV* : 1332B*; 1321VII* : 1319K*; 1321VIII* : 1349B*; 1410* : 1411*; 1431* : 1430; 1431* : 1341; 1431* : 1291; 1541I* : 1476A*, 1547A*; 1729* : 1775A*; 1883* : 1889E.

French: 22D : 122A; 317 : 314A; 317[1] : 321; 713* : 717*; 942* : 1676; 1184* : 1187; 1844* : 1804B; 2045* : 2010.

Spanish: 52* : 51A; 57* : 56; 64* : 34B; 66B* : 67; 128* : 127B*; 135C* : 154; 244 : 235C*; 275A* : 1074; 278* : 1030; 290* : 155; 327D* : 451*; 340* : 1164A; 340A* : 312C; 345* : 750H*; 445A* : 891A; 445A* : 437; 445B* : 894; 445B* : 437; 449* : 934; 449* : 437; 557* : 402; 792* : 774G; 819* : 1860A; 835* : 470A; 836A* : 830C; 836C* : 1682; 925A* : 2040; 936* : 506*; 945A* : 935**; 970* : 879; 970* : 956C; 973* : 958D*; 980A* : 982; 983* : 933; 1019* : 1562D*; 1149A* : 1162*; 1355* : 1351*; 1374* : 1373; 1375* : 1377*; 1389* : 1387A; 1410* : 1516C*; 1424* : 1406; 1482* : 1449*; 1550A* : 1548A*; 1555* : 1567F; 1532 : 1654; 1532* : 1740B; 1534 : 1536;* 1535A* : 1534; 1546* : 1553; 1550A* : 1862A; 1550B* : 1641B; 1550C* : 1551*; 1583* : 1843A; 1583* : 1860B; 1587* : 1534D*; 1593* : 518*; 1621* : 870D*; 1654* : 1341A; 1684 : 1337C;

1690* : 1691A*; 1693* : 1681A; 1696A* : 1381B; 1697A* : 1699B; 1800B* : 1853A*; 1805A*, B* : 759B; 1836* : 1848C; 1842ABC : 1833; 1848* : 1525L; 1848* : 1526A; 1850* : 1525R*; 1852* : 1529; 1855* : 1806; 1868* : 1853B*; 1940A* : 1562A; 1940B : 1545; 1940H* : 1717*; 2020 : 2019*; 2023* : 2022; 2026* : 2037; 2030D : 2034B; 2225*, 2226*, 2227*, 2228* : 2014.

Dutch: 891A* : 1534; 905* : 1375; 924*, B* : 1676; 943* : 1676B; 1183* : 1091A; 1212* : 1242A; 1528** : 1527A.

Flemish: 6** : 122B; 6**** : 122C; 50* : 51; 160* : 248; 471* : 470B; 752B* : 759; 771* : 7J9; 773* : 761; 790* : 791; 922* : 921; 924* : 927; 946* : 982.

Walloon: 2A* : 2D; 61B*, 61C* : 122B*; 78* : 136; 79* : 132; 79* : 154; 138* : 122E; 200CDE : 200A; 218* : 207A; 779I, II : 555; 923, 923C* : 875; 1030A* : 1045*; 1030B* : 1047*; 1205* : 1242B; 1207* : 1287*; 1214* : 1310B; 1214A* : 1282*; 1215* : 1290*; 1221, 1221B : 1225A; 1223* : 1331A*; 1229* : 1212*; 1275B* : 1337A; 1317* : 1316****; 1335A : 1335; 1357* : 1420B; 1380A : 1284A; 1383B* : 1284; 1385A* : 1555A; 1552* : 1641B; 1553* : 778; 1554* : 1553B*; 1557* : 1555; 1588* : 1585*; 1594* : 1641C*; 1613* : 924; 1636* : 1572H*; 1655A : 1655; 1677* : 1347*; 1686A* : 1682*; 1711* : 1676; 1884* : 1965; 2036* : 2021*.

German: 61* : 56D; 149* : 161; 317* : 468; 362* : 846; 725D* : 774J; 815* : 826; 845* : 846; 1205* : 1260A; 1388* : 1349M*.

Italian (Tuscan): 41b : 3; 152a, b : 1093; 301b : 780; 313d : 402; 333b : 1199; 360 : 1697; 402 : 653; 510b : 403; 554a—d : 851; 555c : 1689A; 563a, 1 : 1960G; 563i : 851; 563d, i, o : 853A; 571 : 513A; 707u : 1960G; 950A : 1737; 955 : 956B; 1000a : 1775; 1525A : 1737;

1642 : 1313; 1875 : 1348; 2016 : 1586. —
[208] : 715; [301] : 550; [304]b, e : 403;
[307] : 518; [310] : 451; [312] : 514;
[315]d : 853A; [315]e, g : 851; [315]f :
854; [316] : 709; [316]c : 403; [317] :
514; [317]e : 401; [324] : 461; [329] :
567; [333] : 750C; [752] : 751; [753] :
750C; [756] : 751A; [760] : 774E; [850] :
956B; [851] : 956B; [852] : 931; [854] :
434; [855] : 513A; [860] : 501; [863] :
956B; [864] : 302; [869] : 451; [870] :
567; [872] : 401; [880] : 432; [890] : 567;
[891 sexies] : 432; [892] : 434; [894] : 403;
[895]b : 403; [897] : 403; [900] : 432;
[901] : 518; [904] : 1641; [908] : 500;
[916] : 302; [917] : 710; [918] : 401;
[902] : 879; [932] : 425P; [932]b : 401;
[933] : 302; [934] : 302; [950]a : 1737;
[1004] : 1176; [1005] : 1049; [1206] :
1586A; [1212] : 1334; [1219] : 1408**;
[1220] : 1691, 1775; [1222] : 1643;
[1224] : 1876; [1226] : 1677; [1227] :
1696; [1228] : 1696; [1354] : 1920G;
[1355] : 1710; [1359] : 1371**; [1367] :
1725; [1440] : 751B; [1442] : 934;
[1453] : 1457; [1529] : 470; [1532] :
810; [1563] : 1525E; [1566] : 1792;
[1618] : 1539; [1736] : 1562A; [1739] :
1620; [1741]a, b : 1735A; [1757] : 922;
[1762] : 1775; [1763] : 1775; [1767] :
1785*; [1771] : 1551, 1538; [1779] :
1419G; [1783] : 1931.

Sicilian: **516 : 425D; *552C : 425*;
*651 : 652A; *674 : 672C*; *708 : 788;
755 : 938A; 750 : 753; *752D : 774P;
*752E : 928; *785A : 753A; *786 :
774N; 828 [14e] : 759A; *872 : 874;
*874 : 1419E; *876 : 1533; *878 : 891;
902* : 879A; *926 : 922B, 921A; *927 :
851; *947 : 1534; *948 : 947A; 980 :
982; *1374 : 1373; *1380 : 1725; *1406 :
1419E; *1541 : 1653F; *1653 : 1654;
*1661 : 1736A.

Rumanian: 16* : 64; 33I* : 105*,
105B*; 58* : 122B; 54III : 154; 92* :
70; 122D* : 47E; 131* : 155; 133* : 155;
202* : 200D*; 212 : 281A; 213I* :
219B*; 216 : 922; 243II* : 76*; 254* :
253; 255* : 137; 300I*C : 530; 308* :
401A; 315C* : 712; 403D* : 531;
562II* : 653; 827* : 1168C; 876* : 875*;
877 : 875**; 886I : 792; 902 : 903C*;
904* : 901*; 905* : 901C*; 910F* : 981;
921I* : 922A; 921III* : 920A; 932* :
934A; 948* : 938B; 949* : 844; 953* :
956D*; 961* : 926D; 963* : 956D;
968* : 969; 1285A : 1294A*; 1366* :
1367*; 1374I* : 1453A*; 1380II :
1355A; 1380III : 1360C; 1380V* :
1362; 1380VII : 1725; 1388* : 1392;
1389* : 1362B*; 1459* : 1453A*; 1481* :
1349G; 1615* : 1082A; 1654* : 1355AC;
1700* : 1372; 1701* : 1698; 1705* :
1592B; 1706 : 1643*; 1778* : 1728A*;
1825E : 1848A; 1846* : 1842A; 1849* :
1811A; 1903* : 1656; 1963 : 2022B.

Hungarian (Berze Nagy): 63* : 154;
106* : 103*; 124* : 123A; 123* : 124;
133* : 125B*; 134* : 125C*; 135* :
125D*; 160** : 160A*; 162* : 327C;
163* : 47*; 286* : 2030; 286* : 2021A;
286B* : 2022; 286B* : 2022A; 286C* :
2018; 286D* : 2018*; 319* : 328A*;
320* : 463A*; 332I* : 332F*; 332I* :
735A; 332II : 332E*; 334* : 1188;
340* : 361; 342* : 470; 343* : 313J*;
344I* : 480B*; 345* : 336; 365I :
407B; 368* : 934B; 400I* : 410A;
403B* : 480; 404 : omitted; 404* : 709;
411* : 401A; 419 : 307B*; 465I : omitted; 468* : 425A*; 520* : 516; 530I :
468; 523* : 519; 546 : 480; 577** : 879;
577** : 883B; 588* : 987; 614* : 653;
615* : 613C*; 678* : 1391; 721* : 970;
726** : 958; 727 : 723*; 728* : 550;
728* : 322*; 729* : 298; 754 : 774F;
764* : 774E; 766* : 830B; 769* : 822;
772* : 774L; 773* : 774C; 776* : 934;
779III* : 774A; 779V* : 724B; 779VI* :
785A; 779VII* : 795; 779VIII* : 751;
779IX* : 779A*; 779XII* : 774D;
779XIII* : 774K; 779XXVII* : 980D;

779XXVIII* : 774H; 779XXX* : 774M;
803** : 899;   819 : 820A;   823* :
920A*;   842* : 470B;   891* : 1419E;
926 : 1660;   928* : 1621*;   932* : 725;
949B* : 550; 975* : 980A; 975* : 980C;
977* : 1426*; 1016** : 1010; 1141* : 1137;
1229* : 1290; 1232* : 1210; 1289* : 1225A;
1293 : 1371*;   1294* : 1327A;   1295* :
1698C*;   1299* : 1326; 1321* : 1319L;
1325* : 1336; 1331* : 1349D*; 1332* : 1255;
1332* : 1322A*;   1333* : 1699;   1340* :
1203;   1341* : 1349F;   1344* : 1319A*;
1346* : 1324**;   1347* : 1534;   1349* :
1273C*;   1349II* : 1288A;   1349VII* :
1349J*;   1349XIII* : 1310;   1349XIV* :
1349H*;   1349XXVIII* : 1349K*;
1349XXXI* : 1293;   1371* : 1351A*;
1409* : 1284;   1410* : 1423;   1412* :
1408; 1459* : 1510; 1479* : 1453****;
1542* : 1533;   1543* : 1529;   1565* :
853; 1566* : 853; 1566* : 1545; 1614* :
1531;   1616* : 1691;   1626* : 1678*;
1628* : 778;   1631* : 1381D;   1643* :
1654; 1645** : 1381E; 1645** : 1644;
1646* : 1643;   1654* : 1335B;   1654* :
1240;   1655** : 1355C;   1686* : 1628;
1688* : 1341A;   1688* : 1341;   1689* :
1681A; 1693* : 1676*; 1694* : 1313A;
1698* : 1696A*; 1699* : 1833B; 1726A* :
1536B;   1727B* : 940;   1752* : 571B;
1789* : 1829A*;   1961A** : 1882A;
1961B** : 1961A*;   1961C** : 1961B*;
1961D** : 1961C*;   1961E** : 1961D*;
1961F** : 1965; 1962E* : 2013; 1962C* :
2017;   1962H* : 2200;   1962I* : 2200;
1962F** : 2205; 1962A* : 2251; 1962G* :
2275; 1962B* : 2300; 1964 : 2201.

Hungarian (Honti): 320 : 322*; 320 :
550;   332II : 476*;   361I* : 361*;   467 :
468;   480A : 480;   753I : 830B;   753I :
830C; 775 : 774M; 825 : 759A; 917 :
1531;   926* : 1534B*;   1069 : 1083;
1231* : 1291B;   1410 : 1691;   1535I :
1689; 1620* : 1634C*; 1621* : 1634D*;
1752* : 1733A*.

Hungarian (Kovács): 8^I : 2D; 54* : 154;
58 : 51***;   59* : 133*;   66* : 59;   79* :
132; 202* : 214; 203* : 200E; 205B* : 81;
215* : 214*;   216* : 207B;   218* : 219F;
222^I : 272B;   255* : 137;   278* : 277A;
287 : 293F*.

Slovenian: 1b : 1*; 650 : 810A; 752ab :
830C*; 763 : 837; 785C : 774N.

Serbocroatian: 58** : 51**; 411 : 401A;
425* : 470B; 787 : 960B; 821A* : 813C.

Polish: 11 : 34B; 72A : 81; 84 : 61A;
107 : 101*; 154A : 161; 169 : 179; 176 :
49;   202 : 200B;   276 : 298;   282 : 825;
299 : 282A*; 309 : 307A*; 317A : 313E*;
320 : 319B*; 322* : 311A; 336* : 332D*;
337A : 325*; 338* : 332G*; 339* : 328B*;
340* : 366*; 341* : 934A**; 342 : 325**;
354* : 326D*; 355* : 331*; 356* : 956C*;
372* : 815;   377* : 500*;   404 : 570B*;
412 : 934D; 412 : 862*; 414 : 402; 417 :
550;   420 : 402A*;   421 : 409A;   431A :
480;   443* : 445;   453 : 307C*;   462 :
653A;   469 : 470*;   472 : 471*;   474 :
471A*;   515 : 570;   521 : 406A;   525 :
406A;   568 : 590A;   656 : 875A;   662 :
1225A;   666A : 554C*;   667* : 666*;
668* : 671C*;   669 : 671D*;   672D :
672B*; 675 : 570*; 678 : 300B; 706A :
706; 714 : 712; 733 : 920A*; 734 : 780;
742* : 729.

Russian (Andrejev): 30* : 35B*; *56C :
248A*;   72** : 156A;   126* : 125A;
160I : 163B;   162* : 163;   162* :
2028B*; *176 : 1147*; *242 : 6; *242I :
227*; *282 : 283B*; *284 : 282A*; 288* :
282B*;   291* : 292*;   333B* : 2028;
*400B : 437;   *533B : 437;   559I : 945;
716 : 782;   747* : 790*;   751I : 960B;
758 : 756F*; *762 : 756A*; 770* : 822;
790* : 1416;   *796I : 751C*;   *804I :
471; 812B* : 2010; *816 : 819*; 821C* :
1186; *834B : 745A; 881I : 976; *894 :
921B; *901I : 905A*; *905 : 920; *914 :
910G; 931I : 938B; 931II : 938; *932I :
934A; 932* : 934; 934* : 930A; 959A* :
956D; 959*B : 958; 959I : 956E*; 965 :
955A*; *966 : 969; *967 : 969; *981II :

983; *981I : omitted; *981IV : omitted; 982* : 980A; *992 : omitted; 1084I : 1199B; 1136* : 1137; 1162I : omitted; 1165 : 1353; 1178* : omitted; 1183* : 1188; 1213* : 1242A; *1277I : omitted; 1292* : 1293*; *1356 : omitted; *1360A : 1358C; *1375I : 1378A*; 1406*B : 1419J*; 1406*C : 1419K*; 1406*D : 1419L*; *1440I : 1441A*; *1442 : 1441C*; 1465* : omitted; *1480 : 1456*; 1541I : 1540A; 1544A* : 1545B; *1547 : omitted; *1563II : 900B*; *1570A : 1544; *1570B : 1544B*; *1606 : omitted; *1609 : 1543; *1610I : omitted; *1616 : omitted; *1618 : omitted; *1630 : 570; *1636 : 1590; 1637* : 1557; 1660 : 1534; *1696B : 1690*; *1701 : 1545; 1710* : 1339E; *1730I : 1536B; *1730II : 1359D; 1730IV : 1358C; *1730IV : omitted; *1731I : 1745*; *1734 : omitted; 1744 : omitted; 1776* : 1319; *1789 : 1642; 1843** : 1833C; *1885 : 804A; *1896I : 1895C*; 1940 : 1562A; 1960G* : 2044; *1960G^I : 218B*; *2000 : 2400; *2008 : 1698; *2008II : 1699; *2008 : 1702; *2014II : 1702; 2015I* : 2016; 2015II* : 2016*; 2020* : 2300; *2028A : 1468*; 2050 : 1702A*; 2054* : 1867; 2063 : 1288*; 2067* : 1867; *2103B : *1705B*; *2132 : 921C*.

Russian (Afanasiev): 72** : 81; *119 : 47D; *119 : 117*; 222*B : 313B; *241I : 2021A; 241II : 2021B; *241II : 2022; *241II : 2032B; *241III : 2022B; 296* : 2025; 480BDEF : 480; *722 : 313E*; *813B : 445; *841I : 862; *847 : 1642A; *884V : omitted; *855 : omitted; *894 : 875F; *895 : 1426; 925* : 655; *1012II : 1685; *1013I : omitted; 1084I : 1082A; *1360I : 1725; *1360I : 1358A; *1361I : 1360C; *1375 : 1378B*; *1425 : 804A; 1525*J : 1624B*; 1528* : 1528B; *1545 : 1544A*; *1545 : 1636; *1563III : 1423; *1567I : 1562B*; *1567 II :1562C*; *1580 : 1533; 1625 : 778*; 1665* : 1644; 1696*B : 1691B; 1720* : 1690*; 1789* :

1642; *1825D : 1694; 1876B* : 1881; 1877B* : 1882, 1882A; *1885 : 1889K; *1912 : 1889F; 2003* : 1656; 2009* : 1348; *2014I : 2040; *2060 : 1334; *2065 : 1446; *2076 : 1295; *2082 : 1628; *2104 : 1634A*; *2140 : 1699B.

Greek: 2* : 41**; 2B* : 68B; 402* : 898; 590* : 591*; 770* : 822; 735** : 938A; 816* : 1645B; 874* : 707A*; 880B* : 879A*; 883B* : 879A; 884*** : 891A; 888* : 938; 925 : 655; 927* : 1534; 928* : 927; 933* : 930F; 933** : 934E; 936* : 461; 950* : 920A; 955 : 655; 1228* : 1586A; 1240** : 1250A; 1284* : 1327; 1294* : 1354A*; 1316* : 1740A; 1316* : 1319D*; 1318** : 1319C*; 1318** : 1319D*; 1319* : 1318B*; 1322* : 767; 1322** : 1320*; 1324* : 1334; 1325* : 1335A; 1325** : 1336; 1326* : 1336A; 1340* : 1337B; 1406** : 1419E; 1409* : 1359*; 1431* : 1433*; 1460* : 1362*; 1527* : 1654; 1544** : 1545A; 1570* : 982; 1587* : 1543; 1610* : 1331; 1651*, 1660* : 1530*; 1677** : 1225A; 1696** : 1691A; 1699 : 1692A*; 1705* : 1689*; 1736* : 1341B; 1841* : 1848B; 1844* : 1653A*; 1846** : 1810B.

French Canadian: 40* : 40A*; 1184* : 1187; 1386* : 1260A*; 1541* : 1376C*; 1702* : 1698N.

Spanish-American: 51**A : 49; 59**AB : 58*; 74**A : 78A; **169 : 1095; **203AB : 200B; **216 : omitted; **218AB : 105A; 246**A : 132; 275*A : 1074; **289 : 286*; **296 : omitted; 303**A : 550; 326*A, *B : 326; 340*A —*H : 312C; **416 : 413B*; 425**D : 433D; 425**F : 433B; **429 : 425B; **438 : 431B*; **439A—F : 431C*; **448 : 444C*; **446 : 444E*; 452**A : 450; **459 : 452D*; **542 : 511A*; 556**A : 551; **596 : 595B*; **775 : 760**; **778 : omitted; *823AB : 1950; **823C : 1951; 836**A : 830C; 836**G : 836B*; 836**I : 836C*;

836**K : 836D*; *835 : 472A; 876** : 891A; *926 : 924A; **939 : 935**; 970* : 956C; 970* : 879; **982 : omitted; **1152 : 1063; **1191 : 1180; **1392 : 1381*; **1549 : 1540B; 1532**A : 1740B; 1535 : 1689; 1535 : 571A; 1535*A : 1534; 1550E : 1641B; **1554 : 1578A; 1558D*, E* : omitted; 1556**A : 1807A*; 1556**B, **C : omitted; 1588** : omitted; *1618 : 1543; 1631**A : 1387; **1648AC : 1645A*; **1676 : 1341A; **1677 : 1676B; **1682 : 1699; 1686ABC 1685; *1692 : 1681B; *1693 : 1681B; **1704 : 1681B; **1706 : 1681B; **1709A : 1341B*; **1709B : 1676*; **1709A : 1703*; 1940**A : 1562A; 1940**B : 1545; 1940**I, **J : 1138; cf. *1942 : 1626; 1940*A : 1717*; 1835D : 1828*; *1852 : 1529; **1858 : 1806B*; 1889**ACJ : 1888*; 1889**D : 1892; 1889**F : 1920; 1889**H : omitted; 1889**N : 1960D; 1889**P : omitted; 1920**G : omitted; 1920**S : omitted; 1940*D : 1530*; **2045 : 2010; **2050 : 2046*; **2052 : 2010I A.

India: 929D : 875; 936 : 934D$_I$; 948 : 736A; 1338* : 1349L*.

INDEX

References are to type numbers.

Abandoned bride in male disguise, 881A; children escape from burning barn, 327E.
Abandonment in boat of fated bride, 930CD; on golden mountain, 936*; on island, 1118*.
Abbot gets substitute to answer king's questions, 922.
Abducted girl kills robbers with poisoned grass, 850**.
Abduction in »singing bag» (substituted animals), 311B*.
Abraham worships (chain tale), 2031B.
Absurdity of task shown, 875, 875B, 875B$_1$, 875B$_2$, 875B$_3$, 875E, 875B$_4$*.
Accidental discharge of gun, 1890.
Accidents (lucky, 1640—1674).
Accursed daughter, 813A.
Accusation of murder (blackmail), 1536—1536*.
Accuser is madman, 1587**.
Achikar, 922A.
Acorn crop, 1185.
Actor in passion play, 1687*.
Adam's vision of future, 840A*.
Adder upsets poisoned porridge and saves woman, 285A*.
Adulteress and lover (eat goose prepared for guests), 1729A*; (caught by »himphamp»), 511B; makes equivocal oath, 1418.
Adulteress's spoiled food, 1359*.
Adultery betrayed by alleged speaking animals, 1750, 1750A; in pear tree, 1423; revealed by bird (bird punished), 243, 243A.
Adventure told as dream, 1364.
Adventures as a dog (man has been transformed), 1898*; of prince and three hosts, 726**; related to save robber sons, 953.
Adversity pursues couple, 735B*.
Advice of devil, 823*; of fox (when you have a fox don't let him loose), 150; of frog, 278C*, 150.

Advocate and devil, 1186; is devil, 821, 821A, 821B.
Ages of men and animals readjusted, 173.
Agreement not to scratch, 1565.
Air journey on helpful eagle's back, 537.
Aircastles, 1430, 1681*.
Aladdin, 561.
Alcestis, 899.
»All stick together», 571.
All depends on how you take it, 915, 915A; these are mine (whiskers of penniless wooer), 859D.
Amicus and Amelius, 516C.
Ammunition wasted by robber, 1527A.
Amor and Psyche, 425A.
Anchor large enough, 1277**.
Androcles and the lion, 156.
Anecdotes, 1200—1999; about clergy, 1725—1824; of women (misc.), 1500—1524; of men, 1525—1874.
Angel and hermit, 759.
Angels on widow's roof, 796*.
Anger bargain, 1000.
Animal bride, 402; brothers as helpers, 465D; brothers-in-law as helpers, 552—552B; in chest substituted for lover, 1419B; languages learned, 671—674; languages understood (inquisitive wife), 670; (ring and corpse), 670A; tales, 1—299; sons-in-law and their magic food, 552B; talk imitated in tale, 106, 206, 2075; tied to another for safety (fatal), 78; troops to be sent against army, 1302*; turned inside out, 1889B.
Animals as helpers, 530—539; build road (dig well), 55; eat each other, 20, 231*; (grateful) help hero perform task, 554; go a-journeying, 130, 210; in night quarters, 130, 130A—130C, 130D*; learn to fear men, 157—157D*; rebel against work, 207; ransom selves, 159; warm selves at fire, 130D*, 159A; saved from pit, 160; with queer names (henny-penny), 2010 IA.

Animals' foolish interpretation of human action (rape), 152B*.
Answers of boy to priest (impertinent), 1832C*D*F*G**H*J*K*.
Ant and lazy cricket, 280A; carries large load, 280; finds penny, (chain tale), 2023; plants chickpeas (chain tale), 2030A.
Anticipatory whipping, 1674*.
Antlers and legs (stag), 77.
Appearances maintained by poor girl, 1459**.
Application of sermon, 1833.
Apprentice invokes ghost (in vain), 325*.
Ariadne-thread wins prince, 874*.
Aristotle and Phyllis, 1501.
Ark admits devil, 825.
Arrogant mole refused fire (given to polite quail), 287*.
Artificial child made by childless couple, 703*.
Aschenputtel, 510, 510A.
Asinus vulgi, 1215.
Ask and you shall receive (hermit asks for princess), 862.
Asking the large fish, 1567C.
Ass as mayor, 1675; boasts of having kicked sick lion, 50C; carries found money to master, 1645B*; carries wolf to village to be mayor (wolf beaten), 122N*; envies horse fine trappings, 214*; frightens lion by turning ears back, 125D*; has charter in his hoof, 47E; hoisted to tower (hanged), 1210*; imitates dog (may not caress master), 214; in lion's skin, 214B; overawes lion, 125B*; pulls down tree top (bluff), 125C*; refuses to drink when full, 1621A*; relieved of burden (rider takes sack on shoulders), 1242A; rescued from well, 1225*; taken for hare, 1316****; (transformed) disenchanted, 430; tries to get cricket's voice, 292; with hay caught between bushes, 1294B*; without a heart, 52.
Ass's egg (pumpkin), 1319.
Asses loaded with salt and with feathers 211.
Attack on hare (flight from fierce animal), 1231.
Attempted murder with hatchet, 1115.
Attempts to murder hero, 1115—1129.
Attention drawn by old maid, 1485A*.
Attentive donkey, 1213*.
Auctioneer persuades man to buy back worthless cow, 1214.
Automatic saw and wagon make princess laugh, 675.

Avaricious priest outwitted, 1842A*.
Axe demanded to cut whole forest, 1049; in stream falsely claimed, 729.
Axes thrown away, 1246.
Baba Dochia, 368C*.
Bad luck (follows man), 947, 947A, 947A*; (imprisoned), 735B.
Bad rearing blamed, 838; woman punished, 750C.
Bad-luck boots exchanged, 735C*.
Badger leaves den befouled by hedgehog, 80.
Bag for food, 1088.
Bake-house imprisons greedy fox, 66**.
Balancing mealsack with rock, 1242B.
Baldak Borisevich, 946A*.
Baldness of Peter, 774J.
Ball of thread as magic help, 934E.
Balloonist falls (digs self out), 1882.
Balls followed into adventures, 431A*.
Banana fruit thrown away, 1339B.
Banished wife or maiden, 705—712.
Bank robbery, 951B.
Baptism (anecdotes), 1823.
Barber discovers ass's ears, 782; substituted for smith hanged, 1534A*.
Bargain of three brothers with devil, 360; not to become angry, 1000; to act as God one day (runs after goat), 774D; with devil: not to sleep three nights, 813*.
Bargains good and bad, 1642; (lucky) made by animal, 170A.
Barking dog's head, etc., 572*.
Barn (burning) escaped by children who return home, 327E; is burning, 1562A.
Basil maiden, 879.
Basin (magic) catches lover, 571A.
Basket stolen by fox, 1*; tied to wolf's tail, 2B.
Basketmaker husband recognized by peculiar basket, 888A*.
Basketwork learned by gentlemen so as to marry lowly girl, 949*.
Bat in war of birds and quadrupeds, 222A.
Bath in dragon's blood, 650C.
Bath-house kept to learn of vanished husband, 425D.
Bathing garments kept until promise of marriage, 400, 413, 425M; or warming grandmother, 1013.
Battle of serpents, 738*.
Bauer schickt den Jockel aus, 2030E.
Bayberry child, 407A.
Bean king (youth's boast), 545D*; planted by cock and hen, 218*—218B*; straw and coal, 295.

Beans break old maid's tooth, 1478; in pocket (for counting days), 1848B.
Beanstalk to sky, 328, 555, 804A.
Bear and honey, 49; and man (misc.), 179*; breaks leg repeatedly crossing bridge, 163C*; chases robbers, 957; falls from roof and is beaten, 3*; fishes through ice with tail, 2; food, 154; goes to monkey for gold chain, 48*; (wolf) harnessed, 1910; helps fox's mother get berries but fox eats them, 39; in various conflicts, 171B*; mistaken for preacher, 116; pelts wolves with logs, 87A*; persuaded to have new tail made of glowing iron, 40B*; riding horse sinks claws into his flanks, 117; taken for dog, 1312; taken for log seizes man, 1630B*; taken for St. Martin, 1705B*; two girls and dwarf, 426; whispers in sham dead man's ear, 179; will eat the butter, 51*; with wooden leg avenges injury, 161A*.
Bear-skin, 361, 361*.
Bear-trainer and bear, 1161.
Beard of ogre caught (haunted castle), 1160; gilded, 1138.
Bearded head presented daily to adulteress, 992A.
Bear's son, 301; testament, 164*.
Beautification by painting: dupe burned, 8; promised: dupe injured, 8A.
Beautiful and ugly twin, 711.
Beauty and beast, 425C.
Bed the most dangerous place, 921D; rolls robber's treasure into cellar, 963*.
Bee and beehive (lie), 1920G; saved by dove (repays by stinging hunter), 240A*.
Beehive goes to wolf irrespective of age, 80A*.
Beer brewed by birds, 234A*; brewed by man and animals, 176**; runs while woman chases dog, 1387.
Bees punished for stinging Peter, 774K.
Beet presented to king (later a horse), 1689A.
Beetle fried by fox, 65*.
Beggar disguise for robber, 958D*; dressed up obtains credit, 1526; in night lodgings leaves money, 842A*; on cross, 800A; trusts God, not king, 841.
Behavior at table (foolish), 1691—1691B.
Belfagor, 1164.
Believing oneself dead, 1313—1313A*.
Bell alarms robbers, 965*; falls into sea, 1278; on slain horse rung by fox, 40; on wolf's tail rings alarm, 40A*; put on salmon, 1208*.
Belle aux bois dormante, 410.
Belling the cat, 110.
Bells give bad advice, 1511*.
Belly debates with members, 293.
Beloved of women, 580.
Below the sea, 677*.
Belt around neck to keep life in, 1293**; gives hero strength, 590, 590*.
Bending tree (trickster shot to sky), 1051.
Berries meant for fox's mother go to fox, 39.
Berry (transformed girl), 702B*.
Best friend, worst enemy, 921B.
Betrayal of hidden animal when he is induced to make movement, 66B.
Better game to be provided, 122D.
Bewitched palace collapses, 321*.
Bible leaves pasted, 1835B*.
Biblical repartee, 1847*.
Big bird or little bird (argument), 1365H*; cake for Lent, 1565*; Claus and Little Claus, 1535; 'Fraid and Little 'Fraid, 1676A; shoes in front of barn (overawe ogre), 1151, 1151*; wedding, 1963; wind (thief's excuse), 1624.
Binding devil in chains in hell, 803; midnight, dawn, etc., 723*.
Bird and hunter's skull, 244D*; and jackal as friends, 223; disguises of lover, 432; husband sought, 425N; indifferent to pain (chain tale), 2041; language learned, 671, 671C*, 517; lover (healed), 432; (disenchanted), 432*; mouse and sausage, 85; of truth, 707; seeks mason to free its young (chain tale), 2034E; (enchanted prince) steals girl's jewel, 425F; sought by king's sons, 550; thrown from cliff as punishment, 1310C; to be made tastier before being eaten (escapes), 122D*; waits until hunter has shot, 246.
Bird-heart eaten (magic), 567.
Bird's pea gets stuck (chain tale), 2034D.
Birds, 220—249; and the net, 233—233C; and quadrupeds at war, 222—222B*; as symbols of princes' character, 920B; break rope and drop fox, 58*; discuss trap, 245*; elect king, 221; fly off with net, 233B; have council, 220; have court, 229A*; in net sham death and escape, 233A.
Birthmarks of the princess, 850.
Biting a grain in half (chain tale),

2044A*; doll, 571C; stone (deceptive), 1061; the foot, 5.
Black and white bride, 403; animal to be washed white, 1312*; princess to be disenchanted, 463B*.
Blackmail of princess, 850.
Blacksmith never finishes work for ogre, 1163*.
Blemishes of women reflected by magic, 870D*.
Blessing at grave (parson's ox), 1840; of God not asked, 830, 830B, 830C; to be asked before eating (fox and cock), 61.
Blind bride and her fiancé, 1456*; couple's eyes restored, 321; fiancée, 1456; lame and deaf in court, 1673*; men and elephant, 1317; men cheated, 1577—1577*; men duped into fighting, 1577; robber paid back, 1577*; wolf deceived into releasing captive ox, 122L*.
Blinded man learns secrets, 613.
Blinding ogre by glowing mass stuck into eye, 1135, 1137; the guard, 73.
Blindworm trades eyes, 234.
Blood and brains shammed, 3; of children for disenchantment of friend, 516—516C.
Blood-brother's wife, 1364.
Blood-brothers, 303.
Blowing house in, 124.
Blue band gives hero strength, 590.
Bluebeard, 312, 955.
Bluff wins contests, 1611, 1612.
Bluffing ogre, 1149.
Boar climbs tree and falls on bear, 171A*.
Boast of having kicked sick lion, 50C.
Boaster about wife imprisoned, 880; wins bride, 545C*.
Boastful deer-slayer denies God's help, 830A; servant, 2404.
Boasting of dowry, 1930B*; goat at watering place apologises to wolf, 132; punished by loss of property, 830, 836.
Boat gets tired, 1277; of bread-crust for mouse, 135*; on fire quenched from shore, 1330; needs bailing out (plug removed), 1746*; tarred by ogre, 1156; to be put in water (deceptive), 1053**.
Boiling milk runs over, 1328*.
Bone in wolf's throat removed by crane, 76.
Bones (singing) reveal murder, 780; traded for reindeer, 8*.
Bonhomme Misère, 330D.
Booty left by dupe and stolen, 15*, 15**.

Boots sent by telegraph, 1710.
Borma Jarizhka, 485.
Born of a fish, 705; of three mothers (riddle), 927B*.
Borrowed coat claimed by witness, 1642, 1642A; feathers for raven, 244.
»Both?», 1563.
Bottle imp, 331, 331*.
Bottomless boat, 1963*.
Bow bent by hunter, 246; rebounds and kiils meddler, 180.
Box holding maiden to be brought into seducer's room, 894; (magic) stolen but recovered by cat, 560B*; on the ear (bought), 1372; on ear (gives sparks to light fire), 1344; on ear (returned), 1557.
Boy adopted by tigers, 535; answers priest, 1832*—1832P*; applies the sermon, 1833; as hero of stories, 1525—1874; at witch's house, 327, 334; in hollow tree, 1877*; on wolf's tail, 1875; raised in eagle's nest, 554B*; refuses food to angels, 766*; with many names cheats and seduces, 1545; with hat of butter, etc., 1880; with active imagination, 2411; who had never seen a woman, 1678; who learned many things, 517.
Boy's disasters, 1681.
Boys with extraordinary names, 883C.
Brahman and mongoose, 178A.
Branch of tree cut by man sitting on it, 1240, 1240A.
Branches of tree grow together over lover's graves, 970.
Brave tailor, 1640.
Bread hits bear's nose (fatally), 1890B*; poisoned eaten by poisoner's son, 837; played with (girl punished), 962**; returned for stone, 1696A*; taken to hell (kind and unkind), 480C*; with gold unwittingly exchanged, 841.
Breadloaf followed leads to adventures, 431B*.
Breath for both warm and cool, 1342; in cold air taken for tobacco smoke, 1320
Breathing tree (full of animals), 1916.
Breeches jumped into, 1286.
Bremen city musicians, 130, 210.
Briar-patch punishment for rabbit, 1310A.
Bribed boy sings wrong song, 1735A; judge, 1861A.
Bridal chamber and monster, 507B; couple stutterers, 1702B*.

Bride won in tournament (grateful dead man), 508.
Bride's false eyes (teeth), 1379*.
Bridegroom is robber, 955; puts dog in soup (etc.), 1685.
Bridegroom's foolish acts, 1685.
Bridegrooms exchanged, 855, 856.
Bridge to be built, 1005; to otherworld, 471.
Bringing unheard-of riding-horse, 1091.
Broken image, 1643.
Brother and sister heal the king, 613C*; freed from prison by clever sister, 879C*; or sister*, 450—459; rescues sisters, 312—312D; to hang himself (treasure under tree), 740**; to be saved rather than husband or son, 985; transformed to snake, 450A.
Brothers (four skillful), 653; (three), 654; (three lucky), 1650; (wise), 655; sought (7, 9, or 12), 451, 451A; in tree (door dropped on robbers), 1653B.
Brunhilde, 519.
Bucket in well (fox rescued) 32.
Buffalo herd helped by buffaloes, 534.
Building bridge for ogre (deceptive), 1005; the church, 1246*.
Bull's milk (calves), $875B_1$, $875B_4$*.
Bullock saves captive children, 314A*.
Bundle of twigs and quarreling sons, 910F.
Buried sheep's head, 1381C; tail, 2A; wife (still disagrees), 1365F*.
Burned and underbaked bread, 1448*.
Burning escaped (hero bluffs), 1116; house to get rid of (cat), 1281, (insects), 1282; of Lanka, 1693; ogre's wife in oven, 1121.
Burying the mole, 1310B.
Bushel to be level, 1182.
Butcher as devil, 750G*; catches fox, 67**.
Butter on altar-bread, 1836*; to fill cracks, 1291B; weighed with bread, 1566**; cask taken for dead, 1314.
Buying an island (drunk man), 1671*; dream of treasure, 1645A; good weather, 1296A; wood (deception), 1048.
Cabbage fed meat, 1386.
Cake for peasants who have no bread, 1446.
Calendar for priest (egg-shells and seeds), 1848A—D.
Calf and parson, 1739; has eaten man all but feet, 1281A.
Calf's head reveals murder, 780C; head in pot, 1294.

Calling tree-names on wager, 7.
Calumniated sister, 872*; wife, 707.
Calves not to be looked over by wolf, 165A*.
Camel and ass betrayed by ass's singing, 214A; rider has doorway broken down (instead of dismounting), 1295B*.
Candle (burning) determines life span, 934E, 1187; offered by thief rejected by saint, 848*.
Candles on crayfish, 1740; on goat's horns, 1740A.
Cane left with robber, 961A.
Cannibal (enchanted girl) disenchanted, 406; godfather (godmother) devours girl, 333B; robbers, 955B*; sister, 315A.
Cannibalism pretended to frighten robbers, 958B*.
Cannibalistic brothers, 780A.
Cap of father beaten (head was inside), 1630A*.
Cap o' Rushes, 510, 510B.
Captive animals ransom selves, 159; escapes by deceiving captor, 122.
Carcass of animal hiding place for jackal, 68.
Card game used to illustrate tales, 2340.
Card-playing parson, 1839—1839B.
Cards fall from preacher's sleeve, 1827A.
Carnation (transformed sweetheart), 652.
Carrying the horse (between legs), 1082; the sham-sick trickster, 4, 72; a tree (riding on it), 1052; wolf, goat, cabbage across stream (puzzle), 1579.
Carts as legs for crippled sow (hereditary), 1911.
Case reenacted in court (judge to be kicked), 1327A.
Caskets chosen (gold and fire), 1130*.
Casks hide robbers entering house, 954.
Casting eyes, 1006, 1006*.
Castrating dead horse, 1349H*; ogre to make him strong, 1133; the crucifix (husband and paramour), 1359C.
Castration bargain (wife sent), 153; to make dupe strong, 153, 1133.
Cat and candle, 217, 217*; and others quarrel over food, 219G*; and mouse converse (cat eats mouse), 111; as confessor alone crosses ditch on pole, 136A*; as helper, 545—545B; as inheritance, 1650, 1651; as sham holy man, 113B; as she-fox's husband frightens other animals, 103A; asks about gypsy's lip, 219A*; (bear) has kittens (ogre frightened), 1161; castle, 545A; (enchanted princess) as bride,

402; husband disenchanted, 444D*; kills mice with wooden leg, 1912; loses dog's certificate, 200; overawes wild animals, 103, 103A, 103A*, 103B*; rescues cock from fox and kills young foxes, 61B; reveals treasure, 545E*, stew, 1878*; sets fire to barn (extraordinary names), 1562A; shams death to kill attendant mice at funeral, 113*; to wear bell, 110; washes face before eating (rat escapes), 122B; wins race from careless dog, 200D*; weighed (could not have eaten all of meat), 1373.

Catala, 1515.

Catch tales, 2200—2249.

Catching a noise, 1177*; in cleft tree, 38, 151, 1159; man's broken wind, 1176; rams, 1499*; water in sieve, 1180.

Catechism (anecdotes), 1810—1810C*.

Caterinella, 333A.

Cat's curiosity and single trick, 105A*; funeral, 113*; funeral held by birds, 235A*; only trick (climbing tree), 105, 105A*.

Cats bring firewood, 219C*.

Cattle guarded for ogre (deceptive), 1003*; merchant's voyage (lie), 1887*.

Cave call, 66A.

Cellar hole prevents overfed wolf from escaping, 41.

Certificate of dog lost by cat, 200.

Chain of accidents, 2042—2042D*; of men hanging from limb (top man spits on hands), 1250, 1250B; tales, 2000—2199.

Chains of killings, 2045A*, 2045B*.

Chalk marks (for sins) on heaven's stairs, 1738C*.

Changed order to questions in foreign language brings confusion, 1699B; places in bed to escape murder, 1119.

Changing places with priest (dying man offers), 1806B*.

Chanson de Bricon (chain tale), 2030H.

Chanticleer's crowing makes sun rise, 114.

Chapter of monks disgusting (individually pleasing), 1553C*.

Charcoal-burner Latin, 1641C.

Charity surpasses prayer, etc., 756E*.

Charter in his hoof, 47E.

Chastity of wife guarded by (devil), 1352, (parrot), 1352A; test, 870; wager, 882.

Cheater caught with own words, 1588***.

Cheats in selling (horses), 1631, 1631A, 1632; (oxen), 1538; (various), 978.

Cheese cut thriftily, 1452; dived for (reflection), 34, 34A, 34B*, 1336; sent after another one, 1291.

Cheeses due the minister, 1842B*.

Chernobylnik, 672D*.

Chest as hiding place for spy, 1536A; of (supposed) gold induces children to care for aged father, 982.

Chicken hatched from armpit, 219B*; hides from wolf, 137*.

Chickens from boiled eggs, 821B.

Child and snake, 285; to be borne to absent husband, 891; to be cleaned (killed), 1012; unwittingly betrays mother's adultery, 1358*; weeping in mother's womb promised supernatural wife, 409B*.

Children and ogre, 327—327D*; desire ogre's flesh (bluff), 1149; exchanged, 975*; hidden by Eve, 758; of king, 892; of ogre killed by their father, 1119; preferred are one's own, 247.

Child's head caught in jar, 1294A*.

Chimney stopped forces hospitality, 1527*.

Choosing what food he will have (all), 1388A*.

Chopping contest (deceptive), 1065*—1065B*.

Christ and Peter in barn (thresh with fire), 752A; in night lodgings, 791, (various jests), 774—774P; and the smith, 753; as matchmaker, 822; not married ignorant of suffering, 1516A*.

Christopher, 768.

Church bought in common (each pays full price), 1266A*; moved (away from dung), 1325B, (the stolen coat), 1326; of cheese, 1932; robbers identified (thieves), 1641B*; to be built in hell, 804B.

Churn on back while leaning over, 1408A.

Cinderella, 510, 510A.

Claim to be transformed horse (theft of horse), 1529.

Claw in split tree, 38, 151, 1159.

Claws of bear on horseback sink into horse's flanks, 117.

Clean and tidy (seven-year old porridge), 1462*.

Cleaning the child, 1012, 1012A; (the horse), 1016; out manure (deceptive), 1035.

Clergyman with fine voice (like goat's), 1834.

Clerics (anecdotes), 1725—1849.

Clever acts and words, 920—929; animal

makes fortunate exchanges, 170A; answers, 879C*—879F*; boy with fooling-sticks, 1542; coachman and hungry master, 1572E*; device to get well dug, 1614*; dog milks cows, etc., 201B*; Elsie, 1450; girl at end of journey, 875D; judge and the demon in the pot, 926A; maiden and suitors, 876; maiden kills robbers, 956B; man, 1525—1639; parrot woos for king, 546; peasant girl, 875, 876A*; sparrow helps friendly wolf, 248A*.
Cleverness and gullibility, 1539, 1540*, 1540A*, 1541**, 1541***.
Climax of horrors, 2040.
Climbing after honey (bear falls), 88*; contest with young one (squirrel), 1073; from pit on dupe's back, 31; on top of one another (lowest leaves and all fall), 121; to heaven (lies), 1920D*.
Cloak given stone for warmth, 1271C.
Closing the door tight, 1014.
Cloth instead of sacrament, 1835E*.
Clothing caught in graveyard, 1676B; the servant, 1569**.
Clothes for king imaginary, 1620; welcomed at banquet, 1558.
Cloud marks the spot, 1278*.
Coachman puts hay in front of driven horses, 1576*.
Cock advises how to rule wife, 670; and duck laugh at each other, 211A*; and hen, 2021—2021B; as damages for eaten grain, 1655; as friend but cat as enemy of mice, 112**; bluffs other animals (chain tale), 2027*; crows (and awakens sexton), 1828; crows (and lets sun rise), 114; entices jay from his booty, 15**; has wonderful adventures, 715A; hen, duck, pin, needle on journey, 210; released from fox when latter talks, 6, 61A; sheep, and duck at sea, 204; silent about mistress's adultery saves life, 243A; to crow with closed eyes, 61; strikes out hen's eye with nut (chain tale), 2021B.
Cock's ancestry, 927B*; head hit by nut, 2033; whiskers (chain tale), 2032.
Coconut thrown from tree injures dupe, 74C*.
Coffin-maker cuts off corpse's feet, 1699*.
Coin recovered from offering box, 1735B*; with king's face often seen, 922B.
Coins honestly earned float, 842C*; (four) to be used wisely, 921A.
Cold and wind compete, 298B*; contest (wind and frost), 1097*; May night, 1927; spell has broken (says woman beside fire), 1349G*.
Combined names of brothers (absurd results), 1376C*.
Combing-machine (seduction), 1543A*.
»Come here, lean» (catch tale), 2205.
»Come tomorrow,» inscription tells devil, 1188.
Commanding ship without cursing, 1785**.
Complaint of trapped hare, 72C*.
Concentrated washer, 1465A*.
Condemned soul, 760**.
Confession of sins to fox, 61A; of wolf's depredations, 77*.
Confessional, 1800—1809.
Confessions of pious woman (pleasant memories), 1805.
Confinement to avoid fulfillment of prophecy, 934.
Congregation not to turn around, 1845*; weeps and laughs (person without breeches), 1828*.
Conscript ignorant of right and left, 1679**.
Contagious yawns, 1431.
Contest between man and ogre, 1060—1114; of wind and sun, 298; of wind and cold, 298B*; of frost and hare, 71; in climbing mast, 1611; in cursing, 1094; in eating, 1088; in laughing, 42*, 1080*; in lying, 1920—1920H*; in mowing, 1090; in pulling down tree (ass and lion), 125C*; in rowing, 1087; in scratching, 1095; in sewing, 1096; in shrieking, 1084; in swimming, 1612; in threshing, 1089; in wishing, 1925.
Contract fetched from hell, 756B, 756C*; not to touch bride burned, 1490*.
Contradictions (formula tales), 2335; or extremes (chain stories), 2014.
Convivial fathers-in-law, 903B*.
Conversation of flea and fly, 282B*; of fish, 254*; in half words, 1702A*; in mass antiphonies, 1831.
Cooked rice only accepted, 1951.
Cooking all rice (etc.) for one meal, 1339E; ogre's wife in his own oven, 327C, 1121.
Copper coin contract wears devil out, 1182A.
Cord made of chaff, 1889E, 1889K.
Corn carried away (endless tale), 2301; cut so wind will not blow it away, 1204*.
Cornucopia from cow, 510, 511A*.

Corpse dropped on robbers, 327G, 1653B; killed five times, 1537; to be disposed of, 1536.
Corpse's legs left bring murder accusation, 1537*.
Cost of the ass, 1551*.
Council of birds, 220.
Counsels about traveling, 910H; of fox, 150; given by grateful frog, 150A*; prove wise, 910, 910A—K.
Counterfeit money has been burned, 1592A*.
Countertasks given king by girl, 875B.
Counting stars (sand, etc.), 1172*; out pay (hole in hat), 1130; wrong by not counting oneself, 1287.
Country mouse visits town mouse, 112; visited by city strangers, 1338, 1338A.
Court held for birds, 229A*; physician, 514**.
Courtship of crane and heron, 244A*; of fools, 1688—1688C*; of rich man, 941**.
Covering the cow, 1349A*; wagon with tar, 1017.
Covetous and envious, 1331.
Cow as helper, 511A*; chewing cud thought mimicking woman, 1211; deceitfully shared, 1633; grazes on roof, 1210; helps disenchant prince, 435A*; on pole (how there?), 1225A; sold for three magic objects, 595A*; sold to crucifix, 1643; stolen by parson and sexton, 1790; taken to roof to graze, 1210; without heart, 1218*; divided (which go to old or new stable), 1030*.
Coward not to be trusted (bear whispers to sham dead man), 179.
Cowardly animals in duel, 104; hares find sheep more so, 70; tailors, 1854*.
Crab as name of sham wise man, 1641; thought to be devil, 1310*; walks backwards, 276.
Crack of limb catches birds, 1890A.
Cracks filled with butter, 1291B.
Cradle moved about (seduction), 1363.
Crane and fox invite each other, 60; as traveler learns nothing, 232B*; feeds fox from deep dish, 60; gets no payment for pulling bone from wolf's windpipe, 76; teaches fox to fly (lets him fall), 225; transports fish from drying lake (eats them), 231.
Crane's repeated courtship of heron, 244A*.
Cranes of Ibycus, 960A.
Crayfish breaks promise to crow, 242B*; entices crow into talking (escapes), 227*; to be drowned, 1310.
Creaking frightens fool, 1321A.
Creditor reported insane, 1525L.
Credulity about giving birth, 1739—1739B*.
Crescentia, 712.
Cricket and ant, 280A; loses coin and complains (teller imitates cricket), 292*; suffers in winter because of laziness, 280A.
Criminal confesses because of misunderstanding dialect, 1699A; to lunch with Christ, 1806.
Crocodile carries jackal, 58.
Crooked handle (spoon) preferred to scythe, 1564A*.
Crop of acorns to terminate contract, 1185; division (above the ground, below the ground), 9B, 1030, 1633.
Crosswise loading of logs on sleigh, 1248.
Cross as security for debt works marvel, 849*.
Crow and reindeer meat, 166*; and seal keep house, 247*; and titmouse, 244**; as adviser of magpies, 56A; bespatters swan, 232A*; calls frog but frog waits, 242C*; complains of pains from drinking sour milk, 234B*; drops pebbles in jug so that he can drink, 232D*; helps deer escape from snare, 239; in borrowed feathers at wedding, 224*; marries, 243*; on tarred bridge, 2017; to wash bill (chain tale), 2030B.
Crown of serpent, 672.
Crucifix punished, 1324A*; easier to keep if alive, 1347.
Cruel rich man as devil's horse, 761.
Crying child, 556D*; out permitted captive who thus summons help, 91A*.
Cuckoo confined by high pen (flies away), 1213; imitated by woman in tree, 1029; lays eggs in wren's nest, 240A.
Cuckoo's borrowed skin, 235.
Cumulative pursuit, 2038; tales, 2000—2199.
Cup with two and three handles, 1322**.
Cupid and Psyche, 425A.
Curly hair to be straightened, 1175.
Curse and countercurse, 556B*.
Cursing contest, 1094.
Cut-off hair (nose), 1417.
Cutting cheese as bride test, 1452; wood (magic cat in woodpile), 1001.
Cyclone destroys house (chain tale), 2046*.
Damages demanded (cheat), 1655.

Dance among thorns, 592; for animals given by tiger (but they escape), 74B*.
Danced-out shoes, 306.
Dancing girl's fortune, 879B*; permits hare's escape, 183*; with nun (wager), 1812.
Darkening the flour, 1371A*.
Daughter cursed at birth, 934E*, 934E**; given devil because of mother's foolish talk, 813A; of king and son of peasant, 920A; of the sun, 898; pledged to grieve for father, 884A*; talks too loud, 1486*.
David and Bathsheba, 465.
Days of week counted (formula), 2012; of week told fairies, 503.
Dead (apparent) revives, 990; bridegroom, 365—365B*; child and snake's tail, 285A; child returns, 769; man as helper, 505—508; man speaks up, 1313C; man's bed, 963*; rat in water, 1578A*; watched and overcome, 307A*, 307B*.
Deaf persons and their foolish answers, 1698—1698C*.
Death and luck, 332B*; as godfather, 332; comes to old man, 845; deceived by singing rider, 1082A; feigned (by fox), 1, 33, 56, 56A*, (to be thrown from pot), 33, 33*, 33**; for old couple (woman points to husband), 1354; of the cock, 2021A; of good and bad man (bee and bird from mouths), 808A; of little hen mourned by objects, etc. (chain tale), 2022—2022B; of wife to save husband, 899; postponed by long tale or song, 1199AB; predicted under certain condition, 934, 934A—F, 934**—934D*; prophecy escaped, 506*; refuses to take woman's husband, 332G*; sticks to tree, 330, 330A, 330D; to listener (catch tale), 2201; washes feet, 336.
»Death» and the old maid, 1476C.
Death's messengers, 335.
Debate of animals and objects, 293A*—293G*; of belly and members, 293.
Debt forgiven after confession of theft, 940*; secured by faithful dog (killed by mistake), 178B.
Deceased rich man and devils in church, 815.
Deception of ogre into carrying captives home, 311.
Deceptive tug-of-war, 291; wager, 1559A*—C*.
Deductions from close observation (one-eyed camel, etc.), 655.

Deer (transformed princess) rescued, 401.
Deerslayer punished for boasting, 830.
Defeat of ogre, 300—359.
Defeated king regains throne, 406A*.
Defense of trespasser (on own land), 1590.
Deity (offended) causes hero many misfortunes, 939.
Deliberate toad (turtle), 288B*C*.
Demi-coq, 715.
Demon enters princess, 1164D; helps man against wife, 1164D.
Demons to be brought to life (devil frightened), 1149*.
Depositors must all claim money, 1591.
Descent from sky on sand-rope, 1889E; in one bucket permits escape in other, 32.
Deserted wife to bear child by absent husband, 891.
Detecting poisonous mushrooms, 1287*.
Devil already dead and cannot collect money, 822*; always blamed but God thanked, 846; and advocate, 1186; and angel wait for souls, 808; and iron man, 1162; and man promised to him, 810—814; annoyed by straps on soldier's knapsack crossing, 1166*; as advocate, 821—821B; as creditor cheated, 822*; as host at dinner has long spoon, 821B*; as husband, 1476B; as substitute laborer at mowing (haying), 820—820B; at grindstone, 1178**; at confession 818*; avoids children's picnic, 1162*; borrows money from miser and disappears, 836E*; bound in chains, 803; cannot live with woman, 1164—1164D; challenges farmer to fight, 1047*; fulfills labor contract, 810A; guards wife's chastity, 1352; in chains in hell, 803; in knapsack (hammered), 330B; in Noah's ark, 825; leaves at mention of God's name, 817*; must perform tasks to secure man, 1170—1180*; poses as Jesus (unmasked), 797*; promised man, 810—814; put into hell (seduction), 1425; serves farmer in return for stolen bread, 810A; shears pig 1037; shows wife's unfaithfulness, 824; sits on reversed harrow, 1059*; summoned by careless word, 813, 813A, 813C; to enter girl (doctor to be rewarded for expelling him), 1862B; writes names on cowhide, 826.
»Devilish rake!», 1628.
Devil's bad advice, 823*; bargain, 813*; beard (three hairs from), 461; contract (robber's penance), 756B; help re-

ceived, 656*; horse carries cruel rich man, 761; kindness, 362*; mistress, 407B; riddle, 812; share (cloth thrown out by tailor), 1574C; son as priest, 764; son with his mother at night, 1720*.
Devils and money in church, 815; tempt pope, 816*.
Devout women, 1851.
Diagnosis by observation (ass's flesh), 1862C.
Dialogue of simpleton and jester, 1702C*.
Diamond mountain shown by dragon, 536*.
»Did you see it?», 1588*.
Difficulty alone prompts call on God, 845*.
Digging brings death to dupe from exhaustion, 72A*.
Dinner with the dead, 470.
Direction of wind asked to deceive captor, 6.
Dirty woman takes much washing, 1447*.
Disappointed fisher, 832.
Disasters follow one another, 1680, 1681.
Discovered treasure and talkative wife, 1381.
Disdainful girl punished, 900, 900B*.
Disenchanted husband (witch's tasks), 425B.
Disenchantment of ogress, 871.
Disguise as man to go as soldier, 884A, 884B; as nurse-maid, 37; as police to rob, 1526A*; of woman as man, 880, 881, 881A, 881*; of fox as parson, 36; to rescue enslaved husbands, 888.
Disguised fox violates she-bear, 36; wolf eats young goats, 123; voice gives access to visiting wolf, 123, 123A.
Dish husband hates got rid of, 1390*.
Dishes broken to make place for pot, 1293A*; of same flavor (women), 983.
Dishonest miller unmasked, *1853B*; priest masks as devil, 831.
Disobedient boy (chain tale), 2030J.
Disposing of the corpse, 1536.
Dispute among rescuers of stolen princess, 653—653B.
Dissatisfied cobbler in heaven, 801.
Distressed maidens (misc.), 899*.
Diver and princess, 434*.
Dividing according to scripture, 1533A; eggs (puzzle), 1663.
Diving for reflection, 34, 34A, 34B*, 92, 1168A, 1336, 1336A, 1383.
Division of crops (deceptive), 9B, 1030, 1030*, 1633; of presents and strokes,
1610; of rescued princess demanded, 506—508.
Doctor advises absurd patient, 1543C*; at court is woman in male clothes, 881*; disguise for girl at court, 514**; disguise for woman seeking husband, 434; no longer needed, 1332C*.
Doctor Know-All, 1641.
Doctors, 1862 transfer heart, hand, and eye, 660.
Dog and hog dispute over their children, 219F*; and sparrow, 248; as security for debt (killed by mistake), 178B; as wolf's shoemaker, 102; avenged by friendly sparrow, 248; driven over bridge to evade promise to devil, 1191; eats sausage rather than having it stolen, 201A*; for dinner, 1409*; imitates bear but horse is not frightened (kicks him), 117*; in the sea, 540; language learned, 671; leaders fear defeat because forces are of different breeds, 107; picked up string (chain tale), 2034B; receives blows for cat's theft, 200A*; rescuer of drowning man takes him to bottom of sea, 540; stories (various), 201A*—201E*; tries to imitate wolf (kicked to death), 101*, 119C*; used to strike judge, 1587*; warns master, 554C*; with good and with stingy master, 211**.
Dog's bread stolen, 1562B; certificate, 200; feet shaven, 119A*; cigar (catch tale), 2204.
Dogs with queer names called, 1530*.
Dogs' journey for water, 200E*.
Doll (magic) stolen and recovered, 560C*.
Domestic animals, 200—219; animals and wild animals, 100—149.
Donkey (see Ass); moving ears thought attentive, 1213*.
Door closed tight (nailed), 1014; falls on robbers, 1653; guarded, 1653.
Dornröschen, 410.
Double pension, 1556; pig, 1889L*.
Double-cheating miller, 1853A*.
Dough dropping thought to be ghost, 1318B; three weeks old, 1453***.
Dove to fly in church, 1837.
Dove's egg substitution (two for seven) 240, (race with hen), 240*; keen sight, 238; nest, 236.
Doves in the letter, 1296B.
Dowry given away by foolish bride, 1463A*.
Dragging old man only to threshold, 980C.

Dragon's heart-blood as remedy for king, 305.
Dragon-killers quarrel, 319B*.
Dragon-slayer, 300, 303, 305.
Dream of future greatness, 517, 671, 725; of parishioner in hell, 1738B*; of parsons in hell, 1738; of human punishments, 840; of treasure, 834, 1645B; of treasure (on bridge), 1645; visit to foreign land, 726*.
Dream-bread, 1626.
Dress of gold, silver and stars, 510B.
Drink during sermon, 1827.
Drinking contest, 1088*; from own skull, 1886; girl's reflection in lake, 1141; only after bargain, 1447; up stream to get reflected cheese, 34B.
Driving horse into his collar, 1214*.
Drowning crayfish (turtle), 1310; evaded, 1116*; foretold for certain age, 934A*; the sickle, 1202.
Drunkard's pig replaced by dog, 1692A*; promise doesn't hold (cat and mouse), 111A*.
Drunken man at wedding, 1705A*; man dressed up as rich lord, 1531; man thinks Christ speaks from behind crucifix, 1324*; man thinks he is dead (in hell), 835*, 835A*; parson, 1836—1836B; parson complains about bishop, 1825A; lion learns lesson, 161B*.
Drying candle in stove, 1270.
Duck as peacemaker attacked, 208*; helper (transformed sister), 452C*; sheep and cock at sea, 204.
Duel with bayonet and pitchfork (deceptive), 1083A; with long poles (deceptive), 1083.
Dueling animals easily frightened, 104.
Dumb princess disenchants prince, 435*.
Dung of horse or mare?, 1832B*.
Dungbeetle, 559; enjoys dung, 283F*; taken for bee, 1317*.
Dupe persuaded to substitute in sack (to go to heaven, etc.), 1525A, 1535 (IV), 1737.
Dwarf and giant, 327B—327D*; furnishes magic objects, 595B*; helpers, 403B; removes hump from man, 503; ungrateful, 426.
Dwarfs give magic objects as reward, 611.
Dying between two thieves (lawyers), 1860B; father's counsel, 911*.
Each likes his own children best, 247.
Eagle gives hero magic box (not to be opened), 537; raises boy in her nest, 554B*; teaches tortoise to fly (drops him), 225A; warns shepherd, 229B*.
Earl-king, 367*.
Early pupil finds purse, 1644.
Earrings as price of silence, 1726A*.
Earthworm taken for snake, 1316***.
Easter confused with Christmas, 1848D.
Easy come, easy go, 944*; problem made hard, 1346*—1346A*.
Eaten heart, 992; moon, 1335.
Eating all meals at once, 1561; contest (food into bag), 1088; contest (thought to be lost because of weak legs), 203; moderately (fool starves self), 1691; one another, 20, 20A, 20C; own brains, 21*; own entrails, 21; stingy peasants' butter, 1560*, 1561*, 1562E*; third egg (argument), 1365D*; under difficulties (must keep answering questions), 774N.
Eavesdropping sexton cheated (not one penny less), 1543.
Echo answers, 1701.
Eclipse of moon predicted (cheat), 1627*.
Educating animals (cheats), 1750, 1750A.
Eel filled with sand, 1804*.
Egg broken by mouse (chain tale), 2022B; sat on by general, 1677.
Egg-excreter, 1434*.
Egg-laying bride, 1464A*.
Eggs (boiled) to produce chickens, 920A.
Egyptian Two-Brothers tale, 318.
Ehod mi yodea, 2010.
Eighth deadly sin, 1832A*.
Either ... or (sham threat), 1563*.
Electing mayor by recognition from rear by wife (prearranged signal), 1268*.
Election of bird-king, 221.
Elephant and blind men, 1317; girl, 413C*; sees moon's reflection in troubled water and is afraid, 92A; tramples lark's nest (punished by lark's friends), 248A.
Elephant's tail carries human chain to sky, 1250B.
Elopement with wrong man, 856.
Eloping couple and robbers, 977.
Elves reward hero, 503.
Emperor and abbot, 922.
Emperor's new clothes, 1620.
Emptying mealsack to illustrate emptiness of dispute, 1327.
Enchanted animal husband insulted by guests, 425*; pear tree, 1423; nymph shows man treasure, 412C*; prince disenchanted, 425—449, 444*—444E*; princess (girl) disenchanted, 401—

401A*, 402, 402A*, 405, 405A*, 406, 406A*, 407—407B, 408—409A*.
End of world causes flight of animals, 20C.
Endless tales, 2300—2301B.
Enigmas explained by girl at end of journey, 875D; of suitors understood by clever girl, 876.
Enigmatic expressions bring recognition by fiancée, 926C*; tasks given devil, 1178.
Enmity of lion and man, 159B; of dog and cat, 200—200B*.
Enticing dupe from booty and eating it, 15*, 15**.
Entrails dropped on robbers, 1653E; eaten at trickster's suggestion, 21.
Entrapped suitors, 1730.
Entry into princess's chamber in ram, 854.
Equivocal blessings, 1822; confession (thief is praised), 1807; oath, 1418.
Escape by asking (last kiss), 69**; (respite for prayer), 227; by blinding the guard, 73; by false plea, 122, 122A—Z; by giving three counsels, 150; by persuading animal captor to talk, 6, 6*; by sham death, 33; from animal carcass by trickery 68; from giant's cave, 313G*; from island in ogre's clothes, 1118*; from ogre in glass gourd, 311A*; from robbers (various), 956A*—956E*; from robbers by pretended bathing, 956C, 958E*; from tree stump by holding bear's tail, 1900; from witch's household, 334; in sack on ogre's back, 311; on tree, 315A; through help of ogre's daughter, 313; under ram's belly, 1137.
Esdras chain (stronger and strongest), 2031A.
Etana myth, 313B, 537.
Eulenspiegel's tricks, 1635*.
Eustacius, 938.
Evasion of marriage to predestined wife vainly attempted, 930A.
»Everything» considered as old person's testament, 1407A.
Eve's various children, 758.
Evil fates forestalled by death, 934C; one and his snares, 810; prophecies, 934—934E**; woman in glass case, 1170; woman thrown into pit, 1164.
Exchange of horses, 1529A*; proves profitable, 1655.
Exchanged caps cause ogre to kill own children, 327B, 1119; children, 975*; duties bring misfortune, 85, 1408.
Excuses permit escape, 122, 122A—Z.

Execution escaped by cleverness, 927, 927A; of man for convenience, not guilt, 1534A*.
Expelled brother's success, 740*, 740**.
Expelling devils, 1168; snakes, 672B*.
Experience shows wisdom of precepts, 910, 910A—K.
Explanation of marvelous dream, 759, 840.
Exposure of false magician, 987.
Extraordinary companions, 301—301B*, 513, 514; names, 1940.
Eye of husband covered by adulteress, 1419C; (single) of three giants stolen, 328*.
Eye-remedy (glowing mass put into ogre's eye), 1135.
Eyes closed and good fortune missed; 947A; recovered from witch, 321; stolen from blindworm, 234; to be cast (sheep's eyes), 1006; traded for eyes of a tree, 8***.
Facetiae, 1200—1999.
Fairies give gifts in gratitude, 503.
Fairy son rescues far-away girl, 725*.
Fairy-wife from myrtle, 652A.
Faith put into balance by sinful cleric, 802A*.
Faithful animal rashly killed, 178; John, 516; lion, 156A; servant, 889; wife rescues enslaved husband, 888.
Faithless queen with loathsome lover, 1511; mother, 590; sister, 315; widow, 1510; wife, 318; wife answered by hidden husband, 1380.
Falcon as dove's helper eats young doves, 231**; flatters owl about its children, 247B*—247B***; tears hare (sparrow laughs), 230B*.
Falling on robbers, 1650, 1653—1653E.
False beauty-doctor: dupe injured, 8A; bride takes heroine's place, 408, 425G, 437, 533; horns at animal's dance, 200B*.
Fancy ailment explained in vulgar speech, 1717*.
Far-away princess abducted, 516—516B.
Farmer tricks jackals, 176.
Fart to be caught, 1176.
Farting girl, 1453****.
Fast weaver keeps dropping shuttle, 1453A.
Fasting the first month, 1295A; together (servant girl cheats), 1562A*.
Fat cat (chain tale), 2027; goat waited for (goats escape), 122E; wolf cannot escape, 41.

Fatal bed, 921D; climb for healing plant, 614*; killing of insect, 1586A.
Fate, 930—949.
Fated bride, 930A, 930C, 930D; son-in-law persecuted, 930.
Fates allotted, 947B*, 949; forestalled by death, 934C.
Father and son with robbers (son kills them), 953A*; overhears mother's confession (leaves), 1418*; wants to kill his children, 765B*.
Father-in-law and daughter-in-law, 1441C*.
Father's speech before eating, 1841.
Fatted cow borrowed (bear returned to ogre), 1161A.
Fattening victim permits his escape, 122F.
Fault-finding husband nonplussed, 1408B.
Faults of king to be named by princes, 920D.
Favorite fruit of Peter, 774G; homes for animals, insects and objects, 293C*.
Fear for men learned by animals, 157—157D*.
Fear-test, 326—326D*.
Fearless boy, 326—326*.
Feathers borrowed by raven so as to deceive, 244.
Feet of ox cut off night before slaughter, 1261; without boots on not his, 1288*.
Feigned deafness to get night lodging, 1544.
Feigning death in order to be rescued, 33, 33**.
Felling tree on wagon, 1242*; trees (deceptive), 1050.
Fencer with marvelous speed, 654.
Ferdinand True and Ferdinand False, 531.
Festin de Pierre, 470A.
Fettered monster, 803.
Fever cured by dipping in well, 1349L*.
Fiancée forgotten, 313; forsaken, 884; hardhearted, 1455; lazy, 1454*; is blind, 1456.
Fickle wife and general, 465A*.
Fictitious office pleases fool, 1689*.
Fiddevav, 593.
Fiddle sticks to Peter's back, 774F.
Fidelity and innocence, 880—899; often proved, 881.
Fight on the bridge, 300A; over magic objects (taken by umpire), 518.
Fighting after death as dogs (contentious men), 836D*.
Figs chosen for cleanness (all eaten during test), 1309.

Filling yard with manure, 1183**.
Filthy hog and clean fish, 137.
Finder's right to coin, 1224*.
Fine fellow is father, says dying toad to pregnant paramour, 288A*.
Fine to be paid for saying »That is a lie«, 1920F.
Finger caught in tree-cleft (ogre learns to play fiddle), 151, 1159; to be struck (servant obeys), 1698A*.
Finger-drying contest, 1463.
Fire by stamping on ground (hot ashes prepared beforehand), 1064; far away from meat, 1262; from sparks from box on ear, 1344; made as mock sunrise, 120*.
Fire-steel summons genie, 562.
Fireplace moved to reduce heat, 1325A.
First crop (acorns) delays payment to devil, 1185; to say good morning, 1735; to see sunrise, 120.
Fish, 250—274; caught by fox and both by man, 160A*; caught in boots, 1895; (enchanted girl) disenchanted, 413B*; (enchanted prince) disenchanted, 431C*; in net (small escape), 253,253*; plowed up (absurd truth), 1381A; race, 250, 252; stolen from wagon, 1; swallows man, 1889G; to be hatched from cheese, 1209*; too large for pan discarded, 1221A*; was my father (riddle), 705.
Fish-net stretched on heath, 1220.
Fishs-oup in the sea, 1895B*.
Fisher and his wife, 555; husband of princess, 879A; punished for greed, 832.
Fishing with tail, 2.
Five calves for four teats, 1567F; times murdered corpse, 1537.
Flag made of stolen cloth (tailor's dream), 1574.
Flattering foreman, 1574*.
Flattery used by fox, 57*; causes raven to drop cheese, 57.
Flax destroyed by fool, 1011*.
Flax-field used for swimming, 1290.
Flax-tail burned when dupe turns in wind, 2D.
Flea and fly boast of man's discomfort, 282B*; and fly exchange places to live, 282A*; by jumping betrays louse and bug, 276**; powder (first catch the flea), 1862A.
Fleas drowned by fox, 63.
Fleeing pancake (chain tale), 2025.
Flies chased away but man struck dead, 163A*; on Christ's heart, 772*; thought to have eaten (stolen) food, 1433*.

Flight by magic, 313—313J*, 314—314B*; from sorcerer, 619*; of animals from end of world or war, 20C; of man from own house, 1360A; of ogre, 1132; of woman and lover from stable, 1360B; to forest to avoid marriage, 888*; with help of extraordinary companions, 313J*.
Flood predicted by wife's paramour (Miller's Tale), 1361.
Flounder's crooked mouth, 250A.
Flour in river, 1260A*.
Flower language learned, 671F*; (marvelous) sought, 467; stalk broken, girl disenchanted, 407, 407B.
Flute makes men and sheep dance, 594**.
Fly and flea boast of man's discomfort, 282B*; and flea exchange places to live, 282A*; forgets name, 2013*; killed on judge's nose, 1586; on spider's curtain, 283.
Flying stone as prison, 746*; with magic wings to mistress in tower, 575.
Focus, 921A.
Fog to be pushed away, 1349K*.
Food goes to husband instead of paramour, 1358C; in bag, 1088; not known about, 1339—1339E; offered to crucifix, 767.
Fool as murderer, 1600; gets all backward, 1690*; gives everything away (meat to dogs, etc.), 1681A; guards home and animals (disastrously), 1681B; interrupts sermon, 1691A*; overmounts and falls over horse, 1580A*; spoils work of shoemaker, etc., 1695.
Foolish bargains, 1415; bridegroom, 1685; couple, 1430—1439; killing of insect, 1586, 1586A; man and wife, 1405—1429; parson in trunk, 1725; peasant studies medicine, 1676*; plans for unborn child, 1430A, 1450; talk discredits testimony, 1381—1381*; wife and husband, 1380—1404; wife's pawn, 1385.
Fools, 1200—1349; frightened, 1321—1321D*; warn thief what not to steal, 1341—1341B*.
Fool's errand, 1296; prayer, 1666*; vocation (priesthood), 1834A*B*; wedding (repeats all questions), 1684B*.
Foot bitten said to be root, 5.
Footbridge to heaven, 471*.
For the long winter, 1541.
Forbidden box with magic castle, 313B; to sit in trees, 62*.

Forced gift refused, 1572C*.
Forcing hen to brood chickens, 1284*.
Foreign language misunderstood (absurd results), 1699—1699B.
Foreigners, 1865.
Forgetful man counts days of week, 2012.
Forgetfulness causes useless journey, 1332*—1332C*.
Forgetting much-repeated instructions, 1204.
Forging with sand taught by ogre, 1163.
Forgiven debt, 940*; skeleton, 882B*.
Forgotten cane, 961A; fiancée, 313, 313C*; wind, 752B; word, 1687.
Formula tales, 2000—2399.
Forsaken fiancée disguised as manservant, 884, 884A.
Fortunatus, 566.
Fortune and coincidence contest, 946D*; as end of quest, 460B; of rich and poor man, 735; saves man after money fails, 945A*; through power to win woman's love, 580.
Fortune's source not to be investigated, 832*.
Forty thieves, 954.
Forty-year-old husband advised (wife prefers two of twenty), 1362B*.
Foster children in love, 885**.
Four coins (how used), 921A; men's mistress, 1410; persons in Trinity, 1832G*; skillful brothers display talents, 653, 653*.
Fourteen daughters' birth causes husband's desertion, 891A*.
Fourth story ridden to, 530.
Fowl and thistle contest (chain tale), 2030A*; symbolically carved, 1533.
Fox and bird build boat, 249*; and cat in jumping contest (chain tale), 2030E*; and crane invite each other, 60; and hedgehog (no other justice than that of the stomach), 35C*; and sour grapes, 59; as bluffer, 67; as clever animal, 1—69; as rabbit's riding-horse, 72; as schoolmaster eats chickens, 56D*; as seaman, 67*; as shepherd, 37*; as shepherd's guide, 172A*; as umpire eats all cheese, 51***; asks bird what she does when wind blows, 56D; betrayed into hands of threshers, 56E*; betrayed when peasant points to basket, 161; betrays children, 161*; carried (by crane and dropped), 225; (by wolf), 4; caught (by butcher), 67**; caught (in bakehouse escapes by ruse), 66**; caught (in storehouse and killed),

160**; climbs from pit on wolf's back, 31; converses with his members, 154; deceives bear (wolf), 1—69; divides booty for lion, 51; drinks and laughs, 56B*, 56C*; drowns the pot, 68B; eats his fellow-lodger (accuses others), 170; entices wolf from his booty, 15*; escapes from law court, 53; flatters siren's children (rewarded, wolf punished), 68**; (bear) hangs to horse's tail and is hurt, 42A; in disguise violates the she-bear, 36; in drowning peril claims to be swimming, 67; in orchard overeats, 41*; kills young magpies, 56; leading ass to lion's den is himself eaten, 50B; loses his eye in briars, 135B*; paints (burns) wolf, 8; persuades magpie to bring young into his house, 56B; pollutes wolf who is carrying him, 4*; pulls wolf out of pit, 31*; puts head in sand out of rain, 64**; refuses to be mediator, 51A; rids self of fleas, 63; rings the bell on slain horse, 40; shams death, 1, 33, 56; shams sickness, 4; steals inhospitable wolf's meat, 35A*; stumbles over violin (boasts *about* dancing), 135A*; taught by goose to swim, 226; tries animals' courage, 66*; threatens to push down tree with young magpies, 56A; with pipe ignites barn, 66A.

Franklin's Tale, 976, 976A.

Frau Holle, 480.

Friar adds missing nose (fingers) to unborn child, 1424; unhappy with wealth, 754.

Friends in life and death, 470; unreliable, 893.

Friendship between man, thunder-god and devil, 1147*.

Fright of hawk at snipe's bill, 229; of wild animals at sight of unfamiliar one (cat, ass, goat), 103, 103A*, 103B*, 103C*; from near-incest kills mother, 823A*.

Frightened fools, 1321—1321D*.

Frightening ogre, 1145—1154, 1166**, 1167*; troll from christening, 1165; wolves by falling on them from tree (goat), 126A.

Frog and rat tied together (carried off), 278; as godfather, 332E; as keeper of souls, 476*; (enchanted princess) as bride, 402; enticed from hole, 242; king, 440; language learned, 671, 671B*; races snail, 275C*; rescued from pot of cream (churns butter),

278B*; tries to be big as ox, 277A; will live in puddle (run over), 278A.

Frogs and their adventures, 275C*—278D; decide not to jump into well, 278A*; want king (King Log), 277.

Frost and the hare (contest), 71.

Frost-bitten foot, 2031.

Frostgod and his son, 298A.

Frozen music (words), 1889F.

Fruit tree from deer's head, 1889C.

Fruits (healing), 610; (wonderful), 566.

Full as the nut (empty shell), 1822A; price paid by each partner, 1266A*.

Funeral for cat by birds, 235A*.

Fur coat stroked with whetstone, 1349J*.

Future husband, 737.

Gallows robbed (dead man avenges), 366.

Gambler helped by devil for one task yearly, 408A*.

Gambler's wife wins back losses, 880*.

Game in fox's bag stolen and trash substituted, 67A*; of hanging each other (fatal), 1343, (ogre hanged), 1066.

Gander, drake and boar without money at tavern, 211B*.

Garland of rue, 713A*.

Geese carry man through air, 1881; from Rus, 910F*; given respite for prayer escape from fox, 227; on the line, 1876.

Gelding the bear and fetching salve, 153.

General hatches an egg, 1677.

Gentry, 1867.

Gesture betrays (murderer), 964, (truth), 232C*.

Ghost avenged (girl kills murderer), 512B*; claims stolen property, 366; conquered, 307B*.

Ghosts supposed to be seen (really objects), 1318—1318C.

Ghoulish schoolmaster, 894.

Giant. See also *ogre, dragon*.

Giant carries off girl, 327*; killed or frozen, 1165*.

Giant-killer and dog, 312.

Giant's toy returned (man), 701; treasure stolen, 328—328B*.

Giants fight over magic objects, 518.

Gift of lover regained, 1420—1420G; of the fool (children), 1548*; promised at confession demanded during sermon, 1743*.

Gifts of the (dwarfs), 611; (little people), 503; literally accepted, 1572D*.

Gilding the beard (with tar), 1138.

Gingerbread house, 327A.

Girl as flower disenchanted, 407; as goat, 409A; as helper in hero's flight, 313—

313J*; as jackdaw, 409A; as snake, 409A*; as wolf, 409; behind statue advises mistress, 1388; cursed to remain small, 454*; dressed as man deceives king, 884B*; driven from home (old man helper), 512*, 512A*; hidden tells suitor where she is, 1435*; in fish form as mysterious housekeeper, 413B*; in lagoon, 444C; left in tree (chain tale) 2029A*; shows thrift, 1451; who could not keep secret (of seduction), 886; who eats so little, 1373, 1407, 1458; with ugly name, 1461; without hands, 706.
Girls follow balls and have adventures, 431A*; in robbers' den, 956C; who married animals, 552.
Glass mountains to be ridden up, 530.
Glutton (Red Riding Hood), 333.
Glove, needle, and squirrel, 90; of king left behind in woman's room causes unjust accusation, 891B*.
Gnat chases buffalo from hole when man fails, 281A*; killed in fight of bugs, 91C*.
Gnats meet tragic deaths, 291*; think they have thrown horse down, 281.
Goat admires his horns in the water but lies to wolf, 132; and cabbage taken to market (goat eats cabbage), 212*; always lying, 212; carrying snake over stream threatened (kills snake), 133*; driven from nuts (chain tale), 2030G; eats tree, etc. (chain tale), 2030D*; (enchanted girl) disenchanted, 409A; entices wolf to farmhouse and thus escapes, 122P*; frightened by man's breaking wind, 103D*; will not go home, 2015, 2015*.
Goat's sense not so long as his beard (caught in garden), 127B*.
Goats eaten by wolf when their mother is away, 123; fall into water because of stubbornness, 202.
God and Emperor of Rome, 775*; as beggar denied hospitality, 751A*; bless you will be said only if hero receives princess, 858; can't take a joke, 1718*; called on only in time of trouble, 845*; determines all fates, 934D; died for you, 1833E; help you (silence wager), 1351A; punishes eavesdropping wife (ceases his visits), 775*; repays and punishes, 750—779; sought on quest, 460A; trusted by one beggar (king by other), 841; unknown to shepherd with miraculous powers, 827; will care for all, 1645B*.

Goddess of fate, 947B*.
Godfather death, 332; invitation as excuse for stealing provisions, 15.
God's blessing not asked, 830, 830B, 830C, 830C*; justice vindicated, 759.
Going out to earn wages (chain tale), 2038*.
Gold chain given flattering fox, 48*.
Golden goose, 571; hair sought, 465B*, 531; key (unfinished tale), 2260; mountain, 936*; pumpkin has turned to brass, 1592A; ram, 854; shoe marriage test, 510A*; sons (three), 707.
Goldener, 314.
Good and bad man at death, 808; bargain, 1642; daughter, evil stepdaughter, 403—403**; deeds repaid with paradise, 809**; food brings change in servants' song, 1567G; housekeeping of youngest sister, 1464C*; precepts, 911—915; weather purchased (bees), 1296A.
Goose teaches fox to swim, 226; with one leg, 785A.
Goose-girl, 533, 870.
Gorge silently, 1570*.
Grace before meat, 1841.
Grain thief helped by owner, 1564*, 1564**; harvested with guns (sickle unknown), 1202.
Grain-measure runs away (chain tale), 2029B*.
Grainfields thought to be (the sea), 1290, (marching host), 1290A*.
Grains boast of their importance, 293E.
Granary roof as threshing flail, 1031.
Grandmother to be bathed, 1013.
Grandson given devil because of foolish talk, 813B.
Grateful animals help hero perform tasks, 554; animals and ungrateful man, 160; dead, 505—508; lion, 156, 156A; saint (hero has protected his picture), 506**.
Gratitude only from youngest brother, 550A.
Grave remains unquiet, 760.
Gray hair before gray beard, 921C.
Grazing cow on roof, 1210.
Greasing wheel after journey, 1273B*.
Great animal or object, 1960—1960Z.
Greater bribe wins judge, 1861A; sinner killed (penance ended), 756C.
Greatest fool, 1332.
Greedy fiancée and porridge, 1454*; fisher punished, 832; peasant woman punished, 751—751B.

Green twigs from dry rod, 756; eyes for princess's husband, 836C*.
Gregory on the Stone, 933.
Grindstone to be brought, 1177**.
Griselda, 887.
Groom teaches horse to live without food, 1682.
Ground jumped into (trick), 1086; measured with ox hide, 2400.
Grunting pig thought talking, 1322A*.
Guard blinded so as to escape, 73.
Guardian animal blinded by juice in eyes, 73; of queen kills poisonous snake (accused of molesting her), 916.
Guarding the door (drops on robbers), 1633A; store-room door (carrying it off), 1009.
Guessing girls' names, 445B*.
Guilty man doubts own guilt (eloquent lawyer), 1860C; to speak first, 1351B*.
Gullible husband, 1406; people cheated, 1539, 1539*; woman asks news from home, 1931.
Gun as tobacco pipe, 1157; barrel (bent for crooked shot), 1890E, (looked through by ogre), 1158; bursts (accidental hunting success), 1890B; goes off in church, 1835A*.
Gypsy and Jew (let there be no honor between us), 1632*; boy receives beating, 1707*; tricks,1634*—1634E*.
Gypsy's thefts not sinful, 1638*.
Hair as ladder to tower, 310; (curly) to be straightened, 1175; floating on water induces quest for princess, 516B; in soup (argument), 1365E*; of head gray before beard, 921C; (transformed) speaks and reveals murderer, 780B.
Hairs from devil's beard, 461.
Half-carpet kept for old man, 980A.
Half-chick, 715.
Half-friend, 893.
Hampers piled up to measure tower (lowest removed and all fall), 1250A.
Hand of princess won, 850—869; removed when fool is to hit it (trick unsuccessfully imitated), 1349D*; of maiden cut off, 706.
Hanged man claims stolen property, 366.
Hanging chosen over life with evil woman, 1367*; each other, 1066; game (fatal), 1343; man discovers treasure, 910D; on to leader in race, 250; shammed to cheat devil, 1190*; to horse's tail, 47A.
Hangman as husband refused (girl prefers execution), 907*.
Hans my Hedgehog, 441.

Hansel and Gretel, 327A.
Happy friar (while poor), 754.
Hard-hearted bride (father-in-law as beggar), 1455; horse must assume overworked ass's burden, 207B.
Hare and ram in contest (cause of hare's long ears), 136B*; and tortoise race, 275A; as ambassador of moon, 92A; at third remove, 1552*; attacked (flight from fierce animal), 1231; changes to hawk (escapes), 319A*; enlarges dog's mouth so that he can whistle, 135C*; escapes from owl, 230A*; finds one more cowardly, 70; instructs his sons, 72*; outwits man and fox, 176*; sleeps in race with tortoise, 275A; soup (hare has escaped from pot), 1260A; with rotten ears, 1922*.
Hare's last will (bequeaths members to hunters), 160B*; split lip, 47A, 70; wedding, 96*.
Hares collide, 1893A*; run into bag, 1893.
Harness stretches and shrinks, 1917.
Harnessing bear (wolf), 1910.
Harrow as hair brush, 1019*; as seat for devil, 1059*.
Harvesters stealing crow's grain, 243*.
Harvesting (grain), 1202; (hay), 1053*.
Hat, horn, and knapsack, 569; of butter, 1880.
Hatch-penny always returns to owner, 745.
Hatching chickens from boiled eggs, 821B, 875, 920A; eggs (fool sits on them), 1218, 1677.
Hatchet-murder attempted, 1115.
Haughtiness of king punished (Roderigo, Jovinian), 757.
Haughty girl repaid by deceived suitors, 940.
Hauling of a tree, 1052.
Haunted castle, 1160.
Hawk frightened at snipe's bill, 229; single trick (playing dead), 105B*.
Hay harvest (deceptive), 1053*.
He that asketh shall receive (hermit asks for princess), 862.
Head cut off so as to put on shirt, 1285; in hole of millstone, 1247; in water (peasant allowed to drown), 1293B*; of Peter's created man backward, 774A.
Headless man in bear's den (did he ever have a head?), 1225.
Heads of man and devil exchanged, 1169; of robbers cut off as they enter house, 956B.
Healing the king by secret remedy, 613,

613C*; fruits, 610; the ogre, 1133—1136.
Hearing enormous distance, 1920E*.
Heart of lover must be eaten by adulteress, 992; lacking in ass, 52; left at home (excuse for threatened monkey, cat), 91; of ogre in egg, 302—302B*; (with his whole), 1186.
Heater of hell's kettle, 475, 475*.
Heath for stretching fish-net, 1220.
Heathcock and bird of passage, 232.
Heaven celebrates rich man's arrival, 802; entered by trick, 330C, 330*; forfeited by self-righteous tailor, 800; or palace? (drunken peasant dressed up), 1531.
Heavenly maiden sought, 306A.
Heavy axe (deceptive), 1049.
Hedgehog befouls badger's den so that he leaves it, 80; philosophizes, 293G*; races hare, 275A*; (transformed son) as hero, 441.
Hedgehog's only trick, 105*.
Hell preferred if warm, 1833G.
Heller throws into others' money, 1615.
»Hello, house!», 66A.
Hell's kettle heated, 475.
Help cleverly summoned by girl threatened by robbers, 956D; in escape from robbers by blowing horn, 958; in idleness, 1950A; of God denied by proud man, 830, 830A, 830B, 830C, 830C*; of Virgin's statue, 706A; of the weak, 75; from supernatural beings, 500—559; from three old women, 501.
Helpers, 500—559; (extraordinary companions), 513, 514.
Helpful animals, 530—559; cat woos for hero, 545—545B; dwarfs, 503, 503*; horse, 314, 532.
Hen's death investigated (chain tale), 2022; funeral procession, 2021.
Hens not to be neglected like old maid, 1487*; thrown by bear to fox, 3*.
Herding rabbits, 570.
Hermit escapes devils, 839A*, 839B*.
Hermit's self-righteousness, 756A; three sins, 839.
Hero and Leander, 666*.
Heroine marries prince, 870—879.
Heron transports fish from drying lake (eats them), 231.
Herring given matches for feet, 1567*; sent to bring butter, 1562E*.
Hidden girl tells suitor where she is, 1435*; impostor (in holy image) beaten, 1761*; lover driven out by fire, 1359A; lover escapes, 1419K*;

man observes adultery, 1360; paramour buys freedom, 1358A; paramour carried off in box, 1358B; princess to be found (at bottom of lake), 860A*; son, 937A*.
Hide dropped on robbers, 1653D.
Hiding child to escape fate, 934, 934A, 934B*, 934C*, 937A*; from devil, 329; in ogre's bag to steal goods, 1132; under adulteress's bed, 1355—1355C.
High flying as test for bird, 221A.
Highflown speech persuades ignorant judge, 1534C*.
Hildebrand returns to adulterous wife, 1360C.
Hill-woman robs peasants, 327D*.
»Himphamp» catches lover and adulteress, 571B.
Hog disregards wolf's advice, 106*; in church, 1838; pen for paramour, 1419F; tired of daily food, 211*; undeterred by broken leg, 219D*.
Hog-killing as fatal game, 2401.
Hog-thief's knees cut by companion, 962*.
Hogs in mud and sheep in air, 1004; with curly tails, 1036.
Holding up the rock, 9, 1530, 1731; down the hat, 1528; ship fast on anchor chain, 1179*; up roof as pretense for not working, 9A.
Hole in basket permits theft, 1**; in tree permits violation of she-bear, 36; to be pushed in tree, 1085; to throw earth in, 1255; where he was imprisoned frightens ogre, 1154*.
Holes to tell truth, 1391.
Holidays every day, 1405*.
Holy Ghost has had a calf, 1833D; man has own mass, 759B.
Home preferred over foreign lands by heathcock, 232.
Homecoming husband, 1360C, 1419; (arrives at last moment), 974.
Honesty and Fraud have common housekeeper, 847*.
Honey drop causes chain of accidents, 2036.
Honey-seeking bear caught in wasp nest, 49.
Honor of village saved by peasant (foolish acts), 1349F*.
Hoof is ass's charter, 47E.
Hops and turnips quarrel, 293D*; powerful (intoxicating), 485B.
Horn blown to summon help in escape from robbers, 958; hat, and knapsack,

569; wheedled from goat (chain tale), 2026*.
Horned animals in celebration (dog's artificial horns), 50*.
Horns of stag beautiful but cause of his death, 77; from eating magic apple, 566.
Horse as marvelous hunter, 1892; cleaned (boiling water or sharp razor), 1016; cleverer than priest, 1621*; climbs through his collar, 1895C*; drawn across ice, 1212; frightens lion, 118; helps hero (in flight), 314; (with tasks), 531, 532; kicks wolf in teeth, 47B; painted and sold back to owner, 1631A; repaired (accidentally cut in two), 1889P; substituted for bride, 1440; to find road home, 1291**; to live without food, 1682; weighted down to keep him from blowing away, 1279A; will not go over trees, 1631.
Horse's fault (thief's excuse), 1624C*; new backbone, 1911A.
Horsehead speaks, 533.
Horses exchanged for bones, 1382*.
Horses' defense against wolves (make circle with hindquarters outwards), 119B*.
Horseshoe and cherries (legend), 774C; nail lost, 2039.
Hospitality outweighs sin, 750E*; rewarded, 750B, 750*.
Hospitable widow's cow killed, 759*.
Hot porridge in ogre's throat, 1131; tin under ogre's horse, 1142.
House always answers trickster, 66A; in the wood, 431; is burned down, 2014A; not needed in summer (none built for winter), 81; of feathers and of stone, 124; of my father (penniless wooer), 859C; of ogre repaired (deception), 1010; of robbers, 956A; old man was to build (chain tale), 2035A; that Jack built, 2035.
Household of the witch, 334.
Housekeeping of mouse, bird, and sausage, 85.
Houses of wood and ice (fox and bear), 43.
How men are made, 1110*; much the ass cost, 1551*; the wicked lord was punished, 837.
Human chain let fall (upper man spits on hands), 1250.
Humming bees frighten fool, 1321C.
Hunchback brothers drowned, 1536B; cured of hump, 503; of frog, 278C*.
Hungry fox waits in vain for horse's scrotum to fall, 115; parson hunts food at night, 1775; servant attracts attention by lie, 1567E; servant reproaches stingy master, 1567.
Hunter bends bow (prompt bird escapes), 246; disguise for hare, 70*; with magic gun kills giants, 304.
Hunting for needle lost in sea, 1280; tales, 1890—1909; wolves with rod and line, 1896*.
Husband behind statue advises wife, 1380—1380A*; found in tavern, 1378A*; gets rid of hated dish, 1390*; hoodwinked, 1419; hunts three persons as stupid as his wife, 1384; in chicken house, 1418A; insulted as lousy-head, 1365C; locked out by adulteress, 1377; outwits adulteress and paramour, 1359—1359*; reaches home in time to prevent wife's remarriage, 974; rescued as wife's best possession, 875C; sent for water while lover escapes, 1419J*; sent to would-be seducer in wife's place, 1441B*; (supernatural), 425—449; takes wife's place with paramour (beats him), 1359B; uncertain of own identity, 1419E*; unexpectedly returns home, 1360C, 1419.
Husband's good eye covered, 1419C.
Hymn singing to thwart devil, 1193*.
Hypnotizing the innkeeper, 664*—664B*.
»I can't hear you» (confession not given), 1777A*.
»I don't know», 532; (thought to be a name), 1700.
I killed my grandmother, etc. (chain tale), 2037.
»I know» says dove always to thrush's instructions, 236.
»I preach God's word», 1825B.
Ibycus, 960A.
Ice breaks under bear forced on it by fox, 10*; house and wooden, 43; mill, 1097.
Identities mistaken (various), 1319*—1319M*.
Idler helped, 1950A.
»If God wills», 830C.
If wolf's tail breaks, 1229.
Ignorance of foreign language, 1699—1699B; of own identity, 1284, 1336A, 1382, 1419E, 1531A, 1681; of women, 1545B; of bread baking, 1374*.
Illegitimate son discovered by royal father, 873.
Illustrations from card playing, 1839B.
Image broken (gold within), 1643; of saint smeared with milk, 1829A*.

Imaginative boy sees a hundred wolves, 1348.
Imagined penance, 1804.
Imitating the neighbors (absurd results), 1387*; animals' voice in telling tale, 106, 206, 236, 236*, 292*.
Immortality won through betrayal of death, 332C*, 332D*.
Impaling himself at trickster's suggestion, 23*.
Impertinent answers, 921D*.
Improving on master's statements, 1688.
Inappropriate actions in church, 1831A*.
Incest averted (talking animals), 674, (master and slavegirl), 938*; (mother and son), 823A*.
Incestuous brother, 313E*.
Inclusa, 1419E.
Indoors home for cat in winter, 200D*.
Industrious girl to marry lazy boy, 822.
Inexhaustible purse, 580*.
Infanticide punished, 765A*.
Injuries to ogre (various), 1143—1143C.
Injury remembered prevents friendship, 159B.
Ink on girl to frighten bedmate, 1441A*.
Inn (store) conducted by hare and dog, 200C*.
Innkeeper sent away and robbed, 967**; steals magic objects, 563.
Innocence and fidelity, 880—899.
Innocent slandered maiden, 883A, 883C*, 892; man chosen to fit stake (noose), 1534A.
Inquisitive king, 920A*; wife and the animal languages, 670.
Insect killed, companion killed, 1586A.
Inspecting the daughter, 1573**.
Instructions followed literally, 1562—1562B.
Intelligence or luck, 945.
Intimidation of ogre, 1145—1154.
Intoxicated dragon abducts queen, 422*.
Intruder steals man's clothes, 1360A.
Invisible voices, 727*.
Invitation not needed, 1543B*, 1544.
Inventive coachman, 1576*; beggar, 1578*.
Iron boat tested (sinks), 1349C*; Henry, 440; makes hatchet, etc. (chain story), 2018*; man frightens ogre away, 1162.
Iron more precious than gold, 677; used for oath (trap), 44.
Iron-eating mice, 1592.
Island escaped in ogre's clothes, 1118*.
Itch purchased, 1614**.
»It's a man!«, 1545A*.

Jay borrows cuckoo's skin (keeps it), 235.
Jack (and the beanstalk), 328; (giant-killer), 328.
Jackal as clever animal, 1—69; as schoolmaster, 56C; domineers over tigers, 64*; trapped in animal's hide, 68.
Jackals tricked by farmer, 176.
Jealous queen blinds nieces, 455*; cursed, 748*; suitors maim horses, 1688A*.
Jeering at fox-trap (fox caught), 68*.
Jester-bride, 1538*.
Jew among thorns, 592; punished by ceaseless wandering, 777.
Jewess to bear Messiah, 1855A.
Jews drawn from heaven by auction in hell, 1656; fear sign of cross, 1709*.
John the bear, 301B.
Joint depositors sue banker, 1591; ownership of cow (front or back), 1633*.
Joker poses as ghost (punished), 1676.
Jokes about parson, 1725—1849; and anecdotes, 1200—1999.
Jorinde and Joringel, 405.
Joseph and Mary to leave heaven, 805.
Journey in search of Fortune, 460B; to God, 460A, 461A; to hell, 466**; to other world, 465C; to Rome by animals, 20D*; (useless) caused by forgetfulness, 1332*—1332C*.
Journeying animals, 130, 210.
Jovinian, 757.
Judge appropriates object of dispute, 926D; expects bribe from displayed purse (stone in purse), 1660; kicked (to illustrate case in court), 1327A; outriddled, 927; persuaded by highflown speech, 1534C*.
Judges, 1861A.
Judgment of Solomon, 926.
Judgments in this world discovered, 840B*.
Jug as trap, 68A.
Jukel fetches wine (chain tale), 2030F.
Jumper turns back midway, 1889J.
Jumping from church tower (deceptive), 1075*; into breeches, 1286; into ground (prepared hole), 1086; into river after comrade, 1297*; into sea for fish, 1260**; on dead branch of tree, 1240A; over (fire with basket tied to tail), 2C; over (path cannot get under it), 72B*.
Juniper tree, 720.
Juror asleep votes on wrong case, 1715.
Justice demanded by animals who ring bell, 207C; of God vindicated, 759, 840.
Kaiser's new clothes, 1620.

Keen sight of dove and keen learning of frog, 238.
Keep fox when you have him (good advice), 150; your seats, 1861*.
Keeping warm in bed, 1545*.
Kettle in hell heated, 475.
Key in flax reveals bride's laziness, 1453; to lady's chest (chain tale), 2039*.
Kicking aside riches provided by deity, 842.
Kiddelkaddelkar, 327D.
Killing friendly snake brings misfortune, 285A—D; ogre's live stock, 1007.
Kind and unkind, 403, 431, 480—480C*, 550A, 551, 551**, 556E*, 620, 750**.
Kindness of devil, 362; rewarded, 403, 431, 473, 480, 550A, 551, 556E*, 620.
King and abbot, 922; and lamia, 411; and peasant's son, 921; and robber, 951A; and soldier, 952; covets subject's wife, 465—465B*; discovers unknown son, 873; enriches clothier (prescribes certain clothing) 1639*; of birds elected, 221; of cats is dead, 113A; of fishes, 303, 554A*; of frogs (King Log), 277; of snakes defeated, 300B; in bath, 681; is bastard, 655; joins robbers, 951A, 951C; Lindorm, 433B; Log, 277; saved from robbers, 952; Thrushbeard, 900; transfers soul to parrot, 678.
King's face often seen on coin, 922B; garden guarded by hero, 328*; gloves as false indication of adultery, 891B*; haughtiness punished, 757; new clothes, 1620; sons seek (golden bird) 550, (magic remedy), 551; tasks, 557.
Kiss disenchants animal lover, 433A, 425C; given for goods (help) but later must be repaid, 879A*, 879A**; gives chance for escape, 69**.
Knapsack, hat, and horn, 569.
Knife blade whetted away, 1015; or scissors (argument), 1365B; to cut bread has cut dog, 1578*; with magic powers, 576.
Knoist and his three sons, 1965.
Knots in wood, 774H; to be made from spilled brandy, 1173.
Knotted handkerchief, 466*.
Knowledge (supernatural), 650—699.
Koranski castle, 937*.
Labor contract, 1000—1029.
Lai l'épervier, 1730.
Lake drowns dupe forced into it, 10**; to be pulled together, 1045.
Lamb of God now sheep, 1832N*.
Lamb's heart eaten (by whom?), 785.

Lame man helps blind man, 519.
Lamia as wife, 411.
Lamp (magic) stolen and recovered, 561.
Land and water ship, 513B; of cheaters, 978; of Cockaygne, 1930; of immortals, 313*; of opposites, 1935; where no one dies, 470B, 470*.
Language of animals, 670, 671; of signs, 924, 924A, 924B.
Lard for manuring soil, 1231*.
Large lumps of sugar chosen, 1389*.
Large-headed and large-eyed bird reared, 230.
Larger and larger fish (smaller as bait), 1895A*; deposits expected (banker pays debt), 1617.
Lark reminisces with stork (eaten), 243B*.
Last leaf (oak) never falls (devil cheated), 1184.
Late revenge, 960B.
Latin learned in school (cheats), 1628, 1628*; taught by cutting tongue, 1331D*.
Latin-speaking (cheat), 1641C.
Laughing contest (deceptive), 1080*; fish, 875D.
Laughter contest between fox and bear, 42*.
Law against sitting in trees (fox and grouse), 62*; carries gospel, 1836B.
Lawyer's advice followed with accidental success (credited with wisdom), 1641C*; dog steals meat (twice the damages as fee), 1589; mad client, 1585.
Lawyers in hell, 1860A.
Lazy animals punished in road building, 55; boy and industrious girl, 822; boy has magic powers from salmon, 675; boy makes princess laugh, 675, 675*; dog proves useless, 201C*; fiancée, 1454*; girl doesn't know where spring is, 1454*; horse always waiting for next season, 207A*; husband's success, 986; men boast of laziness, 1950; servant and grain (chain tale), 2030C*; servant reports continuing rain (to keep from work), 1560**; spinning women, 1405; weaving woman and bird's example, 843*; wife disappointed about new dress, 1371**; wife punished, 1370B*; wife punished (must hold cat), 1370; wife reformed, 901B*, 902*, 902A*, wife throws bread out of window-1387A; woman punished, 368*, 368A*, 368B*.

Learn to swim before going in water, 1293*.
Learned son and forgotten language, 1628.
Learning about money, 1385*; to fear men, 157—157D*; to sleep in bed (seduction), 1545A; what fear is, 326—326D*.
Leave of absence given obedient husband, 1409B.
Lecherous father as queen's persecutor, 706C; holy man and maiden in box, 896.
Leeches eaten by patient, 1349N*.
Leg never falls to ground, 1568A.
Legs help stag (horns fatal), 77.
Lending and repaying (progressive bargains), 2034C.
Lenore, 365.
»Let me catch you better game», 122D.
Let them eat cake, 1446.
Letters smaller than in schoolbook (boy cannot read), 1331B*.
Level bushel (cheat), 1182.
Liar will blow out his lantern, 1920H*.
Liberty preferred by dog to food and chain, 201.
Lies (sundry), 1961A*—1965; told princess cause her to say »That is a lie», 852.
Life dependent on sword, 302B; story in week (day, etc.), 2012ABCD.
Life-lights in other world, 332, 332A*.
Life-span of men and animals readjusted 828.
Life-token, 303.
Lifting contest (deceptive), 1045*.
Light for cat to catch mice, 1219*.
Lighted candles lure rabbits, 1891A.
Lighting road for ogre (deceptive), 1008.
Like wind in hot sun, 923A.
Limb cut off by numskull sitting on it, 1240.
Lindorm, 433B.
Lion advised to skin wolf as remedy, 50; and mouse rescuer, 75; dives for own reflection, 92; does not forget injury from man, 159B; follows man in gratitude, 156A; frightened by horse squeezes wolf to death, 118; made drunk, 161B*, 485, 485B*; mourns death of dog companion, 74A*.
Lion's share, 51.
Lip of hare, 47A, 70.
Liquor bottle falls from preacher's sleeve, 1827A.
Lisping maiden, 1457.
Literal fools, 1692, 1693, 1696; imitation of parson quenching fire, 1825D*; instructions followed, 1562—1562B; interpretation of precepts (foolish), 915, 915A; numskull follows instructions, 1696.
Little brother and little sister, 450; Claus and Big Claus, 1535; fish slip through net, 253; goose-girl, 870A; people give gifts, 503; Red Ox, 511A.
Live stock killed, 1007.
Living crucifix chosen, 1347; harp sought, 465B; man wants to see God, 775A*; person as image, 1829.
Llewellyn and his dog, 178A.
Load carried by ant, 280.
Loading wood (if one load then two for horse), 1242.
Loaves large for feeding multitude, 1833H.
Lobsters turning red reveal love affair, 1776A*.
Local moon, 1334.
Long hunt (game chased for months), 1889N; night (fool locked in dark room), 1684A*.
»Long Winter» deceives foolish woman, 1541.
Longevity of men and animals, 173.
Looking for a wife, 1450—1474; through gun barrel (ogre shot), 1158.
Lord above, lord below, 1355A; above will provide, 1355C.
»Lord has risen», 1341B.
Lord's prayer gives respite from death, 1199.
Losing and finding enchanted wife, 400, 401, 425P.
Lost father sought (resuscitated), 369; husband sought (Cupid and Psyche), 425—425*; tongue (silence wager), 1351A*.
Louse and crow as friends (chain tale), 2028A*; and flea to marry (chain tale), 2019*; killed when flea bites man, 282C*; mourns flea (chain tale), 2021*.
Louse-skin as puzzle for suitors, 621.
»Lousy-head» (insulting name for husband), 1365C.
Love adventure told symbolically, 873*; like salt, 510, 923; like wind in hot sun, 923A.
Lover arrives just in time to prevent lady's (man's) marriage to another, 974; hidden in trunk, 1725; in hog pen frightens husband, 1419F; murdered, 1536C; oversleeps at rendezvous, 861.
Lover's gift regained, 1420—1420G.
Lovers as pursuer and fugitive, 1419D.

Loving wife tested by sham-dead husband, 1350; wife to pluck hairs from husband's beard, 1353.
Luck and blessing contest, 946C*; and intelligence, 945; and wealth (fish with jewel), 736; saves man after intelligence fails, 945.
Luck-bringing animal killed (its eaten flesh brings luck), 939*; shirt (shoes), 844.
Luckless man, 947; son and wizard father, 739*.
Lucky brothers (three), 1650; blow at king saves his life, 1646; accidents, 1640—1674; Hans, 1415; wife brings success, 737B*; shot, 1890—1890F.
Lullaby sung by enchanted husband, 425E.
Lump of gold priced (cheat), 1546.
Lumpy porridge, 1458*.
Lying boy disfigured must tell three truths, 570A*; contests, 1920—1920H*; goat, 212; tales, 852, 1875—1999; to princess, 852.
Magic ball of thread, 934E; bird-heart, 567; bird-heart and separated brothers, 567A; bridle, needle, and gun, 594*; doll thrown out bites passing king, 571C; fiddle compels dancing, 592; flight, 313, 314; food of animal sons-in-law, 552B; hammer helps hero win princess, 308*; horse helps hero on flight, 314; knife conquers enemy, 576; mill, 565; mirror (clairvoyant), 709; mirror reflects woman's blemishes, 870D*; object and the trolls, 581; object holds person fast, 571; object stolen and recovered, 560—568; objects, 560—649; objects and wonderful fruits, 566; objects fought over, 518; objects (miscellaneous), 576A*—576E*; objects received from quarreling giants, 518; ox, 511A; pipe as reward, 515*; purse, 564; remedies, 610—619; ring recovered by dog and cat, 560; sickle for devil, 820A; sleep induced by robber, 958D*; staff, 304*; stick, golden feather, etc., 534*.
Magician and his pupil, 325; exposed, 987.
Magnetic mountain, 322.
Magpie to throw down chestnut (chain tale), 2032A; thrown into mud (knows why sow is muddy), 237; killed by fox, 56, 56A, 56B.
Maiden banished, 700—709; in tower, 310; kills robbers, 956B; seeks brothers (the seven brothers), 451; with serpent lover, 507C; without hands, 706.
Maidens in distress, 899*.
Maiden's cleverness, 875, 920—929; »honor», 1542**; lisp, 1457.
Maids must rise earlier (have killed cock who wakes them), 1566A*.
Maimed cattle to recover, 1534B*.
Maiming live stock, 1007.
Mak and the sheep, 1525M.
Make-believe eating, make-believe work, 1560; son (daughter), 459.
Making ogre strong (castration), 1133, 1134; princess laugh, 571—574.
Man (stories), 1525—1874; and his associates, 293C*; and wife build air castles, 1430; and ogre as partners, 1030—1059; and wild animals, 150—199; as God on tree, 1380—1380A*; boasts of his wife, 400, 880; builds air castles, 1681*; caught in log goes for axe, 1882A; does wife's work, 1408; from gallows avenges theft, 366; from tree threatens (debt paid), 1575*, 1575**; hidden in roof, 1360; in heaven, 800—809; is burned up and returned to life, 788; persecuted because of his beautiful wife, 465; promised to devil, 810—814; promised to devil becomes priest, 811; punishes wolf (climbs tree), 162*; seeking midwife has misfortunes, 1680; seeks lost wife, 400; sleeps whole winter in cave, 672D; teaches bear to play fiddle, 151; tells tiger's secret, 181; thinks he has been in heaven, 1531; thinks himself dead, 1313—1313A*; to pick tree to be hanged on, 1587; with unfaithful wife comforted, 1426*; without a member, 1543*; who does his wife's work, 1408; who fell out of balloon, 1882; who flew like a bird and swam like a fish, 665.
Manure to be cleared out, 1035.
Manuring soil with lard, 1231*.
Map produces helpful spirits, 611*.
Mare taken for church, 1315**.
Marienkind, 710.
Mariner changed to bird, 888B*.
Marked coat in wife's room, 1378.
Marking place on boat, 1278; the dream-treasure, 1645B.
Marriage as punishment for wolf, 165B*; by stealing clothing of bathing girl, 400, 413; fee (husband wants to be unmarried), 1516D*; outside parish forbidden, 1475; to she-devil, 424*.
Married daughter as guest, 1292*; couple separated by devil, 821A*; couples, 1350—1439.

Marrying a stranger, 1468*.
Masking as woman to seduce woman, 860B*; as devil punished, 831.
Mass used for conversation, 1831.
Master and pupil quarrel, 1568**; and servant at table, 1568*; more careful than servant (stag discovered), 162; Pfriem, 801; taken seriously when he begins to root out vineyards, 93; thief, 1525—1525R*.
Master's coat burns (servant obedient), 1562; privilege, 1572*.
Match-makers, 1688B*.
Matches all tested by striking, 1260B*.
Matron of Ephesus, 1510.
»May the devil skin me», 813C.
Mayor chosen by footrace (calf victor), 1675*.
Meal of beans, 1478.
Measuring land with **tail** (claim of escaping fox), 67***.
Meat as food for cabbage, 1386; said to be unsuitable for christening, trickster gets it, 32*; springs as toad on face of ungrateful son, 980D; stolen for poor turns to roses, 717*.
Mediation between lion and lioness refused for fox cannot smell, 51A.
Meleager (life while candle lasts), 1187, 934E.
Merchant confused in his calculations, 1592B*.
Merchant's son acquires skill, 654B*; tale, 1423.
Merry wives' wager, 1406.
Messengers of death, 335.
Mice carry an egg by cooperating, 112*; choose cat as king, 113; eat iron, 1592; to put bell on cat, 110.
Midas with ass's ears, 782.
Midas' wish (everything gold), 775.
Middle of bed claimed by each of two, 1289.
Midwife sought (misadventures), 1680.
Milk in the cask (water substituted), 1555; pail stopped so that milk will not flow, 1370C*; smeared on saint's image, 1829A*.
Milking a hen, 1204*.
Milkmaid tosses head, spills milk, 1430.
Mill keeps grinding salt (meal), 565; speaks to wolf (equivocally), 78*; taken for church, 1315A*.
Miller, his son, and ass, 1215.
Miller's tale, 1361.
Millers, 1853—1853B*.
Millpond nix, 316.

Millstone carries off fool with head in its hole, 1247; dropped on robbers, 1653C.
Millstones (hero's mother's pearls), 1146.
Mine darkness makes drunk man think he is in hell, 835A*.
Minister cannot answer people's questions, 1835C*; reinstates self by cleverness (Achikar), 922A.
Ministers (anecdotes), 1725—1849.
Mirror answers questions, 709; reflects women's blemishes, 870D*; frightens demon who sees reflection, 1168A; stolen leads to adventures, 434.
Misadventures of three brothers, 1716**.
Miser and his gold, 1305—1305C; and the eye ointment (blinded), 836F*; and travelers, 1572G*; eats at night, 1562C*; in dying swallows his money, 760A*; lends money to devil and loses it, 836E*; spies on wife, 1407.
Miser's soul disputed over, 773*.
Misfortunes followed by success, 938—939; in youth or age, 938AB.
Missing nose added to unborn child, 1424.
Mistake of breath in cold for tobacco smoke, 1320; of bear for dog, 1312; of big tree for snake, 1315; of buttercask for corpse, 1314; of girl admits youth to her room, 850*; of pumpkin for ass's egg, 1319; of wolf for colt, 1311.
Misunderstood servant transformed, 516, 516A.
Mitten as home of fly, mouse, fox, etc., 283B*.
Mittens chase deer, 1889L**.
Mock stories for children, 2271; sunrise, 120, 120*, 120**.
Modus Liebinc, 1362.
Money in broken image, 1643; in hand (penniless wooer), 859B; in the stick, 961B; to frogs, 1642.
Money-stick of robber found, 961.
Monk and bird, 471A.
Monks appropriate field, 1584*.
Monster as bridegroom (Cupid and Psyche), 425A; fettered, 803; hero (heroine) disenchanted, 708, 711; in bridal chamber, 507B.
Monster's bride (grateful dead man), 507A.
Months and seasons symbolized, 294.
Moon (different) for each place, 1334; dived for, 1336, 34; reflected in pool, 1335, 1335A; rescued (reflected in pool), 1335A; (rising) taken for fire, 1335*; thought to be eaten by cow (reflection in pool), 1335.

More cowardly than the hare, 70; devout, 756D*.
Moslem to be turned into Hindu, 875B$_2$.
Mother dies of fright when about to commit incest with son, 823A*; plots with giant against son, 590; slew me, me, father ate me, 720; wants to kill children, 765; who did not bear me but nourished me, 713; with cannibal brothers, 955B*.
Mother-in-law favors own daughter (absurd results), 1503*; punished for cruelty (reformed), 903D*.
Mound as prison for princess, 870.
Mountain of glass to be ascended by rider, 502, 530.
Mourning dead ass (cumulative tale), 2023*.
Mouse and cat converse, 111; and sparrow at war, 222B; acquires series of things, 2029C*; as devil's bride, 1192*; bird and sausage, 85; bursts when crossing stream (chain tale), 2034A; eats cheese (chain tale), 2030C; (enchanted princess) as bride, 402; frightens man to death, 167*; from country and from city, 112; helps lion, 75; in silver jug, 1416; regains tail (chain tale), 2034.
Mouse-trap for catching light, 1245**.
Moving away from trouble, 1325—1325*; large stone (stretching rope), 1326B*; the church (the stolen coat), 1326.
Mower with prodigious speed (saint), 752C.
Mowing by devil as substitute laborer, 820; contest (deceptive), 1090; grass (destroys field), 1203*.
Mucus and excrement debate, 293F*.
Multiplying the secret, 1381D.
Münchhausen tales, 1889—1889P.
Murder evaded by substituting object, 1115; of child by princess, 781; of hero attempted, 1115—1129; revealed (by bird), 761; revealed (by singing bone, harp, hair), 780—780B; will out, 960—960B*.
Murdered lover, 1536C.
Murderous mother, 765.
Mushroom reviles oak, 293B*.
Mushroom's war, 297B.
Mushrooms from Peter's spittle, 774L; tested by ten-sou piece, 1287*.
Musician in wolf-trap, 160A, 168.
Mustard eaten wholesale, 1339D.
Mutual mockeries of girl and suitor, 1460*.

Naked lover left outside, 1730B*; parson and wife in woods, 1728*; wife sent as riding-horse, 1091.
Name of devil's plant (tobacco) to be guessed, 1091A; of God expels devil, 817*; of helper discovered, 500.
Names absurdly given objects and animals, 1562A, 1940; (extraordinary) given objects, 1940, 1562A; given frogs please them, 278D*; of boys »What was I», etc., 883C; of Holy Trinity (the three cows), 1833D; written by devil on hide, 826.
Naming the child (christening), 1821—1821A; trees, 7; wild game (woman in feathers), 1183*.
Needle, glove and squirrel, 90; in sacramental bread struck by parson, 1785B; prince, 437; pulled from hand (chain tale), 2030B*.
Needles stuck into ice as anchor, 1279; to be made (devil fails), 1194*.
Nera and the Dead Man, 764.
Nests of dove smell, 236.
Net escaped by little fish, 253; of lion gnawed by mouse, 75; to be unraveled, 1178*.
Never heard before, 921E.
New clothes for bird who flies away without paying, 235C*; clothes for king, 1620; Eve, 1416.
News from home (absurd), 1931.
Night-lodgings for Christ and Peter, 790.
Night-quarters for traveling animals, 130, 210.
Nightcaps exchanged, 1119.
Nightingale borrows blindworm's eye (keeps it), 234.
Night's lodging secured by trickster, 1544.
Nine brothers sought, 451A.
Nix of mill-pond, 316.
»No» answer to all questions (princess seduced), 853A, 851, 853.
No time to lie, 1920B; work, no food, 1370A*.
Noah admits devil to ark, 825.
Noblest act (bridegroom, robber, lover), 976.
Nose (hair) cut off, 1417.
Noseless man persuades others to cut off noses, 1707.
Not as I live but as I preach, 1836A; to eat too greedily (cat steps on foot), 1691.
Notary enters heaven, 750H*.
Nothing to cook, 1464D*.
Novelle (romantic tales), 850—999.

Numbers one to twelve (cumulative tales), 2010.
Numskull believes he is married to a man, 1686**; cuts off limb he sits on, 1240; poor hero, and fox as fishermen, 163*.
Numskulls 1200—1349; cannot count selves, 1287; cannot find (own legs), 1288, (ass he is sitting on), 1288A.
Nun who saw the world, 770.
Nurse does not throw child to wolf (wolf waits in vain), 75*.
Nut hits cock's head, 20C, 2033.
Nuts of »Ay ay ay», 860; shoveled with hayfork, 1229*.
Oak leaves to fall before payment is due, 1184; tree to be removed, 577.
Oath on the iron, 44, 44*; with double meaning (Isolde), 1418.
Obedient husband, 1409—1409*.
Object substituted prevents murder, 1115.
Objects displayed overawe ogre (various), 1152; given away lose magic, 572**; to go by themselves, 1291—1291D; with magic powers, 560—649.
Obstacle flight, 313, 314—314B*.
Obstinate wife, 1365—1365J*.
Oedipus, 931.
Offended deity, 939; skull (statue), 470A.
Officious bird punished by monkey, 241.
Oft-proved fidelity, 881.
Ogre afraid of noises, 1145; and children, 327; and tailor at sewing, 1096; blinded, 1135; carries sham-dead man, 1139; castrated, 1133; defeated, 300—359; eats hot porridge, 1131; frightened or overawed, 1145—1154; in haunted castle, 1160; kills own children, 1119; looks through gun-barrel, 1158; makes contract with man, 1060—1114; on ship, 1179; schoolmaster, 707A, 894; tars hero's boat, 1156.
Ogre's beard gilded, 1138; daughter helps hero escape, 313; finger caught, 1159; flight, 1132; heart in egg, 302—302B*; stupidity, 1000—1199; wife (burned), 1121, (killed), 1122 (thrown into water), 1120.
Old and older, 726, 726*; beggar and robbers, 1526; »hen» brought for master, 1623*; Hildebrand, 1360C; maid on the roof, 1479*; maids, 1475—1499; man and Death, 845; man and old woman with cock and hen, 219E*; man at St. John's fire, 773*; man hidden later saves kingdom, 981; man in forest, 442; man mistreated, 980—980D; man sent to school (testimony discredited), 1381E; man with live coals, 751B*; man's blessing for kindness, 750F*; robber relates three adventures, 933.
»Old Saddle» granted by king, 927A*.
Old woman and her pig, 2030; woman as trouble maker (beats devil), 1353; woman in glass case as last commodity, 1170; woman rejuvenated, 406A*; woman who was skinned, 877; woman's dogs (unfinished tale), 2280; women helpers, 501.
Oldest animal, 80A*; on the farm, 726.
One act of charity admits man to heaven, 809*; eye for three old women, 581; Eye, Two Eyes, Three Eyes, 511; vice carries others with it, 839; woman to catch squirrel (falls from tree, etc.), 1227.
One-eyed camel, 655, 655A; man and hunchback, 1620*.
Only one brother grateful, 550A.
Open eyes while asleep, 1140; Sesame, 676.
Opposite of what is wanted always asked, 1365J*.
Oranges are enchanted girls, 408.
Orchard or vineyard of ogre destroyed, 1011.
Ordinary folktales, 300—1199.
Origin of chess, 2009; of physical defects, 758A.
Orphan girl and cruel sisters-in-law, 897.
Other person to pay for supper, 1526A.
Otherworld bridge, 471; ogress disenchanted, 871; journey, 465C, 470, 471.
Ottokar and Alwine, 975**.
Our Lady's Child, 710.
»Out, boy, out of the sack», 564.
Out-riddling (the judge), 927; (the princess), 851.
Outcast queens and ogress queen, 462.
Outwitting fate, 934D$_1$.
Over the Edge, 10***.
Over-hasty toad (beetle), (turtle), 288B*, 288C*.
Overawing the ogre, 1045—1049; the stronger by a bluff, 125, 126, 125A*—125D*.
Overeating in cellar, 33*, 41.
Overseer (fox) punishes lazy animals, 55.
Oversight of thievish tailor, 1574A.
Own children killed by ogre, 1119; children like best, 247.
Owner has refused to accept it (deceptive confession), 1807A.
Ox as mayor, 1675; breaks loose at grave,

1840; carries parson into church, 1786; for five pennies, 1553; helper killed, 511A.
Ox-hide as measure, 2400.
Ox-tongues demanded for dinner: unreasonable wife humbled, 904*.
Oxen before and behind wagon, 1249; (transformed sisters) disenchanted, 452B*.
Padlock on enchanted husband, 425L.
Painted member on trickster, 1547*.
Painter and architect trick each other, 980*.
Painting the bear (burning), 8, 152.
Pan too small for planned cakes, 1221B*.
Pancake flees, 2025.
Paradise mistaken for Paris, 1540.
Paramour carried off in box, 1358B; discomfited by woman's husband, 1359—1359*; poses as crucifix, 1359C.
Pardoner's Tale, 763.
Parents as birds, 452D*; kill son who has returned home unrecognized, 939A; to humble selves before son, 517.
Parody incantation to warn lover, 1419H; sermon, 1824.
Parricide forgiven, 756F*.
Parricide's fate, 761*.
Parrot betrays mistress, 243; helps thief, 1526B*; pretends to be god, 243; tells tales to guard wife's chastity, 1352A; unable to tell details of woman's infidelity, 1422; with lively imagination killed, 100*; woos for king, 546.
Parrots fly away with tree, 1881*.
»Parsley» in soup, 1685.
Parson and sexton, 1775—1799; and sexton (at mass, the stolen lamb), 1831 (steal cow), 1790; as card-player, 1839; carried into churchyard (Is he fat?), 1791; dissatisfied with share of horse sausage, 1741*; dreams of sleeping with host's daughter (gets into trouble), 1775A*; in church on an ox, 1786; in sack to heaven, 1525A, 1535 (IV), 1737; is betrayed, 1725—1774; need not preach, 1826; promises satisfactory weather, 1830; put to flight during sermon, 1785; sees the devil (bear), 1745*; seeks food in house at night, 1775; sexton, and eel, 1776*; sexton, and churchwarden visit beautiful woman, 1730; takes drink during sermon, 1827; to bear calf, 1739; visits the (sick) dying, 1843—1844A; with fine voice, 1834.
Parson's ox, 1840, 1840A; share and sexton's, 1831B; tithes (he prefers share of treasure trove), 1740*; wife seduced (teaching chickens to talk), 1750.
Parsons (anecdotes), 1725—1874.
Partner cheats in returns from common work, 9.
Partnership of man and ogre, 1030—1059.
Pasted Bible leaves, 1835B*.
Patch of land (penniless wooer), 859A; on clothes to recognize oneself, 1531B.
Patelin, 1585.
Patent right lost by dog, 200A.
Paternoster, 1199.
Patience of Job, 1811B.
Patient Griselda, 887.
Paving garden to keep out moles, 1282*.
Pawn of foolish wife, 1385.
Pay counted out (hole in hat), 1130; for bread with beer (cheat), 1555A.
Payment imaginary, 1804—1804B.
Pea in soup sought for, 1562F.
Peace among the animals, 62; for the frogs (stork swallows them), 243A*.
Pear tree for wife and lover, 1423; will not fall (chain tale), 2030D.
Pearls from girl's tears, 836A*.
Peas swept on ice (devil injured), 1180*.
Peasant as parson, 1825; betrays fox by pointing, 161; counts pebbles, 1683*; girl rescues prince from witch, 317A*; girl's cleverness, 875; has sent lawyer's fee by rabbit, 1585*; in heaven, 802; makes master say »You lie,» 1920C; visits city, 1337—1337C; woman (at market), 1382, (greedy), 751.
Peasants need no spoons, 910C*.
Pebble for each sin, 1848.
Pebbles dropped in jug so crow can drink, 232D*.
Peck of grain for each stack (very small stacks), 1155.
Penance until dry branch becomes green, 756—756C.
Penniless bridegroom pretends to wealth, 859, 859ABCD.
Penny always returns, 745.
Pennyworth of wit, 910G.
Pension given both husband and wife, 1556.
Pent cuckoo, 1213.
Peril of sheep, duck, and cock at sea, 204.
Persecuted bride, 403.
Person does not know himself, 1284.
Persuasive auctioneer, 1214.
Peter beaten twice, 791; lets people fall from heaven, 758A; made ridiculous, 774—774P; Ox, 1675.

Peter's mother falls from heaven, 804.
Petrified kingdom disenchanted, 410*.
Physician in spite of himself, 1641B.
Physicians, 1862.
Pif Paf Poltrie, 2019.
Pig blindfolded so that it will take right road, 1212*; eats the money, 891C*; (enchanted girl) disenchanted, 413A*; in apple tree pelts wolf, 136; of stingy parson, 1792; sheared by ogre, 1037; with golden bristles, 530A.
Pigs to walk and not run home (devil cheated), 1185*; build houses of straw, sticks, and iron, 124A*.
Pike and snake race to land, 252.
Pilgrimage vow, 1230*.
Piling up pottery (woman breaks pots), 1371*.
Pillow too high, 1443*.
Pipe (gun) for ogre, 1157; magically calls animals, 570, 570B*; shot from man's mouth, 1708*; smoked by fox, 66A*.
Pit captives eat one another, 20A; escaped by fox on wolf's back, 31; fallen into in race, 30.
Pit-rescue, 30—35.
Pitch on ass's tail to hurry him, 1682*.
Pitfall of ogre catches ogre, 1117.
Placating storm by throwing man overboard, 973.
Place marked on boat where object fell, 1278.
Placidas, 938.
Plans for unborn child (foolish), 1430A.
Plant fails to grow (chain tale), 2047*.
Planting for next generation, 928.
Play at hog-killing, 2401.
Playing-cards symbolically interpreted, 1613.
Pleasing the captain (singer carried on boat free), 1553B*; everyone impossible (Asinus Vulgi), 1215.
Plowing for ogre (deceptive), 1003; without trampling field (horse carried), 1201.
Pointing betrays fleeing fox, 161.
Poison in beggar's bread eaten by poisoner's son, 837; overturned by repentant animal, 168*, 285A*.
Poisoned pot (man lies down for dead), 1313.
Pole planted to catch bear, 1890A*.
Poles used for dueling with ogre, 1083.
Pollution of the animal carrying the trickster, 4*.
Polycrates, 736A.
Polyphemus, 953, 1137.

Poor and rich travel together (poor does deeds, rich rewarded), 520*; boy betrothed to maiden (bride stolen), 885; brother's treasure, 834; man in court (stone in purse), 1660; parson's sermon, 1833*.
Pope tempted by devils, 816*.
Porridge divided unjustly, 9C; in ice hole, 1260; in one room, milk in other, 1263; pot thought to be complaining, 1264*.
Portrait of devil brings master's death, 819*.
Posing as ogre's wife's child, 314*; as saint's statue to enter convent, 1829B*.
Postpone not till tomorrow, 1641C*.
Pot drowned when fox has head in it, 68B; fills house with porridge, 565; has child and dies, 1592B; (magic) steals objects, 591; of gold and of scorpions, 834A, 1645; of meat attracts bird which drops jewel, 1643*; to walk home, 1291A.
Potiphar's wife, 870C*.
Potter pleases king by cleverness and is rewarded, 921E*.
Pound of flesh, 890.
Poverty a good rat poison, 1779A*; attached to man's shoes, 946B*; locked up, 332F*.
Power (supernatural), 650—699.
Prayer for change of wind, 1276*; for food accidentally answered (fool thankful), 1349M*; for husband, 1476; gives respite from death, 122A, 227, 332, 955, 1199; in latrine, 1301*; only when people are in trouble, 774E; permitted allows victim to escape, 122, 227; to be finished (death postponed), 122A, 122B*; to Christ child's mother, 1476A.
Praying without distracting thoughts (wager), 1839D*.
Preachers (anecdotes), 1725—1849.
Precepts prove wise, 910, 910A—K.
Precious cod, 1654*.
Predestined death, 934, 934A, 934A$_1$, 934B, 934D, 934D$_1$, 934E; husband, 930; treasure (always follows man), 745A; wife, 930A.
Prediction of death believed, 1313A.
Preparation of bread (flax) recounted to delay death, 1199A; for wedding (fool gives meat to dogs, etc.), 1681A.
Prescription (chalk) washed off by rain, 1216*.
Present to king brings demand for second, 467, 875.
Presents and strokes divided, 1610; misused and used properly, 620.

Present to lover (girl's eyes, etc.), 706B.
Pretence of ignorance of women (seductions), 1545B.
Pretended corpse at practice funeral, 1653A*.
Pretending cannibalism to frighten robbers, 958B*.
Pretty lips for old maid, 1485*.
Price of wood (»sleeping together»), 1686*.
Pride punished, 836.
Priest cannot be taken by devil, 811; likened to prosecutor (questions about death of Christ), 1806A*; masks as devil to cheat, 831; must bail out boat (plug removed), 1746*; on cow's tail, 1849*; outwits devil (makes cock crow early), 810A*; points out treasure, 1645A*.
Priest's breeches instead of husband's, 1419G; guest and eaten chicken, 1741; pig, 1792A; pretended dream, 1844*.
Priests (anecdotes), 1725—1849.
Prince and arm bands, 590; and clever parson's daughter, 876A*; and storm, 934; and three hosts tell adventures, 726*; as bird wounded and healed, 432; as serpent, 433—433C; exchanged in youth with commoner shows wisdom, 920, 920A; to go courting wakened too early, 1688C*; whose wishes came true, 652; won by heroine, 870—879.
Prince's seven wise teachers, 875D*; wings, 575.
Princess advises poor man to marry, 737A*; and magic fish-skin, 570A; and ogress, 871; as servant girl takes vengeance for mistreatment, 941*; caught with own words, 853; confined to mound, 870, 870A*, 870C*; enamored of woman in men's clothing, 880, 881*, 884A; exchanged in youth with commoner shows wisdom, 920, 920A; flees to forest to escape marriage, 888*; forced to say »That is a lie,» 852; from tower rescues husband, 891A; hidden from, 329; impregnated by wish, 675; in shroud, 307; made to laugh, 559, 571, 621; must say »No», 853; on glass mountain, 530; on the pea, 704; rescued, 300—300A*, 301—301D, 303; rescued from devil, 811C*; rescued (grateful dead man), 506; responsible for own fortune, 923B; the most beautiful thing in the garden, 925*; to love forty Arabs (etc.), 930B; transformed to deer, 401; unable to solve riddle, 851; who murdered her child, 761; won, 300—300A*.
Princess's hand is won, 850—869.
Princesses stolen and rescued, 301.
Problem (easy) made hard, 1346A*.
Prodigal's return, 935.
Profitable exchanges (eaten grain and cock as damages), 1655.
Promise of boy to devil (ogre), 313, 314, 313***; promise to boy to water-nix, 316; of princess to sea-giant, 313**.
Pronouns avoided in tales, 2322.
Property of ogre dissipated, 1002.
Prophecy of future glory, 930; of greatness brings exile and fulfillment, 517; of marriage to princess (rich girl), 461, 930; of prince's marriage to lowly girl, 930A, 930C, 930D.
Protected by the needle, 1279.
Proud king won, 874.
Psyche (and Cupid), 425A.
Puella pedens, 1453****.
Pulling lake together, 1045; on shirt (man's head cut off), 1285; up turnip (chain tale), 2044.
Pulpit sawed (falls as miracle), 1825C.
Puma avenges fox's theft of meat, 66B*.
Pumpkin as ass's egg, 1319.
Pumping out water on ship (whole sea), 1179.
Punished pride, 836; seducer, 883B.
Punishment by drowning (crayfish), 1310; by throwing into bushes (rabbit), 1310A; of wicked lord, 837; of bad woman, 750C; of compassionate angel, 795; for vanity, 833*.
Punishments of Men, 840.
Puns (stupid stories), 1345*.
Pupil surpasses thieves, 1525E.
Puppet bride, 898.
Purchase not him who surpasseth thee, 926A*.
Purchased wife helps husband, 887A*.
Purgatory chosen over return to wife, 1516*; suffered in long marriage, 1516B*.
Purse inexhaustible, 580*; providing money stolen, 564.
Pursuit of heavenly maiden, 306A.
Pushing hole in tree, 1085.
Puss in boots, 545B.
Puteus, 1377.
Quarrel of cow and reindeer, 132*; over air castles, 1430.
Quarreling animals ask man to divide booty, 159*.

Quarrelsome animals fed rethreshed straw, 206.
Queen as gusli-player, 875C; cannot imitate magic of husband's mistress, 1442*; reformed by placing her in cobbler's bed, 905A*; with black lover found in otherworld, 871A.
Quenching burning boat (row to land to get water), 1330.
Quest for father's friend, 463A*; for fear, 326; for good luck, 947C*; for hairs from devil's beard, 461; for living harp, 465B; for lost father, 369; for lost wife, 400, 401; for persons as stupid as his wife, 1384, cf. 1385, 1450; for remedy, 551; for speaking bird, etc., 707; for strawberries in winter, 403B; for strong companion, 650B; for unknown, 465, 465A; for vanished princess, 301A—301D*; for wonderful bird, 550; to the devil, 382*, 461; to morning star, etc., 702A*; to otherworld, 461, 465C.
Question asked to deceive captor, 6.
Questions of king cleverly answered by peasant boy, 921; to be answered, 460—462.
Rabbit borrows money (chain tale), 2024*; catch (extraordinary), 1891; catch (trap on roof), 1226; rides fox a-courting, 72; taken for cow, 1316; to be caught in each net set in trees, 1171.
Rabbit-herd, 570.
Rabbit's split lip, 70, 47A; tail (unfinished tale), 2251.
Rabbits baste themselves, 1920G*; freeze feet to ice, 1891; herded (believed to be cows), 1316; made to sneeze (caught), 1891B*.
Race of birds, 230*—230**; of fox and crayfish, 275; of fox and polar bear, 69*; of fox and wolf (trick), 30; of hare and tortoise (sleeping hare), 275A; of hedgehog and hare, 275A*; with little son (rabbit), 1072; won by hanging on to tail, 250, 275; won by deception (relative helpers), 1074.
Rain kept off hare by spear-grass (hare satisfied), 71*; of sausage (figs, fishes), 1381B.
Rake striking man pretending to have forgotten own language, 1628.
Ram (golden) made to carry hero into princess's chamber, 854; to jump into wolf's jaws (knocks him over), 126C*; to scratch wolf (horns him), 125A*.
Ramrod shot (accidents), 1890D; kills many ducks, 1894.

Ram's belly crawled under to escape ogre, 1137.
Rams deceive ogre at bridge, 122E; kill wolf who is their judge, 122K*, 122M*.
Ransom given by captured animals, 159.
Raparius, 1689A.
Rapunzel, 310.
Rarest thing in the world, 653A.
Rat and frog tied together (carried off), 278; as most powerful (chain tale), 2031C, 2031B*.
Rats or mink (argument over holes in floor), 1365G*.
Raven carries young across lake, 244***; child, 1411*; drowns young who promises too much, 244C*; helper aids in rescuing princess, 553; in borrowed feathers, 244; with cheese in mouth, 57.
Rearing blamed for son's crimes, 838; of large-headed and large-eyed bird (age of owl), 230.
Rebellion of work animals, 207.
Rebounding bow kills meddlesome, 180.
Recipe is saved (though meat is carried off), 1689B.
Recruit flees from suitors, 995*.
Rector's night (with housekeeper), 1842C*.
Red bull fights with giant, 302B*.
Red Riding Hood, 333.
Red-bearded parson, 1835F*.
Red-haired boy returned, 1425A*; children are priest's, 1805*.
Reducing size of lie, 1920D.
Reductio ad absurdum of suit, 920A.
Reeds bend before wind, 298C*.
Reeve's tale, 1363.
Reflection dived for, 34—34B; of girl in lake (ogre tries to drink lake dry), 1141; of self not recognized, 1336A.
Reform of master by servant boy, 1569*.
Reformed wolf still eats goose, 165.
Refusal to tell of propitious dream, 725.
Refusing to eat (servant thinks to deceive master), 1698B*.
Reindeer killed by dupe: trickster drives him away, 8****; to be slaughtered: fox frightens away invited guests, 8**.
Rejected fiancée marries real lover, 900A*.
Relative helpers in race, 1074.
Release from captor by asking questions, 6; from Purgatory, 769*.
Releasing rabbit (hunter shoots string in two), 1876*.
Religions and sects, 1870.
Religious tales, 750—849.

Remarkable companions help hero, 301, 513, 514.
Remedies (magic), 610—619.
Remedy for sick lion (wolf-skin), 50.
Rent receipt fetched from hell, 756C*.
Repairing the house, 1010.
Repartee of deformed people, 1620*.
Repeating instructions so as to remember (forgets), 1204.
Repentant thief pretends to have found stolen cow, 1636.
Repetition of questions instead of answering, etc., 1832L*M*.
Report of cat king's death, 113A.
Reproval of ungrateful son by own son, 980.
Rescue by youngest brother, 303; of animals and man from pit (ungrateful man), 160; (ungrateful wolf), 160A; of maiden (from immortals), 313*; (from sea giant), 313**; (from ogre), 313**; of sister from devil, 452A*; of swallowed persons by cutting open swallower, 123, 333; of three sisters from ogre, 311, 312; of youth by father, 890*; from devils by Virgin Mary, 1168C; from dragon, 300, 303; from ogre by sister, 311; from pit, 30—35.
Rescued princess (grateful dead man), 506.
Respite from death by means of long tale or song, 1199A, 1199B; from death until prayer is said, 61; from devil until old woman is sold, 1170, 1170A; from wooer while he brings clothes all night, 1441.
Restoring blind king's eyes, 541*.
Resuscitation of girl by suitors (who shall have her?), 653B; unsuccessfully attempted (imitation of miracle), 753, 753A, 1535 (IV).
Return of successful prodigal, 935.
Returned soldier unwittingly killed, 939A.
Returning for tools to perform tricks (horse stolen), 1542A; husband hoodwinked, 1419.
Reverse merit, 1579*.
Reynard the fox at court, 53.
Rhampsinitus, 950.
Rich and poor peasant, 1535; man and his son-in-law, 461, 930; man as devil's horse, 761; man (deceased) and devils in church, 815; man disguises as poor to test character of girls he courts, 941**; man pays servant (cumulative), 2010I; man's and poor man's fortunes, 735, 735*; man's courtship, 941**;

man's vision, 802B*; poor, and the diamond, 741*; son-in-law outwitted, 1568***.
Riches as end of quest, 551*, 551**; inadvertently kicked aside, 842.
Rider carries part of load, 1242A.
Riddle of soldier with old woman (stolen cock), 1544A*; propounded by devil, 812, 812*; propounded to princess, 851; revealed by monster, 500*.
Riddles propounded to (devil), 1178, (judge), 927, (suitors by princess), 851A.
Riddling answer betrays theft, 875A; instructions in weaving given ignorant girl, 1463B*.
Riding the leader in race, 250, 275.
Riding-horse (unheard-of) to be brought, 1091.
Ring of Polycrates, 736A; from the dead, 307A*; in sea recovered from fish, 930D; recovered by dog and cat, 560; stolen and recovered, 560, 560A*.
Roasting meat at long distance from fire, 1262.
Robber bridegroom, 955; commiserated (nothing to steal), 1341C; in church taken for ghost, 1318A; Madej, 756A; relates adventures to save sons, 953.
Robber's money-stick found, 961.
Robbers, 950—969; and king, 951ABC, 952; betrayed, 1527; chased by bear, 957; evaded by shepherd boy, 958; frightened (by numskull talking to himself), 1653F, (from treasure by man in tar and feathers), 1527; in death chamber frightened, 1654; take revenge on girl, 956B; under the tree frightened away, 1653.
Robbers' heads cut off as they enter house, 956, 956A, 956B.
Robbery of bank, 951B.
Rock held up (deception), 9, 1530, 1731.
Roderigo, 757.
Roles exchanged in housekeeping (bad results), 85.
Romantic tales, 850—999.
Rome-journey by animals, 20D*.
Roof as hiding place for eavesdropper, 1360; in good and bad weather, 1238.
Rooms in heaven (prepared for man), 802C*.
Root (eldest sister) not branch (youngest), 1465*.
Rope around cow and wolf's neck, 47C; demanded large enough to capture whole flock, 1053A; from sand, 1174.

Rope-maker loses money but finally recovers it, 935**.
Rose-girl and the queen, 708A*.
Round words, 1696B*.
Rounds (stories repeating selves), 2320.
Rowing contest (deceptive), 1087; without going forward, 1276.
Rum and water trade, 1555E.
Rumpelstilzchen, 500.
Run-away crop cut prematurely, 1204*.
Running hare shaved, 654.
Rustling (rattling) frightens ogre, 1145.
Saber (magic) kills enemy, 595C*.
Sacrificing giant candle (needless after danger is past), 778.
Sack for carrying hero, 327C.
Sackful of lies, 570.
Sacks with fugitives on dupe's back, 311.
Sad-faced princess made to laugh, 571—574.
Sailor substitute for lover, 1542*.
Sailor's promise forgotten on land, 1553A*.
Saint Christopher as ferryman, 768; George teaches the poor man, 790*; George's dogs (wolves), 1150; James of Galicia, 516C; killed and resuscitated, 791*; Peter's mother falls from heaven, 804; Peter's wife (with broom), 754**.
Saint's account book (notched stick), 1848C; picture stolen (bad priest?), 1826A*.
Saints blamed for eating cream (lips of effigies smeared), 1572A*; dispute over man's praise or blame, 846*.
Salt for salt-carriers, 1330*; in saltless land, 1651A; in the soup (each puts in some), 1328A*; sowed, 1200.
Same old story told on Good Friday, 1833F.
Sandpiper praises own song, 247A*.
Satans preferred by boy, 1678.
Sausage as revolver used against robbers, 952*; from parson's pocket, 1785A; kept for long winter, 1541; mouse, and bird, 85.
Sausages squeezed out, 1339A; with blood sold devil, 480*.
Saving promised victim from devil by good deeds, 811A*, 811B*.
Savior and Peter in night-lodgings, 791.
Savior's miracles, 750***.
Sawed pulpit, 1825C.
Scalded wolf frightened of housewife, 152A*.
Scalding ogre to make him strong, 1134.

Schlaraffenland, 1930.
Schoolmaster cannibal, 707A, 894.
Schwänke, 1200—1999.
Scornful princess turned into frog, 402*.
Scorpions turn into gold, 834A.
Scratching without detection, 1565; contest (ox-hide protection), 1095A; cotest (woman shows wounds), 1095.
Screaming heard by fox and hare (a frog), 53*.
Scythe cuts off man's head (others imitate), 1203, 1203A; taken for serpent, 1203A.
Sea birds help hero, 554*; burns (etc), 1930C*; burns (many fried fish), 1920A.
Sea-bottom as enchanted dog's kingdom, 540.
Seaman disguise (fox), 67*.
Search for brothers, 451; for golden bird, 550; for husband who commands house, 1366A*; for lost husband (Cupid and Psyche), 425—425*; for man who can rule his wife, 1375; for stolen cow, 313G*; in man's clothing for enchanted husband, 425K.
Seasickness cured (deception), 1532*.
Second cat abed with girl, 1363*.
Secret multiplied by wife, 1381D.
Secrets heard from tree, 613, 613*, 613A*, 613B*.
Seducer led into pigsty, 1730A*.
Seduction avoided by third sister, 883B; by promising magic object, 570, 570A; of girls sleeping in barn, 1498*; of servant's wife by parson, 1726*; with gift of shoes, 1731.
Seeing enormous distance, 1920E*; whole world (adultress to lover), 1355B.
Seeking lost patent right (why dogs sniff at each other), 200A.
Seemingly dead bride revives and marries lover, 885A; dead revives, 990, 990*.
Self not known, 1284, 1383.
Self-righteous hermit (penance), 756A.
Selling old donkey, 1381*; wine to each other, 1447A*.
Serfs congratulate master (absurd misunderstandings), 1698C*.
Series of clever unjust decisions, 1534.
Sermon about the rich man, 1832; illustrated from card-playing, 1839B; parodied, 1824.
Serpent. See *snake*. Serpent at wedding, 842B*; at wedding (leaves crown), 672C; husband disenchanted, 433—

433C; maiden (grateful dead man), 507C; refuses reconciliation, 285D; returned to captivity, 155.

Serpent's crown, 672—672C; flesh eaten brings knowledge of animal languages, 673.

Serpents in battle, 738*.

Servant as trouble-maker, 1573*; eats breakfast, dinner, and supper, then sleeps, 1561; forgets extraordinary names (barn burns), 1562A; gives heavy work to others, 1561**; misunderstood for faithful act, 516, 516A; of giant wins queen, 466A*; sacrifices self to save master's life, 949; sleeps on his job, 1562D*; tempted proves faithful, 889.

Servant's good counsels, 910B.

Servants beat spying master, 1571*.

Service in hell to release enchanted husband, 425J.

Sesame (Open), 676.

Seven brothers sought, 451; magic talents, 513C*; Sleepers, 766; wise teachers, 875D*.

»Seven with one stroke,» 1640.

Seventh cake satisfies (should have eaten number seven first), 1295; cucumber, 1295B; generation will pay penalty, 960B*; has red hair (the only one the husband's), 1425*.

Seventy tales of a parrot, 1352A.

Sewing contest (ogre's long thread), 1096.

Sex magically changed, 514.

Sexton and parson, 1775—1799; carries parson into churchyard (Is he fat?), 1791; falls into brewing-vat (frightens parson and maid), 1776; steals parson's money, 1789*.

Sexton's own wife brings offering (betrays relations with priest), 1781.

Shadow (of self) frightens fool, 1321B.

Shall I tell it all again? (chain story), 2013.

Sham blood and brains, 3; doctor accidentally succeeds, 1641—1641C*; dumb man wins suit, 1534D*; parson, 1825—1825B; physician in league with devil, 1862B; threat, 1563*.

Sham-dead (hidden) animal betrays self, 66B; husband tests wife's faithfulness, 1350; man (carried by ogre — »He smells already»), 1139, (frightens robbers), 1654.

Sham-ghost punished, 1676.

Shamming death to escape, 233A.

Share of (lion is meat but bones for fox), 51, (wolf as umpire — the best parts), 51**.

Sharing sheep with wolf, 156*.

Shaved man uncertain of identity, 1531A.

She-bear demands return of wool and flesh, 163B*.

She-fox's suitors, 65.

Sheep butt each other, 1886*; chases wolf (bluff), 126; duck, and cock in peril at sea, 204; expel shepherds and are eaten by wolves, 203A*; licks her newly-born but wolf may not do so, 129A*; loses eating contest (sheep thinks because his legs are too weak), 203; overawe wolf by boasting, 125, 126; persuades wolf to sing (dogs summoned), 122C.

Sheep's head buried (wife cannot keep secret), 1381C.

Sheeps' clothing for wolf, 123B.

Sheepskin grows on horse and makes wool, 1911A.

Shepherd and three giants, 314A; boy gets magic help, 515; ignorant of God has miraculous powers, 827; in service of witch, 556F*; sought and fox chosen, 37*; substitutes for priest, 922; youth in robbers' power, 958.

Shepherdess in empress's place longs for old home, 949A*.

Shift of sex, 514.

Shifting married couples in bed, 1367.

Ship for land and water, 513B; stronger than reef because new, 1277*.

Shipwreck of bat, diver, and thrush, 289.

Shirt of lucky man, 844; pulled on (head cut off), 1285.

Shoemaker makes devil's shoes, 815*; makes shoes without measuring, 1581*.

Shoes of lucky man, 844; of poverty, 946B*; of princess danced to pieces, 306.

Shooting at father's corpse, 920C; by looking down gun barrel, 1228, 1228A; leader's tail, 1889A; wild boars (bluff), 1053.

Shopkeeper parson mixes business and prayer, 1831A.

Shortest road (thief's excuse), 1624A*.

Shovel turned backward to unload grain, 1572F*.

Show me how (ogre hanged), 327D.

Shrieking contest (deceptive), 1084.

Shroud as disguise for robber, 958C*; (princess in), 307.

Shrewish wife reformed, 900—904; wife

tamed, 901, 901A*, 901B*, 901C*, 903A*.
Shuttle, spindle, and needle, 585.
Sick lion, 50.
Sickle drowned (has cut man), 1202; of magic for devil, 820A.
Sickness feigned (by overworked bullock at ass's advice — ass must do work), 207A, (sham blood and brains), 3, (so as to be carried), 4, 72.
Side-hill beast (short legs on one side), 1913.
Sidi Numan, 449.
Sieve to hold water, 1180.
Sight lost (no butter on bread), 1561*.
Sign language, 924, 924A, 924B; language of the princess, 516A.
Silence impossible for girl at lover's wedding, 886; wager, 1351—1351C*.
Silent man, 1948.
Sinful priest still a priest, 759A; woman throws no shadow, 755.
»Singing bag» carries fugitive to liberty, 311B*.
Singing bone (harp) reveals murder, 780—780B, 780A; of drunken wolf betrays him, 100; like the leader (he is calling for help), 1694; wolf, 163.
Single blanket for quarreling women, 1393; stick of wood in stove (others have burned), 1260*.
Sins confessed by wolf, 77*; of the hermit (one follows another), 839.
Sister as mysterious housekeeper, 451*; Beatrice, 770; becomes cannibal, 315A; driven from home, 512*; enchanted, 450—459; in underground kingdom, 722*; out in the cold, 883D*; plots against brother, 315.
Sisters rescued from ogre by brother, 312—312D.
»Sit still» commands old woman in wolf trap, 168A.
Six brothers seek six sisters as wives, 303A; go through the world, 513A.
Skeleton seeks forgiveness, 882B*.
Skillful brothers, 653; hounds (lies), 1920F*; hunter, 304.
Skinned old woman transformed, 877.
Skins of demons to be brought (bluff), 1154.
Sky-tree holds princess, 468.
Slandered maiden, 883A, 883C*, 892.
Slanderous lover punished, 836B*.
Slaughter of the ox, 1261.
Sledges turned in wrong direction by joker, 1275.

Sleep at the well, 725**; lasting for years, 766.
Sleepers (seven), 766.
Sleeping at the rendezvous, 861; Beauty, 410; in the middle (two fools quarrel), 1289; juror votes on wrong case, 1715; on a feather hard, a sackful harder, 1290B*; on his job (master afraid to punish servant), 1562D*; princess slept by, 304, 550; together as price of wood, 1686*; with God's daughters (nuns), 1807B; with open eyes, 1140; whole winter in cave, 672D.
Sleigh ridden by animals who destroy it, 158.
Slippered husband, 1366*.
Slovenly fiancée, 1453**.
Slow writing for slow reader, 1331C*.
Smallest animal to be eaten first, 20.
Smile from saint's statue encourages altar thief, 1565A*.
Smith outwits devil, 330; tries to imitate Christ's miracle, 753, 753A.
Smoke carried out in sieve, 1245A*.
Smoke-house imprisons greedy wolf, 41.
Snake. See *serpent*.
Snake as girl's guardian, 533*; bites objects (they swell), 1889M; drinks from child's milk-bottle, 285, 285A; enticed out of man's stomach (fed salt and must get water), 285B*; forced to suck out poison from snakebite, 182; (friendly) killed, 285A—285D; in girl's bosom turns to gold, 890A*; killed by servant guarding queen (false accusation), 916; stories, 671—673; trying to surround crab refuses to straighten self, 279*.
Snake-girdle, 403**.
Snake-leaves resuscitate, 612.
Snares of devil overcome by magic circle, 810.
Sniffing dogs looking for patent right or for dog which was sent for pepper, 200B.
Snipe likes own children best, 247.
Snipe's bill frightens hawk, 229.
Snow dried on stove, 1272*; lain on by hare who feigns warmth, 71.
Snow-Child, 884.
Snow-White, 709.
So they speak Latin, 1628*.
Softening bread-crusts, 1567B.
Soldier avenges merchant's inhospitality, 1550; becomes general, 1670*; eating with saber, 1704*; gives snake salted food, 672A*; saved from robber by

alarm, 955A*; saves king from robbers, 952.
Solomon binds devil in chains, 803; Grundy, 2012D.
Solomon's judgment, 926, 926A, 926B, 926C; wisdom in youth, 920.
Some things not for sale, 1559C*.
Somersault of frog before harrow, 276*.
Son bites parent's nose for neglect, 838; made of wood (fox throws it down cliff), 165*; of cow as hero, 532*; of king (Solomon) and smith, 920; of the hunter, 513C; returning home killed by mistake, 939A.
Son-in-law acts stupidly, 1685A.
Song to warn lover, 1419H.
Sorcerer punished, 325**; predicts early death for injurer, 934**.
Sorcerer's apprentice, 325.
Soul in necklace, 412; sold to devil, 1170—1199; transferred to parrot, 678.
Soup-stone, 1548.
Sour grapes for fox, 59.
»Sow» as name for girl resented, 1464C*.
Sower answers Christ discourteously, 752C*.
Sowing salt, 1200; seed all in one place, 1200A.
Spade fetched to dig oneself out, 1882.
Span of life readjusted by man and animals, 828.
Sparrow avenges dog's death, 248; will sing only before open window and escapes death, 20D*.
Sparrows exiled for soiling books, 1325*.
Speaking horsehead reveals truth, 533.
Spectacles teach how to read, 1331A*.
Speech of birds, 517, 670, 671.
Speechless maiden, 898.
Speed in skills (lies), 1920C*.
Spider in house of saving housewife (grows thin), 283C*; invites fly, 283; laughs at slow silkworm, 283D*; reported dead catches flies off guard, 283A*; web saves fugitive, 967.
Spider's disorderly house (no queen like bees), 283E*.
Spiders catch fish in webs, 283G*.
Spindle, shuttle, and needle, 585.
Spinning-women, 500—501; by the spring, 480.
Spirit in blue light, 562; in bottle, 331, 331*.
Spitting into hot porridge (like smith on hot iron), 1262*.
Split dog (legs backward), 1889L; tree catches claw, 38, 151; tree catches she-bear, 36; tree limb (birds caught in crack), 1890A; wood only accepted, 1951.
Spoon with long handle for devil, 821B.
Spoons unnecessary for peasants, 910C*.
Spring and wood debate, 293A*.
Squeezing hand (iron glove), 1060A, 1060A*; (supposed) stone, 1060.
Squirrel as young son, 1073; is gay because good-hearted, 87B*; needle, and glove, 90.
Stag admires self in spring, 77.
Stammering matchmaker, 1457*.
Starving sparrows, 244B*.
Statue avenged for failure to furnish husband, 1479**.
Statue's father, 1347*; smile encourages altar thief, 1565A*.
Staying till he has finished (urinating), 1293.
Stealing serpent's crown, 672A, B; small amount (rope with mare on end), 1800.
Steamship taken for devil, 1315*.
Stepfather as werwolf, 970*.
Stepmother and giantess, 556C*; helps hero, 556A*; woos stepson, 870C*.
Stepmother's dream, 403*.
Stepson as mariner makes fortune, 935*.
Stick from body (fingernail paring) paid devil, 1181; running through animal's body, 167A*.
Stingy bride, 1455*; dead woman corrects laundress's account, 1449**; hostess at inn, 1449*; master (innkeeper) reproached, 1567; parson and slaughtered pig, 1792; parson (may the grass grow up!), 1736; peasant cheated, 1560*; persons, 1704.
Stolen bride, 885; brides, 530C*; coat (ham), 1840B; magic object, 560—568; mirror, 434; princess recovered by four skillful brothers, 653.
Stomach makes life interesting, 716*.
Stone as witness too big to bring to court, 1543D*; bitten (trick), 1061; of pity, 894; of the snake, 672D; squeezed (trick), 1060; thrown (trick), 1062; wall kills man followed by bad luck, 947.
Stones from brook all to be brought, 1172.
Stopper cared for (put in pocket, tar runs out), 1681A*.
Stories to discover greatest fool, 1332.
Stork's daughter, 709A.
Storm placated by throwing man overboard, 973; scorned by man (killed), 934**.

Story of green pig (unfinished), 2275; told to expose thief, 976A.
Storyteller interrupted, 1376A*B*.
Storytelling to buy fire, 1920H.
Straightening the bridge, 1326A*.
Strange foods, 1339—1339E; names assumed (absurd results), 1562A, 1562G*.
Straw and dog with old maid in bed, 1480*; rethreshed, 206.
Strawberries in winter, 403B, 480.
Straying-restraint used on person as on animal, 1349E*.
Stream baled out in nutshell, 1273A*.
Strengthening ogre (by castration), 1133, (by scalding, etc.), 1134.
Stretching the beam, 1244; tree to upper world, 317.
Strokes shared, 1610.
Strong companion sought, 650B; John, 650A—650***; man and his companions, 301B; woman as bride, 519.
Stronger and strongest, 2031, 2031A, 2031C, 2031A*.
Stubborn goats fall into water, 202.
Student as healer, 1845; from Paradise, 1540.
Students and later parson with amorous princess, 1727*.
Stupid man, 1675—1724; ogre, 1000—1199; prince in cave, 524*; son-in-law, 1685A; thief follows instructions (absurdly), 1692.
Stutterers, 1702, 1702B*.
Submarine otherworld, 1889H.
Substitute bedmate provided by wife, 870, 870A; to answer king's questions, 922; bridegroom, 855.
Substituted bride, 403—403**, 408, 437; bride (unmasked), 870, 870B*.
Substitutes in line of race, 1074.
Substitution of old woman as bed mate, 1441*; of trash in dupe's bag, 67A*.
»Such a one» (name deceives ogre), 1138.
Succession of misfortunes but eventual good luck, 938—938**, 939; of old men, 726.
Sugar puppet, 879.
Suit over chickens from boiled eggs, 920A.
Suitor advised by girl in tree, 1462; brings food from home, 1691A; takes offense at word used by girl, 1459*.
Suitors deceived by married woman, 1730; of the she-fox, 65; restore maiden to life (who shall have her), 653B; (unwelcome) locked up and made to spin, 882A*.
Suitors' revenge, 940.

Sukasaptati, 1352A.
Summons to reindeer slaughter, 8**.
Sun as father of girl, 898; brings all to light, 960; (setting) taken for fire, 1335*; to receive girl when twelve, 898*.
Sunbeam upholds holy man's coat, 759B.
Sunlight carried in bag into windowless house, 1245.
Sunrise announced prematurely, 120**; because of cock's crowing, 114; lights trees and hog wins wager, 120.
Superhuman tasks, 460—499.
Supernatural adversaries, 300—399; helpers, 500—559; husband, 425—449; power or knowledge, 650—699; spouse, 400—459; wife, 400—424.
Supper for greatest liar, 1920E; won by a trick (another to pay), 1526A.
Supposed magic spell permits theft, 1629*.
Surprising lovers, 1352.
Swallow advises birds to eat hemp-seeds, 233C.
Swan and swallow to live together, 246*.
Swan maidens, 313, 400, 400*, 465, 465A.
»Sweet death, keep killing me», 1476C.
Sweet word given (honey and Bible), 1437.
Swelling objects (snake bite, bee sting), 1889M.
Swimming contest (bluff), 1612; in flaxfield, 1290; match of fish, 250, 250A, 252; to next town (claim of fox in peril), 67.
Sword for king fetched by transforming self to bird, fish, hare, 665; turns to wood and saves man from execution, 1736A.
Symbolic account of love adventure, 873*; message exchange between girl and king, 874.
Table, ass, and stick, 563; manners get fool into trouble, 1691—1691B; to go by itself, 1291C.
Tail buried (tied), 2A; of glowing iron made for bear, 40B*; of rabbit taken for stick, 74D*; of wolf (attached to bell), 40A*, (nailed to tree), 1896.
Tail-fisher, 2.
Tailless fox tries to get foxes to cut off tails, 64.
Tailor and ogre at sewing, 1096; and smith as rivals, 1631*; as cheater, 1574—1574C; in heaven (throws footstool), 800; succeeds by boasting, 1640.
Tailor's dream, 1574.
Tails in mud, 1004.

Tale of Cradle, 1363.
Tales of fate, 930—949; of magic, 300—749; told as defense against false accusation, 916.
Talkative wife and discovered treasure, 1381.
Talking animals prevent incest, 674; bedlegs warn king, 622; by animal captor permits victim's escape, 6, 6*, 227*; causes fool to be robbed, 1341A; causes slave's recapture, 1341B*; horse and dog frighten man, 1705.
Tall bridegroom enters church by falling down, 1295A*; corn, 1920A*.
Tame bird and wild bird, 245.
Taming of the shrew, 901; wild prince, 877*.
Tar to cover wagon, 1071.
Tarbaby and rabbit, 175.
Tarring hero's boat to injure him, 1156.
Task because of mother's foolish boast, 500, 501.
Tasks, 450—499; assigned husband so as to enjoy his wife, 465—465B*; assigned suitors, 577; given by witch for disechanting husband, 425B.
Tavern at heaven's gate, 804B*.
Tax-exempter, 1605*.
Tea (coffee) wrongly prepared, 1339C.
Tearing up orchard, 1011.
Tears of pearl, 836A*.
Teeth of wolf hold to horse's tail, 47A.
Telegraph to carry boots, 1710.
Tell-tale calf's head, 780C; lobsters turn red, 1776A*; parrot punished, 243.
Teller killed in own story (catch tale), 2202.
Test of princes, 920B, 920C, 920D, 920B*.
Testament of the dog, 1842; of bear, 164*.
Testimony discredited by absurd truth, 1381—1381*.
Tests: luck or intelligence best, 945; for bird-king, 221A—221B.
Ten nights' resistance to princess's temptations, 307C*.
Ten-fold return of goods, 1735.
Tenant promises his daughter to his master (horse substituted), 1440.
»Thank God they weren't peaches,» 1686.
Thankful animals, 156A*, 156B*, 156C*.
»That is all,» (servant leaves), 1572H*.
Theft and recovery of magic object, 560—568; betrayed by riddling answer, 875A; of bacon, 1624B*; of butter (honey) by playing godfather, 15; of fish, 1; of his mother's berries by fox, 39; of the young magpies, 56; from corpse, 366, 366*; from the treasury by its architect, 950; related as dream, 1790; through substitution of horse, 1529.
Thefts, 1525—1525R*.
Thick forest with enormous moose (lawyer's lie), 1860A*.
Thief aided by parrot's instructions, 1526B*; and tiger, 177; as dog, 1341A*; beggar, murderer, 921B*; demonstrates skill (Master Thief), 1525; exposed by a story, 976A; frightened by bagpipe, 1706*; prays for victim (cheat), 1840B; repents and pretends to have found stolen cow, 1636; rescued by devil, 821A; tied· to tree, 958A*; turned into an ass, 753*; warned what not to steal, 1341—1341B*.
Thief's excuse, 1624—1624E*; offer of candle rejected by saint, 848*.
Thieves, 950—969; blessed for hospitality, 751D*; each have special talent (joined by king), 950*; in churchyard and fat parson, 1791; mask as ghosts, 1740B; steal from each other, 1525H; trick each other, 1525N.
Thieving pot, 591.
Think carefully beforehand, 910C; thrice before speaking, 1562.
Thinks he has been in heaven, 1531.
Third sister avoids seducer, 883B; sold for price of fourth, 1266*.
Thorn removed from lion's paw (Androcles), 156.
Thorn-Rose, 410.
Thorns danced in by Jew (monk), 592.
Threat to haul away warehouse, 1046.
Three animals as brothers-in-law, 552A, 552B; billy-goats gruff, 122E; brothers show skill, 654—654A*; brothers trade with the devil, 360; competing wishes, 1925*; counsels of the fox, 150; day tournament, 314, 314A; doctors transfer heart, hand, eye (from hog, thief, cat), 660; golden sons, 707; green twigs, 756; hairs from devil's beard, 461; hunchbacks drowned, 1536B; hundred sixty-five children, 762; joint depositors, 1591; languages (dogs' birds', frogs'), 671; lost children taken by giant, 327C; lucky brothers, 1650; magic objects and wonderful fruits, 566; old women helpers to be invited to wedding, 501; oranges, 408; persons as stupid as his wife, 1384; roads show fates, 840B*; sins of the hermit, 839;

sisters rescued from ogre, 311, 312; sisters to rescue little brother, 480A*; snake-leaves resuscitate dead woman, 612; stolen princesses, 301; wishes, 750A; wishes used to forestall execution, 927A; words at the grave (priest discomfited), 1745.

Three-fold death prophesied, 934A$_1$.

Three-months' child, 1362A*.

Threshing contest, 1089; flail is granary roof, 1031; in stable where fox pretends to hold up roof, 9A.

Thrifty cutting of cheese, 1452; girl saves flax, 1451.

Throwing contest with ogre, 1063—1063B; golden club, 1063; ogre's wife into water, 1120; sham-dead fox from pit, 33; stone (bird), 1062; to sky (man or animals), 1888*.

Thrush gets clothes from grateful peacock, 235B*; teaches dove to build nest, 236; teaches fox to sing, 58**.

Thrushbeard, 900.

Thumbling, 700.

Thunder frightens ogre, 1148—1148B; the rolling of brother's wagon, 1147; to be made in church, 1839*.

Ticking clock frightens fool, 1321D*.

Tidings to king cleverly delivered, 925.

Tiger betrays cow, 131; carries off girls, 312A; ridden by sheep-thief, 177.

Tiger's secret told by man, 181.

Tigers adopt boy and arrange his marriage, 535.

Till the front sweats (pun), 1445*.

Tin under horse's tail makes him wild (ogre riding), 1142.

Titeliture, 500.

Titmouse tries to be as big as bear, 228.

Titmouse's great age, 244**.

Toad (enchanted princess) as bride, 402A*.

Tobias, 507A.

Toes taken for ghosts (shot off), 1318C.

Tom Thumb, 700.

Tom-Tit-Tot, 500.

Tongue torn out for slander, 836B*.

Too cold for hare to build house in winter, 81.

Too much (talk), 1948, (truth), 1691B*.

Topsy-turvy land, 1935.

Tournament with princess as prize, 508.

Tower as abode of princess, 891A.

Tracks into lion's den but not out, 50A.

Trade of three brothers with devil, 360.

Trained horse rolls in the field, 1892.

Transformation flight, 313, 314; to cow's stomach, 404*.

Transformed golden pumpkin, 1592A.

Trap catches jeering fox, 68*; catches old man and animals eat him, 20B; discussed by birds (raven caught), 245*; set up by fool (mother falls into it), 1685A*.

Trapping of animal in animal's carcass (jug), 68, 68A, 68B; of dupe in order to get bait from trap, 35B*; of wolf when he takes oath on iron, 44, 44*.

Travelers and miser, 1572G*; lose way (find selves back home), 1275*; The Two, 613.

Traveling animals, 130, 210.

Treacherous cat, 332H*; companion betrays hero, 531, 613; mother plots against son, 590; wife, 315, 318, 590A.

Treasure and the talkative wife, 1381; always comes to predestined owner, 745A; at home, 1645; of hanging man, 910D; of poor brother, 834; from dream, 834, 834A, 1645B*; through dreams, 1645—1645B*; within foot of ground, 910E.

Treasure-finders murder one another, 763.

Tree from horse shades rider, 1889D; hiding place betrays princess who is seeking trouble, 871*; on mountain (chain tale), 2041*; pulled from cliff, 1241A; refuge (man falls on ogres), 1154; stretches to upper world, 37; taken for snake, 1315; to be bent (deception), 1051; to be carried (deception), 1052; to be chosen for hanging, 1587; to be felled (deception), 1050; to be pulled down for watering (fool with head in branches), 1241.

Tree-demon pays to have tree saved, 1168B.

Tree-names to be called, 7.

Tree-trunks crosswise of sledge, 1248.

Trespasser's defense, 1590.

Trial among animals (chain tale), 2042A*; of crow and eagle, 220A; of Yorsh Yorshovich, 254**.

Trick exchange of magic objects, 518; exchanges (chain tale), 2037A*; of cat better than fox's many (she climbs tree), 105; race, 30, 250, 275, 1074.

Trickster discovers adultery, 1358—1358*.

Trip to hell, 471A*.

Tripe loathed, 1578B*.

Triple tax, 1661.

Troll and christening, 1165; is cut open (chain tale), 2028.
Trouble sought by princess, 871*; now or later, 938A; stirred up by servant, 1573*.
Trouble-maker (in night-lodgings), 1542B*; (jackal), 59*; (old woman), 1353.
True bride, 403; servant saves master's wife (unjustly punished), 516, 516A.
Trusting God or king, 841.
Truth and falsehood debated, 613; comes to light, 780—789; told fails to be rewarded by gold chain (bear and monkey), 48*.
Truth-telling member (gullible wife), 1539*; overdone, 1691B*.
Trying to stretch beam, 1244.
Tsar's dog, 449.
Turandot, 851A.
Turkey and peacock marry, 224.
Turning in wind lets flax-tail be burned, 2D; of princess to suitor at night, 621, 850; over block of stone to find treasure, 926B*.
Turnips called bacon (cat called rabbit), 1565**.
Turtle's war-party, 297A; wedding, 286*.
Twelve brothers changed to ravens, 451; days of Christmas, 2010A; kinds of food, 2010B.
Twixe a fool for marrying twice, 1516C*.
Twigs in bundle hard to break, 910F.
Twining branches over lovers' graves, 970.
Twins, (beautiful and ugly) 711; or bloodbrothers, 303.
Two brothers, 303; brothers (Egyptian), 318; bullets with one charge, 1890C; candles lit (God and devil), 778*; eggs, 1567D; girls, bear, and dwarf, 426; presents to king (beet and horse), 1689A; sold for price of one, 1265*; stubborn goats, 202; travelers, 613.
Tying animals together for safety, 78, 78A; lovers together, 1733A*B*.
Uglier foot (wager), 1559B*.
Ugly name of girl changed, 1461.
Umpire takes all of booty, 51***, 926D.
Unbaptized child stolen by fairies, 412B*.
Unbalanced field, 1296*.
Underground passage to lover's house, 1419E.
Uneducated father defended, 929A.
Unequal crop division, 9B, 1030.
Unfaithful wife as judge, 1355A*; wife exposed by devil, 824; queen discovered in other world, 871A.

Unfamiliar animals frighten wild animals, 103.
Unfinished tales, 2250—2299; work holds off devil, 1187*.
Ungrateful beggar and parson, 1826*; river passenger, 58, 133*; serpent returned to captivity, 155; son reproved, 980—980D; vulture threatens sparrow partner, 76*; wife betrays husband, 612, 612A; wolf threatens crane helper, 76.
Unhappy wife transforms self and flees, 591*.
Unheard-of riding horse, 1091; bird, 1092.
Unibos, 1535.
Unjust decisions, 1534; division of crop, 9B, 1030; partner (dupe works and trickster profits) 9; umpire, 51**, 51***; umpire appropriates disputed goods, 518, 518*.
Unknown animal disposed of, 1281, 1281A, 1651; knight at tournament, 314, 314A; son discovered by king, 873.
Unlaughing fate brought to laughter (transformation), 514*.
Unlucky courtship, 1688.
Unquiet grave, 760.
Unreliable friends tested, 893.
Untidy bride, 1453A*.
Unused sex-organs, 1395*.
Unwilling suitor advised from tree, 1462.
Upstream search for obstinate wife, 1365A.
Uriah letter, 910K, 930.
Urinalysis for diagnosis, 1641A.
Uttering three wise words (king is bastard, meat is dogflesh, one-eyed camel), 655.
Vain waiting for horse's scrotum to fall (fox), 115.
Vampire princess, 307; bridegroom, 363.
Vanished husband found by keeping bath-house, 425D.
Vanity punished, 833*.
Vaticinium, 517.
Vecchia Scorticata, 877.
Vengeance for being cheated, 1538; of magpies on fox, 56; on disdainful girl, 900B*; reversed, 906*.
Verlioka, 210*.
Vices follow one another, 839.
Vidua, 1510.
Vineyard of ogre destroyed 1011.
Viola, 879.
Violation of she-bear by disguised fox, 36.
Virgin Mary and animals, 750****;

thought of saves man from sin, 839B*; to bear a child, 707A*.
Virgin's handkerchief, 754*; statue as protector, 706A.
Voice changed by blacksmith, 327; disguised, 123, 123A; from grave (deception), 1532; of parson reminds woman of goat, 1834.
Voices from graveyard cause fright, 1676C.
Vows deceptively evaded, 1811, 1811A.
Wager about seeing sunrise first (hog sees light on trees and wins), 120; as to calling tree-names first, 7; as to first to speak (close door), 1351—1351C*; as to who can best fool husband, 1406; can supply everything (cheat), 1559C*, of merry wives, 1406; on servant's faithfulness, 889; on wife's chastity, 882; that sheep are hogs, 1551.
Wagers as cheats, 1559A*—C*.
Wages as much as he can carry, 1153.
Wagon covered with tar (deception), 1017.
»Wait till I get dry,» 122H.
Waiting for horse's scrotum to fall, 115; till victim is fat enough, 122F.
Walking home slowly not to intercept wife's lover, 1409C.
Wall collapses (chain tale), 2031A*.
Wanderers seek night lodgings, 1527*.
Wandering husband, 707B*; Jew, 777.
War of (birds and quadrupeds), 222—222B*; (domestic and wild animals), 104.
Warehouse to be hauled away (threat), 1046.
Warming hands and cooling soup with same breath, 1342; the stove, 1271A*, 1271B*.
Warpath of objects, 297.
Warrior trusts faithful wife, 713*.
»Wash me before eating» (victim escapes), 122G.
Washing black animal white, 1312*; black cloth white, 1183; pie, 1273C*.
Wasp nest as king's drum, 49A; nest for parson, 1785C; nest stings bear, 49, 49A.
Watch taken for devil's eye, 1319A*.
Watching supposed corpse, 308*.
Water caught in sieve, 1180; of slander, 1429*; of youth, 550, 551; from the well (human chain hangs down), 1250; thrown on calf's back, 1211*.
»We three,» »for gold», 360, 1697.
Weak animal helps strong and is rewarded, 75; beer served, 1557A.

Wealth of the poor, 1930A*; leads to pride, 751C*; pretended by girl wins prince, 881**.
Weasel and poison, 168*.
Weather predicted by farmer or horse's tail, 921C*; promised as desired, 1830.
Wedding day foretold as death day, 934B; ceremony (absurd answers), 1820; of cricket and fly, 282*; of giant's sixty daughters, 1961; of turkey and peacock, 224; preparations (fool gives meat to dogs, etc.), 1618A.
Wee wee woman, etc., 2016.
Weeping and laughing in congregation, 1828*; bitch, 1515.
Weighed cat, 1373, 1373A*.
Welcome to the clothes, 1558.
Well escaped from in bucket by trickery, 32; to be moved, 875B$_3$.
What does God do?, 1738A*; God gave him, 1572B*; kind of bird, 920B; says David?, 1833A; should I have said (done), 1696.
Where did the Father stay?, 1833B; did Nicodemus go?, 1841*; have you been, goose?, 2011; is warehouse? (chain story), 2018; to put old woman (chain story), 2016*; was Christ?, 1833C.
Whetting the knife, 1015.
Which bird is father, 232C*.
Whipping pupil beforehand, 1674*.
Whiskey and water trade, 1555E.
Whistling contest (deceptive), 1084.
White man believes he is negro, 1284A; serpent's flesh (animal languages learned), 673; sheep-skin as source of light, 1245*.
Whittington's cat, 1651.
Who ate lamb's heart?, 785; can rule wife?, 1375; has lost this? (literal penance), 1807A*; will be her future husband?, 737; will speak first?, 1351.
Why have I nothing?, 737A*; sea is salt, 565.
Wicked lord is punished, 837.
Widow with many children courted (chain tale), 2029D*.
Widow's meal blown away, 759C.
Widowed she-fox, 65.
Widower relieved by wife's death, 1354A*.
Widower's good day, 1354B*; week, 2012A.
Wife as bishop, lover as friend, 1419L*; banished, 705—709; confesses to disguised husband (four men's mistress), 1410; deceived by hidden husband,

1380; disappears and is sought for, 400; disguises and saves enslaved husband, 888, 888A, 890; eats so little, 1373A; immediately ready for new husband, 1350; kept in box deceives husband, 1426; multiplies secret, 1381D; must have lovers (wife confesses), 1357*; not to get angry, 1415; of ogre (killed), 1122; (burned), 1121; (thrown into water), 1120; plots against husband, 318; recovers husband's loss, 1424*; refuses to be beaten, 888A; rescues husband from devil, 813B; sought for upstream, 1315A; talks too much, 1381; tamed of shrewishness, 900—904; undoes curse on husband, 445*.

Wife's feigned disease imitated by husband, 1372*; laziness, 1370; temporary success in mastering husband, 1378B*; work too much for husband, 1408.

Wild animals, 1—149; animals and man, 150—199; animals and domestic, 100—149; animals on seligh, 158; animals other than fox, 70—99; bird and tame bird, 245; boar as husband, 444E*; boars to be shot, 1053; man set free (helps hero); 502; prince tamed, 877*.

Wind and sun contend, 298; and whirlwind, 298D*; greeted (later protects man), 298A*.

Windmill taken for cross, 1323.

Window ledge has knife which wounds prince, 432; worn out by looking through it, 1271*.

Wine in the cask (water substituted), 1555.

Wings (artificial) of the prince, 575.

Winning cards admit to heaven, 330C.

Wisdom of hidden old man saves kingdom, 981.

Wise brothers (king is a bastard), 655; carving of the fowl, 1533; through experience, 910A; words uttered (king is bastard, etc.), 655.

Wishes of prince always come true, 652; granted to fisher's wife, 555; granted good girl, 403A; granted (used well or foolishly), 750A, 750D; (impossible) to be fulfilled by devil, 1173A.

Wishing contests, 1925.

Wishing-hat stolen 581*.

Wit purchased, 910G.

Witch and fisher boy, 327F; turns blood-brothers into stone, 303.

Witch's household, 334.

»With his whole heart» (judge carried off), 1186.

Witness to adultery may keep cows, 1735.

Wolf and Crane, 76; and horses (misc.), 166B*; and pig in race, 121A*; and Red Riding Hood, 333; and reindeer, 95*; and young goats, 123; as dog's guest sings, 100; as stupid animal, 1—69 *passim*; beaten in bath house, 164A*; boasts of having eaten horses, 118; by singing enslaves man and wife and gets possessions (cumulative tale), 163; carries off pig but lion takes it, 91*; converses with he-goat while he is carrying him away, 126B*; cried too often, 1333; cut open and kids rescued, 123; deceived by fox, 1—69; descends into well in one bucket and rescues fox in other, 32; dives into water for reflected cheese, 34; dominates hare, 79*; eats the kids, 123; (enchanted person) disenchanted, 409, 428; flees from wolf-head, 125; gradually eats whole flock of sheep (dies), 162A*; harnessed, 1910; husband disenchanted, 428; in sheep's clothing, 123B; entices goat from cliff, 127A*; kept as old maid's husband, 1477, 1477*; kicked in teeth by horse, 47B, 47D, 47*; loses his prey, 122; made into cheese, 1892*; overeats in cellar, 41; permits wildboar to cry out once, 91A*; predestined to eat sheep, 121B*; punished by being married, 165B*; pursues pig and both fall into well, 121C*; races bee, 275B*; rings bell when he tries to imitate thieving fox, 160***; releases raven healer, 76A*; runs away from his skin, 1896; seeks breakfast but allows too many excuses, 122A; steals the old maid, 1477; taken for colt, 1311; takes best parts of meat, 51**; to go to priest for bread and is chased away, 41**; to pull thorn out of ass's foot (kicked), 122J; tricked into chimney and burned, 124; unjustly accuses lamb and eats him, 111A; vainly comes for cow promised him, 154*; with tail through stable window caught, 166A.

Wolf-head used by sheep to overawe wolves, 125.

Wolf-hunting sheep, 1529B*.

Wolf's and bear's wedding, 91B*; false reform, 165; tail attached to ball, 40A*; tail caught from wolf hole, 1229, 1875, 1896.

Wolves climb on top of one another to tree (all fall), 121; enticed from stable, 1650, 1652.

Wolves' adventures (various), 169*—169L*.

Woman as cuckoo in tree, 1029; betrays bears and escapes, 160*; does not know herself, 1382, 1383; goes for beer, 1387; in the chest, 1536A; in man's clothes wooed by queen, 435K, 512A*, 514, 514**: meets pig (chain tale), 2027A; thrown into pit, 1164; too difficult for devil, 1164—1164D.

Woman's privates betray adultery, 1391; treatment of husband's corpse repels new suitor, 1352*.

Women after squirrel and cooking pot, 1227.

Wonder-child, 708.

Wonderful cock, 715A.

Wood carried up hill to roll it down, 1243; floated for thrush by friendly birds, 249**; (house in the), 431; to be cut, 1001; to be loaded, 1242.

Wood-spirits' foster-son, 667.

Woodcutter kills mock corpse, 1711*.

Wooden drinking cup for old age, 980B; gun explodes, 1228A; house and ice house, 43; saw for building ship, 1274*.

Wooer without money pretends to wealth, 859, 859ABCD.

Wooing the princess, 850—869.

Word contest, 1093; forgotten by stepping into hole, 1687.

Words of princess used to defeat her, 853; in foreign language thought insults, 1322; (unusual) describing hen's death, 2022A.

Wormwood and sparrow (chain tale), 2034A*.

Wren hides in eagle's wings, 221.

Wrestling contest (looks where to throw ogre), 1070, (with old grandfather, bear), 1071.

Written instructions followed (drowning husband left), 1562B.

X-Ray machine (sham doctor), 1641A*.

Yawns contagious, 1431.

You said it, not I, 925; shall see me a little while longer, 1827.

Young suitor robs old widow, 1392*.

Youngest prince betrayed by brothers, 550, 551.

Youth bathes in springs of health, wealth, and wisdom, 412A*; cheated in selling oxen, 1538; seduces with gift of shoes, 1731; shows cleverness, 920—929; sold to devil successfully disguised, 810B*; transformed to a horse, 314; who wanted to learn what fear is, 326—326D*.